Zeitschrift Für Celtische Philologie, Volume 3

ZEITSCHRIFT

FÜR

CELTISCHE PHILOLOGIE

HERAUSGEGEBEN

VON

KUNO MEYER UND L. CHR. STERN

III. BAND

HALLE a. S.

MAX NIEMEYER

LONDON	PARIS
DAVID NUTT	EMILE BOUILLON
57—59 Long acre	67, Rue Richelieu

1901

INHALT.

Seite

Wh. Stokes, The Destruction of Dind Ríg 1
Wh. Stokes, A List of ancient Irish Authors 15
K. Meyer, Mitteilungen aus irischen Handschriften 17. 226. 447
K. Meyer, Brinna Ferchertne 40
R. Thurneysen, Das Alter der Würzburger Glossen 47
J. Strachan, Some Notes on the Irish Glosses of Würzburg and St. Gall 55
H. Zimmer, Grammatische Beiträge, 2. Über verbale Neubildungen im
    Neuirischen 61
E. W. B. Nicholson, The origin of the 'Hibernian' collection of Canons 99
E. W. B. Nicholson, Filius Urbagen 104
V. H. Friedel, Les vers de Pseudo-Nennius 112
E. Anwyl, The four Branches of the Mabinogi, chapter IV 123
L. Chr. Stern, Tec, tegach, teckaf, tecket 135
L. Chr. Stern, Die Visionen des Bardd Cwsc 165
Wh. Stokes, The Battle of Carn Conaill 203
Wh. Stokes, Amra Senáin 220
W. Foy, Zur keltischen Lautgeschichte 264
E. Zupitza, Die Vertretung der u-Diphthonge im Irischen und Ver-
    wandtes 275
J. Strachan, Irish no- in a relative function 283
H. Zimmer, Beiträge zur Erklärung irischer Sagentexte, 2. 285
E. Ernault, Sur les mots bretons get (a), gant, rak, meurbet, a, da,
    douaren 304
E. W. B. Nicholson, The language of the Continental Picts 308
J. K. Zeuss, Briefe an Chr. W. Glück 334
R. Henebry, The Reuehan 'Air' 377
L. Chr. Stern, Über die Formen des Konjunktivs im Britannischen . . 383
Wh. Stokes, Irish Etymologies 467
J. Strachan, Grammatical Notes (Continued) 474
A. Anscombe, The date of the first settlement of the Saxons in Britain 492
V. H. Friedel, Ad versus Nennii 515

  Seite

R. Henebry, The Life of Columb Cille 516

Wh. Stokes, On a passage in *Cath Cairn Chonaill* 572

H. Zimmer, Das Kymrische in 'The pleasant Comodie of Patient Grisill' 574

E. Zupitza, Noch einmal der Diphthong *au* 591

K. Brugmann, Irisch *duine* 'Mensch' 595

Erschienene Schriften

      E. Anwyl 198, H. D'Arbois de Jubainville 19⁴ 434, A. L. C. Brown 444, J. A. Bruun 444, Al. Bugge 622, S. Bugge 621, E. Ernault 438. 623, J. G. Evans 622, Festschrift für Wh. Stokes 432, F. N. Finck 436, E. Gwynn 429, G. Henderson 411, V. Henry 439, E. Hull 189, D. Hyde 192, Irische Texte IV. 1 614, G. Keating 196. 620, J. Loth 623, J. C. MacErlean 620, K. Meyer 620, Oidhe Chloinne Uisnigh 196, Otia Merseiana 195, E. C. Quiggin 436, Dr. Ricochon 619, l'Abbé Rousselot 425, J. Rhŷs 605, Chr. Sarauw 599, Edw. Schröder 199, R. A. Stewart-MacAlister 191, J. Strachan 435. 620, R. Thurneysen 435. 623, Transactions of the Gaelic Society of Inverness XXI. 437, J. Vendryes 383, H. Zimmer 434.

Corrigenda 446. 624

THE DESTRUCTION OF DIND RÍG.

There are three copies of the following tale of treachery, love, self-devotion, and vengeance, one (*LL*) in the Book of Leinster, pp. 269, 270 of the lithographic facsimile, another (*R*) in Rawlinson B. 502, ff. 71, 72, a ms. of the twelfth century in the Bodleian library, and the third (*YBL*) in the Yellow Book of Lecan, cols. 754—756 = pp. 112, 113a of the photolithograph published in 1896. The three copies substantially agree. But *LL* is slightly fuller than the others, and is therefore made the basis of the following edition. The variae lectiones of *R* and *YBL* are given as footnotes.

The tale is now for the first time printed. But it has been noticed, more or less fully, by Keating in his *Forus Feasa air Eirinn,* Dublin 1811, p. 350, by Conall MaGeoghagan in the *Annals of Clonmacnoise,* Dublin 1896, pp. 43, 44, by O'Curry, in his *Lectures* 251, and his *Manners* etc. III, 242—245, by Prof. Atkinson in the Contents to the Book of Leinster, p. 61, and by Prof. d'Arbois de Jubainville, in his *Essai d'un Catalogue de la littérature épique d'Irlande,* p. 184. A tale dealing, very differently, with the same subject is preserved as a scholium on the *Amra Choluimb chille* (YBL. col. 689, Egerton 1782, fo. 9b), and will be published in the *Revue Celtique,* tome XX. Keating (ubi supra, pp. 352, 353) abridges this version.

There seems no ground for doubting the actual occurrence of the final incident of our tale, which is thus chronicled by Tigernach (Rev. Celt. XVI, 378): 'Cobthach the Meagre of Bregia, son of Ugaine the Great, was burnt, with thirty kings around him, at Dind ríg of Magh Ailbe, in the palace of Tuaimm Tenbath precisely, by Labraid the Dumb, the Exile, son of Ailill of Áne, son of Loeguire Lorc, in revenge for his father and grandfather, whom Cobthach the Meagre had killed. Warfare thence between Leinster and Conn's Half' (i. e. the northern half of Ireland).

This warfare is also referred to in the title contained in *R.* viz. Scelśenchas Lagen inso sis. Oʀguin Denna rig inso: Bruiden Tuamma Tenbad ainm aile do, ₇ is *ed* on cetna scel Lagen ₇ tuus a ngliad 'A legendary story of Leinster this below. This is the Destruction of Dind ríg.[1]) The Palace of Tuaimm Tenbad is another name for it, and this is the first tale of the Leinstermen and the commencement of their fighting'.

Orgain Dind ríg.
(Lebar Laignech, 269 a).

1. Cid dia tá orgain Dind ríg?

Ní *ansa.* Bói Cobthach Cóel Breg *mac* Ugaine[2]) Móir ir-rige Breg.[3]) Bái da*no* Loegaire Lorc *mac* Ugaine[2]) ir-rige Her*enn.*[4]) [Mac *sede* da*no* Augaine Mair — R.] Ba *formtech* Cob*thach* f*r*i Loegaire im rige Her*enn,*[5]) cor-ragaib sergg ₇ galar de, co ro śergg a ḟuil ₇ a ḟeóil de,[6]) *con*id de ro bói Cóel Breg fair-sium, ₇ ní[7]) roacht marbad in Loegaire.

2. Ro gaired dó iar*um* in Loegaire co farcbad bennachtain ocai ria n-écaib. INtan di*diu* dolluid a bráthair chucai issin tech brist*er* coss érin chirci[8]) *for* lar in taige. 'Nírb [ś]irsan[9]) do galar',[10]) or Laegaire. 'IS tairisi ón', or Cob*thach.* 'Dochuaid ass uile anísiu et*er* ḟuil ₇ chnáim, et*er* bethaid ₇ indili. Do-

---

[1]) 'This place', says O'Donovan (*The Book of Rights*, Dublin 1847, p. 15 note), 'is still well known. It is situated in the townland of Ballyknockan, about a quarter of a mile to the south of Leighlin Bridge, to the west of the river Barrow. Nothing remains of the palace but a moat, measuring 237 yards in circumference at the base, 69 feet in height from the level of the river Barrow, and 135 feet in diameter at the top, where it presents a level surface on which the king of Leinster's royal house evidently stood'.

[2]) Augaine R.   [3]) Herend YBL. Herenn R.
[4]) Laighen YBL. Lagen R.   [5]) Laighen YBL.
[6]) conid rogab serg ₇ galar de, co luid hi seimnib sirgc de, R.
[7]) for ₇ ni etc. YBL. has c*um*ma roacht marbad ind Laegairi.
[8]) coss erene circe R. coss eirini chirci YBL.
[9]) Nir' forbrisiund duit YBL.
[10]) Nip śirsan indlobra duit, a brathair R.

rónsaid[1]) fuachtain frim,[2]) a gillu, .i. coss na circe do brissiud. Tucaid ille co tucursa cumrech impe.'[3]) 'Fe amai', or Laegaire. 'IS meth[4]) 7 milliud dond fir. IS tabarta i n-éslis.'[5]) 'Tairsiu imbárach', or Cobthach, 'cor' altar[6]) mo fert-sa latt, [7 coro clantar mo lia, 7 coro hagthar m'oenach ñgubae, 7 coro ferthar mo hilach adnaccuil — R], ar atbélsa ar[7]) lúath.' 'Maith', or Loegaire, 'dogéntar'.[8])

3. 'Maith, tra', or Cobthach ria rigna 7 ria rechtaire,[9]) 'Apraidsi ba[10]) marb-sa can fis[11]) do neoch aile,[12]) ocus domberar[13]) im charpat 7 altan scene im láim.[14]) Doraga[15]) mo brathair co dichra [im dochumm R] dom cháiniud [7 dollige form R]. Bés ro sia ní uaimsea hé.[16])

4. Ba fír són. Doberar immach in carpat. Do thaet a brathair dia chainiud. Téit side cona-tailce fair anúas.[17]) Nosclanna[18]) in sciain ind oca fordrund, co tuargaib cend ass i coirr a chride,[19]) conid ro marb[20]) [Loegaire samlaid, 7 ro hadnacht i nDruim Loegairi. R].

5. Foracaib[21]) Loegaire mac .i. Ailill Áine. Ro gab-side ríge Lagen.[22]) Nir'bo lór dano la Cobthach in chétfingal, co tart argat do neoch dorat dig tonnaid[23]) do Ailill co mbo marb de.

6. IArsin ro gab-som rige Lagen. Foracaib dano Ailill Áne mac .i. Móen Ollam. Amlabar side dano co mbo[24]) fer mór.

---

[1]) Doronsáid LL. Doronsaid YBL.   [2]) frinn YBL. R.
[3]) Dos-fucaid domsa co tarat chuimrech n-impe R.
[4]) is meth 7 mell YBL.
[5]) is toirisiu conid meth 7 conid milliud 7 conid tabartha i n-eisleis in fer-sa o éhunn R.
[6]) coro altar YBL. coro claidter R.
[7]) atbélatsa for luath YBL. itbebsa (sic!) co luaċh R.
[8]) Atetha-su na huile sin, ar Loegaire R.
[9]) fria choimmsid n-indmais R.
[10]) bam YBL. am R.   [11]) can a fis YBL.
[12]) cen chomfis do nach ailiu R.   [13]) domfucthar R.
[14]) deis R.   [15]) Dorega YBL.
[16]) 7 ronsua ni huaimse di suidiu R. do ba roiseadh ni uaimse he YBL.
[17]) do thaet cona tarlaic fair di anuas R. teitside cona-teilce fair anuas YBL.
[18]) nus-clandaind YBL. nos-clann R.
[19]) hua chind a chaithre co clár a hocta R.
[20]) i corr a craidi conidh marb de YBL.
[21]) Facbais R. Forfacaib YBL.
[22]) rogab sidhi Laigin fris arisin YBL. congab-sede Laigneo fris afrithise R.
[23]) co rogell innmassa ermasa do scolaige druad ar dig tonnaid R.
[24]) co mbu YBL.

Laa dó did*u* issin chluichimaig oc immáin[1]) dorala camman[2]) dar a lurggain. 'Rom-ánic-se on',[3]) or se. 'Labraid Móen', or na gillai.[4]) 'Labraid' a ainm ond úair sin.[5])

7. Coṅgairther[6]) fir Her*enn* do Chob*thach* do thomailt Fesse Temrach. Luid Labraid da*no* c*u*mma chaich [dia tomailt. R] INtan did*u*[7]) rop ániu dóib ic tomailt[8]) na fesse, batar in t-aes admolta *for* in lár[9]) oc admolad ind ríg 7 na rigna 7 na flathi 7 na n-octhig*er*n.[10])

8. 'Maith did*u*', or Cob*thach*, 'in fetabair cia as ḟéliu [fil R. YBL] i nHer*inn*?' 'Ro fetamar',[11]) or C*r*aptine, '.i. Labraid Loiṅgsech m*ac* Ai*l*ella. Ron-anacsa[12]) i n-erruch, co ro marb a oendam damsa.[13]) IS hé as ḟéliu.' 'Ro fetamar',[14]) ar Ferchertni fili. 'Ron-anacsa[15]) da*no* i ṅgaimriud, co ro marb a oenboin dam,'[16]) [7 ni roib ina seilb *acht* sisi YBL.]

9. 'Eircid-siu lessium da*no*', ar Cob*thach*, 'ar is feliu an-d*ú*sa.'[17]) 'Ni pa[18]) messai-ti seom de sin', or C*r*aiptine, '7 ni pat[19]) fer(r)-dde siu'. 'A Herind[20]) duibsi im*morro*', ol Cob*thach*. 'Mani ḟagbam[21]) ar n-inad inti', or in gilla.

10. Dlomtair iar*um*.[23]) 'Cid ragmait?' or in gilla. 'Síar', or Ferch*er*tni.

11. Tiagait iar*um* cor-ríg Fer Morca .i. fir Mor[c]a[24]) batar immon Luachair úDedad thíar. Scoríath iss hé ba rí dóib.

12. [p. 269b] 'Cid dofor-fuc?'[25]) or Scoríath.

---

[1]) oc immain liathroidi YBL.   oc ain liathroite R.
[2]) adcomaic camm aine R.   [3]) rom[c]omaic he si on YBL.
[4]) ar in fer ba nessom do R.
[5]) Conid [d]e ro lil-seom Labraid ond huair sin R.
[6]) Is iar*um* conac*ra*it R.   [7]) didu YBL.
[8]) rop aine tomailt YBL.   ba hainium doib im thomailt R.
[9]) batar in t-aes dana iarsind aurlar R.
[10]) 7 inna rigna 7 na flaithi 7 inna n-oictig*er*n YBL.
[11]) Rodafetamar R.   [12]) ranacasa YBL.
[13]) a oendam retha air dom daim R.
[14]) Confetamar YBL. rofetar R.   [15]) ran acsa YBL.
[16]) cor' thascair a seilb huile .i. a oenboin dom daim R.
[17]) indnusa YBL. ar itberid is feileo lib he ind*u*ssa R. *Then R inserts* Cia thiasmais leis, ar Cassarn, file Cob*thaig*, rofancamar hil-lathiu teora sín co tarat a oen leind dun.   [18]) Nirbo YBL.   [19]) Nibot YBL.
[20]) assa ind Erind YBL.   [21]) Mini fogbam YBL.
[22]) Do duib a Herind co hog in n-ed bamsa beo R. cein bus id beo YBL.
[23]) Dollotar riam R. Dlomthair iarum YBL.
[24]) Morcca R.   [25]) dof-ucai YBL.

'Ar ñdlomad do ríg Her*enn*.'

'Fochen dúib', or se. 'Bid inund techt no anad dún céin nombeosa. Robar-bia degcommaid', [or in rig. YBL.][1])

13. INgen la Scoríath, Moríath a hainm. No bithe 'co a forcomét col-léir, uair na fríth céili diñgbala di fochetóir.[2]) A mmathair oca comét.[3]) Ni ro chotlaiset a dá súil ríam *acht* indala n-ai[4]) oc aire a ingine. Ro charastar[5]) im*morro* ind ingen inti Labraid. Bái comairle et*er* in n-ingin 7 Labraid. Ro bói urgnam[6]) mór la Scor*íath* do Ḟeraib Morca. IS *ed* comairle[7]) dorónsat, C*r*aiptine do śeinm[8]) suant*r*aige iarsind ól co comtholad[9]) a mmathair-si co roiss*ed*-som in n-imdái. Ba fír son im*morro*. Ni ro cheil C*r*aiptine a chruitte[10]) dadaig, coro chotail in banscál 7 co comarnaic ind lánamain.

14. Nir' bo fota t*r*á iarsin co ro dúsig-si.[11]) 'Erig,[12]) a Scoríath', or si. 'IS olc in cotlud a tái', ol si. 'Anál mnáa lat ingin. Cluinte a hosnaid iar ñdul a menmairc[e] uathi.'[13]

15. At*r*aacht iar*um* Scoríath. 'Fintar cia doróne so',[14]) or se, 'co ro gabtar claidib[15]) dó fóchetoir'. Ni *con* fes cia dorone.[16]) 'A cind[17]) dona druidib 7 dona filedaib', or se, 'mani fintar cia doróne.'[18]) 'Bid anim[19]) duit', or Ferch*er*tne, 'do munt*er* [fessin R] do marbad.' 'Do chend da*no* ditso féin!' ar Scoríath,, 'mani aprai.' 'Apair', or Labraid. 'Is leor mo mudugud m'oenur.'[20])

---

[1]) Techtfaide coibni cein bamsa beo R.

[2]) ar na térglas aithech tige di in Herind R. uair na frith cele ba diñgbala di fochetoir YBL.

[3]) hiccoa in[n]ithim se .i. hicoa haire R.

[4]) Ni ro chotlaiset a da suil ria maitin, YBL. ni ro chomthuilset a da suil se*de* riam, *acht* indara n-ae hic aire R.

[5]) Ro char ind ingen im*morro* Labraid R. ro charastair iudningeu inni Labraid YBL.

[6]) aurgnam R.   [7]) comarcc R.   [8]) sephnad R.

[9]) coro chomthuiled R.

[10]) chruit YBL. Ni derchelt C*r*aiptine i cruittirecht dádaig co ro chomthuil a m*áth*air-si R.

[11]) co ro*n*duisich si YBL. co ro di*u*ssaich-si R.   [12]) Atrae suas R.

[13]) iar techt a menmaircce R. iar ndul a mm[enm]airci uadi YBL.

[14]) ç*ia* rogni in gnim so R. cia doroni so YBL.

[15]) co ro gabthar claideb YBL. co ro claidbither R.

[16]) dorigni R. doronne YBL.   [17]) cenna R.

[18]) noco fessat cia rogni inso R.   [19]) danim LL. ainim YBL.

[20]) mo mugug*u*d ammoenur YBL. is lor mo gabail ind R.

16. IS and asbert Ferchertne:

Ni ceilt céis céol do chruit Chraptine co corastar[1]) for sluagu suanbás consreth[2]) coibnius etir sceo Máin Moriath mac-dacht Morca mo cech[3]) lúag Labraid.

'Labraid', or se, 'condranic frie[4]) iar for tálgud do chruit Chraipthine.'

Ro mertsom a muntir is-suidiu.

17. 'Maith tra', or Scoriath, 'ni con terglansam-ni céli diar n-ingin cosin nocht ara seirc lind. Cia no bemis-ni ica thogu iss é fuaramar and.[5]) Déntar ól istaig',[6]) ol se, '7 tabar a ben for a láim Labrada. Ocus ní scersa fris', or se, 'co rop rí Lagen.'

18. Do thaet iarum a ben chucai 7 foid leis.

19. Ocus doberat[7]) sluagad fer Muman iarsin[8]) cor-roachta-tar[9]) Dinn ríg in cetorcain. Ocus atroas[10]) techt ar in orggain co ndernsat comairli mbrecaig ind oic amuich[11]) .i. Craptine do dul forsin doa[12]) in dúni do seinm[13]) suantraige don téluag innund condarralad[14]) dara cend. Ocus in sluag ammuig[15]) do thabairt a n-aigthe fri lár 7 a mmeóir[16]) ina cluasaib conna cloistis in seinm.[17])

20. Co mbo ed ón[18]) dognithe and, 7 co torchratar ind fír, [thall dara cenn h(i) suan R], 7 co ndechas ar in dún, 7 co ralad ar[19]) in téluaig, 7 co ro hort in dún.

21. Ro bói-si didu for in téluagud[20]) .i. Moriath. Nir'bo miad lési[21]) didu a mméra do chur ina cluasaib ria céol feisin,[22]) co mbói tri thráth ina cotlud, ar ni ro lamad a gluasacht. Unde dixit [Flann R] mac Lonáin:

---

[1]) carsadtar YBL.　　[2]) consreth YBL. consrec LL.

[3]) cech YBL. cein LL.　　[4]) comarnic fria R.

[5]) Cia no bemis ica thoga suidhe dorad Dia duu YBL. is ciau no beinmis 'coa thogu is e dorat Dia dun R.

[6]) isintig YBL. Gaibther ol istich R.　　[7]) doberar YBL.

[8]) doberar slog Muman leis iar suidiu R.

[9]) co rochtatar YBL. co ro ortsat R.

[10]) atroos R.　　[11]) do muich YBL.　　[12]) for dui R.

[13]) senmaim R.　　[14]) conos-tarlad R.　　[15]) immuich R.

[16]) am-mera R.

[17]) arna cloistis in sephain R. con na cloistis in tsenm YBL.

[18]) Combua son R.

[19]) ro lad a n-ar in téluaig YBL. co ro lad ár a sluaig R.

[20]) téluag YBL.

[21]) la Moriath ingin Scoriath la mnai Labrada YBL.

[22]) 7 ni bu mas le am-mer 'na cluasaib riana ceol fessin R.

Feib *conattail* Moriath múad . fiad élúag Morcae, mó *cach* scéol,[1]
dia n-ort[2]) Dind ríg, [p. 270a] réim cen tréis . dia sephaind[3]) céis
[cenntoll[4]) céol.

22. Ro gab-som di*du* rige Lagen iarsin, 7 batar [hi R]
córe 7 Cobthach; *ocus* is and ro bói a sossad[5]) som, i nDind ríg.

23. Fechtas im*morro* ro gab-som 7 lánrige la Cob*thach*. Ro
chuirestar[6]) iar*um* in ní Chobthach do denam a me*n*man 7 do
airiuc[7]) thuile dó. Dorónad teg lesseom da*no* arachind Chob-
thaig. IMchomnart[8]) im*morro* a tech, d'iurn[9]) ete*r* fraig 7 lár
7 chomlada[10]) doronad[11]) a tech. Lagin oco denam bl*iadan* lán,[12])
7 do ceiled athair ar a mac 7 math*air* ar ingin, [7 fer ar mnai,
7 ben ar fiur, con na chuala nech o cheiliu cid imthiagtais 7
cia du tarclamtais a trelmu 7 a n-aicdida R.] IS dó atá[13]) 'nit
lia Lagin rúni'. IS and doronad[14]) a tech i [n]Dind ríg.

24. Ro cured[15]) di*du* Cob*thach* [don lind 7 R] dond irgnam,
7 dolluid[16]) .xxx. ríg imbi do rigaib Her*enn*. Forémdes[17]) im-
morro[18]) o Chobthach dul issin tech *co* *n*digsed máthair Labrada
7 a druth. Is *ed* dorróiga in drúth, be*n*nachtu Lagen 7 soiri a
chlainne[19]) co bráth [de R]. Ar maithi*us*[20]) [im*morro* R] dia
mac dochuaid[21]) in ben. Ésseom féin .i. Lab*raid* oca ferthaigis[22])
[in n-aidchi sin R].

25. Luid-seom arnabarach do chluchi f*r*isna gillu[23]) isin
léna. *C*onaccai a aiti hé.[24]) Imbrid-side oenchossid[25]) sciach
f*or* a druimm 7 f*or* a chind ind Labra*da*. 'IS dochu', or se,
'bid echt la mac echt[26]) latso. Olc duit, a gill*a*', or se, 'rí
Her*enn* do thocoiriud[27]) co trichait ríg[28]) imbi cen bith ria
mbeolu oc airiuc thuili dóib.'[29])

---

[1]) concatail . . . seol YBL.
[2]) diar' ort R.
[3]) diar' sephain R.   [4]) centoll LL, R. cendtoll YBL.
[5]) a longport-som 7 a sosad YBL. hi comfosaud R.
[6]) Ro thocuir-seom R.   [7]) thairiuc R.   [8]) ba himdaingen R.
[9]) Do iurn aithlegtha huile R.   [10]) chomlaid R.
[11]) argniad R.   [12]) bliad*a*in lain 'co a denaim R.
[13]) Unde dicitur R. is de ata YBL.   [14]) rognid R.
[15]) Ro thocuired R.   [16]) dolotar . . . lais R.
[17]) Atroas R. foroemthes YBL.   [18]) YBL. inserts *forro*.
[19]) dia chlaind R.   [20]) Ar mathi*us* YBL. ar a aithius LL.
[21]) doluid R.   [22]) ferdthigsead YBL. ba ferdaigsig R.
[23]) dia chluchu lasin ngillaraid R.
[24]) *co*na facca a aite oc suidiu R.   [25]) oen choisi side sciath YBL.
[26]) ce*ch*t YBL. echt LL, R.   [27]) chuiriud R. thocuiriud YBL.
[28]) ardrig R.   [29]) duind YBL.

26. Gebid imbi iar*um* *ocus* luid chucu issa tech. 'Tene
duib', or se, '7 lind 7 biad isa tech.' 'IS cóir',[1]) ar Cob*thach*.
Nonbur do *for* lár in taigi. Sreṅgait in slabraid bái assin chomlaid ina ndiaid *conda*-ralsat ar in coirthe indor*us* taige,[2]) *ocus*
ro sétea na t*r*i chóicait bolg goband doib immon tech, 7 cethrur
oclách *for*[3]) ca*ch* bulg,[4]) co mbo te don tslúag.[5])

27. 'Do mathair [thall R], a Labraid!' ar na[6]) óic.

'Nathó, a m*a*ccucán', or si:[7]) 'dénasu th'einech thriumsa,
ar atbelsa chena.'[8])

28. Orggthir t*r*a [and sin YBL] Cob*thach* Cóel secht cetaib
7 co[9]) .xxx. ríg imbi[10]) [aidchi notlac mair intsaindriud R]. In*de*
dicitur:[11])

> Trí chet bli*a*dan, buadach rím[12]) . re ṅgein Chr*ist*, comp*er*t nóeb,
>   nirbo bratharda, ba holc . orta Lorc la Cobthach Cóel.'
> Cob*thach*.Cóel co t*r*ichait ríg[13]) ron ort Labraid lirdes muad,
>   mac m*e*ic Loegaire din lind . i nDind ríg ra hort in slúag.

29. *Ocus* is de sin asb*er*t Ferch*er*tne file:

> Dind ríg ropo Thúaim Tenbath[14]) .xxx. fariach ropua find[15])
> bebsait brusi*us*[16]) breósus bure lond Labraid láth ṅgaile[17]) hua
> Luirc Lóeg lond sanb setne sochla coel Cobthach.

> Cond mál[18]) muridach mandras[19]) armu brathar athar Ollam
> Máin m*a*ccu ána Ugaine

.i. Máin ollom-som i tossaig, Labraid Móen iarsin.[20]) Lab*r*aid
Loṅgsech im*m*orro o luid *for* loṅgais[21]) [dia ragaib rige co Muir
n-Icht, dia tuc na gaullu imda leis .i. cc. ar fichet cet gall cosna
laignib lethnaib 'na lamaib, et de quibus Lagin dicuntur. R.]
        Orggain Dind ríg insin.[22])

---

[1]) Maith lind samlaid R.

[2]) conas-ralsat im choirthi ar dor*us* in tige R.   [3]) ar R.   mbolg YBL.

[4]) gach.   [5]) commui the in sluagh, YBL.

[6]) ind R.   [7]) Ni tho a m*e*ic, ar sise R.

[8]) itbelsa olchena R.   [9]) cc LL.

[10]) Oircthir annsain Cob*hach* co .xxx. ardrig, co .uii. cetaib sloig R.

[11]) is de asrubairt YBL.

[12]) R omits the rest of this quatrain.

[13]) R omits the rest of this quatrain.

[14]) R omits the rest of this obscure composition.

[15]) t*r*icha nareach ro bo ron YBL.   [16]) bebsat bruisis YBL.

[17]) elga YBL.   [18]) Connmail YBL.   [19]) mandruas YBL.

[20]) iarsuidiu R.   [21]) o doluid *for* a morloṅgais R.

[22]) *con*id Orgain Dind rig sin for Cobthach Coel Breg. FINIT. YBL.
Orgain Denna rig in sain R.

The Destruction of Dind ríg.
(Book of Leinster p. 269.)

1. Whence is the Destruction of Dind ríg?

Easy (to say). Cobthach the Meagre of Bregia, the son of Ugaine the Great, was king of Bregia, but Loegaire Lorc, son of Ugaine, was king of Erin. He, too, was a son of Ugaine the Great. Cobthach was envious towards Loegaire concerning the kingship of Erin, and wasting and grief assailed him, so that his blood and his flesh wasted away. Wherefore he was surnamed the Meagre of Bregia, and Loegaire's murder was brought about.

2. So Loegaire was called to Cobthach that he might leave him his blessing before he died. Now when Loegaire went in to his brother the leg of a hen's chick is broken on the floor of the house. 'Unlucky was thine illness', says Loegaire. 'This is fitting', says Cobthach: 'all has departed, both blood and bone, both life and wealth. Thou hast done me damage, my lad, in breaking the hen's leg. Bring it hither that I may put a bandage round it.'[1] 'Woe is me', says Loegaire, 'the man has decay and destruction: he is delivered into neglect.' 'Come tomorrow', says Cobthach, 'that my tomb be raised by thee, and that my pillar-stone be planted, my assembly of mourning be held, and my burial-paean be performed; for I shall die swiftly.' 'Well', says Loegaire, 'it shall be done.'

3. 'Well, then', saith Cobthach to his queens and his steward, 'say ye that I am dead, but let none other know it, and let me be put into my chariot with a razor-knife in my (right) hand. My brother will come to me vehemently, to bewail me, and will throw himself upon me. Mayhap he will get somewhat from me.'

4. This was true. The chariot is brought out. His brother came to bewail him. He comes and flings himself down upon Cobthach, who plunges the knife into Loegaire at the small of his back, so that its point appeared at the top of his heart, and thus Loegaire died, and was buried in Druim Loegairi.[2]

---

[1] An action indicating utter destitution: compare *Silva Gadelica* I, 410, line 24, II, 446.

[2] Compare the story of Ragallach and his nephew, *Silva Gadelica* I, 394, II, 429.

Loegaire left a son, even Ailill of Ane. He assumed the kingship of Leinster. The first parricide did not seem enough to Cobthach, so he gave silver to some one who administered a deadly drink to Ailill, and thereof he died.

6. After that, Cobthach took the realm of Leinster. Now Ailill of Áne had left a son, even Móen Ollam. Now he was dumb until be became a big man. One day, then, in the play-ground, as he was hurling, a hockey-stick chanced over his shin. 'This has befallen me!' says he. 'Moen *labraid* ("speaks")', say the lads. From that time Labraid was his name.

7. The men of Erin are summoned by Cobthach to partake of the Feast of Tara. Labraid went, like every one, to partake of it. Now when they were most gloriously consuming the banquet, the eulogists were on the floor, lauding the king and the queens, the princes and the nobles.

8. 'Well then', says Cobthach, 'know ye who is the most hospitable (man) in Erin?' 'We know', says Craiphtine (the Harper), 'it is Labraid Loingsech, son of Ailill. I went to him in spring, and he killed his only ox for me.' Says Ferchertne the Poet: 'Labraid is the most hospitable man we know. I went to him in winter, and he killed his only cow for me, and he possessed nothing but her'.

9. 'Go ye with him then!' says Cobthach, 'since he is more hospitable than I.'

'He will not be the worse of this', says Craiphtine, 'and thou wilt not be the better.'

'Out of Erin with you then', says Cobthach, 'so long as thou art alive!'

'Unless we find our place (of refuge) in it', says the lad.

10. They are then rejected. 'Whither shall we go?' says the lad. 'Westwards', answered Ferchertne.

11. So forth they fare to the king of the Men of Morca, the Men of Morca that dwelt about Luachair Dedad in the west. Scoriath is he that was their king.

12. 'What has brought you?' asked Scoriath.

'Our rejection by the king of Erin.'

'Ye are welcome', says Scoriath. 'Your going or your staying will be the same (to us) so long as I am alive. Ye shall have good comradeship', says the king.

13. Scoriath had a daughter, whose name was Moriath. They were guarding her carefully, for no husband fit for her had been found at once. Her mother was keeping her. The mother's two eyes never slept (at the same time), for one of the two was watching her daughter. Howbeit the damsel loved Labraid. There was a plan between her and him. Scoriath held a great feast for the Men of Morca. This is the plan they made — after the drinking, Craiphtine should play the slumber-strain, so that her mother should fall asleep and Labraid should reach the chamber. Now that came to pass. Craiphtine hid not his harp that night, so that the queen fell asleep, and the (loving) couple came together.

14. Not long afterwards the queen awoke. 'Rise, O Scoriath!' says he. 'Ill is the sleep in which thou art. Thy daughter has a woman's breath. Hearken to her sigh after her lover has gone from her.'

15. Then Scoriath rose up. 'Find out who has done this', quoth he, 'that he may be put to the sword at once!' No one knew who had done it. 'The wizards and the poets shall lose their heads unless they find out who has done it.' 'It will be a disgrace to thee', says Ferchertne, 'to kill thine own household.' 'Then thou thyself shalt lose thy head unless thou tellest.' 'Tell', quoth Labraid: ''tis enough that I only should be ruined.'[1])

16. Then said Ferchertne: 'The lute hid no music from Craiphtine's harp till he cast a deathsleep on the hosts, so that harmony was spread between Moen and marriageable Moriath[2]) of Morca. More to her than any price was Labraid'.

'Labraid', says he, 'forgathered with her after ye had been lulled by Craiphtine's harp.'

In this he betrayed his companions.

17. 'Well then', says Scoriath, 'until tonight we have not chosen[3]) a husband for our daughter, because of our love for her. (But) if we had been choosing one, 'tis he whom we have found here. Let drinking take place within', says the king,

---

[1]) Compare the story of the nun, *Lismore Lives*, Preface X, line 12.

[2]) With *etir sceo Main Moriath* compare *isnaib inscib sco eulis ind ecnai* 'in verbis sapientiae et τῆς prudentiae', Cambray sermon.

[3]) *terglansam* = *to-aith-ro-glendsam*, pret. pass. sg. 3 *térglas* supra 13 R, verbal noun *teclimm* Wb. 1 d 1.

'and let his wife be put at Labraid's hand. And I will never part from him till he be king of Leinster.'

18. Then Labraid's wife came to him and sleeps with him.

19. And thereafter they deliver a hosting of the Munstermen till they reached Dind ríg (for) the first destruction. And they were unable to destroy it until the warriors outside made a deceptive plan, namely, that Craiphtine should go on the rampart of the fortress to play the slumber-strain to the host within, so that it might be overturned, and that the host outside should put their faces to the ground and their fingers in their ears that they might not hear the playing.

20. So that was done there, and the men inside fell asleep, and the fortress was captured, and the garrison was slaughtered, and the fortress was sacked.

21. Now Moriath was on the hosting. She did not deem it honourable to put her fingers into her ears at her own music, so that she lay asleep for three days, no one daring to move her. Whence said Flann Mac Lónáin:[1])

'As great Moriath slept before the host of Morca — more than any tale — when Dind ríg was sacked — course without a fight — when the hole-headed lute played a melody'.

22. Thereafter Labraid took the realm of Leinster, and he and Cobthach were at peace, and his seat was at Dind ríg.

23. Once upon a time, however, when he had taken it, and Cobthach had the full kingship, he induced this Cobthach to do his will and meet his desire. So a house was built by him to receive Cobthach. Passing strong was the house: it was made of iron, both wall and floor and doors.[2]) A full year were the Leinstermen abuilding it, and father would hide it from son, and mother from daughter, husband from wife, and wife from husband, so that no one heard from another what they were going about, and for whom they were gathering their gear and their fittings. To this refers (the proverb): 'not more numerous are Leinstermen than (their) secrets'. Where the house was built was in Dind ríg.

---

[1]) He died, according to O'Curry (*Manners* etc. III, 24), A. D. 891.

[2]) Here should come some words corresponding with the *immárrabatar in da thech claraid* ('round which were the two houses of boards') in *Mesce Ulad*, LL. 268 b 21. Otherwise there would have been no combustible materials.

24. Then Cobthach was invited to the ale and the feast, and with him went thirty kings of the kings of Erin. Howbeit Cobthach was unable to enter the house until Labraid's mother and his jester went in. This is what the jester chose (as his reward for doing so): the benediction of the Leinstermen, and the freedom of his children forever. Out of goodness to her son the woman went. On that night Labraid himself was managing household matters.

25. On the morrow he went to play against the lads in the meadow.[1]) His fosterer saw him. He plies a one-stemmed thorn on Labraid's back and head. 'Apparently', saith he, 'the murder thou hast (to do) is a murder by a boy! Ill for thee, my lad, to invite the king of Erin with thirty kings, and not to be in their presence, meeting their desire.'

26. Then Labraid dons (his mantle) and goes to them into the house. 'Ye have fire, and ale and food (brought) into the house.' 'Tis meet', says Cobthach. Nine men had Labraid on the floor of the house. They drag the chain that was out of the door behind them, and cast it on the pillar-stone in front of the house; and the thrice fifty forge-bellows they had around it, with four warriors at each bellows, were blown till the house became hot for the host.[2])

27. 'Thy mother is there, O Labraid!' say the warriors.

'Nay, my darling son', says she. 'Secure thine honour through me, for I shall die at all events.'

28. So then Cobthach Coel is there destroyed, with seven hundred followers and thirty kings around him, on the eve of great Christmas precisely. Hence is said: Three hundred years — victorious reckoning — before Christ's birth, a holy conception, it was not fraternal, it was evil — (Loegaire) Lorc was slain by Cobthach Coel. Cobthach Coel with thirty kings, Labraid .... slew him (Lugaid). Loegaire's grandson from the main, in Dind ríg the host was slain.[3])

---

[1]) So as to disarm Cobthach's suspicion?

[2]) For the incident of roasting people alive in an iron house see also *Mesce Ulad* LL. 268b, and the reference in the Mabinogi of Branwen (Red Book I, p. 31), where Llassar Llaesgyfnewit and his wife Cymideu are said to have escaped 'or ty haearn yn Iwerdon pan wnaethpwyt yn wynnyas yn eu kylch'. See K. Meyer, *Gael and Brython*, p. 44.

[3]) These quatrains are taken from a poem beginning A chóicid chóem

29. And 'tis of this that Ferchertne the poet said: 'Dind ríg, which had been Tuaim Tenbath,' etc.

i. e. 'Máin Ollam' he was at first, 'Labraid Moen' afterwards, but 'Labraid the Exile', since he went into exile, when he gained a realm as far as the Ictian Sea, and brought the many foreigners with him (to Ireland), to wit, two thousand and two hundred foreigners with broad lances in their hands, from which the Laigin (*Leinstermen*) are so called.

This is the Destruction of Dind ríg.

Chairpri chrúaid, ascribed to Orthanach húa Cællama Cuirrich, a defective copy of which is found in Rawlinson B 502, fo. 50 b 2, where they read as follows:

Coic bliad*na* buadach rim . ria ngein Cr*í*st, ni comrim chloen,
cia do braithirse ba holcc . orta Lorcc la Cobthach Coel.
Cobthach Cæl co *trichait* rig . ronort Labraid, lith co mbuaid,
mac meic Lægaire dond lind . i nDind rig roloisc in téluaig.

(K. M.)

Cowes, Isle of Wight.   WHITLEY STOKES.

A LIST OF ANCIENT IRISH AUTHORS.

(Book of Ballymote, 308 b 12.)

Nai persaind in Senchusa Moir bérla Fene .i. tri rig 7 tri fllid 7 tri naeim .i. Patraic, Beneoin, Cairneach na tri naeim . Laegairi, Corc, Dairi na tri rígh . Ross, Dubthach, Feargus na tri fllid . ut

> Laegairi, Corc, Dairi dur . Patraic, Beneoin, Cairnech coir,
> Ros, Dubthach, Fergus co feib . nói sail[gi] sen Senchuis Moir.

Reraid o thus domain co dilind.
Tuan mac Cairill o dilind co Patraic.
Colum cille 7 Finnia iar Patraic.
Findtan mac Bochra iar Colum cille.
Suide, druidi, fllid iar Finntan.
Dallán hua forgaill in fili . ut .i.

> Dallan mac Alla meic Erc . meic Feradaigh gan timi,
> ardollam Erenn gan on . is e ro mol Colum cille.

Cathbadh primrighdrai.
Na teora Fercertne in fllid.

> Fercertne caem comcubaid . Labradha Luirc lai
> Fercertni i fail Concobair . Fercertni i[c] Coinr[a]i.

Colman mac Coimgellain in sai 7 in fili.
Cennfaelad mac Ailello.
Athairne Ailgisech cona scoil.
Amairgin mac Ecicsalaigh.
Amairgin glúngel mac Miled.
Nera mac Morainn in drai.
Morann mac Main in t-oghmoir.

Ogma mac Elathan meic Delbaid.
Nera mac Findchuill a Sid al[1]) Femin.
Morann mac Coirpri Croimcind.
Morann mac Cairpri Cind chait.
Bresal briuga bochétach.
Cormac mac Airt, hua Cuinn cétchathaig.   [col. 2]
Coirbre Liphechair mac Cormaic.
Sencha mac Ailello in sai.
Concobar mac Nesa in ri.
Fuathach firchestach in fili.
Dubh da conn in righ glam.
Roigní Roscadhach in roth-ogaim.[2])
Baetach hua Buirecháin.
Fachtna mac Senchad.
Laigeach fili Mumu eicis.
Critine fili.
Find hua Baiscni.
Eatan ingen Dencecht, in banfili.
Coirpre mac Etna in fili. Dubthach mac hui Lugair in fili.
Sencan Toirpeist in rigfili.
Senbec hua Ebricc in sai ecsidh.
Fithal Firghaeth laechbriathrach.
Eithne ingen Emangaeth.
Bricni mac Carbri in bilteanga.
IN Morrigan.
IN Dagdha.
.xl. iiii.[3]) staraidhe Gaedel ro cumsat in lebur n-airise a sdaraibh
    7 a n-annalaibh.
Cormac mac Culennain ro[ch]um in Sanais Cormaic.
It eat sin persaind senchusa 7 gabala 7 uraiciptha 7 amhra 7
    genilach 7 imagallama.
Finit.

---

[1]) al for ar.
[2]) See BB. 313: Roth-ogam Roigni Roscadaig. (K. M.)
[3]) Written over staraidhe.

Cowes, Isle of Wight.   WHITLEY STOKES.

MITTEILUNGEN
AUS IRISCHEN HANDSCHRIFTEN.

I.
Aus Rawlinson B. 502.

Auf der oberen Hälfte von fo. 40 b 2 *endigt der* Saltair na
Rann *mit der Notiz* fēil Maire hi fogomur indiū. *Dann fährt
derselbe Schreiber fort wie folgt.*

Panechte incip*it* .i. tintūd Duiblitrech h*ūi* Hūathgaile[1])
forsin pandecht Cīrine[2]) trīa gōedeilg inso sīs. Do ardgabalaib
in domuin 7 do chrōebaib coibniusa in domain 7 dia hilchenēlaib
7 do numir a mbērla 7 do āissib a n-airech 7 dia n-anmannaib
7 do æssaib in domuin 7 do numir cacha āesse.   5

Do rēir in septīn inso.

1 Cētna amser bethad bind,   ō thūs domuin co dīlinn,
  dā cēt cethracha immalle,   dā blīadain is dā mīle.

2 Is d'æs tānaissi, nī tár,   ō dīlinn co Abrahám
  nōi cét ō chīanaib, is cet,   dā blīadain is dā fichet.   10

3 Ochtmoga blīad*an* co mblaid,   fiche blīadan[3]) do blīadnaib,
  cēt ar thrī mīlib namān[4])   ōn chētchrut[h]ad co Abrām.

4 Ō Abrām co tempul ūDē   nōi cēt blīad*an*, būan in rē,
  do rēir rīagla, is lōr a fat,   cethri blīadna ochtmogat.

5 Atāt cōic blīadna is cōic [c]ét   ō Abrām, nī himmarbréc,   15
  cor'dluiged Muir Romuir rūad   rīa Mōise cona mōrslūag.

---

[1]) *Siehe Atkinson in der Einleitung zum Faksimile des Book of*
Leinster, S. 32.

[2]) *i. e. Pandecta Hieronymi.*   [3]) *Zu lesen* cethri blīadna.

[4]) == nammá; n *ist müssiger, gleichsam deminutiver Zusatz des Reimes*
wegen. *Vgl.* trán, *S.* 18, *Z.* 12.

6 Ō Mōisi co tempul trēn   cethri chēt blīadan atbēr,
   a nōe sechtmogat fri sein,   is ceirtidde[1]) in chomāirim.
7 A cūic sechtmogat trī chēt   ō rotoglad Trōe na trēt,
   īar n-āis Mōise, īarair lat,   in chūiced blīadain trichat.
8 Tricha *ocus* cethri blīadna   ar ocht cētaib cōemrīagla
   ō Abrām co togail Trōe   cen imroll, cen immargōe.
9 Ō rotoglad Trōe na tor   co rochumtaiged tempol
   do blīadnaib, nī sæb in sēt,   ōenc[h]ōeca ar ōen fri ōenchēt. C.

Dēbi na fīrinni ebraide frisin *sechtmog*ait tintūdac*h* inso sīs.

1 Cétaimmser in bethad bind   ōthā Ādam co dīlinn
   sē blīad*na* cōicat, rād ūglō,   ar sē cētaib ar mīle.
2 Ind aimser thānaisse tr*á*n   ō dīlinn co Abarām
   a dō nochat, guth ūglūair ūgrinn,   ar dā cēt *m*blīad*an* *m*blāithbind.
3 In tress amser, fēg co fīr,   ōthā Abrām co Dauīd,
   a dō cethrachat cen ail   ar nōi cētaib do blīadnaib.
4 In chethramad chnbaid chōir   ō *s*hain[2]) co brait[3]) *m*Babilōin
   trī blīad*na* *sechtmog*at sain   ar chethri cētaib cōemaib.
5 In chūiced ōn brait blāith bil   co gein maic Dē i mBethil,
   a nōe *ochtmog*at fīl ann   ar cōic cētaib, cāin cumaūg.
6 In tsessed ō gein Crīst chōir   co lathe brātha bāgmōir,
   nī fītir nech *acht* Dīa dil   cid bīas isind aimsir sin.
7 In tsechtmad, is gnīm glan glē,   i comsīniud friu huile
   ō Abēl, fīriāl a dath,   cosin fīriān ūdēdenach.   [fo. 41 a]
8 Ind ochtmad ō *s*hain imach   is ī side in tsīrsæglach,
   innisimm, is nī brēc dam,   nā bīa crīch ar a cētmad. Cēt.
9 Crīst ar cara rochain cess,   Crīst co rala frim arddless,
   [Crīst] roncuinnig ō chēin chain,   Crīst ar cuiniud īar cētaib.
                            Cētaimser in bethad binn.

Sex aetates sunt mundi, *id est* ō Ādam co dīlinn in chētna
æs, ō dīlinn co Abrām ind æs tānaisi, ō Abrām co Dau*i*d in
tres æs &c.

De Babilonia *h*oc carmen.   [fo. 43 b 2]

1 Babilōin roclos hi cēin,   dind rochumtaig Nīn mac Bēil
   ar sīr-ecla slait na slōg,   cathir dīrecra dīmōr.
2 Cethrochair in chathir chain,   dona flathib fōt n-ortain,
   sūairc solus, sēt co nglaine,   co cēt ūdorus n-umaide.
3 Sesca mōr-mīli immacūairil,   rob hē a tomus, nirbu dūairc,
   do chēm*en*daib ūird ellaig   īar rēm*en*daib rothennaib.

---

[1]) *Ueber dem zweiten d und unter e puncta delentia.*
[2]) *Ueber o*s*hain ein Zeichen* (··), *welches auf* co Dauid *in* V. 3
zurückweist.
[3]) braith *MS.*

4 Cōica cubat tigi am-mūir, annsa a thogail do nach dūil,
 dā cēt cubat, comul ūglē, sūas i n-aēr in-hairdde.
5 Fichi cetharrīad, cōem dūib, talldais *for* mulluch am-mūir,
 gnīm cen nach cleith *cumuing* lib, *etir* dā sreith do thigib.
6 Nī dernad rīam tīar *nó* thair *etir* selbaib sīl Ādaim, 5
 foclaim, ar is caṅgen chōir, dūn daṅgen mar Babilōin. Babil.
7 Tic sruth nĒofrait dar a lār, de bæ glēo-throit is glēo-dāl,
 conde roforbad a fōir is rotoglad Babilōin. Babil.
8 Dodechaid Cīr līn a slūaig dochum in tsrotha ruitrūaid,
 roscāil, rofadail 'masech, *co mba* sēt soraid soinmech. 10
9 Luiditar trīa brīg ṁbrotha innund for slicht in tsrotha
 co dorus in tigi mōir i mbāi in rī 'sin Babilōin. Babilōin.
10 Īar sin roairg cathraig Nīn cona rīgraid, cona rīg,
 Ballasair, ba hardd a blad, robo mac do Negussar.
11 Negussar co lūathi a hech, mac *side* Labudsardech, 15
 Labudsardach crūaid i cath ba mac Euilmoradach.
12 Euilmoradach fodēin ba mac Nabcodoin nār fēil,
 is hic Nabcodon cen fell roairggeth[1]) ar thūs Salem.
13 Ruc brait móir a cathraig ūDē *ocus* romill a aidme,
 rosīachtatar lais dia thaig, læchaib, clēirchib, mnāib, *maccaib*. 20
14 Sechtmoga do blīad*naib* dōib i ndōire 'sin Babilōin,
 co tānic Cīr, comul ūglē, co rofūaslaic a ndōire.
15 Atrubairt friu Cīr Iar sin: 'Ēirgid dia bar tīr feissin,
 ocus imthigid co tenn co rissid Hierusalem'.
16 Īar sin dochūatar fodes dochum a tīre cen chess, 25
 cor'chumtaigset cathraig ūDē *etir* aidmi *ocus* tige.
17 Iar sin insaigis Cīr cain rīge for feraib domuin
 tricha bl*iadan* bāi a glōir 's a hardrīgi i mBabilōin. Babil.
18 Luid Iar sin Cīr līn a slūaig cosin Scithia n-ūabrig n-ūair,
 ic Iarair chāna nī is sīa romarb rīgan na Scithia. 30
19 Cethri flathi*usa* cen on ar mēit neirt, ba cain comol,
 rogabsat in domun ūdōid, am*al* innises canōin.
20 Flathi*us* na nAsarda n-ān co tānic Cīr mō *cech* māl, [fo. 44 a 1]
 flathi*us* Med is Pers, ba glicc, conastānic mac Pilipp.
21 Flathi*us* na nGr*ēc* ūgr*i*bda a ūgāir conastāncatar Rōmāin, 35
 Rōmāin raid²) hir-rīgi Iar sain co tici dēad in domuin.
22 Inad in tuir Nemrūaid nāir ar lār in maige Šennāir,
 sluind im sruth nĒofrait co ūglōir rocumtacht in Babilōin. Ba.

Imrāit*er* sunn da*no* do aidedaib na prīmflatha 7 dond lucht
foneblatar 7 dona hinadaib in raadnaicthea &c. 40

In diesem Abschnitt (44 a 1) *wird die Entfernung zwischen
Himmel und Hölle auf* 365 *Tagereisen* (cōic huidi sescat ar .ccc.)
angegeben: ar iss *ed* sain fil ōn Babilōin sīansaidi .i. ō ifurn hi

---

¹) roairggech *MS.* ²) *Zu lesen* Rōmānrad?

fail cach cummasc 7 cach ṁbūadrech cosinn Hierusalem nemda
hi fail cach sīd 7 cach sonmigi. Acht chena filet .clxxui. passe
in cach uide 7 dā staid ar fichit[1]) in cach huidi.

Secht cōicat huide co ṁbrīg,	a cōic déc cen immarīm
ō Babilōin[2]) duiscthi drenn[3])	co cathraig Hierusalem:[4])
sechtmoga sē passe ar chēt[5])	in cach uidi adbul-mēt,[6])
dorīmet ēcnaide, is glē,	acht sain cenēl cech phasse.[7])

5 (line 5)

Es folgt nun (44 b 1) unter dem Titel Dūan Dublitrech *inso
forsin panechte das aus LL. 141 b und BB. 7 b bekannte Gedicht:*

10 Rédig dam, a Dé do nim,   co hémid, ní hindeithbir,
     éirniud mo chesta, is gním glan,   corop espa olloman.

Es endigt auf fo. 45 a 2 mit dem Verse:

Missi don Chūachmaig ōn chill   hūa Hūathgail[e] a Husenglind:
romruca sech sæbi snēid   torud æne ind Rīg rorēid! Rēdig.

15 *Das nun folgende, dem* fer légind *von Ross Ailithir Mac
Coisse zugeschriebene Gedicht* Rofessa hi curp domuin dúir *ist
von Th. Olden nach der in LL. befindlichen Kopie mit Angabe
der Lesarten unseres Kodex in den Proceedings der R. I. A. 1883,
SS. 219—252 herausgegeben worden. Es folgt oben auf fo. 46 a 1
20 ein Gedicht, dessen Anfang lautet:*

Fichi rīg, cia rīm as ferr?   rogabsat Hierusalem
Iar Saūl sāsaid ar son   co rofāsaig[8]) Nabcodon.

Es endigt fo. 46 a 2 mit dem Verse:

Serntair Hestras dara n-ēis   ocht ṁbliadna Artartarxēs,
25 ocus nī reilced dia thig   Nemias cosin fichetmaid.

*Dann folgt das lange Poem, ebenfalls von Mac Cosse und
zwar im J. 982 (s. V. 34 u. 36) verfasst, dessen einleitendes Gebet*
A Dé dúlig adateoch &c. *ich im ersten Bande dieser Zeitschrift
auf S. 497 abgedruckt habe. Es enthält zunächst den versifizierten
Psalmenkommentar, aus dem ebenda schon einiges mitgeteilt ist.
30 Ich lasse ihn hier vollständig folgen:*

1 Cethrur doræga, nī dalb,   Duid fri cētal na salm:
     Asaph, Eman, ētrocht rūn,   Ethān ocus Ithithūn.

---

¹) fichet *MS.*   ²) .i. ō iffurnn.   ³) .i. crithnaiges dētu.
⁴) .i. co nem in sein.   ⁵) .i. līn fers na biate in sein.
⁶) .i. in cach cēmmim don biait.
⁷) .i. pais stairidi 7 pais sīansaide.   ⁸) rofasaid *MS.*

2 Radascōraigset fōu clais   in *cethrar* co cēill cainmais,
  cīasu Du*i*d rodascan,   is dōib-seom daaselbtar.   [fo. 46 b 1]

3 Deich c*et* i ndīaid cech fir dīb,   ba slūag dīrecra dīrīm,
  fond ōenchlais ic molad Dē,   cia ceōl bad ferr for bith chē? C.

4 Cinnas rochanta in cec*h* thur,   in trīa prōis nō in trīa met*ur*?   5
  is trīa met*ur*, medar úglē,   feib asindfēt Cīrine. Cethr*ur*.

5 Ōr hesriud bātar, cīa bē,   i n-amair mōir-ma*ic* Iasse
  ina mblogaib la cec*h* droúg   do mebuir lasin popoll.

6 Estras dosīarglam īar tain   i n-ord n-ōentad n-ōenlibuir,
  rosuidig rempu, rēil mod,   argum*ent* ocu*s* titol.   10

7 Cid nād gaib*ter* in cach dū   a tituil rīasna salmu?
  dāig is dō thuctha, is dāil úglain,   do sluinn sīansa asna salmaib.

8 Ardosroet eclai*s* Dē   i n-ord n-etal n-airnaigthe,
  conid de gaibdi cen chol   fīr domuin a hur i n-or. Ōr.

9 Cetharda i salmaib, sēol úglē,   cētna stair, stair tān*aise*,   15
  fogabar indib,[1] nī *gus*,   sīan[s] sōer ocus morolus.

10 Is friu be*rair* cētna stair,   fri Du*i*d, fri Solamain,
  fri hingrintide na slōg,   fri Saūl, fri Abisolōn.

11 Stair tāna[i]se sluint*ir* sunn   fri Ezech*i*as, frisin popull,
  frisna rīgu, rēil in clū,   fri Mōise, fri Machabdu.   20

12 Sīansa na salm cona snais   fri Cr*ist* cāid, frisin n-ecla*is*,
  morolus īar sin for leth   fri cach fīriān find figlech.

13 Sechtmoga b*li*adan ar bith chē   bæ Isaias ic fāithsine,
  fri rē *cethri* rīg, nād chēl,   bātar for tīr nIsrahēl.

14 Ozias, Iotham, ētrocht dīas,   Achaz ocu*s* Ezech*i*as,   25
  co luid martrai[2] ar Dīa   i nderiud flatha Ezech*i*a.

15 Nōi b*li*adna dēc,[3] brīg roclos,   ō martrai mōir-ma*ic* Amos
  is *ed* sain do bl*i*ad*n*aib bīas   co fāithsine Herem*i*as.

16 Dorinscan fāithsine ar Dīa   tres b*li*ad*ain* dēc Ioss*i*a
  co mbæ ic fāithsine īar sain   *dā fichit*[4] bl*i*ad*ain* is bl*i*ad*ain*. 30

17 Dorinscanad, cet ō chēn,   fāithsine ard Etzechēl,
  trīa ficheit b*li*ad*an*, būan c*i*s,   būi ic fāithsine ac*ht* rō trī m*i*s.

18 Deichtreib do brith i ndōire   co n-immud a hilmōine,
  dēitreb dīlsigthi ō Dīa   sechtmad b*li*ad*ain* Ezech*i*a.

19 Deichtreb delbda, dingnaib dāl,   ō rosfuc Salmanazār,   35
  a dō *cethrochat* is cēt   cōic b*li*adna sain srethaib sét.

20 Co rucad in dētreb dron   i ndōire la Nab*codon*
  a trī, a *deich* is dā chēt   do bl*i*ad*n*aib sain srethaib sét.

21 Ōn chētdære ar *deichtreb* duind   co trīall athnuigthe in tempuill
  cen chuit merthais, mod[5]) ronsnā,   is fīr senchas, nī sechta. S. 40

22 Dā minfāith dēc derbtait de   ocu*s* *cethri* prīmfāithe
  rodānaigthe a dānaib Dé   trīa *secht* fāthaib fāthsine.

---

[1] indib₃ *MS.*

[2] *Vgl.* dochūatar a martrai 'they underwent martyrdom', *Fél.* cxlvi, 39;
dochōtar martra, *RC.* IX, 18, § 16. *Siehe Stokes, Fél. Index s. v.* martra.

[3] Noi .x. bl. *MS.*   [4] *Oder* cethorcha.   [5] m̄ *MS.*

23 Tría oibriud, aidbliu ca*ch* clū,   tría airdib aidblib iliu,
  tría fissib Dē do gach dū,   tría aslingthiu, tría aiṅgliu,
  tría guth anniūl, nāssad ūglē,   tría thinfisin fāithsine.
24 Fāithsine na salm i fus   do gein Cr*ist* is dia bathius,
  dia frescab*ái*l, in cach dú,   dia cēssud, dia essēirgiu,
25 Do innarba Iudæ cen geis,   do thabairt geinti ar ireis,
  do mōrad fírinni Dē,   do dínsem ca*ch*a clōene,
26 Do messemnacht Cr*ist*, cain clū,   for bíu *ocus* for marbu,
  do heissērgi in betha,   do delmaim in mōrchetha. Cetharda.
27 Cōic thintūda, cain in clū,   atchotaite*r* for salmu:
  tinntūd Simbaig, seōl *co* mbríg,   *ocus* tint*u*d sǣr Septin,
  tintud Círine, cēim ṅdil,   tint*u*d Teothois is Aquil.
28 Tintūd Septin, sāssad ūglē,   is ē side seichmit-ne,
  rotint*ā*iset sūid, seōl ṅdil,   a hebru, a gr*ei*c il-latin,
  rocertaig Du*i*d Iar ceist   fo obil is fo aistreisc.
29 Aurnaigthi dūthrachtach dil,   airēgim ría foichidib,
  deprec*ā*it fri Día, dían mod,   escoine co tairchitol,
  i salmaib sein, seōl as lía,   cibē nosgaba ca*ch* día. A Dē.
30 Trēde dlegair in cach raind,   luic is amsera is persaind,
  atchotaite*r* sunn san chan   ría ṅgr*es*saib athar Solman.
31 Rodascr*i*b Du*i*d ō Día   i tír airmitnech IudÍa,
  roscachain dō dín ca*ch* dū   i n-orddun, i n-arddrigiu.
32 Cipē nosgaba Iar fír   ricfaid ōentaid Hiruphin,
  ní ba mac bāis Iar na*ch* breith,   bíaid it gnāis, a Dē dūlig. A.
33 A nōi no*ch*at, nāssad ūglē,   c*et* comlān la cōic mile
  _ō thosaig domuin, delm ṅdil,   co gein ma*ic* Dē i mBethil.
34 Ō gēnair Cr*ist*, clū cen bēt,   a *do* ochtmog*at* nói cēt
  cosin bl*i*adain bǣ cen chlith   calaind Enair for cūicid.
35 In lín bl*i*adan, milib gal,   ō thūs domuin co cēssad
  fiche dā ch*et* is dā sē   *ocus* ārim cōic mile.
36 Ocht ṁbl*i*adna dēc derbdait de   *acht* fil co dlaid in mile,
  i fail Iar sain, sorcha in tsreth,   ní fitir *acht* Día dūlech. A dē.

*Nun folgen ohne Absatz die schon aus dem Palatinus
Nr. 830 bekannten Verse über die Erschaffung Adams,*[1] *wie
V. 40 angiebt, von Airbertach Mac Cosse aus dem Lateinischen
ins Irische übersetzt. Nach Olden's Untersuchungen*[2] *war Mac
Cosse im letzten Drittel des 10. Jahrhunderts an der Kloster-
schule von Ross Ailithir, jetzt Ross Carbery im Südwesten der
Grafschaft Cork, als* fer légind *thätig. Der Schreiber, welcher im*

---

[1] *Mit Uebersetzung herausgegeben von Stokes in Kuhns Zeitschrift
XXXI, S. 249, und von Güterbock in der Zeitschr. f. vgl. Sprachf. N. F. XIII,
S. 94, kollationiert.*

[2] *Proceedings of the R. I. A. 1883, S. 219. Olden hat aber nicht gesehen, dass unser Mac Cosse identisch ist mit Airbertach mac Coisidobráin,
der als airchinnech von Ross Ailithir im Jahre 1016 (AU.) gestorben ist.*

Jahre 1072—73 *diese Verse auf fo.* 38*a des Palatinus an den Rand geschrieben hat,*[1]) *war gewiss, wie die andern Schreiber desselben Kodex, ein Südire und hat vielleicht in Ross Ailithir seine Bildung erhalten.*

37 Cenn ard Ādaim, ētrocht rād,　　a tīr grinn grīanna Garād,　　　5
　　a bruinnic[h]or, nād brēc brōn,　　a tīr ālainn Ara[dōn].
38 A brū a Lodain is līa,　　a chossa a tīrib Gorīa,
　　is Dīa dorigni dia deōin　　a fuil do usci ind æeōir.
39 A anim do thinfiud Dē　　doridnacht de,[2]) ba gnīm glē,
　　rī condnic brāth buidnib drenn　　is lais cach fāth, cach forcenn. C. 10
40 Airbertach roraith cen ail　　scāiles sūithi sīthamail,
　　a latin i ngoideilgc ūgrinn　　is Mac Cosse rochæmchind. C.
41 In rī rodelb nem im grein　　is darrigne[3]) dia ōgrēir
　　iffern 's in muir medrach mend,　　ocus talam a forcenn. Cenn ard.
42 Innocht fēil Tōmais[4]) cen tlāis,　　ba sūi sōbais fri cach sēis,　　15
　　Tōmas apstal, alt cen bæs,　　ō æs mōr n-astar rochēs.
43 Dīar'cechaing sair, sīd cen meirg,　　i nIndia aird erctha buird,[5])
　　is lais, nirbo lēn in lerg,　　romarb in ferb dia bois buirb.
44 Asbert Tōmas, nirbu dūi,　　athesc do bais dīriuch dōi,
　　bud in crob dia ndernais col　　i mbēlaib coraindiu[6]) læ.　　20
45 Īar sain cing immach in læch,　　cīarbo gæth, fofūair cath crūach,
　　cid ferda rofer a gleō,　　romarb in leō, cīarbo lūath.
46 A lām ind lāich cona lī　　fofūair sār sær for bith chē,
　　dosbeir in cū ar bēlaib cāich,　　feib assebert in fāith Dē.
　　　　　　　　　　　　　　　A Dē dūlig.　　25

Die Midianiterschlacht.

(*Num. cap.* XXXI.)　　　　　[fo. 46 b 2]

1 Rochūala crecha is tīr thair　　etir sretha sīl Ādaim,
　　noco tarla dam cose　　macsamla na crichi se.
2 Iss ī is mō atchū[a]la rīam　　crech ruc Mōisi a tīr Madīan　　30
　　īar n-ār cōic rīg 'sin chath chōir,　　diar'thuit Balam mac Beōir.
3 Cōic mīli sechtmogat sunn,　　is ed lēgthair 'sind lēgund,
　　do chāirchaib, cumnigid lib,　　ar sē cētaib do mīlib.
4 Ārim na n-ech adrīmi　　mīli for sescait mīli,
　　ārim na mbō, finta latt,　　dā mīle sund sechtmogat.　　35
5 Ārim na n-ōg [n]genmnaid ūgrinn　　dā mīli trichat turmim,
　　īar n-ār nam-mac is na mban　　aithle na fer do marbad.
6 Di neoch thānic 'sin gletin　　nī terna ōenfer eter,
　　rīa tūaith Dē, radīan in rath,　　maidid for Madīan meblach.

---

[1]) S. *Güterbock, a. a. O., S.* 94.
[2]) *Mit dem Palatinus* dō *zu lesen.*　　　　[3]) *Vielleicht* dasrigne.
[4]) 21. *Dez. Zu der folgenden Erzählung vgl. das Original in Acta Thomae, ed. Bonnet, S.* 99.　　　　[5]) *i. e.* baird.
[6]) a *unter der Zeile hinzugefügt.*

7 In lín rothuit 'sin chath crūaid   ní fitir nech tess nā tūaid,
   āirim na mac is na mban   ní fíl nech rofessadar.

8 Ro-imred ferg forsna mnāib,   badb derg dochūaid 'na comdāil,
   cona maccaib immalle   ní fūaratar condercle.

9 Dā míle dēc bæ 'sin chath   di thūaith Dē, dāna in teglach,
   dodeochatar ass huili   slān cen esbaid ōenduine.

10 Īar sin tucad asin tír   íarna indriud rēil romín
   crech croda, buidni brassa,   is ī is mō rochūalassa. R.

11 Ana tucsat leō do fadbaib,   d'ētuch, d'argut, d'ōr, d'armaib,
   di chrud blāith builid, sūairc sēis,   is lía turim is aisnēis.

12 Īar n-ēc Mōisi mō cech mūr   ba tōisech dōib Īsu[1] mac Nūn,
   co crīch mbetha, būan a blad,   a crecha rochūalammar. R.

13 Tricha ríg rīmtir ratha   rosmarb Īsu[1] a clēith chatha
   cona slōgaib, borb in plāg,   di thūathaib crōdaib Cannān.

14 Fecht robris chath n-ard n-amra   for cōic rígu rochalma,
   diar'fosta grīan, glēo mbūada,   cía bēo rīam nā rochūala? R.

15 Trīar tenn darala dam-sa,   bad ferr lim coamblad m'am-sa,
   Īsu[1] mac Nūn trēnfer tricc,   Duid, Machabíus mōrglicc.

16 Ní rucsat rīam traig for cūl   for teched, demnigthir dūn,
   ní ragaib friu nert læch lonn   cocad nō cath nō comlonn.

17 Ní rarīm dōib Día ar peccad   guin na geinti dia seccad,
   olcc ar olcc, ba grēs glan glē,   ba hē bēs a n-amsire.

18 Ō thānic Crīst i colainn,   maith ar olcc, is ed molaim,
   dílgud, is gairgiu cach gal,   ar chairdin rochūalamar. R.

19 Ālim, aittchim mac Dē bí,   guidim nōebaūgliu nimi,
   co rís in flaith feib atā   is mo maith rochūala-sa. Rochūala.

II.

Aus Rawlinson B. 512.

Von den Todsünden.

[fo. 39 a 2] Conæmdetar sruithe Ērenn a rīaglaib na screptræ
pennatōir dílgind frepthæ cech pecthæ ō biuc commór. Air rosui-
digthe na hocht n-airig sūalach cona fodlaib fri hícc 7 slānugud
na n-ocht n-airech ndūalchæ co neoch gainedar ūaidib.

Mesrugad co n-ainmneit fri craos 7 mesci. Congbaideta co
ngenus fri sártoil 7 adaltras. Easlabrai co cartōit fri saint 7
cāindūthracht cride fri format 7 meisci.[1] Cennsa co n-āilgeni
fri ferc 7 debthaige. Fāilte spirdalta fri dogailse ndomanda.

Uaman bãis 7 airchræ fri indōcbãil n-ũaibrigh. Fĩr-umoldōit *co*
n-uaman in Coimded fri dĩum*us* 7 ũaill.

It ĕ da*no* nom*in*a na n-erech ndũalachæ indso trĩasmbĩ bãs
cuirp 7 an*m*a cech duine .i. crōes 7 ĕtrad 7 rl.

It ĕ indso anman*n* na fodladh genither ō chræs .i. fãilte 5
nemmeasraigthe, ilar comlabrai, [fo. 39 b 1] b*æ*s cēdluda, daoscaire
imrãiti, inglaine menman, derchãinedh, deogh cen comm*us*, meisci
cen frithgabãil.

It ĕ *immorro* fodlai genethar ó ainmnit .i. fãilte spiral-
taide [*sic*], sochraide cuirp, glaine an*m*æ, tó co toiscide, cētfaide 10
ecnai, immed n-indtliuchta, saigid for rũna Dé.

It ĕ andso freptha in craóis .i. ãine mesraigthe, congain
cride, ũaite séire, mence cestaigthe, frithaire, fled do bochtaib,
dĩdnad ce*ch* goirt, timargna fri ōentrãtha, *c*ummessair saingnũstæ,
ainmne fri cech rēt cor imrãiter.   15

Incip*it* de luxoria.

Luxoria (.i. drũis) tra iss *ed* ainm na dũalchæ tánaisi marbas
anmain duine. Is ĩ tra cland gainethar ōn dũailche si .i. dronua
brĩathar, fursi dochraite, daille menman, ainbsithe aicnith, comlabra borbæ, cuitim hi crinder, ilar comairli, tarngaire cen folta, 20
cētlud fri sochraithe, dethiden do duine, fall fri Dĩa.

Is ĩ da*no* sũalaich roerbath frisin ndũalaich se dia dĩbduth
.i. congbaidet[u] hi ngenus *co* neuch genedar ũaid .i. for*us* comairle,
comlabrai cobsaid, fostai fri anfontai, tairngaire fĩr, fĩr do comal-
lath, imrãdud Dē, fēle aicnid, nertath n-irisi, miscais an ceann- 25
tair, searc in alltair.

It ĕ indso freptha in ētraidh collnaide .i. damnath craois,
pr*o*ind mesraigthe, mesrugud dige, imgab- [fo. 39 b 2] ãil mesca,
miscais cēlithe, brisiuth aicnith, faitiges i n-ũathad, roithinche
hi sochaide, lenv*m*ain do sruithib, imgabãil ōcbada, airchēimniug*ud* 30
di lebair [*sic*] nō da lēgund nō ernaigthe, miscais daescaire co
mbrĩathraib anglanaib, menma sochraithe co nglaine comlabra
searc fochraice ara n-ascnama, pĩana do imchaisiu ara n-imgabãil.

Incip*it* de auaritia.

Auairitia (.i. saint) da*no* iss *ed* nom*en* inna treisi dũalchæ 35
marbas anmuin duine. Is hĩ tra cland 7 geneluch genedar ōn
dũalaigh se .i. accobar cen mesrug*ud*, rocholl *co* nderchōined,
inrath cen cumsanad, airchelad cen trōcaire, gũa cen imcomm*us*,

ēthech cen erchōiliud, faithbe¹) cech maith, airer cech uilc, daille
menman, dīultad aicnid, *forbrissed* cech trūaig, aslach cech triūin,
sant im talma[i]n, brēc uman²) anmuin.

    Is ī tra sūalach roherbad do chathug*ud* frisin ndūalaich se
5 .i. easlabra *co* ndēirc *co* neuch gainedar ūaidi .i. trōcaire *co* ndīl-
gadaig, dīrge co fīrinde, tidnacul co n-áilgine *cen* ūaill, *cen*
grāin, *cen* inire, airchissecht *co* ndígairse *cen* mbrath, cen togāis,
cen tochailche, cāindūthrucht *co* *n*-eslabræ cen gōi, cen ēthech,
cen ēcmailte.

10   It ē andso da*no* freptha inna sainte .i. frestal nūide*n* Cr*ist*,
fled do bochtaib, treabad imthairic, men*m*æ im bochtæ, tōeb *fri*
bennachtain, reimdēicsiu pēne, [fo. 40 a 1] freiscisiu fochraice,
idnaide mbrithe³) ar gnūis an duilemun il-laithiu brāthæ.

Inuidia (.i. formad)

15 iss *ed* ainm inna cethramthæ dūalchæ marbas anmain duine.
Iss ī tra clann 7 genelach geneth[ar] ōn dūalaich se .i. miscais
coimnesam, fodord um cach maith, altugad ce*ch* uilc, tathbiuch
carat, brón *fria* n-airmitin, fāilte fria ndīmess.

    Is ī sūalaich roherbad do chathug*ud* fr*i*sin ndūalaich se .i.
20 cāindūthracht cride cen inire *co* neuch gainethar ūaide do śūail-
chib .i. serc brātharda, *fort*acht cech coimnesaim, degteist di cāch,
miscais écnaig, indarba fodoird,⁴) mōrath cech maith, tāinsium
cech uilc, brīathar āilgean, menmæ airchisech di ce*ch* duine acht
nī b*us* dīr⁵) pecath.

25   ## Ira (.i. ferg)

iss *ed* ainm inna cōicthe dūalche⁶) marbas anmain duine. Amal
tregdas anmain duine fōebur trīa corp, is amlaid tregdas rinn
na fergai in anmain co n-imfolngai bās do suidiu. Is ī tra clann
7 geneluch gainethar ōn dūalaich se na *fe*rcai .i. duinorcain cen
30 dōenchaire, crād ce*ch* coimnesaim cen airchissecht, borrfad men*·*
man cen tairniud, nūall mbrīathar ce*n* trōethad, deabthaige cen
erdībduth, cossaite cen condarclei, athisi cen imrádudh, ēcndach
cen imcom*us*.

---

¹) *Zu lesen* faitbe.   ²) *Zu lesen* im.
³) idnaidę mbrithę *MS.*   ⁴) fodoirt *MS.*
⁵) *Dahinter* et *durchstrichen und mit punctis delentibus.*
⁶) dualchęa *MS.*

Is ī dono sūalach roherbath do cathugad frisin ndūalaig si
.i. censa co n-ailgine co neuch gainethar ūaidi .i. slāine cride,
imgabail debtha, [fo. 40 a 2] brīathar ailgen, timarcain borrfaidh,
sochoisce aicnidh, tūa fri labrai, ainmne fri fochaide, miscuis
ēcndaig, dīlachtai cen athchossan, cāindūthracht cen togais, cuim- 5
liuch cen iníre.

Tristitia (.i. tuirse)

iss ed ainm inna sesside dūailche marbas anmain duine. Atāt
dā gnē forsan dūalig se .i. dogailse domando co nderchōiniud 7
aimiris, dogailse dēoda co ndēeirc 7 cāin-iris. Indalana imfolngai 10
bithfailte i mbithbetha for nim, araile immefolngai bithbrōn i
mbithpīanaib inferno. Hiss ī didu in dogailse imfolngæ faoilte
na hanmæ for nim innī bīs trìa chói pectha co n-iris dīlguda 7
indī bīs tria airchisecht caich triūin 7 cech trūaigh 7 caich
coimnessaim bīs ar obur pecthæ 7 dūalchæ 7 co tuit i ndoescaire 15
7 i trōigi cen iris cen aithrige. Ar antii conessa a pecthæ
fadeisin 7 pecthæ a coimnesaim bīd failid side la Dīa for nim.[1]
Is de asbeir Crīst:[2] Beati qui lugent nunc[3] quoniam ipsi[4] con-
sulabuntur.[5]

In dogailse domunda immorro, atāt trī gnē for suidiu .i. 20
dogailse 7 brōn scartha frisna cardiu calnaide ar ingnais a dōen-
nachta 7 ar a seirc 7 ar a n-inmaine, nō fobithin etarscartha
fria a māine 7 a feba talmandai, nō fobithin etarscartha fria col
7 pecath 7 a tola calnaidi. Is ed dano an gnē tānaise inna
dogailse domundai .i. brōn 7 derchōiniuth di cech accobar atcobra 25
duine cen a orba acht tol Dé namā.

Is ed[6] dano in tres gné ina [fo. 40 b 1] dogailse domundae,
brón 7 dérchāined di cech feib fogaib duine ar homun a foxail
airi 7 a erchra 7 ar omun scartha fria cith iarmaul conna [sic] co
mbī cen brōn 7 dogailse cēin bas mbeō, co tēit īarum ar ceann 30
mbithbrōin dochum péine suthaine cen forcend.

Is hī tra cland 7 geneluch gainethar ón dogailse domundai
.i. serbai co n-inire, anseirce co n-ēcmailte, cruine co foichlighe,
rolabrai co tōi, forlūaman easpæ cen taiscithe, anbsaide aicnith,
utmaille chuirp, foindletha menman fri cech dæscair im tinnscetal 35

---

[1] nimm MS.   [2] x̄p.
[3] nunc steht nicht in der Vulgata.
[4] ipse MS.   [5] Matth. V, 5.   [6] Is s̄s̄ MS.

cech uilc, toipliun 7 laxa fri cech maith, derchōined co tercmenmain i timnaib Dé, fōilte co sonairte i ngnīmaib deabail.

Hit ē *tra* frepthai inna dogailse domundai .i. fāilte spiraltai
co roithinche cride 7 menman fria dogailse ndomunda, grᴇscha
5 ernaigthe co n-āine 7 frithaire fri toifliun 7 cotaltaige, easlabra
col-let[h] *men*man im Dīa fri tercmenmain, mod airchiund di
lubair 7 ernaigthe *fri* forlūamain n-esbæ, hires co ngnīm, fāilte
co n-āilgine fri derchāiniuth 7 inire menman.

Uana gloria (.i. indōcbāil ūaibrech)

10 iss *ed* ainm ina¹) sechtmad dūalchæ marbas anmain duine. Is ɪ
tra clann 7 geneluch gainethar ōn dūalaig si .i. anerlatu co
tairisium, hūall co mōrmenmain, airrecht debtha, [fo. 40 b 2] ecosc
sechta, cosnam éris cen dliged, mōideam deggnīmraid, *cu*mtach
labartha, saobath ēcuisc, saorath cuirp, doerath anmæ.

15   Hit ē da*no* frepthæ roherbath dia hīcc .i. erlatu cen tairisium, humaldōit co fēthamla, imgabāil debthæ, rᴇide²) cen tᴇechtai,
foglaim la sruithe, cobsaithe aicnith, *men*mæ īseal, i*m*chaisiu Dé.

Regula Choluimb Chille.

Diese 'Regula Eremitica seu præscripta fratribus in eremo
20 *degentibus', wie Colgan sie bezeichnet, ist von Reeves im Anhang*
zu seiner Ausgabe von Primate Colton's Visitation of the Diocese
of Derry,³) S. 109, nach einer Abschrift von Michael O'Clery⁴)
mit einer Uebersetzung von Curry herausgegeben worden. Die
Wichtigkeit dieses alten Schriftstückes rechtfertigt den Abdruck
25 *einer zweiten Kopie, die sich auf fo. 40 b 2 des Oxforder Kodex*
befindet, zumal da mehrere fehlerhafte Stellen in O'Clery's Ab-
schrift oder Reeves' Ausgabe hier ihre Besserung finden.

Incip*it* Regula Colaim Cilde.   [fo. 40 b 2]

1. Bith inn-uathad il-lucc foleith hi fail prīmcathrach, minap
30 inill lat cub*us* beth i coitchennd*us* na sochaide.

2. Imnochta do sechim dogrēss ar Crīst 7 ar na soiscēla.

---

¹) ana *MS.*   ²) reide. A *MS.*
³) *Dublin, For the Irish Archæological Society, MDCCCL.*
⁴) *In der Handschrift 5100—4 der Bibliothèque Royale zu Brüssel*
(*S.* 23).

3. Cach bec nō cech mór nomuinichither di cech rét etir locc 7 ēdach 7 dig 7 bīad, rop de forcongrai tsenōra a comair-lecad. Ar nī hinill do crāibdech[1]) airbera bith nach cruth la śōerbrāth fēin.

4. Locc umdaingen umat cona ōendorus.[2]) 5

5. Uathad crāibdech[1]) umarāidet Dīa 7 a timna do tathigid cucat il-laithib līthaib, dot imnertad a timnaib Dē 7 a sgēlaib sgrebtræ.

6. Duine immorro olchenai conscēlaigetar do brīathraib esbaib nó domandaib nó fodordad anní nad cumcat do íocc nó 10 do cuimriuch, acht is mōite fofera sāeth dait ma condístai etir carait 7 escarait, nī rofāemtha cucut, acht berat bennachtain mādroillet.

7. Mog gor̈ crāibdech[1]) nemscēlach dianeta do bith ocut timthirecht. Do sæthar mesraighthe bidh [fo. 41 a 1] cosmail is 15 ed as inill.

8. Comus forēir neich nach aili. Bescna bus cráibdech.[1])

9. Menma irlam fri dergmartrai.

10. Menma fossaid fedil fri bánmartra.

11. Dīlgud ō cride da cech aonduine. 20

12. Aurnaigthe grēsach ar in muintir do tōisigh.

13. Lēire gabāla ēcnairci amal bid sainchara duit cech marb ireseach.

14. Imna anma hi sesam.

15. Do coitchend figell ōn trāth co alaile forēir[3]) neich 25 nach aili.

16. Trī torba isind ló .i. érnaigthi 7 lubair 7 legund.

17. Ind lubfur [sic] do fodail i trī .i. do thorba fadēine .i. do torba do luic do neuch bas fīr-tóis[c] dó, araill do chuit inna . mbrāthar, araill do gor ina coimnesam .i. rop d'forcetul nó scrībend 30 nó cecip tarba arnābeither ind espa, id est ut Dominus ait: Non apparebis ante me uacu[u]s .i. cech nī ina urd chóir.

18. Nemo enim cor[o]nabitur nisi qui legitime certauerit .i. secheam dērce rē cech rēt.

19. Nī airbertha biudh co mba guirt. 35

20. Nī cotalta co mba ēim lat.

21. Nī acallta nech co mba fri toiscc.

---

[1]) craidbech MS.   [2]) doerus MS.   [3]) forēior MS.

22. Nach forcraid no sechna do dīles praind nō do ētach fúir, tabair fri airchisecht inna mbrāthar dochoiset nō do bochtaib olchenai.

23. Serc Dē ō uilib craidib,¹) ō uilib nertaib.

5   24. Searc do coimnesaim amlut fodein.

25. Feidliugud a timnaib Dē tresin uili aimsir.

26. Do mod ernaight[h]e co taothsad do déra, nō do modh di obair tórbaigh nó do slechtan- [fo. 41 a 2] aib co tī th' allas co menic, menbat solma do déra. Finid.

10   *Von heimlichen Sünden.*

[fo. 41 a 2] Imrorāid Grigoir Rómæ, fer ind raith, do pecdaib inclithib na ndōine nā tabrad²) i cobais. Cīid fri Dīa 7 ferais nemēli fris corrofaillsigthe dó an cruth noīcfaitis. Tāinic aingel adochum 7 asbert fris: 'Is mōr do brón 7 do[t] dīdnad tānac-sa
15 ō Día, 7 an duine dia ndéni-siu deithidin, taibred a choibseana fīa[d] Dīa cona dúilib 7 tailced déra 7 bad edh indso chanas: 'Domine quis habitabit'³) et 'Domini est terra',⁴) 'Te decet',⁵) 'Deus in nomine',⁶) 'Deus misereatur',⁷) 'Deus in adiutorium',⁸) 7 'Deus in adiutorium' usque 'Festina' etir gach dā salm et
20 'Appropinquatur' 7 pater 7 'Ascendat usque ad tronum'. 'In fil anaill?' ol Grigoir. 'Fil', ol in t-aingel. 'Trī sailm .i. 'Dominus illuminatio',⁹) 'Judica, Domine, nocentes',¹⁰) 'Exurgat'.¹¹) Doémat na trī sailm sea ar format 7 demnaib 7 erchotib, acht rogabthar gach dīa 7 'Deus in adiutorium' usque 'Festina' etir cech dā
25 salm¹³) 7 pater. Mad dīan-adrige, dā psalm 7 cantaic, 'Confitemini Domino in æternum',¹⁴) 'Super flumina'¹⁵) 'Benedicite'¹⁶) 7 'Ante faciem tuam' usque 'Confirma me'. Nī fil do pecdaib dognē nech ina colainn nā hīcat na harra sa acht ēcndach ạụ Spiruta Naeib.'

---

¹) craide MS.	²) Zu lesen tabrat.	³) Ps. XIV.
⁴) Ps. XXIII.	⁵) Ps. LXIV.	⁶) Ps. LIII.
⁷) Ps. LXVI.	⁸) Ps. LXIX.	⁹) Ps. XXVI.
¹⁰) Ps. XXVI.	¹¹) Ps. XXXIV.	¹²) Ps. LXVII.
¹³) cech da cech da MS.		¹⁴) Ps. CXXXV.
¹⁵) Ps. CXXXVI.	¹⁶) Ps. CXXXIII?	

Die Verwandlungen des Tuán mac Cairill.

(*Vgl. Imram Brain II, Appendix A.*)   [fo. 98 b 2]

1 Tuān mac Cairill roclos[1])   dorad Ísu for anfos,
   dorumalt cēt mblīadan mbúan   a richt duine, ba degdūal.

2 Trī cēt blīadan dó i richt daim   allaid forsna mōrmuigib,
   dorumailt cēt mblīadan mbil   a richt antrellaig allaid.[2])   5

3 Trī cēt blīadan dō for feōil,   dia raibi i richt in tseneōin,
   dorumailt cēt mblīadan mbind   i richt bratāin bodair-chinn.

4 Co fūair lascaire 'na līn,   co tuc leis do dún an ríg,
   ō'tces an t-ēcne glé glan,   romīanaig an banrígan.

5 Rofuineth dī é for ruth,[3])   gu rotomail a hōenur,[4])   10
   rotoirrched an rīgan rán,   is de rochoimpred Tuān. T.

6 Tuān mac Stairn sdiurda slōig,   é mac brāthar Partolōin,
   ba hē Finntān, ferrdi a rádh,   frisi n-abairthea Tuān. T.

7 Is dō atchūaid an scēl sa īar fīr   co nach raib nech 'na imsnīm,
   Finnēn Maige Bile bāin   rōbai [a] acallāim Tuāin. Tuān.   15

Prophezeiung Sétna's.

*Die hier dem Sétna im Zwiegespräch mit seinem Sohne (?)
Finnchú von Brí Gobann in den Mund gelegte Prophezeiung ist
im 12. Jahrhundert geschrieben, da V. 10 die Vertreibung der Hui
Carthaig aus Cashel (A. D. 1139) und V. 14 ff. die englische Er-* 20
*oberung Irlands erwähnen. Mit Uebersetzung herausgegeben von
N. O'Kearney, The Prophecies of SS. Columbkille, Maeltamlacht,
Ultan, Seadhna &c. Dublin 1856, SS. 110—117.*

1 'Apair rim, a Sētna,   scēla deiridh betha:
   cinnus bīas an líne   nách lorg fíre a mbretha?   25

2 'Cinnus bīas an popal   'ga mbīa cocar mebhla?'
   'Nī racha díbh ænnech   andsa rígt[h]ech nemda.

3 'Adeirim-si rit-sa,   a chlēirigh chāidh chunnla,
   ní tēit ar nem nīamda   acht fer dīada[5]) is umla.

4 'Adeirim-si rit-sa   cach rí tic is tír si,   30
   cach rēim tic ar Ērinn,   ní hé grind dochím-si.

5 'Lenfaid fallsacht bunaid   breithemain andligid,[6])
   etir mac is athair   rachait síat da sligid.[7])

6 'Lenfaid clēirigh næmchell   adhaltras is écāir,
   nī fāghat dá taradh   ní asa fāghat étáil.   35

7 'Trēicfit na mná a mbandacht   ar cēilibh gan pósadh,
   dogēnait gan chagar   ní basgfas a nóssa.

---

[1]) roclas *MS.*   [2]) allaig *MS.*
[3]) ruth = rith. *Siehe SR. Ind.* for rith '*eilends*'; *vgl. Imr. Brain II,
S. 304, Anm. 8.*   [4]) hoenar *MS.*   [5]) díaghda *MS.*
[6]) *Oder* andligthig.   [7]) *Oder* sligthib.

8 'Trēigfidh talam toradh   don rēim sin aderim,
    budh fás cach lis lomlān,   budh hé in comhrád neimmbind.
9 'Ticfat plágha troma   ar síl Ádhaim uili,
    rachdait . . ¹) a n-anrēim   trē aimseir Mic Muiri.
10 'Scrisfuighther a Caisel   clann Carrthaig, clann Eogain,
    co ná bía 'na falaid   acht danair is deóraidh.
11 'Teilcfidhther síl sœr Bríain   tar an Sinainn sribhghlain,
    docīm mar a fuilim   a tuitim 'na cinntaibh.'
12 'Cīa scrisfus in líne   atá 'san tír ibraigh?
    abair rim, a Sétna,   na scéla nách inmain.'
13 'A ticfa 'na n-inadh   dogēbhthar a fīss agam,
    a Finnchú BríGobhann,   in slūagh rothrom echtrann.
14 'Ticfa cobhlach Saxan   a crislach cúain Erend,
    terc ré ndingnet míne   ar áidhe a nglérend.   [fo. 121 b 2]
15 'Beit nōi fichit blīadan   a rīghi clāir Fodla,
    nogu ndernat fingail   gan bidbaid dá fógra.
16 'Fellfait ar a chēile   co scáilter a flaithius,
    dergfait cloidbe is túagha,   beit úada gan maithius.
17 'Ticfa mac ríg Saxan   cuca-san tar sáili,
    scéraid sé ré ríghe   Goill in tíre itáim-ni.
18 'Goill is Gáidil Erenn   donīad œnlam daingen,
    a n-agaid slūag Saxan,   nī scarthar a caingen.
19 'Toitfid mac rīg Saxan   a tosach na slūagh sain,
    ō cumusc dā chéili   bíaid Ēiri gan ūamain.
20 'Ríghait énrí ar Ērinn   Goill is Gāidil glana,
    ó ríghait in fer soin,   ní bía esbaid arra.'²) A b.

Mochuta und der Teufel.

[fo. 142 b 2] Mocuta Rathin dorōine roinn dia comtinōl 7
dia āigedhaibh adhaigh³) n-ann. Cach bīad frisi comruicedh a
lām,⁴) rocuimledh a lāma ana brōgaib bīdis uime, co ndechaid
dīabal isin brōig ar in lethcumaid sin. 'Is mōr in rīghe si a
fuilim-si', ar Mocuta, '.i. mōrseiser 7 secht fichet 7 secht cēt, 7
imacallaim fria hainglib da gach treas fer dīb-sin 7 abdaine 7
cennus acam-sa forro-sin uile 7 conad mesa misi oldās ga[ch]
fer dīb-sin. Et nī slighe nime dam-sa sin 7 nī bīu amlaid', ar
Mocuta, 'acht ragad isin luing fil oc himtecht a Hērinn, co nā
rabar dā hadaig a n-aeninad ac oilithre ar fud in domain mōir.'
Ocus ro-ēlo lānmochtrath īarnamāirech co rāinic go hairm a
mbāi Comgall Tighe Teille. Bennachais cāch dīb dia cēle.
40 'Suidh',⁵) ar Comgall. 'Nī hāil lem', or Mocuta. 'Atā tinninus

---

¹) rachdait mit einem Haken unter dem t.   ²) Aus orra korrigiert.
³) aghaidh MS.   ⁴) alam lama MS.   ⁵) suigh MS.

orm.' 'Suidhfidh[6]) im*morro*', ar Comgall. 'Suidhid[7]) Mocuta 7 bentur a brōga de. 'Tair amach asin brōig, a trōig, a dīab*ail*!' ar Comgall, '7 nocha bēra lat an ētāil roforbr*ais*.'[1]) Lingis dīab*al* amach a brōig Mocuta. 'Ni seachmaidh',[2]) ol dīab*al*, 'do tegmail-si annso, ar nī lēicfinn-si do b*eth* dā oidche a n-āeninad ar in l*eth*c*u*maid dorōine sé ar a brōgaib fēin sech brōgaib na manach'. Conad ann dorōine Comgall in rann la fostud Mochuta:

'Maith do cl*ēirech* b*eth* abus *ocus* atāidhe 'na trāth,
dobeir demon cuitmide[5]) spirat utmaille *for* cāch.'

Ocus anais Mocuta oc a muinnt*ir* īar sin 7 nir'fēd dīab*al* ercoit do dēnam dō ōsin amach. Finit. Amen.

III.

Aus Laud 610.

Danklied einer erlösten Seele.

[fo. 9 a 1] I n-araile domnuch do ṡenóir nóemh a ǽnur, co faccaidh in duini círdubh am*al* gūal gobhond cuice isin tech. 'Cūich tussa ale?' forsin senōir. 'Domnach indiū', for sē, '7 nīdampīant*ar*-sa ann 7 nī gabt[h]ar dím dul cech conair is áil dam isin domnuch, 7 ar Día dia foghnai, geib m'écnairc 7 guidh in Coimdhi[dh] lem im deliug*ud* damh re hiff*er*n 7 im rochtain na fochraice nemda.' 'Dagēntar', ar in senóir. Acus doní sumh irnai[g]the cech trātha fair co cend *fichet* lā. Ticed s*um* do*no* cech domnaigh[3]) d'acallaimh in ṡenóra 7 ba gili 'sa gile hé cech tan dorochedh, 7 roatlaigh isin tres domnuch a scaradh re hiff*er*n 7 a bith glēgeal uile 7 isbert: 'Ben[d]acht fort fēin 7 bendacht for th'irnaigthi' 7 dorōine na runna so sís *con*debuirt [fo. 9 a 2]:

1 Bennacht for in n-irnai[g]the, mochin do neoch nodnāile,
maith dontī darrogathar, maith dontī arnodāili.[7])

---

1) suighfidh *MS.* 2) suighid *MS.* 3) roforbrȝ *MS.*
4) *Besser* seachbaidh. 5) *Besser* cuitbide. 6) domnaid*h* *MS.*
7) *Vielleicht* arrodaili?

2 Bennacht ar in n-irnaigthe,   baüaramur[1]) a cennsa,
  demna duba dinsigthe   nobītis imom cenn-sa.
3 Bennacht for in n-irnaigthe   rodingaib dīm in füath sa,
  demna ocus pluic teintide[2])   nobītis ocom lüad-sa.
4 Bennacht for in n-irnaigthe   ruc üaim-si demna is cruma,
  luc[3]) ifernnach ēcāinde,[4])   is ann do[g]nīn-si dubha.
5 Bennacht for in n-irnaigthe   roscar misi re temel,
  cruma crüaidh[i] cennmōra   nomberdis isin teined.[5])
6 Mōr do phecdaib gnīu-sa,   tardis orum ...[6])
  slutaig demna co n-erduibi   bītis im dīaid[7]) a n-iffirn.
7 Süsta imda īarnaide   nogeibdis dam im dīaid,[7])
  in uchd[8]) marbda meirbligi   nobīn-si naddiaig.[9])
8 In irnaigthe atberim-si   romsær ar iath[10]) namabr ...
  is duit-si doberim-si   co brāth īar mbrāth mo bennacht.

Dochüaid as īarsin co n-ëtrochf[a] grēne la hainglīu.

König Fedlimids Rache.

(Vgl. die Annalen der Vier Meister, A. D. 832.)

1 In matra,   cía beith do gairbe a gotha,   [Ib.]
  curthar fīrchenn a srōna   i fīrcenn tōna in tsrotha.
2 In sruith,   cía beith do lēithi a finnai,
  curthar fírcend a srōna   i fircend tōna in gillai.
3 In gilla,   bidsi mur atā,[9])
  curthar fírcenn a srōna   i fírcenn tóna na mnā.
4 In ben   dobí do ghairbhi a freacra,
  curthar fírchenn a srōna   i fírcenn tōna in matra.

Feidhlimidh mac Crimthain rī Mumhan dorōine in lāid so
iar [n-]arcain Clúana mic Nóis 7 īar marbad srotha do mhuinntir
Clúana lais 7 a mná 7 a gillai 7 a matra a ndīghail dīultaidh
dorōine in sruith reim Feidlime 7 a ben 7 a gilla 7 a cú, 7
Feidhlime a richt duine boicht ag taiscelad for Leith Cuinn. Is
amail so dorōine friu ag a marbad nō ag a crapall.[11])

---

[1]) = íofüarammar.   [2]) teintige MS.   [3]) = loc.
[4]) Gen. von ēcāiniud.   [5]) Sic; leg. teinid.
[6]) Ich lese etwas wie nangph..., vielleicht 'na ng[ri]ph ...
[7]) diaig MS.   [8]) Zu lesen lucht?
[9]) Augenscheinlich unvollständig.
[10]) Zu lesen úath?
[11]) crapall 'fesseln, Fessel'. Vgl. i cengul 7 chrapull 7 chuibrech,
LL. 67 b 29. acum chrapull, LB. 235 m. sup. crapall for a ndornaib fria
ndruimm, ib. 156 b 10.

Wunderthaten des Dúnchad húa Bráin in Armagh.

[fo. 14 a 1] Dúnchad húa Bráin .i. comarba Cīarān docūaid
do ailithre co hArdmacha i n-aimsir Mælsechloind Mōir[1] 7 Bríain
maic Cennētig,[2] cu raibi .XIII. blīadna i lumma crābaid i nArd-
macha, cur'līn rath 7 onōir na cathrach hé, cur'fūabrat[3] [fo. 14 a 2] 5
som cu meinicc Ardmacha do fácbāil ar a mēt lais a hanōire
and, co ticed cech droṅg ar timchill do muintir Arda-macha da
fostud, 7 noanad som blīadain o[c] cach droing dīb, ar nīr' āil
dōib a thaissi do brid[4] dō ūaithib, ar donīthea ferta 7 mír-
boile co follus. Ōen di mirbuilib andso sīs.   10

Fect n-ōen dō ina ṡuidi[5] lēigind lá fēil Andrēas apsta[i]l
dorōine sium rand la tothlugud feōla 7 leanna ar in Coimdi[d],
condebairt:

'Da ibaind dig do ūachtur mesrach[6]   do lāim coicci basglain,
   do caithfind feōil do glanmēis   hi fēil Andrēis[7] apstail.'   15

Co ūdechaid a timthirid[8] -sium in lá sin do bein birt lūachra, co
tarrla i tech lānāibind hé 7 dīas and. Rofersit fáilti frisin timthirid[8] ar a tigerna. 'Feōil 7 lind roīar do tigerna andiū' ar-
sīat, 'ar in Coimdid.' 'Is ed', ar in timthirid.[9] 'Do muintir
in Coimdid[10] dūindi', ar sīat, '7 fogēba sium sin ūaindi'. Ocus 20
roceṅglad tocht senṡailli 7 mesair senbrogoitti isin mbert lūachra
7 nīr'doirted hí co ráinicc co hairm i mbói Dúnchad. Roatlaig
Dúnchad sin 7 asbert: 'Bennacht ar in Coimdid', ar sé, 'doratt
dūin proind in læ indiū', 7 rochaith in proind īar sin.

Is ē dono Dúnchad clērech rataithbeōg marb fodeōid i 25
nĒrinn. Bandscal bói i ūdorus in reclesa 7 mac becc aici, cu
fūair bás in mac ócc. Ro-indlaicc in máthair hé co dorus tigi
Dúnchada 7 bói oc a ḟarcsi a hinad ele. Dorīacht Dúnchad co
hairm i mbói in corpān 7 tuc aichni coro do iarraid a taith-
beóghaid tuccad cuicci hē. Dorōini sium irnaigthi[11] lándīc[h]ra 30
7 rachí 7 racēirig[12] in mac. Tāinic in māthair 7 roatlaig do

---

[1] *Oberkönig von Irland* † 1023.
[2] *Oberkönig von Irland* † 1014.
[3] = fúapart.   [4] = brith.   [5] suigi *MS.*
[6] *Gen. von* messar *oder* messair gl. phiala, *O' Mulc.* 223.
[7] Andreas *MS.*   [8] timthirig *MS.*   [9] timtirig *MS.*
[10] *Zu lesen* Choimded.   [11] iirnaigthi *MS.*
[12] raeirid *MS.*

Dīa 7 do Dūnchad. Conid hé sin marb rotaithbeūgad fodeōid i nEirind.

Is fair tucc Eochaid hūa Flandacān in teisd mōir .i. co nach dechaid co hAird-macha rīam nech bud ferr inā Dūnchad, con-
5 debert:

Macāmh molbthach medrait mūaid   salmthech a slūaigh selbait ') nāim,
nī tarla mūrclad a muir   dar tuil mar Dūnchad hūa mBrāin.

Gregor und die Oblatenmacherin.

[fo. 14 b 2] Araile domhnach do Griguir oc edbairt cuirp
10 Crīst. O robūi cāch ac dul do lāim, tāinic fedb irisech dognīd ablundu dō-sum cuicce co tīsad di lāim. Intan īarum dorat in clēirech dīssi corp Crīst, adubairt amal is béss: 'Corpus Domini nostri Iesu Christi conseruæt animam tuam', 'rocoimēta corp ar tigerna Īsu Crīst t'anmuin'. Is andsin rogab fūailfed²) 7 dorōine
15 gāire ūdermāir. Tuc in clērech focétoir a deissi³) ūada 7 ros-fuirimh corp Crīst forsiūd altōir 7 nirlēic dīa caithim. Rofiar-faig īarum di cid ima ūderrna gāire intan tucad in corp di. 'Hiūgnad' ar sī, 'lim in bairgen dorōnus com lámaib arbhu iūdé, a rād duit-si conidh corp Crīst soin.' Roslecht Griguir iarum
20 hi fiadnaisi na haltōire cosiūd uile popul himaille fris do dícur dícreidmi na mnā. Atracht⁴) Griguir 7 fūair in pars⁵) tuc forsin altōir i mbloig feōla dergi. O'tconncatur na huile in mirbuile mōir sin, rocreit in bandscal. Conid ē fīrcorp Crīst edbur[ar] ar cech altōir .i. corp rogēnir ō Muire ōig-ingin, 7 rocalmaiged iris
25 in popuil rōmānaig huile. Roslecht Grigoir dono Iarsin co rusæth⁶) hē ina gnē tosach, ar nīrba dir co mbeith gnē feōla dirgi fair oca caithem. Rosærad dó fochétoir i ngnē ablainne.

Gedicht vom Schweine des Mac Datho.

(Vgl. Windisch, Irische Texte S. 108.)   [fo. 58 b 1]
30 1 Muc Maic Dāt[h]ō, lactmūad torc,   nocorb ī ind attrūag imnoct,
co cenn secht mblīadan cen brath   sesca gamnach coa bīathad.

') selbiait MS..   ²) O'R.'s fuailfeadh 'leaping, skipping'.
³) deisse 'die Rechte'. O'Mulconry 307.   ⁴) Attrachth MS.
⁵) 'Partes dicuntur divinae Eucharistiae vel panis Eucharistici parti-culae', Ducange. Aisl. Maic Congl. S. 23, 7. cūic parsa di obli coitchinn, Stowe Missal.
⁶) = rosæ, altir. rosōi.

2 Ba hairdairc in moltach mas,   feib sontair trīasin sencas,
    cen cleith mbratha, roscan clú,   cethracha dam dia fothu.[1]
3 Fiadnaib cōraib *for* cert[2]) cairr   ere nōnbair 'na tromtairr,
    cēin bāi ic rainn robailc co rath   dosromailt Conall Cernach.
4 Cē ruslu Ailbe im grād nglan   cū dia ndeocha*id* cach cosnam,   5
    cē dorairg *gressa* don phurt,   nīrbo messaide in mōrmucc.
5 Lotar dō[3]) īar ndōtib drenn   *cōic cōicid ina Erenn,*
    dosfuc a combāg cucca   corbo oldam ōenmucca.
6 Mesgegra, Mesrōeta rān,   dā *mac* Dāthō na tromdām,
    in Mesrōida fri fēth fuit,   is ē romēth in mōrmu[i]c. M. u.   10

Tri cēt do Chonnachtaib romarbtha i mbruidin M*aic* Dāthō
7 *cōica* do hUltaib. Gilla Ailella romarb in coin i Comor
Chinncon. U*nde* Connachta d*icuntur.*

Scandlán Mór cecinit.   [fo. 92 b 1]

1 Is ē mo sāmud re mnāi   am*al* bīs cámull hi ceó,   15
    cen co hana lim is cet,   cet lim cid marb, cet cid beō.
2 Cett lim cīa rabur 'na gnáis,   cet lim cīa hanur dia hēis,
    is *ed* rofācbad do mnāi,   is cet cía thái, cet cīa théis.

Gedicht auf Cúrói Mac Dári.

Dieses im Metrum crō cumaisc etir rindaird ocus lethran- 20
*naigecht (Thurneysen, Irische Verslehren S. 83) abgefasste Gedicht
auf Cúrói mac Dári spielt auf mehrere bekannte und einige sonst
unbekannte Abenteuer dieses mythischen Heros an. Am Schlusse
wird auf Papst Gregor als aus seinem Geschlechte entsprossen
hingewiesen. Vgl. Félire Oengusso S. LXIII, wo Strophe 14 und* 25
15 *unseres Gedichtes citiert werden.*

1. Atbēr mōr do mathib   [fo. 117 a 1]
   . rīg Ērend[4]) na n-īath:
Cūrúi mac dil Dáre,
cīa ba mō is ba hālle   30
is ba náre im bīath?[5])

2. Beti a scēla il-lāidib
i nHērind ciatgēis,
nī thānic rīam reime,
nī tharga īar creitim   35
nech amlaid dia hēiss.

---

[1]) fotha *MS.*   [2]) *Zu lesen* cret *mit H.*
[3]) doib *mit punctis delentibus unter* ib.
[4]) Erind *MS.*   [5]) = bíad 'Speise'.

3. Rotairchanad d'Erínd
   rí ar domun rodet
   Cúrúi,[1] in léoman lasrach,
   claideb sliged Saxan,
5 crod Assia cen aslach
   sair dar glasmach[2] Gréc.

4. Rochroid descert domain,
   cath Conchend roblogaig
   Cúrúi dar Muir Robuir
10 ar dágin a homuin
   inn Afraic rombíad,
   díles Lúachra is Lemna,
   ardrí tulcha Temra,
   cingid catha cerba,
15 in longportach lerda,
   in t-Ebra rodríar.

5. Míle carpat corcra
   imba húatiu a slúaig,
   deich míle ruirech[3]
   co failgib óir uilech,
20 ba buidech in búaid.

6. Míle Fomoir fortrén
   'na longport for leith,
   Cígloisti[4] 'na comair,
25 níbtis omain neich.

7. Nír'mó leis crod caindlech
   ocus bíad do airlech,
   húa Dedaid,[5] in claidbech,
   andá ailbech cloch,
30 amal gainem mara
   nó usce na haba
   is a ndís dorala
   fri ré Con na cloth.[6]

---

[1] Cúirui MS.   [2] = glas-mag.
[3] Vielleicht zu lesen: deich cét míle ruirech.
[4] Zu lesen Cíchloiscthi.   [5] Dedaig MS.
[6] i. e. Cúchulinn.

8. Coire dub Chonrūi,   is fīr, is ni gō,
   tricha dam 'na crōes,[1]   nīrba luchtlach dó.[2]

9. A dabach dond dairech,
   ba mairech al-lān,
   cét trebarglan trēnfer   5
   tēged for a lār.

10. A chorn chrōes[3]-toll tana,
   nīrbo mada in mind,
   ōl cēt and ic comōl,
   ba romōr im lind.   10

11. Mīas Conrūi mic Dāre
   arget uile is ór,
   ēoin ōir imma huru
   cen guba, cen glōr.

12. Arpetitis rīgu   15
   is dæscurslóg dond
   ceōl na n-én dorīrib
   a tīrib na tonn.

13. Ticfa brāthair būada
   a fine Chonrūi,   20
   Grigoir ōthā tairbri
   cīa saidbri nach sūi.

14. Hūa Dedaid maic Sin
   Grigoir carta máil,
   abb Rōma, lām[4] Letha,   25
   i nHērinn atetha
   arís ina dāil.

15. Ár Hēriu ard-ailēn   [fo. 117 a 2]
   i mbīa Grigoir gér,
   cend na nGædel nglanmas,   30
   sīl nGōedil gil gablas,
   cid amnas, atbẽr. Atb.

---

[1] croés *MS.*

[2] *Cf. R. C.* VI, *p.* 187 *und LU.* 114 b 20:
        tricha aige inna crōes   nīrbo luchtlach dō.

[3] chroés *MS.*   [4] *Zu lesen* lūam *oder* láin *mit Fél. S.* LXIII?

Liverpool.   KUNO MEYER.

BRINNA FERCHERTNE.

The following poem is now for the first time published from the only manuscript copy in which it has reached us, that contained on fo. 117 b 1 — 118 a 2 of the Bodleian codex Laud 610. As the title indicates, it is a vision[1]) by Ferchertne, the poet of Cúrói mac Dári,[2]) of the storming of Curói's fort by Cúchulinn and the men of Ulster, of the death of Cúrói himself and of various members of his household, of the defeat of the Éraind in Argat-glenn, and, lastly, of Ferchertne's own death and that of Blathnait, Cúrói's faithless wife. Its contents are therefore the same as those of the tale known as *Aided Conrói* or the Tragical Death of Cúrói. This tale has long been accessible to English readers in Keating's account, as translated by O'Mahony (pp. 282 —284), O'Conor (I, pp. 100—102), O'Dermot (I, pp. 302—310) and Haliday (pp. 398—405). A very short Irish version from Laud 610 fo. 117 a², where it immediately precedes our poem, was published by me in the *Revue Celtique* vol. VI, pp. 187—188.[3]) More detailed versions are found in the Yellow Book of Lecan pp. 123 a — 125 a, and in Egerton 88, fo. 10 a 1 — 10 b 1. I should have liked to print the former *in extenso* from the facsimile published by the Royal Irish Academy, but for reasons stated in vol. I, p. 494 of this *Zeitschrift*, that is impossible without a previous collation of the facsimile with the manuscript. I must

---

[1]) *Brinna*, n. pl. of *brinn* 'vision'. See O'Mulconry's Glossary, Archiv f. celt. Lexikogr., ed. Stokes, no. 158.

[2]) Ferchertne fili Conrói, YBL. 124 a 45.

[3]) Here, on p. 188 l. 12, instead of *ceni mále* read *cen imále*, and in l. 15, for *Briathra* read *Brinna*.

therefore confine myself to quotations illustrating certain passages
in our poem. The Egerton version is quite independent from
that of the Yellow Book. Unfortunately, it is very corruptly
and carelessly written,[1]) and consequently not easy to understand.
   If I may venture a guess I should assign our poem to the
10th century. The name Cúrói still scans as three syllables, as
in Cinaed húa Hartacáin's poem beginning *Fianna bátar i
nEmain,*[2]) while it makes two syllables in Broccán Cráibdech's
poem in LL. 43 b[3]) and in the poem printed above, p. 37.

Brinna Ferchertne inso trÍana codl*ud.*

1. Atch*i*u d*a* choin ac congail   ferda comraim co n-áne:
   is C*u*cul*aind* conm*a*ide   b*a*s Chonr*u*i mic Dáre.

   I see two Hounds[4]) *manfully   fighting a glorious combat:
   Cuchulinn is boasting   of the death of Curoi, Dare's son.*

2. Héraind rogabsat H*e*rind,   b*a*tir l*i*nmair a fini,
   gabsat c*o*iced cen tu*s*led   corrice Uisnech Mide.

   The Eraind[5]) *seized Erin,   numerous were their families,
   They seized a province without mishap*[6]) *as far as Usnech in Meath.*

3. Fichsetar m*o*r do chathaib,   b*a*tir cr*o*dai na saithi,
   contolsat aidchi i Temair   oc saiged d'Emain Machi.

   *Many battles they fought,   hardy were the troops,
   They slept a night in Tara   on their march to Emain Macha.*

4. Ba di cherddaib Chonrói   dia ngeoga*i*n f*e*nnid Fliuchna,
   ba hed bunad a ch*e*sta   dia n-acht na hercca Iuchba (*sic*).

   It was one of Curoi's feats   when he slew Fliuchna the champion:[7])
   That was the origin of his suffering   when he drove off Iuchna's kine.

----

[1]) The following opening sentences will give an idea of the state of
this text: Ad*h*aig*h* Conrói. Amba*t*ar Uola*i*d and Emain có*n*facadar fer edien-
caill doib*h* ta*r* mach int Eam*ain*. coniet*h* Blaithine i*ngen* Conchobuir con-
depe*r*t diadhaim*h* n*o* carusa inamu*ψ* 7 incorrguine Cónruio m*a*ic Daire. Ba
he Ec*h*de Ecbel dogene in*n*sin 7 nach fiti*r* nec*h* dUl*t*aib iugi Có[i]*n*roi namae &c.
   [2]) LL. 31 b 6: Lecht Conrúi i Sléib Mís,   lecht Lug*dach* fo lecaib lis.
   [3]) LL. 43 b 35: Lecht Conrúi, lecht Fergusa,   lecht Conculaind cr*u*aid
                                                        [eubail.
   [4]) i. e. *Cú-Chulaind* 'Culand's Hound' and *Cú-rói* 'Hound of the
Battlefield'.
   [5]) A Munster tribe, to which Cúrói belonged. See O'Mulconry's Glossary 417. n. pl. Éraind, LL. 213 a 14. acc. Érnu, v. 7. dat. Érnaib, Dinds. 80.
   [6]) Lit. 'without falling'.
   [7]) I can find no other reference to this incident.

5. Dia sāraigestair Ultu,   ba scēl fota fri turaim,
   Iar feis fri curach codail   bert Blathnait ō Coinchulaind.

   When he had outraged the men of Ulster,   it were a long story to tell,
   After feasting, in a coracle of hide,   he carried off Blathnait from
   [*Cuchulinn.*

6. Bāi Cūchulaind for Iarair,   blīadain lān dó hi tói,
   co fitir eōlas athlam   dochum chathrach[1]) Conrói.

   Cuchulinn was a-searching,   a full year he passed in silence,[2])
   Till he knew ready guidance   towards Curoi's city.

7. Dia mert a ben Coinrói,   ba holc in gnīm dogēni,
   sech nī thērna hi sēgdu,   fācbas Ērnu fo mēli.

   When his wife betrayed Curoi,   evil was the deed she did,
   While she did not escape unscathed[3])   she left the Eraind under dis-
   [*grace.*

8. Romert Blathnait ingen[4]) Minn   in argain inn-Argatglind,
   olc gním do mnái brath a fir,   dáig ba maith donderuidir.[5])

   Blathnait, the daughter of Menn, by treachery brought about the slaughter
   [*in Argat-glenn:*
   An evil deed for a wife to betray her husband, since . . .

9. Cumrecht a folt do hailib,   do cholbaib, cródu scélaib,
   atract foraib, Cúrói,   ropo chomērgi trēnfir.

   She tied his hair to rails,   to bed-posts[6]) — cruellest of stories!
   Curoi arose against them,   'twas the rising of a champion.

10. Docher cēt fer dia hērgiu   Iarna cuimriuch i n-ailib,
    trī chōecait fer cen śodain,   ocus cōeca hi fuilib.

    A hundred men fell from his rising[7])   after he had been tied to rails,
    Thrice fifty men besides,   and fifty with bloody wounds.

----

[1]) chathram MS.

[2]) YBL. Bui Cuchulaind Iar sin blīadain lāin for imgabāil Ulad.

[3]) Literally 'in a blessed or happy state'.

[4]) ingin MS.

[5]) Thus in YBL. 125 a 24 (differently, but corruptly in LL. 169 b 56, and in the Rennes Dindśenchas, fo. 107 b 15):

      Roort Blathnad ingen Mind   la horcain ōs Aircedglind,
      mōr gním do mnái brath a fir,   dóig is friss rodamidir.

[6]) Cf. YBL. 124 a 15: ocus rochumrig a folt dona cholbaib 7 dona tuireadhaib '*and she tied his hair to the bed-posts and pillars*'.

[7]) Cf. YBL. 124 a 20: marbaid cēt fer dīb col-lūib 7 co ndornaib '*he kills a hundred of them with kicks and blows of his fist*'.

11. Cid[1]) tarraid[2]) Cûchulaind   cona claidiub fadessin,
conidfargaibh i cossair   for formnaib særa sessir.

However Cuchulinn came upon him   with his[3]) own sword,
And left him in a litter   upon the noble shoulders of six men.

12. Sīactatar as for slēbib,   dīgalsat fēnnid Fliuchna,
sech bertatar a cathle,   actatar erca Iuchna.

They went out upon the mountains,   they avenged Fliuchna the champion,
Besides carrying off their . . .,   they drove away Iuchna's kine.

13. Tarraid Senfīaccail Setnach,   dīmelta lecthi[4]) a chnāmi,
gabsi fulung co ndēni   īar ndīth anma mic Dāre.

Senfiaccail Setnach came,   worn out, decayed were his bones,
Quickly he got support   after the destruction of Mac Dare's life.[5])

14. Ced fer gāire na flatha,   ba maith fri hētacht catha,
tescais coica[i]t fer n-armach,   īar sain damair a marbad.

As for the crier of the prince,   he was good in the thick (?) of battle,
He cut down fifty armed men,   then he allowed himself to be slain.[6])

15. Dosrelic Tredornán dall   for slúag nUlad, nīrb inmall,
nertlia nóethech, núall nād bæth,   marbais trí fichti fīrlǽch.

Tredornan the blind flung himself   upon the Ulster host, he was not slow,
A famous stone of strength, no foolish cry!   three score true warriors he
                                       [slew.

16. Comram Echdach mic Darfind,   fil a thindrem issin glind,
bec a fis do neoch ar atá   cair cia rolá lecca ind.

The combat of Eochaid son of Darfind,   its final scene is in the glen,
'Tis little known to any one that is asked   who put flag-stones there.

---

[1]) Here fo. 117 b 2 begins.

[2]) Read *donfarraid*, or *dosfarraid* 'came upon them'?

[3]) *i. e.* Cûrói's. Blathnait had taken it from him (YBL. 124 a 16: dofall in claideb asa thrūaill).   [4]) Leg. legthi.

[5]) Cf. the Rennes Dindsenchas fo. 107 b 1, 19:

    Fer Bregda *ocus* Senīacail   ropdar araid do thrīathaib,
    Fer gāire a Frǽchmaig a fat,   mar do lǽchaib roortsat.

In YBL. 124 a 48 the name of Curoi's charioteer is Fer Becrach.

[6]) YBL. Atracht a . . . . dōib in fer gāire robāi istaig co romarb tricha lāech dīb. Is de rochēt:

    Cid fer gāire na flatha,   fa sær oc imbirt chatha,
    geguin tricha fer n-armach,   īar sin dāmair a marbad.

Senfīacail cēta-taraid fona ēgim, dia n-ebrad:

    Taraid Senfīacail Siring,   marbais cēt fer dia fairind,
    cīarbo mōr a nert a colaind,   fūair a leacht le Coinculaind.

17. Comram Echdach mic Darfind   ōtha [rind corrici in n-][1] glind,
     marbais cét fer fo chomlond   con[d]atarraid écomlonn.

The combat of Eochaid son of Darfind,   from the promontory as far
                                                      [as the glen,
He slew a hundred men in fair fight   until an overwhelming number[2])
                                                           [fell upon him.

18. Īar sain tucad écomlond   for Echdaig, nī fo chumlond,
     co fil a charnd for Maig Rois   a lín[3]) robói deas anfois.

Then Eochaid was overwhelmed by numbers,   not in fair fight,
So that his cairn is on Mag Rois, ...

19. Dosfarraid Cairpri Cūanach,   marbais cét fer, dál mbrígach,
     robága fri Conchubor   mani bad a muir mílach.

Cairpri Cuanach came upon them,   he slew a hundred men, a vigorous
                                                     [encounter,
He had boasted to Conchubor,[4])   if the monsterful sea had not drowned
                                                          [him.[5])

20. Dosfarraid Cló co mbarainn,   marbais cét fer dia fairind,
     cid mór a nert hi colaind,   fúair a lecht la Coinculaind.

Cló came upon them with fury,   he slew a hundred men of their host,
Though great his strength in the body,   he found his grave through
                                                           [Cuchulinn.

21. Dosfarraid Rus mac Dedad,   ocus tailc trén a bunad,
     ba di dígail a curad   gegnatar ócu[6]) Ulad.

Russ the son of Deda came upon them,   who was of a race stout and
                                                      [strong,
To avenge their heroes   the warriors of Ulster slew him.

22. Īar sain tarraid Nemtes drúi,   rofitir ní aridmbái,
     cethri dechenbuir robí,   atherracht ind co fo trí.

Thereupon came Nemthes the druid,   he knew what was in store for him,
Four times ten men he slew,   thrice he repeated it.[7])

23. Dosfarraid Foraí fīanach,   fer nad gillad ar gári,
     dosfarraid Dēdornd dúalach,   cartais na slúagu a háni.

Forai of the Fian came upon them,   a man who would not serve for
                                                      [laughter,
Dedornd of the curly locks came,   he ousted the hosts from glory.

---

[1]) Sic YBL. 124 a 35.   [2]) Lit. 'unequal combat'.

[3]) alin alín MS.   [4]) Or, 'he would have fought with C'.

[5]) Leg. min báded. Cf. YBL. Robāghai fri Conchobar mā nobāded muir mīlach .i. ō robūi ōcbaid fri Conchobar co n-acai a chathraig for lasad fri muir athūaid. Luid didu isin muir dia thesarcain inna cathrach. Mōr in snām, co robāided and.

[6]) Perhaps originally óaic.

[7]) As to the use of *aitherraigim* with the preposition *i n-* cf. ceni bad i n-olc n-aill n-aithirsed, Laws I, 10, 6.

24. Tarraid Ferdomon, ferais   debaid, ar bodb[d]a bron[n]ais,
  bí a dornd ar comlond cain   do Fiachaig mac Concobair.

  Ferdoman came, he gave battle,   he wrought a terrible slaughter,
  In fair fight he cut off the hand   of Fiachaig the son of Conchobar.

25. Dosfarraid[1]) mac Riangabra,   Ingeilt a hainm co n-áni,
  bert Carpre mac Conchoboir   fo tonnaib serba sáile.

  The son of Riangabra came upon them,   Ingeilt was his glorious name,
  He put Carpre the son of Conchobor   under bitter waves of the salt-sea.

26. Lugaid ocus Lóegaire   fersat debaid dar dā bran,
  fácbaid a charpat dia chur   is a faraid[3]) ina scur.

  Lugaid and Loegaire   made combat fiercer than two ravens,[4])
  He leaves his chariot to its hero,   and its charioteer in its paddock.

27. Cotgart Lóegaire don tslúag,   mida mín ticed úad:
  'Brissem fír fer forsin lōech   dús in dersamis ar sāeth'.

  Loegaire cried to the host ......
  'Do not let us grant the warrior fair fight,   to see if we avenge our
                                                          [trouble.'

28. Gabsi Fergus for a grúad   arnach romarbad in slúag,
  Iar sain rosīach(t) cert curad   for ócu amra Ulad.

  Fergus took hold of his cheek,   lest the host should slay him,
  Then he obtained fair fight   against the famous warriors of Ulster.

29. Trí fichit lǽ dó for leirg,   fer cecha lá inna cheird,
  bátir hé sein a hélaing[5])   con[d]atánc[at]ar Héraind.

  Three score days he was on the field,   every day a man (fell) by his skill,
  Those were his ...   until the Eraind arrived.

30. Iar sain táncatar Héraind   dia r[é]ir ar-ríg domrímid,[6])
  secht fic[h]et ar secht cétaib,   secht cét míle do mílib.[7])
  Thereupon came the Eraind   according to the will of their king ...,
  Seven thousand seven hundred   and seven score of thousands.

---

[1]) Here fo. 118 a 1 begins.

[2]) Cf. YBL.:
  Fer Becrach co n-imāle   bēs nī brēg immaraīde,
  bert Cairpre Mac Conchobair   fo thonda searba sāile.

[3]) Read araid; cf. *farradnacht*, LU. 113 b 28, for *aradnacht* 'charioteership'.

[4]) Literally, 'exceeding two ravens'. For this use of *dar* cf. dám nó tascur tar dá fer décc, Laws I, 48, 5.

[5]) O'Brien has *ealang* 'a fault, flaw', a meaning which will hardly suit here.

[6]) domrimŗid MS., with punctum delens under the second *r*.

[7]) Thus in YBL.:
  Arsin tarraid cland Dedaid   dia raidh a rīg da rímid,
  cōic fichit ar trī chētaib   deich cētaib ar dí mīlib.

31. Scortside[1]) for maig Henaig,   ba hann cotricht in debaid,
    acta fri alla argait,   conid de attá in cath charpat.[2])

    . upon Mag Enaig,   'twas there the combat reached,
    They were driven against the silver rocks,[3])   whence is the chariot-fight.

32. For leirg lectaig fersat núall,   ba hand cotránic in slúag,
    is ed a hainm foridtá   ocus nocha n-ed nammá.

    Upon a grave-covered slope they raised a shout,   'twas there the host
    [came together,
    That is the name that is on it,   and not that only.

33. Is trúag a comrac amne   Blathnaite ocus Fercertne,
    co fil a lecht[4]) di[b]línaib   hi Laind Chindbera assin rind.

    Sad truly is the encounter of Blathnait and Ferchertne,
    The graves of both of whom are in Land Cindbera above the promontory.

34. Atchīu teor erca Echdai,   ní meirb docengat latha,
    adchīu daglaechuin (?) beth,   adchīu graige cach[5]) datha.

    I see the three kine of Echda,   not slowly do they march through sloughs,
    I see a noble warrior (?) . . .,   I see studs of horses of every colour.

35. Atchīu curchu la habaind,   adchīu galaind forsngabther,
    atchīu dírim dar magthech,   adchīu læch forsnalamt[h]er.

    I see coracles along a river,   I see enemies that are being seized,
    I see a host across a great house,   I see a warrior that is not to be dared.

36. Atchīu gin húi Nessa   cessa fri fiansa forbair
    diasnad Hériu ergair,   atciu[6]) -sa hi congail.[7]) Atchiu.

---

[1]) scortside, with punctum delens under d, and nó t written over it.
[2]) Leg. carpait.
[3]) From which Argat-glend 'Silver-glen' takes its name.
[4]) lecth MS.   [5]) cacha MS.
[6]) Here fo. 118 a 2 ends.
[7]) This quatrain is evidently corrupt, and I cannot translate it.

Liverpool.   KUNO MEYER.

DAS ALTER DER WÜRZBURGER GLOSSEN.

In der Vorrede zu seiner Ausgabe der Glossen aus der Würzburger Handschrift M. th. f. 12 zeigt Zimmer, dass von den drei Händen, die diese Glossen unterscheiden lassen, diejenige, die durch die ganze Handschrift hin nur wenige, kurze Einträge gemacht hat, die älteste ist; er nennt sie daher nicht mit Zeuss *manus tertia*, sondern *prima manus* und hält für möglich, wenn auch nicht für sicher, dass sie dem Schreiber des lateinischen Textes selbst angehöre. Dagegen den S p r a c h - charakter dieser ersten Glossen bezeichnet er als j ü n g e r als den der später eingetragenen Hauptglossenmasse.[1]

Was das absolute Alter der Handschrift betrifft, beschränkt er sich darauf zu konstatieren, dass der Text dieselben Buchstabenformen zeige wie andere von Iren im achten und neunten Jahrhundert geschriebene Denkmäler, während Zeuss in der Vorrede zur Grammatica Celtica sie für gleichartig und gleichaltrig mit den Mailänder Glossen gehalten hatte, welche *uiri docti quidam* dem achten Jahrhundert zuschrieben (und noch zuschreiben). Zeuss war damit der Ansicht Eckhardts entgegengetreten, der sie ins neunte oder zehnte Jahrhundert hatte setzen wollen. Später hat aber d'Arbois de Jubainville doch wieder als einstimmiges Urteil von de Wailly, Quicherat und Delisle angegeben, die Handschrift müsse um 900, am Ende des neunten oder am Anfang des zehnten Jahrhunderts geschrieben sein.[2] Da hiezu die junge Sprache der zuerst eingetragenen Glossen

---

[1] Glossae Hibernicae p. XIV, XV.
[2] Essai d'un catalogue de la littérature épique de l'Irlande, p. CXXIX f.

gut stimmen würde, habe ich mich früher dieser Taxierung an-
geschlossen;[1]) die übrigen Glossen wären somit als aus einer
sehr viel älteren Handschrift kopiert anzusehen.   .

Eine genauere Prüfung der *prima manus* führt nun aber
zu einem ganz andern Resultat: ihre Abweichungen vom gewöhnlichen Irisch in Sprache und Schrift sind kein Anzeichen
von Jugend, sondern von allerhöchstem Alter. Auf Grund
mehrerer Kriterien, welche die Schreibung irischer Eigennamen
in datierbaren lateinischen Texten an die Hand giebt, konnte
ich in dieser Zs. I, 348 f. einige Sprachdenkmäler, besonders das
Irische der Handschrift von Cambrai, der zweiten Hälfte des
siebenten Jahrhunderts oder dem Uebergang zum achten zuweisen. Auch die Namen in der von Adamnan († 704) verfassten *Vita Columbae* bestätigen diesen Ansatz durchaus. In
diesen Kreis gehören nun eben die Glossen der *prima manus*
in Wb.

Man findet sie bequem zusammengestellt bei Zimmer,
Glossae Hibernicae p. XIII und *Glossarum Hibernicarum Supple-
mentum* p. 6. Ein Versehen ist dort nur *túercómlasat* gegenüber *túercómlassat* im Text p. 42, wie auch Stokes (Wb. 7 a 7)
liest. Die Stokes'sche Lesung weicht in folgenden Punkten ab:
7 a 7 Zimmer *cómtinól* Stokes *comtinol* (ohne Accente); 7 c 11 Zi.
sech St. *[ir]isech*; 11 b 19 Zi. *icundrattig* St. *icundrathtig*; 12 c 18
Zi. *farcanit* St. *forcanit*; 14 a 24 Zi. *dilmain* St. *dilmain* (ohne
Punkt); 14 b 23 Zi. *toncomrit* St. *toncomra*; 15 b 22 Zi. *frisbrúch-
mór* (oder *-bráchmór*) St. *frisbrúdémor*; 15 b 23 Zi. *ni dergemar*
St. *ní derge . . . .met*; 15 d 8 Zi. (p. 287) *dubsi* St. *dúbsi*; 17 d 1
Zi. *cetarco . .* St. *cetarcoti*; 22 a 7 Zi. *cith* St. *cithisse*; 22 b 16 Zi.
dronei, Stokes scheint am Ende etwas zu fehlen; 22 d 10 Zi.
aithirgaliu (oder *-lia*) St. *aithirgabu*; 23 b 19 Zi. *aircur* St. *airchur*.
Ausserdem scheinen drei Glossen bei Stokes zu fehlen: *p(ro)umthe*
neben 7 b 17, *manam* 17 c d, *rectire* neben 17 d 13.

Als sprachliche Kriterien jener frühen Texte haben wir
kennen gelernt, dass *e* und *o* noch nicht diphthongiert sind. Für
jenes fehlen hier Beispiele; aber *o* bleibt in *soos* (= *suas*) 20 a 8;
coirt-tobe (= *cuairt-*) 'Kreisschnitt' (gl. *circumcissio*) 23 d 24; *boid*
(= *buaid*) 24 a 16. Unbetonte *e* und *o* vor dunkler Konsonanz
sind nicht zu *a* umgefärbt: *esbetu* 9 b 15 (vgl. *esbataid* Ml. 130 c 23);

---

[1]) Revue Celtique VI, 318.

fugell 9 c 5 unmittelbar neben der Schreibung *fugall* des Haupt-
glossators (9 c 4); *fresdel* 24 c 11 doch wohl gleich dem späteren
frestal; *frisbrudemor* (gl. aporiamur) 15 b 22; *folog* 17 b 23 wohl
gleich dem späteren Substantiv *fulach*, ungenaue Glosse zu 'sub-
portate', wie gleich darauf das Substantiv *het* 17 b 25 das Verbum
'aemulor' glossiert.[1]) Aus der Handschrift von Cambrai lernen
wir ferner, dass damals die Präposition *to do* vortonig vor Verben
immer mit *t* anlautete: *tu-thegot, tu-esmot, amcul* (lies *amail*) *tond-
echomnuchuir* (aber vor Substantiven und Pronomina stets mit
d: *du cach oin, du duiniu, dundaib abstolaib, do*); ebenso lesen
wir hier *tu-ercomlassat* 7 a 7, *ton-comra* (gl. ut tederet nos)
14 b 23. Auch dass die Konjunktion 'wie' hier wie dort immer
amail heisst (21 c 10, 22 c 14) gegenüber dem *amal* des Haupt-
glossators und späterer Texte, darf angeführt werden (Glossae
Hibern. XIV). Alles dieses zusammen genommen, lässt sich an
dem altertümlichen Sprachcharakter nicht zweifeln; ja, wenn
man sich auf die Endung von *frisbrudemor* neben *manos comal-
nnamar* Cam. 38 b stützen darf, ist die *prima manus* des Wb.
älter als die Vorlage des Camaracensis.

So erklärt sich auch die unsichere Orthographie. Wir
haben offenbar die ersten, tastenden Versuche vor uns, irisch
mit lateinischen Buchstaben zu schreiben. Die nicht spirantischen
Mediae hinter Vokalen sind bald durch Mediae bezeichnet: *ro-
slogeth* (gl. absorpta est) 13 d 24, *adob-ragart* 19 b 5, bald durch
Tenues *het* 17 b 25, *téte* (gl. luxoria) 20 b 17, *hœcosc* 27 d 17. Die
dentalen und gutturalen Spiranten sind wohl häufig, wie später,
durch *th d, ch g* wiedergegeben, daneben aber mehrfach durch
blosse Tenues (ähnlich wie in altkymrischen Texten); vgl. *comtinol* 7 a 7, *forcanit* (gl. prophetetis) 12 c 18, *cetarco(ti)* 17 d 1,
fulget (gl. portate) 20 c 5, *rigteg* 23 b 8; *tuercomlassat* 7 a 7, *aincis*
17 d 15, *adcumbe* 23 d 22; einmal — zwischen zwei *i* — ist dagegen für späteres *ch* blosses *h* geschrieben: *menmnihi* (gl. de-

---

[1]) Dass auch der *e*-Vokal in *fulget* (gl. portate) 20 c 5 neben *i* im
i-Verbum *dilgid* (gl. donate) 18 a 11 eine Altertümlichkeit bewahre, ist wegen
forcanit (gl. ut prophetetis) 12 c 18 unwahrscheinlich; vgl. auch den Plural
nitam toirsech (gl. non angustiamur) 15 b 21. Eine vereinzelte Umfärbung von
e zu *a* scheint in *amail ata* 22 c 14 vorzuliegen, das nach dem Zusammenhang
3. Plural sein muss (so Strachan, *Subst. Verb* 1084); als älteste Endung ist
doch wohl auch hier *-te* anzusetzen. Aber es handelt sich hier nicht um den
Einfluss folgender Konsonanten, und *atta* steht auch Cam. 38 b.

sensiones) 18 a 21.[1]) Auffällig sind ferner die Schreibungen
dersciddu (gl. potiora) 23 b 3 und *dronei* (gl. turpitudo) 22 b 16,
die zum Teil Zimmers Altersbestimmung veranlasst haben. Aber
dersciddu für *derscigthu* kann nicht als junge Form bezeichnet
werden, da *gth* oder *chth* auch später nicht zu *dd* geworden ist;
es beruht entweder auf individueller Aussprache, oder viel eher
ist es eine Verlegenheitsschreibung. Näher liegt es von moderner
Lautgebung zu sprechen, wenn Zimmer mit Recht *dronei* dem
späteren *droch-gné* gleichsetzt (doch vgl. oben Stokes). Aber
mich dünkt, sie wäre zu modern, selbst wenn wir die Handschrift ins zehnte Jahrhundert hinabrücken; denn das Resultat
der Doppelspirans *ch + g* könnte auch damals noch nicht völlig
verklungen gewesen sein. So werden wir das Fehlen des
Gutturals entweder der Nachlässigkeit des Glossators oder seiner
Unfähigkeit zuschreiben müssen, den Lauten in der Schrift völlig
gerecht zu werden. Andere Eigentümlichkeiten sind für die
Altersbestimmung ohne Belang, so das mehrfache *ai* für *ẹ* vor
palataler Konsonanz: *praidchas* 12 c 27, *aipthi* (gl. ueneficia)
20 b 20, *saichi crud* 23 b 22; diese Vorliebe für *ai* zeigt sich auch
in *maidem* 17 c 14 (Hauptglossator *móidem*), das wohl nur
äusserlich an mittelirische Schreibung erinnert. Wir ersehen
daraus zunächst nur, dass die spätere relativ feste Orthographie
noch nicht erfunden war.

Diese alten Glossen dürften nun wohl geeignet sein, die
Diskussion über gewisse Kopulaformen zwischen Pedersen und
mir zum Abschluss zu bringen.[2]) Hatte ich wegen des Vokalismus von *con-id*, der Pluralformen *nun-dem* etc. den Zusammenhang mit der Wurzel [*s*]*tā*- nicht nur für diese Formen, sondern
auch für die negierten *ni-ta ni-tat* (*ni-dat*) etc. in Abrede gestellt,
so suchte ihn umgekehrt Pedersen für beide Klassen aufrecht zu
erhalten. Nun steht neben *oire nun-dem* im Camaracensis und
ce nu-ded, don-nat-det im Turiner Palimpsest in unseren mindestens
gleich alten Glossen *ni-tam* 15 b 21. Also da, wo nach Pedersens
Untersuchungen die Relativpartikel *d* (*id*) zu erwarten ist,
e-Vokalismus; nach der Negation *ni*, wo sie keine Stelle hat,
a-Vokalismus und im Anlaut *t*. Die zwei Klassen sind somit

---

[1]) Schreibfehler ist *din dib oiprib* (gl. nolite fru dare inuicem) 9 d 19
für *dindib-oiprid* 'dass ihr euch betrügt'.

[2]) Pedersen KZ. 35, 359 und in dieser Zs. II, 378; Verf. ebend. I, 3 f.
und Indogerm. Anzeiger IX, 191 f.

ursprünglich streng geschieden; nur die zweite gehört zur Wurzel
[s]tā- und liefert zur 3. Sg. *ní* 'non est' die übrigen Personen;
die erste enthält die Partikel (*i*)*d* = mkymr. *yd* und vokalisch
anlautende Verbalformen. Die spätere Gestalt dieser Klasse, -*dan*
-*dad* -*dat*, ist im Vokalismus regelmässig entwickelt; aber dass
man dann auch mit Tenuis *ce nu-tad* und umgekehrt mit Media
ni-dan ni-dad ni-dat sprach und schrieb, beruht auf sekundärer
Vermischung beider Reihen. Auch möchten unsere Stellen für
höheres Alter des -*m* in der 1. Plur. sprechen gegenüber späterem
con-dan ni-tan etc.

Wenden wir uns nun zum Alter der ganzen Handschrift,
so ist klar, dass, wenn die Glossen der *prima manus* der Zeit
um oder eher vor 700 n. Chr. angehören, auch der lateinische
Text nicht jünger sein kann. Denn es ist nicht wohl denkbar,
dass zwei oder drei verschiedene Kopisten (die *prima manus* und
die beiden Hauptglossatoren) Glossen aus zwei verschiedenen
älteren Quellen geschöpft und alle ganz buchstabengetreu, ohne
den Sprachcharakter irgend zu verwischen, in eine späte Handschrift eingetragen hätten, zumal die Kleinheit der Glossenschrift
eine solche philologische Akribie ungemein erschwerte. Aber,
wird man fragen, darf man s o w e i t von dem Urteil der
französischen Paläographen abweichen? Da auch mich solche
Zweifel plagten, wandte ich mich damit an Herrn Dr. Ludwig
Traube, dem so manche irische Handschrift älteren Datums
durch die Hände gegangen ist. Seiner Antwort entnehme ich
Folgendes. Die insulare Paläographie ist noch so dunkel, dass
äussere Indicien für die Altersbestimmung viel mehr Gewicht
haben als blosse graphische Schätzungen. Ohne meine Darlegung würde er die Würzburger Handschrift nach dem Faksimile vielleicht dem achten Jahrhundert zugeteilt haben; doch
könne er jetzt sehr wohl auch siebentes bis achtes Jahrhundert
ansetzen. Somit scheint mir sicher, dass die drei Schriftarten,
die der lateinische Episteltext, die Einleitungen und die Glossen
der *prima manus* zeigen, schon gegen 700 in Irland ausgebildet
waren.

Und die Hauptglossenmasse? Ihrer Sprache nach ist sie
merklich jünger als die *prima manus*, aber bedeutend älter als
z. B. der zwischen 795 und 808 gedichtete Heiligenkalender des
Oengus und als die, freilich nicht sicher datierten, Mailänder
Glossen. Die Annahme, Glossen einer viel älteren Handschrift

4*

seien in Wb. sehr genau kopiert worden, ist, wie wir gesehen,
jetzt nicht mehr nötig, war überdies an und für sich wenig
wahrscheinlich. Denn wie sollten wir das Verfahren des zweiten
Glossators begreifen, der von fol. 33a an den ersten abgelöst
hat? Obschon er wesentlich dieselbe Sprache schreibt wie jener,
weicht er, wie bekannt, doch in der Orthographie mehrfach von
ihm ab. Die überaus grosse Korrektheit der Glossen versteht
sich dagegen leicht, wenn die Glossatoren eben die Sprache ihrer
eigenen Zeit schrieben. Ob sie dabei einem Vorbilde durchaus
gefolgt sind oder selbständig kompiliert haben, wäre noch zu
untersuchen. Die jüngsten ihrer sicher datierbaren Gewährs-
männer sind Gregor der Grosse und Isidor; es spricht also nichts
dagegen, dass ihre Arbeit dem achten Jahrhundert angehört.
Der von Gagney dem Bischof Primasius von Hadrumetum (um
551) zugeschriebene Kommentar der paulinischen Briefe, der eine
ihrer Hauptquellen zu bilden scheint,[1] ist diesem zwar von
Haussleiter[2] abgesprochen worden, der vielmehr Gallien als
Ursprungsland vermutet; wann er aber entstanden ist, ist unbekannt. Gerade unsere Glossen, die wir im achten Jahrhundert
nicht zu weit hinabrücken dürfen, können einen *terminus ad
quem* abgeben.

Altertümlich sind auch die irischen Glossen in der *Ex-
planatio Iunii Filargirii in Bucolica*, die Stokes nach zwei
Handschriften des zehnten Jahrhunderts herausgegeben hat, nach
dem Laurentianus plut. XLV cod. 14 in Kuhns Zeitschrift 33, 62 ff.
und 313 ff. und nach der Pariser Handschrift Bibl. Nat. ms. lat.
7960 in der Revue Celtique 14, 226 ff. Beide — ich nenne jene
L, diese P — sind von kontinentaler, des Irischen unkundiger
Hand geschrieben, und viele gemeinsame Fehler weisen darauf
hin, dass dasselbe schon für ihre Vorlage gilt. So erklärt sich
die Erhaltung alter Wortformen in so späten Quellen.

Unbetontes ĕ und ŏ bewahrt: *fors .i. toceth* (*toc eth* L 13 r 31,
tochet P 11 r 1); *electra .i. or-arget* (*orar get* P 10 r 36, *orget*
L 12 v 4); *anser .i. gigren* L 13 v 14 (*gigrem* P 11 r 18); *palus .i.*

---

[1]) Nach Thomas Olden, The holy scriptures in Ireland one thousand
years ago (Dublin 1888) p. VII und 120.
[2]) Leben und Werke des Bischofs Primasius von Hadrumetum (Erlangen
1887).

cethor L 16 r 6, *cetor* P 13 r 4, nach Stokes *cechor* zu lesen und dem späteren *cechair*[1]) gleich zu setzen. Vortoniges *tu-* in *mentiri* .i. *tucrecha* L 8 r 8, P 6 v 21; die Ueberlieferung schwankt bei *deerrauerat* .i. *dodihel* P 9 r 22, *todidel* L 11 r 3, wo es sich aber vielleicht um die vortonige Form von *di* handelt. Langes *o* ist bewahrt in *frontem* .i. *grode* P 8 r 22, L 9 v 23; *hiias hilas* (d. i. *Hylax*) .i. *conbochuil* L 13 r 23, *conbochuili* P 10 v 33, *conbocail* L 21 v 27, P 17 v 32 = *con-buachaill* Ancient Laws I, 126; *uini(a)tor* .i. *finbondid* L 14 r 28 (*finbondio* P 11 v 19) von *fin-buain* 'Weinernte'; aber einmal diphthongiert: *minio* .i. *ua fordinn* P 18 r 29, L 22 r 28. Ebenso ist in *labruscas* .i. *feadinne* L 8 v 1, P 7 r 13 wohl *ea* als diphthongiertes *ē* zu betrachten, vgl. *dea* Cam., *Druim Leas* Tir. (Zs. I, 348 f.); denn wenn auch Stokes' Deutung des Wortes als *fiad-fini* 'wild vines' kaum das Richtige treffen kann, so wird er doch den ersten Bestandteil mit Recht dem späteren *fiad* = kymr. *gwydd* 'wild' gleich gesetzt haben. Scheinen die zuletzt besprochenen Glossen zu einer späteren Sprachperiode hinüberzuleiten,[2]) so ist anderseits eine sehr alte Form bewahrt in *exuias* .i. *inda fodh* L 13 r 6, *inda foht* P 10 v 21. Stokes hat das zweite Wort richtig in *fodb* verbessert, das in der Bedeutung genau *exuviae* entspricht. *Inda* hatte er zuerst (KZ. 33, 75) als 'die zwei' gefasst, was aber der Zusammenhang des Textes (Ecl. VIII, 91) ausschliesst. Darum sieht er ib. p. 314 und Rev. Celt. 14, 233 in *inda* den Plural von *ind* und übersetzt 'ends (or edges) of vestures', auch eine sehr gezwungene Deutung, die der Text nicht an die Hand giebt. Vielmehr ist *inda* einfach die ältere Form des Artikels *inna* und *fodb* neutraler Accusativus Pluralis, wie schon Hogan, *The Irish Nennius* etc. p. 105, erkannt hat. Dieselbe Form des Artikels erscheint nun auch in einer Glosse der *prima manus* in Wb. Dort werden die paulinischen Worte Gal. VI, 17: *ego enim stigmata Iesu in corpore meo porto* glossiert durch: *indá* (oder *in dá*) *érrend* .i. *turmenta flagill(lorum)* 20 d 5. Stokes übersetzt 'the two marks'. Aber schon die beigefügte lateinische Erklärung zeigt, dass an eine Zweizahl hier nicht gedacht ist; auch würde neutrales *dá* ein *n-* hinter sich

---

[1]) Belege bei Stokes, *On the metrical glossaries of the mediaeval Irish*, Glossarial index s. v.

[2]) Auch die Schreibung *oe* dürfte dahin zu rechnen sein in *muscosi* .i. *coennich* L 11 r 29 (*coenhic* P 9 v 11), vgl. neuir. *caonach cúnach* gäl. *còinneach* manx *keanagh* 'Moos'.

verlangen. Somit ist *inda* blosser Artikel und die Accente, wie
oft, bedeutungslose Zeichen, die nur die irischen Wörter markieren
sollen. In diesem Punkt sind also unsere Denkmäler älter als
der Camaracensis, der zwar noch *dundaib abstolaib*, aber schon
inna tre chenel martre so schreibt; etwas anderer Art ist eben-
dort *isnaib inscib, issnib colnidib*, da ein Konsonant vorhergeht.
Man kann also sagen, dass der Wandel von *nd* zu *nn* im Innern
vortoniger Wörtchen etwa um den Uebergang vom siebenten
zum achten Jahrhundert eingetreten ist, während er sonst erst
ein Jahrhundert später erfolgt.

Freiburg i. B.   R. THURNEYSEN.

SOME NOTES ON THE
IRISH GLOSSES OF WÜRZBURG AND ST. GALL.

Würzburg Glosses.

1 a 3 *húare rocreitset ardlathi inbetho cretfed cách iarum* et *intí cretfes ní agathar dngreim.*

Here *cretfed* cannot be the secondary future, which would have been *nocretfed*; it is written for *cretfid* as *sóirfed* 32 d 13 represents *sóirfid*. This observation will, I think, remove the difficulty in *nipridched hiris* 33 d 1. Here *pridched* has been taken as passive, but, apart from the fact that the gloss has then no obvious connexion with the text, *hiris* should have been *hires*. Rather *pridched* is for *pridchid*, either 'ye do not preach faith', or 'ye shall not preach faith'. The latter translation seems the better. The sense would be: it is not the time now to lay the foundation by preaching faith, that has been done already; rather it is the time to hasten onwards to perfection. Cf. also *bed* for *beid* Wb. 3 c 10, 12 b 10, Cod. Cam. 37 d. In Wb. 20 a 15 *doforbadsi* has been taken for *do-b-forbadsi* 'excisi estis', but that is not how these glossators interpret. Rather *excídistis* was mistaken for *excídistis,* and this is rendered by *doforbadsi = doforbaidsi*. In the end of the gloss *greim* is 'sway, power', cf. Wind. s. v., *ingremmae* g. sceptri Ml. 110 d 3.

2 b 22 One might supply et *nibad coscrad* legis.

2 c 6 *isderb linn is ní nim͏̈ atruirmed hiresche do.* The sentence as it stands is impossible; *is* and *ní* are mutually exclusive, and the *n* after *ní* is inexplicable. Read probably *is derb linn ní inimdibiu atruirmed hiresche do,* 'we are sure it is not in circumcision that faith was imputed to him'. Probably the glossator wrote *is* and then added the correct *ní* without deleting *is.*

3 d 10 *issí indainim aslam dochomalnad recto.* Read *asairlam* 'which is ready'. *air* was omitted from its similarity to *as*.

4 a 6 *ciabeid Crist indibsi trefóisitin hirisse* in babtismo et *isbeo indanim trisodin.*

For the subjunctive followed by the indicative in the conditional sentence cf. 13 a 12 *mabeidní dirúnaib dothéi armenmuin indfir bíis innasuidiu* et *adreig achele.* To the interpretations suggested for this passage by Stokes and by Ascoli (Gloss. Pal. hib. CCI) I would venture to add another: 'if there be any mystery that comes to the mind of a man who is seated, and his fellow (i. e. the fellow of the man who is speaking) rises'. The sentence is awkwardly expressed, for, if my interpretation be right, the *fer bíis innasuidiu* and the *céle* are one and the same. In any case the interpretation does not affect the syntactical observation. *intí* etc. seems an independent gloss on *prior*.

4 a 16 *dorbe fri Crist.*

The correct interpretation of this has been pointed out to me by Professor Thurneysen. The words really belong to the following gloss, *cororannam dorpe fri Crist,* an explanation of *coheredes Christi.*

4 b 14 *india indoichside do náde nídoich ar* qui iustificat *isdochu do* quam contempnere.

In Gramm. Celt.[2] 349 *side* is taken as a neuter pronoun 'num simile hoc ei?', a usage which, so far as I have observed, would be without a parallel; cf. Windisch s. v. Now in LL. 61 b 15, cf. ll. 28, 36, we have *cia bad dóig diar tiachtain,* 'who would be likely to have come to us?' *indoichside do* may be similarly translated, 'is He likely to it?', and the whole gloss would mean: 'Is it God? Is He likely to do it?' Nay, He is not, for *qui iustificat*; He is more likely to do that (*iustificare*) *quam contempnere.* The alleged neuter *sode*, Gram. Celt. l. c. comes from a misinterpretation; *ciadsode lat* means 'though thou keep him with thee', *ciatasode lat* 'though thou keep her with thee'. In Sg. 66 a 20, *atsuidi* is rightly referred by Ascoli to *adsuidim*, but at 64 b 3 *atasuidi = ad-da-suidi* is wrongly translated.

7 a 2 ne super alium fundamentum aedificarem, sed sicut scriptum est: quibus non adnuntiatum est de eo, uidebunt, g. .i. *isdímsa tairrchet adcichitis genti dindí sin* per mé. As it stands, *dindí sin* has no meaning, and *genti* is most awkwardly separated

from *per mé*. The sense becomes clear if we refer the gloss to *de eo* and emend: *dindí sin* .i. *isdíimsa tairrchet adcichitis genti per mé.*

7 a 11 per uos proficiscar in Hispaniam. Scio autem quoniam ueniens ad uos in abundantia benedictionis euangelii Christi ueniam, g. *rofetar nímirchói* (leg. *nímirchói*) *nachgéin libsi.*

24 d 11 *horbí accobur læ nebud dó innoidenacht nachgéin.*

In these two passages *nachgéin* still requires explanation; that they are both corrupt is unlikely. I would suggest that *nachgéin* stands for *nachncéin* 'for any long time'. The eclipsis would be expressed as in *oldáu*, according to the most probable explanation of the word. In the second passage that sense is clearly appropriate: 'since she wishes him not to be in infancy for any long time'. And in the former it also suits: 'it will not delay me among you for any long time'. The subject is not altogether clear; perhaps it is *abundantia benedictionis euangelii Christi*; in any case the general sense is that St. Paul will soon finish his work in Rome and then set out for Spain. For *-irchói* here the sense of 'hinder' is doubtfully suggested by Thurneysen, KZ. XXXI, 74. Cf. *arachoided* g. impedientis Ml. 83 d 2, *erchót* 'hindrance' or 'impediment' Ml. 42 c 19, 56 a 13. Further in Ml. 31 d 10 *arachoat* probably means 'which hinders'. For the two senses of 'impeding' and 'injuring' may be compared Gr. βλάπτω. With the phrase *nachgéin* compare *nachmór* 'to any great extent' Wb. 11 d 5, Ml. 64 d 13.

8 c 19 Fundamentum enim aliud nemo potest ponere, .i. *cia-fasásat sóibapstil.*

Ascoli, Gloss. Pal. hib. CCCI, rightly denies the connexion of *fasásat* with *fás*, but he substitutes no other explanation. The word may be analysed *f-a-sásat*, subj. of *fo-sagim* with infixed pronoun, 'though false apostles try it'.

9 b 19 *armain bed accuiss napreceptesin* debueritis *nótresstæ dithír* et *talam náni sin.*

Here the difficulty is *nótresstæ*. That it should come from *trécim* is improbable for two reasons; (1) *trécim* is a weak verb, and so would not have a sigmatic aorist, (2) *trécim* in the sense of to 'leave' a place is followed by the accusative case.[1]) Per-

---

[1]) In the sense of 'yield to' *trécim* is found intransitively followed by *do*, BB. 462 b 84.

haps *nótressta* should be corrected to *nótessta*, 'ye should have fled from the earth and land of those people'. Nearer to the MS. would be *no-d-restæ*, but *rethim* is not so appropriate as *techim*.

9 d 2 *is bésad inna flatho doeme dofich.*

Here *doeme* is unintelligible; what is wanted is the 3. sg. pres. ind. Read accordingly *is bésad inna flatho doem* et *dofich*, 'it is the custom of a prince to protect and punish'. As according to Stokes' sandhi-rule, KZ. XXXVI, 273, *et* would have been pronounced *ed*, it is really only a matter of writing one *d* for two. As to the syntax, *is bés, is bésad* is often followed by an indicative without a conjunction (the above literally means, 'it is the custom of a prince, he protects' etc.), e. g. Tur. 120, Wb. 24 d 11, where *berad* should, with Stokes, be corrected to *bésad*.

10 c 2 hic cognitus est ab eo, g. *is . . . . sius dodia.*

Here *sius* is probably an error for *fius*. To supply the lacuna might be suggested *ishé asfius dodia.*

11 c 18 mulierem non uelatam, g. *nocht* Zimmer, *nochit* (leg. *noicht*) Stokes. Perhaps *nocht* i. e. *nochtchenn*, cf. 11 c 12.

11 c 19 *niforcain aicned.*

Pedersen, KZ. XXXV, 342, objects to Stokes' *ní forcain* and takes *ni* for the negative. If so, the glossator has misunderstood his text. On the other hand *ní forcain aicned* is perfectly good Irish, and an excellent explanation of *lex naturae.*

12 b 34 .i. in mortem *ardagní sochuide báas aracharit nesso assanesso ɔdidtanicc fessin.*

Here there are two glosses, or, at least, two sentences, (1) 'for many die for a friend', (2) 'nearer and nearer till he comes to himself' (i. e. his own body). The latter is a general gloss on verses 1—3; Paul first speaks of diverse gifts, prophecy etc., then he speaks of giving his goods to the poor, and finally he speaks of sacrificing his own life. In KZ. XXXV, 407 Pedersen translates 'bis er auch dazu kam', which seems hardly to account satisfactorily for the *fessin.*

12 d 16 leg. *don doiscar.*

12 d 39 *trissinprecept bésti ituiremar bestatu cáich.* For *ituiremar* read *ituisemar.*

15 a 23 *preceptori nuiadnissi mór ní as dénti ní airriu.* Pedersen, KZ. XXXV, 317, would reject the second *ní* as dittography, but the sentence is capable of translation as it stands:

'teachers of the New Testament, greatly is somewhat do be done for them'. In Ml. *mór ní* is common, especially in the connexion *ciafiu* .i. *mór ní.* For *as dénti asndénti* might rather have been expected, cf. Pedersen, KZ. XXXV, 391, and perhaps it should be restored.

15 b 23 *ní derge . . . met* g. non distituimur.

Cf. Stokes' note on the passage. Perhaps we should supply *ní dergemar* (which Zeuss and Zimmer read) and correct *met* to *ni et* i. e. *ni etir. dergemar* is a curious translation of the passive *destituimur*, but it is supported by the preceding *frisbrúdémor* which glosses *aporiamur*.

17 b 5 *iarríchte ní barscéuil si.*

'After getting some tidings of you', Stokes. The only difficulty is *ní*; I can find no evidence that it was used as a genitive. One might suggest tentatively *iarnarríchteni barscéuilsi,* 'after tidings of you have reached us'. Cf. *farríchtu* 7 a 3.

17 d 18 si gloriari oportet, non expedit quidem mihi, .i. *ní torbanad.*

There is nothing in the Latin context to justify an imperfect. Should we read *ní torban and*?

18 c 11 *arniba maith a áidlea dúib anétsecte.*

In this sentence it is clear that *áidlea* is a noun, on which the genitive *étsecte* depends. The preceding *a* may be explained as the possessive pronoun anticipating the genitive. The general sense required is, 'the consequence to you of hearkening to them will not be good'. But *áidlea* is not clear. Can it be for *aithle* the noun which appears in the phrase *as a haithle*? If so, for the spelling may be compared *foirbthea* for *foirbthe* 19 a 11.

20 b 1 Only *forsarobith* is possible, since *no-* is not used with particles that take the enclitic form of the verb.

21 a 13 For *arailiu* one would expect in full *madiarnarailiu* or the like.

26 a 12 *cinidaccastar ni nachthised agním arandogenadsom íartichte* etc.

This seems to mean: 'though he be not seen. Not that his work has not come; for what he would do after coming' etc.

26 b 22 *indualib.*

Can this be for *indual lib*, 'do ye think it proper'? If so, it is not a translation of any particular word in the text, but a general gloss.

27 c 11 *ma* : : : *d irlaithi.*

The sense must be, 'if ye be not obedient', and the mood required is the subjunctive. Hence we may probably supply *ma*[*nba*]*d* or *ma*[*inba*]*d*, according to the number of letters for which there is space.

Saint Gall Glosses.

63 b 17 Ascoli remarks, cancell.: *tindrem.* In Ml. 48 c 11 occurs *béstindrim* g. tropologiam; which may have been in the writer's mind.

136 a 1 um. *doglanad inderiud ferso.* Rather *doglanad as,* cf. 136 a 2.

188 a 19 fere *cétnide* .i. *é amess limm.*

Rather fere *cétnide* .i. *isé amess limm.* The last words seem to be an explanation of the meaning of the 'primary' *fere.* For the 'derivative' *fere* cf. Prisc. XV, 14, where *fere* = *iuxta* is derived from *ferus.*

188 a 22 *neph denom rainne di foleith acht aram la ainm.*

Read *aaram,* 'in not making of it a separate part (of speech), but reckoning it with the noun'.

188 a 23 in participiis *techtite* proprias transfigurationes uerborum *hicach aiccidit* absce personis 7 modis 7 *notechtath dano in aimsir indsainriud.*

Leg. *notechtat* (= *no-d-techtat*), 'which have it in time in particular.

199 a 5 *gniid sem nachnaile.* Leg. *for nach naile,* cf. 199 a 2, 3.

209 b 30 Ascoli has corrected *diacumachtachtaigther* to *diacumachtaigther* (Gloss. Pal. hib. CI), but 'quo potiaris' hardly expresses the meaning of the Irish. *Cumachtaigim* is coined to express *potior* on the assumption that it comes from the comparative *potior.* Here one might translate literally: 'till thou knowest for whom thou art powerful, whether for thyself or for another, i. e. it is uncertain whose the slave is till thou sayest *mei,* i. e. it is shewn therein that he is my own'.

217 b 16 *echtarecht* g. cis naturae leges.

Cf. Stokes, CZ. II, 479. But may not *echtarrecht* be a compound like *echtarchathraig, sechtarchathraig* Ml. 54 c 18, 20?

Bowdon, Cheshire.   J. STRACHAN.

GRAMMATISCHE BEITRÄGE.

2. Über verbale Neubildungen im Neuirischen.

§ 1. Das Neuirische hat im Indikativ, sowohl des Aktivs wie Passivs, als Erbe aus älterer Zeit fünf Tempora überkommen: 1. ein Präsens (*caithim* 'ich verbrauche', *caitheann sé* 'er verbraucht'); 2. ein Imperfekt, in der altirischen Grammatik nach seiner Bildung 'Praesens secundarium', in neuirischen Grammatiken nach seiner hauptsächlichsten Verwendung 'Habitual Past' oder 'Consuetudinal Past' genannt (*chaithinn* 'ich pflegte zu verbrauchen', *chaitheadh sé* 'er pflegte zu verbrauchen'); 3. ein Präteritum (*chaitheas* 'ich verbrauchte', *chaith sé* 'er verbrauchte'); 4. ein Futur (*caithfead* 'ich werde verbrauchen', *caithfidh sé* 'er wird verbrauchen'); 5. einen Konditionalis, altir. nach seiner Bildung 'Futurum secundarium' genannt (*chaithfinn* 'ich würde verbrauchen', *chaithfeadh sé* 'er würde verbrauchen'). Von diesen fünf Tempora haben besonders 3 und 5 ausgedehnte Gebrauchssphären, worüber man in neuirischen Grammatiken gar nicht oder nur mangelhaft unterrichtet wird. Es hat 3 die Bedeutung von Aorist-Perfekt und Plusquamperfekt im Griechischen (von historischem und wirklichem Perfekt und Plusquamperfekt im Lateinischen; von Passé défini, Passé indéfini, Plusqueparfait, Passé antérieur im Französischen); und Tempus 5 hat noch die Bedeutung des französischen Conditionnel antérieur (Plusquamperfekt Konjunktiv).

Gerade die Vereinigung der beiden Bedeutungen in Tempus 5 fällt einem Deutschen am meisten auf. Man sagt also, um einen Satz wie 'wenn ich davon würde Kenntnis gehabt haben (hätte

Kenntnis gehabt), würde ich früher geredet haben' auszudrücken, neuir. *dá mbeidheadh fhios agam sin, do laibheórainn
nios luaithe* d. h. 'wenn ich davon würde Kenntnis haben
(Kenntnis hätte), würde ich früher sprechen' (Leabhar sgeulaigheachta, le Dúbhghlas de H-Ide S. 229). So heisst es dann
auch Joh. 11, 21 in Übersetzung der Worte Marthas (*Domine!
Si fuisses hic, frater meus non fuisset mortuus*) in der
irischen Bibel: *A Thighearna, dá mbeitheasa annso ní bhfuigheadh
mo dhearbhráthairsi bás* 'o Herr, wenn du hier sein würdest,
würde mein Bruder den Tod nicht finden'. In einer modernen
Connachterzählung heisst es: *Rinne an seanduine gáire, O, ar
seisean, dá bhfeicfeá an bóithrín seó dá fhichid bliadhain o
shoin nuair bhí mise am ógánach, dheurfá nach raibh ann acht
cosán coinínidh* 'der alte Mann stiess ein Lachen aus, o, sagte
er, wenn du gesehen hättest diesen Nebenweg vor 40 Jahren
als ich ein junger Bursche war, dann würdest du gesagt
haben, dass nur ein Kaninchenpfad da war' (Leabhar sgeulaigheachta S. 76, 6 ff.). Ganz gewöhnlich trifft man in Erzählungen die Formen des Konditionalis in den beiden Bedeutungen neben einander: *A Fhinn Mic Chumhail, arsa Déirdre,
shaoil mé nach n-déanfá breug liom. Cia an fáth nár chuir tú
na bratacha dubha suas dam? bhí faitchios orm, a Dhéirdre, go
g-cuirfeá ceó draoidheachta orm dá bh-feictheá na bratacha
duba shuas againn. Dá m-béidhdís shuas agat, ní leigfinn in
tíre thú go d-tabharfá Murchadh beó chugam.* 'O Finn
Mac Cumail', sagte Deidre, 'ich dachte, du würdest nicht
Betrug an mir ausüben. Weshalb hast du die schwarzen
Flaggen nicht für mich aufgezogen? Ich fürchtete mich, o
Deirdre, du würdest Zaubernebel über mich bringen (aus-
giessen), wenn du bei uns die schwarzen Flaggen oben sehen
würdest. Wenn du sie oben gehabt hättest, würde ich
dich nicht ans Land gelassen haben, bis du Murchad lebend
würdest zu mir gebracht haben' (Siamsa an Gheimhridh,
S. 11, 1—6).

　　Ebenso gewöhnlich ist, dass Tempus 3 neben der Bedeutung
des lateinischen Perfekts — also des Aorists (historischen Perfekts)
und wirklichen Perfekts — die Bedeutung des lateinischen Plusquamperfekts hat. So heisst es in einer Munstererzählung:
*D'iontuigheadar aghaidh ar áit go glaodhann siad Céim
Cairrige uirthe, i n-aice Sráide an Mhuilinn. Nior chuireadar*

puinn bothair díobh nuair bhuail sluagh saighdiúrí umpa 'sie
gingen auf einen Ort zu, den man Céim Cairrige nennt, in der
Nähe von Millstreet; sie hatten keine grosse Strecke Weges
zurück gelegt, als ihnen eine Schar Soldaten begegnete'
(Fáinne an lae 3, S. 59, 2); in einer Mayoerzählung heisst es:
*Leis sin thosuigh sí ag caoineadh go bog, gur imthigh an
chumhaidh dithi comh sgiobtha agus tháinic si* 'bei diesen
Worten begann sie sanft zu schluchzen, bis der Schmerz sie so
rasch verliess wie er gekommen war' (Irisleabhar Gaedhilge
9, 289, 1). Noch sei aus einer Galwayerzählung angeführt:
*D'éirigh Goll go marbhóchadh sé Osgar, mar gheall gur mharbh
sé an Bhean Mhór* 'Goll erhob sich, um Oskar zu töten, weil
er die grosse Frau getötet hatte' (Annales de Bretagne 13, 54);
*nuair fuaradar amach go ceart gur b'é Bric na Buaire dubhairt
an sgeul sin agus do chuir amach orra é, níor bhfiú leó é
mharbhadh, acht sé do rinneadar, é do chur asteach i soitheach
agus a chathadh amach 'sa bhfairrge* 'als sie heraus bekommen
hatten, dass es Bric na Buaire war, der diese Geschichte
erzählt hatte und über sie in Umlauf gesetzt hatte, da
dünkte es sie nicht der Mühe wert, ihn zu töten, sondern sie
thaten dies, ihn in ein Fass setzen und es hinaus ins Meer
werfen' (l. l. 13, 78). Da ich im weiteren Verlauf in anderem
Zusammenhang noch weitere Belege beibringe, mögen die angeführten vorläufig genügen.

§ 2. Diese Vieldeutigkeit der Tempora 3 und 5 (Präteritum und Konditionalis) ist schon mittelirisch und beruht auf
Entwicklungen des Altirischen, deren Darlegung mich hier zu
weit führen würde. Der Versuche, in einzelnen Fällen, wo eine
genauere Ausdrucksweise wünschenswert erschien, der Vieldeutigkeit abzuhelfen, finden sich im Mittelirischen und älteren
Neuirisch mancherlei. Dem heutigen Neuirischen, wie es im
Norden, Westen und Süden von Irland gesprochen aber noch
nicht von Grammatikern dargestellt wird, blieb es vorbehalten,
einen festen Ersatz zu schaffen in einer umschreibenden
Konjugation mit 'haben' für die transitiven Verba. Ein
Verbum wie gr. ἔχω, lat. habeo, germ. (got.) *haban* besitzen bekanntlich die keltischen Sprachen nicht, sondern suchen durch
mannigfache Umschreibungen dem Begriffe gerecht zu werden.
An zwei Punkten des keltischen Sprachgebietes hat sich aus der
Mannigfaltigkeit der Umschreibungen je eine durchgerungen und

zu einem Verb '*haben*' ausgebildet: im Bretonischen (Kornischen)
und Neuirischen. Im Bretonischen hat sich die gemeinkeltische
Redensart '*est mihi, est tibi, est ei*' etc. für *habeo, habes, habet*
zu einem Verbum durch alle Tempora verdichtet (s. ZE. 565—572;
Ernault, Revue Celt. 9, 258—266); im Neuirischen andererseits
ist die Redensart *est apud me* (*penes me*) die Grundlage für ein
Verb 'haben' durch alle Tempora geworden. So also neuir.
Präsens *tá agam* (enkl. *níl agam, go bhfuil agam*) 'ich habe',
tá agat 'du hast', *tá aige* 'er hat', *tá aici* 'sie hat', *tá againn*
'wir haben', *tá agaibh* 'ihr habt', *tá aca* 'sie haben'; Imperfekt
bhíodh agam 'j'avais'; Prät. *bhí agam* 'j'eus' (*ni raibh agam, go
raibh agam*); Futur *béidh agam* 'ich werde haben'; Konditionalis
bhéidheadh agam 'ich würde haben'; Infinitiv *bheith agam, agat,
aige* etc. 'haben', je nachdem das im Infinitiv liegende Subjekt
ein 'ich, du, er' etc. ist. In analoger Weise, wie das Bretonische
schon seit 500 Jahren mit Hilfe seines neugeschaffenen Verbes
für '*haben*' die ihm mit dem Kymrischen gemeinsam als keltisch-
britannisches Erbe überkommenen Tempora ergänzt (s. ZE. 543 ff.),
hat das gesprochene Neuirisch unter Anlehnung an das Verb
'*haben*' auf Grund umschreibender Tempora des Passivs neue
Tempora zu den eingangs genannten 5 überkommenen Tempora
des Aktivs gestellt, wie wir im Verlauf noch näher erörtern
werden. Es hat dadurch mit einem Schlag für einzelne Fälle
eine Genauigkeit des zeitlichen Ausdrucks erreicht, die man im
Deutschen oder Englischen nur durch Hinzunahme einer weiteren
Umschreibung wiedergeben kann, und die sich der Präzisität
des Französischen vergleicht. Es stellt sich daher in dem
heutigen gesprochenen Irisch die Flexion des eingangs als Beispiel benützten transitiven Verbs *caitheamh* 'geniessen, verzehren,
verbrauchen' im Aktiv so dar, wenn ich der Kürze wegen die
gewöhnlichen französischen Bezeichnungen der Tempora wähle:
1. Présent *caithim* 'je consume'; 2. Imparfait *chaithinn* 'je con-
sumais'; 3. Passé défini *chaitheas* 'je consumai'; 3 a. Passé indéfini
tá caithte agam 'j'ai consumé'; 3 b. Plusqueparfait *bhíodh caithte
agam* 'j'avais consumé'; 3 c. Passé antérieur *bhí caithte agam*
'j'eus consumé'; 4. Futur *caithfead* 'je consumerai'; 4 a. Futur
antérieur *béidh caithte agam* 'j'aurai consumé'; 5. Conditionnel
chaithfinn 'je consumerais'; 5 a. Conditionnel antérieur *bhéidheadh
caithte agam* 'j'aurais consumé'; ferner tritt zum Infinitiv des
Präsens *caitheamh* 'consumer' ein Infinitiv des Präteritums *bheith*

(*a bheith*) *caithte agam, agat, aige* etc. 'avoir consumé' und zum alten Imperativ das Präsens *caith* 'consume' ein Imperativ des Präteritums *biodh caithte agat* 'aie consumé' etc.

§ 3. Die neuirischen Grammatiker schweigen sich über diese wichtige Neubildung des neuirischen Verbes vollständig aus, soweit ich sehe, obwohl man kaum eine Seite genuinen Neuirisch lesen kann, ohne einem Beleg für die eine oder andere Form zu begegnen. Ich sehe mich daher genötigt zuerst durch eine Materialsammlung Umfang und Gebrauch der Neubildung festzustellen, ehe ich weitere ergänzende Bemerkungen vorbringen kann. Der Raumersparnis wegen citiere ich die hauptsächlichsten Quellen für diese Materialsammlung mit den im folgenden ihnen vorgesetzten Chiffern.

A. *Cois na teineadh. Sgeulta Gaedheilge cruinnuighthe agus curtha le chéile le Dúbhghlas de H-Ide.* Dublin 1890.

B. *Leabhar sgeulaigheachta cruinnuighthe agus curtha le chéile le Dúbhghlas de H-Ide. Baile-ath-cliath* 1889.

C. *An sgeuluidhe Gaodhalach. Cuid I, II. Le Dubhghlas de H-Ide.* Rennes 1895, 1897.

D. *Annales de Bretagne.* Tome 13, 14. Rennes 1898, 1899. Enthalten in einzelnen Nummern Fortsetzung von C.

E. *Siamsa an gheimhridh no cois an teallaigh in Iargconnachta. Do chruinnigh Domhnall O' Fotharta. Baile-Atha-Cliath* 1892.

F. *West Irish folk-tales and romances. Collected and translated by William Larminie.* London 1893. Enthält S. 239 ff. den irischen Text, phonetisch geschrieben, von einigen Erzählungen.

G. *Sgeuluidheacht chúige Mumhan. Ag Pádruig O Laoghaire. Baile-atha-Cliath* 1895.

H. *Irisleabhar na Gaedhilge.* Dublin 1882—1899. Es kommen besonders Band 5—7 in Betracht, in deren Nummern der erste Teil der unter *I* genannten Erzählung erschienen ist.

I. *Seadna. An dara cuid. An t-athair Peadar ua Laoghaire do shaothruig.* Dublin 1898.

K. *Fáinne an lae. Páipéar seachtmhaine dá theanga chum Gaedhilge do chur ar aghaidh.* Dublin 1898 ff.

L. *An claidheamh soluis* (*The Gaelic League weekly*). Dublin 1899.

Die Quellen unter *A* bis *F* repräsentieren Connacht- und
Donegal-Irisch (Galway, Roscommon, Mayo, Sligo, Donegal); die
Texte sind fast alle in den letzten 10 Jahren aus dem Munde
des Volkes gesammelt, nach den Angaben der Herausgeber oft
von alten Leuten, die Englisch gar nicht oder nur mangelhaft
verstehen. Wir haben also genuines West-Irisch heutigen
Tages in ihnen. In *G* bis *I* liegen uns Quellen genuinen
heutigen Südirisch aus Cork vor: den Texten in *G* merkt
man den Erdgeruch an, und über das Irisch in *H* und *I* ver-
sichert uns P. O'Leary in *I*, S. I 'there is not a single word,
nor a single turn of expression, which has not been got directly
from the mouths of living people who knew no English. There
has been no word-building. Not a single phrase has been either
invented or introduced from any outside source. The reader can
rest assured that while reading the story he is reading the
actual speech of living Irish people who knew no
English'. Von den im folgenden gegebenen Belegen stammen
76 aus *A* bis *F* und 90 aus *G* bis *I*; ein Unterschied zwischen
West- und Süd-Irisch tritt in Bezug auf Umfang und Gebrauch
der Neubildungen nicht zu Tage; ein im Verlauf zu erwähnender
kleiner formeller Unterschied im Futur antérieur hat mit der
Neubildung als solcher speziell nichts zu thun, sondern entspringt
einer allgemein dem Verb angehörigen Differenz zwischen West-
und Süd-Irisch. Es war daher auch nicht nötig für die rund
50 Belege aus *K* und *L* die Herkunft genauer zu bezeichnen,
was bei der guten Hälfte leicht möglich wäre. Ich gebe zuerst
bei jedem Tempus der umschreibenden Konjugation ein Paradigma und dann die Belege, wobei ich nicht belegte Formen im
Paradigma einklammere.

§ 4. 3 a) Passé indéfini.

    α) Sing. 1. *tá caithte agam* j'ai consumé.

            2. *tá caithte agat* tu as consumé.

            3. *tá caithte aige* il a consumé.

            tá caithte aici elle a consumé.

    Plur. 1. *tá caithte againn* nous avons consumé.

            2. [*tá caithte agaib*] vous avez consumé.

            3. *tá caithte aca* ils ont consumé.

Mit der einfachen direkten Negation muss sich das Paradigma so gestalten:

β) Sing. 1. [*níl caithtc agam* je n'ai pas consumé.

      2. *níl caithte agat* tu n'as pas consumé.

      3. *níl caithte aige* il n'a pas consumé.

      níl caithte aici elle n'a pas consumé.

Plur. 1. *níl caithte againn* nous n'avons pas consumé.

      2. *níl caithte agaibh* vous n'avez pas consumé.

      3. *níl caithte aca*] ils n'ont pas consumé.

Nach *go* (dass), *nach* (dass nicht), *an* (ob) und in anderen Fällen der Enklise haben wir:

γ) Sing. 1. *a (go) bhfuil caithte agam* ai-je consumé?

      2. *a (go) bhfuil caithte agat* as-tu consumé?

      3. *a (go) bhfuil caithte aigc* a-t-il consumé?

      a (go) bhfuil caithe aici a-t-elle consumé?

Plur. 1. *a (go) bhfuil caithte againn* avons-nous consumé?

      2. [*a (go) bhfuil caithte agaibh*] avez-nous consumé?

      3. *a (go) bhfuil caithte aca* ont-ils consumé?

§ 5. Die Belege zu *α* sind: Sing. 1. Person. *tá mo gheall gnóthaighthe agam* 'ich habe meine Wette gewonnen' (C, 44, 2); *tá an geall gnóthaighthe agam* 'ich habe die Wette gewonnen' (C, 136, 1); *tomhais cia mheud meur atá tóigthe agam* 'rate, wie viel Finger ich in die Höhe gehoben habe' (E, 17, 22); *tœœ tjriiăn don iine bonty oiam, ers ă maq rjii* 'ich habe ein Drittel deiner Tochter gewonnen, sagte der Königssohn' (F, 248, 16); *tœœ do niin ălig bunty oiam, ers ă maq ă rjii* 'ich habe deine Tochter ganz gewonnen, sagte der Königssohn' (F, 249, 37); *cad i an choir seo atá déanta agam?* 'was ist das für ein Verbrechen, das ich begangen habe?' (G, 80, 4); *ar choingoill ná tráchtfair choidhche ar an margadh so atá déanta agat féin agus agamsa le chéile* 'unter der Bedingung, dass du nie über dies Geschäft sprechen wirst, das du und ich mit einander gemacht haben' (H, 5, 180, 1); *pé tairbhe tá déanta agam, is ar aon aighneadh amháin do rinneas é* 'was immer Gutes ich gethan habe, nur in einer Absicht that ich es' (H, 7, 27, 2); *tá an gnó do thug mé déanta agam* 'ich habe das Geschäft, welches mich herführte, gethan' (H, 7, 35, 1); *tá cleamhnas déanta agam duit* 'ich habe eine Verlobung für dich zu stande gebracht' (H, 7, 52, 1); *tá rud déanta agam cheana féin, arsa Donnchadh ... tá ainm nua límnighthe ar clár agam agus cuirfidh mé suas é amáireach* 'ich selbst habe schon etwas gethan, sagte Donnough, ... ich habe einen neuen Namen auf eine Tafel geschrieben und ich werde sie morgen aufstellen' (K, 3, 2, 1); *tá sé buaidhte agamsa* 'ich habe sie (die Wette) gewonnen' (K, 3, 131, 3).

Sing. 2. Person. *tá do mhac gnóthaighthe agad* 'du hast deinen Sohn verdient' (C, 21, 12); *tá an geall gnóthaighthe agad* 'du hast die Wette gewonnen' (C, 36, 4); *sgaoil mé, tá mo chaol-droma briste agad* 'lass mich los, du hast mein Rückgrat gebrochen' (D, 14, 274, 4); *ar choingioll ná trachtfair choidhche ar an margadh so atá déanta agat féin agus agamsa le chéile* 'unter der Bedingung, dass du nie über diesen Handel sprechen wirst, den du gemacht hast und ich mit einander' (H, 5, 180, 1); *tá aos óg an bhaile loitthe agat* 'du hast das Jungvolk des Ortes verdorben' (H, 5, 181, 1); *cad tá déanta agatsa?* 'was hast du gethan?' (H, 6, 153, 2); *tá pádh an lae indiu tuillte agat* 'du hast den Tagelohn heute verdient' (H, 6, 178, 2); *is iomdha maith atá deanta agat leó na beidhcadh déanta agat dá mbadh na feicfa riamh iad* 'manches Gute hast du mit ihnen gethan, das du nicht würdest gethan haben, wenn du sie nie gesehen hättest' (H, 7, 35, 2); *tá dearmad déanta agat* 'du hast einen Irrtum begangen' (K, 2, 155, 1); *is iomdha peacadh marbh atá déanta agat* 'du hast viele Todsünden gethan' (K, 3, 19, 1); *tá siad meallta agat go deimhin* 'du hast sie sicher betrogen' (K, 3, 138, 3).

Sing. 3. Person. *mise am' bhanna go gcúiteóchamuid leis an dá bheart so atá imrighthe aige orrainn* 'ich verbürge mich, dass wir ihm diese beiden Streiche heimzahlen werden, die er uns gespielt (angethan) hat' (E, 26, 9); *tá bréidín casta aige air gharmain C. A.* 'er hat Loden gedreht auf dem Webstuhl von C. A.' (E, 95, 2); *atá a dhóithin faghálta feasta aige* 'er hat jetzt genug abbekommen' (G, 24, 24); *cad é an tuathal is deire-annaighe atá déanta aige?* 'welches ist die letzte (neueste) Thorheit, die er begangen hat?' (H, 6, 153, 2); *ní saoráidighe atá sgartha aigesan le Máire* 'nicht leichter hat er Marie aufgegeben als ...' (H, 7, 118, 2); *is dóich liom gur sa Mhumhain a dhein sé pé cuir atá deanta aige* 'ich glaube in Munster beging er, was er immer für ein Verbrechen begangen hat' (I, 38, 19); *is amhlaidh tá ceaptha aige colláisde do chur ar bun i g-Cartoum* 'er hat beschlossen, eine höhere Schule in Khartum zu gründen' (K, 2, 177, 3). — *tá buaidhte aici ort* 'sie hat dich besiegt' (H, 7, 101, 2); *ní saoráidighe atá sgartha aigesan le Máire 'ná atá sgartha aici leis* 'nicht leichter hat er Marie aufgegeben als sie ihn aufgegeben hat' (H, 7, 118, 2).

Plur. 1. Person. *tá an uair seó gnóthaighthe againn* 'wir haben diesmal gewonnen' (C, 22, 28); *tá an cluiche buaidhte againn* 'wir haben das Spiel gewonnen' (K, 3, Beilage zum 18. März, S. 2, 2); *ar maith leat an chaint chéadna so, atá caite againne le chéile indiu, d'aireachtaint?* 'möchtest du diese Unterhaltung da, welche wir heute mit einander gepflogen haben, hören? (L, 1, 29, 2).

Plur. 3. Person. *tá mé cráidhte acca* 'sie haben mich gequält' (A, 1, 26); *tá an t-aonach creachta accu* 'sie haben den Markt geplündert (ruiniert)' (H, 7, 165, 2); *tá caogad míle punt cruinnighthe accu chuige* 'sie haben 50000 Goldkronen dazu gesammelt' (K, 2, 178, 1); *tá buaidhte acca orainn* 'sie haben uns besiegt' (K, 3, 2, 2); *tá ainm mór onórach tuillte acca do línéadach na hEireann* 'sie haben einen grossen ehrenvollen Namen für das irische Leinen erworben' (K, 3, 18, 1); *tá cuid mhaith dá n-iarrtóiribh ceaptha amach aca cheana féin* 'sie haben schon selbst einen guten Teil ihrer Kandidaten in Aussicht genommen' (K, 3, 33, 2); *is ar éigin atá leithead a mbonn de na hoileánaibh buaidhte aca fós* 'kaum haben sie eine Fussbreite von den Inseln schon erobert' (K, 3, 50, 1); *tá ceaptha aca anois ar chúig breitheamhnaibh agus dá fhichid do chur i mbun na cúise* 'sie haben sich jetzt entschlossen, 45 Richter für die Sache zu bestellen' (K, 3, 50, 2); *tá cuaird ceapuighthe aca do feisiribh Sasana* 'sie haben einen Besuch der englischen Abgeordneten in Aussicht genommen' (K, 3, 57, 1).

§ 6. Für β habe ich für die im Paradigma vorgesehenen Fälle, dass das Subjekt ein Pronomen ist, keinen Beleg, wohl aber für die im Verlauf (§ 14) zu behandelnden Fälle, dass das Subjekt durch ein Nomen repräsentiert wird. *Ní'l puinn buaidhte ag Riaghaltas na Stát agus is beag a bhfuil caillte ag na hinnseoiribh go dtí so* 'die Regierung der Vereinigten Staaten hat nicht das Geringste gewonnen, und die Insulaner haben wenig bisher verloren' (K, 3, 58, 1).

§ 7. Die Belege zu γ sind wieder zahlreich. Singularis 1. Person: *ceapaim anois ná*[1]*) fuil an ceart déanta agam*

---

[1]) *ná fuil* ist Munsterdialekt für *nach bhfuil* des Connachtdialektes.

'ich glaube jetzt, dass ich nicht recht gethan habe' (H, 7, 34, 2);
béidh buidheachas mór agam ort acht insinn do lucht léighte do
'Thuairisg bliadhanamhail' go bh-fuil an leabhar do sgriobh
Seathrun Ceitinn, ar a dtugthar mar ainm 'Eochair-sgiath an
Aiffrinn' anois clodhbhuailte agam 'ich werde dir sehr
dankbar sein, wenn du den Lesern deines Jahresberichtes mit-
teilst, dass ich G. Keatings Buch, welches Eochair-sgiath an
Aiffrinn genannt wird, jetzt gedruckt habe' (Report of the
Society for the Preservation of the Irish Language 1898,
S. 36).

Sing. 2. Person. *tá faitchios orm go bhfuil anachain*
déanta agat 'ich fürchte, dass du Unheil angerichtet hast
(A, 36, 21); *feicim go bhfuil d'obair lae deanta agad* 'ich sehe,
dass du dein Tagewerk gethan hast' (C, 81, 23; 82, 20; 118, 12)';
muna bhfuil mé gearrtha agat 'wenn du mich nicht ge-
schnitten (geritzt) hast' (E, 52, 5); *a bhfuil do dhóithin faghál-*
tha fós agat? 'hast du schon genug bekommen?' (G, 13, 24);
cuimhnimh ar a bhfuil déanta as an tslighe agat 'denke daran,
was du Unrechtes gethan hast' (G, 21, 13); *agus ní beag a*
bhfuil déanta cheana agat 'es ist nicht wenig, was du schon
gethan hast' (G, 70, 11); *chím go bhfuil an phuiblidheacht*
meallta agat 'ich sehe, dass du das Publikum betrogen hast'
(K, 3, 138, 3); *muna léigheadsa amach as an bpáipér so dhuit an*
uile fhocal dh'á bhfuil raidhte anso indiu agat 'wenn ich
nicht aus dieser Zeitung dir jedes Wort lesen werde, das du
heute hier gesagt hast' (L, 29, 2).

Sing. 3. Person. *cia an sluagh a bhfuil an báire gnó-*
thaighthe aige? 'welche Schar hat das Spiel gewonnen?' (C,
65, 29); *i dteannta a bhfuil faghaltha aige* 'zu dem, was er
bekommen hat' (G, 29, 3); *tá eagla orm go n-eirgheáchaidh a*
chroidhe ar Dhiarmuid muna bhfuil eirighthe cheana aige
air 'ich fürchte, dass sein Herz gegen Dermot revoltieren wird,
wenn es nicht schon gegen ihn revoltiert hat' (I, 2, 19). — *'s*
dócha go bhfuil sé ithte um an taca so aicci 'ich vermute,
dass sie ihn jetzt schon aufgegessen hat' (H, 6, 5, 1).

Plur. 1. Person. *do réir mar chím ní dóich liom go*
mbeadh slígh don sgéal an turus so i dteannta a bhfuil ráidhte
againn 'nach dem was ich sehe, ist mir nicht wahrscheinlich,
dass diesmal Raum für die Geschichte wäre zu dem, was wir
geredet haben' (L, 108, 1).

Plur. 3. Person. *is dóigh liom nach fuláir nó go bhfuil rud éigin fóghanta beirthe uaidh acu* 'es scheint mir, dass sie irgend etwas Wertvolles ihm entführt haben müssen' (H, 7, 179, 1); *an mhuintir go bhfuil a gcuid caillte acu* 'die Leute, welche ihr Eigentum verloren haben' (H, 7, 179, 2); *is mór é ár meas ar mhaighisdiríbh sgoile na hEireann, cé gur beag a bhfuil déanta fós ar son na Gaedhilge acu* 'wir hegen grosse Hochachtung vor den Schulmeistern Irlands, obwohl sie erst wenig fürs Irische gethan haben' (L, 113, 1); *agus ní séantar gur i n-olcas atá an aicíd ag dul tár éis a bhfuil ráidhte acu* 'und es wird nicht geleugnet, dass die Krankheit zu einem Übel wird nach dem, was sie gesagt haben' (L, 1, 113, 2).

§ 8.   3b) Plusqueparfait.
Sing. 1. [*bhíodh caithte agam*] j'avais consumé.
    2. [*bhíodh caithte agat*] tu avais consumé.
    3. *bhíodh caithte aige* il avait consumé.
Plur. 1. [*bhíodh caithte againn*] nous avions consumé.
    2. [*bhíodh caithte agaibh*] vous aviez consumé.
    3. *bhíodh caithte aca* ils avaient consumé.

Belege hierfür sind folgende.   Sing. 3. Person. *nuair bhidheadh ceann no beirt ceaptha aige, bhidheadh an chuid eile air siúbhal nuair thigeadh sé* 'jedesmal wenn er eins oder zwei von ihnen eingefangen hatte, pflegte der andere Teil wegzulaufen, wenn er wieder zu kommen pflegte' (B, 139, 3, 4); *i dtreo gur dhóich leat gur geall abhíodh curtha aige* 'in der Weise, dass du glauben solltest, dass er eine Wette eingegangen hätte' (I, 15, 2). — Plur. 3. Person. *'nuair bhíodh roinnt capall ceannuighthe accu agus díolta asta agus iad féin agus an giollaidhe curtha ar bhóthar Bhaile Atha Cliath acu, d'fhillidís* 'so oft wenn sie eine Partie Pferde gekauft und bezahlt hatten und (wenn) sie dieselben und ihre Burschen auf die Strasse nach Dublin gebracht hatten, pflegten sie zurück zu kehren' (H, 7, 165, 1); *'nuair bhíodh a sáith magaidh déanta ag daoinibh fé Dhiarmaid agus fé Shaidhbh, do bhíodh nidh eile ar siubhal aco* 'so oft wenn Leute genügend ihren Spott an Dermot und Seive ausgelassen hatten, pflegten sie etwas anderes im Gange zu haben' (H, 6, 116, 1).   Die geringe Anzahl der Belege im Vergleich zu dem betrachteten Passé indéfini und zu dem sofort zu betrachtenden Passé antérieur erklärt sich aus der speziellen Bedeutung dieses Tempus, die eine häufige Verwendung in den zu Grunde liegenden Quellen einfach ausschliesst.

§ 9. 3 c) Passé antérieur.

Hier haben wir zwei Reihen von Formen zu unterscheiden: α) Formen in direkter unabhängiger Rede (Orthotonese) und β) Formen abhängig von *ni, nach, go, an* und anderen Bedingungen der Enklise.

α) Sing. 1. *bhí caithte agam* j'eus consumé.
    2. *bhí caithte agat* tu eus consumé.
    3. *bhí caithte aige* il eut consumé.
     bhí caithte aici elle eut consumé.
  Plur. 1. [*bhí caithte againn*] nous eûmes consumé.
    2. [*bhí caithte agaib*] vous eûtes consumé.
    3. *bhí caithte aca* ils eurent consumé.

β) Sing. 1. *ni raibh caithte agam* je n'eus pas consumé.
    2. [*ni raibh caithte agat*] tu n'eus pas consumé.
    3. *ni raibh caithte aige* il n'eut pas consumé.
     ni raibh caithte aici elle n'eut pas consumé.
  Plur. 1. [*ni raibh caithte againn*] nous n'eûmes pas consumé.
    2. [*ni raibh caithte agaibh*] vous n'eûtes pas consumé.
    3. *ni raibh caithte aca* ils n'eurent pas consumé.

§ 10.

Belege zu α sind: Sing. 1. Person. *is ar éigin a bhí sé tabartha dó agam* 'kaum hatte ich es (das Geld) ihm gegeben' (I, 41, 6); *nuair a bhí cúig no sé de thurasaibh eile tabhartha agam, bhí na focail móra agam* 'als ich 5 oder 6 weitere Touren (Versuche) gemacht hatte, hatte ich die grossen Wörter' (L, 29, 1).

Sing. 2. Person. *cheapas go mb'éidir gur braon beag do bhí olta agat* 'ich dachte, es könnte sein, dass du einen kleinen Tropfen (Schluck) getrunken hattest' (H, 5, 132, 1); *cad do bhí ceapuighthe agat le déanamh?* 'was hattest du beschlossen zu thun?' (K, 3, Beilage zum 18. März, S. 4, 2).

Sing. 3. Person. *air bhárr na hoibre a bhí déanta aige* 'oben auf die Arbeit, die er gemacht hatte (A, 3, 22); weitere Belege für *bhí déanta aige* 'er hatte gethan' finden sich: A, 4, 17; B, 7, 6; 60, 17; C, 10, 27; 141, 26; H, 5, 164, 2; 6, 71, 1; 7, 134,

1; 7, 147, 1; I, 11, 85; K, 3, 115, 1; 3, 123, 1; *táinig mac ríogh Éireann ᚇ shiubhail sé na trí mhíle agus bhí a bhean gnóthuighthe aige* 'es kam der Königssohn aus Irland und ging die drei Meilen und er hatte seine Frau verdient' (A, 21, 13); *nuair bhí sé réidh sgríobhtha aige, chuir sé a ainm faoi* 'als er ihn fertig geschrieben hatte, setzte er seinen Namen darunter' (B, 22, 4); *sul bhí na focla sin cumtha aige ann a intinn, dubhairt glór ann a chluais* 'bevor er diese Worte in seinem Sinne gebildet hatte, sagte eine Stimme in seinem Ohr' (B, 120, 1); *bhí cuid mhaith draoigheachta fóghlamtha aige* 'er hatte ein gut Teil Zauberei gelernt' (B, 150, 14); *nuair bhí an suipéar ithte aige* 'als er zu Abend gegessen hatte' (C, 5, 23; 115, 19; 118, 5, 28); *do léigh an sagart sin an t-aifrionn agus nuair bhí sé leighte aige* 'es las dieser Priester die Messe und als er sie gelesen hatte' (C, 6, 27); *nuair bhí sgathadh caithte i gConnachtaibh aige* 'als er eine Weile in Connacht zugebracht hatte' (D, 13, 76, 5); *thosaigh Murchadh ag obair agus bhí an bád críochnuighthe aige sul má ndeachaidh an ghrían faoi an tráthnóna sin* 'Murchadh begann zu arbeiten und er hatte das Bot fertig gemacht, bevor die Sonne am Abend unterging' (D, 14, 96, 12); *chomh luath agus bhí sé ólta aige* 'sobald er es getrunken hatte' (D, 14, 280, 15); *chuir sé síos an teine agus nuair bhí sí deargtha aige dubhairt sé* 'er legte Feuer unter und als er es angezündet hatte, sagte er' (E, 9, 2); *nuair do bhí an cath tugtha, gnódhuighthe aige, thriall sé air an g-caisleán* 'als er die Schlacht geliefert und gewonnen hatte, schritt er auf die Burg zu' (E, 13, 21); *nuair bhí an fathach marbhuighthe aige* 'als er den Riesen getötet hatte' (E, 65, 13); *do bhí an lá buaidhte aige* 'er hatte den Tag gewonnen' (G, 101, 17); *ní túisge bhí an méid sin cainte raidhte aige, ná thug sé fé ndeara* 'sobald er diese Worte gesprochen hatte, bemerkte er' (H, 5, 118, 2); *nuair bhí an dá fhéire bróg críochnaighthe aige* 'als er die zwei Paar Schuhe fertig gemacht hatte' (H, 6, 85, 1); *mar bhí an áit geallta aige do dhuinè eile* 'denn er hatte den Ort einem Anderen versprochen' (H, 6, 153, 1); *nuair bhí a chuid bídh caithte aige* 'als er seine Nahrung verzehrt hatte' (H, 7, 3, 1). *D'imthigh air an rud do bhí tuillte aige* 'es widerfuhr ihm das, was er verdient hatte' (H, 7, 86, 2); *nuair bhí gabhtha go maith aige uirthi* 'als er sie ordentlich geprügelt hatte' (I, 26, 15); *thug sé fógra amach: fear ar bith do*

*thiocfadh isteach agus do chaithfeadh a phíce san teineadh mhór
do bhí faduighthe aige i sráid an mhargaidh, go maithfidhe
dho a chortha* 'er liess den Befehl ausgehen: wer immer herein
käme und seine Pike in das grosse Feuer werfen würde, welches
er in der Marktstrasse angezündet hatte, dem würden seine Ver-
gehen verziehen werden' (K, 3, 43, 1). — *D'éirigh Páidín agus
chuir sé an méid óir a bhí cruinnighthe aici ann a phóca*
'es erhob sich Páidín und steckte, was sie von Gold zusammen
getragen hatte, in seine Tasche' (A, 35, 22); *nuair bhí an
crúisgín lionta aicci* 'als sie den Krug gefüllt hatte' (C, 33, 6);
ann san áras do bhí deunta aicci 'in dem Wohnorte, den sie
gemacht hatte' (D, 13, 52); *chengail sí iad agus nuair bhí siad
uile ceangailte aicci* 'sie band sie und als sie sie alle gebunden
hatte' (D, 13, 52); *ní túisge bhí ólta aice 'ná bhí sí in-a sán-
rith* 'sobald sie getrunken hatte, war sie ganz gesund' (G, 5, 7);
sul ar shroich leission bheith ithte aige, bhí an loch taosgtha aicci
'bevor er dazu kam gegessen zu haben, hatte sie den See ausgeschöpft' (G, 84, 10); *nuair chonnaic sé, cad a bhí déanta
aicci* 'als er sah, was sie gethan hatte' (H, 6, 117, 1); *ni túisge
bhí an focal déidheanach ráidhte aici si* 'sobald sie das letzte
Wort ausgesprochen hatte' (H, 7, 36, 1); *do bhí rún chomh mór
leis tabhartha aici do Shiobháin cheana* 'sie hatte schon ein
so grosses Geheimnis der Siobháin anvertraut' (H, 7, 85, 2); *bhí
sé leathta ar fuaid na dúithche aici* 'sie hatte es durch die
Gegend hin verbreitet' (H, 7, 117, 2).

Plur. 3. Person. *nuair bhí sé ithte aca* 'als sie es gegessen hatten' (A, 4, 30); *do bhí an oircad sin de'n chorda
ithte aca faoi dheire, go ndearna sé iarracht láidir le n-a bhri-
seadh* 'schliesslich hatten sie so viel von dem Strick abgefressen,
dass er einen kräftigen Versuch machte, ihn zu zerreissen' (B,
85, 10); weitere Belege für *bhí ithe (olta) aca* 'sie hatten gegessen (getrunken)' finden sich noch C, 9, 9; 122, 21; F, 240, 23;
is ar éigin do bhí aghaidh tabhartha aco ar an mbaile 'kaum
hatten sie ihr Antlitz nach Hause gewendet' (H, 5, 164, 2); *nuair
bhí an chogarnach críochnuighthe acu* 'als sie das Geflüster
beendigt hatten' (H, 6, 162, 2); *do thuigedar 'na n-aighneadh nár
imthigh ortha acht an rud a'bhi tuillte acu* 'sie merkten in
ihrem Sinn, dass ihnen nur widerfuhr, was sie verdient hatten'
(I, 5, 17); *mar gheall ar an ngníomh abhi déanta acu* 'wegen
der That, welche sie begangen hatten' (I, 10, 27); *nuair tháinig*

deireadh na bliadhna bhí níos mó tairbhe déanta aca i gcaitheamh na bliadhna sin ná dorinneadar riamh roimhe sin ar feadh an taca chéadna 'als das Jahresende gekommen war, hatten sie grösseren Gewinn gemacht im Laufe dieses Jahres als sie je vorher während eines gleichen Zeitraumes machten' (K, 3, 50, 1); *bhí an cath críochnuighthe acu* 'sie hatten den Kampf beendet' (L, 84, 1).

§ 11. Die Belege für die Formenreihe β dieses Tempus sind: Sing. 1. Person. *dubhairt sé liom go raibh págh an lae seo tuillte agam* 'er sagte zu mir, dass ich den Lohn für diesen Tag verdient hatte' (H, 7, 3, 1); *níor chuimhnigheas orm féin go raibh an focal raidhte agam* 'ich dachte nicht an mich selbst, bis ich das Wort gesagt hatte' (H, 7, 74, 2); *ní raibh mo chuid airgid tabhartha agamsa dhó an uair sin* 'ich hatte damals ihm mein Geld noch nicht gegeben' (H, 7, 179, 2); *go dtí go raibh mo chuid airgid tabhartha agamsa uaim* 'bis ich mein Geld weg gegeben hatte' (H, 7, 179, 2); *ba ghearr go raibh páipéar fada curtha le chéile agam* 'in kurzer Frist hatte ich eine lange Abhandlung zusammengestellt' (K, 2, 154, 1).

Sing. 3. Person. *Shaoil an fathach go raibh sé ólta aige* 'der Riese dachte, er hätte es getrunken' (A, 5, 8); *ní raibh na trí choiscéim siúbhalta aige* 'er hatte die drei Schritte nicht gegangen, als ein Mann kam' (A, 9, 26); *chuaidh Páidín abhaile agus d'innis d'á mhnaoi go raibh teach mór agus gabháltas talmhan ceannuighthe aige* 'Páidín ging nach Hause und erzählte seiner Frau, dass er ein grosses Haus und ein Pachtgut erworben hätte' (A, 38, 31); *níor sguir sé dhe go raibh leath an chupáin ólta aige* 'er liess nicht davon ab, bis er die Hälfte des Bechers getrunken hatte' (B, 47, 5); *níor sguir sé no go raibh teud fada garbh deunta aige* 'er liess nicht ab, bis er ein langes, rauhes Seil gemacht hatte' (B, 60, 13); *ní raibh sé móimid ithte aige go raibh sé chomh slán a's bhi sé ariamh* 'er hatte es nicht einen Moment gegessen, als er so gesund war wie er früher war' (B, 167, 26); *dubhairt si go dtáinig agus go raibh aifrionn léighte aige* 'sie sagte, dass er gekommen wäre und dass er die Messe gelesen hatte' (C, 6, 11); *níor bhfad go raibh an méad a bhi ann san sgiobol buailte aige* 'in Kürze hatte er so viel in der Scheune war gedroschen' (C, 28, 1); *go raibh fiche piosa deunta aige de'n*

maide 'bis er 20 Stücke aus dem Stock gemacht hatte' (C, 35, 1);
ni chorróchadh sé go raibh a sháith ithte aige 'er würde sich
nicht von der Stelle bewegt haben, bis er sich satt gefressen
hatte' (C, 135, 31); *d'innis sé dhó go raibh an bád criochnuighthe aige* 'er erzählte ihm, dass er das Bot fertig
gemacht hatte' (D, 14, 96, 15); *duurtj maq ă rjii cŏ roo çœœ
djriiĕn an iine bontj enjiuh egĕ* 'der Königssohn sagte, dass
er zwei Drittel der Tochter heute gewonnen hätte' (F, 248, 36);
*mar shil sé cóirmáireach[1]) go raibh an bhean-uasal caillte
aige* 'da er sich einbildete, dass er die vornehme Dame verloren hatte' (G, 100, 26); *do bhí ag déanamh amach ar eadarthra
um an dtaca go raibh a mhachtnamh criochnuighthe aige*
'es ging auf die Zeit zwischen hell und dunkel zu um die Zeit
als er seine Betrachtungen beendigt hatte' (H, 6, 133, 1); *ni
raibh dá ghreim curtha aige* 'er hatte nicht zwei Stiche
gethan' (H, 6, 163, 1); *ni raibh an triomhadh greim curtha
aige* 'er hatte nicht den dritten Stich gethan' (H, 7, 51, 1);
*má's amhlaidh d'innis sé dhi go raibh geallamhaint tabhartha
do Shaidhbh aige* 'wenn er ihr erzählte, dass er der Seive ein
Eheversprechen gegeben hatte' (H, 7, 118, 2); *níl agam le rádh
leis acht ... gur leig sé air liomsa ná raibh oiread airgid aige
agus dhiolfadh as a raibh ceannuighthe aige* 'ich habe
ihm nur zu sagen, dass er mir gegenüber vorgab, er habe nicht
genügend Geld zum Bezahlen dessen, was er gekauft hatte' (I,
37, 29; 41, 4); *nior leig sé air, go raibh pioc déanta aige*
'er liess nicht merken, dass er etwas gethan hatte' (K, 3, 123, 1).
níor imthigh leath a raibh tuillte aici 'es widerfuhr ihr nicht
halb, was sie verdient hatte' (I, 25, 24); *mar go raibh comaoin
mhór curtha aici air* 'da sie ihm eine grosse Gefälligkeit
erwiesen hätte' (I, 43, 29).

Plur. 3. Person. *nuair mheas seisean go raibh a sáith
ithte aca* 'als er dachte, dass sie sich satt gegessen hatten'
(C, 25, 1); *nuair ba dhóigh leis na hinnseoiribh go raibh díogh-
bháil a ndóthain déanta aca* 'als es den Insulanern schien, dass
sie genügend Schaden angerichtet hatten' (K, 3, 97, 3).

---

[1]) Für *Shil cóirmáireach* giebt O'Leary in den Noten zu G, 75, 16 als
Erklärung *shaoil go ceart acht bhí sé meallta.* Darnach löst sich *cóirmáireach*
auf in *cóir* und *máireach* (*muna bheidheadh*) 'wenn nicht wäre', worüber
Pedersen in Kz. 35, 365 gehandelt hat: 'er dachte richtig (*cóir*) ausser dass
(*máireach*) er nicht dies und das in Betracht zog'.

§ 12. 4a. Futur antérieur.

In diesem Tempus macht sich ein kleiner Unterschied zwischen Westirisch und Südirisch bemerkbar. Im Westirischen existiert neben der 3. Sing. des einfachen Futurs von 'sein', *béidh* 'er wird sein', eine relative Form *bhéidheas,* die auch nach gewissen Konjunktionen steht; im Munster-Irisch ist diese relative Form auf *-as* sowohl im Futur wie in anderen Temporibus fast unbekannt und es steht die gewöhnliche 3. Singularis dafür. Infolgedessen hat das Südirische auch nur eine Form für das Futur antérieur der transitiven Verba, während das Westirische noch eine relative Form kennt.

Sing. 1. *béidh caithte agam* j'aurai consumé.
 2. *béidh caithte agat* tu auras consumé.
 3. [*béidh caithte aige*] il aura consumé.
 [*béidh caithte aici*] elle aura consumé.
Plur. 1. [*béidh caithte againn*] nous aurons consumé.
 2. *béidh caithte agaibh* vous aurez consumé.
 3. *béidh caithte acu* ils auront consumé.

Hierzu tritt im Westirischen die relative Form:
 nuair bhéidheas caithte agam
 nuair bhéidheas caithte agat u. s. w.

Belege für das Tempus sind: Sing. 1. Person. *Fan go fóil go mbéidh mo dhinéar ithte agam* 'warte ein wenig, bis ich werde mein Diner gegessen haben' (C, 118, 26); *béidh an obair déanta agam* 'ich werde die Arbeit vollbracht haben' (D, 14, 274, 22); *tabhair spás beag cile dam 7 béidh sé dearmaduighthe go glan agam* 'gewähre mir noch eine kleine Weile und ich werde es rein vergessen haben' (K, 3, 50, 3). Ein Beleg für die relative Form ist *nuair bhéidheas sé deunta agam* 'wenn ich ihn werde gemacht haben' (C, 107, 10).

Sing. 2. Person. *fan go fóil go mbeidh mo mhála agus a bhfuil ann reamhruighthe agat* 'warte nur bis du meinen Sack und was darin ist gewalkt haben wirst' (G, 25, 27); *nuair bheidh do sgeal inste agat* 'wenn du deine Geschichte erzählt haben wirst' (I, 38, 2); *nuair bheidh na ba crúithte agat, beir chugham mo mhealbhóg* 'wenn du die Kühe wirst gemolken haben, bring mir meinen Rucksack' (G, 18, 22); *nuair bhéidh sé claoidhte agad, rachaidh mise leatsa* 'wenn du ihn besiegt

haben wirst, werde ich mit dir gehen' (D, 14, 274, 18), wo also
die relative Form in einem Connachtext nicht steht. Dafür
findet sie sich in *nuair bhéidheas an t-iasg ceannaighthe
agad* 'wenn du den Fisch wirst gekauft haben' (C, 7, 7).
    Plur. 2. Person. Das einzige Beispiel hierfür ist ein
Beleg für die relative Form: *ithigidh bhur ndinéar, adubhairt
an sean-fhear, agus nuair bhéidheas sé ithte agaibh, inn-
seóchaidh mise* 'esst euer Diner, sagte der alte Mann. und wenn
ihr es werdet gegessen haben, werde ich erzählen' (C, 122, 14).
    Plur. 3. Person. *Gan stad dá saothar go mbeidh an
beart déanta aca* 'nicht abzulassen von ihrer Mühe, bis sie
die Sache werden gethan haben' (K, 3, 33, 2); *gan dearmad, beidh
mórchuid díobh so oireamhnach ar déunamh go maith ag an
dtriail do'n Chlár léighinn ansa bh-fóghmhar so chúghann nuair
a bheidh a mblíadhain caithte aco dá fóghlaim* 'es wird ohne
Zweifel die Mehrzahl von ihnen fähig sein bei der Prüfung der
Unterrichtsbehörde im nächsten Herbst gut zu bestehen, wenn
sie ihr Jahr werden mit Lernen desselben (des Irischen) verbracht
haben' (Report for 1898 der Society for the Preservation of the
Irish language, S. 31; der Schreiber des Briefes stammt aus Grafschaft Cork). — Relative Form: *nuair a bheas a dtéarma
caithte aca* 'wenn sie ihre Zeit werden abgesessen haben'
(K, 3, 10, 1).
    § 13. 5a. Conditionnel antérieur.
    Sing. 1. *bhéidheadh caithte agam* j'aurais consumé.
        2. *bhéidheadh caithte agat* tu aurais consumé.
        3. *bhéidheadh caithte aige* il aurait consumé.
    Plur. 1. *bhéidheadh caithte againn* nous aurions consumé.
        2. [*bhéidheadh caithte agaibh*] vous auriez consumé.
        3. *bhéidheadh caithte aca* ils auraient consumé.

    Belege sind für Sing. 1. Person: *bhí eagla orm go mbhei-
dheadh cuid de caillte agam* 'ich hatte Furcht, ich würde
etwas davon verloren haben' (H, 5, 131, 1).
    Sing. 2. Person: *is iomdha maith tá deanta agat leó na
beidheadh deanta agat dá mbadh ná feicfeá riamh iad*
'manches Gute hast du mit ihnen gethan, was du nicht würdest
gethan haben, wenn du sie nie würdest gesehen haben' (H, 7,
35, 2); *nuair ná beadh aon nídh deanta as an slígh agat*
'wenn du nichts Unrechtes würdest gethan haben' (I, 26, 29).

Sing. 3. Person. *nuair bheidheadh sé déanta amach
ó'n gcaint aige* 'wenn er es aus der Unterhaltung würde heraus
gebracht haben' (H, 6, 85, 1); *tá súil agam anois go dtuillfidh
Miceal an t-airgead sain chomh macánta agus dá mbadh ná
beidheadh sé faghálta roimh ré aige* 'ich hoffe nun, dass
Michel das Geld so ehrlich abverdienen wird, als wenn er es
nicht vor der Zeit erhalten hätte' (H, 6, 162, 1); *chomh dána
agus dá mbhadh ná beidheadh a leithéid deanta aige* 'so kühn
als ob er nichts dergleichen gethan hätte' (H, 7, 134, 2); *dá
mbeidheadh sí árduighthe leis go Baile Átha Cliath aige*
'wenn er sie würde mit nach Dublin genommen haben' (H, 7,
148, 2); *nuair bhéadh gnó an aonaigh críochnuighthe aige*
'wenn er das Marktgeschäft würde beendigt haben' (I, 11, 29);
nuair do bheadh a thoil imeartha aige ortsa 'wenn er seine
Lust an dir würde ausgelassen haben' (I, 12, 5); *feuch ansain
nách deas an obair a bheadh deanta aige* 'sieh nun, was für
ein prächtiges Werk würde er gethan haben' (I, 19, 33); *dá mb'
aige beadh an gníomh deanta* 'wenn er die That würde gethan
haben' (I, 22, 8); *nuair a gheóbhadh sé ceann, ni shílfeadh se
dadaidh fanacht na shuighe oidhche agus lá da sgríobh go
m-béidheadh leabhar úr deánta aige fhéin as* 'wenn er
(Columba) eins (Buch) erlangt hätte, dann würde er für Nichts
geachtet haben Tag und Nacht dazusitzen um es abzuschreiben,
bis er selbst ein neues Buch aus ihm würde gemacht haben'
(Cuimhne Columcille, or the Gartan Festival, Dublin 1898, S. 128).

Plur. 1. Person. *da mbeadh sain déanta againn* 'wenn
wir dies würden gethan haben' (K, 3, 41, 2); *ni bheadh réim na
n-ainm sin rithte amach againn*[1]) 'wir würden die Liste dieser
Namen nicht beendigt haben' (K, 3, 140, 1).

Plur. 3. Person. *bhí siad ag deunamh lúthgháire le chéile
ag rádh nach fada anois go mbeidheadh an turus sin críochnuighthe acca faoi dheire* 'sie freuten sich mit einander,
sagend, dass jetzt nicht mehr fern wäre, bis sie schliesslich
diese Reise würden beendigt haben' (B, 76, 17); *nuair bhei-*

---

[1]) *rithim amach* 'ich beendige' ist Anglicismus *run out*, wie *techt suas
le* 'erreichen' = *come up with* und vieles andere. Das Neukymrische strotzt
in gleicher Weise von Anglicismen wie das Neubretonische von französischen
Wendungen. Herr Quiggin wird fürs Irische und Kymrische die Anglicismen
behandeln.

dheadh an obair deunta acca 'wenn sie die That würden
vollbracht haben' (C, 50, 26); *cheap lucht na nOileán go bhfuigh-
dis saoirse o Riaghaltas na Stát nuair do bheadh na Spáinnigh
ruaigthe aca* 'die Insulaner dachten, sie würden von der
Regierung der Vereinigten Staaten die Freiheit erhalten, wenn
sie die Spanier würden vertrieben haben' (K, 3, 26, 1); *ar coin-
gioll cána bliadhna do thabairt do'n Riaghaltas go dtí go mbeadh
na feilme ceannuighthe glan amach aca* 'unter Verpflichtung
der Zahlung einer jährlichen Abgabe an die Regierung, bis sie
(die Erbpächter) die Pachtgüter vollständig würden ausgekauft
haben' (K, 3, 41, 2).

§ 14. Zur Beleuchtung der fünf neuen Tempora habe ich
mich von § 4 bis § 13 auf die Fälle eingeschränkt, wo das
Subjekt ein Pronomen ist. Darauf ist natürlich die Bildung
nicht eingeschränkt, und es muss in den vorgeführten Formen
statt *agam, agat* etc. *ag* mit dem betreffenden Subjekt eintreten,
sofern dasselbe durch ein Nomen repräsentiert wird. Ich wähle
eine kleine Anzahl von Belegen aus in der Reihenfolge der be-
handelten Tempora.

Passé indéfini. *má tá an teine seo tuillte ag aonne,
is liomsa tá* 'wenn irgend jemand dies Feuer verdient hat, so
bin ich es' (G, 81, 10); *mar gheall ar an obair atá déanta ag
Connradh na Gaedhilge ar feadh na dtrí no ccathair de bhlia-
dhantaibh seo chuaidh tharainn* 'infolge der Arbeit, welche die
Gaelic League gethan hat im Verlauf der drei oder vier ver-
gangenen Jahre' (K, 3, 146, 3; H, 9, 287). Enklitisch: *muna
bhfuil buaidhte ag an méidsin gnótha ar a bhfacasa riamh
de neithibh iongantacha* 'wenn diese Arbeit nicht das, was ich
je von wunderbaren Dingen sah, übertroffen hat' (H, 6, 54, 1);
*ní'l amhras ná go bhfuil mórchuid déanta ag beagán daoine
le deidheanaighe do chúis na Gaedhilge* 'es unterliegt keinem
Zweifel, dass seit kurzem einige wenige Leute viel für die Sache
der irischen Sprache gethan haben' (K, 2, 178, 2); *ní'l puinn
buaidhte ag Riaghaltas na Stát agus is beag a bhfuil
caillte ag na hinnseoiribh go dtí seo* 'die Regierung der
Vereinigten Staaten hat nicht das Geringste gewonnen und die
Insulaner haben wenig verloren bis jetzt' (K, 3, 58, 1).

Plusqueparfait. *nuair bhíodh a sáith magaidh déanta
ag daoinibh fé Dhiarmuid agus fé Shaidhbh* 'so oft wenn

Leute genügend ihren Spott an Dermot und Seive ausgelassen hatten' (H, 6, 116, 1).

Passé antérieur. *Fuair an marcach é féin agus an t-each air an talamh tirim acht bhí a leathbhróg caillte aig an marcach* 'der Reiter fand sich und das Pferd auf dem trockenen Lande wieder, aber der Reiter hatte einen Schuh verloren' (E, 125, 22); *do bhí an gnó déanta ag Diarmuid chomh botúnach* 'Dermot hatte die Sache so tölpelhaft gethan' (H, 6, 116, 1); *bhí sé leathta ar fuaid na dúithche ag Saidhbh gur gheall sé i féin do phósadh* 'Seive hatte es durch die Gegend verbreitet, dass er versprochen habe, sie selbst zu heiraten' (H, 7, 133, 2); *bhí bean óg pósta ag fear críona fad ó* 'vor Zeiten hatte ein alter Mann eine junge Frau geheiratet' (K, 3, 58, 1); *dubharthas ann leis gur maith an rud a bhí ceapuighthe ag an gComhaltas Ríoghamhuil* 'man sagte auch, dass gut wäre, was die königliche Kommission in Aussicht genommen hatte' (K, 3, 129, 2); *nuair abhí an dinneur ithte ag Jack, cá bhfuil an bára óir anois, adeir an sagart* 'als Jakob das Diner gegessen hatte, sagt der Priester, wo ist der Goldklumpen jetzt' (L, 1, 69, 1). Enklitisch: *bhí gach re mbuille aca araon go raibh buille agus fiche buailte ag cách díobh* 'sie schlugen abwechselnd, bis jeder von ihnen 21 Schläge geschlagen hatte' (G, 13, 18); *bhí sé buailte isteach ina aigneadh go raibh geallamhaint phósta tabhartha ag Séadna do Shaidhbh* 'er war fest überzeugt bei sich, dass Seadna der Seive ein Heiratsversprechen gegeben hatte' (H, 7, 117, 2); *dubhairt sé aon lá amháin le Seorsa agus bhí m'athair i láthair, go raibh a chroidhe briste ag a bheirt mhac* 'er sagte eines Tages zu Georg, während mein Vater zugegen war, dass seine beiden Söhne sein Herz gebrochen hätten' (K, 3, 34, 3).

Conditionnel antérieur. *is iomdha bróg bhéidheadh deunta ag duine i gcaitheamh an mhéidsin aimsire* 'manch einen Schuh würde ein Mann im Verlauf dieser Zeit gemacht haben' (H, 5, 132, 2); *do bheidheadh an feall deanta ag Séadna badh mheasa d'ár deineadh riamh* 'dann würde Seadna den schlimmsten Betrug, der je ausgeführt wurde, geübt haben' (H, 7, 51, 2); *d'fhág sé an chuid eile de na caorchaibh gan ainmniughudh go dtí go mbeadh an méidsin foghlamtha ag Seaghán* 'er liess den übrigen Teil von den Schafen ohne Benennung, bis dass John dies würde gelernt haben' (K, 3, 91, 2).

§ 15. Infinitiv des Perfekts.

Die Bildung ist einfach und klar: *bheith caithte ag-* mit Subjektnomen oder Subjektpronomen, das natürlich suffigiert wird (*agam, agat, aige, againn, agaibh, aca*). Belege sind: *sul a shroich leission bheith ithte aige, bhí an loch taosgtha aicci* 'bevor es ihm gelang gegessen zu haben, hatte sie den See ausgeschöpft' (G, 84, 10); *níor leig an gaisgidheach air, blúire a bheith déanta aige* 'der Ritter liess sich nicht merken, das Geringste gethan zu haben' (K, 3, 123, 2); *é bheith tuillte againn* 'es verdient zu haben' (H, 6, 100, 1); *shaoil siad é bheith ithte aca* 'sie dachten ihn gegessen zu haben' (C, 24, 33).

§ 16. Imperativ des Perfekts.

Das Paradigma ist anzusetzen als *bíodh caithe agat* 'habe verbraucht', *bíodh caithte aige (aici), bíodh caithte againn, bíodh caithte agaibh, bíodh caithte aca.* Ich habe mir zwei Beispiele für die 2. Person Sing. angemerkt. *Gháir an righ ar Pháidín agus dubhairt leis: taodhm an loch sin shíos agus bíodh sé deunta agad seal má dtéidh an ghrian faoi an trathnóna so* 'der König liess Páidín rufen und sagte zu ihm: mache den See dort unten leer und habe es gethan, wenn die Sonne heute Abend untergeht' (C, 28, 21); *thug sé an mac righ go bruach locha agus thaisbeán sé dhó sean-chaisleán agus dubhairt leis: caith gach uile chloch san gcaisleán sin amach 'san loch agus bidheadh sé deunta agad seal ma dtéidheann an ghrian faoi tráthnóna* 'er brachte den Königssohn zum Ufer eines Sees und zeigte ihm eine alte Burg und sagte zu ihm: wirf jeden Stein an dieser Burg hinein in den See, und habe es gethan, wenn die Sonne zu Abend untergeht' (C, 81, 4 ff.).

§ 17.

Wer das Material von § 5 bis § 16 überschaut, wird zugestehen müssen, dass die Zahl der Belege für die einzelnen Tempora und die einzelnen Personen innerhalb der Tempora in dem Verhältnis steht, wie wir es im allgemeinen erwarten dürfen, wenn es sich um überkommene, alte Bildung handelte. Belegt ist im Vorhergehenden die umschreibende Konjugation mit 'haben' von folgenden Verben, wobei ich bei den häufiger vorkommenden die Zahl der Belege in Klammern beisetze: *árduighim, beirim, brisim, buailim, buaidhim* (8), *casaim, caillim* (5), *caithim* (5), *ceanglaim, ceannuighim* (5), *ceapaim* (4), *ceapuighim, claoidhim, clodhbhuailim, cráidhim, creachaim, críochnuighim* (7), *crúithim,*

cruinnighim, cuirim (6), *cumaim, deargaim, dearmaduighim, díolaim, dobheirim (tabhartha,* 8), *doghním (déanta,* 60), *eirighim, fogheibhim (faghaim), foghlamaim, faduighim, gabhaim, geallaim, gearraim, gnóthaighim* (8), *imrim, innisim, ithim* (16), *leathaim, leighim,*
- *líonaim, límnighim, loitim, meallaim, mearbhuighim, ólaim* (5), *pósaim, ráidhim* (6), *reamhrighim, rithim amach, ruaigim, sgaraim, sgríobhaim, siubhlaim, taosgaim, tógaim, tugaim, tuillim* (8). Es sind also 57 **transitive** Verba oder solche, die durch Zusatz eines Adverbiums transitive Bedeutung erhalten; und unter den 212 Belegen von 57 Verben befinden sich allein 60 Belege für die umschreibenden Formen von *déanamh* 'thun', eine Erscheinung, die vollständig im Einklang damit steht, dass die Quellen für das Material volkstümliche Rede in einfachster Form bieten, worin ja in allen modernen Sprachen die Verwendung von Verben wie 'machen, thun' vor allen anderen Verben hervorragt.

§ 18. Vergleicht man die altüberkommenen Tempora des Aktivs eines Verbs wie *caithim* 'ich verzehre', *buailim* 'ich schlage' mit den § 4 bis 16 betrachteten Neubildungen, dann ergiebt sich ein bemerkenswerter Unterschied, sobald das Objekt des transitiven Verbs ein Pronomen wie 'ihn (eum), sie (eam), es (id), sie (eos, eas, ea)' ist. Man sagt *caithim é* 'ich geniesse es (das Essen)', *chaitheas é* 'ich genoss es' oder *buailim í* 'ich schlage sie (eam)', *bhuaileas iad* 'ich schlug sie (eos)', aber: *tá sé caithte agam* 'ich habe es gegessen', *bhí sé caithte agam* 'ich hatte es gegessen' oder *tá sí buailte agam* 'ich habe sie (eam) geschlagen', *bhí siad buailte agam* 'ich hatte sie (eos) geschlagen'. In ersterem Fall hat das Objekt auch wirklich die Form des Accusativs (*é, í, íad*), während es in letzterem Fall — bei den umschreibenden Formen — die Form des Nominativs hat (*sé, sí, síad*). Dies ist lehrreich für die Entstehung der umschreibenden Konjugation mit 'haben' im Neuirischen. Sie baut sich auf den entsprechenden Tempora des Verbsubstantivs mit dem sogenannten Partizip Präteriti Passiv auf.

Im Passiv hat das Neuirische dieselben fünf Tempora des Indikativs überkommen wie im Aktiv (s. § 1): 1. *caithtear mé* 'ich werde verbraucht', *caithtear é* 'er wird verbraucht' oder *buailtear mé* 'ich werde geschlagen', *buailtear í* 'sie wird geschlagen'; 2. *chaithtí mé, chaithtí é* oder *bhuailtí mé, bhuailtí í*; 3. *caitheadh mé* 'ich wurde verbraucht', *caitheadh é* oder *buaileadh*

mé, buaileadh í; 4. *caithfear mé* (*caithfidhear mé*), *caithfear é* 'ich
werde, er wird verbraucht werden', oder *buailfear mé, buailfear
í* 'ich werde, sie wird geschlagen werden'; 5. *chaithfí mé* (*chaith-
fidhe mé*), *chaithfí é* 'ich, er würde verbraucht werden', oder
bhuailfí mé, bhuailfí í 'ich, sie würde geschlagen werden'. Hier
haben die Tempora 3 und 5 dieselbe ausgedehnte Gebrauchssphäre wie die entsprechenden des Aktivums (s. § 1); abgeholfen
ist der Vieldeutigkeit der beiden Tempora im Neuirischen durch
Umschreibungen des Verbums 'sein' mit dem Partizip Passiv,
sodass dieselben umschreibenden Tempora entstehen, wie wir sie
in § 2 und § 4 bis § 14 fürs Aktivum kennen lernten. Also
3a) Passé indéfini *tá mé caithte* 'ich bin verzehrt worden', *tá sé
caithte* 'er ist verzehrt worden' (*tá mé buailte* 'ich bin geschlagen
worden', *tá sí buailte* 'sie ist geschlagen worden'); 3b) Plusqueparfait *bhídhinn* (*bhídheadh mé*) *caithte* 'j'avais été consumé',
bhídheadh sé caithte 'il avait été consumé' (*bhídhinn buailte*
'j'avais été battu', *bhídheadh sí buailte* 'elle avait été battu');
3c) Passé antérieur *bhíos* (*bhí mé*) *caithte* 'j'eus été consumé',
bhí sé caithte 'il eut été consumé' (*bhíos buailte, bhí sí buailte*);
4a) Futur antérieur *béidhead* (*béidh mé*) *caithte* 'ich werde genossen worden sein', *béidh sé caithte* 'er wird genossen worden
sein' (*béidhead buailte* 'ich werde geschlagen worden sein', *béidh
sí buailte* 'sie wird geschlagen worden sein'); 5a) Conditionnel
antérieur *bhéidhinn* (*bhéidheadh mé*) *caithte* 'ich würde genossen
worden sein', *bhéidheadh sé caithte* 'er würde genossen worden
sein' (*bhéidhinn buailte* 'ich würde geschlagen worden sein',
bhéidheadh sí buailte 'sie würde geschlagen worden sein'). Diese
die Gebrauchssphäre der Tempora 3—5 des Passivs ergänzenden
umschreibenden Tempora (3a, 3b, 3c, 4a, 5a) sind im Passiv
im Neuirischen so gewöhnlich, dass auch einzelne neuirische Grammatiker (O'Donovan, John O'Molly) Notiz von
ihnen nehmen, wenn auch nur flüchtig und zum Teil verkehrt.
Sie lehren (s. O'Donovan, Irish Grammar S. 187; John O'Molly,
Grammar of the Irish language S. 97) die Bildung formell richtig,
aber nach ihrer englischen Übersetzung der Tempora muss man
annehmen, dass die umschreibenden Tempora nicht die alt
überkommenen temporell ergänzen, sondern sie ersetzen.
O'Donovan giebt nämlich S. 184 für das Präsens *glantar mé* 'I
am cleansed', *glantar é* 'he is cleansed' und für das Präteritum
glanadh mé 'I was cleansed', *glanadh é* 'he was cleansed' und

ebenso S. 187 für das Passé indéfini *tá mé glanta* 'I am cleansed' und für Passé antérieur *bhí sé glanta* 'he was cleansed'. Demnach wäre Tempus 3a Ersatz für Tempus 1 und Tempus 3c Ersatz für 3. Dies widerspricht allem Sprachgebrauch. Neuir. *glantar é* (*buailtear é*) und *tá sé glanta* (*tá sé buailte*) sind ebenso geschieden wie griech. τύπτεται und τέτυπται, neuir. *buaileadh é* ist griech. ἐτύφθη und *bhí sé buailte* ist ἐτέτυπτο (*verberatus erat*). Die allem irischen Sprachgebrauch widersprechenden Angaben O'Donovans und O'Molloys über die Tempusbedeutung der 5 altüberkommenen Tempora des Passivs und der 5 umschreibenden neuen Tempora des Passivs sind einer der vielen Belege wie die neuir. Sprache von Grammatikern misshandelt wird, indem sie von englischen Erscheinungen ausgehen. In den englischen Grammatiken wird in Übereinstimmung mit Sprachgebrauch folgende Passivbildung gelehrt: Präsens *I am loved* 'ich werde geliebt', Imperfekt *I was loved* 'ich wurde geliebt', Perfekt *I have been loved* 'ich bin geliebt worden', Plusquamperfekt *I had been loved* 'ich war geliebt worden' etc. Von diesem Standpunkt aus ist es ganz richtig zu sagen neuir. *buailtear é* bedeute 'he is beaten' d. h. 'er wird geschlagen' (verberatur) und *buaileadh é* 'he was beaten' d. h. 'er wurde geschlagen' (ἐτύφθη). In der gesprochenen Sprache sagt man aber um die andauernde Handlung auszudrücken im Präsens *I am being beaten* 'ich werde geschlagen', Imperfekt *I was beeing beaten* 'ich wurde geschlagen', und demnach im Perfekt *I am beaten* 'ich bin geschlagen (worden)' für *I have been beaten* und im Plusquamperfekt *I was beaten* 'ich war geschlagen (worden)' für *I had been beaten*. Von diesem Standpunkt aus ist es ganz richtig zu sagen, neuir. *tá sé buailte* bedeute 'he is beaten' d. h. 'er ist geschlagen (worden', verberatus est) und neuir. *bhí sé buailte* bedeute 'he was beaten.' d. h. 'er war geschlagen (worden, verberatus erat, ἐτέτυπτο). Diese Verschiedenheiten zwischen gesprochenem Englisch und Grammatikerangaben geben aber doch kein Recht — wie O'Donovan und O'Molloy thun — irisch *buailtear é* und *tá sé buailte*, *buaileadh é* und *bhí sé buailte* gleich zu setzen; sie sind geschieden wie τύπτεται und τέτυπται einerseits und ἐτύφθη und ἐτέτυπτο andererseits. Wird für *tá sé buailte* als engl. Übersetzung 'he is beaten' gegeben, dann muss für *buailtear é* 'he is being beaten' gegeben werden, und wird umgekehrt für *buailtear é* gegeben 'he is beaten', dann muss für *tá sé buailte* gegeben werden 'he has been beaten'. Die umschreibenden Tempora 3a, 3b, 3c, 4a, 5a des Passivs ersetzen also die altüberkommenen Tempora 1—5 des Passivs im Neuirischen nicht, sondern ergänzen sie in der oben angegebenen Weise.[1])

Zum Verständnis der Entstehung der aktiven umschreibenden Tempora, wie wir sie in § 5 bis 16 kennen lernten, muss ein weiterer Punkt beachtet werden. Eine charakteristische Eigentümlichkeit des Neuirischen im Gebrauch der 5 alten überkommenen Tempora des Passivs (1. Präsens, 2. Imperfekt, 3. Präteritum, 4. Futur, 5. Conditionalis) besteht nun darin, dass sie in der Regel nur dann verwendet werden, wenn der Urheber der Handlung ganz allgemein gedacht ist und nicht durch eine bestimmte Person ausgedrückt wird; also man sagt *buailtear mé* 'ich werde geschlagen', *cuirtear mé annso* 'ich werde hierher geschickt', wenn man meint 'man schlägt mich, man schickt mich hierher'. Soll der Urheber bezeichnet werden (lat. *a* mit Ablat., deutsch 'von', engl. *by*, franz. *par*), so wendet man im Neuirischen gewöhnlich aktive Konstruktion an, indem der Urheber in dem Nominativ als Subjekt steht. Also *buailtear mé* 'ich werde geschlagen = man schlägt mich', aber 'ich werde vom Vater geschlagen' ist in idiomatischem Neuirisch *buaileann an t-athair mé* 'der Vater schlägt mich'; so *cuirtear é annso* 'er wird hierher geschickt = man schickt ihn hierher', aber 'er wird vom Vater hierher geschickt' ist *cuireann an t-athair annso é* 'der Vater schickt ihn hierher'. Dasselbe gilt für die übrigen altüberkommenen Tempora. Also *buaileadh mé* 'ich wurde geschlagen = man schlug mich', aber 'ich wurde vom Vater geschlagen' ist *bhuail an t-athair mé* 'der Vater schlug mich', oder *cuireadh annso é* 'er wurde hier-

---

[1]) Wem diese Meisterung und Misshandlung der Sprache, wie sie O'Donovan und O'Molloy begehen, wunderbar erscheinen sollte, den möchte ich erinnern, wie die irischen Grammatiker von O'Donovan bis Joyce über die Bedeutung der 3. Sing. Präs. auf *-ann* (*eann*) geflunkert (*buaileann sé*) und ein Tempus *buaileann mé* neben *buailim* mit gesonderter Bedeutung aus den Fingern gesogen haben (Präsens der Gewohnheit). Und wo konnte man in neuir. Grammatiken lernen, dass 'ich bin nicht' regelmässig, wie man erwarten soll, lautet *nílim* (aus *nifilim*), bis ich Kelt. Studien Heft I, S. 77 Anm. meine Stimme erhob? wofür mir der gewohnte Dank von Schuchardt und K. Meyer gezahlt wurde.

her geschickt = man schickte ihn hierher' aber 'er wurde vom
Vater hierher geschickt' ist *chuir an t-athair annso é* (*is é an
t-athair dochuir annso é*) 'der Vater schickte ihn hierher'.
Dies ist ideomatischer neuirischer Gebrauch (vgl. auch
An Claidheamh Soluis 1, 13).[1]

---

[1] Der Umstand, dass das sogenannte Passiv des Neuirischen in der Regel
nur gebraucht wird, wenn der Urheber der Handlung allgemein gedacht
ist ('man, sie'), ferner dass die begleitenden Pronomina die Accusativform
haben (*buailtear é, buailtear í, buailtear iad* 'er, sie wird geschlagen, sie
werden geschlagen' = man schlägt ihn, man schlägt sie (eam), man schlägt
sie (eos), ferner dass man bei einem bestimmten Urheber aktive Konstruktion
verwendet: diese drei sich ergänzenden Umstände zeigen deutlich, dass
meine KZ. 30, 224—256 versuchte Erklärung der Entstehung des sogenannten
keltischen Passivs in den entscheidenden Punkten richtig ist. Das, was
Thurneysen bei Brugmann, Grundriss II, § 1080, Anm. 1 bemerkt, widerlegt
doch nichts. Als leitende Gesichtspunkte scheinen mir nach wie vor in
Betracht zu kommen: 1. dass das Gemeinkeltische etwas mehr als eine
Person im Passiv besessen habe (altir. *noberr*, kymr. *gwelir*), etwa eine volle
Flexion wie Latein, ist reine Willkür anzunehmen, da das Indogermanische
sicher eine solche Flexion nicht besessen hat. Italisch und Keltisch müssten
ganz andere gemeinsame Neubildungen aufweisen, dass wir annehmen dürften,
sie hätten eine gemeinsame passive oder deponentiale Flexion ausgebildet, und
ein Recht hätten, die keltischen Sprachen auf das Prokrustesbett des Latein
zu zwängen. — 2. Die allein in den keltischen Sprachen vorliegende angebliche
3. Person Passivi im Präsens (altir. *noberr, noberar,* kymr. *gwelir,* korn. *gweler,*
bret. *gweler*) ist aus einem Zustand wie im Latein (*legitur, ducitur*)
formell unerklärlich, vielmehr ganz klar die alte 3. Pluralis Aktivi
Präsentis auf -*r* neben der paradigmatischen auf -*nt*. — 3. Diese sogenannte
dritte Sing. Passivi des Keltischen trägt in allen keltischen Dialekten zu
allen Zeiten bis heute ein Janusgesicht: in der erdrückenden Mehrzahl der Fälle wird sie konstruiert und verwendet im Sinne einer 3. Pluralis
Aktivi 'sie ...' im Sinne von 'man' (altir. *nomberar, notberar, nonberar,
nobberar* 'man trägt mich, dich, uns, euch' = 'sie tragen mich, dich, uns,
euch' = 'ich werde, du wirst, wir werden, ihr werdet getragen', kymr.
ymgelwir, korn. *ym gylwyr,* nbr. *em garér* und die eingangs dieser Anmerkung
berührten neuirischen Erscheinungen); verhältnismässig seltener wird sie als
3. Sing. Passivi 'es wird ...' und 'er wird ...' (altir. *asberar, doberar in-
dalmsan,* Kuhns Ztschr. 30, 249; und neukymr. *dysgir dyn* nicht *dysgir ddyn*!)
verwendet. Sollen wir nun annehmen, dass die gewöhnliche Verwendung
und Konstruktion der *r*-Form im Keltischen etwas Altes und erklärlich ist
aus ihrer Entstehung aus einer 3. Pluralis Aktivi und dass die seltene Verwendung und Konstruktion als 3. Sing. Passivi eine leicht erklärliche Weiterentwicklung ist ('sie tragen, man trägt, es wird getragen')? oder ist es wahrscheinlicher, dass die keltische *r*-Form formell der letzte Rest eines stattlichen Luftschlosses ist und dass die seltene Verwendung und Konstruktion
der letzte Rest der ursprünglichen Verwendung ist und dass die von den

Nunmehr sind wir in der Lage verstehen zu können, wie
im Neuirischen Bildungen, die auch ihrem Ursprung nach ent-

ältesten Zeiten an gewöhnliche Verwendung und Konstruktion eine nicht
leicht zu erklärende Weiterentwicklung ('er wird getragen, es wird getragen, man trägt') ist? Ich denke, wer recht beherzigt, 1. dass die Annahme einer Passivflexion fürs Urkeltische ein Luftschloss ist, 2. dass die
keltische r-Form sich von selbst als reguläre Fortsetzung einer 3. Plur.
Aktivi auf -r im Indogerm. ergiebt, und 3., dass die keltische r-Form
lautlich aus einer Form wie lat. *legitur, ducitur* nicht kann entstanden sein
— der kann nicht zweifelhaft sein, wie er sich entscheiden soll. — 4. Durch
die Weiterentwicklung des 'man trägt', 'es wird getragen' trat die alte
3. Plur. Activi in der Bedeutung neben 'es ist getragen worden' (altir.
doberar: dobreth), also neben eine ursprüngliche Passivform, bestehend
aus Particip Perf. Passivi und dem hinzu zu denkenden Verb substantiv.
Dieser Parallelismus hat dann dazu geführt, dass man auf die ursprüngliche
Passivform des Präteritums die alten, fest eingewurzelten aktiven Wendungen
der sekundär erst passivisch gewordenen Präsensform übertrug (altir. *dobrograd,
donrograd*, neuir. *buaileadh é*, kymr. *fe'm dysgid, fe'm dysgwyd*). Oder sollen
wir annehmen, dass das Keltische eine volle Passivflexion im Präsens besessen, dass alles bis auf die 3. Sing. verloren gegangen sei, dass diese
ursprüngliche Passivform sich zu einer 'man'-Form entwickelt habe, dass
dann die Sprache diese 'man'-Form aktiv gefühlt und mit ihr durch Umschreibung (altir. *nomberar*, kymr. *fe'm dysgir*) in aktiver Weise die verloren
gegangenen anderen Passivformen ersetzt habe und dass schliesslich diese
Analogiebildung dann das passive Präteritum in seine Analogie gezogen habe
(ir. *donrograd*, kymr. *fe'm dysgwyd*)? Mir fehlt der Glaube an das urkeltische
Luftschloss, um alle diese Konsequenzen schlucken zu können. — 5. Im Kymr.
besteht die Regel, dass wenn das Verb als Prädikat den Satz beginnt — was
gewöhnlich ist — und das folgende Subjekt ein Nomen im Plural ist, das
vorangehende Verb nur im Singular steht (*daeth y dynion* 'es kamen die
Menschen', nicht *daethant y dynion* s. ZE. 933); im Irischen entwickelt sich
vor unseren Augen immer mehr an Stelle der alten synthetischen Verbalformen (altir. *berim* 'ich trage', *berid* 'er trägt', *berme* 'wir tragen', *berit*
'sie tragen') eine analytische Flexion bestehend aus 3. Sing. und den persönlichen Pronomina (neuir. *beir mé, beir tú, beir sé, beir sinn, beir sibh, beir
siad* neben — besonders im Südirischen — altem *beirim, beirir* etc.). Beide
Erscheinungen sind weitere Schlussfolgerungen aus dem Janusgesicht der
keltischen r-Form. Wurde im altkymr. *gwelir y dynion* 'man sieht die
Menschen' = 'es werden die Menschen gesehen' *gwelir* als 3. Sing. Passivi
gefasst, so liegt die aktive Konstruktion *gwel y gwŷr* 'die Männer sehen',
gwelodd y gwŷr 'die Männer sahen' an der Hand. Ebenso ergiebt im Irischen
eine Auffassung von *nomberar* 'man trägt mich' *buailtear* mé 'man schlägt
mich' als 'es wird ich getragen, es wird ich geschlagen' ein *beir* mé 'es trägt
ich', *beir tú* 'es trägt du' für *beirim* 'ich trage' etc. Diese in den neu-
keltischen Sprachen vor unseren Augen nach Analogie der Passiv-
konstruktion sich entwickelnde 'unpersönliche' aktive Flexion heran zu

schieden passivisch sind — was *buailtear, cuirtear, caithtear é,
i, iad* ursprünglich nicht sind, wie in Anmerkung gezeigt ist —,
im Sprachgefühl als aktive Tempora zur Ergänzung aktiver
Tempora aufkamen. Der Wechsel im Irischen zwischen *cuirtear
é* 'er wird geschickt', *buailtear i* 'sie wird geschlagen' und
cuireann an t-athair é 'er wird vom Vater geschickt' (der Vater
schickt ihn), *buaileann an t-athair i* 'sie wird vom Vater geschlagen (der Vater schlägt sie)' ist ursprünglich gar kein
Wechsel zwischen Passiv und Aktiv, da die sogenannte passive
Form im Präsens eine im aktiven Paradigma obsolet gewordene
dritte Pluralis Aktivi Präsentis ist; es sind beides ursprünglich
aktive Wendungen ('sie schicken', 'er schickt'), woher auch
verständlich, dass im sogenannten Passiv die Person, an der die
Handlung zum Ausdruck kommt, durch den Accusativ des
Pronomens (*é, i, iad*) ausgedrückt wird. Thatsächlich wird
aber *cuirtear é* oder *buailtear i* im Verhältnis zu *cuireann an
t-athair é* oder *buaileann an t-athair i* im Neuirischen wie
Passiv zu Aktiv bis zu einem gewissen Grade gefühlt.
Solchen Bildungen nun wie dem alten *buailtear é, cuirtear i,
caithtear iad* gegenüber sind die temporalen Neubildungen
des Passivs (3a, 3b, 3c, 4a, 5a) wie *tá sé buailte, tá siad
caithte* 'er ist geschlagen worden, sie sind verzehrt worden'
wirkliche Passivbildungen; sie bedeuten also ursprünglich
'er ist (*tá sé*) geschlagen (*buailte*), sie sind (*ta siad*) verzehrt
(*caithte*)' und nicht erst sekundär. Tritt zu ihnen eine nähere

---

ziehen, um im Urkeltischen den Verlust der vermeintlich vorhanden gewesenen
vollkommenen Passivflexion bis auf die 3. Singularis zu erklären, heisst
doch in einem bedenklichen Zirkel sich drehen: ganz abgesehen davon, dass
dann die Konstruktion und Verwendung der *r*-Form im Keltischen wesentlich
passivisch sein müsste — was nicht der Fall ist —, so muss doch auch die
'Neigung' der keltischen Sprachen zu unpersönlicher Konstruktion in der angegebenen Weise irgendwo ihren Ausgangspunkt haben.

Ob die keltische *r*-Form schon in urkeltischer Zeit oder gar in kelto-
italischer Zeit den Januskopf hatte, ist ziemlich nebensächlich, da sich letzteres
kaum wird ausmachen lassen; das Entscheidende bei der Frage ist: ist die
gewöhnliche aktive Konstruktion und Verwendung der *r*-Form in den
keltischen Sprachen das Ursprüngliche und die seltenere passive Verwendung daraus entstanden, oder ist das Umgekehrte der Fall? Da halte
ich nach wie vor jedes Ausgehen von einer 3. Singularis Passivi im
Keltischen oder gar die Annahme einer urkeltischen Passivflexion für eine
ebensolche Liebhaberei wie die Annahme einer gemeinsamen italo-keltischen
Verschiebung des indogermanischen Accentes und ähnliches der Art.

Bezeichnung des Urhebers 'vom Vater, von mir', so muss bei diesen Formen der Urheber direkt ausgedrückt werden und so entstehen *tá sé buailte ag an athair* 'er ist vom Vater geschlagen worden', *tá sé buailte agam* 'er ist von mir geschlagen worden', *tá siad caithte ag an athair* 'sie sind vom Vater verzehrt worden', *tá siad caithte agam* 'sie sind von mir verzehrt worden'. Diese Gruppen von Bildungen, von denen die jungen (3a, 3b, 3c, 4a, 5a) die altüberkommenen (1—5) temporell ergänzen, und die beide (alte und junge) die Unterabteilungen von 'Urheber allgemein' und 'spezieller Urheber' aufweisen, beeinflussten sich so, dass die neu aufkommende Bildung (3a, 3b, 3c, 4a, 5a) bei letzterem Unterschied von der altüberkommenen Bildung (1—5) in Analogie gezogen wurde. Nach dem Verhältnis von *buaileann an t-athair é* 'der Vater schlägt ihn' (Ersatz für 'er wird vom Vater geschlagen'): *buailtear é* 'er wird geschlagen' erhielt in *tá sé buailte ag an athair* 'er ist vom Vater geschlagen worden' : *tá sé buailte* 'er ist geschlagen worden' das erstere die Bedeutung 'der Vater hat ihn geschlagen'. So entstand im Neuirischen für das Sprachgefühl die aktive Flexion *tá sé buailte agam* 'ich habe ihn geschlagen', *bhí sí buailte agat* 'du hattest sie geschlagen', *béidh siat caithte againn* 'wir werden sie genossen haben' bei formell passiver Bildung. Wie die neuirische passive Flexion *buailtear é*, *buailtear í* 'er, sie wird geschlagen' noch in dem *é*, *í* verrät, dass eine alte formelle aktive Grundlage vorhanden ist, so bezeugt die neuir. aktive Flexion *tá sé buailte aige* 'er hat ihn geschlagen', *tá sí buailte againn* 'wir haben sie geschlagen' in den *sé*, *sí*, dass eine formelle passive Grundlage vorhanden ist.

Dass nun die § 4 bis § 16 belegte Neubildung trotz der durchsichtigen passiven Grundlage bald und vollständig — wie wir in § 22 sehen werden — im Sprachgefühl die Geltung einer aktiven Bildung zur Ergänzung der 5 altüberkommenen aktiven Bildungen erhalten hat, daran hat wohl einen wesentlichen Anteil, dass die Redensart *tá sé agam* 'es ist bei mir', *tá sé agat* 'es ist bei dir', *tá sé aca* 'es ist bei ihnen' die Bedeutung eines selbständigen Verbs 'ich habe es, du hast es, sie haben es' u. s. w. im Neuirischen erhalten hatte. Wurde *tá sé buailte ag an athair* 'er ist vom Vater geschlagen worden' neben *tá sé buailte* 'er ist geschlagen worden' nach Analogie von

buaileann an t-athair é 'der Vater schlägt ihn' für 'er wird
vom Vater geschlagen' neben *buailter é* 'er wird geschlagen'
gefasst als 'der Vater hat ihn geschlagen', dann musste eine
Beziehung zu dem Verb *tá agam* 'ich habe' von selbst sich ein-
stellen und die aktive Festsetzung der passiven Redeweise begünstigen.

§ 19. Diese Entstehung der umschreibenden Konjugation
mit 'haben' im Neuirischen erklärt uns auch schön gewisse dem
Munsteririsch eigene Formen, die in § 4 bis § 16 noch nicht zur
Sprache gekommen sind. Ein wesentlicher Unterschied zwischen
heutigem Munsteririsch und Connachtirisch besteht auf verbalem
Gebiet darin, dass in Munster in der Flexion die alten Formen
vielfach bewahrt werden, wo im Connachtirisch die aus 3. Sing.
und Pronomen bestehenden jüngeren analytischen Formen verwendet werden, also südirisch oft *táim, táir, támaoid, táid,* wo
man westirisch fast nur *tá mé, tá tú, tá sinn, tá siad* sagt, und
so südirisch oft *bhios, bhiodar, béidhead,* wo westirisch gewöhnlicher *bhí mé, bhí siad, béidh mé* etc. gilt. Auf die umschreibenden Tempora des Passivs angewandt, ergiebt dies, dass
man südirisch auch noch *táim buailte* 'ich bin geschlagen worden',
támaoid buailte 'wir sind geschlagen worden', *bhiodar buailte*
'sie waren geschlagen worden' sagt, wo westirisch nur *tá mé
buailte, tá sinn buailte, bhí siad buailte* gesagt wird. Wird nun
in solchen Fällen noch die bestimmte Person des Urhebers
hinzugefügt, dann bekommt man südirisch die Formen *táim
buailte agat* 'ich bin von dir geschlagen worden', *támaoid buailte
aca* 'wir sind von ihnen geschlagen worden', *bhiodar buailte
againn* 'sie waren von uns geschlagen worden' neben den westirischen und südirisch ebenfalls gewöhnlichen *tá mé buailte agat,
tá sinn buailte aca, bhí siad buailte againn.* Bekommen nun
diese Formen aktive Verwendung in der S. 88 ff. dargelegten
Weise, dann können im Südirischen neben den § 4 bis § 16 vorgeführten Formen der mit 'haben' umschriebenen Tempora Neben-
formen auftreten, sobald das Objekt des transitiven Verbes
ein 'mich, dich, uns, euch, sie (eos)' ist. Also neben den gewöhnlichen *tá mé meallta agat* 'du hast mich betrogen', *tá sinn
meallta aca* 'sie haben uns betrogen' können im Munsteririsch
táim meallta agat, támaoid meallta aca vorkommen. Dies ist
thatsächlich der Fall. Belege sind: *táim creachta acu* 'sie
haben mich ruiniert' (J. 2, 7); *táimíd múchta acu, táimíd curtha*

amú acu 'sie haben uns erstickt, sie haben uns vernichtet'
(L. 1, 3, 1); *is uirthi féin do thuitfidís nuair na beidís tuillte
agat uaithi* 'auf sie selbst (die Flucherin) würden sie (die Ver-
wünschungen) zurückfallen, wenn du sie nicht würdest verdient
haben (*nuair na beidheadh siad tuillte agat* gewöhnlich nach
§ 13) von ihr' (J. 26, 32); *b'fhéidir gur dhóich liom féin na
beidís tuillte agam agus b'fhéidir, ar a shon sain, go mbeidís.
Pe 'cu bheidís tuillte agam no ná beidís, níor maith liom í
bheith 'ghá ndeanamh orm* 'es könnte sein, dass ich dächte, dass
ich sie nicht verdient hätte, und es könnte trotzdem sein, dass
ich sie hätte; ob ich sie nun würde verdient haben oder nicht,
angenehm wäre es mir nicht, dass sie solche über mich thue'
(J. 26, 35 bis 27, 3).

§ 20. Ferner erklärt die § 18 vorgetragene Entstehung
der umschreibenden Konjugation mit 'haben', warum im Irischen
weder eine umschreibende Konjugation bei den Verben 'sein'
und 'haben' selbst noch bei den intransitiven Verben überhaupt
vorkommt, wie wir dies im Deutschen, Französischen und
Englischen treffen ('*ich habe gehabt, bin gewesen, j'ai eu, j'ai
été, I have had, I have been*' oder '*ich bin gekommen, I am
arisen, je suis venu*'). Die irischen aktiven Neubildungen mit
'haben' für Passé indéfini, Plusqueparfait, Passé antérieur, Futur
antérieur, Conditionnel antérieur sind ja aus einer Unterabteilung
der passiven Neubildungen gleicher Tempora hervorgegangen,
wenn ein bestimmter Urheber beim Passiv ausgedrückt war.
Diese Kategorie ist aber bei 'haben, sein' und allen wirklichen Intransitivs fürs Passiv ausgeschlossen, wie diese Verba
im Irischen ja auch alle kein Partizip Perfekt Passiv haben.
Es giebt, soweit ich sehe, im Neuirischen nur eine Ausnahme,
das Verb *imtheacht* 'weggehen', Präsens *imthighim* 'ich gehe
weg'. Hier finden sich neben den fünf altüberkommenen Temporibus (1. *imthighim* 'ich gehe weg'; 2. *d'imthiginn* 'ich pflegte
wegzugehen'; 3. *d'imthigheas* 'ich ging weg'; 4. *imtheóchad* 'ich
werde weggehen', *d'imtheóchainn* 'ich würde weggehen') die 5
Neubildungen: 3a) *tá mé imthighthe* 'je m'en suis allé'; 3b) *bhidheadh mé imthighthe* 'je m'en étais allé'; 3c) *bhí mé imthighthe* 'je
m'en fus allé'; 4a) *béidh mé imthighthe* 'je m'en serai allé'; 5a)
bhéidheadh mé imthighthe 'je m'en serais allé'. Die Belege sind
ziemlich zahlreich und ich hebe nur einige aus: *nuair bhí na
daoine uile imthighthe 'nna suaimhneas, tháinig an dá fhathach*

'als alle Menschen zur Ruhe gegangen waren, kamen die beiden Riesen' (A, 4, 7); *andiu atá na daoine imthighthe agus na seanráidte do chleacht siad atáid aig imtheacht 'na n-diaidh* 'heutigen Tages sind die Leute dahin gegangen und die Sprichwörter, die sie gebrauchten, gehen ihnen nach' (E, 5, 1); *tá sé imthighthe thorrain anois acht gcobhmuid greim air arís* 'er ist uns jetzt entkommen, aber wir werden ihn wieder zu fassen kriegen' (E, 26, 7); *ní'l na geinti glinde imthighthe as amharc gohuile fós orrainn* 'die Thaldämoninnen sind noch nicht vollständig uns aus dem Gesichtskreis gegangen' (E, 28, 25); *d'imthigh an gabha ó'n mbaile lá, agus chomh fhad as bhí sé imthighthe, do thosuigh an bheirt bhuachaill ag troid* 'eines Tages ging der Schmied von Hause fort und sobald er weg gegangen war, begannen die beiden Burschen zu streiten' (E, 5, 18); *chomh fad agus do bhí tusa imthighthe chum an aonaigh, tháinic fear mór agus bhailigh sé leis airfad é* 'als (während) du weggegangen warst zum Markte, kam ein grosser Mann und er sammelte es (das Geld) sich zusammen' (E, 49, 13); *muna mbéidheadh gur chnuasuigh sinn an dán so shíos dobheidheadh sé imthighthe as cuimhne go goirid* 'hätten wir nicht das nachfolgende Lied gesammelt, so würde es bald aus der Überlieferung weggegangen (verschwunden) sein' (E, 43, 20). Das Verb *imtheacht* 'weggehen' hat im Neuirischen sehr oft den starken Nebengeschmack 'der Gewalt weichend oder einem Befehl nachgebend weggehen' (*imthigh leat* 'scheer dich zum Teufel'), sodass *imthigheann sé* 'er geht weg' gefühlt wird als 'er wird weggegangen', wenn ich so sagen darf nach der scherzhaften Redensart 'er wird abgegangen'. Von dieser Bedeutung aus ist *tá sé imthighthe* für das Sprachgefühl eine 3. Sing. Passiv des Passé indéfini 'er ist weggegangen worden' wie *tá sé buailte* 'er ist geschlagen worden'. Es ist also der einzige neuirische Beleg einer umschreibenden Konjugation im Aktiv zum genaueren Ausdruck der Tempora 3a, 3b, 3c, 4a, 5a bei einem anderen als transitiven Verb vollständig verständlich aus der Art und Weise, wie die Umschreibung der genannten 5 Tempora im Aktiv des neuirischen Verbs beim Transitivum zu stande gekommen ist (§ 19).

§ 21. Schon aus den S. 62 ff. vorgeführten Belegen für die Verwendung des Conditionnel im Sinne des Conditionnel antérieur und des Passé défini (Aorist, histor. Perfekt) im Sinne des Passé

antérieur (Plusquamperfektum) ist ersichtlich, dass durch die von
§ 4 bis § 20 erörterte Neubildung im Aktiv von 5 Temporibus
(Passé indéfini, Plusqueparfait, Passé antérieur, Futur antérieur,
Conditionnel antérieur) bei transitiven Verben der altüberkommene
weitere Gebrauch besonders bei dem Präteritum und Conditionalis im Neuirischen nicht vollständig beseitigt worden ist,
da ja die Hauptbelege S. 62 ff. denselben Texten entstammen,
denen die Belege § 5 bis § 16 entnommen sind und transitive
Verba unter ihnen vorkommen. Ich möchte gemäss dem am
Schluss von § 1 gegebenen Versprechen noch einige weitere Belege beibringen. *D'éist an déirceach leis go cúramach agus
nuair chríochnuigh sé an sgeul uile, d'fhiafruigh sé dhe* 'es
hörte der Bettler ihm aufmerksam zu und als er die ganze Geschichte beendigt hatte, fragte er ihn' (A, 26, 34 ff.); nach *nuair*
steht das Passé antérieur (Plusquamperfekt), wie aus zahlreichen
Belegen auf S. 72—75 ersichtlich ist, und *criochnuighim* lieferte
uns in § 5 bis § 16 nicht weniger als 7 Belege für die umschriebenen Tempora (D, 14, 96, 15; H, 6, 85, 1; H, 6, 162, 2; L,
1, 84, 1; I, 11, 27; H, 6, 133, 1; B, 76, 17), worunter zwei besonders
lehrreich sind: *nuair bhí an dá fhéire bróg críochnaighthe
aige* 'als er die beiden Paar Schuhe beendigt hatte' (H, 6, 85, 1),
nuair bhí an chogarnach criochnuighthe acu 'als sie das Geflüster beendigt hatten' (H, 6, 162, 2). Es ist also *nuair chríochnuigh sé* (A, 26, 34) die ältere ungenauere Ausdrucksweise für
die präcisere *nuair bhí críochnaighthe aige* (H, 6, 85, 1; 162, 2) der
jüngeren umschreibenden Konjugation. Ein anderes Beispiel ist
*nuair ghnóthuigh sluagh Connacht an cath, thangadar ar
ais go Cnoc Matha agus thug an righ Finbheara sporán óir do
Pháidín O Cellaigh* 'als die (Feen-)schar von Connacht die
Schlacht gewonnen hatte, kamen sie zurück nach Cnoc Matha
und der König Finbheara gab dem Pádín O'Kelly eine Börse
mit Gold' (A, 42, 26 ff.); auch *gnóthuighim* ist ein gebräuchliches
transitives Verb, von dem § 5 bis § 16 nicht weniger als 8 Belege für die umschriebenen Tempora aufgeführt sind (A, 21, 13;
B, 21, 12; 22, 28; 35, 1; 36, 4; 65, 28; 136, 1; E, 13, 21), von denen
wieder einer im Vergleich zu der aufgeführten Stelle besonders
lehrreich ist: *nuair do bhí an cath tugtha gnódhuighthe aige,
thriall sé air an g-caisleán* 'als er die Schlacht geliefert und
gewonnen hatte, ging er auf die Burg zu' (E, 13, 21 ff.). — Ein
anderes Verb, von dem zahlreiche Belege in § 5 bis § 16 für die

umschriebene Konjugation gegeben sind, ist *ithim* 'essen' (H, 6, 5, 1; C, 115, 19; 118, 5. 26. 28; 122, 14. 21; 135, 31; A, 4, 30; B, 85, 10; C, 9, 9; B, 167, 26; C, 25, 1; 24, 33; F, 240, 23; L, 1, 69, 1), darunter mehrere für *nuair a bhí [an dineur, a sháith] ithte aige* 'als er (das Diner, genügend) gegessen hatte'; dem gegenüber steht die ältere Ausdrucksweise *nuair d'ith agus d'ól sé a sháith, dubhairt sé* 'als er genügend gegessen und getrunken hatte, sagte er' (B, 181, 20; 196, 7; 197, 24; 198, 23; 200, 4; 204, 21).

Der neuirische Gebrauch stellt sich also so dar: alle intransitiven Verba mit Ausnahme von *imthighim* 'weggehen' sowie 'sein' und 'haben' kennen im Neuirischen im Aktiv nur die 5 altüberkommenen Tempora (s. oben S. 61), von denen besonders die beiden Tempora Präteritum und Conditionalis die S. 61 ff. nachgewiesene weite Gebrauchssphäre haben, sodass also z. B. ein neuir. *tháinig sé, 'chuaidh sé* bedeutet sowohl 'er kam, er ging' als auch 'er ist, er war gekommen, gegangen'; die transitiven Verba haben in der § 19 erläuterten und in § 4 bis § 16 belegten Weise auf Grund von umschreibenden Tempora im Passiv sich 5 umschreibende Tempora im Aktiv geschaffen, mit deren Hilfe die Vieldeutigkeit der beiden Tempora Präteritum und Konditionalis eingeschränkt wird: das alte Präteritum behält die Aoristbedeutung (Passé défini), und die übrigen Funktionen desselben werden i n d e r R e g e l durch die 3 neuen umschreibenden Tempora *tá caithte agam* (Passé indéfini), *bhíodh caithte agam* (Plusqueparfait), *bhí caithte agam* (Passé antérieur) übernommen, wie neben Futur und Conditionalis ein *béidh caithte agam* (Futur antérieur) und *bhéidheadh caithte agam* (Conditionnel antérieur) treten, um die Vergangenheitsfunktionen dieser Tempora zu übernehmen. Ausgeschlossen ist jedoch bei den transitiven Verben nicht, dass die alten Tempora Präteritum und Konditionalis auch noch in alter Weise, wie es bei den intransitiven Verben ja Regel ist, die Funktionen von Passé indéfini, Plusqueparfait, Passé antérieur resp. Conditionnel antérieur mit übernehmen können. Die § 20 erläuterte Umschreibung bei dem intransitiven *imthighim* 'ich gehe weg' geht in Verwendung und Nichtanwendung mit den neuen Tempora der transitiven Verba Hand in Hand.

§ 22. Ich denke, das in § 4 bis § 16 vorgelegte Material spricht für sich selbst laut genug, dass die umschreibende Konjugation mit 'haben' bei den transitiven Verben im Neuirischen heutigen Tages ebenso integrierender Teil der aktiven Konjugation dieser Verba ist wie die entsprechenden Tempora mit 'haben, have, avoir' im Deutschen, Englischen, Französischen, wenn auch die neuirischen Grammatiker, einer den andern mehr oder weniger paraphrasierend, keine Kenntnis davon nehmen, und die Grundlage der neuen umschreibenden Konjugation thatsächlich keine aktive ist, wie wir § 18 gesehen haben. Besonders belehrend dafür sind die zahlreichen in § 5 bis § 16 vorgekommenen Stellen, wo umschreibende Formen in vollem Parallelismus zu den alten ursprünglich aktiven Tempora stehen (vgl. auch § 21), wozu noch ein Beleg möge hinzugefügt werden. K, 3, 115, 1 lesen wir in einer Munstererzählung: *Fé deireadh do fuair an gaisgidheach an ceannsmách air agus do dhin sé dá leath dhe le cros-iarracht dá chlaidheamh; nuair bhí an méid sin déanta aige, do thóg sé leis leath dhe is gach aon lámh go dtí an báid agus tháinig abhaile; dubhairt sé le n-a bhean dul agus a rádh leis na fir eile teacht amach agus an collach a thógaint isteach* 'schliesslich gewann der Ritter die Oberhand über ihn und er machte mit einem Kreuzhieb seines Schwertes zwei Hälften von ihm; als er dies gethan hatte, trug er in jeder Hand eine Hälfte von ihm zum Bote und kam nach Hause; er sagte zu seiner Frau zu gehen und den andern Männern zu sagen, heraus zu kommen und den Leichnam hinein zu tragen'. Lehrreich ist auch das Verhalten der Iren selbst, wenn sie heutiges Neuirisch in Englisch wiedergeben. Douglas Hyde hat seinen ursprünglich nur mit irischen Einleitungen und irischen Noten versehenen *Abhráin grádh chúige Connacht* (Dublin 1895) nachträglich eine englische Übersetzung von Text und Beigaben mitgegeben, worüber er sagt: 'my English prose translation only aims at being literal, and has courageously, though no doubt ruggedly, *reproduced the Irish idioms* of the original' (Preface S. IV); er schreibt (S. 52, 4 ff.) bei Erzählung einer Geschichte von dem Verfasser eines der Liebeslieder *mar shaoil sé go n-ólfadh sí sláinte ar an bhfear saidhbhir sin do bhí leagtha amach aige mar chéile dhí* und übersetzt dies englisch 'because he thought she would drink the health of the wealthy man he had laid out for her as a consort' (a. a. O. S. 53, 4 ff.): es ist also *bhí leagtha amach aige* so sehr entsprechend einem 'er hatte bestimmt', dass Hyde das Ideom gar nicht beibehält in der Über-

setzung. Noch lehrreicher ist Peter O'Leary in seiner Ausgabe
von Seadna (erster Teil in H, 5. 6. 7; zweiter Teil I) und einigen
Aufsätzen in K, denen eine die irischen Idiome berücksichtigende
englische Übersetzung und Noten für den Lernenden beigegeben
sind. Es sind in § 4 bis § 16 im ganzen 40 Belege aus den
genannten drei Quellen genommen zur Illustration der umschreibenden aktiven Konjugation, und in allen Fällen übersetzt
O'Leary schlankweg im Englischen 'I have, had, would have
made' etc. ohne auch nur ein einziges Mal das Bedürfnis zu
fühlen, in einer Note die eigenartige irische Bildung der umschreibenden Tempora zu erklären. Einige Beispiele seien angeführt: *is iomdha bróg bheidheadh deunta ag duine i gcaitheamh an mhéid sin aimsire* 'Tis many a shoe a man would
h a v e m a d e in the lapse of the portion of time' (H, 5, 132, 2);
's dócha go bhfuil sé ithte um an tacaso aicci 'I suppose, she
h a s h i m all but eaten by this' (H, 6, 5, 1); *nuair chonnaic sé
cad a bhí déanta aici* 'when he saw, what she had done'
(H, 6, 117, 1); *mar bhí an áit geallta aige do dhuine eile* 'for
h e h a d the place promised to another person' (H, 6, 153, 1),
nuair bhí a chuid bídh caithte aige 'when he had taken his
food' (H, 7, 3, 1), *ní raibh an triomhadh greim curtha aige*
'h e h a d not the third stitch put' (H, 7, 51, 1); *bhí sé leathta
ar fuaid na dúithche ag Saidhbh* 'Seve had it published through
the country' (H, 7, 133, 2); *ní raibh mo chuid airgid tabhartha
agamsa dhó an uair sin* 'I had not given him my money at
that time' (H, 7, 179, 2); *táim creachta acu* 'they have ruined
me' (I, 2, 7); *nuair bheidh do sgéal inste agat* 'when you will
h a v e your story told' (I, 38, 2); *do réir mar chím ní dóich liom
go mbeadh slígh d'on sgéal an turus so i dteannta abhfuil
ráidhte againn* 'according as I see I dont think there would
be room for the story this time along with what we have
said' (L, 1, 108, 1); *nuair bhéadh gnó an aonaigh criochnuighthe aige* 'as soon as he should have finished the
business of the fair' (I, 11, 29); *b'fhéidir gur dhóich liom féin na
beidís tuillte agam* 'perhaps I may imagine that I would
n o t h a v e deserved them' (I, 26, 35); *is ar éigin abhí sé
tabhartha dhó agam* 'I had it hardly given to him' (I, 41, 6);
*nuair a bhí cúig nó sé de thurasaibh eile tabhartha agam,
bhí na focail móra agam* 'when I had given five or six
rounds more, I had the big words' (L, 1, 29, 1); *ar maith leat*

*an chaint chéadna so, atá caite againne le chéile indiu, d'aire-
achtaint* 'would you like to hear this same talk which we
have addressed to each other to-day' (L, 1, 29, 2).

Für das Sprachgefühl von Peter O'Leary, der nach meinem
Gefühl der idiomatischste neuirische Schriftsteller ist und mit
einer erfrischenden Derbheit überall für die Rechte der heute
gesprochenen irischen Sprache gegenüber den Schulmeistereien
der Grammatiker eintritt, ist also auch die umschreibende Konjugation bei den transitiven Verben, wie sie in § 4 bis § 20
gelehrt ist, ein fester Teil der aktiven Flexion dieser transitiven Verba im heutigen Neuirischen. Es ist daher Zeit, dass
neuirische Grammatiken, die die gesprochene Sprache lehren
wollen, davon gebührende Notiz nehmen.

Greifswald. H. ZIMMER.

THE ORIGIN
OF THE 'HIBERNIAN' COLLECTION OF CANONS.

The collection of canons which is known as the Hibernian or Irish was edited in 1874 and 1885 by Prof. Hermann Wasserschleben. Henry Bradshaw also spent 'several years' work upon the origin and earliest history of the collection'. A letter about it, from him to Wasserschleben, is printed in the latter's second edition, and by Mr. Jenkinson in the 'Collected Papers' of Bradshaw. Two other papers of his about it, unfinished, were published, under Mr. Jenkinson's editorship, in 1893.

That the collection was made late in the 7th or early in the 8th cent. is beyond doubt, for (says Bradshaw) in the more primitive form of its text the latest author quoted is Theodore, who died in 690, while in the less primitive form the latest author quoted is Adamnan, who died in 704. But in neither form is the name of the compiler or the place of compilation given. Loofs, in 1882, thought the collection was made in Northumbria — his only at all plausible reason being that the Irish would hardly have known Theodore's Penitential so early. Bradshaw, in 1885, thought 'it was compiled by an Irish monk or abbat of Dairinis in the south-east of Ireland', and 'must have originated in some locality where' Irish synodical decisions 'were accessible; in other words, in Ireland'. And Wasserschleben, in the same year, thought it originated either in Ireland or Wales — for it contains Welsh canons as well as Irish. The object of this paper is to show that it almost certainly originated at Iona, and was almost certainly compiled by its great abbat Adamnan, who died in 704.

7*

'The most primitive', says Bradshaw, 'although not perhaps the oldest' of the MSS., is MS. Lat. 12021 in the Bibliothèque Nationale, written in the 9th or 10th cent. by a Breton cleric named Arbedoc, at the direction of a Breton abbat named Hael Hucar. And at the end of his copy of the collection he writes

Hucvsq; nubeɴ & cv · cuiminiæ · & du rinis

— only that, of course, he doesn't dot his *i* 's. It 's from this colophon that Bradshaw sought the evidence of the collection's origin, and that, after recording what others have made out of it, I shall produce direct evidence of the connexion with Iona.

Bradshaw was the first to throw light on the colophon. He identified 'du rinis' with Dairinis. Let me add that both Durinis and Dairinis are variations of an earlier Darinis. There was a Durinis (now Duirinish) in Skye: but it isn't known to have had a monastery — only a church. There was a Darinis with a monastery in Wexford, but Archdall knows nothing of it after about 540. So that the much longer-lived monastery of Darinis above Youghal is doubtless meant.

Then in 1888 came Mr. Whitley Stokes. *r* and *n* are so like each other in some early mediaeval hands that they are continually confounded in MSS., and Mr. Stokes suggested that for 'nubeɴ' we should read 'rubeɴ'. And the Rev. B. Mac Carthy presently put the suggestion beyond doubt by pointing out that Irish annalists mention the death of 'Rubin scribe of Munster' as taking place in or about 724 (725). The difference of final vowel is quite unimportant, for the name is an adjective from the stem *rub-* 'hair', and might be formed in either *-in* or *-en*.

Mr. Stokes discovered another thing, which, in ignorance of his discovery, I myself found out ten years later — that the second person mentioned in the colophon is Cu Cumine, otherwise Cu Cuimne, whose death is put by Irish annalists between 742 and 747. He is called 'sapiens', wrote a Latin hymn to the Virgin (which is still extant), and is the subject of an epigram said to have been addressed to him by Adamnan, wherein he is chaffed for reading his authors only half through — to which he replied in other verses that he would read them right through for the future. We do not know what his local connexions were: that he was not abbat of Darinis is practically certain from the fact that in the very year of his death Irish annalists also chronicle the death of Ferdacrich, abbat of Dairinis.

But what no one, so far as I know, has yet seen is that the colophon also contains the place-name 'iæ', that is to say, the genitive, dative, or locative case of Ia, our modern Iona. Ia and Iae are the ordinary Latin nominative and genitive used by Irish annalists. Consequently, in the original from which our colophon was copied, we get two place-names, 'Iæ & Durinis' parallel to the two person-names 'Ruben & Cu Cuimni', and the line ran

'Thus far Ruben & Cu Cuimni at Ia & Durinis.'

Before pointing out to what this irresistibly leads us, I must justify my reading of 'Cu Cuimni' instead of 'Cu Cuimne'. *Cú*, which means Hound, was a common Irish name, and those who bore it generally had some distinguishing surname, which often consisted of another man's name in the genitive — implying that Cu was the son, or servant, or pupil of another man. Now *Cumine* (Cuimne) was also a common name, and to my mind it is morally certain that Cu Cuimni's name means 'Cumine's Cu'. And the genitive of Cumine (Cuimne), at the period we are dealing with, was not (as often in later Irish) the same as the nominative, but ended in -*i*.[1])

And now for our conclusions. As Ruben died some 20 years before Cu Cuimni, and as Ia is mentioned before Durinis, it's pretty clear that the first of the two copies was made by Ruben at Ia. We don't know to what religious foundation Ruben was specially attached, but we do know that it must have been in Munster — and Durinis was in Munster. Consequently, it's pretty clear that the copy he made at Ia was made for Durinis, and that the copy made at Durinis by Cu Cuimni was transcribed from it for some other foundation. What that foundation was we don't know, because we haven't the least clew to Cu's local connexions. But it's clear that he wrote a colophon in which he said his transcript was made at Durinis from a copy taken by Ruben at Ia.

----

[1]) Cu's name is commonly, but I think far less probably, supposed to mean 'Memory Cu'. The final -*in* the Paris MS. also suggests an original -*ni*, but not -*ne*.

The pedigree, then, of our Paris MS. is this:

A) MS. at Ia, written before 726,
B) MS. at Durinis, copied at Ia from A by Ruben before 726,
C) MS. copied at Durinis from B by Cu Cuimni before 748,
D) The Paris MS. — copied in Brittany from C, or from an intermediate MS., by Arbedoc in the 9th or 10th cent.

The collection, then, of canons, hitherto known as the Hibernian, makes its first appearance, before 726, at Ia. Is there any reason to suppose that it was compiled anywhere else than at Ia? So far as I know, absolutely none. On the contrary, the internal evidence seems to suit Ia far better than Ireland. That Irish synods should be quoted in an Ia collection is just as natural as that they should be quoted in an Irish one, for Ia was the principal and most revered foundation of the Irish church. That Welsh synods and a Northumbrian book (the Penitential of Theodore) should be quoted in an Irish collection is immeasurably less likely than that they should be quoted in one made at Ia — for the Dalriad Scots were next neighbours to the Welsh of Alclyde and Loch Lomond, and Adamnan, abbat of Ia, had come back in 688 from a visit to the Northumbrian monasteries. [1])

I go further: I believe that the collection was made by or under the direction of Adamnan himself. It was certainly compiled by a strong Romanizer: Adamnan was such from 688 to his death in 704, but his community of Ia refused to accept the Roman Easter or the Roman tonsure till about 716. Again, if the collection was made after his death, why is he himself never cited? He was the foremost man of his time in the Irish church — and the absence of all allusion to his decisions in the earliest type of our text would be very difficult to understand, if it were not due to his own reluctance to cite himself as an ecclesiastical authority. And here I must add that in our Paris MS. and four others the collection is actually followed by a collection of

---

[1]) The quotations from Theodore's Penitential seem to call for some uch explanation: for Bede doesn't mention the book, so that in England its would appear to have been still almost unknown as late as 731.

'Canons of Adamnan' — so that it would seem that, after his death, the monks of Ia insisted on supplementing the collection with those decisions of Adamnan which his own modesty had excluded from it. And in the later type of text he is also quoted in the collection itself (the text of the quotation being the same as in these supplementary Canons).

As regards the name to be given to the collection for the future, I suggest 'Hiiensis', the adjective of *Hii* (Ia), used by Bede. *Hi* and *Hii* are early Irish forms of the name of the isle,[1]) and the initial *H* almost undoubtedly represents an original initial consonant.

---

[1]) The authority on the subject is Reeves in his editions of Adamnan's Life of Columba. *Iona* is a misreading of *Ioua*, an adjective agreeing with *insula*.

Oxford.   E. W. B. NICHOLSON.

FILIUS URBAGEN.

On my way back to Oxford in October 1898 from the St. Gallen Conference of Librarians I visited various libraries in order to examine manuscripts of Keltic interest. Among those which I saw was the Chartres MS. 98, commonly called Nennius. I found that the proper name of an author given in the first line was (as it ought to be) FILI URBAGEN, and not as it had previously been read.[1]) I also found to my surprise that the MS. was much later than anyone had placed it — that in fact it was later than 1040 and quite possibly later than 1070, though doubtless earlier than 1100. It is in continental Caroline minuscules, and I know of no MS. written in that hand so early as 1040 in which the tops of tall letters are forked, as they frequently are in the Chartres MS.: the point is one to which I have given special attention.[2])

I then began to consider for the first time what the Chartres MS. really was, and came to certain conclusions of which I communicated some to Prof. Mommsen. I afterwards learnt that several at least of these had been anticipated in print by Prof. Thurneysen, but in preparing the present paper I purposely abstained from reading his articles, in order that such of my arguments as confirmed his own might have the weight due to absolute independence. At Prof. Stern's request I have now looked at those articles, and have made special mention of Thurneysen's anticipations.

---

[1]) Thurneysen, however, had conjectured 'fii (d. i. filii) Urbagen' (*Zeitschrift f. deutsche Philologie* 28, 83).

[2]) In *Hiberno-Saxon* minuscules this forking begins to appear some $3^1/_2$ centuries earlier, in a charter of which the date is either 700 or 715.

I hold, I. that the Chartres MS. contains not Nennius, but a work which is one of the sources of Nennius; II. that this work is itself a compilation; III. that it was written in the territory of the Northern Kymri; IV. that the latest part of it is not earlier than 752; V. that the earliest part may have been compiled by Run the son of Urbgen, from whom Nennius states that the Northumbrians received baptism; VI. that the Urbgen in question may be the British king mentioned by Nennius; VII. that Run may just possibly be a prae-ordination name of Paulinus, bishop of York.[2])

I. The MS. does not contain anywhere the name of Nennius or that of any of the persons mentioned by 'Nennius' as his instructors. And a comparison with Mommsen's critical edition of Nennius shows that the Chartres text not only presents wide differences of order, and in some places wide differences of text, but is also very much shorter. Except that, like Nennius, it introduces the miracles of Germanus by the words 'aliquanta . miracula quae per illum fecit dominus scribenda decreui', it lacks all Nennius's personal notes. And it lacks all his references to prae-existing documents — e. g. on p. 159 'Aliud experimentum inveni de isto Bruto ex veteribus libris veterum nostrorum', on p. 161 'hanc peritiam inveni ex traditione veterum', and on p. 162 'Et redeam nunc ad id, de quo digressus sum'. The first of these three passages is specially remarkable. It states that what is about to follow is discovered from 'old books of o u r old authors', that is of much earlier British writers, and I hold that the Chartres text represents the actual source of the discovery.

II. The title of the Chartres text (as far as it can be represented without special type) is as follows:

INCIPIUNT · exberta · FILI VRBA GEN ðe LIðRO SčI
GERMANI · INUENTA & ORIGINE · & GENELOGIA
BRITONÛ · DE ÆTATI BUS · MUNðI ·

---

[1]) *Zeitschrift f. deutsche Philologie* 28, 80 und *Zeitschrift f. celt. Philologie* 1, 157. The former article I first heard of from L. Duchesne, *Revue Celtique* 17, 1: both are mentioned by Dr. Ludwig Traube, *Neues Archiv der Gesellschaft f. ältere deutsche Geschichtskunde* 24, Heft 2, in an article which kindly refers to my communications to Mommsen.

[2]) Of these contentions I find I, II, V, VI by Thurneysen in the *Ztschr. f. deutsche Philologie.*

The words 'De ætatibus mundi', though written as large as the rest, are really no part of the title, but are only the heading of the opening section,[1] just as subsequent sections are headed 'ᴅᴇ qua · ꝺaᴍ ᴘɪᴛɪa · aʙʀɪᴛaɴɪa · ɪɴѕvle' and 'ᴅᴇ ɢᴇɴᴇ · ʟоɢɪa · ʙʀɪᴛо · ɴꝒ · The true title I write and punctuate thus in modern fashion:

Incipiunt exberta. (*exberta* being a misreading of *excerpta*
[written monogrammatically)
Fili Vrbagen de Libro Sēi Germani inuenta, & origine   .
[& genelogia BritonꝒ.

The archetype, in fact, was professedly a collection of excerpts such as Nennius himself speaks of. The first of these excerpts was 'The son of Urbagen's discoveries relating to the book of St. Germanus and the origin and genealogy of the Britons.' Possibly other excerpts, such as the Saxon genealogies, followed — for the Chartres text is incomplete and breaks off in the middle of a sentence.

I cannot see the force of Traube's objection to 'excerpta': I cannot see why Nennius should not speak of these 'excerpta' as having been thrown down[2]) by British stupidity. And I believe that 'exberta' arose out of a monogram in which the c of 'excerpta' was expressed in the righthand half of the x, while the second E and the R were written back to back on a single stem, and below the centre of the R was added the loop of a P. The form might be

Every palaeographer knows of such compendia in titles,[3]) and that the original title was compendiously written is indicated by the facts that 1. the first *i* in 'Fili' is hung on to the lower cross-stroke of the *F*', and 2. the first *i* in 'origine' is very small, and joined to the tail of the *R*.

III, IV. The evidence that this particular collection was made in the territory of the Northern Kymri lies in the inter-

---

[1]) This Thurneysen has seen (*Ztschr. f. d. Philologie* 28, 86).

[2]) 'deiecerat' suggests that he found them lying on the ground.

[3]) The original of the Chartres text was apparently written, as we shall presently find, in the second half of the 8th cent.: for compendia in titles of that date see the Bodleian MS. Lat. th. d. 3.

polation respecting the date of the Saxon invasion of Britain, where a date is given 'fič libine · abafiæ · inripū ciuitate · inuenit · ł repit', i. e. sic*ut*¹) (S)libine abas Iæ²) Inripum ciuitate inuenit (*vel* repe*r*it)'. Inripum, now Ripon, was in ancient Northumbria; Ia is the ordinary ancient Latin name for what is now incorrectly called Iona; Slebine became abbat of Ia about 752 and died 767. Doubtless his journey to Ripon was to see the pastoral staff given by his great predecessor Columba to St. Kentigern — which was kept in the church of St. Wilfrid at Ripon (Reeves's ed. of Adamnan's Columba, 1874, p. XC).

Zimmer (*Nennius Vindicatus*) has already argued that our 'Historia Britonum' is partly based on a North Kymric chronicle of 679, which received additions down to the period 737—758. Slebine's supposed discovery cannot have been made after 767 (when Slebine died), and there is little doubt that the person who mentions it was a Briton: had he been a Saxon or Angle he would hardly have failed to know or mention Baeda's statements as to the date of the invasion. He probably wrote in Alclyde or Carlile — through both of which Slebine's road would almost certainly pass (at any rate through Alclyde).

V, VI. The reasons for identifying 'Filius Urbagen' with Run map Urbgen, and for identifying his father with the British King Urbgen are these. The name Urbgen is of extreme rarity in Britain — so rare that I doubt there being any authentic instance of it except in the case of King Urbgen.³) And the presence of the connecting vowel in Urb*a*gen is evidence that the person alluded to lived at least prior to 731. For in 731 Baeda finished his Ecclesiastical History, in II, 2 of which he writes not 'Brocomaglus' but 'Brocmail' — an evidence that

¹) The oldest forms of the name of Ripon consist of the preposition *in* followed by a dative plural in -*is* (Lat.) or -*um* (Eng.).

²) This identification was sent by me to Mommsen in ignorance that it had been anticipated by Mr. A. Anscombe in the *Zeitschrift f. celtische Philologie* I, 274—6. Anscombe, however, has not seen what special object Slebine might have in visiting Ripon.

³) A name Urbien was fairly common in Brittany, and is apparently a later form of Urbgen, though the number of Breton names which began with Ur- makes me just the least bit doubtful. In a document of 869 (*Cartulaire de Redon*, p. 83) an Urbien is mentioned in a pedigree, who might have been born in the 6th cent. and named after the British King Urbgen. He had a son Urban (= Urbanus?).

the connecting vowel had already been dropped in British.[1]) I
am inclined to derive the name from the stem of the Latin *urbs*,
as if 'born in the city', and to suppose that King Urbgen was
born in the city of York ('urbs Ebrauc' of the *Annales Cambriæ*):
the derivation from Stokes's stem *orbio-, orbo-*, 'Erbe' (as if 'son
of the heir'), also occurred to me, and is given by Stokes himself (*Urkelt. Sprachsch.* 40), but Stokes furnishes no examples of
the passage of this stem into a form beginning with *u*, and I
do not see where the phonetic justification would be.

I do not regard the mention of Run map Urbgen in Nennius
as evidence in favour of identifying Filius Urbagen with him.
Obviously the passage respecting Run, beginning with 'si quis
scire voluerit', is no part of the work of the Filius Urbagen.
But Run map Urbgen is mentioned less than 20 lines after a
laudatory account of Urbgen himself, and — seeing, as I have
said, the extreme rarity of that name in Britain — it is natural
for a reader to suppose that the same Urbgen is referred to.

VII. According to Baeda the Northumbrian English received
baptism, in 626 and onwards, from Paulinus, who had been sent
by Pope Gregory in 601 (with Mellitus, Iustus, Rufinianus, and
others) to help Augustine, and whom Augustine's successor Iustus
had sent in 625 in the suite of a Kentish princess whom the
Northumbrian king was about to marry. With Paulinus went
a deacon Iacobus, who remained in the country in 633, when
the king was killed and Paulinus took the queen back to Kent.

According to the 'Historia Britonum', however, it was from
Run map Urbgen that the Northumbrians received baptism, and
I find that the suggestion of his identity with Paulinus has been
made by others before me.

It was common to change a non-Latin name to a Latin
name at ordination — at any rate on ordination to the office of
bishop. For instance, Berctgils, consecrated in 652, with his see
at Dunwich, is surnamed Bonifacius; Deusdedit, archbishop of
Canterbury (655), was originally Frithona; and Damianus of

---

[1]) Cf. in the same chapter the Welsh place-name Bancor (modern
Bangor), in which the connecting vowel is equally lost. Cataracta is no
instance to the contrary, any more than its modern name Catterick would
be; for when Baeda wrote it had been an English town for nearly 130 years,
and the English kept the connecting vowel as they have kept final -s in the
pronunciation of 'Calais' and 'Paris'.

Rochester (655) was a Sussex man whose Saxon name has been lost altogether.

If Run *did* go to Rome and *did* take a Latin name, Paulinus was an appropriate one to take; for a saint of that name, who (unless tradition has confounded the two Paulini) 'had been a disciple to a bishop at Rome', had founded a collegé in Caermarthenshire (Rees's *Lives of the Cambro-British Saints*, p. 405). Ricemarch, who died in 1096, calls this earlier Paulinus 'Paulinum scribam discipulum Sancti Germani' (Rees, p. 122). And, if this was so, Run map Urbgen would be attracted to the 'book of St. Germanus' by the connexion of his namesake with that saint. If it was *not* so, then apparently Ricemarch has anticipated me by eight centuries in identifying Filius Urbagen with Run, and Run with Paulinus of York, and has confused the latter with the teacher of St. David.

Let me add that the name of Paulinus's deacon, Iacobus, is suspiciously British. I doubt if Iacobus was a common name in West Europe at the beginning of the 7th century. As an Anglo-Saxon name Iacob seems to be absolutely unknown. But as a Welsh name (starting *before* the 7th century and passing through Iacob, Iacou, Iaco, into Iago) it was quite common.

Of course, if the archbishop of Canterbury had among his clergy two Britons, one of them son of the king who had been the chief antagonist of the Northumbrians, the choice of them to accompany the Kentish princess north would be an act of excellent policy; it might lead to the conciliation of international enmities, to the introduction of Roman usages among the Britons who lived in or on the borders of Northumbria, and to their coöperation in the work of converting the English.

The objections to identifying Paulinus with Run seem to me to be, I. the fact that Baeda gives no hint of either Paulinus or Iacobus being of British birth, II. the improbability that Britons of that period would have gone to Rome at all, III. a statement by Alcuin.

I. That Paulinus should have been of British birth, and Baeda not know it, does seem unlikely. That he should have known it, and omit to mention it, also seems unlikely — in spite of his great prejudice against the un-Romanized British church. Yet, if St. Patrick was a real person and a Briton — as I fully believe — the fact that Baeda never mentions *him* (but does mention Palladius's mission from the Pope to Ireland) would be equally curious.

II. That in the latter half of the 7th cent. a British king's son should have gone to Rome for his religious training also seems unlikely. Yet at that very time we have in Gildas a Briton whom residence in Brittany seems to have made a strong Romanist (see Mommsen's ed., p. 88, XI). If we were able to trust the life of Gildas written by the monk of Ruys, Gildas himself might just possibly have taken young Run to Rome. According to that life, Gildas when in Ireland 'collegit monachos ... ex nobilibus ... omnem denique regionem Hibernensium et Anglorum' (Northumbria?) '.... suo instruxit exemplo', after which he went to Rome (Mommsen's ed., p. 95). Gildas's death is placed by the *Annales Cambriæ* in 570: Paulinus died in 644.

III. Alcuin in his *Carmen de Pontificibus Eccl. Eboracensis* (l. 135) calls Paulinus 'civis clarissimus urbis Romanæ'. That is a very curious description — so curious that I think I see what gave rise to it. Alcuin had read or heard that the baptizer of the Northumbrians was called by the Britons Run map Urbgen, or was 'filius Urbigenæ (*or* Urbigenii)', and had supposed that his father was born in the *urbs* Roma. Perhaps even the name Run — which (through Rū) has come to be written Rum in the manuscripts HK of Nennius — was supposed by him to mean 'Roman'.

It is clear to me that the writer of the account of the Northumbrian baptisms was partly indebted to a blundered version of Baeda, or a source of Baeda, for some of his statements. He says 'Eanfled filia illius *duodecimo die post* pentecosten baptismum accepit cum universis hominibus suis de viris et mulieribus cum ea' (§ 63). Baeda (II, 9) says that the king 'filiam suam Christo consecrandam Paulino episcopo adsignavit; quae baptizata est die sancto pentecostes prima de gente Nordanhymbrorum, cum XI aliis de familia eius'. One 8th cent. MS. reads XII for XI, and it looks as if this XII has been written in the margin (as the number of persons baptized) and has been wrongly associated with Pentecost.[1]) The '12' persons baptized with Æanfled seem also to crop up in the statement that 'X̄I̅I̅ hominum', i. e. 12 000 persons! 'in uno die baptizati sunt cum

---

[1]) So also Thurneysen, *Ztschr. f. deutsche Philologie* 28, 85.

eo', i. e. with her father. And I strongly suspect that the words
of Baeda 'de familia eius' had been construed in two ways,
1. as meaning 'from *her* household', which is wrong, and 2. 'from
his household', which is right.

Again, we are told in the manuscripts HK that Run 'per
quadraginta dies non cessavit baptizare omne genus ambronum',
and Baeda (II, 14) tells us how Paulinus (when at a certain
place with the king and queen) 'XXXVI diebus ibidem cum eis
cathecizandi et baptizandi officio deditus moraretur': and the
change from 36 to 40 days looks as if there was a statement or
belief that the days in question were the week-days in Lent,
which at the beginning of the 7th cent. would be 36, and at
the end of the 8th cent. would doubtless have risen to their
present number of 40.

In 635, only 10 years after the first Northumbrian baptism,
and only 2 years after the flight of Paulinus, a second mission
to Northumbria was begun by Aidan of Ia. 'Exin coepere
plures per dies de Scottorum regione uenire Brittaniam atque
illis Anglorum prouinciis quibus regnauit Osuald .... gratiam
baptismi, quicunque sacerdotali erant gradu praediti, ministrare'
(Baeda III, 3). Was Run only one of this later mission, a
Strathclyde Briton who had joined it on its way from Ia to
Northumbria?

And is not the 'Renchidus episcopus' (who, together with
'Elbobdus', attributed the Northumbrian baptism to Run) simply
bishop Senchan or Senchai, of Emly in Ireland? In the Hiberno-
Saxon hand *ſ* and *r* are easily, and frequently, confounded, and
ui (= *ai*) might well be misread as *id*. Senchai died in 781,
and from the beginning of § 15 (a passage not in the Chartres
text) we know that 'peritissimi Scottorum' gave information to
the compiler of the Historia Britonum.

Oxford.   E. W. B. NICHOLSON.

LES VERS DE PSEUDO-NENNIUS.

Codd. Cantabb. Corpus Christi 139 (s. XIII, C de l'éd.) et Bibl. Univ. Ff. 1. 27
(s. XIII, L de l'éd.) — Ed. San Marte (Stevenson) p. 22; éd. Mommsen p. 144.
— The Irish Version of Nennius, éd. p. J. H. Todd, Dublin, Arch. Soc. 1848,
p. 11 de l'introduction de A. Herbert.[1]

A   B   C   D   E   F
1. Adiutor benignus cari|s doctor effabilis fonis.

G sit H   I .i. Samueli K L   M
2. Gaudium honoris isti katholica lege magni.

N   O   P   Q R S T   V
3. Nos omnes precamur qui ros sit tutus utatur.

X   .i. beulan
4. Xpe tribuisti patri Samuelem leta matre.

Y   .i. mater   .i. Samuel
5. Hymnizat h̄ semper tibi longeuus ben seruus tui.[2]

Z |||||
6. Zona indue salutis istum tis pluribus annis.

7. Fornifer qui digitis scripsit ex ordine trinis.
8. Incolumis obtalmis sitque omnibus menbris.
9. Eu uocatur ben notis litteris nominis quini.

---

[1] Voyez: Nennius und Gildas, éd. p. San Marte (A. Schulz), Berlin, 1844;
— Nennius Vindicatus, Ueber Entstehung, Geschichte etc. der Historia Britt-
tonum, p. H. Zimmer, Berlin 1893, et les articles critiques sur cette étude
magistrale de MM. D'Arbois de Jubainville, Revue Celtique, tome XV, pp. 126
—129; L. Duchesne, Nennius retractatus, ibid. pp. 174—197; R. Thurneysen,
Zeitschrift für deutsche Philologie, tome XXVIII, pp. 80 et suiv.; — Mommsen,
Neues Archiv, tome XIX, pp. 285 et suiv.; — enfin, l'édition de ce savant:
Gildae Sapientis de excidio et conquestu Britanniae etc. et Historia Brittonum
cum additamentis Nennii, Berlin 1894.

[2] C'est bien au-dessus de 'longeuus' et non de 'tibi', comme l'a cru
M. Zimmer et que l'ont imprimé MM. San Marte et Mommsen, que se trouve
la glose '.i. Samuel'. Voyez ci-dessous p. 119.

Voilà comment sont disposés et écrits — sauf les quelques abréviations que nous avons résolues — ces fameux vers dans le plus ancien des deux MSS., celui de Corpus Christi Cambridge (no. 139, s. XIII, *C* de M. Mommsen). Texte et gloses sont de la même main. Cette main a écrit tout ce qu'il y a sur ce feuillet du MS. Nos vers s'y trouvent non pas en marge, sur le côté ou en bas, mais dans le corps du feuillet, pour ainsi dire, sur les dernières lignes de la 2e colonne, séparés par un espace libre de la fin de l'énumération *de bonis naturis gentium* etc. qui commence dans la colonne de gauche.

Les détails graphiques s'appliquent également au MS. Ff. 1. 27 de la bibliothèque de l'Université de Cambridge (*L* de l'éd. Mommsen). Ce MS. est un peu plus récent. MM. Zimmer et Mommsen n'ont pas hésité à le considérer comme une copie de celui de Corpus Christi. M. H. Bradshaw va plus loin, trop loin, à mon humble avis, en concluant d'une certaine ressemblance dans l'écriture, 'que *C* et *L* ont été écrits par le même copiste'. Celui de *L* est beaucoup plus soigneux, d'abord, et veut faire beau. Dans *C,* il n'y a que les lettres de l'alphabet au-dessus des mots correspondants qui soient en rouge.[1]) *L* (ou son rubricateur) prodigue les couleurs; ses titres sont en rouge, les initiales de chaque vers alternativement en rouge et en vert; quand, faute de place, le vers est brisé, il marque l'alinéa d'un trait en couleur. Il est vrai que le scribe de *L* a reproduit fidèlement le *tis* (ligne 6) inexpliqué et peut-être inexplicable, et c'est seulement plus tard qu'un lecteur, ne sachant qu'en faire, l'a barré. Il omet, cependant, *sit* au-dessus de *Gaudium,* parce qu'il comprend que ce n'est pas une glose et qu'on n'en a pas besoin; il écrit *tibi* (ligne 6), en toutes lettres, à la place *t́* de *C,* *hec* (ligne 6) pour *h́* de *C,* enfin, il abrège *quini* de *C* en *q́ni* (ligne 9).

Mais, ce MS. donne des titres, où *C,* le soi-disant modèle, a des espaces libres. Or, ces titres sont une addition tellement considérable qu'il est difficile d'admettre qu'un même copiste (ou

---

[1]) Si *L* est copié sur *C,* et si dans *C* on n'avait pas pris la peine d'indiquer la suite alphabétique, *L* ou son rubricateur aurait pu, à la rigueur, insérer les lettres dans *C*; elles y sont, en effet, en rouge, et la ressemblance avec celles de *L* est grande. C'est cela qu'a voulu dire, ce semble, M. Bradshaw. Mais, si cela était, pourquoi ce scribe n'aurait-il pas ajouté aussi les titres, puis qu'il y trouvait la place nécessaire, spécialement réservée?

son rubricateur) ait pu les oublier une fois et les placer soigneuse-
ment dans une copie postérieure. Quant au texte même, celui
qui copie, si copie il y a, c'est *L*; il est scribe d'autant plus
fidèle qu'il entend moins ce qu'il transcrit; il reproduit con-
sciencieusement, nous dit-on, jusqu'aux plus simples erreurs
d'orthographe de *C*.[1] Mais alors, il y aurait eu une autre
source pour les titres — nous n'en connaissons plus aujourdhui —,
ou bien, *L* aurait écrit ou fait écrire de son invention: *Versus
Nennini* (sic!) *ad Samuelem filium magistri sui Beulani presbiteri
viri religiosi ad quem historiam istam scripserat*, en tête des
lignes 1—6 incl., et *Versus eiusdem Nennii*, au-dessus des lignes
7, 8, 9. Pour ma part, je m'arrête à la première hypothèse.
D'abord, je préfère supposer que *nennini* soit un simple lapsus
et que *L* ait reproduit, sans s'en apercevoir, une fois *nennini*,
puis, quelques lignes plus loin, *nennii*. C'est discutable, car, ce
nom a été écrit par certains scribes de la même façon,[2] et il
est encore possible que l'original, d'où *C* + *L* ont tiré cet addita-
mentum, ait eu lui-même cette singularité. Peu importe, ces
titres sont là, et nous avons à nous demander où celui qui les
a écrits le premier en tête de ces lignes, a puisé ses in-
formations. Sûrement ce n'est pas dans les gloses, encore moins
dans les vers eux-mêmes, comme le croit M. Zimmer, p. 48.
Celles-là ne mentionnent que Beulan et Samuel, et pour formuler
de ces maigres indications une attribution aussi complète à
Nennius, il aurait encore fallu qu'il fût renseigné sur les rapports
de Nennius avec ces deux hommes. C'est donc l'inverse qui a
eu lieu: les gloses découlent des titres ou elles ont la même
origine; dans l'un et dans l'autre cas, ils datent de bien plus
loin que nos MSS.

Occupons-nous d'abord des titres, ou plutôt du premier
seulement; car, le second n'a même pas droit à être pris en
considération, la ligne 9 n'ayant absolument rien à faire avec le
distique qui précède, de même qu'il est fort probable que celui-ci
soit étranger au carmen, c'est à dire aux v. 1—6.

Je suis de l'avis de M. Zimmer, que cette strophe n'a pas

---

[1] Éd. Mommsen p. 125. Il ne faudrait peut-être pas insister sur ce
genre de ressemblances entre *C* et *L* au point de faire de celui-ci une copie
de celui-là. Voyez ci-dessous p. 4.

[2] Voyez Thurneysen, dans sa critique du *Nennius Vindicatus* p. 82 et
95. Le traducteur irlandais, par ex., a lu *nemnius* ou *nemnus* (= neninus?).

appartenu à la première rédaction de Nennius. M. Zimmer a également raison de dire que son titre provient des derniers mots de deux additions (éd. San Marte [Stevenson] § 10 l. 18 et § 56; éd. Mommsen p. 151 et p. 207) d'une rédaction postérieure. Ces passages les voici:

1. *Sic inveni ut tibi, Samuel, id est infans magistri mei id est Beulani presbyteri in ista pagina scripsi. Set haec genealogia non scripta in aliquo volumine Britanniae, set in scriptione mentis scriptoris fuit.* (Cod. G: *scriptorit*, Zimmer: *scriptoriter*).

Cette addition ne se trouve pas dans *L*, précisément le MS. qui seul a conservé le titre de nos vers; c'est une preuve de plus que le scribe n'a pas suppléé lui-même le titre qu'il n'avait pas trouvé dans *C*, mais que ce titre se trouvait bien dans le modèle commun, ou, en tous les cas, dans un MS. antérieur du même groupe ayant et les vers et ce passage en entier. Pour tout autre que M. Zimmer ce passage signifierait, non pas *malgré*, mais *à cause* de la mauvaise latinité, ceci: *Si ai trouvé comme j'ai écrit dans cette page pour toi, Samuel, c'est à dire enfant de mon maître, c'est à dire du prêtre Beulan.* M. Zimmer voit bien, ce qui est facile d'ailleurs, que l'auteur de cette phrase est un élève de Beulan; il a tort de ne pas voir en *Samuel* un vocatif, à *tibi*, mais un cas sujet à *scripsi*; cela l'a amené à rapporter *tibi* à *Beulan*; il fait dire, ainsi, à un élève qui écrit pour son maître ou sur la demande de celui-ci, — ce n'est pourtant pas tout à fait la même chose — une platitude de ce genre: *Si ai trouvé [maître] comme j'ai écrit pour toi, en Samuel, c'est à dire enfant de mon maître, c'est à dire de Beulan.* 'Pour ne pas blesser les susceptibilités de Beulan en le comparant au faible Eli, il dit *magistri mei* au lieu d'*Eli mei*, ainsi que l'idée évoquée par le parallèle avec Samuel eût fait prévoir.' M. Thurneysen trouve 'inutile' cette interprétation artificielle (p. 97). Nous verrons tout à l'heure quel sens elle a fait découvrir à M. Zimmer dans nos vers.

2. Dans le deuxième passage le latin est plus clair. L'auteur, évidemment le même, s'excuse de ne pas 'écrire' certaines généalogies: *Set cum inutiles magistro meo id est Beulano presbytero visae sunt genealogiae Saxonum et aliarum genealogiae gentium, nolui eas scribere, set de civitatibus .... ut scriptores ante me scripsere, scripsi.*

On comprend mieux, mais l'abus de *scribere* et des dérivés dans les deux passages, tout en caractérisant le même auteur

8*

d'une façon irréfutable, ne rend pas meilleur son latin. J'approuve
entièrement M. Zimmer qui voit dans la mauvaise latinité de ces
passages un raison suffisante pour ne pas en affubler Nennius
(p. 52): '*So kann doch der Nennius nicht schreiben, der mit Ego
Nennius sancti Elbodugi discipulus anhebt*'.   M. Thurneysen
reconnaît la difficulté et, pour la tourner, semble admettre
qu'après tout le latin du deuxième passage n'est pas si mauvais
qu'on veut bien le dire, et qu'il est, en tous les cas, meilleur
que celui du premier; celui-ci aurait été écrit, dit-il, à la hâte
et au hasard de la mémoire. Pour ne pas nous arrêter à des
subtilités qui abondent dans l'épineuse question de Nennius, je
crois, d'accord avec M. Zimmer, que l'élève de Beulan n'est pas
Nennius. Sur ce point, MM. Duchesne, Mommsen et Thurneysen
sont trop indulgents (p. 97).   Cet élève de Beulan prétend avoir
reçu un renseignement de '*l'évêque Renchidus*' et '*du plus saint
de évêques Elbobdus*', éd. Mom. p. 207.[1]) Or, comme Nennius
se dit lui-même, dans sa préface, disciple '*sancti Elbodugi*',
M. Thurneysen fait de Nennius le disciple de l'évêque de Bangor
(† 809) et de Beulan. C'est à croire qu'il n'a ni longtemps ni
beaucoup travaillé avec le célèbre Elbobdus, puisqu'il reste dans
une condition inférieure, et que, en homme déjà âgé, il se dit,
de préférence, l'élève d'un prêtre Beulan, dont nous ne savons
rien. Aussi, ce savant en conclut-il qu'il a commencé l'Historia
(réd. Harley.) après la mort du premier maître; *âgé* alors, ainsi
le suppose M. Thurneysen (p. 96), *de 18 ans*, il y aurait travaillé jusqu'en 859, dernière date fixe de son ouvrage; après
cela, en *homme très âgé*, il en aurait fait un abrégé pour son
maître Beulan, et c'est alors et dans cet ouvrage qu'il aurait
inséré les deux indications en question.   On comprend que
M. Thurneysen ne veuille pas de l'explication de M. Zimmer:
il n'a que faire d'un *Nennius vieux* s'appelant le *Samuel de
son maître*; pour ma part, je ne comprends pas un Nennius,
qui, tout en sachant écrire convenablement, perd son style
en faisant un abrégé de son grand ouvrage, et qui n'est jamais

---

[1]) Les paroles *sic mihi Renchidus episcopus et Elbobdus episcoporum
sanctissimus tradiderunt* ne nous obligent nullement à croire qu'il s'agisse de
traditions *orales*. Voyez M. Zimmer, p. 51. Il n'y a aucune conclusion à tirer
de là, si ce n'est que l'interpolateur invoque des sources connues à Beulan.
Tout au plus, un homme de sa trempe pourrait-il s'être approprié une paren-
thèse de sa source, de Nennius.

sorti d'une situation apparemment très humble. Il est beaucoup plus naturel que Beulan ait eu un fils Samuel, et qu'il
ait confié l'éducation de ce fils à un de ces anciens élèves;
celui-ci accepte avec empressement cette occasion de rendre
au maître ce qu'il lui doit. Ce n'est pas beaucoup, dira-t-on;
mais enfin, il arrange pour ce Samuel une histoire nationale,
celle de Nennius, en ajoutant ce qui peut intéresser l'élève plus
particulièrement et en laissant de côté ce que le père ne juge
pas nécessaire. Ainsi les *généalogies des Saxons et d'autres
peuples* sont supprimées. Par contre, ce fils doit savoir que Run
map Urbeghen a baptizé *omne genus Ambronum.* Certes, notre
clerc-pion n'est pas un esprit très critique. Il se tient à la tradition courante parmi les gens d'église; car, tout comme Beulan,
son maître, lui, le disciple, est homme d'église; ce n'est pas
à des Jérôme, des Eusèbe, des Isidore etc. qu'il s'adresse, ainsi
que le ferait le savant Nennius, le disciple du savant Elbobdus.
D'éducation classique, il en a une trace. Sa généalogie des
Troyens (éd. Mom. p. 151—2) est une réminiscence, probablement,
des commentaires de Virgile. *C'est un homme de ce genre, mais
pas un Nennius qui est, à notre avis, l'auteur de nos vers,* et
M. Zimmer a raison.

Maintenant, venons aux vers eux-mêmes. Il y est question
d'un père, d'un fils qui a nom Samuel, et d'une mère qui est
contente de ce que Dieu leur a donné ce fils. Sans aucun
doute, il y a eu là une quasi-répétition de l'histoire biblique.
L'auteur des vers l'exploite. Le père, homme d'église, implorait
le ciel de lui donner un fils. Ce fils lui est accordé sur le tard;
on l'appelle Samuel; la mère, comme Anne, s'en réjouit. Ce
fils, ce Dieu-donné, est voué au service de Dieu. Il est élevé
et instruit par celui qui fut le disciple du père déjà vieux, par
l'auteur de nos vers, qui a vieilli lui-même et qui est heureux
d'être, à son tour, le maître dévoué, le *serviteur,* dit-il modestement,
du *ben de Dieu,* de Samuel. Comme il a appris à faire des vers,
il promet de louer Dieu toujours de cette grâce accordée aux
parents, ses amis. A qui le promet-il? Au fils, à ce même
Samuel; car, c'est à lui qu'il souhaite bonne santé pour de
longues années encore. Il profite pour cela d'une occasion.
Samuel a été élevé à un grand honneur selon la loi catholique.
S'agit-il de son élection à l'épiscopat? Nous ne le savons. Il
doit régner, être un chef, c'est tout ce que son maître nous

indique. Car, Samuel est devenu lui-même un savant, et il paraît qu'après la mort de son père il est demeuré le protecteur de son vieux maître. Celui-ci, par son âge plutôt que par sa science, est devenu quelque chose comme le doyen d'une communauté, au nom de laquelle il adresse ses souhaits à son ancien élève; car, Samuel est un des leurs, et, s'il mêle à ses souhaits le souvenir des parents, c'est qu'il se rappelle que le père de Samuel avait été, jadis, son maître à lui.

Voici, maintenant, ses vers tels que je suis d'avis de les disposer et de les lire métriquement, si cela se peut:

1. α Ádiutór benígnus cáris ⎫
   β Dóctór effábilis fónis ‖ ⎭
2. α Gaúdiúm honóris ísti ⎫
   β Kathólica lége mágni ‖ ⎭
3. α (?) Nós omnés precámur ⎫
   β Qui rós sit tútus utátur ‖ ⎭
4. α Christe tríbuísti pátri ⎫
   α Sámuélem léta mátre ‖ ⎭
5. α Hýmnizát hec sémper tíbi ⎫
   α Lóngeuús ben séruus túi ‖ ⎭
6. α Zóna índué salútis ⎫
   β (?) Ístum (tis) plúribus ánnis ‖ ⎭

Il y a, si l'on veut, du rhythme et de l'assonance, même de la rime, autant qu'un clerc, qui par 'Xriste' et 'Hymnizat' fait commencer ses lignes en X et Y, peut en avoir appris dans les hymnes qu'il avait l'habitude de réciter ou de composer. Je les traduis ainsi: [Samuel est un] *Aide bienveillant, qu'on peut dire docteur en sons chers. La joie d'un grand honneur lui [est échu] selon .la loi de l'Eglise. Nous prions tous: celui qui (ou puis qu'il) est chef, qu'il [en]jouisse en sécurité. O Dieu, tu as accordé Samuel au père, à la joie de la mère. Toujours, le vieux serviteur de ton ben te loue pour cela. Ceins-le d'une ceinture de santé pour plus d'années encore.* Le *vieux serviteur,* c'est l'auteur des vers; *iste*[1]) c'est Samuel, le *ben de Dieu,* le Dieu-donné, le protecteur de l'auteur, son élève, enfin, qui est devenu un savant

---

¹) '*tis*', que *L* a reproduit fidèlement, ne paraît être qu'une correction de *istum* en *istis* = istos; ce serait aux parents encore vivants que l'auteur souhaiterait, dans ce cas, encore bien des années de santé; cela ne changerait beaucoup au sens général.

.

docteur de l'Eglise. '*Tui*' et '*tibi*' se rapportent à la personne
apostrophée, à Dieu, qui, à cause de l'alphabet, est appellé
Christ. Sans doute, le peu de clarté qu'on peut attendre d'un
poète de cette force, est encore obscurcie par la contrainte de
la suite alphabétique, volontaire, et, par cela même, bien caracté-
ristique pour le talent déployé. Voici, à titre de curiosité, l'interprétation de M. Zimmer:[1]) 'Samuel est un pseudonyme, c'est lui
l'auteur des vers; (il est vraiment peu modeste en priant, ainsi,
pour lui-même devant la postérité); le père c'est Beulan; la mère,
c'est l'Eglise'. J'avoue que je ne comprends rien à cette interprétation qui 'se présente naturellement' à M. Zimmer; l'éditeur
de l'Historia Brittonum n'en a pas voulu; il a préféré écouter
M. Thurneysen. M. Zimmer fait bon marché des gloses, que
M. Mommsen, au contraire, laisse à Nennius *non ignorans versus
se composuisse interpretatione vel maxime indigentes.* Avec les
gloses '*isti .i. Samueli*' et '*longeuus .i. Samuel*', — le MS. n'a
pas: *tibi .i. Samuel* — on n'arrive pas à grand'chose. Si,
la première fois, le glosateur a raison, si, ensuite, '*patri .i.
beulan*' a du sens, il s'est certainement trompé en entendant
par *longeuus servus* Samuel et par *hec* la mère, *.i. mater.* Je
n'accorde aucune importance aux gloses, et je m'étonne que
M. Zimmer, en trouvant suspecte l'une d'entre elles, ne les ait
pas rejetées en bloc. Sûrement, le glosateur et l'auteur de ces
vers ne font pas un seul et même personnage; par contre, il est
assez vraisemblable que le glosateur soit aussi l'auteur des titres:
gloses et titres se valent.

Le glosateur n'est donc qu'un scribe qui a trouvé ces vers
à la fin du Nennius interpolé; comme il y est question d'un
Samuel et qu'il vient de copier les deux passages ajoutés par le
maître de Samuel à l'édition de Nennius 'in usum discipuli', il
fabrique les titres et il glose de son mieux, en ne désignant, toutefois, que les personnages; sur l'occasion et sur les circonstances
de ce curieux poème il ne savait pas plus que nous. Je crois
pourtant qu'il veut nous montrer son savoir en expliquant, dans
le vers 9, pourquoi et comment Samuel — qui est devenu *ros*
— est appelé *ben. ros* est bien transmis,[2]) et ne peut être que

---

[1]) Nennius vindicatus p. 50—51; au fond, elle est de M. A. Herbert.
[2]) Dans un vieux glossaire de Chartres (Anc. No. 90, Xᵉ siècle), que j'ai
l'intention de publier un jour, j'ai trouvé: ros : capud.

ראש, *chef*: Samuel est devenu un chef; c'est le 'grand honneur' dans l'Eglise, dont l'auteur du carmen le félicite. '*Notis litteris nominis quini*', par lesquelles il est *justement* (εὖ) appelé '*ben*', me reste incompréhensible. L'auteur aurait-il relu l'histoire de Samuel? aurait-il remarqué que Samuel a eu comme nom particulier ראה, *vates*, nom qu'il a imparfaitement compris; aurait-il pensé à ראובן, *Ruben* (= *voyez un fils*! cf. Gen. 29, 32), et aurait-il voulu indiquer quelque rapport de son invention entre ce mot et les noms donnés à Samuel dans le carmen? Quoi qu'il en soit, la ligne énigmatique n'a rien à faire avec le distique héxamétrique qui la précède; elle a, au contraire, tout à fait l'aspect d'une glose. Comme elle était trop longue, il n'était pas possible de l'insérer, au-dessus de la ligne, à l'endroit voulu; le glosateur l'a donc placée à la fin de ce qu'il venait de copier. Cela prouve encore que le glosateur est postérieur à l'auteur des vers, et, de plus, qu'il a déjà trouvé le distique à la suite du carmen. Ce qui semble confirmer cette conclusion, c'est que le jeu du chiffre dans l'explication de *ben* de la ligne 9 peut bien être inspiré par *digitis . . . trinis* de la ligne 7. Je ne crois pas que les lignes 7 et 8 aient aucun rapport avec les précédentes; elles en sont séparées par l'espace libre d'une ligne dans les deux MSS.; *L* y a même inscrit en guise de titre: *Versus eiusdem Nennii*. Cependant, ni l'idée exprimée ni la forme héxamétrique ne nous empêcheraient de les supposer l'oeuvre du même auteur. Ce souhait de scribe pour une bonne vue et pour une bonne santé générale est formulé de façon à permettre la supposition qu'il est adressé à un homme vivant, que l'auteur a connu, et qui a écrit quelque chose que celui-ci vient de lire.

Malheureusement, la clef de l'énigme, le sens du mot *fornifer*, n'est pas encore trouvée. Tel que les MSS. donnent ce mot, il nous échappe. M. Gutschmid s'est rappelé *fonis* de la ligne 1 et a proposé de lire *fonifer*; j'avoue que je n'en vois pas le sens. Faut-il ou ne faut-il pas admettre une défiguration du mot par le copiste? puis, veut-on ou ne veut-on pas admettre que ces vers aient quelque rapport avec les précédents? c'est d'après ces considérations qu'on devra chercher à expliquer ce composé bizarre. Si l'on en fait abstraction, pour un instant, il ne reste qu'un simple souhait de scribe. Faute de pages blanches à gâcher, les clercs qui apprenaient à écrire, s'exerçaient sur les marges des

livres profanes en y griffonant des alphabets, des prières etc.
A la pratique insuffisante on suppléait par des règles versifiées,
p. ex. sur la façon de tenir la plume, ou bien sur la préoccupation
et les soins qu'exigent l'art de l'écriture. Ainsi, on a dû reprocher
à des clercs travaillant à la reproduction des livres que leur
occupation n'était pas fatigante, ou du moins, on se l'imaginait;
cette fausse idée, peut-être le reproche, a inspiré à un scribe les
héxamètres suivants, que j'ai trouvés dans un MS. d'Irlande, à
la fin d'une prière assez mal écrite (D. 4, 18, Trinity College,
Dublin):

> *Tres digiti scribunt et cetera membra laborant.*
> *Scribere qui nescit nullum putat esse laborem.*
> *Dum digiti scribunt, vix cetera membra quiescunt.*

Que l'on compare à ces vers les lignes 7 et 8 attribuées à
Nennius:

> *Fornifer qui digitis scripsit ex ordine trinis,*
> *Incolumis obtalmis sitque omnibus membris.*

L'auteur se rapelle ses leçons d'écriture: il faut [pour écrire]
trois doigts *ex ordine*: le pouce, l'index et le doigt du milieu, de
bons yeux et des membres sains. Le verbe 'scripsit' n'a pas de
régime directe, un *hoc* ou un *haec*, qu'on serait en droit d'attendre,
si ces vers devaient nécessairement s'adresser au scribe des lignes
précédentes — car, cela se pourrait après tout —; mais, il n'est
pas moins possible que ce soit un de ces additamenta que les
scribes traçaient d'un texte, au hasard de la plume au-dessous
même bien écrit: *Que (le scribe?) qui a écrit avec les trois doigts
selon l'ordre, soit sain des yeux et de tous ses membres.* 'Fornifer'
serait, dans ce cas, une désignation tirée de je ne sais où pour
'scribe', celui qui tient la plume (cf. *forīnae, tube?*) Si le mot
est déformé, on peut penser à *foruifer = furuifer (porteur de
noir)*, c'est à dire *plume = scribe* (plutôt que *prêtre*). Enfin, *for-
mifer (= calligraphe?)* ou *formiter (selon la formule, selon la
règle)* resteraient dans le même ordre d'idées. On en sort et on
rattache le distique aux vers précédents, en supposant que *fornifer* soit une désignation qui contienne une allusion que nous
ne comprenons plus, ou qu'en lisant *fronifer (φρόνις + fer*, la

quantité de l'*o* n'aurait pas arrêté le rimeur) il faille entendre *le maître* ou *l'homme intelligent* = φρόνιμος.[1]

On arrive donc à conclure ceci:

Le carmen a accompagné une Histoire dite de Nennius abrégée; il est l'oeuvre de l'abréviateur lui-même. Cet abréviateur n'est pas Nennius, le disciple d'Elbodug: il se dit l'élève d'un prêtre Beulan et travaille pour le fils de celui-ci, qui a nom Samuel. Le travail de cet anonyme n'a pas touché au fond de l'oeuvre de Nennius, et son nom ne s'est pas substitué à celui de Nennius. Ce fut, selon toute vraisemblance, un homme insignifiant et modeste. En tenant compte des dates, à peu près certaines, obtenues par les critiques pour les différentes versions de l'Historia Brittonum, il y a toute probabilité que cet abréviateur et son oeuvre appartiennent à la fin du IXe siècle; nous réussirons peut-être une autre fois à dire s'il a vécu dans le Nord ou dans le Sud du pays de Galles. Le distique héxamétrique n'a qu'une importance tout au plus secondaire. Les deux pièces circulaient au XIIe siècle, et sans doute avant, sous le nom de Nennius.[2]

---

[1] φρόνιμος, qui peut avoir suggéré cette curieuse formation, n'est pas rare dans le Nouveau Testament. Je pense notamment à ὁ πιστός δοῦλος καὶ φρόνιμος ὅν κατέστησεν ὁ κύριος ἐπὶ τῆς οἰκετείας αὐτοῦ etc., Matth. XXIV, 45, ce qui pourrait s'appliquer à l'auteur de nos vers.

[2] Mon aimable collègue, M. Kuno Meyer, m'a signalé depuis une assez curieuse introduction à des vers irlandais dont certains mots sont expliqués par les équivalents latins (MS. lat. 67, Bibl. Publ. de Leyde). M. Whitley Stokes a réimprimé les mots glosés dans ses *Goidelica* (2e éd., Londres 1872) p. 56. Le scribe de ses vers s'appelle Dubthach; il a fait son travail en 808, ainsi qu'il resort de la souscription suivante:

Dubthach hos uersus transcripsit tempore parvo,
Indulge lector quae mala scripta uides,
tertio idus apriles,
tertio anno decennio cicli,
tertio die ante pascha,
tertia decima luna incipiente,
tertia hora post meridiem,
tribus degitis,
tribus instrumentis: penna, membrano, atramento,
trinitate auxiliatrice.

Cette souscription est intéressante pour nous parce que le scribe mentionne dans son jeu bizarre avec le chiffre *trois* les *trois doigts* qu'il lui faut pour écrire, et les trois instruments: la plume, le parchemin et l'encre.

Liverpool.   V. H. FRIEDEL.

THE FOUR BRANCHES OF THE MABINOGI.

Chapter IV.
Their structure.
(Continued.)

In their present arrangement and with their present divisions the 'Four Branches of the Mabinogi' form a unified whole, worked together with considerable skill by a writer to whom the materials seem to have been thoroughly familiar from frequent narration. This writer seems to have been well acquainted with some of the leading local legends especially of Gwynedd, Dyfed and Gwent on the one hand, and, on the other, with stories and triads of the isle of Britain. Of the stories in question of the 'Ynys Prydain' type we have specimens in 'Lludd a Llevelys' and 'Breuddwyd Macsen Wledig'. In the 'Four Branches' we find that the first and the fourth branches consist very largely of local legends, while the second and the third contain, in the stories of the Llyr-cycle, a narrative which has many affinities with stories of the 'Lludd a Llevelys' and 'Macsen Wledig' types. The story of the Llyr-family here given, contains indeed some local allusions to certain parts of Wales, but, as it is a story concerning the family of a 'brenhin coronawc ar yr ynys honn', its scene ranges over the whole of 'Ynys y Kedyrn' and implies relations of the isle of Britain with Ireland and France. Similarly, the geographical area implied in the narrative is much wider, in the case of such stories as 'Macsen Wledig' and 'Lludd a Llevelys', than in the case of more narrowly local legends such as those of Pryderi and Gwydion. It is clear, too, that the mind

of the writer of the 'Four Branches' in their present form is
dominated by ideas derived from the Feudal system of the Anglo-
Norman period and the personages who play prominent parts in
these stories come to be grouped in relation to one another
accordingly. Thus, while Bendigeitvran fab Llyr is a 'brenhin
coronawc', Pwyll, Pryderi, Teyrnon and Math ab Mathonwy are,
in the final form of the narrative, only 'arglwyddi'; who may
on occasion have to do homage (hebr6ng g6rogaeth) to the ruling
king. The legends concerning the 'arglwyddi' in question have
a more purely local colouring than those concerning the royal
families of Llyr and Caswallawn fab Beli. For some reason or
other the Mabinogi refers to no lord of any portion of Powys,
and thus we have in it no Powys legends of the Dyfed or the
Gwynedd type. This may possibly have been accidental, for the
Mabinogi in its final form does not ignore the existence of Powys,
There appears to be a similar accidental absence of any reference
to Rhiannon in the Book of Taliessin, for it is difficult to believe
that poets so familiar with the Pwyll, Manawyddan, Pryderi,
Gwydion and other legends should not have known the name
which seems to have been familiar enough at any rate in the
expression 'Adar Rhiannon'. Powys was not entirely ignored
by the composer of the Mabinogi in its final form, as testified
by the expressions 'Kym6t ym Powys a elwir Mochnant' and
'minheu a baraf ... dygyuori Gwyned a Phowys a Deheubarth
y geissa6 y uor6yn'. In like manner, too, it would be rash to
infer that the omission of the Taliessin legends from the Mabinogi
implies ignorance of them on the part of their final composer,
for Taliessin is mentioned as one of the seven men who carried
the head of Bendigeitvran to London. Nevertheless the fact
remains that the districts whose local legends seem to have
been most clearly incorporated in these stories are Dyfed, Gwent
and Gwynedd, and these clusters of legends, that were closely
connected in the mind of their narrator with certain definite
localities, may, for the purpose of this article, be called respectively
legends of the Rhiannon and the Don-cycles. It should be noted
that some of these localities are definitely named while others
such as 'Llyn y Morwynion' near Festiniog (alluded to in the
Mabinogi of Math ab Mathonwy) are tacitly implied.

In order to bring out as clearly as possible the contrast
between the Rhiannon-cycle, the Don-cycle and the Llyr-cycle

in the Mabinogi a general analysis is here given of these respective legendary cycles into their probable component legends with special reference to their topographical allusions.

1. The Rhiannon-cycle.

The Rhiannon-cycle as contained in the 'Four Branches' may be broadly analysed into the following component parts.

a) The story of the meeting and marriage of Pwyll and Rhiannon (related in Pwyll, Pendefig Dyfed) and the subsequent vengeance of Gwawl fab Clut, on whose behalf Llwyt fab Kil coet lays Dyfed under a spell (Yr hud ar Ddyfed). This latter story, the sequel to that of the marriage of Pwyll and Rhiannon is given in the third branch of the Mabinogi, Manawyddan fab Llyr.

b) The story of the birth, loss, discovery and restoration of Pryderi, together with an account of Rhiannon's punishment for her supposed murder of her own child.

c) The story of the fosterage of Pryderi by Pendaran Dyfed. In the Mabinogi there is but a brief and passing allusion to this story.

d) The story of the marriage of Pryderi to Kicua. Here again the Mabinogi affords but a fugitive suggestion of the local affinities of this story.

e) The story of the second marriage of Rhiannon to Manawyddan fab Llyr.

f) The story of Pryderi's death (given in Math ab Mathonwy). To this story the account given in 'Pwyll Pendefig Dyfed' of the growth of friendly relations between Pwyll and Arawn may be considered as forming a prelude. To these stories of the Rhiannon-cycle may be added the passing allusion to the birds of Rhiannon, mentioned in Branwen ferch Llyr.

On taking these stories and carefully scrutinising them, the following appear to be their main topographical affinities. The narrative (a) is mainly associated with Arberth and the surrounding district. Arberth is doubtless the modern Narberth in Pembrokeshire; Arberth being the form of the name still in use among the Welsh-speaking inhabitants of the district. Then again, the story of Llwyt fab Kil coet, represented in the story of Manawyddan as a bishop, was no doubt associated in the

narrator's mind with the place now known in English as Lud-
church, but in Welsh as 'Eglwys Lwyd', not far from Narberth.
Not far distant, too, is the stream called the 'Cilgoed'. These
facts must be taken into account in any identification of Llwyt
fab Kil Coet (in Manawyddan fab Llyr) or Llwyteu fab Kelcoet
(in Kilhwch and Olwen) with the Liath mac Celtchair of Irish
legend.   Furthermore, in the reference to the story called
'Mabinogi Mynweir a Mynord' there is not improbably an
allusion to Minwear near Narberth.   It will be noted that
Rhiannon herself is not represented as a native of Dyfed, for it
is said of Pwyll and Rhiannon after their marriage at the court
of Eueyd Hen — 'wynt a gerdassant trannoeth part a dyuet'
(Oxford Mab. p. 17). Whether in the account of Heveyd there
is any implied reference to Maesyfed = Maes Hyveyd, it is impossible to say, for the story affords no clue.

In b) we have, in the story of Pryderi's birth and Rhiannon's
.punishment, a reference to Presseleu in Dyfed, (possibly, as
Professor Rhys has suggested, some spot near the Precelly
range of mountains), where the nobles of Dyfed desire Pwyll to
divorce Rhiannon for want of issue, and to Arberth, where
Pryderi is born.   In the account of Pryderi's restoration the
narrator refers to the district of Gwent-is-coed, between New-
port and Chepstow in Monmouthshire.   Teyrnon Twrf Vliant
was doubtless connected in his mind with Nant Teyrnon, now
known as Llantarnam, in this district.   Why Pryderi should be
associated in the Mabinogi with this locality it is difficult to
say.   Possibly legends were current in Gwent which treated
Rhiannon (Rigantona) as the female partner of Teyrnon (Tiger-
nonos).   The identification of Pryderi with Gôri (or Gôare, see
Kilhwch and Olwen) Wallt Euryn may have been an after-
thought.   Apart from any question of local allusion, it should be
noted that the story of the loss of Pryderi is closely associated
in the narrator's mind with the derivation of the name from
pryder, *anxiety.*

In c) we have but a meagre reference to a personage
about whom legends may have been very plentiful at one time
in Dyfed.   The story of the fosterage of Pryderi by Pendaran
Dyfed was probably much more important than we should
imagine it to be from the Mabinogi; for example, the Triad
referring to 'Tri Gwrdd feichiad Ynys Prydain' speaks of

Pryderi as the swineherd of his foster-father Pendaran Dyfed
·in Glyn Cuwch (= Cuch) in Emlyn. To this story the Mabinogi
does not even allude.

In d) the relation of Kicua, the wife of Pryderi, to *Gloy6*
Wallt Lydan, her grandfather, according to the Mabinogi of
Pwyll, suggests that into the original legend Gloy6 the eponymous
founder of Caer Loyw (Gloucester) entered. The story of Pryderi's
connection with Gloyw may possibly be a fragment of the Gwent
cluster of legends concerning Gwri Wallt Euryn, afterwards
identified with Pryderi. Owing to the meagreness of the narrative
one can only conjecture this connexion, but it is noteworthy that
Caerloyw did not lie outside the purview of Welsh local legend,
as we see from the story of Kilhwch and Olwen.

In e), the story of the second marriage of Rhiannon with
Manawyddan, there seem to be no special local allusions which
might help to suggest its origin. In Branwen ferch Llyr, the
.three birds of Rhiannon are connected with Hardlech, but
whether the local legends of that place spoke of Rhiannon as
the wife of Manawyddan son of Llyr, it is impossible to say.
The story of Rhiannon's second marriage is not unlike an attempt
·to reconcile two divergent accounts of her wedded life (Vid. Nutt,
Voyage of Bran, Vol. II, p. 16. 17), but it may after all be a
mere invention of the narrator in order to give sequence to the
narrative.

The story f) is the connecting link between the legends of
the Rhiannon-cycle and those of the Don-cycle, so far as the
Four Branches are concerned, though, from the fact that the
.birds of Rhiannon were associated with Hardlech and the grave
of Pryderi was shewn at Maentwrog, we may well suppose that
there were current other Rhiannon legends, which formed similar
links. This narrative, as given in the Mabinogi, is rich in local
allusions. Several of these allusions are to place-names containing the word 'moch', and some of them are not introduced
in a very relevant or natural manner. The prelude in Pwyll,
to which reference has already been made, mentions Arberth,
Pen llwyn Diarwya and Glyn Cuch. Pen llwyn Diarwya has
not yet been identified with certainty, but it may possibly be
another name for Pen llwyn gaer, which lies a little to the east
of Llanboidy, a place through which Pwyll might naturally pass
on his way from Arberth to Glyn Cuch. In the portion of this

story given in 'Math ab Mathonwy', reference is made to a
court belonging to Pryderi at 'Rudlan Teiui', a place corresponding, according to the Ordnance Survey Map, to Highmead
near Llanybyther, Cardiganshire, the house of the present Lord
Lieutenant of the country. Rhuddlan Teifi was known by that
name in contrast to Rhuddlan Tegeingl, the better known
Rhuddlan on the river Clwyd. In the narrative of Gwydion's
flight with the swine into Gwynedd, the local allusions appear
to be the following. 'Mochnant yg góarthaf keredigyawn' is
probably one of the two streams known as Nant y Moch to the
West of Plinlimon. 'Elenit' is the range of mountains between
Cardiganshire and Radnorshire, to which Giraldus Cambrensis
makes several references in his Itinerary. Mochtre, between
Keri and Arwystli is the place now called Moughtre, a little to
the east of Llandinam, Montgomeryshire. Mochnant in Powys
is familiar in the name Llanrhaiadr-yn-Mochnant. Mochtref in
Rhos now forms with Pabo the station called 'Mochdre and
Pabo' on the Chester and Holyhead Railway. Creuwyryon ('y
dref uchaf yn Arllechwedd') is the place now generally known
as Cororion in the name 'Llyn Cororion', not far from the
Bethesda Slate Quarry district. Caer Dathyl, also known as
Caer Dathal (as in Cynddelw Brydydd Mawr), has not yet been
identified with certainty. It is clear from the Mabinogi that it
was located in Arvon. Pennard and Coet Alun are the modern
Penardd and Coed Helen (a mistake for Coed Alun) respectively.
Nant call should be Nant coll and Dol penn maen is still familiar
in the name Garn Dolbenmaen, not far from Portmadoc. Y
Traeth Mawr is still the name of one of the two beaches from
which Penrhyndeudraeth derives its name, and y Felenrhyd is
still the name of a farm near Maentwrog, the beautiful valley
on the river Cynwal, in the Mabinogi mis-called 'y maen
tyuyaóc'.

2. The Don-cycle.

The stories of the Don-cycle seem to have been chiefly, if
not entirely, connected, in the mind of the narrator of the
Mabinogi, with the districts of Arvon (possibly also Arllechwedd)
and Dunoding, containing Eifionydd and Ardudwy. The following
is a broad classification of these narratives.

a) The story of Giluaethwy's love for Goewin and the sub-sequent vengeance of Math ab Mathonwy.

b) The story of Gwydion's introduction of swine into Gwynedd, already given under the Rhiannon-cycle.

c) The story of the birth of Dylan eil ton.

d) The story of the birth of Llew Llaw Gyffes and Lleu son of Aranrot.

e) The story of Gwydion's success in obtaining for Lleu a name, arms and a wife. The legend describing the formation of Blodeuwedd, Llew's wife, out of flowers appears to have been an account of one out of many successes in sorcery attributed to Math ab Mathonwy and his magic wand called in the Book of Taliessin 'Hutlath Vathonwy'. Portions of the story, too, are pieces of old folk-lore explaining the peculiar appearance and habits of the owl.

f) The story of the infidelity of Lleu's wife with Gronw Pefr, lord of Penllyn, and the treacherous death of Lleu with his subsequent vengeance upon Gronw.

Taking these stories in order, we find that in a) the places to which reference is made are Caer Dathyl, the centre of Math's administration, and Dol pebin, the home of Goewin, now known in the district as Dol bebi. It may be noted that there is a place of the same name (similarly pronounced) in Ardudwy, not far from Harlech, but no connexion between the two places has been hitherto traced. This narrative is interesting as containing an old *englyn* of the *triban* type referring to 'bleidwn', 'hydwn' and 'hychtwn'. In the Mabinogi in its present form this story is closely connected with the story of Pryderi's death. This may not have been originally the case, but it was probably closely connected with the narrative of the birth of Dylan eil ton.

Of b) enough has been already discussed under the Rhiannon-cycle. It is probably one out of many stories at one time current to explain the introduction of swine into Gwynedd.

In c) the story of the birth of Dylan eil ton, we have only a fragment of a large mass of legend. In the narrator's mind, the story of Dylan was doubtless closely connected with the grave of Dylan, which was, according to 'Englynion y Beddau', in Llanbeuno, in Clynnog, and also with the headland called Maen Dylan which juts out into the sea close by.

In d) we have the first of a group of stories connected

with Lleu, not improbably, as Professor Rhys has pointed out in his 'Celtic Heathendom', the same as the Irish Lug and the Gaulish Lugus of Lugudunum. In connection with this story the original narrator had in mind certain spots in Arvon into which the name of Lleu entered, viz. Dinlle = Din Lleu and Nantlle = Nant Lleu. Gwydion is similarly thought of in connection with the place still known as Bryn-y-gwydion in Arvon. In this district, too, the graves of Gwydion and Lleu were shewn. The exact spot meant by Caer Aranrot is uncertain, and the same uncertainty exists in the case of Cefn Cllutno, but Bryn Aryen (also called in 'Englynion of Beddau' Bryn Aren) may possibly be the present Bryn Eura, now a farm near Clynnog. For the loss of '*n*' one may compare the local pronunciation Dol bebi for Dol bebin. The story here given, it should be noted, implies a reference to a triad which names Gwydion as one of 'Tri Eurgrydd Ynys Prydain'.

In f), the story of the infidelity of Lleu's wife, the scene changes to the districts of Trawsfynydd and Festiniog. The references are to Mur y castell near Trawsfynydd, probably the present 'Tomen y Mur'; to Bryn Cyfergyr near Festiniog, now known as Bryn Cyfergyd and explained locally as Bryn Cyfer Ergyd; and to Llech Gronw, a large pierced stone once visible near the river Cynwal, less accurately called in the present version of the 'Four Branches', Cynuael. One of the most important spots, however, which the narrator had in view while writing is not expressly mentioned, viz. Llyn y Morwynion near Blaenau Festiniog. This story like that of the vengeance of Math upon Gwydion and Giluaethwy is of interest as containing specimens of old 'tribanau', the spelling of which shews that they were written originally in an orthography similar to that of the Venedotian Code of the Welsh Laws.

3. The Llyr-cycle.

The stories of the Rhiannon-cycle and the Don-cycle refer, in the Four Branches in their present form, to the families of 'arglwyddi' and to certain places within their supposed domains. The Llyr story, on the other hand, is given as an account of the members of the family of a 'brenhin coronawc' and naturally the scope of its topography is much wider. The stories of the

Llyr-cycle, as they are given in the Mabinogi, may be broadly classified as follows:

a) The story of 'Y Trydyd Anfat Palfawt' beginning with an account of the marriage of Branwen and describing her ill-treatment in Ireland. Branwen is here called 'tryded prif riein yn yr ynys honn'.

b) The story of 'Yspadawt Bran' when he went over to Ireland to avenge the insult to his sister.

c) The story of 'Yspadawt Urdawl Benn', containing an account of the adventures of the men who bore the head of Bendigeitvran to London. Here again the narrative is connected with triads: 'a h6nn6 uu y trydyd mat cud pan cudywyt, a'r trydyd anuat datcud pan datcudywyt; kany doey ormes byth dr6y vor yr ynys honn tra uei y penn yn y cud h6nn6'. In this narrative several stories have probably been fused together.

d) The story of the mischief-making Efnissyen, a kind of Welsh Bricriu, closely interwoven with the other stories of this branch of the Mabinogi.

e) The story of the conflict for the sovereignty of the isle of Britain between Caradawc fab Bran and Caswallawn fab Beli.

f) The story of the death of Branwen.

g) The story of the settlement of the five provinces of Ireland.

h) The story explaining the place-names having reference to 'Gwyddel' and 'Gwyddyl' in Anglesey and elsewhere.

i) The story of the term 'Trydydd Lleddf Unben' as applied to Manawyddan fab Llyr.

j) The story of the appellation 'y Trydydd Eurgrydd' as applied to Manawyddan fab Llyr.

k) The story of Manawyddan's relations with Pryderi and Rhiannon.

In a) the main story implies relations between the Isle of Britain as a whole with Ireland as a whole through their ruling families. It is significant, too, that the purely local allusions are to Aberffraw and Talebolion in Anglesey. At the time when this story was formed Aberffraw was doubtless at the height of its glory as the seat of the chief court of the Gwynedd princes. In the Mabinogi of Branwen there are references to two other places in Wales connected with the

9*

government of the Llyr family, viz. Hardlech yn Ardudwy,
where Bendigeitvran is said to have had a 'llys', and Kaer
Seint yn Aruon, where he held a 'dadleu'. For the term
'dadleu', one may compare 'a dadleu brenhined a oed arna6
diwarnaot', said of Maxen Wledig. It is doubtful whether the
introductory reference to Hardlech found a place in the original
story of 'Palfawt Branwen'. The local allusions which connect
Branwen closely with Anglesey seem to suggest forcibly that
the story of her life was especially popular at the court of
Aberffraw.

In b) we have a fragment of what was probably at one
time a much longer story. Apart from the reference to Bendigeitvran and his 'dadleu' at Caer Seint yn Arfon, a place which
tends to figure very prominently in the 'Ynys Prydain' stories,
there are no allusions to definite and clearly identifiable places.
The rivers Lli, Archan and Llinon were probably mentioned in
the older 'cyfarwydyt', but the narrator of the Mabinogi in its
present form seems to have felt some difficulty in locating them.
These stories which deal with adventures in Ireland are clearly
of a different type from those in which the narrator has before
his mind's eye certain definite Welsh localities. The form which
the story of 'Yspadawt Bran' took probably varied a great deal
with different narrators. For example, the reference in the
Book of Taliessin, Poem XIV, seems to imply that the death of
Mordwyt Tyllyon played a very prominent part in the story,
whereas in Branwen ferch Llyr the only reference to him is in
the words 'Ac yna y dywaot mord6yd tyllyon — Gwern g6ng6ch
ui6ch uordwyt tyllyon'.

In c), the story of Yspadawt Urdawl Benn we have also,
not improbably, only fragments of a much longer and fuller
narrative. The spots named as the halting-places of the bearers
of Bendigeitvran's head seem to suggest that, in its original
form, the story was that of a voyage or Imram. For example,
the bearers of the head stay at Hardlech and proceed thence to
'Gwalas ym Penuro', i. e. the island of Gresholm, off the coast
of Pembrokeshire. The reference to the bride of Rhiannon at
Harlech is interesting as apparently connecting the Rhiannon
story with that place. It is noticeable that, according to
Poem XIV of the Book of Taliessin, an 'yspydawt' was held at
'ebyr henvelen':

Keint yn yspyda6t uch g6ira6t aflawen,
Keint rac meibon Llyr in ebyr henvelen.

The final resting-place of Bendigeitvran's head, according to this
story, is 'y Gwynfryn yn Llundein'. London, it need scarcely
be said, tends to figure very prominently in all the 'Ynys
Prydain' stories.

In d) we have probably only a few out of many instances
of the mischief wrought by Efnissyen. There appear to be no
points of special topographical interest connected with him.

In e) the Mabinogi gives us but a short account of what
must have been a much longer and fuller story, viz. the passing
of the sovereignty of Britain from the hands of the family of
Bran into the hands of the family of Beli. In the stories of
Branwen, Lludd and Llevelys, and Macsen Wledig, the island of
Britain is represented as being, successively, in the hands of the
families of Bran, Beli and Macsen. It is interesting to note, too,
that all these stories agree in giving prominence to Carnarvon
and the neighbouring district, though the town itself is not
expressly mentioned in Lludd a Llevelys. So far as the conflict
of Caradawc and Caswallawn has reference to Wales, the narrator
seems to be pre-occupied with the district of 'Seith Marchawc'
in Edeyrnion, where there is still a place known as 'Bryn Saith
Marchog' near Gwyddelwern. It would appear that legends
about Bran were prevalent in the neighbouring districts. Near
Llangollen there is a conspicuous ruin still known as Castell
Dinas Bran, while a portion of the Llangollen district itself is
called Dinbran. On the other side of Gwyddelwern, too, there
is a lake near Nantglyn called Llymbran (i. e. Llyn Bran), from
which a stream called the Brenig (apparently a diminutive of
Bran) flows.

In f) we have a story connected with Glan Alaw and Aber
Alaw in Talebolion in Anglesey, where a grave, said to be that
of Branwen, was shewn.

In g) we have a story which has naturally no Welsh local
allusions. The story classed as h) implies that it is the explanation of certain facts with regard to the population of
Britain, in the words, 'pa del6, argl6yd, yd erbynneist ti 6ynt6y.
Eu rannu ym pob lle yn y kyuoeth, ac y maent yn lluossa6c
ac yn dyrchauel ym pob lle, ac yn kadarnhau yn y uann y bont
o wyr ac arueu goreu a welas neb'. It is not improbable that

the narrator had here in view the place-names which contain the word Gwyddel, and among them, doubtless, that of Gwyddelwern. For a list of these place-names and their distribution, see Basil Jones, Vestiges of the Gael in Gwynedd, pp. 35, 36, 37.

In the stories classed as i) and j) we have references to the triads of 'Trydydd lleddf unben' and 'Trydydd Eurgrydd Ynys Prydain' respectively. Some of the local allusions in these stories are to well known places in England such as Oxford, Kent and Hereford.

To the story k) reference has already been made under the Rhiannon-cycle. In addition to the points to which reference has already been made, it may be noted that it is in the stories of the Llyr-cycle alone that we find references to Kymry, Lloegyr, and Ynys y Kedyrn, Iwerdon and Freinc. These indications are alone sufficient to shew that the Llyr-cycle belongs to a different type of narrative from that of the Rhiannon-cycle or the Don-cycle. In many respects it approximates closely to the 'Lludd a Llevelys' and the 'Macsen Wledig' stories.

Aberystwyth.   E. ANWYL.

TEC, TEGACH, TECKAF, TECKET.

Die welsche Grammatik stellt die Regel auf, dass die Adjektiva auf *g, d, b* vor den Endungen der Steigerungsgrade ihre auslautende Media zur Doppeltenuis verhärten. Von *teg* 'schön' heisst also der Komparativ *teccach*, der Superlativ *teccaf* und der sogenannte Aequalis *tecced*. So bildet Griffith Roberts, Welsh grammar 1567, p. 117, auch von *caled* 'hart' *calettach, calettaf, caletted* und von *cyphelyb* 'ähnlich' *cyphelyppach, cyphelyppaf* u. s. w. Desgleichen lehrt J. Davies, Antiquae linguae britannicae rudimenta, Londini 1621, p. 60: 'Hic autem consonae finales leviores seu mediae *b, g, d* mutantur in duriores seu tenues, easque duplices *pp, cc, tt*', und so auch die spätern Grammatiker.[1]

Nur J. Davies und nach ihm J. Williams ab Ithel, The ancient Welsh grammar 1856, p. 58, führen *tegach* als eine gelegentliche Ausnahme an; auch Zeuss, GC.[2] 153, belegt die Form. Und wenden wir uns der alten Sprache zu, deren Quellen uns heute voller fliessen, so finden wir, dass freilich der Superlativ auf *-af* und der Aequalis auf *-et* ausnahmslos die Tenuis geminata der erwähnten Adjektiva auf *g, d, b* haben, dass aber der Komparativ auf *-ach* ebenso regelmässig die einfache Media aufweist. Jenes bedarf keiner Beweise, denn alle sind darin einig; dies aber wird durch Beispiele aus der mittelwelschen Litteratur zu begründen sein. In ihr erscheint ausserdem die auslautende Muta des Positivs nicht als Media wie in der heutigen Schrift, sondern, wie bekannt, in den allermeisten Denkmälern als Tenuis, also *tec, kalet, kyffelyp*.

---

[1] W. Gambold, A Welsh grammar 1724, p. 20; Th. Richards, Grammar 1753, p. 19; Rob. Davies, Gramadeg Cymraeg 1808, p. 46; W. Spurrel, Grammar 1848, p. 64; Th. Rowland, Grammar 1853, p. 45; D. S. Evans, Llythyraeth yr iaith Gymraeg, Caerfyrddin 1861, p. 135; E. Anwyl, Grammar 1898, 1, 20.

Man steigert in der alten Sprache so:

Tec 'schön'	tegach[1]	teckaf	tecket
Karedic 'geliebt'	karedigach[2]	karedickaf	karedicket
Tebyc 'wahrscheinlich'	tebygach[3]	tebyckaf	tebycket
Kyvoethawc 'mächtig'	kyvoethogach[4]	kyvoethockaf	kyvoethocket
Kalet 'hart'	kaledach[5]	kalettaf	kalettet
Rat 'billig'	radach[6]	rattaf	rattet
Reit 'nötig'	reidyach[7]	reittyaf	reittyet
Tlawt 'arm'	tlodach[8]	tlottaf	tlottet
Drut 'kühn'	drudach[9]	druttaf	druttet
Hyfryt 'froh'	hyfrydach[10]	hyfryttaf	hyfryttet
Kyffelyp 'ähnlich'	kyffelybach[11]	kyffelyppaf	kyffelyppet

[1]) Red Book 1, 164. 229. 278, Hengwrt Manuscripts 1, 66. 120. 218, D. G. 8, 60. 221, 50, I. G. 32, 123. 70, 58, Psalm 45, 2 Morgan; neben *teckaf* HM. 1, 218, D. G. 59, 16. 62, 66. 93, 5; *tecked* D. G. 80, 20. 26, 24. 118, 18. 221, 1. p. V, aber 193, 18 falsch *deged* statt *decced*. Ebenso *breisgach* RB. 1, 148; *chwegach* MA. 843 a, *whegach* Skene 2, 155 neben *chwechach* RB. 1, 121 und *chweccaf* KB. 7, 233.

[2]) RB. 2, 217. 245. HM. 1, 298. 431; ebenso *pethedigach* RB. 1, 170, *digach*, *penedigach*, *arbennigach*, *bonhedigach*, *yskymunedigach*, wo sie vorkommen.

[3]) RB. 1, 30. HM. 1, 3. I. G. 46, 14; aber D. G. 171, 34 falsch *tebycach*.

[4]) RB. 1, 279; ebenso *mawrweirthogach* HM. 1, 120, *gwerthvawrogach* RB. 2, 50. 207 (verdruckt *gwyrvawrockach* MA. 530b und *gwerthvoroach* ibid. 588 an einer Stelle, wo RB. 2, 183 *gwell* liest), *rudvogach* 1, 303, *enwogach* Ceinion 1, 195 b, *bywiogach* 1, 340 a; ebenso *diogach*, *chwannogach*, *rhywiogach*, *llidiogach* neben *llidiockaf* HM. 1, 283.

[5]) *Caledach* HM. 1, 44 neben *calettaf*, *calettet* 1, 54; aber später *caletach* IM. 258. MA. 61 a; die Bibel schreibt *calettach* Jerem. 5, 3.

[6]) Davies, Gr. p. 60; ebenso *gwastadach* zu *gwastattaf* RB. 1, 83, *giradach* zu *girattaf* RB. 2, 232.

[7]) HM. 1, 29. 306, *rheidiach* D. G. 207, 27. In den Dentalen sind die Schreiber mitunter unsicher: *reityach* HM. 1, 252, *direitach* 298 neben *reityaf* 1, 299, *direittyet* 1, 306, *cynrheitied* D. G. 149, 55. So bildet man auch (G. O. 2, 86) *diniweitiach*.

[8]) Davies, Gr. p. 60, *tylodach* IM. 308 zu *tlottaf* HM. 1, 197, *tlottet* 1, 249; *gnodach* Skene 2, 285. I. G. 24, 65. Cein. 1, 193 a von *gnawt*.

[9]) Llyvyr yr Agkyr 36, 4. IM. 322, neben *druttet* RB. 1, 147. 150. D. G. p. XVII.

[10]) HM. 1, 150. 409. RB. 2, 50, neben *hyfrytted* G. O. 1, 74; ebenso *ynfydach* (neu *ynfyttach* BC. 25, 31) zu *ynfyttaf* D. G. 163, 18; *gwydnach* D. G. 73, 15 (nicht *gwytnach*, Welsh Orthography 1893, p. 46), wozu auch der Superlativ *gwydnaf* heisst, Karls Reise 11, 34. HM. 2, 12.

[11]) Davies, Gr. p. 61; so müsste es *gwlybach* zu *kynwlypet* RB. 1, 150 heissen. Übrigens schreibt das Rothe Buch den Positiv neben *kyffelyp* 1, 165. 2, 12. 29 auch *kyffelyb* 1, 99. 180. 202.

Dem verhärteten Auslaute der übrigen Grade gegenüber zeigt die vorstehende Liste durchweg die Media des Komparativs. Damit nun niemand diese Eigentümlichkeit der Unart fahrlässiger Schreiber beimesse, so mögen die Barden, die Hüter des Sprachschatzes und des lautern Ausdrucks, vortreten, sie durch das Cynghanedd croes zu bestätigen.

Dafydd ab Gwilym 8, 60: Drud fudd dei*gr* nid oedd de*g*ach;
    256, 38: Yn de*g*ach, Gwen, na deu*g*ain;
    207, 27: Nid rhei*d*iach i'm byd rhy*deg*.

Iolo Goch 70, 58: De*g*ach o ddwr bendi*g*aid.

Rhys Goch Eryri (Iolo mss. 308): Tal o*dl* ni byddwn tylo*d*ach.

Meredydd ab Rhys (ib. 322): Pysgy*d*wr pw*y* esgu*d*ach.

Gytto'r Glyn (Ceinion 1, 195 b): Llan E*g*wst lle enwo*g*ach.

Tudur Aled (ibid. 1, 340 a): Dan fi*g*wrn dyn fywio*g*ach.

Hier antwortet der Media des Komparativs die Media, während den andern Steigerungsgraden die Tenuis sicher ist.

Dafydd ab Gwilym 59, 16: Decca' o ddyn fal da*cc*w ddydd;
    26, 24: Ei the*cc*ed ac ni thy*cc*ia,

welchen Vers Griffith Roberts p. 254, auch lehrreich, so liest:
    Ai the*g*wch ag ni thy*g*ia.

Einer Media des Superlativs und des Aequalis wird man in sprachreinen Texten nicht begegnen.[1]) Offenbar hat die neuere Sprache *teccach* nach der Analogie des korrekten *teccaf, tecced* gebildet und erst im 16. Jahrhundert hat sich die Form eingeschlichen und festgesetzt. Und in dieser Entartuug ist dem Welschen das Armorische gefolgt; es bildet *pinvidikoc'h* 'reicher' von *pinvidig* oder *pinvidik* (Ernault, Grammaire bretonne § 40), und schon im Mittelarmorischen kommt *penhuikoh* vor (Ernault, Glossaire p. 492), d. i. welsch *pendevigach*, wozu der Superlativ

---

    [1]) Eine Ausnahme würde ein Wort Taliessins bilden, wo er vom Winde sagt:
        Ef ymaes, ef ygkoed,
        Heb law a heb troet,
        Heb henaint, heb hoet,
        Heb *eidigaf* adoet —

Skene 2, 160, wenn die letzte Zeile 1, 536 richtig übersetzt wäre: 'without the most jealous destiny'. Aber es heisst: 'Er ist auf dem Felde, er ist im Walde, ohne Hand und ohne Fuss, ohne Alter, ohne Verweilen, ohne dem Tode zuzustreben'. *Eidigaf* ist ein Infinitiv (= *eidigafu* Zs. 1, 140) zu *Nyt eidigafaf* 'Ich will nicht begehren', Skene 2, 286 (vgl. 1, 456).

pendevickaf lauten würde; ebenso im Cornischen *tecah tecke* 'schöner', *wheccah whekke* 'süsser', *lacca lacke* 'schlechter'.

Noch merkwürdiger gestaltet sich dieser Lautwandel, wenn wir den Positiv in seine Erörterung einschliessen. Die neuere Sprache schreibt *teg* und bildet *teccach, teccaf*; die ältere schreibt *tec* und bietet *tcgach, teckaf.* Waltet hier die Willkür und ist es ein Zufall, dass die Alten für die auslautende Muta, sobald sie inlautend wird, hier die Tenuis und dort die Media wählen? Gewiss nicht, denn sie unterscheiden in dem Nachdruck, den sie einer aus- und inlautenden Muta geben, scharf und bestimmt. Mitunter ist das ganze Gewicht der Bedeutung auf diesen einen Buchstaben gelegt: es heisst *tebygaf* 'ich meine' und *tebyckaf* 'ähnlichst' auf derselben Seite RB. 1, 237; *kyvoethogaf* 'ditabo' und *kyvoethockaf* 'potentissimus' wiederum auf derselben Seite RB. 2, 132; ebenso im Mittelarmorischen *caledaff* 'härten' und *caletaff* 'härtest' (Ernault, Dictionnaire p. 240).

Zum Verständnis dieser Erscheinungen ist es räthlich, dass man sich die Verhältnisse der auslautenden Muta im Welschen vergegenwärtige, und das kann nicht besser geschehen, als wenn man sie in einem gesamten Überblicke denen im gälischen Zweige der Sprache gegenüberstellt. Denn jedes welsche Wort bleibt uns nur halb verstanden, so lange wir nicht den irischen Zwilling kennen. Es ist kaum paradox, dass sich die neuirische Sprache für solche Vergleichung besser bewährt, als beide die altirische und die mittelirische. Einmal lässt es die alte Sprache, wie unentbehrlich sie uns zur Nachprüfung der neuern Formen auch ist, in den in Frage kommenden Punkten an strenger Gleichförmigkeit, an organischer Orthographie fehlen, wie sie denn z. B. ir. *cerdd, cerd, cert* für dasselbe Wort, *bocc* 'Bock' nicht anders als *bocc* 'weich' und *borb* mit keinem andern Auslaute als *garb* schreibt, und andrerseits ist die welsche Sprachform, auf die wir in der Hauptsache angewiesen sind, jener um Jahrhunderte vorausgeeilt und stellt, nach viel Unsicherheit in den Zeiten des Mittelalters, nun eine abgeschlossene Bildung dar, die mit der neuirischen auf gleicher Höhe steht. Selbst die Rudera des Altwelschen zeigen schon Fortschritte, die das Irische erst viel später erreichte. Weiter befindet sich das Mittelwelsche gerade in einem seiner ältesten Monumente,[1]) dem Schwarzen Buche von

---

[1]) Die Schrift des Llyfr Du, dessen Zeit sich aus dem Inhalte kaum genau

Carmarthen, in einem völlig haltlosen Zustande, indem es z. B. für das neuwelsche *dd* mit Vorliebe *t* schreibt, wie in *prit* BBC. 10 b 1 (neben *prid* 12 a 13), *bet* 13 a b. 15 b 5. 21 b 1 (neben *bed* 10 b 1), *bit* 16 a 2. 2 b 8 (neben *bid* 10 a 1. 13 b 6. 11), *but* 4 b 4 (neben *bud* 19 a 5), *gwaret* 20 b 6 (neben *guared* 21 b 3), *gulet* 'Fest' 20 b 6 (neben *gulad* 'Land' 15 b 12), *yt oet* 23 a 11, *argluit, bart, beirt, bartoni, buchet, kert, diwet, gwirt* gwyrdd, *haut, naut, het, hit, fit, gorset, hoffet, y gilit* etc. Und dieses *t* des Schwarzen Buches hatte ganz gewiss die Geltung des nw. *dd*, wie die Variante *forth* 17 b 16 für *fort* 17 a 12. 22 b 5 (vgl. *gosgeth* LA. 66, 1 neben *gosged* 57, 18) lehrt; ja, es hatte schon die schwache Aussprache der neuern Zeit, denn neben *yssit* ysydd (altw. *issid* KB. 7, 405) 9 b 6. 18 a 6. 21 a 6 steht *yssi* 18 b 12. 19 a 10. 21 a b, *issi* 19 b 6. 20 a 11. 21 a 10, *isy* 19 b 5. Im Verlaufe der Litteratur sind nun diese und ähnliche Schwankungen allmählich zum Stillstande gekommen und die beiden celtischen Schwestersprachen durch ebenmässige Entwickelung, trotz aller Ungleichheit der Anlagen, endlich ins schönste Einvernehmen gelangt.

---

bestimmen lässt, gehört (mit Ausnahme natürlich von Bl. 35 a 14 ff.) dem 12. bis 13. Jahrh. an. Gegen die allzu frühe Datierung innerhalb dieser Grenze sprechen das weit überhängende Dach des *a*, die ziemliche Länge des zweiten Federzuges vom *h* unter der Linie, die fast eckige untere Schleife des *g*, die starke Gabelung der Stämme von *l, b* etc. oben und ihre schwunghafte Umbiegung nach rechts unten, namentlich beim *r*, das Ineinanderschreiben zweier Buchstaben wie *de, bo, do* (z. B. 28 a 9. 41 b 1. 8. 42 b 10 f. 13), sowie die vielen Accente über dem *i*, mit denen man im 12. Jahrhundert in den Codices erst allmählich beim *ii* zum Unterschiede von *u* beginnt. Diese Merkmale bedeuten nicht viel, wenn sie einzeln auftreten, aber sie fallen ins Gewicht, wenn sie sich wie hier vereinigt finden. Die Schrift des Schwarzen Buches ist, um einige ähnliche Proben zu vergleichen, entschieden älter als Nr. 17 in W. Schums Exempla (vom Jahre 1258), Delisle 40, 3 (vom Jahre 1247) und auch wohl als Nr. 53 in W. Arndts Schrifttafeln (vom Jahre 1241); aber sie erscheint mir jünger als Schum Nr. 9 (von 1147), Palaeogr. Soc. 2, 42 (eine Urkunde aus Shropshire von 1156), ibid. 2, 132 (ein Psalter von 1158), Sickel 3, 7 (eine Urkunde von 1160), Palaeogr. Soc. 1, 194 (eine Urkunde von 1174), Ecole des chartes Nr. 74 (desgleichen von 1175), Palaeogr. Soc. 1, 37 (ein Leviticus aus Shropshire von 1176), die Hand *D* im Buche von Llandâv (1160—1180) und selbst Sickel 5, 18 (eine Bulle von 1208), sowie der cod. Berol. lat. qu. 324, der bald nach 1192 geschrieben wurde. Gleich dem letztgenannten auffallend ähnlich ist die undatierte Nr. 14 bei Schum, sowie Palaeogr. Soc. 2, 219 (ein Missale von 1218) und Sickel 7, 5 (eine Urkunde von 1237). Nach der Schrift zu urteilen würde das Buch also etwa in das erste Drittel des 13. Jahrh. gehören; die erste Hand scheint die eines alten Meisters der Schreibekunst zu sein.

Was eigentlich den Unterschied zwischen Tenuis und Media bildet, ob Quantität oder Intensität oder Stimmton, darf man der Entscheidung der Phonetik anheimstellen: die Grammatik ist nicht Naturwissenschaft, sondern Historie. Und da zeigt die gälisch-britannische Sprachgeschichte, dass die Muta, vom Stärksten und Starken zum Schwachen und Schwächsten (von starken Explosiven zu stimmhaften Spiranten) herabsinkend, vier Stufen durchschreitet: *cc gg c g, tt dd t d, pp bb p b.* Die starken Konsonanten *cc gg, tt dd, pp bb,* etwa den langen Vokalen zu vergleichen, sind die eigentlich festen Radikalen, die selbständigen und widerstandsfähigen; die schwachen *c g, t d, p b* unterliegen dem vokalischen Einflusse, den wir mit dem Worte Lenitio oder Lenierung bezeichnen. Wenn auch die Schrift der Theorie niemals völlig gerecht geworden ist, so erscheinen doch die Starken, die 'schweren' der welschen Grammatiker, von den Schwachen, gemilderten oder lenierten (sie heissen den Welschen 'leicht') deutlich geschieden. Die Starken erster Stufe können in der Regel nicht in die der zweiten übergehen, die Schwachen erster Stufe nicht in die der zweiten, da sie aus Prototypen von verschiedener Qualität entspringen. In der lebenden Sprache stellen sich nun diese vier Arten der Mutae bei den Iren und Welschen zwar in ihrer allgemeinen Lage zu einander unverschiebbar, aber im besondern, kraft der Infectio, die bald Aspiratio und bald Destitutio ist (so bezeichnet Zeuss diese phonetischen Wirkungen), durchaus verschieden dar.

Um das Bild des bewegten Wechsels der Mutae für unsere Betrachtung in das rechte Licht zu rücken, ordnen wir sie in vier Reihen und stellen zu der prähistorischen Einheit, auf die wir schliessen, die daraus hervorgegangene Doppelform des Irischen und des Welschen, so wie sie die neuere Sprache anerkennt.

CC	bac : ba*ch*	TT	ca*t* : ca*th*	PP	cea*p* : cy*ff*
GG	thu*g* : du*g*	DD	crei*d* : cre*d*	BB	sgua*b* : ysgu*b*
C	dro*ch* : drw*g*	T	ca*th* : ca*d*	P	nea*ch* : ne*b*
G	ma*gh* : ma	D	mo*dh* : mo*dd*	B	trea*bh* : tre*f*, tre.

Obwohl diese Verhältnisse ja nicht unbekannt sind, so werden sie doch durch Ordnung und Mehrung der Beispiele anschaulicher und durch Anmerkung einiger Abweichungen bestimmter werden. Unter die celtischen Auslaute sind im folgenden auch Fremdwörter und einige Fälle des Inlauts eingereiht, wenn auch

das allgemeine Gesetz nicht bis in alles einzelne verfolgt
werden soll.

CC, TT, PP. Die welsche Aspirata entspringt, wie die erste
Reihe zeigt, aus ursprünglicher Tenuis geminata, die das Irische
oft noch schreibt. Beispiele: (*c : ch*) *ir.* bacc bac : *w.* bach 'Haken';
m fracc : gwrach 'Weib'; cac : cach 'caccare'; leac : llech 'flacher
Stein'; peacadh : pechod 'peccatum'; breac : brych 'bunt'; *m* secc :
sych 'siccus'; minic : mynych 'manchmal'; béiceadh : beichio
'brüllen'; broc : broch 'Dachs'; *m* clocc : cloch 'clocca'; *w.* coch
'coccus'; boc : bwch 'Bock'; soc : swch 'Schnauze'; roc : rhych
'Furche'; ioc 'Heilung: : iach 'gesund'; *w.* bwch 'bucca'; muc :
moch 'Schwein'; ebenso nach *l*, wie in cailc : calch 'calx'; bailc
'stark' : balch 'stolz'; *w.* gwalch 'Falk'; cylch 'circulus'; sylch
'sulcus'; folcadh : golchi 'baden'; und nach *r*, wie in marc : march
'Pferd'; airc : arch 'arca'; airc 'Not' : arch 'Bitte'; searc : serch
'Liebe'; dearc : *arm.* derch 'Auge'; oirdhearc : ardderch 'angesehen';
torc : torch 'torques'; *m* orc : porch 'porcus'; carcair : carchar
'carcer'; gleichsam für *lcc, rcc*; — (*t : th*) cat : cath 'cattus'; slat :
llath 'Stab'; brat 'Mantel' : brethyn 'Wolltuch'; feat (fead) :
chwyth 'sibilus'; Britt : Bryth 'Britto';[1]) lite : llith 'Suppe'; *m*
got 'blaesus' : gyth 'murmeln'; croit : croth 'Wampe'; cruit : crwth
'crotta, Buckel'; *w.* saeth 'sagitta'; both 'buttis'; leitir : llethr
'Klippe'; so auch nach *r* in art : arth 'Bär'; ceart 'certus' : certh
'wunderbar'; ceart : parth 'Richtung'; neart : nerth 'Stärke';
feart : gwyrth 'virtus'; gort : garth 'Garten'; tort : torth 'torta';
frith 'Gewinn' : gwerth 'Wert'; frithbhac : gwrthfach 'Wider-
haken'; so auch in *ct*, d. i. ir. *cht* (nir. meist *chd* geschrieben) und
welsch **gtt* und mit weiterer Lenierung *eth, ith, yth*, wie in tracht :
traeth 'Strand'; cacht : caeth 'captus'; cumhacht : cyfoeth 'Macht',
etc.; breacht : braith 'bunt'; feacht : gwaith 'Fahrt, That, Mal';
reacht : raith 'Recht'; créacht : craith 'Wunde'; teacht 'kommen' :
taith 'Reise'; téachta : teithi 'Gebühr'; *m* necht : nith 'Nichte',
'rein'; riocht : rhith 'Gestalt'; bliocht : blith 'Milch'; icht (iochd) :
iaith 'Stamm, Gesittung, Sprache'; nocht : noeth 'nackt'; nocht :

---

[1]) Der Singular *Bryth* ist nicht gebräuchlich, sondern nur der Plural
Brython, Brythyon (Skene 2, 294) 'Brittönes'; er ist von diesem ebenso abzuleiten, wie *Sais* 'Saxo' von *Saeson* 'Saxönes' und *lleidr* 'latro' von *lladron*
'latrones'. Diese Wörter zeigen deutlich den Ursprung der Pluralendung *on,*
ion, die in der Sprache zum allergrössten Teile dem Persönlichen vorbehalten
blieb.

-noeth 'Nacht'; *m* mocht : mwyth 'sanft'; ocht : wyth 'acht';
brucht 'Auswurf' : brwth 'Aufruhr', brytherio 'vomere'; lucht :
llwyth 'Last'; lucht : llwyth 'Familie, Volk'; beannacht : bendith
'benedictis'; *w.* ffaeth 'factus', 'bestellt'; doeth 'doctus'; coeth
'coctus'; ffrwyth 'fructus'; ähnlich *pt* in scriptuir : ysgrythur
'scriptura'; *w.* pregeth 'praeceptum'; aber Egipt : Aipht 'Aegyp-
tus', als Eigenname in seiner Form geschützt. — (*p* : *ff*) ceap :
cyff 'cippus'; corp : corff 'corpus'; *w.* cloff 'cloppus', 'lahm'; sarff
'serpens'; Alpin : Elphin n. pr.; so auch *w.* chwalp chwalff 'Bruchstück'; cwlff 'Stück'; twlff 'ungestalter Mensch'.

Auf Gemination kommen auch einige andere Doppelkonso-
nanzen heraus, die die welsche Aspirata vertritt, wie **ux*, uas :
uwch 'über'; *m* basc 'Halsband' : baich 'Bürde', fascia; feascar :
ucher 'Abend', vesper; is tu : *ac ti*, a thi 'und du'; is t'ár : a th'aer
'und deine Schlacht'; a cath : ei chad 'ihre Schlacht' aus *'ης cat*,
e ccat; a tír : ei thir 'ihr Land' aus *'ης tir, e ttir*; a pian : ei phoen
'ihr Strafe' aus *'ης pĕn, e ppĕn*. — Der welschen Aspirata stellt
das Irische einige male wieder eine Aspirata an die Seite, wie
in dem Fremdworte manach : manach 'Mönch' so in moch 'mox' :
mwch 'hastig'; dreach : drych 'Gestalt, Ansehen'; *a* foich 'vespa' :
aarm. guohi 'Drohnen' (KZ. 33, 275); meath : meth 'defectus';
ruathar : rhuthr 'Angriff'; luaithre : lluthrod (nach Rhŷs, sonst
lluttrod, llytrod) 'Asche'; sgíth 'müde' : chwith 'linkisch'; bith :
byth : *corn.* bys 'immer' (vgl. AC. V. 12, 267). Das welsche *byth*,
zu dem einerseits ein Substantiv *pyth* und andrerseits die adverbiale Form *vyth* tritt, ist möglicherweise eigentlich das irische
choidche, alb. chaoidhe 'immer' (aus *co-oidhche : *py-yth*), dessen
Gebrauch dann nach der Analogie von *bith : byd* über die nächste
Bedeutung ausgedehnt worden wäre. — Eine verhältnismässig
späte Erscheinung ist es, dass die Endung der abstrakten Nomina
auf w. *-wch* wie in tegwch 'Schönheit', die vermutlich der von
fid*u*cia und aer*u*ca neben aer*u*go zu vergleichen ist, mitunter die
Form *-wg* annimmt, wie in tywyllwch tywyllwg 'Finsternis',
trythyllwch trythyllwg 'Wollust', tawelwch 'Stille' neben poethwg
'Hitze' u. a. m.

Wo sich die Muta mit einem vorhergehenden Konsonanten
(*n, l, r, s*) verbindet, da wird sie von ihrem gewöhnlichen Wege
vielfach abgelenkt, so dass Tenuis und Media oft schwer auseinander zu halten sind. So zeigt sich statt der welschen
Aspirata die dentale Tenuis beharrlich in (*nt* : *nt*), wie mant : **mant**

'Kiefer'; sant : chwant 'Begierde'; *w.* gwynt 'ventus'; in (*lt* : *llt*),
wie folt : gwallt 'Haar'; molt : mollt 'Widder'; alt : allt 'altum';
in (*st* : *st*), wie *m* lost : llost 'Ende, Spitze'; tost (tosd) 'gewichtig'
: tost 'streng'; teist : tyst 'testis'; piast : bwyst 'bestia'; súist
: ffust 'fustis'; feis : gwest 'Bewirtung'; cluais : clust 'Ohr'; *w.*
gast 'Weibchen'; cist 'cista'; trist 'tristis'; ffrwst 'Eile'. Dagegen scheint *rt* : *rt* ganz auf Fremdwörter beschränkt zu sein,
wie cart : cart 'charta'; cúirt : cwrt 'court'; *w.* dart, gwart, pert,
cort, gort, hort etc.

GG, DD, BB. Die radikale Media wird wieder durch die
Beständigkeit des Anlauts im Falle der Gemination erwiesen,
wie in — a gort : a gardd 'ihr Garten', a dorus : ei drws 'ihre
Thür', a bun : ei bon 'ihr Stamm', statt *'ης gort, e ggort* u. s. w.
(cf. GC. 59). So sind *g : g, d : d* auch im Inlaute einem *gg, dd*
gleich, wie agus : agos 'nahe'; cudaim : codwm 'Fall'. Die auslautende Media nach Vokalen ist im Irischen häufig (z. B. brag,
bog, grug, gróg, léig 'lass', fad, cnead. tread, grod, broid, troid,
rud etc.), aber im Welschen begegnet sie selten. Es gehören
hierher thug 'gab' : dug 'brachte'; bréag : breg 'Lüge, Trug';[1]
carraig : carreg craig 'Fels'; *a* sebocc (seabhag) : hebog 'Habicht';
m blonac (blonóg) : blonag 'Speck'; creideamh : credu 'glauben';
carbad : cerbyd 'Wagen'; *m* tadaim 'aufhäufen' (LL. 207 b 50) :
todi 'aufbauen'; oinmhid : ynfyd 'Thor'; sguab : ysgub 'Besen',
scopa; reabaim : rheibio 'reissen', rapere. Sonst aber neigt das
Welsche zur unorganischen Verhärtung des Auslauts, wie schon für
lag 'schwach' : llag 'slack' heute llac gewöhnlicher ist; ebenso
súd : hwt hwde 'dort'; gob : gwp 'Schnabel'. Es greift hier auch
eine Regel der Aussprache ein, wonach die Media (die im Welschen
zugleich die lenierte der ersten Stufe ist) dem langen Vokale
(*cōg, bȳd, māb*), die Tenuis aber dem kurzen folgen soll (*llăc, ăt,
chwăp*), Es giebt aber einige Fälle, in denen der irischen Media
im Welschen die Aspirata entspricht, namentlich beag (*a* becc) :
bach 'klein'; fothragadh : trochi 'baden'; cuid : peth : *arm.* pez
'Teil, Sache'; brod : broth 'Stachel'; nead : nyth : *arm.* nez 'Nest';
seid : chwyth : *arm.* c'houeza 'blasen'; dergleichen aus dem lautlichen Bestande der Ursprache meist seine Erklärung gefunden
hat (vgl. KZ. 32, 570).

---

[1] Das welsche Wort kommt nicht selten in der Bedeutung des irischen
vor; Dafydd ab Gwilym hat: twyllfreg 42, 11; dullfreg 122, 3; mewn breg a
brâd 133, 14; breg na brâd 207, 18. Vgl. AC. V. 12, 266.

Ein vorhergehender Konsonant (*n, l, r, s*) erweist sich auch im Bereich der Media von Einfluss. Nach N kommt vor allem die Gutturalis in Betracht, aber es bleibt dem eigentlichen *ng* die Media erhalten, wie in ing : ing 'Enge'; cumhaing : cyfyng 'enge'; mong : mwng 'Mähne'; tualaing 'fähig' : teilwng 'würdig'; *m* tongim : twng 'schwören'; auch wo der Nasal im Irischen geschwunden ist, wie in éag : angau 'Tod'; éigean : anghen 'Not'; *m* tocad 'Glück' : twg 'Glück', tynghed 'Schicksal'; ähnlich steht iangh-wr neben iang-wr 'Kerl';[1]) mit einem lenierten *c* verbindet sich der Nasal in deich : deg deng, durch Metathese aus *decem*. In andern Fällen entspricht der nachvokalischen ir. Media die welsche Tenuis mit vorhergehendem, meist wurzelhaftem Nasal (vgl. KZ. 24, 526. 27, 450; Brugmanns Grundriss 1, 379). So in (*g* : *ngc*) comhrag : cyfrangc 'Kampf'; géag : caingc 'Zweig'; óg : ieuangc 'jung'; tréigean 'verlassen' : trangc 'Ende'; slugadh : llyngcu 'schlucken, schlingen'. Die Barden unterscheiden nicht immer streng zwischen *ng* und *ngc* (caingc = cang etc.); vgl. z. B. D. G. 154, 14. 15. 72. — (*d* : *nt*) téad : tant 'Seite'; céad : cynt : *corn.* cyns 'erst'; céad : cant : cans 'hundert'; déad : dant : dans 'Zahn'; éad : iant 'Sehnsucht'; formad : gorfynt 'Neid'; séad : hynt 'Weg'; méad : maint 'Grösse'; siad : hwynt 'sie'; braghad : breuant 'Hals'; sealad 'Weile' : helynt 'Zustand'; caraid : ceraint 'Freunde'; *m* niit : niaint 'Neffen'; gaibhne : goffaint 'Schmiede'; molaid : molant 'sie loben' etc.; auch cead : cennad caniad 'Erlaubnis' (KZ. 33, 154) und (*nd* : *nt*) cland clann : plant 'Kinder';

---

[1]) Es findet sich *ianghwr* 'der Kerl' RB. 1, 219, oder *iangwr* G. R. 369; D. G. 254, 39; I. G. 38, 74. 41, 72; und dazu das Femininum *iangwraic* I. G. 73, 41, und der Plural *iangwyr* D. G. 94, 14, wo die Ausgaben eangwyr, cangwyr haben. Von diesem Worte gänzlich verschieden ist *gwrêng* BC. 106. 143, das im Gegensatze zum bonheddig 'dem Edelmann' und cardottyn 'dem Bettler' den Mann von mittlerm Stande, d. i. den Bürger und den Bauer, bezeichnet. Daher *mab gwreng* 'der Bauernsohn' IM. 194; *gwreng a brodawr* 'Bürger und Bauer' ib. 236; *gwyr gwreng* 'freie Männer' R. Prichard p. 445. Dasselbe ist *gwreang* HM. 1, 58 etc., D. G. 124, 23. 154, 15 und *gwrangc* (einsilbig) 154, 69. Die alte Form des Wortes ist *gwraenc* RB. 1, 146 oder *gwraync* 1, 72, im Plural *gwyreeinc* RB. 1, 61, *gwyreeingk* HM. 1, 175 etc., *gwyreeing* 1, 119; hier scheint der Ausdruck dem *gwr da* der Gesetze zu entsprechen und zum *taeog* und *aillt* oder *caeth* oder *bilain* den Gegensatz zu bilden. Es wird schwer halten das Wort *gwrangc* zu deuten, wenn man es halbiert, denn es ist ohne Zweifel das lat. *francus*, franz. *franc* 'frei', und seine Bedeutung ist die des 'francus homo'. Siehe Ducange.

swnd : hwnt 'dort', schliessen sich an; — (*g* : *mp*) cúig : pump 'fünf'; *w.* camp 'Spiel', campus; clamp 'Masse', engl. clump.

Nach L hat die auslautende Media im Welschen verschiedene Behandlung erfahren. Das *g* hat nach dieser Liquiden zunächst der Lenierung unterlegen, ist dann vokalisch geworden und schliesslich abgefallen, ein Verlauf, den das Altwelsche deutlich erkennen lässt, wie in sealg : helgha helcha hely hel 'jagen'; bolg : bola boly bol 'Bauch' (neben bolgwd); colg : cola col 'Spitze'; cealg : celg cel 'Trug, List'; aber tolg 'Bett' : twlc 'Koben' D. G. 108, 30; tolg 'Welle' : tolc 'Runzel'. Dagegen hat sich *d* (wie *t*) mit *l* zu *llt* vereinigt, wie in swllt 'solidus', 'Schilling'; aber maledictio hat mallacht : melldith 'Fluch' ergeben. Ähnlich ist wohl für *lb* im Welschen *lp* zu erwarten, wie in tailp : talp 'Haufen'; desgleichen bleibt auch *lm* unverändert in psalm : salm 'Psalm'; tailm : talm 'Schlinge'; *w.* talm 'Weile'; ffalm 'Westwind'.

Nach R wird *g* wiederum abgeworfen, wie in lorg : llwrw llwry llwr 'Spur, Richtung'; *m* bargen : bara 'Brot'; und in den Fremdwörtern *w.* llara llary 'gemächlich' von largus; gwyra gwyry (dann gwyryf) 'Jungfrau' von virgo; ebenso meadhg : maidd 'Molken', gallolat. mesga. Für ir. dearg, fearg, learg, searg, mairg u. a. fehlt das Welsche. Das ir. *d* nach *r* wird im Welschen leniert, wie in ord : urdd 'ordo'; ord : gordd 'Hammer'; bárd : bardd 'Barde'; bord : bwrdd 'Tafel'; dord 'Gesumme' : dwrdd 'Geräusch'; ceard : cerdd 'Kunst'; und analog *w.* gardd 'Garten' statt gort : garth; doch findet sich *rd* in godard 'Becher', sard 'Zurückweisung', dwrd 'Schelte', twrd 'Zober'. Die Labialis scheint als Tenuis aufzutreten in lurga : llorp 'Schenkel', gleichwie in *w.* llarp 'Fetzen', tarp : torp 'Klumpen'. Ebenso bleibt auch das *m* nach *r* unleniert in gairm : garm 'Schrei'; gorm : gwrm 'dunkelbraun'; *w.* gorm 'Füllung'; torm 'Anhäufung'; aber es fällt ab in cuirm : cwrw 'Bier', wie in ainm : enw 'Name'.

Nach S hat sich der neuere Schriftbrauch bei Iren und Welschen für die Media der Gutturalis entschieden, also (*sg* : *sg*) leasg : llesg 'lässig'; measg : mysg 'Mitte'; seisg : hesg 'Binsen'; iasg : pysg 'Fisch'; rusg : rhisg 'Rinde'; losgadh : llosgi 'brennen'; taosgadh 'ausschütten' : twysg 'Haufen'; faisgeadh : gwasgu 'pressen'; fosgadh : gwasgod 'Schutz'; *w.* cwsg 'quiescere'. Als Labialis wäre wohl die welsche Tenuis zu erwarten, wie in cosg 'Unterweisung' : cosp 'Strafe'; seasg : hysp 'unfruchtbar';

w. diasp 'Schrei'; aber die Schreibart schwankt und in der Welsh Orthography 1893 p. 21. 45 wird neben *cwsg* auch *cosb* empfohlen.

C, T, P. Die Lenierung erster Stufe führt die Sprache mit grosser Regelmässigkeit durch, indem sie die unter vokalischem Einflusse stehende gemeinceltische Tenuis im Irischen zur Aspirata [1]) und im Welschen zur Media mildert, ganz so wie es die Mutation des Anlauts lehrt, nämlich — a chath : ei gad 'seine Schlacht', a thir : ei dir 'sein Land', a phian : a boen 'seine Strafe', aus 'εο *cat* u. s. w. Beispiele: (*ch : g*) nach : nag 'nicht'; tosach toiseach : tywysog 'Fürst'; marcach : marchog 'Reiter'; coileach : ceiliog 'Hahn', etc.; tormach 'Zunahme' : magu 'aufziehen'; curach : cwrwg 'curuca'; luireach : lluryg 'lorica'; braich : brag 'Malz'; deich : deg 'zehn'; cioch 'mamma' : cig 'Fleisch'; tiach : twyg 'theca'; cloch 'Stein' : clogan 'grosser Stein'; droch : drwg 'schlecht'; loch : llwg 'schwarzgelb'; caoch 'blind' : coeg 'eitel', caecus; fraoch : grug 'Heide'; laoch 'Held' : lleyg 'Laie', laicus; laiches : a leeces (KB. 4, 410) 'laica'; much : mwg 'Rauch'; luch : llyg 'Maus'; luach : llog 'Lohn'; cuach : cog 'Kuckuck'; cuach : cawg 'caucus'; cruach : crug 'Haufen'; ebenso inlautend in urchur : ergyr 'Wurf'; buachaill : bugail 'Hirt'; luacharn : llugorn 'lucerna'; *m* cocholl : cwgwll cwcwll : *c.* cugol 'cucullus';[2]) — (*th : d*) cath : cad 'Schlacht'; rath : rhad 'Gnade'; roith : rhod 'Rad'; srath : ystrad 'Thalgrund'; brath : brad 'Verrat'; calath (caladh) : caled : *corn.* cales 'hart'; lathach : llaid 'Schmutz'; ath- : ad- 'wieder'; áth : odyn 'Ofen'; láth : llawd 'Brunst' (RC. 2, 326); bláth : blawd 'Mehl'; bráth : brawd 'Gericht'; bráthair : brawd 'Bruder', slaw. brat; gnáth : gnawd

---

[1]) In der Aussprache ist das irische *th* guttural geworden (*h*) und hat sich dem *ch* genähert, ebenso wie *dh* die Aussprache des *gh* (*g*) angenommen hat. Die Veränderung hatte vermutlich noch nicht stattgefunden, als man in alter Zeit die Regeln des *Uaim* aufstellte. Hätte ir. *th*, *dh* schon damals die Aussprache *h*, *g* gehabt, so würde die Alliteration, die auf der Wiederholung von anlautenden Buchstaben desselben Organs, ohne Rücksicht auf Eklipse und Aspiration, beruht (vgl. Windisch, Kunstgedicht p. 224), also *th* dem *t* und *dh* dem *d* gleichstellt, eine unvollkommene gewesen sein. Vielmehr werden ir. *th*, *dh* einst dem welschen *th*, *dd* ähnlich gewesen sein. Z. B.
Ollmas fa *th*ocaid *t*ugaib, WT. p. 320.
Ceile acht *d*iot ni *dh*inguntair, Zs. 2, 348.

[2]) Ab Gwilym hat die Form *cwgwll* 124, 32 und im Cynghanedd *cwcwll* 198, 22, und in einem andern Gedichte (p. VIII) spielt er mit den beiden Formen.

'Gewohnheit', *m* fáth : gwawd 'Gedicht'; tláith 'matt' : tlawd
'arm'; scáth : cysgod 'Schatten'; maith : mad : *corn.* mas 'gut';
raith : rhedyn 'Farn'; caitheamh 'consumere' : peidio 'absolvere,
cessare' (schwerlich von *pati*); flaith : gwlad 'Herrschaft, Land';
leath : led 'halb'; beith : bedw 'Birke'; breith : bryd 'Urteil,
Meinung'; sgeith : chwyd 'vomitus'; féith 'Sehne' : gwdan 'Weiden-
gerte' (?); ith : yd 'Korn'; íth : uwd 'Brei'; bith : byd 'Welt';
sith : hyd 'Länge'; *m* clith : clyd 'warm'; liath : llwyd 'grau';
cliath : clwyd 'Hürde'; sgiath : ysgwyd 'Schild'; rioth : rhed
'Lauf'; both : bod 'Hütte', 'sein'; loth : llwdn 'Junges'; loth
'lutum' : lludedig 'beschmutzt'; saoth : hoed 'Zeit', 'Verzug';
bruth : brwd 'Glut'; sruth : ffrwd 'Strom'; cruth : pryd 'Gestalt'; tuath : tud 'Volk'; luaith : lludw 'Asche'; ebenso inlautend
satharn : sadwrn 'Saturnus'; párthas : paradwys 'Paradies'; máthair : modr-fydaf 'Mutter' (des Bienenschwarms); athair 'Vater' :
edr-yd 'Verwandtschaft'; leathar : lledr 'Leder'; seathar : hydr
'kühn'; leathain : llydan 'breit'; Leatha : Llydaw 'Letavia';
meithiol : medel 'Schnitter'; ceathair : pedwar 'vier'; riathar :
rhaiadr 'Wasserfall'; arathar : aradr : *arm.* arazr 'Pflug'; tara-
thar : taradr : tarazr 'Bohrer'. — Eigentümlich steht die
Labialis in dieser Reihe; denn da der Celte ein indogermanisches
p nicht gesprochen hat, so würde es auch hier als *ph : b* nicht
erscheinen können. Aber an seine Stelle tritt gewissermassen
das *qu*, das der Ire regelrecht zu *ch*, der Welsche zu *b* lenierte.
(*ch : b*) cách : pob 'jeder'; each 'Pferd' : ebol 'Fohlen'; neach :
neb 'jemand'; seach : heb 'ohne'; *m* sechaid : hebyr heby heb
'er sagt'; *m* sechim 'folgen' : hebrwng 'begleiten'; praiseach :
preseb 'praesepe'; fliuch : gwlyb 'feucht'; uch : wb 'ach, pfui!';
toich : tyb 'Natürlichkeit, Wahrscheinlichkeit'; *m* enech : wyneb
'Gesicht'; auch die welsche Endung *yb* (lat. aequus?) in modryb
'Tante' vom ir. máthair 'Mutter' und in cyffelyb 'ähnlich' von lat.
copula[1]) und corn.-arm. hevelep von samhail : hafal 'ähnlich',
wird hierher gehören. Vereinzelt stehen mac : mab 'Sohn' (aus
maqu) und seiche : hif 'Haut' mit der Lenierung zweiter Stufe
im Welschen.

Da die lenierte Tenuis im Welschen mit der radikalen
Media zusammenfällt, so kann nur die Vergleichung des gälischen

---

[1]) 'Non video quomodo ista tam diversa in eandem copulam coniiciantur',
sagt Seneca. — Von *copula, cupla* 'Koppel' hat vermutlich auch *ceffyl* statt
cafall 'caballus' seinen Inlaut *ff* angenommen.

Dialekts lehren, ob die Media in jedem Falle (in der alten
Schreibung die Tenuis) auf eigentlicher Doppelmedia oder auf
einfacher Tenuis beruht. Die Tenuis der Fremdwörter behält
das Irische entweder bei (nir. meist mit vokalischem Nachschlag,
wie in coca 'cook', cota 'coat', rata 'rat'), oder es leniert sie zur
Media wie das Welsche, wenn ein langer Vokal vorhergeht; z. B.
draic draig : draig 'draco'; *m* coic : cog 'cocus'; pic : pyg 'picem';
cloca : clog 'cloak'; *w.* gwag 'vacuus'; bád : bâd 'boat'; staid :
ystâd 'status'; *w.* ffawd 'fata'; grod 'groat'; gwyd 'vitium' (pl.
gwydyeu LA. 34, 28), davon diwyd 'fleissig'; cyrchyd 'circuitus';
aber hap 'Glück' D. G. 170, 12 u. a.; als Fremdwort würde sguab :
ysgub 'scopa' auch hierhergehören; mitunter ist auch der Inlaut
im Irischen leniert, wie in sagart 'sacerdos', madain 'matutina',
ladrónn 'latronem', piobar : pib 'piper'; — cubhad : cufydd 'cubitus'
ist eine Ausnahme. Die welsche Adjektivendung -*ig* von bonheddig
ist die lateinische von civ*ic*us, ebenso meddyg 'med*ic*us'; die Endung -*wd* (in hugwd 'Gespenst', yscerbwd 'Skelett', bolgwd 'Dick-
bauch', hwgwd 'Dickkopf') ist die des lat. cornu*t*us, nas*ut*us etc.;
die Endung -*tawt, -dod* von ciwtawt ciwdod etc. ist die lateinische
von civi*tat*em; die kollektivische Endung -*awt, -od* in pyscawt
pysgod 'Fische' ist die des lat. pisca*tus*; die ähnliche Endung
-*et -ed* von pryfet pryfed 'Würmer' die des lat. formi*cet*um
'Ameisenhauf'.

Im Irischen steht die Lenierung erster Stufe der der zweiten
Stufe näher als im Welschen; sie wechseln mit einander, wo
Mollierung und Accent eingreifen, häufig, z. B. toiseach pl. toisigh :
tywysog 'Fürst'; *m* tich LL. 216 b, d. i. *tioch : teg 'schön', éi-digh :
annheg 'hässlich', sothigh : hydeg 'stattlich' (Bezz. 21, 127); neben
air. ró-sárichset steht rosariged (G. C. 74); ir. deabhaidh 'Streit'
bildet das Adjektiv deabhthach, etc. Dergleichen ist im Welschen
selten, aber aw. tig 'Haus' verhält sich zu nw. ty, wie ir. teach
zu tigh; ebenso verhält sich ir. maitheamh 'vergeben' zu w. madden
(aus *madjem*); maothalach 'erweichend' : meddal 'weich'.

G, D, B. Die zweite Stufe der Lenierung bildet die letzte
Schwächung der Muta, die im Welschen wie im Vulgäririschen
teilweise bis zum völligen Schwunde des Konsonanten geführt
hat. Im Anlaute beobachtet man sie in — a ghort : ei 'ardd 'sein
Garten', a dhorus : ei ddrws 'seine Thür', a bhun : ei fon 'sein
Stamm', statt 'εο gort u. s. w.. Beispiele: (*gh : spiritus lenis*) magh
'Feld' : ma 'Ort'; deagh : da 'gut'; ri rígh 'König' : rhi 'Herr';

brigh : bri 'Wesen, Würde', ital. brio; léagh : lle 'lies'; graigh :
gre 'grex'; plaigh : pla 'Plage'; aigh : ia 'Eis'; laogh : llo 'Kalb';
figh : gweu 'weben'; tiugh : tew 'dick'; *m* liag (liach) : llwy
'Löffel'; mogh : mau-ddwy 'Diener Gottes' : *corn.* maw 'Knabe';
dóigh 'wahrscheinlich' : do 'ja'; luighe : llw 'Eid'; tuighe : tô
'Dach'; bogha : bwa 'Bogen'; *m* brugh : bro 'Land'; ugh : wy
'Ei'; truagh : tru 'elend'; sluagh : llu 'Volk'; dlighe : dyly
'Pflicht'; reoghadh : rhew 'Frost'; *m* starga : taryan 'Tartsche';
so auch im Inlaute faighin : gwain 'vagina'; *m* laighen : laïn
'Lanze'; droighin : draen 'Dorn'; traoghadh : treio 'ebben';
m feugadh 'Welkheit' : gwyw 'welken'; troigh : troed (aus
*traged?) 'Fuss'; und in den Fremdwörtern *w.* ystaen 'stagnum',
swyn 'signum', llwyn 'lignum' (H. Schuchardt, Lbl. f. germ. und
rom. Philol. 14, 103), wenn das letzte nicht vielmehr das ir. lian
in lianmag (SR. 679) ist; — (*dh* : *dd*) cladh : cladd 'Graben'; grádh :
gradd 'gradus'; rádh 'sagen' : adrodd 'erzählen'; -fadh : gwedd
'Art und Weise'; *m* fedan : gwedd 'Joch'; slaidhim : lladd
'tödten'; báidhim : boddi 'ertrinken'; snáidhim 'stützen' : nawdd
'Schutz'; meadh : medd 'Meth'; fleadh : gwledd 'Fest'; sneadh :
nedd : *arm.* nez 'Niete'; *m* clé : cledd 'link'; *m* bled : blaidd
'Wolf'; meadhg : maidd 'Molken'; geadh : gŵydd 'Gans'; réidh :
rhwydd 'eben, frei'; faoidh : gwaedd 'Geschrei'; fiodh : gwŷdd
'Gehölz'; sidh (síth) : hedd 'Friede'; criadh : prydd 'Thon'; fiadh :
gŵydd 'wild'; fiadh : gŵydd 'Gegenwart'; modh : modd 'modus';
ruadh : rhudd 'rot'; snuadh : nudd 'Gestalt'; buaidh : budd 'Sieg,
Vorteil'; nuadh : newydd 'neu'; crábhadh : crefydd 'Religion';
snáthadh : nodwydd 'Nadel'; *m* robud : rhybudd 'Warnung'; *m* costud 'Gebahren' : cystudd 'Beschwerde'; ráidhe 'radius' : rhaidd
'Speer'; *a* déad : diwedd 'Ende'; damhna : defnydd 'Stoff'; airdhe :
arwydd 'Zeichen'; Dáibhi : Dewi Dafydd; *w.* cybydd 'cupidus';
buidhean : byddin 'Schar', etc. Einige male entspricht dem irischen *dh* die unlenierte Media, z. B. peacadh (alt peccath) :
pechod 'peccatum'; moladh (alt molath) : molad 'Lob', etc.;
biadh : bwyd 'Nahrung'; meanadh : mynawyd 'Ahle'; cúigeadh :
pummed 'fünft'; seachtmhadh : seithf-ed 'siebent', septimus; con-
nadh : cynnud : *corn.* cynys 'Brennholz'; foludh 'Macht' : golud
'Reichtum'; colcaidh : cylched 'culcita' Mitunter schwindet das
welsche *dd* (ir. *dh*, gesprochen wie *gh*) ebenso wie *gh* nicht
nur im Auslaut, wie in *sy* statt iseadh : sydd 'der ist'; *y* Verbalpartikel == *yd ydd* vor Vokalen; sondern auch im Innern des

Wortes, wie in meadhon : mewn 'innen'; rhoddi rhoi : *arm.* rei
'geben'; oeddwn : *corn.* esen : *arm* oann == vulgärwelsch *ûn*, etc.;
— (*bh : f*) treabh 'Stamm' : tref 'Wohnung'; *w.* barf 'barba'; sil-
labh : sillaf 'syllaba'; gobha : gof 'Schmied'; saobh 'thöricht' :
hyf 'kühn'; gabháil : gafael 'nehmen'; meabhul : mefl 'Schande';
lobhar 'leprosus' : llwfr 'feig'; *m* odb : oddf 'Knoten'; oftmals
schwindet die auslautende Labialis im Welschen, namentlich nach
Konsonanten, wo sie indess eine vokalische Spur zu hinterlassen
pflegt, wie in dubh : du 'schwarz'; taobh : tu 'Seite'; luibh :
llu-arth 'Kraut'; so auch oft tre statt tref, hy statt hyf etc.;
dealbh : delw (statt delwf) 'Bild'; sealbh : helw 'Besitz'; garbh :
garw 'rauh'; marbh : marw 'tot' (*manx* marroo); tarbh : tarw
'Stier' (*m.* tarroo); searbh : chwerw 'herb' (*m.* sharroo); moirbh :
mor 'Ameise'; bearbhadh : berwi 'sieden'; banbh : banw 'Schwein'
(*m.* bannoo); feadhbh : gweddw 'Wittwe'; *m* medb : meddw
'trunken', woneben *w.* meddf 'weibisch'; *w.* syberw 'superbus'.
Dem lenierten B ist durch gleiches Schicksal das lenierte M verbunden: (*mh : f*) samh-radh : haf 'Sommer'; neamh : nef 'Himmel';
claidheamh : cleddyf cleddeu 'Schwert'; riomh : rhif 'Zahl';
primh : prif 'primus'; omh : of 'roh'; clúmh : pluf 'pluma';
cruimh : pryf 'Wurm'; umha : efydd 'Erz'; *w.* ffyrf 'firmus';
lámh : llaw (statt llawf) 'Hand'; caomh 'sanft' : cu 'lieb'; *m*
nemed 'Vorrecht', 'Heiligtum', 'Edler' : neu-af 'vortrefflichst'
IM. 327, wozu aw. nouod-ou 'palatia', nw. neuadd 'Halle' nicht zu
gehören scheint (Sprach. 194); ughaim : iau 'Joch', eine radix
multifarie infirma. Wegen der Schwäche ihrer Aussprache
wechseln die spirantischen Mediae nicht selten, wie aus dem
Irischen wohl bekannt ist. Daher sugh : sudd 'sucus'; crodha
'tapfer' : cryf 'stark'; cubhachail : cuddigl 'cubiculum'; fréamh :
gwreiddyn 'Wurzel'; saoghal : hoedyl (Skene 2, 72) == hoeddl,
später hoedl 'Lebenszeit' (wie aos : oes 'Alter'), in das, wie es
scheint, zugleich ir. saothar 'Arbeit' aufging. Häufig ist der
Wechsel auch innerhalb des Welschen, wie gwyryf, gwyrydd statt
gwyry 'virgo' (RC. 12, 143).

Dieses sind die Verhältnisse der auslautenden Muta im
Neuceltischen, die im wesentlichen auch in der ältern Sprache
bestanden, obschon sie sich hier unter weniger streng geschie-
denen Formen offenbaren. Die Korrespondenz, die die Lenierung
erster Stufe darstellt, kommt schon innerhalb des Altirischen

vor, wie *doig* neben *doich, rad* neben *rath, madramil* von *máthair*
(GC. 73 ff.). Im Irischen hat das *ch, th,* im Welschen das *g, d*
prävaliert. Aber das Mittelwelsche scheint unsere Reihen zu
stören, indem es für droch : drwg, cath : cad, cách : pob vielmehr
drwc, cat, pawp ziemlich allgemein festhält (es musste daher
TEC als erstes Wort über diesem Aufsatze stehen). Ebenso hat
die ältere Sprache für die Media der zweiten Reihe die Tenuis,
thuc : duc, oinmhit : ynvyt, und auch im Inlaute schrieb der Ire
cretim, étig etc. und das Altwelsche des Martianus gar *cueeticc*
statt gweedig (KB. 7, 395), gerade so wie sich im Neuirischen
cc für *g, tt* für *d* geschrieben findet. Zu solcher Schreibweise
wurde man geführt, weil *g, d* vor der Erfindung des ir. *g d,*
w. *d dd* die Lenierung zweiter Stufe, die Spiranten, ausdrückt.
Das Schwarze Buch erkennt denn auch der Media als der Lenierung der ersten Stufe seine Stelle zu und schreibt: *diag* 13 a 7,
ysprid 23 a 12, *priaud* 21 b 16, *braud* 20 b 5. 21 a 15, *faud* 9 b 11,
cnaud 10 a 14, *mad* 5 b 5. 22 a 10, *anuad* 22 a 1, *amhad* 5 a 7. 8 a 3,
brid 10 a 8, *drud* 10 a 9. 16 a 7, *diwawd* 21 b 13, *diwod* 23 a 2,
diwad 22 a 7, *diwed* 22 b 12, *kid* cyd 2 a 4, *kyhid* 5 b 1, *kyhidet*
8 b 4, *meib* 3 a 8, *paub* 21 a 16 (neben *a fop* 19 a 12), etc. Die
auslautende Media bezeugt auch das Cynghanedd der Barden:

> D. G. 1, 15: Caeth y g*l*er cywaetho*g l*yw;
> 1, 26: A hyd y g*w*lych hoywde*g w*lith.
> I. G. 4, 118: Tan *g*astyll te*g* ei ystum;
> 10, 73: A gwrai*g* orau o'r gwrae*g*edd,
> 69, 59: Ef yn de*g* a fendi*g*awdd.

Hier ist kein cywaethoc, tec, gwraic am Platze. Die organische
Media kommt zum Vorschein, so oft eine vokalische Endung antritt. So heisst das Femininum von mw. marchawc marcho*g*es,
der Plural von bonhedic bonhedi*g*ion, der von ynvy*t* ynvy*d*yon
(RB. 2, 4) u. s. w. Es unterliegt daher keinem Zweifel, dass der
irischen Aspirata mit Fug die welsche Media gegenübertritt.
Die mittelwelsche Tenuis hat ein durchaus entsprechendes Gegenstück im Mittelhochdeutschen, wo für das nhd. *tag* vielmehr *tac*
geschrieben wird; das Althochdeutsche hat regelrecht *tag* und nur
selten und ohne Belang die Varianten *tagh, tach, tac, tak.*
Es ist ein Gesetz der welschen Wortbildung, dass zwei zu-
sammentreffende gleiche Mediae die Tenuis (die Schrift verdoppelt
sie meist) ergeben, wie *ad-dal* = attal, *lugaid-du* = lugeittu

(IM. 237), ganz ähnlich wie aus *digder* die empfohlene Schreibung dicter entstanden ist; ebenso die Media mit folgendem *h*, wie *dryg-hin* = dryccin, *ad-heb* = atteb, *eb-hil* = epil. (Vgl. J. Rhys, Welsh Philology[2] p. 71; Welsh Orthography 1893, p. 20.) Hierauf beruht die alte Bardenregel, wonach zwei gleiche Mediae oder eine Media mit *h* der entsprechenden Tenuis gleichzuachten sind.

I. G. 25, 37 *C*lyswriaeth de*g* *g*lwys oroer;
     10, 8 Ni*d* *d*rwg yno y *t*rigaf.
Gr. Roberts p. 257 Po*b* *b*ron fal y pa*p*ur yw;
Ibid.   Golw*g* *h*onn o gil y *c*yrch;
Ibid.   Cau 'r *t*y no rhag caria*d* *h*ir;
Ibid.   Anha*p* oedd i wyne*b* *h*onn.

Diese Lautregel lässt sich auch im Mittelwelschen an einigen grammatischen Formen beobachten, deren Ursprung noch im Dunkeln liegt. In ihnen lässt ein antretendes *h* auslautende Spiranten und Liquide unberührt, aber es verbindet sich mit der Media zur Doppeltenuis. So in der Bildung der Denominativa (GC. 506. 833), z. B. *ufudhau* 'gehorchen' RB. 2, 43. 75, rydhau 'befreien' 46. 120, arafhau 'sanft werden' 1, 152, edivarhau 'bereuen' 2, 75, cadarnhau 'stärken' 45. 51, llawenhau 'sich freuen' 107, truanhau 'bemitleiden' 78, ofynhau 'fürchten' 108, gwrhau 'ein Dienstmann werden', gwra 'heiraten' RB. 1, 178, etc.; und daneben gwreicka 'ein Weib nehmen', teckau (aus *teg-hau*) 'verschönern' RB. 2, 40. 78, ardunockau 'disponere' 10, buchedockau 'leben' 59, chwaneckau 'vermehren' 102, gwastattau gwastatta 'ebnen', kanhatau kennattau kennattahu LA. 101 'senden', trugarhau 'sich erbarmen' und dazu trugerehe LA. 42, 3, u. a. m. Dieses *h* des Infinitivs behalten die abgeleiteten Formen bei; es giebt indess Ausnahmen, von denen oben eine bemerkenswerte mitgeteilt worden ist. — Ein solches *h* und statt seiner die Provectio mediae zum Ersatze zeigt auch der Konjunktiv (GC. 512), im Aktiv, wie in ladho (RB. 1, 189), talho, digonhom (Skene 2, 10) und tebyckych, dycko, cretto (RB. 1, 189), crettoch (1, 131), mynaccont (LA. 168, 7), etc.; und ebenso im Passiv, wo es G. Dottin, Les désinences verbales en R, p. 158 ff. nachweist, wie in barnher, gwelher, tebycker etc. Der Konjunktiv der Denominativa begnügt sich mit éinem *h*, wie rwydhao RB. 1, 17, rydhaer 1, 65. Dass dieses *h* hier, wie in andern Fällen und namentlich im Neuwelschen, lediglich die Tonsilbe bezeichne (wie in brénin, brenhínes) und dass die Doppeltenues *ck, tt* nur eintreten, um die Mutae von den Aspiraten *ch, th* zu unterscheiden, ist nicht wahrscheinlich.[1])

Fragen wir aber nach dem Ursprunge dieser Bildungen, so müssen wir gewärtig sein, dass das welsche *h* keineswegs immer aus einem *s* hervorgeht. Oft beruht es auf einer Tenuis, die Farbe und Klang verloren hat, wie nach dem Nasal[2]) in: fy n*h*ad

[1]) Dass die Texte in der Anwendung des konjunktivischen *h* unbeständig sind, lässt sich nicht leugnen; aber ein Charakter der Form bleibt es trotzdem. Es scheint mir auch nicht ausgemacht, dass das Mittelwelsche keinen Conjunctivus imperfecti habe, wie PRIA. III 3, 460 gesagt wurde. Vgl. *ny thebygwn* 'ich meinte nicht', R.B. 1, 176, und: *bei na thebyckwn ... mi a vanagwn* 'wenn ich nicht meinte, würde ich sagen' 1, 165. Gibt es nicht von bod 'sein' solche Form: *bawn, bait, bai, baem, baech, baent*, die nach *pe* 'wenn', *oni* 'wenn nicht', *o na* 'o dass doch' gebraucht wird?

[2]) Das Mittelwelsche hat die Eklipse noch nicht streng geregelt, da es ym penn, ym benn, yn mhenn und ymhenn neben einander gebraucht; sonst hat es *gg* für *ng*, und *gk* oder *gh* für *ngh*. Erst im Neuwelschen ist die Eklipse durchgeführt, aber zugleich zu einer Plage in der Orthographie geworden, da sie zwischen *anmarch, anmharch, anmarch, ammharch, amarch, amharch* hin und her rät (Zs. 2, 599). Wo es sich um ein deutlich gesondertes Wort, wie *fy* 'mein' handelt, gibts keine Schwierigkeit; denn wie man im Irischen *ar gcuirt* 'unser Hof' schreibt, so im Welschen *fy nghwrt* 'mein Hof'. Das eklipsierende *n* bewirkt nicht eine Veränderung des folgenden Konsonanten, sondern verbindet sich mit ihm zu einem neuen Laute, eine konsonantische Krasis. Dass in den Fällen der Eklipse des *yn* loci (ir. *i n-*) nur eine Nasalis geschrieben werden sollte, zeigt das Irische und geht aus dem Verlaufe der lautlichen Umbildung deutlich hervor. Zunächst nimmt die auslautende Nasalis die organische Qualität der folgenden Muta an: *n* vor *t d*, *ng* vor *c g*, *m* vor *p b*; dann stösst sie diese aus, die Media völlig, während vom explosiven Charakter der Tenuis ein *h* bleibt.

Ir. *i ncath*	*i gcath*	W. *yn cad, y-ng-c-ad*	y' ng-h-ad
i ntir	*i dtir*	*yn tir, y-n-t-ir*	y' n-h-ir
i npein	*i bpein*	*yn poen, y-m-p-oen*	y' m-h-oen
i ngort		*yn gardd, y-ng-g-ardd*	y' ng-ardd
i ndorus		*yn drws, y-n-d-rws*	y' n-rws
i nbun	*i mbun*	*yn bon, y-m-b-on*	y' m-on.

Welche Berechtigung hat da ein *yng nghad*? Niemand spricht so; der Bischof Morgan schreibt *yng had* und ein Schreiber, der im Anfange des 17. Jahrhunderts *ꝟ* für *ng* einführen wollte, hat y *ꝟlan̄*, y *ꝟhaer*, aber nicht *yꝟ ꝟlan̄, yꝟ ꝟhaer*. Auch im Cynghanedd wird der nasalierte Laut einfach gerechnet, z. B. Broch y' *ngh*ôd braich *angh*adarn, D.G. 125, 46; Y' *mh*oen yddwyf am *h*yny, id. 205, 2; Mam *h*irffawd, mae y' *mh*orffor, id. 33, 39. Es wäre folgerichtig, was uns *fy* und *yn* lehren, auch auf den Inlaut der Composita mit *an-* und *cyn-* anzuwenden; dann könnte *an+porth* nur *amhorth*, *an+parch* nur *amharch* geben. Es muss aber wiederholt werden, dass sich die Regel in der älteren 'mein Vater' von *t*ad, **fy** m*h*en*n* 'mein Kopf' von *p*enn, bren*h*in 'König' von brain*t* 'Vorrecht', pimhed 'fünft', eine alte Form (BBC. 27 b 3), von pum*p*. In andern Fällen kommt das nach-konsonantische *h* der Gemination gleich, z. B. canhwyll 'candela'; prynhawn für das alte prytnawn = prydnhawn BC. 5. 94.[1]) Dass das Denominativ *sarháu* oder vielmehr sarháad 'beleidigen' dem irischen *sárughadh* gleichgebildet sei (RC. 6, 32; Brugmanns Grundriss 2, 1128), will nicht recht einleuchten; vielmehr scheint das irische -*ughadh* im Welschen -*io* zu lauten. Wichtiger als das *h*, das die Schrift leicht ganz aufgiebt, ist das stets be-tonte *ā* der welschen Denominativa auf -*hā-u*, und so erscheint es mir glaublich, dass darin das irische *tá* 'es ist, es steht, es giebt' von der Wurzel *stare* enthalten ist, das das Welsche sonst in Partikeln wie *nid, nad, neud*, aber auch, wie es scheint, in *mae* 'es ist', *maent* 'es sind', aus *imm-thá, imm-tháid*, und vielleicht auch in *mai* 'dass ist' (vgl. E. Anwyl, Grammar 2, 177), bewahrt hat. So schon im Altwelschen: lemhaam, eig. ich bin scharf, 'arguo'; parhau 'bereit sein, dauern' von par 'bereit'; und der Übergang von der neutralen Bedeutung in die transitive, wie glanhau 'reinigen' (ir. glanadh), möchte auch nicht allzuschwer zu finden sein. Was aber die Konjunktive *talho, talher* betrifft, so scheinen sie, im Hinblick auf die gleichen Formen gwypo, gwyper (neben gwybu) von *gwydd-*, mit den Konjunktiven *bo, baer* von bod 'sein' zu-sammengesetzt zu sein. Die Verhärtung des Anlauts, die auch der mir. Konjunktiv *pa* hat, ist noch im welschen Imperativ *poed* statt boed sehr gewöhnlich, z. B. D. G. 29, 43. 33, 5. 76, 47. 137, 29. 143, 18. 192, 51. Und wie der Anlaut des Verbs bod schwindet, zeigt anschaulich *pettwn* 'wenn ich wäre' statt ped bawn (pawn, hawn) D. G. 39, 8. 127, 9. 208, 27; *pettaem* 'wenn wir wären' 213, 11.

Sprache noch nicht durchaus befestigt hat, und dass die Dichter eine Aussprache wie *anmarch* zulassen. Anmarch a oedd hy*n* imi, D. G. 21, 53; *Merch* i *g*oed, anmarch i *g*au, id. 46, 6; — aber: Diwyd anmorth yn dad imi, id. 127, 28, ist falsch ediert für: *Diwyd* amhorth yn d*a*d imi.

[1]) Dass die aus prytnawn hervorgegangene Form *prynhawn* lautet, be-zeugt das Cynghanedd: I byrn*h*awn a bery '*n* hir, D. G. 40, 30; Ac wy*bren* *h*oyw | ar brynhawn, id. 116, 23; Barn he*n* oe*dd* | brynha*w*n iddaw, id. 215, 8; wo die Ausgaben zum Teil falsch lesen.

Indem wir nun in der Erklärung der Steigerungsformen fortfahren, so ist uns die Endung des indogermanischen Komparativs *jes, jos* (vgl. Brugmann 2, 125. 420) im irischen *iu, u,* später *e,* noch erkennbar; aber im Welschen sind nur spärliche Reste davon übrig geblieben. Nämlich siniu sine : hyn RB. 1, 163, hyyn LA. 4, 26 'senior' von sean : hen 'alt'; máá móo mó : moe BBC. 11 b 1, mwy 'maior' zu mór : mawr 'gross', 'viel'; sia : hwy 'serior' zu sír : hir 'lang'; óa : ieu 'junior' zu óg : ieuangc 'jung'; *m* laigiu lugha : llai : *c.* lê 'levior' zu beag : bach 'klein'; *m* leithiu leathne : lled Job 11, 9 Morgan, llet HM. 1, 231 zu leathan : llydan 'breit'; *w.* haws 'leichter' von sádh-ail 'behaglich, easy' : hawdd 'leicht' (wie feas : gwys 'scitum est' D. G. 22, 19. 119, 39 von finnaim : gwydd-; llas 'er wurde getötet' von lladd 'töten'). So würde man also von *teg* etwa (dem *hŷn* analog) ein **tŷg* gebildet haben.[1]) Da die Komparativform im Welschen dermassen geschwächt war, dass sie zum Ausdrucke ihrer Bedeutung kaum noch taugte, so hat die Sprache sie durch die nota augens *ach* verstärkt, ähnlich wie sie die Positive *isel, uchel* von den Komparativen *is, uwch* durch eine adjektivische Endung unterscheidet. Von dem vokalischen Ansatze musste natürlich die auslautende Media Media bleiben, also *TEGACH.* Der Umlaut des *w* im Positiv zu *y* in Komparative und Superlative (trwm, trymach, trymaf) ist der sonstigen Wirkung der Suffigierung gemäss.

---

[1]) Die Steigerung des Adjektivs 'gut' hat auch im Welschen ihre eigene Art. Man hat für das w. *gwell* 'besser' und *goreu* 'best' Stämme aufgestellt, die dem Gälischen fremd wären. Ich meine, man soll an Zeussens Gleichsetzung des w. *gwell* mit dem ir. *ferr, fearr* (GC.[1] 286) festhalten, da der Wechsel des *r* und des *l* im Celtischen nicht zu den Seltenheiten gehört. Man hat im Gälischen ol = or, ar 'inquit', im Albanogälischen aillis statt aithris 'sagen', cuilm statt cuirm 'Fest', searbhag neben sealbhag 'Ampfer' (Scott. Rev. 8, 356); ferner iolar : eryr 'Adler'; biolar biorar : berwr 'Kresse'; alaile araile : arall 'anderer'; saor 'frei' : hael 'edel' (wie maor : maer, saor : saer); síreadh : chwilio 'suchen'; féar : gwair 'Heu', gwellt 'Gras' u. a. m. Was den Superlativ *goreu* (auch *gworeu, goraf,* RC. 6, 31 f.) anbetrifft, so hat er, wie es scheint, gleiche Endung mit cynneu 'vormals', deheu (alt dehou) 'links'. Dieses *eu, ou* ist vermutlich das ir. *omh, amh* von iaromh 'postea', riamh 'antea', von denen Ebel sagt: 'videntur ad superlativi formam derivata e praepp. *iarn, ren*' (GC. 613). Demnach steht w. *gor-eu* für ir. *for-amh,* das vielleicht in der Bedeutung 'Trefflichkeit, Tüchtigkeit' in dem altertümlichen Ausdrucke *forom nglé* erhalten ist; indess findet sich neben jüngerem *forumh* auch einmal *foromm* (SR. 3225). Wie dem auch sei, so scheint es von foramh 'jagen' (WW. 566), foram-rioth (Lism. 2971), foram-les (WT. 1, 217) verschieden zu sein.

Selbst einige noch deutliche Komparative haben sich durch die Endung wieder gefestigt, wie hynach, mwyach : *arm.* muioh, lledach (llettach Job 11, 9. BC. 139). Die Vulgärsprache bildet indess solche Komparative vom Positiv aus, wie ieuangach (spr. *jengach*) = ieuanghach HM. 1, 66, hirach, islach, ähnlich den Elativen agosad, hawddad, hirad, uchlad — aber (nach der Analogie des Superlativs) hynach, isad (TPhS. 1882—84 p. 440). Im Cornischen ist das Suffix *ach* von *tecach tecah* bis zu *teca tecé* geschwächt worden, so dass sich die Form vom Superlativ oft nicht mehr unterscheiden lässt.

Der Ursprung der Endung *ach* ist nicht ohne weiteres erkennbar. Keinesfalls darf man eine Urform *-hach* annehmen, die J. Rhŷs, Welsh Philology p. 231, auf das falsche *teccach* gegründet hat. Die Endung *ach* findet sich in weiterm Sinne gebraucht: amgenach 'vielmehr', hayach 'beinahe', llessach 'besser' RB. 1, 11 von dem Substantive leas : lles 'Vorteil'. Auch scheint ihre sonstige Verwendung von der, die hier in Rede steht, nicht allzu weit abzuliegen. Mitunter drückt sie Geringschätzung oder doch die Andeutung einer Absonderlichkeit aus (RC. 2, 189): poblach 'Pöbel' G. O. 2, 120; dynionach 'elende Menschen' 1, 32; deiliach 'wertlose Blätter' BC. 144; swbach 'Knirps' ibid. 63. G.O. 1, 209 von sop : swp oder sôb D. G. 253, 43 'Haufe, Bündel'; bwbach 'Popanz', blythach 'aufgeblasene Person', ffollach 'kurzer dicker Mensch', buach 'Tölpel', celach 'Fant', um von einigen andern Bedeutungen der Endung (GC. 851) abzusehen. Ich darf wohl erwähnen, dass z. B. die semitische Sprache durch dieselbe grammatische Form sowohl den Komparativ als auch Farbe und körperliche Eigenschaft ausdrückt, wie arab. *akbar* 'grösser', *aswad* 'schwarz', *a'wag* 'krumm', *a'mā* 'blind'; das 'andere' ist auch im Deutschen ein Komparativ und 'ein älterer Mann' bezeichnet einen Mann in einem gewissen Alter. Im Grunde ist fracc : gwrach 'Weib, Vettel' (neben *frech : gwraig : *corn.* freg 'Frau') von fear : gwr 'Mann' keine andere Bildung; sie zeigt zugleich, dass dem welschen *ach* regelrecht das irische *acc, ac* entsprochen hat, das freilich wenig im Gebrauch gewesen ist (GC. 812). Es bleibt daher fraglich, ob, wie Siegfried vermutet (KB. 6, 10), in dem welschen *ach* des Komparativs ein irisches *ass* 'ex eo' zu finden sei.

Brugmann berührt die britannische Komparativbildung auf *ach* im Grundriss nicht, wie sie denn vielleicht als eine innerceltische Angelegenheit anzusehen ist. Wenn der lettische Kom-

parativ, z. B. *labb-ák-s* 'besser' von *lab-s* 'gut', den A. Bielenstein
(Die lettische Sprache 2, 60) mit den littauischen *did-oka-s* 'ziemlich gross' von *didi-s* 'gross' zusammenstellt (vgl. Grundr. 3, 411),
auf dem Suffixe beruht, dessen Form im Celtischen *ach* : *awc, og*
lautet, dann kann er mit dem Suffixe *acc* : *ach*, das den welschen
Komparativ bildet, nicht unmittelbar zusammenhängen. Indess
wird der Unterschied zwischen *ach* : *awc* und *acc* : *ach* nicht grösser
sein als etwa der zwischen lat. *civicus, mordicus* und *mordex,
audax, loquax* oder althochdeutsch *durstac, mahtig, steinig* und
steinoht, steinicht, die im engl. *stony* wieder in eins zusammenfielen (J. Grimm, Grammatik 3, 382). So ist es möglich, ja wahrscheinlich, dass *acc* : *ach* in Form und Bedeutung von *ach* : *awc*
differenziiert ist, um mich des Ausdruckes eines unvergessenen
Lehrers, Theodor Benfeys, zu bedienen.

In der Bildung des Superlativs scheinen die celtischen
Sprachen wiederum den italischen sehr nahe zu stehen. Einige
alte Formen beruhen auf dem indogerm. -ṃmo (lat. *min-imus*),
namentlich *m* moam máam : mwyaf 'grösst'; *m* síam : hwyaf :
aarm. hoiam (RC. 15, 94); óam : ieuaf 'jüngst'; *m* lugam lugimem :
lleiaf : *aarm.* leiam 'geringst'; *m* tressam : trechaf 'stärkst' (vgl.
lassar : llachar); *m* nessam : nesaf 'nächst', osc.-umbr. *nessimŏ.*
Dazu finden sich (entsprechend den Komparativen uachtar 'Ober-
teil' : uthr 'wunderbar'; ir. íochtar 'Unterteil'; *m* echtar : eithr
'extra') wenige Spuren der Form mit *t*, wie *echtam : eithaf :
aarm. héitham 'ex-timus'; *m* ointam aontumha : *arm.* intaūv
'einzeln' (Sprachsch. 47); ir. Sualtam n. pr. m. von sual-ach 'be-
wundrungswürdig', und vielleicht noch andere. Eine dritte Bildung ist die mit *s*, die im lat. *maximus*, pulcerrimus (aus *polcri-
sumus*, KZ. 33, 552), gall. uxellim (KB. 6, 12) vorliegt. Diese ist
im Britannischen die üblichste geworden und das älteste Zeugnis
dafür im Oxoniensis posterior ist *hinhám* (GC. 1063) aus *seni-sam*
von hen 'alt', eine wichtige Form, mag sie nun altwelsch oder
altcornisch sein. Wie in *hynhaf hynaf*, so tritt die Endung *haf* :
arm. *haff aff* : corn. *a* an den Komparativ auch in ieuhaf RB.
1, 193 (neben ieuangaf D. G. 154, 72); mwyhaf : c. moychaf : *arm.*
muyhaff; so dass sie hier thatsächlich auf *isam* zu beruhen
scheint. Ich vermute aber, dass das Indeclinabile *sam* oder
hám, haf vielmehr mit ἅμα, *sem-per*, ir. sam-ildánach 'einer der
viele Künste zumal hat' (RC. 12, 123), samhail : hafal 'similis'
etc., zu verbinden ist. In diesem Falle wäre das welsche *-haf*

eine Verstärkung des Komparativs. Das Neuwelsche hat den
Hauchlaut nirgends bewahrt, aber in der ältern Sprache erscheint
er, wie im Armorischen (GC. 299), nicht selten, z. B. in haelhaf
Skene 2, 177. 185; duhaf RB. 1, 232; glewhaf Skene 2, 192; goreuhaf
2, 195, oreuhaw BBC. 21 b 2, etc. Tritt diese Endung an die Media,
so kann aus *g-h, d-h, b-h* nur *cc, tt, pp* entstehen, also *TECKAF*
nach der Schreibweise der Alten, wofür teccaw BBC. 21 b 3 eine
Variante ist. Ähnlich bildet man von diwedd 'Ende' den Superlativ diwethaf 'letzt'. Die Wirkung des *h* reicht mitunter selbst
über eine Liquida hinweg, wie in rheitiaf von rhaid 'nötig';
hyttraf RB. 1, 255 (aber auch hytrach 'vielmehr') von hydyr
'kühn'; hackraf RB. 1, 232, hacraf von hagr 'hässlich' (corn.
hager, hacra, hacré); hyotlaf von hyawdl 'beredt'. So lebendig
ist noch das Gefühl für eine Form, von der im Gälischen, wie es
scheint, nicht einmal die Spur zu finden ist.

Was nun die ganz eigene Bildung des 'Gradus aequalis'
anbelangt, so hat Zimmer überzeugend nachgewiesen, dass ihr die
Bedeutung eines Substantivs zukomme. Es ist keine Frage, dass
das Nomen auf -*ed* (vormals -*et*) gelegentlich andern Ausdrücken
des Abstrakten ohne bemerkenswerten Unterschied parallel steht,
wie z. B. *duet* y vran a *gwynder* yr eiry a *chochter* y gwaet,
RB. 1, 211. In der Regel scheint allerdings in der Bildung eine
gewisse Steigerung des Begriffs zu liegen, wie: och Duw vyn
direittyet 'O Gott! mein grosses Unglück!' HM. 1, 34; gwiw oed
y Arthur *dahet* y gwely 'würdig war für Arthur die grosse
Trefflichkeit des Bettes' RB. 1, 174. Einige Verse Ab Gwilyms
werden das noch deutlicher erkennen lassen: Breuddwyd yw
ebrwydded oes! 'ein Traum ist die grosse Raschheit des Lebens!'
103, 35; Gan glywed *digrifed* tôn Y gog las ddigoeg leision
'beim Hören der grossen Lieblichkeit der Stimme des grauen
Kuckucks von gehaltvollen Tönen' 98, 13; Na cheisied, a'i *fawed*
fo, Hon eiddig ei hun iddo! 'es soll sie nicht, bei seinem grossen
Unwert, der Eifersüchtige für sich selbst begehren!' 89, 11, und
ähnlich 90, 6. 163, 43; *digon uched* y dringaist 'hoch genug bist
du gestiegen' 95, 23.

> Ac ni chanaf a'm tafod,
> Yn neutu glyn, ond dy glod,
> I'th ganmol, ferch urddolwaed,
> Dy wedd — dos! a dyddiau *daed!*

'Und ich werde mit meiner Zunge im Thale hier und dort nur

deinen Ruhm singen, dich zu preisen, o Maid von vornehmem Blut, deine Art — o komm, und wie schöne Tage werden wir haben!' 191, 45.

> Dy wên yw 'r pum' llawenydd,
> Dy gorph hardd a'm dug o'r ffydd!
> A'th *fwyned* fal nith Anna
> A'th liw yn deg a'th lun da;
> Dy *fwyned* dan do fanwallt,
> Dy *decced!* dyred hyd allt!
> Gwnawn wely fry yn y fron,
> Bedeiroes mewn bedw irion,
> Ar fatras o ddail glas glyn,
> A'i ridens o'r mân redyn,
> A chwrlid rh'om a churwlaw —
> Coed a ludd cawod o wlaw.

'Dein Lächeln ist die fünffache Freude,[1]) dein herrlicher Leib hat mich vom Glauben gebracht, und deine Holdseligkeit wie die einer Anverwandten der heiligen Anna, und deine hübschen Farben und deine stattliche Gestalt. Wie anmutig du unter deinem feinen Haar — Wie schön du bist! komm in den Wald! Lass uns uns lagern auf dem Hügel droben, vier Zeitalter lang im Birkengrün, auf einem Pfühl vom grünen Laub des Thales mit seinen Gardinen vom zarten Farn,[2]) mit einer Decke gegen den tröpfelnden Regen; das Schauer werden die Bäume abhalten' 118, 13 ff. — Wer die Zeilen des Dichters mit Bedacht liest, der merkt die Prägnanz, die in den Ausdrücken auf *-ed* liegt und in der Übersetzung angedeutet ist.

Dieser Elativ, wenn ich ihn so nennen darf, verbindet sich nun gern mit einigen Präpositionen, namentlich *gan* 'bei' (das den folgenden Anlaut leniert), wie: gan *decced* yr ha' 'bei der grossen Schönheit des Sommers' D. G. p. V; gan *daered* y gwr durawl 'bei der grossen Strenge des stählernen Mannes' 64, 38;

---

[1]) Diesen Vers hat sich ein späterer Barde, Gwilym ab Ieuan Hen, angeeignet, der seinen Gönner anredet:

> Dy wên yw 'r pum' llawenydd,
> Dy galon yw ffynnon ffydd.

Gorchestion Beirdd Cymru 1864 p. 156. Es liegt vielleicht eine Anspielung an die Geschichte Josephs darin, der seinen Bruder Benjamin durch ein fünffaches Gastgeschenk vor den andern auszeichnete: 'Majorque pars venit Benjamin, ita ut quinque partibus excederet', Genesis 43, 34.

[2]) Dieser Vers ist nach der Lesart im Report on manuscripts in the Welsh language 1, 84 gegeben.

gan *gyflymed* yr oeddynt yn hedeg 'bei der grossen Geschwindig-
keit, (womit) sie flogen' Bardd Cwsc 7; gan *ddaed* ganddynt
dwysoges stryd arall 'bei ihrem Gefallen an der Fürstin einer
andern Strasse' 13. 14; gan *serthed* a *llithricced* ydoedd 'bei der
grossen Steilheit und Schlüpfrigkeit, (wovon) er (der Weg) war,'
88; gan *dywylled* a *drysed* yw 'r wlad a maint sy o'r elltydd
heirn tanllyd ar y fford 'bei der Finsternis und Verworrenheit,
(wovon) das Land ist, und bei der Grösse der feurigen Eisen-
klippen, die auf dem Wege sind' 117; A Duw, gan *hyfryted* oedd,
Dywedai mai da ydoedd 'Und Gott sagte, da er zufrieden war,
dass es gut wäre' G. O. 1, 74; — nach *er* 'für, trotz' : er *amled*
ei brenhinoedd 'trotz der grossen Menge ihrer Könige' (nicht
amlder oder amledd) BC. 16; er *daed* y rhain oll 'trotz der Vor-
trefflichkeit dieser aller' 145; er maint, er *cryfed* ac er *dichlined*
yw 'r mawr hwn, etto mae un sy fwy nac ynteu 'trotz der Bedeutung, der grossen Stärke und des grossen Eifers, (wovon)
dieser Grosse ist, giebt es doch einen, der noch grösser ist als
er' 17; er *gwyched* yr olwg arnynt nid yw ond ffug 'trotz des
trefflichen Aussehens, (das) sie haben, ist's doch nur Trug' 40;
er eu *perycled* 'trotz ihrer grossen Gefährlichkeit' 73; er *hawsed*
dyfod i wared yma, etto nesa i amhossibl yw myned yn ôl 'trotz
der Leichtigkeit hier hinabzukommen, ist es doch fast unmöglich,
zurückzugehen' 117; er *cywreinied* gwniadyddes a *glewed* yw
'trotz der grossen Geschicklichkeit als Nähterin und der grossen
Kühnheit, (die in ihr) ist' 144; Nid oes y' Ngwynedd heno, Er ei
galled, a'i gallo 'Nicht ist heute abend in Nordwales, wie klug
er sei, einer der das vermöchte' D. G. 185, 27; Er *ised* oedd yr
Iesu, O *inged* yw Angau du! 'Trotz der Tiefe, zu der Jesus
hinabstieg, wie zwingend ist noch der Tod der arge!' G. O. 1, 206,
d. h. (der Herausgeber versteht es nicht richtig) der Heiland
konnte trotz der Niedrigkeit seiner Leiden die Macht des Todes
nicht brechen; — nach *rhag* 'vor, wegen' : rac y *drymhet* ef y
syrthyawd 'vor seiner grossen Schwere fiel er hin' HM. 1, 60;
rhag ei *chyfynged* 'vor ihrer grossen Enge' D. G. 161, 38. 150, 28
etc.; gelegentlich auch nach andern Präpositionen, wie y *rwng*
RB, 1, 281. Es zeigt sich also, dass die Form zwar das Pronomen possessivum und einen abhängigen Genitiv, aber keinen
Artikel verträgt, und es entgeht nicht, wie die Präpositionen
gan und *er* mit dem Nomen auf *-ed* syntaktisch ineinander
laufen, gleichsam zu einer Konjunktion werden, die die relativische

Anknüpfung entbehrlich macht. Llygad dichwant nis gwel er
amlycced y peth 'das Auge eines Gleichgültigen sieht nicht trotz
der Deutlichkeit des Gegenstandes' IM. 157, und: er *amlycced* y bo
'wie deutlich er auch sei' ibid., und noch kürzer in der alten
Sprache: yr *drycket* bo 'so schlecht er auch ist' HM. 1, 31; vgl.
KZ. 34, 188. Diese zusammengesetzten Ausdrücke sind in derselben Weise konjunktional wie *o achos* oder *o herwydd* 'aus dem
Grunde dass, weil' (GC. 734) oder *o eisiau* 'mangels, weil nicht',
deren *o* auch ausgelassen werden kann. Ähnlich ist daher wohl
die folgende Stelle zu deuten: *kadarnet* (statt gan gadarnet?) y
dywedy di dy vot 'bei der Stärke, (wovon) du bist, wie du sagst'
RB. 1, 221.

Der bekannteste, namentlich aus der mittelalterlichen Litteratur reichlich belegte Gebrauch der Form auf *-ed* (*-et*) ist der
mit vorgesetztem *cyn* oder seltener *cyf* oder *cy* 'mit, gleich' (ir.
comh) und nachfolgendem *a* 'und, als wie', z. B. comháluinn agus
tu : kyndecket a thi RB. 1, 221, cyn *decced* a thi D. G. 222, 4 'von
gleich grosser Schönheit', 'so schön wie du'; cyn *farwed* a chi
'so tot wie ein Hund' D. G. 218, 34; cyn *dynned* a rhisg 'so dicht
wie Borke' 74, 31; cyn *laned* a'r aur 'so rein wie das Gold'
BC. 123 (cf. 36. 45. 95. 98. 123 etc.).

> Cyn *rheitied* i mi brydu
> Ag i tithau bregethu;
> A chyn *iawned* i mi glera
> Ag i tithau gardota.

'Mir ist so nötig zu dichten als dir zu predigen, und mir so
billig ein fahrender Sänger zu sein als dir zu betteln' D. G.
149, 55. Nach dem Präfix *cyn, cyf, cy* ist die Lenierung des
folgenden Anlauts geboten; nur bei *rh* (mitunter auch bei *ll*)
scheint sie zu unterbleiben. Das Verglichene ist mitunter zu
ergänzen, wie in: cyn *erwined* 'so schrecklich' D. G. 65, 28; am
fatter cyn *lleied* 'wegen einer so geringfügigen Sache' BC. 93.
Eine Ergänzung 'wie der, wie die, wie das' ergiebt sich in solchem
Falle von selbst.

Es wird aber in dieser Formel nicht nur das Verglichene
ausgelassen, sondern auch die Partikel der Gleichheit *cyn, cyf, cy*.
Sie fällt aus, aber hinterlässt ihre Spur in der Lenierung des
Anlauts des Elativs, den sie regierte. Ni chair y loyw grair o
gred, Duw ni luniodd dyn *laned*! 'Es giebt kein glänzenderes
Kleinod der Christenheit, Gott hat keinen Menschen so rein ge-

bildet!' D.G. 256, 14. Und diese Unterdrückung des *cyn* ist das
gewöhnliche im Ausrufe, wie beim Bardd Cwsc: O *odidocced* oedd
ei flâs a'i liw! 'O so vortrefflich' oder 'o wie vortrefflich waren
sein Geschmack und seine Farbe!' 87; Oh! *barotted* yr oedd yr
hen sarph yn eu hatteb hwytheu 'o wie schlagfertig die alte
Schlange ihnen antwortete!' 123; O *fonddigeiddied* y tyngant i
gael eu coelio ... o *goegced* yr edrychant 'o wie vornehm sie
schwören um Glauben zu finden, o wie leer sie blicken!' 98; och
drymmed genni gip o'i atco! 'ach! wie schwer ist mir eine augen-
blickliche Erinnerung daran!' 152; och fyth *erwined* oedd weled
cêg Annwn! 'ach! wie ewig schrecklich war's den Schlund der
Unterwelt zu sehen!' 147. Und bei David ab Gwilym: Och fi!
ddaed awch ei fin! 'Weh mir! wie gut die Schärfe seiner Spitze
war!' 236, 44; O *lawened* gweled gwydd! 'O wie freut's den Wald
zu sehen!' 198, 29; Doe ddifiau, cyn dechreu dydd, *Lawned* fum
o lawenydd! 'Gestern Donnerstags vor Tagesanbruch, wie war
ich von Freude voll!' 54, 9; Gwae ni, hil eiddil Addaf, Fordwy
'r hin, *fyrred* yr hâf! 'Weh uns, dem armen Geschlecht Adams! o
stürmisches Wetter, wie kurz ist der Sommer!' 201, 1; Nid hawdd
godech na llechu, A *glewed* yw y gwlaw du! ·Nicht leicht ist's
unterzuschlüpfen und sich zu verkriechen, und wie heftig ist der
abscheuliche Regen!' 135, 4; Gwae fardd oferddysg edlym! *Afrwy-
dded* fu 'r dynged im! 'Weh dem witzigen Barden von eitler
Gelehrsamkeit, wie unglücklich war das Schicksal mir!' 253, 1;
Post oer, *anhapused* oedd Rhodio 'n y man yr ydoedd 'Ein kalter
Posten, wie unglücklich war's an dem Orte zu spazieren, wo sie
war!' 253, 35; und endlich sagt er vom Winde:

> Uthr wyd, mor aruthr i'th roed
> O bantri wybr, heb untroed,
> A *buaned* y rhedy
> Yr awr hon dros y fron fry!

'Ein Wunder bist du, wie wunderbar du losgelassen aus dem
Vorratshause der Luft, ohne Fuss, und wie geschwind du jetzund
droben über den Hügel dahinläufst!' 69, 5.

Aber diese Ellipse ist keineswegs auf den Ausruf der direkten
Rede beschränkt, sondern wird mit derselben Freiheit im ab-
hängigen Satze angewandt. Beispiele: Nebydded *flined* fy nhro,
Wb o'r hin o'r wybr heno! 'Wissen soll sie, wie kläglich meine
Lage — pfui über das Wetter in der Luft diese Nacht!' D.G.
53, 17; Diommedd y'm gommeddwyd, Diriaid im' *ddiweiried* wyd!

'Ohne Rückhalt wurde ich zurückgewiesen; unselig mir, wie ehr-
bar du bist!' 215, 25; tan syn-fyfyrio *decced* a *hawddgared* oedd
y gwledydd pell a *gwyched* oedd gael arnynt lawn olwg 'über-
denkend, wie schön und lieblich die fernen Länder wären und
wie hübsch es wäre einen Überblick über sie zu erhalten' BC. 5;
myfyrio 'r oeddwn i ar ryw ymddiddanion am fyrdra hoedl dyn
a *siccred* yw i bawb farw ac *ansiccred* yr amser 'ich dachte an
einige Gespräche über die Kürze des menschlichen Lebens und
wie sicher jedem zu sterben und wie unsicher die Zeit ist' 54;
y rhyfeddwn *uched, gryfed* a *hardded, laned* a *hawddgared* oedd
pob rhan ohoni 'ich wunderte mich, wie hoch, stark und schön,
rein und lieblich jeder Teil des Baues war' 45; basei rhyfeddach
gennit *ddeheued* yr oedd y Fall fawr 'du hättest dich noch mehr
gewundert, wie geschickt der grosse Böse war' 123; ähnlich auch
p. 28. 49. 75. 96. 108. 122. 123, etc. etc.

Der Ausdruck des Wie liegt demnach im lenierten Anlaut
des Nomens auf -*ed*, wie denn die Lenierung des Anlauts im
Welschen ein wichtiges Mittel bildet, die Unzulänglichkeit der
Wortbeugung syntaktisch auszugleichen. Ganz so wie *gan* und
er mit folgendem Elativ zur Konjunktion werden, ebenso *cyn* in
dieser Verbindung, obschon nur eine leichte Mutation noch seine
Stelle bezeichnet. Man könnte *byrred yr haf* nur als 'die Kürze
des Sommers' verstehen, aber *fyrred yr haf* heisst: 'wie kurz ist
der Sommer!' oder 'wie kurz der Sommer ist!' Man könnte versucht werden, dieses *fyrred* als Vocativus zu deuten: 'O die
Kürze des Sommers', aber im abhängigen Satze würde diese Erklärung versagen. Man könnte daran denken, ob etwa das
Fragewort *pa* vor dem lenierten Elative unterdrückt sei, wie es
in *pa faint, pa leied* vorkommt (Ernault, Glossaire p. 542). Aber
ein solches *pa* würde kaum so regelmässig fehlen und *beth?* 'was?'
(ital. cosa?) steht zu vereinzelt da, auch würde diese Annahme
so manches, was ich angeführt habe, unerklärt lassen. Es versteht sich von selbst, dass die Lenierung des Elativs nur statt-
findet, wo sie möglich und grammatisch zulässig ist; so wird sie
durch *a* 'und', wie unsere Beispiele zeigen, aufgehoben. Es
kommt auch vor, dass ein Dichter sie dem Cynghanedd zu liebe
vernachlässigt, weil die Bedeutung der Form ohnehin Wurzel
gefasst hat. So sagt Siôn Tudur (übrigens auch sonst nicht ganz
korrekt):

Bywyd tawdd yw 'r byd diddim,
Byrred yw! heb barhau dim.

11*

'Ein zerfliessendes Leben ist die nichtige Welt. Wie kurz ist's, ohne irgend welche Dauer!' E. Jones, Welsh Bards 1, 50.

Nun ist es verwunderlich, dass man dem Nomen auf -ed nach der einen Art seiner Verwendung den Namen einer 'forma aequalitatis' beilegen konnte. Wenn man bedenkt, dass es überhaupt eine Steigerung des abstrakten Begriffs ausdrückt und dass es sich ebenso durch *gan* und *er* als durch *cyn* ergänzt, dann möchte ein allgemeinerer Name wie Elativ (der in der Grammatik schon üblich ist) seinem Wesen besser entsprechen.

Nicht in den Komplementen liegt die Grundbedeutung der Form, sondern in dem -ed (vormals -et). Zimmer leitet diese Endung von einem altceltischen *etā*, das dem sanskritischen *átā* entsprechen würde (KZ. 34, 154); aber es sind Bedenken gegen die Annahme laut geworden, namentlich von Loth (RC. 18, 398), und, wie es scheint, sind sie begründet. Die alte Form des Elativs lautet *TECKET*, und wenn wir den Superlativ *teckaf* aus *teg-haf* vergleichen, dann ist es mehr als wahrscheinlich, dass sie aus *teg-het* (später *teg-hed*) entstanden ist. Das *h* wird nicht selten noch geschrieben, wie in *duhet* RB. 1, 214, *gwynnhet* 1, 149, *kyvawhet* ib., u.s.w., und äusserst selten schwanken die Texte in der Provectio der auslautenden Media vor -et (-ed), wie in *kynvreisget* RB. 1, 21 neben *kynvreiscet* 1, 69. Entsprechende Elative hat das Armorische: *goazhet* 'wie schlecht', *guelhet* 'wie gut', *caezrhet cazrhet* 'wie schön', und im Vannetais *caërraet*, *caeret*, ferner *calettet* 'wie hart', *peurraet* 'combien pauvre' (Ernault, Glossaire p. 268); dazu kommen Formen auf -at, -ad, die auch das Vulgärwelsche liefert. Mit den Lehnwörtern *ciwed* civitas, *caethiwed* captivitas, *syched* siccitas (D. G. 70, 55) u. a. hat die Bildung schwerlich etwas zu thun. Was könnte das welsche *het*, *hed* nach den Erfordernissen der Form und der Bedeutung wohl anderes sein als das irische *sáith*, *sáth* 'Genüge, Fülle'? und dieses ist das lat. *satis*, *sat* 'genug'. Ebenso ist das irische *saithe* 'Schar, Schwarm' im Welschen *haid*, wie in: *heit wenyn* 'ein Bienenschwarm' LA. 105; davon lautet der Plural *heidiau* D. G. 162, 16. 18, und auch ein Verb *heidio* 'schwärmen' D. G. 48, 29. 87, 32 ist bekannt. Irre ich nicht, so steht *tecced, tecket* für ein altirisches *tich-shaith* und für ein noch älteres *tico-sati* und heisst eigentlich 'eine Fülle vom Schönen, des Schönen genug, grosse Schönheit'.

So sehen wir an die Stelle der Derivation einer ältern

Periode die Komposition treten. Dessen ist aber der Elativ nicht
das einzige Zeugnis in der welschen Sprache. In ihrer Accidenz
hat sie, als liege das Zeitalter der Suffixe hinter ihr, eine Reihe
von Zusammensetzungen, denen das Irische nur wenig an die Seite
zu stellen hat. Mit Leichtigkeit bildet sie Komposita wie dryg-
arfer, drygfoes, drygfyd, drygnaws, drygwaith etc. und verleiht
ihnen die allgemeine Bedeutung von drygedd. Die Bildungen
auf -fa (von magh 'Feld' : ma 'Ort'), auf -wedd (von *m* -fad :
gwedd 'Art und Weise') und auf -radh -redh : *rwydd,* gleichfalls von abstrakter Bedeutung, hat schon Zeuss p. 856. 890 verzeichnet. Es ist auch wohl wenig zweifelhaft, dass das welsche
Suffix -red, wie in gweithret LA. 106, 10, nw. gweithred, das irische
m ret, *n* rud 'Sache' ist, und dass das Suffix tra, wie in uchdra
'Höhe', oerdra 'Kälte', eondra 'Kühnheit', cyfleustra 'Gelegenheit',
von dem cornisch - armorischen *tra* 'Sache' nicht verschieden ist.

Eine weitere Bildung der Art liegt in den Abstrakten auf
-ter vor, wie trymder 'Schwere', oerder 'Kälte', cryfdwr 'Stärke',
mw. praffter 'Kraft' (GC. 829). Ist dieses w. *twr, ter* nicht dasselbe wie das irische *tur, tor* 'Masse, Wucht'? *Tor gach tromm,*
sagt Cormac; *tor* .i. imat, O'Davoren; *tura* .i. iomad, O'Clery. So
entspricht w. *trymder* buchstäblich dem ir. *tromthur.* Im Saltair
na rann heisst es: co tuilib tromthúr 906, tolaib tromthúr 5266
'mit Fluten, eine schwere Wucht' oder 'von schwerer Wucht',
und in einem anderen alten Gedichte: iarthur tromthoraib 'der
Westen mit schweren Massen', WT. p. 69.

Ein Abstraktum wie purdeb 'Reinheit' weist ebenso wie
ardeb 'Bild' auf ein Nomen *teb* (vgl. GC. 838) und dieses ist vermutlich das ir. *toich* 'natürliches Recht', 'was angeboren ist und
eignet', .i. duthaigh, sagt O'Clery, cf. Lismore lives 749; is toich
dom 'es ist mir natürlich', 'es kommt mir zu' findet sich in den
alten Glossen.

Statt des welschen porfa 'Weideplatz' heisst es auch porfel
und neben oerfa 'ein kalter Ort' giebt es auch oerfel 'Kälte',
wie: y gwrês a'r oerfel 'die Hitze und die Kälte' BC. 119, ein
häufiges Wort.[1]) Der Bardd Cwsc hat auch poethfel 'Hitze' in:

---

[1]) Vgl. z. B. RB. 1, 136; LA. 52, 5. 152, 18; MA. 27 a; Ceinion 2, 109 b;
D. G. 58, 30. 70, 73. 116, 41. 254, 35. Das Wort kommt namentlich im Fluche
vor: Oerfel uwch ben ei wely! A phoeth fo dy feistr o ffy! 'Kälte über seinem
Lager! und heiss werde deinem Herrn, wofern er flieht!' D. G. 134, 17, und:
Oerfel iddi! 'Ungemach treffe sie!' I. G. 48, 8; D. G. 38, 45. 44, 61. 65, 41. 73, 35.

taflod fawr o boethfel uwch ben uffern 'ein grosser Hitzboden über der Hölle' p. 39, und: i rostio fel poethfel 'zu rösten wie ein Braten' p. 91. Der letzte Herausgeber bringt poethfel gewiss nicht richtig mit dem celtischen *bel* 'Feuer' (Sprsch. 163) und dann selbst mit dem w. *ufel* 'Feuer' (= mir. óibel, nir. aibhle, manx aile) zusammen. Vielmehr enthält arfel 'zeichnen' den gleichen Stamm. Das welsche *-fel, bel* ist unweigerlich das irische *bale, baile* 'Ort, Stätte', neben dem ein Femininum besteht: *bail* 'die Art und Weise' (Keating, Trí biorghaoithe s. v.), und w. *fel* 'wie' und *y felly* 'so', gleichsam ir. an bhail-se, gehören zu derselben Verwandtschaft.

114, 13. 117, 61. 133, 33. 253, 47. 257 a 30. Davon abgeleitet ist oerfelog, Llwyd, Archaeol. brit. p. 61.

Berlin.   L. CHR. STERN.

DIE VISIONEN DES BARDD CWSC.

Die Visionen von Ellis Wynne sind unlängst in 23. Auflage erschienen.[1] Ein Buch, das so oft gedruckt und zweimal aus dem Welschen ins Englische übersetzt worden ist, wird seinen Wert haben und uns rechtfertigen, wenn wir seiner Stellung in der Litteratur sowohl wie seiner Sprache einige Blätter dieser Zeitschrift widmen.

Ellis Wynne, 1671 in Glas-Ynys geboren und 1734 als Pfarrer in Llanfair bei Harlech in Merionethshire gestorben, veröffentlichte 1701 eine welsche Übersetzung von Jer. Tailors 'Rule and exercises of holy living' und 1703 ohne seinen Namen 'Gweledigaetheu y Bardd Cwsc'. *Y Bardd Cwsc* ist der angebliche Dichtername eines der *Cynfeirdd* oder Urbarden, den der Verfasser gewisser Prophezeiungen im 16. Jahrhundert annahm (vgl. J. G. Evans, Report on manuscripts in the Welsh language 1, 108. 111), und Ellis Wynne eignete ihn sich als Pseudonym für ein Werk an, das für einen Geistlichen stellenweise zu weltlich war. Der Ausdruck wird daher wohl nicht ganz deutlich mit 'schlafender' und jedesfalls unrichtig mit 'eingeschlafener Barde' wiedergegeben; denn *cwsc* scheint nicht den Zustand oder die Thätigkeit (*y bardd y' nghwsc* oder *yn cyscu*), sondern die Eigenschaft oder die Gewohnheit zu bedeuten, und nach der Analogie von *diod gwsc* 'Schlaftrunk' wäre, in unserer Sprache wenigstens, 'Schlafbarde' vielleicht zutreffender.

In drei Visionen sieht der Dichter erst den Lauf der Welt, dann die Herrschaft des Todes und endlich die Schrecken der

[1] Gweledigaetheu y Bardd Cwsc gan Ellis Wynne dan olygiaeth J. Morris Jones. Bangor, Jarvis & Foster, 1898. LXXVI + 207 pp. 8°.

Hölle. Das Werk ist eine Nachahmung der Sueños des Don Francisco de Quevedo Villegas oder vielmehr der englischen Bearbeitung davon. Die 'Träume' des spanischen Lucian (ich ergänze ein wenig die Auskunft, die uns Charles Ashton in seiner schätzbaren Hanes llenyddiaeth Gymreig p. 112 darüber giebt) wurden 1608—27 verfasst und ihre erste Gesamtausgabe erschien 1627. Don Francisco ist fein, witzig, gelehrt, fanatisch und ganz ein Spanier. Schon die erste Übertragung durch den Franzosen Sieur de la Geneste, die 1633 erschien, hat an seinen Satiren ziemlich viel geändert. Auf dieser schwächlichen französischen Fassung, die auch Moscherosch zum Philander anregte, beruht die englische Übersetzung des Polygraphen Sir Roger L'Estrange von 1667, und nur auf der, wie man sogleich erkennt, wenn man sie gegen das Original hält. Der englische Bearbeiter hatte die Visionen auch in der Sache, d. h. vom Römischen ins Protestantische, zu übertragen und den Anschauungen seiner Landsleute anzupassen. So sind denn Ellis Wynnes Gesichte in ihrer Tendenz das gerade Gegenteil des Originals geworden, indem sie die Rolle des 'maldito Lutero' dem Papste zuweisen.

Die 'Träume' Quevedos, der die Anregung durch einen Vorgänger anerkennt, indem er sagt: 'habiendo cerrado los ojos con el libro de Dante', sind nicht ursprünglich als ein Einheitliches gedacht; und der welsche Dichter drängte die sieben Visionen des Originals in drei zusammen, und diese wollte er als einen ersten Teil angesehen haben, denn die Freuden des Paradieses (kein Gegenstand des spanischen Satirikers) hatte er sich für einen zweiten Teil aufgespart, auf den er p. 123 selbst verweist, der aber nie erschienen ist. Im Einzelnen hat er manche Züge und Ausdrücke seinem englischen Vorbilde entlehnt, manche Stellen sogar wörtlich übersetzt, anderes hat er aus Miltons Verlorenem Paradiese herübergenommen, und auch Bunyans Allegorieen sind von Einfluss gewesen, aber gleichwohl hat er noch viel Eigenes an dem Werke. Der Herausgeber verteidigt (p. XXIV) das Verfahren des welschen Dichters gegen den Vorwurf des Plagiats, indem er sich namentlich auf Goethe beruft. Dessen Ausspruch lautet in Eckermanns Gesprächen 1, 151: 'Und überall was können wir denn unser Eigenes nennen als die Energie, die Kraft, das Wollen? Wenn ich sagen könnte, was ich alles grossen Vorgängern und Mitlebenden schuldig geworden bin, so bliebe nicht viel übrig'. Aber hören wir, was der Schlafbarde von seinen Gesichten zu erzählen weiss.

An einem Sommernachmittage verweilt er auf einem Berge seiner welschen Heimat und verfällt, in Gedanken über die grossartige Fernsicht versunken, in einen festen Schlaf. Aber seine Seele bleibt wach. Da gewahrt er einen Spielplatz, auf dem eine Schar von Wichtelmännern in blauen Röcken und mit roten Hüten einen Tanz aufführt. Er hält sie zunächst für Zigeuner. Als er sie aber anspricht, heben sie ihn unversehens auf ihre Schultern und tragen ihn über Land und Meer in ein Luftschloss, das von einem grossen Graben umgeben ist. Er erkennt nun Elbe von dem 'guten Volke' (*tylwyth teg*), Kinder der Unterwelt (*plant Annwfn*), in den Gestalten und macht sich auf Schlimmes gefasst. Während sie aber noch beraten, was mit ihm zu thun sei, erscheint ein Engel, der sie verscheucht und sich bereit erklärt, dem Dichter den Lauf der Welt, so wie er es sich gewünscht hatte, aus einem erhabenen Standpunkte zu zeigen.

Nun schaut der Barde eine grosse Stadt, die drei lange Strassen nach Norden zu und eine kleinere Querstrasse in östlicher Richtung durchschneiden. Der Engel belehrt ihn, dass es die Stadt Belials ist, der in seinem 'Castell hudol' sitzt, und dass in den zu den drei Strassen gehörigen Türmen die drei bestrickenden Töchter Belials hausen und, jede in ihrem Gebiete, herrschen. Sie heissen Hoffart, Vergnügungssucht und Gewinnsucht, und die Stadt ist die 'Stadt des Verderbens' (*Dinas ddihenydd*). Höher gelegen ist die Stadt des Königs Immanuel, der häufig Boten in die Stadt Belials schickt um deren Bewohner zu sich zu ziehen und manchen eine Salbe für ihre Augen darreichen lässt, den Glauben.

Indem der Barde nun mit dem Engel in die Strasse der Hoffart hinabsteigt, sieht er zuerst verfallene, nur noch von Eule, Krähe und Elster bewohnte Schlösser, deren Besitzer, die Einfachheit der heimatlichen Sitte verachtend, sich nach England oder Frankreich gewandt haben; dann schöne Häuser mit Fürsten, Edelleuten und Damen; hier bemerkt er neben der Zierdame und der Koketten auch die Schlumpe, die es ihnen gleichthun möchte und wie ein Pfau aufgeputzt einhergeht; weiter neben dem Alderman, der sich vor Schmer und Gicht kaum bewegen kann, aber darauf hält bei Titeln und Würden gebührend angeredet zu werden, auch den jungen Streber, der den Leuten nach dem Munde redet, um das Ziel seines Ehrgeizes zu erreichen. Es zeigt sich auch das päpstliche Rom und gegenüber der Palast des Türken und in der Nähe das Schloss Ludwigs XIV. Die beiden Herrscher umwerben die älteste Tochter Belials vor andern, während die Spanier, Holländer und Juden der Gewinnsucht und die Engländer und die Heiden der Vergnügungssucht den Hof machen; aber der Papst möchte sie alle drei für sich in Besitz nehmen. Alle finden sich in der Absicht zusammen die Stadt Immanuels zu zerstören. Einige sieht man den Turm der Hoffart bestürmen, der eine Vorratskammer der Eitelkeit ist.

In der Strasse der Gewinnsucht ist die Geschäftswelt vertreten, namentlich auch die grossen und kleinen Diebe, denen gehörig der Text gelesen wird. Weber, Schmiede, Müller und die nass und trocken messen, sind hier zu finden. Man will einen Schatzmeister für den Turm der Fürstin wählen,

und Verwalter, Geldmänner, Sachwalter, Kaufleute drängen sich zu dem
Posten.

In der dritten Strasse sieht man die Fürstin der Vergnügungssucht,
mit Wein in der einen, mit Fiedel und Harfe in der andern Hand. 'Da sind
schöne Häuser mit sehr gefälligen Anlagen, volle Obstgärten, schattige Haine,
für heimliche Zusammenkünfte jeder Art geeignet oder um darin Vögel und
hier und dort ein weisses Kaninchen zu fangen, zierliche klare Bäche zum
Fischen, prächtige weite Felder, passend darin den Hasen und den Fuchs zu
jagen. Längs der Strasse sieht man Puppenspiele, Zauberkünste, allerlei
Mummenschanz, jede Art wollüstiger Musik für Stimme und Saite, Balladen-
singen und sonstige Ergötzung. Schöne Jünglinge und Mädchen jedes Standes
singen und tanzen, und viele von der Hoffartstrasse kommen dahin um sich
preisen und verehren zu lassen' (p. 23). Da sieht man sie in den Häusern
auf seidenen Lotterbetten der Lust fröhnend, an Spieltischen schwörend und
fluchend, würfelnd und Karten mischend, bei Schmausereien und Trinkgelagen
und in Tabaksqualm gehüllt. Da ist auch eine lärmende Gesellschaft von
fünf Handwerkern, einem Priester und einem Barden, die unter zerbrochenen
Flaschen und Thonpfeifen über ihre Tüchtigkeit in der Schwelgerei mit
einander streiten, und der Barde erhebt zum Schluss seine Stimme:

'Wo sind euch noch im weiten Land
So durst'ge sieben Mann bekannt?
Die Besten sind beim braunen Bier
Das Pfäfflein und der Barde hier.'

Der Dichter wendet sich von diesen betrunkenen Schweinen ab und sieht
weiter, wie Cupido mit seinen giftigen Pfeilen die Triebe weckt, und
beobachtet das Getändel der Verliebten (bei ihnen spielen auch Tränke mit
Fingernägelabschnitten eine Rolle) und die Stätten der Unzucht.

Am Ende der drei Strassen gelangt der Dichter zum Schlosse der vierten
Tochter Belials, der Heuchelei, in deren Kunst sich Männlein und Weiblein
eifrig unterweisen lassen. Alsbald beobachtet er das Gebaren einer Witwe im
Leichenzuge ihres Gatten und eine Hochzeitsgesellschaft, in der einer den
andern hintergeht. Weiter zeigen sich der Tempel des Unglaubens und des
Aberglaubens, eine Moschee, eine Synagoge und eine römisch-katholische
Kirche, in der eine Gattenmörderin für Geld und eine Kindsmörderin für
Zärtlichkeit von dem Pater Vergebung ihrer Sünde erlangt und wo zur sinnlichen
Darstellung des Überirdischen schnöder Betrug geübt wird. Nach dem Gottes-
dienste der Quakers und Dissenters erscheinen auch die englische und die
welsche Kirche. 'Da sahen wir einige wispern und flüstern, einige lachen,
einige nach hübschen Mädchen schielen; andere musterten die Kleidung des
Nachbars vom Scheitel bis zur Sohle, andere stiessen und keiften um den
Vortritt, andere schliefen und nur wenige waren bei ihrer Andacht, aber
auch von diesen einige heuchelnd' (p. 36). Auch die Art und Weise, wie die
Leute zum Tische des Herrn treten, wird der Kritik unterzogen.

Nun suchen manche den Weg zur Stadt Immanuels, aber sie werden
darob verhöhnt und belästigt. Nur einer lässt sich in seinem Entschlusse
nicht irre machen: 'Friede und Zufriedenheit sind des Menschen Glück, aber
in eurer Stadt ist davon nichts zu finden. Denn wer ist mit seinem Zustande

zufrieden? Höher, höher will jeder in der Strasse der Hoffart; gebt, gebt mehr! schreit jeder in der Strasse der Gewinnsucht; wie süss, noch einmal! ruft jeder in der Strasse des Vergnügens. Und wo ist Friede? wer hat ihn gefunden? Wer vornehm ist, den töten fast die Schmeichelei und der Neid; wer arm ist, den lasst jeden treten und verachten. Wenn du in die Höhe kommen willst, so sei bedacht zu intrikieren; wenn du Ehre willst, so sei ein Ruhmrediger und Prahler. Willst du fromm sein, Kirche und Altar besuchen, so wirst du ein Heuchler genannt; wenn du es nicht thust, bist du ein Antichrist und ein Ketzer. Wenn du fröhlich bist, so heisst du ein Spötter; wenn still, ein giftiger Hund. Wenn du Redlichkeit übst, so bist du nur ein Narr, der zu nichts taugt; wenn du gut gekleidet bist, so bist du stolz; wenn nicht, ein Schwein. Wenn du in deiner Rede sanft bist, so bist du falsch und ein Schelm, der schwer zu durchschauen ist; wenn grob, ein frecher, unleidlicher Teufel' (p. 37 f.).

Nun langen sie beim Thore des Lebens an, dem Eingange zur Stadt Immanuels. Da sehen sie die zehn Gebote angeschrieben und darüber: 'Du sollst Gott von ganzem Herzen lieben', 'Liebe deinen Nächsten wie dich selbst' und 'Liebt nicht die Welt und was in der Welt ist'. Ein Geiziger, der das liest, kann das harte Wort nicht hinunterbringen; einen Verleumder schreckt das achte Gebot, und als die Ärzte lesen 'Du sollst nicht töten', machen sie Kehrt. So mancher hat keinen Zutritt zu dem bewachten Thore, weil er sich von dem, was ihm lieb ist, nicht trennen kann; und wer hinein will, muss sich zuvor tüchtig an der Quelle der Busse waschen. Aber wie ruhig und friedlich geht es in der Stadt Immanuels zu! Hier befindet sich die eigentliche katholische Kirche, namentlich die Kirche Englands, über der die Königin Anna thront, mit dem Schwerte der Gerechtigkeit und dem des Geistes, vor sich das englische Landesgesetz und die Bibel. Hier hat der Papist mit den Traktaten der Väter und den Konzilien der Kirche keinen Zutritt, noch auch der Quaker, der mit dem Hute auf dem Kopfe einzudringen sucht.[1]

Plötzlich verfinstert sich die Luft; unter Donner und Blitz greift man zu den Waffen. Belial mit seinen Verbündeten, dem Papste, dem Könige von Frankreich, den Türken und den Moskowitern rüsten sich zum Angriff der Kirche und ihrer Königin, aber sie lassen ab, als das Schwert des Geistes weht. Jetzt verschwindet der Engel im Äther, der Dichter erwacht und fasst seine Gedanken in einer Poesie über den Wunderbau der Welt zusammen.

In einer kalten Winternacht wird der Dichter vom Schlafe, der sich in Begleitung seiner Schwester, der Nachtmahr, einstellt, wiederum zu einer Wanderung in die Stadt des Verderbens abgeholt um den Tod, beider Bruder, zu besuchen. Er sieht darauf unzählige Gemächer des Todes, vor denen je ein kleiner Tod steht, als da sind Hunger, Kälte, Furcht, Galgen, Liebe, Neid, Ehrsucht. Dann kommt er in das Land der Vergessenheit (tir anghof), das

---

[1] Nach dem Vorgange des Bardd Cwsc hat ein späterer welscher Dichter, Thomas Edwards gen. Twm o'r nant (1738—1810), die Stadt des Verderbens in Versen geschildert in seinen Bannau y byd; vgl. O. Jones, Ceinion llenyddiaeth Gymreig 1, 314.

durch die unübersteigliche Mauer (*y wall ddiadlam*) abgeschlossen wird, ein endloses Thal ohne alles Grün, mit garstigen Tieren erfüllt. Unter den unzähligen Schatten, die sich hier bewegen, begegnet der Dichter einem alten Barden, der, über die Störung seiner Grabesruhe unwirsch, ihn hart anlässt. Auf Befragen giebt er sich dem Alten als der Bardd Cwsc zu erkennen. Der aber fährt ihn an: 'Herr, wisset, dass nicht ihr der Schlafbarde seid, sondern ich, der ich seit 900 Jahren hier ruhe, nur durch euch gestört'. 'Seid ihr unterrichtet', fragt er weiter, 'in den 24 Metren? Könnt ihr den Stamm Gogs und Magogs und den des Brutus, des Sohnes des Silvius, bis auf ein Jahrhundert vor Trojas Zerstörung zurückverfolgen? Könnt ihr vorhersagen, wann und wie die Kriege zwischen Löwen und Adler, zwischen Drachen und Hirsch[1]) enden werden? Ha?' (p. 60 f.). Hier trifft er auch Myrddin und dann Taliessin, der ihm den tiefern Sinn eines seiner Verse auslegt (eine Nachahmung Quevedos), und endlich den unglücklichen grossen Unbekannten, dem alle Lüge in der Welt angehängt wird (*Rhywun*, 'Some body', 'L'autre — les Latins m'appellent Quidam').

Nun wird der Dichter zu dem Schlosse des Todes geleitet, das aus Knochen und Schädeln aufgebaut und mit Schleim, Eiter und Menschenblut gefügt ist. König Tod, unablässig frisches Fleisch verschlingend, thront zwischen dem Schicksal zu seiner Rechten und dem Dämon der Zeit zu seiner Linken und waltet hier als Richter. Vier Fiedler, ein papsttreuer König, ein Trunkenbold, eine Dirne und sieben 'recorder' oder Rechtsverwalter werden von ihm in das Land der Verzweiflung (*tir anobaith*) gewiesen. Als noch sieben Gefangene vorgeführt werden, wird auch ein Schreiben Lucifers verlesen, worin der König der Hölle bittet diese Sieben der Welt zurückzugeben, wo sie ihm mehr nützen könnten als in seinem eignen Reiche, aber auf ernste Vorhaltung des Schicksals lehnt der Tod das Ansinnen ab. Die Sieben sind aber 'Finger-in-jeder-Brühe', *alias* Hans in allen Gassen, der Verleumder, der Prahler, Madame in Hosen (von dieser, der *Marchoges*, hat der Dichter die allerschlechteste Meinung), der Ränkeschmied und der Angeber. Zu ihnen gesellt sich der Querulant. Nachdem der Dichter noch einen Blick auf die Richtstätte der Gerechtigkeit geworfen hat, erwacht er und erleichtert seine geängstigte Seele durch ein Gedicht auf den Tod.

An einem schönen Aprilmorgen verfällt der Dichter am Ufer des Severn über Bayleys 'Practice of Piety' in einen Schlaf. Abermals erscheint sein Schutzengel und führt ihn durch den unermesslichen Weltraum über alle Sterne hinaus in das Land der Ewigkeit und in die Hölle, die unsagbar rauh und hässlich, mit Rauch und Gestank erfüllt ist. Schon hört er die Teufel und die Verdammten und sieht den Fluss des Bösen (*afon y Fall*), worin der Mensch zum Leiden erneut wird und jeden Schimmer der Hoffnung verliert. Und nun die Strafen der Hölle! 'Was ist das Pfählen oder Zersägen lebendiger Menschen, das Zerreissen des Leibes in Stücke mit eisernen Zangen oder das Braten des Fleisches gliederweise mit Kerzen, was das Zerdrücken der Schädel zu Platten in einer Presse und alles Grässliche, was man je auf Erden er-

---

[1]) Mit solchen Namen bezeichnen die Barden ihre Helden gern, wenn sie sich prophetisch über den Ausgang politischer Kämpfe aussprechen; vgl. Iolo Goch, ed. Ch. Ashton, p. 211.

sonnen? Alles ist nur ein Spass gegen eine von diesen Strafen. Hier tausend hunderttausendfach der Aufschrei, das heisere Ächzen, das tiefe Gestöhn; dort antworten wütende Klagen und gelles Gekreisch. Das Geheul der Hunde ist eine liebliche, anmutige Musik gegen diese Stimmen' (p. 90). Vom Feuer ins Eis, vom Rauch und Schwefel zum eklen Gezücht der Amphibien, ohne Unterlass, ohne dass sich jemandes Kräfte erschöpften. Dazu die giftigen Spottreden der widrigen Teufel und die bohrenden Schmerzen des gequälten Gewissens. 'Ach! wenn ich doch hätte!' (*Gwae fi na baswn!* 'O that I had!' 'O qui aurait!' 'O quien hubiera!'), sagen einige, 'Wo bleibt die Barmherzigkeit Gottes!' andere. Da sind die, die das Gebet und die Kirche verachteten, und die, die sich über ihre Schandthaten mit dem Hurentroste zu beruhigen pflegten: 'Oho! ich bin der Erste nicht'. Da sind weiter die Atheisten, Ketzer, Tyrannen und 'die zuerst Stammbäume geführt und die Wappen aufgebracht haben' (p. 99). Unter den letzten muss auch, viel verlacht, ein Halbblut-Squire Platz nehmen, der sein Geschlecht von so und so vielen der funfzehn Stämme von Gwynedd ableitet und es aus einem Pergament nachweisen will, ebenso ein anderer Edelmann, der auf eine lange und vornehme Ahnenreihe zurückblickt, aber sich sagen lassen muss, dass alle Menschen auf demselben Wege 'inter lotium et stercus' zur Welt gekommen sind. Da sind weiter die Koketten und die Weiber von schlechtem Lebenswandel, die letztern als Reptile in einem See, der grösser als Llynn-Tegid, d. i. der See von Bala, ist.[1]) Da sind endlich Diebe (mit Judas unter ihnen) und Kaufleute, Ärzte und Apotheker, Schwelger und Unbarmherzige, Zanksüchtige und Geizige u. a. m.

Der Dichter kommt nun zum Schlosse Lucifers, der hier als Fürst der Hölle richtet; aber er ist angekettet und eine gewaltige Faust über ihm hält einen Donnerkeil. Die vier Töchter Belials bringen ihm ihre Opfer herbei. Es ist wenig Eintracht in der Hölle; Lucifer ist mit seinen Teufeln unzufrieden und die Verdammten hadern unter sich. Mahomet, Cromwell und der Papst streiten über die Frage, wer Lucifer am meisten nützt; so zanken sich auch die Soldaten mit den Ärzten, die Wucherer mit den Juristen, die Betrüger mit den Edelleuten u. s. w. Alle Bösen empfangen ihre Strafe und es wird nicht viel Federlesens mit ihnen gemacht. Mehrere Könige (darunter Ludwig XIV.) mit ihren Höflingen und Schmeichlern werden in den locus sordidus geworfen, wo neben den niedrigsten Teufeln die Hexen hausen, 'wie vormals in der Donnerstags Nacht so nun hier immerdar[2]) osculantes daemones in anis suis' (p. 120). Zu ihnen werden auch die Zigeuner gesteckt: 'Werft sie zu den Hexen in den Abort oben, da ihre Gesichter der Farbe des Kotes so ähnlich sind. Hier giebt's für sie weder Katzen noch Binsenfackeln, aber lasst sie unter sich alle zehntausend Jahre einen Frosch haben, wenn sie stille sind und uns nicht mit ihrem Kauderwelsch betäuben' (p. 122). Auch die oben erwähnten Acht finden hier ein Ende mit Schrecken.

---

[1]) 'Llyn Tegyd, lle pesgyd pysg', sagt Dafydd ab Gwilym 206, 6. Der See von Bala ist sechs Kilometer lang. Bei La Geneste p. 231 befinden sich die Dollegnas als Frösche in einem See, 'un lac qui me semblait beoucoup plus grand que celuy de Geneue'.

[2]) Vgl. Jac. Grimm, Deutsche Mythologie[3] p. 891.

In den Verhandlungen vor dem Throne Lucifers kommen Dinge zur
Sprache, wo einige der ausgesendeten verdammten Menschenkinder und unter-
geordneten Teufel auf der Erde ihre Pflicht verabsäumt haben. Ein Ankläger
tritt auf und spricht: 'Hier ist ein Schalk, der jenem in Shrewsbury ähnlich
ist, als neulich das Interludium von Doktor Faustus[1]) aufgeführt wurde. Da
trieben einige mit den Augen Unzucht, andere beschwatzten sie und wieder
andere setzten zu gleichen Zwecken eine Zusammenkunft fest, und dergleichen
mehr zum Frommen deines Reichs. Als sie nun am eifrigsten waren, erschien der Teufel selbst seine Rolle zu spielen und jagte damit alle vom Vergnügen zum Gebet. So auch dieser. Auf seiner Wanderung durch die Welt
hörte er einige davon reden, sie wollten um die Kirche herumgehen um ihre
Liebsten zu sehen.[2]) Und was that der Narr? Er zeigte sich den einfältigen
Leuten in seiner natürlichen Gestalt, und obwohl ihr Schrecken gross war, so
schworen sie doch diese Thorheit hinfort ab. Er hätte sich doch in gemeine
Vetteln verwandeln sollen, dann würden sich jene gebunden gehalten haben
diese anzunehmen; und so hätte der schmierige Unhold der Hausherr bei den
Paaren werden können, da er die Hochzeit angestiftet hatte. Und hier ist
ein andrer, der letzten Dreikönigsabend zwei Mädchen in Wales besuchte, als
sie ihre Hemden wendeten,[3]) und anstatt die Jungfrauen in der Gestalt eines
schmucken Burschen zur Wollust zu verlocken, brachte er eine Bahre um die
eine zu ernüchtern. Zu der andern ging er mit Kriegslärm in einem höllischen
Wirbelwinde um sie noch mehr von Sinnen zu bringen als vorher, was gar
nicht nötig war. Und das war noch nicht alles, sondern nachdem er in das
Mädchen gefahren war und es hingeworfen und arg geplagt hatte, schickte
man nach einigen unserer gelehrten Feinde um für jenes zu beten und ihn
auszutreiben. Anstatt sie nun bis zur Verzweiflung zu prüfen und einen der
Prediger zu gewinnen zu suchen, fing er an zu predigen und die Geheimnisse

---

[1]) Einige solcher welschen Interludia sind erhalten geblieben, wie
M. Nettlau, Beiträge p. 20 Note, angiebt. — Es scheint fast, dass der Bardd
Cwsc in dem Teufelsglauben seiner Zeit befangen war; p. 93 spricht er auch
von einem Teufel, der im Schornsteine sitzt.

[2]) Die welschen Herausgeber führen an, dass am Abend des Totenfestes
(2. November) die Mädchen mit einer brennenden Kerze zur Kirche zu gehen
pflegten, um aus dem Flackern der Flamme die Aussichten des kommenden
Jahres zu erkennen. Dann gingen manche zwei- oder dreimal um die Kirche
herum ohne ein Wort zu reden und darauf zu Bette, wo sie im Schlafe ihre
künftigen Männer zu sehen hofften. Aber im Texte sind es offenbar die
Männer, die um die Kirche gehen.

[3]) Man legte ein Hemd an einen besondern Ort in einer Ecke des
Zimmers und ging dann feierlich in eine andere Ecke. Darauf kam der zu-
künftige Gatte herein und wendete das Hemd, die innere Seite nach aussen.
Ich kenne eine Farm, erklärt der Gewährsmann des Herausgebers, wo man
diesen Brauch noch vor weniger als 20 Jahren übte, und einige von denen,
die zugegen waren, leben heute noch und glauben, sie hätten jemanden das
Hemd wenden sehen, der zur Zeit wenigstens 20 Meilen entfernt war. Einen
ähnlichen Aberglauben verzeichnet Jac. Grimm, Deutsche Mythologie 3, 470
unter Nr. 955.

eueres Reiches auszuplaudern, indem er so, statt sie zu hindern, ihre Errettung
förderte' (p. 131 f.).

Lucifer beratschlagt mit seinen Oberteufeln, Meistern von sieben Todsünden, hin und her, wie wohl England und seiner tugendhaften Königin beizukommen sei. Die einzelnen bieten ihre Dienste an, Cerberus den Tabak,[1]
Mammon das Geld, Apollyon den Stolz, Asmodai die Wollust, Belphegor die
Trägheit, Satan den Betrug mit seinen Euphemismen, Belzebub den Un-
verstand. Obwohl sich Lucifer vom Zusammenwirken der Sieben guten Erfolg
verspricht, so ist er doch überzeugt, dass die Nährmutter aller und seine
eigene Vertreterin auf Erden, die Prosperitas, noch mehr erreichen würde.
'Der folget' (p. 147). Nach ihrer Sitzung werden die Teufel wieder in die
äusserste Hölle zurückgeworfen.

Wie aber dem Dichter noch ein Überblick über das ganze Reich des
Schreckens gestattet wird, da gewahrt er eine Riesin, die durch die Welt
reicht und alles überragt. Sie hat drei Gesichter, deren eines trotzig dem
Himmel, das andere lächelnd der Erde und das dritte grausig der Hölle zu-
gekehrt ist. Sie allein ist nicht von Gott geschaffen. Sie ist die Mutter der
vier Töchter Belials, die Mutter des Todes und die Mutter alles Bösen, die
ihren Griff nach jedem Menschen ausreckt, und sie heisst die Sünde.

Eine ernste Poesie schliesst das Werk ab.

Obwohl es in den Visionen des schlafenden Barden nicht
an lebendiger Schilderung fehlt, so sind sie doch in ihrer Anlage,
um einen Augenblick dabei zu verweilen, nicht eben glücklich.
Was der Dichter im 'Laufe der Welt' darstellt, wiederholt sich
zum Teil in dem zweiten und dritten Gesichte; das Reich des
Todes liess sich kaum gegen das der Hölle abgrenzen. Ursprünglich gedachte Ellis Wynne wohl nur eine Übersetzung
Sir Rogers zu geben; es ist schade, dass er sich von seinem Vorbilde nicht gänzlich frei gemacht hat. Der spanische Mantel, in
den sich der welsche Dorfgeistliche hüllt, ist aus Stücken zusammengesetzt und man erkennt noch überall die Nähte darin.
Die Allegorie ist ein Ingrediens der poetischen Schöpfung, von
dem ein Zuviel leicht ermüdet. Der grimmige Hass des Dichters
gegen alles, was Lüge, Ungerechtigkeit und Laster heisst, ist
gewiss das Zeugnis einer lauteren, unabhängigen Gesinnung, aber
reifere Jahre würden seiner Meinung über die Dinge dieser unvollkommenen Welt vielleicht einen menschenfreundlichern Ausdruck verliehen haben. Manch derbes Wort entfährt ihm in
seinem Zorn und einigemale (wie p. 70, 100) scheint er sich in

---

[1] Schon Quevedo kennt einen Dämon des Tabaks, obwohl er ihn nicht
Cerberus nennt. Zu derselben Zeit nahm König Jacob I. im 'Counterblast'
zu diesem Geschenke der neuen Welt Stellung.

der Schrankenlosigkeit seiner Rede zu vergessen. Aber sein
Werk ist immerhin eine bemerkenswerte Erscheinung in der
Litteratur. Zwar haben uns schon Homer und Virgil das Reich
der Schatten geschildert, aber erst die christliche Moral hat die
Lehre von der 'duplex poena' im Jenseits ausgebildet, indem sie
es sich bald als einen Ort, wo Heulen und Zähnklappen ist, und
bald als ein ewiges Feuer dachte.[1]) Man kennt die Apokalypse
des Apostels Paulus (die Beda in der 100. Homilie betrachtet)
und die der Maria, die Visionen des Abba Sinuthios, dann die
des Furseus und Drycthelm (wieder beim Beda), Adamnans,
Brendans und Laisréns bei den Iren, Karls des Dicken und
Albericos, des Tnugdalus (1149) und des Knaben Wilhelm im
Speculum historiale, das Fegefeuer des heiligen Patricius von
Henry von Saltry (1153) mit seinen Nachahmungen, die Vision
des Mönches von Evesham (1196) und Thurcills (1206), die
Träume des Raoul de Houdaing und des Rutebeuf und den ge-
waltigen Abschluss dieser Dichtungen in der Divina commedia.
Nach ihr war für den Gegenstand nur noch in der Satire Raum.
Ellys Wynne ist ein Satiriker.

*   *   *

Wertvoller noch als durch seinen Inhalt sind uns die
'Gesichte des schlafenden Barden' durch die Sprache, die ihnen
in der neuwelschen Litteratur einen hohen Rang sichert. Goronwy
Owen, der sinnige Dichter, der den Bardd Cwsc bewunderte
(Works ed. R. Jones 2, 53) und zu Zeiten als Vademecum führte

---

[1]) Die celtischen Dichter nennen die Hölle häufiger kalt als heiss. So
sagt ein welscher Dichter: 'Uffern oer gwerin gwartret', Skene 2, 110; und
öfter noch sprechen die gälischen Dichter in Irland und Schottland von Ifreann
fuar, vgl. Keatings Tri biorghaoithe; Oss. 4, 118; Zeitschrift 1, 322; Inv. 11, 330;
Mackenzie, Beauties p. 182. Die Missionäre wurden angewiesen auf den Färöern
eine kalte Hölle zu lehren. Aber auch den Orientalen ist sie bekannt; bei
den Arabern heisst sie *zamharir*, wie Ibn Raǵab († 1393) in seinem gelehrten
Werke über die muslimische Hölle erwähnt (MS. Peterm. I, 107, Bl. 20b).
Nach rabbinischer Vorstellung müssen die Verdammten sechs Monate im
Feuer und sechs Monate in der Kälte zubringen, aber am Sabbath haben sie
(wie auch nach christlicher Darstellung) eine Erholung von ihren Leiden, und
wenn man dem Elia de Vidas im Reschit chokhma Glauben schenken darf, so
kommt es manchmal vor, dass einer dieser Unglücklichen aus der kalten
Abteilung ein Stück Eis unter dem Arme mit sich schleppt um hernach in
der heissen Kühlung zu haben.

(2, 90. 126), hat sich von seiner Schreibweise ersichtlich be-
einflussen lassen. Die Ausgabe, die diese Besprechung veranlasst
hat, macht uns mit dem Werke in seiner ungekürzten und un-
verfälschten Form von 1703 bekannt. Dagegen werden andere
neuere Drucke, die alles und jedes mit Willkür behandeln, nicht
aufkommen können.[1]) Ausgelassen hat auch die neueste Übersetzung des Buches, von der sonst nur Gutes zu sagen ist.[2]) Es
hat unsern Beifall, dass J. Morris Jones, dem wir bereits zu
Dank verpflichtet sind, sich von dem genauen Abdruck der editio
princeps nicht hat zurückhalten lassen; denn zuverlässige Texte
sind das Unum necessarium aller Philologie. Nur darüber kann
man vielleicht streiten, ob auch alle Druckfehler wiederholt
werden mussten, so getreu als ob es sich um eine alte Inschrift
handelte. Ellis Wynne, der schon in der Orthographie ungleich
ist und den Druck, wie es scheint, nicht gehörig überwachen
konnte, würde vermutlich keinen Wert darauf gelegt und anders
gedacht haben als A. Schopenhauer, der, seiner Schärfe im Grossen
wie im Allerkleinsten sich bewusst, letztwillig bestimmt: 'Meinen
Fluch über jeden, der, in künftigen Drucken meiner Werke, irgend
etwas daran wissentlich ändert, sei es eine Periode, oder auch
ein Wort, eine Silbe, ein Buchstabe, ein Interpunctionszeichen'.
Jedesfalls würde man im Bardd Cwsc auf die zahlreichen Sphal-
mata des Setzers gern verzichten.[3])

---

[1]) Zwei Ausgaben dieses Bardd Cwsc 'des familles' erschienen 1898,
die eine in Caernarvon, die andere in Liverpool. Mit ihrem moralischen Werte
steht der sprachliche leider nicht auf derselben Höhe, wie denn die letzt-
genannte z. B. *Prydain* beharrlich in *Brydain* korrigiert.

[2]) The Visions of the Sleeping Bard, translated by Rob. Gwyneddon
Davies. London 1897. XXIX + 130 pp. 8°.

[3]) Folgende in den Anmerkungen nicht verbesserte Druckfehler sind mir
aufgefallen: 7, 27 *mawn* statt mawr; 9, 18 *fell* fel; 10, 20 *Frainc* Ffrainc;
12, 5 *he* hi; 13, 4 *a crefydd a chededl* a chrefydd a chenedl; 13, 16 *Srryd*
Stryd; 19, 14 *ceibddeilwyr* crib-; 20, 19 *stiwardiad* stiwardiaid; 25, 3 *a'r* ar;
28, 11 *ymhem* ymhen; 29, 23 *ym ddangos* ymddangos; 31, 29 *er Angel* yr
Angel; 34, 25 *Ypspryd* Yspryd, 27 *Uffernl* Uffern; 36, 18 *'myfc* 'mysc; 38, 21
dyleferydd dy leferydd, 22 *dyddirnad* dy ddirnad; 39, 27 *losci* llosci; 42, 17
rhagofn rhag ofn; 44, 25 *ddhienyd* ddihenyd; 46, 5 *amddeffyn* amddiffyn;
47, 29 *a Taraneu* a tharaneu; 48, 5 *goelceth* goelcerth (vielleicht wie aelgeth
neben aelgerth, S. Evans, Dict. 1, 67), 27 *dechruodd* dechreuodd, 31 *digalloni*
digaloni; 49, 21 *y hyn* yr hyn; 56, 5 *attolw* attolwg; 58, 7 *Augeu* Angeu;
59, 10 *adfeidrol* anfeidrol; 60, 5 *fel y fynnoch* fel y mynnoch, 9 *gen* gan;
65, 27 *fawn* fawr; 68, 8 *Agendorr* Agendor; 73, 13 *dûr a a* dûr a; 74, 14 *creft*

Anders steht es mit seiner Orthographie, die etwas Wesent-
liches ist. Sie weicht von der heutigen nicht unerheblich ab
und spiegelt deutlich den Dialekt des Verfassers wieder, sowohl
in der Aussprache der Vokale als einiger Konsonanten. Einige
Eigentümlichkeiten des Dialekts von Merionethshire hat M. Nettlau
in seinen Beiträgen p. 35 angemerkt, mehr lernen wir aus E. Wynnes
Schreibart kennen. Die Sprache des Bardd Cwsc ist sowohl reich
als rein, gedrungen und idiomatisch, weit entfernt vom heutigen
Zeitungsstile und, da sie unablässig aus der Redeweise des Volks
schöpft, nicht immer ganz leicht zu verstehen. Einige ihrer
Eigentümlichkeiten werden wir vielleicht zu gelegener Zeit in
Verbindung mit der Vulgärsprache erörtern, wie sie uns nach
der Mundart von Carnarvonshire H. Sweet beschrieben hat und
wie wir sie nach der von Denbighshire aus den Briefen des
alten Farmers und andern Schriften vernehmen.

Gut welsch wie er ist, wird man doch manche Anglicismen
im Bardd Cwsc beobachten. Dahin gehört z. B. Beth oedd y
matter *what was the matter* 20, 113; pa fodd yr oedd eich
matterion chwi 'n sefyll *how did your matters stand* 128; i
chwarae ei bart *to play his part* 132; oni basei i hwnnw
rhwng têg a hagr dorri 'r cae 'wenn es diesem nicht gelungen
wäre mit Güte und Gewalt die Hecke zu durchbrechen', *by fair
and foul* 100; i gadw eu haddolwyr mewn awch 'um ihre An-
beter willig zu erhalten', *on edge* 25; a wnaeth i mi feddwl fod
rhyw ffrae gyffredin ar droed 'das liess mich denken, dass ein
allgemeiner Aufstand im Gange wäre', *a-foot* 20; yn atteb eu
coeg-escusion hyd adref 'ihre leeren Entschuldigungen zurück-
weisend', cf. *home-thrust* 123; y dyn a ymgadwo rhag ei swynion

---

crefft; 76, 13 *na arbedwch* nac arbedwch, 17 *yrwythfed* yr wythfed; 77, 24 *yn
ymysc* ymysc; 79, 8 *Corsedd* Gorsedd; 80, 14 *ai* a'i; 81, 14 *y gwelláu* a gwelláu;
82, 9 *au* a'u; 85, 16 *ei fynu* i fynu; 86, 28 *Gagoniant* Gogoniant; 88, 10 *llawr*
llawer; 89, 14 *dieieithriaid* dieithriaid, 21 *affon* afon; 91, 20 *ei* i; 94, 25 *gym-
meiriad* -aid; 103, 29 *trigfu* trigfa; 105, 1 *brenhinghwrt* -gwrt; 104, 30 *erchyll-
cod* erchylldod; 109, 18 *mor* mo'r, ult. *i fynd* ei fyned; 110, 14 *yngorfod* yn
gorfod, 22 *gwenwym* gwenwyn; 115, 5 *gosynnodd* gofynnodd; 116, 2 *uncant*
o'r ddeg* ar ddeg; 118, 7 *meistr* meistri; 119, 15 *i tràd* i dràd, i'r tràd; 120, 25
ymoroll ymorol; 126, 24 *atrodwr* athrodwr; 127, 25 *gwasanethwr* gwasanaethwr;
129, 7 *eu amser* eu hamser; 131, 3 *pan ei gwelodd* pan y'i gwelodd, 12 *gystall*
gystal; 136, 13 *orphwystro* -tra; 138, 12 *snafedd* llysnafedd wie 103; 144, 9
perthynaseu a ph.; 148, 15 *a'i* âi; 152, 8 *y* ei, ult. *trynderau* trymderau. Von
der ganz elenden Interpunktion zu geschweigen.

mwynion hi gellwch daflu 'ch cap iddo 'wer sich vor ihren holden
Reizen bewahrt, den könnt ihr aufgeben', *you may cast your
cap at him* 147; y dydd arall '*the other day*' 130 f.; troi dalen
arall '*to turn over a new leaf*' 92; troi allan 20, troi ymaith 47,
scheinen dem englischen '*to turn out*', syrthio allan '*to fall out*'
nachgebildet, u. a. m. Aber es ist wenig im Vergleich zu dem,
was die welsche Tageslitteratur sich erlaubt.

Die englischen Lehnwörter sind dagegen bei E. Wynne
recht zahlreich. Goronwy Owen (Works 2, 120) tadelt den Dafydd
ab Gwilym wegen seiner Vorliebe für Fremdwörter; Lewis Glyn
Cothi gebrauchte deren nach 150 Jahren noch viel mehr, und
nach dem gleichen Zeitraume war die Invasion, wie das Canwyll
y Cymry zeigt, wieder erheblich vorgeschritten; freilich war Rees
Pritchard ein Südwelscher und auf die Reinheit der Sprache
weniger bedacht. Gerade die Lehnwörter sind ein Beweis, dass
die Sprache des Bardd Cwsc in der des Volkes wurzelte, wie
H. Sweet hervorgehoben hat. 'The superiority of such a work
as the Bardd Cwsg consists precisely in its style being founded
(as shown by the numerous English words) on the every-day
speech of the period.' TPhS. 1882—84 p. 484. Ich habe in
meiner Sammlung aus dem Bardd Cwsc 270 und einige englische
Lehnwörter, doch sind manche darunter alter Besitz und ihre
Form aus dem Mittelenglischen zu deuten.

Abl, mittelengl. *able*, 15. 97. D. G. 239, 10.
aer, me. *heir eir*, 97.
ail *aisle*? fr. *aile*, 51.
alderman (jetzt aldramon) 15.
as *ace*, fr. *as* 6.
Bailiaid, me. *bailif baili*, 120.
baledeu *ballads* 23, vom prov. ballada.
banc *bank* 52.
bandieu *bonds, bands* 20.
baner 10. 16.
bargen 33. 88, bargeinion 62. 123. 146, me. *bargain*, afr. *bargaine*.
barr 67. 70. 117.
bastardiaid 144.
bilieu *bills*, me. *bille*, 20.
bir *beer*, 'cerevisia lupulata', 144.
bôllt *bolt* 107. 109. 147.
bostid, von me. *boste* 'boast', 93, oft bei D. G. .

bribis *bribes* 81, breibwyr *bribers* 19.
Britaniaid *Britains* 22.
briwlio, me. *broile*, afr. *bruiller*, 90; sw. brwylian, R. Prichard p. 92. 142. 318. 396.
brwmstan, me. *brunston* (brwnstan RB. 2, 46, brwîistanawl LA. 31, 28), 'brimstone', 88. 91.
brywes *brewis*, von me. *brewe* 'Brühe', 74.
burgyn, ist vielmehr ins engl. *morkin* übergegangen.
bwrdd byrddeu, me. *bord*, 120.
Canel *kennel* 100. 114.
cancr, me. *cancre*, 31; verwandt ist crancod 34.
canon *cannon* 107.
cap 66. 121, capieu 16; schon bei D. G.
cardieu 23. 102, cardiwr 119; me. *carde*.
cario, me. *carien*, 120. .

12*

carl *carl* 146 (D. G. 65, 41. 66, 7. 94, 58. 253, 32); cerlyn 140; ae. *ceorl*, me. *cherl* churl.

caroleu, me. *carole*, 27; celt. Wort.

cart *chart*, lat. charta, 97.

cast 24. 26 f. 34. 63. 107. 131; cestyn 140. 143; castiau D. G. 171, 54, von me. *caste*, an. *kasta.*

ceisbwl 19. 131. D. G. 99, 18; *ceisbyliaid* 120, von me. *cacchepol.*

cêr 42. 57, von me. *gere.*

ceremoniau (= seremoniau) 18.

cêst 15, von me. *cheste*, lat. *cista.*

clai 47. 65 (D. G. 50, 9. 194, 49. 230, 40), von ae. *claeg* 'clay'.

clarc *clerk*, 74, clarcod 62. 120.

cleimio 46. I. G. 4, 127, klaim 59, 37, von me. *claime cleime*, von afr. *claimer cleimer.*

clep *clap* 'clack' 96, von me. *clappe*, ae. *claeppian.* D. G. hat clep 216, 87 und clap 146, 30. 151, 15. 196, 51. 159, 51.

clipwyr *clippers* 19.

clir 20. 135 (D. G. 13, 41. 130, 16), clirio 116. 118, von me. *cler*, fr. *clair.*

clos, small-*clothes*, 75. 117. 127.

cnâ, me. *knaue*, 21. 75; 'cna' diarab' nennt D. G. 182, 38 den Fuchs, wo andere 'cnu' lesen.

cnap 60, von me. *knop knap.* RB. 1, 164.

coeten *quoit* 62.

cofenant *covenant* 117.

cogiwr 21, von cogio 'to cog', W. L. Jones, Caniadau p. 17.

considrio 'to consider' 141.

copr *copper* 67.

cortyn 58, cyrt 57, me. *corde.*

costio 'to cost' 93.

crab *grab* 30. 148; cf. arm. crap, grap 'appui'.

crefft, ae. *cræft*, 75, crefftwyr 31.

crêu *crave* 37.

cri 90, crio 24, criwr 75, von me. *crie*; cri D. G. 44, 42. 93, 71. 85, 6. 123, 51.

croesi 'to cross' 123.

cwacer 100, cwaceiriaid 47. 105, 'quakers'.

cwcwaldiaid 102. 125, von me. *cuke-wold.*

cwerylon 119, von me. *querele.*

cwestiwn *question* 10. 61.

cwestiwr 'questman' 41, cwestwyr 124.

cwil *quill* 21.

cwmbrus 75 f., cwmbrys 128, *cumbrous*, von me. *cumbre.*

cwmpas *compass*, -og 9. 23. 106.

cwmpaseu *compasses* 57.

cwmpni 107, cwmnhi 29. 49. 64. 72. 75. 93. 96. 147, cwmpeini 64. 72, von *company.*

cwncwerwr *conqueror* 73, cyncwerwr 21, -wyr 102.

cwppan *cup* 147; cf. ir. copán.

cwrs *course* 86, cyrsieu 13; oft bei D. G.

cwrt, me. *curt*, 69. 105, cyrtieu 75. 120; cyrtiwr 127, cyrtwyr 121.

cwsmeiriaid 'customers' 119, cwsmeriaeth 22. 74.

cynfaseu *canvas* 94.

cypres-wydden *cypress* 65.

chwap *whap* 56. 118. 141. 143. 149; whap D. G. 196, 51; von me. *quappen.*

chwarter *quarter* 46.

chwippyn 8. 59. 135; = *whip* (yn ebrwydd), R. Prichard p. 259.

Dainteithion 23. 27, von me. *dainte*, deinteth (von lat. *dignitatem*).

damnio, me. *damne*, 93. 123. 146.

Demigorgon *Demogorgon* 114.

diemwnt *diamond* 73. 106.

dis *dice* 21. 102, disieu 23, disiwr 119; dreimal bei D. G.

dwbl *double* 70.

dyfeis 62, dyfais 75 *device*, dyfeisieu 27. 75.

dyfeisio 25. 3. 63. 84. 110. 114, dyfeisiwr 38. 127.

dyfosiwn *devotion* 36. 14.

Ecclips 47.

empriwr, me. *emperour*, 109. 115. 135 (statt ymmerawdr).

escus *excuse* 123. 128, oft bei D. G., ymescusodi 123.

Ferdit, me. *verdit*, 130.

ffafr 15. 68. 108, ffafer 85 *favour*, ffafrau 'wedding favours' 29.

ffair *fair* 'Markt' 22. 43. 136, bei D. G. und I. G., von me. *feire*, fr. *foire* (feria).

ffals *false*, ffeilsion 102, ffalsder 28.

ffardial *fardel*, afr. *fardel* = *fardeau* 102.

ffarwell *farewell* 147.

ffei, me. *fy* = *fie*, 140; cf. ffei ffei = ha ha, Psalm 40, 15 Morgan.

ffest, me. *fest*, 140. D. G. 72, 7. 107, 20. LA. 123, 20.

ffidil, ffidler 42. 67 (statt ffil, ffilor), vom me. *fithel*.

ffls *fees* 122.

fflagenni 57, von *flagon*.

ffollt *fold* 112.

fforestwyr 19. 102. 105 (Ceinion 1, 200 b) von fforestwr D. G. 222, 34, *forester*; das welsche Wort scheint einen weitern Begriff zu haben als das englische, da *fforesdu* = cadw 'custodire' ist: y gweirgloddiau a fforesdir rhag y moch bob amser yn y flwyddyn, canys llygru y tir a wnant, Wotton, Leges wallicae p. 290.

ffortun *fortune* 122.

ffrae *fray* 20.

ffrâm *frame* 14.

ffrio, me. *frie*, 43.

ffrind, friend *friend* 63.

ffwl *fool* 38. 68.

ffwrdd '*forth*' (= away!) 67. DG. 21, 49. 149, 92. 197, 24.

ffwrnes, me. *furneis*, fr. *fournaise*, 99.

ffyrling 30 f. 63. 117, von *farthing*.

Gapio, me. *gapen*, 29.

garlleg, me. *garlek*, ae. *gár-léac*, 31.

gibris *gibberish* 122.

gowt *gout* 15.

gras *grace* 23, grasusol 107.

gwarant, me. *waraunt*, 18. 140.

Happus 125, happusrwydd 37, von hap D. G. 170, 12 (skandin.).

help 8. 78. 110. 144, helpu 5. 39. 131, so auch 133, 3 zu lesen statt help (D. G. 223, 6), me. *helpe*; dihelp 57.

heretic 33. 96.

hettieu 47, von het, me. *hat*, ae. *hæt*.

hislan *hatchel*, *hetchel* 91; cf. hislengarth D. G. 173, 51.

hopran *hopper* 66.

hulio 28. 31 (Ceinion 1, 345a) 'verhüllen, decken' von 'to hill'.

hwndrwd *hundred* 6.

hwsmyn *housemen* 57, von hwsmon D. G. 197, 22. 200, 10.

Interlud 23. 131.

'Lecsiwn *election* 20. 136.

lêg *league* 117.

lifrai *livery* 11. 83, oft bei D. G., I. G. etc.

locustiaid *locusts* 59.

lwcusach 67, von *lucky*.

Madam 75.

maeden *maiden*, ae. *mægden*, 33.

maentumio 31. 98, von me. *maintene*; R. Prichard hat neben maintumio 127 auch maintainio 107. 165. 303. 425. Aber nifaintinieid Sk. 2, 5 ist für nisaintinieid BBC. 5 a 12 verlesen.

maersiandwyr 20, marsiandwyr 19. 57, von me. *marchaund*.

malis *malice* 44. 109, maleis 40, (malais D. G. 179, 3), maleisgar 134, difalis 119 (fehlt bei S. E.).

marcio 136, D. G. 171, 53, *to mark*, me. *merke*.

mastiff 34.

matter, me. *matere*, 17. 113. 115. 121. 124. 125. 134, matterion 128, difatter 62.

medleiwr *meddler* 74. 126, von medlai *medley* D. G. 17, 28.

meincieu 57, mainc 66. 76, von me. *benche*, ae. *benc*.

milein *villain* 34, mileiniach 110; bilein = taeog in den Gesetzen, bilein llu RB. 2, 110. 122; die Form milein ist alt (HM. 1, 267), vgl. y meiddiwn 85 = y beiddiwn.

munud *minute* 4. 68. 73, munyd 91. 104. 146.

muwsic 58. 90, jetzt miwsic.

mwrdwr, me. *murther*, 112. 119; mwr-
driwr 78. 97, mwrdrwyr 58. 102.
Onest *honest* 122, gonest 70. 146, onest-
rwydd 38.
ordeinio *to ordain* 146.
Pacc *pack* 101, paccieu 122; pac D. G.
142, 33.
paentio, me. *painte peinte*, 14.
papist 46.
papur, me. *papér*, 84. 121; lliw papir,
D. G. 149, 22.
pardwn, me. *pardown*, 53. D. G. 10, 30.
256, 34.
parliament 107. 128 f.
parlwr, me. *parlour*, 25. 65. D. G.
78, 26. 80, 6. 258, 49.
parsment *parchment* 121.
part 132.
pastai, me. *paste pastie*, 18.
pedler *pedlar* 14, pedleriaid 102.
perlau *perle* 14, schon bei D. G. 207, 3
und I. G.
person *person* 109, *parson* 67. 94, me.
beides *persoun*.
perswadio *to persuade* 12.
perwigau 41, vom me. *periwigge,
-wicke*.
phansi *fancy* 6.
phlem *phlegm* 65.
physygwr 102, physygwyr 19, physyg-
wriaeth 22, von *physicus*.
pib *pipe* 27; cf. ir. píob.
pigwr-pocced *pick-pocket* 21.
'piniwn *opinion* 31. 143, d. h. 'per-
versity', cf. ymhob pen y mae piniwn, MA. 866 b.
pinneu *pins* 14.
piso, me. *pissen*, 70.
pistol 24, für 'Pfeife'.
pleser *pleasure* 12. 22. 132.
possibl 45. 107.
pot 24. 42. 57. 104.
potecari 102, potecariaid 19. 21. 119,
von *apothecary*.
pris, me. *pris*, 80 f. 121. D. G. 34, 2.
185, 41; prisiwr 169, 30. 200, 14.
prolog *prologue* 48.
pshaw 109.

pulpyd *pulpit* 134.
punt, me. *pund*, 143, punneu 63. 121.
pwff *puff* 76.
pwrpas, me. *purpos*, 22. 58. 132. 134.
136, pwrpaswr 144.
pwrs, me. *purs*, 21, byrseu 57.
pwynt *point* 41.
Recordor *recorder* 70, recordwyr 120.
redi *ready* 74 f.
renti *rents* 19, von ae. *rente*; cf. rhent
D. G. 154, 10, rrent hafaidd I. G.
7, 21.
rowndiad *round-head* 86. 100, rown-
dieid 115.
rheoli 12. 15. 18, rheolwr 71, rheolaeth
107. 141, von me. *reule*, afr. *riule*
'regula'.
rheswm, me. *resoun*, rhesymmeu 17 f.
29. 123; davon ymresymmu 123.
rhidyllio 14, von rhidyll D. G. 54, 17.
235, 1 'riddle', me. *riddel*, ae.
hridder, ahd. *hritara*.
rhôst 40. 69. 103, rostio 91. 121, me.
roste, ymrostio 93.
rhwd *rood* 47. 104; D. G. 134, 26. 230, 70.
rhwymedi, me. *remedie*, 28.
Sawdwr, me. *soudiour*, 21, sawdwyr
114; sawdiwr I. G. 9, 41.
sawyr, me. *sauour*, 27. 73; I. G. 191
(heute sawr, wie D. G. 202, 39).
scarlad, me. *scarlat*, 66; ysgarlad D.
G. 118, 11. 233, 76. HM. 1, 211.
259.
sciabas *scab*, *skab* 58.
scithell *scud*, *scuttle*? 124.
scorpionau 111.
Scotyn 'Scott' 116, Scotsmyn 122.
scum 98.
scweir *squire* 97.
scwrs *scourge* 92; yscwrs HM. 1, 191,
ysgors 1, 237.
scwtsiwn *scutcheon* 18.
seler *cellar* 7. 26. 51. 94. 104; D. G.
211, 32. 232, 90. HM. 1, 222. 326.
serio 91, 'to sear', me. *seeren*.
sessiwn *session* 120, = assize 136.
siacced *jacket* 24; D. G. 190, 29. I. G.
9, 36.

siampleu 93. D. G. 42, 48, vom me. *saumple*.

siarpwyr *sharpers* 19.

siars *charge* 45. 107. 118.

siccr, me. *siker*, 24. 62.

siêl *jail* 34; cf. sieler, D. G. 11, 14; R. Prichard p. 59.

simnei, me. *chimnee*, 34, simnai 93. 103. 121; simneiau I. G. 10, 48.

siop, me. *schoppe*, 14, siopwyr 19. 98.

sipsiwn *gipsies*, 6. 122; *sipswn* R. Prich. 391.

sir *shire* 7, siroedd I. G. 27, 9.

siri *sheriff*, 36. 97; sirif suri I. G. 7, 13; me. *scherefe*.

siwglaeth *jugglery* 23.

siwrnai, me. *journee*, 55; D. G. 69, 36. 121, 44. 144, 29. 45, 5. HM. 1, 159.

smottieu 27, ysmottieu 58. 91, von *spot*.

sobr, me. *sobre*, 140, sobrwydd 24. 43.

spectol *spectacles*, 32.

spio, me. *spie*, fr. *espier*, 14. 25. 28. 32. 145; yspio 9. 125. HM. 1, 387, yspi 71. 126, spiwyr 126.

stâd, me. *estat*, 5. 143. (D. G. 44, 2); stât 21. 29. 38. 141; sonst ystad.

splent *splint* 117. 124. 126.

stalwyn, me. *stallone stallion*, 131.

stent *extent* 97.

stiwardiaid 19. 102; ystiwardaeth D. G. 76, 37, von me. *stiward*.

stori *story* 23. 134, storiau 18. 64. 146; sonst ystori.

stormoedd *storms* 146.

strîp *stripe* 11.

stryd, me. *strete*, 9. 139; ystryd D. G. 101, 35. I. G. 74, 52.

studio, me. *studie*, 41. Cein. 1, 147; studiwr 144.

swpper *supper* 6.

swrffedig *surfeiting* 145.

sydyn *sudden* 73. 89. 134. 153; me. *sodain, soden*, afr. *sudain*.

syr *sir* 8.

syre *sirrah* 34.

Tabler *tables* (mir. táiplis) 23, von *tablier, tabularium*.

taclus 123, tacluso 26, von *to tackle*.

taeliwr, me. *taillour* 21. D. G. 8, 10; taelwriaid 18. 31. 102.

tafarnwyr 19, von tafarn *tavern*; bei D. G. oft, tafarnwriaeth 229, 22.

tasc *task* 17. 25; D. G. 107, 34. 230, 23.

tenentiaid *tenants*, 98. D. G. 179, 18.

temtio, me. *tempte*, 113. 127. 129. 132. 145.

titlau *titles* 15. 17 (heute teitlau).

tobacco 23. 141, tybacco 135, tobeccyn 142.

trafaelio, me. *trauail* 'to travel', 6. 80. 87; dagegen trafael 'Mühe' D. G. 38, 13. 143, 21. 208, 89; trafaelu 4, 9.

trâd *trade* 119. 124. 131. 133.

trolyn *roll*: a chanddo drolyn mawr o femrwn sef ei gart acheu 'und er hatte eine grosse Pergamentrolle bei sich, nämlich seinen Stammbaum' 97.

trwnc *trunk*, tryncieu 57; aber trwnc 98 = *trwngc*.

trwp *troop* 41. 102.

twrneiod *attorneys* 62. 120.

Ustus, me. *iustice*, 60. 97, D. G. 241, 21; ustusiaid 19. 120.

Wal *wall* 69. 81.

wâr *ware* 102.

weir *wire* 34.

widw, me. *widwe*, 28.

winwyn *onion* 31. Cf. mir. uineamhain, Irish glosses 862.

wingo *to wince*, me. *wincen*, 91.

witsiaid *witches*, 7. 120. 122.

Ymharneisio 47, vom me. *harneis*.

yscowl *scold* 14, yscowliaid 14. 101. 119.

yscwîr, me. *squiere*, *squyer* (escuyer), 25; ysgwir D. G. 42, 38. 130, 26. 155, 13. 189, 27. 203, 2; ysgwier HM. 1, 18. I. G. 7, 11; ysgwiar 6, 11; ysgwiair 5, 27.

J. Morris Jones hat seiner Ausgabe ein nützliches Verzeichnis der heute nicht allgemein verständlichen Wörter bei-

gegeben, an das ich noch einige etymologische Erörterungen an-
knüpfe.

Annwn 58, 71, 112, 147, oder Annw'n 51, 73, 106, oder Anw'n
113, ist nach Wynne dasselbe wie Annwfn, wie er auch
schreibt, 8, 39, 71, 134, und bezeichnet nach ihm die
äusserste Hölle. Schon im Mittelwelschen entsprechen die
Formen *Annwn* und *Annwvyn*. Gegen die Ableitung von
anima, die H. Gaidoz auf das armorische *anaoun* gründet
(Zs. 1, 30), hat J. Loth manches eingewendet (Annales de
Bretagne 11, 488). Es kann m. E. nicht bezweifelt werden,
dass annwfn annw'n für *an-dwfn* steht, sowie annuw
'gottlos' für *an-duw*; ob das aber 'tief' oder 'sehr tief'
heissen kann, ist eine andere Frage. Von Evans' '*an*-
intensivum' ist, scheint es, nicht viel zu halten, und der
Belag, den er für ein solches annwfn 'sehr tief' giebt: nyt
oed *anydyfnach* y gwaet udunt yn eu hymlit noc y deuei
yr budugolyon hyt ym bras eu hesgeiryeu, HM. 2, 37 (in
der Ystoria de Carolo Magno p. 16 entspricht dem Ausdruck
kyn amlet . . . ac), gehört, wenn er überhaupt korrekt ist,
gewiss nicht zu annwfn. Wenn es ein Adjektiv *annwfn*
giebt, so kann es nur 'untief' bedeuten, was uns den
Namen Annwn durchaus nicht verständlicher macht; auch
scheint sich *dw'n* für *dwfn* 'tief' selbst kein Dichter zu
gestatten. W. *dwfn* ist das irische *domhain* 'tief', aber es
ist vermutlich auch das Substantiv *domhan* 'Welt', das
freilich aus der welschen Litteratur nicht mehr nachweisbar ist. Wie bod 'das Sein' und anfod 'das Nicht-
sein', fodd 'das Gefallen' und anfodd 'das Missfallen' bedeuten, so wird Annwfn (aus *a ndwfn*) 'die Nicht-Welt,
die Unterwelt', 'the other world' heissen. So ist w. annynog
'unmännlich' und ir. anduine 'ein Bösewicht' (von *duine*
: *dyn* 'Mann'). Also kein 'bottomless pit', und auch die
Bedeutung 'Hölle' liegt nicht eigentlich in dem Worte und
passt in den Mabinogion ganz und gar nicht. Dafydd ab
Gwilym nennt den Nebel: enaint gwrachiod Annwn 'die
Salbe der Vetteln von Annwn' 54, 28; und: mwg ellylldân
o Annwn 'den Rauch des Gespensterfeuers aus Annwn'
39, 19; und abermals: mor wyd o Annwn 'du bist ein
Meer aus Annwn' 39, 44. Und in seinem Gedichte über
den Fuchs sagt er:

Nid hawdd i mi ddilyd hwn
I'w dŷ annedd hyd Annwn.

'Nicht leicht ist's für mich diesen zu seinem Wohnhause
bis in die Unterwelt zu verfolgen', 182, 43 f. Bei demselben
Dichter spricht aber der Sommer:

Dyfod tri mis i dyfn,
Defnyddiau llafuriau llu;
A phan ddarffo do a dail
Dyfu a gwau y gwiail,
I ochel awel auaf,
I wlad Annwfn ddwfn ydd âf.

'Drei Monde kommen für das Wachstum, das der Leute
Ernten in sich birgt; und wenn Dach und Laub aus-
gewachsen sind und das Gezweig sich ausbreitet, dann
gehe ich, des Winters Hauch zu meiden, ins Land der
tiefen Unterwelt', 162, 35 ff.

Dwylyw 'die beiden Parteien' 132 wird wohl richtiger dwyliw
geschrieben, es reimt auf *rhiw*, D. G. 75, 17. Der Herausgeber s. v. erklärt *deuliw sêr* nicht richtig als 'eine zweite
zu' oder 'vergleichbar mit der Farbe der Sterne'; es heisst
'doppelt sternenfarbig', sowie *wyth liw sêr* 'achtfach sternenfarbig' D. G. 10, 8.

Ffristial ist wohl kaum ein dem Schach ähnliches Spiel, wenn
gleich Ab Gwilym neben chwarau ffristiol 2, 37 auch gwerin
ffristial 208, 69 hat (gwerin y wyddbwyll = *mir.* foirend
fidchille). Salesbury giebt: ffrustial 'a myse, mase' (= mease,
w. *mwys*?). Es ist eines der vier gogampeu oder kleinern
Spiele der Cymry (MA. 872b), das Würfelspiel, nach Davies
fritillus, i. e. 'in ludo aleae vasculum infundibuli speciem
referens, in quo agitantur tali et unde jaciuntur in
alveolum', d. h. ein Würfelbecher. Ducange hat ausserdem:
'Fritillum est sistrum vel tuba, quo vocantur ad ludum'.
Das welsche Wort scheint von fritillus abgeleitet zu sein,
mit Anlehnung an altfr. frestele 'Pfeife, Flöte' von fistella
für fistula (aw. *fistl*).

Haro 'oho!' Haro! nid fi yw 'r cynta p. 94, eine Interjektion,
die vielleicht mit *aro* gleichbedeutend ist: dyre yma, aro
dyre 'komm her, he! komm!' S. Evans s. v.; aro etto, I. G.
4, 100. Es ist das cornische *harow* 'sad! alas!' und das
altfranzösische *haro, harou, hareu, harau, hero* und einmal

harol alarme, 'exprimant l'appel ou la détresse' (Godefroy
4, 426). Haro! la gorge m'art! 'Hallo! mich brennt's in der
Kehle!' war früh und spat das Wort des guten Meisters Jean
Cotard. Diez leitet *haro* aus dem Deutschen und giebt ihm
die Grundbedeutung 'hierher'. Wenn man aber bedenkt,
dass das franz. *haro* uns von dem Bretonen Noël du Fail
(Oeuvres facétieuses, 1874, 1, 253) aus der Bretagne bezeugt
wird und hier eine Volksetymologie veranlasst hat (ha
Raoul), so ist es nicht unwahrscheinlich, dass es celtischen
Ursprungs ist. Es lebt noch im heutigen irischen *hurroo*
fort, womit vielleicht der Kriegsruf der Alten zusammenhängt: 'Totus autem tam equitatus, quam peditatus, quoties
ad manus et pugnam venitur, alta voce *Pharro, pharro*
inclamat. Utrum a rege Pharaone, Gandeli socero, an ab
alia caussa clamor iste natus sit, parum ad rem attinet
explicare'. R. Stanihurst, de rebus in Hibernia gestis, 1584,
p. 43. Ob dieser Ausruf von *faire o* abzuleiten ist, wie
Keating in der Einleitung seiner Geschichte sagt, und ob
er dem Vulgäririschen von Munster *airiú* 'aroo' (GJ. 5, 151.
163. 6, 4. 70 etc.) entspricht, bleibe dahingestellt.

Hwndliwr 'Schwindler, Händler': hwndliwr a'th siommei mewn
rhyw hen geffyl 'ein Schwindler, der dich mit einem alten
Pferde betrog' 21; y pedleriaid a'r hwndlwyr ceffyleu 'die
Trödler und die Pferdehändler' 102; mae 'r cwestwyr a'r
hwndlwyr ar falu y bon'ddigion 'die Denuncianten und die
Schwindler fallen über die Edelleute her', 124. Das Wort
scheint eine Wallicisierung von *swindler* (**chwindlwr*) und
erinnert an das deutsche *händler*, d. i. namentlich 'der
Pferdehändler oder Rosskamm'. Das Wort *pedlar*, un-
bekannter Herkunft im Englischen, ist möglicherweise das
deutsche *bettler*; cf. der *bettel*, d. i. die wertlose Sache.

Llumman in *noeth lumman* 7 sollte lymman geschrieben werden,
denn es entspricht dem ir. *lom-nocht* (w. noethlom) oder
lomán. Salesbury hat: noeth lymyn 'stryp naked', Walters:
noeth-lummyn 'stark-naked', G. Owen: noeth lyman (2, 77)
und noeth luman (2, 266).

Mâd felen 'die gelbe Pest' 61; cynddrwg a'r vad velen, MA. 842b;
chwaer undad, chwyrnad, hirnos I'r oer Fad felen o Ros,
D. G. 139, 50 (I. G. 77, 47). 'Flava pestis quam et physici
ictericiam dicunt passionem', sagt Giraldus im Itinerarium.

Diese Mortalitas suchte sowohl England als Irland heim, zuerst 547—550, sodann 664 'tempore Finani et Colmani episcoporum' (Beda, Hist. eccl. 3, 27), diesmal durch Jahrzehnte. Sie heisst bei den Iren Galar buidhe (Reeves, Vita Sancti Columbae p. 182) oder Buidechair oder Buide (auch *cron*) Chonnaill. Vgl. Liber Hymnorum 1, 25; 2, 113. Das welsche *mad* ist vielleicht der Name eines Tieres, wie Jones bemerkt, dem irischen *math* (WT. p. 279) entsprechend, dessen Bedeutung nicht feststeht, von dem aber mathgamain 'Bär' abgeleitet ist.

Mursen 14, 99, 140 wird von Salesbury 'a calat' (d. h. callet) erklärt; vgl. D. G. 79, 25. 48; 139, 55; 202, 42. Ein dunkles Wort, gewiss nicht = *virgin*, denn es giebt auch ein Masc. *mursyn*.

Scithredd 'Zähne, Hauer' 117, ist der Plural von *yskithyr* RB. 1, 122. 135 oder *ysgithr*; ysgithred y baed 'die Hauer des Ebers' HM. 1, 411. 2, 148; esgithred I. G. 2, 51, var. ysgythred; eskydred, Laws p. 152; in übertragener Bedeutung: drwy yskithred kerric 'per abrupta saxa' RB. 2, 59; und davon abgeleitet: y baed yskithrawc 'aper dentosus' 2, 151; kythreul ysgithrawc 'ein Teufel mit Hauern' LA. 153, 20; cf. MA. 157 b (altw. *schitrauc*, KB. 7, 415); und: wylo ac ysgythru a chrynnu dannedd 'weinen und Zähne fletschen und knirschen' BC. 192. Dem Worte kommt eigentlich der Vokal *i* zu, aber daneben steht ysgwthr, ysgythr in der Bedeutung 'Spitze, schneiden': brid ysgwthrlid ysgythrlem, D. G. 173, 74, cf. 85, 4; ysgythru 'schneiden' LA. 87; ysgythrwr cad 'ein Hauer in der Schlacht' I. G. 2, 49; yskythredic 'impictus' d. h. gemeisselt RB. 2, 189; ysgythrat 'Meisselung' Karls Reise 8, 15, wozu ir. sgathara 'hewing' O'R. und alb. sgatharra, sgathaireachd in gleicher Bedeutung erwähnt werden mögen. Mir scheint *ysgithr* gleiches Stammes mit *air.* cinteir 'calcar', *gr.* χέντρον und *w.* cethr 'Spitze, Nagel' (cf. cythraul von contrarius, cythrudd von contrudere, cythrwfl von contribulatio, athrywyn von intervenire, etc.) und zu der begrifflichen Entfaltung des Wortes möchte *sculptura*, wovon Jones es ableitet, in Anschlag zu bringen sein. Vermutlich hängt mit ysgithr, ysgythr auch *yscethrin* zusammen, das bald als 'impetuous' und bald als 'horrible' erklärt wird, BC. 87, 97, 107, 113, 150; es ist

nach S. Evans, Dictionary p. 1611 = disgethrin, dysgethrin
'rauh, hart', und in einem Gedichte Iolo Gochs 2, 51 lesen
die einen: baedd disgethring, die andern: baedd ysgethring
'ein hauender Eber'.

Ymleferydd 'das Zusammenreden' 46, 56, 93 setzt eine Mehrheit
voraus und sollte daher nach Simwnt Fychan (Cyfrinach y
Beirdd p. 105) nur mit einem Plural verbunden sein. Er
tadelt daher selbst den Vers des Dafydd ab Gwilym: 'Mil
fawr yn ymleferydd O darannau sugnau sydd' 44, 32, wo
andere 'o gadwynau' oder 'o gertweiniau' lesen. Ebenso
gut könnte der Pedant an 'Aml ferw yn ymleferydd'
I. G. 76, 10 (= D. G. 146, 14) Anstoss nehmen.

Ich kann diese Bemerkungen über den Bardd Cwsc nicht
schliessen ohne die Ausstattung zu rühmen, in der er diesmal
vor uns erschienen ist. Das Streben der Herren Jarvis und
Foster in Bangor verdient alle Förderung. Es ist im Werke
uns mit ihrer Hilfe in der Guild Series of Welsh Reprints
namhafte Bücher der ältern Litteratur, wie Morgan Llwyds
Schriften, mehreres von W. Salesbury, das Drych y Prif Oesoedd
von Theoph. Evans und anderes Gute wieder zugänglich zu
machen. Dem sehen wir gern entgegen. Inzwischen ist schon
der Bardd Cwsc in solcher Ausgabe uns ein werter Besitz in
unserm 'twysg o lyfrau'.

Berlin.   L. CHR. STERN.

ERSCHIENENE SCHRIFTEN.

The Cuchullin Saga in Irish Literature. Being a Collection of Stories relating to the Hero Cuchullin, translated from the Irish by various Scholars: compiled and edited with Introduction and Notes by Eleanor Hull. London, D. Nutt, 1898. 8°. Pp. lxxx + 316.

Obschon diese Sammlung von vierzehn irischen Heldensagen in englischer Bearbeitung sich an das grosse Publikum wendet, so enthält sie doch auch für den Fachgelehrten gar manches Neue und Beachtenswerte. Vor allem sei auf Miss Hulls Einleitung hingewiesen, in welcher die Fragen, die sich an Entstehung und Überlieferung dieser Texte knüpfen, klar und einsichtig behandelt werden. Im Anschluss an eine Besprechung des Stils dieser Sagen und des Kulturzustandes, der sie hervorgebracht, hebt die Verfasserin mit Recht im Gegensatz zu Atkinsons Bemerkungen in der Einleitung zum Yellow Book of Lecan die Reichhaltigkeit der älteren irischen Litteratur hervor, die vollendete Erzählerkunst, die in den Sagen zu Tage tritt, und die Ideale edler Sitte, die aus ihnen hervorleuchten. Warme Empfindung und feine Beobachtung zeichnen diesen Teil von Miss Hulls Arbeit vor vielem andern aus, was über denselben Gegenstand geschrieben ist. Die Wiedergabe der Sagen selbst hält sich im ganzen treu an die Übersetzungen, die von O'Curry, Stokes, Windisch u. a. herrühren und in der Revue Celtique und anderen Zeitschriften zerstreut sind. Auch das in der eingegangenen Archaeological Review schwer zugängliche 'Wooing of Emer' ist hier mit einigen Kürzungen wieder abgedruckt. Was aber dem Buche in unsern Augen seinen grössten Wert verleiht, ist die meisterhafte Übersetzung der *Táin Bó Cúalnge* und des *Brislech Mór Maige Muirthemne*, die von O'Grady herrührt, der, wenn er auch in Einzelheiten öfters irrt, wie kein anderer Idiom und Stil dieser Litteratur beherrscht. Besonders seine Übertragung der Schlacht von Muirthemne ist vielleicht das Beste, was er uns je geboten hat. Obgleich er uns auf S. 110 durch Miss Hull zu wissen thut, dass diese Übersetzungen 'for English readers, not for Irish scholars' seien, so glaube ich doch, dass es keinen noch so guten Kenner des Irischen giebt, den ihre Lektüre nicht belehren kann. Und wenn ich im folgenden einige Mängel der Übertragung rüge, so hoffe ich, dass weder er noch Miss Hull mir das verargen werden. Bei dem heutigen Stande unserer irischen Sprachkenntnis sind auch die Fehler eines Kenners wie O'Grady lehrreich.

Auf S. 114 ist *lóthommar* mit 'brewer's trough' übersetzt, während doch Aisl. Meic Conglinne S. 11, 3. 22 zeigt, dass es 'Waschtrog' bedeuten muss. Ebenda ist *órdúse* durch 'thumb rings' wiedergegeben, als ob es mit *ordu* 'Daumen' zu thun hätte; es ist aber der Plural von *ór-dúis* 'Goldgeschmeide'.

S. 120, 'in unison they both lifted their feet and put them down' = LL. 55 b 8: *i n-óenfecht dostorbaitis a cossa*, also besser: 'in unison they checked their feet'.

S. 121, *mendchrot* 'peaked harp', als ob *mend* für *bend* stünde. Stokes hat gezeigt, dass das Wort 'kleine Harfe, Laute', wörtlich 'kid-harp' bedeutet.

Warum O'Grady auf S. 123 *fer fínd*, von Cuchulinn gebraucht, mehrfach mit 'a small man' übersetzt, verstehe ich nicht.

Auf S. 131 muss es statt 'on its side he cuts his name in Ogham' heissen: 'on its side he put an inscription in Ogham' (*dobreth ainm n-ogaim 'na tæb*). Vgl. diese Zeitschrift Bd. II, S. 214.

S. 139 ist 'the land into which the little boy is come' in 'the land out of which' u. s. w. zu ändern (*tír asatánic*, LL. 63 b 1).

S. 146 übersetzt O'Grady *co ndechaid a mdel asa gúalaind* mit 'so that his mouth is brought over one shoulder', indem er *mdel* als für *bél* verschrieben nimmt. Aber *mdel* bedeutet 'Nacken', und es ist zu übersetzen 'so dass ihm der Nacken aus der Schulter ging'. In LL. 29a ist *mdel* das Nackenstück eines Tieres, das dem *rannaire* und *rechtaire* zukommt.

S. 153. Levarcham ist nicht die Tochter Aeds, sondern von Ae und Adarc (*ingen saide Aí ocus Adairce*, LL. 67 b 24).

Auf S. 155 sollte es statt 'Do the trimming, said the driver' heissen 'I will gather them, for it is easier', [said the driver]. (*Dogén a n-imtheclamad, dáig is assu*, LL. 68 a 42).

S. 163 statt Buic lies Buide.

S. 164 statt LL. 74 a lies LU. 74 a.

S. 178 ist 'moles' keine gute Übersetzung für *tibri*, vielmehr 'tufts of hair', wie Rev. Celt. XVI, S. 89 gezeigt ist.

S. 179 giebt O'Grady *sciath digrais* (LL. 79 a 5) mit 'a trusty special shield' wieder. Das Wort *digrais* hat bisher keine befriedigende Deutung erfahren (s. Windisch). Ich möchte es als aus privativem *di* und *gréis* zusammengesetzt erklären. So wird **so-réid* zu *soraid*, **do-réid* zu *doraid* u. s. w. Es hiesse dann etwa 'unwiderstehlich'. BB. 236 a 5 wird die Sündflut so genannt (*ó theibirsin truim na dilend dighraisi*) und LL. 107 b 40 sagt Cuchulinn: '*Cían úad ... ó ná lud do chur chúardda im Murthemniu 7 is digrais lend techt indiu*' d. h. 'es

ist lange her, dass ich keine Rundfahrt in M. gemacht habe und heute
lockt es mich unwiderstehlich'.

Derartiges könnte noch manches ausgestellt werden; doch thun
solche Versehen dem hohen Werte der Übersetzung keinen Abbruch.
Ich schliesse mit dem Wunsche, dass auch bald einmal bei uns ein des
Irischen Kundiger die wichtigsten und schönsten Sagen des alten Irlands
in ebenso gelungener Übertragung dem deutschen Publikum zugänglich
machen möge.

On an Ancient Settlement in the South-West of the Barony
of Corkaguiney, County of Kerry. By R. A. Stewart-
Mac Alister, M.A. (Transactions of the Royal Irish
Academy, vol. XXXI, part VII.) Dublin, March 1899.
Pp. 209—344. Plates XVII—XXV. 6sh.

In diesem stattlichen mit mehreren Abbildungen geschmückten
Heft handelt der unsern Lesern wohlbekannte Verfasser von den Überresten einer alten Ansiedelung an der Küste zwischen Ventry Harbour
und Dunmore Head. Er giebt zunächst eine eingehende Beschreibung
der natürlichen und künstlichen Höhlen, Steinkammern u. s. w. mit
ihren den heutigen Umwohnern geläufigen Namen (*clochán, liss, dún,
cathair*). Er berechnet, dass nach niedriger Schätzung die Ansiedlung
etwa für tausend Menschen Unterkunft bot. In einem zweiten Teile
werden dann die Fragen erörtert, die sich an die Bewohner, das Alter
und den Zweck der Niederlassung knüpfen. Herr MacAlister verwirft
O'Curry's Idee einer klösterlichen Ansiedlung (laura), besonders wegen
der clocháns mit mehreren Kammern, der weiten Zerstreuung über
mehrere englische Geviertmeilen, des Mangels einer einschliessenden
Mauer und einer grösseren Kapelle, und kommt zu dem Schluss, dass
wir es mit einer heidnischen Ansiedelung zu thun haben, die aber bis
in die Zeiten des Christentums gedauert hat. Auf die Nahrung der
Bewohner lassen Überreste von Muscheltieren, Hasen, Kaninchen, Schafen
und Ziegen sowie einige kleine Handmühlen schliessen. Eine Wasser-
mühle (*muilleann maol* 'a wheelless mill') stammt wahrscheinlich aus
späterer Zeit. Von Waffen oder Hausgerät hat sich nichts gefunden.
Schliesslich sei noch eine rätselhafte Ogaminschrift (LMCBDV) erwähnt,
die an eine ähnliche auf einem Bernsteinamulet erinnert (LMCBTM,
Journ. of the Kilkenny Archaeol. Soc. III. S. 339). K. M.

H. D'Arbois de Jubainville, La civilisation des Celtes et celle
de l'époque homérique. (Cours de littérature celtique,
Tome VI.) Paris, A. Fontemoing, 1899. XVI + 418 pp. 8⁰.

Was von dem Staate, der Religion, der Familie und der Kriegs-
führung der alten Celten von Griechen, Römern und Iren überliefert
wird (es ist zum Teil schon in frühern Bänden des 'Cours' behandelt),
stellt der Verfasser hier der Civilisation des homerischen Zeitalters
gegenüber. Wenn die Allgemeinheit des gewählten Themas überraschende Resultate nicht liefern kann ('l'esprit humain a partout les

mêmes lois', p. 104), so ist es doch nützlich, dass man die celtischen
Realien, die aus den Alten herangezogen werden, beim Fortschritte der
sprachlichen Studien wieder durchgehe. Dahin gehört namentlich, was
in einem *réimhsgéal* über den celtischen Zweikampf, den Heldenpart und
den Kriegshund zusammengestellt wird, so wie die Nachrichten über
celtische Söldner, die Götter der Celten, ihren Glauben an die Un-
sterblichkeit, ihre Menschenopfer, ihre heiligen Zahlen u. a. m. Als die
Träger der Kultur in der altceltischen Gesellschaft erkennt der Verf.
die drei Personen, die Strabon in den Worten βάρδοι τε καὶ οὐάτεις
καὶ δρυΐδαι namhaft macht, und die bei Homer ἀοιδοί, μάντεις und
ἱερεῖς heissen; das sind die Dichter (poetae), die Seher (vates) und die
Priester (magi). In der uns bekannten celtischen Sprache entsprechen
den drei Klassen offenbar das gallo-britannische *bard*, das irische *fáith*
und das irische *drui*, *draoi*. Den ersten Ausdruck haben, wie ich vermute, erst später die Iren (vgl. Thurneysen, Verslehren p. 107) und das
Wort *dryw* sehr spät die Welschen entlehnt, die auch der Wurzel *fáth*
: *gwawd* eine andere Bedeutung gaben. Des geheimnisvollen Zauber-
wesens hatte vermutlich jeder der drei Stände viel und der Unterschied
scheint früh aufgehoben zu sein. Jedenfalls ist das irische *file* 'Dichter'
(in den Glossen einmal 'comicus') ein, wie es scheint, alles umfassender
Ausdruck (vgl. O'Curry, Materials p. 2. 461) und es überzeugt nicht,
wenn er hier (dem welschen *gwelet* 'sehen' und der Seherin *Veleda* zu-
liebe) als der *vates* der Alten gedeutet wird, wofür die celtische Sprache
ein entsprechendes Wort hat. Das von Augustin überlieferte *dusius*
'incubus' wird als Bachgott gedeutet, aber gleichzeitig auch mit dem
niederdeutschen Worte *dusel* (p. 184) und seinen Verwandten in Verbindung gebracht.

D. Hyde, A Literary History of Ireland from Earliest Times
to the Present Day. London, T. Fisher Unwin, 1899.
XVIII + 654 pp. 8°.

Inschriften von hohem Alter, lateinische Psalterien und Evangelien
in der Halbunciale des 6. und 7. Jh., lateinische Gedichte aus dem frühen
Mittelalter und ein Anteil an der wissenschaftlichen Litteratur dieser
Zeiten; altirische Glossen in lateinischen Codices des 8. und 9. Jh. nebst
Resten theologischer Traktate in gleicher Sprache; dann im Mittelirischen des 10.—15. Jh., eine überreiche Fülle von Sagen des mytho-
logischen Zeitalters und der Heroen von Ulster, Erzählung, Didaktik
und Lyrik in zahllosen Gedichten, Bibelhistorie, Legenden der Heiligen,
Homilieen und andere Theologica, Weltgeschichte, Annalen, historische
Skizzen, Topographie, Genealogie, Gesetz und Recht, Medizin, Schul-
schriften der Barden, Übersetzungen aus lateinischen und französischen
Autoren u. a. m.; endlich vom 16.—19. Jh. in neuirischer Sprache,
wiederum Sagen aus den frühern Cyklen und aus dem ossianischen
Kreise in Poesie und Prosa, die Erneuerung der veralteten Texte dieser
Art, christliche Lehre und Erbauung, Predigten, die Werke Keatings,
geschichtliche Darstellungen, Märchen, eine lange Reihe von Barden und
Dichtern in alten und neuen Formen — das ist die ungeheuer umfang-

reiche Litteratur Irlands, das einst, als es sich die Kultur Roms aneignete, eine 'Schule des Westens' gewesen ist, dann aber, in sich selbst zurückgekehrt, an seinem altüberlieferten geistigen Besitze unabhängig gearbeitet hat. Dieses Schriftwesen zu beschreiben hat, nach dem unvollkommenen Versuche von W. Harris 1746, als erster vor 80 Jahren der wackere 'Compilator' Edward O'Reilly unternommen. Sein Werk wurde aus dem Mittelalter durch E. O'Curry ergänzt, der ihn an irischer Sprachkenntnis weit übertraf, aber seine Arbeit nicht entbehrlich machte. Den Gegenstand nach den Forschungen der letzten dreissig Jahre vollkommener, zuverlässiger, präciser zu behandeln, ein Handbuch zu schaffen, aus dem man die gedruckte irische Litteratur mit ihren Kommentaren (von dem noch nicht verzeichneten Inhalte der Manuskripte ganz abgesehen), namentlich die Autoren in chronologischer Ordnung und die Titel oder Initia der Werke, bequem und möglichst vollständig übersehen könnte, wäre wahrlich ein Desideratum, zu dessen Leistung sich freilich so leicht kein 'Compilator' bereit finden wird. Auch D. Hyde hat darauf verzichtet das Werk O'Reillys und O'Currys in der angedeuteten Weise fortzuführen; sein indes ziemlich dick geratenes Buch ist für Analphabete im Irischen berechnet, indem es aus den Darstellungen und Übersetzungen der Celtisten auswählt, was für die Unterhaltung am geeignetsten erschien. Wer das Studium eines Buches mit seiner Inhaltsangabe beginnt, wird von der Disposition des vorliegenden keine günstige Meinung gewinnen; indes hilft ein Index nach. Der Verf. hat eine grosse Zahl von Büchern benutzt und daraus mitgeteilt, was in den Rahmen seines Werkes zu passen schien, darunter genug des Wissenswerten und wenig Bekannten, leider aber meist ohne die erforderliche Quellenangabe. Was er dagegen nicht benutzt hat, ist mehr, darunter die fünf edierten irischen Codices des Mittelalters mit ihren höchst verdienstlichen Inhaltsangaben und das meiste, was seit 100 Jahren in Zeitschriften sehr zerstreut niedergelegt worden ist. Der Verf. erfasst die Aufgabe vom Standpunkte der neuirischen Litteratur, in der er bewandert ist. Hier und dort teilt er einiges aus Handschriften der neuirischen Dichter mit und bildet ihre Metra in englischer Übersetzung mit Meisterschaft nach.

Das Buch ist voll Vindikation, so namentlich in der historischen Einleitung; aber in der Liste der Wörter, die die Deutschen, 'less intellectually cultured than the Celts', den Celten verdanken (p. 12 f.), ist das meiste (wie *frei*, *held*, *herr*, *sieg*, *beute*, *flur*, *furt* etc.) unbedenklich zu streichen. Der Verf. hat von Anfang bis zu Ende festinante calamo geschrieben. Z. B. nennt er p. 267 als Herausgeber der altirischen Glossen: der Mailänder Ascoli, Zeuss, Stokes, Nigra; der St. Galler Ascoli, Nigra; der Würzburger Zimmer und Zeuss; der Karlsruher Zeuss; der Turiner Zimmer, Nigra, Stokes; der Wiener Zimmer und Stokes; des Sermo von Cambrai Zeuss. Die älteste Erzählung über den Kampf Cuchulinns mit seinem Sohne Conlaoch oder Conla hat nicht Keating (p. 300), sondern das Yellow Book of Lecan p. 214 a. Das Gedicht des Königs Alfred von Northumbria (p. 221) steht schon, wiewohl nicht vollständig, im Buche von Leinster p. 31 a.

Cormacs Rat an seinen Sohn im Buche von Ballymote p. 62a ist leider nicht 'heavily glossed' (p. 246), sondern hat nur einige wenige Glossen, und ein älterer Text steht LL. 343a; es war auch zu erwähnen, dass die Übersetzungen, die der Verf. giebt (p. 247 ff.), die O'Donovans sind, im Dublin Penny Journal 1, 214. 231 (vom Jahre 1832 f.). Nicht Cormac 'an eigeas' heisst der Barde Muircheartachs (p. 428), sondern Cormacan eigeas, wie sein Herausgeber in den Tracts relating to Ireland, vol. I, Dublin 1841, ihn richtig nennt; vgl. Oirchel eces RC. 5, 202; Aedh eiges SG. 249. Dass der Dechant von Lismore in einem wohlbekannten ossianischen Gedichte nicht *ni nelli fiym* schreibt (p. 509), war aus Camerons Reliquiae Celticae 1, 2 zu ersehen; was der Verf. über ossianische Poesie überhaupt sagt, zeugt nicht von sehr grosser Kenntnis dieser Litteratur. Die Anzahl der MacWards und der O'Mulconrys bei O'Reilly (p. 524) ist nicht richtig gegeben; Bonaventura O'Hussey (p. 534) ist derselbe wie Maelbrigte O'Hussey (p. 612). Entgegen der Angabe p. 564, erwähnt O'Reilly das Leben des Aodh Ruadh in seinen Irish writers p. CXC allerdings und sagt, dass er es abgeschrieben und fast ganz übersetzt habe (seine Arbeit wird sich wohl in Cheltenham befinden); das MS. gehörte damals W. M. Mason, und was der Herausgeber des Werkes D. Murphy in seinem Vorworte p. III darüber sagt, ist falsch. *Snigid gaim* heisst nicht 'winter roars', sondern 'der Winter giebt Schnee' (p. 409). Dass nir. *aibéil* in den Tri biorghaoithe p. 145. 151. 153 'rasch' bedeutet, ist schon gesagt worden (GJ. 6, 80); aber schwerlich kann man damit (p. 407) das mir. *abéla* LU. 6 a 41 (var. *abbeli* RC. 20, 144) im Amra Choluimchille erklären (vgl. K. Meyers Contributions p. 6).

Der Verfasser kennzeichnet die irische Litteratur gewiss richtig so, dass darin grosse dominierende Namen und Werke fehlen, dass aber die Masse des überlieferten Stoffes der litterarische Besitz des ganzen Volkes geworden ist, es durchdrungen und auf seine geistige Bildung den bedeutendsten Einfluss geübt hat. Wenn sie so mehr in die Breite als in die Höhe und in die Tiefe gewachsen ist, so sind doch ihre Formen höchst eigenartig, ursprünglich und bemerkenswert.

J. Strachan, The Substantive verb in the Old Irish Glosses. (Transactions of the Philological Society 1899.) 82 pp. 8⁰.

Eine Sammlung der Stellen, an denen in den altirischen Texten die Copula *is* und die Verba substantiva *atá, fil, biid* mit ihren Formen vorkommen, nebst Erläuterungen ihres Gebrauchs. Auch die in ähnlicher Bedeutung angewendeten *rongab, dicoissin* und das rätselhafte *dixnigedar* sind in die Übersicht aufgenommen. Dazu gehören die Tabellen in RC. 20, 81—88. Mir scheint, die Annahme eines Zusammenhangs zwischen ir. *fil* und welsch *gwel* ist nicht ohne weiteres zu verwerfen (p. 56); ohne mich auf semasiologische Erörterungen einzulassen, möchte ich es doch für möglich halten, dass ir. *fil, fail* 'es ist', welsch *gwel* 'sieh', lat. *vel* 'oder', engl. *well* 'wohl' im Grunde dasselbe Wort sind, dessen ursprüngliche Bedeutung *velle* 'wollen' bewahrt hätte.

Otia Merseiana, The Publication of the Arts Faculty of University College, Liverpool. Volume One. London, Th. Wohlleben 1899. 152 pp. 8⁰.

Wenn wir es nicht wüssten, dass in jenem blühenden Emporium an der Irischen See, der zweiten Stadt des vereinigten Königreichs, abseits vom geschäftigen Verkehr der Völker, den Musen ein Tempel geweiht ist, so würde uns dieser erste Band gelehrter Arbeiten, den wir der Arts Faculty an der Universität Liverpool verdanken, darüber belehren. Unter den zehn Beiträgen nehmen wir den meisten Anteil an den Stories and Songs from Irish MSS. von K. Meyer (p. 113—128), die zwei Inedita darbieten. Das eine ist ein sehr merkwürdiges Fragment von Laisréns Vision der Hölle aus Rawlinson B. 512, Bl. 44a, das der Herausgeber, durch einige altertümliche Formen bestimmt, der Zeit um 900 zuweist; der Urheber dieser Höllenfahrt möchte der Abt Laisrén von Leighlin sein, der 638 starb. Der andere Beitrag Prof. Meyers ist das Lied des alten Weibes von Beare, das er nach zwei Texten in H. 3. 18 TCD. ediert und übersetzt. Einiges ist davon schon in der Vision des Mac Conglinne p. 208 ff. mitgeteilt worden. In 35 Strophen, von denen einzelne allerdings vielleicht nicht zu dem ursprünglichen Gedichte gehören, gedenkt eine verwelkte Alte, die in reifen Jahren den Schleier genommen hat, ihrer Jugend, als sie schön, lebenslustig und von Liebhabern umringt war. Das Poem, dessen Überlieferung nicht über das 16. Jahrhundert zurückreicht, ist altertümlich und schwer; an seine Übersetzung konnte sich nur ein mit der mittelirischen Litteratur so vertrauter Gelehrter heranwagen. *Caillech Berre buoi* oder *Berrao baoie* versteht der Herausgeber nachträglich als 'die Alte von Bera-buie', was nach O'Grady der einheimische Name für Dursey Island ist. In Strophe 21 übersetzt er *ruscar* nun vielmehr als 'spread' (statt 'loved'). *Finān q.* (p. 121) heisst vielleicht 'quidam' oder 'quaeritur', da es unbestimmt gelassen wird, welcher Finán gemeint ist. — Es kommt uns nicht zu die übrigen Artikel dieses Bandes zu loben, aber erwähnt sei, dass nach J. A. Twemlow die irische Bulle 'In dispensatione ministrorum ecclesie Dei', die man dem Papste Urban V. beigelegt hatte, vielmehr Urban IV. gehört; dass V. H. Friedel über den Cod. Calixtinus in San Jago de Compostella, der unter anderem den Pseudo-Turpin enthält, beachtenswerte Mitteilungen macht; und dass R. Priebsch über die verschiedenen Formen der alten Homilie über die Sonntagsheiligung, die namentlich in drei angelsächsischen Fassungen überliefert ist, belehrt. Von der ersten Form, einem vom Himmel gefallenen Briefe Christi, druckt der Verfasser das lateinische Original aus dem Wiener Codex 1355 ab. Die zweite Form, die die Epistel mit den Visionen des Iren Niall († 854) verknüpft, weist auf einen lateinischen Text, mit dem der Angelsachse in Irland bekannt wurde; seine irische Redaktion findet sich LB. 202a, YBL. 215a und sonst (Zs. 1, 495). Die dritte gekürzte Form, die der Bischof Peter von Antiochia angeblich verbürgt, haben sich ausser den Franzosen die Welschen zu eigen gemacht; der welsche Text ist gedruckt im Cymmrodor 8, 162 ff., im

13*

Llyvyr yr Agkyr p. 157 und in R. Williams' Selections from the Hengwrt
Manuscripts 2, 289, Zeile 6 ff., mit Übersetzung 2, 638, Zeile 7 ff. In
dem letzten Druck ist er von der vorhergehenden Vision des Apostels
Paulus nicht getrennt worden.

**Geoffrey Keating, Eochair-sgiath an aifrinn. An explanatory
defence of the Mass. Dublin, P. O'Brien, 1898. XVI
+ 128 pp. 8⁰.**

Der einzige Autor neuirischer Prosa, der einen Namen hat, ist
Keating. Dieser Geistliche, von anglo-normannischer Herkunft, hat sich
durch seine Werke, die einst in zahllosen Exemplaren verbreitet waren,
um die Iren das grösste Verdienst erworben. Seine Geschichte ist ein
unentbehrliches Handbuch für jeden, der sich mit dem irischen Altertum
beschäftigt; seine 'drei Wurfspiesse des Todes' sind ein anderes Meister-
werk neuirischen Stils, mit dem uns eine vortreffliche Ausgabe vertraut
gemacht hat. Er hat noch mehr dergleichen geschrieben, was Andrew
MacCurtin 1709 in einer wertvollen Abschrift mit dem letztgenannten
Werke vereinigt hat (PRIA. III. 3, 1893—96, p. 218 ff.), nämlich ein
Werk über die Messe; *Iomagallma an anma agus an chuirp le cheile*
'Gespräche zwischen Seele und Körper'; und endlich (nach GJ. 9, 312)
ein Werk über den Rosenkranz und das Officium der heiligen Jungfrau.
Das Werk, von dem uns jetzt ein Abdruck geboten wird, ist gewiss
eines von Keatings frühesten und durchaus theologisch; er erwähnt es
in den Trí biorghaoithe p. 124. Eine Abschrift aus dem 17. Jh. liegt
in Cheltenham (cod. Phillipp. 10275). Er behandelt in dieser 'Clavis
clypeus missae' nach einem Vorworte in 18 Kapiteln mit der Gelehrsamkeit, die wir an ihm kennen, die Geschichte der Messe, ihre Bedeutung und ihre Namen, das Messgewand, den Messkanon, die Trans-
substantiationslehre, Beichte und Abendmahl und die segensreiche
Wirkung der Messe, die er namentlich gegen die Lehren Luthers und
Calvins verteidigt. Das Werk enthält manche Wörter, die in den
andern gedruckten Werken Keatings nicht vorkommen. Dazu gehört
z. B. auch *na hiobhail* oder *hiubhail* oder, wie dafür in den Text gesetzt
ist, *na huidhil* 'die Juden' (p. 35), wo man dem Worte *jew* (das auch
in das ältere Manx übergegangen ist: *Iú-yn* Phillips p. 76) die Pluralendung von *Gaoidhil* gegeben hat. Schade, dass die sehr nützlichen
Corrigenda und Varianten nur bis p. 49, 2 reichen; aber nach p. 128
fehlt nichts, wie uns der Herausgeber bestätigt.

**Oidhe Chloinne Uisnigh. Fate of the children of Uisneach,
published for the Society for the Preservation of the Irish
Language, with translation, notes, and a complete vocabulary.
Dublin, M. H. Gill and son, 1898. VIII + 150 pp. Kl. 8⁰.**

Wenn wir uns in den weiten Bahnen der mittelirischen und der
neuirischen Litteratur der Willkür der Schreiber annoch auf Gnade oder
Ungnade ergeben müssen, so ist uns nichts erwünschter, als dass uns
der Grammatiker einmal wieder in seine straffe Disciplin nehme. Wir

sind erleichtert, wenn uns ein Text vorgelegt wird, der es weniger auf
diplomatische Wiedergabe einer fehlerhaften Handschrift als auf sprachliche Korrektheit absieht, und uns alsbald das Gefühl überkommt, dass
der Herausgeber deklinieren, konjugieren, aspirieren und eklipsieren
kann. Wenn ein strenger Kritiker sagt, dass in dem vorstehenden
kurzen Titel ebenso viel Fehler als Wörter sind, so werden wir inne,
wie schwer das ist. Der Text dieser Erzählung ist aus dem späten
Mittelirischen ins Neuirische übertragen, schon mit viel Unsicherheit
und Zweifel in den Sprachformen. Wenn man indessen die besten der
siebzehn vorhandenen MSS. gewissenhaft zu Rate zieht, so darf man
hoffen daraus die Norm der Sprache zu gewinnen. Freilich ist ein
Apparatus criticus eine mühevolle Arbeit und nicht jedermanns Sache.
Auch der Herausgeber der Society hat selbst von dem einzigen MS.,
das ihm zugänglich war, nur sehr spärlichen Gebrauch gemacht und
sich begnügt O'Flanagans mangelhaften Text der Deirdri nach seiner,
wie das Vokabular zeigt, unvollkommenen Kenntnis der Sprache zu
revidieren. Daher ist denn des Zweifelhaften und Unrichtigen so viel
geblieben und das Ganze, wie die erwähnte Anzeige im Gaelic Journal
darthut, unbefriedigend ausgefallen. Ich füge nur einige Beispiele
hinzu. Wenn gleich auf der ersten Seite O'Flanagan hat: *Ró eirghe
an aes chiuil óirfidedh* acas *eladhna*, do sheinm a *ccruitedha* ceolbhinne
caeinthédacha acas a *ttiompána* taithnemhacha taidhuire, acas do *gabhail*
a *ndréchta* fīlidhachta, a *ccraebha* cóimhnesa acas a *ngéga* geinelaidh —,
so ist gewiss *ro éirigh a naos ccoil* mit dem Herausgeber zu lesen;
aber wir wünschen durch die Übereinstimmung der Handschriften bestätigt zu sehen, dass *oirfide* der dem mir. *airfite* entsprechende Genitiv
von *oirfideadh* ist und nicht etwa *oirfidthe* oder *oirfididh*. Der Genitiv
von ealadha 'Kunst' ist *ealadhan* (nicht ealadhna), vgl. KZ. 33, 148.
Der Accusativ pl. nach 'do sheinm' und 'do ghabháil' bei O'Flanagan
ist ein Solöcismus, aber der Genitiv sg., den der Herausgeber überall
einsetzt, ist nicht minder hart; es muss, wie übrigens der ältere Text
in WT. II, 2, 122 und Cameron, Reliquiae 2, 464 erkennen lässt, *a
gcruit gceoilbhinn gcaointéadach* und *a ndréacht filidheachta* etc. heissen.
Statt 'a ngéige geinealaighe' ist m. E. *a ngéag geinealaigh* zu
schreiben, denn geinealach ist ein nom. msc.; cf. a ngluine geinealuigh,
Keating, History p. CVIII; go na ghabbluibh geinioluigh, id. p. 356.
So bedarf der ganze Text der Superrevision, denn der Herausgeber ist
in allem unsicher. *A haithle na laoidh sin* schreibt er immer wieder,
obwohl er doch weiss, dass *laoidh* ein Femininum ist und den Genitiv
laoidhe bildet. Was die Verse anbetrifft, so können sie niemals
korrekt werden, wenn man nicht hier und dort einen altertümlichen
Ausdruck stehen lässt. 'Gleann Laoidh! ón, a nGleann Laoidh!' (p. 18)
hat eine Silbe zu wenig, 'Gleann Eitche! nch ón Gleann Eitche!' (p. 19)
eine Silbe zu viel; das hat auch 'Ann do thógbhas mo cheudthighi'
(p. 19). Hier muss es *mo cheudthigh* heissen, denn der Dativ *tigh* (von
teach) steht für den Nominativ-Accusativ, wie im Albanogälischen gewöhnlich. Dies Gedicht 'Ionmhuin tír an tír úd thoir' (nicht *t-shoir*)
ist in Schottland entstanden, wie die topographischen Namen zeigen

(vgl. Al. Stewart, Nether Lochaber 1883, p. 416). Dún Suibhne kommt im Dean's book p. 96 vor: *Down Swenyth* und ist das Castle Suine in Argyle, das ebenso wie 'the Castle of Duntroone' (Dún Treoin, p. 38 des Textes) in einem Schreiben vom Jahre 1685 ernährt wird (Highland Monthly 1, 474); er giebt auch Sliabh Suine (Inv. 14, 354). Baile gréine, *recte* Buaile gréine (p. 19), ist die 'Sonnensenne', ein sonst vorkommender Ausdruck, wie in dem Namen Buaile na gréine, südlich vom Berge Callan (PRIA. II. 1, 271). Wenn der Herausgeber p. 25 liest:

O nach bhfuil eagla orrain-ne
Ní dhéanfam an chomhairle —

so zerstört er den Vers; statt orrain-ne (*recte* orain-ne) muss die albanische Form *oirnne* beibehalten werden, damit er im Debide bleibt. Das Gedicht 'Sóraidh soir go Halbain uaim' p. 38 ist oft gedruckt (O'Flanagan, Deirdri p. 108; WT. II, 2, 115; Neilson, Grammar III, p. 18; Highland Monthly 2, 247; Cameron, Reliquiae 1, 120. 210; 2, 451), aber der Wortlaut ist noch nicht befriedigend hergestellt. Líonas mo cheann lán do'n éad 'my head fills full of jealousy' kann einem durchaus nicht gefallen; eine Edinburger Handschrift liest *lingis um chen* und das weist auf das Richtige: Lingis a'm cheann lán do'n éad 'es sprang, es kam mir in den Kopf eine Fülle der Eifersucht'. (Vgl. Zs. 1, 137.) Go ndeachadh uaim ar shluagh na marbh 'until he would go from me among the host of the dead' (p. 38) kann nicht richtig sein, ebensowenig wie *no go rachadh* der erwähnten Handschrift, da der Vers 8 Silben hat; man muss *uaim* mit Neilson auslassen oder O'Flanagans go *tteigh* beibehalten, womit *go dteidh* 'bis er geht' gemeint ist. ''S do ghuilfinnse léi fó seacht' (p. 39) ist willkürlich umgestellt; es muss *fó seacht léi* heissen, damit es auf 'i gcré' reimt. Doch das sind der Beispiele genug um zu beweisen, dass auch der neuirische Herausgeber die Handschriften benutzen, mit Verständnis und Urteil benutzen muss. Thut er es nicht, so mag er sich nicht wundern, wenn sich Stimmen vernehmen lassen, dass er überhaupt keine Litteratur besitze und dass seine Sprache ein Jargon ohne Regel sei.

E. Anwyl, A Welsh Grammar for schools. Part II — Syntax. London, Swan Sonnenschein & Co., 1899. pp. 81—187. 8⁰.

Der erste Teil dieser Grammatik ist in der Zeitschrift 2, 409 angezeigt worden. In diesem zweiten werden die Konstruktion des Satzes, dann der zusammengesetzte Satz und endlich die Bedeutung der Formen behandelt. Ein Anhang enthält anregende Bemerkungen über die gewöhnliche Wortstellung und die Inversion. Der Index hätte auch auf den ersten Teil ausgedehnt werden müssen. Der Verfasser ist ein gründlicher Kenner der Sprache und aus seiner Grammatik ist viel zu lernen; doch hat er manches übergangen, was Rowland beachtet. Etwas, worin ich mich schwer finde, das ist die Anordnung des Stoffes, wie sie nun in den beiden Teilen zu übersehen ist. Meines Erachtens sollte man von der natürlichen Dreiteilung der Grammatik nicht abgehen: die Lehre von den Buchstaben, die Lehre vom Worte und die Lehre vom Satze.

Edw. Schröder, Zeuss, Johann Kaspar. Sonderabdruck aus der Allgemeinen Deutschen Biographie, Band XLV. 1899. 5 Seiten. 8°.

Der schlichte Lebenslauf des Begründers der celtischen Philologie, den, mit Würdigung seiner Verdienste, diese Schrift einem weitern Leserkreise zu schildern bestimmt ist, wird den Freunden seiner Wissenschaft aus der Skizze von H. Gaidoz in der Revue Celtique 6, 519, die auf Chr. W. Glücks 'Erinnerung an Kaspar Zeuss', München 1857, beruht, bekannt sein. 1856 starb der vortreffliche Mann 'in Folge eines langwierigen Lungenleidens', nur erst 50 Jahr alt. Was er in diesem kurzen Leben an Unvergänglichem geleistet, ist ausserordentlich, und daher begleiten wir jeden Bericht über seinen Bildungsgang, über sein grosses Talent, über sein stilles Forscherleben mit regster Teilnahme. Zeuss war einer der namhaftesten Germanisten, als er, mit unvergleichlicher Ausdauer die grössten Schwierigkeiten überwindend, ein ganz neues Fach der Sprachwissenschaft schuf. Durch mannigfaltige Studien hatte er seine Erfahrung bereichert und seinen Blick geschärft. Im Lateinischen und Griechischen wohl gegründet, bezog er die Universität München als Studiosus der Theologie und der Philologie; er hörte hier Vorlesungen über Philosophie, Physik, Chemie, Mineralogie, Astronomie; dann über Theologie, namentlich bei dem berühmten Döllinger, dazu Hebräisch, Arabisch, Sanskrit; und endlich altklassische Philologie bei Thiersch. Er erwarb die Befähigung zum Gymnasiallehrer (als solcher war er anfangs Lehrer des Hebräischen) und, durch seine historischen Untersuchungen, die zum Universitätslehrer. In den Fächern, in denen er Grosses geleistet hat, ist er sein eigener Lehrer gewesen. Befriedigung scheinen ihm die verschiedenen Lehrstellen, die er inne gehabt hat, zunächst in Speier, nicht gewährt zu haben. 1840 bittet er den König, er möge geruhen, 'ihm das in Würzburg noch nicht vertretene Lehrfach der deutschen Sprache und Altertumskunde und zugleich der altindischen Sprachwissenschaft allergnädigst zu übertragen'. Erst 1847 erlangte er dann eine Münchener Professur für Geschichte, aber die akademische Jugend hatte kein Verständnis für die geistige Grösse dieses Gelehrten. Er kehrte an das Gymnasium, nun nach Bamberg, zurück, bewarb sich 1849 um die Stelle des Oberbibliothekars in Würzburg und verblieb, als sie ihm nicht gewährt wurde, bis an sein frühes Ende bei der Schule. In den vierziger Jahren ergriff er das Studium der celtischen Sprachen. Keine grössere That in seiner wissenschaftlichen Laufbahn als die Erforschung der altceltischen Glossen, von denen vor ihm wenige etwas wussten und niemand etwas verstand.

Da es mich hintrieb einen Blick in die Werkstätte dieses schöpferischen Geistes zu thun, so bin ich der K. B. Hof- und Staats-Bibliothek zu München dankbar, die mir ihre 'Zeussiana', den handschriftlichen Nachlass des grossen Gelehrten, mit der allen bekannten Liberalität zur Durchsicht verstattete. Welch erstaunlicher Fleiss auf diesen Tausenden von Quartblättern! Ich kann die Menge der Excerpte

aus lateinischen und griechischen Historikern, aus den Monumenta
Germaniae, aus Petries Monumenta britannica, aus den Bollandisten,
aus den Hisperica famina u. s. w. nur eben erwähnen; mehr zog mich
an, was auf die celtischen Sprachen im besondern Bezug hat: da ist
eine Abschrift von O' Reillys irischer Grammatik von 1817, Auszüge aus
Katalogen irischer Handschriften, aus O' Conors Scriptores, eine Abschrift
des zweiten Bandes der Mabinogion, ein Vocabularium zu den drei
Bänden der Ausgabe der Lady Guest in drei Teilen, Auszüge aus dem
Liber Landavensis, die Stücke des Llyfr Du aus der Myvyrian Archaeo-
logy, Excerpte aus dem Chartularium Rhedonense und sonstige Vor-
arbeiten zur Grammatica Celtica und das MS. derselben, dazu vieles
andere, was erkennen lässt, wie Zeuss unablässig nach allen Seiten
Umschau hielt und sich das Gebiet seiner Wissenschaft so vollständig
unterworfen hatte. Da ist auch manches Persönliche und flüchtige Ent-
würfe einzelner Briefe. [1] Was aber meine Wissbegierde aufs höchste
spannte, das waren die Glossen. Zeuss schrieb unter dem 27. November
1855 an Glück, er habe zweierlei Glossensammlungen: die einen enthielten die Glossen, die er unmittelbar aus den von ihm benutzten
irischen Handschriften abgeschrieben habe, und eine andere, worin die
irischen Glossen alphabetisch geordnet seien, nämlich die Sanktgaller,
Mailänder, Karlsruher und Würzburger und ein Anhang von Vocabula
obscura. Glück hat den Nachlass offenbar nicht sehr genau gemustert,
da er auf einem beiliegenden Blatt berichtet, dass er die ersten Abschriften der Glossen 'während seines Aufenthaltes in Vogtendorf und
Kronach im September des Jahres 1857 unter den Zeussischen Handschriften, die nicht nur durch ihre Fortschaffung von Vogtendorf [wo
Zeuss geboren und gestorben ist] in das Kronacher Pfarrhaus in die
grösste Unordnung geraten, sondern zum Teile verschleppt waren, leider
vergebens gesucht' habe. Alle sind sie da — die irischen Glossen sowohl wie die britannischen, mit rascher, sicherer Hand von Zeuss aus
den Originalen abgeschrieben, 160 Quartblätter, auf denen unendlich oft
sein forschendes Auge geruht haben muss. Auch einige Schriftproben,
auf Pflanzenpapier durchgezeichnet, finden sich, darunter die Incanta-
tiones Sangallenses und die GC.[1] p. XXXIII erwähnte charta pellucida.
An zweifelhaften Stellen wird man diese Abschriften noch immer gern
zu Rate ziehen; z. B. liest Zeuss in den Würzburger Glossen: fol. 11c
(1. Cor. 11, 6) roberrthe; 14c (2. Cor. 1, 15) cate; 17d (2. Cor. 11, 24)
madaessoir; 22b (Eph. 4, 26) irascemini et nolite peccare (irascē .i. fribar
pecthu arnarobat lib alit ished iarum torad forferce bad cenpeccad);
26b (2. Thess. 3, 4) confidimus .i. ammi torissig; 33a (Hebr. 3, 5) alit
isdim dar moysi .sintegdais ishe som im orotaig integdais. In einer
Zusammenstellung, die er flüchtig zu Papier gebracht hat, sagt Zeuss,
wann er die celtischen Codices excerpiert hat, nämlich in Würzburg (er
hat die Glossen des Cod. Paulinus von 1—1344 numeriert) vom November
1843 bis Februar 1844, in St. Gallen vom 30. März bis 13. April 1844,

---

[1] Die Briefe, die Zeuss in den Jahren 1853 bis 1856 an Glück geschrieben hat, lege ich für ein künftiges Heft der Zeitschrift zurück.

in Karlsruhe vom 3. bis 5. Mai 1844, in Mailand von Ende August bis
Anfang September 1844 und wieder im August 1846, in London und
Oxford vom 5. bis 11. Oktober 1844. Da ist noch das lateinische
Originalblatt, womit er sich in der Bodleiana vorstellt und um Vor-
legung der cambrischen und etwaigen irisch glossierten Codices der
Bibliothek bittet. Dies war 1844; nach dem horazischen Zeitraum von
neun Jahren erschien die Grammatica Celtica.

Niemand war in der Lage eine Kritik dieses Werkes tiefster
Gelehrsamkeit zu liefern. Ein Ungenannter (wohl M. Haupt) gab in
einer Anzeige im Litterarischen Centralblatt (die den Verf. so sehr
erfreute, dass er sie sich abschrieb) seiner Bewunderung Ausdruck und
bedauerte nur, dass das Buch lateinisch geschrieben sei. A. F. Pott,
der selbst keltizierte, sagte in der Deutschen Wochenschrift 1854:
'Ohne Übertreibung glaube ich versichern zu können, zwar einiger-
massen in dem Sinne, aber nicht mit dem zu schäbig gewordenen
Worte der durch Buchhändler-Panegyriken in Verruf gekommenen
Phrase von befriedigten Bedürfnissen: Das Buch füllt ein Loch, nein
vielmehr einen wahren Abgrund aus auf der grossen Heerstrasse der
historisch-philologischen Wissenschaft und auf der Seitenbahn der Sprach-
disciplin insbesondere'. Nicht minder aufrichtig war die Anerkennung,
die die Sachverständigen in den celtischen Ländern dem Werke zollten.
Ein welscher Gelehrter schrieb: 'Truly it is an unparalleled acquisition
to Celtic literature, whether we regard the importance of its object —
the plan on which it has been conducted — or the consummate skill
and sound learning which are displayed in its compilation'. (Cambrian
Journal 1854, p. 291). O'Donovan urteilte nach dem Tode des Verfassers so: 'Germany regrets in him one of those men who have raised
to its present height her position among learned nations in this age;
and Ireland ought not to think of him without gratitude, for the Irish
nation has had no nobler gift bestowed upon them by any continental
author for centuries back than the work which he has written on their
language. It is pleasing to record that the greatest acknowledgment
ever made to him came from Ireland. A short time before his death,
an invitation to visit Dublin was sent to him by Dr. Todd, President
of the Royal Irish Academy, in a manner which could not fail to be
most gratifying to him, and which was done with the ultimate intention
of conferring deserved honours on him.' (Ulster Journal of Archaeo-
logy 7, 12.)

Die Beschreibung der celtischen Sprachen hat schon 1706 Edward
Llwyd unternommen und seiner grossen Leistung gebührt das schönste
Lob. Andere haben nach ihm mehr oder minder richtig die Stelle
erkannt, die die celtischen Sprachen im weiten Kreise der indogermanischen einnehmen, Sir William Jones, Prichard, Pictet, Bopp.
Was aber verleiht einem Manne wie Zeuss den Vorrang vor allen Vorgängern? Er hat das wichtigste Material, das diesen unbekannt geblieben war, erst mühsam zu Tage gefördert; dann hat er den weit-
schichtigen Stoff mit eisernem Fleisse im einzelnen durchgearbeitet,
indem er mit dem klaren Verständnisse des gesamten Gebietes eine

bewundernswerte Sicherheit linguistischer Methode verband; sein Sinn war nur auf ein Ganzes gerichtet, und er war ein Meister in der Beschränkung. Dass die Grammatica Celtica in allen ihren Teilen, namentlich durch Verfolgung der Entwickelung der Sprache in die neuern Zeiten, wesentlich erweitert und selbst in manchen Punkten berichtigt werden kann, wer möchte das heute nach fast 50 Jahren in Abrede stellen? Das hat schon Ebels preiswürdige Arbeit vor 30 Jahren gezeigt. Zeuss hat den unerschütterlichen Grund gelegt, den Aufbau der Nachwelt überlassend. Bis zuletzt hat er seine Forschungen fortgesetzt, wie sein Nachlass zeigt, hat er sein Werk gepflegt, wie aus H. Ebels Programm 'De supremis Zeussii curis positis in Grammatica Celtica', Schneidemühl 1869, und aus der Vorrede zur zweiten Auflage hervorgeht.

Zeuss war ein Gelehrter von seltener Begabung und er lebte ganz in der Welt der Wissenschaft. Man kann ihn 'nur mit Hochachtung und Verehrung nennen', sagt Glück, der ihn gut kannte, in einem Nachrufe im Abendblatte der Münchener Zeitung vom 25. November 1856. 'I paid a visit', erzählt Siegfried, 'to this remarkable man in the vacation of 1856, when his health was fast sinking. He was a tall, well-made, rather spare man, with black hair and moustache, giving me on the whole more the impression of a Slavonian or a Greek than of a German'. Diese Schilderung ist zutreffend. Zeuss war von sehr hohem Wuchs (in seiner Reife 6' 2"), Haar, Bart und Brauen waren schwarz, die Augen braun, die Stirn hoch und nicht breit, die Nase gross, das Kinn rund, das Gesicht oval und von gesunder Farbe. Man hat ein Bildnis von ihm, das freilich den durchgeistigten Ausdruck seiner Züge nur schwach wiedergiebt. Er war von fränkischem Stamme, im Herzen Deutschlands geboren. Freilich gehört er, wie O'Donovan sagt, zu den Gelehrten, die ihrem Vaterlande zum Ruhme gereichen. Insbesondere ist er einer der ausgezeichneten Männer, die das Studium der Grammatik bedeutend gemacht haben: Jacob Grimm, der unsterbliche Finder, Begründer und Gesetzgeber der neuern Sprachwissenschaft — Franz Bopp, der geniale Entdecker — Friedrich Diez und Franz Miklosich, die vollendeten Meister — und Kaspar Zeuss, der so scharfsinnige, so tiefe und so besonnene Forscher.   St.

Druck von Ehrhardt Karras, Halle a. S.

THE BATTLE OF CARN CONAILL.

The following tale is taken from the lithographic facsimile of the Book of the Dun (LU., *Lebor na hUidre*), a MS. of the end of the eleventh century, in the library of the Royal Irish Academy. Another copy, somewhat abridged, is found in the Book of Leinster (LL., *Lebor Laignech*), a twelfth-century MS. in the library of Trinity College, Dublin, pp. 276b — 277b of the facsimile. A third copy, or rather another recension, is contained in ff. 59b — 61a of Egerton 1782 (Eg.), a MS. in the British Museum, written in 1419, and has been edited, with an incomplete translation, by Mr. S. H. O'Grady in his *Silva Gadelica* I, 396—401; II, 431—437. Keating embodied much of this recension in his *Forus Feasa ar Éirinn*. Lastly, a copy of the legend contained in §§ 11—20 of our tale is found in the Yellow Book of Lecan (YBL.), col. 795 (p. 132 of the photolithograph). All important various readings of LL., Eg. and YBL. are given as footnotes.

The battle of Carn Conaill was gained, according to the Four Masters, in the year 645, by Diarmait, son of Aed Sláne, over Gúare, king of Aidne, a district in Connaught, [1]) and his Munster allies. And the following account of the battle is interesting, first, from the fragments of archaic poetry imbedded in the text; secondly, from the instances of fasting upon saints and of submission at the sword's point which the tale contains; thirdly, from the mention of *Céli Dé* (Culdees); fourthly, from its legends of the generosity of Guare, the Irish counterpart of the Arabian Hátim-et-Tái; fifthly, from the rare words found in the tale, such as *adnuu* 'I promise', *athlad* 'change', *bualta* 'merdae', *dubchenn* 'sword', *etla* 'penance', *féccad* 'morsel', *findne* 'shield', *furec* 'feast', *forreith* 'hospitality', *riamnach* 'fishing-line', *trist* 'curse'; and lastly, from its grammatical forms, such as *ata-biu*, *cingth-e*, *dor[o]ecairt*, *doidnais*.

---

[1]) O'Donovan, *Four Masters* I, 260, says that Aidhne was coextensive with the diocese of Kilmacduagh in the county of Galway, and that Carn Conaill is probably now called Ballyconnell in the district of Kilbecanty, near Gort.

Cath Cairnn Chonaill.

(Lebor na hUidre, p. 115 b.)

Cath Cairnd Chonaill ria Diarmait mac Aeda Sláni
for Guari Adni.

1. Diarmait mac Aeda Sláne, Sinech Cró rodn-alt. No
bertis Con[n]achtai a bú-si, co tarat-si imchosait móir eter Diarmait
7 Guaire Aidne. Is and asbert-si:

A Diarmait, a mallchobair ꞏ úamun[1]) Gúare fón-fodair,
ar it anmand cluithe[2]) cath ꞏ tair chucund a dunebath.

Leic do[3]) Diarmait na raid[4]) fris ꞏ in cath ni héol ní firdis,[5])

dénid cóir[6]) dó mar atá ꞏ foid chuci dotathlebá.[7])
Rúanaid atberthe[8]) cosse ꞏ frisseom ar met a náne,[9])
indiu is lobrán[10]) im-Míde[11]) ꞏ Diarmait mac Aeda Sláne.
Tricha tinne, tricha bó ꞏ furec[12]) ceneóil Fergusso,
icdai[13]) dartaid hi cind gait ꞏ inna forreith[14]) do Diarmait. A.

Beit fir móra[15]) ar macáin bic ꞏ co tí ar cobair co Grip,[16])

bit daim ríata láig[17]) ar mbó ꞏ co tí cobair Diarmato.

                                                A Diarmait.

---

[1]) uamain LL., Eg.
[2]) clóithe LL. cláite Eg.   [3]) do LL. Eg. de LU.
[4]) na raid LL. Eg. mairid LU.
[5]) ni heol nirradais LL. ni hord irradais Eg.
[6]) Denaid choirm LL. dena coirm Eg. 'Make ale for him' — to give
Diarmait what is called in English 'Dutch courage'.
[7]) do thaideba LL. do toideba Eg. Leg. do t-adleba, 3d sg. b-fut.
of do-ad-ellaim with infixed pron. of sg. 2, and cf. to-sn-aidle LU. 96 b 38.
[8]) asberthe LL. asberti Eg.   [9]) sic LL. ainé Eg. náire LU.
[10]) sic LL. lobran Eg. lobrand LU.   [11]) gunál-li Eg.
[12]) .i. oigidecht LL.   [13]) icdái LL.
[14]) inna forreith .i. ina oegidecht LL.   [15]) móir LL. Eg.
[16]) nomen equi Diarmata, Eg. ainm eich (Diarmat)a, LL.
[17]) ríatai lóig LL.

The Battle of Carn Conaill.

The Battle of Carn Conaill (gained) by Diarmait, son of
Aed of Sláne, over Guare of Aidne.

1. Diarmait, son of Aed of Sláne, Sinech Cró fostered him.
The Connaughtmen used to carry off her kine, so she brought
about a bitter quarrel between Diarmait and Guare of Aidne.
Then she said (to her fosterson):[1]

O Diarmait, thou slack in help, fear of Guare destroys[2] (?) us
since thou art weak[3] in winning battles, come to us out of the
[manslaying!
Let Diarmait alone: speak not to him of battle, nothing truly
[small is known:
Do right (?) to him as he is, send to him, he will come to thee.
Hitherto he was called a hero from the greatness of his splendour;
today a weakling in Meath is Diarmait, son of Aed of Sláne.
Thirty flitches, thirty cows was the feast of the kindred of Fergus,
a yearling at the end of the prey was paid to Diarmait for
[his guesting.
Our little boys will be big men before[4] our help comes with
[Crip,[5]
the calves of our kine will be trained oxen before[4] help comes
[from Diarmait.

---

[1] Eg. begins thus: Hí sechtmad bliadain flatha in Diarmata sa dorónad
tinól les d'indsaighid Guaire Aidhne 'arna imcháined co mór o hSinigh Chró
'ar mbrith a bó do Guaire Aidne, 7 is ed atberith si fri Diarmait Ruanaid oc
tabairt immchosaiti eturro 7 Guaire. 'In the seventh year of this Diarmait's
reign a muster was made by him to attack Guare of Aidne because of his
having been sorely lampooned by Sinech Cró, whose cows had been lifted by
Guare of Aidne; and this is what she used to say to Diarmait the Champion,
bringing about a bitter quarrel between him and Guare.'

[2] fo-n-fo-dair, cogn. with Ir. dar-cabaltith (gl. particeps), Gr. δέρω,
Goth. ga-taíran.

[3] I take anmand to stand for anfann.

[4] Lit. until.

[5] The name of Diarmait's horse. As the three MSS. have Grip, I have
not here corrected the text. But the true reading is certainly Crip, allite-
rating with cobair, and probably cognate with Gr. κραιπνός.

14*

2. Ro ícc[1]) ní dissi immorro[2]) in cossait sin.[3])   Ro thinoil Diarmait slúagu 7 sochaide leis do inriud Con[n]acht.

3. ISs ed iarom ludi Diarmait oc techt hi Con[n]achta co Cluain maic Nóis. Dorigensat íarom samud Cíaran cona n-abaid .i. Áed-lug mac Commain, etla fri Dia fair co tísad slán d'inchaib a coraigechta-som.   Ro idbair in ri iarom Tóim nEirc cona fodlaib feraind .i. Líath Manchan, amal fód for altóir do Dia 7 do Chíaran. 7 dobert teora trísti for ríg Midi dia cathed nech dia muntir [p. 116 a] cid dig n-usci n-and. Conid de-sin na laim rí Midi a ascin 7 na laim nech dia muntir a biad do chathim.

IS de sin dano doráegart[4]) Díarmait a adnacul hi Cluain maic Nois, conid iarom ro adnacht inti.

4. Dorat Diarmait laim dar Con[n]achta remi co ránic Aidni. Ro thinol Gúairi firu Muman dia saigid. Roptar iatso rig tancatár hi forithin Gúari .i. Cuan mac Ennai ri Muman 7 Cuan[5]) mac Conaill rí Húa Fidgente, 7 Tolomnach rí Húa Líathan. Doratad iarom cath Cha[i]rnd Chonaill etorro il-lo cengiges, co ráemid for Gúari, corro lad ar cend and, im Chuan mac Énnai, rí[g] Muman 7 im Cuan mac Conaill, ríg Húa Conaill [leg. Fidgente?] 7 im Tholomnach rig Húa Líathán.[6])

5. Cammini Insi Celtra iss é dorat brethir for Gúari con

---

[1]) Ro hícc LL. Ro ícc Eg. Róic LU.

[2]) ṁi LU. facs.

[3]) LL. omits the rest of § 2 and the whole of § 3.

[4]) Read doroccart or dorecart, as in Tigernach A. D. 648: from to-ro-aith-gart, root gar.

[5]) In marg. over cid ... rí is written the following quatrain commemorating this Cuan and Tolomnach:

         Mac da certa cecinit.
   Gort maic Cu-cirb cruth rod-gab · ni adas nach Mumanchlár,
   Ni fil Galand ro sói dath · dirsan son ar Talomnach.
   Rí da Chonchend, ri dá Chí · docher hir-rói Cendfotai,
   Atá a lecht isind fan · inti mac Conaill Chuan.

[6]) For § 4 LL. has only: Dorat Diarmait láim dar Connachta co raimid riam for Guaire Aidne co ro giall-saide dó fri rind claidib.

2. Howbeit this setting at loggerheads paid her somewhat, for Diarmait mustered hosts and multitudes to invade Connaught.

3. Now when entering Connaught Diarmait went to Clonmacnois, and S. Ciarán's community, with their abbot Aed-lug, son of Cumman,[1]) did penance to God for him that he might come (back) safe by virtue of their guarantee. So the king (after returning in triumph) offered Tuaim n-Eirc with its subdivisions of land[2]) — i. e. Liath Mancháin[3]) — as a 'sod on altar'[4]) to God and to S. Ciarán, and he bestowed three curses on the king of Meath (for the time being) if any of his people should consume (as a right) even a drink of water therein. Wherefore no king of Meath ventures to look at it, and none of his people ventures to partake of its food.

Hence it is that Diarmait requested his burial in Clonmacnois, wherefore he was afterwards interred therein.[5])

4. Diarmait overcame Connaught till he came to Aidne. Guare gathered to him the men of Munster. These were the kings that came to succour Guare, to wit, Cuan, son of Enna, king of Munster, and Cuan, son of Conall, king of Húi Fidgenti,[6]) and Tolomnach, king of Húi Liatháin.[7]) Then the battle of Carn Conaill was fought between them on the day of Pentecost, and Guare was defeated, and a 'slaughter of chiefs' was inflicted there, including Cuan, son of Enna, king of Munster, and Cuan, son of Conall, king of Húi Conaill, and Tolomnach, king of Húi Liatháin.

5. St. Cámmine of Inis Celtra,[8]) 'tis he that had set a curse

---

[1]) He died A. D. 651, according to the Four Masters.
[2]) 'appurtenances', Annals of Clonmacnois, A. D. 642.
[3]) Now Lemanaghan, in the barony of Ballycastle, King's county.
[4]) i. e. land belonging to the altar, church-land, O'Don. Four Masters I, 261.
[5]) For § 3 (which occurs also in Tigernach's Annals, Rev. Celt. XIX, 190, and see O'Mahony's Keating p. 477) Eg. tells how Guaire sent S. Cummin the Tall to ask a day's truce from Diarmait, and how the king refused in spite of the superiority of the forces arrayed against him. 'Nach fetruidh-si, a chlerigh', ar Diarmuit, 'nach ar lin na cruth brister cath, acht amail is ail ra Dia?' 'Knowest thou not, O cleric, that a battle is gained neither by number nor outward form, but according to the will of God?'
[6]) A territory in the county of Limerick.
[7]) A territory in the county of Cork.
[8]) An island in the N. W. of Lough Derg.

ná gébad fri ócu.[1]) Ar ro bói Cámmini tri trath oc troscud fair
im slanaigect hi tarat hé, ar ro sáraig Gúari hé.

6. 'Mad cóir la Dia', ar Cámmine, 'in fer fil hi comthairisim[2]) frimmsa ní ro-thairise fri námtiu [. Conid ann atbert
in t-aingel re Caimin inso, co ndebuirtt — *Eg.*

IN cath i n-Inis Celtra · feras lobur (.i. fri Camin) fri nerta
(.i. fri Guaire)
is e in lobur bus[3]) tren · is e in tren bus techta[4]) — *LL.*]

7. Do tháet Guaire do aurgairi Chammini, 7 sléchtaid dó.
8. 'Doreilce[d] didu t'irchor-sa,[5]) or Cámmine: 'ni chomraim
a ostud. Comluath sin, dano', for Cammine, '7 dobérat do réir
duit in lucht máidfit maidm fort .i. dobérat do réir duit
fochetóir.'[3])
9. Is de asbert Cammin:

I mbíat fáebra fri fáebra · ocus fin[d]ne fri fin[d]ne,[6])
bi[d]at[7]) aithrech, a Guairi · cléirchin fris'[8]) tarlais tinne.

IAR réir[9]) doarbart Mac De · fri athlad na óenúaire[10])
cride Guaire fo chi[u]nu[11]) · inna tri[u]nu[12]) fo Gúairiu.[13])

---

1) Ar foracaib Cámine Indse Celtra do Guairiu uad gebad fri hócu, LL.
2) comthairisim LL. comthairisium Eg. comtairisem LU.
3) bui LL. facs.
4) tetta LL. facs.
5) Doreilced in t-aurchorsa, or Cámmin. Comlúath sin dano, or Cámmine,
7 doberat doréir, LL. Ni fuil festa, ar Cáimin, a chumang dam gin buaid do
brith dot naimtib dít, acht chena is comluath sain 7 doberat do réir féin duit.
6) IMbiat faibra fri faibra 7 findne fri findne, LL. IMbiat foebra fri
foebra ocus indnae fri hindnae, Eg.
7) bidit LL. bidat Eg.
8) clerchen fri LL. clerchen fris Eg.
9) Eg. omits.
10) fri hathlad uáire, LL. fri hathlath uáire, Eg.
11) chiunu LL. triuna Eg. ciunu is acc. pl. m. of ciun .i. coem, Maelbr. 4;
compounded in ciun-tonn, O'Cl. s. v. macht.
12) triunu LL. triúna Eg.
13) Guaire LU., LL. Ghuaíre Eg.

on Guare, that he should not withstand warriors. For Cámmine had been for three days fasting upon him concerning a guarantee which the saint had made him give; for Guare had outraged him.

6. 'If God see fit', says Cámmine, 'the man who is stubborn against me shall not stand fast against (his) foes.' Whereupon the angel declared this to Cámmine, saying:

'The battle in Inis-celtra which the weakling fights against
[strengths,
'tis the weakling that shall be strong, 'tis the strong that shall
[be put to flight.' [1])

7. Guare went to entreat Cámmine, and kneels to him.

8. 'Thy cast hath been hurled', says Cámmine: 'I cannot help to stay it. [2]) But this is as swift as that', says Cámmine, 'and those that shall inflict a defeat upon thee will straightway give thee thy desire.' [3])

9. Thereof said Cámmine:

When edges shall be against edges and shields against shield, [4])
thou wilt be penitent, O Guare, as to the poor cleric to whom
[thou hast shewn stiffness.
According to (His) will God's Son in the change [5]) of a single
[hour has brought
Guaire's heart under gentle ones, the strong ones under Guare.

---

[1]) A guess. I take *techta* to be the part. pass. of *techim* 'I flee', here used as if the verb were transitive.

[2]) Another guess. I take *chomraim* to stand for *chobraim*, and *ostud* for *fóstud*, the verbal noun of *fosta[i]m*, O'Br.

[3]) The corresponding passage in Eg. is: acht chena is comluath sain 7 doberat do reir fein duit, which S. H. O'Grady renders by 'yet [so much I may procure: that] this once done they in turn shall submit to thee.'

[4]) *findne* is cognate with O'Clery's *finnell* .i. sgiath, *finnén* .i. sgiath, *finden* Ir. Texte 1, 81. It may also be cognate with Ahd. *want*, now *wand*, wall'.

[5]) *athlad* is rendered 'vicissitude' by S. H. O'Grady.

10. 'Troisc limsa da*no*', *for* Gúaire fri Cammin, 'fri Dia co tarda itchi dam.'

11. Lotár iarom a *t*riur isin n-eclais .i. Cammini 7 Guairi 7 C*u*mmini Fota. Eclas mór dorónad la Cámmin, is intí bátar. Batar iarom na clérig oc tabairt a chobsena *for* Gúari.[1]

12. 'Maith, a Guair[i]', ar iat, 'cid bad maith lat do linad na ecailsi-sea hi tám?'

13. 'Ropad maith lim al-lan di or 7 d'argut, 7 ni ar [p. 116b] saint in tsáegail,[2] *acht* dia thindnacul ar m'anmain do náemaib 7 ecailsib 7 bochtaib in domain.'[3]

14. 'Dorata Dia fortacht duit, a Gúaire!' ar iat. 'Dob*é*rthar in talam duit doidnais ar t'anmain, 7 bát nimidech.'

15. 'Is bude lend', or Guaire. 'O*cus* túsu, a Chammini', or Gúare, 'cid bad maith lat día linad?'

16. 'Ropad maith lim a linad do sáeth 7 gal*ur* 7 cech aingcis bad messo do duini, co mbad *for* mo chorp dobe*r*tais uli.'[4]

17. 'O*cus* t*us*su, a Ch*u*mmine', or Guaire, 'cid bad maith lat día línad?'

18. 'Ropad maith lim al-lán di lebraib .i. dia tudecht do áes légind, 7 do silad brethre De hi clúasaib cach duine dia thabairt a lurg Díabail doch*u*m nimi.'[5]

19. Ro firtha t*r*a uli a n-imráti dóib. Doratad in tal*am* do Gúaire. Doratad ecna do Ch*u*mmin. Dorata sóetha 7 galra *for* Cammine *con* na deochaid cnaim de fri araile hi talam, *acht* ro legai 7 ro lobai ri aingces[6] cech galair 7 *c*ach threblaiti.

20. Co ndeochatar ule dochum nimi lía n-imratib.[7]

---

[1] Badar som di*du* oc tabairt a n-anmchairdeasa *for* Guaire, YBL.

[2] domain YBL.

[3] Ro bud maith lium al-lan oir oc*us* airc*it* acum, 7 ni dá thaiscith acht da tidnucol ar m'anmuin do boch*t*aib 7 adailgnecha*ib* in Cuimd*ed*, Eg.

[4] Robad maith liumm a lan do éaeth 7 do ghalur fam' ch*u*rp, ol Cáimin, *con*a dicsigh cnaim re chele i talmain di, Eg.

[5] ... do lurg Diabail doch*u*m in Choimded, YBL. Ro bud maith lium, ol Cuimin, a lan do leabruib do bith occum, 7 a tuidhecht do aes leghinn co ro fo*r*chantais in ciniuth daendoi, Eg.

[6] ro ha*n*ces, YBL.

[7] lia n-imrate ina n-eclais. Finit. YBL.

10. 'Fast with me then', says Guare to Cámmine, 'unto God, that He may grant my prayer.'

11. Then the three of them entered the church, to wit, Cámmine and Guare and St. Cummine the Tall. A great church built by Cámmine, therein they were. Then the clerics were causing Guare to confess.[1]

12. 'Well, O Guare', say they, 'with what wouldst thou like to fill this church wherein we stand?'

13. 'I should like its fill of gold and of silver; and not for worldly greed, but to bestow it for my soul's sake on the saints and the churches and the poor of the world.',

14. 'May God give thee help, O Guare!' say they. 'The earth which thou wouldst bestow[2] for thy soul's sake shall be given to thee, and thou shalt (after death) be a dweller in heaven.'

15. 'We are thankful', saith Guare. 'And thou, O Cámmine', saith Guare, 'with what wouldst *thou* like it to be filled?'

16. 'I should like to fill it with pain and sickness and every ailment that is worst to man, so that all of them might be inflicted on my body.'

17. 'And thou, O Cummine', saith Guare, 'with what wouldst *thou* fain have it filled?'

18. 'Fain would I have its fill of books, for students to repair to them, and (then) to sow God's word in the ears of every one, so as to bring him to heaven out of the troop of the Devil.'

19. Now all their musings came to pass.[4] The earth was given to Guare. Wisdom was given to Cummin. Pains and sicknesses were inflicted on Cámmine, so that no bone of him came to another earth, but it had dissolved and decayed with the anguish of every illness and every tribulation.

20. So they all went to heaven according to their musings.[3]

---

[1] According to YBL. 'they were giving their spiritual direction (lit. soul-friendship) to Guare.'

[2] do-idnais s-subj. sg. 2 of *do-idnacim.*

[3] This interesting legend has been edited, from LU., in Lismore Lives, p. 304: see also O'Mahony's Keating, p. 440. A version of it, said to be a scholium on the Félire of Oengus at March 25, was printed by Dr. Todd, in his edition of the *Liber Hymnorum*, p. 87. There is another in Rawl. B. 512, fo. 141 a 2, and another in the Book of Lismore, fo. 44 b 1.

[4] Literally: were verified by them.

21. Techid *t*ra Gúaire assin cath *for* leith 7 a gilla irraith.[1])
Ro gab in gilla bratan ríamnaige, ro fon 7 dorat do Gúari.
*Con*id and asbe*r*t Gúari:[2])

Atloch*u*r do Dia i n-étad[3]) · innocht dom feis óenfeccad:[4])

rom-bui-se adaig aile · dombe*r*t secht mbú[5]) Mac Maire.

22. Dolluid-seom *t*ra do gíallad[6]) *f*ri claideb do Diar*mait*
intí Gúari.

23. 'Maith', or Diar*mait*, 'cid ara ndéni Guairi in féli[7])
ucut? .i. inn ar Dia fá inn ar daini?[8]) Mád ar Día dobé*r*a ní
innossa. Mad a*r* dáine[9]) ni thibre, ol ata co feirg 7 lond*us* mór.'[9])

24. Do tháet chucu.[10]) 'Ni dam! a Gúaire', ol in druth.
Cingthe secha.[10]) 'Ni damsa, a Gúaire!' or in clam. 'Rot-bia',
or Guaire. Focheird a goo[11]) dó. 'Ní damsa!' or a chéli.
Focheird a sciath dó. 'Ní damsa!' or a chéli aile. Focheird a
brat 7 a delg 7 a *c*ris dó.[12])

25. 'Nit-ain', or Diar*mait*. 'Tair fón claideb.'

26. 'Ni damsa, a Gúaire!' *for* in céli Dé. 'An bic, a
Diar*mait*', or Guaire, 'co tallur[13]) mo lene dim don chéle[14]) Dé.'

'Maith', or Diar*mait*, 'ro giallaisiu do rig aile .i. do Mac
Dé. Asso mo giallsa duitsiu im*morro*.'

27. Slechtaid [p. 117 a] da*no* Diar*mait* fo thrí do Gúari. 'Nip
anchobrai[15]) trá', or Diar*mait*, 'co ndigis ar mo chend-sa do

---

[1]) Taich di*du* Guaire *for* leith assin chath 7 a gilla, LL.
[2]) unde Gúaire dixit.
[3]) LU. Facs. metad. LL. inetad. Eg. anétad.
[4]) hénecad LL. einécad Eg. óenfeccad LU.   [5]) deich mbuu Eg.
[6]) giall LL.   [7]) rofeili LL.   [8]) duine LL.
[9]) 7 luinne LL.   [10]) Ciṅgthe sechai LL.   [11]) gáo LL.
[12]) Focheirt in sciath, in delg, in ṁbratt, in criss, LL.
[13]) tall LL.   [14]) cheiliu LL.   [15]) ancórai LL.

21. Guare flees out of the battle on one side with his servant only.[1]) The servant caught a salmon with a line, broiled it, and gave it to Guare. Whereupon Guare said:

I thank God for what has been gained to-night for my feast,
     [a single morsel.
I have had (many) another night (when) Mary's Son gave me
     [seven cows.

22. Then Guare went to make submission to Diarmait at the sword('s point).[2])

23. 'Well', says Diarmait, 'why does Guare practise that generosity (for which he is famed)? Is it for God's sake or for men's? If it be for God's sake he will now bestow somewhat. If it be for men's, he will give nothing, because he is in anger and great bitterness.'

24. He went to them. 'Something to me, O Guare!' says the jester. He passes by him. 'Something to *me*, O Guare!' says the leper. 'Thou shalt have', says Guare. He flings him his spears. 'Something to *me*', says the leper's fellow. Guare flings him his shield. 'Something to *me*!' says his other fellow. Guare flings him his mantle and his brooch and his girdle.

25. 'This will not protect thee', says Diarmait: 'come under the sword.'

26. 'Something to *me*, O Guare!' says the Culdee. 'Wait a little, O Diarmait', says Guare, 'till I strip off my shirt for the Culdee'.

'Well', says Diarmait, 'thou hast submitted to another king, even to God's Son. Here, however, is my submission to thee.'

27. So Diarmait kneels thrice to Guare. 'Let it not be unpeace now', says Diarmait, 'that thou shouldst go to meet

---

[1]) *irraith* (leg. *ir-ráith*) is, I suppose, synonymous with *do ráith* 'only', Wind. Wörterb. 741.

[2]) IS he in giall*ad* sin .i. rinn in ghai no in chloidim do thabuirt i mbel itir i fiacluib in neich no giall*ad* ann 7 se fáen 'this is that (manner of) submission, i. e. to put the point of the spear or of the sword into the mouth between the teeth of him that made submission there, and he supine', Eg. And see O'Mahony's Keating, p. 436. For other forms of submission, see *The Academy*, May 14, 1892, p. 470, and July 2, 1892, p. 15: Frazer's *Pausanias* III, 331: and Darmesteter, Chants populaires des Afghans, clxxiv.

áenuch Tallten, *co* nda[t]ragbat[1]) fir Her*enn* do chomarlid'[2]) 7
do chind athchomairc dóib.'

'Dogéntar', or Gúaire [facs. *gúnar*].

28. Is andsin ro chan[3]) Sinech in molad-sa do Diarm*ait*:

Cach m*a*c tigirn tim*c*raidi · tathut airle limsa de,
dothe desell in brogo[4]) · leis fudell mo rúanado.[5]

Ní *for* brágtib dam na bó · clóthir colg[6]) mo ruanado,
is *for* rigaib focheird feit · indiu dubchend[7]) la Diar*meit*.[8])

[p. 117a] Gúaire m*a*c Colmain in ri · ro chacc[9]) *for* craibu[10]) Adní,
ro lá búalta méit cind bó · ar óman mo ruanadó.

O ro breca bróenán cró · léni nde[n]dg*uir*m[11]) nDíarmató,
erred fir cluas[12]) catha · ni comtig cen ildatha.

O ro breca bróenán c*r*ó · brunni gabra Diar*m*ató,
usce asa negar G*r*ip[13]) · ni l*u*sta[14]) fri sacarbaic,[15])

O doleict*er*[16]) immasech · c*r*anna f[i]anna *for* ca*ch* leth,
ní po decmaic[17]) casal[18]) c*r*ó · *for* c*r*and a duir*n*d[19]) Diar*m*ató.

---

[1]) *conatrogbat*, LL. [[2]) ríg LL. [3]) *asbert* LL.
[4]) *moroga* LU. Facs. (leg. mbroga?). broga LL. in brogha Eg.
[5]) ruanada LL. rúanodo Eg.
[6]) .i. claideb LL.
[7]) in dubcend .i. claideb LL. in duibgenn Eg.
[8]) Thus in O'Clery's *Foclóir*:
Ní for bhraighaibh damb na bó · promhthar colg mo ruanadhó
for bhraighdibh riogh focheard feid · a níth a duibhgeann ag Diarmaid.
[9]) alíís rothéig, LL. *in marg.*
[10]) cróibu LL. craeba Eg. craibiu LU.
[11]) ùdendgorm LL. dhendgorm Eg.
[12]) chlo*us* Eg.   [13]) .i. ech Diarm*a*ta LU.   [14]) .i. ni glan LU.
[15]) 'gan sacarbig Eg.   [16]) légith*er* Eg.
[17]) decmait LU. Facs. decmaiṅg LL. decmuing Eg.
[18]) caisel *nó* crott *nó* all, LL. *In marg.* In alí*is* or atu gai casai cró.
[19]) *for* crund a durn LL.

me to the Assembly of Talltiu, so that the men of Erin may take thee for their adviser and their chief of counsel.'

'It shall be done', says Guare.

28. Then Sinech sang this praise to Diarmait:

Every faint-hearted son of a lord,[1]) a counsel I have for thee
[about him,
he shall walk righthandwise round the mark: he shall have
[my champion's leavings.
Not on necks of oxen or cows is my champion's sword blunted,
'tis on kings that the sword in Diarmait's hand today makes
[a whistling noise.[2])
Guare son of Colmán, the king, befouled the trees of Aidne:
he cast forth ordures[3]) as big as a cow's head, for dread of
[my champion.
Since a shower of blood has bespattered Diarmait's blue-coloured
[shirt,
the dress of a man who turns back battles is not meet without
[many colours.
Since a shower of blood has bespattered the breast of Diarmait's
[steed,
the water with which Crip[4]) is washed is not clear for the
[Sacrifice.[5])
When in turns the warlike shafts are hurled on every side
a bloody mantle were not strange on the shaft from Diarmait's
[hand.

---

[1]) *macc tigirn* seems = Br. *mach-tiern*.

[2]) *feit* acc. sg. of *ind fet* Sg. 3 a 7 = Cymr. *chwyth*. In his *Foclóir* O'Clery explains this quatrain thus: Nach ar bhraighdibh damh na bó, dearbhthar cloideamh an roíeinnedha, acht as ar bhraighdibh riogh a gcath [he reads *a nith*, for *indiu*] do ní a cloidheamh fead.

[3]) *búalta* 'merdas' cogn. with *búalthach* (leg. *búaltach*?) and *búaltrach* 'cowdung', O'Br. Aristophanes has a similar joke.

[4]) Or Grip, king Diarmait's horse.

[5]) i. e. is not fit for mixing with the sacramental wine.

O do[1]) sernatár gai bic · hi tossuch an[2]) imairic,
is í dias cíta ric · a gabair *ocus* Diarmait.[3])

A[r] Guairi:

Adnuu ón, adnuu · da reis Sinich[4]) co *cr*uu,[5])
nocos-faicéb[6]) la biu · ata-biu com luu.

Or si:[7])

Adnuu · ní ric Sinech co cruu,
ni fil occu 'cá im[ḟo]-chaid[8]) · cid náci[d]-fitir nuu.[9])

Diar*mait* rúanaid, maith in ri · *for*brid ar cách t*r*ia lunni,
*for*brid ar cach n-óen co gnáth · in rí co cuir broén ar cách.[10])
[*Cách.*

29. Luid-seom iarom inti Gúairi do áenuch Talten arcend
Diarm*ata*, 7 míach árgit leis día thabairt do feraib Her*enn*.

30. 'Maith', or Diar*mait*, 'in fer dotháet chucaib atethaid
a innili oc a thig. Is [s]árugud damsa t*r*úag *nó* trén isind óenuch
do chuingid neich cuci.'

31. Luid-seom di*du* co mbói *for* láim Diarm*ata* *for* *for*adaib
bith[11]) isind óenuch. In la sin, t*r*a,[11]) ni chuinnig[12]) nech ní
cuca[i] *som*. Bá machdad leiseom aní-sin.

32. [Medón lái arnabarach, LL.] 'Maith, a Diar*mait*', or
Guar*e*, 'epsc*op* do gairm cuc*um*sa co tard-sa mo choibsena dó.'
[7 co rom-ongthar'][13])

---

[1]) ro LL.   [2]) in Eg.

[3]) *sic* LL. *The LU. facs. has*: is í cétní and arric a gai, is a gabair
la Diar*mait*. is iat dias ceta rig, a ghabar *ocus* Diarmait, Eg.

[4]) rís sinich LL. ris sínech Eg.

[5]) com cruu Eg.

[6]) ni cos faicéb LL. nocos fáecebad LU. noch*us* fuigeba Eg.

[7]) In the MS. these words follow *adnuu* in the next line.

[8]) ni fil óca cu himochaid LL. ni fil occu 'ca imfochaid, Eg.

[9]) cid na cid nach a fiter (nó can co toractatar) nuu, LL. cid naccid-
fit*er* nuu, Eg.

[10]) LL. and Eg. omit this quatrain.

[11]) *for* foradaib bít and al-laa sin, LL.

[12]) comtich LL.

[13]) Epsgob chugam, ar se, co ndernar m'faisitin dó 7 gu*rr*om-ongthar, Eg.

When the small javelins are loosed at the beginning of their
[conflict,
the pair which first meets (them) is Diarmait's steed and himself.

Saith Guare:

'I promise this, I promise, if Sinech reach a fold
I will not leave her alive, I will slay her[1]) with my kick.'

Saith she:

'I promise. Sinech reaches not a fold:
there are no warriors. ... why dost thou not know it ...?
Diarmait the hero, good the king, outgrows every one through
[boldness,
the king usually outgrows every one, so that he causes sadness
[to all.

29. Then Guare went to the Assembly of Taltiu to meet
Diarmait, having with him a sack of silver to bestow on the
men of Erin.

30. 'Well', says Diarmait, 'the man that has come to you,
ye seize his cattle at his house. 'Tis an outrage to me if
(anyone), wretched or strong, in the assembly ask aught of him.'

31. So Guare went and stayed on Diarmait's (right) hand on
the ... highseats[2]) in the assembly. On that day, then, no one
asks aught of him. This seemed to him a marvel.

32. At midday on the morrow, 'well', says Guare, 'let a
bishop be summoned to me that I may make my confessions to
him and be anointed.'[3])

---

[1]) *atabiu* = *ad-da-biu*, fut. sg. 1 of *ad-benim* (with infixed fem. pers.
pron. sg. 3), as *as-ririu* is fut. sg. 1 of *as-renim*.

[2]) *bíth* (if this be the right reading) may be gen. sg. of *bí* 'threshold',
O'Dav. 57 (cf. *conice in crand mbith ... iar ndul dar crand mbith*, LB.
277 a 54/55, here used for 'entrance'. The *bít* of LL. should probably be the
imperf. pl. 3 *bítis*.

[3]) See O'Mahony's Keating p. 437. The story shews that the Old-Irish
bishops sometimes heard confessions and administered extreme unction. As
to their other spiritual functions, see *Lismore Lives*, pref. CXVII.

'Cid so?' or Diar*mait.*

'Cid nách mana éca letso damsa, a Diar*mait,* áit hi tát fir Her*énd,* et*er* t*r*uag 7 t*r*en, na*ch* cuinnig uech díb ní chu-c*um*sa.'

33. 'Ní rogebthar¹) *fort',* or Diar*mait,* [p. 117b] 'miach argait duit sunn út.'

'Atá airget im*morro* limsa', ol Gúairi.

34. At*r*aracht im*morro* Gúairi, 7 nos-tairb*ir* assa díb lamaib, 7 asb*er*at-som ba lethfota a lám ónd úair sin oc rochtain na céli nDé.

35. Dogniat iarom ógsid .i. Diarmait 7 Guaire, 7 ro gabsat fir Here*nn* intí Gúairi do chomarlid 7 do chind athchomairc dóib²) ond uair sin t*r*ia bithu cein ro bo béo.

36. Bá maith iarom intí Guairi: is dó doratad t*r*ia ráth féli in bó *co* *n*-aib ítha 7 inna sméra 'sind fulliuch.

37. IS é doróni in firt n-am*r*a hi Clu*ain* ma*i*c Nóis día rucad-som dia adnacol di.

Tánic in drúth dia saigid, 7 ro gab algais de im athchuingid fair. Dorat-som a laim darsin for*b*aid im*m*ach, 7 ro gab lán a duirnd don ganium, 7 ro dibairc i n-uch[t] in d*r*uad, *co* *n*d*er*na[d] bruth óir dé. *Co*n*id hé sin enech dedenach Guairi.³)

*Co*n*id Cath Diar*mata* 7 Guairi Adni a scel sin anúas.

---

¹) raigebthar LL.

²) Here LL. ends, and there is nothing in Eg. corresponding with §§ 36, 37.

³) A tale of the post mortem generosity of Háṭim-eṭ-Tái is translated by Lane, *The Thousand and One Nights,* 1859, vòl. II, p. 295.

'Why is this?' says Diarmait.

'Deemest thou not, O Diarmait, that it is an omen of death to me that in a stead where stand the men of Erin, both wretched and strong, not one of them asketh aught of me?'

33. 'Nothing shall be taken from thee', says Diarmait. 'Here is a sack of silver for thee.'

'But *I* (myself) have silver', says Guare.

34. So then Guare rose up, and flings it out of his two hands. And men say that from that hour one of his arms was longer than the other from reaching out to the 'servants of God' (*Culdees*).

35. Then they, Diarmait, to wit, and Guare, make a perfect peace. And the men of Erin took Guare for their adviser and their chief of counsel, from that time forward so long as he was alive.

36. Good, then, was that Guare. 'Tis to him that through grace of generosity was given the cow[1]) with beauty of fat, and the blackberries in the ...

37. 'Tis he that wrought the wondrous miracle at Clonmacnois when they were bearing him thither to his burial.

The jester came to him and asked a boon of him repeatedly. So he (the dead king) put his hand out over the ground, and took his handful of the sand, and flung it into the jester's[2]) bosom, and made a glowing mass of gold thereout. So *that* is Guare's last deed of bounty.

This tale above is (also called) the 'Battle of Diarmait and Guare of Aidne.'

---

[1]) *bó co n-aib ttha*; cf. *bo co n-æib nitha*, Lism. Lives, pref. XXVII. Obscurum per obscurius!

[2]) Here, as often, *drui* and *druth* are confounded.

London.   WHITLEY STOKES.

AMRA SENÁIN.

The following eulogy of S. Senán of Inis Cathaig is ascribed to Dallán, the alleged author of the eulogy of S. Columba.[1] Three copies are known: one in the fourteenth-century *Lebor Brecc*, p. 241a of the lithographic facsimile published by the Royal Irish Academy in 1876: another in columns 832—835 of H. 3. 17,[2] a MS. in the library of Trinity College, Dublin, written partly in the fifteenth, partly in the sixteenth century, and a third, from the hand of Michael O'Clery,[3] in the Brussels MS. 4190—4200, fo. 269a. None of them has hitherto been published.

The present edition is made from a good photograph of the copy in H. 3. 17, the obvious inaccuracies of the *Lebor Brecc* facsimile[4] rendering its reproduction inexpedient. It is to be hoped that some Continental Celtist will edit the Brussels copy with its gloss, and that some Dublin scholar will tell us what the *Lebor Brecc* copy really contains. It will then, perhaps, be possible to translate the text of this obscure *amra*. Meanwhile,

---

[1] Edited by Crowe, Dublin 1871: by Atkinson, *The Irish Liber Hymnorum*, London 1898, and by the present writer, *Goidelica²*, pp. 156—173, and *Revue Celtique*, t. XX, pp. 30, 132, 248, 400. As to its date, see Strachan, *Rev. Celt.* XVII, 41.

[2] For pointing out this copy I am indebted to Professor Thurneysen.

[3] He died about 1644.

[4] Consider, for instance, *la siada* .. for *la fiadait*, *dg* for *dx.* (i. e. dixit), *buaid* for *bruaid*, *carson* for *curson*, *mogaigthe* for *moaigthe*, *Rue* for *Ruide*, *findaigib* for *findmaigib*, *faib* for *fail*, *moain* for *moam*, *sánlige* for *súilige*.

the following transcript of the photograph, with a literal version
of the preface and epilogue, may be acceptable to some of the
readers of this journal.

Preface.

The Eulogy of Senán, son of Gerrchenn, here.

This Senán was a famous saint. One day as he was
a-praying to God, Nárach the wright went with a number of his
household under the saint's protection, so that he, Nárach, might
go safely by the monster[1]) that dwelt in the lough, and he
'bound his defence'. So the wright fared forth. The monster
attacked him and devoured him with the whole of his company.
This was made known by God to Senán. The monster is summoned to Senán, who hung her, and out of her was put the wright
and his company. Wherefore Oengus says (*Félire*, March 8):

> 'Senán of Inis Cathaig hung Nárach's enemy.'

i. e. her who was a foe of Nárach's.

Senán questioned Nárach: 'did she give thee (back) all?'
'She gave', quoth Nárach, saying:

> 'She gave it all (back) to us', quoth the wright; 'we render thanks —
> no rude renown — that she had taken from us at the rough sand, save a
> high caldron and a sledgehammer.
> From the time that my saint perceived her, her mouth became pale:
> with the hook of the cold caldron she spewed a fragment of her strong liver.'

Now Dallán composed this eulogy for Senán that his
(Dallán's) sight might stay with him after he had made the
other eulogy (the *Amra Choluimb chille*) for Columba.

Epilogue.

So God caused Dallán's eyes to remain with him until his
death, because of the honour and respect of the praise and dirge
of Senán. Heaven and healthy sight to him that hath this
eulogy of Senán, both body and sense (i. e. text and gloss).
More numerous than grass or a wood's hair[2]) (i. e. the leaves)
are the many graces of this holy dirge. Whoso hath it is not
sore here (on earth) or there (in the other world).

---

[1]) See a bombastic description of this monster (whose name was Cathach),
in *Lismore Lives*, ll. 2212—2227.

[2]) Cf. the metaphorical use of κόμη (Od. XXIII, 195) and *coma*.

Amra Senáin.

(H. 3. 17.)

[col. 832] Amrad[1]) Senáin[2]) maic Geirrchind inso.

Ba sanct n-amra inti Senan. Laithiu[3]) n-óen do Senan ina urnaigthi la Fiadait doching Nárach cerd (lín a m)untire for a chomairchi ar(a) co r(ised)[4]) slan sech in peist bói 'sind loch, (7) nenaisc a dín. Dochomlai iarma[5]) in cerd. Dothic in peist chuccai 7 no[n]-ithi uile[6]) lín a mbúi. Ro fes o Dia do Senán andisin.[7]) Dogarar in peist co Senan 7 nodus-croch 7 doberta in cerddai (?)[8]) lín a mbói eisi. Conid de sin asbeir Aengus:

Senan Inse Cathaig · crochais ecrait Náraig.

.i. intí ropo[9]) écraiti do Nárach.

Comarcais Senán do Narach: In tuc duit uile? Tucc, ol Narach · ut dixit:

Tucc dúin uile, ol in cerdd · berma buide, ni blad borb,
na rucc uaind fri gainim úgarg · acht agen ardd ocus ordd.
Uand uáir forsrathaig[10]) mo noeb · ro chuir for bánfaid a bél,
la corran ind again[11]) uáir · ro scé bruaid[12]) dia tromman trén.

Dallan dono doroine ind amra-sa do Senán do fossugud a ruisc lais iar ñdenam ind amra[13]) aile do Colum cille.

1. Senan soer[1]) · sídathair[2]) silem soailche[3]) · sainemail · suib sreith amra[4]) · curson[5])*) · cadb calb[5]) · cletharda[6])**) · cuipe co fín.[7])

[1]) .i. soer · uais.   [2]) .i. ar n-athair sída Senán.   [3]) .i. oc silad soailche do cach.   [4]) .i. is[s]ainnrethach in suí co n-áib oc suidigid dligid do cach.   [5]) .i. is coir son Dé.   [6]) .i. ar cáincend.   [7]) .i. ar cleth ordan.
[8]) .i. amal tulcuma fína.

2. Fo lún lainderda loo · laissium[1]) luamna · assallais[2])***)

[1]) .i. is lais is dagsoillsigad taitnemche · lun o luna .i. amal esca il-lo [is laissium LB.] lansomain in molta.   [2]) [.i. ondi is laus, LB.].   [3]) .i. is

---

[1]) Amra LB.   [2]) .i. Inse Cathaig .i. do Chorco Baiscinn.
[3]) la LB.   [4]) for a comarc-sium co rised LB.
[5]) iarum LB.   [6]) nonithe uli LB.   [7]) innísin LB.
[8]) dobertha in cerd LB.   [9]) rop LB.
[10]) hon uair ros-rathaig LB.   [11]) in aigin LB.
[12]) buaid LB.   [13]) amrad LB.

*) carson LB.   **) clethard LB.   ***) asallais LB.

luan · lan fuach firinde[3]) [col. 833] forosna iltuatha Herend[4])
uasmaig.[5])

lan focal fursaintech firinde.   [4]) .i. foruaisligfider he etir iltuathib Erenn
ar-mo ruscu dam.   [5]) .i. uas cach.

3. Man moaigthe*) dagdaíne[1]) danaib do Crist cáinmuinter ·
cumachtaig[2]) eter cond sceo colt.[3])

[1]) .i. matan métaigthe na ñdagdaine .i. na cristaige.   [2]) .i. ro danaiged
no ascedaighed do Crist cona muintir caemichtaig biad 7 édach.   [3]) .i.
enech no biad.

4. Cob n-uile**) n-adamra · cona ecalsib i n-ilgradaib[1]) im
riched[2]) rith raas.[3])

[1]) ro bo buaid adasmar uile gach gnim dognid fo ilgradaib n-ecailsi.
[2]) .i. im iath ind rig.   [3]) .i. cen mair raithestar rith.

5. Ruide***) im rochorp carcrastar[1]). cen chais[2]) modeat[3])†) ·
mugsaine is††) macc Geirrgind[4]) · gart.[5])

[1]) .i. ruanaid ro carcrastar a rochorp.   [2]) .i. cen carthain.   [3]) .i. a
maethadbair.   [4]) .i. dognith mogsine Dé ic fognam do Dia in mac so
Geirrchind.   [5]) .i. ba grian a inech.

6. Glainidir gol[1]) go noam som súi[2]) · dian sossad sid-
lotha[3]) sine i[4]) · Cathaig caur.[5])

[1]) .i. is glaine ol na dér.   [2]) .i. (er)draci som c(ach) súi.   [3]) .i.
dianad soistad sid .i. in sid(loth sin).   [4]) .i. ro deil idu liter da insin.
[5]) [ro]sinestar a sáethar cathaisi co(coir) inna (hindsi).

7. Cáin n-ard n-orddon[1]) n-adamra · assa orddon[2]) · ar-
chaingel†††) hi findmaigeib§) fil.[3])

[1]) .i. is cain conid ard oirdnide adamra aige.   [2]) .i. intí asa hardainm
nó ard anim .i. fil eter arcanglib .i. eter uassalteachtairib.   [3]) hi maigib
(na find) .i. na firian, fuil S(enán).

8. Fiadh fochraice follnathar[1]) · amru§§) cach ór oeibli-
gad[2])§§§) ina ma[3]) (ni mo).*†)

[1]) .i. is e fiadugad airmitin ro follamnaig.   [2]) .i. is ferr lais olda cech
or iarna oebelgo(rad) nó iarna bruindid.   [3]) .i. in log mor (fofuair) .i. nem
(.i. is) do foch(raicc).

---

*) mogaigthe LB.   **) hulide LB.   ***) Rue LB.
†) modeta LB.   ††) as LB.
†††) asa hordan n-archaingel LB.   §) findaigib LB.
§§) sic LB. amra H. 3. 17.   §§§) oeibligud LB.
*†) sic LB.

9. Mor ua Dubtaig *) drongo(blaig) [1] [col. 834.] dom ro[f]oir dom rusc reil-cobair ar a molta miad. [2]

[1] .i. is mór intí ua Dubthaig dronchoíbnes(saig *nó* dron)diglaig.
[2] dom ro foire dom suilib soluschobair ar miadamlataig a molta *nó* a moaigthi.

10. Moai mo rosc [1] · rigfotha [2] mo da n hed **) n-ard n-imchaissen uassnaib nim-conbeb[a] ***) blái. [3]

[1] .i. rop limm mo radarc. [2] is fotha rigi. [3] .i. mo [dá] súil co rabat ic arddeiscin cacha rodeirc ocum, 7 ni raibe ní uassaib nodus-beba do dorchu blaisg.

11. Bleasc†) amrosc ilarda [1] co mbrosnaigib uath [2] uas mo luirgnib langlassaib is forru mada fail. [3] ††)

[1] .i. ni rofuirme daille ni lernalaig dam. [2] [.i.] co cnuassaigib grainechta. [3] [.i.] air isat langlas dom luirgnib daille mo súl, ár is *fris* benaid [leg. friu benait] beimenn.

12. Deaith [1] · doerchrau hi crichaib caincailb [2] co tarchan ainm in chanand caidb. [3]

[1] .i. diaith .i. ni haith. [2] .i. do ercrasait mo súile hi cáincrichaib mo chind · calb .i. cenn. [3] .i. co ra tircanus a ainm in chano achantaid cendchaeim†;†) .i. Seanan cadb . 7 calb cenn insin.

13. Cain teasbann§) teim essgal [1] sceo [2] ni ain ni hain · ai§§) is mo hae is moam§§§) mo ain. [3]

[1] .i. is taithnemach doesbann dorchatu esgail[e] na daille form. [2] [.i. sceo ar ocus, LB.] .i. i[s]focus rom-cobuir ar in anim*†) ro bi form. [3] .i. mo rosc ar focus mo hai is lim indí as moo dom ainius.

14. Mod roglanad mo blus [1] · cach ambe [2] · bui liath [3] · cen blæ [4] amsom bui diach die. [5] *††)

[1] .i. intan ro glanad mo bloesc dailli. [2] .i. cach a mbóe de form. [3] .i. ba liath mo indtliucht lam daille.*§) [4] .i. cen landeche do brith uaim ar mo rosc. [5] .i. dé.

15. Dommrofoir fiadu firinde fallnathar [1] · triath [2] trethnaig · na bi sæthach sen. [3]

Senán s. s.

[1] .i. dom-foire tigherna firinde follamnaighes rigi na tri teglach .i. nem 7 talam 7 iffern. [2] .i. treiath .i. triath ri · triath tír · triath mucc. [3] .i. ni fil sæth na sentu *for* Crist.

---

*) Senán's grandfather was Dubthach: see his pedigree in LL. 337, col. 2, *Lismore Lives*, p. 887.

) mo da n-ed LB.   *) conbea LB.   †) Bleach LB.
††) faib LB.   †††) sic LB. in chanon chantaidcēd chaím H.
§) tesband LB.   §§) ni hainai LB.   §§§) moain LB.
*†) anai LB.   *††) dihe LB.   *§) .i. am daille LB.

Ro fossaig *tra* Dia do Dall*án* a súile có a bás ar anóir 7 ar airmidin molta 7 marbnaide[1]) Senáin. Ro geallad nem *ocus* slansúilighe[2]) don tí la[sa] mbiad etir chorp 7 chéill in t-ámrad sa Senáin. Is liriu feor *nó* folt fidbaide[3]) [col. 835] ilratha in marbnaid noeb siu[4]) · ní bi[5]) goirt hi fuss na thall inti lasa mbia. Finit.[6])

----

[1]) marbnada LB.   [2]) slánsánlige LB.
[3]) Cf. etir fld 7 a folt .i. etir fld 7 a duilli, Rawl. B. 502, fo. 61 a 2.
[4]) in marbnada noibsea LB.
[5]) Niba LB.
[6]) 7 rl. LB., the scribe adding: Do scrib*us* in amra a n-oenlo et*er* cheill 7 fogur, i. e. 'I have transcribed the *Amra* in one day, both text and gloss.'

Cowes.   WHITLEY STOKES.

Corrections.

(Ztschr. f. celtische Philologie, Band III.)

P. 9, l. 10. Here YBL. is translated. LL. means 'but he did not (yet) attain to killing Loegaire.'
„ 9, „ 11, *for* leave him his blessing *read* bid him farewell (Henebry).
„ 9, „ 15, *for* all has departed *read* this goes beyond all (Henebry).
„ 9, „ 18, *for* the man has *read* this is (a sign of) the man's (Henebry).
„ 9, „ 20, *for* is *read* may be.
„ 9, last line, *read* thus he killed Loegaire, who was (then) buried in Druim Loegairi.
„ 10, § 8. More literally thus: 'Well then', says Cobthach, 'know ye who is more hospitable in Erin?' 'We know', says Craiphtine; 'it is Labraid Loingsech, son of Ailill. I went to him in spring, and he killed his only ox for me. *He* is more hospitable.' Says Ferchertne the Poet: 'We know. I too went to him in winter, and he killed his only cow for me, although he possessed nothing but her.'
„ 11, l. 14, *for* he *read* she.
„ 11, „ 15, *after* daughter *insert* (now).

MITTEILUNGEN
AUS IRISCHEN HANDSCHRIFTEN.

IV.
Aus Harleian 5280.

Diese wichtige Handschrift ist oft beschrieben worden, zuletzt von mir in der Einleitung zu Hibernica Minora. *Ich füge noch folgende von den Schreibern herrührende Marginalien hinzu:*

fo. 40 b *marg. sup.* dies luna [*sic*] re feil Babloir[1]) odie .i. fer fuaslaicthi giall la Gaidhelai.

fo. 41 b *marg. sup.* mairt inidi ódie.

fo. 46 a *marg. sup.* Baili Bricin sund. Mesi an Gillo Ríabach.

fo. 49 b sechtmain o aniug luan hinide.

fo. 57 a *marg. sup.* is imresnach mo menma rim hodie.

fo. 58 b Agsin deitt a Túathuil o Fiorfessa mhac Conchabair maille re gradh occus re beannachtain occus da mbeith dithchell bud ferr ina sin agam-sa dogeptha-sa uaim hé. Ni beg sin do dimaoines briathar ach cuimnighugh orum-sa *gach* uair docifir so.

fo. 61 b *letzte Zeile* Misi an Gilla Riabach scriuhus an lebar so.

fo. 74 b In cedain ria feil Muiri na sainse[2]) odie. Et a cuirr Lessa Conaill dam. Mesi an felmac on cill dianadh leathnomen an sechtmad soerlaithi na sechtmaini.[3]) Tuicedh Sencan sin.

Wunderbare Heilung Kaiser Konstantins.

Diese Erzählung findet sich auch auf S. 137 *des Gelben Buchs von Lecan* (L), *aus dem ich Varianten beifüge.*

---

[1]) Babloir .i. ainm do Pátraic, Corm.
[2]) d. h. *Mariä Verkündigung* (25. *März*).
[3]) Cell Sathairn?

[fo. 26 b] In Consaitin mac Elinæ imráitir sund, indtan rob áiniom ndō, rotgab acais mōr. Do[bretha]¹) a lege quca dia Ioc. IS *ed* legios atpertot*ar* hi²) legi pris: lind lūaide di legad 7 fuil trī *cet* mac n-enocc de testin isan lind lūa*ide* 7 fot*h*racad ass. Dincōid Ier*um* di atcoma*rc* die m*ā*thai*r* d*ū*s hi²) ndingn*ed*. 'Olc sen', ol i²) m*ā*t*h*ai*r*, 'oir derat Diæ mait[h] det, nac[h]idbaid hinn-ulc. Dorine rī crōda būi reumot sunt ingrem na crist*aidi* .i. tr*i*cha mag fon mBet[h]il 7 *cet* gachae moigi 7 .xl. ar *cet* hisin mBet[h]il f*ē*n do m*a*ccoib do marba*d* les, dāig co tōet[h]sad *Crist*. Tresiu c*u*muctæ Crīst olt*ā*s qum*a*ch*t*a Irūaith .i. dochua*id* Irūaith³) *etir* ū*ir* 7 ifr*inn*, at*ā* an macra*d* *immorro* for nimh. T*u*ssa *immorro* n*ā* quind*i*g ifr*enn*, n*ā* bīth ad lenmoin⁴) in gair 7 ind gubha ferfuidit fīr 7 mn*ā* hoc cōined a mac*ā*n, 7 na h*ē*rcc⁵) anddīaid Irūaid a n-ifr*inn*. Ar is usao leom b*eth* fo croic[h] 7 martor⁶) det sunt an*ā*s do dol amol docōid Erūaid *etir* ū*ir* 7 ifr*inn*. At*ā* nī is dēoda liom dīt⁷) .i. edpair edparta mōra don fīr dorat cobuir doid hi tosaich⁸) .i. do Cr*ist* mac Dē bi 7 dia nōeba*ib*. Bīd legi*us* sōn *immorro* die⁹) c*u*rp 7 die⁹) anm*ain*.' 'Cinn*us* dogēnt*ar* ōn?' ol *Consatin*. 'Dēntor coibl*ed* mōr leat-sa do Rōm*ā*nch*aib* 7 intan uh*us* áiniu doiph¹⁰) tomoilt na fl*edie*, abai*r*-sie ru cie lūag dob*ē*rdaois ar h'Ioc. Atp*e*rot som dno¹¹) am*ail*¹²) do s*erc* leō, die mba[d]¹³) leōu in vili dom*un*, dop*ē*rdaois ar h'Ic. Tabai*r*-sie did*iu*¹⁴) do cath*air* .i. Rōm L*etha* do Dīe 7 do P*etur* 7 do Pōl co br*ā*th 7 nī fūasnabat íer*um*.' Dorōnad amlaid 7 dohedprad Rōm do Dīe 7 do Petor 7 do Pōl.¹⁵) Int*an* ier*um* at*racht* īernab*ā*r*ach* antī *Consatin*, nī raibe bainni sōethae¹⁶) foair, *acht* rol*ā*d de forsin tr*ā*t[h]¹⁷) *co* mbo for an *ē*duch.¹⁸) *Co* ndeocha*id* īer sīrsōeg*ul* doc*um* nime. Is mairc n*a*cha n-erbæ¹⁹) don Comdied, mairc n*ā*²⁰) taba*ir* a edbort*a* 7 a almsana dō 7 doa²¹) nōeba*ib*, oir is ē ōenliaig an c*uir*p 7 na hanmo é. Is aire is cōir dá *gach* duine nī do dēn*um* ar a liaigh nemdao .i. ar anmcaraid cr*ā*ibd*ech*.²²)

---

¹) *Sic L.*	² = a.	³) Irhuait *MS.*
⁴) id diaid *L.*	⁵) heirc *L.*	⁶) martra *L.*
⁷) duit *L.*	⁸) 7 i toicedh*us* do beathad *add. L.*	
⁹) dot *L.*	¹⁰) ic *add. L.*	¹¹) iar*um* *L.*
¹³) ata *add. L.*	¹³) dia mbad *L.*	¹⁴) iaram *L.*
¹⁵) co bráth *add. L.*	¹⁶) ná galair *add. L.*	¹⁷) in trath sin *L.*
¹⁸) co mbái slán forsinn édach *L.*		¹⁹) nachnearba *L.*
²⁰) nach *L.*	²¹) dia *L.*	

²²) bis do réir Dé do glanad a cuirp 7 a anma for nim. Finit. *add. L.*

Göttliche Bestrafung der Sonntagsübertretung.

Die folgenden drei Erzählungen finden sich als warnende Beispiele der Sonntagsentheiligung am Ende der irischen Übersetzung des Sonntagsbriefes (Forus Cána Domnaig) fo. 38a eingeschaltet. Sie fehlen in den übrigen Handschriften des Traktats, die ich Ztschr. I, S. 495 aufgezählt habe.

1. Alaili cēli Dē and fechtus dīe domnaig co n-aco nī: an gilli mbec docum in luic i rabī 7 prosna connaid les. 'Cid dingēntar frisan gilla sa?' ol a muinter risan sruidh. 'Mesiumnacht Dē fair!' ol in sruidh. Co n-acotar nii: rolas in brosna ind ēdach bō[i] immon mac, co n-erbailt an mac de. Unde dicitur:

In macān dīa domnaig · tuc in brosna co nglanbail
loisccis an brosna a bratān · bōi an macān gan anmuin.

2. Bōi dno sruid eli ann inna regles. Ticid aingel[1]) Dē cucoi cegh nōna cona cuid. Oc timciul relci dō dīa domnaig fuceird mberridi mbeg cona bachuill din conair bōi fuirri. Tallad airi Ierum in timt[h]irecht nemdho sen ōn trādh sin [c]o alaili. Unde dicitur:

An sruit[h] ruglan in conair · dīa domnaig badid n-aithreg
nī tāinic an cuid nemdho · ba roscremda ind aithbiur.

3. Bāi dno alaili popul oc timchiul relci dīa domnaig co n-acotar in tāin folaid[2]) issan gort ina fīnemna. 'Berar an tāin isan[3]) gurt!' ol in popul. 'Nī co mbertur', ol in sruith, 'dēg an domnaig.' Luid alali alithir do Gāidiulaib isan mancuini do tabuird na tāna assan gort. Adfīadur din tsruith annī sin 7 nī bo maith les. Espeurt an sruidh: 'Tabraid trī baco tairis isan trācht baili ina tora tond tuili.' Toghnī[th] andī sin. An cēdna tonn doāinic nī farcaib findo fair, an tonn tānaisse nī farcaib croconn foair, an tress tonn nī farcaib feōuil for cnāim ndó. Unde dicitur:

Luid alali 'san fīni · dīa domnaig co n-āine
donāncatar teveoir[4]) tonna · comtar lomma hi[5]) cnāma.

---

[1]) aingil *MS.*
[2]) folad *hier 'Rinder'. Vgl.* co folodaib 7 indilib, LU. 65 b 9.
[3]) *Zu lesen* asan.   [4]) *Besser* teoir.   [5]) = a.

Tochmarc Emire la Coinculaind.

Von den acht Handschriften, in denen uns diese Sage erhalten ist, habe ich Rev. Celt. IX, S. 433 ff. gehandelt. Ich drucke hier den Harleyschen Text, den einzig vollständigen ausser dem des Stowe-Manuskripts, ab und füge aus den anderen Handschriften wichtige Varianten bei. Zugleich verweise ich auf meine Über-setzung in der Archaeological Review I, S. 68 ff., von der Miss Hull in ihrer 'Cuchullin Saga' neuerdings einen verkürzten Abdruck veröffentlicht hat.

[fo. 27a] 1. Poi ri aumrau airegdai and-Emain Macho fecht n-aild, edon Concopor[1]) mac Fauchtnae.[2]) Bai mar de amro ina flaith lie hUlto. Poie siod ocus same 7 suboidhe,[3]) boi mess 7 claus[4]) ocus murtorad, poi smacht 7 recht ocus dechflaitius rie remess[5]) lia hUllto, boi mor d'ordan 7 d'oirecus 7 d'imad isan rictoig and-Emoin.

2. As amloid ierom boi in tech soin, edon in Craebruad Concoboir, fo intamoil tige Midhcordai. Noi n-imdodhai o ten co fraic.[6]) Triucho troiccid ind-airdiu cech airenoicch credumai boi isan[7]) tig. Errscor di dercciuhar and. Stial[l] ar cabor hee ier n-ichtar 7 tugai slindid[8]) ier n-uachtar. Imdae Concoboir ind-airienech in tighe co stioaldoib arcait, co n-uaitnip credumai,[9]) co ligrud oir for a cendaib, co n-gemoib carrmocail intib, comma[10]) comsoloss laa 7 adoicc inte, gona steill aircid uasan riog co airdlius an rightighi. In n-am nobualed Concobor co flesc[11]) rigdoi an ste[i]ll, contaitis Ulaid ulie ris. Di eimghai[12]) dec[13]) in de erraid dec[13]) imon imgoi[12]) sen ima cuaird.

3. Nothelldis immorro laith galie[14]) Ulad ac ol isan rigtoig sen 7 ni bid neuch dib a comcetboidh alailie. Ba han airctech[15]) nobidis laith gailie fer nUlad isan ticc and-Emoin. Boi mar do

---

U = LU., S = Stowe MS. 992, F = Book of Fermoy, B = Betham 145 (vellum), b = Betham 145 (Papier), R = Rawlinson B. 512, E = Egerton 92.

[1]) Coincopor MS. [2]) Fathaig add. BS.
[3]) Lies subaige. — cáinchomrac U. [4]) claiss U.
[5]) fria remis U. [6]) o thenid co fraigid and U.
[7]) is U. [8]) Lies slinded (U). [9]) crédumaib U.
[10]) Lies co mba (U). [11]) fleisc U. [12]) Lies imdai (U).
[13]) deac U. [14]) fer n-add. U. [15]) aircech U.

immod ceuc turcomroicc isann rig*t*ig 7 de airfedaib adamroib.
Arclisde 7 arsendtee 7 arcante ann, edon arclisde[1]) errid, ar-
cantis[2]) filid, arsendis c*r*utirie 7 timpanoic.

   4. Die mba*t*ar 'diu Ulaid fechtus n-ann and-Emoin Machie
ic ol ind iarngualai.   Ced mbrothai noteged ind di lionn[3]) cechi
nonai.   Ba sis*i*de[4]) ol ngolai.   Is*i*de[5]) nofurad[6]) Ul*t*u ulie ind-
oensisd.   Noclisdis errid Ul*a*d ar[7]) suainemn*a*ib[8]) an[9]) dorus
[c]o'roile[10]) isan toicc and-Emhoin.   Coic traigid dec[11]) ar noi[12])
ficteb med an tige.   Tri clessai[13]) dengnidis an errid .i. cles
cletinech 7 cless ubhall 7 foeb*a*rcles.

   5. At e and errid degnedis ina clessai sen .i. Conold Cernoch
ma*c* Airmirgen,[14]) Fergos mac[15]) Rossai[16]) Rodanai, Loeccoirie
Bua*d*ach ma*c* Condoig,[17]) Celt*c*har mac Uthir,[18]) Dubtoch ma*c*
Lucd*a*ch, Cucul*a*ind ma*c* Soal*d*aim.   Scel mac Bairdine, a quo
Belocch Bairdine nomena*t*ur, doirseid Emno Machie.   As dee ata
sceul Sce*ó*il, ar ba prasscel*a*ch side.

   6. Dorosce[19]) Cu*ch*ulaind diuh ulie ocon cli*u*ss ar aine 7
athlame.   Ruscarsad[20]) mna Ulod co mor[21]) ar[a] aine ocon clios,
ar atlaime[22]) a leme, ar febas a ergno, ar bindie a erlapra, ar
coime a[23]) ghnuse, ar sercaide[24]) a dreiche.   Ar ba*t*ar secht
mec imblesan ina rigroscoib .i. a cethair isan dalai suil, a tri
isan tsuil n-ali[25]) ndo.   Secht meoir cech*t*ar a da coss 7 a secht
cechtor a di laime.   Ba*t*ar buado imda foair.   Bu*ai*d do ced*u*s a
gois noco ticced a lon laich,[26]) bu*ai*d clesomnochtai, buad mbuan-
fa*ig*, bu*ai*d fi[d]ceallechtai, bu*ai*d n-airdmessai, bu*ai*d faidsene,
buad [fo. 27b] crotai.   Tri lochtai Concul*ai*nd: a bieth roocc, ar
ni rofasota*r* a rengai rodaim, ar bo moide concesdis oicc anait-
nig[27]) foir, et a biith rodanai, roaloind.

   7. Boi comair*l*ie lia hUltai fodiag Concul*ai*nd, ar r*u*scarsod
a mna 7 a n-ingena co mor e, ar ni boi setig a fail Concul*ai*nd
an tan sen.   Ba si comoirli co n-irsad, set*ig* ba[28]) togai la

---

[1]) *Lies* arclistis (*U*).	[2]) nochantais *U*.	[3]) im tráth *add. U*.
[4]) sisin *U*.	[5]) issi *U*.	[6]) nofired *U*.
[7]) for *U*.	[8]) tar*s*nu *add. U*.	[9]) *Lies* ón (*U*).
[10]) diarailiu *U*.	[11]) deac *U*.	[12]) ba hé *add. U*.
[13]) trichles *U*.	[14]) Amorgeni *U*.	[15]) maic *MS*.
[16]) Roich *U*.	[17]) Connad *U*.	[18]) Uthidir *U*.
[19]) dirósced *U*.	[20]) rocharsat *U*.	[21]) Concl. *add. U*.
[22]) athlaimecht *U*.	[23]) ai *MS*.	[24]) *Lies* sercaigi (*U*).
[25]) aile *U*.	[26]) láith *U*.	[27]) *Lies* anaichnid (*U*).
[28]) bad *U*		

Coincul*aind* de tochm*arc* ndo, ar bo derb leo conod[1]) lucchaide rosoigfed[2]) millid a n-ingenr*aide* 7 foemod sercie a mban *fer* dia mbe[3]) set*ig* a coimfrestoil occo, 7[4]) ba soédh[5]) leu mochercrai ocai,[6]) corb acobar leo ar an foáth sen toab*air*t mna ndo, fodég co farcbod comorbo. Ar rofedat*ar* is vadh bodesin nobíad a athcin.[7])

8. Dobreta ier*um* Con*ch*obor nonbur uad cevca cuiccid a nEr*inn* de cung*id* mna de Coincul*aind* d*ús* in faigepdis indach[8]) pr*imbaili no primdunod a nEr*inn* ingen[9]) rig no rofl*ath*av no prugad de nech bud ail do togai 7 de tocm*arc* ndou. Tancotor ulie na teachtai diblionoip[10]) 7 ni fuarot*ar* ingen[11]) bud[12]) togai la Coincul*aind* de tocmarc ndo.[13])

9. Luid C*uchulaind* feisne[14]) de tocm*arc* ingine ro*fitir* al-Luglocht*aib* Logai, edon Emer inccen Forcoild Monoch.[15]) Lod C*uchulaind* feisne 7 a aræ Læcc mac Riaengapr*ai* ina carp*ut*. Ass e oencarp*at* in sin nad foglendis dirmonnoa[16]) na echr*aidie* do cairpt*ib* Ul*ad* arodene[17]) 7 áne[18]) in carboid 7 an errid arid-suided ann.

10. Forranic C*uchulaind* in ingen[19]) ina cluichemag cona comolt*aib* impe. Ingenai son na mbrugad bautor im dun Forg*aill*. Bot*ar* side oc foclaind[20]) druine 7 decclamdai la hEmir. Is iss*ide* ingen pas[21]) fiu lai[s]-sem de ingen̄oib Erionn do acaldoim 7 de tochmorc. Ar is iss*ide* congaib na *sé* bu*adha* fuirre .i. bu*aid* crotha 7 buad ngothai, bu*aid* mbindi*ussai*, bu*aid* ndruine, bu*aid* ngoisse, bu*aid* ngensai. Atbert C*úchulaind* acht ingen pad comad*us*[22]) ndo ar aois 7 cruth 7 cinel 7 cles 7 solme, bad deuch lamdai de ingenaib Er*enn* nad ragad lais 7 na bad coimdich[23]) ndou do bancelib Er*enn*[24]) mona beth saml*aid*. Ar as is*ide* oeningen congepied[25]) na modai sen. Is airie is die tocm*arc* sa[i]nr*ud* lod[26]) C*uchulaind*.

---

[1]) co mbad *U.*
[2]) nosaigfed *U.*
[3]) mbeth *U.*
[4]) dan*o* add. *U.*
[5]) sáeth *U.*
[6]) do bith do Choincl. *U.*
[7]) athgein *U.*
[8]) *Lies* in nach (*U*).
[9]) *Sic U, lies* ingin.
[10]) *Lies* día blíadna (*U*).
[11]) *Lies* ingin (*U*).
[12]) ba *U.*
[13]) om. *U.*
[14]) iarom add. *U.*
[15]) Manaich *U.*
[16]) dirmann *U.*
[17]) *Lies* ar a déni (*U*) oder ar rodéni.
[18]) ar a áni *U.*
[19]) *Lies* in n-ingin (*U*).
[20]) foglaim *U.*
[21]) is i sin dan*o* áen ingen ba *U.*
[22]) chomadais *U.*
[23]) chomdi *U.*
[24]) *Lies* do banchéli (*U*).
[25]) uli add. *U.*
[26]) ludi *U.*

11. Ba cono timtocht oenoicc luid [1]) Cúchulaind [2]) de acoldaim Emire 7 de taidbsene [3]) a crotai dii. A mbatar na hingena ina suide [4]) for forad oenaic an duine, concolatar andi ina ndochum: bascoire na n-euch, culgaire na carbod, [5]) siangoil [6]) na tet, dresacht na roth, im[f]orran [7]) in laith goilie, scred[g]airie [8]) na n-arm. 'Fechadh [9]) oen uaib', for Emer, 'cia [10]) dotaed inar ndochum.'

12. 'Atciu-ssa em ann', for Fial ingen Forgaill, 'di ech commorai comailde comcrothai combuadai [11]) comlemnechai biroig airdcind aigenmair allmoir goblaid [12]) gobchoil dualaig tulleathain forbreco fairseggai fo- [fo. 28 a] lethna [13]) forranc[h]ai cassmongaid [14]) casscaircich. Eoch liath leslethon [15]) luath luaimnech lonnmar luthmar luglemnech leobarmongach maiccnech toirnech trostmar [16]) tuagmong ardcend uchtleathan. Lassaid fod fondbrass focuirse focruaid fo[a] cruib coluth [17]) cetharda. Dogrind elmo [18]) enlaithe luthbuadai. Beraid rit[h] for set. Foscain uathai edh [19]) n-análche. Oibliuch tened tricimruaidie [20]) tendiuss a craess glomorcind fil fo [21]) dessfertis an carpait.

13. 'Aroilie ech cirdub cruaidcenn cruinn caelcossach cae-lethan [22]) cobluth dian dualmar dualach [23]) dronchoechech maignech aignech bairnech bhailccemnich [24]) lemnech [25]) lebormongach cas-mongach scuableabor drondualach tulleathan grind imaaig ier ndith [26]) aige ech i n-iath. Moscigg srathai sreg [27]) serge, sechid [28]) moige midglinde, ni facoib ann imdoraid etir omnoib riad [29]) rout.

14. 'Carpat fidgridn fet[h]aide dia n-droch findoi umaidhe. Sidbe finn finnarcaid co fet[h]anoib [30]) findrune. Cret urard iraibidn, [31])

---

[1]) dolui U.   [2]) allásin add. U.
[3]) Lies taidbsin. thaidbred U.   [4]) i sudiu U.
[5]) Lies in charpait (U).   [6]) siangal U.
[7]) imorrain U.   [8]) scretgaire U.   [9]) fecced U.
[10]) cid U.   [11]) comchróda comlúathu U.
[12]) Lies gablaig (gablaich U).   [13]) fosenga forlethna U.
[14]) Lies cassmongaig (U).   [15]) lond add. U.
[16]) trosmar U.   [17]) calath U.   [18]) almai U.
[19]) úathu ech U.   [20]) trichemruaid U.   [21]) do U.
[22]) calethan U.   [23]) druimlethan add. U.
[24]) Lies balccémnech (U). balcbéimnech add. U.
[25]) om. U.   [26]) Lies iar níth (U).   [27]) Lies sréid (U).
[28]) sétid U.   [29]) hitir omnáriád U.   [30]) fethain U.
[31]) drésachtach U.

si credoa cromglindie. Cuing druimniech dronordai. Da n-all dualcho dronbuidie fertse cruaidie colcdirge.

15. 'Fer broenach duub isan carp*ut* ass aildium di feroip Er*enn*. Fuan cain coir[1]) corcordai[2]) imbe, osse coicdiapail. Eou oir indtslaidie uassa banbruindiechair[3]) ina turscloc*cud*[4]) rie mben luthai lanbuildie. Lene gealculpudach co nderccindlid oir oirlasrauch.[5]) S*echt* ngemou d*er*cca[6]) dracandai for lar *cecht*ar a da imcassen. Da ngruaid ngorm ngelai[7]) crodergai difich oibliech tened 7 analc[h]e.[8]) Dofich ruithnie[9]) serce ina dreich. Ata lem bo f*ras* de nemonnoib rolaad ina cinn. Dubit*hir* let[h] dubfoloch *cecht*ar a di p*rai*.[10]) Cloidem orduirn i n-echraiss[11]) sestai for a dib sliast*aib*. Gai gormruad glactomseip[12]) la fogai fé[i]g foephartoch for crandoib ruis ruamanndai a cengall die cre[i]t croi[13]) an[14]) carp*ait*. Sc*iath* co comroth aircid, oosse corcorda co tuadmilaib[15]) oir oss a dib n-imdadhoib. Focerd ioch n-err*ed* n-indiee,[16]) imad cless comrum[17]) ossa err*id* oencarpaid.

16. 'Arai ar a belaib isan carpod sen, aralie fer seng fanfodoa forbrec. Folt forcass forordai[18]) forruad for a muldoch, gipne findrune for a edon na leccid[19]) a f*olt* fo aigid. Cuaiche do or for dib culib[20]) a taircellad a f*olt*. Coichline etrich[21]) imbe co n-aursollccud for aa dibh n-ullinnoib. Pruidne die derccor ina laim dia taircillid[22]) a eocha.'

17. Doricht[23]) C*uchulaind* co hairm a mbat*ar* and ingenr*ad* foi sen 7 bendochaiss doib. Tocb*aid* Emer a gnus cain[24]) crut*haig* a n-ardo 7 dobert[25]) aichne for C*oinculaind*, con*idh* admbert:[26]) 'Dess imriadam duib!' ar si (.i. Dia do rediuc*cud* duib, ol sii). 'Slan imroisc[27]) duib-se!' ol sesem (.i. rop slan sib-se o cach aiscc). [fo. 28 b] 'Can dolot-sai?'[28]) al si. 'Do Int[id]e Emno', ol se (.i. din machi na hEmno). 'Cia hairm a femhir?'[29]) ol si. 'Femir' ol se, 'a tig fir adgair buar moicche Tethru' (.i. a tic

[1]) *om. U.*	[2]) corcra *U.*	[5]) bánbruinnechur *U.*
[4]) áthaurslocud *U.*	[5]) forlasrach *U.*	[9]) deirg *U.*
[7]) gruad gormgela *U.*		[8]) analaich *U.*
[9]) ruithen *U.*	[10]) a da bruád *U.*	[11]) *Lies* ecr*us* (*U.*).
[12]) *Lies* glacthomside (*U.*).		[13]) crón *U.*
[14]) *om. . U.*	[15]) *Lies* túagmilaib.	[16]) n-indnæ *U.*
[17]) comluith *U.*	[18]) *om. U.*	[19]) nád leced *U.*
[20]) for a díb cúladaib *U.*		[21]) ettech *U.*
[22]) taircelland *U.*	[23]) doriacht *U.*	[24]) gnúis cáim *U.*
[25]) dobreth *U.*	[26]) conid andaide asbert *U.*	
[27]) imreisc *U.*	[28]) dolluidisiu *U.*	[29]) hi febair *U.*

fir acla[i]d[1]) buar moige Tetra.[2]) 'Cia bur[3]) fess ann?' ol side.
'Fonoad (.i. rohimfuined) cul[4]) carbait dun ann', ol se. 'Cisse
conair deloud-sai?' al side. 'Etir da codat feda', ol se. 'Cid
atgaibsid[5]) ierum?' ol si. 'Ni ansa', ol soide. 'De teme marai
for amrun fer nDeaa, for uan di ech nEmno, for gort na
Morrignai, for druim na mormhuice, for glend an mardaim etir
in dia 7 a faith, for smir mna Fedilmai, etir an triath 7 a
setig,[6]) for toinge eech[7]) nDea etir rig nAnond 7 a gnied, do
mandculie[8]) cethorculie domoin, for Oilbine, for tresc in marim-
dill, etir dabaic 7 dabcine, do ingentib niad Tetrach rig Fomorie
do luglochtaib Logai (.i. do gortaib Loga).

18. 'Cate[9]) do slondad-sai, a ingen?' ol Cuchulaind. 'Ni
ansa emh', al and ingen. 'Temair ban, báine ingen, ancing[10])
gensai, ges[11]) nad forfoemthar (.i. amoil ata Temair os cech
tulaicc, sic atu-ssa os cech mnai a ngenass), dercoid na dexinech[12])
(.i. nomdechar o cac ar mo caime 7 ni dechaim-si nech), doirp a
ndopor[13]) aindir[14]) imnar[15]) (.i. an tan dechtar an doirb is a
n-ichtar usce tet), tetra[16]) tetrai dá luá, luacoir nad imtethar[17])
(.i. ar a cáime), ingen rig richiss gartai (.i. enech), conair nad
foróemter do conair coil ermoim, gonad fri suan senbath sretaib
cerd adpclossaib errid. Atcotaim trenfer[18]) tiarmoirset (.i. atad
lim trenfir dogenad[19]) m'iarmoirecht, cebe nomberai tar a ter-
togai[20]) cin foruss mo caingne cucai[21]) 7 co Forgoll.'

19. 'Cidne trenfir detiarmoirset, a ingen?' al Cuchulaind.
'Ni ansa', ol Emer. 'Da Lui, da Lauth, Luath 7 Lath Gaiblie
mac Tethrach, Triath 7 Trescad, Brión 7 Bolar, Bas mac Omna,
ochtar Conlai, Cond mac Forcaild. Ceuch fer diib co nirt ced[22])
7 co cliuss nonbair. Forcoll fesne dno, andso airim a cumochtai.[23])
Tresse cech gnied,[24]) eolchai cach drui,[25]) amainsi ceach filid.

---

[1]) arclaid U.   [2]) iasc immuir ethiar .... U.   Vgl. Strachan,
Archiv I, S. 33.

[3]) ce bú U.   [4]) col U.   [5]) adgaibside U.
[6]) setchi U.   [7]) Lies ech.   [8]) mondchuilib U.
[9]) cade U.   [10]) inching U.   [11]) gass U.
[12]) nad decsenach U.   [13]) a ndopor om. U.   [14]) ainder F.
[15]) imnair FU.   [16]) Vgl. tethrai .i. ben, Hib. Min. S. 47.
[17]) imthegar U. umdecthar F.   [18]) trénfir FU.
[19]) dodigenat FU.   [20]) dia raiter togai F.   [21]) chucu U.
[22]) and add. FU.   [23]) ilchumactai FU.   [24]) gniaid FU.
[25]) druid FU.

Bid forfinach[1]) dit-se cluche caich fria tresaib[2]) Forgoild fesne,
ar idcodai[3]) ilcumochtai occo fri coibled fergnim.'

20. 'Cid nachimm-airme-se,[4]) a ingen', ol Cu*chu*laind, 'liasna
tré*nf*eroib[5]) sen?' 'Madcodo[6]) do gnioma fesne',[7]) ol an ingen,
'cidh im nach airmebaind[8]) etorra?' 'Forglim fen em, a ingien',
ol Cu*chu*laind, 'comad[9]) luiet mo gniomaie eti*r* clot[h]aip n*ert*
n-erridaie.'[10]) 'Caidie do neurt-so di*diu*?'[11]) ol Em*er*. 'Ni *ansa*
em', ol *sé*. 'Argair fichid fauth[12]) mo comroicc, lor de trichaid
triean mo galie. Roferai .xl.[13]) mo comlond[14]) m'oenar. Argair
cé*t* mo commairge.[15]) Imgaibt*ir* athai ⁊ irgolae rem err*ud*[16])
⁊ rem úath. Techid sluaicc ⁊ socaide ⁊ ilor fer n-armach re
huatg*rá*iene mo dreche ⁊ mo gnusse.'

21. 'At mait[h]e na comrume moethmacaim sen', ol and ingen,
'act nat ranic go hoes[17]) n-erred beo*uss*.' [fo. 29a] 'Maith emh
romepled-sai, a ingen', ol *sé*, 'liam popoa Con*chobo*r. Ni hama*il*[18])
atfochne[19]) aithecan urbodad[20]) a claindie eti*r* leic ⁊ lossait no
ó ten co fraiecch.[21]) Ni[22]) for blæ oenurlaindie romalt-sæ la
Con*chobo*r, acht eti*r* erridib ⁊ anradaib Uludh,[23]) eti*r* drut[h]aib ⁊
deogbairib ⁊ druidib, eti*r* filiduib ⁊ fisidib, eti*r* brugadoib ⁊ biata-
choip Ul*ad* romforbaig*ed*-sai, co fuilid a mbesa ⁊ a ndana ule
lium-sai.'

22. 'Cidnie and em[24]) rodeblatar isna gniomaib maithe
sen?'[25]) ol Emir. 'Ni *ansa* em', al *sé*. 'Romebail Senca sober-
laid,[26]) conid am[27]) tren trebor an at[h]om athirgaib.[28]) Am goeth
a mbret[h]aibh, nidim dermodoch *cusc*.[29]) Atgair[30]) neuch re tua[i]t
trebair trebour.[31]) Arfoiclim a indscee,[32]) coicertaim brethai
Ul*ad*[33]) a n-ainsist ⁊ nininsorcc[34]) tria oilim*ain* tSenchoa formb.

---

[1]) f*o*rmach *FU*.　　[2]) tresai *F*.

[4]) nacham imraide-si *F*.

[6]) ma atchotat *U*.　[7]) da*no* add. *U*.

[8]) cid dam nachat airmébaind *U*.

[10]) neirt n-erred *U*.　[11]) da*no U*. fein *F*.

[13]) cethrachait *FU*.　[14]) einfir *add. F*.

[16]) er*ud U*. eirret *F*.

[18]) amal *U*. hamlaid *F*.

[20]) *Lies* orbugud (*U*).

[22]) nó *U*.　　　[23]) om. *U*.

[25]) isna gnímaib sin máidi *U*.

[27]) conam *F*.　　[28]) athargaib *FU*.

[30]) adgadur *U*. adgadair *F*.

[32]) a n-insce *U*.　[33]) uli *add. U*. a mbrethai uili *F*.

[34]) nisninsorg *UF*.

[3]) atchota *U*.

[5]) trénfiru *FU*.

[9]) co mba *FU*.

[12]) fand *U*.

[15]) coimeirge *F*.

[17]) nad ránac co nert *U*.

[19]) fogni *U*.

[21]) ó thenid cu froigid *F*.

[24]) di*diu FU*.

[26]) sobelraid *F*.

[29]) om. *FU*.

[31]) túaith treabair *FU*.

Romgab Blai bruccaid cucai for aice a treibe corroferadar[1])
mo techtai occo, gonad ierum adgairim firu coiccid Conchoboir
imma ricc. Nosbiathaim fria re sechtmaine. Fossaidier[2]) a
ndano 7 a ndamai 7 a ndiberccai farrid a n-eniech 7 a n-enech-
gressai.

23. 'Romalt Fergass, gonad rouba[i]m trenógai trie nert.[3])
Am amnus ar gail 7 gaisciud, conid o[m] tualaigg oirer criche
di coimed[4]) 7 di imdidien ar echtrandoib.[5]) Am dín cech
dochair,[6]) im sunn slaide cech sochraide.[7]) Dongniu socair[8])
ceuch truaigh, dongniu dochair[9]) cech triuin trie oilimain[10])
Fercussa form.

24. 'Rosiachtsu[11]) glun Aimirgin filid[12]) corromolaim rii[g]
as ceuch feip[13]) a mbí, go ndingbhaim oinfer ar gail, ar gaisced,
ar goeis, ar aine, ar at[h]laime, ar amanse, ar ciurt, ar calmodus.[14])
Dingbaim cech n-errid. Ni toillim buide di neoch acht do
Conchobor.[15])

25. 'Romirgair Findcoem, conid comoltai cartanacha[16]) com-
luid daum Conall Cernach coscoruch. Romtecuisc Catfad coem-
oinech diaig[17]) Dectirie, gonid am fisied fochmairc i cerdaib
dei druidechtai, conid am eoluch i febaib[18]) fiss. Ba cumma
romaltsad Ulaid etir aroidh 7 errid, etir ricch 7 ollamoin, gonid
am carua sluag[19]) 7 sochaidee, ganad cumma difichim a n-enech-
gresa ulie. Is soer em doroegartus-sa[20]) o Lug mac Cuind maic
Etlind de echtrai dén[21]) Dectirie co tech mBuirr in Broghai.
Et tussai didiu, a ingen', ol Cuchulaind, 'cindus rodalt-sai il-
Louglochtaib Logai?'

26. 'Romalt-sa em', ol side, 'la febai fenee i cossdud for-
caine, a foghart ngenussai, a congraim[22]) righnai, and-ecusc
sochraid, gonad cucom arbaigtir[23]) cech ndelb soer sochruid etir
iallaib ban buaidnide.'[24]) 'At mait[h]e em na febha sen, a ingen',
ol Cuchulaind. 'Cindus didiu', ol Cuchulaind, 'nachar commdicc

---

[1]) coroferad UF.   [2]) fossudiur UF.   [3]) gaili add. U.
[4]) do cosnam F.   [5]) fri ecratu echtrand U.
[6]) dochraid FU.   [7]) sochraid FU.   [8]) sochor UF.
[9]) dochor U.   [10]) altram U.   [11]) rosiachtus FU.
[12]) Lies filed.   [13]) asa feb F.   [14]) chalmdatus F.
[15]) cách add. U. Vgl. Zimmer, Kelt. Stud. I, S. 38.
[16]) om. U; lies carthanach.   [17]) diág UF.
[18]) fedaib F.   [19]) cara slúaig UF.   [20]) domrimgart-sa U.
[21]) dián UF.   [22]) comgraim UF.
[23]) bagthir U. bagthar F.   [24]) buágnithi U.

dun diblinaib comríacht*ain*?[1]) Ar ni fuar*us*[2]) cose ben[3]) follongad and-aires dala immacall*aim* [fo. 29b] fon sam*ail* sen[4]) frim.'
'*Ceist*: an fil bancelie laut', ol in ingen, 'ar foimdidin de trepe dit-see?'[5]) 'Nato emh', bar Cu*chulaind*. 'Ni techtai damh', ol iss*ide*, 'dolai fri fer[6]) a fladn*usse* na sethar is sine innú[7]) .i. Fial ingen Forgaild adcii am farrud sunn. Iss í roben beim foraiss for an lamt[h]orud.' 'Ni hi rodcaur*us*-sai[8]) em', for Cou*chulaind*, '7[9]) ni rofoem*us*-sai[10]) did*iu*[11]) mnai atgneed feur remonn[12]) 7 adcoss dam co rofoi and ingen uc*ut*[13]) la Coirprie Niefeur feuchtus n-aill.'

27. A mbat*ar* ier*um* fora n-imraitib,[14]) atcii Cu*chulaind* brundiu na hingene tar sedlauch[15]) a lened, conadh ann aspert in[16]) so: 'Cain an mag so, mag alcuing.' As and aspert and ingen na briathra sai[17]) oc frecc*rai* Concul*aind*: 'Ni ralie[18]) an mag so', ol Emiur, 'nad rubann comainm n-arcaid for ceuch n-ath ó Ath Scene Mend for Ollbine cu*ssan* mBancuing n-aircid[19]) ara mbruindenn[20]) Breaa diantoss Fedlime.'[21]) 'Cain an[22]) mag sai, mag alcuing', ol Cu*chulaind*. 'Ni ralie in mag sai nad rolo genid granne a loig bo briuine co tabhairt fir co cutrume aroile co mbem tr*í* nonbor d'aenbeim co n-*a*nacal fir a medhon cacha nonbair.' 'Cain an mag sa, mag alcuing', ol Cu*chulaind*. 'Ni raili a mag sa', ol s*ide*, 'nad ecmongai benn Suain m*aic* Roiscmilc o sam*é*uan co hoimhelc, ho oimhelc co beldine, ho beltine co brón trogain.' 'Asper*tar*, dogentor', ol Cu*chulaind*. 'Forreghtar, forimregt*har*, gebt*har*, arfoemt*ar*', ol Eim*er*. '*Ceist* caide do slonnad?' 'Am nia fir dichet a n-aili[23]) i Ross Bodbai', ol essemh. 'Cia h'ainm-se dno?' ol sii. 'Am nuadai tedmai tataigh[24]) conai', ol sesemh.

28. Deluid ier*um* uaidib iarsan tsegdou mbriat*har* sen Cu*chulaind* 7 ni rogensad[25]) ni bud[26]) moo de imacollaimh isen

---

[1]) comrichtain *U*.   [2]) fuar-sa *U*. fuaramar *F*.
[3]) ingin *U*.   [4]) samail se *U*. samla sa *F*.
[5]) do threib dit eisi *U*.
[6]) dul cu fer *F*. dál fri fer *U*.   [7]) andú *U*. nu *F*.
[8]) rocharusa *U*.   [9]) da*no* add. *U*.   [10]) forfæmusa *U*.
[11]) om. *U*.   [12]) remum *SF*.   [13]) ben ut *F*.
[14]) sin add. *S*.   [15]) sedlachaib *SF*.   [16]) om. *F*.
[17]) briath*ussai* *MS*. briathra so *S*.   [18]) ruale *S*. ruaili *F*.
[19]) n-aircit *F*.   [20]) mbruigend *SF*.   [21]) diandoss Fedelm *SF*.
[22]) a *S*.   [23]) i n-ail *SF*.   [24]) taithig *SF*.
[25]) forgensat *SF*.   [26]) bu *S*.

16*

laithe sen indasen. An tan boie Cu*chu*laind ierum oc eraimm
do Bregai,[1] imcomaircid a arai, edon Loeg, ndou: 'Ailee', bar
essem, '7 na briatrae immacloisset 7 an ingen, edon Emiur, cid
dieraidset[2] ann?' 'Nach fedor-sae', ol Cu*chu*laind, 'mo beth-se
òc tochma*rc* na hingenee? 7 is airee rocelsom ar cobrun,[3] arna[4]
tuicdis na hingenai conid oc a tochrai at*ú*-sai. Ar dia fessai
Forgold, nicondricfom dia deoin.'

29. Tanic Cu*chu*laind a tossag na himacallmou dia aroidh[5]
7 boie occa miniougu*d* ndo de irgairdiugu*d* a seta. 'And
Entidai Emno isruba*rt*-sa an tan isp*ert* s*i*de can diluidesie,[6]
iss *ed* donraidi*us*-sai:[7] o Eomain Machai. Is dei imoru asperour
Eomon Machou ndii .i. Machou iongen tsanrith m*ai*c Inbothai,
ben Cruindchon mic Agnoma*in* rou*s*sreth fri die gauboir and rig
ier caur ailgi*us*sou fuirrie, co ndeochoid diob ar-rith 7 arsibseis[8]
(.i. beris) manc [fo. 30a] occ*us* ingen die oentoirbe*rt*, conid din
eoma*in* sen asp*er*or Ema*in*[9] dii 7 conid on Macho sen raiter
Eomon no Mag Machai.

30. No dno is dei ata Emoin Machou am*ail* ata isan scel
soa.[10] Tri rig russbata*r* for Ultoib i comflaitess for Erind .i.
Dit[h]orba mac[11] Dimain a hUissneoch Midie, Oed Ru*ad* mac
Baduirn maic Aircetmair[12] a Tir Oedai, Cimboet[h[mac Findt*ain*
m*ai*c Aircidmoir a Findobair Moige hInes. Is ee rosnalt Ugaine
Mour mac Eo*ch*dach Bua*daig*. Dongnied corie ieru*m* ind fir, secht
mblia*dna* cech fir diib ir-rige. Tri secht rathai etarrou:[13] *secht*
ndruid, *secht* filid, secht n-octigernai; na druthie dia ngrisad trie
bithai, na filid dia nglamodh 7 die n-erfocc*r*aie, na taiss*ig* die
nguin 7 die lousc*ud*, monatseched[14] an feur nat[h]ai i cionn secht
mblia*dan* co coimed fir fla*th*ua .i. meus cecha blia*dna* 7 gen
meuth ruamnai in*a*[15] datha 7 cin mna de ecaib die banda[i]L
Timcellset teora cuar*da* cech fir diib and rige .i. lx.ui.[16] Aed
Ru*ad* adbath diib ar t*ús* .i. bagad[17] robaided a n-E*us* Ru*aid*,

---

[1] dar Bregu S.   [2] doraidsed S.   [3] cobra SF.
[4] arnar S.   [5] dia rad SF.   [6] doluidsiu S.
[7] roraidi*usa* S.   [8] arsisbis SF.
[9] *Dahinter* macha *ausradiert.*
[10] *Vgl.* Dindsenchas 161 (*Rev. Celt.* XVI, S. 279 *ff.*).
[11] maic H.   [12] Airgetmail F.
[13] *So zu lesen* Rev. Celt. XVI, S. 280, Z. 3, *wo* mblia*dna* *zu streichen ist.*
[14] mane teched S.   [15] cech SF.
[16] *So auch* LL. *Lies mit Stokes* lxiii.   [17] *Lies* bádud.

contuccad a coland isan siod, conid dei ata Sid Oedai os Euss
Ruaid feisne. Et ni farcaib side de cloinn acht oeningen .i.
Maucho Moggruad a hainm-side. Conataich side and rige i
n-aimser[1]) techtai. Isbert Cimboet[h] 7 Dithorbo na tibretis rige
die mnai. Fechtai cat[h] etarro 7 mebus forro-sim.[2]) Dierimalt
secht mbliadna irrige. Derochoir Dithorbo i Corand foisim.[3])
Forfacaib side macua matha .i. Brass 7 Boeth 7 Bedach ocuss
Uallac 7 Borrcass, go n-atcetar rige. Aspert Mauchai na tibred
doib, 'ar ni ó rathaib tuctai',[4]) al side, 'acht ir-roe cata ir ecin.'
Fecta cath etorra. Brises Machui for macoib Ditarba, co far-
caibsed ár cenn ace, co mbatar[5]) a nditruib Connacht. Tucc
Macai ierum Cimboeth cucie do céile dii 7 do toissigect a hamus
immbe. O robtar oentadaig tra Machai 7 Cimboet, lod Macai
d'ioarrair mac nDitorbo ir-richt claimsidie[6]) .i. toeus secail 7
rotai ruscoimledh immpee, conusfuair a mBoirinn Condocht ac
fune tuirc allaid. Iórfaidid[7]) ind fir scelai dii ocus innissid[8])
scélai doib 7 denberad biad dii ocon tened.[9]) Atbert feur diib:
'As aloind a ruscai na clamsige. Aentaigem friee!' Nusbert-
se[10]) leis fon cailde. Cengloid sii an feur sen al-luss nert[11]) 7
facbaid e isan caillid. Tic side dirise din tenid. 'Catie an feur
dechoid laut?' al sied. 'Mebol leis tiechtain cucaib-se ar oento-
gaudh[12]) [fo. 30b] ria clamsig.' 'Ni ba meobol', ol iet-sam, 'ar
degenam-ne ule andi sen an cednai.'[13]) Nuspeir ceuch feur fon
caillid. Cenglaid sii cech feur dib iar n-urd[14]) 7 nosber a n-oen-
cengal leaa co hUlltaib. Isbertatar Ulaid a marbad. 'Nito', ol
side, 'ar is coll fir flathu dam-sai; acht a ndoerad fo doirie 7
claided raith imbom-sai, conob[15]) sii bus primcathir Ulad co
brath. Co rotoraind si doib a ndun gona heo oir imma muin .i.
Emain .i. eo-muin, edon eo 'ma muin Machai, gonid de-sin ata
Emain Machai.

31. 'An feur isrubort-sai ir-rofaideamar[16]) thig, iss e
iascaire Conchoboir in sen (.i. Roncu a ainm). Iss e atclaid

---

[1]) *Lies* ina aimsir (*S*).
[2]) 7 brisis Macha forro *S*.   [3]) *Lies* fóisin *SF*.
[4]) tucus *S*.   [5]) for indarba *add. SF.*
[6]) *Lies* chlaimsige.   [7]) *Lies* iarfaigit.   [8]) si *add. S.*
[9]) *Lies* tenid.   [10]) *Lies* si (*S*).   [11]) *Lies* nirt (*F*).
[12]) ar n-oentugud *LL.*   [13]) uli a cétna *LL.*
[14]) ar niurt *LL.*   [15]) curub *S.*
[16]) irrofoiimar *S.* irrooiamar *F.*

na[1]) hiasco fo[2]) [s]náad fo moirib,[3]) ar iss e buair an marai a hiascaie[4]) 7 as i an moir Mag Tetrai (.i. ri di rigaib[5]) Fomore Tethrai .i. mag ríg Fomóre).

32. 'An fulacht asrubart-sai fo[r] rofonad[6]) dun lurcaire (.i. serrach) ann sen, iss e is coul[7]) carbaid co cend teorai nomad fo bit[8]) fo rigaib 7 as geis do[9]) a combairge .i. geis dien carbod co cend teurai nomad ier n-ithe feulai eich duine de doul ind; fodaigh[10]) ar is each folloing an carpait.

33. 'Etir da cotadh feudai asruburt-sai, edon[11]) an da sliab in sen etir a d[t]utcamar .i. Sliab Fuaid friunn andess[12]) 7 Sliap Cuillind rind anoir. A nDorcel[13]) (.i. in coill fil etarro) didiu ronbammaur[14]) etorrai, edon forsan set dorumenar etarrai andiss.

34. 'An conair asrubart de temheu moarai .i. de Moich Murteme. Ass aire adberar teime marai do-sside, fobith dodet moir foir tricaid mbliadan ier ndilind, gonad teme marai .i. ditiu no foscemhiel marai ee. No didiu[15]) as de ata Mag Murteme foir .i. moir druidechtai rusba[16]) foir co murseilce n-ann co n-aicned suidich[17]) leis, gonsuided[18]) an feur cona armbgaisced for laur a ustodbuilcc,[19]) co tanic an Dacdai 7 i[20]) lourg aine (nó anfaid) laiss, cor'caun na briathrai-ssai ris, cor'traighie fochétuair, edhon: 'Tai do cend cuasachtach, tai de corp cisach-tach, tai de thul tagebaitai!'[21])

35. 'For amrun (.i. run 7 cocar amrae) Fer nDea (.i. run 7 cogaur amraie), is side Ccrellaidh[22]) Duollaid indiu. Is fuirre geogoin[23]) Duollud mac Coirpri Niedfir la matau. Coticc[24]) sin[25]) ba hAmrun Feur nDea a ainm, fobith[26]) ba hand cétna

---

[1]) ina SF. [2]) sa SF. [3]) muir SF.
[4]) hiascach SF. [5]) na add. F. [6]) forrofonad SF.
[7]) col SF. [8]) bith S. beith F. [9]) doib StF.
[10]) Lies do dul ind fodeoid. — co cend tri .IX. duin edo dul ind iar n-ithi feola eich do fodeoig SF.
[11]) it e SF. [12]) aniar SF.
[13]) A n-Oircel S. i n-Orcel F.
[14]) dobadmar S. dobamar F. [15]) dna F. dano S.
[16]) robai S. [17]) suithech S. suidheach F. Lies suigthech.
[18]) Lies co suiged (F).
[19]) a hustadbuilc F. Zu lesen itsadluic? [20]) Lies a.
[21]) Rasuren hinter b und dem ersten i. taigi baig thaig FS.
[22]) grellach FS. [23]) geodna S. [24]) cotici FS.
[25]) immorru ad. F. [26]) fobithin FS.

rohimraidedh toichestal[1]) cata Moigee Tuiredh lia Tuaidh Dea
Donand fodegh dicair an cissa conaitcietar Fomoire forrau .i. da
trian ethai 7 blechtai 7 cloinde.

36. 'For uan di aech nEmnai. Bai oclach amru la
Gaidiulaie i rigi. Batar da ech aigi oc a n-ailimain do a Sid
Ercmon a scáthaib aba Cennman[2]) do Tuaid Dea. Nemed mac
Namha ainm an rig sin. Delecthie[3]) duo ierum in di ech asan
tsidh 7 demebhaid sruaim sain- [fo. 31 a] emhail asan tsid 'na
ndegaid et bui a huan már forsan sruaim sin 7 lethais darsen
tir and uan moar sen fri re moir 7 boi samhluidh go cend
mbliadna, gonad aire isrubrad a huanab din uisce sen .i. a uan
far[4]) in uisce 7 is side[5]) Uanabh[6]) insen andiu.

37. 'An gort na Morrignai asrubort-sai, iss ed Ouchtar
Nedmon in sen. Donbert an Daghda din Mhoirrigain an ferond
sen. Rohaired[7]) e ierum. An bliadain ronort Iubor Bochlid
mauccuu Gairb ina goirt-see botar[8]) moela[i]n mulce[9]) docorustair
a goirt se dee in[10]) bliadain sen, fobith ba coïbdelach disse
maccu Gairbh.

38. 'An Druim na Marmuice asrubart-sai, at e Druimne
Breg andsen, ar ba deulb muce doadbhas de maucaib Milid for
cech tulaicc 7 for cech ndingne[11]) a nErinn an tan imbersed 7
adcobraissed gabáil tiri ar egin inte ier cor brechta fuirre do
Thuaid De Danann.

39. 'Glenn an Mardaimh asrubart, iss e Gleund
mBreogaind[12]) .i. o Breogai mac Breogaind[13]) sendsir maic
Milid rohainmniged[14]) Gleunn mBreogaind 7 Mag mBregh.
Glend an Maurdaim dorad de, edhon Dam Dile mac[15]) Smirgaild
maic Tetrach ba rii for Erinn no aitrebodh[16]) and. Adbath[17])
an Dam sen oc toidhin mna fuada oc esscrad Muighe Breg siar
co beoulai dun.

40. 'An Conair isrubart etir an dia 7 a faidh .i. etir
an Mauc Oc asSidh an Brogaie 7 a faidh .i. Bressal Bofaid and-

---

[1]) tochetal S. toicetal F.
[2]) Von batar bis hier auf dem unteren Rande der Seite.
[3]) doleicthea S.   [4]) fair mit punctum delens unter i — fair FS.
[5]) issi FS.   [6]) Uanuib S. Uanaib F.
[7]) leai add. FS.   [8]) batir FS.   [9]) moelain muilchi S.
[10]) isin FS.   [11]) dinngnai S.   [12]) indsin add. FS.
[13]) o add. B.   [14]) ainmnigther B.   [15]) om. FS.
[16]) aitrebait FS.   [17]) dno add. FS.

airteur in Brogai. Is etarra boi an oinben,[1]) bean an gaband.
As [ed][2]) dolotarmar-ni,[3]) etir cnoc Sidi in Progæ i fil Oencuss
7 Sid mBressail druadh.

41. 'For Smiur mna Fedelma isrubart-sæ .i. Bounn in
sen. Is de atá Boann furrie .i. Boann ben Nechtain maic
Laurada luid do coimed in tobuir diamair boi[5]) a n-orlaind an
duine lia tri deogbairib[6]) Nechtain .i. Flessc 7 Lessc 7 Luam.
Ni ticed neuch cin aithiss on topur, mona tissed[7]) na deugbairi.
Luid and rigan la huaill 7 dimus docum in tobair 7 ispert nad[8])
raibe ni nocoillfed a deulf no douherud aitiss uirri. Tainic
tuaithbel[9]) in topair di airiugud a cumacht.[10]) Romefatar ierum
teeora tonno tairrse corr[o]imid[11]) a di ssliassaid 7 a desslaim
7 a lethsuil. Rethid si for imgabáil na haithesse sen assan tsid
co ticce[12]) moir. Cech ni roreth si, doreth in tobur ina diaidh.
Segais a ainm issan tsid, Sruth Segsai on tsid co Linn Mocoe.
Rig mna Nuadat 7 Colbtai mna Nuadat iersen, Boann a Midie.
Mannchuigg Aircit i o Finnoib co Tromaibh, Smiur mna Fei[d]-
limai o Trommoif co moir.[13])

42. 'In Triath isrubart et a sétigh,[14]) Cletiuch 7 Fesse
inn sen, ar iss triath ainm do torc taiseuch na tret. Is
ainm didiu[15]) triath[16]) do rig[17]) toisseuch na morthúath. In
Cletiuch dno is clethbuidig catha. Inn Fesse dno is ainm din
crain mair aithechtaigi tuirc 7 a seitich. Etir torc 7 a crain
dno lotmar.[18])

43. 'An ri nAnond isrubart 7 a gniæ, iss e Cernæ inn
sen tarsa tutchamar.[19]) Ba si Cirine a ainm o cein. [fo. 31 b]
Cernai a hainm o geugain in fuacurthai .i. Enno Aigneuch Cerno
ri[20]) nAnonn inssan[21]) di[n]gnae (.i. sid) sen 7 geugain i[22])
rechtairi ind-oirther in fuirt[23]) sen. Gniæ a ainm-side. Is de
atá Raith Gniad i Cerno degréss. For Geise for rig mac

---

[1]) oenbe S. [2]) sic FS.
[3]) *Lies* dolodmair-ni (FS).
[4]) *Vgl. Dindsenchas* 19 (*Rev. Celt.* XV, S. 315).
[5]) om. FS. [6]) deogbairi FS. [7]) tisad FS.
[8]) nach F. na S. [9]) tuaithbil FS. [10]) cumachta FS.
[11]) corraemaig FS. [12]) ticed FS. [13]) i add. FS.
[14]) setchi FS. [15]) dna F. dano S. [16]) om. FS.
[17]) drig MS. [18]) dolodmair S. dolotamair F.
[19]) tarsan deochamair SF. [20]) *Lies* rig (SF).
[21]) *Lies* isin (SF). [22]) *Lies* a (S). [23]) *Lies* phuirt.

nEmnoe dogeniu Ennæ inn sen,[1]) ar (*nó* fo) bith[2]) bvi carat*rad*
mor et*ir* Geise et Cerno.

44. 'In Toingi Euch nDea isrub*art*, ass hi Ange[3]) in
sen. Ba Tonge .i. tonach euch[4]) a ainm ar tos, fobith is innti
conega*tar* fir Deuai nDeud cedamus a n-euchai ier tie*ch*t*ain* o
cath Moigi Tuired. Aingi (.i. amn*us*) dorad di iarsandi rig-
nigsed Thuatae Dei Donand inn-eochæ innte.

45. 'An Manncuili cetharcuili isrub*art*, iss e Muincilli
in sen. Iss ann boi Mann b*ri*ugæ. Bai di*diu* buár mar ind-
Er*inn* i flaith Uressail B*ri*c m*ai*c Fiacho Fobric di Laignib.
Dogeni 'diu Mannach (.i. prop*ri*um no*men* uiri) domanchuili[5])
moræ fo talm*ain* issan inad atá Muincilli dia ngart*her* Óchta*r*
Muincilde 7 docoisse*cht*[6]) (.i. doronta) esstadæ indib do foichill
na plagæ. Digeni ier*um* cai[7]) (.i. f*ri*tailim) in righ cetheoræ
lanamna *fichet* co cenn se*cht* mblia*dan*. In Manncuili di*diu* .i.
cuili Mandaich Óchta*r* Munchilli.

46. 'An Oillbine[8]) dno isrub*art*, is si*de*[9]) Ailuhine inn
sen. Bai ri aum*rae* svnn a nErie .i. Ruad m*ac* Ri[g]dvinn .i.
di Mum*ain*. Doboi iriss (.i. comdal) laiss do Galluib. Luid
do*cum* a irisse do Galla*ib* timcel nAlp*an* andess teuora noaib.
T*ri*cho in cech noi dib ier*um*. Gaba*is* a cobla*ch* tasst[10]) foaib i
medon na fairci. Ni boi ni nodfuaislaiciud di setaif no moinif
dia cor issa trethan. Fo*c*r*essae* crannchor[11]) leou d*ús* cie dib
die ross*ed*[12]) techt dia fiss fon[13]) fairce cid notfosst.[14]) Doralæ
in cranncor forsan rig[15]) feisne. Eibling ier*um* in ri .i. Rvad
m*ac* Ri[g]dhuinn forsan[16]) moir. Diclethar[17]) fair ier*um*[18]) am-
muir. Focard i machairie.[19]) Fosrainic dno[20]) is-suide noi
mbaindelbæ oiminnai. Atdamna*tar* (.i. doraidsedar) doba*tar* se
fotrerga*tar*[21]) (.i. difosta*tar*)[22]) na longa contissed[23]) som cucthae,[24])
7 dobe*r*tatar[25]) noi longæ oir ar noi n-oidcib dia fess leu .i.

---

[1]) in bith *SF*. [2]) *om. SF*. [3]) Angne *S*. Angen *F*.
[4]) nDea *add. SF*. [5]) domcuili *FS*. [6]) dochoiseat *F*.
[7]) cauin *FS*. [8]) *Vgl.* **Dindsenchas** 5 (*Rev. Celt.* XV, *S.* 294).
[9]) is i *S*. [10]) tasad *SE*.
[11]) comairle crandchair *SE*. [12]) cia dia roised dib *S*.
[13]) for in *SE*. [14]) nosfost *SE*. [15]) for ri *SE*.
[16]) isin *SE*. [17]) diclith*er* *S*. [18]) foc*é*toir *SE*.
[19]) mór *add. SE*. [20]) *om. S*. [21]) foderergatar *SE*.
[22]) rofostatar *SE*. [23]) *co* tisad *E*. [24]) chucu *SE*.
[25]) do *add. SE*.

aidci[1]) cech æi dib. Dognith[2]) samlaid. Ni boi cumang[3]) la
muintir coleic dianglossacht la cumachtae na mban. Isbert beun
uaidib ba hi n-am compertæ dii 7 nusberud mac 7 ardotaidlid
oc tinntod indoir[4]) cuctai-som for cend in mic. Doluid seom
ierum co a muintir 7 loutar seom i fechtus. Batar co cend secht
mbliadan laa caraid et doluotar afrithisse conair n-ali 7 nintaid-
lidis[5]) in maigin cétno, co ngabsad a maigin[6]) ind-Inbeur nAilbine.
Iss[7]) and dusfairthetar na mna. Rocolatar ind fir ind amar[8])
ina nói umaidi. In tan batar som[9]) oc télach a coblaig, iss ann
dolotar-som na mna a tir 7 docuirset[10]) in mac n-uaduib assa
noi issan port[11]) a mbatar ol suide. Ba clochach acus ba cairr-
cech in port. Adrumidir ierum in mac cloich dib conidappath[12])
di suidiu. Dotruinfitsetar[13]) na mna cotgartatar uli: Ollbine!
ollbine!

47. 'A Tressc in Máirimtill isrubart, iss e Tailne in sin.
Is and dogeni Lug Scimmaig an fleid moir do Luog mauc Ethlend
do dignad[14]) ndou ier cath Moicchi Tuiriud. Ar ba si-sen a
banaiss rigi. Ar rorigsat Tuatai Dea iar marbad Nuadat inti
Lug. Ait in rocuiriud a treusc dorigne cnoc[15]) nde. Ba he a
ainm Tressc[16]) in Marimtill .i. Taillne andiu.

48. 'Do ingentaib niad Tethruch isrubart .i. Forcoll
Monach nia side Tetrach rig Fomore .i. mac a fedar,[17]) ar iss
inond nia 7 mac fethar[17]) 7 dono atberur nia trénfeuur.

49. 'In slonnad isrubart riut, atat da uisque i Crich Roiss.
Concupor ainm indalanai, Dofolt (.i. moel) ainm aroili. Teid 'diu
Concopor a nDofolt. Fandiched (.i. cotmesscæ)[18]) fris, conid oen-
sruth ieud. Am nia-sæ didiu ind fir sen', al sé, '.i. am mac
seuthor Concopuir Dectiri. Nó am nia, im trénfeur Conchobuir.

50. 'Hi Ross Bodbo .i. na Morrighno, ar iss ed a ross-
side Crich Roiss 7 iss i[19]) an bodb catha hi 7 is fria idbeurur
bee Neid .i. bandee in catæ, uair is inann be[20]) Neid 7 dia[21])
cathæ.

---

[1]) adaigh SE.	[2]) dogni SE.	[3]) cumaing SE.
[4]) Lies anair.	[5]) ni taidlitis SE.	[6]) a maigin om. SE.
[7]) conid E.	[8]) a n-amhor SE.	[9]) son SE.
[10]) docuirsetar SE.	[11]) i tír SE.	[12]) co n-apaid SE.
[13]) dothruinfethsitar SE.		[14]) Lies didnad.
[15]) mór add. SE.	[16]) cnocc SE.	[17]) sethar SE.
[18]) cotmesta S. comesta E.		[19]) dano add. SE.
[20]) Mit SE auszulassen.		[21]) in add. SE.

51. 'And ainm isrub*art* daum, am nuatai tedmo taith*ig*
conæ. As fir sen, uair angbaide*cht* feoch*r*ai iss *ed* teidm tai-
tidid[1]) conæ. Am nuada-ssao .i. am c*u*mnid t*r*én an tedma sin
.i. am feochair 7 im angbaid i cataib 7 i congalaib.[2])

52. 'An tan isrub*art*: cæin an mag sai, mag alcuing,
ni he Mag mBre*g* romol*us*-sæ ann sen, *acht* iss i devlb na hingene. Ar cuiṅg a da cich dar der*c*[3]) a lened *con*facusæ 7 is fr·iss
conerb*art* mag alcuing, fria bruinde na hingene.

53. 'An tan itisrub*art*: ni rali neuch an maug sæ nad
ruband comainm n-arcaid .i. arcadd a mbel*r*a na fil*ed* c*ét*,
iss *ed* et*er*c*er*tar 7 iss *ed* fil issuide: nach ruássæ an in*gin* do
tap*air*t ar[5]) aitheth [fo. 32a] conrubar ceut feur for cach n-ath
o Albine co Boann im Scennmenn Manuch, fiur ath*ar* disse,
nusdelbabud in cech ric*ht* and sen do mild*iud* mo carboid-se 7
do taidb*r*iud mo bais.

54. 'In genid grainde isrub*art* .i. ni ticfad[7]) si leum-sæ
conid rolaaind-se ich n-errid dím t*ar* na tri lissæ die saighid-
s*i*de, ar nompiad tri brait*h*ri disse oc a imc*o*med .i. Sciuhar 7
Iubar 7 Caut 7 nonbur cechæ dib et conecmoing-se bem[9]) for
cech nonb*ur* dia n-eplie[10]) an t-ochtar 7 ni aidleúpæ[11]) n*a*ch
mbem[12]) oen a braith*ir*-si eut*ar*ro 7 cototuccusæ[13]) ass isse 7 a
comaltæ cona comt*r*om leu di or 7 airc*et* dunaid Forgaill.

55. 'An Benn Suain isrub*art* m*ai*c Roiscmilc, iss inond
on sen .i. conrubar-sæ cin cotl*ud* o šam*ui*n, edhón sam-fuin .i.
fuin an tsamr*ai*d ann. Ar is dé roinn nobid for an[14]) mpl*ia*dain
and[15]) .i. in samraid[16]) o beltine co samfuin 7 in gem*r*ed o
samf*ui*n co beltine. *Nó* samsun[17]) .i. sam-svan .i. is ann sin
f*er*aid sam svana .i. sam són. Co hóimolcc .i. taiti and err*a*ig
.i. imme-folc[18]) .i. folc ind erraig 7 folc in gemrid.

Nó aimelc .i. u-melc. Oi issan éxi ainm ina cæirech, iss de
isp*er* oi-ba, ut d*icitur* coinba,[19]) echba, duineba, amol iss ainm
do bas ba.[20]) Oimolc 'diu is hi aims*er* inn sen a ticc as cæiriuch

---

[1]) taithige*s* *SE*.   [2]) a n-irgalaib *SE*.   [3]) deir*c* *SE*.
[4]) ina *S*.   [5]) for *E*.   [6]) siur *SE*.
[7]) ticfed *S*.   [8]) Catt *SE*.
[9]) 7 decmaingindsi beim *SE*.   [10]) ebela *SE*.
[11]) aidleba *S*.   [12]) dib *add. SE*.
[13]) *condattucusa S*. cotucasa *E*.   [14]) forsin *S*.
[15]) anall *SE*.   [16]) *Lies* samrad.   [17]) samfuin *SE*.
[18]) ime a łolc *SE*.   [19]) comba *S*.   [20]) bath *S*.

7 i mbleugaur coirich, unde oissc .i. oi-sesc .i. coeru seisc. Co
beldine .i. bil-tine .i. tene soinmech .i. da tene[1]) dognidiss la
hæss rechtai no[2]) druid co tincetlaib moraib 7 dolecdis na cethra
etarræ ar tedmonnaib cecha bliadna. Nó co beldine 'diu, [.i. bel
dono][3]) ainm de idail. Is ann doaselbti dine gacha ceathra for
seilb[4]) Beil. Beldine iarum bel-dine, dine cecha cethrai. Co
prón trogein .i. lugnusad .i. taide fogamuir .i. is and dobroine
trogain[5]) .i. talom fo toirtip. Trogan didiu ainm do talvm.'[6])

56. Luid 'diu[7]) Cuculaind reme ina ermaim[8]) 7 fess and-
Eumain Machæ an aidce sin. Atflatatar didiu[9]) a n-ingenu
dinaib prugadaib ind oclæch donfánicc[10]) ina carbut sainemail 7
an imacallaim dorigensid[11]) etorrai 7 Emir 7 natfetatar son cid
forcansad etorro 7 a impod budene tar Mag mBreg vaidib fotvaid.
Atfladat dno na brugaid do Forcald Monach indi sen 7 conide-
pert[12]) in ingen fris. 'As fior sin', al Forcall. 'In riasstardi o
Eamain Machi tanic ann di acoldaim Emiri 7 ruscarustar[13]) and
ingen esseom 7 iss aire sin donacolt[14]) cach alali dib. Ni ba
cobair doip-sim on ceni',[15]) al sé. 'Dororbius-[s]a (.i. tairmiusc)[16])
co na manairceba doib indii is acobar[17]) levo.'

57. Is de sen doluid Forcoll Monach docum nEumno[18])
Machi isna Gaillecuscaib, amail batis iatd[19]) techtæ rig Gall
tissed[20]) di acaldoim Concvboir co n-imcomarc do di orduisib
Finngald 7 cechai maithiusai arceuna. Triar bá ssed a lin.
Feurthar[21]) failti moir fris ierum. O rola iarum a muindterus
dia in tress læi, molaigter[22]) Cichulaind 7 Conald 7 errid Ulad
arcena fladai. Aspert com[23]) ba fir 7 ba hamro conclissed na
herrid. Acht ceno nama, dia rissed Cuculaind Domnall Milde-
mon[24]) ar Alpi, robad amraide a cliss 7 die rissed Scathaig de
morfoclaim anmilti,[25]) roderscaidfed[26]) curæ[27]) Eurpæ uli. Acht

---

[1]) tenid S.   [2]) la — no om. S.   [3]) sic S.
[4]) fo selb S.   [5]) Lies trogan (RS).   [6]) sic R. talmain S.
[7]) om. S.   [8]) erim S.   [9]) dono S.
[10]) dodanaicc R. dotfainic S.   [11]) dorigensat S.
[12]) cechidepirt R.   [13]) rochar R. rocharustar S.
[14]) cotnacalt R. dotnacallat S.   [15]) om. S.
[16]) doroirbisa .i. tairmisefedsa S.   [17]) ocobair S.
[19]) docum na hEmna S.   [19]) amail ba thisad S.
[20]) om. S.   [21]) ferthai R.   [22]) molta R. molaitir S.
[23]) dano add. R. S.   [24]) mildemal S.   [25]) do foglaim inmillti S.
[26]) Lies roderscaigfed (S).   [27]) curu S.

cenæ ba do focerd[1]) som anni sen for Coinculaind, fodeig arna contissed ina friteng doridesse, ar ba doich leiss die mbeth Cuculaind ina carutrad, commad tremit nogabad bas ar anserc[2]) 7 lunde ind erred ucud 7 ane[3]) boi do-ssom on.

58. Foemaiss Cuculaind techt frissin 7 fonaisciss Forgall fair araige forna techtais is[in] aimsir sen. Cotsela iarum Forgall ho araill for Coinculaind inni rob ocabur laiss. Luid[4]) ierum Forcold dia tig 7 atregad in la[i]th gali arabaruch 7 debertad die n-óidh techt frisna gnimo rogellsad. Luidset[5]) comboi[6]) Cuchulaind iarum 7 Logaire Buadach 7 Concupor 7 airmid foirind Conoll Cernach do techt aræn ru.

59. Is ed luid[7]) Cúchulaind 'diu[8]) dar Bregu de[9]) adald na hingeni. Atglatustar som iarum Emiur ria[10]) techt ina noi. Roraid ind ingen fris ba sse Forcoll dorat an ailgius fair-som and-Emain do techt do foglaim in milti, ar daig na comristais Emiur 7 esseom. Et aspert[11]) ara mbiad 'na foicill ar nobiad oc admillid Conchulaind cech conair conricfed. Tincellaid cach dib da céile comed a ngenaiss,[12]) acht mana fagbaud nechtar dip bas foi, co comristis dorisse. Timnaiss cauch dib celiubrad di alaili 7 imdisoat go Alpi.

60. Ho raucatar[13]) ierum Domnall, forcetai leis aill for liic dercain 7 fosetiud cetharbolc foithi. Noclisstis fuirri conabtar duobai na glassæ a fonn.[14]) Aill for slig frisdringtis,[15]) conclisstis for a rind[16]) na feurad for a n-indib.[17]) Carais iarum Cuculaind[18]) ingen Domnailll. Dorndoll[19]) a ainm, old-dorna. Ba forgranno a delp. Batar mora a gluine, a salu rempe, a traicthi ina diaig. Svili duibliathai mora ina cinn. Duibighthir[20]) [fo. 32 b] cuach ceru[21]) a gnuis. Tul fortreun fuirrie. Folt forgarb forruad ina

---

[1]) fachairt R. fochart S.
[2]) anserge S.
[3]) ane is ed S. [4]) atluid S.
[5]) luid R.
[6]) Lies cammæ (R). [7]) luide R.
[8]) om. R. iarum S.
[9]) ar R. S. [10]) oc R.
[11]) si add. S.
[12]) comeit a ngenais S.
[13]) roancatar RS.
[14]) fonna S. [15]) frisndringtis R. frisindringtis S.
[16]) .i. fonaidm niad for rindib sleg add. S.
[17]) ferad for a fonnib R. (fonnad S). [18]) Lies Coinculaind (R).
[19]) Dornolla S. [20]) Lies duibithir.
[21]) cera, gen. von cir 'Pechkohle'. Vgl. batir dubidir cir, LL. 252b. Zimmers Deutungen von cir-dub 'pechkohlenschwarz' als aus ciar-dub 'schwarz-braun' entstellt oder gar dem kymr. purddu nachgebildet sind also beide verfehlt.

gibn*ib* foa cend. Opp*ais* Cucul*aind* a comleub*aid.* Tingevllaid
si¹) a degdigail sin fair-seom. Asp*ert* fria Coincul*aind*²) nad bai
foiside (.i. forv*s*) forceut*ail* Concul*aind* co rissed Scathaig³) fri
Alpi allaanoir. Notlot*ar* ⁴) 'diu a cetar⁵) .i. C*úchulaind* 7 Concup*or*
ri Emno⁶) 7 Conold Cernach 7 Laog*aire* Buad*ach* tar Albo. Is
and doadbas doib Emoin Machu ar a suilib. Ni rofetad 'div
Concub*or* 7 Conall 7 Laeg*airi* seocha sein. I*ngen* Domn*aill*⁷)
du*s*fuc an taidbse,⁸) fodíaic a scartai Concul*aind* fria muinntir
daig⁹) a admilti.

61. Iss *ed* airmid araili sleuchta comad e Forcoll tucc an
taidbse doib ar daig a n-impuid co nar'comallad Cucvl*aind* indi
rogeuld fris a nEmain fodeig a impaid, comad melacht*ach* de 7
dno, da thecm*ad* dou teucht sair do foclaim anmilti (.i. an gaiscid
gnáth*aig* 7 ingnataich, co mbad moide fogebad bas bith a oenur.

62. Luid Cucul*aind* uaidib iar*um* dia daim (.i. dia deoin) i
conair n-indeurb,¹⁰) ar bat*ar* herdruch (.i. maith) a cumachtæ ni
hingine 7 fofeur ircoduch¹¹) (.i. olc) do-*s*som, conscarad fria a
muint*ir.* O tacoid¹²) ier*um* Cucul*aind* tar Alpie, ba pr*ó*nach 7
ba scithlond¹³) de dith a coiceli friss 7 ni fit*ir* cid notragad do
iarraid¹⁴) Scaitci. Ar rogell som dia coicelib na tinntaigfed¹⁵)
afrithesse co hEmain noco rosseud¹⁶) Scatoich no co fogbaud
bass. Anais iarum dissuide,¹⁷) ó roairigesst*ar* a imarcor 7 a
aineol*us.*

63. A mbai ann iar*um* co n-acai biastæ vathmair máir ina
docum am*ail* levmon. Poi occa feitheum 7 ni rogenair¹⁸) nach
ercoid¹⁹) ndou. Cech conair iar*um* notegiudh ticciud in beisd
for a cinn 7 doberiud a sliss friss beos. Focerd²⁰) iarum bedg
dee co mboi for a muin. Ni boi sseom 'diu i comus fuirfi²¹)
acht²²) a teucht alledh²³) pud meulluch lei fen. Lotarset²⁴)
cetri lau fon cruth sin condotarrlat*ar* fri²⁵) crich a mbat*ar*
aitrebt*haig*i 7 i missimbert²⁶) na maucruide (.i. ic imáin locain)

¹) did*iu add. S.*   ²) asbert Domnall *S.*   ³) bai *add. S.*
⁴) nalotar *R.*   ⁵) cethror *S.*   ⁶) Ul*ad S.*
⁷) i*ngen* Domnaill *S.*   ⁸) taidbein *S.*   ⁹) ardaig *S.*
¹⁰) ni gat ni de *add. S. Vgl. R.*   ¹¹) foferad codach *S.*
¹²) dochoid *RS.*   ¹⁸) lonnscith *S.*   ¹⁴) ciad ragad fo iarair *S.*
¹⁵) tindtaifed *S.*   ¹⁶) noco res*ed S.*   ¹⁷) asuidiu *S.*
¹⁸) forgenair *S.*   ¹⁹) nach n-ercoit *S.*   ²⁰) fochart *S.*
²¹) *Lies* fuirri (*S*)   ²²) at*ch H.*   ²³) leth *S.*
²⁴) lot*ur*sat *S.*   ²⁵) fo *S.*   ²⁶) *sic H. Vgl. R.*

and,[1]) condotibsetor[2]) and ar ingantus[3]) lev in mbést eurcoidiuch
ucat di bit[4]) a ngíallæ do duine. Tarblengaid iarum Cvcvlaind
dii iarum[5]) 7 scaruiss an mbest friss 7 bennochais som di.

64. Luid iarum reime 7 focard[6]) for teuch mor n-ann a
nglinn mouar. Is ann foráinic ingin coim cruthaig astig. Atid-
gladustar and ingen eei 7 feraid failti fris. 'Foceun do tiuachtæ,
a Cvculaind!' ol si.   Aspert som can boi di athne[7]) fair.[8])
Aspert si bautur comdaltai cartanachai diblinuip la hUlbecan
Sæxu,[9]) 'dia mbamur mad tu leis ic foclaimb bindiusai', ol sie.
Dobeurt and ingeun dicc 7 mir ndo 7 imdosoi vaithi iarum.

65. Immaricc[10]) dno for[11]) occlæch n-aumrui n-aili. Ferais
sidie an failti cetno friss. Imeclæchlaissent athiusc etarroib.[12])
Boi Cucvlaind oc iarraid eoulussæ[13]) do dvn Scathqi. Incoisscid
an t-oclæch eulus ndo tar an[14]) maug ndobail boi aro cinn. A
leth in moigi noseichtis[15]) doine ndei .i. nolendæis a cossai,
al-leuth n-aill cotaocbad for an feor.[16])   Tobeurt an t-oclæch
ruoth ndo leis 7 ispeurt friss araressed amol in roth sin[17]) tar
leuth an maige ar na roseichiud.[18])   Donbeurt 'div[19]) uball ndo
7 ismbeurt friss araliad di laur amal noliad ind ublau[20]) sen 7
co mbad fond innus sen rosessed tarsan[21]) mag ut. Cotela (.i.
docvaid) samlaid[22]) Cuculaind darsa mag fortainic ar a cinn iar
suidiv. Aspert an t-oclaech fris iarum[23]) bai gleunn maur ar a
cinn 7 æntet[24]) coel ar a cinn tairiss 7 se lan d'urtrachtaib (.i.
d'fuathaib) iarna foidiud do Forcoll dia admilliud-som, 7 ba si sen
a conair-siom do tig Scathqu tar a[r]d[25]) leicthi n-uatmair son dno.

66. Bennochaiss cach dia celi dip iarum, Cvculaind et an
t-oclæch .i. Eouchai Bairci esside 7 iss e rustecaisse é[26]) amail

---

[1]) inis a mbatur na maccrada ann .i. ic imain lochain SE.
[2]) conidtibsitur SE.   [3]) ingnathaigi S.   [4]) do beth S.
[5]) iarsuidiu SE.   [6]) .i. dorala add. SE.
[7]) dia aithgne R. dia aichne SE.   [8]) om. RSE.
[9]) Saxa R. Sexae SE.   [10]) imarnic R.
[11]) fri R.   [12]) eturru S.   [13]) iarair eolais de SE.
[14]) darsa R. tarsa S. tarsin E.
[15]) noseccdis R. nosectais SE.
[16]) corocongbad for rind a feóir add. SE.
[17]) araliad do lar othsin SE.
[18]) rosecceath R. secad SE.   [19]) dano S.
[20]) Lies uball (RSE). [21]) forsa SE.   [22]) samlaich H.
[23]) beos SE.   [24]) ointeit SE.   [25]) art SE.
[26]) rothecaisc hé SE.

dogenad[1]) a airmidin a tig Scathqi. Rotairngir 'diu in t-oclæch cétno ndo ina césfath de drennaib 7 di drofélaip for tanaid uo Cuailngi et roindiss dou di*diu* ina ndingniud d'olcaif 7 d'aigbenaif 7 comramhaib for feraif Erenn.

67. Lvid Cúchulaind 'diu in[2]) sed sein darsa maug ndophail 7 tarsan gleunn ngaibtiuch amal roforchan[3]) ind[4]) oclæch ndo. Is ed[5]) conair rogaub[6]) Cúchulaind issan longfort araibe[7]) daltai Scathci. Roiarfacht som cie hairm a mbæi ssi. 'Isinn oilen ucut', ol siet. 'Cisse conair dodloutar cuici?'[8]) or sesseum. 'Do droiched na n[d]alta',[9]) ol iedd, '7 ni ricc neuch esside noco forpai a gaissciud,[10]) ar iss amlaid boi sidie 7 di cenn issliu ocai 7 medon ard 7 intan nosaltrad neuch for a cenn, cotnocfad a cenn n-ali foair cotacorad inna[11]) ligiu. Iss ed airmid aroili slechtai inn so co mbatar drem di laithaib gaili fer nErenn[12]) issan dunad so ic foclaimb cleuss la Scathaig .i. Ferdiad mac Damain 7 Noisse mac Uissneuch 7 Luóchmor[13]) macu Egomaiss[14]) 7 Fiamhain mac Forai 7 dreum diairmide elie [fo. 33a] olcenai. Acht cenu ni hairimtir iersan slicht so a mbith ann and inbaid sen.

68. Dinbert Cuculaind ammull fo trí ierum de techt in drochid 7 forfeimdig.[15]) Nuscaineud ind fir. Riastarda iarum imbi 7 saltraiss for cenn in drocid 7 dimpert[16]) cor n-iach n-erred de co tarlo for a medon, co na tarnaic den[17]) droiched a ceunn n-ali de tocbail antan ranic-som é,[18]) co ndocor[19]) nde co mboi for laur issan inse. Lvid don dún co mbi in comlaid co n-eu a sligi conlod trithi.[20]) Asperthur fri Scathaig innsin. 'Fir', ol sise, 'neuc ier forbo[21]) gaiscid i n-inat aile sin.' Et cartaich[22]) a hingin hvaithi dia fiss coich in gildo. Lvid 'diu Vathach ingeun Scathqi ar a cenn. Doneci 7 ninaicaill[23]) ar a meud dit inbeurt in deulp derrscaithiuch,[24]) co faco ar an gildie

---

[1]) doenad S.　　　　[2]) forsin SE.　　　　[3]) doforcan SE.
[4]) Lies int (S).　　　[5]) i S.　　　　　　[6]) dogab S.
[7]) a mbatur S.　　　　[8]) dolotursa chuca SE.　[9]) an alta S. indaltai E.
[10]) forba gaisced Sb.　[11]) a Sb.　　　　　[12]) na Herenn S.
[13]) Lochmor S.　　　　[14]) mac Egomais S.　　[15]) Lies forémid (S).
[16]) dobeir S.　　　　　[17]) don S.　　　　　[18]) he S.
[19]) condacor S.　　　　[20]) co luid trea R. treith S.
[21]) forbaid E.　　　　　[22]) Lies cartaid S.
[23]) danecachae. ninacaldastar R.
[24]) ar met dombert tol di an delb R. ar a met dobert in delb derscaig-
thech SE.

dia hóidh a toil ndii.[1]) Tafaissig (.i. doeric) combvi[2]) co hairm[3])
a mboi am-máthair. Molustar si[4]) fria a máthair in fer con-
facoi. 'Rotolustar[5]) an feur amne', ol a máthair, 'adciu laut.'
'Is fír on', al ind ingen. 'Tofeit am toil[6]) se dno', or si, '[7]
foi[7]) less d'adaig, mássed condaighti.' 'Ni scith leum-sa emh',[8])
ol si Scathach, 'mássed dotaed a toil[9]) fen.'

69. Donimtirenn iarum and ingeun co n-usqi 7 piad 7
fecid ac[10]) airfitiud. Feraiss eussoman (.i. failti)[11]) fris fo delp
cofarig[12]) (.i. la gabáil grema de[13])). Craidsiusai Cvcvlaind co
mbobith[14]) a meur. Egiss and ingeun. Faraith (.i. rosiact) isan[15])
dvncairi vili, co n-ergetar lucht an duncaire[16]), cotnerracht dno
a treunfeur doa .i. Cochar Cruibne cathmilid Scathaige. Araselig
sem 7 Cuculaind 7 feraid glieid fri ree fottæ. Luid iarum in
trenfeur a muinidin a cless ngaisscid 7 nusfrithail Cuculaind
amail pid foglaim ndou ho æis iead 7 dofiche an trénfeur laiss
7 consevla a cenn de. Ba bronoch an uhen Scathach dissuide
co n-epert Cuculaind fria congeupad moda et mamma ind fir
dusceur co mba toissech sloig 7 co mba trenmilid dii esseom
dia eis. Et dофициced[17]) hUathach iersin co mbid ic comrad fria
Coinculaind.

70. [fo. 33 a 2] Dombeurt iarum ind ingen comairli ndov
Co[i]nculaind dia in tress læi, ma bud do denaim laochdachtæ
doluid, ara tessed docum Scathcie co[18]) maigin a mboi ic forcetul
a da mac .i. Cvar 7 Ceut, arincuorud[19]) ich n-errid nde isand
iubaur dossmor i mbæi ssi 7 si foen[20]) adn, gonidfurmed etir a
da cich cona claideb, co tartath a tri drinnroisc[21]) ndo .i. a
forcetol cin diciull 7 a hernaidm-si[22]) co n-icc[23]) tinnscrae 7
epirt friss in neich bai do-som ar cinn,[24]) ar pa faid si.

---

1) co n-accai for an ngilla a toil di *SE*.
2) *om. E. Lies* cammaib (*R*).   3) comhairm *H*.
4) molsi *R.* si *om. SE*.
5) ruttolnastair *R.* rotholtanustar *SE*.   6) *Lies* tolc (*R*).
7) foid *R.* fai *S*.   8) inni sin *add. RSEb*.   9) duit *add. SEb*.
10) oca *SEb*.   11) esomni *R.* failti esomnai *Sb*.
12) cobari *R.* cofairig *Sb.* cufairid *E*.   13) ass *SEb*.
14) conbobig *R*.   15) sin in *ES*.   16) *Lies* dúnaid (*ES*).
17) dothiced *S.* ticeth *E*.   18) *om. ES*.
19) arincorad *RS*.   20) foin *E*.   21) indrosc *RS*.
22) errsnaidm *E*.   23) *sic R.* can ic *S.* cen icc *E*.
24) fris nech aridbai *SE*.

71. Lvid ier*um* Cu*ch*ulai*n*d co hairmb i mboi Scatoig. Dobir
a di coiss for da mbordaib[1]) in clep cliss 7 nochtaiss in cloid*eb*
7 dobretha[2]) a rinn fo comair a c*r*ide 7 isp*er*t: 'Bas hva*ss*ut!'
ol se. 'To tr*í* drinnroisc[3]) dait',[4]) al si, 'fep ti*ss*e*d* liat anail.'[5])
'Gebt*h*ar!' ol Cuculai*n*d. Fonaiss*c*id uirri iar*um*. Is *ed* airmid
araili sle*ch*ta annso, co ruc Cvculai*n*d Scat*h*ai*g* laiss issan tr*ach*t
7 co comranic f*r*ie ann 7 co rocot*ail*[6]) ina farr*ud*, conid annsidie
rocachain indi seu oc a taircet*ul*[7]) ga*ch* neich[8]) aridbíad, co
n-ep*er*t: 'Focen, a scithbvaidn*ig*e' 7 rl. Acht ni hairmit*h*ir iarsan
sli*ch*t so sen olceno.[9])

72. Foidis[10]) Uat*h*a*ch* la Coinculai*n*d 7 nu*s*forcedlæ [Scá-
tha*ch*][11]) immon milti.[12]) Isan aimseir sin tra[13]) boi seom la
Scathaich 7 a muint*er*us hUat*h*qu a hingene, is and diluid aroili
f*er* aumrae boi la M*u*main .i. Lug*a*id mac Nois *mac* alamaic in
ri soinem*ail*, coicceli (.i. comalta) Concvlai*n*d. Dilli*g*h[14]) indiar
7 *dá* err*ig*[15]) deucc imbi[16]) do errig*aib*[17]) na M*u*man di tochm*ar*c
da n-ingeun dec Níaidhf*er* m*ai*c R*u*sa. Arnassa sen di feraib
vili r*e*mib-seum. An tan iar*um* rocaula som Forcall Monuch
indi sein, forr*u*mai[18]) do Teumr*ai*g 7 isp*er*t fri Lug*a*id boi oca-
seum ind-oent*u*mæ ingen is dech bai ind-Eriu et*ir* cruth 7 gen*us*
7 lamdæ. Aspert Lug*a*id ba maith laiss inn sen. Arnaiss iar*um*
Forculd a ingeun dind rig 7 da ingin deuc na dí mbriug*ad* ndecc
olceno uá[19]) Bre*g*hu den di err*ig*[20]) n*déac* bot*ar* aræn la Lug*a*id.

73. Dotaet an ri den banfeis ar oen lia Forgauld dia dunat.
An tan iar*um* de- [fo. 32 b 1] br*e*t*h*au Emiur di Luccti*th* do*ch*um
ind ionaid a mbai oc[21]) ssuidiu f*or* a laim, digabaid si a *dá*
ngruad. 'F*or* f*l*or h'oinich 7 h'anmo daum!' ol si 7 adamair[22])
ba Cuculai*n*d carust*ar* 7 f*or* a g*r*eiss bui 7 ba coll oinigh cibe
dob*er*ud isse. Ni forlamair iar*um* indti Lugaid feis la hEmir ar
omon Conculai*n*d 7 imdosæi afr*i*tesse dia tigh.

---

[1]) for da bort *E.*   [2]) dob*er*ra *E.* dob*er*ar *S.*
[3]) rindroisc *S.*   [4]) huaim-si *add. SE.*
[5]) .i. do tr*í* rogain ruisc feb conaitecht lat anail *SEb.*
[6]) curcatail *E.*   [7]) dó *add. SE.*   [8]) ni *SE.*
[9]) chena *SE.*   [10]) faiis *SE.*   [11]) *sic SE.*
[12]) .i. imonn gaisc*ed* *add. SEb.*   [13]) sin tra *om. SE.*
[14]) doluid *RS.*   [15]) errid *Sb.* airrig *R.*
[16]) leiss *RS.*   [17]) airrigaib *R.* airdrigaib *S.*
[18]) far*u*mai *R.* forr*u*amaid *S.*   [19]) la *Sb.*
[20]) don da airrig *Sb.*   [21]) do *R.* a *S.*
[22]) 7 dosb*e*ir for fir a enigh 7 a anma 7 adamair &c. *S. Cf. R.*

74. Bai cauth *for* Scath*aig* dno issan aims*ir* sene *f*ria tuatai ali 7 is *f*o*r*ra *ss*i*d*e ba banflaith Aifl. Rotinoilset iar*um*[1]) ce*ch*tarda líno do tab*air*t in cauth*æ*, co re*ch*t (.i. docengl*ad*) lia Scath*aig* [Cúchulaind][2]) 7 imdisai i*f*ritesse 7 debreuth deug suain ndo riam ar na tess*ed* isan cath, ar na riss*ed* ní do ann. Ar choimainmche[4]) dognith se[5]) sein. Dofochr*ass*tar[6]) 'diu ellam inti Cv*ch*ul*ai*nd assa cotlad iar n-var foch*é*toir; ar a mba mithesse ceteourai n-var *f*ichet do neuc ali din digh svain i cotlad, ba hoenúar ndo-ssom innsin.

75. Lvid iar*um* la da mac Scathqu din cath ar cinn tr*í* m*ac* Ilsvanaigh .i. Cuar 7 Cet 7 Cr*u*ifne iat side tr*í* milid Aifl. Arossanaic sim a tr*í*ar a oenur 7 deceurtar[7]) laiss. Bai dal in catho 'arnauharuch 7 dotoegat[8]) in tslvaig ce*ch*tardai co mbat*ar* in da n-idhn*æ* drech ria dreich. Lotar 'div tr*í* mic Esse Enchinne 7[9]) Ciri 7 Biri 7 Bailcne, tr*í* mil*id* *ai*li di Aiffe 7 forfvacarsad[10]) comlonn *for* dá m*ac* Scatqui. Dolotar side for an ted cliss. Foceurd Scath*ach* essnaid dissvidi, ar ni *f*it*ir* cid nopiad de. Aill on bad[11]) bith [cen][12]) in tress feur la da mauc Scathce frisan triar amne 7 do*no* ba homon[13]) le Aiffe in bainfendig, fodeug is s*id*e ba hannsom bvi issan doman. Lvid 'div Cuchul*ai*nd fria a da mac-si 7 n*u*sleublaing *for* an tet 7 immacomarnic[14]) ndo-ssom friu i tr*í*ur 7 beuhsat*ar* lais.

76. Focraiss Aiffe comlo*nn*[15]) *for* Scath*aig*. Lott[16]) Cvcvl*ai*nd ar cinn Aeiffl 7 iermofoa*ch*t qid ba moam s*er*c[17]) bui aicti riam. Aspert Scath*ach*: 'Iss *ed* ba moom s*er*c lei,[18]) 'ol si, 'a dá heuch 7 i carp*at*.'[19]) Dilotar di*diu* for in tet cliss Cvchul*ai*nd 7 Aiffi 7 fersaid c*u*mleng[20]) fair. Docombai (.i. briss*id*)[21]) iarum Aiffi a hairm[22]) for Coincvl*ai*nd, co *n*a pa sia dornd a clai*d*e*b*. Is ann asmpert [fo. 33 b 2] Cuculaind: 'Aill amai!' ol s*é*, 'derochair arau

---

[1]) dano ·S. [2]) sic S.
[3]) ar na riass*ed* ni ann S. Cf. R.
[4]) choimainchi R. coi*n*mainchi S. [5]) Lies si (S).
[6]) dufochtrastar R. [7]) docer*t*har S. [8]) rotheccait F.
[9]) Lies .i. (RSF). [10]) forfuarsat S. [11]) ba RS*b*.
[12]) sic RS. [13]) homain S. [14]) imcomarnic S.
[15]) comrac S. [16]) luid S. [17]) seirc S.
[18]) is moo seirc S.
[19]) a da hech 7 a carp*at* 7 a ara carp*ait* S. ara a carp*ait* F.
[20]) comlann SF. [21]) .i. dobris S.
[22]) arm RS.

17*

Aiffi 7 a da heuch carp*ait*[1]) fon gleunn conidnapat*ar*[2]) ulie.' De-
cid Aiffi lassotain. Foss*dicet*[3]) Cucul*aind* la sotain 7 gabth*us*
foa dib cichib 7 domp*ert*[4]) tarsnai amail assclaing,[5]) conatulaid
gona slvagu bodein C*ú*culaind leis hi,[6]) gonrat*ustar*[7]) a beim fri
talm*ain* dii 7 dobeurt claideb urnocht vasti. Asbert Aifl: 'Anmoin in anm*ain*, a Cuc*h*ulaind!' al si. 'Mo tr*í* drinnrvisc[8]) damsa!' ol se. 'Rotbiad amoil[9]) notistais lat anail', or si. 'It e
tri drinnroisc',[8]) ol *sé*, 'giallnæi do Scat*h*aig cen nach frithorgain
fria iar*um*, mvinter*us* frium d'ádaig ar belaibh di dunaicch[10]) fen
7 co rucai m*ac* dam.' 'Atmaur-sa aml*aid*',[11]) ol si. 'Digent*ar*
airiut[12]) foan inn*us* sin.' Lvid di*diu* Cuc*h*ulaind la hAeifi 7
fæidiss[13]) lee in aidqi sin. Asb*ert*[14]) iar*um* inti Aiffe ba torruch
7 mac n*us*berad.[15]) 'Cvirfed-sai 'div dia se*cht* mbl*iadan* co
H*é*rinn he', ol si, '7 facaib-se ainm do.' Facbaiss[16]) Cvchul*aind*
dornnaisc n-oir ndo 7 ispert frie gontissad dia cving*id*-seum co
H*é*rinn in tan bvd lan in dornnaisc dia meor 7 isp*ert* co mbad
é a ainm dobr*et*ha ndov *C*onlui 7 aspert frie nachaslonnad[17])
d'oin*fir* 7 nac*h*ambeurad oinf*er* dia slig*id* 7 na rodob*ad*[18]) com-
l*onn* ainfir.

77. Ataninntai Cvcvl*aind* coa muindt*ir* n-iar*um* fessne 7
iss*ed* tanic, for an t*ét* c*é*tnoi. Co farnoic sentvinn tuathcæich
for a cinn[19]) *for* an teid. Atbert som[20]) fr*is*-som ara f*or*chaine[21])
ar na beth *for* a cinn iersan teid. Asp*ert* som nad mbvie occo
conar diroisevd[22]) ac*ht* fon[23]) ald mor[24]) roboi foi. Aidchisi fr*is*
an conair do legivd[25]) ndii. Dolec seum din tet ac*ht* gi*u*il a

---

[1]) a da ech 7 a carpat *SF*.
[2]) conidaptha *R*. conidapadar *S*. conabatar *F*.
[3]) .i. rosoich *add. SF*.
[4]) do*s*mbert *R*. dobeir *SF*.
[5]) asclaind *SF*. aires *R*.
[6]) contulid coa sl*ú*agu fadeisin *R*.
[7]) aconrodastair *R*. c*on*radu*s*tar *S*.
[8]) indrosc *R*. rindroisc *SF*.
[9]) feib *SF*.
[10]) *Lies* do d*ú*naid (*RSF*).
[11]) samlaid uile *SF*.
[12]) samlaid *SF*.　　　[13]) faiis *SF*.
[14]) si *add. RSF*.
[15]) 7 is mac doberad *SF*.
[16]) facbaid *SF*.
[17]) nachasloinned *S*.　　[18]) roopad *SF*.
[19]) *for* a cinn *for* a cind *H*.
[20]) si *SF*.
[21]) ar ferchaire *R*. ar fr*i*chaine *SF*.
[22]) nach boi ocai leth dochoised *SF. Vgl. R.*
[23]) isind *SF*.　　　[24]) *Lies* mora (mara *SF*).
[25]) lecen *SF*.

ladair[1]) aire namaa. A ndolvid si vassæ fornessæ a ordain di
cor den tetd dia chor foan ald. Airiges som dno indni sen 7
focerd ich n-errid nde svass doridesse 7 benaiss[2]) a cend din
caillig. Ba si sen mathair na tri caurad ndegennach doceurthur
lessum .i. Ess[3]) Enchinne, 7 fodeicc a admillte-sevm tanaic ar a
cind. Doloutar iarum in tslvaig la Scathaig dia crichaibh feisne
7 dibrethai gellnai o Aiffl le 7 anais [fo. 34 a 1] Cuculaind
denas[4]) taithslainti i fuss.

78. O russcaich iarum de Coinculaind lanfoglaim in milti do
denum la Scathaig etir uballclius 7 torandcless 7 foebarcless 7
foencless 7 cles cletinech 7 tetcless 7 foerclius[5]) 7 corpcless 7
cless caid 7 ich n-errid 7 corndeliud[6]) 7 gai bulgai 7 bai braisse
7 rothcless 7 otharcless 7 cless for analai 7 brud ngeunai (no
gemi)[7]) 7 sian curad 7 bem fo commus 7 taithbeim 7 fodbeim 7
dreim fri fogaist co ndirged creiti for a rinn 7 carbad serrdhai
7 fonaidm niadh for rinnib sleg, tainic timgairi do tiachtain dia
toig[8]) fesin iarum 7 timnaiss celiubrad 7 aspert iarvm Scathach
fris iarsen inni arudbai dia forcenn 7 rocachain ndo tria himus
forhossnai, conad ann ispert na priathru sai ndou.

79. 'Foceun, a sciath bvaidnige[9]) bvadaigh
         badhaig[10]) uarcra[i]daig[11]) urbataich,[12])
         taissceá corraib fortacht fort!
      Ni ba furtacht cin reicne,
      Ni ba reicne cin decne.
      Imbe err[13]) ængaili,
         arutossa ollgabad,
         vathad fri heid n-imleubair.
      Óicc Crvachnai concirriusai,[14])
         cotad cura[i]d cellfitheur,[15])
         fortat braigid beufsatar,[16])
         bied do colg culbemnioch[17])

---

[1]) ladar *SF*.   [2]) benaid *SF*.   [3]) Eisi *S*.
[4]) denais *F*.   [5]) *om. SF*.
[6]) 7 léim tar nem (néim *U*) 7 filliud erred náir *add. USF*.
[7]) ngeme *U*.   [8]) tíchtain día crích *U*. tiacht dia tír *SF*.
[9]) scíthbuágnigi *US*.   [10]) *Lies* bágaig (*U*).
[11]) úarcraidi *U*. uarcraidig *S*.   [12]) *Lies* urbágaig (*U*).
[13]) imbé eirr *U*. eir *R*.   [14]) rascéra-su *U*.
[15]) cotut curaid cellfetar *U*. chaurith ceillfetar *R*.
[16]) bibsatar *RUE*. bebsatar *S*.   [17]) cúlbémenn *RUE*.

cruach fri sruth Setantai, [1])
sennaid fria rod [2]) rvadtressai
rinnib *ru*sclæifíd cnaimredaig [3])
clarad im buaib benncuirde [4])
tithiss fidach [5]) firamn*us* [6])
fethail feulai fedclessaib, [7])
feurba do Breug brathfíter, [5])
braigdiu do tuaith [9]) tissethar [10])
tren [11]) cithach caictigiss
cichiss do buaib [12]) -mbealta.
Bat hoin [13]) ar sloig sirechtach [14])
sirdochar [15]) sirdemin sirdupai, [16])
asealfai [17]) do fuil flanntedhmann
fernaip ilip ildlochtaib
armbaib sceo mnaib de*r*gdeurcaib
crodergæ airmb airmeud [18]) mellgleou
fiaich fothai firfítheur [19])
arathar croich crosfaigt*ir* [20])
recur serech sarlathaur [21])
gætar luinne losscaide [22])
lin dofedat [23]) ildamaib
ilar fuili firfaidt*ir* [18])
ar Coincvl*aind* [24]) cencolinn
cesfe alad [25]) n-encraidhe
ana dolath tetharbæ [26])
digern brodercc [27]) brufidhir [28])
prón ar cach dot brathbreislig

---

[1]) Setinti *U.* Sétantæ *E.*
[3]) risclóifet cnámreda *U.*
[5]) fidoch *U.* fithóg *E.*
[7]) ferchlessaib *E.*
[9]) *Lies* thúath *(U).*   [10]) *Lies* tithsitir *UE.*
[12]) *Lies* búar *(UE).*   [13]) ba hóin *UE.*
[15]) sírdochair *U.*   [16]) sírguba *U.*
[18]) cródergía arm armeth *U.*
[20]) arath croich crosfaiti*r* *U.*
[22]) cúan dia eilis losccannaib *E.*
[24]) fort Choinchaulainn *E.*
[26]) al de dalaib dedarbe *E.*
[27]) dideirn (.i. dot gráin) bródeirg *U.* dedirn brodirc *E.*
[28]) brisfith*ir* *U.*

[2]) sennait rout *U.*
[4]) bendcr*u*di *U.*
[6]) fæburamnas *UE.*
[8]) *Lies* bratfitir (bratfat*ar* *U*).
[11]) trean *UE.*
[14]) sírrechtach *U.*
[17]) sifis .i. selfa *U.*
[19]) *Lies* firfitir (*U*).
[21]) sárlatir *U.*
[23]) difedat *U.*
[25]) césfe álag *UE.*

diathaib maigib Murtemhe[1])
dia mbia cluiche tregdaighti[2])
bruthaig fria tuinn trechtaigi[3])
risa mbeliun[4]) mbandernach
belaig uathaig ochtclessaig
be- [fo. 34 a 2] lenn dichet clesamhnoch[5])
cichid biit[6]) banchuri
baigt[h]i Medb sceo Ailella
aruttosa otharlighie
ucht fri hechtgai irgaige.
Adciu firfe[7]) Finnbeunnach[8])
fri Donn Cuail[n]gie ardburuch,
cuin doregai, cuin doraidhfie[9])
ross do gaili gnat[h]geiri.
Benfaid[10]) beimenn fiarleabra[11])
mic Roich rvaidrennaich ardurgnæ
naisceta[12]) n-ollach n-oindelloch[13])
lochta do tam doscura cetha
erich do loch luirechdai
cuchtach ecé ilcrothoch[14]) (nó comraic)[15])
scelaib thanaigh[16]) trubud
co tir nUlad ogerigh
de mnaib Ulad centomaip[17])
do sciath cnedach comramuch,
di gai truagach tairbertach trentuirig,
do colg ded dathfaigthir[18])
a donnfolaif.[19])
Rosia ainm[20]) Albanchu
ciach di gair gemadaig.
Aiffe Uathach iachtafid,[21])
aloinn sethnoch svanaichfe[22])

---

[1]) diataib maigi Murthemni U.
[2]) tréchtidi UE.   [4]) frisin mbelend UE.
[6]) cichit biet UE.   [7]) firfid U. firfeith RE.
[8]) Ai add. RE perperam.
[10]) benfait U.   [11]) iarlebra U.
[12]) nóenellach U.   [14]) écsi thilcbennaic U.
[16]) selaig tanaig U.   [17]) óentomaim U.
[19]) andondálaib U.   [20]) th'ainm U.
[22]) sóermilfa U.

[3]) tregaigi U.
[5]) clesamna U.

[9]) doriidfea U.
[13]) naiscseta U.
[15]) om. U.
[18]) dathbuthair (?) U.
[21]) iachtfaitit U.

[étrocht sóebrocht súanaigfe].[1])
Teouru bliadna ar trentrichud
bad neirt ar do lochnaimhdip.
Triuchai bliadan bagaim-seo
guss de gaili gnathgeirie,
oasin amach ni indessimb,[2])
do soeccol ni fuillim-se[3])
itir bvaduib bancuirie,
gé gairidd, ge etgene,
dit alaib mocen.'[4])   Mocen.

80. Dodeuchaig iar sen Cvcvlaind ina longa do saigid
Herenn. Iss iatt robo lucht oenlongai ndov .i. Lvgaid 7 Lvan
da mac Loich 7 Feur Boeth 7 Lairine[5]) 7 Feur Diadh 7 Drúsd
mac Seirb. Lotar iarumh do tig Ruaid ri[g] na n-indsse aidci
samnoo. Is ann bai[6]) Conall Cernach 7 Lægairi Buadach ic
tobuch an[7]) cissa. Ar bai cioss a hinnsib Gall do Uldtoib an
tan sin.

81. Atcloss do Co[i]nculaind[8]) an mbron ar a cind i ndun[9])
ind ricch. 'Qise nuall so?' for Cúchulaind. 'Ingeun Ruaid
doberur a ciss[10]) do Fomorip', ar ieat. 'Iss airiu fuil an mbron
sa issan dunadh.'[11]) 'Cait a fuil an ingen sen?' al sé. 'Fil
isan traig tiss',[12]) ol iad. Ticc Cuculaind co mboi i comair na
hingine issan tracht. Immafoacht Cuculaind scélo di. Atfet an
ingen do leri[13]) ndou. 'Canus assa[14]) tegaid in[15]) fir?' ol se.
'Onn innsiu etercein tall', ol si, '7 na bi-sse sunn' ol si, 'ar cinn
na n-eclann.' Tarustar[16]) ann iarum for a cinn-som 7 romarb
na tri fomori ar galaifh oinfir. [fo. 34 b 1] Rocrecht[17]) an fer
ndegenoch[18]) dib essim ar a doid. Rorad[19]) in ingen breid dia
hedach do-ssom imin[20]) crecht. Tet seum ierum ass can a slonnad
dind ingin.

82. Ticc an ingen den dunad[21]) 7 adfet dia hathair a[22])

---

[1]) sic U.   [2]) ni fullim-sea U.   [3]) ni indisim-sea U.
[4]) fochen U.   [5]) Lárin U.
[6]) bátar issudiu for a cind U.   [7]) a U.
[8]) atchluin Cucl. íarom U.   [9]) oc dún U.
[10]) berair hi cís U.   [11]) 'sin dún U.   [12]) thís U.
[13]) du léir U.   [14]) can assa U.   [15]) na U.
[16]) tarrasair U.   [17]) rochrechtnaig immorru U.
[18]) Lies dédenach (U).   [19]) dorat U.
[20]) ma U.   [21]) don dún U.   [22]) in U.

scel n-uli. Tic Cuculaind den dunad[1]) ierum amail cech n-óigid.
Feraid failti fris ierum Conoll 7 Lægairi. Moidid sochaide issan
dun[2]) marbad na fomóre dano, acht nirrocreid and ingen doib.
Mosronad[3]) fothraccud don[4]) rig 7 dobreta cach ar uair chuice.
Tainic Cuculaind dno cumai caich 7 rorad[5]) an ingen aithne[6]) fair.
'Dombeur an ingen dit', for Ruad, '7 icfad fein a tinnscrai.'
'Nato', ol Cuchulaind. 'Ticceud dia bliadna imm deugaid-se co
Hérinn mad ail ndi 7 fogepai messe ann.'

83. Tanic Cuchulaind co hEamain iartain 7 atfed a scelai
ann. O rocuir a scis nde, tanic reme co dunad[7]) Forcaill do
cuingid Emiri. Bliadain lan ndo oice-ssin 7 ni roacht ammus
fuirre lia himmad na forairi. Tic iarum cenn[8]) mbliadna. 'Iss
aniu, a Læig, rodailseum[9]) fri ingin Ruaid, acht nad fedamor
ind inath airithe,[10]) ar ni gaeth robamar. Tair riunn tra', ol
sé, 'la hairiur an tíri'.

84. O robatar la haireur Locha Quan iarum atciat dá n-en
forsan muir. Dombert[11]) Cuchulaind cloich issan[12]) tailm 7
nusdibraicc na heuna. Reithid an fir cucai iersin iar mbeim
andara heoin dib. O rancatar ierum,[13]) iss ed botar ann, da
mbandeilb is cóimhe boi forsan mbith. Is ed bai ann, Derbfor-
caill ingen Rvaid 7 a hinailt. 'Is olc in gnim doronais, a
Cuchulaind!' ol si. 'Iss tot indsaigid tancamar cia romcráidis.'[14])
Suidiss[15]) Cuchulaind in cloich esti cona loimb folai imbpe. 'Ni
coimraiceb-sai festai friut', ol Cuchulaind, 'arintibiss[16]) t'fuil.
Dombéur cenai dom dalta sunn .i. do Lugaid Reondercc.' 7
dignith[17]) samlaid sin.

85. Et bvi Cuchulaind bliadain doridisi ic saigid dunaid[18])
Forcaill 7 ni rooacht an ingen beus la feupus a coimhetai.
Luidie 'diu Cuchulaind aitherruch do Luglochtaib Logha do dun
Forgaill 7 indiltir in carbat serrgaie[19]) lessom in la ssin 7
dobreth seul trom foair .i. torannclius trí cét 7 nonbair 7 ass e
an tress laa rohindliodh[20]) in carpat serrgæ[19]) do[21]) Coinculaind

---

[1]) don dún U.	[2]) dano add. U.	[3]) dorónad U.
[4]) lasin U.	[5]) dorat U.	[6]) Lies aichni (U).
[7]) ratha S.	[8]) cind S.	[9]) rodailsimar S.
[10]) dairithi S.	[11]) dobeir S.	[12]) ina S.
[13]) iat S.	[14]) romcraidis S.	[15]) Lies suigis (S).
[16]) aratibus S.	[17]) dognither dono S.	[18]) raith S.
[19]) Lies serrda (S).	[20]) doindled S.	[21]) ra S.

7 iss airi asmperadh[1]) ona serruib iarnaidib [fo. 34 b 2] bidis i
n-indiull ass, no ona Serdaib tucad[2]) a bunadus ar tos.

86. Rancatar dunad Forcaill[3]) 7 focertt ich n-erred de co
mboi tarna trí lissa[4]) for lar in dúine[5]) 7 bithais trí bemenn[6])
issan liss co tochair[7]) ochtar cecha beme ndib 7 anacht fer i
medon cacha nonbuir .i. Scibar 7 Ipur 7 Cat, tri braithri[8])
Eimere. Focerd Forcoll bedc nde tar[9]) dua na rátha imach[10])
for teiched Conculaind, cor'tuit[11]) co farcoib cen anmain. Tobert
Cuchulaind Eimiur leis cona comdalta cona n-eredaib[12]) d'or 7
d'airced 7 focerd som bedc de aitherruch tarsan tredua[13]) cona
dib n-ingenaib 7 dotæd reme. Eighteur impe do cach aird.
Berid Scenmend foraib. Marbaid Cvchulaind e[14]) oc a áth,
conidh de dogarur Áth Scenmenn. Toecaid[15]) assaidi co Glonnath.
Marbais Cvchulaind cét fer ndib ann. 'Is mor in glonn dorinnis',
[ol Emer][16]) 'in cet fer n-armmach n-incomlainn do marbad.'
'Pidh Glonnáth a ainm didiu co bráth olcena',[17]) or Cuchulaind.

87. Doroich Cuchulaind co Crufóid. Ræ ban a ainm coruici
sin.[18]) Bentai sium a brathbemendai mora for na slogaib issand
inad sin, corromoigseut[19]) na srothai fola tairrsib tar[20]) cech
leuth. 'Is fod cró an telach so laut indiu, a Cuchulaind!' ol and
ingen. Gonad de sin diráiter[21]) Croofoit dii .i. fod cro. Toroich
in t-iarmoracht forro co hAth an Imfoit[22]) for Boinn. Teit
Emiur assan carbat. Tobeir Cvchulaind tofonn for in toir cor-
rosceinnsit na foit a cru na n-ech tar ath fothuaid. Dobeir
tafond aili fothuaid co scenndis na foit a cruib[23]) na n-each for
ath bódess. Gonad de sin atá[24]) Ath n-Imfoid de dona foitib
adiu 7 anall.

88. Cid fil ann tra [acht][25]) marbaiss Cvchulaind cét fer for
cech áth o Ath Scenmenn for Ollbine co Boind mBreg 7 comal-
lustar uli na gnima sin dorairngert ind[26]) ingeun 7 teid slan

---

[1]) atberthai serrda de S.	[2]) frith S.
[3]) ranic sium tratha ratha Forgaill S.	[4]) co mbai add. S.
[5]) dunaid S.	[6]) bemenda S.		[7]) torcair S.
[8]) derbraithre S.	[9]) for S.		[10]) sechtair S.
[11]) co rofuit S.	[12]) n-errib S.		[13]) tres dua S.
[14]) he S. Lies hí.	[15]) tiagait S.		[16]) sic US.
[17]) om. US.	[18]) ar tús cotici sin US.
[19]) co romaidset US.	[20]) tarsi for U. tairis for S.
[21]) dogarar US.	[22]) co hÁth nImfuait U. ac Ath nImfuait S.
[23]) crúib U.	[24]) dogarar US.		[25]) sic US.
[26]) dond U. in S.	

iar*um* conranic Emvin Machai bo deme[1]) in adhaic[2]) sin. At-
nagar Eimeur issan Cræbruaidh Concopu*ir*[3]) co maithib Ul*ad*
arcenai 7 ferait failti frie.   Boi fer dvaig dotengai[4]) do Ulltaib
asstoig .i. Bricne[5]) Nemtengai m*ac* Carb*ad*.[6])   Conad and isp*ert*
side: 'Bid doilig eim', ol *sé*, 'la Coincul*aind* anni dogent*ar* and
ano*cht* 7 an ben tucc laiss a feis la Concop*ar* ano*cht*, ar is less
coll c*ét* ingen ria nUlltaib dogr*éss*.' Nu*s*fvassnaig*ther* im [fo. 35 a 1]
Coincul*aind* annsin occa cloisste*cht* sin 7 nu*s*bertaigenn[7]) co
reoimhid[8]) in coilcid boi foi co mbat*ar* a cluma for foluamain
immon teuch imacuairt 7 teid amach lassodain.

      89. 'At*d* doiligh mor and', ol Cathf*ad*, 'a*cht* as geis don rig
cen a ndoraid[9]) Br*i*cne do denam. Dobith*us* Cu*chulaind* imm*orro*
antí foidis[10]) léa mnai', ol se. 'Goir*ther* Cùchul*aind* dund!' ol
Concvp*ar*, 'd*ús* an fedfamæis talgadh a brotha.'   Tic iar*um*
Cu*chulaind*. 'Eircc damh', ol *sé*,[11]) '7 tuc laut dam evlma[12])
failit[13]) a Slep Fvaid.   Teid iar*um* Cv*chulaind* 7 nu*s*timaircc
leis ina fvair di mucaib 7 d'aigib allt*aib* 7 d'ernvilib gacha fiada
folvaimn*ige* olcena i Sleip Fvaid 7 nu*s*beir[14]) a n-oinimain leis
co mbvi f*or* faithce na hEmno. Teidi di*diu* a f*ercc* lass*ot*ain
for cvla do Coincvl*aind*.

      90. Dognitheur imagall*aim* ic Ullt*aib* immon caingin sen.
Is *edh* iarmho[15]) comarli irri*cht* leu: Emer do feis la Concob*ar*
an ad*aigh* sen 7 Fercus 7 Cathf*ad* a n-oinlep*aid* friv do comhed
enich Concul*aind* 7 benno*cht* Vl*ad* don lanam*ain* ar a fæmadh.
Foemaid anni sin 7 dognieitheur saml*aid*. Íca*id* Conc*h*ubor
tinnscrai Emirie iarnamaruch. Dobre*thai*[16]) enicl*ann* do Coincvl*aind* 7 foidis lia a baincéile 7 nir'scarsatar[17]) ier suide co
fvarut*ar* bas diblinaip.

      91. Atnadhar[18]) cenn*acht* macr*aidi* Vl*ad* do Coincvl*aind*
iarsin. Iss iad sen[19]) robo m*acrad* ind-Em*ain* and inbaid sin,
die ndeb*ert* an fili oc taba*irt* a n-anmond oss aird:

---

[1]) fo demi *U.* bude*in* (!) *S.*		[2]) aidchi *U.*
[3]) co Concobar 7 *U.* [4]) dothengtha *U.*		[5]) Bricriu *U.*
[6]) m*ac* Arbad *U.*	[7]) no*s*ber*t*naigend *U.*	[8]) rémid *U.*
[9]) ce*n* an roraid *U.*	[10]) féefes *U.*	[11]) Conc*h*obar *U.*
[12]) almai *US.*	[13]) fil dam *U.* filet *S.*	
[14]) dosb*eir* *US.*	[15]) sic *H.* om. *S.*	[16]) dobre*th* a *S.*
[17]) ni roscarsat *US.*	[18]) *Lies* atnagar (*U*).	
[19]) so *US.*		

Macra*d* Emno, ailli[1]) slua*ig*, inb*aid* bat*ar* 'sa[2]) Craeprvaidh,
  im F*u*rpai*d*i, finn in tslat, im Cumscra*id* is im Corm*ac.*
Am Conaing, im G*la*sne nglan, im F*iachaig* iss am Findch*ad,*
  im Coincul*aind* cruadach ngle im m*ac* mbva*dach* nDecht*ire.*[3])
Im Fiac*hn*a, im Follam*ain* and, imm Cacht, im Maine, im Ill*and,*[4])
  im *sech*t Maine a[5]) Sleph in Chon, im Pres, im Nár, im Lot*hu*r.
Im *sech*t mic Fergus[a][6]) ann, im Ilarcless, im Crimtand,[7])
  im Fiamhain, am Bvidne,[8]) am Bri, i*m* [M]al claidm*ech,*[9])
                                    [im C*o*[i]*n*ri.
Lægairi Cas, Conall Clæn, is in da Ethiar ardcæm,
  Mesdiad iss Mesdeadh[10]) dil, clan*nv* amra Aimirgin.[11])
Concr*ai*d m*ac* Caiss a Slep Smoil, Concr*ai*d m*ac* Baid be*r*nad broin,
  Conchr*aid* mac an D*eirg* m*aic* Finn, Concr*aid* Svana m*ac*
                                    [Salcinn.
Aed m*ac* Finderg o Loch Brec,[12]) Aed m*ac* Fidaig, fo*r*mna ne*r*t,
  Aed m*ac* Conaill cirr*id* cath, Aed m*ac* Duinn, Aed m*ac* Dvach.
Fergus m*ac* Leidi, lith ngle, Fergus m*ac* De[i]rc m*aic* Daire,
  Fercus m*ac* Rvis lvaidid rainn, Fercus m*ac* Duib m*aic*
                                    [Crimt*hainn.*
Tri m*aic* Traigle*th*ain t*rén* bl*adh* Sidvath, C*u*rrech is Carmon,
  tri m*aic* ic Uslenn na n-ágh, Noisi, Ainnli *is* Ard*án.*
[fo. 35 a 2] Tri Flainn, tri Finn, tri Cuinn civil, anmonn do nói
                                    [m*acc*aib Scivil,
  tri Foelain, tri Colla cain, tri mic Neill, tri m*ic* Sithgail.
Lon is Iliach, ailli fir, *ocus* t*ri* Corm*aic* c*r*ithaidh,[13])
  tri m*aic* Donngaiss m*ic* Rossa,[14]) tri Dungaiss, tri Dælgusai.
Aess dana do Corm*ac* civil noi m*ic* Lir m*ic* Ete*r*scivil,
  a tri c*u*slenna,[15]) cain bann,[16]) Finn, Eoch*aid ocus* Illann.
A cornairi civil iar sin im da Aed is am Fing*in,*[17])
  a t*ri* druid denmo glam ngér Aith*ir*ne is Dreuch is Droibel.

---

[1]) inmain *S.*   [2]) 'sin *US.*   [3]) Dechtine *S.*
[4]) Crimthand *U.*   [5]) i *U.*
[6]) se maccaib Fergais *U.*   [7]) Illand *U.*
[8]) Bu*n*ni *U.*
[9]) im Mul im Chlaidbech *U.* im Mal claidmech *S.*
[10]) Mesdedad *U.*   [11]) clanna Amargin giunnaig *U.*
[12]) Find deirg ollach mbrec *U.*
[13]) comaltai Corm*aic* crichid *U.*
[14]) tri Dondgais m*aic* m*aic* Rossa *U.*   [15]) c*u*slendcha *US.*
[16])˙cǽm in band *U.*   [17]) Firgein *U.*

A tri dailim*ain* co mbloid   Finn, Iruath is Faitimhain,
 tri va[1]) Cleit*ig,* comal ngle,   Uath, Uruath iss Aisslinge.
Aed, Euch*aid* air*derc* Emhno,   *dá* mac ailliu Ilgauhla,
 mac Bricrenn dobronnad ba[2])   air*derc* ic m*a*craid Emna.

[M. c. r.[3])

[1]) ú *U.*
[2]) robrunned bla *U.* do brondud bai *S.*
[3]) conidh e Tochmarc Em*i*ri ann siu. Fiuit. *S.*

Liverpool.   KUNO MEYER.

ZUR KELTISCHEN LAUTGESCHICHTE.

---

1. Idg. *au* im Inselkeltischen.

Unter idg. *au* begreife ich auch den von den meisten Indogermanisten mit *əu* bezeichneten Diphthong. Pedersen, KZ. XXXVI, 75 ff., hat es nicht unwahrscheinlich gemacht, dass *a* und *ə* im Idg. éin Laut gewesen sind. Für unsre Frage ist es übrigens ganz gleichgültig, ob er damit das Richtige getroffen hat oder nicht; denn das postulierte *əu* ist auf dem ganzen idg. Sprachgebiete mit idg. *au* gleich behandelt worden.

Für idg. *au* führt nun Brugmann, Grdr. I², 200, zwei Belege aus dem Inselkelt. an: ir. *ōs uas* 'oben', *uasal* 'hoch, erhaben', nkymr. *uch, uchel* zu gr. *αὔξω* 'ich mehre', lit. *áukstas* 'hoch' oder zu gr. *ὑψηλός* 'hoch, erhaben', *αἶπος* 'steile Höhe' aus *auqos* (Thurneysen, KZ. XXX, 492); ir. *ō ua* 'a, ab' = lat. *au-*, ai. *ō-* neben ai. *ava* 'ab, herab'. Dagegen soll idg. *ău* vielleicht durch mir. *au ō* 'Ohr' vertreten sein.

Dazu ist zunächst zu bemerken, dass, wenn die für idg. *au* angeführten Beispiele richtig wären, ir. *au ō* sicherlich (nicht nur „vielleicht") *ău* enthielte. Denn der idg. Diphthong dieses Wortes wäre im Ir. ganz anders vertreten als idg. *eu, ou* und *au*, sodass er von ihnen unterschieden, d. h. *ău* gewesen sein müsste. Idg. *eu, ou* ist im Inselkelt. in *ou* zusammengefallen und wahrscheinlich auch schon in derselben Periode zu geschlossenem *ō (ǫ)* geworden (vgl. abrit. *Bōdicos* 'Victor', kymr. *Budic* zu ir. *buaid* 'Sieg', kymr. *budd* 'utilitas, commodum, quaestus'); im Brit. wurde *ǫ* zu *ū (u)*, im Ir. dagegen blieb *ǫ* als *ō* und wurde weiterhin zu *ua* diphthongiert (vgl. Brugmann, Grdr. I², 199).

Mit inselkelt. *ou* müsste auch idg. *au* zusammengefallen sein, wenn Brugmanns Belege dafür richtig wären; denn nach diesen wäre es gleichfalls ir. zu *ō ua*, brit. zu *u* geworden. Dagegen erscheint in ir. *au ō* 'Ohr' ein Diphthong *au*, der nie bei idg. *eu, ou* und den für *au* angeführten Beispielen auftritt, und andrerseits neben *ō* kein *ua*. Diese Thatsache lässt sich nur daraus erklären, dass in diesem Worte inselkelt. der Diphthong erhalten blieb, während aus idg. *eu, ou* und angeblich auch aus *au* ein *ọ̄* entstand, und erst später gleichfalls zu *ọ̄* wurde, nachdem jenes *ọ̄* schon zu *ua* weiterentwickelt war, oder in offenes *ō (ọ̄)* überging.

Es ist nun aber ganz unwahrscheinlich, dass die sich am fernsten stehenden Diphthonge idg. *au* und idg. *ou (eu)* im Inselkelt. zusammengefallen sein sollten, während *ǝu*, i. e. *ọu*, bewahrt blieb und dann ev. zu *au* wurde. Lautphysiologisch ist nur der Fall denkbar, dass *ǝu* zu *ou* wird, während *au* bewahrt bleibt, oder dass alle drei Diphthonge zusammenfallen (zunächst *au* mit *ǝu* und dann *ǝu* mit *ou*). Vertauschen wir nun Brugmanns Beispiele für idg. *ǝu* und *au*, so werden wir dieser lautphysiologischen Forderung gerecht, ohne gegen die Ablautslehre zu verstossen. Es verhalten sich ir. *au ō* : gr. *οὖς* = gr. *ἄκρος* 'spitz' : *ὄκρις* 'Bergspitze' und ir. *ōs uas* resp. *ō ua* : gr. *αὔξω* (oder *αἶκος* aus **auqos*) resp. lat. *au-* (wenn nicht aus *ǝu*, worüber unten) = gr. *ὄκρις* : *ἄκρος*; ir. *ō ua* entspräche lautlich genau gr. *οὐ* 'nicht' (vgl. dazu Horton-Smith AJPh. XVIII, 43 ff.). Idg. *au* ist also im Keltischen bis in einzeldialektische Zeit hinein als Diphthong erhalten geblieben, und idg. *ǝu* wäre im Inselkelt. mit idg. *eu, ou* in *ou*, weiterhin *ọ̄* zusammengefallen, wenn es ein idg. *ǝ* überhaupt giebt. Jedoch scheint mir Pedersen, KZ. XXXVI, 86 ff., vollkommen recht zu haben, wenn er die Existenz eines idg. *ǝ* neben *o* leugnet. Danach liegen in ir. *ōs uas*, nkymr. *uch* und ir. *ō ua* nur weitere Beispiele für idg. *ou* vor. Für lat. *auris* ist, wie für ir. *au ō*, idg. *au* (resp. *ǝu*) anzusetzen, ebenso für lat. *au-*; denn idg. *ou* wurde lat. *ū (ō)*.[1]) Für got. *ausō*, lit. *ausìs*, aksl. *ucho* ist idg. *ou* und *au* möglich.

---

[1]) Dadurch dürfte auch die Frage über das Verhältnis lat. *lavo* : gr. *λούω* etc. (Brugmann, Grdr. I², 155) ihre Erledigung finden. Im Lat. liegt idg. *a* (resp. *ǝ*) vor, im Griech. *o*. Lat. *ovis* enthält jedenfalls idg. *oṷ-*, da auch Brugmanns Gesetz von der Dehnung eines idg. *o* in offener Silbe im

Auf gleicher Stufe mit *ōs uas* und *ō ua* stehen folgende Worte: ir. *guaire* 'edel' gegenüber gr. *γαῦρος* 'fröhlich, stolz', *γαυριάω* 'stolz sein'; ir. *cuaille* 'Pfahl' gegenüber gr. *καυλός*, lat. *caulis* 'Stengel'; ir. *lōg luag luach* 'Lohn, Preis'[1]) gegenüber gr. *ἀπολαύω* 'geniesse', lat. *Laverna* 'Göttin des Gewinnes'; ir. *ōthad uathad* 'Einzahl, geringe Zahl, Seltenheit' gegenüber lat. *pau-cus* 'wenig' (vgl. Stokes, Urkelt. Sprachschatz S. 53). — In ir. *guala* 'Kessel, Loch' gegenüber gr. *γαυλός* 'Eimer', *γαῦλος* 'Kauffahrteischiff' (mit *au* resp. *əu*), ahd. *chiol* 'Schiff' (mit *eu* oder *ēu*) würde wegen des Ablauts ein idg. *eu, ou* und nicht *āu* angenommen werden, selbst wenn es idg. *ā* geben sollte. Derselbe Ablaut liegt vor in ir. *luad* 'Gespräch, Rede' (*eu, ou*): lat. *laus, laudis* (*au* resp. *əu*), ahd. *liod* (mit *eu* oder *ēu* und *to*-Suffix).[2])

Mit idg. *au* müssen im Inselkelt. *au* aus *āu* und das *au* der lat. Lehnwörter zusammengefallen und, wenn das Beispiel für idg. *au* richtig sein soll, gleich behandelt worden sein. Das ist auch wirklich der Fall. Auch für diese *au* erscheint, wie für idg. *au, ō* (wo daneben *ū*), aber nie *ua*, und im Britannischen entspricht ein Diphthong (akymr. *ou*, mkymr. *eu*, nkymr. *au*), nicht etwa *u* (aus inselkelt. *ọ*). Über *au* aus *āu* siehe Verf., Festschrift W. Stokes S. 26 f.; zu beachten ist namentlich ir. *bō*, mkymr. *beu* (in *beuch, beudy*) 'Kuh' aus *baus : idg. *gōus* neben ir. *bō- bua-*, brit. *bu-* aus *bou-, idg. *gou-* (in ir. *buachail*, nkymr. *bugail*, korn. bret. *bugel* 'Hirt' etc.: gr. *βουκόλος* 'Rinderhirt', ai. *gō-caras* 'Weideplatz für Rinder'). An Beispielen für lat. Lehnwörter mit *au* führe ich an: ir. *augaist* GS. = lat. *Augusti* (Monatsname); ir. *ōr*, akymr. *Our-* (in Namen), mkymr. *eur*, nkymr. *aur* = lat. *aurum*; air. *Pōl* (*Pool*) = lat. *Paulus*; air. *cōis* AS., *cūisi* GS. zu NS. *cōs* = lat. *causa* (vgl. GC.³ 33 f.). Wenn ein ir. *ua*, kymr. *aw* einem lat. *au* entspricht, wie z. B. in ir. *cuach* 'Becher', mkymr. *cawc*, nkymr. *cawg* = lat. *caucus* 'eine Art Trinkschale' (vgl. gr. *καύκη*), so müssen wir für das

---

Arischen nach der Beschränkung von Kleinhans-Pedersen, KZ. XXXVI, 87 ff., nicht dagegen spricht (vgl. auch Uhlenbeck, PBrB. XXII, 545, wogegen Bartholomae, Woch. f. klass. Phil. 1898, Sp. 1054, Anm. *; Buck, AJPh. XVII, 445 ff., wozu Brugmann, Grdr. I², S. XLIII f.).

[1]) Über ir. *folad*, kymr. *golud* siehe Zupitza, KZ. XXXV, 267 ff.
[2]) Über die Stufe *a* resp. *ə* in der *e-* : *o*-Reihe siehe Brugmann, Grdr. I², 505. Vgl. auch Pedersen, KZ. XXXVI, 100.

Inselkeltische eine dialektische lat. Nebenform mit $\bar{o}$ voraussetzen (vgl. Thurneysen, Keltoromanisches 55 und zum Lat.: Conway, IF. IV, 215 ff.; Stolz, Hist. Gramm. der lat. Sprache I, 210 f.). Denn auch sonst entspricht einem lat. $\bar{o}$ ein ir. $\bar{o}$, ua (aus $\bar{\varrho}$), mkymr. aw (aus $\bar{\varrho}$ = inselkelt. $\bar{a}$): z. B. ir. $\bar{o}r$ uar, mkymr. awr = lat. $hora$; ir. $n\bar{o}na$ $n\bar{o}n$, mkymr. $nawn$ = lat. $nona$; ir. $scuap$ = lat. $scopa$; ir. $gluass$ = lat. $glossa$ (gr. $\gamma\lambda\tilde{\omega}\sigma\sigma\alpha$).[1]

Im Irischen ist ferner mit dem aus dem Inselkelt. überkommenen au der aus inselkelt. $\breve{a}\mu$- entwickelte Diphthong[2]) zusammengefallen und in gleicher Weise, wie inselkelt. au, behandelt worden. Man vergleiche: ir. NS. aue ($haue$), $\bar{o}a$ ($h\bar{o}a$), $\bar{u}a$ aus *$a\mu\underset{.}{i}os$ 'Enkel, Nachkomme', GS. (h)$\bar{u}i$, DP. (h)$\bar{u}ib$: lat. $avia$ 'Grossmutter' zu $avus$ 'Grossvater'; ir. $l\bar{a}ine$ (i. e. $l\bar{o}ine$) 'Fröhlichkeit' aus *$la\mu en\underset{.}{i}\bar{a}$: akymr. $leguenid$, nkymr. $llawenydd$ 'Freude' aus derselben Grundform, vgl. gr. $\dot{\alpha}\pi o\lambda\alpha\acute{\upsilon}\omega$ 'geniesse'; ir. $caur$ (GS. $caurad$) 'Held' aus *$ka\mu aro$-[3]) : gall. $K\acute{\alpha}\nu\alpha\varrho o\varsigma$, $Cavarillus$, ai. $\acute{s}av\bar{\imath}ra$- neben $\acute{s}\bar{u}ra$- 'mächtig, stark, Held' u. s. w.; ir. $c\bar{u}a$ 'Winter' aus *$ka\mu at$: mkymr. $cawat$ u. s. w. 'Regenschauer'; ir. $d\bar{o}im$ 'ich brenne' aus *$da\mu\underset{.}{i}\bar{o}mi$: gr. $\delta\alpha\acute{\iota}\omega$ 'zünde an', $\delta\alpha\acute{\iota}o\mu\alpha\iota$ 'stehe in Flammen', ai. $dun\acute{o}ti$; ir. con-$\bar{o}i$ 'servat' aus *$a\mu et$: lat. $aveo$, ai. $\acute{a}vati$; ir. $lour$, $l\bar{o}r$ 'genug, hinreichend'[4]), $loure$ 'sufficientia' (GC.[2] 33): mkymr. $llawer$ 'grosse Menge, grosse

---

[1]) In das Brit. müssen die Worte gelangt sein, als $\bar{\varrho}$ schon zu $\bar{a}$ und $\bar{a}$ zu $\bar{\varrho}$ geworden war. Doch können die brit. Sprachen lat. Wörter mit $\bar{o}$ auch schon zu einer Zeit entlehnt haben, als noch $\bar{\varrho}$ bestand. Dann musste daraus in betonter Silbe $\bar{u}$ (u) werden, was Zimmer, KZ. XXXVI, 437, ohne Grund ganz allgemein als Vertretung von lat. $\bar{o}$ anzunehmen scheint.

[2]) Im Irischen (Gälischen) hat sich $\breve{a}$, $o + \mu +$ Vokal zunächst zu u-Diphthong $+ \mu +$ Vokal entwickelt (vgl. ogm. $avvi$ = ir. aui, (h)$\bar{u}i$, GS. zu aue u. s. w. aus *$a\mu\underset{.}{i}os$ 'Enkel'), weiterhin ist μ geschwunden und der Diphthong monophthongisch geworden ($\bar{a}u$ über au). Wenn Brugmann, Grdr. I[2], 326, meint, dass interson. μ im Ir. hinter jedem langen Vokal völlig geschwunden sei, so ist das im Hinblick auf $\bar{a}\mu$- ein Irrtum.

[3]) Ir. cur (GS. $curad$) kann auf *$kurat$ oder auch *$k\bar{u}rat$ (wenn u ungenaue Schreibung für $\acute{u}$ ist) zurückgehen; $caurad$ scheint nach $curad$ gebildet zu sein. Mkymr. $cawr$ (pl. $cewri$ mit i-Umlaut, wie $llewni$ 'implere' zu $llawn$ 'voll'), korn. $caur$ 'gigas' sind wohl aus dem Irischen entlehnt, da man sonst im Mittelkymr. *$cawar$ (vgl. $llawer$ 'grosse Zahl' ohne Elision des Vokals zwischen w und r) erwarten sollte.

[4]) Daneben giebt es eine Form $le\bar{u}r$ (vgl. Windischs Wörterbuch); die Grundform des Wortes ist mir unklar. Nach dem Kymrischen zu urteilen, muss hinter ir. ou, $\bar{o}$ aus au ein e verloren gegangen sein, vgl. ir. $caur$.

Zahl'; ir. *lō* 'Wasser' aus **laγos* : kymr. *glau* (Loth, Rev. Celt.
XX, 351), *gwlaw* 'Regen', korn. *glau* 'pluuia', nbret. *glao* (kymr.
-lau, korn. *-lau*, nbret. *-lao* ebenfalls aus **laγos*, vgl. akymr. *Litau*,
mkymr. *Llydaw* aus **pḷtaγi-* : gall.-lat. *Letavia*, gr. *Πλάταια*), lat.
lavo, gr. *λούω*; ir. *nōi* n- 'neun' aus idg. **naγṇ* resp. **nₐγṇ*, nicht
aus **neγṇ*, wegen mkymr. *nau naw*, nkymr. *naw*, korn. *naw*,
mbret. *nau*, nbret. *nao*[1]) : gr. *ἐννέα*, lat. *novem*, got. *niun* u. s. w.
aus **néγṇ*; ir. *tō* 'still, schweigend' aus **taγos*, älter **tausos*, und
daneben ir. *tua* (i. e. *tūa*) für **tōe* oder **tūe* (vgl. *nua*, i. e. *nūa*,
neben *naue*, *nūe* 'neu') aus **taγios*, älter **tausios*[2]), wozu GS.
tuæ, *tua* (zweisilbig, vgl. Windischs Wörterbuch) wie *nemda* zu
NS. *nemde*, *nemda* 'himmlisch' etc.: mkymr. *taw* 'schweig' aus
*taγe, älter **tause*, akymr. *taguel*, nkymr. *tawel* 'schweigend' aus
*taγelo-, älter **tauselo-*, ai. *tuṣyati*; ir. *clō* (NP. *clōi*, *clūi*) 'Nagel'
aus **klāγos* : lat. *clāvus*, *claudo* 'ich schliesse' etc.; ir. *nōi* (DS.
zu *nau nō* 'Schiff') aus **nāγai* : ai. *nāvé*, lat. *nāvī*; ir. *broon*,

---

[1]) Zu dem *a* dieser Form vgl. man arm. *tasn* 'zehn' gegenüber gr.
δέκα, lat. *decem* (Brugmann, Grdr. I², 117, § 117 Anm. 2). Nicht richtig Foy
IF. VII, Anz. 208; das dort angedeutete Gesetz von der keltischen Dehnung
eines idg. *ŏ* in offener Silbe vor dem Übergange von idg. *ō* zu *ā* halte ich
nicht mehr aufrecht. Mein Ausgangspunkt waren die inselkeltischen Perfekta
mit ir. *ā*, kymr. *au aw* in der Wurzelsilbe: mir. *ro rāᵗth*, akymr. *guaraut* 'er
lief' zu ir. *rethim* (aus **retō*: Brugmann I², 468); air. *ro gáᵗd* 'er bat' zu
-gᵘᵗdᶦu: gr. *ποθέω* etc.; air. *ro tāᶦch* 'er floh' zu *techim*, lit. *tekù* etc.; mir.
faᶦg, i. e. *fāᶦg* 'dixit': gr. *εἶπον*, *ἔπος* etc.; akymr. *gwaut*, mkymr. *dywawt*
'dixit' zu *dywedut* 'sagen' (ir. *fet-* in *aᶦsind-fedat* 'conserunt verba': Zimmer,
KZ. XXX, 194); mir. *ro scāᶦch* 'praeteriit' zu *scuchim* 'ich weiche' (mit *u*
aus *o* vor mouilliertem Konsonanten — vgl. *foscoᶦchim* 'ich entferne mich,
weiche ab' —, nicht mit Strachan, BB. XX, 5 aus **scaciō*, wonach auch mir.
scēn 'Schrecken' aus **skeqno-*, nicht **skaqno-* zu erklären ist), aksl. *skokū*
'Sprung' etc. Doch liegt hier entweder idg. langer Vokal (*ŏ*) vor (vgl.
Brugmann, IF. VI, 91), oder die Länge erklärt sich durch Analogiebildung,
wie Buck den damit jedenfalls in Beziehung stehenden langen Vokal der
3. Sg. Pf. des Arischen im AJPh. XVII, 445 ff. zu deuten sucht. — Übrigens
ist nicht das *a* von neukymr. *naw* das Entscheidende und zunächst Unklare
(Brugmann, Grdr. I², 125), sondern das *a* von mittelkymr. *nau*, *naw*. Denn
ein **neγṇ* wäre über **noγṇ* zu akymr. **nou*, mkymr. **neu*, nkymr. **nau* geworden (vgl. unten S. 271). — Ferner sei hier darauf aufmerksam gemacht,
dass in ir. *nōi* n- ein sicheres Beispiel für idg. *ṇ* vorliegt, das Zupitza,
KZ. XXXVI, 70 f., bei seiner Annahme, dass *ṇ*, *ṃ* im Ir. möglicherweise *an*,
am ergeben habe, nicht verwertet hat.

[2]) Dazu sind die Verben *contōᶦsim* und *contūaᶦsim* 'ich höre zu' gebildet worden.

i. e. *brōn* (GS. zu *brō* 'Mühlstein'), aus inselkelt. **brā̆u̯onos* : kymr. *breuan* 'Handmühle', ai. *grā́van-* 'Pressstein'; ir. *blā* 'gelb', i. e. *blō* (vgl. z. B. *bā*, i. e. *bō*, AP. 'Kühe'), aus **bhlāu̯o-* [oder **ınlāu̯o-*] : lat. *flāvus* 'gelb' [vgl. dazu Prellwitz, BB. XXV, 285].

Der Entwicklung von *ău̯-* im Irischen geht diejenige von inselkelt. *ou̯-* (= idg. *eu̯-*, *ou̯-* und ev. *ău̯-*) parallel. Vgl. z. B. ir. *naue nūe nūa* 'neu' aus **néu̯i̯os* : kymr. *newydd*, ai. *návyas* got. *niujis* u. s. w.; ir. *cōir* 'gerade, recht, angemessen' aus urkelt. **ko-u̯eros* : kymr. *cywir*, gall. *Dumno-covēros*; ir. *crou crāo crō crū* 'Blut' (mkymr. *creu*, nkymr. *crau*) aus **kréu̯as* : gr. *χρέας*; ir. *gau gāo gō* (*gōo*) *gū* 'das Falsche, die Lüge' (mkymr. *geu*, nkymr. *gau* 'falsch') aus **gou̯os* (Loth, Rev. Celt. XVIII, 93) : lit. *pri-gáuti* 'betrügen'; ir. *bou bō* aus **bou̯ós*, GS. zu NS. *bō* 'Kuh'; ir. *lōathar* 'pelvis' (woraus *lōthur, lothor* wie *ōc* aus *ōac*), aus **lou̯etró-* resp. **lău̯etró-* : bret. *louazr*, gr. *λουτρόν* aus **λοϝετρόν*.

In historisch unbetonter Silbe ist inselkelt. *ău̯-* und *ou̯-* irisch über *au, ō* zu *a* geworden (vgl. ir. *teglach* : *slōg sluag*): mir. *Letha* aus **pl̥tau̯i-*, vgl. gall.-lat. *Letavia*; ir. *tana* 'dünn' (bret. *tanau*) aus **tanau̯os* : gr. *ταναός*; ir. *ro chuala* 1. Sg. Pf. 'audivi' aus inselkelt. **kūklóu̯a*[1]); ir. *sochla* 'berühmt' aus *su* + **clō* (historisch *clū*), letzteres aus idg. **kléu̯os*, inselkelt. **klou̯os* : gr. *κλέος*. Dagegen spräche ir. *fedb* 'Witwe', wenn dies bei Brugmann, Grdr. I², 328, richtig aus idg. **u̯idhéu̯ā* erklärt wäre. Dem ist jedoch nicht so: eine solche Form müsste im Nkymr. **gweddau* lauten (vgl. das Pluralsuffix akymr. *-ou*, mkymr. *-eu*, nkymr. *-au* aus *-eu̯es*, Suffix des NP. der *u*-Stämme), es giebt aber dort nur ein *gweddw* 'Witwer'. Folglich setzt Stokes, Urkelt. Sprachschatz S. 280 richtig **u̯idu̯ā*, **u̯idu̯os* als urkelt. Formen an (vgl. got. *widuwō* etc. aus idg. **u̯idhuu̯ā*: Brugmann a. a. O. 257).[2])

---

[1]) Mit *ū* in der Reduplikationssilbe, vgl. mkymr. *cigleu* 3. Sg. Pf. 'audivit', wo *i* nur aus *ū* entstanden sein kann (zu Brugmann, Grdr. II, 1246; vgl. auch Loth, Rev. Celt. XVIII, 92). — Das *-f* der mkymr. 1. Sg. Pf. *ciglef* ist unerklärt; wahrscheinlich ist es analogisch von der 1. Sg. Praes. bezogen, und die Form steht für **cigleuf* (statt *cigleu*, das daneben vorliegt).

[2]) Ebenso wie in ir. *fedb* liegt idg. *-du̯-* auch in mir. *badb-scēl*, *Bodb* vor; im Akymr. entspricht *Bodu*, i. e. *bodu̯*, aus **bodu̯os*, wozu *Boduoc* mit der Ableitungssilbe *-auc*, *-oc* gebildet worden ist. Folglich ist idg. *du̯* nur anlautend inselkelt. zu *d* geworden, dagegen inlautend ir. zu *db*, kymr. zu *dw*. Vgl. auch Pedersen, Aspirationen i Irsk (I) 149.

Da sich ir. *au* nicht nur für inselkelt. *au* (= idg. *ău*, lat.
au) und *ău-* (= idg. *ău-*, *ŏu̯-*), sondern auch für inselkelt. *ou̯-*
(= idg. *eu̯-*, *ou̯-*) findet, so ergiebt sich daraus, dass es nicht *au*
ausgesprochen worden ist, vielmehr wird es zur Darstellung von
ǫu dienen sollen, wie daneben *ou* (in *lour*, *crou*, *bou*). Aus *ǫu*
ist zunächst *ǭ* (offenes langes *o*) entstanden, was wohl auch
durch *āo* (in *crāo*, *gāo*) neben *ō*[1]) bezeichnet werden soll, und
daraus weiterhin *ū*. Die Bedingungen, wonach *ō* oder *ū* erscheint,
sind allerdings noch nicht klar (vgl. Brugmann, Grdr. I², 327).
Nicht undenkbar ist es, dass ein Teil der Fälle von *u* aus *ō* vor
folgenden mouillierten Konsonanten resp. vor dem als Übergangs-
laut zu ihm entwickelten *i* entstanden ist, wie ja *o* unter gleicher
Bedingung zu *u* wird. So erklärt sich z. B. *tu̇isech* neben *tōisech*
'Führer' (vgl. *cūiced* neben *cōiced* 'der Fünfte'); ebenso *clūi*
neben *clōi*, NP. zu *clō* 'Nagel', aus **clū* **clōi*, älter **klāui(u̯)ī*
aus **klāu̯ī* (nicht klar Brugmann, Grdr. I², 242). Natürlich haben
dann mannigfache Ausgleichungen stattgefunden. Ferner scheint
ō vor erhaltenem *a* der nächsten Silbe zu *ū* geworden zu sein,
vgl. *cūa* 'Winter' (mkymr. *kawat*), *ūan* 'Schaum' aus **pou̯eno-*
(nkymr. *ewyn* 'spuma', abret. *euonoc* 'spumaticus' : lit. *putà*, lett.
putas 'Schaum' nach Bezzenberger bei Stokes, Urkelt. Sprachschatz 53), *ūa* 'Enkel' neben *ōa*, *nūa* 'neu' neben *nūe* (statt
*nōe nach *nūa?*); beachte auch *nūna* neben *nōine* 'Hungersnot'
aus **nou̯eni̯ā* : nkymr. *newyn* aus **nou̯eno-*, got. *nauþs* 'Not'.
Ebenso wie *a* hat ein folgendes *u* auf *ō* eingewirkt, vgl. *tūus*,
tūs 'Vorrang, Führerschaft, Anfang' aus **tōus*, dies aus **tóu̯essus*
(zu *u* aus *e* vgl. Brugmann, Grdr. I², 244): nkymr. *tywys* 'Führung'.

Im Kymrischen ist mit inselkelt. *au*, für das in vorhistorisch
betonter Silbe (d. i. die Ultima der historischen Zeit, vgl. Zimmer,
Gurupūjākaumudī S. 82[2])) akymr. *ou*, mkymr. *eu*, nkymr. *au*
erscheint, derjenige Diphthong zusammengefallen, der sich durch

---

[1]) Für *ō* findet sich auch die Schreibung *ōo*, *oo*, wie für *ā* die Schreibung
āa (vgl. z. B. *scāath* 'Schatten'), für *ī* die Schreibung *ĭi* (z. B. *rĭi* 'König'
= lat. *rēx*) etc. Brugmann ist daher Grdr. I², 846 im Unrecht, wenn er *broo*
'Mühlstein' zweisilbig auffasst. Ebenso ist wohl *biid*, GS. zu *biad* 'victus',
als *bīd* aufzufassen.

[2]) Aus der Geschichte der brit. Betonung ergiebt sich m. E., dass Hirt,
Indogerm. Akzent S. 44 f. und Brugmann, Grdr. I², 977 ff., beide im Anschluss
an Thurneysen, mit Unrecht die gälische Anfangsbetonung in die urkelt. Zeit
rücken.

Schwund der Endungen aus inselkelt. *oṷ-* + Endung ergab. Beispiele sind: das Pluralsuffix akymr. *-ou*, mkymr. *-eu*, nkymr. *-au*[1] — oder, mit *-i* komponiert, *-iou, -ieu, -iau* — (GC.[2] 284 ff.) aus **-éṷes*, Endung des NP. der *u*-Stämme, z. B. akymr. *lloggou*, mkymr. *llongeu* 'Schiffe', nkymr. *llongau* 'Gefässe' : ir. *long* 'Gefäss, Schiff'; die vollbetonten Possessiva mkymr. *teu*, nkymr. *tau* (Rhys, BB. XVIII, 270) 'dein' aus **téṷe* (ai. *táva*) und die Analogiebildung dazu mkymr. *meu*, nkymr. *mau* 'mein' (GC.[2] 387; Brugman, Grdr. II, 823 f.), vgl. die vortonig verkürzten Formen ir. *do, du* aus **tō* (aspirierend: Stokes, Kuhn-Schleichers Beitr. I, 470) und ir. *mo, mu* aus **mō*[2]); mkymr. *creu*, nkymr. *crau* 'Blut' aus **kréṷas* : ir. *crou* (*crāo, crō, crū*), gr. χρέας; mkymr. *cigleu* 3. Sg. Pf. 'audivit' aus inselkelt. **kūklóṷe* : ir. *ro chuala*; mkymr. *geu*, nkymr. *gau* 'falsch' (vgl. *dieu, diau* 'wahr, sicher') aus **goṷos* : ir. *gau* u. s. w., lit. *prigáuti*. Beachte auch die als Plurale fungierenden alten Singularformen wie nkymr. *cnau* (sg. *cneuen*) 'Nuss' aus **knoṷā* : ir. *cnū*, lat. *nux*, an. *hnot* (Grundform nicht richtig bei Pedersen, KZ. XXXII, 251, vgl. auch Noreen, Urgerm. Lautlehre 225) und mkymr. *llau* (sg. *lleuen*) 'pediculus' aus inselkelt. **loṷos* : ahd. ags. *lūs*, nhd. *laus*. Eine Ausnahme würde nkymr. *clyw* 'Gehör' bilden, wenn es bisher mit Recht dem air. *clū* 'Ruhm' gleichgesetzt und auf idg. **kléṷos* zurückgeführt worden ist. Doch ist dies schon der Bedeutung wegen ganz unwahrscheinlich; vielmehr wird *clyw* eine Neubildung zu den Verbalformen mit *clyw-* (z. B. 3. Sg. Impf. mkymr. *clywei* 'er hörte') sein, nach einem Verhältnis wie mkymr. *attebei* 'er antwortete' : *atteb* 'Antwort'.

Der Übergang von mkymr. *eu* zu nkymr. *au* steht auf gleicher Stufe mit dem von mkymr. *ei* zu nkymr. *ai* (z. B. in akymr. mkymr. *seith* = nkymr. *saith* 'sieben'), vgl. auch akymr. *leguenid* : nkymr. *llawenydd* 'Freude', mkymr. *cennyat* : nkymr. *caniad* 'Erlaubnis' u. s. w. Überall scheint es sich mir um ein mkymr. *ę* (d. h. offenes *e* oder *ä*, in den zuletzt genannten Fällen durch Umlaut aus *a* entstanden) zu handeln, das nkymr. zu *a* wird. Wie nun aber im Nkymr. für mkymr. *ei* in vorhistorisch unbetonten Silben (d. h. in Silben, die historisch nicht die Ultima bilden) gleichfalls *ei* erscheint (z. B. akymr. *gueirclaud*, mkymr.

---

[1]) Daneben nkymr. *-eu* und *-e*, vgl. z. B. Rhys, Rev. Celt. I, 358.
[2]) Über weitere Verkürzungen siehe z. B. Brugmann, Grdr. I², 688.

gweirglawd, nkymr. *gweirglawdd* 'Wiese' neben nkymr. *gwair*
'Heu' aus *$\underset{\cdot}{u}$egro-* : ir. *fér*), so auch in denselben Silben *eu* für
mkymr. *eu*: z. B. mkymr. *eureit*, nkymr. *euraid* 'goldig', mkymr.
eurawc, nkymr. *eurog* 'freigebig' neben mkymr. *eur*, nkymr. *aur*
'Gold'. Hier lag jedenfalls mkymr. *ę* (d. h. geschlossenes *e*) vor.
Welcher Lautwert dem akymr. *ou* zukommt, wage ich nicht zu
bestimmen.

Inselkelt. *au* und *o$\underset{\cdot}{u}$-* + Endung ist nicht die einzige Quelle
für akymr. *ou*, mkymr. (und auch schon akymr.) *eu*. So ist z. B.
mkymr. *peunyd* 'täglich', *peunoeth* 'jede Nacht' aus **popnyd*,
*popnoeth[1]) entstanden und setzt ein akymr. **pounyd*, **pounoeth*
voraus. Akymr. *toulu*, mkymr. nkymr. *teulu* aus **togo-slougos*
(neben nkymr. *telu*, air. *teglach* aus **tego-slougos*, vgl. Stokes,
Urkelt. Sprachschatz 126 f.) haben *u* aus *g* entwickelt, und
mkymr. *teulu* lautet im Nkymr. gleich, weil *teu* in vorhistorisch
unbetonter Silbe steht. Ebenso ist akymr. *louber*, mkymr. *lleuver*,
nkymr. *lleufer* 'Licht' aus **logber*, älter **lokber* (**lok* aus **lukā*
— vgl. gr. ἀμφιλύκη 'Zwielicht' — mit *ā*-Umlaut) und nkymr.
iau F., akorn. *iou* (Vokab. *ieu*), mbret. *yeu*, nbret. *geo*, *ico* 'Joch'
aus **$\underset{\cdot}{i}$og*, urkelt. **$\underset{\cdot}{i}$ugā* (vgl. die Plurale von gr. ζυγόν, lat.
jugum) zu erklären[2]); ferner mkymr. *meudwy* = air. *mugdē*
'Klausner' (mkymr. *meu* = air. *mug* aus **mogus*) u. s. w. In
gleicher Weise geht mkymr. *peu* (korn. *pow*, abret. *pou* in
Poutrecoet) = lat. *pāgus* auf vorhistorisches **pōg*, akymr. **pou*
(aus **pōu*) zurück, wonach wir auch für inselkelt. *ā$\underset{\cdot}{u}$-*
(+ Endung) regelrecht akymr. *ou*, mkymr. *eu*, nkymr. *au* erwarten dürfen; doch fehlen Beispiele dafür (über nkymr. *clo*
aus **klā$\underset{\cdot}{u}$os* : ir. *clō*, lat. *clāvus* siehe unten). Ich kann Zimmer,
KZ. XXXVI, 437, nicht darin folgen, dass es sich in den zuletzt

---

[1]) Nicht **peupnyd*, *peupnoeth*, wie K. Meyer, Peredur ab Efrawc S. 42
als Grundform ansetzt; vgl. *pop* adj. 'jeder' neben *pawp* subst. 'jedermann'.

[2]) Akymr. *louber* und nkymr. *iau* lassen sich nicht etwa aus vorhist.
*lōgber und **$\underset{\cdot}{i}$ōg* (mit inselkelt. *ō* aus *ou* = idg. *eu*, *ou*) erklären, weil *ōg*
kymr. zu *u* geführt hat, vgl. ir. *slōg sluag* 'Schar' : nkymr. *llu* 'exercitus'
(vgl. akymr. *te-lu* 'Haushalt, Familie'), ir. *trōg truag* 'elend, unglücklich'
: kymr. *tru*. *ō* war also schon zu *ū* geworden, als *u* aus *g* entstand, sodass
g in dem vorangehenden *ū*-Laut spurlos aufging, während es mit *ō* zu dem
Diphthongen *ou* verschmolz (vgl. korn. *pow*, abret. *pou-*, mkymr. *peu* = lat.
pāgus, worüber oben im Text). Loth, Rev. Celt. XX, 350 will *louber* aus
*lo$\underset{\cdot}{u}$o-ber- herleiten; was soll aber **lo$\underset{\cdot}{u}$o-* sein?

genannten Fällen von mkymr. *eu* um *ei* mit *e* aus *o* durch Umlaut und mit *i* aus *g* handelt. In nkymr. *treio* 'ebben' : mir. *trāgᵃim*, worauf er sich vor allem beruft, gehört das *i* nicht zum Stamme, sodass es aus *g* entstanden sein müsste, sondern zur Endung, die die bekannte Infinitivendung mkymr. *-iaw, -yaw*, nkymr. *-io* ist, woneben sowohl *-i* wie *-aw* (nkymr. *-o*) vorliegt (vgl. GC.² 536 f.). Neben *treio* giebt es ja auch mkymr. nkymr. *troi* 'vertere' und nkymr. *tro* 'versio, gyrus'. Letzteres, aus **trǫg-* (vgl. mir. *trāgᵃim*) zu erklären, sollte allerdings regelrecht mkymr. **treu* (vgl. *peu* = lat. *pāgus*), nkymr. **trau* lauten; doch findet sich auch sonst (dialektisch?) *o* für zu erwartendes mkymr. *eu*, nkymr. *au*: z. B. nkymr. *clo* (pl. *cloeu*) 'sera, clausum' (woneben *cloi* 'obserare, claudere', wie *troi* neben *tro*) aus inselkelt. **klāu̯os*: ir. *clō*, lat. *clāvus* 'Nagel'; *gro* 'sabulum, saburra, glarea' neben korn. *grou, growyn*, mbret. *grouanenn*, nbret. *grouan*: lit. *grúdas* 'Korn', an. *griót* 'Steine', ahd. *grioz* 'Gries' (idg. Anlaut *gh*-: gr. χέραδος 'Griess'); *to* 'tectum' (woneben *toi* 'tegere') aus **tog-*, vgl. ir. *tu̯ige* 'stramen' aus **togi̯ā*. Die Geschichte des intervok. *g* im Britannischen ist noch genauer zu untersuchen; jedenfalls scheinen die umgebenden Vokale dabei eine Rolle gespielt zu haben.

Zum Schlusse noch einige chronologische Bemerkungen über den Wandel von inselkelt. *au* zu *ou* im Britannischen, spez. Kymrischen (wo *au* = akymr. *ou*, mkymr. *eu*, nkymr. *au*). Da inselkelt. *au̯-* + Endung mit dem Schwunde der letzteren im Brit. zu *-au* geworden ist (Beispiele siehe oben S. 268),[1] so ergiebt sich, dass der Übergang von inselkelt. *au* zu *ou* vor dem Schwunde der Endungen stattgefunden haben muss; denn sonst müsste auch *au̯-* + Endung brit. *ou* ergeben haben. Das aus inselkelt. *a* entwickelte kymr. *au, aw* ist natürlich noch jünger als der Schwund der Endungen, weil einzeldialektisch, und konnte daher erst recht nicht mit inselkelt. *au* zusammenfallen. Dagegen folgt aus mkymr. *taw* aus **tause* über **tau̯e* u. s. w. (worüber oben S. 268), dass der Wandel von inselkelt. *au* zu brit. *ou* erst nach dem völligen Schwunde des intervok. *s* vor sich gegangen sein kann.

---

[1] Hierher gehört auch korn. *frau* 'Krähe', bret. *frau* 'Eule' aus **sprau̯ā*, wie Stokes, Urkelt. Sprachschatz 317 mit Recht als Grundform ansetzt (nicht richtig Foy, IF. VI, 320).

2. Urkelt. *sk̑u* im Britannischen.

Nach Pedersen, Aspirationen i Irsk (I) S. 177 (im Anschluss
an Zimmer, KZ. XXXIII, 276, wogegen ich IF. VI, 316 — vgl.
auch VIII, 202 — polemisiert habe) soll idg. *sq-* über *sk̑u̯-*, *ksu̯-*
zu *chu̯-* geworden sein (Beispiel: nkymr. *chu̯edl* = ir. *scēl* aus
idg. *sqetlo-*). Ich glaube an der angeführten Stelle (IF. VI, 316)
deutlich genug gewesen zu sein, um meine Verwunderung über
Pedersens Bemerkungen aussprechen zu können.[1]) Urkelt. *sk̑u̯-*
(aus idg. *sk̑u̯-* und *sq-*, vgl. IF. VIII, 202) kann zur Zeit der Umstellung von *-sk-* zu *-ks-* im Brit. und Gall. (IF. VI, 323 f., 327 f.)
nicht zu *ksu̯-* geworden sein. Die verglichene Umstellung von
-sk- zu *-ks-* hat nur nach Vokalen, d. h. also bei der Silben-
grenze nach dem *s*, stattgefunden, und daher erscheint anl. *sk-*
im Brit. als *sc* (IF. VI, 315), weil *sk-* im Satzzusammenhange
häufig auf Konsonanten folgte. *sk̑u̯-* könnte also nur nach Vokalen
Metathesis zu *ksu̯-* erfahren haben; dann müsste dies aber auch
inlautend zwischen Vokalen geschehen sein, wo jedoch nicht *chu̯*
aus *ksu̯*, sondern *sp* erscheint (vgl. nkymr. *cosp*, IF. VI, 325 f.).
Danach erklären sich die anlautenden *sp-* im Brit. (und Gall.)
aus urkelt. *sk̑u̯-* in der Stellung nach Vokalen im Satze (IF.
VIII, 202).

Während also urkelt. *sk̑u̯-* nach Vokalen brit. (und gall.)
zu *sp* wurde, wird es zu *χu̯-* (*chu̯*) nach Konsonanten und im
absoluten Anlaut entwickelt worden sein, und zwar über *sχu̯-* zusammen mit idg. *su̯-*[2]) (vgl. *sp-* über *sf-* zu *f-*, IF. VI, 319, was sich
sowohl bei 'aspiriertem' wie 'unaspiriertem' *s* erklären würde).

Kann ich auch in den angeführten Punkten Pedersen nicht
beipflichten, so muss ich doch gestehen, dass durch seine wichtige
Schrift die von mir IF. VIII, 205 ff. gegebene Chronologie der
das *s* betreffenden Lautgesetze im Keltischen zum Teil antiquiert
worden ist. Doch halte ich den Zeitpunkt noch nicht für geeignet, sie durch eine neue zu ersetzen.

---

[1]) Allerdings in gerechterer Weise als Pedersen a. a. O. 145 gegen meine
Bemerkungen IF. VI, 314, wo ich, wie ich selbst angebe, nur diejenigen brit.
Worte mit *s-* anführe, die sich mir am wenigsten als Entlehnungen aus dem
Lat., Ir., Ags. erklären liessen.

[2]) Pedersens Ansicht über die Entwicklung von *su̯-* a. a. O. 177 ist nach
dem über *sk̑u̯-* Gesagten insofern unhaltbar, als ein *sχu̯-* nicht zu *γsu̯-* hat
führen können.

Dresden.   WILLY FOY.

DIE VERTRETUNG DER *U*-DIPHTHONGE IM IRISCHEN UND VERWANDTES.

Die indogermanischen Diphthonge *eu ou au* sind im Britannischen in *u,* im Irischen in *ó ua* zusammengefallen. Das Altgallische hält sie noch auseinander. *eu* wird erst spät zu *ou* (vgl. die *Teutones* : *Toutones*), desgleichen *au.* Letzteres liegt z. B. vor in dem hispanischen Stadtnamen *Auxuma* (Florus 2, 10, 9), vgl. das italische *Auximum,* später Οὔξαμα, *Uxama,* vgl. des Pytheas Οὐξισάμη (*Ouessant*), auch in *Uxellodunum* ist gegen Brugmann, Grdr.² I, 200 *au-* anzusetzen, vgl. altir. *úasal,* kymr. *uchel.* Ferner tritt *au* verhältnismässig oft in Suffixen auf, so in *Vellaunodūnum, Cassivellaunus* (vgl. venetisch *Volsouna,* illyr. *Dripponius*), wo gr. κεραυνός für das Alter des *au* Gewähr leistet; in *Nemausus, Carausius* (slav. *-uchŭ*) u. dergl. Im Hinblick auf Bremers Versuch, den Namen der *Taurisci* mit dem der *Teurisci* in Nordungarn zu verbinden (Pauls Grdr. d. germ. Phil.² III, 778), sei bemerkt, dass *au* keine Durchgangsstufe des *eu* in seiner Entwicklung zu *ou ō* etc. gewesen ist; vielmehr ist der Wechsel von *eu* und *au* ein Kennzeichen dakischer Lautgebung (vgl. Kretschmer, Einl. i. d. Gesch. d. griech. Spr. 228).

Im Irischen erscheinen also *eu ou au* als *ó* : *ua.* Die Ursache dieser Doppelheit ist noch unbekannt. Ihre Parallelisierung mit der Doppelheit *é* : *ía* hat sich als trügerisch erwiesen (vgl. Strachan, BB. XX, 12, Anm. 3); auch die durch 'Ersatzdehnung' entstandenen *ō* partizipieren an der Spaltung.

Zunächst ist klar, dass zum Teil zwischen *ó* und *ua* einfach ein zeitlicher Unterschied besteht. *ó* ist eben das ältere und erscheint daher in einigen der ältesten Denkmäler an Stelle des

späteren *ua*. So in den Namen der Vita Columbas von Adamnan
von Hi (Zimmer, KZ. XXXVI, 476): *Tothal* (sp. *Tuathal*), *Cloni*
(= *Cluain*), *Moda fluvius* (*Muad*), in den Noten Tirechans
(Thurneysen in dieser Ztschr. I, 348): *Boin, Booín, Boonrigi,
Gosacht, Clono, Crochan, Coona* neben seltenerem *ua* in *Buain,
Thuaithe, Chonlúain, Ruaid, Muaide, Buás*, in der Hs. von
Cambrai: *ood, oire, onni*. Es muss auffallen, dass bei Tirechan
ausser in *Buás ua* durchweg vor palataler Konsonanz steht,
während dem erhaltenen *o* überwiegend 'harte' Laute folgen.
Vielleicht gestattet dies Verhältnis einen Schluss auf die Be-
dingungen, unter denen im vorhistorischen Irisch einmal ein
lebendiger Wechsel zwischen *ó* und *ua* stattfand; das historische
Irisch weiss nichts mehr davon.

Der Würzburger Kodex hat folgende Fälle von erhaltenem *ó*:
óg 'integer' mit Ableitungen 1 a 9. 3 d 22. 9 d 25, 26, 27.
10 a 12, 18, 20, 26. 10 b 14, 20, 21 (2 mal), 24.

lóg 'Preis', verschiedene Kasus: 1 c 3. 3 c 1. 5 d 35. 6 a 5, 11.
10 d 23, 26, 27, 29, 31. 11 a 12. 14 c 8, 10, 11, 12. 14 d 38. 15 b 11.
16 c 77, d 4. 23 c 25. 24 d 1, 2. 27 c 10, 12. 29 a 14.

tróg 'miser' 19 b 4. 21 b 5, *trócaire* 'misericordia' 4 c 38.
5 c 17. 15 b 8. 23 c 10.

conóigset 'sie nähten' 19 a 1 (bekanntlich ein böses Miss-
verständnis des Glossators, der consuesco und consuo verwechselte).

ócht 'Kälte' 10 d 24, 25. 15 d 29.

óre 'da' stets ausser 1 a 3. 2 a 18, 19. 5 d 5.

ón, són 'id' stets.

ó als proklitische Präposition und in Verbindung mit dem
Artikel (*ónd* etc.), dagegen *huaimse* 5 d 37, *uáit* 6 c 7, *húad*
7 c 15, *huanni* 5 a 7 (*ónni* nur 4 b 19), *huáib* 7 b 4, *úadib* 4 c 2.

ós als Präposition, auch *ósib* 2 b 7, aber *anúas* 10 d 2.
15 a 22. 16 d 7. 23 c 23, *túas* 3 d 10. 10 a 15. 11 b 5. 12 c 17.
33 a 21.

hómon 'Furcht' 6 a 7. 16 a 21. 29 d 15.

docoith 'ging' 11 a 22, *doc(h)oid* 14 c 20, d 30. 21 a 12,
dochood 17 d 7, *docoadsa* 18 d 6, *docotar* 29 a 8, *docói* 29 a 28.

chródatu 'Tapferkeit' 31 b 21.

loun 'Proviant' (später *lón*) 29 b 14. *tó* = *to* + *fo* in *tóbe*
'Beschneidung'. *fó* = *fo* + *ód* in *fócre* 'monitio'.

ua erscheint dagegen in:

adcuaid 'explicavit' 21 d 11.

chluas 23 c 2.

sruáim 'Fluss' 11 a 19.

buáid 11 a 4, 6, 7, 10 (2 mal). 26 a 34. 27 a 22, c 20. 30 b 13,
buade 24 a 17 (aber *boid* 24 a 16).

uáisliu 19 d 21. 21 a 13. 23 c 15. 24 b 4, *foruáistigem* 17 b 17.

fúath 'Gestalt' 24 a 8. 32 c 9.

uain 'Borgen' 31 c 5.

uáin 'Musse' 14 a 25.

fúan 'Rock' 30 d 19.

luaith 'schnell' 32 c 16.

guássacht 'Gefahr' 13 c 7.

suánemuin 'Stricke' 24 d 14. 26 b 17.

uall 'Übermut' 10 b 27. 15 d 40, *uáilbe* 14 c 21.

uabar 'vanitas' 13 b 14 (aber *obar* 27 a 9).

huáthad 'raritas' 4 d 4, 5. 5 a 26. 25 a 38.

glúas 'Glosse' 4 d 25. 8 c 4. 17 d 21. 32 d 2. 33 a 21.

túath 4 d 1. 5 b 24 u. s. w.

Einige Punkte sind ohne weiteres klar. *ó* ist vor folgendem
Guttural geblieben, während es vor andern Lauten zu *ua* geworden ist; mit *hómon docoith chródatu loun* hat es, wie gleich
gezeigt wird, eine eigene Bewandtnis. Ferner bleibt *ó* in Worten,
die vermöge ihrer Funktion im Satze unbetont sind (vgl. die
Erhaltung von *ō* in ahd. *dō, salbōta* u. dergl.).

hómon, mittelir. *óman, úaman*, neuir. *uamhan* enthält auf
keinen Fall einen alten Diphthong.   Die Gleichung *hómon*
: kymr. *ofn*, gall. *-obnus* ist eine von denen, an deren absoluter
Evidenz eine lautliche Schwierigkeit nichts ändern kann, nach
solchen Gleichungen haben sich eben unsere 'Lautgesetze' zu
richten.   Nach Pedersen, Aspir. i Irsk S. 129, ist in kymr. *ofn*
ursprüngliche Länge unter dem Einfluss des vorhistorischen
Accents gekürzt worden.   Andrerseits scheint es auch ein irisches
ŏmun gegeben zu haben (vgl. diese Ztschr. II, 211).   Wie dem
auch sein mag, in *hómon* ist *ó* offenbar unter dem Einfluss des
folgenden *m* aus *á* entstanden; dass es sich länger als Monophthong
gehalten hat, als *ó* = ursprünglich *eu* u. s. w., kann nicht auffallen; das in späterer Zeit n a c h *m* aus *á* entstandene *ó* (*mór*)
ist ja überhaupt nicht diphthongiert worden.

códatu erscheint auch Ml. 42 b 2, ferner im Mittelir. und
Neuir. durchgehend mit *ó*, es gehört zum Adjektiv *crúaid*. In
códatu ist *ó* ein Kontraktionsprodukt, denn es ist mit lat. *crūdus*

auf *kroved- oder dergl. zurückzuführen, vgl. gr. κρέας, altind. kraviš. Ähnlich steht es mit docóid, dessen scheinbare Wurzelsilbe -cóid aus der Präposition co und der Verbalwurzel feth- 'gehen' besteht, vgl. fethid 'geht' LL. 121 a 21, dofaith 'adiit' Fiaccs Hymn. etc., BB. XXIII, 55. Was schliesslich loun anbetrifft, so zeigt ja schon seine Schreibung, die an loan Ml. 39 c 33, lóon Sg. 70 a 7, loon 125 a 1, weitere Stützen hat, dass es ursprünglich zweisilbig gewesen ist; in der That stellt sich ein keltisches *lara*n- neben *laϝερ- in gr. λᾱρῑνός 'fett' wie altind. udnás neben gr. ὕδωρ u. s. w.

Der Mailänder Kodex zeigt einen etwas fortgeschritteneren Sprachzustand. Er hat ó ausschliesslich oder überwiegend in:

lóg 36 a 32. 84 c 12. 87 b 9. 129 a 1. 130 a 3, d 15.

óg 100 a 3, ógai 94 b 4. 144 c 7.

tróg mit Kas. u. Abl. 20 a 1. 23 b 5. 33 b 1. 38 d 11. 39 d 3. 40 b 8. 51 c 20. 54 a 12. 55 d 2, 5. 71 a 2. 75 a 14. 77 a 4/5. 77 d 2. 86 c 2. 87 b 1. 96 a 7, 8. 98 c 6 (aber truag 118 c 5 (2 mal). 133 a 8, truaig 36 a 32).

slóg 51 a 5. 55 c 1. 62 b 20. 90 c 10. 111 b 19. 115 a 8. 130 d 14 (sluag 55 c 1. 95 c 12).

crodatu 42 b 2.

Die Präposition ó überwiegt bis etwa S. 50 des Ml. gegenüber ua, sowohl selbständig, als zusammengesetzt; später ist es umgekehrt, von 56 an kommen nach meiner Zählung 245 ua auf 40 ó. huare herrscht ausnahmslos statt hóre des Wb., ebenso uas. Statt ócht heisst es in Ml. huacht 76 d 14. 90 d 3. 94 b 23, statt ochtur 'pars superior' des Cod. Bedae Carolisr. 32 a 3. 33 c 9 hat Ml. uachtar 42 b 10; 42 b 19. 107 c 16. 130 b 4, ferner luaichtidiu 'fulgida' 40 d 4. Hier hat also die Diphthongierung die in Wb. noch verschonten ó unbetonter sowie durch ch geschlossener Silben erfasst, während g noch so ziemlichen Schutz gewährt.

Zu Wb. stimmt ómun 33 c 7. 42 d 9. 55 c 10. 59 a 18. 79 b 2. 96 a 10. 128 d 7, 8, ferner ducoid mit 7 Belegen (32 d 10. 38 b 2. 43 d 27. 63 c 19. 74 a 12. 84 c 9. 124 c 26), doch vgl. ducuaid 65 c 4, ducuatar 66 c 16. Altes ove steckt auch in erchót 'Schaden' 39 c 20. 42 c 19. 56 a 13. 61 c 8. 121 d 4, vgl. erchoat 47 c 4, arachoat 31 d 10, arcói 46 d 11, erchoitech 31 d 14. 35 b 25. 68 c 21. 74 c 6. 83 d 2; erchót gehört m. E. zweifellos zu abret. arcogued 'nocivos' kymr. argywedd 'Beschädigung', wie Stokes früher lehrte (KZ. XXVI, 457). fót 'Rasen' 37 d 14. 84 a 5.

126 a 15 ist etymologisch dunkel, enthält aber keinesfalls einen alten Diphthong.

Im übrigen stimmt Ml. im Gebrauch von *ua* zu Wb.: *buadarthu* 2 b 3; *cluas* 24 a 18. 60 b 16. 112 b 12; *fuath* 38 c 6; *buad* 33 c 13 u. ö.; *guasacht* 35 c 4; *huath* 40 c 11, 16. 42 b 12; *nuall* 40 d 18, 20. 67 b 19 u. ö.; *luaithfider* 57 c 7; *luaithred* 49 c 2; *gluaistis* 96 c 13; *huáin* 'Musse' 100 a 3 u. dergl.

Der Sanktgaller Kodex bietet folgende *ó*-Belege: *óg* 16 a 14. 25 b 2. 52 a 9. 59 b 10. 73 b 1. 75 a 5, b 2. 98 a 1, 2. 157 b 4, 5 (2 mal), 6.

óigthidi 'sartores' 186 b 1.

trogan 48 a 11 (*truag* 229 a — b).

(*h*)*óthud* 41 a 8. 49 a 14. 56 b 3. 92 b 2. 163 b 6. 198 a 22, b 3. 203 b 9 (gegen *úathad* 51 b 11. 71 b 3 [2 mal], 12, 15. 72 a 1, 4. 90 b 2. 137 b 2. 162 a 6. 186 a 2).

lochairnn 24 a 16 (*luacharnn* 47 a 9).

hó ist etwas zahlreicher als *hua* (88 : 72).

huare wie in Ml.; vgl. ferner *luach* 'foenus' 41 b 5, *tuag* 'Bogen' 107 b 1, *sluag* 20 b 1.

Das Material ist sehr dürftig; am meisten fällt der starke Prozentsatz der *ó* im Worte (*h*)*óthud* auf. Wie diese hohe Altertümlichkeit in den Sg. Kodex hineingeraten ist, entzieht sich unserer Kenntnis.

Im Mittelirischen findet sich bei altem Diphthong einheimischer Worte ein Schwanken natürlich nur vor Guttural, denn die übrigen betonten *ó* = *eu* etc. sind ja längst zu *ua* geworden. Vor Gutturalen scheint aber ganz regellos bald *ó*, bald *ua* zu stehn, *slóg* wechselt mit *sluag*, *slóig* mit *sluaig*. Die Bedingungen, unter denen hier *ua* zuerst aufgekommen ist, sind nicht mehr zu erkennen (s. o.). In neuir. *óigh* 'Jungfrau' : *sluagh* liegt eine Regelung der Doppelheit vor, ob das etwas altes ist, lasse ich dahin gestellt; vor anderen Lauten als Gutturalen schien *ua* gerade durch Palatalisierung hervorgerufen zu sein. Unbetonte *ó* sind neuir. wieder monophthong.

Auch in Fällen von 'Ersatzdehnung' schwankt das Resultat zwischen *ó* und *ua*, doch mit dem Unterschiede, dass nie beides in demselben Worte auftritt, und dass ferner *ó* keineswegs im Laufe der Zeit durch *ua* verdrängt wird. *ó* und *ua* stehen hier von vornherein nebeneinander und sind bis auf den heutigen Tag so geblieben. Strachan hat darauf aufmerksam gemacht

(a. a. O.), dass *ua* weit häufiger ist, sowohl vor *n* (*úan* 'Lamm'
: kymr. *oen, súan* 'Schlaf' : kymr. *hun*), als vor *r* (*úar* 'kalt'
: kymr. *oer*, gall. *ogro-* im Kalender von Coligny; vielleicht zu
griech. ὠχρός 'blass', vgl. zur Bedeutung engl. *bleak winds* 'kalte
Winde' : *to look bleak* (Shakspere) 'vor Kälte bleich aussehen'
: nhd. *bleich*) und *l* (*cúala* : **cuclova*). Das scheinbar abweichende
móin 'Morast' kann, wie auch Strachan für möglich hält, *ó* statt
á (kymr. *mawn* 'Torf') durch den Einfluss des *m* bekommen
haben. Aber *srón* f. 'Nase' : k. *ffroen, tón* f. 'podex' : k. *tin,*
brón 'Kummer' : k. *brwyn* sind nicht aus der Welt zu schaffen.
Eine rein mechanische Regel lässt sich ja hier gewinnen: *ukn-*
und *ugn-* ergeben *ón*, dagegen *okn-, ogn-, opn-, upn-* etc. *uan*;
cúanéne ist als Fremdwort nicht massgebend, *dúan* 'Gedicht',
wenn es wirklich zu τεύχω gehört, kann altes *ou* haben, desgleichen *lúan* 'Licht' (altir. Ml. 67 c 18).[1] Eine wirkliche Erklärung vermag ich aber nicht zu geben.

Im vorhergehenden sind einige Wörter zur Sprache gekommen, die in der Frage nach der Behandlung des intervokalischen *v* eine Rolle spielen. Bekanntlich sind die mit
dem teilweisen Schwunde des *v* zusammenhängenden Laut-
veränderungen noch nicht genügend aufgeklärt (vgl. Brugmann,
Grdr.[2] I, 326 f.); einige Punkte seien hier kurz besprochen. *ava**
ergiebt im sekundären Auslaut in den ältesten Quellen *áo*, später
ó : *gáo* 'Lüge' (k. *gau*) Wb. 14 c 22. 17 d 12, *gáu* 14 c 23, 24, 27,
31; *gláosnathe* 'linearum' Sg. 3 b 20: *glosnathe* ebda., Ml. 33 d 10.
72 c 8. 99 d 2. 145 b 5; *nau* 'Schiff' Cod. St. Pauli IV, 1: *noe* Gen.
Sg. Sg. 69 a 24, *noa* Gen. Pl. Ml. 67 d 23. Inlautend ist *ó* wohl
schon früher eingetreten, vgl. *lóur* = k. *llawer, loon* = gr.

----

[1] Dazu führen Strachan und andere eine Doublette *lón* an. An die
Existenz dieser Form vermag ich vorläufig noch nicht so recht zu glauben.
Parallel mit der bekannten, von Windisch angeführten Stelle LU. 80 a 12 ff.
atracht in lúan láith asaétan hat LL. 78 a 9 f. *atracht inlond láith asaetun*,
vgl. Togail Troi[1] 1706 *co raeirgetar a n-eoin gaile ósa n-analaib, co rachom-*
thócbaiset a lonna láith ósa cleithib. Weiter heisst es *atrachtatar badba osa*
cennaib (TT.[1] 1708), anderswo (600) *atrácht a én gaile ósa anáil co m-búi for*
foluamain immachend, LL. 120 a 44 *lon gaile*, TT.[2] 1473 *lon láich*. Verschiedene Vorstellungen und Wörter scheinen hier vermischt zu sein. Bei
lond láith ist doch wohl sicher an *lond* 'wütend' zu denken, bei *lon* an *lon*
'merula', vgl. *én gaile, badba* u. dergl. Einen Anhalt für ein *lón* = *lúan*
finde ich hier nirgends.

λαϝϱ-. *ú* statt *ó* beim Antritt von Endungen: *gue* 'falsi'
Wb. 14 c 29, Ml. 31 b 12; *guaigedar* 31 b 1, *guigter* 51 c 14, *guaigitir*
31 b 1 (vgl. unten *úa*, und *Duid* = *David*) und in der Komposition, vgl. *guforcell* Wb. 13 b 15, *gubrithemnachtae* Ml. 103 c 10,
14, *gúbrethach, gúchomram* Windisch Wb. Die Grundform **avio-*
entwickelt sich über *aue* (vgl. Ascoli Gloss.) zu *óe óa* und *úa*;
bemerkenswert ist hier, dass das *-io* hinter dem *v* seine pala-
talisierende Kraft nicht zur Geltung bringen kann, wir haben
genau dieselbe Erscheinung in altir. *núe* 'neu' aus **nevio-*,
mittelir. *núa*, neuir. *nuadh.*

    ova* ergiebt im allgemeinen *ó*, vgl. *bó* : ahd. *kuo*, lat. *bōs*;
ói 'Schaf' : *ovis* (in der Komposition in alter Zeit *au-* und *u-*
Ascoli Gloss. 19); *cró* 'Blut' : k. *crau*; *tóisech* (Abl. von *tuus* s. u.)
: k. *tywysog*; *bói* = **bhovet*; *lóthur* 'canalis' = *λόϝετϱον*; *cóir*
= k. *cywir*; *erchót* : k. *argywedd*; *ducóid* (s. o.); *astóidi* 'strahlt'
Ml. 40 c 15, d 4. 56 c 3. 99 a 4. 115 d 3 : kymr. *tywydd*, altbulg.
vedrŭ 'hell, heiter', *vedro* 'gutes Wetter', nhd. *Wetter*; *doe*
'tardus' Sg. 66 a 1, *doi* 'tardi' Ml. 20 a 26 : dor. *δοᾱν* (**δοϝᾱν*)
'lange', gr. *δηϑύνω* 'zaudere', abg. *davě* 'einst', *davĭnŭ* 'alt' u. s. w.;
cródatu s. o. Vor palataler Konsonanz ist so entstandenes *ó*
später zu *ua* gespalten worden, vgl. *dochuaid* = altir. *docóid*,
cruaid neben *cródatu*. In *buachaill* = *bóchaill* Sg. 58 b 6 steckt
altes *ou*, vgl. k. *bugail* und altind. *gōpālá-*. Enthielt die ursprünglich dritte Silbe ein *u* oder *ū*, so ist das Kontraktionsprodukt *ú*, älter *uu, tuus* 'Anfang' : *tovessu-, duus* = do *ṗuss.*
Natürlich lautet der Dativ von *cró crú*, der Acc. Plur. von *bó*
bú u. dergl.

    Anders als altes *ova** scheint sekundäres *ova** = altem
eva* behandelt worden zu sein, vgl. den Gegensatz zwischen *bó*,
cró (?) und *clú*, zwischen *doe* und *núe*. Es würde daraus folgen,
dass die beiden *o* in der Aussprache nie zusammengefallen sind.
Für *eva** stellt sich nunmehr die Regel so dar: *ev* wird zu *ó*
vor hellem Vokal, sonst zu *ú*. Also *nói* 'neun', k. *naw* : lat.
novem, got. *niun* u. s. w.; *rói* 'planities' Ml. 133 b 7: lat. *rūs* (aus
*reuos, vgl. Solmsen, Stud. z. lat. Lautgesch. S. 60); *nóidiu* 'Kind'
aus **nevid- νήπιος*; *cnói* 'Nüsse', k. *cnau*; *nóine* 'Hungersnot'
: k. *newyn*, aber *núe* 'neu', mittelir. *núa*, k. *newydd* : got. *niujis*,
gr. *νέϝος*; *clú* 'Ruhm', k. *clyw* : gr. *κλέϝος*; *núna* neben *nóine*;
cnú 'Nuss'; *úan* 'Schaum', k. *ewyn* (zur Basis *pewā-* nach dem
Ansatze Hirts, idg. Ablaut 104).

Einfache Worte, die die Lautverbindung *uva** enthalten, sind *óac* 'jung' = lat. *juvencus*, und altir. *cróa* = *ingen* Sg. 46 b 13. Unter welchen Bedingungen letzteres im Mittelir. als *crú* erscheint, ist bei den spärlichen Belegen nicht deutlich zu ersehen. Die Zusammensetzungen **suvid- druvid-* ergeben *súi drúi*, heute diphthongisch *saoi draoi*. *sóir* und *dóir* sind vermutlich aus **sovir- *dovir-* entstanden, mit bereits zu *o* 'gebrochenem' *u*.

Berlin, Friedenau.   E. ZUPITZA.

IRISH *NO-* IN A RELATIVE FUNCTION.

The Irish language is rich in devices for the expression of relativity in the verb, cf. Thurneysen, CZ. II, 73 sq., Pedersen, KZ. XXXV, 315 sq. In the present and the future indicative, and in the present subjunctive, the distinction of non-relative and relative forms in the third persons of the orthotonic simple verb has long been familiar. Thanks to Thurneysen, l. c. pp. 78 sq., and Pedersen, l. c. pp. 374 sq., a distinction has been established likewise for the first person plural of these tenses. What of the remaining persons, the first person singular and the second persons singular and plural? Was the language here contented with a single form, or did it here too invent some special means for the expression of relativity? As might have been expected, the latter is the case; the means adopted is the prefixation of *no-*, naturally with aspiration.

Ebel, GC.[2] 415, had already remarked that *no-* appears 'in sententia relativa qualicunque, frequenti usu, etsi non necessario', but he does not attempt to define the limits of its usage. For the use of *no-* in the orthotonic forms of the aforementioned tenses of simple verbs the following rules may be laid down.[1]

(1) Where there is an infixed pronoun, *no-* is always used.[2]

(2) Where there is no infixed pronoun, *no-* is used with the first person singular and the second

---

[1]) In § 82 of my paper on the Irish Subjunctive rule 2 requires accordingly some modification.

[2]) In Ml. 16 a 18 *noberat* should be corrected to *nodberat*.

persons singular and plural, when these have a relative sense.

Rule (1) needs no illustration. Of rule (2), omitting doubtful cases like Wb. 9 a 22, 11 a 15, 17 b 20, 28 b 27, 29 b 3, where there is the possibility of an infixed relative, I have noted the following instances in the Glosses.

Sg. 1 *annupridchim, anopridchim* 'what I preach', Wb. 8 d 26, 19 d 17; *ished inso nochairigur* 11 d 1; *ished noadamrugur* 16 c 3; *ished inso noguidimm* 21 a 8; *innahí noguidim* Ml. 21 b 8; *nothoris-nigiur* g. fidentem 126 d 19; *nani nogigius* 46 b 12. In *is dosochidi noprithchib* Ml. 45 a 8 the relative form is improperly used,[1] but Pedersen has pointed out a considerable number of irregularities in Ml.

Sg. 2. *forsani nothechti* Sg. 148 a 9.

Pl. 2. *ished inso anaithesc noberid uaimm* Wb. 9 d 15; *annogessid* 'what ye pray for' 24 b 3.

Unfortunately the examples are very few, particularly in the second persons. But there is a considerable number of instances of non-relative forms, and in these *no-* is regularly absent, a fact which of course helps to confirm the rule.

---

[1] Unless it is to be emended *notprithchib*. Regularly *is tri Ísu pridchimse* Wb. 1 d 9.

Bowdon, Cheshire.   J. STRACHAN.

BEITRÄGE
· ZUR ERKLÄRUNG IRISCHER SAGENTEXTE.

---

2. *Batórniud dodergór* LL. 55 a 48.

Im Verlaufe der Erörterung in meinem ersten Beitrage (s. diese Ztschr. 1, 74 ff.) glaube ich eine ganze Reihe gesicherter Belege aus dem alten Sagentext Fled Bricrend dafür beigebracht zu haben, dass wir in den irischen Sagentexten, die hinsichtlich ihrer ersten Aufzeichnung in die altirische Sprachperiode hinaufreichen, Entstellungen gewärtigen müssen, die unserer gesamten Überlieferung voraus und zu Grunde liegen und deren Heilungsversuche vielfach neue Entstellungen in unserer Überlieferung zur Folge hatten (s. a. a. O. S. 88—93). Die in der Überschrift angeführte Stelle scheint mir ein ganz besonders lehrreicher Beleg für beide Punkte aus dem Sagentext Táin bó Cualnge, sodass es sich aus methodischem Gesichtspunkt lohnt, ausführlicher auf sie einzugehen. Sie findet sich in der Schilderung der Vorbereitungen Medbs zum Kriegszug. Zu Medbs Hilfstruppen gehörten auch die in Connacht als Verbannte lebenden Ulsterleute unter Führung von Conchobar's eigenem Sohn Cormac Condlongas und des alten Fergus Mac Róig; die Zahl dieser Ulsterleute betrug 30 Hundert und sie kamen in 3 Scharen zu je 1000 Mann zu dem Sammelplatz des Heeres in Rath Croghan in Connacht in folgendem Aufzug (LL. 55 a 46 — 55 b 10).

Incetna lorg cetamus forthí berrtha forro. bruit úanidi impu. delggi argait intib. lénti órsnaith friacnessaib. batór-niud dodergór. claidib gelduirn léo conimdurnaib argit. Inné Cormac sút forcách. Nadé om for Medb.

Inlorg tan(aise) berrtha nua leo. bruitt forglassa uli impu. lénti glegela friacnessaib. claidib comuleltaib óir 7 conimdurnib argit leo. Inné Cormac sút forcách. Nadé omm bar Medb.
Inlorg dedenach berrtha lethna leo. moṅga findbuide forórda forscailti forru. bruitt chorcra chumtaichthi impu; delgi órdai ecorthi ósochtaib dóib. lénti sémi setai sítaidi cotendmedon traiged dóib; innoenfecht dostorbaitis acossa 7 dofairnitis arís. Inné Cormac sút arcách. Isé ón ém ar Medb.

'Der erste Trupp zuerst: sie trugen lang herabfallendes Haar;[1]) sie hatten grüne Mäntel um, in denen Silberspangen sich

---

[1]) Eigentlich 'Übermäntel (forthí) waren die Haare (berrtha) auf ihnen.' Das Substantiv berrad, das wohl Nomen actionis zu berraim 'ich scheere, schneide die Haare' ist, findet sich in den alten Sagentexten ziemlich häufig in der Bedeutung 'Haarschnitt, Haartracht' und konkret 'Haar': cruindberrad 'Rundschnitt' heisst LU. 88 a 27 die Haartracht, wobei das Haar gleichlang (comlebar) nach Nacken und Stirn (forcúl 7 étan) hängt; weitere Stellen sind LU. 68 a 9, 78 a 1 (= LL. 76 a 23), 86 a 3, 90 a 20, 91 a 15, 93 a 4. Windisch, Ir. Texte III, 1, S. 239, Z. 138 u. Anm.; O'Curry hat Manners and Customs 3, 107 Anm. 68 eine Stelle, wo a berrath erklärt ist mit mullach a chinn, und so wird das Wort LL. 93 b 4. 42 (odaberrad coabonnaib 'von seinem Scheitel bis zu seinen Fusssohlen') verwendet. — Was forthí anlangt, so ist tí in der Stelle Silva Gadelica 74, 30 und Windisch, Ir. Texte III, 1, 239, Z. 136 sicher ein Wort für 'Mantel'. Wie nun zu brat 'Mantel' ein forbrat 'Übermantel' existiert (LU. 79 a 4 = LL. 77 a 5), so kann man zu tí ein fortí 'Übermantel' annehmen: in dieser Bedeutung kommt das Wort in zwei klaren Stellen eines alten Sagentextes vor (LU. 87 b 8, 93 a 4), und LU. (55 a 14) schreibt an der LL. 55 a 46 entsprechenden Stelle fortti (Plur. zu fortí wie tíi Silv. Gad. 74, 30 Plur. ist) für forthí von LL. Dies zur Rechtfertigung meines Übersetzungsversuches, der von O'Curry und O'Grady abweicht. Ersterer sagt (Manners and Customs III, 91) 'The first party came with black uncut hair' und O'Grady hat in E. Hull, Cuchullin Saga S. 119 'they had on them black heads of hair.' Hier ist jedoch zu bemerken, dass O'Grady gar nicht LL. übersetzt oder analysiert, wenn auch die Seitenzahlen von LL. den einzelnen Abschnitten vorgesetzt sind, sondern die Londoner Hs. Add. 18748. Diese ist a. 1800 von einer 1730 geschriebenen Hs. kopiert (!), bietet zwar die Rezension von LL., ist aber sprachlich vollständig modernisiert und liest an der in Rede stehenden Stelle p. 63 An cead bhuidhean diobh iomora fuilt dubha forra, also was O'Grady übersetzt und O'Curry, der die Hs. auch benutzte, mit im Sinne hatte. So lange nicht stichhaltige Gründe vorgebracht werden, dass das forthí berrtha forro von LL. (= fortti bértha foraib in LU.) bedeutet 'sie trugen schwarze Haare', haben wir gar keinen Wert darauf zu legen, ob ein Ire um 1800 oder 1730 die Worte als fuilt dubha forra fasste. Der älteste Beleg für eine solche Auffassung der Stelle scheint mir bei O'Clery vorzuliegen, der in seinem Wb. den Artikel hat foirtchi .i. dubh no dorcha, foirtchi bearrtha .i. monga dubha no gruaga dubha (Rev.

befanden; (darunter) auf ihrer Haut hatten sie Hemden (Unter-gewänder) mit Goldfaden durchzogen ....; sie führten weiss-griffige Schwerter mit silbernen Bügeln. Ist dies Cormac dort, sagte ein Jeder. Nein, sagte Medb.

Der zweite Trupp: sie trugen frisch geschnittenes Haar; sie hatten tiefgrüne Mäntel alle um; (darunter) auf ihrer Haut hatten sie glänzend weisse Hemden; sie führten Schwerter, deren Elfenbeingriffe vergoldet und deren Bügel silbern waren. Ist der dort Cormac, sagte ein Jeder. Nein, sagte Medb.

Der letzte Trupp: sie trugen breit geschnittenes Haar, dessen blondgelbe, tiefgoldige Mähnen auf ihnen wallten; sie hatten purpurne, schön geschmückte Mäntel um, in denen goldige Spangen über ihrer Brust sich befanden; (darunter) hatten sie

---

Celt. 4, 422). Da O'Clery unter seinen Quellen nachweislich eine Sammlung schwieriger Wörter der Táin bó Cualnge hatte, so scheint mir ziemlich sicher, dass mit *foirtchi bearrtha* unsere Stelle gemeint ist. Das Adjektiv *foirtchi* findet sich in der Bedeutung 'dark, black, swarthy' bei O'Brien und O'Reilly: so lange jedoch nicht Belege aus mittelirischer Litteratur oder aus modernen Dialekten vorliegen für dasselbe, haben wir allen Grund zu der Annahme, dass beider Quelle einfach O'Clery ist, schon wegen der auffallenden Form des Adjektivs auf *i* (*foirtchi* nicht *foirtche* wie man doch erwarten sollte). Aber auch wenn ein Adjektiv *foirtche* 'schwarz' existierte — was ich blos auf die Trias O'Clery, O'Brien, O'Reilly hin nicht glaube — und wenn sich O'Clery's Auffassung noch um 200 oder 300 Jahre früher nachweisen liesse, so wäre die wirkliche Bedeutung der in Rede stehenden Stelle dadurch nicht sicher gestellt, da sich in der gesamten Überlieferung der Tain, so weit ich sie überschaue, ein *foirtchi* oder *fortchi* an der Stelle ni cht findet, sondern nur *fortii, fortti, forthi*: es wäre dann *foirtchi berrtha* bei O'Clery oder seinem Gewährsmann der erste Versuch, ein unverständliches, überliefertes *fortii* (*forthi*) *berrtha* umzudeuten. Gegen diese Umdeutung spricht aber bei einiger Überlegung der ganze Zusammenhang aufs Entschiedenste. Es herrscht in der Schilderung der 3 Scharen hinsichtlich der einzelnen Punkte, die genannt werden (Haupthaar, Mäntel, Hemden, Schwerter), ein voll-kommener Parallelismus. Da nun bei der zweiten und dritten Schar ganz deutlich vom Haarschnitt, der Haartracht (*berrad nua, berrad lethan*) die Rede ist, so ist es wenig wahrscheinlich, dass bei der ersten Schar die Haar-farbe angegeben ist. Auch daran darf man erinnern, dass in den Sagen-texten die Ulsterhelden — und Ulsterhelden sind die beschriebenen Krieger — als 'blond' (*find*) oder 'hellgelb' (*fegbuide*) erscheinen, aber nicht als 'schwarz'. Ich bin daher auf Grund der Überlieferung und der thatsächlich belegten Be-deutung von *forti* der Ansicht, dass die Stelle besagt 'Übermäntel-Haare waren auf ihnen' oder 'Übermäntel waren die Haare auf ihnen' d. h. die Haare waren ungeschnitten und hingen wie Übermäntel über die Schultern herab.

feine, lange, seidene Hemden, die ihnen gingen bis zur festen
Mitte (Spanne) der Füsse; gleichzeitig erhoben sie[1]) sowohl als
setzten sie wieder nieder ihre Füsse. Ist der dort Cormac, sagte
Jeder. Er ist's gewiss, sagte Medb.'

In der Schilderung der 3 Scharen scheint mir ganz deutlich
ein Parallelismus beabsichtigt zu sein. Bei jeder Schar werden
der Reihe nach genannt 1. Haartracht, 2. Mäntel (Oberkleidung),
3. Hemden (Unterkleidung), 4. Schwerter. Man darf daraus wohl
schliessen, dass das oben unübersetzt gelassene *batórniud dodergór*
in der Schilderung der ersten Schar eine weitere Ausführung zu
der Beschreibung der Hemden bringen soll, wie *delggi argait
intib* zum vorhergehenden *bruit úanidi impu* ergänzend gehört.
Einen irgendwie befriedigenden Sinn in die Worte *batórniud
dodergór* zu bringen, scheint mir jedoch nicht möglich. Die
nächstliegende Trennung ist ja *ba tórniud dodergór* 'es war ein
tórniud von rotem Gold'; aber was soll *tórniud* bedeuten? Nomen
Verbale zu *tairnim, turnim* (neuir. *turnaim*) 'niederlassen, niederdrücken' liegt nach Form und Bedeutung fern, ebenso Verbalnomen zu mittelir. *tóirndim* (gleich altir. *dofoirndim*), da dies
alt- und mittelir. *tórand* heisst; es bliebe also übrig, an ein
Verbalnomen zu mittelir. *toirnim* neuir. *tóirnim* 'ich donnere,
mache ein Geräusch' zu denken: allein ist es wahrscheinlich,
dass von Hemden, die mit Goldfaden (*órsnáth*) durchwebt sind,
gesagt wird 'es war ein Donnern (Rauschen) von rotem Golde'?
Weder zu bekannten Wörtern in herkömmlicher Orthographie
noch zu befriedigendem Sinn kommt man bei den möglichen
Trennungen *ba tór niud* oder *bat órniud do dergór*. O'Grady
giebt entsprechend den Worten *lénti órsnaith friacnessaib batórniud dodergór* in LL. in seiner Übersetzung der Stelle (E. Hull,
Cuchullin Saga S. 119) 'next to their skins, shirts of gold thread
bearing raised patterns of red gold'. Dies ist jedoch keine
Übersetzung von LL., sondern der Versuch, die Lesart von
Addit. 18748 p. 63 *leinte orsnaithe fria ccneasaibh bhadar a
niamdha do deargor* wiederzugeben. Bei dem klaren Charakter

---

[1]) Es ist *dostorbaitis* wohl für *dostorcbaitis* verschrieben und dafür zu
bessern *nostorcbaitis*, da ja in dem Táintext von LL. die vortonigen Silben
promiscue verwendet werden. Additional 18748 p. 63 hat *a naoinfheacht
iomora nothargbhadaois a ccosa 7 nósthoirnitis doridheadaois*, was hinsichtlich
der Verbalformen nach Bewahrung von Altertümlichem und nicht nach neuirischer Besserung einer Lesart wie in LL. aussieht.

der ganz modernen Hs. Addit. 18748 (s. Anm. S. 286) wird man a priori unbedingt annehmen müssen, dass *bhadar a niamdha* weiter nichts ist als ein Versuch, möglichst im Anschluss an eine Überlieferung wie *batórniud* in LL., der Stelle durch Besserung einen Sinn abzugewinnen. Dasselbe gilt von einem weiteren Repräsentanten der LL.-Rezension H. 1. 13 (Trinity College Dublin), nach d'Arbois, Catalogue de la littérature épique de l'Irlande p. 215 zwischen 1743 und 1746 geschrieben; hier lautet die Stelle *leintibh orsnaithe fria ccnesibh bad(ur) niamhdha*[1]) *do derg or* (p. 199, 19), also 'Hemden von Goldfaden auf der Haut, die glänzend waren von rotem Gold.' Weitere Hss. der LL.-Rezension, die die in Frage kommende Stelle enthielten, sind mir nicht bekannt.

Die definitive Entscheidung darüber, ob wir die Lesungen der jungen Hss. des 18. Jahrhunderts als das nehmen dürfen und müssen als was sie sich nach dem ganzen Charakter derselben gegen LL. ergeben, nämlich als junge Versuche in die Lesart der 600 Jahre älteren Hs. einen Sinn zu legen, oder ob diese zwar die LL.-Rezension repräsentierenden aber von LL. direkt nicht abhängigen jungen Hss. in diesem Fall die bessere Lesart der Rezension bewahrt haben gegenüber einer Verderbnis in der ältesten Hs. der Rezension[2]) — die definitive Entscheidung hierüber kann nach einem Einblick in die Lesart der LU.-Rezension an dieser Stelle nicht zweifelhaft sein. Ich muss wegen der im Verlauf anzuknüpfenden Erörterungen die ganze aus LL. vorhin ausgehobene Stelle nach LU. geben; sie lautet LU. 55 a 12—26 folgendermassen:

In cetna lorg broitt brecca iforcipul cofilliud impu; Fortii bértha foraib; léini fothair inniuth cotanglun ocus fotalscéith foraib ocus manais lethanglas forcrúnd midšing illáim cechfir.

---

[1]) In der Hs. steht *niam* mit Aspirationszeichen über *m* und der Abkürzung für lat. *est* mit Aspirationszeichen. In jungen Hss. wird diese Abkürzung für lat. *est* ganz gewöhnlich für die irische Silbe *ta* (*tá = est*) verwendet und mit dem Aspirationszeichen für die irischen Silben *tha* und *dha*.

[2]) Abgesehen davon, dass eine Entstellung von so gewöhnlichem Irisch wie *batar niamda dodergór*, was für Vorlage von LL. müsste angenommen werden, in *batórniud dodergór* für eine Hs. wie LL. sehr unglaublich ist, kommt hinzu, dass wir in den alten Sagentexten in Schilderungen der Kriegerausrüstung nie einen Zusatz *batar niamda dodergór* bei den Untergewändern begegnen, wohl aber andern, aus denen durch Zwischenstufen eine Entstellung wie in LL. herauskommen konnte.

In lorg tánaisi broit dubglassa impuside ocus lénti con-
dercintliud cohorcnib sís, ocus monga taracenna star ocus lubne
gela foraib ocus slega coicrinné innalamaib. Nihé Cormac beus
or Médb.

Tic intres lorc dano, broitt chorcra impu ocus lénte culpa-
tacha fodérgintshlaid cotraigthe ocus berthai slechtai coguaille ocus
cromscéith cofœbraib condúala impu ocus turre rígthige illaim
cachfir. Isé Cormac inso hifechtsa or Médb.

'Der erste Trupp hatte bunte Mäntel in Faltung[1]) um
sich; sie trugen die Haare als Übermäntel; das Hemd .... bis
zum Knie und *fotal*-Schilde trugen sie, und auf einem in der
Mitte dünnen Schaft in der Hand eines jeden Mannes befand
sich eine breitgrüne Speerspitze.

Der zweite Trupp hatte dunkelgrüne Mäntel um, und rotdurchwobene Hemden reichten nieder bis zu den Waden, und
Mähnen auf ihren Häuptern nach rückwärts, und weisse Schilde
(hatten sie) über und fünfspitzige Speere in ihren Händen. Das
ist Cormac noch nicht, sagte Medb.

Es kommt der dritte Trupp nun: Purpurmäntel um sie, und
mit Kaputzen versehen rotdurchwobene Hemden reichten bis zu
den Füssen, und geschnittenes Haar bis zu den Schultern, und
sie hatten Krummschilde mit ciselierten scharfen Rändern um
selbige und (Speere so lang wie) Pfeiler eines Königshauses in
der Hand eines jeden Mannes. Das ist Cormac jetzt, sagte
Medb.'

Vorausschicken will ich der weiteren Erörterung die Lesarten der übrigen Hss. dieser Rezension für die in Frage
kommende Stelle *léini fothair inniuth cotanglun ocus fotal-*
scéith foraib. Es hat[2]) Egerton 1782 (Brit. M.) fol. 88 *leni*
fotairindiu cotanglun ocus fotalsceth foruib; H. 1. 14 (Trinity
Coll. D.) p. 3, 12 *leni fotarindiu cotanglua 7 fotal sceth foraib*;
endlich Egerton 114 (wohl Abschrift von Egert. 1782) S. 3 *leni*
fotharrindiu cotanglun acas fotalsceth foraibh. Die Überein-

---

[1]) Gewöhnlich steht nur *hiforcepul* (LU. 93 a 29; 133 b 26; 70 a 36; 78 a 3
= LL. 76 a 25; LL. 267 a 35; 90 a 33. 45); LL. 266 b 13 hat zu *iforcipul* die
Glosse *ifilliud* und LL. 78 b 4 steht *ifilliud*, wo LU. (70 a 36) hat *hiforcebul*.
[2]). Die nach LU. und LL. ältesten Hss. bis zum 15. Jahrhundert —
H. 2. 16, T. C. D. (Yellow Book of Lecan), H. 2. 17, T. C. D. und Egert. 93
Brit. Mus. — sind leider alle im Anfang fragmentarisch. Die Mitteilungen
aus den Hss. des Trinity College verdanke ich Prof. Atkinsons Freundlichkeit.

stimmung ist also in dem von LL. entscheidend abweichenden Punkte in der Überlieferung der Rezension LU. vollkommen.

Betrachtet man nun die beiden gegebenen Partien LL. 55 a 46 bis 55 b 10 = LU. 55 a 12 — 26 und zieht das Verhältnis der beiden Rezensionen LL. und LU. in allen Stellen, in denen sie im Gange der Erzählung zusammen gehen, mit in Betracht, so scheinen mir 3 Punkte sicher: 1. LU. und LL. gehen trotz mancherlei Abweichungen in Einzelheiten in der Stelle LU. 55 a 12 — 26 = LL. 55 a 46 — 55 b 10 auf eine gemeinsame Quelle zurück; 2. LU. ist altertümlicher und wird im grossen und ganzen das Ursprüngliche besser gewahrt haben; 3. dem *léni fothairinniuth* (*fotairindiu*) in LU.-Rezension entspricht *lénti ... batórniud* in LL. Was den zweiten Punkt anlangt, so fällt namentlich das Verhältnis der LL.-Rezension zur LU.-Rezension in zahlreichen anderen Stellen mit ins Gewicht, die klar zeigen, dass der Text der LL.-Rezension vielfach nur mittelirische Umgestaltung, manchmal Verunstaltung eines altirischen Textes ist, wie er in LU. noch vorliegt. Zwei Belege seien aus Dutzenden heraus gegriffen für solche, die mit dem Verhältnis der beiden Texte nicht näher vertraut sind. In dem Gedicht der Seherin Fedelmid entspricht der Zeile LU. 56 a 8

Doich lim isse dodobsaig Cuchulaind mac Sualdaim

in LL. 56 a 47 folgende Zeile:

Donchomlund isé farsaig Cuchulaind mac Sualdaim.

Hier ist nicht nur *farsaig* eine offenkundige mittelirische Umgestaltung des altirischen *dodobsaig*, sondern es ist bei einer genauen Betrachtung des Zusammenhangs auch *donchomlund* nach dem vorangehenden *donchath* vergröbernd eingetreten für *doich lim*, um die fehlende Silbe zu ersetzen. Als zweiter Beleg diene LL. 58 a 32 = LU. 57 a 39. Sualdam fragt Cuchulinn, was er in der Zwischenzeit, während Sualdam nach Ulster mit Warnungen geht, machen werde: *Amécensa tocht inherus inalta Feidilmthi noichruthaige fodess co Temraig* 'ich muss gehen zum Stelldichein der Dienerin der Feidilmid nóichruthach südlich nach Tara' erwidert Cuchulinn; als Sualdam wegen der Unzweckmässigkeit im Augenblick Vorstellungen erhebt, schneidet ihm Cuchulinn das Wort ab mit *Ammecensa tra techt* 'ich muss nun einmal gehen' (LL. 58 a 37). Wir haben also zweimal kurz hinter einander *amécensa* für 'ich muss', wie man weder im Altirischen, noch Mittelirischen noch Neuirischen sagen

kann. Was zu Grunde liegt, ist jedem mit dem Altirischen
vertrauten klar: prätonische Kopula und Substantiv oder Adjektiv
wird im Altirischen hinsichtlich der Infigierung von Pronomina
behandelt wie eine komponierte Verbalform in Orthotonese (ZE.
346, 13 ff.); wie also gleichwertig mit *dobèir dom* ist *dombèir*
so mit *isécen dom* 'est-necessitas mihi' gleichwertig *issumécen*
'est-mihi-necessitas', ebenso dem negativen *niécen dom* gleichwertig *nimécen*, wie durch altir. *issumecen precept armetiuth*
'es ist mir Notwendigkeit predigen wegen meiner Kleidung'
(Wb. 10 d 25) und *nibécen lóg* 'nicht (ist) euch Notwendigkeit
Löhnung' (Wb. 16 c 17) belegt wird. Die schriftliche Aufzeichnung der Táin bó Cualnge geht nun in eine Zeit zurück,
in der derartige Infigierungen noch ganz gewöhnlich waren; dies
beweist nicht nur der Text in LU. (*isimégen tra* LU. 73 b 13),
sondern auch in LL. liegen noch Zeugnisse vor, die der Umgestaltung des Redaktors nicht zum Opfer gefallen sind; *isa-
mecensa tra imbarach comrac fri Coinculaind* 'es ist mir eine
Notwendigkeit nun morgen Kampf gegen Cuchulinn' LL. 71 b 50;
maditecen 'wenn ist dir Notwendigkeit' LL. 83 b 41; *indat-
mebairsiu iter* 'num tibi memoria omnino?' fragt Fer Diad
(LL. 84 a 46) und Cuchulinn antwortet *isammmebair ám écin*
'est mihi memoria certo' (LL. 84 a 48). Es kann daher auch
a priori gar kein Zweifel sein, was an den beiden Stellen
LL. 58 a 32. 37 für *amécensa techt* ursprünglich stand, nämlich
isumécensa techt, und so bietet auch LU. thatsächlich noch
an der in Rede stehenden Stelle *isimécensa techt indáil
Fedelma nóichride .i. indáil ahinailte* 'es ist mir Notwendigkeit
zu gehen zum Stelldichein der Fedilm nóichride d. h. zum Stelldichein ihrer Dienerin' LU. 57 a 39. Um zu verstehen, wie der
Redaktor der LL.-Rezension zu seinem *amécensa* kam, muss
man neben den Umstand, dass *isamécensa* für ihn obsolet und
grammatisch — nicht dem Sinne nach — unverständlich war,
hinzunehmen, dass die Emphasierung nicht nur von Wörtern,
sondern auch von Satzteilen durch vorangestelltes *is* 'est' gewöhnlich war wie *isatlomthru* 'du bist ganz elend' LL. 85 b 6
für *atlomthru* oder *isatscítha arneich* 7 *itmertnig arnaraid* 'es
sind müde unsere Rosse und es sind schwach unsere Wagen-
lenker' LL. 85, 20 für *itscítha arneich* etc. So wird er denn
auch in dem grammatisch unklar gewordenen *isumecensa* (*isa-
mecensa*) *techt* mit dem Sinn 'ich bin gezwungen zu gehen' das

is als emphatisierend gefasst und in dem *am* die erste Sing. des Verb substantiv 'ich bin' gesehen und eine Flexion *am écensa* 'ich muss', *at écensu* 'du musst' gefolgert haben, obwohl ein Adjektiv *écen* nie im Irischen existiert hat. Es liegt also nicht eine korrekte Umgestaltung des altirischen Textes ins Mittelirische in dieser Stelle vor, sondern eine auf halbem Wege stehen gebliebene Verunstaltung des alten Textes, wie wir sie auf anderen Sprachgebieten beim Volkslied vielfach beobachten können.

Unter diese Gesichtspunkte muss man nun *lénti ... batórniud* LL. 55 a 48 = *léni fothairinniuth* LU. 55 a 14 rücken, dazu aber noch eine weitere Eigenheit des Redaktors der LL.-Rezension hinzunehmen. Für ihn waren schon wie heutigen Tages überall in Irland in der gesprochenen Sprache die vortonigen Silben *do, ro, fo, no, at, as, ar* etc. soweit reduziert, dass es schwer fiel oder unmöglich war, sie mit dem Ohr genau zu unterscheiden und aus der Aussprache ihren ursprünglichen Lautwert festzustellen, infolgedessen er sie nicht nur gelegentlich, sondern sehr oft durcheinander wirft, also *ra* für *do* und *as, fo* für *do, da* und *ra* für *at* u. a. m. schreibt, wie ich schon Kuhns Ztschr. 30, 72 mit Anm. 2 und 32, 216 bemerkt habe. Die Vorführung weiteren Materials kann ich mir ersparen, da Herr Quiggin demnächst in seiner Dissertation das gesamte Material der LL.-Rezension der Táin bó Cualnge vorlegen wird.[1]) Hier genügt es darauf hinzuweisen, dass der Redaktor der LL.-Rezension es besonders liebt *ba-* für *fo-, do-, ro-* zu schreiben: so hat er *b a snetarraid* LL. 73 a 51 zu dem bekannten *doetarraid, tetarraid*, wo in der entsprechenden Stelle in LU. 70 b 18 *that-*

---

[1]) Bei der Abneigung derartige Erscheinungen des gesprochenen Irisch bis ins 12. Jahrh. hinauf reichen zu lassen, möchte ich darauf hinweisen, dass wir ganz ähnliche Erscheinungen schon im frühen Mittelenglisch, ja schon im Altenglischen vorfinden. In letzterem schon *a-* für unbetontes *ar-* (= ahd. *ur, er*), *on-, of-, af-*; in mittelengl. Adverbien (altengl. *a-bútan*) *a high* = *on high, a night* = *on niht; a front* = *in front, a cross* = *in cross, a shore* = *on shore, alate* = *of late, akin* = *of kin* etc. (s. Franz, Shakespeare-Grammatik § 92 ff.). Die altir. *oc tócbáil* und *do thócbáil* sind neugälisch *a tógail* und *a thógail*, ebenso im Neuir., obwohl man hier noch *ag tógail* und *do thógail* schreibt! Für Shakespeares *aboard, afire, afoot* etc. schreibt man heute lieber *on board, on fire, on foot*. In dem sogenannten engl. Gerundium *a fishing* ist *a* (ə) aus *on* entstanden wie in dem gälischen *a togail* aus *oc*.

sächlich *do snetarraid* steht; *ba cóistis* LL. 69 b 28 zu *dochuaid*,
wo wieder LU. 65 a 42 hat *do choestis*; *obariachtatar* LL. 73 b 37
für *odoriachtatar*; in vollständig parallelen Stellen steht *focherd-
setar aclessrada uathaib illamaib anarad* LL. 84 b 11 = *ba-
cheirdset anairm uathu illamaib anarad* LL. 84 b 28 und
bacheird clessrada ána LL. 86 a 21 = *focheird clesrada ána*
LL. 86 a 38; ebenso *badrí* LL. 102 a 53 = *fothrí* 102 a 38; besonders lehrreich sind Stellen wie *léine glégel chulpatach badergintliud dodergór friagelchness* 'ein ganz weisses mit Kapuze
versehenes Hemd rot durchwoben (*fo-dergintliud*) von rotem
Golde auf seiner weissen Haut' LL. 97 a 29 (ebenso 97 a 39) verglichen mit *fodergintlaid* LU. 55 a 22, oder gar *léne desrólríg
badergintliud dedergór frigelchness* LL. 100 a 5 = *léne desrólríg madergfilliud dedergór frigelchness* LL. 98 b 24, wo *badergintliud* und *madergfilliud* für *fodergintlaid* dieselbe Aussprache wiedergeben. Ich denke, dass *batóirniud* LL. 55 a 48 für
fothairinniud LU. 55 a 14, soweit der Wandel von *ba* für *fo* in
Betracht kommt, damit hinreichend klar gestellt ist.

Rekapitulieren wir die Erörterungen von Seite 289 bis
hierher, so ergiebt sich: 1. die Lesart *badur niamhdha* (*bhadar
a niamhdha*) der jungen Hss. der LL.-Rezension ist gegenüber
dem *batórniud* der 600 Jahre älteren LL. ein wertloser Besserungs-
versuch; 2. *batórniud* LL. 55 a 48 ist ein mittelirischer Besserungs-
versuch oder Wiedergabe einer älteren Form, die mit *fo-* begann
wie *fothairinniuth* LU. 55 a 14. Ehe ich mich nun den weiteren
Differenzen zwischen LU. und LL. in der Stelle zuwende, ist es
zuerst nötig zu prüfen, ob in dem *fothairinniuth* von LU. das
Original unverdorben vorliegt, und was die Bedeutung ist.

Rein für sich betrachtet giebt die Stelle LU. 55 a 14 *léini
fothairinniuth cotanglun* von altirischem Standpunkt aus einen
leidlichen Sinn. Wir haben Beda Carlsruh. 33 d 4 die Glosse
intairinnud zu lat. *dejectio*. Dies altir. *tairinnud* entspricht
mittelir. *tairniud* (LL. 284 b 29; Windisch, Ir. Texte II, 1, S. 5,
Z. 63), Verbalnomen zu dem sehr gebräuchlichen Verb mittelir.
tairnim trans. 'niederdrücken, herunter lassen' und intr. 'sich
niederlassen, herunter fallen' (LL. 263 b 16; LU. 43 a 34; Ir.
Texte II, 1, S. 59, Z. 1921 *rotheraind Antenoir for a glúinib*; Rev.
Celt. 10, 226, Z. 185 *na tairinnfit*). Es könnte demnach *léini
fothairinniuth cotanglun* wohl bedeuten 'ein Hemd herabfallend
(sich herab erstreckend) bis zum Knie.' Die Frage ist nur, ob

es wahrscheinlich ist, dass so etwas ursprünglich an dieser
Stelle gestanden hat, und da fordert mancherlei zu Zweifel
heraus. Vergleicht man die Schilderung der 3 Scharen, so sieht
man, dass sowohl in LL. wie LU. ein Parallelismus beabsichtigt
ist, der in LU. auch dahin geht, dass an allen drei Stellen
bei den Hemden (Untergewand) ein Zusatz· steht: 1. *léini
fothairinniuth cotaṅglún*, 2. *lénti condercintliud cohorcnib sís*,
3. *lénte culpatacha fodérggintṡlaid cotraigthe.* Der Zusatz ist
in der Schilderung der zweiten und dritten Schar ganz klar:
indṡlaid, intlaid, inlaid ist der 'Einschlag' im Gewebe, also
'Hemden mit rotem Einschlag' (vgl. LU. 68 a 11; 68 b 9; 78 a 4;
94 a 19. 28; 96 a 20; LL. 97 a 29. 39; 100 a 5 u. s. w.; Windisch
Wb. S. 642 s. *inliud*, Ir. Texte III, 1, S. 264, Anm. 31). Bei dem
offenkundigen Parallelismus der drei Stellen drängt sich doch
die Vermutung auf, dass *fothairinniuth* an erster Stelle aus
fothair-intliud oder *fothair-indliud* entstellt ist, also eine ein
Adjektiv vertretende Apposition zu *léne* da stand, wie in den
beiden anderen Stellen. Diese Vermutung bekommt dadurch
Stütze, dass das in der Überlieferung von LU. in *fothairinniuth*
fehlende *l* in einem anderen ganz nahe dabei stehenden Worte
in LU. anscheinend zu viel ist. Die Schilderung fährt nämlich
direkt fort *ocus fotalscéith foraib* 'und *fotal*-Schilde auf ihnen
(ihren Schultern)'. Was soll ein *fotalsciath* sein? Ein Kompositum
fotalbéim '*fotal*-Schlag' findet sich in der Táin bó Cualnge von
LL. öfters (72 a 22; 87 a 17; 63 a 5), dessen prägnante Bedeutung
in der erst genannten Stelle klar ist. Cuchulinn will den Kampf
mit dem sich herausfordernd betragenden Etarcomal vermeiden,
da er ihn, als unter Fergus Schutz stehend, nicht verletzen will;
als aber Etarcomal. immer unverschämter wird, sieht sich
Cuchulinn gezwungen, ihm einen Denkzettel zu geben: *tuc
Cuchulainn fotalbéim dó gorothesc infót bói fobund achossi
conidtarla bolcfæn isafót forabroind* 'Cuchulinn versetzte ihm
einen *fotal*-Schlag, sodass er den Rasen (die Erde), welche unter
seiner Fusssohle war, wegschnitt, sodass er ausgestreckt wie ein
Sack auf dem Rücken lag[1]) und sein Rasen auf seinem Bauch'.

---

[1]) Zu *faen, foen* vergleiche K. Meyer, Aislinge maic Conglinne S. 137
zu 24, 19 und LU. 17 a 38; 38 a 36; 76 b 16; 89 a 19; 91 b 7; LL. 280 b 42;
100 b 25. 30; 102 b 36. 43; 79 b 53; 263 b 48. In LU. heisst es an der betreffenden Stelle *benaid Cúchulaind infót bai fochossaib cotorchair inalige* 7
afót foratairr 'Cuchulinn schnitt die Erde unter den Füssen weg, sodass er

Als Etarcomal davon keine Warnung nahm, versetzte ihm
Cuchulinn einen 'mächtigen *fœbar*-Schlag', mit dem er ihm das
Haar von Nackengrube bis Stirn und von einem Ohr bis andern
glatt abrasierte, ohne ihm auch nur eine blutige Schramme zu-
zufügen; da Etarcomal auch jetzt noch dringend nach ernstlichem
Kampf verlangte, versetzte ihm Cuchulinn einen *muadal-* (Mittel-)
Schlag, der den Etarcomal in die Gegend des Nabels (*imbliu*)
tötlich traf. Hier ist neben dem Schlag, der die Haare wegschnitt und neben dem den Nabel treffenden Schlag offenbar
fotalbéim ein gegen die unteren Extremitäten gerichteter Schlag.
Hierein fügt sich die Stelle LL. 63 a 5 sehr schön, wo gesagt ist,
dass der wütende kleine Cuchulinn die Knappen von Emain
dothulbemmennaib 7 *muadbemmennaib* 7 *fotal(bemmennaib)* 'mit
Stirnschlägen, Mitte-Schlägen[1]) und *fotal*-Schlägen' traktierte.
Endlich wird LL. 87 a 17 von den *bráthbalcbemmennaib* 7 *fótal-
bemmennaib* 7 *muadalbemmennaib* 'den todbringenden wuchtigen
Schlägen und den Erdschlägen[2]) und den Mittelschlägen' Fer
Diads gesprochen.   Eine ungezwungene Deutung von '*fotal*-
Schild' giebt sich nach der in den angeführten Stellen vorliegenden Bedeutung von *fotal* nicht.   Sieht man sich nun in
den Sagentexten nach Schildarten um, so treffen wir in der zur
Diskussion stehenden Stelle die dritte Schar *cromscéith* 'Rundschilde' tragen (LU. 55 a 24); bei der Musterung der Ulster-
streitkräfte trägt Eogan mac Durthachta einen *cromsciath* 'Rundschild' (LL. 98 a 5) und der Führer einer anderen Schar einen
crundsciath 'Rundschild' (LL. 98 a 48), ebenso Fergus mac Róig
einen 'Rundschild' (*cromsciath* LU. 68 b 9); als Cuchulinn und
Fer Diad am dritten Tage zum ernsten Schwertkampf übergehen, nimmt jeder von ihnen einen *leborsciath lánmór* 'sehr
grossen Langschild' (LL. 85 b 29).   Kurz 'Rundschilde' und
'Langschilde' sind die beiden Schildtypen in der ir. Heldensage

---

hinfallend zum Liegen kam und seine (unter ihm weggeschnittene) Erde auf
den unteren Teil seines Bauches' (LU. 69 a 1).

[1]) In der Hs. stehen unter *be* in *muadbemmennaib* Punkte und ebenso
unter *al* in *fotalbemmennaib*, was wohl andeuten soll, das für *muadbemmennaib*
zu korrigieren ist *muadalbemmennaib*, was auch noch LL. 87 a 17 steht.

[2]) Man beachte, dass hier *fótal-* in der Hs. ein Längezeichen trägt,
weil man offenbar das Wort zu *fót* zog wie *muadal* zu *muad* 'Mitte'.
Welche Art Haartracht *fotolberrad coclais addchúlad for cachfir dib* LU. 86 a 3
genannt wird, ist mir unklar.

(s. O'Curry, Manners and Customs I, S. CCCCLXIV ff.). Da nun
die dritte Schar 'Rundschilde' trägt, da *fota* das gewöhnliche
alt- und mittelir. Adjekt. für 'lang' ist, und *fotal-* in *fotalscéith*
keinen rechten Sinn giebt, wie wir sahen, so liegt es doch ungemein nahe, in LU. 55 a 15 zu schreiben *fotascéith* 'Langschilde' für *fotalscéith* der Überlieferung. Dann erhalten wir
das *l*, welches wahrscheinlich in einem kurz vorhergehenden
Wort derselben Stelle fehlt, wie wir S. 295 sahen. Die Entstehung der Verderbnis lässt sich leicht verstehen durch die Annahme, dass in einem Archetypus des Textes ungefähr so stand:

> *léini fothairindiud co*
> *tanglún* 7 *fotascéith for*

und das ausgelassene *l* zwischen beide Zeilen nachträglich zu-
gefügt war. Ein Abschreiber, dem das *fotalbéim* bekannt war,
zog mechanisch das *l* zur unteren Zeile und schrieb *fotalscéith*.

Haben wir nunmehr mit *léini fothairindliud cotanglún* 7
fotascéith forru die ursprüngliche Lesart endgültig gewonnen?
Ich glaube nicht. Es ist, wenn der Gedankengang von S. 294
an richtig ist, doch *léini fothairinniuth cotanglún* 'ein Hemd
herabfallend bis zum Knie' ein Versuch eines Schreibers in den
nach Wegfall des *l* in *-indliud* unverständlich gewordenen Zusatz
zu *léne* einen Sinn zu bringen ohne Rücksicht auf den Parallelismus in der Schilderung der beiden anderen Gruppen. Es
ist daher wahrscheinlich, dass in *fothairinniuth* noch eine weitere
Änderung, wie sie nach irischer Aussprache möglich war —
vgl. *badergintliud* LL. 100 a 5 und *madergfilliud* LL. 98 b 24 für
fodergintlaid —, vorgenommen ist. Eine Vermutung, welche
Änderung eingetreten ist, liegt sehr nahe. Wie die dritte Schar
Hemd mit rotem Einschlag (*dergintliud*) und Rundschild trägt,
so die erste Hemd mit braunem Einschlag (*odor-* oder *odarintliud*)
und Langschild. Es wären demnach die ursprünglichen Lesarten
fodorintliud (*fodorindliud*) und *fotascéith* gewesen, woraus durch
mechanische Versehen in der oben vermuteten Weise *fodorindiud*
und *fotalscéith* entstanden; ersteres wurde in einer Hs., auf der
die gesamte Überlieferung der sogenannten LU.-Rezension zurück
geht, zu *fothairinniuth* umgestaltet, um einen Sinn in die Stelle
zu bringen.

Für die von S. 295 ff. angestellte Erwägung, dass in dem
fothairinniuth von LU., obwohl es einen leidlichen Sinn giebt,

nicht das Original der Stelle unverdorben vorliegt, kann man auch die Lesart von LL. anführen, dessen *batóirniud* einerseits von dem *fothairinniuth* in LU. nicht getrennt werden kann, wie wir S. 291 ff. sahen, und die doch einerseits als Ganzes (*lénti órśnaith friacnessaib batórniud dodergór*) schwer aus LU. (*léini fothairinniuth cotanglún*) verständlich ist, wenn dies das Original darbietet. Anders steht dies, wenn LU. selbst, wie angenommen, nur eine Besserung eines mechanischen Versehens in einem Archetypus repräsentiert. Es kann und wird die Umgestaltung von LL. parallel mit der von LU. bei demselben Versehen einsetzen, da ja die LL.-Rezension weder auf Handschrift LU. sich aufbaut noch auf der Vorlage dieses kontaminierten Textes. Dann aber lässt sich für die Abweichung von LL. als Ganzes die Möglichkeit einer Erklärung gewinnen. Ein so alter Text wie die Táin bó Cualnge war schon im 11. Jahrhundert in Bezug auf viele alte Wörter und Formen in Irland unverständlich, wie die vielen in LU. als Glossen übergeschriebenen Erklärungsversuche zeigen. Für den Text in LL. ist es nun charakteristisch, dass in zahlreichen Stellen derartige Glosseme einer vorausgehenden Handschrift einfach im Text neben den durch sie zu erklärenden Wörtern und Formen stehen. Ich führe einiges an. Wenn es LL. 74 a 35 ff. heisst *isandsin tincais Cuchulaind fair isinund ón 7 nofégand ocus isandsin torgaib 7 tarlaic nahocht nubla* etc., so kann über das Verhältnis von *isinund ón 7 nofégand* zu den vorhergehenden Worten (*isandsin tincais*) kein Zweifel bestehen. Ebensowenig LL. 69 a 14, wo es von dem wütend angestürmt kommenden Dond Cualnge heisst *ocus foclassa búrach dó isinundsón 7 focheird úir daluib taris* 'und er wühlte sich (mit den Füssen) eine Grube, es ist dasselbe wie er warf die Erde mit seinen Füssen über sich.'[1] Auch LL. 57 a 43 *Atá ní ar Fergus nibatecra indfirsin isinund ón 7 ni deceltar dam* können die Worte von *isinund* an nur Glossen sein, zumal wenn man LU. 56 b 45 hinzunimmt.

Etwas anderer Art, aber darum nicht weniger bezeichnend

---

[1] LU. hat an der betreffenden Stelle (64 b 45) einfach *ocus ocechlaid búrach* 'und er wühlte auf eine Grube'; man vergleiche noch LL. 103 b 51 und 101 a 52 (*claidet búrach*) sowie neug. *búrach* 'searching or turning up the earth, delving, digging', *búraich* 'dig lightly or irregularly'; zu *daluib* vgl. altir. *sal no lue* gl. zu *calx* Pr. Sg. 50 a 20 und LU. 19 b 19. 20. LL. 79 a 35; 90 b 48. 49.

und sicher, sind andere Stellen von LL. Cuchulinn gerät in eine Wutverzerrung[1]) *gomba metithir rafomóir na rafer mara inmilid mórchalma* 'sodass der sehr tapfere Krieger so gross wurde wie ein *fomóir* (Riese) oder ein Mann des Meeres' (*fer mara*) LL. 86 b 36 ff. Wer die Vorstellungen der irischen Sage von den *fomóir* kennt und sich erinnert, dass in demselben Sagentext die Wörter *fomóir — fomórach* und *allmuir — allmarach* synonym verwendet werden (cf. LL. 254 a 36; 254 b 5. 51; 255 b 21. 23. 43; 256 a 41. 42; 256 b 5. 41; 257 b 27; 259 a 7 mit 254 b 33. 38), kann nicht zweifeln, dass in der Stelle LL. 86 b 37 *na rafer mara* ursprünglich nur Glossem zu *rafomóir* war. — Als Nathcrantail dem Cuchulinn entgegen tritt, dünkt er sich seines Sieges so sicher, dass er überhaupt keine Waffen mitnimmt *acht tri nói bera culind até fuachta follscaide forloiscthi* 'ausser dreimal 9 Stechpalmenspiesse, die *fuachta, follscaide, forloiscthi* waren' LL. 72 b 28. An einer anderen Stelle, wo geschildert ist, wie Cuchulinn einen frischgehauenen Schoss mit 4 Gabeln so zubereitet, dass er ihn in die Erde schleudern kann, wird die Zubereitung gegeben mit den Worten *rosfuacha 7 rosfallsce* LL. 59, 33; zu diesen beiden Verbalformen sind *fuachta* und *follscaide* in erster Stelle Participia Perf. Passivi. Was nun das letztere Wort (*follscaide*) anlangt, so findet sich dasselbe auch noch Fis Adamnáin (LU. 29 b 28), wo der ganze Zusammenhang keinen Zweifel lässt, dass es das r e g u l ä r e Particip Perf. zu

---

[1]) Die ir. Bezeichnung ist *riastrad*; das Verbum ist *riastraim*, der in Wut geratene Cuchulinn heisst *inriastarthe* (LU. 57 a 25; 81 a 44; 70 a 18; 72 a 28; 73 b 42; 74 a 8 u. o.). Wie dem ir. *briathraim* entspricht kymr. *brwydraf* und ir. *criathraim* ein kymr. *crwydraf*, so dem ir. *riastraim* Laut für Laut *rhwystraf*. Im Kymr. bedeutet *rhwystr* 'Hindernis' und *rhwystro* 'ein Hindernis in den Weg legen', und dies ist meines Erachtens auch die ursprüngliche Bedeutung von ir. *riastraim, riastrad*. Cuchulinn gerät in seine Wutverzerrungen, wenn ihm ein anscheinend unüberwindliches H i n d e r n i s im Wege stand, wenn er infolge eines Hindernisses im Vorhaben nicht ausführen konnte (vgl. LU. 103 b 1) oder wenn ein mächtiger Gegner ihn am Siege hinderte: *in riastarthe* ist 'der (in Ausführung seiner Absicht) gehinderte Cuchulinn' und dann 'der (infolgedessen) in Wutverzerrung geratene'. Diese sekundäre Bedeutung übertrug sich dann auf die anderen Formen im Irischen und verdrängte die ursprüngliche ganz, wie analoge Vorgänge für Kymrisch und Irisch in Kuhns Ztschr. 36, 447—454 von mir nachgewiesen sind. Vielleicht darf man die reguläre Konstruktion *riastartha immi, roriastrad immi* noch aus der Grundbedeutung des Verbs erklären 'es wurde ein Hindernis ihm bereitet' = 'er geriet in Wutverzerrung'.

foloscim oder vielleicht *forloscim* 'ich brenne, verbrenne' ist, wie denn auch LBr. 255 a 28 an der Stelle *foloisthi* (l. *foloiscthi*), also die nach den orthotonierten Formen restituierte Form des Part. Perf. hat. Nehmen wir dazu noch, dass Cuchulinns Kunststückspeer heisst *bunsach bunloscthe* 'ein am unteren Ende gebrannter Schoss' (LL. 62 a 48), so ist klar, was *follscaide* als Beiwort zu *bir culind* 'dem Stechpalmenspiess' sagen will: er war mangels anderer Instrumente durch Anbrennen oder Ansengen in primitiver Weise zugestutzt oder eben gemacht worden. Es ist aber auch klar, dass das LL. 72 b 28 neben *follscaide* stehende weitere Epithet *forloiscthe* nicht nur genau dasselbe aussagt, sondern wahrscheinlich nur die auch Ml. 31 c 28 vorkommende restituierte Form für das durch Wirkung der Lautgesetze etymologisch undurchsichtig gewordene *follscaide* ist. Dann ergiebt sich der Schluss von selbst, dass *forloiscthe* nur ein in den Text geratenes Glossem ist. In der That liest denn auch LU. 69 b 11 einfach *berid nói mbera culind fuachta follscaidi laiss*, also ohne *forloiscthi*.[1]) — Eine weitere ganz gleiche Stelle findet sich LL. 84 b 19 = 84 b 15: Cuchulinn und Ferdiad kämpfen mit *slegaib snaitti snasta slemunchruaidi*. Zu dem kymr. *naddu* 'schnitzen, behauen, von Holz und Stein' entsprechenden ir. *snadim* gehört regulär als Nom. verbale mit Suffix *tu*: mittelir. *snass* 'das Behauen, Beschneiden' (LL. 68 a 45 *snass 7 slemnugud*); das Part. Perf. Pass. muss *snasse* lauten, wie es LU. 23 b 29 (*bunsaig snaisi* 'einen abgeschälten Zweig') vorkommt; mit sekundärer Wiedereinführung des *t*, wofür wir Belege in altir. *frescastu, imcasti, tinfesti* (Windisch, Gramm. § 357. 361 b) haben, entspricht *snaste* 'geschnitzt, geglättet', wie es in den beiden in Rede stehenden Stellen und in dem neuir. Adjektiv *snasta* 'ornamental, dainty, neat, elegant, brave' vorliegt. Auch dies *snaste*, worin die in dem regulären alten *snasse* eingetretenen Lautgesetze wenigstens hinsichtlich des Anlautes des Suffixes wieder rückgängig gemacht sind, wurde in jüngerer Zeit, als im Präsensstamm starke und schwache Konjugation zusammenfielen, nicht mehr als reguläres Particip Perfekti zu *snaidim* gefühlt; wie zu *foidim* ein *foitte* (*remfoite*), zu *cathim* ein *catte*,

---

[1]) Yellow Book of Lecan, das ebenfalls LU.-Rezension bietet, hat *berid noi mbera culind fuaighthe* (gebessert aus *fuigthe*) *follscaithi lais* (29 a 21), also gleichfalls kein *forloiscthe*.

so trat zu *snaidim* scheinbar regulär *snaitte*, wie ja die gäl.
Wörterbücher ein *snaidhte* 'cut down, hewn, dressed as a stick'
neben *snaidh* 'v. reduce by cutting with a knife, hew stones'
haben. Dass in den beiden angeführten Stellen (*slegaib snaitti
snasta slemunchruadi*) das *snaitte* ursprünglich nur ein übergeschriebenes Glossem war zu dem seiner Bedeutung nach ver-
standenen aber nach seiner Bildung als Partic. Perf. Pass. unklar
gewordenen *snasta*, scheint mir keinem Zweifel zu unterliegen. —
In LL. 98 b 50 führen die Haken oder Heften (*stuaga*), mit denen
das blaue Untergewand (Hemd) eines Kriegers über Scham-
gegend und Brust zusammengehalten ist, mehrere Beiwörter: *go
stuagaib fíthi figthi féta findruini*. Hier ist *figthe* (d. h. *fighthe*)
klar das Partic. Perf. Pass. von *figim* (d. h. *fighim*) 'ich webe',
und seine Aussprache kann nur *fíhe* gewesen sein, was auch
orthographisch mit *fíthe* wiedergegeben werden kann. Ich denke
nach dem, was von S. 298 an vorgeführt ist, liegt die Annahme
an der Hand, dass in einer älteren Hs. der LL.-Rezension im
Text nur stand *costuagaib fíthi féta findruini* und dass über
fíthi ein *figthi* übergeschrieben war, wie LL. 72 b 28 über *follscaide* ein *forloiscthe*, um anzudeuten, dass dies *fíthi* für *figthi*
stehe und 'gewebt' bedeute.

Wir lernen also aus den angeführten Stellen, die sich noch
vermehren lassen, für LL. Folgendes. Es ging eine Überlieferung
voraus, die in zahlreichen Stellen, wo ein Verständnis des Sinnes
wirklich oder traditionell vorhanden war, wo aber die Wörter
und Formen, sei es absolut oder durch Lautgesetze oder Entstellungen undurchsichtig geworden waren, etymologisch durch-
sichtige Sacherklärungen übergeschrieben hatte, die im Verlauf
bei weiteren Abschriften oder Bearbeitungen ein integrierender
Teil des Textes neben den zu erklärenden Wörtern wurden.
Wenden wir dies auf das Verhältnis von LL. 55 a 48 zu LU. 55 a 14
an im Lichte der S. 291—297 gewonnenen Ergebnisse, so können
wir das *lénti órsnaith friacnessaib batórniud dodergór* in LL.
dafür anführen, dass in dem einen leidlichen Sinn ergebenden
léini fothairinniuth cotanglun in LU. das Original nicht erhalten
ist, sondern eine Besserung einer S. 294—297 erklärten Entstellung bietet. Setzt nämlich Rezension LL. mit seinem *batórniud* bei der Lesung der LU.-Rezension *fothairinniuth* ein, dann
bietet sich, wie schon S. 298 bemerkt ist, keine Möglichkeit oder
Wahrscheinlichkeit, die Gesamtabweichungen von LL. an der

Stelle zu erklären; wohl aber bietet sich eine solche Möglichkeit
durch den S. 298—301 gewonnenen Gesichtspunkt, wenn LL.
nicht bei der Lesung unserer LU.-Rezension, sondern bei der
dieser Besserung vorausgehenden Entstellung *fodorindiud einsetzt. Dass in dem verderbten und wie es dastand unverständlichen léne *fodorindiud in der unserer LL.-Rezension vorausgehenden Überlieferung ein Redaktor, der entweder ein tra-
ditionelles Verständnis der Stelle besass oder aus Vergleich mit
dem Zusatz zum Hemd bei der zweiten und dritten Schar einen
Sinn hineinlegte, als Erklärung órsnaith überschrieb, und dass
dies Glossem im weiteren Verlauf in den Text geriet — also
ein léne órsnaith *fodorindiud (dodergór) cotanglún entstand —,
hat in den S. 298—301 erörterten Stellen von LL. seine Entsprechungen. Ein solches übergeschriebenes órsnaith verbunden
mit léne giebt aber in der That den Sinn des ursprünglich an
der Stelle stehenden *fodorindliud in Verbindung mit léne gut
wieder. Ob der Zusatz dodergór, der charakteristischer Weise
in LL. überall bei vorhergehendem fodergintliud beigefügt ist —
s. S. 294 einige Belege — von demselben Schreiber oder Redaktor
herrührt, der órsnaith übersetzte, also letzteres genauer *fodorindiud dodergór glossieren sollte, oder ob der Zusatz später
eintrat als eine Folge des glossierenden órsnaith, lässt sich nicht
ausmachen; ebenso wenig, ob die weitere Umgestaltung der
Stelle — Weglassung der Länge des Hemdes und Zusatz friacnessaib — von dem Redaktor herrührt, der hier wie an anderen
Stellen die Glosseme in den Text aufnahm, oder ob es die Arbeit
des Mannes ist, der aus *fodorindiud das der Überlieferung der
LL.-Rezension zu Grunde liegende batórniud schuf. Die Reihenfolge derartiger vor der Überlieferung liegender Umgestaltungen
können wir ja überhaupt selten feststellen. Es ist dies hier
auch nur ganz nebensächlich neben der Erkenntnis, dass einerseits fothairinniuth der LU.-Rezension und batórniud der LL.-
Rezension nicht von einander zu trennen sind, und dass andererseits das leidlich verständliche léini fothairinniuth cotanglún nicht
der Ausgangspunkt sein kann, von dem wir die Zusätze órsnaith
und dodérgor in LL. verstehen können, sondern dass wir zu
letzterem Zwecke von einer durch die LU.-Rezension selbst
nahegelegten (s. S. 295—297) Entstellung eines ursprünglichen
léne *fodorintliud ausgehen müssen. Von diesem rekonstruierten
léne (lénte) *fodorintliud — entsprechend dem lénte condercintliud

bei der zweiten und *lénte fodergintslaid* bei der dritten Schar
— bis zu *leinte* (*leintibh*) *orsnaithe ... bhadar a niamdha* (*badur niamhdha*) *do deargor* der jungen Repräsentanten der LL.-Rezension (s. S. 288) ist allerdings ein weiter Weg, den wir nur teilweise überblicken.

Greifswald.   H. ZIMMER.

SUR LES MOTS BRETONS *GET* (*A*),
GANT, RAK, MEURBET, A, DA, DOUAREN.

———

1. Le vannetais *get* combien, ordinairement *get a, ged a* que de, sous-dialecte de Batz (Loire-Inférieure) *ked a* est expliqué *Mémoires de la Société de linguistique de Paris* X, 330—332, cf. ici-même II, 494, 495, comme extrait de **naket, naget,* lequel pris instinctivement pour *na* oh! et *get* avec, était en réalité *nag-(h)et*. Ainsi (*na*)*get a inour* que d'honneur serait une combinaison de *nag a inour* id. avec *nag inouret-et* combien honoré.

On pourrait opposer à cette explication la seconde des trois traductions que le P. Grégoire de Rostrenen donne dans son dictionnaire, p. 391, de la phrase 'que de façons': '*Hac a fœçzounyou. gad a fœçzounyou.* (Van. *gued a fœçzonyëu*)'. En effet, ce *gad a* nous montre hors de Vannes un correspondant de *get* (*a*) qui semble identique à *gad*, variante de *gand, gañt* avec.

2. L'objection paraît d'abord appuyée par le léonais *gant ar vez*! 'quelle honte!' *Nouvelles conversations* [par G. Milin], St.-Brieuc 1857, p. 122, 'tu devrais avoir honte!' 58, *gand ar vez*! 'c'est honteux!' 55. Mais il y a là une ellipse; c'est quelque chose comme '(vous devriez rougir) de honte'; comparez en anglais (*fie*) *for shame*, gallois (*ffei* ou *ffwrdd*) *rhag cywilydd*. On dit en petit Tréguier, par un emploi analogue de *rak, koach rag ë véz* (*hag ë goñpasion*) cache-toi pour ne pas faire honte (et pitié). L'expression familière dans le même langage, *arsa ganac'h(wi ie)*, qu'on peut traduire 'ah! quel homme vous êtes!' est une abréviation de *me zo estoñnet ganac'h* 'je suis étonné de vous', qui est également usitée. Le P. Grégoire donne, v.

appaiser: *Habasqaït da-vianâ, ha ne véz nemed gand ar vez,*
litt. 'calmez-vous . . ., ne fût-ce que par honte'.

3. Un lien plus vraisemblable entre *get* (*a*) et *gañt* se
trouve dans l'idée 'tant, tellement', qui peut en pet. Trég. se
rendre par *gañt a, gañd ë* devant un adjectif, un infinitif ou un
nom: *n'allañ ket labourat gañd ë skwiz oñ, gañd a c'houézañ rañ,
gañd a drouz a ret* je ne puis travailler, tant je suis las; tant
je sue; tant vous faites de bruit. Il suffirait d'une transposition
de cette dernière phrase pour reproduire en van. la formule
exclamative qui nous occupe: *ged a drouz e hret! n'ellañ qet
labourat* que de bruit vous faites! je ne puis travailler.

4. Le brittonique **mōr* grandement a pris aussi d'autres
sens qui le rapprochent tantôt de *gañt a,* tantôt de *get* (*a*):
1⁰ moyen bret. *meur claf* très malade, etc., *Glossaire moy. br.*
2e éd. 411, 412; 2⁰ mbr. *mar*[1]) *cruel* si cruellement 545, van.
mar pihuig et *mar a bihuig é* il est si riche, tant il est riche
393, trécorois *gañd a binvig e;* 3⁰ mbr. *nac eu mar fier* si fier
qu'il soit (cf. μινυνθάδιόν περ ἐόντα *Iliade* I, 352, moi qui ai
une existence très courte, bret. *n' 'm euz ket pell-meur da vewa
Gloss.* 411, à côté de ἀγαθός περ ἐών *Il.* I, 131 si brave que tu
sois, ce qui se dirait en mbr. *nac out mar cadarn);* 4⁰ vieux
gall. *morliaus* combien nombreux! cf. van. *get a dud* combien de
gens, ou absolument *get,* comme en français *combien* id.; 5⁰ gall.
edrych mor wyn yw'r eira regarde comme la neige est blanche,
van. *sell mar guenn é enn erh, Gloss.* 541.[2])

5. Le 4e emploi de **mōr* a laissé en bret. moderne des
traces remarquables: *meur da galon* que de cœurs, *meur da hini*
combien, *meur da hini all* combien d'autres *Gloss.* 273, 543; et
aussi *meurbet à garuu eo* qu'il est dur 412; cf. *ac a galon* et
ac a bet calon que de cœurs, *ac a hini* et *ac a bet hini* combien

---

[1]) Le van. et le tréc. disent *mar a* plusieurs (léon. *meur a),* cf. tréc.
sal, léon. *seul* d'autant (plus); voir *Gloss.* v. *mar* 3. Une variation analogue
s'observe dans le bret. moy. et mod. *arauc* en avant, adverbe accentué sur la
finale, et *rac* devant, préposition et préfixe. Je crois maintenant que *speur*
cloison *Gloss.* 642 ne tient pas à *sparl* barre, mais au vieux franç. *spuer*
(angl. *spur,* proprement 'éperon', etc.).
[2]) Le cornouaillais *N'euz nemed Doue a oar mar zo keun em c'halon*
'Dieu seul sait ce que j'ai de chagrin au cœur!' *Barzaz Breiz* 236, paraît
venir de *mar braz keun zo;* une traduction du français 'Dieu sait si j'ai du
chagrin!' devait donner *hag-éñ* (allemand *ob*) plutôt que *mar* (all. *wenn).*

(de gens) 5. C'est, en effet, l'exclamation qui justifie l'*à* de *meurbet à garuu*, comme le *da* après *meur*.

6. A ses rapprochements, on peut répondre par d'autres comparaisons qui appuient la première étymologie de *get a*. Telle est la dérivation du tréc. *bennak-et* quelconque *Gloss.* 276, 544, *Mém. Soc. ling.* X, 338, 339. Il y a aussi dans l'expression *na da pad bell* qu'il dure longtemps! si elle est bien expliquée *Gloss.* 543, une curieuse ressemblance avec le van. *gucd é câranmé* que j'aime! interprété par *(na)g-et*, *Mém. Soc. ling.* X, 331.

Une tournure elliptique: 'que (le chemin est) pour durer longtemps!' n'est pas probable. Je ne vois par ailleurs *da* employé comme conjonction devant un indicatif que dans les expressions du pet. Trég. telles que *bop dë kresk* à mesure qu'il grandit, *bop të hés* à mesure que tu vas (cf. *bep ma teufet en oad* à mesure que vous avancerez en âge *Gloss.* 479). Mais ceci est tout différent de *na da bad*.

7. Quant au *gad a* du P. Grégoire, son isolement permet de le tenir pour suspect. Il pourrait bien être dû, non pas même à une 'étymologie populaire', mais simplement à une association qui se sera faite, dans l'esprit de l'auteur, entre le van. *get a* et le léon. *gad* avec. Lui-même nous apprend, dans sa Préface, qu'il a parlé d'abord un breton 'peu intelligible, sinon dans l'évêché de Vannes, où il avait passé ses premières années'. Ce genre de méprise qui consiste à introduire dans le dialecte de Léon un mot purement vannetais n'a donc chez lui rien que de naturel.

8. On doit convenir pourtant qu'il est beaucoup plus rare dans son œuvre, que ne l'est le défaut inverse dans les dictionnaires vannetais de Châlons. Le P. Grégoire s'est plutôt embrouillé en donnant au vannetais quelques *h* de trop au lieu de *s*, *z*, cf. *Mém. Soc. ling.* XI, 114, 115. Cette variation dialectale est une pierre d'achoppement pour les vannetisants d'occasion, voir *Revue Morbihannaise* II, 241, 242; cf. *e vousc'hoerzin* souriant, *a garantec'h* d'amour, pour *vushoarhein, garañte*, etc., *An Hirvoudou* St.-Brieuc 1899, p. 101, 102.

Dans le plan général de son dictionnaire, le P. Grégoire n'accorde qu'un rang secondaire au dialecte de Vannes, ce qui aide à comprendre qu'il ne l'ait pas plus souvent mêlé au léonais. Voici toutefois un cas qui peut servir à confirmer l'explication de *gad a* par une réminiscence inopportune du van. *get*.

D. Le Pelletier donne *doüaren* petit-fils, fém. *-és*, comme
'du Breton de Vannes, et inconnu dans les autres Cantons', bien
qu'il écrive, par inadvertance, au pluriel *douarenou.* Roussel
ms. a: 'Douaren [vennes] petit-fils'. C'est aussi l'avis de Le
Gonidec et de Troude; l'absence du mot dans le *Nomenclator,* et
chez M. du Rusquec, doit s'interpréter dans le même sens. Or
le P. Grég. ne se contente pas de donner d'abord *douaren* pl.
ed, et son fém. *douarenès,* sans les noter comme vannetais, mais
il les emploie en dehors de ce dialecte, avec l'article léonais, et
à l'exclusion des expressions les plus usuelles, *mâb-bihan, merc'h-
vihan* Le Gon. Il y a lieu de croire qu'en cela il s'est laissé
influencer par ses souvenirs vannetais, et que j'ai eu tort d'expliquer le fait autrement, *Gloss.* 193. Cependant il n'est pas
exact que le mot soit propre au dialecte de Vannes. G. Milin
a écrit sur deux exemplaires du dictionnaire de Troude ces notes:
(*doarenn*) 'Ce mot est aussi du Léon où je l'ai entendu'; (*doa-
rennes*) 'Ce mot est de Léon où on le dit encore dans quelques
cantons'. C'est donc peut-être simplement la rareté de *douaren*
en Léon qui a échappé au P. Grégoire; *gad a* est, je crois, une
distraction plus grave, inspirée par le van. *get a.*

9. Le van. *get* est quelquefois séparé de son complément:
guæd e zou a Grechenion haval doh combien il y a de chrétiens
semblables à ... *Instructioneu santel* 1848, p. 230.

10. Il est suivi d'un singulier au sens pluriel, dans *guèd a
huéh* que de fois, *Mis Mari,* Vannes, N. de Lamarzelle 1841,
p. 295 (cf. *mar-a-huéh* quelquefois *Vocabul.* 1863, p. III, hors de
Vannes *meur a veach, meur a veich* plusieurs fois Gr.).

Poitiers.   E. ERNAULT.

THE LANGUAGE OF THE CONTINENTAL PICTS.

We all know that Poitiers (once Pictavi) and Poitou (once Pagus Pictavus) receive their name from a people called the Pictones, Pictavi, or Pectavi. In the recently published section of the *Corpus inscriptionum Latinarum* (XIII. 1, 1) which relates to Aquitania are various Latin inscriptions found within their territory, and containing proper names which are doubtless native; but the only ones yet discovered which are written entirely in the vernacular of the district seem to be the following:

1. A pyramidal *menhir* between the ruins of Vieux Poitiers and the river Clain. Stokes (Bezzenberger's *Beiträge* XI, p. 129) reads it thus:

RATIN BRIVATIOM

FRONTV . TARBEISONIOS

IEVRV.

The C. I. L. reads RATN and gives the idea that 2 or 3 letters have been lost before the following B. It also reads TARBELSONIOS. After looking at the facsimile in the *Dict. archéologique de la Gaule* I have no hesitation in abiding by Stokes's reading, except that the C. I. L. is apparently right in placing the first stop above the line and omitting the second.

Stokes has rendered the lines:

Propugnaculum pontilium

Fronto, Tarbeisoni filius,

fecit.

Of the approximate correctness of this rendering there can be no serious doubt. *Ratin* is the acc. sing. of 'râtî-s, râti-s, râto-n, Erdwall, Erdbank', which gives in Irish *ráth* (Stokes, *Urkelt. Sprachschatz*, p. 226). *Brivatiom* is the gen. pl. of an adjective of which the nom. pl. would have been given in Latin as Brivates, from the stem of 'Gaulish' *briva*, 'bridge' (ib. p. 184). *Frontu* is a man's name borrowed from the Latin Fronto. *Tarbeisonios* is an adj. formed from *Tarbeisonos*, which is a nickname denoting a man 'who bellows like a bull'. For the general form of the name cf. Latin *raucisonus*; *tarbei-* represents *tarbeio-*, *ταυρειο-* from *tarb-* 'bull', O. Ir. *tarb-* (cf. *κραται-* for *κραταιο-* in Greek compounds); and *sonos* represents the stem of Lat. *sonus*, Ir. *son*, Welsh *swn* (Pictet, *Rev. archéol*. XV, p. 395). And *ieuru* is the word so frequent in 'Gaulish' inscriptions, governing the name of some material object in the accusative.

I render:

> *The embankment of the people at the bridge*
> *Frontu the son of Tarbeisonos*
> *put up.*

My reasons for translating 'embankment' and not 'rampart' (= *propugnaculum*) are these. The position — according to Longnon's atlas — was not on or near a frontier, and if it had been we can hardly suppose that the Pictones would have been in danger from any neighbouring tribe: the Romanization of the country is manifest both from the character of the engraving and from the borrowed name Fronto. It seems to me far more likely that the embankment was erected to protect the houses near the bridge from floods.

Pictet takes *brivatiom* to signify not 'people at the bridge' but 'the bridge and its appurtenances': Stokes from the fact of his translating in Latin (instead of, as usual, in English) perhaps meant to leave that an open question. When Pictet says '*Brivates*, au pluriel, a dû signifier *pontilia*', I cannot believe that this signification would have been conveyed by a masculine termination,[1] and the abundance of 'Gaulish' names in *-ates*, signifying dwellers at or in, seems to furnish a presumption in favour of a masculine sense here.

---

[1] No neuters are known of 'Gaulish' or Latin adjectives in *-atis*: place-names like Brivate are always possible locatives masculine.

My reason for translating *ieuru* 'put up' is that I believe
it to be from a stem answering to that of ἀιωρέω and ἐωρέω,
'I raise, I suspend'. It would thus have the double sense of
'to erect' and 'to set up as a votive offering' (cf. ἀνατιθέναι),
which would suit every case in which it occurs.[1]

The inscription is clearly in an ancient Keltic language,
but of what exact class it does not show; for it contains no
stems in which Indo-European *p* or *q* were ever present. It
does, however, contain the stem *tarb-* 'bull', which appears on
an altar at Paris as *tarv-* (in the nom. *tarvos*). Had the Paris
inscription been late, we might have attributed the difference to
an 'infection' of *b* into *v*; but it is assigned to the time of
Tiberius (Desjardins, *Géographie de la Gaule* III, pl. XI). Consequently there is a presumption that the language of the Picts
differed at least dialectally from that of the Parisii.

2. There[2] has, however, been published by M. Camille
Jullian in the *Revue Celtique* for Ap. 1898 a Pictavian inscription
which I venture to say will revolutionize most current beliefs as
to the history of the Keltic languages. It actually bristles with
Indo-European *p*, and thereby conclusively shows that Pictavian
was not a 'Gaulish' dialect at all.

It is engraved on the two sides of a leaden tablet, 9 centi-
meters in height and 7 in breadth, found in 1887 in a well at
Rom, about 38 kilometers SW. of Poitiers. In the same well
were 15 similar tablets, but uninscribed. M. Jullian says:
'C'était l'usage, dans l'antiquité gréco-romaine, de confier non
seulement à des tombes, mais à la mer, aux fleuves et même
aux sources des puits les tablettes adressées aux divinités in-
fernales et sur lesquelles les dévots avaient tracé leurs souhaits

---

[1] The undoubted forms are IEVRV (8 times) and ΕΙΩΡΟΥ (once), and
the latter, as being in Greek characters, is presumably the older. IOREBE
is probably from the same verb, though the division of words may be
contested.

Is not the name of the Jura range (Iura, Ἰουρα, Ἰορα) from the same
stem, with the meaning 'Highlands'?

[2] I pass over the charm numbered 28 in Stokes's list because I am
satisfied that M. d'Arbois de Jubainville is right in reading that part of it
which is not obviously Latin as Greek written in Latin letters. As a matter
of palaeography, I am certain that, if the facsimile can be trusted, there is
no *d* in the entire inscription. But I agree with Stokes that 'bis' is a
direction to say the following words twice.

ou leurs exécrations'. He regards the inscriptions on the tablet as unquestionably of this nature, but beyond suggestions as to the meaning of a few words has attempted no translation. I myself never examined them till March 1899, when I communicated an almost complete rendering of them to a distinguished Keltic scholar. In arriving at this rendering I was not in the smallest degree influenced by any preconceptions of M. Jullian as to the nature of the inscriptions; but it will be seen that the rendering confirms his theory to the fullest degree.

The well was connected with a goddess named Imona: an invocation to her from two persons unnamed fills one side of the tablet, and implies that the supply of water was sometimes stopped or delayed. The other side of the tablet contains invocations to two other goddesses, Caticatona and Dibona, the former from persons unknown, the latter from Sueio(s) and his female servant Pontidunna Vouseia. It is possible that these two may be the authors of all three of the invocations, the writing of which M. Jullian conceives to be not earlier than the 3rd cent., while he thinks the *m* sometimes found points to the 4th. He will, however, find similar *m*'s in a Latin document of the year 293, facsimiled in Grenfell and Hunt's *Greek papyri*, ser. 2, plate V and Wessely's *Schrifttafeln z. älter. lat. Palaeographie*, tab. VI.

As regards the names of the goddesses invoked, -*ona* was a common termination of the names of goddesses in Gaul. Devona or Dibona (see Holder) was the name of the town of Cahors, and in the 4th cent. Ausonius celebrates the fountain of Bordeaux, named Dīvŏnă: it was 'urbis genius' and its name meant 'Celtarum lingua, fons addite divis'. Imona is, of course, from an *im*- or *eim*-stem, and, as she was a well-goddess, that of the Lat. *im-us* suggests itself. Caticatona remains, shown by the epithet *clotuvla* to be another water-goddess, and her name seems to mean 'very white'. All three names will be discussed later.

The original is in cursive Latin letters, without capitals, division of words, or apparently stops.[1] I here divide it into

---

[1] M. Jullian's facsimile shows a dot high up at the end of A 1 and an acute accent after the end of B 8; but, as he does not include them in his transcript, they may be accidental marks either on the plate or on the tablet.

words, add hyphens and stops, and give *the most literal rendering possible*. Had I allowed myself the ordinary freedom of translators, the version would have been much more effective.

A.

1. *Ape cialli carti,*	For thought's love,
2. *eti-heiont Caticato-*	ever-continuing Caticato-
3. *na, demtis sic clotu-*	na, to- [thy-] servants be flow-
4. *vla; se demti tiont.*	strong; since [thy-] servants
	honour [-thee].
5. *Bi cartaont, Dibo-*	Be gracious, Dibo-
6. *na. Sosio, deei pia!*	na. With-this, goddess kind!
7. *sosio, pura! sosio,*	with-this, pure-one! with-this,
8. *gorisa! Sucio tiet:*	joyous-one! Sueio honours [-thee]:
9. *sosio, poura he(i)o(nt)!*	with-this, maiden continual!
10. *sua demtia Po(n)ti-*	his servant Ponti-
11. *dunna Vouseia.*	dunna [daughter-] of-Vouso(s).

B.

1. *Teu! oraiimo:*	Swell! we-pray:
2. *chzia ata[n?]to te, hei-*[1])	today forthstretch thee, to-
3. *zio atanta te, com-*	day forthstretch thee, to-this
	(*sosio,* l. 4) be-
4. *priato sosio derti!*	loved tribute!
5. *Noi pommio at cho*	We-two drink at this
6. *tis-se potca: te pri-*	thy-own well: thee have-
7. *avimo — atanta! Te[i]-*	we-loved — forthstretch! Ho-
	nour-
8. *onte ziati mezio*	ing daily at-mid
9. *ziia, 'Teu!' oraiimo:*	day, 'Swell!' we-pray:
10. *ape sosio derti,*	for this tribute,
11. *Imona, demtis sic*	Imona, to- [thy-] servants be
12. *uziictiao[nt] pa[dv]a.*	outreachi[ng] qu[ic]k.

---

[1]) 'HEI (liés) est douteux, il n'y a de certain que les deux hastes extrêmes.' The facsimile suggests E in the middle of H, i. e. HE, EH, or HEH. Fortunately the meaning of the word is beyond doubt, and only the phonetic form is in question.

The letters inside ( ) are M. Jullian's conjectures. In B 12 the [*nt*] and [*dv*] are my own, M. Jullian not being able to conjecture the missing letters. The [*n*?] in B 2 is inserted because the second *at* are a ligature, 'il est difficile de distinguer les ligatures AT et ANT', and the word occurs with an *n* in the next line: on the other hand see under Caticatona in my glossary for the possibility of two forms — with and without the nasal. The [*i*] in B 7 is quite plain in the facsimile, though M. Jullian has overlooked it in his transcript. The Roman i's in B 2, 3, 8, 9, 12 are cases in which *di* has been modified to *si* before a following vowel and the *i* has been written horizontally across the *s*. M. Jullian has admitted the possibility of its being an *i*, but, not having the linguistic clew, has not seen that it *was* one, and has represented the digraph in his transcript by simple *s*. In the Vieux Poitiers inscription a similar ligature occurs, the I in RATIN being laid horizontally across the T and N, and unligatured horizontal I above the line is common in British Christian inscriptions.

I now proceed to give a full glossary of the tablet, which will put the substantial accuracy of the translation beyond doubt. My references to Stokes's indispensable *Urkeltischer Sprachschatz*, Macbain's *Etymological dict. of the Gaelic language,* and Lindsay's *Latin language* will be so frequent that I shall abbreviate them to the author's name followed by the number of the page: Holder's *Alt-celtischer Sprachschatz* I refer to in the same way, and also Z² i. e. Ebel's (2nd) ed. of Zeuss's *Grammatica Celtica.*

ăpĕ (A 1, B 10). 'For'. Preposition governing dative, = (Stokes 24—5) Sansk. *ápi*, Gr. *ἐπί* (Lithuanian *api- ap-*, Lat. *op-*, Oscan *op*?). For its meaning here cf. Gr. *ἐπί* with dat. signifying the price for which or condition on which a thing is done.

ăt (B 5). 'At'. Preposition (governing accusative?), O. Ir. prefix *ad-* (Stokes 9), *at-* (in *atomaig* &c., Z² 430), Lat. *ad*, also *at* (Lindsay 577, 77). Not to be confounded with '*ati* darüber' (Stokes 8), 'Gaulish' *ate*. But an alternative is to read *at'* = *ate*, and suppose the meaning 'over, at top of' given to *áti* with the gen. in Vedic Sanskrit.

atăntă (B 8)
ata[n]tŏ (B 2) } 'Stretch forth, reach forward'. 2nd pers. sing. imper. act. of transitive verb, governing acc. *te.*

These are compressed either from *ăt-tăntă, ăt-ta[n]tŏ* (see above under a t) or more probably from *ăd-tăntă, ăd-ta[n]tŏ.* Cf. in Belgic 'Atrebates pro

Adtrebates, assimilatione eadem, quae hibernice invaluit in ... *atreba'* (Z² 866, comparing *adrothreb*): Irish instances of *at-* for *adt-* can be multiplied from Stokes and Windisch.

The main stem is *tan* 'stretch'; for parallels see Stokes (127) under 'tenô „extendo"' : Lat. *ten-do* and Gr. τείνω are of course among them.

The terminations *-tā* and *-tō* = the Latin 2. sing. imper. in *-tō(d)*, O. Ind. *-tāt* (see Lindsay 516). The corresponding Irish form is *-the*, where the *th* of course arises from earlier *t*, but the *e* according to Macbain (p. xlvii) represents *-es*. For Gadelic *ā* = Lat. *ō*, Gk. ω, cf. the vocative particle *a*; and for interchange of *ā* and *ō* in Irish¹) cf. *mār* and *mór* (Z² 17). It is doubtful whether we should read *atănto* or *atāto*: see under Caticatona.

bī (A 5). 'Be'. 2nd pers. sing. imper. from stem of 'beiô ich lebe, bin' (Stokes 165). The corresponding person of the imper. is *bí* in Irish, but in Welsh *byd* (mod. *bydd*), Corn. *byth*, Bret. *bez* — in which, however, the final consonant is not a person-ending but part of an extended form of the stem.

cārtăŏnt²) (A 5). 'Gracious'. Nom. sing. pres. part. act. of *cārtāō*, from stem *cārt-* — see carti. Cf. from the shorter stem *cār-* Stokes's 'karaô ich liebe' (70) and 'karaont- liebend, Freund' (71).

cārtī (A 1). 'Kindness'. Dat. sing. of *cārtis* (masc.) from stem *cārt-*. *cārt-* is lengthened from the stem of 'karo-s lieb' (Stokes 70) = Lat. *cārus*. The stem is found in Irish in the Milan glosses — '*carthaig* (gl. amantes) Ml. 52r. *carthacha* (gl. affecta) 66r.' (Z² 810) — and the Lebor na hUidre — *cartach* (Windisch's *Wörterb.*).

With the form of substantive cf. derti, which suggests that *cār-tis* is formed direct from *cār-*: for suffix *-tis* added to a nominal stem cf. Lat. Carmen-tis. The same stem, apparently the same noun, enters into the name of the British queen Cartimandua or Cartismandua.

Catīcatŏna (A 2). Name of a goddess, 'Very white'. Voc. sing. of *Catĭcatŏna*, which is possibly the fem. of an adj., as the corresponding masc. ending *-onu* occurs in Sequanian names of months.

I regard this as representing an earlier Cŋtacŋtona, from 'kŋta mit' (Stokes 94) and 'kŋ[s]to-s weiss' (Stokes 90). *kŋta* = 'Gaulish' *canta-*, *cata-* (Stokes 94), Ir. *céad* in *céadfadh*, O. Ir. *cét*, O. Welsh *cant*, Corn. *cans*, Breton *gant*, *-cent*, Gr. κατά. *kŋ[s]to-s* = 'Gaulish' *canto-* in 'Canto-bennicus Name eines Berges in der Auvergne' (Stokes 90), Welsh *cann*, Corn. *cant-*, Breton *-cant*.

In the Brythonic languages *n* does not go out before *t*: in the Goidelic it does, with lengthening of previous vowel. In continental Pictish of the date of our tablet, *n* still remains in terminations (*hei-ont*, *ti-ont*, *tei-ontes*, *carta-ont*, *uziietia-o[nt]*), also in *atan-ta* and *Pontidunna*. Its absence in *Caticatona* may be due either to the commencement of a tendency to disappear (cf. *atato*, if rightly read), or to the possibility that in Pictish *ŋ* was *never* represented by *an* but only by *a*.

---

¹) In the insular Pictish inscriptions on the Shevack stone we have this adjective in the masc. gen. sing. both as *uaur* (= mhaur) and *vor* (= mhor).

²) The signs over vowels here and elsewhere are only meant to be their original time-values: *cārtăŏnt* may have become *cărtăŏnt*.

The Brythonic representative of the stem should be *Canticant-*, and we find that in the name of Canticantus, now Arcueil-Cachan (Holder) just south of Paris. The meaning of it should consequently be equally applicable to a village and to a fountain-goddess, and this condition is fulfilled by our derivation (with Canticantus cf. Alba Longa 'the long white street').

For the intensitive force of *cati* cf. Greek κατά in composition with adjectives: indeed Liddell and Scott give, though without reference, a Byzantine κατάλευκος 'very white'. The change of *cata* to *cati* is due to dissimilation.

cĭăllĭ. 'Of thought'. Gen. sing. of *ciallo(s)*, subst. The nom. is found in Sequanian (Coligny calendar, Espérandieu's restoration, top of col. 9) in a sentence beginning CIALLOS B[V]IS, '(The) aggregate is' or, less probably, '(The) meaning is.' In Irish we have *cíall* (fem.), gen. *céille*, 'Verstand, Sinn' (Stokes 58) and *ciall*, 'sammeln' (Stokes 85). The former of these Stokes refers to an earlier *qeislâ*, from '*qeitô verstehe', which again is from '*qei scheinen, wahrnehmen'. The latter he refers to an earlier **qeislo-*, from *ki* or *qi* 'sammeln'. But is not 'putting together' the root-meaning of both?

Prof. J. Morris Jones tells me that the change of *ei* to *ia* in Irish is only before a 'broad' vowel, not before *e* or *i*. But (1) as, under influence of English, Highland Gaelic tends to substitute the stem-vowel of the nominative for that of the genitive, so may continental Pictish have done under influence of Latin: (2) *ciallicarti* may perhaps be a single word, arising out of *ciallocarti*.

The *p* of Welsh *pwyll*, Corn. *pull*, Breton *poell* (Stokes 58), proves a q- root for *ciall*, gen. *céille*, and for *cialli* here. So that Sequanian and continental Pictish agree with the Goidelic languages (against 'Gaulish' and the other Brythonic languages) in not changing Ind.-Eur. initial *q* to *p*. In Irish it is now represented by *c* (as here), but the inscriptions also give *q*. *Q* is likewise found in Sequanian (Coligny calendar), interchanging with Indo-European *c* (*Qutios* and *Cutios*), and also in *quimon*, which I take to be an adjective from the same stem as Lat. *quin-us*: but comparison with *ciallos* suggests that as early as the date of the Coligny calendar (1st cent. A. D.?) Sequanian *q* was becoming *c*.

clōtuvla (A 3—4). 'Flow-strong, strongly flowing'. Nom. sing. fem. of adj. *clotuvl-o(s)*, -*a*, (-*on*?). The first element in the compound is a subst. *clōtus*, akin to 'kloutâ Flussname' i. e. Tacitus's Clota, Ptolemy's Κλωτα, Welsh Clut, Ir. Clúath, Cluad, our Clyde (Stokes 102, Holder 1046): this is assigned to a root found in Gr. κλύ-δων, κλύ-ζω, Lat. *clu-o* (= *purgo*), *cloaca* (also *clouaca*). The second element is the stem '*vala : *vla mächtig sein' (Stokes 262), found in Lat. *valere*, and yielding *flath* 'lord' in Highland Gaelic, *flaith* in Ir., &c.: hence 'valo-s mächtig' (Stokes) which gives an ending to various Keltic person-names.

The Old British person-name *Clotual-os*, later *Clutuual*, must not be compared except for its second element, the first being the stem *clot-* 'fame' (see Stokes 102).

cŏmprĭātō (B 3—4). 'Beloved'. Loc.-dat. sing. masc. of past participle *compriat-o(s)*, -*a*, (-*on*?). The first element is the preposition and prefix com (= Lat. eom-) found in 'Gaulish', Irish, Old British, Old Breton — Welsh cym-, cyf-, &c. (Stokes 86, Z¹ 871, 901). For the second element see below under priavimo.

deei (A 6). 'Goddess'. Voc. sing. of deei(s) = deis. For the de- stem cf. (Lat. dē-us) in Irish the following cases of dia 'god' — gen. déi, dat. and acc. dea, voc. dé, gen. pl. dea, dat. pl. déib, acc. pl. deo. Deis seems also to be found in the Umbrian or early Latin inscription quoted by Conway, Italic dialects I, p. 434 (no. 6), where we have the dat. sing. fem. dei.

dĕmtī (A 4). 'Servants'. Nom. pl. masc. ⎫
(= dĕmtYī) ⎪
    dĕmtYa (A 10). 'Servant'. Nom. sing. fem. ⎬ of adj. demti-o(s), -a,
    dĕmtYs (A 3, B 11). 'To servants'. Dat. pl. ⎪ (-on?).
masc. (= dĕmtYīs) ⎭

The stem is given by Stokes (141) as '(*dama), damnô bändige, damô dulde'. Gr. δᾱμάω, Lat. dŏmo, Ger. zahm, Eng. tame are related.

The adj. is formed from a past part. demtos, which is either derived directly from the stem dem- or else syncopated for demētos, (cf. Gr. ἀ-δάμᾱτος, Lat. domĭtus).

Among the Keltic derivatives of the stem may be mentioned Highland Gaelic damh 'ox' (also 'stag'), O. Ir. dam 'ox', damnaim 'I bind to', O. Welsh dometic 'gezähmt' (cf. DOMETOS on a London inscription -- Holder 1302). I believe it to be also present in the name of the Demetae of South Wales, and their country Demetia (now Dyfed): they were the subject-race. Ptolemy indeed is made to call them the Δημῆται, but the shortness of both e's is shown by the mediaeval Welsh Dyuet — see Z¹ 85, 96.

The gen. Demeti in a British Latin inscription quoted by Holder from Rhŷs gives a nom. Demet(i)os or Demet(i)us.

dērtī (B 10). 'Tribute, due'. Loc.-dat. sing. of masc. subs. dertis. The primary stem is dĕr-, Stokes's 'dēro-s gebührend, schuldig': for -tis see above under carti (at end). Hence Ir. dír 'proper' (later díor) and díre 'a due'. And in Welsh there is dir 'certain, necessary' and dirwy 'a fine'.

Dībŏna (A 5—6). Name of a fountain-goddess, 'Brilliant'. Voc. sing. of Dibŏna, which is possibly the fem. of an adj. (see above under Caticatona).

This is Ausonius's fountain-deity Dīvŏnă (see above, p. 4), but we cannot be sure that the quantity of the -a was not accommodated by him to Latin practice and the exigence of the metre. He explains the name as 'Celtarum lingua fons addite divis' — in other words he derived it from the stem of 'deivo-s, dívo-s Gott', and so does Stokes (144), taking this from earlier '*dei strahlen'.

The b demands attention, and is paralleled by the stem tarb- found in continental Pictish where Parisian seemingly had tarv- (see above, p. 3). The question of the relations of b and v in ancient Keltic names is much too large to be approached here; but I suspect that in tarv- and Divona the sound of Lat. v (Eng. w) is meant, and in tarb- and Dibona that of Eng. v.

Compare Ptolemy's Δηούα (= Dewa), the name (in gen. case) of two rivers in Britain, the Pictish Dee and the Welsh.

ĕho (B 5). 'This'. Loc.-dat. sing. masc. of *eho-(s)*, *-a*, *(-on?)*, or else acc. sing. masc. for *ĕhŏn*. The stem is seen in Lat. *ec-ce* (Lindsay 617, 432), Gr. ἐχεῖ, Oscan *eko-* 'this', fem. *eka-* (Conway, *Italic dialects* II, pp. 614, 478). The passage of the original *c* through *ch* into *h* is illustrated by the case of the insular Pictish name Necton (for which see Stokes in Bezzenberger's *Beiträge* XVIII, p. 107). On a stone at Lunasting in Shetland that name appears in the genitive as Nehhtonn: see my *Vernacular inscriptions of the ancient kingdom of Alban*, pp. 4, 30, 57, where I have guessed the date at about 680 or so — that it is at least as early is suggested by its preserving a genitive in -*s*. In 731 Bede gives the same name as Naiton, from which even the *h* has disappeared. Compare also the Vacalus of Caesar (IV, 10. 1) and the Vahalis of Tacitus (Ann. II, 6).

ĕhzīā (B 2)
(?) h-ĕ(i)zio (B 2—3) } 'To-day'. Adv. of time.

The first element in these is the stem referred to in the last paragraph. For absence of connecting vowel cf. Lat. *ec-ce*, and it may be mentioned that Oscan has a fem. sing. *ek* (Conway, *Italic dialects* II, p. 614, I, p. 111).

The initial *h* — if correct — in *h-e(i)zio* is merely to prevent hiatus: other instances are *eti h-eiont* (A 2), *poura h-eiont* (A 9): see h —. If the rest of the word is to be read *ezio*, the middle *h* has simply disappeared: if with M. Jullian we read an *i* before the *z*, then the disappearence of the *h* has been accompanied by compensatory diphthongizing of the *ĕ*. But the true reading may be *ehzio* or *hehzio*.

The second stem in the form before us is *zia* or *zio* = 'day', i. e. *dia* (for *diya*) or *dio*. Continental Pictish changes *di* before a vowel to *zi*: see under mezio, uziietiao[nt], ziati, and ziia. The variation between the endings -*zia* and -*zio* may be due either to substitution of vowel (cf. *atanta* and *ata*[n?]*to*) or to the one representing an -*a*- and the other an -*o*- stem. Stokes (145) gives two stems (1) 'dijas- (dejes?) Tag', whence Ir. *die*, *dia*, and (2) 'divo- Tag', whence Ir. *in-diu* 'hodie' and Welsh *dyw* — cf. also Lat. *dīū* 'by day'.

In Highland Gaelic and Irish the 'infection' of *d* is to *dh*, now pronounced as *gh* or *y*, but doubtless originally as *ð*, between which and *z* the distance is very slight — thus our English 'the', = *ðə*, is liable to be pronounced by foreigners as *zə*.

h-eiŏnt (A 2, 9). 'Continuing, continual'. Nom. sing. fem. present part. of 'eimi (gehe), bin' (Stokes 25) or rather of the -*o* form *eiō*. The corresponding Greek and Latin participial stems are ἰοντ-, ἰent-, ĕunt-, but Lat. *eo* is 'from *ĕy-ō* instead of I.-Eur. *ei-mi*, (Lindsay 456) — cf. (ib.) '*īs*, older *e-is*', '*it*, older *e-it*', '*ī-mus*, older *ei-mus*', *ī-tis*, older *ei-tis* (with *ei-* again for *ī-*)'. Mediaeval and Modern Keltic derivatives of this stem are given by Stokes, and by Macbain (under *eith*).

The initial *h* is merely to prevent hiatus: see h —.

ĕtī (A 2). 'Still, ever'. Adv. of time. Cf. Sansk. *ati* 'over', Gr. ἔτι, Lat. *et*. It is worth considering whether *etic* in the Alise inscription (Stokes's no. 18) does not = this word + -*c* 'and', Lat. (-*que* and also) -*c* in *nec* and *ac* (Lindsay 122), Ir. -*ch* in *nach* (Stokes 62).

gŏvĭsa (A 8). 'Joyous'. Voc. sing. fem. of gŏvĭso(s), -a, (-on?). Cf. Lat. gāvĭsŭs, -ă, -ŭm, past part. of gaudeo 'for *gāvĭ-d-eo' (Lindsay 479). The same root gives in Greek γηθέω (Dor. γαθέω), ἀ-γανός, γαῦρος &c. (see Prellwitz), and in Ir. guaire 'noble' from original gourios (Stokes 112).

h- (A 2, 9). Insertion to prevent hiatus between two words forming a single idea (A 2 eti h-eiont 'ever-continuing', A 9 poura h-eiont 'maiden-continual = ever-virgin'). Its insertion in B 2, where they do not form a single idea, is doubtful.

Imŏna (B 11). Name of a goddess, 'Deep-dwelling'. Voc. sing. of Imŏna, which is possibly the fem. of an adj. (see Caticatona). The stem is that of the Lat. ĭmus, 'lowest', which probably = inf-mus, as quīnus = quincnus, and as (I hold) in Sequanian quimon = quincmon.

mĕzĭŏ (B 8). 'Middle'. Temporal-dat. of mezio-(s), -a, (-on?), for medios &c. For the stem see Stokes 207: in 'Gaulish' as in Latin it is medio-, in Ir. med-, mid-.

nŏi (B 5). 'We-two'. Nom. dual of pronoun of 1st person. Sansk. nāu, Gr. νῶι, νώ. And Irish has a gen. náthar 'of us two' equated by Stokes (194) with Gr. νωΐτερος, the adj. of νῶι.

ŏraiĭmŏ (B 1, 9). 'We-pray'. 1st pers. pres. ind. act. of ŏraiŏ. From the root of 'ŏro- (ŏrā?) Gebet' (Stokes 51), i. e. of Lat. ŏrō (= ŏrāyŏ).

pă[dv]a (B 12). 'Quick'. Nom. pl. neut. (used adverbially) or nom. sing. fem. in apposition with uziietiao[nt].

The stem is Stokes's '[p]advo-s schnell' (28), whence the river-name Adva (now Adda) in Cisalpine Gaul (ib.). I suggest that we are to refer to it also the name of that rapid river the Pădus with its southern outlet the Padua or Padva (see Holder), and that there were p-preserving Kelts even in N. Italy.

pĭa (A 6). 'Kind'. Voc. sing. fem. of pio(s), -a, (-on?). Lat. pius is the same word, the i being originally long (Lindsay 131, referring to Oscan Piĭhioi = Pio).

pommĭŏ (B 5). 'We-drink'. 1 pers. pl. pres. ind. act. of '*[p]o, *[p]ŏ trinken' (Stokes 46).

The difference of termination between this and the plurals oraiimo (B 1, 9), priavimo (B 6—7) is analogus to that in Sanskrit, where the 1st pers. pl. has both 'Primary -mias and -masi, and 'Secondary and Perfect -ma' (Brugmann, Comp. gr., Eng. tr. IV, § 1002). In O. Ir. the former termination is represented by -mi, -me-, -mmi, -mme, arising out of '*-mesi, (or -*mĕsi)', used in 'conjoined' forms: the latter by '-m for *-mo or *-mos', used in 'absolute' forms (ib. § 1006). In continental Pictish the two are represented respectively by -mmio (present ind. absolute) and -mo (perfect ind. absolute and conjoined). The explanation of the mm in Irish is (Brugmann) that the consonant was 'a hard, not a spirant m'. That of the io in pommio is more difficult: I suggest that it = pommi with o added under the influence of the other termination in -mo.

Pŏ(n)tĭdŭnna (A 10—11). Name of a woman-servant, 'Dun-robed'. Nom. sing. fem. of pontidunno(s), -a, (-on?).

The first element is *pontis* 'raiment', a subst. in *-tis* like *car-tis* and *der-tis* from the root. given by Stokes (32) as '*[p]en kleiden', by Macbain (16) as *pan*, found in Highland Gaelic and Irish, but apparently not as yet in the Brythonic languages. The weight of evidence both in Goidelic and in other languages (e. g. Lat. *pannus*) seems to be for *pan*. Three of the Irish derivatives exhibit a *-ti-* suffix.

The second element is *dunno(s)*, *-a*, (*-on?*), 'dun', Stokes's 'donno-s braun, dunkel' (152), Irish *donn*, Welsh *dwn*. A derivation is suggested by him from *dus-nos* (comparing Lat. *fus-cus*, Sansk. *dhūsara*, Eng. *dusk*), which favours *dunnos* as an earlier form than *donnos*. Holder derives from **dunno-s'* in this sense the proper name Dunni(us) found in an inscription at Lyon.

pŏtĕa (B 6). 'Well'. Loc.-dat. sing. or acc. sing. (for *potean*). The root is that of the word last mentioned: the stem is that of the Lat. *pŭtĕus* 'well', and Prof. Lindsay has repeated to me the remark of some other scholar, that an alternative *pŏtĕo-* stem in Italic is suggested by *Ποτίολοι*, used in Greek (as well as *Ποντεόλοι*) for Lat. Puteoli.

It is difficult to say whether the Pictish substantive is of a masculine *-a-* stem, *putea(s)* like Lat. *paricida(s)* (Lindsay 373) or whether *potea = poteo* — cf. *atanta* and *ata[n?]to*, *ehzia* and *e(i)zio*.

poura (A 9). 'Maiden'. Voc. sing. of *poura*. Cf. Lat. *puera*, of the same meaning.

The root is '(*[p]u, *[p]ou (Basis und Bedeutung zweifelhaft)'. — So Stokes 53, giving Urkelt. (p)uero-s, Welsh *wyr* 'nepos, neptis', and equating Lat. *pucr*. It is found in Greek dialects in the word for 'child' as *πούς*, *παύς*, whence *πά(F)ις* (Prellwitz). Stokes (22) has equated with this the O. Ir. *haue* 'grandson', which has the gen. *avi* in Ogams, but has treated them both as from a distinct stem '[p]avio-s Enkel', which is unnecessary.

In insular Pictish the same word as *haue* is found in the gen. sing. *ui* (Lunasting stone), loc.-dat. sing. *o* (Kilmadock stone), *u* (the same). I believe also that forms with initial *p* are found in the Burrian stone (*pevv = aibh*), the St. Vigean's stone (*pev = aibh*), and the Shevack stone (*pua*).

prīavĭmŏ (B 6—7). 'We-have-loved'. 1st pers. pl. perf. ind. act. from *priăŏ* or *priămĭ*.

The root is that given by Stokes (233) as '*[p]ri lieben', whence Ir. *riar* 'will, pleasure', Sans. 'prinăti erfreuen, priyate befriedigt sein', Old Slav. 'prijati günstig sein', and Gothic *frijōn* 'to love'.

The same verb compounded with *com* is found in *compriato* (B 3—4). And, as the root does not exist in Latin, the two forms cannot be alleged to be borrowed thence (as *pia*, *potea*, *poura*, *pura* might be) but are decisive proofs of the conservation of Indo-Eur. *p* in continental Pictish.

pūra (A 7). 'Pure-one'. Voc. sing. fem. of adj. *puro(s)*, *-a*, (*-on?*). The Lat. *purus* is of course identical. The root is given as 'pū reinigen' (Fick, *Vergleich. Wörterb.* I, p. 483) and Sansk. 'punăti reinigen' (Stokes 55) is connected.

sē (A 4). 'If, since'. The form represents an earlier *sei* = O. Lat. *sei* (later *si*), which is also found as *-se* in *nise* (Lindsay 611). The use of the Lat. particle with the indicative, implying that the condition is a fact, is analogous to the use of *se* here, where it is followed by an indicative.

The root is the pronoun *so- (Lindsay 610), for which in Keltic see Stokes (292) and Macbain (269).

sĭŏ (A 3, B 11). 'Be'. 2 pers. sing. pres. opt. from root es 'to be', for earlier sĭes = O. Lat. sĭes (Lindsay 513). For the root in Keltic see Stokes (44) and Macbain (197, under is).

The difference between the use of bi and sie — which may or may not be accidental — is that the former is used absolutely, and the latter as the sequel to a condition fulfilled.

sŏsĭŏ (A 6, 7, 9, B 4, 10). 'This'. Instr.-loc.-dat. sing. masc. of sosios, -a, (-on?), demonstr. adj.

This adjective is already well-known from 'Gaulish' inscriptions: the following are the instances in those interpreted by Stokes. (6) COCIN NEMHTON 'this temple', 'for sosion' (Stokes, comparing O. Lat. alis, alid for alius, aliud): (18) SOSIN CELICNON 'this tower' (25) BVSCILLA SOSIO LEGASIT 'Buscilla placed this' (neut. for sosion — not 'Buscilla Sosio placed (this)', as Stokes).

The word is reduplicated from the pronominal stem 'so(sjo)' (Macbain 291, under sin): cf. Eng. 'this here', Fr. ceci. For 'sjo, Fem. sjâ Pronomen demonstrativum' in Keltic see Stokes 317.

sŭa (A 10). 'His'. Nom. sing. fem. of possessive pron. suo(s), -a, (-on?). Lat. suus is of course the same word, and Gr. ἑός (= σεϝός) related, the stem being Ind.-Eur. *sĕwŏ- (Lindsay 426).

This pronoun seems to be lost in the mediaeval Keltic languages; and, although we have Ir. -s- 'he', sí 'she', su 'them', and similar forms (Stokes 292), they are referred to a se- (swe-) or so (swo) stem, with Lat. sui, sibi, se (see Stokes, Lindsay 424, Fick, Vergleich. Wörterb. I, 578).

Sŭeĭŏ (A 8). Name of a man, 'Boarlike'. Nom. sing. masc. of sueio(s), -a, (-on?). The root is that of Lat. sū-s, Gr. ὑς, O. H. G. sû: in the mediaeval Keltic languages it seems only to appear in the secondary stem sukku- (Stokes 305, Macbain 301), giving Ir. socc 'snout', mod. Ir. suig 'pig', Welsh hŵch, Corn. hoch, Bret. houc'h. For the termination see Holder under -eio- and cf. Tarbei- for Tarbeio- above, p. 2.

tē (B 2, 3, 6). 'Thee'. Acc. of pron. of 2nd pers. sing. Lat. te is the same word, the nom. being Ind.-Eur. *tū, preserved in O. Ir. tū, Welsh ti, Corn. ty, te, Bret. te (Macbain 341, Stokes 134). But in these other Keltic languages the oblique cases have been lost.

teu (B 1, 9). 'Swell!' 2nd pers. sing. imper. act. The Ind.-Eur. root is 'tevă: tû schwellen; stark sein' (Fick, Vergl. Wörterb. I, 61), which gives in Irish 'teo Stärke, Kraft' (Stokes 131), and the tu-meo group in Latin, while in Lithuanian 'tvanas, Fluth' (Fick l. c.) it is applied to the swelling of water.

For the unthematic bare tense-stem as imperative act. in Greek, Latin, and O. Irish see Brugmann, Comp. gr., Eng. tr. IV, 497.

teĭŏnte (B 7— 8). 'Honouring'. Nom. dual or pl. masc. pres. part. act.

tĭĕt (A 8). 'Honours [-thee]'. 3rd pers. sing. pres. ind. act.

tĭŏnt (A 4). 'Honour [-thee]'. 3rd pers. pl. pres. ind. act.

} of teiŏ, tĭŏ, 'I honour'.

The root is found in Gr. τίω, with the same meaning, Arcadian τείω (Brugmann, *Comp. gram.*, *Eng. tr.* IV, 236).

The presence of this verb in continental Pictish makes it practically certain that the attempts to connect τίω with a *k*- or *q*-stem must be given up, as there is no evidence of initial *k* or *q* being changed to *t* in Pictish or any other Keltic language.

tis-sĕ (B 6). 'Of thyself, thy-own'. Gen. of pron. of 2nd pers. sing. *tū-sĕ*.

For the first part of this pronoun see te above, and for the form of the gen. cf. O. Lat. *tis*.

The second part is the suffix so often attached to *tū* in O. Ir. in the forms *su*, *so* (Z² 325), and to the first person in the forms *sa*, *se* (Z² 324, Macbain 269).

uẓiietiăŏ[nt] (B 12). 'Outreaching'. Nom. sing. fem. pres. part. act. of *uẓiietiao = ud-iietiao*, as *ẓiia = diia*.

The first part of the compound is 'ud, od aus, Präfix' (Stokes 54). In Highland Gaelic *ùd* = 'out' is referred by Macbain to Norse *út*. But in O. Ir. *ud-* is found in *uccu* (Stokes, 'aus *ud-gus'), and *-od-* in various compounds (Z² 885). Breton has *ut-*. The Sansk. is *ud*.

The second part is a vb. *iietiăō* from the root '*jat streben' (Stokes 222), found in 'gall. Ad-iatunnus, Add-iatu-marus' and Welsh *add-iad* 'desire' (ib.). A *iet-* stem is also found (see Holder) in *Ad-ietuanus*, king of the Sotiates (Sos, dep. Gers., S. W. France) and *Su-ietius*.

As regards the *ii*, it cannot in this case stand for *ei* as in *ẓiia*, the root being *yat-*; it probably = *iy-*.

Vouseia (A 11). '[Daughter-] of-Vouso(s)'. Nom. sing. fem. of adj. in *-eio(s)*, *-a*, (*-on*?) from *Vousŏ(s)*.

The latter name may just possibly = an earlier *vouksos* (cf. *ehẓia* for *ek-ẓia*). Can that = 'Ir. oss (aus *uksos) ... 'cervus', which Stokes (267) derives from a root '*veg (: *ug)'?

ẓIăti (B 8). 'Daily'. Adv. of time = *ẓiăti(n)*, representing an older *diătin* analogous to a possible Lat. *diătim*. For the stem see ehẓia.

ẓIiă (B 9). 'Day'. Temporal-dat. of stem *ẓiia = diya* 'day' (see under ehẓia).

So much for the story told by the inscriptions commonly so called. I come next[1]) to the coins of 3 Pictish princes, as described in Muret and Chabouillet, *Catalogue des monnaies gauloises de la Bibliothèque Nationale.*

The first of these, following the order of the catalogue, is VIREDISOS or VIREDIOS, which suggest that intervocalic *s* had already begun to disappear — as it has in Irish — though

---

[1]) I omit the Keltic names found on Latin inscriptions, or on pottery, in Poitou on account of the uncertainty that the persons who bore them were native to the district.

doubtless it previously became *h*. The name is doubtless connected with *Virdu*marus, *Virdo*marus, *Virido*marus, *Virido*vix, and perhaps with Lat. *viridis* (see Stokes 281 under 'virjó-s grün': the root-meaning might be 'to grow').

The name of the second prince appears as DVRAT and on the reverse of the coin is IVLIOS, which identifies him as the Pictish king Duratius who was an ally of the Romans. The full name of the king would be *Duratios*, which would mean '[chief-] of-the-fort-dwellers'. The stem 'dûro- hart, Festung' (Stokes 151), = 'gall. dûron 'arx' in Augusto-d., Boio-d., Brivo-d., Epo-manduo-d.' (ib.), with the ethnic suffix *-ate-* would give Durates 'Fort-dwellers', whence the adj. Duratios.

The name of the last of the three was either[1]) Vepotalo(s) or Viipotalo(s), whose coins have the legends VIIPOTAL or . . . POTALO. It means 'Raven-browed', and is also found in a Styrian inscription which begins ADIATVLLVS · VEPOTALI · F · (*Corp. insc. Lat.* III, 5350). The second part of it is from 'talo-s Stirn' (Stokes 124), whence 'gall. talos in Cassi-talos, Dubno-talos' (ib.), Welsh and Cornish *tâl*, Bret. *tal*. The first part is from Indo-Eur. *veipo-s* 'raven', given by Stokes as 'veiko-s Rabe' with reference to 'ir. fiach M. Rabe' (263).

The ascertainment of the true prototype of *vepo-* and of various allied forms will lead to such remarkable results that the reader must forgive me for going into it in detail.

The stem is the same as that of 'véipô schwinge' (Fick, *Vergl. Wörterb.* I, 126) whence Sansk. 'vep . . . zittern', O. Norse 'veifa vibrare agitare', O. H. G. 'weibôn schweben, schwanken' (ib.): in Lat. *vibrare*, however, the *b* is difficult (ib.). The name == Flapper.

The word appears first in Italy in the Verona inscription (Stokes's no. 3), where we have '*Vepisones*, gen. sg. of *Vepi-sona*' i. e. 'Raven-voiced'. The inscription is written from right to left, and is consequently very early: I find in it strong confirmation of my suspicion (see above under pa[dv]a) that there were *p*-preserving Kelts in Cisalpine as well as in Transalpine

- - -

[1]) *II* was common for *E* in Roman inscriptions. Pauli, who regards it as ii in Venetic (*Altit. Forschungen* III, p. 91), takes it to = *i* in the Alise inscription (Stokes's 18) in the names DVGHONTIO and ALISIIA (ib. p. 88).

Gaul. For the meaning of the name cf. Tarbeisonos 'Bull-voiced' implied in Tarbeisonios.

That the *vēpo-* or *vĭpo*-stem indicated a bird is also confirmed by the fact that Pliny (X, 49 [69]) mentions *vipiones* as a kind of birds in the Balearic isles: 'sic vocant minorem gruem', he says — and the *vipio* may have been so called from looking like a long-legged raven.

Coming to Gaul, we find the genitive *Vepi* at Landecy, a league S. of Geneva (*Corp. inscr. Lat.* XII, 2623), and at Geneva itself the adjectival form *Vipius* in the name of a freedman (ib. 2590): Geneva is only 41 miles from Coligny, where Indo-Eur. *p* was preserved.

Stokes[1]) (Bezzenberger's *Beiträge* XVIII, p. 112) and Holder (under *mulo-*) give Vepomulus, but without reference. And, if from the analogy of Epomulus (= equo-mulus) it be argued that *vepos* is the name not of a bird but a quadruped, let me observe that the derivation of *mulus* is still unknown.

In Britain we find VEP CORF i. e. VEP . COR . F . on coins discovered in Yorkshire, which may contain the stem — if any non-Brythonic Kelts lived in that part. But an undoubted instance of it is found in the Colchester engraved tablet, of which a photograph is reproduced on p. 326 of Prof. Rhŷs's paper previously mentioned, put up by a NEPOS ˙ VEPOGENI ˙ CALEDO between the years 222 and 235. *Vepogen(us)* of course means 'Raven's offspring', and Prof. Rhŷs[2]) admits the Caledonians to have been Picts (ib. p. 329).

Not only was Vepogen(us) an insular Pictish name, but among the lists of insular Pictish kings we find *Uip* (Skene, *Chronicles of the Picts*, pp. 5, 26, 325, 397) i. e. 'Raven', and a later one whose name is given variously as *Vipoig namet, Uipo ignavict, Poponcuet, Wmpopwall, Verpempnet, Vipoguenech* and *Uipo ignauit* (ib. pp. 6, 27, 149, 172, 200, 285, 398). I will not discuss here the origin of these forms, but it is quite clear that they contain the stem Uip- or Vip-. Now in three of these cases the name is followed by the name of another king who

---

[1]) I owe my references for all the proper names quoted either to Stokes (loc. cit.) or to Rhŷs (*Proc. of the Soc. of Antiquaries of Scotland* XXXII, p. 328, in a paper he has kindly given me).

[2]) He does not, however, admit that the insular Picts were Kelts, but supposes this name to be borrowed from a Gallo-Brythonic source.

reigned just the same number of years (30), and who is called 'Fiacua albus' (p. 149), 'Fiacha albus' (p. 172), and 'Fiachna le blank' (p. 200), and Stokes has seen that these entries are really only glosses on the preceding name (Bezzenberger's *Beiträge* XVIII, p. 112). It is obvious that insular Pictish *vip-* = Ir. *fiach-*, and we know that one of the meanings of Ir. *fiach* is 'raven'.

Now *veik-* would naturally become *fiach*, and, if *fiach* does *not* stand for *veik-*, what *does* it stand for? My suggestion is that it stands for *veipak-*. I have called *veip-* 'raven', but it may be 'rook' or 'crow', and from it may have been formed the secondary stem *veipak-* = 'crow-like' and so = 'raven', giving Ir. *fi[p]ach*. If anyone asks for a parallel, let him turn to Stokes 64, where he will find 'ka[p]ero-s Bock' followed by the secondary 'ka[p]erak-s Schaf' i. e. a horned breed.

I pass to the place-names found in Longnon's map of Gaul under the Romans (*Atlas hist. de la France*, pl. II).

Aunedonacum is a derivative of the man's name Aunedo(n) found at Reims (Holder), and that from the stem of 'aunio-s grün' (Stokes 4) with the common suffix -edo (see Holder). For similar colour-names cf. Candiedo, Donnedo, Vindedo, Viredo. Modern name, Aulnay (-de-Saintonge).

Brigiosum is from 'brgi Berg' (Stokes 171) and means 'Hilly'. Modern name, Brioux.

Lemonum or *Limonum* is the neut. of an adj. in -ono-, -onu-, from the stem of 'leimâ Linde' (Stokes 242, Macbain 203), and means Lindenham: cf. Welsh *llwyf*.

The stem of *Locodiacus* is found also as Logotigiac- and Locoteiac-, all three forms appearing to be of the 6th cent. It is *lucot-* 'mouse', for which see Holder (303) and Stokes (244), and the site either swarmed with mice or was named after a chief Lucoteios. Modern name, Liguge.

Ratiate quite obviously means 'the place of the embankment' or 'the place of the earthen wall' (see the beginning of this paper). Modern name, Rézé.

Rauranum has not been reached by Holder, and I see no fitting stem for it in Stokes. It is probably Raur-ănum, with the stem of Raur-acum and the adjectival suffix (= Gr. -ăvo-) seen in Rodănus and Sequăna. Modern name, Sainte-Soline.

Segora is either from '*seg säen' (Stokes 294, quoting Lat. seges) or from 'sego- Gewalt, Sieg' (id. 297) which forms such a common part of 'Gaulish' proper names, e. g. Segobriga and Segomaros. For the suffix -*or*- or -*ur*- see Z^2 779 (e. g. Lesora, Lactora).

To these must be added, from Longnon's *Géographie de la Gaule au VIe siècle*, as probably Pictish:

Arbatilicum (Herbauge), inhabited apparently not by Picts but by Lemovices. The name seems to be late for Atrebatilicum, 'the immigrants' land', as we have Caleba Arbatium for C. Atrebatium in the Ravenna geographer (5, 51 — Holder 271).

Becciacus (Bessay). Doubtless, as Holder takes it, named from a man Beccius = 'Beaky', from *beccos* 'beak' (Holder 364, Stokes 166).

Castrum *Sellus* (Chantoceaux). 'Usque ad Sellus castrum' (p. 574) suggests an acc. pl. of Sellos, like Parisius, Pictavus. The place is on a hill 79 m. above the sea, and I suspect that the Selli were 'look-out-men', from Stokes's 'stilnaô (oder stilniô) ich sehe' (313) which gives in Irish 'sell Auge, sellaim ich sehe an'.

Vogladensis campus. If the *g* is radical, I can only look to '*veg ... netzen' (Stokes 266), which gives 'vegro- Gras' and 'voglo- Harn' (ib.), and suppose that the place had a system of irrigation. But there is another form Voclad-, and, although the 7th cent. MSS. of Gregory of Tours do not support it, they have both Mecledonensem and Miglidunensem. Hence Ir. 'fochlaid Höhle' (Stokes 82), which postulates earlier Voclad-, may be akin. But in that case continental Pictish would have lost medial *p* in *upo*- before 576.

Vultaconnum (Voultegon). Cf. 'Mediconnum', just outside Pictish territory (now Mougon). Both are in the angle of a confluence; *Medi*- should mean 'middle'; and the inference is that *conn*- = *cond*- in *Condate*, which is recognized by Holder as meaning a place at the junction of two rivers. And we now see that *Condate* is an adj. in -*atis* from a stem *cond*- 'junction', formed from *con*- 'together' and the shortened stem *d*- 'put' seen in Lat. *con-do*. The loss of root-vowel in Latin is certain in *cond-o, -is, -it, -unt* (Brugmann, *Comp. gram.*, *Eng. tr.* I, 71) and possible in all other parts of the verb, while it is equally clear in the derived Plautine substantive *condus* = 'qui condendis cibis præpositus est'. Consequently *Vulta*- = *Volta*- from

Stokes's '*vel ... umgeben' (275), and the entire name means 'encircled by the confluence'.

The following are quoted by Holder (989—90) from Gregory of Tours and Fortunatus, both 6th cent. writers:

'G(C)racina Pictavensis insula' (*Greg. Tur., Hist. Fr.* 5. 30 [48]). From the context it seems that the slave of a fiscal vine-dresser lived there. Against the older *Cracina* Arndt gives *Gracina* without various reading: does it = the 'graci-lis ager' of the Elder Pliny, or the 'graci-les vindemiae' of the Younger?

'In villa Suedas (*Saix*) Pictavo territorio' (*Fort., Vit. Radegund.* 1, 15, 35). Probably from *sū-* 'swine', seen above in *Sueio*, and the stem of '*edō* ... ich esse' (Stokes 29) — 'the place where swine feed'. *sū-* 'swine' may also be present in Suessiones (*ss = dt.* 'Swine-eaters'?), and certainly is in S[u]-belino, 'Bright-coloured boar' — cf. Cunobelinus 'Bright-coloured hound'[1]) — and probably Suobnedo, 'Terrible boar'.

The name of the people themselves remains. They were the[2]) Pīctŏnes, Pĕctŏnes, Pīctăvī, or Pĕctăvī. The termination -ŏnes was common in names of Keltic peoples: Z^2 772 gives Lingŏnes, Senŏnes, Turŏnes, Santŏnes, Rhedŏnes, Kentrŏnes. The termination -āvo- was also extremely common — for its use in tribal names cf. Nemetavi and Segusiavi (Z^2 783 and Holder). We are accordingly reduced to a stem Pīct- or Pĕct-. These two forms suggest Ind.-Eur. *peik-*; is there such a root? There is. In Fick's *Vergleichendes Wörterbuch* vol. I we have a 'Wortschatz der westeuropäischen Spracheinheit (der Griechen, Italiker, Kelten, Germanen)', and therein on p. 472 we have 'peik- stechen, sticken', among the derivatives of which are ποικίλος, πικρός, and Sansk. *piç.* The name of the Picts, whether continental or insular, means 'Tattooed'.[3]) Have we any evidence that they did

---

[1]) The real meaning of Cuno- and its correlatives in proper names is shown by Gildas, who (writing before 548) is made by the MSS. — the earliest of which is 11th cent. — to address Cuneglasus as 'Cuneglase, Romana lingua lanio fulve' (32). I pointed out in the *Academy* for Oct. 12, 1895 that *lanio* is corrupted from *canis*, written with square [which was mistaken for L. The staghound, boarhound, and wolfhound were the ancient Kelt's types of swiftness, strength, and bravery, and in Old Irish the proper name Cú 'Hound' is well-known.

[2]) The length of the ī is shown by an early 2nd cent. Poitiers inscription (CIL, XIII, 1129 and Holder 1001) which writes cĪvitas pĪcTonm.

[3]) Cf. the opening words of the Pictish Chronicle (Skene's ed. p. 3),

tattoo? As regards the insular Picts we have the most convincing. Prof. Rhŷs, who has observed in his *Rhind lectures* that 'the word Pict . . ., whatever it may have meant, is hardly to be severed from the name of the Pictones of ancient Gaul', and has given excellent reasons why it cannot be derived from Lat. *pictus,* brushes aside the testimony of Claudian

ferroque notatas
Perlegit exsangues Picto moriente figuras

as probably suggested by a false derivation.[1]) But there is earlier and far stronger evidence than Claudian's. The Greek historian Herodian was a contemporary of Severus, whose expedition against the North Britons he describes, and, as he wrote best part of a century before the name of the insular Picts is found in literature, he is not likely to have been influenced in his physical description of the people by a false derivation of that name. These are his words (III, 14 § 8):

> τὰ δὲ σώματα στίζονται γραφαῖς ποικίλαις καὶ ζῴων
> παντοδάπων εἰκόσιν· ὅθεν οὐδ᾽ ἀμφιέννυνται, ἵνα μὴ
> σκέπωσι τοῦ σώματος τὰς γραφάς.

After this few, I think, will doubt that *Cruithne,* the Irish for Pict, has the meaning given to it by Duald Mac Firbis:

> Cruithneach (Pictus) neach do gabhadh crotha no
> dealbha anmann, eun, agus iasg, ar a eineach, .i. ar
> a aighidh: agus gidh ní uirre amhain acht ar a chorp
> uile (at end of Ir. trans. of Nennius, p. VII)

that is

> 'Cruithneach (Pictus) one who takes the *cruths* or
> forms of beasts, birds, and fishes on his visage, that
> is, his face: and yet not upon it only but on his
> whole body.'

'Picti propria lingua' — not 'Latina lingua' — 'nomen habent a picto corpore; eo quod aculeis ferreis cum atramento, variarum figurarum stingmate annotantur'. Isidore of Seville had derived the name in the same way centuries earlier, but had not specified the language of it (Holder 995).

[1]) But his 'nec falso nomine Pictos', in another passage, ought to mean that he *knew* them to be 'pictos'. And for the meaning of *that* cf. his 'Membraque qui ferro gaudet pinxisse Gelonus' (*I in Rufin.* 318).

Now this word *cruth* represents earlier 'qrutu-s Gestalt' (Stokes 60), and of course in Brythonic this q becomes p, so that the modern Welsh analogue is '*prġd* M. „forma, species, vultus"' (ib.). Hence the Brythonic Gauls of the neighbourhood of Massilia who informed the early Greek travellers and merchants would speak of the people not as the Qɹtanoi, whence 'Cruithne', but as the Pɹtanoi, whence the νῆσοι Πρετανικαί and Old Welsh Priten, modern Prydain.

Prof. Rhŷs in his Rhind lectures has called attention to the fact that in the Wessobrunner Codex at Munich, written before 814, a name equivalent to Cruithneach 'was another name for Gallia, or a part of it'. The exact entry and those on each side of it are as follows (Steinmeyer and Sievers, *Die althochdeutschen Glossen* III, p. 610):

'Gallia uualholannt' i. e. Gallia welsh-land
'Chorthonicum auh uualholant' i. e. Chorthonicum also welsh-land
'Equitania uuasconolant' i. e. Equitania gascon-land

and I have no doubt that the Cruithneach territory which is placed with the Gauls on one side and the Aquitanians on the other is, or includes, that of the Pictones.

Unless the work from which the scribe took these names of countries which he glossed was written by an Irishman, the name Chorthonicum must have been derived from a continental Goidelic source, other of course than that of the Pictones themselves (who did not call themselves Cortones but Pictones). Were there other Goidels in Gaul? Undoubtedly: the Sequani were Goidels, or at least the people who named the river Sequana (Stokes 295) were such, and so were the people among whom the Coligny calendar was engraved.

In 1898 I published a little treatise, called 'Sequanian', upon the Coligny calendar.[1]) Since then Captain Espérandieu has succeeded in settling the order of the fragments, and I find the following corrections necessary.

---

[1]) Being abroad a little later, I hoped to work on the fragments themselves; but M. Dissard informed me that this was impracticable, as he should be away and they were being repaired. I continue to deplore the want of a photograph of them, in the order restored by M. Espérandieu.

The calendar was for 5 years only, 3 being years of 355 days, and 2 having an intercalary month which raised the number of days to 385. The intercalary month is inserted once in the winter (before Giamon(us)), when it seems to have been called by a name beginning with X, and once in the summer (before Samon(us)), when it may have been called by one ending with -cantaran. The order of the last 5 months in our solar year was Rivros, Anagantios, Ogron(us), Qutios or Cutios, and Giamon(us). The calculations that Oct. 14 was intercisus at Coligny as well as at Rome, but Aug. 22 not, were erroneous. The position of Qutios or Cutios makes my explanation 'Threshing-month' impossible, and shows me that it should be 'Wet' or 'Cloudy', the stem being Stokes's 'kavat- Schauer' (74), which gives 'ir. cúa, Gen Sg. cúad, Winter . . . . cymr. cawad, cawod, cafod „imber, nimbus", acorn. couat (gl. nimbus) . . . bret. couhat glau „ondée de pluie", jetzt kaouad' (ib.). That this is not a q-stem is shown by the Brythonic forms beginning with c, not p; but I maintain my derivation of quimon from a q-stem, and hold that ciallos is from one.

Captain Espérandieu's restoration shows that the word beginning with PET, which when written in full turns out to be PETIVX, and the words BRIC, CO, and OCIOMV, occur only in Rivros or the month after it, and that each time they are followed by the nom. Rivros, the gen. Rivri, or an abbreviation of that month's name. It is clear to me that these 4 words represent different dates connected with 'Harvest' (Rivros) and the internal evidence for the order of the 4 dates shows it to have been Bric (thrice on Rivros 4), Petiux (once on Rivros 25, once on Rivros 23), Co (once on Rivros 25, once on Rivros 13, once on Anagantios 2), and Ociomu (once on Rivros 4, thrice on Anagantios 4). The meaning of Bric is quite clear to me — it is the 'Whitening' of the harvest, from '*brak blinken' (Stokes 170). The first part of Petiux is certainly from the stem of Stokes's '[p]itu-, [p]ittu- Korn, Getreide' (45), which yields 'ir. ith, Gen. etho + cymr. yd „frumentum, seges", îth in gwenith (= vindittu) „triticum, far, ador", corn. yd (gl. seges), bret. id, ed, eth „blé"' (ib.), and I suggest that all these forms may be explained from a single stem petiu-. In the case of Co, its special association with Harvest is shown by the fact that when it occurs on Rivros 25 the mutilated entry against that day has [ʀ]ɪᴠʀɪᴏʙɪᴠʀɪ i. e. 'Rivri Co Rivri', where I erroneously took the first 5 letters visible to represent Lat. *iurid(icus dies)*.

And I now believe that ᴘʀɪɴɴɪ and ʟᴀᴄɪᴛ, so often occurring together, and each so often associated with ʟᴏᴠᴅ or ʟᴏᴅ, do not represent any Latin words but are pure Sequanian. *Loud-* is the Sequanian analogue to Lat. *ludi*. *Lacit-* I take to = *spectacula* from Stokes's stem 'lakato-, lokato- Auge' (237); cf. the double sense, active and passive, of our English 'spectacles' and 'sight'. *Prinno* and *prinni* I take to be sing. and pl. of *prinnos* from the stem of Stokes's '[p]rannâ Teil' (227) —? cf. Lat. *prand-ium*. The days so marked were in fact days when games and spectacles were exhibited in the amphitheatre of the colony[1] ('Coligny') and public 'doles' (cf. Lat. *prandia*) given.

Whether Sequanian and continental Pictish were absolutely identical the materials do not enable us to deceide, but any difference between them was obviously no more than a very slight dialectal one. Both preserve Ind.-Eur. *p*, and represent initial Ind.-Eur. *q* by *c*,[2] reducing an original *qeislos* to the

---

[1]) See Holder (1067), Longnon (*Atlas hist. de la France*, pl. VII and p. 175). Scribes wrote 'Coloniacum' as late as the end of the 13th cent., and 'Colognacum' centuries later still (see Bernard, *Cartulaire de Savigny* &c. II, p. 1116).

[2]) In the *Revue Celtique* for Jan. 1899, pp. 108—9, M. d'Arbois de Jubainville points out that '*Epamanduodurum*, Mandeure, et *Loposagium*, Luxiol' were in Sequanian territory, and regards each as an instance of *p* for *q*. But the name of the Sequani suggests that they had once lived on the Sequana (Seine) and had migrated E. Hence these two places may have been originally Brythonic settlements.

M. d'Arbois argues that the agnomen Poppilli (gen.) of a Sequanian citizen of Lyon shows a Sequanian Poppillos, with mutation of *q* to *p*: to me it is merely the gen. of the Latin name Popilius, Popillius. Surely the *q* in the name of the Sequanians themselves is good evidence that 'le *q* médial se serait maintenu'.

Whether we derive the name of the Sequana from the root of Ind.-Eur. *seikô* 'I gush out' (Fick, *Vergl. Wörterb.* I, 137), as does Stokes (295), or from Ind.-Eur. *seik-* 'to dry up' (Fick ib.), whence Lat. *siccus*, it first got that name at or above Châtillon-sur-Seine: for 'en certains étés il n'y a plus d'eau dans son lit aux approches de Châtillon; mais là-même, d'une grotte, sort une douix supérieure aux autres, onde éternelle . . . au-dessous de laquelle on n'a jamais vu sécher le fleuve de Paris (Vivien de Saint-Martin, *Nouv. dict. de géog. univ.* V, p. 777). Châtillon is a little N. W. of the position of the Sequani in Caesar's time.

same form *ciallos*. These are conclusive tests of a Goidelic language: in Irish *qeisl-* has given *ciall*, *q* has become *c*, and, though single *p* has been lost or mutated, *pp* is apparently still represented by *pp* or *p*.[1])

We have seen reason to trace the *p*-preserving Kelts also on the Po and at Verona. In fact the inscriptions and proper names of the entire ancient Keltic-speaking area require to be examined from a totally changed standpoint. Hitherto it has been generally assumed that every *p* was a mutated *q* (unless borrowed from a Latin gentile name), and that on the Continent Ind.-Eur. *q* was lost altogether: it now seems that as regards a considerable part both of Gaul and of N. Italy this assumption is the direct reverse of the truth. What the result of the re-examination may be on the history of the Keltic races and speeches and of those most nearly related to them it is impossible to foresee.

I have reserved to the end the question whether there is any evidence that the continental Picts tattooed, because I do not for a moment allow that the derivation of their name should be considered as depending on my ability to produce such evidence. But I can produce it. In the catalogue of the Gaulish coins in the Bibliothèque Nationale the obverse of a coin of the Pictones, no. 4439, is described as 'Tête à droite, les cheveux divisés en grosses mèches; croix en relief sur la joue.' The coin is depicted in the atlas: the cross is not an ear-ornament, but is well on the cheek, and has a knob at each of its four ends. A similar cross is used as a symbol on coins of the Osismii and Coriosopites of Aremorica ([6522], 6537, 6578, 6584), the Caletes at the N. of the Seine's mouth (7352), the Ambiani of Amiens (8472, 8476, [8503, 8505]), the Viroduni of Verdun (8990, 8993), emigrant Senones (9275), 'Germani' (9366, 9367, carried by soldier in right hand ? meant for a caltrop), 'Gaulois en Pannonie' (10 157). Moreover a X is cut on the cheek in D 19 on the last plate in the atlas (Collection Danicourt, Musée de

---

[1]) Stokes derives Ir. *ceapach* (Highland Gaelic the same) from 'keppo-s Garten' (76), Ir. *gop* from 'goppo-s Mund' (114), Ir. *timpán* (Highland Gaelic *tiompan*) from 'temppu- Saite' (129), and Ir. *ropp* from 'ruppo-s ein stössiges Tier' (236). He also gives Ir. *rap* (cf. Highland Gaelic *rapach* [Macbain]) as from '*re[p] packen, reissen' (226) through *rapnó-* (with intermediate *rappo-*, no doubt).

Péronne) and a + on the hind-quarters of a horse on a British coin of Cunobelinus struck at Camulodunum (Evans IX, 9) figured on pl. XLIV.

I have run my eye over the thousands of coins in this atlas for other apparent cases of tattooing, and have found some very interesting ones. In 5318, a coin of the Sequani, a figure like a Greek ɐ is cut on the bottom of a jaw: it lies on its side with the round end towards the chin. In 6913, an Aremorican coin, a head shows a design reaching from the eye to the neck: it consists of waving lines with circles at their upper end. In 6933, a coin of the Unalli, who inhabited the Cotentin, a head has on it a short sword with the hilt on the neck and the point level with the nostrils. In 6897, a coin of the 'Aulerci Cenomani' of Maine, almost an entire cheek is scooped out into a circle, with an inner circle of dots, inside which is a cock with 3 dots at the back of his head. In 6954, a coin of the Baiocasses of Bayeux, a circle is also scooped out of the cheek, and inside it are A and 3 dots. The coins found in Jersey abound in heads with figures on the cheek. Sometimes these are merely concentric circles with dots in the middle, and may have been imitated by the moneyer from the dots used on some Gaulish coins to indicate whiskers, but from a comparison of various obverses and reverses it is clear that he meant them to represent astronomical bodies. In other cases (J. 15, 10387, J. 49, J. 50) the figure is quite certainly a three- or four-tailed comet.

It is to be noticed that except as regards the Sequanians, whom we have already had to pronounce Goidels, all these examples come from regions in the W. of Gaul — the southermost being Poitou, which we know to have been Goidelic. Are they signs of a Goidelic race?[1] If so, the Aulerci Cenomani were Goidels, and, if they, then doubtless the Cenomani of Cisalpine Gaul. Now the Cenomani of Cisalpine Gaul dwelt on the Po and in Verona, and we have already seen reason to believe

---

[1] Cf. Isidore of Seville, *Etymolog.* IX, 2 § 103, '*Scoti* propria lingua nomen habent a picto corpore, eo quod aculeis ferreis cum atramento variarum figurarum stigmate annotentur' — the passage from which the opening words of the Pictish Chronicle have been adapted by substituting 'Picti' for 'Scoti'. The derivation of 'Scot' from a stem meaning 'cut', 'tattoo', has been suggested also in modern times: see Rhŷs, *Celtic Britain*, pp. 237—8, and Macbain 855.

that the name of the Po (Padus) was given to it by *p*-preserving Kelts, and that *p*-preserving Kelts lived in Verona!

And a singular confirmation as regards Verona is supplied by the new part of Holder. Gregory of Tours, an Auvergne man by birth, is describing an incident which happened at Clermont in Auvergne, and mentions 'urceum, qui anax dicitur' (*Mirac.* 2, 8 — Holder 137). Stokes (46) suggests that *anax* and Ir. *án* F. 'Trinkgeschirr' are from '*[p]o ... trinken'. *Now* Holder on col. 925 prints the following epigram of Martial (14, 100):

Panaca

Si non ignota est docti tibi terra Catulli,
　potasti testa Raetica vina mea.

I cannot end without paying the profoundest homage to the zeal, patience, and acumen exhibited by M. Jullian in deciphering the Rom tablet. Nor must the name of M. Blumereau, whose excavations led to its discovery, be forgotten. They have given us a new and wonderful illustration of the saying that 'Truth lies at the bottom of a well'!

Oxford.　　　　　　　　　　　　E. W. B. NICHOLSON.

Den vorstehenden Artikel haben wir wegen seiner sachlichen Ausführungen den Lesern der Zeitschrift nicht vorenthalten wollen, obgleich wir die sprachlichen Deutungen des Verfassers nur als einen Versuch betrachten, der bei dem dermaligen Stande dieser Forschungen gesicherte Ergebnisse noch nicht haben konnte.　　　　　　　　Die Herausgeber.

BRIEFE VON J. K. ZEUSS AN CHR. W. GLÜCK.

Vorwort.

Christian Wilhelm Glück, der Sohn des Erlanger Juristen Christian Friedrich und selbst ein gelehrter Jurist, wandte sich nach politisch aufgeregten Lebensjahren dem Studium des Celtischen zu und ist als Verfasser namentlich eines tüchtigen Werkes über die bei Cäsar vorkommenden celtischen Namen rühmlich bekannt. Er starb als Sekretär der K. B. Hof- und Staatsbibliothek zu München 1866 im 56. Lebensjahre, war also nur 4 Jahre jünger als Zeuss. An diesen richtete er, durch den Germanisten und Freund Franz Pfeiffers Alois Jos. Vollmer († 1876) eingeführt, 1853, ehe noch die Grammatica Celtica erschienen war, einige wissenschaftliche Fragen, an die sich ein bis in Zeussens Todesjahr fortgesetzter Briefwechsel anschloss.

Der verehrlichen Direktion der K. B. Hof- und Staatsbibliothek in München bin ich für die wohlwollende Mitteilung der Zeussischen Briefe dankbar, die ich nun den Lesern der Zeitschrift vorlege. Es sind 29 Briefe (zu dreien, Nr. 9. 10. 22, finden sich in dem Nachlasse auch die mit Blei geschriebenen Konzepte) und einige Beilagen, und sie betreffen in der Hauptsache das Altceltische. Wenn solche Schriftstücke nach fast einem halben Jahrhundert für die celtische Philologie Neues kaum noch ergeben, und einen Wert vielleicht nur für ihre Geschichte haben, so sind sie uns doch als die Reliquien eines bedeutenden Mannes wichtig. Hier und dort lassen diese Briefe die Persönlichkeit des untadeligen Gelehrten durchscheinen, die uns in der unnahbaren Strenge seiner Werke verhüllt bleibt. Hier redet, freimütig auf seine Wissenschaft vertrauend, der ernste und gütige Meister zu seinem wissbegierigen, dankbaren Schüler, der diese Lehrbriefe pietätvoll aufbewahrt und uns überliefert hat.

Der folgende wortgetreue Abdruck ist mit erläuternden Anmerkungen versehen, wo solche für das unmittelbare Verständnis nötig oder nützlich erschienen.

Berlin. Ludw. Chr. Stern.

1.

Bamberg, den 3. Mai 1853.

Verehrtester Herr!

Wenn Sie für Ihre Arbeit noch einige Zeit vor sich haben, so wird es Ihnen vielleicht nicht unangenehm sein, wenn ich Sie statt einer eigentlichen Antwort auf Ihre wissenschaftlichen Anfragen auf meine in ein paar Monaten erscheinende Grammatica celtica verweise, wo Sie unter dem Diphthong AU ausser dem norischen Lauriacum auch ein westgallisches, den gallischen Mannsnamen Lauro, aus bretonischem Chartularien die Mannsnamen Louran, Lourone, Louronui, aus altirischen Glossen das Adj. *loor, lour*, das Subst. *loure* (aus gallischem *laur*, was aber nicht 'Wasser' bedeutet haben kann), ferner unter der Ableitung ÂC, JÂC (altkymr. -auc, -iauc) die Deutung der gallischen Ortsnamen mit *-acum, -iacum* finden werden.

Die gallische Endung *-acum, -aco* etc. kann unmöglich ein Plural sein; Sie haben das selbst schon gefunden und aus den Träumereien Mone's sich schön hinausgearbeitet.[1] Ich freue mich deshalb, Sie hiermit als einen feinen, gründlichen Forscher zu begrüssen.

Hrn. Vollmer grüssen Sie mir freundlichst und melden Sie ihm, dass ich alsbald nach Vollendung der Arbeit (und ich denke, es soll das bis zu Anfang der Herbstferien geschehen sein) auf kurze Zeit nach München zu kommen gedenke. Da soll es mich freuen, Ihre Bekanntschaft zu machen, und Ihre Frage vielleicht auch mündlich zu besprechen.

Entschuldigen Sie die Verzögerung meiner Antwort, woran aber die jetzt mehr als sonst drängende Arbeit schuld ist.

Hochachtungsvoll

Ihr

ergebenster

Zeuß, Prof.

Sr. Wohlgeboren
Herrn Chr. W. Glück, Literat
in
München
Schwanthalerstrasse Nro. 28a.[2]

---

[1] Vgl. Glücks Keltische Namen p. XIV.

[2] Die Briefe sind von Nr. 8 an nach der Schwanthalerstrasse Nr. 25c, von Nr. 15 nach derselben Strasse Nr. 27 adressiert.

.2.

Bamberg, den 23. Juli 1853.

Hochgeehrter Herr und Freund!

Vielleicht ist es Ihnen möglich, mir in folgender Angelegenheit auszuhelfen. Ich wünschte die Einsicht von ein paar Stellen in folgenden zwei Werkchen, die weder hier noch in Erlangen auf-zutreiben sind: 1. Peyron, Ciceron. orat. fragm. inedita, Stuttgart 1824; 2. Lateinische Gedichte des 10. und 11. Jahrh., von J. Grimm und A. Schmeller, Göttingen 1838.

Dass das erste, von Peyron, auf der k. Hofbibliothek in München vorhanden ist, weiss ich, da ich es daselbst schon benützt habe; ohne Zweifel ist es auch das andere. Sie würden mich Ihnen sehr verbinden, wenn Sie dieselben herausnehmen und mir durch die Post zuschicken könnten. In ganz kurzer Zeit, in acht Tagen, haben Sie sie wieder zurück.

Im Laufe des Septembers, hoffe ich, werde ich selbst in München erscheinen können, und ich freue mich darauf.

Hochachtungsvoll
Ihr
ergebenster
Zeuß, Prof.

3.

Bamberg, den 11. August 1853.

Hochgeehrter Herr und Freund!

Ich schicke hiermit die zwei Bücher, die Sie so gefällig waren mir zu übersenden, wieder zurück, und danke schönstens für Ihre Güte. Ich werde nun in kurzer Zeit die gelehrten Herren in München selbst sehen; sollten Sie vorher noch mich mit einem Schreiben beehren, wie Sie in Ihrem letzten Briefe äussern, so würde es mich sehr freuen.

Die Stelle, die Sie in Martène[1]) nicht finden, ist in meinen Excerpten so notiert: Tom. I, p. 51. Praec. Caroli Magni a. 797, res sitas in Andecavo, villas nuncupatas Lauriaco et Catiaco.

---

[1]) Dom Edmond Martène, Veterum scriptorum et monumentorum am-plissima collectio, Paris 1724.

Sollten Sie mir bald schreiben, und ich wünschte das, so möchte ich Sie ersuchen, mir folgende excerpierte Stelle aus dem Werke, das auf der Staatsbibliothek vorhanden ist, zu ergänzen. O'Conor, Rerum hibernicarum scriptores, Tom. III, p. 648, ad a. 1085: *Gilla na naomh Laighen*, ... 7 *Cennmanach iar sin in Uairisburg* (Gildas sanctorum Lageniensis, ... et caput monachorum postea Herbipoli, obiit).

Ich habe früher die Bedeutung der Stelle nicht gekannt.[1] Ich vermuthe hier, da das Schottenkloster in Würzburg erst 1134 gegründet ist, eine Verwechselung mit Marianus Scotus, der in Würzburg die Priesterweihe erhalten hat, möchte aber doch alles, was von diesem *Gilla* oder *Gildas* im irischen Text und in der Übersetzung von O'Conor (das Ganze wird sehr wenig sein) dasteht, kennen.

> Hochachtungsvollst
> Ihr
> ergebenster
> Zeuß, Prof.

4.

Bamberg, den 25. September 1853.

Geehrtester Herr und Freund!

Er lässt von sich nichts hören und nichts sehen, werden Sie von mir denken. Wirklich wahr. Seit Ihrem letzten Schreiben wechselte eine Korrektur mit der andern, und wenn eine kleine Pause blieb, so war sie für Untersuchungen in Anspruch genommen. Erst jetzt, nachdem das Gedränge vorüber und nur die Korrektur von den letzten paar Bogen noch übrig ist, kann ich ans Briefschreiben denken. Die Sache hat sich also ungeachtet des Drängens des Verlegers, der die Erscheinung des Werkes schon auf die Mitte des Septembers angekündigt hatte, ziemlich verzögert, und erst in den ersten Wochen des Oktobers wird meine Abreise Statt finden können. Näheres weiss ich auch jetzt noch nicht anzugeben.

Auf den Wunsch des Hrn. Vollmer werde ich natürlich Rücksicht nehmen. Der Preis des Buches ist ziemlich hoch, wie

---

[1] Vgl. Grammatica celtica[1] p. XXIII ff.

Sie vielleicht schon in der Ankündigung des Leipziger Blattes gelesen haben, auf 8 Thaler für die 2 Bände, die zugleich ausgegeben werden, festgesetzt. Auf den Verleger einwirken, dass er einzelne Exemplare wohlfeiler abgebe, kann ich wohl nicht; allein ich bin bereit, aus dem Vorrathe meiner Freiexemplare an Sie und Hrn. Vollmer zwei gratis abzugeben, wenn Sie mir versprechen, neue Beobachtungen und Erfahrungen, die Sie im Umfange dieses Zweiges machen werden, aufzuzeichnen, und mir einmal bei etwaiger neuer Auflage des Buches zur Benützung zu übergeben.

Über die gelehrten Untersuchungen, deren Sie in Ihrem Schreiben gedenken, werden wir uns am besten in nächster Zeit mündlich besprechen. Nur über die Bedeutung des Namens *Vindobona* will ich, weil Sie es ausdrücklich wünschen, meine Ansicht angeben. Sie werden vielleicht grosse Augen machen, wenn ich sage, dass ich vermuthe, er bedeute 'Weissenbrunn'. Die Form Vindobona muss wohl als die reinste und sicherste gelten; die übrigen sind der Entstellung verdächtig. Das gallische *vind*, ausser den von Ihnen angegebenen auch noch in andern Namen, wie *Vindonissa, Vindomagus, Vindesca* etc., vorkommend, ist von Buchstab zu Buchstab das ir. gäl. Adj. *fionn*, alt *find*, kymr. *gwynn, gwenn* 'weiss'. Sie werden die Umbildung dieser Laute von mir nachgewiesen finden. Möglich dass *Vind* auch als Mannsname gebraucht war; da habe ich nichts dagegen. Das Wort *bona*, das ausser den von Ihnen angegebenen sich auch in Ratisbona (gall. *ratis* 'Farrenkraut'), mit Ableitung in Bononia in Italien und Nordgallien zeigt, ist nicht mehr so erreichbar: da bleibt nichts übrig als Wagen. Aus der Wurzel abgeleitet sind wohl kymr. *bonedd*, ir. *bunad* 'origo'. Wie, wenn die Wurzel *bon* nichts wäre als buchstäblich das lat. *fon* in *fon-s, fon-tis*? Lateinischem *f* entspricht fast regelmässig kelt. *b*, z. B. in *fráter*, ir. *bráthir*, kymr. *braut*, u. in andern, die Sie von mir erwähnt finden werden. Auch den Namen Vindobona werden Sie von mir an mehreren Stellen erwähnt finden.

Hochachtungsvoll

Ihr

ergebenster

Zeuß.

5.

Bamberg, den 8. November 1853.

Verehrtester Herr und Freund

Sie erhalten hiemit die 2 Exemplare der Grammatica celtica. Sie früher zu schicken, war mir nicht möglich: Letzten Samstag vor 8 Tagen war ich von meiner Reise hier wieder angekommen und hatte sogleich nach Leipzig um Freiexemplare geschrieben, aber erst gestern Abends ist das Paket hier angekommen.

Meine Reise über Ulm und Friedrichshafen nach St. Gallen, wo ich 3 Tage war,[1]) und zurück über Lindau und Kempten ist vom schönsten Wetter begünstigt gewesen.

Ich bin aufmerksam gemacht worden auf ein Bruchstück aus einem vatikanischen Codex, überschrieben Fragmentum Scoticum, in Angelo Mai's Auctores classici, in dem Bande, der um das Jahr 1832—33 erschienen sei. Es sei das Bruchstück in barbarischem Latein geschrieben mit unverständlichen Wörtern, die vielleicht aus dem Irischen erklärt werden könnten. Ich habe dieses Werk des A. Mai bis jetzt auf keiner Bibliothek auftreiben können. Es wäre mir sehr angenehm, wenn Sie auf der Staatsbibliothek darnach suchten, und wenn Sie das Stück fänden, mir den Band nur auf ein paar Tage zuschicken möchten.

Meine Grüsse an Vollmer.

Hochachtungsvoll
ergebenster
Z e u ß.

6.

Bamberg, den 30. November 1853.

Verehrtester Herr und Freund!

Ich schicke hiermit die 2 Bände der Mai'schen Sammlung wieder zurück, und danke Ihnen schönstens, dass Sie mir beide geschickt haben. Ich habe für den altkeltischen Sprachvorrath zwar keine Bereicherung, jedoch sonst einige hübsche Sachen darin gefunden.

---

[1]) Die Notizen, die sich Zeuss damals über die Sangaller Codices machte, befinden sich in seinem Nachlasse. Sie bestätigen meist nur die Lesungen in seiner Grammatik (GC.[1] p. XIII ff.).

Den Virgilius grammaticus[1]) habe ich schon in der Vorrede
meines Werkes (p. XLVIII) abgewiesen. Ich kann in all den
bei ihm erwähnten Wörtern auch jetzt nichts Keltisches finden,
sondern nur ein gemachtes Geheimlatein (z. B. S. 99 quoque-
vihabis = *coque-vi-habis*, i. e. quod coquendi vim habet [*quo-
quere* für coquere auch in Mai's 8. Bd.] und andre ähnliche für
ignis, die Zahlwörter auf S. 125).

Desselben Gehalts, nur irischen (schottischen) Ursprungs,
jedoch auch kein einziges irisches Wort enthaltend, sind die
Hisperica famina, die ohne Zweifel Greith[2]) in St. Gallen mir
mit seinem Fragmentum scoticum gemeint hat (er hat nur die
Überschrift nicht mehr gewusst). Aber einigen Dienst hat mir
dies Stück geleistet, da es Licht auf einige dunkle lateinische
Wörter unter meinen altkymrischen Glossen wirft.

Da ich nun einmal angefangen habe, mich mit diesem
sonderbaren Latein zu befassen, so wäre es mir wirklich lieb,
wenn ich ein anderes Produkt dieser Art auch einsehen könnte,
worauf A. Mai verweist. Es ist dies von Atto Vercellensis und
zwar im sechsten Bande seiner Scriptores veteres. Es muss das
eine andere Sammlung von A. Mai sein, weil dieser Atto im
3ten Band der gegenwärtigen, der Auct. classici, die ich wohl
kenne, citiert wird.[3]) Es wäre mir sehr angenehm, wenn Sie
mir auch jenen 6ten Band der *Scriptores veteres* von A. Mai noch
auf ein paar Tage zuschickten. Ich werde Sie dann nicht weiter
plagen.

Matuinus, Saltuinus können allerdings keltische Namen sein
und Ableitungsbildungen, wie Nantuates, Bituitus, Meduana,
Arduenna (*nant* vallis, *bit* mundus, etc.), und andere, die ich auf
S. 725 anführe. Die deutschen Eigennamen auf *-uinus* (= *win*)
sind freilich davon fern zu halten, auch die Ableitung *-ên*, da
der Übergang des ursprünglichen *ê* in *oi*, *ui*, *wy* wohl im
Kymrischen Regel ist, aber doch nicht auch für Gallisches
geltend gemacht werden kann. Gegen Ihre Zusammenstellung

---

[1]) Classicorum auctorum e Vaticanis codicibus editorum tom. V cur.
Angelo Maio, Romæ 1833, p. 1 ff.

[2]) C. J. Greith, der Verfasser der 'Geschichte der altirischen Kirche als
Einleitung in die Geschichte des Stifts St. Gallen', Freiburg 1867. Die hier
erwähnten Hisperica Famina stehen in A. Mai's Classic. auct. 5, 479—500.

[3]) Des Bischofs Atto satirische Schrift 'Polypticum' in ungebräuchlicher
und mystischer Latinität (10. Jahrh.) steht in A. Mai's Scriptorum veterum
nova collectio e Vaticanis codicibus edita, tom. VI, 1832, part. 2, p. 43 ff.

des Namens Mansuinivus mit Primanivus habe ich nichts zu
erinnern; nur ist bei so einzeln stehenden Inschriften-Namen
Vorsicht zu empfehlen, da sie falsch gelesen und selbst falsch
eingehauen sein können, wie Beispiele vorkommen, und Sicherheit
nur bei öfterem Vorkommen oder weiterer Bestätigung erreicht
werden kann.[1])

Wenn Sie wieder schreiben, wäre es mir angenehm, wenn
Sie mir andeuten möchten, wo Sie Nachricht von einem Schotten-
kloster in Constanz, von der Sie bei meiner Anwesenheit in
München sprachen, gefunden haben.[2])

Grüsse an Vollmer. Hochachtungsvollst

Ihr

ergebenster

Z e u ß.

[Auf besonderm Zettel.]

N. S. Die seltenen lat. Wörter, die in den von Mone ent-
deckten altkymr. Glossenbruchstücken vorkommen,[3]) finden nicht
nur durch die Famina Hesperica bei Angelo Mai (wovon Sie mir
den Band überschickt haben), sondern auch durch eine kleine
von Hoffmann v. Fallersleben aus einer Hs. zu Neuwied vor
einigen Jahren herausgegebene mittelalterliche Schrift[4]) Aufklärung.

Forschen Sie über den Ptol. Namen χαιτονωροι (ungefähr
in der südlichen Oberpfalz) weiter nach. Ich halte καιτονοροι
aus den verschiedenen Lesarten für das Rechte, Cait-vori, aus
kymr. caead, alt caeat 'Decke' und -vor, das in zusammengesetzten Mannesnamen, wie Matuuor, Bedwor etc., vorkömmt,
und der Bedeutung des griechischen -φόρος zu sein scheint.
(Mynwar, mynwor ist 'collare', d. i. Halstracht, wor also 'Tracht'
und 'Träger'). Also Caetvori 'Deckenträger'. In derselben

---

[1]) In der That heisst der Name richtig vielmehr Masuinnus, was Glück
von w. masw 'lascivus, mollis' ableitet und dem Namen Arduinna vergleicht.

[2]) Das Schottenkloster in Constanz wurde 1142 gegründet; es war eine
Kolonie des Mutterklosters in Regensburg. Vgl. W. Wattenbachs Abhandlung
'Die Kongregation der Schottenklöster in Deutschland' in der Zeitschrift für
christliche Archäologie und Kunst I, 1856, p. 49.

[3]) Die Luxemburger Glossen; s. Mone, Die gallische Sprache, Karlsruhe
1851, p. 76. Vgl. jetzt H. Zimmer in den Nachrichten der Göttinger Gesellschaft der Wissenschaften, philol.-histor. Klasse, 1895 p. 119.

[4]) Epistola Adami Balsamiensis ad Anselmum ex codice Coloniensi edidit
Hoffmannus Fallerslebensis. Neowidæ (1853).

Gegend stehen in der Tab. Peut. Armalausi[1]) d. i. 'Armellose',
wohl deutsche Benennung desselben Völkchens, da das Wort
armalaus 'ohne Ärmel' auch im Altnordischen noch vorkömmt.

7.

Bamberg, den 12. Januar 1854.
Verehrter Herr und Freund!

Hiermit sende ich den Band der Mai'schen Sammlung, den
Sie mir zu schicken die Güte hatten, wieder zurück und will
Sie vor der Hand nicht weiter belästigen. Möglich, dass ich
später einmal mich daran mache, den O'Conor wegen einiger
Sachen noch einmal zu durchlaufen.

Für Ihre Mittheilung über Tragiva flum. danke ich Ihnen,
ebenso über Arlape, wo ich jedoch nur Arel. It. citiere, so dass
sich die Form Arelape in dem einen oder andern Itinerar (Itin.
Ant. oder Tab. Peut.) im Texte oder den Varianten finden muss.
Das spätere Erlafa ist wohl deutsche Umformung des kelt.
Namens nach dem Subst. *erla* 'alnus'. Mit dergleichen Beobachtungen und Untersuchungen bitte ich schön fortzufahren.
Mit Ihrer Untersuchung[2]) des Namens Merc. Tourenus bin ich
ganz einverstanden, weniger mit Merc. Cissonius, der schnelle
(Götterbote), da der keltische Merc. (Teutates) seiner Stellung
nach ebensowenig Götterbote sein konnte, als der germanische
Mercurius (Wodan). Unter meinen altirischen Glossen kömmt
cissi 'Haarlocken' vor; also Cissonius = Cincinnatus?

Für Ihr nächstes Schreiben ersuche ich Sie um gütige
Mittheilung des Titels des Herrn A. Peyron aus seinem Buche:
Ciceron. Orat. fragm. ined., Stuttg. 1824.[3]) Hat Vollmer am
Keltischen schon angebissen oder steckt er noch im Gothischen?

Hochachtungsvoll

Ihr

ergebenster

Zeuß.

----

[1]) Oder Armilausini, vgl. K. Müllenhoff, Deutsche Alterthumskunde 3, 316.

[2]) Später veröffentlicht in den Münchener Gel. Anz., Hist. Cl., 1854,
Sp. 42 f.

[3]) Dieser Titel war 'In R. Taurinensi Athenaeo ling. orient. professor,
colleg. theolog. XXX vir et R. Scientiarum Academiae socius'.

8.

Bamberg, den 24. Januar 1854.

Verehrtester Freund!

Meine letzte Sendung, den Quartband von A. Mai, werden Sie erhalten haben. Ich ersuche Sie, sobald es für Sie thunlich ist, mir den Titel des A. Peyron, wie er auf dem Titelblatt seines auf der Staatsbibliothek vorhandenen Werkes: Ciceronis orat. fragmenta inedita, Stuttg. 1824, sich findet, mittheilen zu wollen.

Etwas für Hrn. Vollmer. Ich erhielt vor ein paar Tagen unter Umschlag mit meiner Adresse ein Schriftchen: 'Heinrich von Stretelingen. Ein altdeutsches Gedicht. Den Freunden älterer deutscher Dichtung dargebracht auf Neujahr 1854', ohne Angabe des Druckortes, des Herausgebers und die mindeste Andeutung seiner Herkunft.[1] Es sei dem Leipziger Packet beigelegen gewesen, erfuhr ich nur in der Buchhandlung. Das Gedicht, eine Romanze von 39 Strophen im Nibelungenversmasse, ist aus der Mitte des 13. Jahrhunderts. Weiss Vollmer etwas davon? Hochachtungsvollst

ergebenster

Zeuß.

9.

Bamberg, den 3. Februar 1854.

Verehrter Herr und Freund!

Ich danke sehr für Ihre gütige Mittheilung dessen, was ich gewünscht habe. Ihre Bemerkungen über verschiedene Punkte und Namen, z. B. Cobeperdus,[2] Caractacus, Bagaudae etc., sind mir ganz willkommen, und ich werde sie in Zukunft nicht ausser Acht lassen; für jetzt sind mir nur die Autoritäten, auf die Sie sich stützen, nicht immer sicher genug. Steininschriften haben bekanntlich öfter ganz nachlässige Schreibung, deren Grund in der Unwissenheit und Unbildung der Steinmetzen zu suchen ist;

---

[1] Dieses Gedicht über die Stretlinger Haussage ist, auf Wunsch einer Dame, von Franz Pfeiffer verfasst, der es an Freunde zu verschenken pflegte. Vgl. seine Germania 13, 253.

[2] Wohl Cobnertus gemeint.

ihren Namen traue ich nur bei weiterer Bestätigung. Den Etymologieen, die Sie aus O'Reilly machen, traue ich auch nur bei
weiterer Bestätigung. Wie, wenn z. B. *bágh* 'Band', aus dem
Sie Bagaudae erklären, für *bádh*, mit der nicht seltenen Verwechselung zwischen *gh* und *dh* stände, und *á* für *an*, so dass
bádh ganz das deutsche *band*, sanskr. *bandh* wäre? In *troigh*
'Fuss', welches mit *troidh* wechselt, ist *gh* das Richtige (Gramm.
celt. p. 6). Im gälischen Lexikon der Highlands' Society finde
ich: '*Bagh* 1. a promise, a bond, a tie, or obligation : promissum,
vinculum, adstrictus; 2. kindness, respect, friendship : benignitas,
observantia, amicitia'.[1] In dieser letzten Bedeutung steht *bádh*
bei O'Reilly; wie also, wenn hier umgekehrt *dh* das Richtige wäre?

     Unter Ihren Erklärungen des Namens Giegeus ist un-
bedenklich die der Ableitung vorzuziehen. Vergleichung mit
kymr. Wurzeln *gwg, gygu* ist unzulässig, da diese auf früheres
guc zurückgehen, früheres *g* aber im späteren Kymrisch in der
Mitte und am Ende immer verloren geht. Ferner ist *ie* kein
gallischer Wurzellaut, wenn nicht etwa es für *i* steht, und dem
heutigen kymr. *gi* 'nervus' = *gi* altes *gig* zu Grunde liegt, so
dass Giegeus = Gîgeus, i. e. nervosus, wäre.

     Die Erklärungen des Namens *Fitacit:* haben bedeutende
Schwierigkeiten. Mir scheint *fil. Tacit:* immer noch das Ein-
fachste;[2] und kommt denn sonst der Genitiv ohne filius vor?

     Für Sero, Serro etc. kenne ich nichts aus ältern Quellen.

     Die Endung *ius* neben *us* in alten gallischen Namen als
etwas Besonderes bezeichnend aus dem Keltischen erklären zu
wollen, wer möchte das versuchen? Dass die keltischen Völker
keine Geschlechtsnamen gehabt haben, weder vor noch nach den
Römern, ist wohl offenbar, ebenso, dass sie unter der römischen
Herrschaft keine gehabt haben. Zugegeben kann werden, dass
einzelne, die in römischen Staats- oder Kriegsdiensten standen,
die römische Sitte nachgeahmt haben, dass etwa einige statt
nach gallischer Sitte sich *N. fil. N.* zu nennen, um den Schein
eines römischen Geschlechtsnamens zu haben, die lateinische
Endung *ius* an den Namen ihres Vaters angehängt hätten, so
dass z. B. Meddignatius so viel gewesen wäre wie Meddignati

---

[1] O'Reilly hat unter *bágh* die Bedeutungen von *bág* 'Kampf', wovon
bagaudae, und von *báid* 'lieb', wovon das schottisch-gälische *bagh*, vereinigt.

[2] Hierüber handelt Glück in den Münchener Gel. Anz., Hist. Cl., 1854
Col. 52 ff.

filius, Nertomarius = Nertomari filius. Sonst wüsste ich in
diesem Augenblicke für den Unterschied der Endung in *-gnatius,
-marius* von der gewöhnlichen *-gnatus, -marus* nichts anzugeben.
Ob es in mehreren Fällen passt, werden Sie in dem Inschriften-
vorrath, den Sie vor sich haben, finden können; ich habe jetzt
von diesem Material gar nichts in den Händen.

So wenig wir von einer altgallischen Endung *i*, werden
wir mit Sicherheit von einem altgallischen *a* im Auslaute etwas
sagen können. Da übrigens die Endung *au*, *av* in gallischen
Eigennamen häufig genug ist, so ist immerhin am wahr-
scheinlichsten, dass der helvet. Name Cattaus = Cattavus ist.

Wenn Sie etwa das altir. *cissi*, *cissib* irgendwo zu erwähnen haben, können Sie genauer die Stelle aus dem Würzburger Codex selbst auf S. 1046 der Gramm. celt., Glosse 10, wo
es das lat. 'tortis crinibus' glossiert, bezeichnen.

Auf Ihre Recension des Hefnerschen Buches[1]) freue ich
mich. Sie werden mir wohl ein Exemplar derselben zukommen
lassen können?

Ich muss endlich Ihre Güte wieder mit einigen Anfragen
in Anspruch nehmen. Einmal, ob auf der Staats-Bibliothek die
Transactions of the Irish Academy vorhanden sind? Ferner, ob
auf derselben kein Handschriftenverzeichniss der Königl. Bibliothek in Kopenhagen vorhanden ist? Wenn dies der Fall, so
ersuche ich Sie nachzusehen, ob keine irischen Handschriften
mit verzeichnet sind; es sollen nämlich solche dort liegen. Um
Antwort darauf bitte ich in Ihrem nächsten Schreiben; es drängt
übrigens nicht so sehr damit.

Hochachtungsvoll
Ihr
ergebenster
Z e u ß.

10.

Bamberg, 15. März 1854.

Verehrtester Herr und Freund!

Ich danke Ihnen für Ihre gütigen Aufklärungen über
meine Anfragen. Ich bedurfte der Sachen selbst nicht, und

---

[1]) Jos. v. Hefner, Das römische Bayern in seinen Schrift- und Bildmalen.
3. Aufl. München 1852.

bedarf derselben auch jetzt noch nicht. Die Verzögerung Ihrer
Antwort hat also nichts Nachtheiliges oder Unangenehmes zur
Folge gehabt. Dass kein gedrucktes Verzeichniss der Hss. der
Kopenhagener Bibliothek existirt, glaube ich selbst, nachdem ich
einige Werke über dieselbe (v. Molbech und Ratjen, Abrahams)
auf hiesiger Bibliothek eingesehen habe. Wegen einiger Bände
der Irish Transactions werde ich mich später an Sie wenden.

Bei Durchlesung Ihrer Arbeit habe ich es lebhaft empfunden,
dass es doch recht wünschenswerth wäre, gründlichere Wörterbücher der keltischen Sprachen zu besitzen als die vorhandenen.
So müssen Sie sich z. B. wohl in Acht nehmen, die Phantasieen
und Abstractionen des Owen[1] für Wirklichkeit und Wahrheit
zu halten. Die unter Ilara vorkommenden kymr. *il, iliaw* bedeuten in der wirklichen Sprache nichts anderes als 'Gährung,
gähren' (ferment); das Vorausgeschickte: 'that is in motion, to
put in motion', sind Owens Phantasieen zur Erklärung des
Sinnes der Wörter, die nicht als Auktorität aufgestellt werden
können! Diese Phantasieen können wohl richtig sein, häufig
aber auch irrig. Der Art sind fast immer die ersten Erklärungen
dieses phantastischen Wörterbuchs, die sich sehr oft verhalten,
wie die Antwort des hochberühmten Etymologen Koch-Sternfeld[2]
auf die Frage, was der Name des Flusses Inn bedeute (wie uns
ein Student, der die Frage stellte, selbst erzählte): 'Inn ist in,
innen, ein-, hineingehend, Inn bedeutet tiefer Fluss!'

Den altkymrischen Mannsnamen Tacit, mit der gegenüber-
stehenden neuen Schreibung Tegid, finden Sie in der Ausgabe
der Gesetze Hywel Dda's von der Rekordkommission (der ganze
Titel in meiner Vorrede XLII) in einem kleinen kymr. Chro-
nikon, welches der Vorrede der Ausgabe einverleibt ist, auf
Seite V.

Damit Sie dem Hrn. Hefner wegen seiner deutschen Ein-
wohnerschaft des alten Vindeliciens recht zusetzen, habe ich noch
ein paar Beiträge beigelegt, von denen Sie, wenn es Ihnen taugt,
meinetwegen unter meinem Namen Gebrauch machen können.
Ich könnte so bei dieser Gelegenheit einiges, Forschern vielleicht

---

[1]) Will. Owen, Geiriadur Cynmraeg a Saesoneg. A Welsh and English
Dictionary. London 1793—1803.

[2]) Joh. Ernst v. Koch-Sternfeld hat veröffentlicht 'Rückblick auf die
Vorgeschichte von Bayern' 1853 und anderes in den Abhandlungen der
Münchener Akademie der Wissenschaften.

willkommenes, aus dem Codex des Cozroch,[1]) den ich einmal verglichen habe, an den Mann bringen.

Hochachtungsvollst

Ihr

ergebenster

Zeuß.

[Beilage.]

Isara. Es gibt bekanntlich ausser der baierischen noch
eine südgallische Isara von den Alpen, heute Isère, und eine
nordgallische, heute Oise, die in den Legenden noch Isara heisst
und so schon im Itin. Ant. in Ortsnamen Briva Isarae (i. e. pons
Isarae; vergl. Samarobriva bei Caes.), heute Pont-Oise bei Paris.
Die Wortform ist ganz dieselbe wie die von Ilara, mit der Ableitung -ara,*) und mit kurzem Wurzelvokale i, den die Volkssprache erhält, welche *Iller, Iser* spricht, nicht *Eiler, Eiser*, wie
in *Eile* aus *ila, mein* aus *min, Eis* aus *is, Eisen* aus *isarn, isan*.
Auch die französische Form *Oise*, mit verlorenem *r* etwas
entstellt für *Oisre*, deutet kurzen Wurzelvokal an, da sie ganz
sich verhält, wie *Loire* aus *Liger* mit kurzem *i*, wie *toise* aus
tisa (Gramm. celt. p. 105). Kurz ist endlich *i* in Isara, dem
alten Namen der südgallischen (in deren neuerem Isère die süd-
französische Mundart das *i* erhält), beim Dichter Lukanus,
Pharsal. 1, 393. Die Bedeutung wird keinem Zweifel mehr
unterworfen sein, wenn aus alten Denkmälern noch nachgewiesen sein wird, dass das heutige ir. und gäl. *eas*, Gen. *easa*
'cataracta' (*ea* vertritt die Stelle eines kurzen *e*) aus altem *is*,

---

[1]) Codex Traditionum Frisingensium (Freising 3a, olim 187), jetzt im
K. allg. Reichsarchiv zu München. Vgl. C. Meichelbeck, Historia Frisingensis,
Aug. Vindel. 1724. 2 voll. fol.

*) Bemerkenswert ist das Schwanken dieser Ableitung in *-ura* mit *u*
in den ältesten baierischen Handschriften, wie im Traditionscodex Cozrochs
und auch in andern (Schmellers Baier. Wb. 1, 121). Der älteste Freisinger
Codex, von Cozroch noch vor 850 geschrieben, hat z. B. in einer Urkunde aus
dem Jahre 763 *isura* (im Cod. S. 133b, bei Meichelbeck Nr. 12), allein eben-
derselbe hat in einer Urkunde vom Jahre 846 (im Codex S. 360a, bei Meichelb.
Nr. 638) die Stelle: 'in loco qui dicitur ad holze inter fluuiis *isaurie* et filusa',
aus der man wohl schliessen darf, dass der Schreiber im Originale oder im
Sinne *isare* oder *isarie* gehabt, und im Schreiben noch sein *u* hinzugefügt
habe. Jedenfalls wird dieses Schwanken nicht höher anzuschlagen sein, als
das zwischen Isana und Isna. [Anmerkung von Zeuss.]

Gen. *esa* entstanden ist. Es gibt noch mehrere altirische Wörter
dieser Bildung: *ith*, Gen. *etha, etho* 'frumentum'; *fid*, Gen. *fedo*
'arbor, lignum' (gall. *vidu-*); *bith*, Gen. *betha* 'mundus' (gall. *bitu*
in Bituriges); *rind*, Gen. *renda* 'stella'. Hier ist das ursprüngliche Wurzelwort *i* immer bei folgendem *a* oder *o* der Beugung
in *e* übergegangen, das ausser diesem Verhältnisse von *i* getrennt
ist; ebenso wegen des *o* oder *u* in der folgenden Sylbe im altir.
etal = Italia; *lethan* = altkymr. *litan* 'latus' (Litana silva,
Liv.); *felsub* = philosophus. Im Nom. der erwähnten Wörter
behalten auch die neuen Mundarten das *i*: *ith, bith, fiodh* (lies
fidh), *rionn* (lies rinn = rind). Nur *fcadh* (lies fedh) findet sich
neben *fiodh* auch im Nom. bei O'Reilly angesetzt; es fragt sich
nur, ob mit Recht. Ist dies der Fall, so kann auch ir. gäl. *eas*
'der Wassersturz' für *ios* stehen und gleich altem *is* mit kurzem
i sein, und der Name Isara bedeutet 'die stürzende'. Bei
O'Reilly und in den gälischen Wörterbüchern stehen auch die
Formen *easar, casach, easard* in derselben Bedeutung wie *eas*.
Aus derselben Wurzel mit Isara werden wohl auch die Namen
der Flüsse Isana, Isna (*Isana* in einer Urkunde v. J. 777 bei
Meichelbeck N. 54, ferner ebendaselbst N. 163. 589, *Isna* in
Urkunden von den Jahren 772, 792. 793 bei Meichelb. N. 26. 35.
102. 107, heute *Isen*, Nebenfluss des Inn; vergl. den Ortsnamen
Isinisca aus oberbaierischen Gegenden in den Itin.), Isontius
(Isonzo), Isarcus (Eisack, diesmal mit *ei*) sein. Der böhmische
Flussname *Iser*, böhm. *Gizera* (lies Jisera mit *j* und weichem *s*)
ist vielleicht eher aus dem Slawischen (altslav. *jezero*, böhm.
gezero, russ. *ozero* 'lacus, stagnum') zu erklären als für ein
Überbleibsel aus der Sprache der gallischen Bojen, der ältesten
bekannten Bewohner Boiheims, zu halten.

G l a n a (die Glan, Glon, Name mehrerer baierischer
Flüsschen). Schmeller sagt im Baier. Wörterbuch 2, 93: 'der
Name Glana schon ad 914 in Cod. diplom. ratisb.' Er findet
sich bereits in viel älteren Urkunden, welche der Codex Cozrochs
enthält, z. B. einer vom J. 772 (im Cod. auf S. 36a, bei Meichelbeck N. 29): 'locus quae dicitur clanae (sic) secus fluenta ipsius
fluminis', und einer v. J. 784 (im Cod. 37b. 38a, bei Meichelb.
N. 97): 'in loco in ripa fluminis quod uocatur clana uilla nuncu-
pante uualdkereshoua'. Ferner in einer vom J. 834 (im Cod.
S. 366a, bei Meichelbeck N. 576) steht *clana* im Texte geschrieben und *glana* in der Überschrift. Das *c* in Clana verhält

sich also wie das *c* oder *p* für *g* oder *b* in den Mannsnamen *cozroch, cozroh, cozpald, cundpato, uualdker, rekinperht* u. a. in demselben Codex für Gozroch, Gozbald, Gundbato, Waldger, Reginberht. Im Testamentum S. Remigii (6. Jahrh.) bei Pardessus 1, N. 119[1]) kömmt die Stelle vor: 'cum Coslo et Gleni', wo die Plätze Kusel und Altenglan am Flusse Glan in der baierischen Rheinpfalz bezeichnet sind. Der Name ist unbedenklich aus dem allen keltischen Mundarten heute noch geläufigen Adj. *glan* 'purus, clarus', neben welchem altirische Glossen auch das Subst. *glaine* 'puritas', das Verb *glainim* 'purgo' darbieten, zu erklären, und also derselben Bedeutung mit dem ebenfalls häufigen, deutschen Flussnamen Hlutra, Hlutraha, Lutara, Lutra 'die Lauter' aus dem Adj. *hlûtar* 'lauter' (purus, clarus, liquidus).

11.

Bamberg, den 25. März 1854.

Verehrtester Herr!

Ich kann in Beantwortung Ihres letzten Schreibens nur das Wichtigste ausheben.

YS .... that is active, violent ...., aus welchem Sie den Namen Isara erklären wollen, ist pure Owenische Phantasie, ohne sprachliche Wirklichkeit und Wahrheit.

YL, welches Sie zu Ilara stellen wollen, ebenso.

YS in der Erklärung 'that is active, violent, or consuming; a combustible principle' ist aus dem Verb *ysu* abstrahiert, dessen Bedeutungen bei Owen belegt sind: 'to itch, to corrode, to consume, to devour, to eat.' Ferner aus *ysawl* 'consuming, caustic', *ysadwy* 'consumable, ignitible', *ysyn* 'firebrand'. Was verzehrt, verbrennt, brennt, ist thätig und greift an, also die Abstraktion 'that is active, violent', die als allgemeineres Dekokt vorausgesetzt werden muss!

Die erste Erklärung dieser Visions-Formel YS, unter welcher auf Owenische Weise im allgemeinen die Bedeutung aller mit *ys* anfangenden Wörter erklärt werden soll, ist 'that is'. Diese ist abstrahiert aus dem gleich darauffolgenden *ys*

---

[1]) Diplomata ad res gallo-francicas spectantia, Paris 1843.

'est', dem Verb. defect., das nur in dieser Form und Bedeutung
vorkömmt. Von einer substantivischen Bedeutung 'that is',
etwas das ist, Existirendes, ist keine Rede, die Angabe also
Owenische Phantasie. Und so alle folgenden Angaben unter
dieser Formel YS.

Mit YL, wenn Sie den ganzen Absatz durchgelesen hätten,
würden Sie gesehen haben, dass der fürchterliche Etymologus
die Ableitungssilbe -yl, wobei er an das allgeläufige el, elu
'gehen' gedacht haben mag, erklären will.

Mich wundert, dass Sie auf die Leerheit dieser Sachen
nicht durch die grossen Buchstaben der Rubriken, in denen gewöhnlich der etymologische Unfug Owens zusammengedrängt ist,
und durch das sonderbare 'that —, what —, that is —, what
is —' aufmerksam geworden sind.

Der Unfug findet sich freilich auch unter den besondern
Posten, z. B. ysyn 'that is all in agitation', das Sie wieder als
Autorität anführen, das aber nichts bedeutet als 'Feuerbrand'
nach dem beigegebenen Beispiele (welches, die Hauptsache, Sie
gar nicht ansehen!): mae wedi myned yn ysyn gwyllt 'er ist
geworden ein wilder Feuerbrand', wo es figürlich gebraucht
allerdings einen Mann bedeutet, oder etwas 'that is all in
agitation'. Aber das bedeutet es nicht seiner Wurzel nach,
sondern einen brennenden Stoff, oder Fackel, wo ein andrer
Phantast auch setzen könnte: 'that is all in conflagration,
illumination' oder wer weiss noch was!

Bei Spurrel, der nur die nackten Bedeutungen aufzählt,
finde ich einfach: ysyn n. m. a firebrand.

Das ist Owens Art, und ich muss mich sehr wundern, dass
Sie sie nicht durchschaut haben und derselben so blindlings
folgen. Selbst die lateinischen hinübergenommenen ysbryd
(= spiritus), ysgol (= scola) behandelt er so, z. B. 'ysgol (col)
That matures (!!); a school'. Also bei ihm zusammengesetzt aus
ys- ('It is a common prefix in composition'! sagt er am Schluss
der etymologischen Vision YS) und aus col, wo er an col 'foetus'
und colaeth 'a nursing' gedacht haben muss!

Welche Lexikographie und welche Autorität, auf die Sie
sich stützen!

Die Form Aenus[1]) ist allerdings die sicherste; Oenus war

---

[1]) d. i. der Fluss Inn, s. A. Holders Sprachschatz 1, 71 s. v. Ainos.

von mir Gedächtnissfehler, ich hatte nicht nachgesehen; aber sie ist darum nicht zugänglicher.

Das Wort *easarg* 'tumultus', dass Sie mit Isurgus zusammenhalten, kenne ich wohl. In den alten Glossen kommt vor *esarcim* 'ich haue, schlage', woraus leicht die Bedeutung 'tumultuare' entstehen konnte, zusammengesetzt aus dem häufigen *arcim* und der Präposition *es-*, welche gallisch *ex-* war. Ich kann also jene Zusammenstellung nicht billigen.

Aus Ihrem Schreiben ersehe ich, dass Sie, wo ich Beiträge zu geben glaubte, schon selbst gearbeitet hatten, ich mich also in Ihre Arbeit eindrängte. Da mir aber nichts weniger eigen ist als Ein- oder Zudringlichkeit, so nehme ich meine vermeintlichen Beiträge wieder zurück, und ersuche Sie, mir das Blatt gelegentlich wieder zuzuschicken.

Ergebenster

Zeuß.

12.

Bamberg, den 30. März 1854.

Verehrtester Herr!

Sie haben meinen letzten Brief zu schwarz gesehen.[1]) Zu Ihrer Beruhigung beeile ich mich deswegen, Ihr Schreiben zu beantworten. Ich hätte es schon gestern gethan; aber wir hatten den ganzen Tag hindurch Semestralprüfung.

Ich habe den letzten Brief allerdings mit Unwillen geschrieben, und zwar nicht Ihretwegen allein, sondern auch meinetwegen. Warum Ihretwegen, wissen Sie; die Lektion wird Ihnen nicht geschadet haben, Sie wissen jetzt, wie Sie dran sind. Warum haben Sie statt dieses unsichern Owen nicht von Anfang an den alten ehrlichen Davies,[2]) der auf der Staatsbibliothek vorhanden ist, benützt?

---

[1]) Die Wirkung des Briefes, womit ihm Zeuss über Owen die Augen öffnete, beschreibt Glück in dem Vorworte seines Buches über die Keltischen Namen p. XX: 'Obstupui, steteruntque comae, vox faucibus haesit'.

[2]) Antiquae linguae britannicae nunc vulgo dictae Cambro-Britannicae, a suis Cymraecae vel Cambricae, ab aliis Wallicae: et linguae latinae dictionarium duplex: accedunt adagia britannica. Londini 1632. Ein kurzer Auszug aus dem Werke findet sich in Marci Zuerii Boxhornii Originum gallicarum liber, Amstelodami 1654.

Von meiner Seite war Schuld daran, abgesehen davon, dass
ich mich allerdings in Ihre Arbeit eingedrängt hatte, dass ich
mit unserem *eas* zu Isara nicht vorwärts, sondern rückwärts
gekommen war. Es steht nämlich bei O'Reilly auch die Form
as 'cataracta', und diese deutet, wie heutiges *gan* 'sine' aus
altem *cen* entstanden ist (kurzes *ea* in der heutigen Sprache
wird auch wie *a* gesprochen, z. B. in *deas, neart,* welche alt *des,
nert* sind, vgl. O'Donovan, Gramm. S. 18), auf altes *es* zurück
und nicht auf *is*. *E* und *i* sind aber in den Wurzeln wohl geschieden, z. B. in Vergobr*e*tus (= ir. breth), B*i*turiges (= ir. b*i*th),
und wurzelhaftes *e* bleibt in alten Namen, z. B. in Su*e*ssĭones,
nie Su-*i*ssiones; wie in ir. *air-ess,* gen. *air-isse;* in Genava,
Genauni, nie Ginava, Ginauni; wie ir. *gen* 'os', Dimin. *ginán.*
Aus *es* (= *eas*) wäre also *Esara* zu erwarten, nicht *Isara,* was
anderer Wurzel sein könnte. Die Sache war mir zu schwankend,
ich wollte dieselbe zurückhaben.

Allein ich habe die Erklärung aus *eas* nur bedingungs-
weise gestellt, und wer weiss, ob sich doch nicht noch manches
zu ihrer Unterstützung wird aufbringen lassen? (z. B. *Litana* etc.
neben kymr. *llyt* und *llet* etc., was ich noch genauer untersuchen will).[1]

Unter solchen Umständen gebe ich Ihnen volle Freiheit
mit meinen fatalen Beiträgen zu thun was Sie wollen. Passen
sie Ihnen und wollen Sie Gebrauch davon machen, so habe ich
nichts dagegen; passen sie Ihnen nicht (und ich hatte auch
gemeint, meine geschichtlichen Nachweise würden nicht zur
eigentlichen Sache gehören) und setzen Sie Ihr Früheres dafür,
so ist es mir auch recht, und nur in diesem Falle würde ich
Sie bitten, mir das Blättchen wiederzuschicken, für etwaigen
anderweitigen Gebrauch wegen der Zusammenstellung, da ich
keine Abschrift davon habe.

Ergebenster

Zeuß.

---

[1] Später hat man andere Erklärungen des Namens der Isar aufgestellt,
von denen zwei erwähnt seien. Nigra (Glossae cod. Taur. 1869 p. XVIII)
leitet ihn von *is* 'infra', D'Arbois de Jubainville (Premiers habitants de
l'Europe 2, 134. 138) von ἰερός; vgl. RC. 19, 87.

13.

Bamberg, den 17. Mai 1854.

Verehrtester Herr und Freund!

Die Stille, die nach unsern letzten Briefen auf einmal zwischen uns eingetreten ist, thut mir beinah ungewohnt. Ich muss sie zuerst wieder unterbrechen und Sie ersuchen, mir folgendes in England erschienene Werk, wenn es auf der k. Bibliothek vorhanden ist, gütigst zu überschicken: Monumenta historica Britannica ed. Petrie and Sharpe. Vol. I. 1848. Published by command of her Majesty. Sollte seit 1848 davon noch Weiteres erschienen sein, so bäte ich es auch beizugeben.

Wie steht es mit Ihren Arbeiten? Wird bald etwas erscheinen? Ich bin sehr neugierig, und hochachtungsvollst

Ihr

ergebenster

Zeuß, Prof.

14.

Bamberg, den 30. Mai 1854.

Verehrtester Herr und Freund!

Dass die Mon. hist. Brit. in München vorhanden sind, ist mir sehr lieb, ich bedarf ihrer aber jetzt nicht sogleich, und bitte Sie also zuzuwarten, bis sie zurückgegeben sind, und mir dann das Buch zuzuschicken.

Grimms Erklärung von *ambactus, andbahts* und seinen Ausfall auf die meinige kannte ich schon.[1]) Anfangs etwas aufgebracht, freue ich mich jetzt vielmehr darüber, da mich nun ein so grundloses Benehmen, wie z. B. mit Ambigatus, Ambiorix, lateinischem ambactus, auch jeder Rücksicht bei seinen Schwächen überhebt. Dass das Wort der Grimmschen Erklärung bei den Galliern *andebactus* gelautet haben müsse, bemerken Sie sehr richtig; ich habe das immer auch gedacht. Ambactus halte ich aber jetzt für zusammengesetzt, da ich nicht nur für das persönliche *-actus* und das abstrakte *-actio* (S. Diez, Etymol. Wörterbuch der roman. Sprachen S. 14. 15) entsprechende altirische Beispiele habe, sondern dazu noch die Wurzel kenne. Bei

---

[1]) S. Deutsches Wörterbuch von J. Grimm und W. Grimm I (1854), p. L, und Kleinere Schriften J. Grimms 8, 359.

Vollmer, unserem gründlichen Gothen,[1]) den ich freundlich zu
grüssen bitte, ersuche ich Sie anzufragen, ob im Gothischen noch
andere Adj. auf -ts, unmittelbar vom Subst. abgeleitet, wie *bahts*
aus *bak* 'Rücken', vorkommen; die in Grimms Gramm. 3, 193 flg.
aufgeführten scheinen mir nur aus Verben zu fliessen.

Die Wurzel *al*, nach der Sie wegen der Namen Alaunus,
Alauni etc. fragen, kömmt allerdings in alten Denkmälern vor.
Altirisch in der Gramm. p. 337: *ishé no-t-ail* 'ipse te alit' und
p. 823 abgeleitet *altram* 'nutritio'. Auch im Vocab. corn. p. 1104
werden *altrou* 'victricus', *altruan* 'noverca', Stiefvater, -mutter,
eben 'Nährvater, -mutter' bedeuten. Sollte *alaun*, aus dieser
Wurzel abgeleitet, auch in weiterer Entfaltung ihrer Bedeutung
nicht befruchtend (z. B. von Flüssen), wohlhabend, Reichthum
gebend (Mercurius bei den Galliern wie Wodan bei den Germanen Gott des Handels und des Reichthums: hunc ad quaestus
pecuniae mercaturasque habere vim maximam arbitrantur,
Caes.) etc. haben bedeuten können? Was Sie sonst noch anführen, geht auf altes *éula* 'sapiens' (Gramm. p. 42), oder auf
elathan (cf. Ogma Elathani fil., Gramm. p. 2 not., p. 1140 not.)
zurück. Das kymr. *al* bei Owen ist aus *ael, ail, el*, wie es in
kymrischen Denkmälern heisst, und dieses aus *agel, angel* = angelus
(Gramm. p. 165. 1100); da haben Sie wieder ein Pröbchen Owenscher
Etymologie. Das kymr. *awen*, wenn gesichert, könnte allerdings
mit *awel* derselben Wurzel sein; allein es fragt sich, ob es nicht
umgestellt das anderswoher vielbestätigte *anau, anaw* (Gramm.
praef. VII) ist. Bei Owen sind bei beiden Wörtern fast dieselben Bedeutungen angegeben.[2])

Bei Diez (Etymol. Wörterb. S. 129) finde ich Richards
Welsh dictionary angeführt.[3]) Ich kenne es noch nicht; ist es

---

[1]) Als solcher hatte sich Vollmer durch seine Besprechung der Ausgabe
des Ulfilas von 1846 (Münchener Gel. Anz. 1846, Nr. 163 ff., 245 ff.) einen
Namen gemacht.

[2]) Ir. *ahél aial* : w. *awel* ist dem gr. ἄελλα, lat. *aura* gleichgestellt
worden. W. *awen* 'Phantasie' scheint das irische *áine* zu sein, das O'Cl. als
'gute (*án*) Kunst oder Wissenschaft' erklärt; *ni aine fodruair* 'nicht Phantasie hat es geschaffen', Fel. ep. 97, steht parallel mit *ni soas dorigne* 'nicht
Gelehrsamkeit hat es gemacht', ib. 89. Cf. *áine* 'amusement, play', Meyer,
Contributions p. 41.

[3]) Thomas Richards, Antiquae Linguae Britannicae Thesaurus, Bristol
1753, ein nützliches Buch, von dem 1839 die vierte Auflage erschienen ist.
Goronwy Owen urtheilte abfällig über das Werk, das ihm des Südwelschen zu

in München vorhanden? Wohl schwerlich! Kennen Sie dieses von 'Erfolgen triefende' Buch von Diez, wie ich es in der Beurtheilung meiner Grammatica von Pott, mit anderswoher entlehntem Ausdrucke, bezeichnet finde (Deutsche Wochenschrift 1854, 15. Heft)? Auffallend ist, dass Diez durch sein ganzes Werk den ersten Band des meinigen, noch ehe es erschienen war, wie es scheint durch buchhändlerische Begünstigung, benützt hat; seine Vorrede ist vom Juli, meine vom August 1853 datiert.

Hochachtungsvollst
ergebenster
Zeuß.

15.

Bamberg, den 28. Juni 1854.

Verehrtester Herr und Freund

Ich danke Ihnen für die gütige Übersendung des kymr. WB. von Thom. Richards. Obwohl ich mich jetzt erinnere, dass ich es in München schon in Händen gehabt habe (ich war nur der Meinung, das bei Diez erwähnte könne ein anderes, erst erschienenes Werk sein), so ist es mir doch lieb, dasselbe jetzt genauer kennen zu lernen, und ich ersuche Sie noch, dass Sie mir auch den Titel von dem von Will. Richards angeben möchten.[1] Ich werde auf meiner Reise in England, die ich für nächste Ferien vorhabe, auf solche Sachen Acht haben.

Da unsere Ferien möglicherweise schon am 7. August, gleichförmig mit den Gymnasialferien anfangen (die Sache liegt noch zur Entscheidung beim Ministerium), und ich sobald es möglich ist, abreise, so wäre es mir sehr lieb, wenn Sie das engl. Werk, Mon. hist. Brit., mir in etwa 8 Tagen schon überschicken wollten.

Für ihre weiteren mir sehr willkommenen Mittheilungen über *ambacti* danke ich Ihnen schönstens. Von dem keltischen

---

viel aufgenommen hatte, und er liebte die Sprache der *Hwyntwyr* nicht. 'I wish he had nothing to do with Moses Williams, H. Salisbury, and Baxter. I am sure it had been better, but especially his own *Glam.*: what have *Glam.* words to do with Welsh?' (Works ed. R. Jones 2, 96). Gleichwohl liess er sich das Buch durchschiessen, hübsch in zwei Theile binden und trug fleissig ein (2, 157).

[1] An English and Welsh Dictionary, Carmarthen 1798. Es giebt neuere Drucke dieses Wörterbuchs.

Ursprung des Wortes *ambactus* bin ich so überzeugt, und war
von der Grimmischen Erklärung vor Ihrem Schreiben so abgekommen, dass ich daran war, das was Grimm für unmöglich
halten zu müssen glaubt, für das Richtige zu nehmen, Hinüber-
nahme durch die Germanen und Verwandlung des *amb* in *andb*
durch die Gothen nach ihren Analogien, zumal da sonderbarer
Weise in den althochd. Denkmälern immer nur *amb, amp,* nie
antb, antp, was man erwarten dürfte, vorkömmt. Ich dachte an
das Wort *gabel,* das auch bei allen deutschen Stämmen sich
findet, meines Wissens im Deutschen keine Etymologie hat, aber
im Keltischen, wo es auch vorhanden ist, sich einfach an das
Verb *gabim* 'sumo, capio' anschliesst. Was meint Vollmer von
dem Worte *gabel?* Nach seiner Beigabe, für die ich schönstens
danke, ist ohne Zweifel deutsche Erklärung von *andbahts* noch
haltbar. Nur kömmt mir die Bedeutung 'entgegengebückt', die
gut auf einen geschniegelten Kellner oder feinen Komplimenten-
macher unserer Zeit passt, für den gewöhnlichen Volksgebrauch
im hohen deutschen Alterthume etwas zu vornehm vor; nach
meiner keltischen Etymologie bedeutet das Abstrakt *ambactio*
einfach 'Umgebung', das persönliche *ambactus* 'einen von der
Umgebung'.

Eine weitere Begründung von meiner Erklärung dieses
Wortes, auf die Sie passen, habe ich anfangs allerdings beabsichtigt, in einer Zeitschrift, etwa bei Haupt, zu geben, allein
ich bin wieder davon abgekommen, und will es lieber auf eine
weitere Arbeit versparen.[1]) Dass Grimm noch andere von
meinen Etymologieen anfällt, und auf ähnliche Weise, vermuthe
und wünsche ich; dann geht es in einem hin.

Wenn Sie wegen des Namens Tacitus das kymr. *tec, teg* in
Ihrer Gleichung so stellen, das neukymr. *teg* = altem *taci* (nicht
tac!) sei, so habe ich gar nichts dagegen; *i* verschwindet auch
sonst ohne weitere Spur als eines in *e* umgelauteten *a*, z. B. im
kymr. *enw* 'nomen', altir. *ainm,* plur. *anman,* wo wohl ein
ursprüngliches *anim* oder *anmi* zu Grunde zu legen ist.

Hochachtungsvollst

Ihr

ergebenster

Zeuß.

_____ _____

¹) Vgl. den unten unter Nr. 30 veröffentlichten Aufsatz Zeussens.

16.

Bamberg, den 24. Juli 1854.

Verehrtester Herr und Freund!

Ich schicke hiermit Richard's Welsh Dictionary wieder zurück. In wenigen Tagen wird auch Petrie, Mon. hist. Brit., nachfolgen. Dieser starke und schwere Band macht Ihnen mehr Mühe wie gewöhnlich, wie mir mehr Auslagen; aber er hat mir auch sehr willkommenen Stoff geboten, und ich bin deshalb für dessen gütige Übersendung Ihnen sehr zu Danke verpflichtet.

Wenn ich vor meiner Abreise Sie noch mit einer Bitte belästigen darf, so wäre es, nachzusehen, ob nicht folgendes Werk in München vorhanden ist, und, wenn der Fall, es gütigst auf ein paar Tage zu überschicken: A descriptive catalogue of the manuscripts in the Stowe Library, by Charles O'Conor, Buckingham 1818. 4⁰, 2 voll.

Vor Anfang der Ferien, die für uns, nach alter Weise, gegen das Ende des Monats August beginnen, werde ich ohne Zweifel auch noch Ihre Recension zu lesen bekommen.

Hochachtungsvollst

Ihr

ergebenster

Zeuß.

17.

Bamberg, den 7. August 1854.

Verehrtester Herr und Freund!

Hiermit schicke ich Petrie, Mon. Brit. zurück und danke Ihnen für die Mühe, die Sie mit dem schweren Buche gehabt haben und noch haben. O'Conor, Biblioth. Stowens., habe ich erhalten, und werde sie vor meiner Abreise, die in 14 Tagen ungefähr stattfinden wird, wieder abschicken.

Die Beobachtungen, die Sie mir in Ihrem Schreiben mittheilen, sind mir sehr willkommen. Darunter war mir die Schreibung *Dubnorex* befremdend, wegen des *b*, da ich *m* in Dumnorix für sicherer gehalten hätte, wegen des Adj. *domun* 'tief' und des Subst. *domun* 'Welt' (= *mund*us mit versetzten

Konsonanten?), die beide doch desselben Ursprungs sein werden, und überall mit *m* geschrieben sind in den alten Hs., die nie *b* und *m* mit einander verwechseln. Dagegen werden *bh* und *mh* wegen der gleichen Aussprache in der neuern Schreibung häufig regellos mit einander vermengt, so dass *dubhaig[é]in* bei O'R.[1] nichts entscheiden kann. Aber interessant ist jene Schreibung und neben dem germ. *diup, dup* darauf hindeutend, dass das ableitende *n* auf das wurzelhafte *b* seit uralten Zeiten schon Einfluss gehabt habe.

Über die Casses dii (deae?), Viducasses etc. wüsste ich durchaus nichts Haltbares oder Entscheidendes anzugeben. Früher meinte ich, die Wörter könnten mit dem franz. *chasse, chasser*, mit dem deutschen *Hassi, Hasu* (als Gauname öfter gebraucht) in Verbindung zu bringen sein, mochte es aber nicht als sicher hinstellen. Neben dem franz. *chasse* steht ital. *caccia, cacciare*, und Diez, Etym. WB. S. 79, giebt die lat. Etymologie *capt(i)are*. In meiner Gramm. S. 1095 finden Sie das altkymr. *casgoord* mit meiner Erklärung. In Südirland liegt die Stadt Cashel, deren alten irischen Namen ich eben in dem Werke O'Conors, das Sie mir überschickt haben, finde, in einer Inschrift aus dem 11. Jahrh.: rig Cassil 'rex C.', im Append. p. 3.[2] Bei O'R. steht *cassal* 'a garment', in altir. Glossen *casal* (gl. tunica, gl. lacerna, s. Gramm. p. 976, Anmerkung, Schluss), ursprünglich 'Jagdkleid'???[3] Ir. *cais*, kymr. *cas* 'odium, inimicitia' wird wohl verschieden sein.

Man behauptet hier wiederholt, die Cholera herrsche in München. Es werden wohl doch nur übertriebene Gerüchte sein.

Hochachtungsvollst

Ihr

ergebenster

Zeuß.

---

[1] *Dubhaigein* steht in der schottisch-gälischen Bibel (Iob 38, 16) für 'abyssus', 'depth' und wird mit *doimhne* glossiert; die Volkssprache hat auch *dubhagan*. Damit ist doch vermutlich *dubhaigéan* 'der schwarze Ocean' (w. *eigion*) gemeint. Vgl. *'s gu'm fan air an aigein dhubh-dhonn*, Al. Macdonald, Poems 1874, p. 26.

[2] Caiseal, das Cormac von '*casula*' oder von *cís-ail* 'Zins-Felsen' ableitet, ist zweifellos das lateinische *castellum*. Vgl. P. W. Joyce, Irish Names of Places 1, 286.

[3] 'Casula, vestis cucullata, quasi minor casa', sagt Du Cange, 'eo quod totum hominem tegat, unde cuculla, quasi minor cella.' Noch Ebel GC. 768 verzeichnet das altir. *casal* unter den Ableitungen auf *-al*.

18.

Bamberg, den 12. August 1854.

Verehrtester Herr und Freund!

Sie werden sich über gegenwärtige Sendung wundern. Es ist, wie Sie sehen, nichts anderes, als ein Reisepass, der nach England lautet. Dieser Sache habe ich jetzt eine ganz andere Wendung gegeben. Nach den neuesten Zeitungsnachrichten hat die Cholera in Paris in den letzten Tagen des Juli, und in den ersten des August sehr bedeutend zugenommen, und sie gewinnt in England, namentlich in London, immer mehr Ausbreitung. Unter solchen Umständen muss ich natürlich Bedenken tragen, die Reise dahin zu unternehmen.

Ich habe auch in Mailand, wegen des dortigen Codex, noch eine Ferienzeit zuzubringen und hatte dies auf das nächste Jahr vor. Ich richte nun die Sache so ein, dass ich umgekehrt England auf das nächste Jahr verspare, und nun zuerst Mailand vornehme, — wenn auch da die Cholera nicht entgegentritt. Sie wüthet zwar in Genua und ist in Rom ausgebrochen, ist aber noch nicht über die Apenninen gegangen und hat selbst das Genua zunächst liegende Turin noch verschont.

Nach Mailand bedarf ich nun aber noch der Visa der österreichischen Gesandtschaft in München, und ich darf Sie wohl ersuchen, mir diese Angelegenheit zu besorgen. Im Pass ist der deutschen Bundesstaaten schon gedacht, und Sie brauchen nur anzugeben, dass ich noch österreichisches Gebiet betreten wolle. Das österreichische Gesandschafts-Büreau war seit Jahren im Eckhause vor der Theatiner Kirche gegen die Ludwigsstrasse, und wird wohl jetzt noch dort sein. Etwaige Geldauslagen bitte ich zu besorgen und mir zu melden. Heute nach 8 Tagen, nach Beendigung unserer Schulsachen in der nächsten Woche, werde ich wohl schon reisefertig sein.

Ich gedenke geradenwegs über Augsburg, Lindau, dann über Splügen nach Mailand zu reisen, und auf der Rückreise Euch in München besuchen zu können.

Ich sehe nun im Laufe der nächsten Woche der Rücksendung dieses Passes, und auch Ihren sonstigen Sendungen entgegen. Hochachtungsvollst

Ihr

ergebenster

Zeuß.

_____

19.

Bamberg, den 19. August 1854.

Verehrtester Herr und Freund!

Ich schicke hiermit O'Conor, Bibl. Stow., wieder zurück und danke Ihnen für alle Ihre Bemühungen, die Sie meinetwegen bisher gehabt haben.

Meine Reiseangelegenheit wird, scheint es, abermals eine andere Wendung nehmen. In Turin ist nun auch die Cholera ausgebrochen und es wäre wie ein Wunder, wenn Mailand, nun die nächstliegende grosse Stadt, davon verschont würde. Mir ist inzwischen der Plan gekommen das zweite Semester des nächsten Schuljahres für mich ganz frei zu gewinnen (meinen Lyceal-Rektor[1]) habe ich schon auf meiner Seite; Näheres ein andermal), und jetzt nur den Ausflug über Prag nach Wien zu machen, den ich schon im vorigen Herbst vorhatte. Das österreichische Visum, für dessen Besorgung ich Ihnen schönstens danke, ist mir also auch so nothwendig.

Die Cholera wird wahrscheinlich nach und nach auch unsere Gegenden erreichen; in Nürnberg ist sie schon verbreiteter, in Erlangen, Baireuth und auch hier in einzelnen Fällen aufgetreten.

An Hrn. Vollmer, dessen Schreiben ich gestern erhalten habe, meine Grüsse. Seine Angelegenheit werden wir bald schriftlich oder mündlich weiter besprechen können; jetzt nur soviel für ihn, dass Graf Castiglione, der eine mächtige Hand auf der Ambrosiana in Mailand gehabt hat, gestorben ist, und zwar im Exil, wie ich von Leipzig benachrichtigt worden bin, da ich den Auftrag gab, an ihn ein Exemplar meiner Grammatik zu schicken.[2]

Ich gedenke jedenfalls noch im Laufe dieser Ferien, wenn vielleicht nicht mündlich, doch schriftlich mit Euch zu verkehren.

Hochachtungsvoll

Ihr

ergebenster

Zeuß.

---

[1]) Der Rektor des Königl. Lyceums in Bamberg war Dr. Gengler. Die Anstalt, an der Zeuss Professor der Geschichte war, ist der katholischen Theologie und Philosophie gewidmet, ein Überrest der 1803 aufgelösten alten Universität.

[2]) Carlo Ottavio Graf Castiglione (geb. 1784) ist bekannt als der Heraus-

20.

Bamberg, den 21. November 1854.

Verehrtester Herr und Freund!

Ich hoffe, dass diese Zeilen Sie bei gutem Wohlsein antreffen werden, unangetastet von dem unheimlichen Gaste, der Seuche, die unsere Gegenden heimgesucht hat, und ersuche Sie, sowohl von Ihnen als von unseren Freunden in München mir baldige Nachricht zukommen zu lassen.

Dass die Seuche meine Pläne für die Ferienzeit durchkreuzt habe, ist Ihnen schon bekannt. Die Reise nach Wien habe ich durchgeführt, zwar mit geringer Ausbeute, in Wien selbst und in Klosterneuburg, jedoch so dass es der Mühe werth war, sie zu machen.[1]) Ich bin nämlich auf derselben auch zur Gewissheit gelangt (namentlich, von Karajan in Wien dazu veranlasst, durch Hoffmann von Fallersleben, den ich auf der Rückreise in Weimar besuchte), dass in Kopenhagen altirische Handschriften liegen, von denen ich früher nur unsichere Spuren hatte. Da gäbe es für das nächste Semester genug zu thun, in Mailand, England und in Kopenhagen, wenn ich meine Absicht durchsetzte, die ich Ihnen schon mitgetheilt habe. Mein Rektor ist, wie ich Ihnen schon damals meldete, auf meiner Seite, und er äusserte neulich noch, ich solle, um die Sache um so sicherer durchzusetzen, noch zuvor mit den Münchner wissenschaftlichen Herren, die an geeigneter Stelle für mich sprächen, darüber mich benehmen. Ich wüsste nur nicht recht mit wem, etwa mit Thiersch?

---

geber der gothischen Fragmente in der Ambrosiana zu Mailand; er starb 1849 in Genua.

[1]) Zeuss machte sich damals, im August 1854, in Wien und in Klosterneuburg nur wenige Notizen. Aus den Lesarten des Wiener Codex des Marianus Scottus (Zimmer, Glossae hib. p. 284) ist etwa zu erwähnen: *feil comgaill indiv fain diden . . . do muiredach trúg . . . do muretach trój*. Aus dem Codex des Eutychius verzeichnet er eine Glosse (auf fol. 67 a), die Nigra (RC. 1, 59) und andere übersehen haben, nämlich: *benim* gl. pinso. Von dem Klosterneuburger Codex regularum Nr. 587 (er enthält auch unter anderm Proverbia S. Evagri episcopi, Isidori Hispalensis lib. synon.) sagt Zeuss: 'Die Handschrift ist von der des Codex des Marianus Scottus in Wien völlig verschieden. Irische Orthographie des Lateinischen nicht wahrzunehmen. Die Hand des irischen Gedichtes etwas schwerfällig, unbehülflich.' An Haupts frühern Lesungen (GC.[1] 933) findet er wenig zu verbessern. Vgl. RC. 2, 113.

Ihre Recension ist wohl schon erschienen, und ich darf ein Exemplar davon erwarten? Ich erlaube mir Sie zu ersuchen, dass Sie bei dieser Gelegenheit mir den ersten Band der Mabinogion der Lady Guest aus der Königl. Bibliothek auf ein paar Wochen mit[zu]schicken möchten.[1])

Meine Grüsse an Vollmer. Ist er wohl und hat er Lust mit nach Mailand? Ich bin recht neugierig auf Ihre Nachrichten.

Hochachtungsvollst

Ihr

ergebenster

Zeuß.

21.

Bamberg, den 4. December 1854.

Verehrtester Herr und Freund!

Meinen letzten Brief, der Ihrer letzten Sendung auf dem Wege begegnet sein muss, werden Sie erhalten haben. Dass der 1. Band der Mabinogion, um den ich Sie ersuchte, nicht kömmt, daraus schliesse ich, dass er ausgeliehen sein wird, oder gar, dass Sie den Brief nicht erhalten haben. Ich bin jetzt in dem Falle, Sie zu ersuchen, mir nebst dem 1. auch zugleich den 2. Band der Mabinogion zu übersenden.

Ihre Recension[2]) hat mir in mehrfacher Hinsicht Freude gemacht. Einmal, dass sie eine so schöne Anwendung meiner Arbeit, deren Gegenstand uns ferne zu liegen scheint, auf unsere eigenen Gegenden und unsere nächsten Umgebungen gemacht haben, und ferner, dass Sie in derselben anzeigen, eine besondere Schrift über das keltisch-römische Baiern zu bearbeiten, eine prächtige Aufgabe, für die Sie, ausgerüstet mit den hiezu nöthigen juristischen und sprachlichen Kenntnissen, mit Genauigkeit und Kritik, ganz geeignet sind, und durch welche Sie

---

[1]) Zeuss besass die Mabinogion nicht selbst; zu seinen grammatischen Arbeiten waren sie ihm von M. Haupt und früher, schon 1845, ebenso wie The Myvyrian Archaiology, aus der Darmstädter Hofbibliothek geliehen.

[2]) Die Besprechung des Hefnerschen Buches von Glück erschien in den Gelehrten Anzeigen der k. bayerischen Akademie der Wissenschaften zu München, Historische Klasse, 1854, col. 25—68. Manches, was in dem Briefwechsel mit Zeuss erörtert ist, hat Glück in dieser Anzeige verwertet.

sich ohne Zweifel ein schönes Verdienst erwerben werden. Den altbaierischen Philistern, die nicht wissen, was rechts oder links, keltisch oder deutsch ist, werden Sie mit jener Ankündigung keinen kleinen Schrecken eingejagt haben. Auch hat es mich gefreut, dass Sie den alten Philister und Sünder Mone gehörig gewürdigt und an den Pranger gestellt haben.[1]) Das hätte ich schon längst gewünscht; mir konnte es wegen meiner Stellung zu ihm nicht zukommen, für Sie hat es sich gut gepasst.

Auf Ihre Anfragen erwidere ich Folgendes. Die Annahme, dass die Endung *is* bei Eugippius in den Namen Faocanis, Batavis, Cucullis, Asturis, Quintanis etc. keltisch sei, scheint doch sehr wenig Anhalt zu haben, da *is* in Civismarus etc. (vgl. das deutsche Sig*is*mund) doch wohl ableitend sein wird, und zugleich das nicht viel später auftretende *-as,* wie in Baias, Pesonas etc., auf Verstümmelung lateinischer Kasusendung deutet. Das in der Gramm. S. 783 angeführte *Lauri* (noch in 2 Stellen derselben Quelle finde ich *Laur*) ist wohl zu *lâr* zu stellen, nicht zu Lauro, Louroni etc.

Für Mogontiacum und das ir. *mogán* (so wird bei O'R. stehen sollen, nicht *mógan*) wüsste ich jetzt nichts als das altir. *mug,* gen. *moga* (Gramm. S. 17) anzugeben, das zuletzt doch mit dem kymr. *mail* = maglus, magulus (Gramm. S. 121) zusammengehören wird. Und wäre denn das *a* in Magontiacum, wie meines Wissens die Hss. des Tacitus haben, wegen der Inschriften so gewiss zu streichen? Über die Entwickelung des Begriffes 'Held' aus diesem Worte mögen Sie Diez, Etym. Wb. S. 366, Art. vassallo, nachlesen, wo gesagt ist, dass aus *gwas* sich die Bedeutungen 'junger Mann, Diener, streitbarer Mann' entwickelt haben und das altdeutsche *degan* die drei Bedeutungen 'junger Mann, Diener, Held' in sich vereinige. Als Beiname des Apollo, dächte ich, wäre letztere Bedeutung ganz passend, da der Sonnengott bei allen alten Völkern als jugendlicher Held gedacht ist. Da kymrisch auch *-iauc* und *-iaun* abwechselnd in

---

[1]) Franz Joseph Mone (geb. 1796 zu Mingolsheim, gest. 1871 zu Karlsruhe) hat sich durch vielseitige Thätigkeit auf dem Gebiete der Geschichte und der Litteratur des Mittelalters sehr verdient gemacht. In der Kritik schwach, zeigt er sich in seinen 'Keltischen Forschungen' 1837 und in den 'Untersuchungen über die gallische Sprache' 1851 von der Keltomanie ergriffen. Zeuss war mit ihm seit seiner Speierer Zeit bekannt, wie ein Brief an ihn vom 16. April 1841 (jetzt in der Berliner Bibliothek) beweist.

Eigennamen gebraucht ist, wie in Brecheniauc (Gegend des
Brachan, Gramm. S. 773) und Guorthigirniaun, Cereticiaun
(Gegend des Guorthigirn, Ceretic, Gramm. S. 792), so bin ich
ganz einverstanden, wenn Sie Mogontiacum und Mogentianis[1])
zusammenstellen.

Dass Sie mich auf das Vorhaben Holtzmanns aufmerksam
machen, ist mir sehr angenehm, und ich ersuche Sie, wenn
Ihnen dergleichen wieder vorkömmt, es immer zu thun. Mir ist
es recht, Hr. Holtzmann soll mir kommen, wir wollen ihn schon
holzen. Ein solcher Narr ist neulich auch in der Person eines
Engländers Barber aufgetreten, mit einem ziemlich dicken Octav-
band unter dem Titel 'Suggestions on the ancient Britons, London
1854', welchen der hochgelahrte Mann mir selbst überschickt
hat, der im Eingange des Buches naiv erklärt, dass er nicht[s]
kymrisch verstehe, und dann in hochtrabendem, breiten Vortrag
kymrische, ja auch angelsächsische Namen aus dem — Hebräischen
erklärt.   Hochachtungsvollst
                                   Ihr
                                ergebenster
                                   Zeuß.

                         _____

                            22.

                Bamberg, den 19. Januar 1855.

       Verehrtester Herr und Freund!

Ihr letztes geehrtes Schreiben vom 21. Dec. v. J. habe ich
erhalten und mit Vergnügen daraus ersehen, dass Sie fleissig mit
der kritischen Sichtung der alten keltischen Namen fortfahren.
Dieses rüstige Fortarbeiten ist das Beste, was wir thun können
zu noch grösserem Verdruss für jenen altbaierischen Idiotismus,
von dem Sie mir so erbauliche Proben mittheilen, und von dem
ich selbst auch eine erhalten habe durch die Übersendung des
Ihnen schon bekannten Buches von Siegert,[2]) mit der Auf-

_____

[1]) Die richtige Form ist Mogetiana, A. Holder 2, 608. 'Mogontiâcon
hat seinen Namen von einem Gallier Mogontios (der grosse, mächtige, starke),
der sich dort ansiedelte und den Ort nach sich benannte.' So erklärt Glück
in seiner Abhandlung über Rênos, Moinos und Mogontiâcon in den Sitzungsberichten der Münchener Akademie 1865, p. 1—27.

[2]) Carl Siegert, Grundlagen zur ältesten Geschichte des bayerischen
Hauptvolksstammes und seiner Fürsten. München 1854. Er verficht die

forderung, 'die von ihm geführten Beweise anerkennend seine Anschauungen zu theilen' etc.

In Betreff des scheinbaren Vorwurfs wegen der Codices von Mailand und Turin von jener Seite muss ich Sie selbst für etwaige andere derartige Fälle aufklären, dass in Turin nur ein paar Blätter, kein Codex, mit irischen Glossen liegen, die Peyron gesammelt hat, von welchem falschen Menschen (er ist ein 'geistlicher Herr') ich sie zu erhalten jetzt wohl aufgeben muss, da er mich schon das erste Mal, bei meiner Anwesenheit in Turin, mit falschen Vorspiegelungen und Versprechungen angelogen,[1]) und nachdem ich ihm mein Werk überschickt und

Meinung Aventins, dass die Bevölkerung Baierns in der Hauptsache keltisch-bojoarisch sei, gemischt mit germanischen und anderartigen keltischen Stämmen. Zeuss hat bekanntlich 1839 eine Schrift veröffentlicht, in der er, auf den Anonymus Ravennas gestützt, die Herkunft der Baiern von den Markomannen nachzuweisen suchte. Freilich ist die Forschung dabei nicht stehen geblieben. — Auch Jacob Grimm neigt sich in einem Briefe an einen baierischen 'Mitbruder' vom 19. März 1856 (er hat sich in seinem Nachlasse gefunden und ist vermutlich nicht abgeschickt worden) der ältern Annahme zu: 'Allmälich hat man gelernt einsehen, dass zwischen Kelten und Germanen tiefere Berührung stattgefunden hat, in Sprache und Volksverhältnissen. Die Kelten sind keine Germanen, aber beide Völker haben einzelne Stämme in einander geschoben und mit einander vermischt. Die Boji sassen lange in der Donaugegend, die Tectosagen hausten mitten unter Germanen. Die Boji werden häufig neben Norici gestellt, oder im ager Noricus genannt, z. B. bei Cäsar, bell. gall. 1, 5; unser Mittelalter, wenn man Gewicht darauf legen will, verdeutscht aber noricus ensis durch „beierisc swert". Auch Langobarden treten auf in Noricum, wie später neben Baiern. Dass die Boji unter den Germanen deutsch geredet haben, kann man vermuthen.'

[1]) Dasselbe erzählt Zeuss in einem Briefe, dessen Entwurf sich in dem Nachlasse befindet. Der Adressat (ich vermute A. F. Pott) hatte ihn nach dem Erscheinen der Grammatica Celtica auf den Leidener Codex des Priscian und den Codex epist. Pauli Boernerianus aufmerksam gemacht, wofür er dankt und hinzufügt: 'Es lässt sich vielleicht erwarten, dass noch mehr dergleichen zum Vorschein kommen wird, und ich werde mich nächstens um derartiges noch einmal an Peyron wenden, den Bösen, der bei meiner Anwesenheit in Turin seine Glossen unter dem Vorwande, ein Freund habe sie auf die Insel Korsika mitgenommen, (mir) vorenthalten und mich mit dem Versprechen abgespeist hat, er werde sie mir auf diplomatischem Wege durch die Regierung zukommen lassen'. — Der Abbé Victor Amedeus Peyron (1785 in Turin geboren und 1866 daselbst gestorben) hat sich vor allem als Lexicograph und Grammatiker der koptischen Sprache grosses Verdienst erworben. Mit den irischen Glossenhandschriften scheint er sich nicht beschäftigt zu haben. Die Turiner Fragmente wurden erst 1866 von Stokes, 1869 von Nigra und 1881 von Zimmer ediert.

24*

mich auch schriftlich an ihn gewendet habe, keine Sylbe ge-
antwortet hat; ferner, dass ich den Mailänder Codex ja schon
zum grossen Theile benützt habe und die Sprache desselben
kenne. Ja, ich habe, weil der lat. Text dieses Cod. ungedruckt
ist, und ich ihn nicht ganz habe abschreiben können, die deswegen schwieriger zugänglichen von mir abgeschriebenen Glossen
bei meiner Arbeit nicht einmal alle benützen mögen, habe sie
aber seit dem Erscheinen des Buches genau durchsucht und
nichts Neues gefunden; nur hie und da könnte ich den von
anderen Quellen her schon hinlänglich belegten grammatischen
Regeln und Formen daraus noch ein Beispiel zufügen. Und den
ganzen Vorrath der alten Sprache enthält auch der ganze
Mailänder Cod. und noch andere dazu noch nicht, so wenig die
althochd. oder goth. Denkmäler den ganzen Vorrath dieser
Sprachen enthalten.

Nachdem ich die Herbstferien nicht Gelegenheit gehabt
habe zu Euch zu kommen, so denke ich jetzt, dass es Ostern
geschehen werde, vorzüglich wegen meiner Ihnen schon bekannten Absicht. Sollte ich sie auch nicht durchsetzen, so würde
mir jetzt deshalb weniger daran liegen, weil ich seit ein paar
Tagen Nachricht von Kopenhagen habe, nach welcher dort soviel
wie keine Ausbeute für mich zu machen wäre. Bibliothekar
Worlauff theilt mir mit, dass sich da nur ein Fragment einer
Pergamenthandschrift der Brehon Laws finde,[1] dergleichen auch
in England existiren, und von welchen Gesetzen in England
bald eine Ausgabe erscheinen soll, wie vor einiger Zeit die
Allgem. Zeitung gemeldet hat.

Wegen der Mabinogion muss ich Sie jetzt ersuchen, dass
Sie mir weder den ersten noch den zweiten, sondern nur den
dritten Band derselben übersenden, und diesem auch das Werk
'Iolo Manuscripts' gütigst beilegen möchten. Ich freue mich
schon auch auf die Nachrichten und Notizen, die von Ihnen mit-
folgen werden.

                    Hochachtungsvollst
                        Ihr
                    ergebenster
                        Zeuß.

---

[1] Dies ist das Fragment Thorkelins, über das in dieser Zeitschrift
2, 324 f. einige Mittheilungen gemacht worden sind.

23.

Bamberg, den 26. Februar 1855.

Verehrtester Herr und Freund!

Für Ihre gütige Mittheilung der Holtzmannischen Neuigkeit danke ich Ihnen schönstens.[1]) Die paar Proben, die Sie zugleich geben, lassen mich schon auf die ganze Art des Mannes schliessen: ex ungue leonem. Ich habe auch nichts anderes erwartet, oder vielmehr war es mir bisher immer noch unglaublich, dass jetzt wirklich jemand, der auf Sprachgelehrsamkeit Ansprüche machen will, solchen Wahnsinn unternehmen könne; es ist also doch so. Ich werde das Produkt auch bald in Händen haben. Dass Sie ebenso wie Vollmer Lust haben, sich dagegen zu erheben, freut mich recht sehr, und ich zweifle nicht daran, dass Euer vereinigter Widerstand, der Ihrige von Seiten der keltischen Sprachüberreste, der Vollmers von Seite der ältesten deutschen Lautverhältnisse, schon vollkommen hinreichen wird, dem Unfug den Garaus zu machen. Dass auch ich meine Streiche führen werde, versteht sich von selbst, ob aber gleich für den Anfang, weiss ich noch nicht.

Über die altbretonische Endung -ac, iac kann ich Ihnen nichts anderes angeben, als dass sie eben auch mir räthselhaft war und noch ist.[2]) Aber das, dächte ich, dürfte behauptet werden, dass sie mit dem ja auch bretonischen -ôc nicht für eins gehalten werden darf; vielleicht steht in einigen Beispielen -ac mundartlich für das kymr. -ec (z. B. in carrec, carreg 'Fels', Cymraec, Ffrancec 'lingua cambrica, francica', heute -eg), vielleicht ist es in andern von den französischen Herausgebern, die leider ziemlich unzuverlässig sind, falsch gelesen für -oc. Ob die Form des Mannesnamens, der dem Ortsnamen Viriziaco zu Grunde liegt, Viritius, Viricius, Viridius sei, ist wohl auch schwer zu entscheiden, da Sie für jede Analogie Belege angeben; für z aus d

---

[1]) Es handelt sich um das Buch 'Kelten und Germanen' (Stuttgart 1855) von Adolf Holtzmann (geb. 1810 zu Karlsruhe, gest. 1870 zu Heidelberg). Der Verfasser stellt darin die beiden Sätze auf: 1. die Germanen sind Kelten; 2. die Kymren und Gälen sind keine Kelten. Den Namen der Germanen hielt er für lateinisch; vgl. Germania 9, 1 ff.

[2]) Die berührten Fragen hat W. Glück in seiner Abhandlung über die norischen Bistümer p. 110 ff. behandelt.

(und wenn ich nicht irre, ist der bekannte Name Virdomarus
in Hss. auch Viridomarus geschrieben) finden Sie auch in der
Gramm. S. 72 Anm. einige alte Beispiele. Die in der Gramm.
gebrauchte Abkürzung *Mor.* bezieht sich auf das in der Vorrede
S. XLII erwähnte Werk von Dom Morice, und zwar, denke ich
(ich besitze es selbst nicht), nur auf den 1. Band, da im folgenden
nur neuere Urkunden enthalten sein werden.

Vor meiner Abreise nach München gedenke ich noch einmal
Nachricht zu geben; vielleicht finden Sie bis dahin auch noch
Einiges zu berichten. Meine Grüsse an Vollmer.

Hochachtungsvoll
Ihr
ergebenster
Z e u ß.

N. S. Die 2 Werke aus der k. Bibliothek werde ich wohl
noch ein paar Wochen behalten und dann selbst mit überbringen
können?

⸻ ⸻

24.

B a m b e r g, den 26. März 1855.

Verehrtester Freund!

Ich liege schon über 8 Tage auf dem Krankenbette, und
werde wohl erst nach ebensoviel Zeit selbst zu schreiben im
Stande sein. Ihrem ersten Vorschlag über das bewusste Buch,
das ich jetzt kenne, stimme ich vollkommen bei. Jetzt durch
fremde Hand nur soviel: Sekundieren Sie von Seite der Inschriften,
Vollmer von Seite des Altdeutschen.

Ihr ergebenster Freund
(gez.) Z e u ß.

⸻ ⸻

25.

B a m b e r g, den 23. Mai 1855.

Verehrter Herr und Freund!

Ich hatte um die Mitte des Märzes das Concept einer
kleinen Schrift: 'Die keltische Nationalität. Gegenschrift gegen
Holtzmanns ... Von ... Mit Beiträgen von ... und ...' bereits

fast vollendet, da ergriff mich das Fieber, dessen Name auch in München bekannt genug ist, gegen dessen Nachwehen ich immer noch zu kämpfen habe. Ich soll mich wissenschaftlicher Beschäftigung soviel möglich fern halten, nur der Sammlung frischer Kräfte leben. Doch so Gott Gesundheit und Rüstigkeit wieder schenkt, so wird auch Leichteres wieder vorgenommen werden können. Haben Sie, wie ich Sie durch fremde Hand auffordern liess, zum 'Sekundieren' gesammelt, so heben Sie es noch einige Zeit auf.

Bücher, überschickte Briefe von Gelehrten lese ich vor der Hand noch nicht. Ich gedenke Ihnen selbst nach einiger Zeit wieder Nachricht zukommen zu lassen. Meine schönsten Grüsse an Vollmer.

Ihr

ergebenster

Z e u ß.

26.

K r o n a c h, (den) 27. November 1855.

Verehrtester Herr und Freund!

Ihr letztes Schreiben enthält recht viel Schönes, und ich bin mit allem einverstanden, was Sie vortragen, ausser dass ich Aduatuannus, Aduatumarus etc.[1] von *ad-iatu-* trennen würde, aus *ad-* (verstärkend?) und *iat*, kymr. *iad*, das vorkömmt, wenn ich nicht irre. In *rian* = *rên* ist wohl die Erklärung des Flussnamens Rhenus = trames zu suchen? Das ir. *geig, geag*, aus altir. *géic* 'membrum', woraus Pictet irrig gall. *gigarus* erklärt, ist kymrisch *geinc*. Jakob Grimm[2] billigt dies und setzt hinzu: 'man vergleiche unser Knöterich von Knote, Gelenk, Glied'. Dass die Aquitanier nicht gallisch, sondern iberisch sprachen, sagt meines Wissens Strabo ausdrücklich; es müssten also diese Formeln eher aus dem Baskischen erklärt werden. J. Grimms sein sollende Rechtfertigung ist also nichts als hochfahrende Unwahrheit,[3] und es bleibt die Behauptung, dass in den Formeln

---

[1] Gemeint sind Adiatunnus, Adiatumarus bei Glück, Die bei Cäsar vorkommenden Namen p. 1 ff.

[2] Kleinere Schriften 2, 159.

[3] Dies soll nicht übel gedeutet werden. Es ist eine Anspielung auf Jacob Grimms zweite Abhandlung, wo er, Zeussens Ansicht über die

nach seinem Ausdrucke 'auch nicht ein Sterbenswörtchen keltisch stecke'.

Der Verleger der Grammatica celtica, Herr Reimer, früher der zweite Theilhaber an der alten Firma 'Weidmannsche Buchhandlung', jetzt mit eben dieser Firma nach Berlin übergesiedelt,[1]) gibt mir die Nachricht, dass wenn der bisherige Absatz bleibe, immerhin 100 Monate bis zum völligen Verkauf verfliessen würden.

Arbeiten Sie nur fleissig fort; Sie können einmal, da meine Gesundheitsumstände sehr ungünstig sind (ich werde auch den Winter hier bleiben),[2]) eine zweite Ausgabe meiner Arbeit besorgen. Unter meinen Büchern in Bamberg befindet sich ein durchschossenes Exemplar mit vielen Beispielen und Verbesserungen, die im vorigen Jahre eingetragen sind; unter dem Handschriftlichen ausser den altirischen Glossen der Codd. auch das Lexicalische der irischen Codd., der Mab. etc. Über die Ossianischen Verse am Schlusse des Werkes muss ich bemerken, dass diese den altirischen nur nachgemacht sind. Die Ossianischen Gedichte sind, wie schon die Irländer dargethan haben (vgl. die Schrift der Talvj über Ossian), unächt, d. h. von Macpherson gedichtet, nicht aus dem Alterthum stammend. Also fleissig fortgearbeitet!

Ihr
ergebenster
Zeuß.

N. S. Ihre Abhandlung über die norischen Bisthümer[3]) erhalte ich eben, sie macht mir wegen ihrer Gediegenheit ausserordentlich viel Freude. In Bezug auf das im beiliegenden Briefe erwähnte -cent, -gent bemerke ich, dass im Ir. und Kymr. be-

---

Marcellischen Formeln (GC.[1] p. XLVIII) anführend, hinzufügt: 'Dem Eindrucke dieses Werkes erliegend und eigne Forschung hintansetzend haben die Berichterstatter nicht gesäumt, die hochfahrende Stelle schadenfroh auszubeuten'. (Kl. Schriften 2, 154).

[1]) Die erste Ausgabe der Grammatica Celtica erschien 'Lipsiae apud Weidmannos 1853'.

[2]) Da sich Zeussens Gesundheit nach Ablauf des Winters nicht gebessert hatte, so wurde er vom 1. April 1856 an auf ein Jahr in den Ruhestand versetzt; sein Aktivitätsgehalt von 1000 fl. wurde dadurch auf 800 fl. des Jahres vermindert.

[3]) 'Die Bistümer Noricums, besonders das lorchische, zur Zeit der römischen Herrschaft' in den Sitzungsberichten der Wiener Akademie der Wissenschaften, Philos.-histor. Klasse, XVII, 1855, p. 60—150.

ständig *cenéel* = *kenetel, kenedyl* 'genus' vorkommt, während die Verbalwurzel *gen, gan* bietet. Ein anderes Beispiel derartigen Wechsels ist bekanntlich ir. *gabail, gabal,* kymr. *cafael.*

27.

Kronach, den 22. December 1855.

Verehrtester Herr und Freund

Was die Hauptsache anlangt, die Sie am Schlusse Ihres letzten Schreibens vortragen, nämlich die Übersendung Ihrer Erklärung der gallischen Namen bei Caesar, so bin ich ganz damit einverstanden; ich freue mich darauf.

Ich habe nichts, was ich gegen irgend etwas von den Ihnen vorgelegten Erklärungen in Ihrem Schreiben einwenden könnte; *adiatu* bleibt auch mir nach dem von Ihnen Mitgetheilten noch dunkel.

Meine schönsten Grüsse an Vollmer; auf seine Anfrage die traurige Meldung, dass allerdings ein Brustleiden, eine Verschleimung, immer weiter sich ausbreitet. Der Buchhändler habe bis jetzt weder geschrieben, noch Rechnung abgelegt. Für Sie lege ich auf Vollmers Aufforderung eine Anweisung auf ein gratis-Exemplar meiner 'Deutschen' bei.

Hochachtungsvoll

Ihr

ergebenster

Zeuß.

N. S. Wissen Sie, dass das altgallische *esseda* das altkymr. *estit* sedile Gl. Oxon. (heute *eistedd* 'sedere') ist? *t* ist eingeschoben wie in kymr. *gwystyl* 'Geisel' obses, für *gwysyl*. Im korn. Passional kommt *esethe* 'sedere', *asethva* 'sessio' vor. Vgl. *Suessiones.*

28.

Sie erhalten hiermit Ihre Blätter wieder zurück, von welchen aber zwei fehlten, nämlich N. 7 und 9, die Sie also wohl einzulegen vergessen haben werden. Ich finde, dass Sie viele schöne Sachen zusammengestellt haben; ich freue mich auf Ihre weiteren Arbeiten.

18. Febr. 56.   Zeuß.

_____

29.

Kronach, den 2. April 1856.

Verehrtester Herr und Freund!

Sie erhalten hiermit Ihre letzte Sendung zurück und dazu die paar vermissten Blätter der vorigen, die sich bei mir vorgefunden haben, von dem aufräumenden Mädchen in die Schublade verlegt.

Mit Ihrer Ansicht über die Präposition *vo* in Vobergensis bin ich vollkommen einverstanden und habe auch bemerkt, dass auch in *veredus* dieselbe Präp. anzunehmen sei, *vorêdus*. Sie lässt sich vielleicht noch in andern Wörtern auffinden, kaum in Vogasus oder Vosagus oder in Vodgoriacum Tab. Peut., wofür Vogodorgiacum (heute Waudrez) gesetzt wird, s. Grandgagnage's Abhandlung über die ostbelgischen Ortsnamen (T. 26 der Mémoires couronnés de l'Acad. royale de Belgique 1855, S. 89). Hier wird wohl die Wurzel *vog* Statt haben.

Als Neuigkeit kann ich Ihnen angeben, dass ich jetzt der Meinung geworden bin, dass die Marcellischen Formeln denn doch gallisch sind.[1]) Was mich dazu gebracht hat, ist die Entdeckung, dass diese Sprüche in poetischer Form, derselben die ich in altirischen und altkymrischen Sprüchen nachgewiesen habe, der Form des Anklangs, In- oder Ausklangs, abgefasst sind, z. B. *ex|ci |cuma |criosos*, Anklang,

    |*crisi |crasi |con|crasi*, An-, In- und Ausklang.

Die Formel *exci cuma criosos* ist ferner von Pictet[2]) auf eine Weise erklärt, dass sich kaum an der Richtigkeit zweifeln lässt; statt *cuma* könnte man vielleicht *cumba* lesen: 'Durch-

_____

[1]) Am 3. April 1856 las Jacob Grimm in der Berliner Akademie der Wissenschaften eine Erklärung Zeussens, 'dass er nunmehr an die Kelticität der Marcellischen Formeln glaubt und sein in der Grammatica celtica darüber ausgesprochenes Verdammungsurteil streicht'. (Sitzungsberichte 1856, p. 187).

[2]) In Jacob Grimms Abhandlung 'Über die Marcellischen Formeln' 1855, p. 57 (Kleinere Schriften 2, 159).

schaue die Krümmung, Höhlung des Gürtels!'*) Der Pictetschen
Erklärung der übrigen kann ich aber nicht beistimmen. Merkwürdig ist, dass die angegebene poetische Form sich nun als
allgemein keltische herausstellt. Machen Sie sich nun darüber,
diesen altgallischen poetischen Sprüchen, namentlich mit Hülfe
des Kymrischen (unter den in der zweiten Abhandlung J. Grimms
vorkommenden finde ich auch den gallischen [= kymrischen]
Plural *grilau*), auf eine gründliche Weise beizukommen!

Ihr

ergebenster

Zeuß.

*) Exspice curvaturam cinguli! Zu *exci* stellt sich das altir.
adci 'adspicit, adspice!' *adcither* 'adspicitur'; *criosos* steht offenbar für *crisos*, mit eingeschobenem *o* wegen des *o* der folgenden
Endung *os,* der altkeltischen Genitivendung, aus welcher die
irische auf *-o, -a* (mit abgestossenem *s,* wie in der Komparativ-
endung *-iu* für *-ius*) erklärt werden muss. — Ich habe nur die
neuere Abhandlung J. Grimms bei der Hand; es wäre mir angenehm, wenn Sie mir auch die übrigen in derselben nicht besprochenen Formeln, etwa aus dessen früherer Abhandlung,[1]
gelegentlich mittheilen könnten.

N. S. Sie hatten die Sendung frankiert. Auf dem Umschlag
finden Sie hier neben 'frei' 11 Kr. notiert, und mein Bruder legte
16 Kr. aus. Wie kommt das?

30.[2]

[Beilage.]

Jak. Grimm stellt in seiner Abhandlung über die Marcellischen Formeln das Gallische noch dem Irischen zur Seite.
Dass aber Gallisches zunächst aus dem Kymrischen erklärt
werden müsse, dafür dächte ich hätten wir Beweise genug:
Allobroges (alienae terrae possessores) mit *brog* 'Land', aus
dem das urkundliche *brogilum* 'Landstück', unser *Brühl* (s.
Schmeller s. v.), kymr. *bro,* ein Wort, das dem Irischen ganz

---

[1] Die andere akademische Abhandlung Jacob Grimms 'Über Marcellus
Burdigalensis' erschien 1847. (Kleinere Schriften 2, 114 ff.).

[2] Das Datum dieser gegen Jacob Grimm gerichteten kritischen Bemerkungen lässt sich nicht feststellen. Das Papier, auf dem sie geschrieben
sind, ist dasselbe wie das des 27. Briefes. Vgl. oben Nr. 15.

fehlt.[1]) Eporedici (boni equorum domitores), kymr. *ebrwydd*
'celer', eigentlich 'pferdeschnell' aus *ep*, *eb* 'equus' und *rhwydd*,
welches auch im gallischen Volksnamen Rhedones vorliegt. Pe-
torritum bei Gellius, richtiger petorrotum (kymr. *rod* 'rota',
alt *rot* in Rotomagus aus der Wurzel *ret* 'currere', so dass sich
auch das lat. *rota* als keltisch erweist), ferner pempedula;
beide von den Zahlwörtern *petuar*, *pemp*, die im Irischen andere
Konsonanten zeigen. Ferner Nàntuates (Vallenses), kymr. *nant*
'vallis', welches wieder dem Irischen abgeht, und so eine Menge
andere. Was Pictet bietet, das einzige *grilau*,[2]) was der kymr.
Plur. *au*, in alten Hss. *ou*, sein könnte, von ihm sonderbar aus
dem ir. *ibh* erklärt, genügt noch nicht. Grimms[3]) Erklärung
von uisumarus kann nicht gebilligt werden, da neben dem ir.
aui vom Sing. *áu*, heute *ó*, im Gall. nie *ui*, wohl aber *avi* hätte
Statt finden können; denn Vibisci, welche Form auch der Orts-
name Viviscum, heute Vévey am Genfersee, zeigt, ist wohl ohne
Zweifel aus dem Adj. kymr. *gwiw*, ir. *fiu* 'aptus', dem altgallisch
viu entsprochen haben muss, und also doch abgeleitet.

Das Wort ambactus müsste *andebactus* lauten, wenn es
das goth. *andbahts* wäre, da die Gallier *ande-* besassen; es ist
amb-actus zusammengesetzt aus *amb-*, kymr. *am-* oder *ym-*, und
act-, das kymr. nach den grammatischen Gesetzen *aeth* (wechselnd
mit *eith*, *euth*), irisch *-acht* (wechselnd mit *echt*, *achte*) lautet und
dem die einfache Wurzel *ag* 'ire' zu Grunde liegt. So irisch
tocht (der Bürge, qui adit, für *do-acht*), *sechmadachte* (praeteritum,
aus *sech-do-achte*, *sechm-* seltenere Compositionsform, in der
Gramm. nicht erwähnt). Kymrisch ist *ymdeith* aus *ym-* (= *am-*)
do-eith, qui circuit, plur. *kedymdeithon* 'socii', noch wieder zusammengesetzt *kyt-ym-do-*, häufig in Mab. Das heutige kymr.
amaeth (= *amb-act*) bedeutet colonus 'Landmann', eigentlich
einen aus der Umgebung. Das Abstraktum muss es auch bedeutet haben; denn im Armor. ist *amez* wohl auch nicht üblich,
aber in *amezek* 'vicinus' enthalten.

Merkwürdig, wie Grimm in seiner Geschichte der deutschen
Sprache das dakische βουδάλλα 'lingua bovis' missdeuten konnte.[4])

---

[1]) Mittelirisch *mruig*, *bruig*.
[2]) In den Marcellischen Formeln; s. J. Grimms Kleinere Schriften 2, 170.
[3]) Kleinere Schriften 2, 156. 171.
[4]) Geschichte der deutschen Sprache 1848, 1, 212, wo das dakische *-δάλλα*
'Zunge' mit nnl. *lel* 'Zunge' und mit *lallen* verglichen wird.

Es muss βουδάγγα gelesen werden, auch wenn Dioskorides βουδάλλα geschrieben hätte; λ und γ sind schon in den alten griechischen Handschriften ganz ähnlich. *Danga* ist dakisch, also thrakisch das bekannte Wort, goth. *tungo*, ir. *tenge* (für *denge*), lingua = *dingua*; *bu* ferner wieder thrakisch das ebenso verbreitete *bos*, βοῦς, irisch *bu* und βουουίνδας bei Ptolem., *inis bon finde* 'insula vitulae albae' bei Beda, sanskr. *go* mit *g*, wie im Slav. Germ. *go, ko* mit wechselndem Laute derselben Stufe (*b* = *d* = *g*, wie *p* = *t* = *c* in petuar, τέσσαρες, ketur), wie auch liquidae thun, wie in *harud*, Harudes schon bei Caes. gegenüber kelt. Caledonia, ir. *caill* 'silva', korn. *kelli* 'nemus' (= calid, celid), germ. *hart* gegenüber kelt. *calet*. Ein Volk, das *bû, bô* sagte, nicht *gu, go*, oder *cu, co* ist gewiss kein germanisches. Dieses einzige Wort macht einen vernichtenden Strich durch Grimms Behauptung, dass die Geten Germanen seien; dass damit auch seine dakisch-danische Zusammenstellung fällt, versteht sich von selbst. Eben dieses Wort beweist auch, dass die Thraker zur indisch-europäischen Verwandtschaft gehören.

Noch im deutschen W.B.[1]) stellt Grimm Perkunas, Fiörgyn,

---

*) In einem Briefe an J. Grimm vom 4. August 1846, dessen Entwurf im Nachlasse befindlich ist, dankt Zeuss für die Einladung zur Germanistenversammlung in Frankfuit a. M. (der Grimm präsidierte) und für die ihm übersandte Abhandlung über Jornandes und die Geten. Über diese sagt er: 'Ich bin überzeugt, dass Sie mir meine Offenheit nicht übel nehmen werden, weil ich weiss, dass auch Sie in Ihren Schriften sich offen und ohne Scheu über die Ansichten anderer aussprechen. Mit der Sache selbst in dieser Abhandlung, der Verbindung der Geten und Gothen, bin ich ganz und gar nicht einverstanden, schon deshalb nicht, weil ich alte Zeugnisse, die mir und sicher auch anderen nicht so unbedeutend scheinen können (wer wird gegen solche einen Jornandes oder gar [einen] sprachlich und geographisch verwirrten Kopf im späten Mittelalter höher anschlagen und vertheidigen wollen?) nicht beachtet sehe. Strabo zeigt sich in sprachlichen Verhältnissen immer besser als irgend ein anderer alter Schriftsteller unterrichtet; er weiss z. B. besser als Cäsar, welche Völker in Südgallien gegen die Pyrenäen nicht dem gallischen, sondern dem iberischen Sprachstamme zugehören.' Weiterhin heisst es: 'Ich freue mich, dass Sie sich bald öffentlich über die Celtomanie einiger Schriftsteller erklären wollen, und habe es gern gelesen, dass Sie in mir einen Gegner derselben voraussetzten; ebenso würden Sie mich als Gegner der Slavomanie Schaffariks finden, aber auch der Germanomanie. Jedem Volke das Seine.' Der Brief ist übrigens durchaus in dem Tone gehalten, der sich dem verehrungswürdigen Manne gegenüber gebührte.

[1]) Unter *B*, Band 1, Sp. 1052. Schon früher, in der Deutschen Mythologie (1835) 1, 117 und in den Altdeutschen Blättern (1837) 1, 288, hatte

Hercynia zusammen. Aber lith. Perkunas steht für *Perunas* mit
eingeschobenem *k,* wie im lith. *auksis* 'aurum' für *ausis,*[1]) oder
besser durch Einfluss des slav. Perun für Kerunas mit vor-
geschobenem *P* und vorgesetztem *K*; denn lith. *keru* 'hauen'
(wozu auch goth. *hairu,* Cherusci) ist slav. *peru,* kymr. *taraw*
(wovon Taran = Perun, Perkunas = germ. Thonar, mit *k* = *p*
= *t,* wie im Zahlwort). Hercynia ferner ist nicht durch röm.
Mund geändertes *Fiörgyn,* denn schon bei Aristoteles steht
Ἀρκύνια, nicht aus römischem Munde, sondern aus gallischem,
offenbar aus Massilia, nach Griechenland gekommen. Diese drei
Wörter sind also völlig von einander verschieden.

Grimm Perkun mit Thors Mutter Fiörgyn zusammengestellt. Am aus-
führlichsten aber kommt er in seiner Abhandlung 'Über die Namen des
Donners' (1853) auf diese Etymologie zurück, die Glück p. 12 seines Buches,
Zeussens Argumente gebrauchend, bestritten hat. Vgl. J. Grimms Kleinere
Schriften 2, 416.

    [1]) Lit. *duksas* 'Gold' entspricht dem preussischen *ausin,* lat. *aurum* (aus
*ausom).

THE RENEHAN 'AIR'.

The following copiously glossed 'air' occurs in MS. Renehan, 70. Battles, etc. in Maynooth College Library. This, together with another of the Renehan MSS. containing a magnificent collection of Munster Poetry, is the work of one O'Rielly, a careful and accurate scribe. He was a carpenter in Enistymon, Co. Clare about 1847.

The piece here published is evidently the work of some-body who had access to the old glossaries. It has interest as being one of the sources of O'Clery. His quotation (s. v. luan) 'ge atá na luan ag tadhg' puts this beyond doubt. Happily it also enabled me to understand the false reading 'geata na luan' in my source, a matter that would otherwise have sorely puzzled me.

I append an attempted translation and a list of the glosses.

I take this occasion of directing the attention of enquirers to the very good collection of modern MSS. in Maynooth College Library. Besides the small Renehan set, and a few odd books, there is the Murphy collection, amounting to over 100 volumes, transcribed from various sources at the instance of Dr. Murphy, Bishop of Cork, circa 1820. An index to the whole is very much to be desired. This would be the easier to compile as most of the volumes are already equipped with a full table of contents.

Ceoir Oda¹) radad ris. Ainm nar mol mmm.²)

Aithnidh dhomh homo re haoi, uios do ghres ar caoi na ndalb,
Cia nach laithfeadh siansa an duar, acht geata na luan ag tadhg.
Da mbeith in tis ag teinm fuach, acht giodh iomdha asnuad mar
[dhonn,
Ní bhoingfedh cairche as anad, acht feibh do bheith sal for onn.
Iomdha gun cia sin mos fi, ar neasgoid ni bhfionn a chail,
Nomen bu gairid omhal, nir cagaidh sin do dha fair.
Fuath do bharcuibh caise dfeis, imtearc sin o bheith na bhár,
Seang a thost qs cudh a cín, engach sa caoi a mbíd mna.
In dae sin cidh dubh a ghlór, i ccedfuidh a fo da mbeith,
7 búc tion ina mhad, ni aitheonadh .a. seach .b.
Eccosg in sgail eanfad i, dha lua is leth reann diobh go losg,
Fédhnach eidigh is tearc cua, beara nac lang is cuar crob.
Uinnsi a caput fliuc do greann, as a ós is cearr gach creath,
Fi on Rex ar chuchtin chia, do theimh is dia a innsi a dhearc.
Faolfadh a nomen do chach, do gach earnaidh len ma a eatt,
Nae at comhnaic barr beag, na raibh tuis na bfeart da eur.
Fios manma tre dhil do den, se gan guidhe ader om theing,
Baedan fearb gan flaitri me, neach osgar ní fhéad mo teinm.
Donn na ndul domutaing fein, dom noadh rem re go raibh,
Neach le naigfedh me as a ae, nar léigidh se am dae do shaic.
[Aithnidh.

Translation.

I know a man of science, who is ever on the way of lies,
A man who would not put sense in (understand) a quatrain although
[he is as a son to a poet.
If the man understood a word, although great his hair like a poet,
He would not harvest bristles off his podex, but as dross upon a stone.
Many by that man — a sad condition — are the keepings of the
[histories of the Irish (?),
A name near to a poet, such it is not seeming to give him.
Hatred of books, love of feasting, that is far from being a sage,

---

¹) The MS. has a small oi written within this o. The whole is probably
a compendium for Fáloi, as o did the duty of a fál or hedge around the
enclosed letters.
²) mmm. — muinter.

Long his silence over his book, garrulous in a house where women
[are.
That man though great his noise, in the presence of his king if
[he were,
And an easy book in his hand, he would not know A from B.
The man's guise I will set it forth: two feet and one of them lame,
An ugly body sparest of flesh, hands not long and a narrow fist.
His head is full of beard, dumb is every science from his mouth,
Evil from the king (that he is) in form of the man (?), it is enough
[of death to see his eyes.
I will make known his name to all, to every wise one that wishes
[to get it,
He is a person of scant hair, may the king of miracles hold him
[not in keeping.
A knowledge of my name through art I will give, without dumbness
[I shall say it from my tongue,
The calf of a cow without milk am I; an ignorant person cannot
[understand me.
The king of elements keep myself, may he be a-keeping me for life,
The person by whom I should be put out of his possession, may
[he not leave in my hand thy wealth.

The MS. gives glosses on the list of words here collected:

ae .i. seilbh. ai, Meyer, Archiv
p. 32; possession O'R.
aigfedh .i. ccuirfedh. againm, ich
treibe, W.
haoi .i. ealadhain. áe, áei, ái,
Archiv, Lec. gl. p. 67.
at comhnaic .i. comainm. Cf.
Wb. 6 b 13.
baedan .i. laogh, a calf, O'R.
bár .i. saoi, a learned man, O'R.
Lec. gl. p. 70.
bharcuibh .i. leabhraibh, barca,
a book, O'R.
barr .i. gruag, Archiv, O'Mul.
gl. p. 281. Sg. 70 a, gl. tiaras.
beara .i. lamha. Pl. of bior?

boingfedh .i. fásfadh. Misunderstood?
búc .i. leabhar. O. E. bóc. Still
so pronounced in Waterford
in the phrase 'book-muslin'.
chagaidh .i. chomhadais, meet,
fitting. Vid. Hogan, Latin
Lives, Index.
chail .i. coimhead, O'Mul. gl.
p. 285.
cairche .i. fionfadh, hair, fur.
fionfad o. g. O'R.
caise .i. gradh, cáise, love, affection, O'R.
caoi .i. slighe, cae, Lec. gl. p. 72.
caoi .i. teagh, cai, a house, O'R.

caput .i. cean*n*.

cearr .i. balbh, mute, dumb, O'R.

ccedhfuidh .i. feagranais (?).

cia .i. fear, (ter), id, O'C.

chin .i. leabhar, O'Mul. gl. p. 286.

creath .i. ealadha, science, knowledge, O'R.   creth .i. hai,
Cormac, W.

cua .i. feoil, cua, flesh meat,
O'D. Supp. and cuadh .i. feoil,
ibid.

cuar .i. cúmhang.   Plunket's
Dict. (Vid. O'R. p. 556) gives
cuar .i. depravate .i. cam, and
cuar .i. cumaisg, ni fa gcuairt
no cruinn. But cuac .i. cum-
hac no cumhang.

chucht in .i. gne, cucht .i. gne,
O'C. Farbe, äussere Er-
scheinung, W. cuchtair mode,
manner, O'D. Supp. Perhaps
the word should be divided
cucht in, in being the article.

cudh .i. cean*n*, cudh, cuth .i.
cean*n*, O'C. cud .i. cenn, W.

dae .i. lamh, id, O'C. righ no
guala, O'Dav.

dalb .i. na mbreag, .i. brég, O'C.
So Cormac, W.

dearc .i. súl, súil, O'C.

dia .i. leor, plenty, abundance,
lór, o. g. O'R.

dil .i. eigse, eigsi, o. g. the li-
terati, O'R.

domutaing .i. cumhdach, conu-
taingim, ich schütze, W.

donn .i. righ, uasal no brithem
no ríg, O'Dav. W. a king,
O'R.

duar .i. rann, draoigheacht .i.

carmen, duar file .i. dialecticus,
Plunket. Cf. duarfine, O'D.
Supp. Lec. gl. p. 78. ag tinm
duar .i. tuicsin focal no rann,
H. 3. 18, p. 210; Stokes, O'Mul.
gl. p. 322.

dubh .i. mor, mór, O'C. great,
O'R. Cf. rug se go dub ar
a sgórnach, Eachtra an iom-
fhorráin.

eanfad .i. foillseochad. eanfaidh,
declaring, explaining, O'R.

earnaidh .i. eolach, earna, know-
ing, experienced, O'R.

eatt .i. faghail (fághbhail). Cf.
étaim, Wi.

eccosg .i. dealbh, cuma, O'C.
model, shape, likeness, O'R.

eangach .i. caiteach, a babbler,
talkative, O'R. The gloss is
therefore to be corrected to
cainteach. Procax, Hogan,
Lat. Lives, Index.

eidigh .i. granna, édigh .i. granna,
O'C. granna o. g. O'R.

eur .i. coimhéd, euróg .i. im-
pedimentum, remora, Plunket.

fair .i. do tabhairt.

faolfad .i. foillseochad, faolad .i.
foghlaim, O'C. faolaim, I
track, O'R.

fearb .i. bo, bó O'C. ferb, Kuh,
W. from Cormac. fearb, a
cow, O'R.

fédhnach .i. corp.

feibh .i. amhuil.

fi on Rex .i. olc ón righ, fi .i.
olc, O'C.

ni bhfionn .i. na Gaoidhiol.

flaitrime, leg. flaitri me, .i.

bainne. flaith .i. cuirm no
lionn, O'C. Milch, W. from
Cormac. flaith, milk, and
flaithri, a calf; i. e. laeghbó,
o. g.; milk; i. e. bainne, o. g.,
O'R.

fliuc .i. lán.

fo .i. rig, flaith, tighearna no
ri, O'C. a king, prince, O'R.

(do)greann .i. d'fulchadh, greann
.i. ulcha no fésóg, O'C. a
beard, O'R. greann ainm
dulchain, lith nach locht, For.
Foc. ib. in voc. crom.

gres .i. do ghnath.

guidhe .i. bailbhe, dumbness,
o. g. O'R.

homo .i. duine.

imtearc .i. fada, long, i. e. fada,
o. g. O'R.

innsi .i. faicsin.

iomdha .i. fada, vid. Stokes,
Amra Coluimb Cille, R. C.
p. 274.

is, man, from Hebr. îsh. See
Rev. Celt. XIII, p. 226.

laithfeadh .i. cuirfeadh.

lang .i. fada, Lec. gl. also O'R.
from Cormac.

losg .i. bacach, losc (gl. claudus),
O'Mul. gl. p. 313. losc, loscc,
lame, a cripple, O'R. who
quotes the lesc of Cormac.
losg .i. bacach, O'C. losc,
O'D. Suppl.

lua .i. cos. Cris Mobi ro iadad
im lua, W.

luan .i. mac, ge atá na luan ag
tadhg .i. ge atá na mhac ag
fili O'C. quoting from the

second line of our 'air', a
son, a lad, O'R.

ma .i. math, good, i. e. maith,
o. g. O'R.

mad .i. lamh, a hand, O'R.

mos .i. modh, bés, O'C. a mode,
O'R.

nád .i. as a thóin. ton, O'C.
the buttocks O'R.

nae .i. duine, a man or woman,
O'R. .i. duine, O'C. noe .i.
duine, Cormac.

neasgoid .i. seanchus.

(dom) noadh .i. coimhéd, noadh,
watching, protecting, guarding, O'R.

nomen .i. ainm, (bis).

omhal .i. file.

ós .i. a bhél, a mouth, O'R.

onn .i. ar cloich, cloch, O'C.,
O'R. ond .i. cloch, O'Mul.
gl. p. 317.

osgar .i. aineolach, ignorant, i. e.
aineola, o. g. O'R.

reann .i. cos. Cf. Meyer, Archiv,
p. 55, sub voce aires; is tri-
amna (.i. toirsech) mu randa-sa
(.i. mo cosa).

saic .i. ionmhas.

sal .i. uisarus (?), dross, rust, O'R.

seang .i. fada.

(in) sgail .i. fear, scál, a man,
hero, O'R. sgal .i. fear, O'C.
scál, a man, Lec. gl. 93.

siansa .i. ciall, harmony, melody,
O'R.

Tadhg .i. file. file, O'C. a poet,
O'R.

tearc .i. beag, few, rare, O'R.
terc, W.

(do) teimh .i. bas, death, O'R.
   temhe, bás, O'C.
(om) theing .i. om theangaidh,
   ting, a tongue, O'R.
teinm .i. tuicsin, ag tinm duar
   .i. tuicsin focul no rann; O'Mul.
   gl. p. 322. tinm, understanding, O'R.
tion .i. bog, soft, O'R.   tin,

tender, soft, O'Mul. gl. p. 321.
tin .i. méith, bog, O'C.
tuis .i. righ, túis .i. dae uais .i.
   fear uasal, O'C.   id. O'R.
   from o. g.
uinnsi .i. ata, uinsi .i. atá, O'C.
   uindsi thall hé, there he is;
   Lec. gl. p. 100.

Washington, D.C.   R. HENEBRY.

ÜBER DIE FORMEN DES KONJUNKTIVS
IM BRITANNISCHEN.

Obwohl H. Ebel, als er, vor mehr als einem Menschenalter, das Verhältnis des Konjunktivs in den britannischen Dialekten untersuchte, die zuverlässigern Texte, deren wir uns heute erfreuen, entbehren musste, so konnte es dem ausgezeichneten Philologen doch nicht fehlen, dass er Irrtümer der Vorgänger schon damals aufdeckte und den Modus in gewisse unbestreitbare Rechte einsetzte.[1]) Einige Merkmale der Form entgingen ihm freilich, traten auch dann in seiner Ausgabe der Grammatica celtica nicht scharf genug hervor. Noch Atkinsons wertvolle Arbeit über den Modus Conjunctivus im Mittelwelschen hat es, wie ich in dieser Zeitschrift 3, 153 andeutete, darin versehen, dass sie der ältern Sprache den Conjunctivus Imperfecti abspricht.[2]) Eine kürzlich erschienene Schrift von J. Vendryes[3]) stellt denn auch, wie sich gebührt, neben den Konjunktiv des Präsens *carho* 'amet' den des Imperfekts *carhei* 'amaret'. Sie erkennt den letztern auch in den armorischen Dialekten, die

---

[1]) De verbi britannici futuro et coniunctivo. (Jahres-Bericht über das Städtische Progymnasium in Schneidemühl 1866, p. 3—8). Sein Ergebnis fasst der Verfasser p. 8 in die Worte: 'Concordant igitur omnes dialecti britannicae hac re, quod vera futuri specie carent; discordat aremorica a ceteris, quae praesentis forma futurum significant, coniunctivi propriam vim servarunt'.

[2]) Noch Griffith Roberts, a Welsh Grammar 1567, p. 157, kennt einen Conjunctivus Imperfecti, giebt ihm aber eine aus Präsens und Imperfekt gemischte Flexion: pann *garŵn, garyt, garai*; *garom, garoch, garont*.

[3]) De l'imparfait du subjonctif en moyen-gallois. (Mémoires de la Société de linguistique de Paris, Tome XI. 1900.) 10 pp.

carfe oder *carehè* 'amaret' neben dem Indikative *carè* 'amabat'
haben. Beifällig und mit ungeminderter Aufmerksamkeit be-
gleitet man die Darlegung des Verfassers bis auf die letzte
Seite, wo er den Ursprung dieser Formen und ihres *h* bespricht.
Das *h* des mittelwelschen Konjunktivs ist nach seiner Vermutung
das *s* der irischen Futurbildung *fortías* von *fortíagaim* 'ich helfe'.
Auch Thurneysen scheint eine solche Annahme zu begünstigen
(KZ. 31, 71. Brugmann 2, 1299). Aber indem ich die Formen
aufs neue zusammenhielt und überdachte, ist mir ein Zweifel
gekommen. Jenes Futurum auf *s* ist im Irischen, wie nun
Strachans Prüfung aufs neue bestätigt, auf bestimmte Verbal-
auslaute beschränkt und schon im Absterben; das Welsche scheint
nur ganz vereinzelte Reste davon bewahrt zu haben. So ist
w. *gwares* 'er helfe' (von *gwared*) aus dem irischen *fu-m-ré-se*
'mihi succurrat' (von *rethim*) gedeutet worden. Auch w. *duch*
'ducat' BBC. 20 b 5 (= arm. *douc*) hat man ähnlich erklärt
(RC. 20, 79).[1]) Vielleicht giebt es noch andere Beispiele; nämlich
wie dem ir. *doruacht, roacht, toracht* 'pervenit' von der Wurzel
ag- das welsche *aeth* 'ivit', *daeth* 'venit' an die Seite tritt, so
dem ir. *dorua, roa, ró, tora* 'perveniet' das w. *a, aa*: arm. *ay*
'ibit', w. *daw* 'veniet' etc. Dass auch w. *el* 'ibit' ein solches
Futur ist, kann ich nicht bestimmt behaupten (vgl. Stokes,
Sprachschatz p. 43); es spricht dafür möglicherweise, dass *el*
und seine Komposita in der ältern Sprache, wie Atkinson bemerkte, auch ohne die Endung *-ho* modal gebraucht wird.[2])

Von den Grundzügen altertümlicher Sprachbildung, deren
das Irische einzelne bis in die Neuzeit behalten hat, ist dem
Welschen aus vorbritannischer Zeit nur wenig übrig geblieben.

---

[1]) Es ist wohl möglich, dass *duch* eine sigmatische Form ist, einem ir.
*dus entsprechend, für **ducst*, **ducset*; sowie ir. *oss* : w. *ych* ox; *es-* : *ach-*
ex; *uas* : *uch* ux-ellos; *ses-, sé* : *chwech* sex; *dess* : *dehou* δεξιός; *tressa* : *trech*
'fortior'; *lassar* : *llachar* 'igneus' etc. Die Form gehört zu dem w. Infinitive
dygu (statt *dwyn*, arm. *dougen*) von dem celtischen Verbalstamm *uc-*, der auch
in *aduc* 'abstulit', *amuc* 'defendit', *goruc* 'fecit' enthalten ist. Es ist aber
zu bemerken, dass die dem *duch* 'ducat' analog gebrauchte Form von *amygu*
Skene 149, 3 *amuc* 'protegat' lautet, was man als das Futurum zu dem
Präteritum *amwyth* (S. Evans, Dict. 1, 204b) angesehen hat. Ist aber *duch*
wirklich ein Konjunktiv auf *-cs*, so beweist diese Form allein schon, dass der
gewöhnliche Konjunktiv *dycco* andern Ursprungs ist.

[2]) *el* 'eat' RB. 1, 14; *del* 'veniat' 1, 34. 37. 221. 224. Skene 231, 1.
234, 10; *gwnel* 'faciat' RB. 1, 44. BBC. 20 b 4. *gunel* 35 b 14.

Indem die alten Verhältnisse sich lösten und die Analogieen sich lebhaft durcheinander drängten, entstanden hier grammatische Formen, deren wesentlicher Charakter Zusammensetzung ist. Man schuf Tempus-˙ und Moduszeichen, in denen die Urbilder kaum noch zu erkennen sind. Man schuf Personalendungen, indem man selbst Pronomina und Partikeln nutzbar machte, wie *carwn* : arm. *caromp* 'amamus' aus *caram-ni, carom-p-ni* (wie contempno), *cerwch* 'amate' aus *ceri-chwi, carut* 'amabas' aus *caru-ti,* und sogar vielleicht, dem *j'avons* im Patois vergleichbar,[1] ein *cerych* 'ames' aus *cery-chwi* (schwerlich aus *cery-σοι* oder *cery-śva*) nicht scheute. Ein irisches Futur wie *ni im-irchói* 'er wird mich nicht schädigen' Wb. 7 a 11 (von *erchoit* 'Schaden') ist eine starke Formation von indogermanischer Ursprünglichkeit, aber ein welsches *ergyttyo* 'accedat' RB. 1, 103. 267 (von *ergydyaw* 'treffen' HM. 1, 235) steht auf der Stufe eines ir. *erchotigea* oder auf einer noch spätern. Sollte jene vergessene Bildung des sigmatischen Konjunktivs in der neuen Phase der Sprache wieder lebendig werden und ganz überraschend zunehmen, wo man von der altceltischen Flexion so vieles verloren und einige der nötigsten Endungen sogar dem Lateinischen entlehnt hat? Ich halte meine Zustimmung noch zurück, hoffend, es werde die umständliche Erörterung, der ich mich unterfange, das eine oder das andere ergeben, das ins Gewicht falle.

Aus der Formation des irischen Konjunktivs ist von vornherein nicht viel Aufklärung zu erwarten, da er (von den Resten *beth* 'esset', *dogneth* 'faceret', KZ. 27, 183. 31, 66, abgesehen) nur Praesentis ist. Die welschen Konjunktive erscheinen zunächst als ganz unabhängige Bildungen, deren gleichmässiger Charakter ein *h* ist, im Präsens sowohl wie im Imperfektum und im Aktiv wie im Passiv; also in der 3. Sg. von *caru* 'lieben', *tebygu* 'meinen', *gwybod* 'wissen':

Praes. act.   *carho, tebycko* (statt *tebyg-ho*), *gwypo* (statt *gwyb-ho*), zu dem Indikative *car, tebyg, gwyr.*

Imperf. act. *carhei, tebyckei, gwypei,* zu dem Indikative *carei, tebygei, gwybydei,* auch *gwyddai* (D. G. 102, 6 als Konjunktiv gebraucht).

---

[1] Dergleichen kommt auch in andern Sprachen vor; z. B. sagt man im marokkanischen Dialekte des Arabischen *nektub* 'scribam' (eig. 'scribemus') statt *ektub* und unterscheidet *nektub* 'scribemus' davon durch eine plurale Endung: *nektubú.*

Praes. pass. *carher, tebycker, gwyper,* zu dem Indikative *cerir, tebygir, gwybydir* (D. G. 188, 26. 50) oder *gwyddir.*

Imperf. pass. *cerhit, tebyckit, gwypit,* zu dem Indikative *carwyt, tebygwyt, gwybuwyt*; ebenso *adnepit* RB. 1, 70 von adnabod 'erkennen'.

Die Belege sind so zahlreich, dass die Richtigkeit dieser Aufstellungen nicht in Frage kommt, wenn man das *h* der Konjunktive selbst in den alten Texten, die wir haben, hin und wieder vermisst, wie es denn im Neuwelschen fast gänzlich ausser Gebrauch getreten ist.[1]) Auch ist die Bedeutung dieses Buchstaben, die Natur seines Lautes derart, dass er sich oftmals eindrängt, wo er nicht hingehört, z. B. *ny chanhwyt* 'non cantum est' Skene 145, 15. Das lasse ich unbeachtet.

Das *h* der Konjunktive findet sich nach jedem Stammauslaute. Nach Vokalen: *aho* 'eat' RB. 1, 140, *gwnaho* 'faciat' BBC. 35 b 3, von *a* 'ibit'; *foher* 3 a 6 von *ffo* 'fliehen'; *brivher* 3 a 5 von briwo 'brechen'; *clyho* Skene 114, 2, *clywhont* RB. 1, 14, *clywher* Skene 296, 14 (neben clywir ib. 20), von clybod 'hören'; *dylyho* RB. 1, 257. LA. 45, 13 von dylyu 'verdienen'; *dalhyo* RB. 1, 123, *dalyher* LA. 45, 27, von daly 'fassen'; *cudyho* LA. 40, 17 von cuddio 'verbergen'; *coffaho* BBC. 35 b 8 von coffau 'erinnern'; *bwyttehych* RB. 1, 292 von bwyta 'essen'. Dass die Denominative auf *-hau* das konjunktivische *h* sonst vermeiden, habe ich schon bemerkt, also *parhawyf* RB. 1, 24, *parhao* 1, 213, *bwyttao* 1, 289, *rwydhao* 1, 17, *rithao* BBC. 46 b 11, *rydhaer* RB. 1, 65.

---

[1]) Griffith Roberts war der Konjunktivcharakter wohl bekannt, denn er schreibt in seiner Grammatik p. 157 vor, dass man bilde: *pann grettuyf* von credu, *pann dybyccuyf* von tybygu und *pann gyphlyppuyf* von cyphlybu. Wie das Verständnis der Form allmählich verloren ging, dafür liefert Gruffydd von Hiraethog, ein Barde in der ersten Hälfte des 16. Jahrh., ein Beispiel. Er schliesst sein Gedicht 'über die Eifersüchtige' mit den Versen:

> Y mwya' ei dig a'i ddigedd,
> Ei bwrn a'i *dycco* i'r bedd.

'Die sich und ihn am meisten ärgert, möge ihre Bürde sie ins Grab bringen!' Und in demselben Gedichte sagt er, der Allitteration zu liebe:

> Ffei o wraig wych ffriw a gwedd
> A *ddygo* fwrn o eiddigedd.

'Pfui über eine Frau, hübsch von Ansehn und Manier, die eine Bürde der Eifersucht trägt!'

Nach den Liquiden *L, R, N,* wie in: *talho* BBC. 4 a 11, *talhont* Skene 128, 4, von talu 'bezahlen'; *celho* BBC. 4 a 4. Skene 213 von celu 'verhehlen'; *guelher* BBC. 1 b 6 von gweled 'sehen'; ae *dehoglho* 'qui id interpretetur' 4 a 4; *elhont* RB. 1, 61, *elhei* 1, 85, *elhynt* 1, 111, von el 'ibit'; *delhich* BBC. 42 b 7, *delhei* RB. 1, 109, *delher* 1, 61, von del 'veniet'; *gwnelhoch* 1, 140, *gwnelhont* BBC. 30 b 4, *gwnelhit* RB. 1, 105, von gwnel 'faciet'; — *carho* RB. 1, 252 (neben *kerych* 1, 18. 264) von caru 'lieben'; *sorho* Skene 157, 9 (neben *sorro* BBC. 28 b 1) von sorri 'zürnen'; — *canho* BBC. 42 b 5. Skene 129, *canhont* BBC. 17 a 6, *cenhid* 5 b 2, von canu 'canere'; *mynhwyf* Skene 193, 16, *mynho* 206, 2, *mynhont* Cymmr. 9, 62, *mynhei* RB. 1, 277, *mynhut* 1, 213, von mynnu 'wünschen'; *tynho* 1, 222 (neben *tyno* 1, 110) von tynnu 'ziehen'; *prynhom* Skene 116, 26, *prinhei* BBC. 21 a 1, von prynu 'kaufen'; *erlinho* 4 b 8 von erlyn 'verfolgen'; *digonho* RB. 1, 120, *digonhom* BBC. 15 b 3, von digoni 'genügen'; *llunhich* 42 b 7 von llunio 'bilden'; *gwaravunho* RB. 1, 253 (ohne *h* 1, 263) von gwarafun 'verhindern'; *barnher* Skene 158, 22. RB. 1, 256 von barnu 'richten'. Nach den Spiranten *DD* und *F,* wie in: *lladho* RB. 1, 15. 189, *ymladho* Skene 239, 20, *llather* (für llad-her) BBC. 29 a 12, von lladd 'töten'; *dygwydho* Skene 231, 15 von dygwyddo 'fallen'; *eistetho* (für *eistedho*) BBC. 29 b 4 von eistedd 'sitzen'; *rodho* LA. 113, 30 = *rotho* 102, 20. 130, 1 (neben *rodo* RB. 1, 222 = *roto* BBC. 15 a 12), *rodhom* RB. 1, 105, *rothei* (für rodhei) BBC. 22 a 3, *rodher* RB. 1, 258, von roddi 'geben'; *nodho* 1, 126 von noddu ‚bitten'; — *yfho* RC. 8, 21 von yfed 'trinken'; *safhei* RB. 1, 110 von sefyll 'stehen'; *prouher* BBC. 3 b 1 von profi 'probare'.

Nach den Mediae *G, D, B,* wie in: *tebycko* RB. 1, 125, *tebyckych* 1, 120, *tebyckwn* 1, 165, *tebycker* Skene 225, von tebygu 'meinen'; *bendicco* 161, 24 (neben *bendigwyf* 292, 10) von bendigo 'segnen'; *plyccoent* Cymmr. 9, 62 von plygu 'biegen'; *mynaccont* LA. 168, 7 von menegi 'erzählen'; *diwyccom* BBC. 15 b 3, *dywyccviff* 42 a 15, von diwygu 'wiederherstellen'; *dirmycco* 35 b 9 von dirmygu verachten'; *gostecker* RB. 1, 280 von gostegu 'gebieten'; *llosco* Skene 120, 10 von llosgi 'brennen'; *kysco* RB. 1, 122 von cysgu 'schlafen'; *gwascut* 1, 116 von gwasgu 'drücken'; *dyckwyf* LA. 79, 28, *dycko* RB. 1, 109. 124. 127, *dycco* D. G. 149, 34, dazu *an duch* 'er bringe uns' BBC. 20 b 5, von dug- (dwyn) 'bringen'; — *cretto* RB. 1, 189, *crettoch* 1, 131, von credu 'glauben'; *notto* 1, 105. 118. 120. 126, *nottych* 1, 106, von nodi 'bezeichnen'; *dywetto*

1, 217. 222, *dywettych* 1, 113. 276, *dywettei* 1, 237, *dywetter* Skene 242, 2. D. G. 240, 41, *dywettit* RB. 1, 94, von dywedyd 'sagen'; *diaspettych* 1, 114 von diaspedain 'schreien'; *retto* Skene 240, 11, *rettei* RB. 1, 108. 262, von rhedeg 'laufen'; *gattwyf* Skene 168, 28, *gatto* D. G. 114, 56, *gatter* RB. 1, 113. 119, von gadu 'verlassen'; *dotter* RB. 1, 15. 57. 123. D. G. 114, 51 (neben *dodir* 119, 50), *dottit* 1, 13. 153, von dodi 'geben'; *gwatter* BBC. 51 a 14 von gwadu 'leugnen'; *ergyttyo* RB. 1, 103, *erkyttyo* 1, 267 von ergydio 'erreichen'; *cattwo* 1, 123. 177. D. G. 130, 33 von cadw 'hüten'; — *atteppych* RB. 1, 176 von attebu 'antworten'.

Solche Formen liegen vor und sie lassen sich leicht vermehren; ihr gemeinsamer Charakter verbirgt sich uns unter dem vieldeutigen *h*. Dass er ursprünglich überall ein *s* gewesen sei, lässt sich, soviel ich sehe, nicht wahrscheinlich machen. Wenn wir die welschen Konjunktive jeder Art zu verstehen suchen, ihre Formen bis in die ältesten Denkmäler zurückverfolgen, uns bei den verwandten Dialekten Rats erholen, je mehr wir auf den Gegenstand eingehen, desto verwickelter und schwieriger gestaltet er sich.

Eine Frage muss, ehe wir irgend etwas entscheiden, zu allererst beantwortet werden. Kommt dieses *h*, oder auch seine Wirkung, einen vorhergehenden Wurzellaut zu verhärten, in der Konjugation des Verbum substantivum vor?

Der Austausch der Meinungen, der stattgefunden hat (KZ. 26, 423. 27, 165. 28, 55), scheint mir zu ergeben, dass die celtischen Sprachen zwei mit *b* anlautende Wurzeln für das Verb 'sein' verwenden, die in ihren Urformen ähnlich sind, aber doch ziemlich weit auseinander liegen, nämlich: sanskr. *jivâmi*, βιόω, *vīvo*, air. *biuu*, und sanskr. *bhavâmi*, φύω, ahd. *bim*, wozu lat. *fuit* und air. *bói* in gleicher Bedeutung gehören. Wie auf diese beiden Wurzeln die Formen der britannischen Dialekte zu verteilen sind, ist keineswegs leicht festzustellen. Schon darüber sich zu einigen ist schwer, ob das altwelsche *bid*, mittelwelsche *byd*, neuwelsche *bydd*, cornische *byth*, armorische *bez* zu der ersten Wurzel *BÎ* (*BEI*) oder zu der zweiten *BU* gehört? Ist *byd* 'sei' = ir. *bí* 'vive' oder = ir. *ba* (statt *bav*) 'fî'? und ist *byd* 'er ist, wird sein' = ir. *bí* 'vivit', *bia* 'vivet' oder = ir. *bid*, *ba* 'fiet'? Es ist bekannt, dass *byd*, dessen Verständnis Schleicher vergeblich im Slawischen suchte (KB. 1, 505. 5, 318), als ein j-Stamm erklärt worden ist, wie er im äolischen φυίω zu Tage liegt (RC. 2, 116).

Ist das wahrscheinlich? Bedenklich erscheint von vornherein jede Erklärung einer celtischen Wortform, die nicht im Celtischen selbst ihren Grund und ihre Stütze hat; man dürfte diesem Sprachzweige getrost jenen Leitsatz zueignen, den einst Jacob Grimm für den seinigen aufgestellt hat. 'Bei unsern deutschen Wörtern', so sagt er in der Vorrede des Wörterbuchs, 'muss es recht sein vor allem zu versuchen, ob sie nicht auch innerhalb dem deutschen Gebiet selbst sich erklären lassen, das zwar nur engere, der Natur der Sache nach oft sichrere Schritte zu thun erlaubt.' Muss man nicht glauben, dass, wie sich w. *dyd* (alt *did*) : arm. *dez* 'Tag' zu ir. *die, dia* 'dies' (aus *dives*) verhält, so sich auch verhalte w. *byd* (alt *bid*) : arm. *bez* 'sei, ist' zu ir. *bí* 'vive, vivit' oder *bia* 'vivet'? Wie neben *dyd* eine Form *dyw*,[1]) pl. *diev* BBC. 28 b 11 : arm. *de*, pl. *deiou*, liegt, so neben *byd* das Adjektiv w. *byw* : corn. *bew* : arm. *beu* = ir. *bíu, béo* 'vivus' etc. Wird nicht ebenso das ir. *sníim* 'flechte' im Welschen zu *nyddaf*? Analog sind ferner *trydydd* trítîya 'dritt', *rhydd* 'frei', *blydd* 'zart', *toddi* 'tauen'. W. *ydd* geht meist auf ir. *idh* zurück (vgl. *ffydd, cybydd, crefydd, gwydd, hydd*), und eigentlich ist auch *bydd* nicht anders zu verstehen als ein neuir. *bidh* für *bí* oder vielmehr *bij, biv*. So ist auch w. *Ywerydd* 'Irland' aus dem ir. *Ériu* zu erklären (Skene 2, 355. Sprachschatz p. 45), wovon der casus obliquus *Ywerddon* = ir. *Érend, Érind* (wie w. *afon* = ir. *abha, abhand*). Neben *henwyf* 'existo' giebt es auch ein *handwyf* Skene 265, 17, und es scheint, als habe das *i* der ursprünglichen Form **sani* (ir. *sain*) in der erstern Form Umlaut bewirkt, in der andern aber sich zu *dd* verdichtet. Die 3. sg. *handit* 'existit' Skene 115, 16. 270, 7. RB. 1, 178 oder *handid* 1, 71 (gleichsam ir. *sain-atá*) ist bekannt. Ähnlich wird es sich mit *hudwyf* Skene 144, 26 (MA. 33 a) verhalten, neben *hubwyf*. Für die Präpositionen *i, y* 'zu' (ir. *do*) und *o* 'von' (ir. *ó*) hat der südwelsche Dialekt vor Vokalen die Formen *idd* und *odd*, und w. *iddo* : corn. *dozo* : arm. *dezaf* 'ihm' (ir. *dó*) etc. muss vielleicht aus diesem *idd* erklärt werden, obwohl *erddo, hebddo, rhagddo* etc. eher an den

---

[1]) Die Form *dyw* ist in den Namen der Wochentage gebräuchlich, daher in alten Texten wie das Wort für 'Gott' geschrieben: *duw* Skene 158. 173. 189. 207. 222. 270. 298 oder *diw* 83. 105. Statt *duwieu* 'Donnerstag' Skene 207, wo die Aussprache einen konsonantischen Ruhepunkt suchte, ist gewöhnlicher *diuieu* Skene 301, 3 oder *dyv-ieu* BBC. 23 b 4 oder *dyfieu* Skene 158. 170 — ein Zeichen der Verwandtschaft zwischen *dd* und *v*.

Ursprung dieses *dd* aus dem Artikel *ind* denken lassen. Halb
ein Konsonant und halb ein Vokal, erscheint und verschwindet
dies w. *dd* mitunter auf unberechenbare Weise; man denke an
w. *oed* 'er war' = arm. *oa*, w. *oedwn* 'ich war' = arm. *oan*;
w. *gwdost* 'du weisst' neben *gwybuost* 'du wusstest' von *gwybot*
st. *gwydbot*, wie nw. *gwybed* 'Fliegen' = mw. *gwydbet* RB. 1, 54.
112. LA. 10, 23, nw. *gwybwyll* = mw. *gwydbwyll* RB. 1, 84. 220.
235 = ir. *fidchell*; nw. *rhoddi* 'geben' = *rhoi*, arm. *rei* (KZ.
30, 221); arm. *mezeven* 'Mittsommer' = vann. *meheüenn* = w.
mehefin (RC. 16, 189) = ir. *midh-shamhain, meitheamh*; narm. *délez*
'Raa' = marm. *delé*, u. a. m.[1])

---

[1]) Für die Geschichte des welschen *dd*, worüber noch viel zu sagen
wäre, ist auch das Wörtchen *ydd* von Wichtigkeit. Das w. *issid, yssyd,
sydd, sy* scheint doch nicht, wie ich CZ. 3, 149 auch angenommen habe, das
ir. *ished, iseadh* zu sein, da man hierfür eher w. **issed* erwarten sollte und
auch die Bedeutung nicht ganz übereinstimmt. Ir. *ished* ist eine Kopula, die
in der Regel an der Spitze des Satzes steht, franz. 'c'est' und ihre Stelle
nimmt das w. *isem* GC. 398, *yssef* Skene 148, 32 = *sef* ein: altw. *issem i anu*
'das ist sein Name' (KB. 7, 400) = ir. *ished a ainm*. Dagegen ist *yssyd*
eigentlich ein Wort des Daseins, das selten voransteht, franz. 'y est', 'qui y
est'; z. B. *nifer a uu ac a uyd, uch nef is nef meint yssyd* 'viele waren und
werden sein, über dem Himmel, unter dem Himmel giebts eine Menge', Skene
114, 15, ähnlich 292, 34 f.; dann auch als Relativpronomen: aw. *ir hinn issid
Crist* 'dieser, welcher ist Christus', KB. 4, 411. Nach meinem Vermuten ist
issid, yssyd das ir. *is and* 'es ist da'; denn dieses aw. *id*, mw. *yd*, nw. *ydd*
= ir. *and* dient auch zur Verstärkung des Pronomen demonstrativum, wie in
henoid 'cette nuit-ci' (Iuv.); *ir gur hunnuid* im Martianus, d. i. *y gur hwnnw-
ydd* 'dieser Mann da' (KB. 7, 390), cf. arm. *hennez* 'iste'. Vielleicht ist dieses
id, yd, ydd die Verbalpartikel *yd*, die vor Konsonanten das *d* abwirft, vor
Vokalen aber in der neuern Sprache (mit häufiger vorkommendem Lautwechsel)
yr lautet. Sie scheint eigentlich aus *yssyd* verkürzt zu sein, denn w. *y dywawt*
'er sprach da' ist = ir. *is and asbert*, wofür im Mittelirischen auch *ised asbert*
gesagt wird = w. *sef y dywawt*. Selten steht ir. *and* am Anfang des Satzes,
wie: *and seiss Conchobar* LL. 109 a 42, statt *andsin* oder *isand*; auch w. *yd, y*
hat gewöhnlich ein Adverbiale vor sich. Die w. Partikel *y* mit den pronominalen
Suffixen hat mit *yd* vermutlich nichts zu thun (GC. 421), denn sie ist das ir. *do*. —
Neben dem relativischen *issid, yssyd* giebt es im Altwelschen ein selbständiges
Verbum existentiae ('il y a'), das *yssit* lautet und dem ir. *atá* entspricht,
der Form nach aber mit dem ir. -*id* (in *cid, manid, conid* etc.) übereinkommt.
So heisst es: *yssit teir ffynnawn* 'es giebt drei Quellen', Skene 301, 22; *yssit
imi teir cadeir* 'ich habe drei Stühle', 154, 23; *yssit a pryderer* 'es giebt
etwas, was man besorgt', 147, 4; *yssit ym a lauarwyf* 'ich habe, was ich
reden möchte', 262, 10; *yssit rin yssyd uwy* (neuwelsch: *yssid rin ysydd fwy*,
MA. 55 a) 'es giebt ein Geheimnis, das grösser ist', 147, 21; *darogenwch y
Arthur yssit yssyd gynt* 'kündet dem Arthur: es giebt etwas, das zuvor ist',

Ich nehme also an und zweifle nicht, dass der welsche Stamm *byd* zur Wurzel *Bî* gehört. Seine Konjugation ist fast so vollständig wie die des ir. *biuu, biu,* Konj. *beu, beo,* durchgeführt; sein eigentliches Gebiet ist aber das Präsens und Imperfektum: das w. *bydwn* 'eram' entspricht deutlich dem ir. *bíinn* und kann nicht von der Wurzel *BU* kommen, die ir. *bin, benn* : w. *bewn* : c. *ben* : arm. *benn* bildet. Die neugälischen Dialekte fügen dem Imperfekt ein bedeutungsloses *dh* oder *th* ein, das dem welschen *dd* sehr ähnlich ist, nämlich ir. *do bhidhinn,* alb. *bhithinn,* aber manx *vein, veign.* Der Konjunktiv *byddo* 'er sei' und der Imperativ *bydded* 'er sei' scheinen nur der neuern Sprache anzugehören; ebenso die passivischen Formen, wie *byddir* = ir. *bithir* 'vivit vir' = *vivitur* 'man lebt'. Die präsentialen Tempora liefert *byd* auch den mit *bot* zusammengesetzten Verben, wie *gwybyd* 'sci, sciet', *gorfyd* 'vince, vincet', etc. Dieser Stamm hat kein Präteritum, kein Tempus der Handlung und des Geschehens, doch hat man es im Neuirischen (*dobhí* = albanogäl. *bhà,* manx *va,* vormals *vê*) analogisch nach dem Präsens *bí* gebildet. Zu dieser Wurzel scheint auch der im Mittelirischen aufkommende Infinitiv *bith, beith* zu gehören, wovon das Substantivum *bith* : *byt* : *bed* 'Welt' nur wenig verschieden ist.

Der andere Stamm, von dem die Konjugation des Verbs *both* : *bot* (φύσις, skr. *bhûti*) ausgeht, im Irischen wieder fast vollständig durchgeführt und hier meist als Kopula gebraucht, zeigt sich am deutlichsten im Perfekt oder Aorist, ir. *bói, -bu,* w. *bu* (1. sg. *buum*), was dem lat. *fuit,* dem griech. ἔφυ gegenübersteht. Diese Wurzel liefert also das Präteritum, das man von *Bî* nicht bildet, so namentlich auch den Zusammensetzungen, z. B. *dybu* Skene 197 oder *dyfu* 'venit', *gwybu* 'scivit', *adnabu* 'agnovit', *gorfu* 'vicit', *darfu* 'cessavit', *hanfu* 'exstitit'. Die alte Sprache hat, neben dem Plusquamperfektum *buassei* 'fuerat', wie das Cornische ein Praeteritum secundarium, das die Bedeutung eines Imperfekts anzunehmen scheint. Es lautet in der 3. sg.

149, 19; auch wohl: *yssyd* (leg. *yssit*) *wr dylyedawc a lefeir hyn* 'es ist da ein vornehmer Mann, der dieses sagt', 124, 17. Dieses *it* (= ir. *-id*) hat man auch in: *ossit* 'wenn es giebt', Skene 188, 4; *ot* 'wenn es ist' RB. 1, 199; *beyt* 'wenn es wäre', RB. 1, 175; *pet* ... *pet* 'sive ... sive', Skene 133, 4 ff. 174, 25; etc. und sehr ursprünglich in: *kyt yt wo* 'quamquam est ut sit', 286, 20 = *kyt at wo* ib. 22, mit merkwürdiger Häufung des Verbum substantivum (gleichsam ir. *cid atá ropo*).

buei 'erat' Skene 282, 20. Daneben giebt es auch eine Form auf -*at*, nämlich *buiad* 'erat' BBC. 25 b 17, was nach MA. 116 a als *bwyat* zu verstehen ist; und dieses *bwyat* kommt auch sonst in den alten Gedichten vor, Skene 289, 1. 4. 290, 18. Cymmr. 9, 65. Die 3. pl. dazu ist *buyint* 'erant' BBC. 48 b 2, was vermutlich als *bwyint* zu deuten ist. Während *buei* im Codex Hergestiensis ohne Zweifel zu dem Präteritum *bu* gehört, muss *bwyat* vielleicht eher als Imperfektum bezeichnet werden. Beide sind wohl vom Stamme *BU* abzuleiten, und ebenso das Praeteritum (oder Participium) passivi, ir. *both* : w. *buwyt* 'man war', das wiederum in Zusammensetzungen häufig ist. So sagt man: *arganvuwyt* 'perceptum est' RB. 1, 34, *gwybuwyt* 'scitum est'; dann aber in kontrahierter Form: *gwypwyt*; *gwanpwyt* 'transfossum est' Skene 78, 17. 122, 14, *wnaethpwyt* 'factum est' 73, *ry vaethpwyt* 'nutritum est' 63, 20 (cf. AC. IV. 5, 118). Ebenso in der neuern Sprache *claddpwyd* = *claddwyd* (Davies p. 98), *gwelpwyd, dycpwyd, dywedpwyd* (alt und sw. *dywespwyt*), woneben auch unregelmässig *clywsbwyt* LA. 117, 14 und *clywspwt* Cymmr. 9, 77. Offenbar ist also *p* = *bu, bv*.

Die Wurzel *BU* bildete wie im Irischen (*bid, ba*) so vormals auch im Welschen ein Futurum. Hier lautet der Stamm altwelsch vielleicht *boi* 'erit' (in *hacboi* 'excuties' (?), GC. 1056), später aber *bi* oder *pi* (aus *bvi*), und er entspricht, wie es den Anschein hat, dem lat. *fio* (Brugmann 2, 1061). Die Form kommt nur noch bei den alten Dichtern vor, wie: *bi* 'erit' Skene 62, 9. 20, 11. 123, 11; *a ui* 'qui erit' 148, 7 f. 222, 6. 231, 12. 236, 17; *nyt uu nyt vi* 'non fuit, non erit' 199, 25; *nyth vi* 'tibi non erit' 304, 7; häufiger in Zusammensetzungen, wie: *dybi* 'veniet' RB. 1, 119. Skene 111, 8. 128, 10. 292, 7, *dyvi* 303, 34 (== *dybyd* 218. 305, 1), *dymbi* 'mihi veniet' 211, 3. 238 oder *dimbi* 205, 18, von dyfod 'kommen'; *deupi* BBC. 31 a 13 = *deubi* 'veniet' Skene 123, 9. 130, 1; *atvi* 'iterum erit' 127, 9 ff. (= atvyd 296, 6) von adfod 'wieder sein'; *tyrui* 'surget' 115, 19 von tyr-fod; *dyderbi* 'cessabit' 212, 22. 220 (= diderbyd 231, 25. 237, 4) von darfod 'aufhören'; *dorbi* BBC. 31 b 8. 14 von dawr 'es betrifft'; *gwybi* 'sciet' 27 b 9 (= *gwybyd* Skene 161, 25) und, last not least: cat a vi ar Byrri auon a Brython *dyworpi* 'eine Schlacht wird am Flusse Byrri sein und die Britten werden siegen', Skene 237, 4, wo *dy-wor-pi* (von gorfod) das *p* zeigt, das diesem Stamme *bi* eigentümlich ist oder doch, wie in *pwyt*, seinen guten Grund hat. Neben dieser

kurzen Form *bi* giebt es aber eine vollere mit der Endung des
Futurs: *biawt* 'erit' Skene 228, 3. 229, 13 (cf. MA. 112 b. 113 a)
= ir. *bid*, pl. *bit*. Ich denke, auch der Imperativ w. *bit* : corn.
bis 'er sei' ist zu diesem Futurstamm zu stellen = ir. *bad*, vgl.
BBC. 10 a 1 f. 13 b 6. 11. Skene 245 (das Gedicht über die *bidiau*).
261, 19. 305, 16. RB. 1, 147. 246; der Plural dazu lautet *bint* RB.
1, 105. LA. 81, 28. Als Zusammensetzung mit *bit* ist *derffit* 'eveniat'
Skene 279, 18 zu erwähnen.

Nun handelt es sich darum, von welcher Wurzel die Konjunktive von *bot* abzuleiten sind. Geht man von der 3. sg. aus,
so ist es kaum zweifelhaft, dass w. *bo* : c. *bo, bova* 'sit' mit seinem
Plurale *bont* : *bons* 'sint' dem ir. *bo, bat* entspricht und dass
w. *bei* : c. *bei, feve* : arm. *be* 'esset' das ir. *bed, bad* ist, beides
von der Wurzel *BU*. Darin bestärken uns die Zusammensetzungen
mit *bot*, nämlich *gwypo* 'sciat' (aus *gwy-bvo*), *gwypei* 'sciret' (aus
gwy-bvei) und auch *gwypet* 'scito' (aus *gwy-bvet*) neben *gwybydet*
LA. 110, 10; ebenso *dyppo* BBC. 45 b 10, *deupo* 'veniat' Skene
72, 1. 11. 87, 25. Von gorfod lautete der Conj. praes. vormals
gorpo 'vincat' BBC. 9 a 14 (aus *gor-bvo*) und später (nach der
Analogie von *corff* corpus) *gorffo*, dazu das Impf. *gorffei*; ebenso
darffo, darffei; *dyffo* Skene 119, 7 neben *dyfu, dyfyd* 118 etc.
Es zeigt sich also, dass der Indikativ (*gwybyd* 'sciet', *gwybydei*
'sciebat') die Wurzel *Bĩ* 'sein', der Konjunktiv (*gwypo* 'sciat',
gwypei 'sciret') die Wurzel *BU* 'werden' zu Grunde legt. Die
im Neuwelschen aufgekommene Form ('euphoniae gratia', sagt
Davies) *bae* 'esset' (statt *bei, bai*) scheint sich von *pettae* 'si
esset' aus verbreitet zu haben; *pettawn, pettwn* 'si essem' geht vermutlich wie *pet* (nw. *ped*) auf das Verb ir. *tá, atá* 'stare' zurück.

Schwierigkeiten aber bietet noch die Flexion des Conj. praes.:
w. *bwyf, bych, bo*; *bom, boch, bont*, und corn. *beyf byf, by bey,
bo*; *beyn, beugh, bons*. Man kann sie mit Hilfe des Irischen kaum
heben, da dessen Endungen im Conj. praes. von *BU* zum Teil
verkümmert sind: *ba, ba, -bo*; *-ban, bede, -bat*. Es kommt noch
hinzu, dass das Welsche eine alte Flexion des Conj. praes. besitzt,
die zu der 1. sg. *bwyf* stimmt, nämlich: *bwym* 'simus' Skene 181, 6;
bwynt 'sint' 112, 6. 124, 21. 212, 1. LA. 134, 24. 162, 12, *bwyn*
Skene 264, 13; und *bwyr* 'man sei' Skene 114, 21. Die 3. sg. *bwy*
findet sich in *gwypwy* 'sciat' Skene 147, 23 = *gwypo*. Man kann
sich über diese Formen nur mit Vorbehalt äussern. Es ist wahrscheinlich, dass *bwy* auf **boe* beruht und so eine Variante von

bo ist. Möglich aber auch, dass es gewissermassen dem **Präsens**
wyf 'ich bin', *wyt* 'du bist', *wy* 'er ist'[1] etc. analog ist und **dass**
bwyf ebenso zu *bydwn* steht, wie *wyf* zu *oedwn* 'ich war'; **in**
diesem Falle würde *bwy* dem irischen *bé* 'sit' von *Bí* entsprechen.
Jedesfalls dient in der alten Sprache das Präsens *wyf* der Zusammensetzung ebensowohl wie die Formen von *bot*, z. B. **henyw**
'exstat', *gorwyf* 'vinco' Skene 144, 2. Es bleibt aber bei alle-
dem zu bedenken, dass sich schon im Irischen **Konjunktiv**
und Futurum mehrfach nahe berühren und fast vereinigen, **und**
so darf man vielleicht auch w. *bwy* aus dem irischen **Futurum**
bia, w. *bwyf* aus ir. *biam* (LH. 1, 110, mit der spätern Var. *bum*)
erklären, wiewohl dieses Futurum von *BU* erst aus der mittelirischen Sprache nachweisbar ist. Die 2. sg. *bych* : c. *by* 'sis'
ist gewiss von *BU* abzuleiten, da sie in der Zusammensetzung
pych lautet, wie *hanpich* BBC. 18 a 2 oder *hanpych henpych*, jetzt
hanffych; aber die altwelsche Form *hánbíic* (GC. 1063) scheint

---

[1] Diese Form *wy* (für das gewöhnliche *yw* oder *w* wie in *derw* 'cessat')
kommt in einer Stelle des Gododin vor: *ny hu wy ny gaffo e neges* 'nicht
geschickt ist, wer seine Sache nicht erreicht', Skene 78, 15 (MA. 11 a). Vgl.
hubwyf 175, 8, *hubo* 207, 4, *hubyd* 174, 21. 270, 15   Die Form *wy* liefert
den Schlüssel zum Verständnis des 'Verbs' *wyf, wyt, yw*. Man darf für
dieses Präsens einen pronominalen Ursprung vermuten, da es fast nie an
betonter Stelle im Satze steht. Ebenso wie *wy* zu *yw*, wird auch das verbale
Präfix *rwy* (aus *ro-e*, ir. *ro-d-*) zu *ryw* (RC. 6, 51), und ebenso w. *oe* 'zu
seinem' (= ir. *dua*, *dia*) über **wy* zu *yw* (GC. 390); so steht auch *molediw*
(Skene 272, 5) statt *moladwy* 'löblich'. Demnach vermute ich, dass w. *wy*,
yw : corn. *yu* : arm. *eu* 'er ist' dem ir. *ddu*, *dó* 'ihm' entspricht; desgleichen
wyf : *off* : *of* 'ich bin' dem ir. *dom*, *dam* 'mir', *wyt* : *os* : *out* 'du bist' dem
ir. *duit*, *deit* 'dir', und *ywch* : *ough* : *ouch* 'ihr seid' dem ir. *dúib* 'vobis',
während *ym* : *on* : *omp* 'wir sind' = ir. *ammi* und *ynt* : *yns* : *ynt* 'sie sind'
= ir. *at* zu dem alten Verbum substantivum gehören. Im Mittelwelschen
vereinigt *ywch* noch die Bedeutungen 'estis' (nw. *ych*) und 'vobis', aber für
die Dative der sonstigen Personalpronomina traten Zusammensetzungen ein,
wie *ym* aus *y-mi*, *ytt* aus *y-ti*, *ynn* aus *y-ni* und *idaw* aus *i-dd-aw*. Die
Bedeutung *damh* 'ich bin', *duit* 'du bist', *dó* 'er ist' bei präpositionalem oder
adverbialem Prädikat ist im Irischen bekannt: *a gCill Chreidhe dham* 'ich bin
in Kilcrea' RC. 7, 68; *di feraib Gaidel damsa* 'ich bin von den Gälen' RC.
9, 18; *can deit?* 'woher bist du?' WW. 489 a; *is ass dam* 'ich bin daher'
Atk. Gl. 652 a. Allgemeiner ist der Gebrauch dieses *dam, duit, dó* im Welschen
geworden, wie in: *Lunet wyf i* (gleichsam ir. *damhsa*); *hyn gwr wyt* 'du bist
der ältere' (gleichsam ir. *duit*); *pwy wyt?* 'wer bist du?', wofür der Ire sagt:
cia thusa? So sagt auch w. *yttwyf* = ir. *atá dam*. Ob mir. *bidam* 'ero', var.
bidh damh (= w. byddwyf?) RC. 16, 46 und *bidat* 'eris' (Windisch, Gr. p. 104)
eine ähnliche Erklärung zulassen, bleibe dahingestellt.

wieder auf das Futurum zu deuten, dessen 3. sg. *biawt, bi* lautet.
Darnach ist vielleicht auch diese Annahme berechtigt, dass die
Formen *bo, bom, boch, bont* aus dem eigentlichen Konjunktive,
die Formen *bwyf, bych, bwym, bwynt* aus dem Futurum hervorgegangen sind, und dass sich diese gemischte Flexion erst allmählich festgesetzt hat.

   Noch einige andere Formen sind für die Konjunktivbildung
im Welschen von Belang. Die Partikel *po* 'je' würde in diesen
Betrachtungen keine Stelle haben, wenn sie wirklich dem lat. *quo*
entspräche, wie in *goreu po cyntaf* 'je schneller, desto besser'.
Aber *po* mit dem Superlative deckt doch das *quo* mit dem Komparative nicht völlig. Viel wahrscheinlicher, dass *po* mit dem
Konjunktive *bo* 'sit' im Zusammenhange steht ('es sei am
schnellsten, so ist es am besten') so wie *pei* 'wenn wäre' mit
bei 'erat, esset'. Was begründet aber die Verhärtung des
Anlauts? Man könnte auf die Vermutung kommen, w. *po* sei
das ir. *ce bé, ce pé, cia beith* 'was auch sein mag'; auch *pei*
liesse sich allesfalls aus *cia bed* erklären, doch steht daneben
die Form ohne *p*, wie *vei vei* 'gesetzt es wäre, dass wäre',
BBC. 9 b 8; *bei na bei* 'wenn nicht wäre', RB. 1, 189; *beyt uei*
'wenn sie wäre' 1, 175. Auch ist zu bedenken das *p* des Imperativs *poet* 'sit', Skene 78. 91. 96. 109. 110. 125. 129. 178.
179. 203. 259. 299. 304, der neben *boet* BBC. 49 a 5 ff. (augenscheinlich von dem Konjunktive *bo* abgeleitet und noch in
konjunktivischer Funktion vorkommend, RB. 1, 44. 264 f.) und dem
schon erwähnten *bit* besteht. Hier könnte man versucht sein
zu vermuten, dass die Verhärtung im Wesen des Imperativs
begründet liege (etwa nach Thurneysens Annahme durch eine
ausgefallene Interjektion), wie ir. *tabair* 'gieb' neben *dobeir* 'er
giebt', oder w. *tyred* 'komm' = *dyred*, südw. *dyre*. Aber be-
friedigender wäre eine Erklärung für *po, pei, poet* aus der
gleichen Ursache. Sie sollte auch auf corn. *po, bo, pi* und arm.
pe 'oder' (GC. 725) anwendbar sein, womit altir. *robo* (Strachan,
Substantive verb p. 34 n.) gleichbedeutend ist.

   Dass *po, pei, poet* aus *bvo, *bvei, *bvoet* hervorgegangen
sind, dass das *v* der Wurzel *BU* das verhärtende Element ist,
scheint mir sicher. Aber was hat das latente *v* hervorgerufen?
Die annehmbarste Vermutung scheint mir die zu sein, dass es
die Befehl und Wunsch ausdrückende Konjunktivpartikel ist, die
im Irischen *ro*, im Welschen *ry*, im Cornischen *re* und im

Armorischen *ra* lautet. Wenn sie im weitern Gebrauche, wie auch im Irischen gewöhnlich, die Wirkung der Lenitio hat (wie w. *ryvo*, GC. 419), so doch thatsächlich nicht in den in Rede stehenden alten, gemeinceltischen Formen. Ich meine, w. *po* sei der ir. Konjunktiv praes. *ropo*, *rop* und w. *pei* das ir. Futurum secundarium *ropad*. Dass diese Wörter ihr *p* nur für eine bestimmte Anwendung beibehielten, kann nicht auffallen.

Wo ein *p* in der Konjugation des Verbum substantivum *bot* auftritt (der Stamm *byd* hat es nie), da darf man mit einiger Sicherheit schliessen, dass es aus der Wurzel *BU* und nicht *Bî* entsprungen ist. Dass das Präteritum *bói* : *bu* dieses *p* nicht bietet, ist erklärlich, da hier von der Substanz der Wurzel nichts verloren geht. Es ist beachtenswert, dass auch die irische Copula (d. i. der Stamm *BU*) oft, jedoch nur im Status contractus, dieselbe Verhärtung des Anlauts zeigt, wie in: *ni pam* 'non sum', *ni pa* 'non eris', *niptha* 'non eras', *ni po* 'non fuit', *ropsa* 'fui', *ni pâ* 'ne sis', *ropat* 'sint', während sie in den Formen von der Wurzel *Bî*, z. B. *ni piam* 'non vivemus', *ni pî* 'non vivit' (neben *ni bî*), *ro pia* 'vivet' (neben *ro bia*), wie aus Strachans Sammlungen zu ersehen, selten ist. Der Umstand, dass das altir. *b* zum Teil = *p*, *bb* und zum Teil = neuir. *bh* ist, erschwert die Beobachtung. Aber wenn ich nicht irre, so zeigt jenes *p* der irischen Formen noch eine Spur von dem *u* oder *v* der Wurzel, indem z. B. *ropat* ein ursprüngliches *ro-bavat*, *robvat* voraussetzen lässt. Sollte nicht ein ähnlicher Grund der enklitischen Verhärtung in der Präposition *do* liegen (*dobeir* 'dat', *ni tabair* 'non dat'), die doch wohl dieselbe ist wie ahd. *zuo*, engl. *to*? [1])

Ich halte in diesen Spekulationen inne, um eine Tafel (s. S. 397) vorzulegen, auf der ich die Formen des Verbum substantivum von der zwiefachen Wurzel *Bî* und *BU* je an ihrer Stelle versuchsweise eingeschrieben habe.

---

[1]) Der Verfasser des Urkeltischen Sprachschatzes p. 132 scheint es nicht zu billigen. Aber ir. *d* entspricht doch gewöhnlich hochdeutschem *z*, niederdeutschem *t*, z. B. *dá* : *dou* zwei, two; *déc* : *deg* zehn, ten; *dún* : *din* Zaun, town; *dét* : *dant* Zahn, tooth; *dér* : *daigr* Zähre, tear; *dorn* : *dwrn* 'Faust', Zorn; ir. *díth* 'Ende', Zeit, tide? (cf. *díthugad* zeitigen, mit Gegensinn); *did* Zitze, teat; *dial* Zagel, towel; *día* : *duw* Ziu, Tyr; *damnae* : *defnydd* Zimmer, timber; ir. *cride* Herz, heart; w. *dof* zahm, tame; ir. *dabach* Zober, tub; *foddlim* ab-zählen, tell; *dingim* zwingen, twinge; u. a. m.

Die Konjugation des Verbs *both : bot* 'sein' in der 3. Pers. sing.

Bî vivo:

Act.	Irisch	Welsch	Cornisch	Armorisch
Praesens	biid, -bí	byd, 1. sg. bydaf, bydo, 1. sg. bydwyf	byth, bydhaf	bez, bezaff (bezo)
— Conj.	beith, -bé			
Imperf.	bíth	bydat, bydei	bethe, bedhe	—
— Conj.	both, bed			
Praeterit. n.	dobhí			
— Sec.	—			
Futurum	bieid, -bia	bydhawt, 1. sg. bydif	—	bezzo, beziff
— Sec.	biad, bieth			
Imperat. 2. sg.	bí	byd	byth, bedhes, bezens	bez, bezet, 2. pl. bet
3. sg.	biith, bíid	bydet		
Infinitiv	bith, beith	—	—	beza, bezout
Pass.				
Praesens	bithir	n. byddir		bezer
— Conj.	bether	n. bydder		
Praeterit.	—	n. byddid	—	—
— Sec.	—			
— Conj.	—	*bydhawr		bezor
Futurum	—			

BU fuo, fio:

	Irisch	Welsch	Cornisch	Armorisch
	—	—	bo	—
	ropo, rop	po, bo, bwy, bwyat	borva, beva	—
	—		—	—
	bed	bei (bae), bu, bwei, bwassei	be, bove, pue, be, bye, rebee	be, boe, boe, boue, bise
	bói, -bo, -po	bi		2. pl. biket
	—	bei, pei	pe	bihe, 2. pl. bihec'h
	bid, -ba, -pa, bed, -bad, ropad	biawt		
	ba, bad	bit	bis	—
	both, buith	poet, boet, bot	bos, bones	bout
	—	n. beir, n. baer, bwyr	—	boar, boer
	roboth	bwryt		boad
	—	n. bwarid	—	bized, bijed
	—	n. baid	—	bed
	—	—	—	bior

26*

Die allgemeine welsche Konjunktivbildung, wie *carho* und *carhe*, scheint sich an die vom Verbum substantivum *bot* enge anzuschliessen. Sehr bemerkenswert, dass zu *carho* 'amet' wiederum ein *carhwy* sich einstellt. Aus dem Konjunktive auf *ā*, aus dem Wechsel und der Verwechselung des thematischen Vokals, wie etwa w. *o* = ir. *a*, w. *wy* = ir. *ea*, lässt es sich schwerlich erklären. Es findet sich: *molhwy* Skene 161, *dalwy* 75, 24 (= *cynyho* 92, 27), *llanhwy* 117, 10, *canhwi* BBC. 24 b 3, *gorescynhwy* 38 b 9, *tyfwy* Skene 147, 26, *gwledychuy* 147, 30, *guledichuy* BBC. 24 b 1. 30 a 16, *rybuchvy* 38 b 10, *dirchafuy* 30 a 14, *safhwynt* Skene 127, 16, *rodwy* 197, 7 neben *rothwy* 165, 3, dazu das Impersonale *rothwyr* 109, 26 (= *rothwy yr* MA. 81 a), *arhaedwy* 124, 23, *cothuy* BBC. 35 b 6 (zu *a gaut* 41 a 5), *nothwy* Skene 205, 32, *nottvy* BBC. 38 b 7, *gwnelwy* 24 a 15, *rymawy* 5 a 1[1]) und *ae harhowe* 24 b 2 (= *ae harovy* 30 a 17a). Neben *wy* kommt *ve* vor, wie in *eirolve* BBC. 16 b 12; und neben *ve* auch *oe*, wie in *creddoe* 27 a 15; sodass man endlich auch auf diesem Wege zum einfachen *o* gelangt. Darauf hat schon Evander Evans die Aufmerksamkeit gelenkt und auch für die 3. pl. die Formen *wynt, oynt, oint, oent* neben *ont* nachgewiesen (AC. IV. 4, 147). Diese Übereinstimmung des *carho, carhwy, carhei* mit *gwypo, gwypwy, gwypei* scheint kaum denkbar, ohne dass die Konjunktive *bo, bwy, bei* auch auf jene Einfluss gehabt haben, sodass man hier wiederum den Ausdruck des Konjunktivs durch die Wurzel *BU* erreicht hätte. Zu dieser Einsicht war Zeuss gelangt, als er sein Futurum **carboim, carboi, carib carab*; *carbom, carboch, carboint carbont* erschloss (GC.[1] 497), dem er die dann von Ebel als Konjunktive oder Potentiale bezeichneten Formen zuwies. Das *h* könnte in solcher Zusammensetzung als ein geeigneter Vertreter des *b* oder *v* betrachtet werden; jedesfalls hat man im Welschen *kehy* = key (GC. 139), *cahat* = caead RB. 1, 208, von *cael*, arm. *cahout, caout* = ir. *gabháil*.

---

[1]) Die Form ist m. E. zu erklären aus *ry* (= ir. *ro*) + *m* (suff. 1. sg.) + *ā* (d. h. 'ibit') + *wy* (Endung des Konjunktivs). *Deus ren rymawy awen* 'Deus domine, adeat me inspiratio' BBC. 8 a 1, korrig. aus *rymaw*, wofür auch das Impersonale *rymawyr* 'es werde mir zu Teil' Skene 158, 1. 109, 31; *Reen nef rymawyr dy wedi, rac ygres rymgwares dy voli*. 'Herr des Himmels! zu Teil werde mir dein Gebet (d. h. dass ich zu dir bete, d. h. lass mich zu dir beten), vor Gewaltthat schütze mich dein Lob' (d. h. dass ich dich lobe), 304, 8. Ähnlich wird *a* auch mit dem Imperf. *bei* zusammengesetzt: *rymafei* 'mihi contingebat' Skene 201, 26, wie *wnafut* 115, 15.

Eine derartige periphrastische Formation würde der cornische Dialekt erklären helfen, obwohl seine Bildungen von gröberer Textur sind. Konjunktive des Präsens, die den welschen auf *h* entsprächen, sind wohl nur spärlich nachzuweisen: *leuerryf* 'loquar', *leuerry* 'loquaris', *peghy* 'pecces', *carro* 'amet' neben *caro, tokco* 'portet' neben *dogo* (GC. 583), gehören dahin. Hier bleibt die Komposition mit *bot* 'sein' nicht auf wenige Fälle beschränkt, sondern ergreift Verba jeder Art. Man hat *gothfo* 'sciat' (in welscher Schreibung **gwydvo*), *wothfe* = *woffe* 'sciret' (gleichsam **gwydvei*, vgl. *gull* 'facere' = *guthyll*, GC. 598), beides von *gothvos* (gleichsam **gwydvot*, w. gwybod). Man hat aber auch *clewfo* 'audiat' (w. clywho), *wharfo* 'accidat' (arm. *hoarvezo*), *perfo* 'paret'; und dann auch *caruyth* 'amabit' (gleichsam **carvyd*), *taluyth* 'rependet', *talfens* 'valerent' (gleichsam **talvynt*). Vgl. GC. 576.

Einen anderen Verlauf hat die Bildung konjunktivischer Formen im Armorischen genommen. Hier findet man in der Konjugation von *bot* neben den neueren vom Stamme *byd* abgeleiteten Formen noch solche, die zur Wurzel *BU* zu gehören scheinen. Sie erscheint indes in der Aussprache *bi*, selbst im Präteritum *biof* 'fui' (w. buum), *biomp* 'fuimus' (w. buam), *bioch* 'fuistis' (w. buawch), *biont* 'fuerunt' (w. buant), wozu Ernault im Dictionnaire p. 66 die Variante *ez vihont* verzeichnet. Nun hat der Conjunctivus praes. neben den von *byd* abgeleiteten Formen (eig. des Futurs): *bezif*,[1]) *bezi, bezo, bezimp, bezint* die 2. pl. *bihet* (*vihot*, vann. *bêeh*), wozu Ernault im Glossaire p. 229 die neueren Varianten *bizhyt, vezot* anmerkt. Diese sind der übrigen Flexion von *bezif* analog gebildet, aber *bihet* 'sitis' fordert eine Erklärung. Es ist als ein Aorist auf *s* gedeutet worden (KZ. 28, 91), eine Annahme, die das Armorische in einer wichtigen Sache vom Welschen sowohl wie vom Irischen trennt. Ich vermute daher, dass es ein Rest des Futurs von *BU* ist, zu dem

---

¹) Der Form *bezif* entspricht im Welschen nicht die neuere, nach Analogie von *bwyf* gebildete *byddwyf*, sondern die in einem Verse Taliessins aufbewahrte: *ny bydif yn* (var. *ym*) *dirwen na molwyf Uryen* 'ich werde nicht wieder heiter sein, wenn ich nicht Uryen lobe', Skene 184, 2. 185, 27. 187, 16. 189, 10. 190, 8. 191, 32 und 196, 15 mit der Variante *ny bydaf* (cf. 293, 6). Aber auch die Form *bydwyf* in der Bedeutung 'habeam' kommt schon in diesen alten Texten vor: *bydwyf or trindawt trugared* 'möge ich von der Dreifaltigkeit Erbarmen haben!' Skene 180, 2, d. i. ir. *bidh dhamh* (?).

auch arm. *bimp* gehört sowie welsch *biawt* 'erit', *bit* 'esto'; so
heisst es auch arm. *gouzvihet* oder *gouviet* 'sciatis' für w. *gwypoch*.
Das *h* von *bihet* ist nur ein analogisches, wie sich noch weiter
zeigen soll.

Eine andere Erklärung sehe ich auch nicht für das *h* in
dem Conjunct. impf. *vihenn, vihes, vihe, vihemp, vihech,* das *vient*
wieder ausstösst. *Bihe,* vann. *béhé,* ist das Futurum secundarium
und entspricht dem w. *pei,* dem ir. *ropad.* Die dem w. *bydei*
gleichende Form hat unter den armorischen Dialekten nur das
Vannetais *boé,* wiewohl ihnen der Konjunktiv *bezo* (vann. *bou*)
geläufig ist. Der trekorische und der venetische Dialekt pflegen
nämlich das *z* zu elidieren: *beet* 'sit' statt *bezet*; anderswo (RC. 17,
287) wird es zu *h,* wie *beha* 'esse' statt *beza.* Die neuere Sprache
scheint dieses *z* (w. *dd*) im Konjunktive durch *f* zu ersetzen, wie
in *ra vefomp* = *vimp* 'simus', *ra vefet* 'sitis', *ra vefont* 'sint',
ra vefen = *ven* (=*vizen* = *vijen*) 'essem' — ein alter und verbreiteter Lautwechsel.[1]) Arm. *vef-* gehört zur Wurzel *BÎ,* aber
vi- und *vih-* zur Wurzel *BU.*

Auch der armorische Dialekt hat manche rohe, den cornischen
ähnliche verbale Formen, die auf Komposition mit *bot* 'sein' beruhen, so wie in *gouzvezo* 'sciat' (gleichsam **gwydvydo*), *gouez-
himp* 'sciamus' (w. gwypwn), *gouffenn* 'scirem' (gleichsam **gwyd-
vewn*), *goufhemp* 'sciremus' (für **gwydveym*), *gouzvezher* (für
*gwydvydher) 'sciatur', von *gouzuout, gouzout* (w. gwybod); cf.
GC. 578. Im Infinitive sind solche Zusammensetzungen mit *bot*
sehr gewöhnlich, wie in *talvézout, talvout* 'gelten', dann auch
kerout 'lieben' statt *keret,* etc. Der Conj. impf. *ra garfe* 'amaret'
ist eine Zusammensetzung mit *be* 'esset'; die neuere Sprache
vermischt ihn noch mit dem Praet. sec. *ra garze, ra garje,*
dessen *z, j* aus *s* hervorgegangen ist (RC. 19, 184) = w. *carassci,*
wie arm. *bise* = w. *buassei.* Eine Form wie *casfe* 'odisset'
(GC. 521) ist zu neu, als dass sie, wenn es phonetisch möglich
wäre, einem irischen Futurum secundarium auf *F* gleich geachtet werden könnte. Trotzdem hält der von Analogieen über-
wucherte armorische Dialekt an dem *h* der Konjunktive (wie in
bihet, bihe) zäher fest als selbst der welsche.

Der eigentliche Ursprung dieses Konjunktivcharakters lässt
sich aus dem Altwelschen in der Sprache der frühesten Barden-

---

[1]) Vgl. *gwlat Gafis* Skene 214, 2 = ir. *insi Gaid* WT. 302, d. i. *Gadis,* Cadix.

gedichte noch erkennen. Es finden sich darin, wie mehrfach bemerkt worden ist, noch deutliche Spuren der zwiefachen Konjugation, der absoluten und der konjunkten, im Passiv sowohl wie im Aktiv, jedoch nicht mehr mit der strengen Scheidung des Gebrauchs, die das Irische beobachtet. Trotz aller Schwankung der Überlieferung kann man für die 3. sg. praes. die folgenden Formen aufstellen:

Aktiv: *cerit — cari (car)*, Passiv: *ceritor — cerir.*

Was das Aktiv anbetrifft, so entspricht die Endung der 3. sg. *t* (neuw. *d*) hier wie überall dem irischen *d* (neuir. *dh*), wie in *carid* und *nochara, lécid* und *dolléci.* Dass das Schwarze Buch von Carmarthen für dieses *t* beständig *d* schreibt, ist bekannt. Die welsche absolute Form ist, wie Ev. Evans gezeigt hat (AC. IV. 4, 146), nicht selten: *pereid* 'es dauert' — *ny phara* 'es dauert nicht' Skene 289; *trengid* golud, *ni threing* molud, MA. 859 a; *kirchid* 'greift an' BBC. 46 a 7; *dyrcheuid* 'erhebt sich' 41 b 11; *gulichid* 'wäscht' 46 a 3; *chwerit* 'spielt' Skene 305, 3; u. s. w. Die vokalisch auslautende konjunkte Form scheint vorzukommen: *nym cari* 'me non amat' BBC. 25 b 1; aber die gewöhnliche, die im Neuwelschen übrig geblieben ist, hat den Vokal abgeworfen und im Stamme oft Umlaut erlitten, wie *teifl* 'jacit' von *taflu, erys* 'manet' von *aros*, etc., aber zufällig *car* 'amat'. Die ziemlich häufige Endung *a* der 3. sg. praes., wie *doluria* (GC. 508. AC. IV. 4, 147), scheint sich von den Denominativen auf *-hau* auf andere Verba übertragen zu haben. In älteren Fällen der Art kann sich aber sehr wohl der thematische Vokal erhalten haben, den *amat* hat; es ist selbst wahrscheinlich, dass neben der Form auf *-a* eine absolute auf *-awt* gegolten hat: der Futurstamm *bi* scheint in *biawt* 'erit' diese Endung angenommen zu haben. Möglicherweise erscheint dieser thematische Vokal als *a* in *gwelattor* 'conspicitur' (Skene 303, 2) und als *o* in den alten Formen *crihot* 'vibrat' (Luxenb.) und *brithottor* 'variegatur' (BBC. 17 b 5).

Auch das Imperfectum hat die absolute Form, wie in *bydat* Skene 264, 26, *gwydiat* 'sciebat' neben der gewöhnlichen ohne *t*, wie *carei* oder auch *ceri* (AC. IV. 5, 117), *serui* Skene 110, 19, *seui* 182, 5, *gelwi* 90, 13, *lledei* 90, 15, gehabt; beide sind im Irischen *-ad, -ed*, denn hier ist eine besondere absolute Form auf *-aid* nicht genügend belegt, auch kaum annehmbar.

Das Passiv bildet gleichfalls eine doppelte Form, die eine von der absoluten aktiven *cerit* aus, wie *keritor* 'amatur' MA. 177 b

37; *cenitor* oder *kenhittor* BBC. 26 b 7, auch *kaintor* 'canitur';
kwynitor 'defletur' Skene 280, 24; *keissitor* 'quaeritur' Skene 157,
12; *megittor* 'alitur' BBC. 31 b 5; *gwelitor* 'conspicitur' MA. 182 a 3;
clywitor 'auditur'; ebenso *llemittyor* 'calcatur' Skene 305, 4; *peritor*
'efficitur' MA. 105 b = *pervor* Skene 237, 7, etc. Daneben kommen
aber einige Formen auf *etor* vor, wie *kymysgetor* 'miscetur' Skene
181, 72 (cf. ir. *commescatar* 'miscentur'); *cynwyssetor* 'continetur'
200, 8; *tyghettor* 'juratur' (?) 209, 21; *dygettaur* BBC. 13 a 8,
dygetawr Skene 119 'adducitur'; *kynbwylletor* 'mentio fiet' 200, 6.
Das letzte Beispiel hat die ausdrückliche Bedeutung des Futurs,
wie denn überhaupt schon in den alten Texten die Neigung besteht, dem Präsens die Bedeutung des Futurs zu verleihen, die
im Neuwelschen die allein gebräuchliche ist. Die zweite Form
des Passivs, die in der neueren Sprache übrig geblieben ist, geht
offenbar von der konjunkten aktiven aus: car-ir oder vielmehr
cerir, corn. *ceryr, cerer*, arm. *carer, careur*.

Nun ist es merkwürdig, dass das Präsens auf *-it* nicht selten
ein *h* vor der Endung oder die dadurch verursachte Verhärtung
des Stammauslauts zeigt, wie *briuhid ia* 'das Eis bricht' BBC.
46 a 7; *tohid* 45 a 13 = *toid* ib. 3 'er bedeckt' (cf. Skene 116);
aessaur brihuid, torrhid eis 'Lanzen brechen, Rippen werden zer-
schmettert', 50 a 3; *llicrid rid, reuhid llin* 'es verdirbt die Furt,
es gefriert der See', 45 a 2. 12; *gosgupid* 'er fegt darüber hin',
ib.; *mekid* 34 a 19 oder *meccid* 'er nährt' 45 b 3, von *magu*. Diese
Erscheinung ist aus der Form des Präsens unerklärlich, das *h*
muss ihr aus einer anderen zugetragen sein — ohne Zweifel aus
dem Futurum, dessen Charakter es ist.

Das eigentliche Futurum der alten Texte lautet in der 3. sg.
wieder in absoluter und konjunkter Form:

    Akt.: *carhawt* — *carhaw* (*carho*), Pass.: *carhator* — *carhawr*.
Dass das *h* hin und wieder fehlt, ist nicht verwunderlich. Indes
sind einige dieser Formen vielleicht als Praesentia anzusehen, die
als Futura gebraucht sind. Man hat die absolute Form des Aktivs
in: *parahaud* 'manebit' BBC. 50 b 13; *briwhawt* 'franget' Skene
151, 7, *breuhawt* 157, 21; *gwnahawt* Skene 150, 24. 30, *gwnahaud*
BBC. 27 b 4. 30 b 11 'faciet'; *marwhawt* 'morietur' Skene 150, 22;
gyrhawt 'aget' 124, 22; *gwasgarawt* 'dissipabit' 229, 14; *treiglawt*
'percurret' 224, 7; *cannawt* 'canet' 230, 22; *crynnawt* 'contre-
miscet' 224, 8; *golligaut* 'solvet' BBC. 53 b 16; *gwisgawt* 'induet'
Skene 307; *gwledychawt* 'regnabit' 221, 23; *fflemichawt* 'flammabit'

213, 5; *tyfhawt* 'crescet' 151, 13; *dirchafaud* BBC. 27 a 6. 30 b 9,
dyrchafaud 24 b 12, *dyrchafawt* Skene 157, 19, *dirchavaud* BBC.
31 a 5, *dyrchauawt* Skene 223 ff. 'ascendet, eriget'; *kaffaud* 'habebit'
BBC. 26 b 6; *bithaud* BBC. 4 a 1, *bitaud* 28 b 7. 29 b 10, *bydawt*
Skene 292, 30, *bydhawt* 213, 6. 303, 6, *bythawt* 210, 28. 294, 28
'erit' (cf. GC. 516. 1097. KB. 6, 473. AC. IV. 4, 151). Obwohl
diese Form oben dem ir. *bieid* gegenübergestellt ist, so entspricht
sie ihm natürlich formal durchaus nicht (vgl. KZ. 36, 532), denn
das w. *byd* hat die allgemeine Verbalflexion angenommen. Die
verkürzte Form ist selten; *daw* 'veniet' gehört dazu, ferner:
a wnaw 'faciet' Skene 150, 9, *nys gwnaw* 'non faciet' 126, 30; *ny
chaffau ae hamhevo* 'er wird nicht haben, der ihm widerspreche',
BBC. 4 b 9. Für -*haw* erscheint aber schon -*ho* ganz in der Bedeutung des Futurs, z. B. *dideuho, dydeuho* 'veniet' Skene 148, 11.
15. Die 3. pl. auf -*hawnt* hat man in *cuinhawnt* 'deflebunt' GC.
514; *gwnahawnt* 'facient' Skene 124, 2; *bydawnt* 'erunt' 213, 3.

Von den passivischen Formen ist die vollere die seltenere.
Es findet sich: *molhator* 'laudabitur' Skene 131, 12. 137, 11;
canhator 'canetur' 209, 8; *gwelhator* 'videbitur' etc., auch *kwyn-
hyator* 'deflebitur' Skene 86, 8; *traethatter* 'tractabitur' 296, 4.
Desto häufiger ist die kurze Form, z. B. *dedeuhawr* Skene 213, 9,
dydeuhawr 212, 22 'venietur'; *ryglywhawr* Skene 211, 5, *ryglywawr*
221, 8 'audietur'; *galwhawr* 212, 26 'vocabitur'; *divahaur* 'destruetur'
BBC. 29 b 15; *ffohawr* 'fugietur' 126, 34; *molhawr* 'laudabitur'
165, 18; *talhawr* 'rependetur' 128, 6. BBC. 16 a 12; *carhawr*
'amabitur' Skene 117, 19; *canhawr* 'canetur' BBC. 29 b 9; *caffawr*
'habebitur' Skene 235, 27. Dass das *h* in diesen Formen nicht
willkürlich ist, zeigen solche wie: *etmyccawr* BBC. 29 b 13, *dydyc-
cawr* Skene 166, 9 f., *mettawr, dottawr* 136, 28, *crettawr* u. a. m.,
die Dottin, Les désinences verbales p. 169, verzeichnet. An der
ursprünglich futuralen Bedeutung ist kein Zweifel: *kirn a gan-
hawr, briuhaud llurugev* 'Hörner werden geblasen werden, Panzer
werden brechen', BBC. 29 b 9.

Die Flexion des Conjunctivus praesentis mit ihrem durch-
gehenden *ō* ist, wie schon Ev. Evans gesehen hat, mit dem Futurum
auf -*haw* zusammengefallen. Das *h* hat der Konjunktiv *carho,
carhwy* daher nach aller Wahrscheinlichkeit einzig und allein
von dem Futurum auf -*haw*. Ebenso weist der Conj. praes. pass.
carher (corn. *carer*, arm. *carer, carher, carheur*, dann auch *caror,
carfer*) auf das Futurum auf -*hawr* und dieses wird schon in alter

Zeit als Konjunktiv gebraucht, z. B. *eiryaul a garawr hawdweith*
'das Bitten eines, den man liebt, ist leicht', Skene 308, 3, für
sonstiges *a garher* und heutiges *a garer*. In einem südwelschen
Dialekte ist, wie Dottin p. 174 f. anführt, die Endung *-awr* ganz
an der Stelle des sonstigen *-er* noch üblich. Erscheint eine solche
Form ohne *h*, wie hier in *carawr*, so würde man sie von einem
alten Konjunktiv des Aktivs *cara* ableiten können; durch das *h*
wird sie als Futurum gekennzeichnet. Die Flexion des Conj.
praes. von *BU* hat vielleicht die Norm gegeben, namentlich für
die 3. sg. in allen Dialekten: w. *carho*, corn. *caro*, arm. *caro*, vann.
cárou, vielleicht auch für die 3. pl. (*ont : ons : ont*); aber in der
1. und 2. pl. zeigt sich im Welschen (*om, och* = corn. *yn, ough*)
vielleicht der Einfluss des Futurs. Das Armorische hatte vormals
im pl. auch Formen auf *o*, z. B. *labourhomp* 'laboremus', *casont*
'oderint'; aber sie sind durch solche auf *imp, it* (*et*), *int* verdrängt
worden.

Mit dem *h* des Futurs hat man, wie es nach dem oben be-
merkten scheinen muss, ein Präsens-Futur auf *-hit* gebildet, das
im Welschen, als Futur oder Konjunktiv praes., selten ist, z. B.
bythit (d. h. byd-hit) 'erit, sit' Skene 213, 7; *dottint* 'dabunt, dent'
BBC. 29 b 8. Als 1. sg. gehört dazu *bydif*, das vorhin erwähnt
ist, und: *ew kuynhiw iny wuiw in hervit hon* 'ich werde ihn be-
klagen, so lange ich in diesem Verhältnis bin', BBC. 29 b 8;
doch scheint diese Endung *if*: corn. *yf*: arm. *iff* auch zu *-hawt*
die 1. sg. zu bilden. Im Armorischen ist dieses Präsens-Futur
für Futur und Konjunktiv praes. die gewöhnliche Form, z. B.
cleuimp 'audiamus', *veohimp* 'vivamus', neben *clevhet* 'audiatis',
querhet, carehét 'ametis' und, nach Analogie dieser Formen, *bihet*
'sitis'.

Ist also der Conj. praes. *carho* gewissermassen von dem
Futurum abzuleiten, so müsste für *carhei* sich ein Futurum
secundarium darbieten. Eine ältere Form dafür als eben dieses
carhei, arm. *carhe*, vann. *cáréhé* ist nicht bekannt. Das arm.
bihe 'esset' hat sein *h* wiederum nach der Analogie von *carhe*.
Ebenso muss auch das Passiv des Conj. impf. *cerhit* auf einem
Futurum sec. beruhen; das neuarm. *carfet, carfed* ist dagegen
eine Zusammensetzung mit *béed*, der entsprechenden Form des
Verbs *BU*. Denn dieser Dialekt bewahrte den Konjunktivcharakter
im Plural der gesamten Konjugation mit bemerkenswerter Treue,
als das Welsche und Cornische ihn längst aufgegeben hatten, wie

am Verb *gra-* (von *for-ag-*, w. gwneuthur) erläutert sei: *groahimp*
'faciamus', *grehet* 'faciatis', *grahint* 'faciant' (w. *gwnahont* BBC.
31 a 15), neben dem Imperative *greomp, gret, graeñt*; *grahemp*
'faceremus', *grahec'h* 'faceretis', *grahent* 'facerent' (w. gwnaem,
-aech, -aent); *graer* (w. gwneir) 'fit', *graher* (w. gwnaer) 'fiat';
graet 'factum est', *grahet* 'fieret'. Darf man die Formen von
arm. *gra*, w. *gwna* in unmittelbaren Zusammenhang bringen mit
w. *a* 'ibit' = ir. *roa*, wozu der Plural *ri-sam, ri-sta, ri-sat* lautet,
so ist der von Vendryes aufgestellte Satz für diesen Fall erwiesen. Aber es will fast scheinen, als sei *grahint, grahent* etc.
nicht anders zu beurteilen als *rohint* 'dent', *rohent* 'darent',
d. h. es sind Analogieen nach *carhint, carhent*, wo die Ableitung
vom Futurum auf *s* nicht wohl möglich ist.

Aber dennoch giebt uns das Irische die letzte und wichtigste
Aufklärung über diese Bildungen. Die welschen Futura oder
Konjunktive auf *H* entsprechen offenbar den irischen Futuren
auf *F* oder *B*, nämlich:

> w. *carhawt, cerhit* — *carhaw, carho* 'amabit, amet' dem
> ir. *carfid, no charfa*;
>
> w. *carhei* 'amaret' dem ir. *carfad*;
>
> w. *carhator* — *carhawr, carher* 'amabitur, ametur' dem
> ir. *carfaidir, no charfider*;
>
> w. *cerhit* 'amaretur' dem ir. *carfide*.

Wahrscheinlich findet auch w. *bydif*, arm. *bezif* vivebo 'ero, sim'
in der irischen konjunkten Form *no charub, dolléciub* seine Erklärung. Die durch das *h* des Futurs im Welschen veranlasste
Verhärtung einer auslautenden Media der Wurzel (wie *mekit*
'alet' von *magu* 'alere') hat eine ganz merkwürdige Parallele
im Vulgäririschen: hier spricht man *fágaidh* 'er verlässt' wie
fāgĕ, aber *fágfaidh* 'er wird verlassen' wie *fākĕ*; *lúbaidh* 'er
beugt' wie *lūbĕ*, aber *lúbfaidh* 'er wird beugen' wie *lūpĕ*.[1]
Lautliche Schwierigkeiten hat alles dies überhaupt nicht, denn
auch im Irischen schwankt die Vokalisierung der Formen, die
wiederum nur Umschreibungen mit dem Futurum von *BU* dar-
stellen, nämlich *bid, -ba* und seinem Secundarium *bed, -bad*.

Und hier erweitert sich der Blick über die Grenzen des
celtischen Gebiets ins Italische. Denn man kann es nicht dem

---

[1] Vgl. F. N. Finck, Die araner mundart 1, 140. 142.

Zufall beimessen, wenn sich die mit der Wurzel *BU* zusammengesetzten Formen in beiden Sprachen so überraschend entsprechen,
und ir. car*fid* = w. car*hawt* = lat. ama*bit,* ir. car*fad* = w. car*hei*
= lat. ama*bat,* ir. car*faidir* = w. car*hator* = lat. ama*bitur* sind
gewiss des gleichen Ursprungs. Der Einklang der beiden Sprach-
stämme scheint vollkommen zu sein, und ich muss noch eines
hinzufügen.

Obwohl ich den gelehrten und belehrenden Untersuchungen
über den Ursprung des celtischen Passivs zu folgen suchte, so
ist es mir doch nicht gelungen, mir daraus eine Überzeugung
anzueignen.[1]) Es scheint festzustehen, dass diese Bildungen auf
R nicht sehr alt, nicht indogermanisch sind; dass die Deponentia
jünger als die Passiva sind; dass diese Formen sich zum grössten
Teile analogisch über die ganze Konjugation ausgebreitet haben
und dass man, nach ihrem Ursprunge forschend, immer wieder
von der 3. Person ausgehen muss. Und in der That, das ist ja
überall aktive Flexion mit dem Zusatze eines *R,* das sich mit
wechselndem Vokale anhängt. So im Altirischen: *dober* 'dat',
dober-r oder *dober-ar* 'datur'; *doberat* 'dant', *dobert-ar* 'dantur';
oder: *gaibid* 'capit', *gaibthi-r* 'capitur'; *gabait* 'capiunt', *gaibti-r*
'capiuntur'. Dieses *R,* wie man wohl erkannt hat, das eigentlich
Wichtige in der ganzen Erscheinung, ist verschieden gedeutet
worden, bald als aus *S* entsprungen, bald als eine Endung der
3. pl. und bald als aus einem vokalisch auslautenden pronominalen
Suffix gekürzt. Verzeihung, wenn ich, solchen Weisungen wider-
strebend, einen fast unbetretenen Weg einschlage und eine ganz
andere Lösung des Rätsels für möglich halte. Meines Erachtens
liegt das italoceltische Passiv weniger in der Form als in der
Syntax. Zeigen die erwähnten Formen die 3. Person sg. und
pl., so könnte die Endung *R* das Objekt sein, wie in *gaibth-i*
von gaibid oder *gabt-ait* von gabait (KZ. 28, 319); nichts aber
hindert, dass es das Subjekt sei, das sich der 3. sg. und pl.
anhängt wie etwa die Suffixe *s* und *e* der relativen Formen:
bi-s 'qui est', *bit-e* 'qui sunt'. Keine andere Auffassung ist
möglich im lat. *it-ur* 'man geht' und im altlat. *potest-ur* 'man
kann', oder *possit-ur, poterat-ur, posset-ur.* Ich vermute dem-

---

[1]) Vgl. F. Stolz, Lateinische Grammatik² (München 1900), p. 157 ff.;
R. Thurneysen in KZ. XXXVII (1900), p. 92 ff. (während des Druckes dieses
Aufsatzes erschienen).

nach in dem *R* ein nominales oder auch pronominales Subjekt zu der aktiven Verbalform. Da liegt es nahe zu prüfen, ob diese beständig konsonantisch auslautende Endung nicht etwa mit dem lat. Worte *vir*, ir. *fer*, w. *gwr*, *'wr* im Zusammenhang steht. Dann heisst ir. *bithir*, w. *byddir*, lat. *vivitur* (aus bíth-fer, bydit-wr, vivit-vir) 'der Mann lebt, man lebt'. Diese Vermutung hat schon vor vielen Jahren J. Rhŷs ausgesprochen (KB. 7, 57), wenn auch, so viel mir bekannt, ohne sie zu begründen oder zu verfolgen. Sie ist gewiss nicht ganz unwahrscheinlich, wo wir das deutsche *man* (aus *der mann*) und das französische *on* (aus *homo*) vor uns haben. Auch für die Möglichkeit der Verkürzung eines solchen Ausdrucks sind *on* und *man* lehrreich, für welches letztere das Mittelhochdeutsche und Niederländische geschwächte Formen wie *men*, *me* darbieten (J. Grimm, Grammatik 3, 8). Ferner ist *man* schon in der alten Sprache ein Collectivum, das sich sowohl mit dem Singulare seines Verbs als mit dem Plurale verbindet (Grimm 4, 221). Dasselbe dürfte man im urceltischen Gebrauch für das ir. *fer* in Anspruch nehmen.[1]) Wen die formale Erklärung des *R* aus Personalendungen befriedigt, der wird ja freilich einer solchen Hypothese keine Beachtung schenken. Den Beweis ihrer Richtigkeit vermag auch ich nicht zu erbringen; daher soll *fer* 'vir' hier nur als eine Formel gebraucht werden, als ein bekanntes Concretum für ein unbekanntes Abstractum. Darf ich es nach dieser Verwahrung ausführen, so suche ich die Genesis der Formen auf *R* folgendermassen zu verstehen.

---

[1]) Es sei daran erinnert, dass *fer* : *gwr* 'Mann' in den celtischen Dialekten eine allgemeine Bedeutung hat, die einem Pronomen demonstrativum gleichkommt, wie ir. *a fir do chumm in cruinde* 'o Mann, der die Welt geschaffen' LB. 186, 13; albanogäl. *am fear a fhuair i 's leis còir oirre, 's gu bheil ise ann an solas nan gràs* 'der Mann, der sie genommen, hat ein Recht auf sie, so ist sie denn im Troste der Gnaden', Glenbard coll. p. 177 in einer Totenklage; w. *mynn y gwr an gwnaeth* 'bei dem Manne, der uns geschaffen', RB. 1, 190. Die gälische Volkssprache geht in diesem Gebrauche viel weiter, wie man aus einigen Beispielen ersehen mag: *'s an tsaoghal so no 's an athfhear* 'in dieser Welt und in dem andern Es', d. h. in der andern, Campbell, Tales 2, 284; *am fear eile* 'der andere Mann', d. h. hier der Wolf, 3, 105; sonst gesagt von einem Pferde, Nicholson, proverbs p. 342; von einem Vogel; 359; von einem Kuchen, 162; *fear ùr* 'ein neues Haus, Highland Monthly 2, 46; *fear mo làimhe deise* 'das Es', d. i. das Schwert 'für meine rechte Hand', Campbell 3, 343; *fear de na bioran* 'ein Es', d. h. einer, 'von den Spiessen', Mac Innes, Tales p. 80.

Die celtischen Passiva würden von der Vorstellung ausgehen, dass zu der passivisch ausgedrückten Handlung zwei gehören, das Subjekt (d. i. *fer* 'vir'?) und das Objekt, das im Akkusativ steht. Das Irische erweist sich darin ursprünglicher als das Lateinische, das mit dem Passiv den Nominativ verbindet; jedoch hat Ennius noch die ältere Konstruktion: *vitam vivitur* 'man lebt ein Leben'. Es liegen nämlich dem celtischen Satze drei Formeln zu Grunde: *caedit vir* d. h. caeditur 'man tötet', 'er wird getötet'; *caedit vir virum* oder *me, te, nos, vos*; und *caedunt viri viros* 'Mann kämpft gegen Mann; Männer töten Männer'; 'man tötet den Mann, man tötet die Männer'. So ist das paradigmatische ir. *carthir* 'amatur' (w. *ceritor*) = *carid* 'amat' (w. *cerit*) + *fer* 'vir' (w. *wr*); ir. *caritir* 'amantur' = *carit* 'amant' + *fer* 'viri'; *carfaidir* 'amabitur' (w. *carhator*) = *carfid* 'amabit' (w. *carhawt*) + *fer* 'vir'; *carfitir* 'amabuntur' = *carfit* 'amabunt' + *fer* 'viri'. Das Futurum secundarium ist participial und hat daher kein *R*. Das Britannische kennt nur die ursprünglichere Formel *amat vir, amabit vir*, kein *amant viri*. Fehlt einem solchen Ausdrucke das Objekt, so ist er intransitiv oder neutral. Die Zweideutigkeit, die er unter Umständen hätte haben können, wird von der Sprache auch sonst zugelassen; ist es doch z. B. nicht ohne weiteres zu sagen, was in einem Satze wie neuir. *an bhean do bhuail an fear* oder *an bhean nár bhuail an fear* oder 'die Frau, die das Kind schlug' etc. das Subjekt und was das Objekt ist. Der Vokal vor dem *R* schwankt im Irischen zwischen *i, e* und *a*, je nach dem Charakter der durch Vokalharmonie bestimmten, unter den einheitlichen Wortaccent gestellten Form; das Welsche bewahrt in den vollen Formen (*ceritor, carhator*) das dunklere *o* (= lat. *u*), in der geschwächten (*carhawr*) *w*, und beides würde aus *gwr, wr* verständlich sein.[1]

Wie mit dem erwähnten Präsens und dem Futurum auf *B* verhält es sich auch mit den andern irischen Tempus- und Modusformen: sie sind die 3. sg. und pl. Activi mit dem Anhange *R* (*fer*), wie z. B. *berid* 'fert', *berir* (statt *berth-ir*) 'fertur'; *bérid* 'feret', *bérth-ir* 'feretur'; *adchí* (statt **adchíd*) 'conspicit', *ad-*

---

[1] Dürfte man dem ir. Suffixe *ar, er, bar* der Abstracta, wie *dinar* 'Einheit', *cóicer* 'Fünfheit', *nónbar* 'Neunheit', in urceltischer Sprache die Bedeutung und die Selbständigkeit des pronominalen 'man' zuerkennen, so würde es vielleicht eine noch leichtere Erklärung des vermuteten subjektivischen *R* gewähren als *fer*, mit dem es freilich nicht identisch ist.

chith-er 'conspicitur'; *carad* 'amato', *carth-ar* 'amator'; *dlésit* 'merebunt', *dlésit-ir* 'merebuntur', u. s. w.

In den Formen gleicht das irische Deponens durchaus dem Passiv: es sind in allen Personen die aktiven Endungen mit angefügtem *R*; z. B. *carid* 'amat', *labrid-ir* 'loquitur'; *nochara* 'amat', *-labrath-ar* 'loquitur'; *-molat* oder *-molat-ar* 'laudant'; *carais* (statt *caraist) 'amavit', *labrist-ir* 'locutus est'; *carsit* 'amaverunt', *labrisit-ir* 'locuti sunt'; *carfid* 'amabit', *sudigfid-ir*, *noshudigfedar* 'ponet'; *seiss* oder *siass-air* 'constitit'; *tésit* 'ibunt', *fessit-ir* 'scient'; *aithgén* 'agnovi' = w. *adwaen*, *rofhet-ar* 'scio' = w. *gwn* (statt *gwend); *aithgéuin* 'agnovit' = w. *edwyn*, *rofhit-ir* 'scit' = w. *gwyr*, mit Verlust des *t* wie in *cerir* neben *ceritor*. Nur in der irischen Formation der 3. Person praes. weicht das Deponens vom Passiv ab: ersteres knüpft die Endung vokalisch an, wie in *cairigedar* 'reprehendit', letzteres stösst den Vokal aus, wie in *cairigthir* 'reprehenditur'; ebenso *ní labrathar* 'non loquitur', aber *labairthir* 'dicitur' (Sächs. Ges. d. Wissensch. 23, 483). Vielleicht darf man hierin eine Andeutung des verschiedenen Sinnes erkennen, den das *R* des Deponens notwendigerweise hat. Wenn man das *R* des Passivs als das verbale Subjekt *vir* : *fer* 'man' auffasst, so steht doch dieses selbe *vir* : *fer* 'der Mann, die Person, der Einzelne' in den deponentialen Formen als Apposition, gewissermassen in der Bedeutung von 'viritim': *sechur* sequor 'ich folge einzeln, in Person'; *labrur* loquor 'ich rede meinerseits', *midiur* meditor 'ich denke bei mir', *mitter* (statt *midither*) meditaris, vormals meditarus[1]) (statt *meditas-ur), etc. Die 2. sg. praes. depon. *labrither* 'loqueris' lässt auf eine aktive Endung *-ith* schliessen, die vermutlich die in den britannischen Dialekten noch vorkommende ist, nämlich altw. *lleferyd* : corn. *leuereth* : arm. *leuerez* 'du sprichst' (AC. IV. 4, 143). Dass das deutsche *man* auch die 1. Person, den Redenden selbst, und die 2. Person, den Angeredeten, bedeuten kann, brauche ich Kennern der Sprache nicht zu sagen. Ohne Zweifel liegt ein feiner Unterschied darin, wenn das Irische die angeredete Mehrheit nicht als ein 'man' bezeichnet, sondern in der 2. pl. (*sechid*) die aktive Form schlechthin gebraucht, während das Lateinische (*sequimini*) sie participial ausdrückt.

---

[1]) Vgl. W. M. Lindsay, The Latin Language (Oxford 1894), p. 584.

Durch die Apposition *vir : fer* (ich verfolge die analogische Bildung in den andern Formen nicht weiter) wird das aktive Verb zunächst ein intransitives: es drückt den Zustand oder die Thätigkeit aus, die in dem Subjekte bleibt, vor allem die geistige Thätigkeit. *Amat patrem* 'er liebt den Vater', aber ohne Objekt *amat*, est in amore 'er ist im Zustande des Liebens'; *amatur* 'er in Person, seinerseits, in sich, ist im Zustande des Liebens' (ir. *caridir) könnte im Lateinischen, wie die Deponentia beweisen (hortatur filium), noch aktiv gewesen sein; beim Mangel eines Objekts liegt die passive Bedeutung nahe (ir. *carthir*) und in *amatur a patre* ist eine andere ausgeschlossen. Gewiss hat das Lateinische vormals ein Medium besessen, wie man aus *sequere* = ἕπε(σ)ο folgert. Aber wenn lateinischen und celtischen Deponentien in andern indogermanischen Sprachen Media derselben Verba gegenüberstehen (wie lat. *sequitur*, ir. *sechidir* = sanskr. *sacate,* griech. ἕπεται), so beweist das doch nur für die Bedeutung, aber nichts für die Form. Mir ist es wahrscheinlich, dass das Passiv und das Deponens im Celtischen und im Lateinischen vom Aktiv abgeleitet sind. Daraus würde aber folgen, dass die Endung *R* subjektivische oder appositionale Bedeutung hat. Ihre Erklärung durch das ir. *fer* 'vir, viri' ist freilich nur ein Behelf um den geforderten Sinn zu veranschaulichen. Est quadam prodire tenus, si non datur ultra.

Berlin.   LUDW. CHR. STERN.

ERSCHIENENE SCHRIFTEN.

Fled Bricrend, edited, with Translation, Introduction, and Notes by George Henderson. Nutt, London 1899. lxvii + 217 pp.[1])

Twenty years have passed since this interesting but difficult tale was made accessible by Windisch in his *Irische Texte*. In that interval additional manuscript material has been discovered, and the study of the language and literature of Ireland has been making steady progress. An edition published now might be expected to shew a great advance over any edition possible then, and a first glance at the fine volume prepared by Dr. Henderson for the Irish Text Society aroused high hopes. A closer investigation of the book, however, soon shewed how false these expectations were. The editor has evidently spent a great amount of labour on the book, and has striven to make himself acquainted with the work done by others. Yet, on the whole, this edition shews hardly any real advance on that of Windisch; in some respects, it even constitutes a retrogression. It has the appearance of a scientific and scholarly edition without the reality, and, while it may be of use to such as wish merely to learn something of Irish story, the serious student of the language will find in it little help.

---

[1]) A review of this book by Zimmer has already appeared in the Göttinger Gelehrte Anzeigen, 1900 Nr. 5. In the following notice individual errors already pointed out by Zimmer are passed by.

In the Introduction the editor, in accordance with the theories of Zimmer KZ. XXVIII, deals with the different recensions of the tale and their relations; a little more clearness of exposition would have been desirable here. There is also some attempt to fix, from linguistic evidence, the probable date of the text. But the linguistic analysis is not searching enough to lead to any very definite results, nor is the editor's knowledge of Old Irish grammar above suspicion. Thus on p. 1 the *ai* of *atrai, antai* and other verbal forms is put down as an affixed pronoun. In the section on the infixed pronouns there is much confusion, and, to increase the confusion, the relative *n* is in several cases taken to be an infixed pronoun of the third person; it is also something new to explain the *s* of *frisgart* as an infixed pronoun. How *nóithium* comes to mean 'est mihi' (p. lx) I do not understand. On p. lviii the *s*-subjunctive is confused with the *s*-future. On the same page I am charged with 'a singular oversight'. Apparently Dr. Henderson failed to see that my remarks were concerned simply with the timbre of the final *r*; I had certainly no intention of denying that the ending was -*bair*. Since this book was published, Zimmer's investigations in KZ. XXXVI have put a different aspect on some forms that were usually taken as evidence of later composition, the *ro*- less preterite, *dobert* for *dorat*, forms like *gabais*, with corresponding forms like *gabsus* with an affixed pronoun.

The text is edited from the three MSS. used by Windisch, along with the Leyden MS. and the Edinburgh MS. since discovered. The editor has collated afresh the Edinburgh MS.[1]) and the Egerton MS., but apparently not the others.

In the case of Ed. the variants are very imperfectly given, even when they are better than the readings of LU. Thus § 91 for *amal robatar* Ed. has *amal rommbatur*, with the infixed relative which is regular in the old language; afterwards the tendency was to omit the relative *n* after such conjunctions. In the same section the variant *italle* is not noticed, though it points to the correct reading *itella* or *italla* (cf. Rev. Celt. XXI, p. 176). In § 94 Ed. has *attaber* = *addaber* of Eg., and this is right; *atabér* = *ad-da-bér* (*ceist* f.). In the case of H. again all

---

[1]) In § 99 Professor Meyer's transcript has *cid doradsatt*; in Rev. Celt. *tid doradsact* is a mere misprint.

the variants are not given. Many of them are unimportant, but in § 26 *nimatarcomlusa feith* along with the other variants points to an original *nimatarchomlussa fleid* (cf. Zimmer p. 376), in § 59 *conidh tardais* of H. with *conid tárfas* of LU. points to an original *conidtárfais* (Zimmer p. 381).

The text generally is that of LU. In refraining from harmonizing the Irish text (p. xxx) the editor has done wisely. But there was no need to perpetuate all the little carelessnesses of LU., such as the omission of the mark of aspiration. In some cases the readings of the other MSS. have been adopted. In a number of other passages other MSS. have preserved older forms than those of LU. (this is so in other LU. texts; thus the YBL. copies of the Táin and the Togail Bruidne Dá Dergga are in many ways better than those in LU.). We will take some examples of this. § 6 *dogenasib* LU., *dogenasu* H.; the variants point to an original *dogénaesiu.* § 6 *cenco* LU. : *cēi* i. e. *ceni* H. § 7 *atabairecen* LU. : *atibecen* L., *atibeic-* H.; here the original text would have had *atibécen,* cf. also *biditecen* LL. 274 b 7; in LU. -*b*- has been replaced by the later -*bar*- as in *arnáchbaraccais*ter LU. 85 a 4 = *arnachabaccastar* YBL. 94 b 4. § 8 *roimráid* LU. : *immardordidh* H.; here H. points clearly to an older form with *ro*- infixed. § 10 *tíagait* LU. : *tiagta* H., *tiagtha* L.; here H. has preserved the old relative form *tíagtae*; in L. the same is corrupted into *tiagtha,* cf. CZ. II, 488,[1]) and further *fechtha* for *fechtae* YBL. 51 a 45, *retha* LU. 115 a 13 (cf. *rethae* Ml. 68 b 10), *cartha* LBr. 261 a 18, *tiagtha* 261 a 79; in the 3. pl. the relative form was at an early period replaced by the absolute, hence *tíagait* in LU.; *tíagat* is a depravation of the text. § 17 *romboth* is better, as is *domberthar* § 59. § 27 *nodndírgi* LU. : *nod dirge* Eg.; leg. *no-d-dirgea* (*tech* n.). § 46 *más* LU. : *massa* Eg., *masa* H.; O. Ir. *massu,* which appears already as *masa* in the Milan Codex 108 c 16, 118 a 5. A common form of corruption of the text of the Sagas is the addition of an independent pronoun after the later fashion, where there is already an infixed pronoun, e. g. *conachrancatár hé* LU. 59 a 33 (YBL. has not *hé*), similarly LU. 67 b 1, 75 b 25; in our text LU. has

---

[1]) I would here correct an error in CZ. II, 487, note 1. In LU. 128 b 26 *berta* (= *ṁbertae*) is the relative form of the *t* preterite, cf. *baí* (leg. *ba hé*) *in mac altæ* 128 b 14. So in the perfect we find *giulae* Tur. 139.

the added pronoun which is absent in other MSS. in *ní chosna nech frim he* (*curadmír* n.) § 73, *ní ránic hé* (m.) § 81; so § 89 *hé* as the subject of the copula is omitted in Eg. § 86 *rorigi a láim corrici ina cróes* LU. : *roding a lam coricce a gualainn ina crǽs* Eg.; here Eg. has preserved the accusative which is wanted after *corricci.* § 88 *combad ó lemum dochúatar* LU. : *ba do leim dochuatar* Eg.; leg. *combo* (or *ba*) *do lémmim docúatar.*

In some instances conjectural emendations are admitted; where these were made by other scholars, the editor should have given the names. In a few cases the alteration is for the worse. Thus in § 28 *adartha* is corrupted into *adantha.* In § 78 *nosinithar* is changed to *nonsinethar,* as though the infixed pronoun *n* could have remained before *s* (in § 27 *rósini* is allowed to stand). Here *nosinithar,* if there be an infixed pronoun, might represent an O. Ir. *nasínither* (= *n-an-s-*); O. Ir. *-an-* is afterwards replaced by *-n-,* e. g. *rombaist, ronail* LU. 4 a 23, or it might possibly contain an infixed *s,* which in this text as elsewhere in later Irish is used also as 3. sg. masc., e. g. LU. 108 b 18, 109 a 18, 109 b 14. In § 54 there is no need to alter *dodánic; d* is an instance of Pedersen's figura etymologica, KZ. XXXV, 415, and the relative *n* would be out of place. But the most curious perversion of the text is the introduction of Zimmer's inventions *atsraig* 'he, or she, rises', *atsregat* 'they rise'. As *ad-reg-* is transitive, to express the intransitive 'rise' a pronoun is infixed: *ad-d-reig, atreig, atraig*[1]) 'he raises himself', *ad-da-reig, atareig, ataraig* 'she raises herself', *ad-da-regat, ataregat* 'they raise themselves'; with a Mid. Ir. modification of the infixed pronoun LL. 291 a 32 has *atosrerachtatar.* The masculine form of the singular tends to be generalized, *atragat* LU. 37 b 8, *atresat* 34 b 4 etc., *atrachtatár* 101 a 23, cf. 103 a 33, 108 b 15; on the other hand *atafraig* 110 a 12 is used for *atraig.* The origin of the corruptions *affraig, atafregat* I cannot explain.

Here follow some suggestions on the text. § 5 *dofessed,* leg. *dofessid.* § 13 *griánā* LU., *griánā*in Henderson; so far as my reading and my recollection serve me, the genitive of nouns in

---

[1]) Is the change of *atreig* to *atraig* due to the influence of *siag-,* e. g. *atraig : ataregat* = *rosaig : rosegat?* In the preterite the original *e* is preserved in *atrecht* LU. 134 b 19. The change to *atracht* might be explained in the same way, though the prototonic forms may also have helped.

-*án* is very commonly written -*án*. Thus in LU. the titles of the well-known texts are *Fis Adam*nan, *Scél Mo*ngán, and *Tucait Baile Mongán*. Many instances will be found in Vol. II of the Annals of Ulster, where the editor regularly adds *i* within brackets. § 25. *asaithgned* = O. Ir. *ass-id-gned* 'who should know him'. § 32. Leg. *agar imdell*. § 35. Leg. *do imluad dar mési*. § 41. For *noro*curtis of LU. the editor writes *rocurtis no*, a transposition which has little probability. Besides, assuming that in *rocurtis ro* is improperly used for *no*, the imperfect is out of place, as there is no reference to repeated or customary sendings. Leg. probably *nocorochurtis* 'till they should be sent'. § 47 *taraittiu*, leg. with H. *tar raitiu*. § 54. Leg. probably *iar-suidiu bertair i tige condergothaib sainamraib 7 an robo* etc. § 56. Leg. *praind* céit. § 74. For *dobag* leg. *do bág*. § 78. For *ani hisin* leg. *anísin*. § 84. *conidammárb*, leg. *conid a m-marb*, cf. LU. 62 b 33, 35, 63 a 1. § 85. For *inne* leg. *indi* 'in it' (the monster)? § 93. Leg. *for n-Ul*taib, not *for n-Ul*aid, cf. Pedersen, CZ. II, 379; here Ed. has a later form of the expression. § 94. Leg. *lasasétar*? Cf. LU. 68 b 2, 3. § 95. For *sithen* leg. *side*, and for *or ataid-siu* leg. *forataidsi*, or more correctly *forsataidsi*. § 96. *Atfraid suas lasodain 7 docœcmellai suas iarsuidiu 7 teg-mallai a ceann* etc. Here *docœcmallai* and *tegmallai* seem to be an erroneous iteration. Leg. *atraig suas la sodain* (or *iarsuidiu*) *7 doecmallai a chend* etc.? § 96. For *adtaorfas* leg. probably *doárfas*. § 100. *gib* Henderson: *gid* Meyer; the latter is the form wanted here.

The translation is evidently intended to be a free literary version rather than a close rendering of the Irish text. The result is something neither literal nor literary. As a guide to the beginner in making out the construction of the Irish it is of little use, and it has no compensating literary merit. From the character of the translation it is often impossible to see whether the editor really understands the text which he is trans-lating, or whether the slipshod rendering is not a cloak for imperfect scholarship. Still in many passages it is clear that he has misunderstood the Irish. To correct all the errors of the translation would be a tedious task. Some of them have already been pointed out by Zimmer. Here I propose to deal with a few more of them, particularly with passages where it seems possible to contribute something to the understanding of the text. The difficult metrical passages, which are translated throughout, I pass by.

§ 5. *Fergus mac Róig ocus mathi Ulad ar chena*, 'Fergus mac Rōig and the nobles of Ulster also'. The meaning is 'and the rest of the nobles of Ulster'. In other passages *ar chena* is rightly translated.

§ 6. *Bid fír sucut, olse*, „'That will be true', says he" (Bricriu), is left untranslated.

§ 9. *bid lat caurathmír Emna dogrés*, 'the championship of Emain is thine for ever'. Here *bid* is translated as though it were *is*. So *ní bá fír sin* § 14, *bid aingcess* § 16, *ni bá lat* § 73. In § 87 *Bid olc ind adaig* is translated 'Bad night', as though it were a remark about the weather. In § 56 there is another blunder; *ni bá nech bas ferr nodgléfe ém ataisiu*, 'Verily there will be no one who will settle it better than thou', is translated freely 'There is really no better judge', but a note is added: „note modal use of *bá*, 'there were not any one that is better'". But the modal *ba* (for which after *ní bo* or *bu* is the correct form) would have been followed by the past subjunctive, not by the future indicative.

§ 10. *At móra na comrama dait sech ócu Ulad olchena*, 'Great are the victories thou hast already scored over the heroes of Ulster'. The meaning is: 'Great are thy deeds of prowess beyond the other warriors of Ulster'. Here both *sech* and *olchena* are mistranslated.

§ 11. *amal na dernad eter in n-imchossáit*, 'as if no contention had been made among the heroes'. But *amal na dernad* is obviously past subjunctive active (= O. Ir. *amal ní dénad*), and means 'as if he had not made'.

§ 15. *Immanesóirg dóib, co m-bo nem tened indala leth dind rígthig lasna claid*bi (why not *claid*biu?) *ocus la fæbra na n- gái, ocus co m-bo énlaith glegel alleth n-aile di cailc na sciath*, 'At one another they hewed till the half of the palace was an atmosphere of fire with the [clash of] sword- and spear-edge, the other half one white sheet from the enamel of the shields'. Readers will wonder how 'pure-white birds' have been transformed into 'a white sheet', and the editor does not explain. The meaning becomes clear from a comparison of LL. 291 a 10 *amainsi na tadbsin robatar and .i. findnél na cailce* 7 *ind æil*

_dochum inna nél asnaib sciatha ꝛ asnaib boccóitib oc a n-essor-
gain de fǽbraib na claideb ꝛ de imfǽbraib na ṅ-gę etc._ In our
passage, then, the cloud of white dust arising from the shields
is poetically described as a flock of white birds. In the former
part of the sentence the expression _nem tened_ might be illustrated by _ropo nem tened tír Úa Néill impu_, LU. 83 a 22.

§ 16. _techt immi . . . irréir n-Ailella_, 'to decide with reference
to it according to the will of Ailill'. Rather: 'to submit to the
authority of Ailill with reference to it'. cf. _duthluchedar techt
immess inchoim[ded] diafogni_ Ml. 38 d 1, _innáis dutiagat innareir_
Ml. 103 b 16.

§ 17. _Intan iarom roscáig do Bricrind a scrutan ina menmain amal doragad airi ba sí úair insin dolluid Fedelm . . . .
asind rígthig immach_, 'When Bricriu had done examining his
mind, it chanced just as he could have wished that Fedelm . . . .
came from the palace'. Leaving aside _amal doragad airi_, the
rest means: 'When Bricriu had done pondering it in his mind . . .,
that was the time that Fedelm came out of the palace'. In
amal doragad airi doragad airi must have the same sense as in
cinnas doragad ar imchossait na m-ban, where it means 'should
succeed in'. The difficulty here is _amal_ with the secondary
future; so far as I know, _amal_ is not used in the sense of
cindas.

§ 17. _Bá tú theis isa tech ar thus innocht, doroimle caidche áis
banrígnacht úas bantrocht Ulad uli_, 'If thou comest first into the
hall to-night, the sovranty of queenship shalt thou enjoy forever
over all the ladies of Ulster'. Read _bad tú_ and translate: 'let
it be thou that goest first into the house to-night, mayest thou
enjoy the queenship of the women of Ulster forever'. The word
áis is difficult. Dr. Henderson gives it the sense of 'sovranty',
but does not note that _banrígnacht_ should then have been in the
genitive. The variants here are instructive: _co haidne æis_ Eg.
co aidne L., _co aidhne ais banrignochta_ H. (where evidently
banrignochta was taken as depending on _ais_). Note also _adna
.i. ais_ YBL. 257 c 10, _aidhne .i. aos_ O'Cl.; in O'Mulconry a comparison with YBL. shews that we should read _adna .i. ais_. The
following explanation of the variants may then be suggested.
The original text had _co aidne_; in _co aidne ais_ the text has been
contaminated with a gloss; in H. this led further to the change

of an accusative to a genitive; in LU. *co aidne* was replaced by the synonymous *caidche.*[1])

§ 20. *co forcroth a rígthech n-uile*, 'the whole palace shook', The verb is transitive: 'it shook the whole palace'. So § 25.

§ 25. *connabad cutrummus disi frisna mna aili, uair nirbo chutrummus dosom fri cách.* The translation here misses the connexion of the Irish. The sense is: 'that she might not be on an equality with the other women, because he was not on an equality with the rest'.

§ 26. *do lár in tige*, 'from the floor of the house'. Rather 'from the middle of the house'. So in many other passages in the text.

§ 28. *Tancatar a áes cumachta 7 a lucht adartha na dochum.* Here *adartha* is changed to *adantha* (with should at least have been *adanta*), and Zimmer's unfortunate rendering is adopted. The *áes cumachta* and *lucht adartha* ('the people whom he worshipped') are simply names for Cuchulinn's friends in fairyland. Cf. LU. 77 a 40, 78 a 10.

§ 29. *oc imarbaig eter a feraib ocus siat fesni*, 'lauding their men'. Windisch has already given the meaning of the words: 'indem sie wetteifernd sowohl sich selbst als auch ihre Männer rühmten'.

§ 31. *co toracht innaidchi sin cona eoch riata leis co Emain Macha*, 'until on that night Cuchulinn came chasing with his steed (lit. driving horse) to Emain'. The point is that the horse was now tamed and broken to harness, cf. LU. 115 b 32, *bit daim ríata láig ar m-bó co tí cobair Diarmato.*

§ 32. *Ferr cach cless cotlud, diliu lim longud oldás cach ní*, 'and to eat and to sleep it liketh me better than everything'. The first clause 'sleep is better than any play' hardly has its rights here.

§ 32. *diamsa saithech bíd 7 cotulta, conid cless 7 cluchi lim comrac fri óenfer*, 'It would be but fun and frolic for me to fight a duel had I my fill of food and of sleep'. This translation would require the past subjunctive in the subordinate clause, and the secondary future in the main clause. As the Irish stands it means, 'if I be ... it is ...'

§ 37. The word *talchar* seems to be an adjective connected with *tolchaire* Cormac s. v. *diumsach.* If so, it is to be explained from *tol-char* 'loving one's own will', αὐθαδής.

---

[1]) Or was the original form of the phrase *co aidne dis*?

§ 38. '*Fír*', *forse*, '*maith in fer asa eich*'. In the translation 'Yes! a fine fellow he' *asa eich* 'to whom the horses belong' is simply passed by. It may not be superfluous to point out that *asa* is used improperly with a plural subject for *ata*, the grammatical force of the form being no longer felt, cf. *isa cella romill* Ann. Ul. A. D. 1171, similarly 1176; correctly with the singular *isa tech roloiscedh* 1177, *sa altóir rosáraighedh* 1197, cf. 1513. If examples of *ata* 'whose are' are wanted, some will be found in Stokes' Index to the Félire s. v. *ata*.

cid diambá don gillu?, 'What is this you are doing to the lad?' For the meaning of the idiom cf. Pedersen, KZ. XXXV, 391 sq. In the following sentence *hicinta* means not 'by way of penalty', but 'for the offence'.

§ 44. *amal bís curcas fri sruth*, 'like unto rushes in a stream'. Rather 'against a stream', by which the rush would be bent.

§§ 45—51. These chapters contain many difficulties. Similar descriptions appear in many other place in Irish literature, and it might have been expected that the editor would have tried to elucidate the difficulties by comparison with these other passages. That he has not done. I will give one example. In § 45 *Rolasat tri imrothu imma chend cocairse cach œe dib hi taib alaili* is translated: 'Three halos encircle his upturned (is this *cocairse?*) head, each merging into the other'. But cf. LU. 81 a 11, *cáin cocarsi in fuilt co curend teóra imsrotha im claiss a· chúlaid*, and LL. 120 a 47 *cáin cocarus in chind 7 ind fuilt sin co uirend* (leg. *cuirend*) *téora imsrotha de immon chend*. From these it is apparent that *cocarus* and *cocairse* are nouns. With *cocairse* cf. *cogoirse* 'a well ordered system', O'R; apparently it is a derivative from *cocarus* (cf. *cogarus* 'peace, amity' O'R), which itself comes from *con + corus*, cf. *corus bíd 7 etaig* LU. 33 b 40. If the reading of the MSS. is right, *cocairse* here must be nom. pl., for, to judge from the other passages, it must be the subject of *rolásat*.[1]) As for *imrothu* the parallels cited prove that the right form is *imsrotha*, and that the word is feminine. The literal translation, then, would be: 'The harmonious adjustments of each of them beside the other had cast three *imsrotha* about his head'. The exact meaning of *imsrotha* is uncertain. Windisch

---

[1]) Cf., however, *atchiu ardroth n-imnaisse imma chend cocorse* LU. 91 a 15.

suggests 'Kreis', but something more picturesque might be expected.

§ 54. *Lasodain dolluid Medb for fordorus ind liss immach issin n-aurlaind 7 tri coecait ingen lée ocus teóra dabcha uárusci don triúr láth n-gaile dodánic resin sluag do tlathugud a m-brotha.* The last part of this is translated 'with three vats of cold water for the three valiant heroes in front of the hosts to quench their thirst (*lit.* heat)'. Surely Irish hospitality could provide something better than that. A glance at LU. 63 a 28 sq. will shew the real object of the *mná ernochta* and the three tubs of cold water. Usually they are for Cuchulinn alone; cf. also LU. 48 b 28.

§ 56. *Bá iarsudiu dano conacrad Ailill do Chonchobur.* This can surely mean only 'Ailill was summoned to Conchobur'. The following words *cid diarabi arréim*, which are wanting in Eg., are very awkward, and perhaps there is some corruption.

lotar dia crích means 'went to their land'.

§ 61. *iúrthund Cuchulainn día siabairther immi*, 'sorely doth Cuchulainn work on us his fury when his fit of rage is upon him'. But *iúrthund* means 'will slay us', and *dia n-* with the subjunctive means not 'when' but 'if'.

§ 67. *dobretha a armláich leis .i. a claideb* 'took his chief weapon, to wit, his sword, with him'. Here there is no obvious reason for writing *armláich* as one word. The *arm láich* is what distinguished the *láech* from the *midlag*, cf. LU. 75 b 1 sq.

a siriti lethguill, 'you squinting savage'. But cf. Serglige Conculaind, ch. 5; similar descriptions are found in many other places.

Sia[ba]rthar (recte *siabarthair*) *co urtrachta im Choinculainn andaide*, 'Then Cuchulainn was enraged at the sprites'. This *co urtrachta* cannot mean. There is a word *urdrach* meaning 'sprite, spectre', cf. RC. XI, 455. From this might come an adjective *urtrachthae*, and *co urtracht[h]a* is the adverbial use of it qualifying the verb. In the proceding sentence the n. pl. *urtrochta* is peculiar = *urtraig* of Eg. Is it not simply a clerical error, the scribe's eye having been attracted by the *urtrachta* beneath?

§ 68. *ocus a gaisced úas gaiscedaib cáich cenmotha gaisced Conchobuir*, 'Cuchulainn's valour to rank above that of every one else, Conchobar's excepted'. Here *gaisced* means not 'valour' but 'weapons'; Cuchulinn's weapons were to have the place of honour next to those of Conchobur. Cf. LU. 19 a 20 *dobert Cromderoil a n-gaisceda inna n-díaid 7 sudigthi*; 7 *arrocabar gaisced Conculaind úasaib*.

§ 72. *Rolinad iarom ind aradach dabach Conchobuir dóib*, 'Moreover, Conchobar's ladder-vat was filled for them'. This translation does not make it clear that the *Aradach* was the proper name of the *dabach Conchobuir*, cf. Ir. Text. I, 311 bottom. Similar names are *Óchain* the shield of Conchobur LL. 102 b 2, *Caladbolg* the sword of Fergus LL. 102 b 23, *Dubchend* the sword of Diarmait LU. 117 a 9.

§ 74. *Cotnérig cách dib diaraili*, 'They then spring up one after the other'. The meaning is 'each against the other', as might have been learned from Windisch s. v. *do*.

§ 75. *intan na hantai*, 'seeing that ye did not abide'. In the notes *-antai* is explained as 2. pl. sec. pres. But the imperfect would be syntactically out of place here. It is 2. pl. pres., the conjunct form having been replaced by the absolute as in *ni dligthi* § 41, cf. CZ. II, 49.

§ 79. *Bói immorro in ben día reir co fothrocud ocus co folcud*, 'His wife acted according to his wish in the matter of bathing and of washing'. The right meaning is indicated by Windisch: 'the wife waited on them with bathing' etc.; cf. Mod. Ir. *riaraim* 'wait upon, serve'.

§ 84. *ataig in cendáil occo inna sudi faire mod nad mod indessid inna sudiu*, 'He heaped their heads in disorder into the seat of watching and resumed sentry'. The difficulty here is *mod nad mod*. The only other instance of the phrase that I have to hand is LU. 120 b 20, *atchonnarcatar úadib mod nad mod .i. in fat rosiacht ind radairc a roisc* (cf. YBL. 194 b 53), where it is explained to mean 'as far as their eye could reach'. Cf. also *acht modh* explained by *is inbechtain* 'it is hardly', O'Dav. s. v. *modh*, with which are to be compared LL. 77 b 39, 108 a 32. I would venture to conjecture that here *mod nad mod* begins a new sentence and that the meaning is: 'hardly had he sat down when nine others shouted to him'. In LU. 120 b 20 the sense seems to be that they were only just visible.

§ 86. *co torchair beim n-asclaing don pheist asind áer co rabe for lár*, 'Then the beast fell from the air till it rested on the earth, having sustained a blow on the shoulder'. This translation of *béim n-asclaing* is obviously conjectural and is clearly absurd. A somewhat similar phrase appears Ir. Texte II, 2, 241 *conidcorustair cor n-asclaind asa imda* translated 'sodass er wie ein Sack aus seinem Bette ... fiel'. In the Tochmarc Emere CZ. III, 254 we have *gabthus foa dib cichib 7 dompert* (recte *dosmbert*) *tarsnai amail assclaing,* of which the sense evidently is that Cuchulainn took Aiffe under the breasts and threw her over his shoulder. As *asclang* is 'a shoulder-load', *béim n-asclaing* would apparently be a dashing of something from the shoulder to the ground; it may have been a proverbial expression to denote a heavy fall.

§ 88. *Mairg dorumalt a n-imned dorumaltsa*[1]) *custrathsa imma cauradmír', ol Cuculainn, 7 a techt úaim* etc. 'Alas!' Cuchulainn quoth (*sic*), 'my exertions hitherto about the Champion's Portion have exhausted me, and now I lose it.' But *domelim* means 'I eat' and is also used in a figurative sense, e. g. *domel a flaith* LU. 59 a 10. The sense is: 'Woe that I have gone through the affliction that I have already gone through about the Champion's Portion, and that it should pass from me'.

§ 89. '*Ani immátudchabair imresain', olse, 'imma cauradmír, is la Coinculainn íar fírinne ar bélaib óc n-Erenn uile hé,* The Champion's Portion, over which you have fallen out with the gallant youths of Erin, truly belongs to Cuchulainn'. Here there is a variety of blunders. The meaning is: 'That', said he, 'in dispute about which ye have come, the Champion's Portion, rightly belongs to Cuchulainn before the warriors of Ireland'. The idiom *immatudchabair imresain* is not uncommon, cf. *ani díatudchad cuingid* § 93, *donti iraibe láim* (in whose hand) Laws III, 484, *in fer aratánacsa techem,* Silv. Gad. I, 213.

§ 92. *Cid hé mo dán dano, bes cotmidfider cacha bé dim airdi combad coitcenn* (leg. *coitchenn*) *a suillsi don tegluch 7 connábad loscud don tig,* 'whatsoever property may be mine, sooth you will agree, no matter how big I am, that the household as a whole will be enlightened, while the house will not be burned'. In the first place, as it is *cid* not *cip,* the sense must be 'though that be my craft'. What follows is more difficult. Above *cotmidfider* is apparently taken like *cotmidem* § 74; what part it is supposed to be, or what is the force of

---

[1]) If I am right, we should have expected *dorumult, dorumultsa,* but cf. *ciasidrubartsa* Ml. 3 a 15, 66 c 1.

the infixed pronoun does not appear. But *conmidiur* has another meaning, cf. *commidedar* (leg. *conmídair?*) 'fixed, adjusted' Laws IV, 16, *béim co commus* a properly regulated stroke; with a further development of meaning *nad coimmestar* g. nequierit Ml. 127 a 19, *in met conmessamar* Ir. T. II, 2, 228, *commus* 'power'. Here *cotmidfider* seems to be 3. sg. dep. fut., with infixed neuter *d*. One might venture to translate literally: 'Though that be my craft, perchance, whatever may be my height, it (the *dán*) will regulate it that its light might be common to the household, and that it might not be a burning to the house'. Apparently the suggestion was that the giant might serve as a candle by catching fire.

§ 93. *co Grecia* etc. Why should the editor go out of his way to mistranslate, when the correct translation has already been given by Meyer?

§ 94. *arái óenfir do thesbaid díb oc denam a n-einig*, 'because of one man who fails in keeping his (*an?*) word of honour'. The variant *díden* shews the force of *dénam* here, 'for the loss of one man to them in the defence of their honour'.

§ 94. '*bád dóig* (leg. *ba dóig*) *lind dano*', ol *Sencha*, '*mád costrathsa fogebthá óinfer dotdingbad-su* (leg. *do-t-ingbadsu*), 'To us it seemeth likely, if at long last you find such a person, you will find one worthy of you'. What this is supposed to mean must be left to the translator to explain. The sense seems to be: 'we should have thought that even already you would have found here a man to match you (lit. to ward you off)'.

§ 95. *amail rocinnsem as samlaid dogniamm*, 'Let us act according to our covenant'. But that would have required *bad samlaid dognem*.

§ 95. *ni hadlaice* (leg. *hadlaicc?*) *duid eacc samlaid an fer muirfe* (rectius *nomairbfe*) *anocht dialil* (leg. *diadígail*) *ambuaragh* (leg. *imbárach*) *fort*. These words are addressed to the giant: 'in this wise death is not to your liking (i. e. the proposal you make shews that you have no wish to die), that the man whom you shall slay to-night shall avenge it (his death) on you on the morrow'.

§ 102. *cep ce nosdaceannai friut ón trathsa*. Leg. *cip hé nodacosna?* 'whoever disputes them with thee henceforth'. The sentences are rightly divided by Meyer. As *cosnaim* is a compound verb, *cotasena* would be more correct.

The text and translation are followed by four appendices, I Personal Names, II Geographical Names, III Textual Notes, IV Special Notes. In the notes one might expect to find some attempt to clear up the difficulties of the text and to defend the translation of the obscure passages. But of that there is very little. There are some interesting parallels from Scotch Gaelic particularly *dābhigh* p. 154. There is much misplaced etymological speculation, right or wrong, as when *torc* 'boar' is derived from *orc* 'pig'. In the other notes there are a good few mistakes. Thus on p. 148 *nileicfitis* is said to be for *ni-s-leicfitis*, 'the infixed pronoun has dropped out'; of course the infixed pronoun is -*n*-, which before *l* becomes indiscernible. In *cotonmela* (p. 170) the infixed pronoun is not -*on*- but -*don*-. On p. 155 there is a curious explanation of *slān seiss*. But *seiss* is surely the 2. sg. subjunctive of *sed*- 'sit', though the ending is certainly peculiar; cf. *slan seiss a Brigit co m-buaid for gruaid Lifi* LL. 49 b 9. On p. 153 in the SR. verse *neib*, as the rhyme with *grēin* shews, has nothing to do with *nem*, but is the dative of *niam*.

In conclusion it may be permitted to express a hope that this edition will not be taken as a model for other texts of the series.

Bowdon, Cheshire.   J. Strachan.

Les Articulations Irlandaises étudiées à l'aide du palais artificiel: par M. l'Abbé Rousselot (extrait de La Parole, vol. I, Paris 1899).

This important study of Irish, in its modern pronunciation, illustrates for the first time from the physiological side the well-known variety of the sounds of that language. The sole instrument employed is the artificial palate, a contrivance made to cover and fit accurately the palate of the speaker to be observed, from the inner circumference of the teeth to a line about three inches distant from the incisors. The speaker observed in this case was the Rev. Stephen Walsh, native of a district called The Neale, in County Mayo, and at that time a student in the Irish College at Paris.

The use of this instrument is to record the extreme position reached by the tongue in any given articulation. It is first of all coated with some powder or soluble colouring matter: it is then inserted into the mouth of the speaker: the required articulation is executed: the instrument is then withdrawn, and the tongue is found to have removed the coating up to the extent of its furthest contact. The line of extreme contact is generally pretty clear, except in some fricative (frictional) consonants, where the area of perfect contact fringes off into an imperfect contact, which gives only vague indications. Hence the absence of the guttural fricatives from this treatise.

The method is in fact of very different value for different sounds. The instrument covers the hard palate and about half an inch of the soft palate. For sounds which are articulated with the tongue against the hard palate, its indications are of extreme value. But some guttural sounds, and some important vowels, such as *a* and *u*, are produced without any contact of this kind whatever: the instrument remains absolutely blank. Fortunately the Irish *g* and *k* seem just to have touched its backward end. In fact for Irish sounds its indications are unusually instructive: the difference, for example, between the normal *t, d, n, k, g, s* (in *tá, damsa, ná, cad, go* and *san*) and the palatal *t, d, n, k, g, s* (in *teid, deoc, anios, ce, geadh* and *sé*) is shewn to be accompanied by very large differences of articulation: and the diagrams yielded by interdental consonants are also very characteristic and instructive.

Allowance must always be made however for the individuality of the speaker. Every speaker has his own peculiarities of structure and habit. These diagrams, for example, shew a very curious tendency to a closer articulation, and therefore to a larger contact, on the right side of the mouth than on the left: but of course this is not normal; it is not Irish; it is merely individual.

Palates differ a good deal in shape. Some are more arched or vaulted, both longitudinally and laterally, than others: and these differences compel speakers to differences of articulation, in attempting identical sounds. It would be a gain to this method of description if two vertical sections of the palate employed were always given, the one longitudinal and the other transverse. Without this information one is unable, for example, to interpret the diagrams of Mr. Walsh's Irish i with any certainty. The aperture between tongue and palate is shewn to be extremely wide in the lateral direction, for i: but it may be either wide or narrow in the vertical direction, so far as we are told; and this leaves open to us two quite different inferences. It may mean that the i is normal, but that the flatness of the speaker's palate compelled him to give to its articulation a compensatory width: or it may mean that the i is abnormal, 'wide', like the English i in bid — it must mean this, if the speaker's palate is at all vaulted.

Nearly 40 Irish sounds are here given, in 86 diagrams. Some diagrams record several impressions of the same sound, usually in different connexions. The result is at times rather confusing; but in most cases the different outlines of contact can be disentangled, and their comparison is then highly instructive. It would seem that there are few languages where a sound is more liable to be influenced by its adjoining sounds than in Irish. Why the labour-saving tendency, which is the greatest of all causes of phonetic change, should take different directions in different languages, is not always clear: but it is clear that in Irish it takes the direction chiefly of smoothing the passage from every sound to its neighbour as much as possible. The great example, of course, is palatalisation. No sooner do certain sounds come in contact with an e or i than their articulation is carried captive in the direction of that of *e* and *i*, and their sound itself is thenceforth modified, — '*mouillé*'. Many minor phenomena, however, can now be traced in these diagrams. Sound-changes are here to be seen in the making: for they begin to shew in the diagram while their effects are still too weak to be noticed, or even discerned, by the ear.

Diagrams must be interpreted, however, with caution and intelligence. Diagram 70, for example, which is given as a diagram of the palatalised *s* in *sgeamhach*, clearly contains the whole *sg* contact (*sg* = Eng. *shk* here, nearly), and must be read accordingly. The way in which the articulations of *l*, *n* and *r* are carried hither and thither by the adjacent sounds is very remarkable: the *l* and *n*, as also the *t*, can be interdental. The *r*, with back vowels, recedes almost to the 'inverted' or 'cerebral' position. This is also the case in the diagram (N. 50) of the *tr* in *treas*; where it forms a kind of phonetic conundrum, of which the solution is by no means apparent. Diagrams of final consonants shew much weaker articulation than others: the contact is never carried near so far. But this happens equally in other languages.

There are some important things, too, which this instrument never tells us. Its information relates to position attained, not to motion performed: it relates to space and form, not at all to time or speed. Yet the time-relations of an articulation are only second in importance to its space-relations. Take again, as simplest example, the palatalised consonants. The transition from one of these to its following vowel may be quick or slow, or it may begin slowly and then quicken, or *vice versa*: and the sound will vary accordingly. If it begins quickly, the off-glide will not be separately audible; we shall have a true palatal consonant, like French *gn*: but if it begins slowly, the off-glide will be long, and separately audible, offering to the ear a sound resembling the English consonantal *y*, in addition to the simple consonant.

Studies of this kind are so interesting that one could wish to interest all language-students in them. But there is an obstacle which nearly always repels the ordinary reader. Taking up M. Rousselot's article, he finds on the second page that, if he is to understand it, he must learn a new alphabet of phonetic signs; and he probably goes no further. M. Rousselot has done his best, it is true, to make the task a simple one, by taking a large number of his signs from the French alphabet. But there are a good many new signs to be learned, and the French signs themselves are far from unambiguous. There is the sign *r*, for example, which we are told to use with 'the same value as in French'. But what is that value? It possesses three common, besides other not unusual, values in French. Then there is the sign *y*, which is not in itself unambiguous; but in Irish there is an 'explosive *y*' which surely needs to be more scientifically symbolised.

If language-students would only agree to employ, in articles of this kind, a common system of phonetic writing, which could be learned once for all, the number of their readers would be multiplied exceedingly, and the progress of phonetic science would be much accelerated. The alphabet which I like to employ is that of the *Association Phonétique Internationale*, not because it is just the alphabet which I would have drawn up myself, but because it has been established by the common agreement of many phoneticians, and is capable of being extended and amended by the same means. Until some such agreement and common action is adopted the less interested reader will pass over all articles on phonetics as so much jargon.

These are matters, however, which do not affect the substance of the very valuable article here reviewed. The observations there recorded were well worth making, and no body could have made them or recorded them better than the Abbé Rousselot.

Liverpool.　　　　　　　　　　　　　　　R. J. LLOYD.

Poems from the Dindshenchas. Text, translation and vocabulary. By Edward Gwynn, M.A. Dublin. 1900. (Royal
Irish Academy. Todd Lecture series. Vol. VII.)

We regret that we cannot congratulate Mr. Gwynn on what presumably is his first attempt at editing and translating Irish texts.
A critical edition of the Dindsenchas poems would indeed have been
a valuable contribution to our knowledge of the Middle-Irish language
and literature, and we are grateful even for what Mr. Gwynn has given
us. It is evident that much labour has been spent by him upon this
work. But we wish he had approached his task more methodically and
better prepared. It is a pity that he has not in the first place endea-
voured to establish the age and authorship of the various poems which
he prints, and also that he has not been able to consult the Rennes
manuscript which often contains the correct readings.[1] But these are
omissions that may in some measure be rectified as the work advances.
What we deplore most is that he has not made a proper use of the
materials at his disposal in giving us a better text and a fuller list
of variants. In constructing his text he too often sets at naught the
laws both of grammar and metre, and not unfrequently prefers the
faulty reading to the correct one. The following list of the most
annoying errors will show that this criticism is not too severe.

P. 2, l. 15, read *aire-glan* 'of pure temples' (of the head), instead of
  airer-glan. The epithet refers to Étáin, not to Frémand.
  Cf. p. 8, l. 89.

16, for *Banba* read *Banbai* (acc.).

20, for *leith* read *leth* (nom.).

P. 4, l. 41, for *Mes* read *Meiss* (acc. fem.). The word *mess* 'foster-child'
  (meas .i. dalta, O'Cl.) is both masc. and fem. The gen. f.
  occurs e. g. in LL. 292 a 38: Conaire mac Messe Buachalla.

P. 4, l. 42, for *céillig* read *chelig*. It assonates with *Emir* (l. 44), better
  Ebir, the gen. of *Eber*.

50, for *enecland* read *eneclaind*.

P. 6, l. 2, for *drech-fherda* read *decharda* 'distinguished'.

61, read *A ingen, domrimgair-se.*

72, for *Dún Cain Crimthaind* read *Dún cáin C.* 'C.'s fair dún'.

80, for *imon caingen* read *imon caingin* (acc.).

P. 8, l. 1, for *gaid* read *gáid.*

2, for *móles* read *'mó les.*

P. 10, l. 13, for *side* read *síde* 'a blast' or 'attack'.

---

[1] I possess only a few extracts from the Rennes MS., but these seem
to show that it has occasionally preserved the original reading against all
other MSS., as e. g. on p. 22, l. 34 in Gwynn's edition, where it reads *a mind
gel rofitir cách*, preserving the assonance with *ler*.

28*

P. 10, l. 14, for *teithmire* read *téit-mire* 'wanton folly'. Cf. téitmer, 58, 35.

17, for *hErend* read *Hérinn* (acc.).

26, for *ar* read *for*.

P. 12, l. 38, for *ón* read *on*.

45, for *rocurad* read *rocúrad*.

50, for *inmilid* read *in mílid*.

P. 14, l. 14, for *Dún Dronard* read *dún dronard* 'a fort strong and high'.

P. 16, l. 33, for *cu tren-athach* read *cu trén athach* 'strongly a while'.

P. 18, l. 61, for *findfail* read *find Fáil*.

66 and 76, for *Con Chind* read *Conchind*.

82, for *ic Cumall* read *ic Cumaill*.

P. 20, l. 4, read *forsin n-áth*.

6, for *an míl* read *am-míl*; ib., for *cluithi-drenn* read *cluithi drenn*.[1])

12, for *ro-slig* read *ros-líg*.

13, for *in cael* read *in cíl*, with LL., which has *in cail* with punctum delens under the *a*.

P. 22, l. 33, for *hErind* read *Hérenn* (gen.).

P. 30, l. 23, for *ail* read *díl*.

P. 32, l. 35, for *ar clód* read *ar chlód* 'for having overthrown'.

P. 34, l. 11, read *hi tóebnius*.

P. 38, l. 65, for *din d'Albain* read *dind Albain* 'from Alba'.

70, read *la Frigrind Fáil, ferr cech dín*.

P. 40, l. 107, for *dire* read *aire*.

P. 42, l. 1, after *triallaid* insert *nech*, which, in spite of the editor's remark to the contrary, is also the reading of LL.

P. 44, l. 27, read *cen nach cdemna* 'without any sparing'.

35, for *techt* read *techtais*.

P. 46, l. 43, for *hErend* read *Hérinn* (dat.); it assonates with *glébind*.

P. 48, l. 64, for *de arggat* read *de arggut*, which gives assonance with *gargbrut*.

P. 50, l. 4, for *co n-gair* read *congair* and translate 'the green sea shouts against its shoulder' (*congair glasmuir ria gúalaind*).

6, for *ruirthech* read *Ruirthech*. This is an ancient name for the Liffey. See Imram Brain I, p. 47, 9.

16, dele the full stops before and after *Aés*. In the MS., the first serves to mark the end of the half-line, the second belongs to the compendium .m. for *maic*.

28, for *na ré* read *náre*. Tr. 'the gentle chain of Etar's modest wife' (*nasc mall mná náre Etair*).

P. 52, l. 30, for *in cend essiuch* read, I think, *in cech dessiuch*, though *dessech* is a ἅπαξ λεγόμενον to me. In any case, we cannot, as Mr. Gwynn proposes, read *éssium*, as the assonance with *lessium* requires a short *e*.

---

[1]) Similarly dele the hyphen in *ilair-glall* (p. 32, 9), *cridi-crao* (p. 34, 25), *níth-nerth* (p. 36, 34), *Sengaind-sin* (p. 62, 93), *deirb-deithbir* (ib. 94). Conversely, for *toirm thend* (p. 36, 42) read *toirmthend*.

P. 58, l. 26, for *ó selga* read *ós Elgga* 'over Ireland'.

31, for *fianlescaig fothuga* read *fian-flescaig fo thuga* 'hunting-booths of wickerwork under cover'.

52, for *Fremaind* read *Frémand* (assonance with *glémall*).

P. 62, l. 83, for *tech ndeirg* read *tech nDeirg* 'the house of Derg'.

The translation is marred by frequent inaccuracies and much guesswork that cannot be upheld.

P. 2, l. 12, *láthar nena.* In a gloss on this poem in H. 3. 18, p. 467, *nen* is explained by *cumal.*

P. 4, l. 31, *delbda* means 'shapely', not 'transshaped'.

32, *ruibnech .i. robuidnech* (H. 3. 18) 'of great bands'.

P. 5, l. 44, for 'Emir's read 'Eber's'.

P. 7, l. 70, for 'the fort of war' (*in tress dindgna*) read 'one of the three forts'.

P. 11, l. 20, for 'in the form of a fair beast' (*fo cháem-chethair*) read 'four fair times'. Cf. *fo cethair*, RC. XV, p. 306, rightly rendered by Stokes, ib. XVI, p. 311.

P. 15, l. 26, for 'White-neck' (*munchdem*) read 'of the lovely neck'.

P. 17, l. 30, for 'treacherous' (*étig*) read 'uncomely'.

47, for 'pitiable was the garb in which she was' (*ba cáintech cumthach rabdi*) read 'twas plaintful, sorrowful she was'.

P. 21, l. 12, for 'it clave Boyne' (*roslíg Bóinn*) read 'it licked up the Boyne'.

P. 39, l. 63, for 'Cruthmaige Ce' read 'Cé of Pictland'.

68, for 'Fiachu Reil' read 'illustrious (*réil*) Fiachra'.

79, for 'greater than any treasure' (*mó cech mainn*) read 'greater than any manna', i. e. gift. *mainn* assonates with *claind* and cannot therefore stand for *máin.*

85, for 'the tale of every bard' (*senchas cech śin*) read 'every old man's tale'.

P. 41, l. 95, for 'by holiness of strength' (*ar nóebe nirt*) read 'by strength of holiness'. As so often in poetry, the substantive attribute here precedes the noun on which it depends.

101, for 'He is the chief of clerics' (*fuil búaid clérig*) read 'there is the chief of clerics'.

112, for 'I pray God' (*attaig Dé*) read 'in the house of God'.

P. 43, l. 16, for 'the sorrowful Dagda' (*Dagda dulig*) read 'the hard Dagda'.

P. 45, l. 25, for 'he shall lift up' (*tócbaid*) read 'lift ye up'!

39, for 'then some one asked' (*iarfais nech*) read 'some one might ask'.

P. 47, l. 62, for 'for his great force' (*ar a roblaid*) read 'for his great renown'. Here the translator confuses *blad* 'renown' with *blat* 'strength'.

P. 48, l. 65, *ronglenón.* Here *ón* is a suffixed demonstrative which, like the pronominal enclitics *-sa*, *-sin*, *-siu*, *-som*, converts (for metrical purposes) the monosyllables to which it is annexed into dissyllables. See Stokes' remarks in RC. V, p. 353 and in his edition of the Martyrology of Gorman, p. 286.

P.49, l. 69, for 'on earth' (*i crí*) read 'in body'.

P.50, l. 10, *carddis*, translate 'they used to love'.

P.55, l. 81, for 'the slaughter ·of the ravaged harbour' (*dr na cúan créchtach*) read 'the slaughter of the wounded hosts'.

P.57, l. 9, for 'five men of strong fortresses' (*cóiciur ndingna ndocht*) read 'five strong fortresses'. *cóiciur*, like *tríar* sometimes, is here used of things.

21, for 'Told to you' (*adflas dúib*) read 'I shall tell you'.

P.58, l. 35, *nir théitmer*, translate 'he was not wanton, foolish'.

P.59, l. 34, for 'castle' read 'sea' (*ler*). Assonance with *sleg* forbids us to read *less*.

46, for 'or prince' (*is rorús*) read 'tis well-known', literally 'it is great knowledge'.

P.61, l. 65, for 'the grave-stone' (*ail úag*) read 'the perfect stone'

72, for 'without feasting' (*cen esair*) read 'without a litter (of straw)'. Cf. RC. XII, p. 462 s. v. *strophaiss*.

P.63, l. 95, for 'noble as precious stones' (*nóisech néime*) read 'the noble with splendour'. *néime* is the gen. of *niam* f.

103, for 'in possession of the palace' (*fri toiche tig*) read 'for fair possession'.

P.65, l. 106, for 'the loss' (*tesbaide*) read 'the losses'.

119, for 'in that spot' (*ille*) read 'till now'. K. M.

Festschrift Whitley Stokes zum 70. Geburtstage am 28. Februar 1900 gewidmet. Leipzig, Otto Harrassowitz, 1900. VII + 48 pp. gr. 8⁰.

Die Mehrzahl der hier vereinigten Aufsätze gehört zur vergleichenden Sprachforschung: R. Thurneysen verbindet ir. *lith* 'Fest' mit deutsch un-*flat* von der Wurzel *ple-* 'füllen' und *cless* 'Spiel', ursprünglich *cliuss*, mit sanskr. *krīḍati* 'ludit'; F. Sommer erklärt ir. *bibdu* 'schuldig, Feind' als part. perf., von der Wurzel *bheidh*, 'der, welcher bedrängt, beschädigt hat'; W. Foy handelt über die Kürzung indogerm. langer Diphthonge im Keltischen, wie kymr. *dou*, *deu*, *dau* 'zwei' aus indogerm. *du̯ou*, etc.; A. Leskien über die pronominale Prolepsis nominaler Objekte in den macedonisch-bulgarischen Dialekten; K. Brugmann leitet lat. *prope* von sanskr. *prapi-* (πρό - ἐπι) und *proximus* von sanskr. *parc-* 'verbinden' ab; E. Windisch deutet einige gewöhnlich als *S*-Aoriste angesehene mittelir. Praeterita nicht als solche, nämlich *rofhóir* (von **fóirthim* 'succurro'), *forrúmai* (von **foraimh* 'sich wohin begeben'), *dor-écaim*, *do-ecmaing* 'accidit' (von *com-* und der Wurzel *añj-* 'erscheinen'), *arlasair* 'locutus est' (als Perfekt vom Stamme *arlas* von adgládur), *seiss* und *siassair* 'constitit' (vom Verb *sessam* 'stehen'). Andrer Art sind zwei vorangehende Beiträge. K. Meyer interpretiert, nach YBL. 127 b und Rawl. B. 502, fol. 47 a 2, eine Totenklage um König Niall Nóigiallach (c. 400 n. Chr.), deren Abfassung er spätestens in den Anfang des 9. Jahrh. setzt. L. Chr. Stern behandelt eine ossianische Ballade aus dem 12. Jahrh. und in einem Anhange den Namen der Firbholg und den der Tuatha dé Danann. Dem Verf. war ein späterer Text

des Gedichts (LL. 207b), dessen Incipit Wh. Stokes in den Addenda zu
den Lismore Lives p. 405a anführt, nicht bekannt, ist aber nun in der
Lage, eine ihm gütigst mitgeteilte Abschrift des Herrn Stokes nachträglich abdrucken zu können.

Book of Lismore, fo. 153 b 2.

Dámh trír thancat*ur* ille . do chur re Find na féinde
sirdis lind cach moin 's gach magh¹) . in triar uallach ba hingnad.
Dobad*ur* athaigh sa féind . in triar tháinic sund do chéin
sealg léo a cumaidh chaich choidhchi . feis ar leith gach n-aonoidchi.
Áenchú léo ba háille dath . bá cú adhbhul ingantach
caeca fiadh foirrghead do ghail . o trath eirghi co nónaidh.
Luidset in triar sin le a coin . feasc*ur* i Carrn Feradhoigh
tucsat a cú, comall ngle . sís fon tiprait firuisce.
Fín da éis uisci in topair . rob alaind ind urobair
gabhsat ara ol co hán . co tainic chuca Dubhán.
Ro marb*ad* leo, lathar ngle . Dubhan mac Breasail Bhoirne
na tisadh in gnimh na gcend . i fiadhnaisi fian (Erend).
[fo. 154a 1]. Rob ingnad le Find iar soin . líne Dubhain mheic Breasoil
gan fis a oideda²) in fir . robo cheist mhór 'gá mhuinntir.
Adubairt fris a dhéd fis . re mac Cumaill gan éislis
in triar út tainic tar muir . do mharbh Dubhan mac Breasuil.
ISí siut accu in cú cian . issí robhói ac fliuchnud níadh
can fis tucsat*ur* ille . cuilén righ na Hiruaithe.
ISí robúi ac Lugh na lend . tucsat maic Tuireand Bicreand
ré ré cóecat bl*iadan* bil . 'na hibhur áille i fidhbhaidh.
IN cú sin ba haidhbli gluind . fris na gabhthái i cruas comhluind
ba ferr na cach máin coidhci . caor theinedh gach n-aonoidhchi.
Buadha aile ar in coin caoimh . ferr in mháin sin na cach maóin
midh *nó* fín no tsásadh de . da fotraic a firuisce.
Anmanna na tri laoch lán . Sél is Donait is Domhnán
ainm na con co caoimhe chnis . tucadh co Find Failinis.
"A marbad", ar fiann Find Fail . "a cinaidh marbhtha Dubhain".
"ni muirbther", ar Find iar sain, "ma berait íc sa finghail".
"Ata accaind ícc sa fer . a flaithféindidh³) na nGaoidheal
ar cú dhuitsi fein is ferr . ina airdrighi nEireand."
Tucsat ratha ris co fír . grian is ésca, muir is tír
gan béo an chon do breith amach . co brath a tír n-allmharach.
Marbhait iarsain in choin cruaidh . luidset sech Albain sairtuaidh
rucsat craicend in chon sair . co tech Meirce mórghlonn*aig*.
Tinoil*is* Find fianna Fail . gabsat ar muir co morgráin
tinoilter dhuind as'tír thair . Breathnaig, Cruithnigh, Albanaigh.
Rucsam*ur* lind cloich cach fir . in lín tancamar d'fiannaibh
cor' thsáighsem*ur* ar in maigh . re comriachtain da cathaib.
Guth cach aoinfir re Find fein . itir tsen is óc don féin
"ní theichfem co teiche ar clach . ar ecla na n-allmharach".

---

¹) MS. madh. ²) MS. oigeda. ³) MS. flaithfeindigh.

Mairit na clocha astir thair . bhail a mbamar 'nar gcathaibh
ro marbhsum ilar n-aicme . dar' cuirsem cath confaide.
Meircheo *ocus* Maon a[1]) athair . naonmur dóibh riasna cathaib
ní gabhdáis ar n-airm *co* n-ágh . ro ba doilghi na cach dámh.

Dámh.

H. D'Arbois de Jubainville, Les noms de lieu dans le cartulaire
de Gellone. (Extrait des Comptes rendus de l'Académie des
inscriptions et belles-lettres 1900.)

Das 1898 von der archäologischen Gesellschaft in Montpellier
herausgegebene Chartular von Gellone im Canton d'Aniane, Arrondisse-
ment de Montpellier, Hérault, das viele Urkunden des 11. Jahrh. enthält,
giebt dem Verfasser Veranlassung, die geographischen Namen jener
Gegend zu untersuchen, die nach dem Periplus der Scylax in der zweiten
Hälfte des 4. Jahrh. v. Chr. vor den Römern und Galliern von Liguriern
und gemischten Iberern bewohnt war. Daraus wären Ortsnamen auf
-*ascus*, -*nco*, -*nca*, -*átis* zu erklären, während die auf -*ácus* und *Verno-*
dubrum (Verdouble) auf die dann folgende gallische Herrschaft und
andere auf -*ensis*, -*anus* auf die Römer deuten würden.

— Les bas-reliefs gallo-romains du musée de Cluny. (Revue
archéologique 1900. I, p. 66—74.)

Wie das Druidenwesen der alten Gallier dem der Iren ähnlich
war, so finden sich nach dem Verf. auch Spuren der irischen Sage in
den bildlichen Überresten der alten Gallier. Namen wie Donnotaurus,
Deiotaurus und der Tarvos trigaranus 'der Stier mit den drei Kranichen'
erinnern ihn an den Stier in der Táin bó Chuailnge, und Smertullos, ein
Name des Gottes Esus (wie in Esugenus = Eógan), und Cerrunnos
sind nach seiner Annahme das Heldenpaar Cúchulainn und Conall
Cernach.

H. Zimmer, Keltische Studien 17. Ysten Sioned [cf. RC. 5, 500].
(Zeitschrift für vergl. Sprachforschung, XXXVI, 416—458.)

Britannische Etymologieen, nämlich corn. *mar*: arm. *mar*, *arvar*
'Zweifel' aus der Konjunktion *mar* 'wenn'; ir. *eneclann*: w. *gwyneb-*
werth: arm. *enepuuerth* 'die Busse', d. h. die zu zahlende Goldplatte
(ir. *lann*: w. *llafn* 'lamina'), so gross wie das Gesicht, als Genugthuung
für angethanen Schimpf; w. *arglwydd*: corn. *arluit* 'Herr' d. h. hlâford,
lord, von *arlwy* 'die dargebotene Nahrung'; ir. *círdub*, nach Analogie
des w. *purdu*, = pure-*dub*; w. *Seis* aus Saxo, wie *lleidr* aus latro
(cf. KB. 7, 70); ir. *cáin* 'Steuer': w. *ceiniog* 'Pfennig' vom lat. *canon*;
ir. *bág* 'Kampf' = w. *bai* 'Fehler'; ir. *escart* 'Abhuf' etc. nicht
von *scartaim* 'sondere ab', sondern aus *es*-*cart* von *cartaim* 'werfe
aus, schicke'.

---

[1]) MS. an.

H. Zimmer, Keltische Studien 18.   Beiträge zur altirischen
Grammatik. (Ibid., p. 461—556.)

Altir. *giun* ist nom. acc. du. des *u*-Stammes **ginu* 'Mund', dagegen *gin* nom. acc. sg. — Nach eingehender Untersuchung verleiht im
Altirischen die Verbalpartikel *ro* als Zeichen der abgeschlossenen Handlung dem Präteritum die Bedeutung eines wirklichen Perfekts oder
Plusquamperfekts, dem Conj. praes. die des Conj. perf., dem Imperfekt
die des Plusquamperfekts; ausserdem steht sie beim Konjunktiv zum
Ausdruck des Befehls und des Wunsches. Auch die analogen Verhältnisse
in den britannischen Sprachen werden berührt.

— Die keltische Bewegung in der Bretagne. (Preussische Jahr-
bücher, Band IC. 1900, p. 454—497.)

Ein Aufsatz über die Verbreitung und die Pflege der armorischen
Sprache bis auf die neueste Zeit und über die nationalistische Bewegung,
die mit dem Feldgeschrei *Breiz zo d'ar Vreiziz* seit einigen Jahren
auch das französische von Celten bewohnte Gebiet ergriffen hat. Die
allgemeine Verbrüderung, die Iren, Bergschotten, welsche, cornische und
manannische Celten erstreben und durch Kongresse zu fördern suchen,
stösst zur Zeit noch auf ein ernstes Hindernis in dem Mangel einer
Sprache, in der sie sich verständigen könnten. Der hier verzeichnete
Aufsatz des über diese Verhältnisse wohlunterrichteten Verf. schliesst
sich an frühere in derselben Zeitschrift erschienene an: Der Pan-Keltismus
in Grossbritannien und Irland. I. Die heutige nationale Bewegung in
Wales in ihrer geschichtlichen Entwickelung (Pr. Jahrb. XCII, 1898,
p. 426—494); II. Die sprachlich-litterarische Bewegung in Irland und
ihre Aussichten (ibid. XCIII, 1898, p. 59—93); III. Das Wiederaufleben
des Keltentums in seinen Folgen für England (ibid. XCIII, 1898,
p. 294—334).

R. Thurneysen, Zum keltischen Verbum. (Zeitschrift für vergl.
Sprachforschung XXXVII, 52—120.)

Eine Abhandlung über drei streitige Punkte der altirischen
Grammatik, nämlich: die Verbalpartikel *ro*, eine Ergänzung und teilweise Berichtigung des vorhin erwähnten Aufsatzes darüber; Deponens
und Passiv mit *r*, deren Erklärung aus den Formen des Aktivs der
Verf. nicht gelten lassen will (das Passiv geht nach ihm auf einen
Infinitiv auf *r* zurück); und die Entstehung der Formen des *t*-Prae-
teritums.

J. Strachan, The sigmatic future and subjunctive in Irish.
(Philol. Society's Transactions 1900.) 24 pp. 8º.

Eine übersichtliche Verzeichnung der altirischen verbalen Formen
auf *s*, die gesondert sind, einmal nach dem Auslaut der Wurzel (Guttural,
ng, Dental, *nd* und *s*), und sodann nach der Bedeutung die Futura
(diese zeigen noch oft ihre ursprüngliche Reduplikation), wie von *guidim*:
gige-s 'orabit', *ro-gigsed* 'oraturus erat', und in die Konjunktive, wie
-*gé* 'oret', *gessir*, -*gesar* 'oretur', etc.

E. C. Quiggin, Die lautliche Geltung der vortonigen Wörter und Silben in der Book of Leinster Version der Tain bō Cualnge. Inaugural-Dissertation. Greifswald 1900. 62 pp. 8°.

Ein Teil der orthographischen Unsicherheit, die man in mittelirischen Texten wahrnimmt, wird aus dem Widerstreite der überlieferten altirischen Form und der sich heranbildenden neuirischen erklärlich. Wenn namentlich prätonische Partikeln der Kürzung und Schwächung unterliegen, so darf man erwarten, dass eine Handschrift des 12. Jahrh. schon Spuren davon aufweise. An einem der wichtigsten Texte des Buches von Leinster zeigt nun der Verf., wie weit diese Entwickelung schon vorgeschritten war. Es findet sich z. B. *mar* neben *immar*, *gach* neben *cach*, *go* neben *co*, *no* statt *dano*, *andd* und *nd* statt *indá* 'als', *ol* or *ar* for *bar* 'inquit' neben einander. Es werden verwechselt die Präpositionen *ar* und *for*, *ar* und *iar*, *fri* *ri* und *le*, *do* und *di*; es steht *a chétóir* statt *fo chétóir*, *a* statt *ó*, *as* statt *ós* *uas*, und *oc* *ac* *ic* 'c 'g werden ebenso wie *cen*, *can*, *gen*, *gan* neben einander gebraucht. Namentlich zeigt sich diese Verwechselung der Präpositionen in der Komposition mit Verben, denn es werden vertreten: *ad*, *at*, *as* durch *do*, *fo*, *ro*; *do* durch *at*, *fo*; *fo* durch *ro*; *for* durch *ar*; *ro* durch *do* und *no* durch *do*, *fo*, *ro*. Auf die Erscheinung der letzten Art hatte Prof. Zimmer schon vor Jahren aufmerksam gemacht (KZ. 30, 72) und ihm ist auch die Anregung zu Dr. Quiggins Arbeit zu verdanken.

F. N. Finck, Die araner mundart. Ein beitrag zur erforschung des westirischen. Marburg, N. G. Elwert, 1899. I. Band: Grammatik. x + 224 pp.; II. Band: Wörterbuch. 349 pp.

Der zweite Teil dieses Werkes, das Wörterbuch, das hier mit einem Anhange von Nachträgen und Verbesserungen erscheint, ist in dieser Zeitschrift 2, 414 bereits angezeigt worden.[1]) Wir nehmen auch die Grammatik, die in der That den ersten Teil und die Grundlage bilden sollte, dankbar auf. Je rückhaltloser wir das Verdienst ein im allgemeinen zuverlässiges Bild eines gesprochenen celtischen Dialekts aufgenommen und wiedergegeben zu haben anerkennen, desto weniger brauchen wir einige Mängel der grammatischen Darstellung zu verschweigen. Vor allem ist das Buch doch recht unbequem. Die übliche Orthographie des Neuirischen ist für die grammatische Betrachtung in hohem Grade zweckdienlich, da sie sowohl den Zusammenhang mit den ältesten Sprachformen aufrecht erhält, als auch den Forderungen der neueren Aussprache nach Möglichkeit Rechnung trägt. Unsere Bewunderung dafür wuchs, so oft wir uns in die phonetischen Systeme der Macgregor, Macray, Phillips, Kelly, O'Gallagher u. a. einzuleben genötigt waren. So müssen wir uns auch neue Laut- und Wortbilder aneignen oder die Umschrift unablässig in die uns geläufige Schreibweise zurückübertragen, um zu erkennen, dass Laut für Laut in der historischen Orthographie wohl vor-

---

1) In dieser Anzeige beruht der Satz auf S. 415, Z. 33 (zu p. 21) auf einem Missverständnisse und ist zu streichen.

gesehen ist und dass es sich in alle dem nur um Regeln der Aussprache und ihre Ausnahmen handelt, die sich hätten formulieren lassen. Nun geht die Grammatik nicht vom Neuirischen aus, sondern ignoriert es vollständig, als seien wir seit 400 Jahren ohne Nachricht darüber geblieben. Wenn zur Erklärung lediglich alt- und mittelirische Wortformen gebraucht werden, so geht man dadurch des wichtigsten Vorteils verlustig in jedem Falle und sogleich zu erkennen, was die hier behandelte vulgäre oder dialektische Sprache von der neuirischen Schriftsprache unterscheidet. Auch weicht die Ordnung der Grammatik von der gewohnten und bewährten Methode ohne Not ab. Dass der Verfasser nach semitischer Art das Verb vor dem Nomen abhandelt, ist nicht der Rede wert; aber wenn wir in seinem Schema z. B. einen Paragraphen über die Pronomina demonstrativa oder possessiva vermissen, wenn wir kein Kapitel über die Formen des Adverbs, über die Präpositionen, über die Konjunktionen finden, so wird solches Übel zwar durch die Möglichkeit gemildert, dass wir dergleichen in dem Wörterbuche aufsuchen können, aber es begründet die Meinung, dass die Anlage der Verbesserung bedürftig war. Der Fleiss, womit namentlich die Beispiele zusammengetragen sind, muss hervorgehoben werden, und das Ganze ist uns ein schätzbares Hilfsmittel geworden, um uns über das Wesen eines irischen Vulgärdialektes zu unterrichten, dessen Reinheit und Altertümlichkeit J. T. O'Flaherty in einem lehrreichen Aufsatze über die Insel Aran schon 1824 gerühmt hat.

Transactions of the Gaelic Society of Inverness. Vol. XXI. 1896—97. Inverness 1899. XVI + 476 pp.

Aus dem mannigfachen Inhalte dieses Bandes heben wir hervor, was die Sprache und Litteratur des Schottisch-gälischen betrifft. Al. Macbain giebt einen Nachtrag von 19 Seiten zu seinem Etymological dictionary (vgl. CZ. 1, 357), einiges hinzufügend, anderes verbessernd. C. M. Robertson danken wir einen sehr nützlichen grammatikalischen und lexikalischen Bericht über den gälischen Dialekt der schottischen Insel Arran (p. 229—265), über den vor einigen Jahren J. Kennedy einige Mitteilungen gemacht hatte. Hier finden wir auch (p. 240) die richtige Erklärung von *ny lomarcan* im Manx, nämlich: *'n a lom onrachdan* 'ganz allein'. J. L. Robertson liefert eine Übersetzung des Abschnittes über das Schottisch-gälische aus E. Windischs Artikel 'Keltische Sprachen' vom Jahre 1884, und J. Macrury bringt wieder eine seiner gefälligen gälischen Plaudereien über alte Meinungen und Gebräuche. Auch fehlt es nicht an Gedichten: Al. Macdonald und Neil Macleod schöpfen aus neueren Quellen, J. Kennedy aus den von James Maclagan (1728—1805) nachgelassenen Sammlungen, die sich im Besitze der Familie befinden. Immer wendet man sich gern dieser gälischen Poesie zu, wiewohl sie es den *operosa carmina* der Iren nicht gleichthut und sich in einem engeren Kreise bewegt; in jeder neuen Publikation aus den vorhandenen älteren Manuskripten finden wir, was erfreut und belehrt. So steht p. 221 ein Gedicht über das *fuath leam*, von dem der Barde von Lochfyne Evan Maccoll 1890 eine abweichende Lesart mitgeteilt hat (High-

land Monthly 1, 755). Es beruht auf ganz alter Tradition, denn es
stimmt teilweise mit einem Gedichte im Dean's Book (No. 40) überein,
zeigt aber auch, dass diese früheste Aufzeichnung, wenigstens wie sie
Ewen Maclachlan und Thomas Maclauchlan lesen (die ersehnte photo-
graphische Reproduktion des Buches scheint leider in unbestimmte Ferne
gerückt), nicht ganz fehlerfrei ist. Der erstere liest z. B.:

Foyath lam a choggi na heith
nach a leggin a neith mane seach¹
foyath lam κennort gin we chroye
foyath lam sloye nach dany' cath —

während Thomas Maclauchlan *garwe* (st. *gin we*) und *cacht* (st. *cath*) hat.
Die erwähnten neueren Texte lassen, korrupt wie sie sonst sind, keinen
Zweifel, dass, wie Metrum, Reim und Sinn fordern, im Dean's Book zu
lesen ist:

Fuath leam a' chogadh na shith
neach a leigeann nith ma'n seach;
fuath leam ceannard gun bhi cruaidh,
fuath leam sluagh nach deanadh creach.

Seltsam, dass ein so vortrefflicher Kenner des Gälischen wie Maclagan
den Vers 'Is fuath lem Abhal gan ùbhlan' (Unlieb ist mir ein Apfel-
baum ohne Äpfel) so gänzlich missverstehen konnte, indem er Abhal als
Eigennamen der Grafschaft Atholl nahm, die ja an wilden Äpfeln reich
sein mag, deren alter Name aber im Buche von Deir *Athótla* geschrieben wird.

E. Ernault, Une vieille histoire l'épisode de Glaucos. (Bulletin
de la Société des Antiquaires de l'Ouest. 2e trimestre, année
1899, p. 337—352.)

Mit dem Zweikampfe des Glaucos mit Diomedes (Ilias, 6. Gesang)
werden zusammengestellt der Hildebrands mit Hadubrand, Cuchulinns
mit Conlaech, Rustems mit Sohrab, Ardjunas mit Babhruvâhana (im
Mahâbhârata) und ähnliche Kämpfe in einem Lai der Marie de France,
im Rasenden Roland (36. Gesang), im Verlorenen Paradies (2. Gesang),
in der Henriade (8. Gesang) etc. Für die irische Sage, die schon im
Journal des Sçavants 1764, p. 851, besprochen wird, hätte sich bessere
Gewähr bei den Dichtern finden lassen als Macpherson, und wäre es
auch nur Charlotte Brookes Übersetzung oder Drummonds Nachbildung
(Minstrelsy p. 329 ff.) der irischen Ballade oder die schottisch-gälische
im Dean's Book, die Lachlan Maclean (Inv. 5, 59), Al. Macbain (Celtic
Magazine 13, 563) und H. Maclean (Highland Monthly 1, 530; Ultonian
Hero-Ballads p. 65, 138) behandelt haben. Auch J. Smiths Seandàna
p. 158 und Campbells Tales 3, 184 sind zu vergleichen. Die Sage hat
Wanderungen hin und her gemacht. Das incident des Ringes, das sich
in der späteren deutschen Ballade findet, kommt auch in der irischen
Schlacht von Magh-Rath vor (ed. O'Donovan p. 72), und auf die irische
Heroine weist jenes Wort des Alten an den Sohn, wie es die deutsche
Ballade hat: 'Nun sage du mir, viel Junger, den Streich lehrte dich
ein Weib'. Die dunkle alte Geschichte bedarf, nach Edition der irischen

Texte im Gelben Buche von Lecan 214a, in H. 3. 17 TCD. (O'Donovan's Transcripts p. 983) und in den Edinburger Manuskripten (RC. 16, 47), noch gründlicher litterarhistorischer Untersuchung.

V. Henry, Lexique étymologique des termes les plus usuels du breton moderne. Rennes, J. Plihon et L. Hervé, 1900. (Bibliothèque bretonne armoricaine, fasc. III.) XXIX + 350 pp. 8⁰.

Nachdem erst vor wenigen Jahren der Wortschatz des jüngsten gälischen Dialekts etymologisch erklärt worden ist, wird hier dem jüngsten britannischen dieselbe erfreuliche Pflege zu Teil. Mit der Methode der indogermanischen Sprachwissenschaft vertraut, hat der Verfasser die Arbeiten der fachkundigsten Vorgänger gewissenhaft benutzt. Wenn auch sein Wörterbuch kein vollständiges ist, so wird doch der gemischte Bestand des neuarmorischen Dialekts meines Wissens zum ersten Male so vielseitig erörtert, wie es, schon nach den nützlichen Indices des Buches zu urteilen, hier geschehen ist. Man muss der Befriedigung Ausdruck geben, dass man hinfort ein so präcis gehaltenes, übersichtliches Werk bei den celtischen Studien zu Rate ziehen kann. Einigen Bemerkungen, die sich bei der Durchsicht darboten, mag Raum gegeben werden.

Für die armorische Sprache, die sich erst in historischer Zeit von den britannischen Schwestern getrennt hat, wird die reiner überlieferte welsche immer die beste Erklärung liefern. Man sollte ihre Wortformen im Wörterbuche immer anführen, damit es nicht den Anschein gewinne, dass das Armorische ein celtisches Wort allein besitzt, was verhältnismässig selten der Fall ist. Der Verfasser erwähnt das Welsche auch meist, aber nicht immer. Und das vollständige Material zu der Geschichte eines Wortes haben wir auch erst beisammen, wenn wir neben die armorische, cornische, welsche Form auch die irische setzen können. Ohne die Erfüllung dieser Vorbedingung ist jede Etymologie aus dem Indogermanischen überaus misslich. Wer kann z. B. sagen, ob *oad* 'Alter' mit *aevum, aetas* verwandt ist, wenn man nicht die irische Form des Wortes kennt, wenn man selbst die Bedeutungen des entsprechenden welschen Wortes ausser Acht lässt? Das w. *oet* bedeutet eine besondere oder bestimmte Zeit, wie die zu einem Stelldichein festgesetzte (HM. 1, 327. 336; RB. 1, 5); *er-m-oet* 'meiner Zeit', *er-i-oet* 'seiner Zeit' heissen 'je'. Der Begriff Zeit liegt vielleicht nicht ursprünglich in dem Worte, sondern der der Sonderung, der Vereinzelung, so dass man durch die Analogie von *uan:oen:oan* 'Lamm' auf das ir. *uath-ad* 'singularitas, paucitas' geführt wird, wovon auch w. *odid* 'selten' abgeleitet ist.

Namentlich verkennt man leicht den Ursprung grammatischer Wörter, wenn man sich nicht ihre Form in den verwandten Dialekten gegenwärtig hält. So ist *ama* 'hier' zunächst = w. *yma*; *y* ist die Präposition *yn*, und dass *ma* das irische *magh* 'Feld' ist, bleibt nicht zweifelhaft, da von diesem Nomen auch im Irischen Adverbia loci gebildet werden: *amach* 'hinaus', *amuigh* 'draussen'; dies *magh:ma* ist auch p. 192 nicht erwähnt.

Ann, hann 'ici' ist Le Gonidecs Abstraction aus einer Form wie *ac'hann* 'd'ici' = *ac'hanô*; es kommt von einer particula augens wie ir. *som, sin*, hat aber mit ir. *and* 'da' nichts zu schaffen.

Azé 'hier', wofür auch die Formen *sé, zé* verzeichnet werden, kann nicht aus *man-sé* entstanden sein, sondern ist m. E. das w. *ysydd, sydd, sy* 'was da ist' = ir. *is and*. Der Anlaut *z* in *zô* (= mittelarm. *so*) ist keine demonstrative Basis, noch auch *s* in *sioaz* 'leider'; denn das erstere ist wieder w. *sydd*, das letztere w. *sydd waeth*. Ebenso ist auch *zôken* 'selbst' zu erklären = mittelarm. *soquen*; es enthält in seinem ersten Teile das w. *ysydd* und in dem andern das arm. *hôgen* 'jedoch', w. *hagen* 'auch'. Arm. *ez, é* = w. *ydd, y* ist etymologisch kein Relativum, sondern ist wahrscheinlich das ir. *and, is-and* 'da'.

Bété 'bis', vormals *bet*, scheint ebenso wie *fé-nôz, féteiz* die Präposition w. *py* = ir. *co* 'bis' zu enthalten, also vermutlich *py-hyt* = ir. *co-ed*; die Zusammensetzung wäre ähnlich wie ir. *coidche*, worin ich das w. *byth* 'immer' vermute. Dagegen ist *pet* 'combien' wohl = *p-het* (w. *pa-hyt*). Arm. *héd, het* 'longueur' = w. *hyt* ist deshalb nicht das ir. *sith-*, sondern aller Wahrscheinlichkeit nach ir. *ed* 'Raum'.

Hô 'euer' und *hon* 'unser' scheint der Verfasser verschieden zu erklären. Ersteres ist entstanden aus *hoz* und weiter aus *oz, ous* = corn. *as* = w. *awch*, und verhält sich zu *c'houi* 'ihr', wie *hon* 'unser' = corn. w. *an* (ein) zu *ni* 'wir'; die Basis ist also *a-*, die Ausdrücke scheinen eher adjektivisch als genitivisch zu sein. Nun kann arm. *ho* 'leur' nicht zu sanskr. *eṣâm* (= ir. *a n-*) gestellt werden; denn es scheint, man dürfe es nicht von w. *eu* trennen, das wohl ursprünglich auf einen, vor vokalischem Anlaut als *h* erhaltenen Konsonanten, aber nicht auf einen Nasal ausging. Der Ursprung des w. *eu* ist schwer zu erkennen, weil uns die altwelsche Form dafür entgeht. Vielleicht ist es wie *an, awch* gebildet, mit dem Suffix der 3. pl., das im Irischen *-us-* lautet. Wenn aber *eu* 'ihr', 'ihnen gehörig' mit *meu* 'mir gehörig', *teu* 'dir gehörig', *pieu* 'dem gehörig' zusammenhängt, so würde es ein Wort des Besitzes und der Zugehörigkeit sein, also: *eu tir* 'ihr Land', eigentlich 'der Besitz von Land'. Lautete *eu* vormals *ou* (wie *deheu* vormals *dehou*), so würde seine ursprüngliche Form *om* sein. So ist im Altwelschen die Partikel *nou*, z. B. uter nostrum .i. *nou ni* 'zu uns gehörig', spiculae rosarum .i. *nou ir fionou* 'zu den Rosen gehörig' (KB. 7, 887), wofür später *neu* eintrat (Skene 287, 8), aus *nom* entstanden (GC. 1055), dessen *n* vielleicht dem in *neill* zu vergleichen ist. So scheint das w. *ieu*, *ie* = arm. *ia* 'ja' das ir. *am, om, em* 'wahrhaftig' zu sein; so ist auch w. *maddeu* 'verzeihen' das ir. *maithem*.

Es seien noch einige andere Wörter aufgeführt, in denen die Harmonie der Dialekte unvollständig zu sein scheint, da man die welschen oder irischen Formen vermisst.

Annéô f. 'Ambos', vann. *annéan*, vormals *anneffn*, ist w. *eingion*, ir. *indeóin*; vgl. *genn* 'Keil' = w. *gaing*, ir. *geind. Annez* m. 'Gerät' = w. *annedd* f. 'Wohnung'; *anoued* f. 'Kälte' = w. *annwyd* m.; *astud* 'elend' = w. *astud* 'fleissig'.

Aoz f. 'Flussbett' hat den nasalen Anlaut verloren; die ursprüngliche Form ist *naoz*, nicht umgekehrt; denn dies ist das w. *nant* f. in
gleicher Bedeutung. Vgl. marm. *ent effn* = *ez effn* 'directement' (RC. 18,
312. Gloss. 210); *enta* = *eza* 'donc' (RC. 9, 382); und ferner w. *ydd*
: arm. *ez* = ir. *and*; w. *Manawyddan*, Name des celtischen Meergottes
= ir. *Manandan*, etc. In ähnlicher Weise ist vielleicht auch *oaz* 'Eifersucht' (statt *waz*?), w. *add-iant* 'Sehnsucht' = ir. *ét*; denn es ist
kaum das nicht altbelegte w. *aidd* 'Glut' (vgl. w. *blaidd* : arm. *bleiz*;
craidd : *creiz*; *haidd* : *heiz*), und ob w. *eiddig* 'eifersüchtig' nicht von
einem andern Stamme abgeleitet sei (*eidd*- 'zugehörig', also: 'selbstisch'?),
wäre auch zu bedenken.

Azeûli 'anbeten', w. *addoli* hat allerdings, wie der Verf. bemerkt,
mit adorare (ir. *adradh*) keine Verwandtschaft; es ist zusammengesetzt
aus *ad-ioli*, und w. *ioli* ist ir. *ailim* 'bitte', womit möglicherweise
das gr. ζῆλος (es wird von der Wurzel *yá*- abgeleitet) zu vergleichen ist.

Bégin f. 'Blasebalg' ist nicht die ursprüngliche Form, sondern
mégin, wie das w. *megin* beweist. *Breiz* f. kommt von Brittia und gehört zu w. *Bryth-on* und ir. *Britt* (i. e. Britto genere, Todd 5, 56), aber
nicht zu ir. *Bretan*. *Buoch* 'Kuh' ist w. *buwch*.

Kafout 'haben' ist ir. *gabhdil*. *Kaniblen* 'Wolke' scheint mit
ir. *nél*, w. *niwl*, *nifwl* 'Nebel' zusammenzuhängen, *kéô* 'Grotte' mit
w. *cau* 'hohl'. *Kerzu* 'Dezember': wenn arm. *miz du* November bedeutet (nach Le Gonidec sind Oktober bis Dezember die *misiou dû*), so
ist es verschieden vom Welschen, wo *y mis du* (vor oder nach Weih-
nachten) Dezember oder Januar ist. *Kiz* 'recul', *kae* 'geh', *kit* 'geht',
(p. 68) kommen schwerlich von ir. *ro-chim*; eher darf man an ir. *cingim*
'gehe' denken, wozu der Infinitiv *céim* lautet. *Kleizen* 'Narbe' ist der
Singulativ von w. *craith*, ir. *crécht* 'Wunde'. *Kraouñ* 'Nuss', w. *cneuen*,
vgl. manx *cro*. *Kroaz* f. 'crux' ist w. *croes*, *crwys*, ir. *cros*; *kroug* m.
'crucem', 'Galgen' ist w. *crog*, ir. *croch*. *Krouer* 'Sieb', abr. *cruitr*,
ir. *criathar*, ist im welschen *crwydr* erhalten (CZ. 1, 96; HM. 2, 304).
Kudon f. 'ramier' ist nicht ein ir. *ciadcolum* 'Waldtaube', da dies für
fiadcolum verlesen ist (Stokes, Sprachschatz p. 76).

Digwéz 'accident' kommt wie w. *digwyddo* nicht von lit. decedere,
sondern von w. *cwyddo*, arm. *kouez* 'fallen'.

Emzivad 'Waise' = w. *amddifad*.

Faô 'faba' = w. *ffa*; *faô* 'fagus' = w. *ffa-wydden*.

Gélaouen 'Blutegel' ist eine Ableitung vom w. *gel* f. (RB. 1, 119)
= ir. *gel* in gleicher Bedeutung. *Glad* 'Vermögen' = w. *gwlad* 'Land'
ist das ir. *folad* 'pecus'; *gôpr* 'Lohn' = w. *gwobr* ist das ir. *fochraic*.
Gra 'thun' ist vermutlich eine ursprünglichere Form (von *for-ag*-) als
das w. *gwna*, dessen *n* aus *r* entstanden zu sein scheint; dass die welsche
Form mit *gwn* 'ich weiss' zusammenhänge, ist nicht wohl denkbar.
Gwell 'besser' ist schwerlich etwas anderes als das ir. *ferr* (CZ. 3, 155).
Gwenvidik 'glücklich' ist von w. *gwynfyd* abgeleitet, und dies ist das
ir. *findbaid* 'beatitudo'. *Gwéz* 'wild' = w. *gwydd* = ir. *fïad*, das
nicht nur 'gibier', sondern auch 'wild' bedeutet.

Hañter 'Hälfte' kommt nicht von einer Wurzel *sm*, sondern vom ir. *sain*, w. *han* gl. alius 'besonders' und ist eben dem deutschen *sonder* nahe verwandt (CZ. 2, 110). *Héal* 'edel' halte ich für das ir. *soer, saor* in gleicher Bedeutung. *Hévélep* 'gleich' soll für * *kev-he-lep* stehen, d. i. *com-su-liq* 'gute Gestalt habend mit', und dem w. *cyffelyb* 'gleich' entsprechen. Mir durchaus nicht wahrscheinlich, da ein solches *liq : lep*, deutsch *ge-leich*, im Celtischen sonst nicht nachgewiesen ist (arm. *dis-léber* 'défiguré' ist noch dunkler als *hévélep*). Wenn neben ir. *samail*: w. *hafal*: arm. *haval*, *hével* 'similis' im Irischen *cosmail* und im Welschen *cyhafal* stehen, so darf m. E. nicht in Frage gestellt werden, dass *-ep* (w. *-yb*) die Endung ist, die auch *moéreb* = w. *modryb* 'Tante' von ir. *máthair* 'Mutter' hat. Das Suffix *-ep* (*-yb*) hat offenbar die durch ir. *comh-*, w. *cy-* ausgedrückte Bedeutung, weshalb w. *cyffelyb* kaum aus *cy-hafal-yb erklärt werden kann (CZ. 3, 147).

Iéz 'Sprache', w. *iaith*, ist das irische *icht* 'Stamm, Gesittung' und steht dem ahd. *jehan*, *beichte* ganz fern. W. *iaith* heisst noch mitunter 'Stamm', z. B. D. G. 139, 25.

Lavar 'Wort', ir. *labar* 'beredt' — nicht deutsch *flappen* 'klappen' ist zu vergleichen, sondern das die Thätigkeit der Lippen bezeichnende *plappern*, *schlabbern* und *flappe* 'herabhängende Unterlippe'. *Lec'h* s. 'Steinplatte' = ir. *lecc* — hierzu ist das nir. *leg logmar* zu stellen; aber arm. *liac'h* ist ir. *lia*, gen. *liacc*. *Lies* 'mehrere' ist w. *lliaws*, das mit ir. *lia* 'mehr' zusammengesetzt sein mag, sowie albanogäl. *liuth liuthad* aus *lia-uathad*.

Maga 'nähren', w. *magu*, findet sich auch im Gälischen, ir. *tormach* 'auctio'. *Mab lagad* 'Pupille' (w. *mab lygad* 'Augapfel', D. G. 73, 29) entspricht dem ir. *mac imlesen*, und, wenn man vergleichen will, dem gr. *κόρη*, hebr. *ĭšŏn*, arab. *insān al-ʿain* 'das Augenmännlein', etc. *Marth* 'Wunder', w. *gwyrth* = ir. *firt* (virtus); *médi* 'ernten', w. *medi*, ist erhalten im ir. *methil* 'Schnitter' = w. *medel*; *mell* 'Wirbelbein' = ir. *mell*; *mézô* 'trunken' = ir. *medb*; *miz* 'Schüssel' = w. *mwys* = ir. *mias* (mensa).

Oabl 'Himmel', w. *wybr*, ist möglicherweise das ir. *eochair, ochair* 'Rand', d. i. der Horizont. *Or* 'Rand' ist ir. *or*, dat. *ur*. *Ozac'h* 'Gatte' kann nicht das ir. *aithech* sein, da kein Buchstabe ordnungsmässig entspricht; vielleicht ist das Wort mit ir. *aite* 'Pflegevater' oder besser noch mit ir. *óitiu* 'Jugend' verwandt.

Pâd 'Dauer' von lat. *pati* ist eine Etymologie, die kaum viel Zustimmung finden wird; mir ist wahrscheinlicher, dass *pâd* mit w. *peidio* 'abstehen, aufhören' zum ir. *caitheamh* 'verbrauchen, brauchen' zu stellen ist; es würde etwa die Bedeutung 'erledigen, zu Ende führen' zu Grunde liegen. *Piaoua* 'besitzen' von w. *pieu* 'cuius est'; *piden* f. 'phallus', cf. gael. *pit* 'cunnus' (Mackenzie, Beauties 133 b; Inv. 21, 221, 4; s. Armstrong); *poaz* 'coctus', cf. ir. *cuchtair* 'coquina', und *pober* 'Bäcker' = ir. *cocaire* 'Koch'. *Poul'chen* f. 'Docht' kommt kaum von ir. *cuilc* 'Schilf', sondern von *cuirce* 'Knoten', wovon das albanogäl. *cuircinn* 'head-dress' abgeleitet ist.

Rât f. 'Gedanke' kommt nicht von ir. *raith* 'cucurrit', sondern scheint mit dem ir. *rád* 'Rede' zusammenzuhängen. *Roué* 'König' ist w. *rhwyf* und vermutlich ein Superlativ, ob von ir. *rí*, w. *rhi*, gall. *rix*, ist sehr fraglich, und ein ir. *riam* in ähnlicher Bedeutung (Gorman p. 287) ist auch nicht ganz sicher. Vielleicht ist das Wort von ir. *ré n-*, *rem-* *rom-* abzuleiten, gleichbedeutend mit πρό (ir. *ro*), also gewissermassen = πρῶτος, vgl. ir. *ro-duine* 'Edelmann'; dann würde mir. *remain* 'preeminent' das arm. fem. *rouanez* 'Königin' erklären.

Skarr 'Spalte', vgl. ir. *escair*, w. *esgair* 'a ridge'. *Skarza* ist nicht von einer Wurzel *skarto*, sondern von *karto* abzuleiten (KZ. 36, 454).

Tað 'Schweigen', w. *taw*; vgl. ir. *tóaim* 'ich schweige'. *Téôd* 'Zunge', w. *tafawd*, ist von ir. *tenge* f. kaum zu trennen, da der Übergang des *ng* in die Labialis häufiger vorkommt, wie w. *cafell* 'Kanzel' neben *cangell* (cf. CZ. 2, 576). *Teûz* 'Gespenst' hält Le Gonidec für dasselbe wie *teûz* 'Schmelzung' (w. *tawdd*); es ist aber die Frage, ob es nicht dem ir. *taidbse*, *taibhse* 'Erscheinung' zu vergleichen ist.

Das Wort *tonn* 'Welle', das den celtischen Sprachen eigentümlich zu sein scheint und mit lat. *tundere* zusammengestellt wird, gewährt mir die Gelegenheit zu noch einer Bemerkung. Die älteste celtische Form scheint *tonn* zu sein, nicht *tond*, und es fragt sich, ob sie nicht doch deutsche Verwandte habe. In einem in einer Handschrift des 15. Jahrh. (cod. Berol. germ. oct. 210) mit den Singnoten aufbewahrten Liede heisst die letzte Strophe (die Werke über das deutsche Kirchenlied, H. Hoffmann p. 321 und Ph. Wackernagel 2, 694, haben sie nicht ganz richtig):

> Pistu auch guetig vnd diemuetig
> o mueter sey vnß indechtig
> vnd in des lebens tûnnē swer
> vns mit deinem fursprechen gewer.

Das ist die Übersetzung der lat. letzten Strophe eines in derselben Handschrift stehenden Hymnus an Maria Magdalena, beginnend 'Lauda, mater ecclesia, lauda Cristi clementiam' (Daniel 1, 221); sie gehört aber eigentlich zu einem anderen Hymnus 'Aeterni patris unice' (Daniel 1, 287):

> Pia mater et humilis
> nature memor fragilis
> in huius vite fluctibus
> nos rege tuis precibus.

Offenbar bedeutet also dieses *tûnne* (ein Wort, das die Wörterbücher nicht verzeichnen) 'fluctus', Welle. Vielleicht davon abgeleitet ist *dünnung, dünung*, womit der niedersächsische Seemann die Wellen gegen die Windrichtung bezeichnet; dies Wort ist als *dyning* ins Schwedische und Norwegische, als *dønning* ins Dänische übergegangen und wird auf ein friesisches *dinen, thinen* 'schwellen' zurückgeführt. Dass das hochdeutsche *tûnne* mit *düne* zusammenhänge, scheint das ahd. *dûn* 'promontorium' auszuschliessen. Die Verwandtschaft mit dem celtischen *tonn* scheint einiges für sich zu haben, namentlich wenn man *dünne* als die richtige hochdeutsche Form annehmen dürfte; denn dem celtischen

t entspricht sonst hochdeutsches *d*, niederdeutsches *th*, wie in *tú* : *ti*
du : thou; *trí* : *tri* drei : three; *treb* : *tref* dorf : thorp; *tiug* : *teo* dick
: thick; *tuige* : *to* decken : thatch; *tana* : *teneu* dünn : thin; *tart* durst
: thirst; *tuath* : *tud* deutsch; etc.   Aber es kommen Ausnahmen vor,
wie w. *tawdd* = tauen : thaw; u. a.

A. C. L. Brown, The Round Table before Wace.   Boston, Ginn
& Co. 1900.   (Reprinted from vol. VII of Studies and Notes
in Philology and Literature, p. 183—205.)

Über Arthurs Tafelrunde, die zuerst in Waces Roman de Brut
erwähnt wird (la Roonde Table), fügt Layamon um 1200 n. Chr. seiner
Nachbildung eine Erzählung ein, wonach, infolge eines blutigen Streites,
ein Handwerker in Cornwall dem Könige eine runde Tafel gezimmert
haben soll, so gross, dass alle seine Ritter friedlich darum sitzen konnten.
Davon schweigen die welschen Romanciers. Aber nach der Annahme
des Verf., der die Beschreibung irischer Gelage vergleicht, wäre die Tafelrunde eine gemeinceltische Institution gewesen und Layamon hätte sich
auf welsche Darstellungen stützen können, die verloren gegangen seien.

Joh. Ad. Bruun, An Enquiry into the Art of the illuminated
Manuscripts of the Middle ages.   Part I.   Celtic illuminated
Manuscripts.   Stockholm 1897.   (Leipzig, A. Twietmeyer.)
XIV + 87 pp. fol. with 10 plates.   (12,50 M.)

Wem die voluminosen und kostbaren Monumentalwerke, die die
graphische Kunst der Iren im frühen Mittelalter behandeln, nicht erreichbar oder nur schwer zugänglich sind, der wird ein kleines Pracht-
werk willkommen heissen, das das Wissenswerteste darüber in bequemer
und gefälliger Weise vereinigt. Durch recht vollständige Benutzung
der Litteratur wird es zu einer empfehlenswerten Einleitung in den
Gegenstand überhaupt. Die Aufzählung der irischen Prachthandschriften,
die in Frage kommen, lässt sich allerdings noch vervollständigen. So
vermisse ich, suche auch seine Erwähnung in den übrigen neueren
Schriften über die irische Vulgata vergebens, den jetzt in Berlin befindlichen Psalmenkodex aus der Hamiltonschen Bibliothek Nr. 553, über
über den ich deshalb einige Zeilen einfüge. Es ist ein Foliant von
von 64 Blättern, 34 cm hoch und 14 cm breit, ungerechnet was dem
Messer des englischen Buchbinders zum Opfer gefallen ist. Die Handschrift enthält die Psalmen und Cantica und wird auf einem vorgehefteten
Blatte mit den Worten bezeichnet: 'Psalterium S^ae Salabergæ fundatricis
et 1^ae abbatissae huius Monasterii St Joannis Laudunensis; haec meritis
et virtutibus plena obiit anno a natiuitate Christi 655. Hoc psalterium
pene obsoletum in meliorem formam restitutum est, anno 1685.' Diese
Angabe, die den Kodex mit der Gründerin des Klosters in Laon zusammenbringt, beruht auf einer frommen Legende, denn der Psalter ist ein
opus scoticum, den Kellser Evangelien nahe verwandt. Zwar ist er
nicht so reich wie diese und ohne allen figürlichen Schmuck, aber doch
eines der grossartigsten Denkmäler der irischen Halbunciale. Mabillon
hat ihn beachtet (de re diplomatica 1789 p. 375) und nach diesem hat

O'Conor der Enkel ein Pröbchen der Schrift wiederholt (Scriptores veteres 1, p. CCXIX). Es liegen in den Bibliotheken noch manche wenig bekannte Codices derselben Art oder Fragmente aus solchen; hier sei nur an die Maihinger Evangelien erinnert, die uns Wattenbach beschrieben hat (RC. 1, 27).

Welche Bedeutung der gemischte Text dieser irischen Handschriften für die Kritik der Vulgata hat, ist eine Frage für sich. Ihre künstlerische Ausführung können wir recht nur würdigen, wenn wir wissen, welcher Zeit sie angehören. Durch eine einzige Zeile der Aufklärung hierüber wären uns solche Manuskripte fast unschätzbar geworden, aber die weltvergessenen Schreiber haben sie nicht gegeben, und so ragen diese Kunstwerke stumm und wunderbar wie die Rundtürme aus dem Altertume der irischen Kirche hervor.

Nach der Sage gehören die in Rede stehenden Denkmäler der Schrift dem 6. und 7. Jahrh. an, der Blütezeit der Halbunciale. Eine kritische Prüfung hält diese überlieferte Zeitbestimmung freilich nicht aus. Die festen Punkte, die man in der schwierigen Chronologie dieser Schriftgattung hat, sind der Hilarius im Vatikan vom Jahre 510 (Palaeogr. Soc. 1, 136) und der Veroneser Kodex des Sulpicius Severus vom Jahre 517 (Monum. palaeogr. sacra, Torino 1899, pl. IV) und dann das Antiphonarium von Bangor, das durch die Jahre 680 — 697 begrenzt ist. Auch das Buch von Armagh aus dem Anfange des 9. Jahrh. muss als ein altes datierbares Beispiel der irischen Cursive genannt werden. Mit diesem geringen Werkzeug ausgerüstet vermögen wir eines wenigstens mit Sicherheit zu erkennen: es giebt keine irischen Handschriften, die an das Alter des Hilarius und des Sulpicius hinanreichen. Das Antiphonar ist wirklich einer der ältesten irischen Codices; doch scheint ihm der Codex Usserianus prior kaum etwas nachzugeben, und ebenso ist der Cathach sehr alt.

Auch in Hinsicht der eigentlichen Prachthandschriften neigt sich die neuere Forschung, ohne Zweifel mit Grund, der Meinung zu, dass sie dem 6. und 7. Jahrh. kaum angehören können. Die Halbunciale wurde für liturgische Bücher noch immer gebraucht, als in anderen die Cursive schon allgemein üblich war. Dieser hochberühmte Domhnachairgid scheint, schon wegen seiner Compendia scribendi (TRIA. 30, 309), mindestens drei Jahrhunderte jünger zu sein als die Zeit des heiligen Patricius, mit der ihn die Sage verbindet. Auch die Durrower und die Kellser Evangelien und das Psalterium der h. Salaberga, mit der bunten Ornamentik ihrer Initialen, den eigenartigen Umrahmungen mit roten Punkten, den gerundeten Formen für die Buchstaben *d*, *g*, *q*, *r*, *s*, gehören zuversichtlich einer späteren Zeit an als das Antiphonarium von Bangor. Sie stehen einigen Proben halbuncialer Schrift im Buche von Armagh nahe; ja, sie erinnern an den Durhamer Liber vitae (Paleogr. Soc. 1, 238), der um das Jahr 840 geschrieben wurde. Dem Psalterium der h. Salaberga ist auf dem ersten Blatte das Nicaenum beigegeben mit jenem wichtigen *et filio*, das zuerst auf dem 3. Konzile von Toledo 589 eingeschaltet sein soll, in Wirklichkeit aber erst mehrere Jahrhunderte später in den Text der Kirche aufgenommen wurde (J. F. Müller, Die symbolischen Bücher p. XLIX). Nur gehe man nicht zu weit! Jene charakteristischen drei Schlusspunkte des Antiphonars finden sich in dem Psalterium ganz ebenso, und in dem Kellser Buche ähnlich. Vom Liber Hymnorum im Trinity College scheinen die Prachthandschriften der Evangelien und des Psalters immer noch durch einen weiten Zwischenraum getrennt zu sein.

Wenn man so nach langer und aufmerksamer Betrachtung der Schriftzüge im Chronologischen noch schwankend und unschlüssig bleibt, so wünscht man, es möchte sich der Kunstgelehrte der Frage bemächtigen, vielleicht dass sich durch das Studium der Ornamente, der verschlungenen Linien und der Muster, des Rankenwerks, der Farbengegensätze, des Stiles der Figuren und so fort zu bestimmteren Ergebnissen gelangen lässt. Zu einer solchen Behandlung des Gegenstandes hat Bruun einen nützlichen Beitrag geliefert; in mancher Beziehung wird sich die Forschung noch vertiefen lassen. Indem der Verfasser das geometrische, zoomorphische, phyllomorphische Ornament und die unvollkommene Figurendarstellung in den irischen Handschriften bis ins 12. Jahrh. bespricht, hebt er hervor, dass diese Kunst der Iren sogleich fertig ausgebildet auftritt, dass man ihre Anfänge nicht nachweisen und ihre allmähliche Entwickelung nicht verfolgen kann. Da drängt sich denn doch die Frage auf, die der Verfasser kaum gestellt hat: Ist diese Kunst der Schriftornamentik in Irland einheimisch? kann man ihren Ursprung in einer fremden noch erkennen? Es scheint, man müsse den Umkreis der Untersuchung sehr weit ausdehnen. Irre ich nicht, so ist das zoomorphische Element darin von einiger Wichtigkeit, und schon die Darstellung der Evangelisten unter der Gestalt der symbolischen Tiere weist in den fernen Osten. Als Wladimir Stassoff ehemals seine Materialien über die slawische und orientalische Schriftornamentik sammelte, konnte man seine Aufmerksamkeit auf die alten koptischen Pergamenthandschriften in Rom und Neapel lenken. Was er in ihnen fand, übertraf seine Erwartungen, namentlich die Tierpaare in symmetrischer Anordnung, die zu Vögelleibern ausgebildeten grossen Buchstaben, die geflügelten Vierfüssler und andere Wundertiere, wovon er dann manches in seinem 1887 vollendeten, mit kaiserlicher Munificenz ausgestatteten Werke vorgelegt hat. Lässt sich auch die irische Kunst mit der byzantinischen verbinden? lässt sich einzelnes sogar vielleicht bis an die Ufer des Nils verfolgen? Nur die allgemeine Geschichte der Kunst des Mittelalters vermag auf solche Fragen eine befriedigende Antwort zu geben.   St.

Corrigendum.

Zeitschrift III, 195, Zeile 29: Der Name Finan q. ist nach Wh. Stokes *Finan* q (q mit Querstrich) geschrieben, d. h. *Finán quam* oder *camm* (vgl. Gorman p. 363).

Druck von Ehrhardt Karras, Halle a. S.

MITTEILUNGEN
AUS IRISCHEN HANDSCHRIFTEN.

Aus Harleian 5280.

(Fortsetzung.)

Das Apgitir Orábaid des Colmán maccu Béognae.

Die Handschriften, in denen uns dieser altirische, wohl noch dem 8. Jahrhundert angehörige, spätestens aber aus dem Anfang des 9. Jahrhunderts stammende Text erhalten ist, habe ich Ztschr. I, S. 496 aufgezählt. Seitdem ist er von T. Hudson Williams im ersten Hefte der Modern Language Notes, SS. 29—31, besprochen und teilweise herausgegeben worden. Ich drucke ihn hier vollständig mit den wichtigsten Varianten von Rawl. B. 512 (R) sowie einigen aus dem Gelben Buch von Lecan (L) und der Handschrift $\frac{23}{P.\ 3}$ (P) ab.

[fo. 39b] Inncipiunt verba Colmani fili Beognae uiri Dei
.i. Aipgitir[1]) Crābaid.

1. Hiris co ngnīm, acobur co feidli, feťhiumla col-lēri, costud[2]) co n-umlai, áini co n-innmus, bochta co n-eslabra, tva co comlabra, fodail[3]) co cosmali, fofitiu cen indiri,[4]) apstanit co 5 focħraibi, hēt cen aggairbi, cennsa co fírindi, toirsiv cin esliss,[5]) omon cen dercōined, bochta cen dīvmus, fóisitiu cen hurcuitmiud,[6]) forcetal co comalnad, drēim cin tairinned, hīssel fri hard,

---

¹) in *add. R.*   ²) castóth *R.*   ³) *sic R.* fogail *H.*
⁴) iniri *R.*   ⁵) eisleis *R.*   ⁶) erchoitmed *R.*

sleman *fri* garb, gnīm cen fodord, semplæ co trebairi, hvmoldōid
cen *con*naircli,[1]) cressine cen tsecd*h*ai.[2]) Inna hīssiv hvili con-
gaibtiur ann-etlai.

2. Ess ann is[3]) etoil duiniv, an tan is[3]) lān dērcæ,[4]) imthēd
5 co ndēirc, adnais[5]) cech n-olc, cartha cech maith. Is airmidiv
dō for talom,[6]) is indōcbāil for nim. Car Diaa, cechdat[7]) cắch.
Agh*us*[8]) Dia, atutaighfedur[9]) cắch.

3. Ess ē *tra* costad na clērci*ch*tæ[10]) 7 es hī an[11]) lēri mes-
ruight[h]i in[11]) so īer nDīa. Antī fodgiguil 7 nadcomalna-
10 bhat*h*ar,[12]) rombīad[13]) cēddīablai talmon,[14]) rombīaa flaith
nimhe.[15])

4. Ba aslvinti 7 ba gesse do *gach* dvini Coimdi nime 7
talmon im comaltaa a omno[16]) 7 a sercæ ina c[h]ridi, ar is a
n-ailtes[17]) biid duini *con*duidched[18]) hom*on* Dē ina c[h]ridi.

15 5. Cēn b*us* meirb an t-oman, bid meirb an athrigi.[19]) Cēn
b*us* me[i]rbh[20]) in aithrigi, *bid* me[i]rbh[21]) an cressini. Ar lasnā
bī[22]) oman Dē, nī bīa a serc, lasnā bīa a serc, nī bīa comalnad
a timno, lasnā bīa comalnad a timna, nī mbīa betha[23]) for nim.
Ar techtaid an t-oman s*eirc*, techtaid indt[24]) seirc gnīm n-etoil,
20 techt*aid* a[25]) ngnīm n-et*oil* bithbet[h]aid for nim.

6. S*erc* Dē bī fonigh anmoin, sāsaid[26]) menmain, doformaig
foc[h]ruic,[27]) inarben analchi,[28]) arcorbi talm*ain*: fonigh, conrig,
coicli.[29])

7. Ced doghnī s*erc* Dē fri duiniv?[30]) Marb*aid* a tholai,[31])
25 glanaid a cridi, cotnōi, longaid a analchæ, doslī foc*h*raigi,[32])
arcuiredur[33]) sắegal, fonig anmoin.

---

[1]) condarchelli *R*.	[2]) tsechta *R*.	[3]) as *R*.
[4]) dearcæ *R*.	[5]) atnas *R*.	[6]) talmain *RL*.
[7]) cechdut *R*. caur Die cechtat *L*.		[8]) [ag]ais *R*. aghais *L*.
[9]) adagaidfider *R*.	[10]) ina cleirchechtai *R*.	
[11]) ind *RL*.	[12]) nodcomalnabar *R*.	
[13]) rambiet *L* (*sic leg.*). rombia *R*.		
[14]) i talmain 7 *R*. i dtalm*ain L*.		
[15]) gan foircend *add. L*.		
[16]) im comalln*ad* a timna *L*. im tomaltad a omna *R* (*sic leg.*).		
[17]) i n-ailtes *RL*.	[18]) conduidchet a *R*.	[19]) athridi *H*.
[20]) cein bes meirb *R*.		[21]) meirb *R*.
[22]) bia *R* (*sic leg.*).	[23]) ni bi bithbeutha *L*. ni bia betha *R*.	
[24]) *om. R*.	[25]) *om. R*.	[26]) sāsaith *R*.
[27]) fochraicce *RL*.	[28]) innarben analcha .i. dobesa *R*.	
[29]) coiclea *R*.	[30]) dúine *R*.	[31]) tola *R*.
[32]) fochrauici *R*.	[33]) arcuirethar *L*.	

8. Cet[h]eoir īce na hanmo: hom*un* 7 at[h]*rige*, s*erc* 7 fre[s]cse.[1]) A dī dīp cotoat[2]) *for* talmain,[3]) a dī aili foslūatur *for* nem*h*. An t-oman *fr*isīada inna pect*h*a arabīat, a*nn* athr*ige* ardolega[4]) inna pect*h*u remitīagaid.[5]) S*erc* in dūilivm*an* 7 frescsiv a [*f*]latho,[6]) it ē fotalūatar[7]) *for* nem. Nac[h] duine 5 'diu adāigfedur Dīa 7 nodcechr*ae*ar[8]) · 7 comallnabat*har*[9]) a *th*ail[10]) 7 a t[h]imna, b*id* airmidiv[11]) dō fīad dōinib hisíu,[12]) b*id* findfaduch[13]) dō la Dīa hi[14]) tall.

De his q*uae* debet ho*mo* discere.

9. Ced as fogailse[15]) do duini? .i. foss oc etlai, anbata[16]) 10 brīat*har*, brāt*h*irse n-āilgen, ascaid la rēde, rīagol do comalnad cen erchoiltiu, ērgi la cētrēr,[17]) cēim n-erlatad[18]) ar Dīa, dīlgad fūaraigi, forr*u*mai lob*ar*,[19]) lēri hirnaig*ht*hi, āine co comaltai, coicsed *fr*i comnessam, airindiud dīum*u*sa, diūiti ō c*ri*diu, combach tuili, trōithad acn*id*, anmne *fr*i foch*ai*di. Ced*h* dongnī friut in 15 sen? NĪ *anse*. Togairmm co sruit*h*i, svìdi n-er*u*sa,[20]) māin ō neuch nātomnaitiur,[21]) airitiu cen cosnom, cēddīablui ili, a cairti[22]) la brāit[h]ri, bit*h*bet[h]a *for* nim.

10. Ced is imgabt[h]ai[23]) do duine ettail? NĪ *anse*. Hiru-gadh[24]) minic, mōrthai[25]) [fo. 40a] cen dān cen fol*ad*,[26]) dīscri 20 *fr*i haircindiuch,[27]) mailli *fr*i cloc, coicne *fr*i hantestai, imbet*h*[28]) forlūamno, fāitbi brīat*har*,[29]) brīat*hr*a inglano, aggairbiu tait*h*iscc,[30]) toirisem[31]) *fr*i secnabaid, sīthugud[32]) *fr*i cūrsachat[h], comoirb[33]) do manc*h*oib, mence cestaicht[h]i. Ced dognī frit inn

---

<table>
<tr><td>[1]) freiscsiu R.</td><td>[2]) cotaot R.</td><td>[3]) talam R.</td></tr>
<tr><td>[4]) ind aithirigi dolega R.</td><td></td><td>[5]) pectha remitiagat R.</td></tr>
<tr><td>[6]) flatha R.</td><td>[7]) fodaluatar R.</td><td>[8]) nodcechra R (sic leg.).</td></tr>
<tr><td>[9]) comalnabthar R.</td><td>[10]) thoil R.</td><td>[11]) airmidech R.</td></tr>
<tr><td>[12]) om. R.</td><td>[13]) findbodhach R</td><td>[14]) om. R.</td></tr>
<tr><td>[15]) fodailsi R. lenta P.</td><td></td><td></td></tr>
<tr><td>[16]) anbatu R. enbatu P. enfaitiu Lism. L. 4541.</td><td></td><td></td></tr>
<tr><td>[17]) cétrair R. cétbreith*ir* P. Lism.</td><td></td><td></td></tr>
<tr><td>[18]) cet i*nn*erlatad R.</td><td></td><td>[19]) lobair R.</td></tr>
<tr><td>[20]) suide n-erasa R.</td><td>[21]) natomainter R.</td><td>[22]) cairde R.</td></tr>
<tr><td>[23]) ingabtha P.</td><td>[24]) irugad R. fergug*ud P. Lism. Lives 4536.</td><td></td></tr>
<tr><td>[25]) mordhata P.</td><td>[26]) *f*olad .i. cen i*nm*e R. folaid P.</td><td></td></tr>
<tr><td>[27]) discere *fr*i *sen*oire P. senoir Lism.</td><td></td><td>[28]) imad P.</td></tr>
<tr><td>[29]) fáitbe mbraithre R (sic leg.).</td><td></td><td>[30]) tathaisc R.</td></tr>
<tr><td>[31]) toisa*m R.</td><td>[32]) sidhe P.</td><td>[33]) comarb RP.</td></tr>
</table>

30*

sen?[1]) Ni *anse.* Terba fri *sruithi,* monor cen oircess*acht,* lombo
foic[h]l*idi,*[2]) frit[h]airi ō dōinib, ōini cen lūag, airērg*hi* i ndorc*ho,*[3])
dubad ērlama, daiffenn[4]) im nem.

    11. Is dūal[5]) dūn mani[6]) torgōet*hat* in[na][7]) dūailc[h]i hi
5 fail na sūalc[h]e, ar robi togætha: laxe hi fail trōcoiri, mūcnato
hi fail fīrindi, anumolōiti[8]) hi fail dīrgi, homon anetoil cen dītiun
fīrindi, cen fovac*crae,* clōini a fail hvma*lō*iti, nēvit 7 caillti a
fail inm*u*sa, dīum*us* a fail gensa, hūaill a fail apstanit,[9])
malairtc[h]i 7 cait*h*midi[10]) a fail eslabra, fercc nemmesraig*ht*[h]i
10 a fail eōid spirtaidie, rotimme 7 balomlæ[11]) a fail fēthivmlæ,
dūiri 7 glici a fail cobsaidi, cr*i*nner 7 forlūam*ain*[12]) hi fa*il*
áine,[13]) rocholl 7 nemc*u*msanc*hi*[14]) a fail leubra, lescoi 7 dēes a
fail dīlmaine, rom*h*oildi a fail coma*r*li.

    12. Antī bīas a n-ænta[15]) na *h*ecailse catlaice 7 a ndēes
15 ina frescsen nemda 7 comalnab*h*at*h*ar na timno am*ail* donim-
marnad,[16]) rombīad[17]) cēddíablai a tal*main* 7 rombīa bithbethai
for nim.

              De peritia ueritatis.

    13. Mā beith neuch adcobra in fīrinne, is dūal[18]) dō robē
20 d'eol*us* les inna tēchtai, ced dodaceil, ce[d] dodafoillsegor.[19])
D*u*scel in fīrindi ar cāc*h* cotanessa, n*u*sfoillsigedúr[20]) do cāc*h*
nodocomallnat*h*ar[21]) fīrindie.[22])

    14. A cet*h*air fortugat[h]ur[23]) i*n* fīrindi .i. ser*c* 7 hom*un,*
connarcli 7 ad*h*oilcne. Cēn b*us* anfiriēn an dvine, nī c*u*maing
25 forūac*rae* fīrinnde inna tēchta.

    15. A tr*ī* donairt[h]et[24]) occo: hūaill[25]) 7 dīm*us* 7 ferc. Mā
rosoa nec*h* rīam*h* dodī*u*sgai hūaill dō, mā frit*h*mbeuræ dodūsce[26])

---

[1]) *uili add. R.*
[2]) lumba bfoichle *R.*
[3]) airerge ndorchai *R.*
[4]) daithfenn *R.*
[5]) duail *R.*
[6]) mina *R.*
[7]) inna *R.*
[8]) anumaldoit *R.*
[9]) apstainete *R.*
[10]) *Lies* caithmige (*R*).
[11]) balamna *R.*
[12]) fortluaman *R.*
[13]) áne *R.*
[14]) nemcumsantache *R.*
[15]) aontoigh *L.*
[16]) donimarnada *R.*
[17]) rombiat *R* (*sic leg.*).
[18]) duail *R.*
[19]) ced dodafaillsigader *R.* ceudh do foaillsigh *L.*
[20]) *Lies* nusfoillsigedar. nosfaillsigh *L.*
[21]) nodacomalnadar *R* (*sic leg.*).
[22]) *om. R* (*sic leg.*). [23]) fortugadar *R.* fouradtughathar *L.*
[24]) dodnairthet *R* (*sic leg.*). [25]) huall *R.*
[26]) dodiúscai *R.*

ferc 7 dīumus dō, ar id¹) sochaide atā²) étaidi immin fīrindi, acht at ferclaindig³) occo ingi catha ūaiti.

16. A dō ata foimdi⁴) oc éot fīrinne .i. ferc 7 altes, ar is léniud don fīrinde cebē de dotecmo⁵) dī. Air ét inna fīrinne is dūal⁶) inromastar a tēchta: ét cen ferg,⁷) humaldōid cin esliss 5 fīrinde cecruth a fōcairthi la humalōid cen connarclie, ar nī condarcol anfīrinde in homol cammaif. Nī bī fīriēn⁸) nā bī fīrhumol, nī bī fīrecnæ nā bī fīriōn. Air in fīrecno nī rogainn la hanfīrindi an duini, ar is tiug an fīal fīl etorrai, ar is nessa comruc fri hecnai fīrindi 'nās fri fīrinne ecna. Ar is ann is 10 fīrecnæ duine ōr'bī fīriān, co epri fīrindi cen tserbæ cen connarcli⁹) la hanmhnet,¹⁰) la hālgine. Innmus 7 ecna 7 fīretla is himmalle rodosaig¹¹) dvine. Cvin rodosaigh¹²) duine? Intan is ndīlacht a fīrinde. Cuin is¹³) ndīlocht a fīrinde? An taun mbīs a cridhe ina tēchta, is ann is fīrinde hissvidiv, amail nī¹⁴) 15 roichned ō duini.

De uirtutibus animæ incipit.

17. Cōic nert dēac inna hanmo .i. nert n-iresi, nert cennsa, nert hvmoldōiti, neurt n-ainmnet,¹⁵) nert marbtha,¹⁶) neurt n-erlatad, nert cartōid, nert [fo. 40b] fīrindi, nert trōcairi, nert 20 n-eslabra, nert fūarrigi, nert comalti, nert n-inmusæ, nert n-etlai, nert ndēarcai. Na neurt derōne duine di sunt lelaill, digeba a promad a tein, duforma ērlam¹⁷) for nim.

18. Cuin is¹⁸) tūalaing duine rob test¹⁹) for anmonnaib alanaili? Ō robo²⁰) test²¹) for a anmain fadesin indúss. Cuin 25 is²²) tūalaing coisc alanali? Ō chanasca²³) fadesin induus. Duine dosūi²⁴) a anmain fadesin do betha, cē mēd²⁵) anmain doróa fath,²⁶) dōine an domain uili acht²⁷) bidis soc[h]oisce, dodosūifed²⁸) do bethæ comdis flatha nime. In doc[h]osci fadesin²⁹) 7 a n-olc

---

¹) it R.	²) at R.	³) fearglainig R.
⁴) ada foimde R.	⁵) cipe dodecmæ R.	⁶) duail R.
⁷) feirg R.	⁸) firion R.	⁹) condarcilli R.
¹⁰) ainmnit R.	¹¹) rosaigh R.	¹²) rodasaig R.
¹³) as R.	¹⁴) na L.	¹⁵) ainmnit R.
¹⁶) marbtadh R.	¹⁷) dofoirma erlama R.	
¹⁸) as R.	¹⁹) teist R.	²⁰) o rop R. ourob L.
²¹) teist R.	²²) as R.	²³) o cutnasca R.
²⁴) dusói R.	²⁵) mét R. meud L.	²⁶) doroaffath R.
²⁷) om. R.	²⁸) dodasuifed R (sic leg.).	
²⁹) a ndochoisci R (sic leg.).		

7 a n-vallbe[1]) ad*h*arba*n* sech flai*th* Dĕ. Corp *co*nōi anmain, ainim *co*nōi menmoin, menmo conōi *c*ridi, cride conōi iris, hiris conōi Dīa, Dīa conōi dvíne. Am*ail* difuarcoib[2]) lōc[h]rann a soillse a tegdois dorc[h]a, is amlaid dofvarcaib[2]) ind fīrindi a
5 medōn inna hirisse a *c*ridi duine. Cet[h]air dorc[h]a adarban *as*[3]) a ndofvarc*aib*[4]) and: dorc[h]a ngendtlechta, dorc[h]a n-anuis,[5]) dorc[h]a n-amarise,[6]) dorc[h]o pect[h]a *co* nā rogainn nach æ[7]) ann.

19. Trīar ditēt do *ch*resene. Oenne[8]) biid inde, alali bīd ocai, alaili bīd etercēn[9]) ūadi. Nī cuma im*murgu*. Is ferr dondi
10 mbīs[10]) inde oldās dondī bīs occai. Es[11]) ferr dondī bīs oco oltās dondī bīs etircēin ūaide. Iss ē antī bīs inde antī isren[12]) hi cech lait*h*i[13]) a trēdi aran-ëta bet[h]aid a anmo .i. nac*h* fō rocólæ[14]) 7 nach[15]) mait*h* atcondairc rocar 7 rocreti 7 rocomal- nu*star*. Iss ē intī bīs oco .i. antī dosloinde an bit[h] ō bēlaib
15 7 foiset*h*ar[16]) inna cridi, fritidir[17]) frie hāine 7 ernaict*h*i, nī rodlom dorair do saint 7 cailti, alalām do dorm(?), alaili do talam. Ess ē antī bīs etircén[18]) ūadi, antī *forcomh* cresene[19]) 7 nī dēne a mbēsa assa feib a *sæg*ail a fod. Anda less bud[20]) assad[21]) dēnum nac*h* rāt*h*i[22]) alaili.

20 20. Trī nāmaid anmo: doman 7 dīabu*l* 7 forcetl*aid*[23]) anetail. Trēidi inarben[24]) spir*ut* forlūamnai[25]) 7 dognīat mens fossad: frit*h*airi 7 ernaigthi 7 leubar.[26]) Cet*h*ir solaig crābaid .i. anmne *fri* cech n-acobar, fūarighi *fri* cec*h* n-ancride, dīghdi cech[27]) dīubarta, dīlgadh cecha torccabāla. Cet[h]oir brīat*h*ra
25 arindruirfimmis man*u*scomalnamais .i. lēiri fri Dīa, rēdi fri duine, cōendūt[h]racht da gach ænduini, foimdiu ēcco cech ænlat*h*i.

21. Cet[h]arda nā[28]) contecmoing do neuch car*as* Dīa .i. nī fuirsed*h*or,[29]) nī fāt*h*gat[h]ar,[30]) nī ben ēcnach,[31]) nī mītom-
30 nadar ō neoch. Mait[h] seom la cāch, mait[h] cāch lais-sem.

---

[1]) naillbæ *R*.	[2]) dofurgaib *R*.	[3]) adarfan as *R*.
[4]) indufurgaib *R*.	[5]) ánuis *R*, *lies* anfiss.	
[6]) aimirse *R*.	[7]) na hé *R*.	[8]) oenni *R*.
[9]) etirchein *R*.	[10]) *om*. *R*.	[11]) as *R*.
[12]) asren *R*.	[13]) aenlaithe *R*.	[14]) na forrochualai *R*.
[15]) na *R*.	[16]) faisidar *R*.	[17]) frigidir *R*.
[18]) etirchein *R*.	[19]) cresenu *R*.	[20]) i fod anda leis *R*.
[21]) bid assu *R* (*sic leg*.).		[22]) raithe *R*.
[23]) forcetal *R*.	[24]) innarban *R*.	[25]) fortluamnæ *R*.
[26]) leabair *R*.	[27]) gacha *R*.	[28]) nad *R*.
[29]) fuirsedar *R*.	[30]) fathguatar *R*.	[31]) ecndach *R* (*sic leg*.).

22. Cet[h]oir[1] trebairi na mac mbethadh .i. credbad ina tol, oman inna pīan, serc inna fochaidhe, cretium inna foc[h]raice. Mani credbatis inna tola, nī lēcfitis; mani āgitis inna pīana, nī fomnibtis;[2] mani cartais na foc[h]aide, nī fodhēmtis; mani credis na foc[h]raice, nī ricfitis.

23. Cet[h]air glais ina pect[h]ach .i. īadhad a sūili frisan [n]doman,[3] īadat[h] talmon for a corpaib, īadut[h] flatha nimi fria a n-anmonnaib, īadad ifirnn for a[4] suidhib.

24. Cet[h]air dingi [fo. 41a] inna pect[h]uch .i. ding dōib nāt[5] fācbat a tolæ, ding nā tiasat hi[6] pīana, ding cen aithrigi[7] n-īar n-usa,[8] ding cen atriub[9] ina flatha dōivh.

25. Cet[h]arda fobera fīannas do duine .i. doimairg[10] crīcha, toformaig[11] ēcruiti, etirdīben[12] sōegol, arcuiret[h]or pīanai.

26. Cet[h]arda úa roagar flaith Dē .i. foss 7 dīlmaine ōn domon, lēiri 7 feidli.

27. Cet[h]oir flathæ dvine isan centur .i. ōeti 7 soinmige,[13] slāine 7 sochraiti.

28. Cet[h]air ifirnn duine isan centur .i. galur 7 senta, bochta 7 dochraiti.

29. Trēdhi trēsmbī foidherc dīabol trī duini: trīa gnūis, trīa tōchim, trīa labrad.[14] Et per haec tria Deus per hominem intelligitur.

30. Inna teora tonna tīaghtai[15] tar duine a mbat[h]is trē fretiuch fristoing indib .i. fristoing don domun cona adbclossaib, fristoing do[16] demon cona indtledoib, fristoing do tolaib collæ. Iss ed in so imefolngi dvine dendī bes mac bāis co mbī mac bethad, dendii bes mac dorc[h]oi co mbī mac solse. Ochōn abbaing inna trī fretiuch so isna teura[17] tonnaib tiaghta[18] tairis! Mani tudchaid[19] trē drilind[20] afrithisse[21] docōi[22] i flait[h] Dē .i. lind dēr ait[h]rige, lind tofaisct[h]i folai hi pennaind, lind n-aillse hil-lebair.

---

[1] cetheoire R.	[2] foimnebdais R.	[3] frisin ndomun R.
[4] om. R.	[5] na R.	[6] tiagad a R.
[7] aitride H.	[8] Lies īar n-asu (R).	
[9] atrab R.	[10] toimaire R.	[11] doformaig R.
[12] etardiben R.	[13] soinmidi MS.	[14] labradh R.
[15] tiagdæ R.	[16] don R.	[17] teoraib R.
[18] tiagda R.	[19] tudig R.	[20] tria drilinn R.
[21] ni cumaing add. R (sic leg.).	[22] dochoi R.	

31. Cē dech do c[h]resini?[1]) Semplvi 7 diūiti. Cresini dēid dosnī ar mōrśōeth, bid mōr a promad hi tein, bid pecc a fochraic for nimh. Cresine gnīmach dosnī ar mōrdīdhnad,[2]) bed[3]) bec a promad a tein, bed[4]) mōr a foc[h]roic for nim.

5   32. Cē dech do menmain? .i. let[h]ed 7 īsliv, ar rogenn[5]) cach mait[h] for menmain lethain hísel.[6])

33. Cé messam do menmain? Cōili[7]) 7 cróidhi[8]) 7 cumce, ar nī talla nach mait[h] for menmoin cōil crūaidh cumaing.[9])

34. Tal 7 ōeti,[10]) ēc 7 sentai[11]) is ferr bied do cēin[12]) a 10 foimti.[13]) Nī gess,[14]) nī obbais, conóither do innais.[15]) Conetet nāt fūacair, forcongair nād ergair, conceil, contūasse, conpen- fidhir,[16]) conmancha.

De tribus mandatis principalibus.

35. Mā beth[17]) nech adcobra inna timno, gaibet[h][18]) inn 15 belat[19]) forsa tīagat hvili .i. gaibet[h][18]) de[i]rc 7 vmallōiti[20]) 7 ainmnet[21]) inna cridhi, ar is amlaid nī coslebad[22]) ina timno, acht bīt ūaga les vili.

De prvdentissimo homine.

36. Cīa[23]) trebairem? Antī canabeura rē mbāss a n-adais 20 īer mbās. Cain coscaid, nī coin[24]) cūrsachaid, coteraig menmo fri cūrsach,[25]) ar is hissel fri cosc. Is ferr ecno cen sūithi oltās sūithi cin ecna.

37. Cē nessam do Dīa? Antī immorādhi. Cīa frisacongnæ Crīsd? Frisantī dognī maith.

25   38. Cīa a n-aitrebæ an spirut nōeb? Isandii is glaun cen pecad. Is ann is lestar spirto[26]) nōib in duini, ō dondigsed[27]) na sūalchi tar[28]) ēsse na ndūalche. Is ann forbeir tol Dē an

[1]) cresin P.	[2]) móirdígnad R.	[3]) bidh R.
[4]) bid R.	[5]) rogeinn R.	[6]) isill R.
[7]) coile R.	[8]) croithe R.	
[9]) caoil cumaing cruaich R.		
[11]) sentu R.	[12]) bid dichein R.	[10]) oeitiu R.
[14]) geis R.	[15]) indaiss R.	[13]) foimdiu R.
[17]) beith R.	[18]) gaibeth R.	[16]) conpeinnfider R.
[20]) umaldoit R.	[21]) ainmniut R.	[19]) beleot R.
[22]) as add. R.	[24]) cain R.	[23]) choislebat R.
[26]) spiratu R.	[27]) o dodigthet R.	[25]) cursachar R.
		[28]) ara R.

dúine, an tan *sercas* an tal ndomanda.[1]) Is ferr foich*ell*amor[2])
inna cōic dāloi a ricfom[3]) .i. d*al* *fri* cneid,[4]) d*al* *fri* bās, d*al*
fri mu*intir* nDé, dāl *fri* demno, dāl *fri* hesērgi al-lait*h*iu brāt*h*æ.
Finis. Amen.

Zwiegespräch zwischen König Gúaire von Aidne   5
und seinem Bruder Marbán, dem Einsiedler.

Leider ist mir von diesem schönen Gedichte, das wohl noch
dem zehnten Jahrhundert angehört, keine zweite Handschrift
bekannt. Da ich die Absicht habe, es demnächst mit Übersetzung
herauszugeben, beschränke ich mich hier auf den einfachen Abdruck. 10

[fo. 42b]   [Gúaire.]
1 A Maru*áin*, a dīthriub*aig*,   cid nā cotla *for* colc*aid*?
   pa m*enc*i doid fess amoig,   cend[5]) doroig for lár ochtgaigh.

                    [Marbán.]
2 Nicon cotluim *for* colc*aid*   gē bethear com imslānud: 15
   atāid soch*aidi*[6]) amoig   atraicc hocim imrād*ud*.

3 Nī marutt ar comolta,   scar*ad* *fri*u nīnlūaidi:
   acht mād ōinsessior namā   nī ma[í]r nech dīouh, a Gūaire.

4 Orn*ait* *ocus* Lugna lān,   Laidgēn *ocus* Ailirān,
   atā cecht*u*rde fri dān,   Marbān *ocus* Cluit[h]nechān.   20

5 Rochluinis mo tiomna-*sa*   frie hūair tech*t*a don dom*u*n:
   mo qhūach-sa din dīt[h]rebach,   mo c*r*ain do Laidgēn lobhor.

6 Mo scīan is mo spedudhud,   ma treb*ad* i Tūoim Aidhc[h]i,
   mo lourc, mo c*r*ain, mo cūach,   mo tīag let*h*oir, mo cairchi.

                    [Gúaire.]   25
7 A Maru*āin*, a dīthriubaig,[7])   cid dia tiomna doc*ū*aid,
   di d*on* fior cerda a rath,   *acht* a brath do Mac Dūaid.

                    [Marbán.]
8 Atā ūarboith dam hi coild   nisfitir[8]) *acht* mo Fiadai:
   uinni*us* disiu, coll andall,   bili rātha nosnīoadai.   30

---

[1]) tol domanda *R.*   [2]) fochellamar *R.*   [3]) arradfem *R.*
[4]) cneit *R.*   [5]) cedn *MS.*
[6]) *Auf dem oberen Rande hinzugefügt.*
[7]) ditr-uip *MS.*   [8]) nīisfitir *MS.*

9 A *dā* ersainn frāich fri fulong   *ocus fordorus* fēthe:
 feruid in coill imma cress   a mes *for* muca mēthe.[1]

10 Mētt mo boithi becc nāt beg,   ba ili sētt sognath:
 canuid sīen bind die bend   ben al-lenn co londath.

11 Leangoid doim *Droma Rolach*   assa[2] sruth rōeglan:
 fod*erc* essib Roigne rūadh,   Muc*rai*mi mūad, Maonmag.

12 Mennut*ān* dīamuir desruid   die mbī sealb sētrōis:
 die dēxin nī raga liom,   rufinnfet a cētmōuis.

13 Mong celiub*air*   iub*air* ēouglais   noasta cēl:
 cāin in magan,   maurglas dar*ach*   darsin sīn.

14 Aboll ub*ull*,   mār a rath,   mbruignech[3] mbras:
 barr dess dornach   collān cnōbeac[4]   crōeb*ach* nglas.

15 Glēre fīrtip*rat*   es ouisci,   ūais do dig:
 bruindit [b]ioulair,   cōera iob*air*,   fidhvid[5] fīr.

16 Foilgid impe   mucai centa,   cadlaid, oirc,
 muca allta,   oiss airccellti,   bruicnech bruic.

17 Buidn*ech* sīthech,   slū*ag tro*mm tīrech,   dāl d*om* tigh:
 ina erc[h]oill   tecoid c*remt*[h]ainn,   āluind sin!

18 Cāine flat*hu*   tecoid mo teg,   tarcc*ud* tr*ic*:
 uisci iodun,   barrā[i]n bit[h]chai,   bratā[i]n, pric.

19 Barrān cōert[h]ainn,   airne dubui,   *droigin* duind,
 tūari d*ercna*,   cōera loma,   lecna loim.

20 Līne huoga,   mil, mes melle,   Dīa dotrōidh:
 ubla mildsi,   monuinn d*ercui*,   d*ercna* frōich.

21 Couirm co luouh*air*,   logg di śubuip,   somblas snōa,
 sīoluch sclach,   d*ercu* iuech,   airni, cn*óa*.

22 Cūach co medh   collāin condla,   *condal* ndaith,
 durchāin donna,   dristin mongu,   m*ertain* mait*h*.

---

23 Măd *fri* samrad sŭairc snŏbrat   somblas mblas,
    curar orc*ăin*,   foltăin glaise,   glaine glas.

24 Ceŏla *fer* mbrundede*rg forglan,   forom* ndil,
    dordăn smolcha,   cŏei gnăthc[h]ai   uós mo tigh.

25 Tellinn, ciárainn,   certăn cruinde,   cr*ō*năn se[i]mh: 5
    gig*ra*ind, cadhoin,   gair rē sam*uin*,   se[i]nm gairuh cēir.

26 Caincinn gest*lach*,   drŭi donn descc*lach*   don crăib cuild,
    cochvill ăla*inn*,   snaic-ar-dar*aigh*,   aidbli dru*ing*.[1]

27 Tec*ait* căin*fi*nn,   corra, făil*inn*,[2]   foscain cŭach:
    nĭ ceŏul ndocc*rai*,   cercai od*rai*   a fr*ā*ech rŭad.   10

28 Rascach samhaisci a samradh,   svillsiv sĭon!
    nĭ *serb* sŏet[h]r*ach*   ŭas moig mŏethlach   mell*ach* mĭn.

29 Fog*ur* găithi   *frie* flod flesc*ach*   *forg*las nĕol,
    essa abhai,   essnad ealao,   ălaind cĕoul!

30 Căine ailme   ardommpetead   ni 'arna chrec: 15
    do Crĭsd ge*chach* (?)   nĭ mesa dam   olttăs det.

31 Cid m*aith let*-sa   a ndomel-siv   mō cech măin,
    buidech liom-sa   dob*ir* dam-sa   ōm *Christ* căin.

32 Cen hŭair n-aug*rai*,   cin delm debt[h]a   in mo toich,
    buide*ch* don F*laith*   dob*eir* cec[h] m*aith*   dam im boith.   20

                    [Gúaire.]
33 Dob*ér*-sa mo rĭgi răn   lam qhuid comhoirb-siv Colm*áin*,
    a dĭlsiv co hŭair mo băis   ar *beth* at gnăis, a Marbăin.
                        A Marb*ăin* .a.

                    Baile in Scáil.   25

Von diesem wichtigen Texte, an dessen Entstehung sich
manche Probleme knüpfen, enthält unser Kodex nur ein Bruch-
stück. Eine Ausgabe nach der Haupthandschrift in Rawlinson
B. 512, fo. 101 a — 105 b wäre sehr wünschenswert. Ich teile aus

---

[1] draing *MS.*   [2] făilinn *MS.*

*dieser hauptsächlich nur die zum Verständnis des ziemlich
korrupten Harleyschen Textes dienenden Varianten mit. Das
Bruchstück endet mit der Erwähnung Königs Fergal mac Móile-
dúin (709—718), während Rawl. noch 24 Könige aufzählt und*
5 *mit dem fabelhaften Fland Cinach, tigflaith Hérenn (s. O'Curry,
MS. Materials S. 401) endet. Für die irische Geschichte ist die
'Vision des Phantoms' ein wichtiges Denkmal, indem sie mit
ihrer Aufzählung von mehr als 50 Königen, den Angaben über
ihre Regierungszeit und die Umstände ihres Todes, den Schlachten-*
10 *listen und anderen Einzelheiten eine unabhängige Quelle neben
den Annalen[1]) bietet. O'Curry (MS. Materials S. 385—389)
ist der einzige, der bisher eingehender über unseren Text gehandelt hat.*

[fo. 71 a] 1. Laa robói Cond i Temr*aig* iar ndioth dona
15 rigaib atracht mat*in* moch for rí[g]raith na Temrach ria turcbail gréine 7 a tri druith aróen ris .i. Maol, Bloc, Bluicne, et
a trii fil*id* .i. Ethain, Corb, Cesarn.[2]) Fodégh attraige[d]-siom)[3])
cach dia in lion se*n* do airdexin[4]) arna gabdaois[5]) fir side[6]) for
Ērind cen airiug*ud* dō-som.
20   2. In dū[7]) dia ndech*aid* som dogrés co tarlaic cloich and
foa cosaib 7 saltrais f*uir*ri. Rogés an cloch fo cosaib co clos fo
Temr*aig* uili 7 fo Bregaib.[8])
    3. Is andsin roiarfacht Conn dia drūidib[9]) *cid* arusgés[10])
an cloch, cia hainm[11]) 7 can doral*adh* 7 noragadh[12]) 7 *cid*
25 rotaraill[13]) Temraigh. Is *ed* idbert an drāi[14]) fri Conn ni
slondad dō[15]) co cend cōicat laithi 7 a tri.[16]) In t*an* rocin-
diod[17]) an āiriom sin, r*us*Iarfacht Conn don drāi afrīdhisi.[18])

---

[1]) *Ein Citat aus Baile in Scáil findet sich in den Annalen der Vier
Meister, A. D. 773. Fland Mainistrech bezieht sich auf die Scálbaile in seinem
Gedichte über die Könige von Tara (LL. 132 a 48).*
[2]) Eochu 7 Corbb 7 Cessarnd *R.*
[3]) atraigedsom *R.*   [4]) om. *R.*   [5]) ragabtais *R.*
[6]) side side *H. nó* fomoiri *add. R.*
[7]) dua *R.*   [8]) Bregmagh *R.*   [9]) din filid *R.*
[10]) rogéisi *R.*   [11]) a ainm *R.*   [12]) noregad *R.*
[13]) cid frisa táraill *R.*   [14]) in file *R.*
[15]) sluindfed dóu *R.*   [16]) 7 treissi fair *R.*
[17]) ba lan *R.*
[18]) roiarfacht Conn afrithisi dond filid 7 robui side icc scrutan co n-écetar
a eochra eccsi dou *R.*

4. Is ann adbert an drāi: 'Fāl anmaim na cloche,[1]) Inis
Foail asa tardad,[2]) Temair Tīri Fāil i forromadh,[3]) Tīr Taillten
a n-airisfe[4]) co brāth. Et is I an tīr sen[5]) bus ōenach cluiche
cēn uhes flaithios a Temraig 7 lā dēdinach[6]) an aonaigh in[7])
flaith nachusfāigfi,[8]) bid[9]) trú isan bliadain sin. Rogēs fāl foat 5
cosaib-se ann[i]n', ol in drāi, '7 dorairngert. An līn gairm[10])
rogēs an cloch, is ed līon rīg bīas dot[11]) sīol[12]) co brāth. Nī
ba mē nodsloindfe det',[13]) ol in drāi.

5. A mbatar Ierum co n-acotar ciuich mōr[14]) immacūairt,[15])
co nā fedotar cid[16]) docotar ar mēd an dorchu dusnāinecc, co 10
cōlatar trethan[17]) in marcaig ara n-amus.[18]) 'Moar mairc dūinn',
ol Conn, 'dianaruccai a tīr n-ainiūil'.[19]) Ier sin[20]) dollēcci an
marcach trī orchora cucai[21]) 7 is traide dusnāinic in t-orchor
dēdenach[22]) inās 't-orchor tóisech.[23]) 'Is do guin rīg ēmh', or
in drāi, 'cibē dībraicius Conn a Temraig'. Anaid Iar sin an 15
marcach din dībraccud 7 tic cuca 7 ferais fāilti fri Conn et
congart les dia treb.[24])

6. Duscōtar[25]) Iarum[26]) condusrulai isin mag n-ālaind co
n-acatar an rīghrāith isin [maig] 7 bili ōrda ina dorus 7 co
n-acatar tech n-ālaind n-ann fo octæ findruine.[27]) Deich traigid 20
fichit a fod. Lotar Iarum isin [tech][28]) co n-acatar an ingin
macdachta isin toig[29]) 7 barr ōrda for a mullach.[30]) Dabach
aircit co cerclaib[31]) ōrda impe 7 sī lān do derglind.[32]) Escrai
ōir for a ur.[33]) Copān di ór for a beōlai. Co n-acatar

---

[1]) Fal em, ol an fili, a hainm na clocha R.
[2]) torlad R.   [3]) foruirmed R.   [4]) hi tairiss hi R.
[5]) 7 iss ed tir in sein R.
[6]) deginach H. di sechtmain add. R.
[7]) om. R.   [8]) na faigbi R.   [9]) is R.
[10]) ngemind R.   [11]) ditt R.   [12]) for Herinn add. R.
[13]) Attafeid dam amal sodain, ol Conn. Ni dam rothocad a rad fritt R.
[14]) moir R.   [15]) impn R.   [16]) cia R.
[17]) trechan R.   [18]) cend R.
[19]) ma runfucca in ceo sa hi tiri anetargnaide R.
[20]) lasodain R.   [21]) forru R.   [22]) degenach H.
[23]) inds in toisiuch R.   [24]) treiph R.
[25]) docotar R.   [26]) ass add. R.
[27]) condarala assa mag 7 bile n-orda ann. Tech foa ochtaig findruine
and R.
[28]) issa tech R.   [29]) maccthacht i cathair glanidi R.
[30]) 7 brat co srethaib di or impe add. R.
[31]) cernaib R.   [32]) dergflaith R.   [33]) ar a óu R.

an[1]) scāl fodesin isin tigh for a cinn ina rīgṡuide.[2]) Nī frīth
a Temraich rīam fer a mēde nach a caoime ar āille a chrotha,
ar inganta a deuluha.

7. Prisgart side dōib 7 adbert friu: 'Nīdom[3]) scāl-sa ēm 7
5 nīdom[3]) urtrach 7 dom uirdercus dūib īar mbās dodeochadus 7
is do cinēl[4]) Ādaim daum. Iss ē mo slondad Lug mac Ethlend
maic Tigernmais.[5]) Is dō dodechadus[6]) co n-ēcius ded-se saogal
do flathau fēn 7 cech[7]) flathai bīas[8]) a Temraich'.[9])

8. Ocus ba sí an ingen bōi isin tig for a ciond Flaithi[10])
10 Ērenn co prāth.[11]) Ba sī an ingen dobert an diched[12]) do
Cond[13]) .i. damasna 7 torcasnai. Cethri[14]) traigid fichet fod an
damhasna, ocht traigid itir a tuaim 7 talmain.[15])

9. In tan[16]) luid an ingen don dāil, adbert friu: 'Cīa da
tibērthar[17]) an airdeoch sa?'[18]) Frisgart an scāl.[19]) Ō rosluind
15 side cach flaith co brāth,[20]) lotar a foscadh an [fo. 71b] scāil,
co nā rathaic[h]setar an rāth nach an tec[h].[21]) Forrācbad lia
Cond in dabach 7 in t-escrai ōrdao 7 and air[d]ech.[22]) Is de
sin ata Aisling an Scāil et Egtrai 7 Targraide Cuind.

10. 'Cīa fora ndāilfidir an air[d]ec[h][23]) sa cosan derg-
20 laith?'[24]) ol in ingen. 'Dāil de', or in scāl, 'for Cond Cēt-
chathach .i. cēd cathrāi brisflus.

Cōica blīadan namā   dodocaith na doibhdhá.

---

[1]) a R.

[2]) ocus ropu mór a delgnaidhe. Ba dethbir son, ar add. R.

[3]) nimda R.   [4]) de hsil R.

[5]) Ethnen m. Smretha m. Tigernmair m. Fælad m. Etheuir m. Iriail
m. Erimoin m. Miled Espaine R.

[6]) dodeochadsa R.   [7]) cacha R.   [8]) huait add. R.

[9]) co brad add. R.   [10]) flaith R.   [11]) om. R.

[12]) dithait R.   [13]) Chunn R.   [14]) cethair R.

[15]) dá traigh deac fott in torcasnai 7 coic traigid etir a tuaim 7 talmain
add. R.

[16]) didiu add. R.   [17]) tiberthæ R.

[18]) cosin derglaith add. R.   [19]) di iarum add. R.

[20]) cach flaith i ndegaid araile o aimsir Cuinn co brad. Ba trom iarum
la Cesarnd filid an dichetail sin do thabairt fri oinhuair co n-ecmaing tre
oghum hi cetheora flescæ iphair. Cethir traigid fichet fott cacha flesci 7 ocht
ndruimne cacha flesci R.

[21]) ni arrdraigestair a ndun nach a dtech R.

[22]) 7 na flescæi add. R.

[23]) argraige R.

[24]) 7 cia nodasibai add. R.

Firfid catha .i. cath Breg, cath Eli, cath Aiche, cath Machai, cath Cind-Tīri, *secht* cathai Moighi Line, cath Quailgne, *secht* catha Clāirīne' 7 rl.[1]

A com*r*ac am Tibraiti,   cet l*eth*[2] - comnart a n-uidhe,
  is ē gidnit*er* ac dluigi[3])   na slū*ag*[4]) bīas lassuide.   5
Dirsan do Chonn[5]) Chétchathach īar n-ār tened t*ar* [c]ech magh,
gontar[6]) īar timcell cech ruis dīaa Mairt a Tūaith Emruis'.[7]

11. 'Cīa forsa ndāilfidir an air[d]ec[h] sa cusin derg*fl*aith?' or in ingen. 'Dāil de', or in scāl, 'for Art mac Cuind,[8]) *fer* trī ngretha.[9]) Firfid cath Fidruis.[10])   10

Mat*an* [Maige] Muc*r*aime ima tōetsad mairb ili,
  ba dirsan do Art mac Quind cu m*aic* Ail*ell*a Oluim.[11])
Dia dardóin fic[h]id cath a taot*us* la sīl Lug[d]ach,
  tricha bl*iadan* namā in tan nodotibdáa'.[12]

12. 'Cīa *fora* ndāilfidir in air[d]ec[h] sa cusan d*er*claith?' 15
Dāil de', ol in sc*āl*, 'for Lug*daig* mac Con. Cinfid do sīl Cuind.[13]) Doaidleba *cōic* bl*iadna* *fichet* namā docaith nodoibdá. A long*us* co hīath nAlp*an*. Forbrisfi cethri mōrcatha for tūat[h]a Orca.

Dīa domnaich fordu*s*ri hi[14]) dianaitbi[15]) fiac*ail* fidbi.'   20

13. 'Dāil de for an mōirbr*eth*ach, for Cormac ō Cuind. T*rī*[16]) bli*adn*a namā docait[h] *n*ododibdá.

Sīth n-oll co rīan ina rē bīaid t*rī* *fichet* bli*adn*ae.
B*id* rī Temrac[h] comba[17]) trī, arambebad sīabrai.[18])
Tuili tor*ad* ina rē, bid aon do nirt[19]) na flaithe.   25

---

[1]) *Here R gives a much longer list of battles.*
[2]) cith leth *R.*   [3]) gignetar agle *R.*
[4]) in sluagad im suide *R.*   [5]) Chund *R.*
[6]) gentar *R.*   [7]) Imrois *R.*   [8]) quind *H.* oenfer *R.*
[9]) chét gretha *R.*   [10]) .lxxx. catha fir*r*ess *R.*
[11]) *Lies mit R* cin m*ac* nAililla Auluim.
[12]) *fiche* bl*iadan* namma dodacich nodaiba *R.*
[13]) cini di sil Chuind *R.*   [14]) for Ath Hii *R.*
[15]) donaidli *R.*   [16]) *cóica R.*   [17]) co fo *R.*
[18]) arambebat ilsiabrai .i. sithaigi *R.*
[19]) di neort *R.*

Fornaidm mboraime nĒrenn la Cormac fri Fergus airdrī nUlad.
Dotōed Fergus scēo Ēnda dīa mbīa slūag dérach dubach ad-
cumbec. Bid marb[1]) dīa mairt i toaibh[2]) Cletig.[3])

14. 'Dāil de fo fer ilar nglonn,[4]) for Cairpri Lifechar.
5 Tric[h]a cath ina rē. Trī blīadna fichit a flaithius.[5])

Diubairt[6]) Ērenn cota muir,   cath fesar[7]) a Lifemuigh.

In mairt a Lifi arambebais an rīgnía.[8]) Trī maic Coirpri Life-
chair .i. Eochu 7 Eochu Doimlen 7 Fiachu Raibtine la Laighne.
Atorcratar a cath Tuamruis la Bresal mBélach mac Fiachrach
10 Baicedha maic Cathāir. Cōica ar trī mīlib an līon do Laignib
dotuit ann a frit[h]ghuin.

15. 'Dāil de fri Fiachraig Raibtine. Maidion Mide la
saide 7 dā cath[9]) les.

Cōic blīadna fichet a rē   oc[10]) saigid na boruime:
15 cētāin a Cnāmros, bid glē,   a tōeth Fiachu Sroibtine.

16. 'Dāil de for Muiredach.[11]) Cethracha blīadan docaith
no doibhdha.

Cath a Mōrmuig firfid glē   fri Ulltu, fri hAraide:
for brū Dabaill isan cath   dotaoth Muiredach Tīrech.

20   17. 'Dāil de for Eochaig Muidmedhōn,[12]) tōebfoda
Temrac[h], dūnadach Femin,[13]) fostadach[14]) Mōenmaighi, air-
midne armar (?), airsid Life.[15]) Cōic blīadna docaith no doibdá.

Guin Glūnmair,[16]) bid mōr an t-ēcht   guin Concobuir, guin
[Maic Cēcht.

25 Forus[17]) for[18]) Eochaig.[19]) Is ūad gignitir co brāt[h] bunad
na flatha.

---

[1]) mairb H.   [2]) toeb R.
[3]) adcoinfet Goidil add. R.   [4]) iolair glond R.
[5]) biaid .lx. bliadan R.   [6]) dubairt R.
[7]) fhessair R.
[8]) mairt hi Liphimaig arathá | bebaid and in rignía R.
[9]) hi Maig Ratha add. R.   [10]) co R.
[11]) Tirech add. R.   [12]) Mngmedóin R.
[13]) Tlachtgai R. dubartach Femin add. R.   [14]) costudach R.
[15]) After Moenmaighi R has cruind ársid Liphi, toichmech Toirrchi.
[16]) Gluinfind R.   [17]) forus úHer[e]nd R.   [18]) fo R.
[19]) fria ré bid forggu maithe add. R.

A nŪib Conchobuir[1]) fria ré bīaid fotha la suide:[2])
na trī Colla glanfid ār an[3]) taoth Eochu Muigmedán.

18. 'Cīa forsa ndāilfidir?' ol in ingen.
'Dāil de for Nīall Nōigīallach. Noafidhir[4]) tuir, mōr-
faidir[5]) maigi, indsaigfidir[6]) gē[i]ll, firfidir[7]) catha.[8]) Secht 5
mblīadna fichet docaith. Totaim nŌthaili les[9]) antūaidh, bīet
ile a gluinn ar Druim nAlpuind.[10]) Bid adbor mairc truim am
īarnōin[11]) d[ī]a Sat[h]uirnd.
19. 'Dāil de[12]) ...
20. 'Dāil de for Laogairi,[13]) fer ilar nglond.[14]) Roaichfi 10
Libthi 7 īltīre. Cōic blīadna a flaith. Tascor dīan. Secht
mblīadna docait[h] nodoibhda.

Scarfaid fri hardflaith, scēl nglē, do dēnumh na finghaile.

[fo. 72a] Ticfa tāilcend .i. Pātraic, fer grāid mōir, nōifidius Dīa,
mōr breō atandafa, līnfus Ērinn cota muir. Bebaid Lōigire for 15
brū Caisi, flait[h] im bachla, mōr caur cicharda dofortat tāilcend.[15])
21. 'Dāil de for Ailill Molt mac Nathi maic Fīachrach,
fer n-ūallach, fer attcuinti sochuide. Fiche blīadan namā dodacich.

Cat[h]a iliu ina flaith, ar bid hē an rī maith.

Cuiclidhi[16]) Temra, cumuscach Tailltin.[17]) Cath Ātha Talmaigh. 20
Diubertach[18]) Seli, noicech[19]) Aichi. Cath Rātha Crūachan.
Cē[i]m for Sabruldai, cē[i]m for Elpa. Togail an tuiri.[20]) Cē[i]m
for Eolaorcau. Cath Sratha Clūaidi.[21]) Fortuhi Gennedh.[22])
Cē[i]m dar moir nIcht dochum nElpa. Cichsett Ērennmaigh
rē[i]m dīan, atacumbat eachtraind secht mbēl fri firu Gāidel for 25

[1]) i nDubcombair R. [2]) fotha fingaile R.
[3]) hi R.   [4]) nóithfitir R.   [5]) mórfaitir R.
[6]) nensitir R.   [7]) fessaitir R.
[8]) sesaitir sluaigh, mórfaitir flathi, fugeillfi Níel fo thrí daûgega flaith,
ar bidh hé in ri maith add. R.
[9]) friss R.   [10]) nAlban R.   [11]) i nArddmóin R.
[12]) Dail dé for Colla nOss (.i. uais). iiii. bliadna nama dodacííg nodaíb.
Scairfaid fri arddscél do denam na fingali R.
[13]) R places Ailill Molt before Lóigaire.
[14]) ilair glond R.   [15]) tailcind R.   [16]) cucligid R.
[17]) Tailten R.   [18]) dubartach R.   [19]) nóitech R.
[20]) togal in tuir R.   [21]) Cluithi R.
[22]) fortbe nGeinned R.

Ail*ill* and-ōindhidin ar Elpa. Bīt ili atheat mart*r*ai, ba dirsan
do f*e*ruib Ērenn. Is mōr arathá[1]) thoitim la hectranna.

    22. 'Dāil de for Tūathal Mōelgarb .i. mac Cor*m*aic m*a*ic
Coirp*r*i m*a*ic Nēill. *Fiche* bl*ī*a*dan.* Cath Lūachrai Ailue, *cath*
5 Dētnai, toitim n-Ardgail, *cath* Lēgi, *cath* Dromma Arbēla*ig*, *cath*
Bregainn, f*o*rnaidm gīall nGāid*el.* Īar sin, ba[2]) scēl in cech
moig, bebuid aonguine namā Tūatha*l* h*o*c Grella*ig* Elti, gentoir[3])
Mōelmōr dīa dīga*il* hi tūaith Imrois.

    23. 'Dāil de for Lug*d*aig mac Lōegiri. XXVI co toitim
10 dōu do qhūairt f*o*r Ērinn trē dīultad tāilcind inn-Escir Forcha.

    24. 'Dāil de for Muir*c*ertach mac Ercoi, i*d est ingen*
Loairn. Rī cat*h*ach coscrach, attcuinti sochu*i*di. Fonen Ērind,
fīr 7 mnā. Ar bid comurbo Temrai. *Cath* Ātha Sidhi.[4]) Īer
sin līnfus co H*e*rind airbiu. Benuid dubuirt[5]) hi mairt in cairb
15 coscrach col-Laigniu. Mōr atbai.[6]) Beab*a*id M*u*rcertach ēcc
atbai mairt Cletigh.

    25. 'D*āil* de for Ainmir*i*g. Timgēra gīalla[7]) Gāid*el* cech
moigi īartir cinip tair[8]) truimm dofoethsat[9]) ardaig rūad fir-
fit*i*r[10]) catha. Cet*h*ri bl*ī*a*dna* nammā.

20   26. D*āil* de for Bōet*a*n 7 Eocha*ig.* *Cethri* bl*ī*a*dna* namā
do*d*acich *n*otaibha.

    27. 'D*āil* de for Dīarmait .i. mac Fearccusa Cerrbeō*il*,
dub*a*rtach Tailltin,[11]) tairng*e*rtaich Tem*r*ai. Cēnmair ina fl*a*ith,
ar bid hē in rī maith. Dīa *secht* [m]bl*ī*a*dan* īar sin *cath*
25 fōebr*a*ch f*o*r Dīarmait Dremne.

    In sl*ō*g*h* dosía antūaith   glanfaid in rōi co hAthlūain.

Berthair a cathbūaidh.

    Ind-ōinditin a Rāit[h] Bicc   dīth Dīarmata immarricc.

Fiche bl*ī*a*dan* namā do*d*acich notaiobá.

30   28. 'D*āil* de for Fercus 7 Domnall, dá m*a*c Muircertaig
m*a*ic Erca[12]) .i. Brannam[13]) m*a*c Echa*ch* romarb. Dīblīnuib a
comflaith.[14])

    29. 'Dāil de for Oed Ūaridhnec*h*[15]) mac Domn*a*i*ll*,

   [1]) artha *R.*   [2]) bid *R.*   [3]) gentar *R.*
   [4]) *Lies* Sigi (*R*).   [5]) dubart *R.*   [6]) attba *R.*
   [7]) giallu *R.*   [8]) atair *R.*   [9]) dofoeth *R.*
   [10]) firfithir *R.*   [11]) Tailten *R.*   [12]) Ainmirech *R.*
   [13]) Brandub *R.*   [14]) *Lies mit* R dí bl*ī*a*dain* hi comflaith.
   [15]) Úaredach *R.*

mōrfus flaith, fonen Hērind, flait[h] fodbach forranuch, firfíd for-
bassa Hērend. Blīatain īar sin dofuit [1]) Ailill mac Domanguirt.
Bīet[2]) gnīm a Temairmoig.

Iurait Laigin a ndāma   conbibsad a fīrdāla.
Bid garg, bud[3]) coscrach a ree   col-laithi na tangnacté.[4])   5
In mairt hi ndescirt Lifi,   is ann atbeuha[5]) ind rii.

Secht[6]) mblīadna namā.
    30. 'Dail de for Ōett Slāine. Sīth n-oll, flait[h] Gōidiul.
Cāin erni[7]) fini fuata lia mnā.

Dotōet īar sin Aod Slāni   īar līn cath[a] ina ré.   10

Secht[6]) mblīadna namā dodacich notaibhá .i. coirm cat[h]a[s])
prosompni ut dicebat.
    31. 'Dāil de for Ōed Olldān. Secht[6]) mblīadna dodacich
notaibha. Dubartach Fālmoigi. Gēbaid for Lifimoigh, arnenai
gīalla[9]) Gāidil, mōr marb, mōr atbai,[10]) mōr ail cāinfit[11]) Gāidhil. 15
    32. 'Dāil de for Domnall Mend Ulad. Nōi mblīadna
dēac namā. Dracc[12]) ilair band.

Firfíus dā cath a Moig Roth,   mairt is ann tōeth an rīgroth.

Ocus dergmatin Cruithne. Firfíd cath Dūine Cethirn[13]) lia cath
Rātha Almoichi. Cichis īoarum a rē[i]m, mōr ail atbath inn rīg. 20
    33. 'Dāil de for Suibni Menn, dracc[12]) ilair bann.
Blīattain coa secht bīas i flaith. Fonena gīalla[14]) gach rois.
Cath Daithi firfíd in rii.

Is ann dotōet, nī ba gōu,   Colmān Mōr mac Dīarmottou.

    34. [fo. 72b] 'Dāil for Blathmac mac Aoda Slāine. Iss 25
ē notaioba cōic blīadna ar a derbflaith.
    35. 'Dāil de for in rūanaidh (.i. hi[15]) ruidioth hoc gabāil
lāma Mocutta), [for][16]) Dīarmait Dait[h]i. A chétchath
Sēnchua. Cath Rois Corcoi Būain, cath Osruidi, cath Eli, cath
Slebi itir dā inda. Firfíd secht catha Aithne[17]) la cath Selgi 30
īar lō nó nōin arataat dergmaitne Cruichne, bīd crūais cuimnech

---

[1]) dothuit R.
[4]) tangnechte R.
[7]) ernfi R.
[10]) átbai R.
[13]) Dúin Cethernd R.
[15]) Lies a (R).

[2]) Lies bied (R).
[5]) atbela R.
[8]) cath R.
[11]) atcuinfet R.
[16]) sic R.

[3]) bid R.
[6]) ocht R.
[9]) giallu R.
[12]) drauc R.
[14]) giallu R.
[17]) Aidni R.

tūath in cuib. Īar sin in mortlaith for Hērind i mbiatt mūcna
iṅdt slūaig.

36. 'Dāil de for Findachta .i. mac Dunchada maic Aoda
Slāine. Consaidfie for[1]) Mumain mōir. Firfid cath Cūlie Cōilāin
5 scith[2]) i tōib Cithamrae fer mochtaiti.[3]) Atbaild fingail mōir
ind-ōindidin for Dollud. Duthoin a recht. Nī ba rī Aod īarum
.i. mac Dlūthaigh. Fiche blīadna.

37. 'Dāil de for Sechnusach mac Blathmaic. Uno
anno dotacaith. Atbeuba ēcc atbai isin Imbliuch ōs Bōinn.

10   38. 'Dāil de for Cendfōelad. Secht mblīadna i flait[h].
Īar sin an cath i Temuirmaigh. Dotōith Cendfōelad an domnach
Cūili Cōelain.

39. 'Dāil de for Loingsech .i. mac Aongussa maic
Domnaill, cobra[4]) for Fālmoigh, cosdaduch Lifi, buignech Bērriu.[5])

15 Ditōett hoc lecuib finnaib   lasna fianaip[6]) fo minnuib,
ragaid[7]) an imguin fothūaith,   mebuid[8]) for rīg Eassa Rūaid

.i. rīa Celluch Locha Cimbe.

Dīe sathuirn cichis ar cel   itir dā Corann uindsen

.i. fath Corainn Unsen.[9]) Aonblīadain dēac namā dodacich
20 nodaiobha.

40. 'Dāil de for Fogartach n-ān 7 for Congal Cind-
magair mac Fergusa Fanad.[10]) Cethri blīadna dēac namā.
Dotōit idna[11]) isin lūan īer[12]) samain, inddalanae hi tosach in
laithi[13]) 7 alaili ina deriod. Hi Clūain Iraird sepulti[14]) sunt.

25   41. 'Dāil de', for in scāl, 'for Feargal[15]) .i. a n-aondittin
hi cath Almaine. Clethblugaid Ērenn, armach Line, airsid Āi.

Bebhaid la Laigniu ina[16]) rē   Fergal hi cath Almuiné.
Bīaid ár moar isin cath   līnfus co Hērinn airpriu
[hi tōeth ind rīgrad mōinech   immon Cāilech as amru.][17])

---

[1]) fri R.   [2]) sciss R.   [3]) mochtaidi R.
[4]) siabraid R.   [5]) buidnech Beirri R.   [6]) fianna R.
[7]) regaid R.   [8]) memais R.   [9]) cath Coraind R.
[10]) Congal mac Fergusæ Fanat R.
[11]) dathuittet a ndiis R.   [12]) ria R.
[13]) ind lái R.   [14]) sepultus H.
[15]) Lies Dail de forsin cailech, for Fergal (R).
[16]) Lies iarna (R).   [17]) sic R.

Liverpool.   KUNO MEYER.

IRISH ETYMOLOGIES.

búrim 'I strike'.

This verb has hitherto been found only in one passage. LU. 95 b 30: *béim búrit fri teóra sústa iarndœ* 'a blow they strike with three iron flails'. This reminds one of the Welsh *bwrw ergyd* 'to strike a blow', with which Victor Henry connects the Lith. kriuszà *býra* 'to hail'. Windisch suggests a connexion with the Skr. root *bhur* 'sich rasch hin und her bewegen' (Grassmann); and the long *ū* in the Irish word may correspond with the *w* (urkelt. *ŭ*) of *bwrw*, just as Gr. πορφύρω corresponds with Skr. *jarbhŭrīti*, Gr. φῦρω with Lat. *fŭro*, OSlav. *burja* 'storm' with Lith. *būrgs* 'shower'.

canim 1. 'I sing', 2. 'I make'.

The primary meaning of *canim* is 'I sing'. But in Middle-Irish it often signifies 'I make, I do, I perform'. Thus in LL. 144 b 27, cach clessach na chanad cheilg, monach sein isin gaedeilg [MS. manach sein sin gaedilg] 'every player who used to perform a trick, he is (called) a *monach*, „juggler", in the Gaelic'. So in the Laud copy of the Acallam na Senórach, 126 a 1 *ro canad fircháin faeilte friu* 'a truly beautiful welcome was made to them', where, for *ro canad*, the Franciscan copy has *ro ferad*. So again in the Laud copy 136 b 2 *céol ... ro chandais* corresponds with *ceol ... donítis* of the Lismore copy 191 b 1. (The passage refers to the music of a *timpan*.)

This secondary meaning may perhaps be accounted for by the fact that *canim* is employed in connexion with magical spells (*ro chansat brechta druidechta*, Ir. Texte I, p. 226, 25), and this is the regular use of its compound *dochanim* (= *dī* + *canim*, cf. *díchetal*). An inverse development of meaning seems to have occurred in the case of Span. *hechizo*, Port. *feitiço* 'magic', from Lat. *facticius*. Whether the Old Persian μάγος is connected with Ags. *macian*, Eng. *make*, Old Sax. *makôn* I must leave Teutonic philologists to decide.

cét 'a blow'.

céad .i. béim, O'Cl. Old and Middle-Irish *cét*, as in Harl. 1802 (Rev. Celt. VIII, 352) *Éol dam aidid Crist na cét* 'known to me is the tragical death of Christ of the buffets'. This comes regularly from **kento-*, cognate with O. N. *hitta* (Eng. *hit*) from **henþan*.

dega 'stag-beetle'.

The nom. sg. of this word is given by O'Reilly as '*deagha* s. a chafer, a bug; i. e. *dœl*, o(ld) g(aelic)'. Its acc. sg. occurs in the comparison of Ingcél's single eye *duibithir degaid* 'as black as a stagbeetle', LU. 84 b 19. So in comparing the seven pupils of that eye: *Bátar duibithir degaid*, LU. 85 b, where the Egerton copy has: *Ba duibithir déga hi*, and YBL. has, corruptly, *Batar duibithir dethaig*. The meaning of *dega* appears clearly from the description of the hag at the door of the Bruden Dá Derga, where the Egerton copy's *Ba duibithir dega cech n-alt 7 cech n-ági di* ('every limb and joint of her was as black as a stag-beetle') corresponds with LU. 86 a: *Bátár dubithir druim ndáil* 'they [scil. her shins] were as black as a stagbeetle's back'.

Prof. Zimmer, not understanding *dega*, jumps at the conclusion that the scribe of LU. has miswritten *degaid* for *dadaig* (KZ. XXVIII, 573, note), and accordingly translates *duibithir degaid* by 'schwärzer wie zur Nacht', p. 573, 'schwärzer als zur Nacht', p. 570.

dega, acc. *degaid*, is a *t*-stem, urkelt. **digāt-* or **digōt-*, cognate with Eng. *tick*, Germ. *zecke*, with which Kluge connects Arm. *tiz*.

drochta 'tub', *drochat*, *droichet* 'bridge'.

drochta, gen. *drochtai*, LL. 159 b 1 is rendered 'bridge' by Prof. Atkinson, Book of Leinster, Contents, p. 39. But it is glossed by *seinleastar* 'an old vessel' in Corm. Tr. p. 14 s. v. annach, and it really means 'a wooden tub'. See Ancient Laws IV, 310, l. 10, where a mbruigfer's furniture is described as including *ammbur indlait ocus long foilcthe, drochta, cainddelbra, scena buana aíne* 'a washing-trough and a bathing-basin, a tub, a candelabrum, knives for cutting rushes'.

drochta seems radically connected with Eng. *trough*, Germ. *trog*, which Kluge refers to a pre-Germanic *dru-kó-* 'wooden', derived, like Skr. *dróṇa*, 'hölzerner Trog, Kufe', from *dru* 'wood'.

The stem *drukó-* occurs also in the Old-Irish *drochat* (gl. pons) Sg. 46 b 4, and the synonymous *droichet*, Corm., *drochet*, Hy. 6. 4. The former word seems a compound of **droch* 'wooden' and **ot,*[1]) urkelt. **onto-s* = Gr. *πόντος* and cognate with Lat. *pons.* The latter seems a compound of **droch* 'wooden' and **ét,* urkelt. **n̥to-s* (the weak form of **onto-s*), cognate with Pruss. *pintis*, Gr. *πάτος*, Skr. *pathi.* The vowel of the post-tonic **ot* is regularly changed to *ă,* Brugmann, Grundr.[2] § 256. The vowel of the post-tonic *et* is regularly shortened, ibid. § 260.

The gen. sg. *drochit* — oc glanad ur-drochit a thigi LB. 353 a 70 — and the nom. pl. *drochait* — in *tri primdrochait,* Chron. Scot. 322 — prove that the second elements of *drochat, drochet* are not, as native etymologists suppose, *sét* 'way'. For the gen. sg. of *sét* is *séta,* or *siúit* LL. 8 b 43, and its nom. pl. is *seuit* or *séti.* It has two bases, *senti-* and *sento-* = Goth. *sinþs.* In the *i*-infection Ir. *ét* from *n̥t* is clearly distinguished from *ét* from *ent.* See R. Schmidt in Idg. Forschungen I, 64.

inboth 'wedding'.

Pl. gen. *i n-aidchi na n-inboth* .i. *na baindsi,* 'in the night of the nuptials', H. 3. 18, p. 521. Pl. acc. *foruar inna inbotha* 'paravit nuptias', Tur. 48.

The *both* (i. e. *voth*) of this word seems borrowed, as Span. *boda* is descended, from Lat. *vota,* pl. of *votum.* For *vota* = nuptiae cf. ad tertia vota migrare, 'zur dritten Ehe schreiten', Cod. Just., ad secunda vota ire, L. Burg. 42, 1, cited by Diez, s. v. *boda.* But the *in-* remains inexplicable by me. A mediaeval Latin *invotum* is unknown.

---

[1]) Another compound of this **ot* is, apparently, *bélat* (gl. competum) Sg. 24 a 6, which in GC.[2] 804 is regarded as a stem in *-tta.*

múr 'mire'.

This word occurs in the Táin bó Cúalnge in the phrase *ar múr ocus grían*, 'on mire and gravel', LU. 67 b 16, *ar múr is arñgrian* (leg. *ar grían*), LL. 58 a 9.

It is obviously borrowed from the Old Norse *mýrr* 'slime', or Ags. *mýre*, where the *r* is originally *ʀ = s*.

mess 'fosterling'.

meas .i. dalta, O'Cl., enters into many person-names, e. g. *Mess búachaille* 'the cowherds' fosterling', *Mess dead, Mess gegra, Mess réta, Mess róida*. It is compounded with *cú* 'hound' in *mess-chú* (gen. *meschon*, LL. 144 a 42, dat. *meschoin*, Trip. Life 232, l. 21), and *messan* 'lapdog', LU. 91 b, is derived from it.

mess may come from **mesto-, *med-to,* and be cognate with Gr. μαδάω, μαζός, μεστός, and other words cited by Prellwitz.

no in a relative function.

To Strachan's examples (Celt. Ztschr. III, 283) of relativity expressed by the verbal particle *no* I can add the following:

Sg. 1 *Do rígrad no molur, ol is tú mo ruire* ('tis) thy kingfolk whom I praise, for thou art my lord', Fél. Oeng. prol. 13, 14, where Laud 610 has *ro molur*, and LB. has *no molar.*

Atsluindiu lat nóebu frit a n-úag no ráidiu 'with thy saints I appeal to thee by all that I say', ibid. epilogue 357, 358.

Sg. 2 *Bebais in cáid Colmán, mo Líba no rádi* 'the chaste Colman departed (this life), my Líba whom thou mentionest' ibid. February 18.

If there were such a verb as *no chosnagur,* Wind. Wtb. 449, it might be cited as another example of *no* in a relative function. But the true explanation of this form, viz. *nocho-sn-águr* 'I fear them not', has been given by Sarauw, in his *Irske Studier,* p. 139.

rogait 'rock' (distaff).

This word occurs, compounded with *sith* 'long', in LU. 95 b 39: *sithrogait ía[i]rnd sithremithir cuing n-imechtair il-láim cach ae* 'a long bar of iron as long and thick as an outer yoke (was) in the hand of each of them'.

It seems radically connected with the Eng. *rock*, O. N. *rokkr*, Germ. *rocken*. For the suffix *-ait* cf. the adj. *garait* 'brevis'.

The verbal particle *ror*.

As the verbal particle *ro*, *ru* is = Gr. προ, Skr. *pra*, so the reduplicated *ror*, *rur* is Gr. προπρο,[1]) Skr. *prápra*.[2]) I have hitherto found this particle only in verbs compounded with *to* (pretonic *do*), *dí* (pretonic *do*), *eb*, and *for*. Since it is ignored by all the grammars and glossaries, I shall here give the instances I have met.

do-ror-ban (gl. proficit) Ml. 62 a 20, *du-ror-banat* (gl. prosunt) Ml. 43 b 5, pret. *do-ror-bai* (gl. proficeret) Ml. 123 d 5, *da-ror-bai* (gl. cuia interfuit) Sg. 203 a 18, *do-m-ror-bai . . . rith ro raith in slógsa* 'the course which this host (of saints) has run, has profited me', Fél. Oeng. prol. 25. *do-t-ror-bai beist, a Senchain* 'the monster has profited thee, O Senchán', Corm. s. v. *prull*. In this verb the *ror* goes through the whole verbal system, just as *ro* does in *as-ro-choilim*, *im-rui-mdiur*, *r-uccim*, *ro-iccim*. So, apparently, in the verb of which *do-ror-benat* .i. doairmescat, 'they prohibit', O'Dav. 112, is the pres. ind. act. pl. 3.

do-gabim 'profero, emergo': *s*-pret. sg. 3 *du-rur-gaib* (gl. emersit) Ml. 63 a 15, *co du-rur-gaib* (gl. emserserit) 138 d 11. *do-rur-gabsam* (gl. emerserimus) Aug. Carl. 38, *do-rur-gabtha* (gl. sint prolata) Sg. 61 a 15.

*eb-lingim:[3]) perf. sg. 3 *rol-eb-laing* (from **ror-eb-laing*) .i. ro ling, 'saluit', Fél. Oeng. March 5, *fo-rul-eb-langtar* (MS. *forrul-*) gl. subsiluerunt, Ml. 129 c 21. For the prefix *eb-* see KZ. XXXVI, 275. For the assimilation of *r* to the *l* of the root cf. *ro dleb-laing* LU. 72 a 17, where *dleb = dreb = dru + eb*.

for-aith-miniur, *s*-pret. pl. 3 *fo-rur-aithminset* (gl. meminisse) Ml. 135 a 1.

for-benim 'I complete', perf. sg. 3, *fo-ror-bái*, Trip. Life 34, l. 17. 170, l. 9. 178, l. 18. Passive: *ho bu-ror-baither* (leg. *fu-ror-baither*) Ml. 15 a 6 'when it has been finished', *fo-ror-baide*, Trip. Life 104, l. 7.

---

[1]) In προπροκυλινδόμενος Il. 22, 221; Od. 17, 525.

[2]) Grassmann, Wörterbuch zum Rigveda, S. 865, gives six instances of *prápra* with verbs.

[3]) *ebhling no ro eibhling* .i. do ling, 'saluit', O'Cl.

for-biur 'I grow, I increase', *t*-pret. sg. 3 *fo-ror-bairt in cretem*, Fél. Oeng. prol. 173.

for-brisim: *s*-pret. *for-ror-bris* (gl. superauit) Ml. 34 b 16, 67 b 24.

for-cennaim 'I end': pret. pass. pl. 3 *fo-ror-cnait* Fél. Oeng. prol. 87 (Laud 610), where the LB. copy has *forforcennta*: cf. *forforcongair* LU. 25 b 23.

for-con-gur 'praecipio', *t*-pret. sg. 3 *fo-ror-congart*, Trip. Life 198, ll. 11. 18, 228, l. 19, *fo-ror-conggart* 66, l. 17.

for-dingim 'I oppress', deponential *s*-pret. sg. 3 *fo-s-ror-dingestar*, Saltair na rann 5297.

for-gellaim 'perhibeo', pret. sg. 1, *fo-t-roir-gell a briathar na bad nimhe na talman nach aon dogenai, ar is diultad bathis*, Corm. s. v. Imbass forosnae, YBL. p. 271 b 5—8 'his, S. Patrick's, word declared that no one who performed it should be of heaven or of earth, for it is a rejection of baptism'.

In the above compounds of *for*, the *r* of that prefix is (except in the case of *for-ror-bris*) ejected before *ror*. A similar simplification of *r-r* is found in *co-ro-rannam* Wb. 4 a 17, *co-ro-rélam, co-ru-agathar* Ml. 66 a2, which stand respectively for *cor-ro-rannam* (i. e. *con-ro-r.*), *cor-ro-rélam, cor-ru-ágathar*. So in the Middle Irish nominal prep. *faris* for *i farrad ris, farinn* from *i farrad rinn* etc. So in the loanword *Febra* for **Febrar* (cymr. *Chwefrawr*) from Lat. *Februārius*.

selc (seilc?) 'spying'.

I have found this word only in the following passage from the Táin bó Cúalnge, LU. 74 b 45, 46: *tabram fianláech cach n-aidchi do scilc fáir dus in tairsimmis a baegul* 'let us put a champion every night to spy upon him to know whether we might get a chance at him'.

Compare Lith. *stelgiù, stèlgti* 'schauen'. Whether the tenuis of the Irish word is a *g* provected by *l* (GC.[2] 61), or whether there was an idg. root *stelc* beside *stelg* (Brugmann, Grundr.[2] § 701), may be decided by more courageous philologists.

suaitrech 'soldier'.

The modern form of this word is erroneously given by O'Reilly as *suaithreach*. But the *t* is unaspirated, as we see from the glosses, *suaitrech* .i. fer bis ar coinmnedh, O'Dav. 115, *suaitrech* .i. buanna, H. 3. 18, p. 627. So in the *Cogad Gaedel re Gallaib,* ed. Todd, p. 84, l. 13: *Ro daerait imorro a máeir 7 a rectairedha, a suaitrigh 7 a n-amhsaigh* 'their stewards and their bailiffs, too, their billeted soldiers and their mercenaries were enslaved'.

Founded on the Anglo-norman ancestor of the Eng. *soldier,* with provection of *d* after *l* and compensatory lengthening of the preceding vowel.

suartlech 'a Scandinavian warrior'.

This word occurs in Cogad Gaedel re Gallaib, p. 48, where the author, describing the oppressiveness of the vikings, says that they had a king over every territory, a chief over every chieftainry, an abbot over every church, a steward over every village, *ocus suartleach cach tigi* 'and a warrior in every house'. Again in p. 50, though there were only one milch-cow in the house her milk must be kept *do maeir no do rechtair[i] no do suartleach gaill* 'for the foreign steward or bailiff or warrior'. The acc. pl. *suartletu* p. 82, l. 16, is a scribal error for *suartlechu.*

I take this *suartlech* to be based on the O. Norse *svart-leggja,* which Cleasby-Vigfusson explain by '*black leg* or *black stalk,* of a battle-axe with a smoky black handle'.

torc 'boar'.

Ir. *torc* 'boar' (= Cymr. *twrch,* Corn. *torch,* O. Bret. *turch,* Mid. Bret. *tourch*) points to an urkelt. **torko-s.* Sommer, IF. XI, 91, ingeniously suggests that this may be a contamination of **trogos* and **(p)orkos* = Lat. *porcus,* Ir. *orc.* Rhŷs starts from *in t-orc* 'the pig', Ernault from *to-orc.* May not *torc* more probably be explained as for **torgos,* the *r* provecting *g* as in Gaul. *verco-bretus* for *vergo-b.,* and this, by metathesis of *r,* for **trogo-s* cognate with Gr. τράγος and having the same root-vowel as Lat. *troia* from **trogia?*

Cowes, I. W.   WHITLEY STOKES.

GRAMMATICAL NOTES.

11. The Sigmatic Future and Subjunctive.

In a paper in the Transactions of the London Philological Society 1900, (henceforth quoted as Sigm. Fut.) I have attempted to give an account of these formations in Old Irish. Here I propose to deal with their fate in the various texts of the *Lebor na Huidre*. As these texts are of very different ages, it might have been expected that much might be learned from them of the later history of the forms. Unfortunately for the most part the number of occurrences is small, particularly in the later texts, so that, though different texts clearly differ in their conservation and transformation of the old forms, we learn much less about the historical development of the formations than might *a priori* have been expected. In the Tripartite Life, to judge from Stokes' Introduction lxxxviii (I have no independent collections), the sigmatic forms seem to be much as in Old Irish. With few exceptions the same may be said of the Saltair na Rann, a poem which belongs to the end of the tenth century, cf. Verbal System of the Saltair na Rann pp. 16 sq. But it must be borne in mind that of the verbs which in Old Irish have the *s* future and subjunctive only a small number are used in this text, and these are chiefly the verbs in which the *s*-forms are most persistent. It would be rash to assume that in those Old Irish verbs which happen not to occur changes may not have already taken place. For there is no reason to suppose that the sigmatic forms disappeared all at once; those in infrequent use might be expected to go first, those in common use to live on longer. And in fact we find that in a number of common verbs the sigmatic forms survive the general ruin. Thus in the Passions and Homilies sigmatic forms are found from *atracht, -icc, condaigim* (subj. only, the fut. is different), *docúaid* (with some new formations), *-fetar, ithim* (subj. only), *roichim, tecmai, tíagaim* (subj. only), *tidnaicim* (by new formations), *tuitim* (irregular subj.); in the part of the Acallam na Senórach which I have examined I have noted *s*-forms from *do-chúad, -fetar, -icc-, roichim, tuitim* (*co tœthais* 222), with the standing formula *adrae búaid* etc.; for O'Gorman see Stokes' preface xxviii. To speak generally, while we cannot be sure how far the sigmatic forms may have already undergone change in the tenth century, the indications in later texts in LU. point clearly to a great breaking-up of the formations in the eleventh century.

Some new developments within the sigmatic formations have been noted Sigm. Fut. pp. 17, 21. These formations might disappear in three ways. (1) The *s* future becomes a future of another type, commonly a *b* future; the *s* subjunctive becomes an *ā* subjunctive. (2) The whole verb is replaced by a new formation, e. g. O. Ir. *ind-feth-* by *indissim*, *dī-fech-* by *digalim, ara-choat* etc. by *erchóitim, erchóitigim.* (3) The verb disappears from use altogether. In what follows a distinction is made between (*a*) sigmatic forms and (*b*) new formations which have replaced the sigmatic. In two of the oldest texts, where the sigmatic forms are very numerous, and with slight exceptions regular, it has seemed unnecessary to cite them in full.

Nennius.

(*a*) *ni chœmais* 3 b 2.

Commentary on the Amra Coluimbchille.

(*a*) *dech (do-chúad)* 6 b 31; *ní choemsad* 8 a 35; *ɔná heirs̆* 5 a 29; *rosía* (in quotation) 6 a 22.

(*b*) Here are to be noticed only *innisfes* 8 a 29, 31, *noinnis-fed* 6 a 25, 11 b 28, replacing forms of *as-ind-feth-.*

Scél Túain.

(*a*) *co roinnised* 15 b 14.

(*b*) *innisfid* 15 a 42.

On *nisnagsind* 16 a 7 see below p. 478.

Two Sorrows etc.

(*a*) *atreset* 17 b 9.

(*b*) *mani-s-tesorced* ('save') 17 b 16.

Mesca Ulad.

(*a*) *rofestar* 19 b 11; *co n-dérais* (*di-fech-*) 20 b 5; *folilastæ* 20 a 24; *nísnérussa* (leg. *ní-m-érus-sa* 'I will not arise') 20 b 16.

Táin Bó Dartada.

(*a*) *ɔ-digs̃* 20 b 37.

Táin Bó Flidais.

(*a*) *conos-tairsed* 22 a 1. The form is used as a secondary future.

Imram Máiledúin.

(*a*) *co festais* 25 a 34; *ó-tairs̃* 26 b 18; *ní-s-fǽlsad* 26 a 16; *rosesaid-si* 25 b 10, *ní roistis* 26 a 33; *día tiasam* 23 b 27.

At 22 a 36 *fessa* seems corrupt,[1]) YBL. has *cofesar*. At 23 a 25 *nád-roched* is not clear, cf. 43 b 22. Have we here perfective imperfects, cf. 58 a 30?

Fis Adamnán.

(*a*) *ɔnigs̃* (= *co n-digsed*) 31 a 21, *co tí* 28 b 20.

(*b*) *ní innisfea* 28 a 17; *midfid̃* 30 a 17.

Scéla Lái Brátha.

(*a*) *ní thairs̃* 34 a 5; *roses̃* 33 b 8.

(*b*) *noinnisfed* 33 b 23.

Scéla na Essérge.

(*a*) *atchichestár* 37 b 16; *atresat* 34 b 4, 32, 34, 42, 35 b 32, 36 a 1, 37 a 1 (*atrésat*), 37 b 1, *atreset* 34 b 6, 20, 36 b 11, 37 a 36, 37 b 9. At 36 a 44 *dlé* is used irregularly for the relative form of the 3. sg. of the subjunctive.

(*b*) *dliges* 35 a 39, 35 b 22; *midfed* (= *midfid*) 37 a 40; *co timmaircfea* 35 a 40.

Aided Echach.

(*a*) *ro-m-ain* (v.) 40 a 42; *conid-arlasar*[2]) (v.) 40 a 31.

(*b*) *co tudchad* 39 a 31.

Cf. *día tuidchet* 96 a 10 = *día tuidchisead* YBL. 101 b 27. These instances can hardly be explained save as analogical formations starting from the 3. sg. of the primary subjunctive, e. g. *arna tudaich* (from *-todech, -todecha*) LU. 115 a 28.

---

[1]) Or is it gen. of *fis*?

[2]) In the oldest Irish *ad-glddur* has a reduplicated asigmatic future and a corresponding *ā* subjunctive, see below p. 483.

Serglige Conculaind.

(a) *adfíastar* 46 b 37, *arin-festar* (v.) 46 b 32 (irregular *co fíasur* 45 a 26, *co fíastais* 46 a 17); *ní géis* (leg. *geis*)[1] 46 b 18; *co rís* 44 b 20, *co tísam* (v.) 50 a 22, *día tísat* 43 b 31, *tísad* (v.) 47 a 27, 29, *día tísad* (v.) 47 a 36, *nad rissˇ* 43 b 25; *óis*[2]) 46 b 19; *ní sáis* 46 b 7; *ni ettis* (*-tong-*) 46 b 18.

(b) *mani-t-ainge* 45 a 3; *ni irnaidiub* 50 a 31; *ni aisnessea* 46 b 16, *ni frisnesea* 46 b 15.

Senchas na Relec.

(b) *nohadnaicthe* 51 a 44.

Tuccait Innarba na n-Déssi.

(a) *focichret* 54 b 29.

Táin Bó Cúailnge.

(a) The *s* formations are very numerous and, for the most part, regular. All the forms of importance are quoted in Sigm. Fut., and it is needless to repeat them here. Some innovations may be noticed. In a few instances there is confusion of the stem of the future and of the subjunctive: *nocofocher* 63 a 14 (the blurred facsimile of YBL. 22 b 12 seems to have *noconfoicher*), *dofoetsad* 69 b 9, *dofǽthsad* 73 a 18 = YBL. 30 b 28 (in an interpolated remark), *nárthǽth* 76 b 22. In *arciuchlais* 66 b 25, which seems to come from *ar-clech-* the reduplication is irregular; in *fochiuchra* (v., from *fo-cerd-*) 56 a 8 there is irregularity both in the reduplication and in the ending. In *ní théis* 69 b 33 = *ni theis* YBL. 29 a 45 = *ni thechiubsa* LL. 73 a 14 both the mark of length and the *i* are out of place. At 71 a 14 Zimmer, KZ. XXX, 210 explains *-ecma* (for **-ecmas*), to which he is probably right in regarding *nadbenur* as a gloss, as a new formation from the 3. sg.; the passage appears neither in YBL. nor in LL., and it also contains the irregular *bithus*. At 64 a 21 *téis* appears as 2. sg. for *téisi*. At 68 a 33 *atchosse* = *atchoise* YBL. 27 b 38 seems to be an error for *atchóssed*. In the 3. sg. of the past tenses *-ad*, where the termination is written in full, *-ad* commonly takes the place of O. Ir. *-ed*. But *arná teisˇ* 61 b 30 is clearly to be expanded into *arná teised* = *arna teised*

---

[1] Cf. *ni gess, ni obbais* CZ. III, 454.

[2] Cf. *mad ois* O'Dav. 109. It seems to be an *s* subj. from a verb cognate with *óin* 'loan'.

YBL. 21 a 38. In *bad amlaid tíasad* (= *nothéised*) 75 a 20, *arɔ-tíasad* 75 a 19 (both instances in a passage not found in YBL. or LL.) the vocalism of the radical syllable is correspondingly irregular; cf. also *tíasad* in the late passage 78 b 16, where it has the force of a secondary future.

(b) *cé focherded* 79 a 26; *cía nodligthe* 82 b 3 (= YBL. 34 b 32); *oirgfid* (v.) 56 a 11; *slaidfid* (v.) 56 a 8; *snigfid* (v.) 58 a 80; *arná teichtis* 80 b 9. At 78 a 22 *fífatsa* = *firbatsa* LL. 76 a 43, which I once thought might possibly be a misformation from *fech-* 'fight', seems to be a corruption of *fir-fatsa*, cf. *confirend in cath* LL. 101 a 9.

It will be observed that many of these innovations appear in the poem 55 b 34 — 56 a 12, a fact which shews clearly that the verse is a later ornamentation. As to the rest of the text, new formations are most numerous in the late passage beginning LU. 77 b 21.

Togail Bruidne Dá Dergga.

(a) As in the case of the Táin, the important forms will be found cited in Sigm. Fut. There are, however, a few irregularities to be noticed. At 85 a 4 *arnáchbaraccaist* = the correct *arnachabaccastar* YBL. 94 b 5. At 88 b 18 *ni fochriched* = the correct *ni foichred* YBL. 97 a 46. The reduplicated stem appears in the subjunctive in *nád fóelu[s]-sa* 88 a 19 (= *nad rodam-sa* YBL. 96 b 52), *rosía* 91 b 24 (= *rosoa* YBL. 100 a 1), *noírrtha* 87 a 14 (in an interpolated passage not found in YBL.). The future relative *íuras* (*passim* both in LU. and YBL.) is new, cf. Sigm. Fut. p. 24. From this verb some misformations are found: *ni iurfaithe* 88 a 42 = *ni iurtha* YBL. 97 a 26, *cetna-ortábthar* 92 a 5 (not in YBL.). As in the Táin, the 3. sg. of the past tenses is mostly *-ad*. At 85 b 25 *nisnáigsimmis* = *nisnaig-fimis* YBL. 95 a 14. Of course this is simply a blunder due to the similarity of *f* and *s*. Strangely enough this blunder seems to have started some *s* forms in literary Irish. On *nisnagsind* LU. 16 a 7 much stress cannot be laid, but it would not be easy to explain away the subjunctive forms *arand-aigset* 'that they should fear' Rev. Celt. XII, 422 and *ni fuil ni aranddígsind iat* 'there is no reason why I should fear them' LL. 229 b 20 (contrast the genuine subjunctive *ni fetar ni ardotáigthe* LU. 68 b 28). It is to be remembered that the verb *águr* at an early period went out of common use.

(b) *día tuidchet* 96 a 10 (cf. p. 476); *ar-non-sligfitis* 90 a 16 (= YBL. 98 b 18).

In another fragment of this story 99 a 30 — 31 occur two *s* subjunctives which are unintelligible to me.

Fled Bricrend.

(a) *tadbœ* (irregular 2. sg.) 107 b 43; *ɔ-ndechsad* 111 b 17; *ɔ-da-esur* 104 a 14; *tair* 108 a 11, *co comairsem* 104 a 13, *dothí* 106 b 35, *día tísam* 99 b 46, *co tisaid* 99 b 47, *mani thísat* 100 a 4, *-tissad* 101 b 28, cf. 102 a 31, 110 b 46, 111 a 7, *dothisad* 102 a 18; *ɔmestar* (subj.) 104 a 7; *nínortar*[1]) 107 a 5; *at-rai* 110 b 33; *ro-sassad* 112 b 6; *no-don-sel* (from *sladim*) 106 a 42; *ceta-the* 108 a 38, *co tíasat* 100 a 1, *cía thíastáis* 108 a 24, *dotháiset* 111 b 37.

With the future stem in the subjunctive: *cichś* 102 b 4, 18, *rosía* 112 a 26. Note the irregular *th* in *iúrthund* 'will slay us' 108 a 19, cf. *iurthund* Cormac s. v. *rót*; the form is future, not, as Zimmer says KZ. XXX, 52, secondary future.

(b) *cotmidfíd* 112 b 23; *comma-tuaircfe* 100 a 9. At 104 a 6 *-faigbistar* is a barbarous mixture of the *s* and the *b* futures.[2])

Siaburcharpat Conculaind.

(a) *ɔ-écus* (sic, sg. 2) 113 a 17; *arna tudaich* 115 a 28, corrupted into *ná túadaig* 113 b 41.

Cath Cairnd Chonaill.

(a) *ɔ-digis* 117 a 2; *tair* (v.) 115 b 24; *co tí* (v.) 115 b 31, 32, *co tisad* 115 b 38; *doid-nais* 116 b 4.

Comthoth Loegairi.

(a) *co tudchiś* 117 b 36; *amal tísad*[3]) 118 a 11.

Fáistine Airt.

(a) *noco-tí* (v.) 119 b 11, 17, *dánatársind* (v.) 119 a 30; *dofóeth* (v.) 119 a 35. With future stem as subjunctive *cor-ría* 119 b 41.

(b) *ro-m-nigfea* (v.) 119 b 1.

At 119 b 32 *fuigset* is not clear.

Echtra Condla.

(a) *tair* 120 a 19, *ma róismais* 120 b 13, *ɔdrísmáis* 120 b 13 *má chotuméitís* 120 a 21.

---

[1]) Leg. *bess ní-n-orthar* 'perhaps we may not be slain'.

[2]) Cf. *-dingnesta* Mac Conglinne p. 45, l. 14.

[3]) As the syntax requires the secondary future probably *tíasad* should be restored, cf. LU. 78 b 16.

Imram Brain.

At 121 a 7 *ara tía* = *ara tíasad* or *ara tis'* of other MSS. So for *ni tíassat* of YBL. 92 a 52 Eg., Rev. Celt. XII, 248 has *ní tiat.* I cannot explain the forms.[1])

Tochmarc Emere.

(a) *bibsat'* 125 b 16; *cichis* 125 b 22; *sifis* 125 b 23; *tithis* 125 b 19; *tithsitir* 125 b 21 (all in an obscure *retoric*); *rasia* 126 a 4, *tíarmórset* 123 a 15, *do-t-iarmórset-su* 123 a 19.

(b) *follongad* 124 b 22; *nosaigfed* 121 b 38.

Flight of Etáin.

(a) *ɔ-dechos* 129 a 10; *dían-ecastar* 129 b 6.

Tochmarc Etaine.

(a) *cor-clasta* (*cladim*) 130 a 9; *nad fess'* 129 b 36, *día fesmáis* 130 a 18; *co-roorta* (*roortais* might have been expected) 130 a 10; *téisiu* 130 b 12, *totaisiu* 130 a 25.

Tochmarc n-Etaine.

(a) *ni-t-rius* 132 a 34, *día ris* (v.) 131 l. 41, *tís* (sg. 2) 131 l. 25.

Compert Mongán.

(a) *fessa* 'I will fight' 133 a 7.

Scél Mongán.

(a) *con-da-rois* 134 a 17.

Tucait baile Mongán.

(a) *infessed* (that he would relate) 134 b 31, *ara n-indissed* 134 b 11.

12. Reduplicated asigmatic future and $\bar{e}$ future.

These two formations may be most conveniently treated together. For a suggestion as to their relation to one another and to the sigmatic future see Sigm. Fut. p. 15. The reduplicated asigmatic futures have been discussed by Thurneysen, KZ. XXXI, 77 sq., who has pointed out that they are simply $\bar{a}$ subjunctives + reduplication. A brief account of the formations in Old Irish will help to make the statistics that follow intelligible.

---

[1]) Cf. now Sarauw, Irske Studier pp. 93, 94.

The reduplicated asigmatic future is found:

(1) In some verbs that have an *n* suffix in the present indicative, which does not appear in the subjunctive (KZ. XXXI, 84 sq.).

benim 'cut': fut. sg. 3 *fris-bia* Ml. 96 b 15, *du-fóbi* 96 a 7, pl. 3 *ocubiat* 126 b 12, pass. *ocubether* 53 b 17; fut. sec. sg. 3 *nobiad* YBL. 43 a 46, pass. *foindar-paide* Ml. 26 a 1: subj. *-bia* etc. KZ. XXXI, 85.

For the reduplication of the future cf. KZ. XXXI, 89.

to-ror-fen- 'profit': fut. sg. 3 *etira-tórbie* (= 'inter quos profuturus es'?) Ml. 135 d 2, pl. 3 *dund-órbiat* 120 d 14.

di-ror-fen- 'hinder': fut. sg. 1 *doror-biu-sa* (CZ. III, 246), pass. *diroirpiter* YBL. 45 b 12.

Cf. Celt. Ztschr. II, 481, *dororbenat* s. v. *rorba* O' Dav. 112, *nadatorbad* .i. *nachattairmescad* LL. 262 a 21, *dodrorbai*, *derbaid* Ann. Ul. 810.

ad-fen- 'make return': fut. pass. *ad-fether* Wb. 20 b 7, *adfither* LL. 278 a 30.

Cf. *adfenar* Laws I, 256, O'Don. Suppl., Meyer, Ir. Lex. 21.

-crinim 'perish' (fut. stem *cicriā-*): fut. sg. 3 *-airchiure* LL. 346 a 51, pl. 3 *ara-chiurat* Ml. 59 b 9: subj. pl. 3 *-aurcriat* Laws IV, 318.

Cf. *ara-crinat* Ml. 73 c 2.

glenim 'stick' (fut. stem *gigliā-*): fut. sg. 3 *fo-d-giuil* (MS. *fodgiguil*) CZ. III, 448, pl. 3 *giulait* Ml. 65 b 7; fut. sec. sg. 3 *nogiulad* LU.: subj. sg. 1 *-gléu* Ml. 86 b 8, pl. 3 rel. *glete* 127 b 19.

lenim 'adhere': fut. sg. 2. *lileissiu, lilessa, lilesa* Fél. Pr. 309, 311, 3 *do-lili* (MS. *dolin*, corr. Thurneysen) Ml. 30 c 13, rel. *liles* Wb. 10 a 5, pl. 3 *lilit* Trip. L. 180 l. 26: subj. *noliad* CZ. III, 249.

renim 'sell': fut. sg. 1 *as-ririu-sa* Wb. 18 a 14, 3 *as-riri* Wb. 25 b 16, Ml. 30 c 16, *as-rire* LL. 294 a passim, pass. *as-rirther* Wb. 1 c 3: subj. *ni riat* Wb. 28 c 2.

-gninim 'know': fut. pl. 3 *etir-genat* Ml. 68 c 20, 73 a 1, pass. *atat-gentar-su* 122 a 22:[1] pres. subj. sg. 3 *-aith-gné* LU. 71 a 34, pass. *asa-gnoither* Sg. 180 b 2, past subj. pass. *remi-ergnaitis* Ml. 19 b 9.

---

[1] At LL. 346 b 5 is found an archaising malformation *cinnas atgniusa* 'how shall I know?'

-cluniur 'hear': fut. sg. 3 *ro-t-chechladar* Wb. 28 d 16, cf.
Ml. 53 b 27: pres. subj. *-cloor* etc., cf. Phil. Soc. Trans. 1891—4,
p. 450, where should be added sg. 2 *con-dam-chloither-sa* Ml. 21 b 6,
pl. 3 *ro-cloatar* Ml. 70 a 2, which is deponent and not passive;
past subj. pl. 1 *-cloimmis* Wb. 26 b 23, pl. 3 *-cloitis* 5 a 8.

Here may be mentioned fut. pl. 3 rel. *bebté* Wb. 25 b 16 (cf.
ɔ-bebhau-sa Rev. Celt. XII, 113, *bebaid* CZ. III, 462, 463), to a subj.
remim-baat etc. KZ. XXXI, 80, XXXVI, 112, to which no present
indicative is found. To some other of these nasal presents no
futures happen to have been found; without doubt they were of
the same type as the preceding.

(2) Roots ending in a nasal:

gainiur 'am born' (fut. stem *gigenā-*): fut. sg. 3 *gignithir*
CZ. III, 462, *adgignethar* LU. 68 a 2; fut. sec. sg. 3 *nogig[ned]*
Sg. 138 b 1: subj. stem *genā-*; past sg. 3 *roṅ-genad* Sg. 31 a 6.

damim: fut. sg. 2 *fo-n-didmae-siu* Ml. 35 c 33, cf. *atom-didmae*
Fél. Ep. 494, pl. 3 *fo-s-didmat* Ml. 15 c 10; fut. sec. sg. 3 *f-a-didmed*
Sg. 137 b 5. In this verb the subjunctive stem is *damā-*, the *i*
of reduplication and the *e* of *fadidmed* point to a future stem
didemā- (cf. Thurneysen, KZ. XXXI, 71); in the future indicative
we should have expected rather *fodidme, fodidmet*, cf. also *lilmatar* below. In *-fuidema* Ml. 56 c 9 the reduplicated future has
passed into the *ē* future.

Perhaps a similar formation from *-lamur* 'dare' appears in
ni lilmatar Ml. 69 b 3, which would be the simplest correction
of the corrupt *ni lib matar* of the MS.[1]) The regular future
stem in the Sagas is *lēmā-*, but the curious forms *nocholinfaither*
YBL. 22 b 13 (= *noco-lémaither* LU. 63 a 15), *conlindfadar* LL.
102 b 48, 103 a 21, could be better understood as corruptions of
a less common form of the future.

canim 'sing' (fut. stem *cicanā-*); fut. sg. 2 *for-cechnae-siu*
Ml. 114 b 11, sg. 3 *for-dub-cechna* Wb. 9 a 16, rel. *cechnas* (MS.
cechrus) O'Dav. p. 62.

(3) Root ending in *r*:

caraim 'love' (fut. stem *cicarā-*): fut. sg. 3 *no-d-cechra*
CZ. III, 449, pl. 3 *cechrait* O'Dav. p. 66, *nicon-chechrat* Wb. 30 c 4.

---

[1]) Pedersen's suggestion, KZ. XXXV, 391, gives no sense.

(4) Roots ending in *s*:

ces- 'see': fut. sg. 1 *ni-m-air-cecha-sa* LU. 74 b 3, sg. 3 *duécigi* (MS. *duécicigi*) Ml. 111 c 13; fut. sec. sg. 3 *-acciged* LU. 65 a 3, pl. 3 *ad-cichitis* Wb. 7 a 2: pres. subj. *ad-cear* etc. Phil. Soc. Trans. 1891—4 p. 466.

gus- 'choose': fut. sg. 1 *do-gcga* Wb. 33 b 23, pl. 3 *do-n-gegat* 30 d 8; fut. sec. sg. 3 *do-n-gegadh* Ir. T. I, 105, pl. 1 *at-gegmais* Ir. T. II, 2, 246.

(5) Roots ending in an explosive:

ad-gládur 'address': fut. sg. 1 *ata-gegallar-sa* LU. 19 b 30, 3 *ata-gegalldathar* 19 b 33: pres. subj. pl. 1 *immanárladmar* (= *-ad-ro-gládmar*) Wb. 29 d 10.[1]

ib- 'drink' (pres. *ebaid*): fut. sg. 1 *noíb-sa* LL. 279 a 7, pl. 3 *ibait* Ml. 30 c 18.

The reduplication of *íb-* is like the reduplication of *ís-*, used as the future of *ith-* 'eat'; from the association of meaning these futures may have influenced one another in form.

(6) *gníu* 'make': fut. sg. 1 *du-gén* Ml. 69 a 21, *fu-n-gen-sa* 78 d 2, *-digén* Wb. 9 d 4, *-digen* Ml. 37 c 2, 69 a 21, 2 *do-n-genae-siu* Wb. 32 a 25, cf. Ml. 41 b 4, 42 a 8 (MS. *dumgnese*), 3 *da-géna* Wb. 3 d 16, cf. 20 c 10, 26 a 20, 22 d 9, Ml. 53 c 14, Sg. 198 a 19, *-dignea* Ml. 96 a 8, rel. *genas* Ml. 51 b 10, pl. 1 *du-n-genam* Ml. 111 d 3, *-dignem-ni* Wb. 15 d 6, *-digenam-ni* Ml. 30 c 9, 2 *do-n-génid* Wb. 17 a 6, 3 *do-génat* 13 a 13, *-dignet* Ml. 56 b 15, pass. *do-géntar* Wb. 4 d 1, 26 a 8, Sg. 27 a 13, fut. sec. sg. 3 *du-n-genad* Ml. 123 c 1, *-digned* 14 b 4, pl. 1 *do-genmis* Sg. 203 a 6, 2 *darígente* Wb. 11 d 5, 13 b 3, *-digénte* 9 d 9.

The stem is as in the prototonic form of the subjunctive with reduplication, *-dén* (implied in *-dern*), *-déne*, *-déna* etc.

In *ni digenam-ni* of Ml. by *ni dignem-ni* of Wb. the longer form has been analogically reintroduced. In a close syllable apparently *é* did not suffer syncope, cf. *-dingentar* LU. 32 b 20, *na dingentais* 110 b 16. In the last instances *ng* has come from the syncopated forms, cf. Zimmer, KZ. XXX, 65. It will be observed that the other *ē* futures (of *-gninim* there are no instances to the point; it might be expected to behave like

---

[1] Cf. also p. 476, note 2, and Windisch, Festschrift Whitley Stokes gewidmet, p. 43 sq., for later sigmatic forms.

-gníu) in the Glosses never shew syncope. In the LU. texts
the only exceptions that I have noted are *-tibred* 42 a 20, 42 b 16,
ni thibre 116 b 30, *-faigbet* 33 a 7, 37 b 2; there are more in
Atkinson PH. 661 b, cf. Atkinson, Keating XXII sq. The explanation can hardly be any other than that *ber-*, *geb-* etc. are
of later origin than *gēn-*.

In two of the foregoing verbs, *-gninim* and *-gníu*, the
result of the reduplication is a future in *ē, -gēn-*. In Sigm. Fut.
p. 15 it is suggested that these verbs formed the starting point
of the whole *ē* future; at least in none of the other verbs that
we know can the *ē* future be explained from regular phonetic
development.

The *ē* future appears in O. Ir. in the following verbs:

(1) Roots ending in a liquid:

at-bail 'he dies' (subjunctive stem *belā-*): fut. sg. 1 *at-bél*
Wb. 10 d 24, pl. 2 *at-belaid-si* Ml. 29 c 4, 3 *at-bélat* Wb. 1 d 4,
cf. Ml. 102 b 10: fut. sec. sg. 3 *at-belad* Ml. 16 c 10, pl. 1 *at-bélmis*
Wb. 4 d 9.

ebal- 'rear' (see *eblim* Wind.): fut. sg. 3 *no-dn-ebela* LU.
128 b 36, pass. *ébéltair* (leg. *ebéltair*) LU. 61 a 8; fut. sec. sg. 3
noebelad LU. 128 b 27.

celim 'conceal': fut. sg. 1 *-cél* Sg. 203.

melim 'grind': fut. sg. 1 *ɔ-mel* LU. 82 b 31, pl. 1 *coto-mélam*
(leg. *cotonmélam*) 106 b 37, *cotomelat* (leg. *cotonmélat*) 67 b 15.

fogeir:[1]) fut. sg. 3 *fo-gera* Cod. Cam. 37 d.

berim 'bear' (subj. stem *berā-*): fut. sg. 1 *do-béer* Wb. 12 c 35,
cf. Ml. 91 b 10, *-épéer* Wb. 32 a 20, 2 *do-berae* Ml. 44 a 20, *-tibéruc*
77 a 16, 3 *berthi* (= *béraid-i*) Wb. 29 a 19, *as-bera* 9 a 17, cf.
12 d 6, 26 a 6, 1 a 8, 13 b 30, 25 d 13, *-erbera* Ml. 48 b 12, cf.
110 c 2, rel. *bœras* Ml. 94 b 7, pl. 1 *as-béram* Wb. 17 c 23, cf.
29 b 15, 3 *as-bérat* Wb. 12 d 12, 36, cf. 6 b 27, pass. sg. 3 *do-*
bérthar Wb. 10 d 21, 16 a 13, 25 d 12, cf. Ml. 118 d 22, *-tibérthar*
Wb. 18 b 11, rel. *bérthar* Wb. 12 d 27, pl. 3 *-bértar* 15 a 3; fut. sec.
sg. 3 *do-m-berad* Ml. 108 a 5, *-erberad* 48 a 5, *-tiberad* 97 d 10,
pl. 2 *do-sm-bérthe* Wb. 19 d 24, 3 *no·n-da-bértais* Ml. 124 b 6,
-tibertais 15 c 7.

---

[1]) I have no other examples of the verb; the approximate meaning
seems to be 'hurt, injure'.

mer- 'betray' (present *mairnim*,[1]) subj. stem *merā*-): fut. pl. 3 *nu-m-merat-sa* Ml. 140 c 1.

gar- 'call' (subj. stem *garā*-): fut. sg. 1 *ascon-gér* Ml. 126 c 8, 3 *taiccéra* Wb. 6 b 28, pl. 3 *ar-gerat* Ml. 121 b 8, *-tairǹgérat* Sg. 208 b 3.

maraim 'remain' (subj. stem *marā*-): fut. pl. 2 *meraid* Ml. 100 b 4, *ni-mmerat* Wb. 30 c 20.

scaraim 'separate' (subj. stem *scarā*-): fut. sg. 3 *ɔ-scéru* Wb. 26 a 8, cf. Ml. 56 d 6, *etir-scértar* Wb. 8 b 3.

The simple *scaraim* exhibits a *b* future in Ml. 43 a 23.

(2) Roots ending in a nasal:

-em- (*do*-) 'protect' (subj. stem *emā*-): fut. sg. 1 *do-em-sa* Ml. 37 c 20, 2 *du-n-emae* 93 c 18, 3 *du-ema* Ml. 67 c 5, pass. *do-*[*b*]*-emthar-si* 53 b 18.

Also the *b* future: *doemfea* Ml. 128 c 8, *dotemfet-su* 112 c 1.

sem- 'pour forth': fut. pass. sg. 3 *dofuiscémthar* Wb. 4 c 7.

From *cosnaim* comes *-cossena* LU. 107 b 44, which *may* be the O. Ir. future of this verb.

From *gonaim* the regular future stem in old texts is *gēn*-. In the 1. sg. *gegna* is quoted, KSB. VII, 17; the passage is now published Ir. T. II, 2. 246, where it will be seen that there is a variant *gena*; *gegna* then is evidently a corruption of *géna*, cf. the monstrous *gid geogainter* Battle of Magh Rath 122. In LL. 288 b 51 we find *no-t-gignether* 'thou wilt be slain', but this text generally is not of so archaic a character as those in which *gēn*- appears. Therefore, though it is possible that *gēn*- has replaced an older *giyen*-, since *gēn*- is the form found in the oldest texts in which the future appears, this future will in the following lists simply be given among the *e* futures. In the eleventh century *génaid* gives place to *gonfaid*, cf. LU. 117 b 43.

(3) Roots ending in an explosive:

gabim 'take' (subj. stem *gabā*-): fut. sg. 1 *in-geb-sa* Wb. 8 d 12, 3, *gebaid* 8 a 7, *conocœba* Ml. 20 b 5, rel. *gebas* Wb. 11 a 6, pl. 3 *gebtit* Wb. 26 a 8, *ni gebat* 4 c 8, *-foigebat* Ml. 69 a 8, pass. *ni-n-incébthar* Wb. 15 d 27, *conuicgebthar* Ml. 64 b 8, pl. 3 *-digebtar* 73 d 13; fut. sec. pl. 3 *f-a-gebtis* Wb. 8 a 14, cf. Ml. 34 c 8.

---

[1]) Pedersen, Aspirationen i Irsk p. 104; in Celt. Ztschr. II, 210 I was **wrong** in questioning this.

gataim 'steal': fut. sg. 1 *-gét* Wb. 9 d 4; fut. sec. pl. 2 *-gette* Wb. 9 c 8.

For determining accurately the date of the loss of the reduplicated asigmatic future I have no sufficient data; doubtless some lived longer than others; thus *-fuidema* appears already in the Milan Glosses. In the Tripartite Life the formation is still well preserved; in the Saltair na Rann by *gigned* 7524 we find *combenfad* (in one of the following poems) 8070; *nombifud* 5812 is probably only a perverse spelling of *nombíad* under the influence of the *b* future, cf. *bífed* LL. 60, l. 29. We may conclude that in part at least this future survived till the end of the tenth century.

The reduplicated future — so far as the verbs remained in use — was commonly replaced by a *b* future formed from the present stem: *benaid, benfaid; lenaid, lenfaid; as-ren, érnifes; crenaid* 'buys' (which had doubtless a reduplicated future) *crenfaid; arachrinim, -airchranfa* LL. 293 b 3; *-cluinid, -cluinfid; -génar, genfid; canaid, canfaid; caraid, carfaid; ad-cí, -aicfea; togaid* (chooses), *togfaid.* But for the reduplicated *didm- dēm-* comes into use; probably *lem-* has replaced an O. Ir. *lilm-*, and possibly *gēn- (gonaim)* has taken the place of an O. Ir. *gign-*.

In later Irish the *ē* future spreads very widely.

(*a*) In O. Ir. it is the regular future in radical verbs in *l* and *r*, and it is also found in some roots ending in a nasal. Hence in time it becomes the common future from verbal stems in *l, r, m, ng,* cf. Atkinson, Keating XV, O'Donovan 195, and, for dialectical transformations of these forms, O'Donovan 196, J. H. Molloy pp. 92 sq.

(*b*) In later Irish it becomes the regular future from verbs in *-igim.*

(*c*) It appears in some other verbs: e. g. *innisim, inneósat; aithrisim, aithreósat.*

Of (*a*) some instances are found in LU. of (*b*) and (*c*) instances are wanting, as likewise in the Saltair na Rann. In the Passions and Homilies there are still very few examples. In Atkinson's Glossary I have noted from primary verbs *condaigim, cuindegat; érgim, ereochad; toibgim, toibéchar,* to which is to be added *deligim, deléchaid, -deleochar.*

In LU. texts there are some curious transformations of *b* futures of class III; sometimes the *e* is marked long, sometimes

it is not. These are -*áceḃá* 'will see'; -*aidléba*, -*aidlébthai*, *taid-
lébat*, *do-t-athleba* (*ad-ellaim*); *claidbebtair* (*claidbim*); *gairmebtair*
(*gairmim*); *aisnébat* (*aisndisim*); *noairmebad*, -*airmébaind* (*ad-
rímim*); *dofucébad* (*tuiccim*); -*thatnéba*, *taitnébtáit* (*taitnim*); *anéb*
(*anaim* = O. Ir. -*ainib* by -*anub*).[1] Though the mark of length
is not always added, it is probable that the quantity of the *e*
was throughout the same. As to the origin of the formation,
it must be connected in some way with the *ē* future; what the
precise connexion was is not clear.[2] I cannot discover that the
formation was ever a common one; in Passions and Homilies
fuilngim gives *fuilngebad*, cf. Stokes, O'Gorman XXVIII—XXIX
(where most of the instances do not belong here), O'Donovan
195. Here may be mentioned also *nobdidnoba*, cf. *elóbhus*, Silv.
Gad. I, 352, *roderbobmais* s. v. *derbaim* PH., and -*ernába* from
érnaim (= O. Ir. *as-roinnim*). Perhaps fuller collections will
clear up the history of these forms. The spread of the *ē* future
in Irish would probably repay a careful study.

In the following lists are distinguished (*a*) reduplicated
futures (except from -*gninim* and -*gníu*, which are reckoned
among the *ē* futures), (*b*) transformations of the reduplicated
future, (*α*) *ē* futures, (*β*) extensions of the *ē* future. From *ber-*,
gab-, and -*gníu* it would be useless to give the cases where
the accent falls on the *ē*, since these present no points of
interest.

Nennius.

(*a*) *in-dignet* 3 a 22.

The sense seems to demand *un-dogénat* 'what they will do'.

Commentary on the Amra.

(*b*) *nocon-áceḃá* (v. 'shall not see') 5 a 23.

(*α*) *méraid* (v.) 5 b 23.

(*β*) *noairmebad* (*ad-rímim*) 11 b 27; *dufucébad* (*tuiccim*) 6 a 20.

---

[1] In Verbal System of the Saltair na Rann p. 71 I called attention to
the fact that verbs of class I often form their future according to class III.
Further examination of the O. Ir. Glosses has shewn me that this is the pre-
dominant formation in O. Ir. Accordingly in Wb. 32 c 12 Zimmer's old reading
intain neidfider (cf. KZ. XXXVI, 503) would be in accordance with the Old
Irish usage.

[2] As Professor Thurneysen has pointed out to me, the starting point of
the formation may be found in the analogy of compounds of *gab-*, *turcéba* etc.

Scél Tuain.

(a) *ná airbértáis* 15 b 13.

(β) Here may be mentioned *nobdídnoba* 'who shall protect you' 15 a 42.

Two Sorrows etc.

(α) *na dingne* 18 a 9; *ni etarscérthar* 17 a 41.

(β) *claidbebtair* 18 a 3, 15.

Mesca Ulad.

(a) *ata-gegallar-sa* (*ad-gládur*) 19 b 30, *ata-gegalldathar* 19 b 30, *ata-geglathar* 19 b 33. At 20 b 12 the reduplicated -*dercachad* is strangely used as a subjunctive. The reduplicated future of -*cíu* appears in the 1. sg. with the ending of the sigmatic future, *donecuchus-sa* 19 a 2, cf. 19 b 31.

(a) *atbélat* 19 a 3, 19 b 31, *inn-ebél* 20 a 10, *nan-genaind* 20 a 32.

Imram Máiledúin.

(a) *inn-eberam* 25 a 18; *in-dingne-siu* 25 a 21; *ni ib* (leg. *íb*) 22 d 31.

Fis Adamnán.

(b) *ni aicfea* 28 a 25.

(a) *in-fugebtáis* 30 b 41.

Scéla Lái Brátha.

(b) *ni chluinfider* 33 a 13.

(a) *ni faigbet* 33 a 7, *na dingentar* 32 b 20, 38, *o-digniter* 32 b 12; *scérait* 33 a 2.

(β) *gairmebtair* 33 b 28.

Scéla na Esserge.

(b) *carfaidir* (*caraim*) 37 b 17; *atchluinfet* 34 a 44; *ernifes* 36 a 44, 37 a 45; *fodémat* 37 b 4.

(a) *ni faigbet* 37 b 2; *ni dingnet* 36 b 5; *mértait* (= O. Ir. *mérait*) 35 a 33.

(β) *taitnébtáit* 36 a 6, *ni thatnéba* 36 b 15.

Aided Echach.

(a) The reduplicated -*siblad* 39 b 16, improperly used as a subjunctive, cf. *co síblur* LL. 103 a 42, seems to imply a reduplicated future, of which, however, I have no example.

Fotha Catha Cnucha.
(a) *-tibred* 42 a 20, 42 b 16.

Serglige Conculaind.
(a) *atchichither* 'thou shalt see' 49 a 31.
(a) *noco-dingnea* (v.) 50 a 25.

Senchas na Relec.
(a) *meraid* (v.) 51 b 22.
(β) *na aidérad* 50 b 22, *noadérad* 50 b 23.

Tucait Innarba na n-Desi.
(a) *in-dingebad* 54 b 17; *no-s-genat* 54 b 29.
(β) *noco-taidlébat* 54 b 30.

Táin Bó Cuailnge.
(a) *eter-da-bíad* 60 b 17, cf. 60 b 15 (YBL. in each case *-bied*), *forbíad* 61 a 26; *ni-m-aircecha-sa* (*ar-cíu*) 74 b 3 (= *nim aircechsa* YBL. 32 a 14), *in-acciged* 64 a 40, 65 a 3; *noco-dídem* (YBL. *nochodidem*) 63 b 22, *in-didma* 63 b 21; *adgignethar* 68 a 2; *ibait* (v.) 57 a 19; *nír-riri* 68 a 21.

(b) *nobenfad* (so YBL.) 58 b 20 (= *nobíad*); *ni déma* 76 a 25; so probably *noco-lémaither* 63 a 15 (see above p. 482). From *benim* the 1. sg. fut. may have been *bía*; for this we find *bithus* 71 a 23, apparently remodelled after the *s* future, cf. *donécuchus* above p. 487. At 58 b 6 *ɔ-dercaiss* is an *s* subj., whereas *-cíu* has regularly the *ā* subj.

(a) *nocon-imbera* 62 a 44; *ni-n-imgeb* 70 a 5, *ni fuicéb* 62 b 20, *ni faigebthar* 73 b 37, *ni thurcébad* 60 a 12; *ni digéon-sa*[1]) 74 b 43, *ni dingén* 68 a 24, 29, *ni dingned*[2]) 68 a 20; *athelsa* 70 a 15; *ébéltair* (leg. *cbéltair* 'shall be reared') 61 a 8; *ni-t-gén-sa* (*gonaim*) 68 b 32, *genaid* 57 b 41, *no-génad* 58 b 21; *nomertáis* (*maraim*) 61 a 27; *ɔmel* 82 b 31, *cotomélat* (recte *cotonmélat*) 67 b 15.

(β) *nad anéb* (remain I will not) 78 b 34 (= *nad anœb* LL. 76 b 40).

_____

[1]) The *o* is here to be put down the influence of the vanished *g*; cf. spellings like *geoguin* for *geguin* which shew the influence of the velar spirant on a preceding vowel, cf. Pedersen, Aspiratiouen i Irsk p. 4. The form is an interesting one as pointing to the starting point of the *eó*, which later appears for *e* in the *ē* future.

[2]) At 68 a 35 for *forsingénathar* (so YBL.) an unusual form of the 3. sg. we should perhaps restore the pl. *-génatar*.

Togail Bruidne Dá Dergga.

(a) *nogíulad* 84 a 19; irregularly *nogiuglad* 88 b 19 = *ro-giulad* YBL. 97 a 46.

(α) *-fugebmáis* 85 a 5; *atbél* 97 b 7, *atbéla* passim; *nodogéna* (leg. *no-da-géna* cf. YBL. 98 b 40), 90 a 41, *no-dn-géna* 93 b 8, *génait* 88 b 13, *ní génat* 96 b 5, *ni génaiter* 88 b 14, 96 b 5.

(β) *ni-sn-aidléba* 95 b 13 (= *nisnaidleba* YBL. 101 a 43), *ní aidlébthai* 87 b 38 (= *ni aidlebthai* YBL. 96 b 27; the O. Ir. fut. is *doaidlibem* Ml. 14 d 5); *ní aisnébat* 88 a 3 = *ni aisnebet* YBL. 96 b 37 is a mongrel form for O. Ir. *ní aisndiset*; perhaps it came through *-aisnifet* with confusion between *s* and *f.*[1]) Note also *noconérnába* 86 a 20 (= *noconernaba* YBL. 95 a 47) by *doernaba* 92 a 4, from *érnaim*, which in O. Ir. is *as-roinnim*.

Fragment of another version.

(b) *nothogfad* (= *dogegad*) 99 a 37.

Fled Bricrend.

(a) *for-dun-di-b* 106 a 8. At 110 a 45 *ni didemam* is a con tamination of the old reduplicated future with the later *ē* future.

(b) *fodémam* 110 b 10; *no-d-lemad* 110 b 9.

(α) *nocho-dingnium-ni* 100 a 4, *ɔ-digned* 110 b 22, *na dingentais* 110 b 16; *cutan-méla* 106 b 34, *cotomélam* (recte *cotonmélam*) 106 b 37; *ní chossena* 107 b 44.

Cath Cairnd Chonaill.

(a) *ni thibrc* 116 b 30.

(β) *do-t-athlebá* 115 b 26.

Comthoth Loegairi.

(α) *genaid* (*gonaim*) 117 b 43.

Faistine Airt.

(b) *nothogfaind* (= *dogegaind*) 119 a 24.

(β) *digeltar* 119 b 7.

Echtra Condla.

(α) *atgérat* 120 a 44; *ɔscéra* 120 b 6.

Tochmarc Emere.

(b) At 127 a 32 *bithus* is a distortion of the 3. sg. fut. of *benim*, cf. CZ. III, 241.

---

[1]) Cf. *noinrifed* LL. 401 b 39.

(α) *in-faigebtais* 122 a 1.

(β) *nach-at-airmébaind* 123 b 5 (= *nach airmebaind* CZ III, 235).

Compert Conculaind.

(α) *noebelad* 128 b 27, *no-dn-ebela* 128 b 36.

Tochmairc Etáine.

(b) In *noco-ririub* 130 b 8 the reduplicated future is contaminated with the *b* future.

Tochmarc n-Etáine.

(b) *ni-t-ririub* 132 a 36, as above; in *conom-rire* 132 a 34, *dianom-rire* 132 a 35 the reduplicated stem is improperly used as a subjunctive. The curious form *dogignestár* 131 b 19 is probably a transformation of *-gignither* (*gainiur*) under the influence of those verbs that have a sigmatic future passive by a deponential asigmatic future active.

(α) *ni immér* 130 b 40, *inn-imberam* 131 b 20.

Compert Mongán.

(α) *atbéla* 133 a 4.

Scél asamberar etc.

(α) *docechnad* 133 a 36, 38.

(α) *onatibertáis* 133 a 38.

Bowdon, Cheshire. J. STRACHAN.

THE DATE OF THE FIRST SETTLEMENT OF
THE SAXONS IN BRITAIN.

In the first half of the fifth century certain Angles and[1]) Saxons whose leaders are called Horsa, Hengist and Æsc[2]) settled in a district of Britain that had previously been under Roman government. This settlement was the result of an appeal for armed assistance made by a chief who is believed to have been a Briton, and who is called Guorthigirn in British legends, and Uurtigernus and Wyrtgeorn in Saxon ones.[3]) We do not know

[1]) Bede, 'H. E.' I. xv., says: 'Anglorum siue Saxonum gens', where '*sive* = *et*, as constantly in Bede'; compare Mr. Plummer's notes, Vol. II, pp. 73, 82.

[2]) The Geographer of Ravenna (VIIth century) calls the Saxon leader 'Anschis'; V, § 31. Mr. Plummer, vol. II, p. 28, repeats the oftmade assertion that this stands for Hengist, but it seems to me that we should read *auschis*. The Northumbrian 'Oisc' ('H. E.', II, v.) shews that the vowel of the West-Saxon Æsc (*v.* 'Saxon Chronicle') was, at least originally, a long one. It may, therefore, be a condensation of A. S. *eá* which represents the Gothic *au* and the Old Frisian *â*. In that case *ausk* would be the correct Gothic form for A. S. †*eásc* = *Æsc*. The same explanation appears to me to apply to the form Audu(baldus) for Ead(bald) in Pope Boniface's letters in 'H. E.', II. x, xi. Compare the name 'Aschis' in 'Lestorie des Engles' of Gaimar, ll. 524—5 (RB. SS., no. 91, Vol. I, p. 22) and 'Aschillius' in 'Historia Regum Britanniae', Geoffrey, XI, ii. (For the linguistic principles involved in this emendation of *anschis* see Helfenstein's 'Comparative Grammar of the Teutonic Languages', 1870, pp. 42, 414.)

[3]) For the name cf. Florence of Worcester, 1029 (ed. Thorpe, 1848, I, p. 184): 'Canutus . . . . comitem Hacun, qui . . . . Gunnildam sororis suae et Wyrtgeorni regis Winidorum filiam in matrimoniam habuit . . . . in exilium misit . . . .' In William of Malmesbury's 'Gesta Regum', I, xix (RB. SS., no. 90, 1887, p. 23) we have 'Wirtgernesburg' near Bradford-on-Avon. See Mr. Plummer's notes to the 'Saxon Chronicle', Vol. II, p. 24.

with certainty what district this chief ruled over, nor yet what district the invaders first settled in; neither has it been found possible to determine the exact year of their arrival. This point is the most important one of all, and some agreement upon it is fundamentally necessary. But historians are divided with respect to it into two parties which are so clearly and so sharply defined that the differences between them really appear to be irreconcilable. In one camp are gathered together all those who prefer Welsh tradition and believe that Guorthigirn's appeal to Hengist was made or at least responded to in the consulship of Felix and Taurus. In the other are to be found those who prefer English tradition and assign the invasion to the year in which the emperor Marcian ascended the throne, which was twenty-two years later. The later year is the one indicated by Venerable Bede; the earlier one occurs in the Harley MS., no. 3859, in certain chronological memoranda which are printed by Dr. Mommsen as cap. lxvi of the 'Historia Brittonum'. This date is given there quite clearly and it is implied in other statements made in the same work. The doubt respecting the date of the Saxon advent therefore ascends as high as the eighth century, and we may even say that Nennius's teachers and Bede himself were unconscious protagonists in a dispute that is now upwards of a thousand years old.

This dispute still goes on and the two views referred to are alternately advanced and decried. No way out of the difficulty has yet been suggested, and, apparently, if no new criterion is applied to the determination of the question it must remain unanswered, and the attempt to solve important problems in early Anglo-British history must continue to be an affair of partisans. My object, then, is to analyse the chronological position in the hope that the discovery of the true cause of the confusion will indicate the criterion the application of which will harmonise the conflict of opinion and set the antagonists at one. I purpose, therefore, taking into consideration — I. the technical chronology of the data given by Bede; II. the credibility of the 'Excidium Britanniae' with regard to the order of events; III. the technical chronology of the memoranda in the lxvith chapter of the 'Historia Brittonum'. (These preliminary considerations will, I believe, establish the facts that the Northumbrian date is A. D. 450 and the Welsh one A. D. 428).

Lastly — IV. I shall shew that the method of computing the
years *ab incarnatione dominica secundum ueritatem euangelii*,
which is said to have been employed first by Marianus Scotus,
was really in use long before his time; and I shall give reasons
for believing that this method was known in Northumbria before
Bede wrote his 'Historia Ecclesiastica', and that the divergence
of 22 years from Dionysian computation that it presents is the
cause of the retardation in English records of the date of the
first settlement of the Saxons in Britain. This style of computation has not been considered in this connexion by any writer,
and in it such dates as A. D. 428 and 837 (*v.* Historia Brittonum,
cap. xvi., and *cf.* Archiv f. celt. Lexikographie, Bd. I, S. 515) are
given as *A. D. secundum ueritatem euangelii* 450 and 859. These
and similar reasons will lead us to the conclusion that the
annuary numbers 428 and 450 are really computations in
different eras of one and the same year, that, namely, of the
consulship of Felix and Taurus.

I.

In the first chapter an attempt is made to discover the
exact meaning of the date assigned by Bede as that of the
arrival of the Saxons in Britain; and in the course of it the
following points are reviewed and the obscurities connected with
them to some extent, it is hoped, elucidated. In illustrating
these difficulties preference has been given, where possible, to
matters of technical chronology which concern Celtologists. In
§ 1 the objection that Bede's date was not intended to be exact
is considered and the arguments advanced in support of this
view are rebutted. In § 2 the antedating of Marcian's accession
by one year is examined; the by-no-means rare occurrence of
similar phenomena in Bede is pointed out, and the alleged error
explained as the result of difference of system, and shewn to be
dependent upon a very early method of dating events; one,
namely, (§ 3) which ignored the current year entirely and dated
by the number of complete years that had passed away since
the epoch. In § 4 the computations made by Bede in the era
of the Saxon advent are considered. In § 5 the difference of
three years between a date computed in the era of our Lord
according to Bede, in his Chronica, and a date computed in the

era of our Lord according to Dionysius Exiguus is pointed out
and explained; in § 6 the possible cause of the three years' prochronism in the date of the Saxon advent that is implied in
Bede's computations referred to in § 4 is suggested, and in § 7
an attempt is made to discover the source of Bede's report of
the date.

Bede dates the Saxon advent thus:

a) Anno ab incarnatione Domini CCCCXLVIIII. Marcianus
cum Ualentiniano XLVI. ab Augusto regnum adeptus
VII. annis tenuit. Tunc Anglorum siue Saxonum gens
inuitata a rege praefato [sc. a Vortigerno] Brittaniam
tribus longis nauibus aduehitur.

Baedae Historia Ecclesiastica Gentis Anglorum, I. xv.,
ed. C. Plummer, p. 30, 1896.

b) Anno CCCCXLVIIII. Marcianus cum Ualentiniano im-
perium suscipiens VII. annis tenuit quorum tempore
Angli a Brettonibus accersiti Brittaniam adierunt.

Ibid. V. xxiiii. Recapitulatio Chronica, u. s., p. 352.

§ 1. Mr. Plummer in his note upon the date of the first
settlement of the Saxons in Britain (Vol. II, p. 27), says that Bede
never professes to know the exact year in which it happened.
This statement would seem to be contrary to the sense of the
first passage given above, and historians have generally [1]) understood that the word *tunc* in it was used to assign the event to
the year mentioned immediately before, namely, the year of
Marcian's accession. Mr. Plummer dissents from this view and
raises the objection that Bede omits to give the exact year of
the event in his chronological summary where he vaguely refers
the invitation to the times of the emperors already named.
Mr. Plummer regards this omission as proof that Bede did not
claim to know the year, and argues that the incompleteness of
Bede's testimony in one passage requires us to reject the pre-

---

[1]) Lappenberg must be excepted; 'History of the Anglo-Saxon Kings',
Vol. I, p. 96 (Thorpe's transl.). Bede dates the arrival of Columba in A. D. 565
'quo tempore gubernaculum Romani imperii post Justinianum Justinus minor
accepit'; III, iv. This is the true year for the accession of Justin. Are we
to assume that Bede was unaware that he was right because he adds 'quo
tempore'?

sumably exact statement generally believed to be made in the
other. In support of this view of the case it is alleged that
when Bede dates events from the epoch the exact year of which
is in dispute 'he always uses the word „circiter" in reference
to it'. On one hand this is not quite correct: 'circiter' is
always used in the passages referred to with regard to the
intervals themselves, and never in reference to the epoch from
which their duration is computed. On the other hand if the
mere use of 'circiter' in 'H. E.' I. xxiii., II. xiiii. and V. xxiii.
proves that Bede did not pretend to know the date of the epoch
from which he was computing, then the use of 'circiter' in
'H. E.', IV. xxiiii., and in the letter to Archbishop Egbert should
prove the same thing with regard to the events computed from
there. But both these events — namely, the overthrow of
Egfrid in A. D. 685, and the death of Aldfrid in December,
A. D. 704,[1]) occurred in Bede's own lifetime and he gives their
dates. For these reasons I think that Mr. Plummer presses the
word unduly, and that the use of it implies no more than that
the last year of the period qualified by it was current and incomplete at the time when the event referred to took place.

§ 2. It may be assumed, therefore, that Bede dates the
first settlement of the Saxons in Britain in the year of Marcian's
accession, which he antedated, as is well known, by one year.
Now there are other events the dates of which Bede treats in
the same way. In the following table all the events that are
dated by Bede in the era of our Lord from Diocletian's accession
to Marcian's are enumerated. The dates in this series of events
are not identical with those in the 'Chronica Minora', and the
nature of the differences seems to indicate that in the interval
between September, 725, when Bede compiled the Chronica, and
731, when he finished the Historia, either his opinions had
changed respecting some of these dates or his method of dating
had been modified. It will be quite clear from the table that
it was not uniform, and, in order to compare the system used
in the 'H. E.' with that in the 'Chronica', the A. D. of one

---

[1]) The date of Aldfrid's death is disputed. If I am right in assigning
the commencement of Bede's annus ab Incarnatione dominica to September 24
the date given above is the true one. See the *Athenæum*, No. 3804, Sept. 22,
1900, p. 380.

work is tabulated side by side with the Annus Mundi of the other. The Bedane *annus ab incarnatione dominica,* to which I shall hereinafter refer by the initials A. D. I., in order to distinguish it from the Dionysian A. D., is computed by deducting 3951 from the sum of the mundane years.[1]) The Annus Mundi is reduced in this way because Bede assigned the birth of Christ to A. M. 3952 and thus made that year the first of the Sixth Age or Christian Era.

The true A. D.	Historia Ecclesiastica.		A. D.	A. M.	Regnal Years	A. D. I.
				Chronica Maiora.[2])		
284	I. vi.	Diocletian	286	4238	20	287
378	I. ix.	Gratian	377	4332	6	381
382	V. xxiiii.	Maximus	381			
383		[Theodosius]		4338	11	387
395	I. x.	Arcadius	394	4349	13	398
408	I. xi.	Honorius	407	4362	15	411
410	V. xxiiii.	Rome taken	409			
423	I. xiii.	Theodosius II.	423	4377	26	426
431	V. xxiiii.	Palladius	430			
450	I. xv.	Marcian	449	4403	7	452

Seven of the events enumerated in this table are dated in the 'H. E.' one year too early; one, the election of Diocletian, is

---

[1]) I have called this era by Bede's name because I know of no earlier English writer who used it, and not because it is to be supposed that it was unheard of before Bede's time.

[2]) 'Bedae Chronica Maiora ad a. 725; eiusdem Chronica Minora ad. a. 703', ed. Mommsen, 1895, 'Chronica Minora' Vol. III, pp. 223—354 (= Auctt. Antiquiss. tomus XIII, pars II). Mr. Plummer's references to Bede's Chronicle are erroneous at the following places: Vol. I. Introd. p. xxxix, ll. 1—3 (*cf.* S. 508, Note 1, *infra*); Vol. II, p. 14, ll. 18—20; p. 27, l. 24 (*cf.* the similar error of Lappenberg, Vol. I, p. 96, l. 6 from the bottom, Thorpe's transl.), and p. 114, l. 22. The first of these errors repeats the late Joseph Stevenson who says (*v.* 'Opp. Histt. Baedae', 1841, Vol. II, Introd. p. ix) that the Chronicle of Bede is a general summary of history from the Creation to the year 729. All these mistakes are due to the omission to recognize that the chronicle of Bede does not give the A. D. and that the anni Christi were computed by Stevenson from the A. M. and interpolated by him in the margin of his edition. Stevenson does not comment upon the discrepancy between A. Chr. 729 and A. D. 725 and does not seem to have noticed that his anni Christi were three, and sometimes four years behind the true year.

dated two years too low; and only one, namely, the accession
of Theodosius the Younger, is assigned to the true year. When
we compare the A. D. given by Bede in the 'H. E.' with the
A. D. I. of the Chronica (as computed) we find that Diocletian
is dated one year too early; Gratian, Arcadius, and Honorius
four years too early, each; and Theodosius the Younger and
Marcian three years too early, each. Bede's chronology in these
particular instances would thus appear to be greatly at variance
with what we know from the best sources to be the truth. Let
us examine the matter before condemning him, however.

First we will consider the prochronism of one year which
is the most persistent feature of these dates. If there were no
other years given than those of the emperors' accessions the
mistake of dating Gratian in 377 might be supposed to be the
initial one of a series, and we might, conformably with that
view, attribute the other mistakes to the consequences of computing the successive regnal intervals from it. But this reason
is insufficient to account for all the phenomena present in the
table, and it is not applicable to the cases of Diocletian, the
taking of Rome, or Palladius. The latter was sent from Rome
in A. D. 431, and our authority for the data which point to this
year is the same as Bede's, namely, Prosper. Bede, however,
assigns the mission of Palladius to the eighth year of Theodosius II. (I. xiii., p. 28), and dates it A. D. 430 (*u. s.*). He also
assigns the third consulship of Aetius (A. D. 446) to the twenty-
third year of Theodosius (*ibid.*). Mr. Plummer (Vol. II, p. 26) says
that that year would be 446; but that does not coincide with
Bede's view, for the twenty-third year would be 445 according
to the annuary data of Bede who assigns the eighth year to
430. Further, the taking of Rome by the Goths is dated in
H. E.' I. xi., p. 24, thus:

> *c*) Anno ab Incarnatione Domini CCCCVII tenente imperium
> Honorio Augusto ... ante biennium Romanae inruptionis
> ... apud Brittanias Gratianus municeps tyrannus creatur
> et occiditur.

Mr. Plummer (Vol. II, p. 22) says that the date is correct,
and suggests that Bede is probably referring to the first siege of
Rome, 'dating it, as he does the third, a year too late'. But

the date is not correct, because Arcadius did not die, and Honorius did not succeed to seniority until May 1, 408.[1])   If Bede were really dating the event one year in advance, as he did date the six other events, his intention was to point to the correct year of the siege and capture — namely, A. D. 410.

If this antedating really is systematic it must follow that the correctness of the date for Theodosius's accession to seniority is apparent only; because 423 in the system the phenomena of which we are considering really indicates A. D. 424.   It is clear, therefore, that if the date of Theodosius's accession is given correctly it must be given wrongly according to system; while, if it is given in accordance with the alleged system, it is wrong in fact, and this I believe to be actually the case, for the following reasons.   If we ignore Bede's annuary date for Palladius and compute the true year (431), as the eighth of Theodosius, we assume that Theodosius's first year was 424, which is one year too low.   Similarly the twenty-third year from 424 is 446. A. D. 424 would appear, therefore, to have been the year that Bede supposed to be the one in which Theodosius the son of Arcadius became senior.   In further support of this hypothesis there is the fact that Bede assigns only 26 years to Theodosius whereas he should have assigned him 27.   For these reasons I believe that Bede was misled by the writer whose work he reproduced and apparently depended upon.   If it could be shewn that Bede or his predecessor used a copy of the Chronicle of Jerome with the Continuation by Idatius[2]) the point would be established thereby.   For Idatius dated Honorius's death and Theodosius's accession to seniority in the thirtieth year from the death of Theodosius the Elder (395), i. e. in 424, and this is undoubtedly at the root of Bede's mistake respecting the regnal years of Theodosius the Second.   With regard to Diocletian, if Bede or his authority computed the mundane year 4238 as A. D. I. 287, and dated according to hypothesis, 287

---

[1]) Henry Fynes Clinton, 'Fasti Romani', Oxon. 1845, Vol. 1, sub anno. It is singular that Mr. Plummer does not refer to Clinton when treating the chronology of the later emperors.

[2]) Compare the remarks of Clinton, u. s., Vol. I, pp. 600, 604, 634, 636, 640; and of Mommsen, Introd. to 'Hydatii Lemici Continuatio Chronicorum Hieronymianum', 'Chronica Minora', Vol. II (= MG., tomus XI, pars I) p. 5.

would be found noted as 286, and the incomplete or current year would in this case be ignored just as it is in the eight or nine other instances already examined.

This antedating by one year, therefore, is systematic. Consequently, where Bede copied down 449 for the accession of Marcian his authority intended to indicate 450, and similarly in the other cases tabulated. Before considering the causes of the differences of three years that some of the dates present (*v. infra*, § 5) we will endeavour to learn whether the prochronisms tabulated are a solitary group of instances of what is certainly an unusual way of dating.

§ 3. The 'Chronica Minora' which is appended to the 'Liber de Temporibus' was compiled by Bede 'anno quinto Tiberii, indictione prima' (*v.* cap. xiiii., ed. Giles, Patres Ecclesiae Anglicani, Vol. VI, p. 130). The Tiberius referred to began to reign in A.D. 698, and his fifth year fell partly in the indiction which was current from September 1, 702, to August 31, 703, and which was the first of its series. Now in several MSS. of this work there is a chronological note at the commencement of cap. xxii of the 'De Sexta Aetate' which says:

d) Sexta aetas continet annos praeteritos DCCVIII (Giles's edition); DCCVIIII (Mommsen's, *u. s.*, p. 280, at foot).

Bede wrote the little work 'De Temporibus' before August 31, 703; consequently, as the Sixth Age or Christian Era commences with the birth of Christ, this statement could not have been penned by Bede in the year in which he wrote the book. Dr. Mommsen says of this date (*u. s.*, p. 226, note 3): 'numerus p. Chr. 709 .... venit opinor a librario auctoris aequali'. Mr. Plummer (Vol. I., Introd., p. cxlvi) says that DCCVIII is a mistake for DCCIII, the V being, he thinks, wrongly inserted. With regard to the edition dated 709 Dr. Mommsen's remark holds good; with regard to the earlier edition Mr. Plummer has overlooked the connexion between its date, as it stands, and the facts he adduces about Bede and Bishop Wilfrid. Five years after Bede wrote the 'De Temporibus' a charge of heresy which appears to have depended upon something he had written in the 'De Sex Aetatibus Saeculi' was brought against him, and he wrote a letter[1]) to Plegwin, a monk of Hexham, in which he defended himself and begged that his defence might be read 'coram uenerabili domino ... Wilfrido antistite'. Now Wilfrid according to Mr. Plummer (II, pp. 316, 320, 328) died in 709[2]) and the note that says that 'Sexta aetas continet annos praeteritos DCCVIII' means that 708 years had already passed away since the Incarnation, and this indicates that the note was made in A. D. 709, that is to say, in the very year that Wilfrid died in. Bede's defence, written in 708 or 709, would undoubtedly be accompanied by a copy of the work the orthodoxy of which was assailed, and it is very likely that Bede made this addition when dispatching that copy. Be that as it may, we have in the phrase 'anni praeteriti' another trace of a method of counting the years from an epoch, which has long since fallen into disuse, and which consists in ignoring the current year and in dating by the number of years actually completed. This method would appear to be unrecognized by modern scholars. I have only met with it in writers of the IXth century in one or two places. For instance: at the commencement of the Parker MS. of the 'Saxon Chronicle' (v. 'Two of the Saxon Chronicles Parallel', ed. C. Plummer, Oxon. 1892, Vol. I, p. 2) Cerdic's invasion of Britain is dated:

e) Thy geare the wæs âgân fram Cristes acennesse .cccc. wintra 7 .xciiii. uuintra ... [3])

If Cerdic's invasion took place in the annalistic year in which 494 years from the Incarnation had already gone by it should be evident that it could not have occurred before 495. Mr. Plummer, however, overlooks this and says that 'the Preface puts the invasion of Cerdic and Cynric in 494, while the Chronicle places it in 495' (Vol. II, p. 2). The same oversight is present in his omission to treat the datary sentence in the Preface — '7 ccc. 7 xcvi. wintra þæs þe his cyn ærest Westseaxena lond

---

[1]) Apud Migne, Patrol. Cursus, tom. XCIV (1850), coll. 669—675, where it is taken from the 'Complete Works of Bede' edited by the Rev. J. A. Giles, D.C.L. (1843), in 'Patres Ecclesiae Anglicani', Vol. I, pp. 144—154.

[2]) Vide supra, S. 496, Note 1.

[3]) i. e., anno in quo migratus est numerus annorum ab incarnatione Christi CCCCXCIV.

on Wealum geodon'. This means that the Alfredian chronicler
was compiling the work when 396 years had passed away from
the year in which Cerdic arrived. Now *post* 495 *plus* 396
= A. D. 892, and with reference to this very year Mr. Plummer
(Vol. I, p. 83, note 13) says: 'At this point [in the Chronicle],
after writing the number 892 ends the first hand in A', *i. e.,* in
the Parker MS. Other instances of computing *per annos prac-
teritos* may be found in the Chronicle at the years 6, 33, 606, 655.

In the Xth century many instances of the employment of
this method occur. In almost all the MSS. of the 'Historia
Brittonum' we find the formula 'a Passione Christi peracti sunt
anni —'. In MSS. D², G and L, for instance, we get:

f) Ab Adam uero usque ad passionem Christi anni sunt
V̄. CC. XXVIII. A passione autem Christi peracti sunt
anni DCCCLXXIX. Ab incarnatione autem eius anni
sunt DCCCCXII usque ad XXX annum Anharaut regis
Moniae, id est Mon, qui regit modo regnum Wenedotiae
regionis, id est Guennet;[1] fiunt igitur anni ab exordio
mundi usque in annum praesentem V̄I. CVIII.

Chronica Minora III, pp. 145, 146.

Dr. Mommsen objects to the mundane year given here (*u. s.,*
p. 146, note 1) saying that the year of the incarnation 912 is
A. M. 6107. This, however, confirms the statement that it was
intended to rectify. Mommsen has not perceived (*cf.* p. 119,
ll. 1—3) that A. M. 6108 is the only annus praesens or current
year in the indiculus of these MSS., and that 879 a passione,
912 ab incarnatione and 6107 ab exordio mundi are all anni
praeteriti. The Venedotian scribe was actually writing in the
current years A. P. 880, A. D. I. 913, A. M. 6108. That 'a
passione Christi peracti sunt anni DCCCLXXIX' should not be
rendered as if it were in anno passionis 879 will be evident at
once if we deduct 878 years from the mundane annus praesens
in order to get the year of the Passion in the mundane era.
Thus — 6108 *minus* 878 assigns the year of the Passion to
A. M. 5230 which does not agree with what the scribe first told
us — namely, that from Adam to the Passion there were 5228

---

[1] The Cambridge MS., Ff. I, 27 (*L*), has *Guernet*; the Durham MS.,
B II, 35 (*D*), *Suernet.*

years, which assigns the Passion to A. M. 5229. As 879 years had passed away since the Passion when the Venedotian scribe was writing if we deduct 879 from A. M. 6108 we get the A. M. of the Passion 5229, as above. We are not told what were the computistical characteristics of the year of the world to which he assigned the Passion and are unfortunately, for that reason, unable to date the 30th year of Anarawd in the Dionysian era.[1]) All that is certain from the data of the indiculus is that the copy of the 'Historia Brittonum' which bears it was made between Christmas Day and March 25.[2]) We know this because the early Church assigned 33 years and three months to the earthly life of its Founder, and consequently it is only in the first quarter of the Julian year that the annuary numbers of Passion- and Incarnation-years differ from each other to the extent of 33 years. If we assume that the Venedotian scribe dated the Passion in the consulship of the Gemini (A. D. 29), then he wrote in the first quarter of A. D. 909 and Anarawd began to reign in A. D. 879 or 880.

It is in the Chronicle of Ethelwerd,[3]) however, that we find the most regular and consistent use, as well as the greatest number of instances of dates set down according to this method. Ethelwerd wrote at the end of the Xth century, and he dated by the number of years that had elapsed between the birth of our Lord according to Dionysius and the Christmas Day in the annalistic year the events of which he was enumerating — that is, he dated *per annos a Nativitate Dominica praeteritos.* The formulas he employs are very numerous. We find:

| Impletus Factus Transactus Transmeatus Migratus | est numerus annorum | ab Incarnatione a gloriosa Natiuitate a Natiuitate ab aduentu Christi ab origine ab initio a conditione } mundi | Dominica Saluatoris N. I. C. Saluatoris | etc. |

[1]) Prof. H. Zimmer and Dr. Mommsen have treated all years in the 'Historia Brittonum', computed ab Incarnatione, as if they must necessarily be years in the Dionysian era. (*Cf.* S. 507, Note 1, *infra*.)

[2]) Even this depends upon the correctness of the assumption that the year in Gwynedd commenced on December 25.

[3]) Monumenta Historica Britannica I, pp. 500, seqq.

When dealing with dates in Ethelwerd English scholars always treat these formulas as if they were merely variants of *in anno*. For instance, the coronation of Edward the Elder is dated by Ethelwerd on Whit-Sunday when —

> *g*) 'factus uidetur numerus annorum ab aduentu Christi humana sumpta carne nongentesimus pleniter ordo'.

This is heedlessly rendered as if it were in anno DCCCC.[1] Other instances are:

> *h*) The Saxon settlement is dated by Ethelwerd when 'Impletus est numerus annorum ab incarnatione dominica CCCCXLIX'.
>
> *i*) The arrival of Augustine is dated when 'Transactus est numerus annorum ab incarnatione dominica DC. minus quatuor annis'.[2]
>
> *k*) The accession of Egbert is dated when 'Impleti sunt anni ab incarnatione dominica DCCC; ab aduentu Hengest et Horsae CCCL; ab aduentu Augustini ad gentem Anglorum CCIIII', &c.

As the 900th year from the Incarnation was completed in or before the annalistic year in which Edward was crowned it is clear that he could not have been crowned until 901, in which year Whit-Sunday fell on May 31. Ethelwerd, on one of the few occasions when he dates in a current year, says, speaking of the year in which Edward's coronation took place — 'iam defluente siquidem annorum numero centeno ex quo proauus continebat Ecgbyrht praesentia eius regna'. Computations *ex quo* included both terms; hence C anni ex quo is 99 years after,

---

[1] By the Rev. Joseph Stevenson in his translation of 'The Chronicle of Fabius Ethelwerd' in 'The Church Historians of England', (1854) Vol. II, pt. II, p. 437; by Mr. W. H. Stevenson in the *English Historical Review*, January, 1898, and the *Athenæum*, March 19, '98, p. 373, and July 16, '98, p. 99; by Sir J. H. Ramsay, *ibid.*, July 2, '98, pp. 34, 35; by Mr. Plummer, 'Two Saxon Chronicles Parallel', Vol. II (1899), p. 112.

[2] The editors of the Monumenta Historica Britannica suggested that we should read 'DC minus tribus annis'. Joseph Stevenson also mis-corrected Ethelwerd at this point (*u. s.* p. 416), and I am not acquainted with any English writer who renders the formula correctly.

according to modern computation, and the hundredth year before
Edward's coronation is A. D. 802, which agrees with the second
item of *k*. If the Saxons did not arrive until 449 years from
the Incarnation were completed it is clear that they did not
arrive until A. D. 450, and this we have already found to be
the date that Bede's authority had indicated. As Ethelwerd
dates the coming of St. Augustine when 600 years, all but four,
had passed away he dates it correctly *post* 596. In *k* if Egbert
succeeded when 800 years from the Incarnation were completed
he succeeded in 801, and this equals *post* 450 *plus* 350. The
other item in *k*, as I pointed out just now, indicates 802 (*sc.*
post 597 *plus* 204) and the hundredth year from this is 901,
as in *g*.

The discovery and recognition of the early existence of this
method of dating the years enable us to perceive that one of
Bede's authorities, who is unfortunately unknown to us, dated
per annos praeteritos, and that Bede when reproducing his
chronology changed the formula but omitted to make the necessary increase of one year in the annuary figures. If we
regard the nine dates in the table given above, S. 497, as computations which ignore the current year, then all of them except
those relating to Diocletian and Theodosius the Younger are
systematically correct, and the year of Marcian's accession which
is coupled with the first settlement of the Saxons in Britain, is
rightly dated *post* 449.

§ 4. The formula that Bede uses when dating from the
epoch of the first settlement of the Saxons is 'annus ... aduentus Anglorum in Britanniam'. But, when we come to examine
the dates given in this era we find that the intervals are never
calculated from either 449 or 450. It is true it has been
said that the computations in this era are only meant to be
approximate ones, and that we should be wrong to treat them
as if we supposed that they were intended to be exact. This
is Mr. Plummer's position, as we have seen already. In arriving
at it he has overlooked the significance of the fact that in two
passages which we shall examine presently the amount of
variation from A. D. 450 is identical; while in a third there is
a serious error latent. The variation in which two out of the
three computations agree indicates that the annus I of the era

is A. D. 447, which is a year that falls in the reign of Theodosius and Valentinian. In the third passage the computation appears to begin in A. D. 448. In a fourth the battle of Mons Badonicus is dated (I. xvi, p. 33) 'in quadragesimo circiter et quarto anno aduentus (Anglorum) in Brittaniam'. This phrase represents the 43 years and one month of the 'Excidium Britanniae', but as it is not accompanied by any synchronisation we cannot determine either the year of the epoch from it, or the date of the event.[1]) The three passages in which synchronisation does enable us to determine the date of the epoch are:

l) In I. xxiii, p. 42, where A. D. 596 is synchronised with 'anno xiiii (Mauricii Imp.), aduentus uero Anglorum ... anno circiter CL';

m) in II. xiiii, p. 113, where A. D. 627 misrepresents 'ab aduentu Anglorum ... annus circiter CLXXX^{mus}; and

n) in V. xxiii, p. 351, where A. D. 731 is computed as 'annus aduentus Anglorum ... circiter ducentesimo octogesimo quinto'.

When dealing with these dates Mr. Plummer mis-computed the era-year of *l* and *n* as 446, and that of *m* as 447. With regard to *l* the 14th year of Maurice ended on August 12, 596; hence, as A. D. 596 was annus CL of the Saxon era, A. D. 447 (596 *minus* 149) = annus I. Moreover, since annus CL = 596, annus CLXXX in *m* should equal A. D. 626;[2]) but Bede erroneously equates it with A. D. 627 and thus indicates A. D. 448 as annus I. In *n*, also, since A. D. 731 = annus CCLXXXV, A. D. 447 = annus I. In all probability the computations *l* and

---

[1]) M. A. de la Borderie in his article in the Revue Celtique (1883, Vol. VI, pp. 1—13) ignored the computistical change from A. D. 449 to A. D. 447 and miscomputed annus XLIV as A. D. 493. Mr. Plummer, 'Bede', ii. p. 30, assents to this error. It is a very common one and carries its own condemnation with it; for, if 449 be annus I, annus II must be 450, and not 449 *plus* 2, *i. e.* 451. Lappenberg, *u. s.*, I, p. 93 and p. 129, note, correctly computes 449 *plus* XLIV as 492. Polydore Vergil, also, in his Historia, dates Mons Badonicus in A. D. 492.

[2]) This mistake of Bede's is not detected by Mr. Plummer, whose plea that Bede's computations in the Saxon era are not intended to be exact is practically a denial of the necessity for scientific analysis of the chronological data.

m were not made originally by Bede, but were synchronised by him in the Dionysian era after he had adopted them from an earlier author whose work has perished. If Bede really was in error, as I believe, in computing the A. D. of *m*, then all the synchronised dates he gives in the Saxon era show that when practical use of that era was made A. D. 447 was miscomputed as its annus I.

§ 5. We must now return to Bede's statements in § 2 and enquire how it came about that he indicated one year as that of the epoch and yet computed from a date three years earlier. Several instances of dates of the same event computed ostensibly in the era of the Incarnation, but differing from each other by three years, have already been referred to, *v.* § 2. The following may be added to them: in 'H. E.' I. iii. the Claudian invasion of Britain (in A. D. 43) is dated in A. D. [I.] 46; in 'H. E.' I. vi. the election of Diocletian (in A. D. 284) is dated in A. D. [I.] 286.[1]) As Bede in his 'Chronica Majora' dates this event in A. M. 4238, which is A. D. I. 287, it is clear that the A. D. I. was mistaken for the A. D., and the event dated *per annos praeteritos*. In other words Bede omitted to make the necessary addition of one to the annuary figures when he changed the formula.

This difference of three years is the normal measure of the extent to which dates computed in the Christian era by means of the A. M. in the 'Chronica Maiora' differ from the dates com-

---

[1]) Mr. Plummer is occasionally puzzled in his notes (Vol. II) by the existence of dates in both systems. *E. g.*: Degsastan, pp. 66, 77; Mellitus's mission, p. 84; Justus's death, p. 110; Hatfield Chase, p. 116; Ethelwald's consecration and death, p. 297; Acca's death, p. 330; Ethelbald's raid, p. 342. In the 'Two Saxon Chronicles Parallel' the notes (Vol. II) to the following annals and events shew the double date: p. 8, A. D. 84—87; p. 9, 283—286; 443—446; p. 33, 693—696; p. 73, all annals from 829 to 839; p. 77, Beorhtwulf's accession; p. 116, chronology of Edward's reign and Mercian Register; p. 127, 914—917; p. cxxiv. note 3 and text. Some instances are due to erroneous reduction of A. D. years misjudged to be A. D. I. For example: Archbp. Felogild was consecrated 'V. Id. Jun. anes Sunnandages, 829'. June 9 has ferial letter *f*; 829 has Sunday letter *C*. Consequently the data are antagonistic: a day that has ferial letter *f* cannot fall on Sunday in a year that has Sunday letter *C*. In 832 however we get Sunday letter *F* in June, which agrees with the data of the Chronicle, and indicates, that A. D. 832 was wrongly regarded as A. D. I. and reduced according to rule.

puted in the era of the Incarnation according to Dionysius. For instance, the last ten reigns in Bede's 'Chronica' are dated thus:[1])

	Years reigned	Died A. M.	A. D. I.	A. D.
Constantinus F. C.	28	4622 = 671	= 668	
Constantinus P.	17	4639 = 688	= 685	
Justinianus II.	10	4649 = 698	= 695	
Leo II.	3	4652 = 701	= 698	
Tiberius	7	4659 = 708	704	
Justinianus III.	6	4665 = 714	= 711	
Philippicus	1¹/₂	4667 = 716	= 713	
Anastasius II.	3	4670 = 719	= 716	
Theodosius III.	1	4671 = 720	= 717	
Leo Isaurus	9th	4680 = 729	725	

The date of the ninth year of Leo Isaurus differs from 729 *minus* 3 because Bede was writing in the early part of September, 725, that is to say, in the interval between the commencement of the mundane year and the commencement of the Caesarean indiction and annalistic year.[2]) Hence, as the mundane year had increased its figures the A. D. I. and the A. D., when computed from it without correction, do so likewise. The existence of a second era of the Incarnation which commenced three years earlier than that established by Dionysius Exiguus has been a fruitful source of error. We have seen already that Bede himself when dating the Claudian invasion of Britain failed to avoid the error to which it leads, and he made the same mistake when he dated the conversion of certain Irish schismatics in A. D. 714 to the right celebration of the Easter of A. D. 715. Bede dates this in his 'Chronica Maiora' thus:

---

[1]) Mr. Plummer refers to this work of Bede's and says (Vol. I. Introd. p. xxxviii, note 3): 'In chronology Bede has the enormous merit of being the first chronicler who gave the date from Christ's birth in addition to the year of the world; and thus introduced the use of the Dionysian era into Western Europe'. The A. D. is never given by Bede in addition to the year of the world, and it only occurs once in the whole chronicle.

[2]) See the article in the *Athenæum* referred to already, *supra* S. 496, Note 1.

o) [A. M. 4667 to] A. M. 4670: Anastasius an. III. 'Ecbe-
rectus uir sanctus .... plurimas Scotticae gentis pro-
uincias ad canonicam paschalis temporis obseruantiam, a
qua diutius aberrauerant, pia praedicatione conuertit,[1])
anno ab incarnatione domini DCCXVI.'

Anastasius ruled from A. D. I. 716 = A. D. 713, to A. D. I. 719
= A. D. 716. Bede reproduces this reference to Egbert in 'H. E.'.
V. xxii, p. 346, and dates the event in the same year in both
works. In the 'Historia' this dating causes a chronological
difficulty which Mr. Plummer considers (Vol. II, p. 335) but leaves
unsolved. Now, if we restore the formula, and reduce the date
from *post annos DCCXVI. praeteritos ab Incarnatione dominica,*
i. e., from A. D. I. 717 to A. D. 714 the difficulty disappears.
Similarly where Bede dates another event connected with Iona
— namely, the migration of St. Columba, in A. D. 565, if we
restore the formula, and reduce the date from *post annos* 565
praeteritos ab Incarnatione dominica, i. e., from A. D. I. 566 to
A. D. 563, we get a date upon which it is asserted that most
ancient Irish chronologists are agreed. Mr. Plummer prefers
Bede's date, however, (ibid., pp. 130, 131) and rejects the Irish
view. There is another instance of the use of the era of the

---

[1]) In 'H. E.' III. iv. Bede assigns the change of Easter at Iona to 715
and attributes it to the influence of Egbert who remained on the island until
his death on April 24, 729, thirteen years after, we are told. In A. D. 715
Easter fell on March 31, and from that date to April 24, 729, there are
upwards of fourteen years. If Egbert reached Iona in 714 before the date of
Easter Day in 715 was appointed it would have had his early and careful
attention. The year 715 was one in which the Irish schismatics committed
very serious offences against Catholic decency and unity. The Paschal moon
of the orthodox tables was computed full on Sunday, March 24. Though the
schismatics celebrated on moon 14 they would not celebrate before March 25.
Neither would they do so on moon 21. Hence they rejected March 31 and
were not able to find a proper day until April 21, which was computed as
moon 13 by orthodox tables. The Irish schismatics, therefore, celebrated
Easter in 715 in the second lunar month and before the moon was full. It
is not necessary to know exactly how the schismatics really did compute, in
order to recognize their comparative difficulties; for their rules of observance
are sufficient to guide us, while the orthodox priests of the VIIth and
VIIIth centuries could easily foresee when divergences of this kind would
recur. *For* 'XIII' (the number of years that Egbert spent in Iona) *read*
XVI ex quo. 714 *plus* XVI = A. D. 729.

Incarnation that I have styled the Bedane era, in two XIIIth-
century MSS. of the 'Historia Brittonum' (Chron. Minor. III,
p. 169, note), where we get:

> *p*) 'Cuius [*sc.* Maximi] filius Victor eodem anno ab Argabaste
> comite interfectus est in Gallia, peractis a mundi initio
> annis V̄. DC. XC.,[1]) ab incarnatione Domini CCCXCI.'

Here we have the A. D. I. and the A. M. in combination with
the computation *per annos praeteritos.* As 5590 mundane years
and 391 years in the era of the Incarnation had passed away
the son of Maximus was slain in A. M. 5591, A. D. I. 392, and
this mundane year commenced upon September 1, A. D. 388.
The difference of four years instead of three between the A. D.
and the A. D. I. is due to the same cause as that which operated
similarly in the case of Leo Isaurus. Another instance of this
puzzling combination of the A. D. I. with the computation *per
annos praeteritos* is to be found in the 'Excerpta ex Raineri
Miraculis S. Gisleni'[2]) (MG. SS., tom. XV, p. 584), as follows:

> *q*) 'Euoluto   sane   ab   incarnatione   Domini   curriculo
> DCCCCXXXVIII annorum, sexta hora dominici diei,
> XII kal. Septembrium', &c.

As 938 years had already passed away the event thus dated
must have occurred in 939. August 21 (= XII. kal. Sept.) has
ferial letter *b* in the calendar, and the Sunday letter of A. D.
939 is *F*; hence the data are antagonistic: a day that has ferial
letter *b* cannot fall on Sunday in a year that has Sunday letter
F. Let us apply the formula and reduce the date from *post
annos* 938 *praeteritos ab Incarnatione Domini, i. e.,* from A. D. I.
939, to A. D. 936. A. D. 936 had Sunday letter *B* in August;
therefore in this year Aug. 21, *b*, fell on Sunday, which is what
the data require.

------

[1]) 'This date represents 5590; 500 being expressed, as was not unusual,
by the Roman numerals DC instead of D singly'. 'Introductory Remarks on
the Chronology of the Mediæval Historians', Monum. Hist. Brit. I, p. 112, note.

[2]) I take this crux from Prof. Rühl's 'Chronologie des Mittelalters und
der Neuzeit', Berlin, 1897, S. 73, where it is given as an example of dates
which 'auf keinerlei Weise reduziert werden können, weil sie einen Wider-
spruch in sich enthalten'.

If these lines be read in conjunction with the examination of this three years' difference made in the 'Introductory Remarks upon the Chronology of Mediæval Historians' in the Monumenta Historica Britannica, it will, I believe, be perceived that many results of chronological research conducted in ignorance of the existence of a second era of the Incarnation which is divergent from that of Dionysius Exiguus, are in need of confirmation, or, perhaps, even of revision.[1])

§ 6. This difference of era accounts for the parachronism or retardation by three years, of the dates we have been considering, but it does not explain the prochronism or acceleration of three years, visible in the date of the Saxon settlement when calculated from Bede's computations in the era that makes the year of that settlement its annus I. The connexion between the dates 447 and 450 is obvious, and would appear to suggest that the double date for the Saxon settlement is due to the fact that 450 is really in the era that I have referred to above as the Bedane era of the Incarnation. If that were so it must be said that Bede should not have employed it at all in the 'Historia Ecclesiastica', but should have dated the settlement in A. D. 447, throughout. It must, however, be pointed out that Bede had already reduced the annuary figures from A. D. I. to A. D. In his 'Chronica Maiora' he dated the accession of

---

[1]) Prof. Rühl remarks on page 198 of the work just now referred to: 'Ob Dionysius die Geburt Jesu auf den 25. Dezember seines Jahres 1 [a], oder auf den 25. Dezember des vorhergehenden Jahres angesetzt habe, ist für die technische Chronologie gleichgiltig, und [b] ebenso gleichgiltig für diese ist die früher viel behandelte andere Frage, ob seine Rechnung mit der historischen Wahrheit übereinstimme oder nicht.' In a Rühl takes it for granted that Dionysius began the Incarnation-year on the day of the Nativity; he really began it on September 1. Hence, the question is not only important but easy to answer, for Dionysius was not likely to leave eight months of Christ's earthly life out of his computation of the years of the Incarnation. The second assertion, b, is dependent upon the assumption that no attempts were made by those who alleged error in Dionysius's computation to rectify that error, real or supposed. Now, we have eras of the Incarnation differing from that of Dionysius by 3, 5 and 22 years, and it is certainly not a matter of indifference to technical chronology whether Dionysius's fixation is historically correct, if later chronographers who objected to it put forward other systems in which events are dated in the same style as they are in the system of Dionysius — viz., ab incarnatione dominica. V. supra, S. 497, Note 2.

Marcian in A. M. 4403, which is A. D. I. 452, instead of A. M.
4404 (A. M. 4377 *plus* 27) which is A. D. I. 453.   Now these
dates bear the same relationship to each other that A. D. 449
and 450 do, and it is clear, therefore, that when Bede, or his
authority, reduced A. D. I. 452 to A. D. 449, he did so because
he knew that he was dealing with dates that did not tally with
the years of the Dionysian era, and reduced them to that era
by deducting three, according to rule.   It would appear that the
chronographer whose dates in the Saxon era for three events
have been reproduced by Bede, assigned the Saxon settlement,
for reasons which will be considered when we have done with
Bede's share in handing down the tradition, to the year 450,
which was really A. D. but which he treated as if it were
A. D. I.   This mistake imported an error of three years into his
and Bede's calculations which does not reveal itself until Bede
computed another date in the Saxon era — the date, namely,
of the year in which the 'Historia Ecclesiastica' was written.
Bede dated the mission of St. Augustine (in A. D. 596) 150 years
after the Saxons came, and 450 *plus* 150 = 599, which, it is
obvious, must be styled A. D. I.   Now Bede wrote in A. D.
731, A. D. I. 734, which was 135 years after the mission of
St. Augustine, and if he added 135 to the other interval without
inspecting the position, or making the calculations 450 *plus* CL
plus CXXXV, *i. e.*, 450 *plus* CCLXXXV, he, of course, subintro-
duced the error of the earlier writer into his own computations.
Therefore, what he gives as the date of his writing the 'H. E.'
in the Saxon era is either 450 *plus* CCLXXXV, *i. e.*, 734, which
if it be styled A. D. I. is quite correct; or 731, which, when the
interval is deducted, assigns the annus I of the Saxon era to
A. D. 447.   Neither of the years that are implied in Bede's calculations in the Saxon era agrees with the year he gives when
he dates the event explicitly.

§ 7.   The question of where did Bede get the date of the
Saxon invasion is an interesting one, but I do not know of any
evidence that might enable us to answer it with certainty.   The
following indications point to Ripon: (1) We know from the
interpolation made in the 'Historia Brittonum' (Chartres MS.),
presumably by Marcus the Hermit, who was born in Britain
about A. D. 800 but educated in Ireland, that the correct year

of Marcian's accession was given at Ripon in A. D. 744 as the date of the Saxon invasion. At least there is no other way, I believe, of accounting for the date in the Chartres MS., namely, A. D. D., than by the suggestion I made in this Journal in 1897 (Bd. I, S. 275; *cf.* Bd. III, S. 107) to the effect that that numeral is a condensation of CCCCL misread as CCCCC. (2) Ripon is regarded by Mr. Plummer as the abbey at which additional entries in the 'Recapitulatio Chronica' in Bede's 'H. E.' were made: *v.* V. xxiiii, p. 354 at foot, and *cf.* Introd. pp. civ and cv and 'Two Saxon Chronicles Parallel', Vol. II, 1899, Introd. p. lxxi, note 4. These additional entries relate chiefly to Wilfrid, and Mr. Plummer has made out a strong case for Ripon. One of them is: 'A. D. DCLXVII. *Noster* abb*as* scrip*sit*', and in the foot-note referred to just now Mr. Plummer identifies the abbot who wrote in 667 with Wilfrid who was in retirement at Ripon from 666 to 669 owing to the occupation of his see by Chad. To this view there is the objection that Wilfrid was elected bishop of York and consecrated at Compiègne in A. D. 664, and did not retire to Ripon until A. D. 666. Mr. Plummer's view, therefore, requires us to assume that Wilfrid retained the office of abbot after he had been consecrated bishop of York, and that he was still referred to as abbot in after years by a writer of annals at Ripon, although he was really a bishop. There is nothing unreasonable in these assumptions, but we must remember that if 667 be A. D. I., the year indicated, namely, A. D. 664, is not only one to which no objection at all can be advanced, but one the events of which suggest a subject with which Wilfrid, abbot of Ripon, was much concerned and which he was very likely indeed to write about. Wilfrid took a very prominent part in the dispute at Whitby in A. D. I. 667, A. D. 664, respecting Paschal celebration, and he may have prepared himself for the discussion by writing a corrective Paschal epistle like those of Cyril, Victor, Cummián, Aldhelm and others. (3) Mr. Nicholson (*supra*, S. 107) has pointed out that the staff that Columba of Iona gave to Kentigern was preserved at Ripon in the church built by Wilfrid, and we saw above (§ 5) that Bede's date for Columba, if regarded as a computation in A. D. I. *post annos praeteritos*, agrees with that assigned by Irish chroniclers. Mr. Plummer ('Bede', Vol. II, p. 31) says that it is curious that Bede does not seem to have known either Cuimene's

34*

or Adamnan's Life of Columba. Even if Bede had known both Lives the schismatic authors of them would not have given him dates in the Dionysian or orthodox era, and it is possible that he received this date also from Ripon, where, as we have seen reason to believe, the A. D. I. computation was employed as well as the Dionysian one.

For the reasons advanced in this chapter I conclude: (a) that the original form of the statement that Bede had before him when he assigned the first settlement of the Saxons in Britain and the accession of Marcian to A. D. 449, was *post annos praeteritos CCCCXLIX ab incarnatione dominica*; (b) that the prochronism in Bede's explicit date for Marcian's accession is due to his omission to increase these annuary numbers by one when he changed the style from the cardinal number of completed years to the ordinal number of the current year; and (c) that the prochronism of three years in the date of the Saxon advent implied in his computations in the Saxon era, is due to a mistake which was made by an earlier writer upon whom he depended, and which he failed to detect and reproduced unwittingly in his own work.

Hornsey, Middlesex.   A. ANSCOMBE.

AD VERSUS NENNII.

J'ai dit, dans ma note sur les vers attribués à Nennius (voy. vol. III, p. 120) que la dernière ligne 'Eu uocatur ben notis litteris nominis quini' n'avait rien à faire avec le distique héxamétrique qui le précède, mais qu'elle avait tout à fait l'air d'une glose. Cette glose se rapporte, à mon avis, aux vers 4 et 5 du carmen, surtout au v. 5; écrite en marge, elle a été placée à la fin par un scribe qui a déjà trouvé à la suite du carmen le fameux distique 'Fornifer etc.'.

Voici une explication possible de cette glose.

'Ben', dans le vers 5 du carmen, est le fils de Dieu: Ἰησοῦς Χριστὸς Θεοῦ Ὑιὸς Σωτήρ; c'est-là le nom quintuple: on sait l'importance des cinq initiales pour les premiers chrétiens elles étaient connues, surtout les lettres X et l'Y (aspirée). Ces deux lettres commencent les deux vers 4 et 5 du carmen. Les MSS. écrivent même 'hymnizat' au lieu de 'Ymnizat'. Le glosateur veut attirer l'attention du lecteur sur la coïncidence — ou sur l'artifice — qui consiste à faire commencer les vers où il est question de Ben — 'fils' — par des initiales qui désignent le fils de Dieu — Χριστὸς Ὑιός. Les MSS. donnent bien 'eu', mais j'avoue que je préfèrerais 'en', d'accord en cela avec les éditeurs. 'eu' = εὐ ne me plaît guère; d'autrepart, la faute du scribe — si faute il y a — s'explique par le 'uocatur' qui suit. On peut entendre 'uocatur' comme 'inuocatur' ou mieux comme équivalant de 'notatur'. Dans le carmen, 'Ben' est donc un vocatif, comme 'Christe'; celui qui 'glorifie' se dit tout simplement 'le serviteur âgé du Fils de Dieu'.

Liverpool.   V. Friedel.

THE LIFE OF COLUMB CILLE.

On Christmas Day 1896 I received from Whitley Stokes a
photograph of that part of a MS. in the Bodleian Library which
contains the tract called O'Donnell's Life of Columb cille, with
a request that I publish it. For various reasons I have been
unable to undertake the task of making a transcript and translation until now.

Dr. Stokes kindly furnished me with a short description
of this MS. as follows: "The codex is thus described by Macray
in his catalogue of the Bodleian MSS. partis V, fascic. I, p. 734:
'Codex membranaceus, in folio, ff. 78, sec. XVI, binis columnis,
bene exaratus atque asservatus. Olim inter codices Waraei et
comitis de Clarendon, 25; postea inter libros ducis de Chandos,
2567, e cuius bibl. emptus fuit a Rawlinson, pretio viginti soli-
dorum.'

After the Life (which ends on fo. 60) are 18 leaves containing 49 Irish poems in single columns; and, at f. 67b an
entry of O'Donnell's taxations on Ulster, which has been (in
part?) printed by O'Connor in his Catalogue of the Stowe MSS.
p. 398. The names of the poems are given by Macray, ubi supra."

Dr. William Reeves in his edition of Adamnan p. XXXV,
note w, gives the further particulars: 'The leaf measures 17 by
$11^{1}/_{2}$ inches, and there are 60 folios or 120 pages in the Life,
which are followed by 18 folios containing poems on the O'Donnell
family. On the second folio is a large coloured representation
of the saint in episcopal robes. The volume has a slip cover
of undressed skin, which gives the exterior a very hirsute
appearance.' The figure referred to is a fairly tolerable drawing

in full length, showing an abbot vested for Mass, and bearing a mitre and crosier. He stands within a gothic frame of scrolled foliage. The folds of the drapery are conventionalized almost to geometric symmetry, and there is a back-ground in diagonal lines of four-petalled flowers, with two large roses depending from twigs filling the spaces at each side of the head. The whole seems motived by stained-glass designs, and shows no trace of the characteristic Irish intertwining.

The text is valuable for its wonderful variety of matter, and as being a specimen of the literary style of 1532. The codex is very beautifully written.

For illustrative purposes, besides Dr. Reeves's well-known work, I shall make occasional use of the article Columkille in Canon O'Hanlon's Lives of the Irish saints. That is a compilation of wonderful research, and the work of our best Irish topographer since O'Donovan's time.

Betha Coluimb Cille.

1. (T)INNSCANTAR BEATHA AN AB*AD* naemtha 7 an
uas*al*-athar 7 primfaidh nimhe 7 talman andso, edhon Colaim
cilli m*ic* Fheilimthe.   INtí do leig de ar son de gan cheim budh
airde ina abdaine manach n-dub do beith aige sa*n* egl*us*, 7 cliara
Erend 7 Alban 7 iarthair domain ag a togha mar uactaran orra
fein; *et* ni beith an dinite si*n* fein aige, a*cht* do cosnam luaigi-
dechta.   Oir nir b'ail leis i*n* buaidred, *no* an triobloid, bis a
n-diaidh na n-dineteadh ro-ard, do beith eidir se 7 a th*ra*tha,
no a urnaigthe, *no* mol*ad* de do bidh san do denam do gnathach.
Et fos anti do leig rigacht Erind de m*ar* in *ced*na, do cum *ar*
togadh go minic e, 7 budh dual do do beith aige o fholaidecht.

2. IS follas go*r* thuig Colaim *c*illi an briath*ar* ata scribtha
a tegsa an t-shoisc*eil* am*ail* meabraiges G*ri*doir a n-oifiged na
coinfisoired, .i. nos qui plus ceteris in hoc mundo accepisse aliq*u*id
cernimur, ab autore mundi gravi*us* inde iudicemur.   Cum enim
augentur dona, r*ati*ones eciam crescant donorum .i. na daine
gabais na tindlaicthe roa*r*da cuca do taeb an t-shaegail, is
trumaide breithemn*us* dia orra e.   *Et* as se an t-adbor e: an
uair medaighter na tindluicthe, is ecen go medaighter na cundais.

3. Do thuig se fos an briath*ar* adub*air*t Sanct Aug*us*tin .i.
spem quipe omnem seculi reliqueram, non quesiui esse quod sum
7 ab his qui dilig*un*t mundu*m* segreaui me; sed eis qui presunt
pop*u*lis non me coequaui .i. do sgar me re h-ainmian an t-shaog*uil*,
7 nir togh me beith mar ataim.   7 do eidirdel*uig* me adrum 7
an drong le*r* b'i*n*main an saog*al* 7 nir b'ail lim dul a cosmhailes
ris na h-ua*cht*aranuib do bidh os cin*n* na poiplech.

4. Do gab se an tecusc-sa tug an tigerna da deiscibl*ib*
am*ail* mebraighes Matha suib*i*scel sa seisid caibidil dec .i. si
quis uult uenire post me, abneget semet ips*um* et tollat crucem
suam, et sequat*ur* me .i. Gebe lenab ail te*cht* am diaid-si duilt*ad*
se e fein, 7 tocb*ad* se a croch fen 7 lenad se mesi.

The life of Columb Cille.

1. Here begins the life of the holy abbot and of the patriarch and prime-prophet of Heaven and Earth, namely Columb cille the son of Fedlimid; he who for God's sake refused any dignity in the Church higher than an abbacy of black monks, though the clergy of Ireland and of Scotland and of the western world were appointing him for their ruler. And even that minor dignity he would not accept but for assurance of his lowly estate. For he willed not that the anxiety and trouble which follow upon high dignities should interfere with his canonical hours, or his prayers, or the praise of God in which he was ever wont to be engaged. And again, he who likewise renounced the kingship of Ireland, unto which he had often been appointed, and which was his due by right of blood.

2. It is evident that Columb cille understood the word that is written in the text of the Gospel which Gregory mentions in the office of Confessors[1] .i. nos, qui plus ceteris in hoc mundo accepisse aliquid cernimur, ab auctore mundi gravius inde judicemur. Cum enim augentur dona, rationes etiam crescunt donorum, 'those who take to themselves too great worldly endowments, the judgment of God will be the heavier upon them for it. And this is the reason: for when endowments are increased the reckonings must be increased also'.

3. He understood also the saying of Saint Augustine .i. spem quippe omnem saeculi reliqueram, non quaesiui esse quod sum, et ab his qui diligunt mundum segregaui me, sed eis qui praesunt populis non me coaequaui, 'I parted from the inordinate desires of the world, and chose not to be as I am, and I distinguished between myself and those who love the world, and desired not to become like the governors who are over the people'.

4. He accepted the doctrine which the Lord taught his disciples, and the evangelist Matthew mentions in the sixteenth chapter .i. si quis uult uenire post me, abneget semetipsum et tollat crucem suam et sequatur me. 'Whoso desires to come after me, let him deny himself, and take up his own cross and follow me.'

---

[1] Lectione septima in commune Confessoris Pontificis, Breviarii Romani.

5. Do thuig Col*aim* cilli an briath*ar* adub*airt* Bernard IN .xx, ii. se*r*mone super cantica. INcassum p*r*oinde q*ui*s laborat i*n* aq*ui*sscione uirtutu*m*, si aliu*d* ab alio putat quam a dom*i*no uirtutu*m* .i. is dimhai*n*ech subailche d'iarraid a m-bethaidh eli *acht* a m-beath*aid* rig na subailche. Oir do threig se beatha an t-sao*g*ail ar a smuaintighib do beith go comnaightech a m-bea-thaidh an tig*er*na, 7 ar a beith go sir aga hol ina deoch*a* ro-millsi; oir do lean se Crisd in a beth*aid*, o thoil 7 o ghnim, 7 o anum glan, 7 o smeroidighib tendtighe a g*r*ada do beith i*n* a croidhe go comnaigthech.

[fo. 1 a] 6. *ET* fos do thuig se an briath*ar* eli adubairt Bernard, IN. lxi. sermone super cantica. Tolerantia martyrii p*r*ovenit quod in *Chr*i*st*i unleribis tota deuocione uersetur, et iugi meditaconem illis demoret*ur* .i. as o smuaintighib duthrach-tachta na mairtirech a cr*echt*aib Cri*sd* tainic a b-faidhide in a m*ar*tra; 7 ar a med do bad*ar* crechta Cri*sd* in a n-a*n*mo*nn*aib nar mothaighetar na h-iaraind ga snoidhe 7 ag gerradh a corp.

7. *ET* adeir Bern*ar*d nach iad na m*ai*rtirigh amháin do rinde an foidhide-so, *act* go n-dernat*ar* na confesori hi. *Et* as follas dui*nn* go n-derna an confisoir uasal .i. Col*aim* c*illi*, foidhide sa m*ar*tra shuth*ain* do cuir se *ar* a corp fen, do reir m*ar* ata sc*r*ibta a n-deredh an leabair-si a tu*ar*uscb*ail* a crabaidh fein. 7 ni hedh amain do bidh aige foidhide in a galruib 7 in a t*ri*-bl*ói*d*i*bh *acht* do bidh se go luthgairech, solasach; 7 doberidh buidhechus mor do dia *ar* a son. 7 as se an t-adhbhar é, nach a*nn* fein do bi a anam, *acht* a m-bethaidh in tig*er*na, *ar* a med do cnedhaig sí a croide. Gonadh airi si*n* nach mothaig*edh* se na piana ro-pendaidecha, ro-gh*r*uama, do cuiredh se *ar* a corp fen.

8. *ET* bidh a fhis ag lu*cht* legtha na bethadh-so go n-deach*aidh* si a m-bathad o cein mhair, 7 nach roibe ar f*ag*b*ail* di *acht* bloidh m-big don lebar do de*cht* Adh*am*nan naemtha a Laidin, 7 becan eli a n-Gaidilg, ar na dechtadh go ro-c*r*uaid d'fhile*d*uib na n-Gaid*el*, *et* fos an cuid eli i*n* a scel*aib* a fad ó cheli *ar* fud t-shenlebar Erind. *Et* as doig lemsa gorub é dob adb*ar* do so: IN uair tancut*ar* dan*air* 7 allm*ar*aidh do denam gabaltuis *ar* tus a n-Erinn, do milled*ar* 7 do loiscet*ar* *air*d-cella Er*enn* uili, 7 do millet*ar* a sc*ri*ne 7 a screbt*ra*, 7 rugat*ar* moran do taisib na naem leo da tirth*ib* fen, am*ail* mebraighid senleb*air*

5. Columb cille understood the saying of Bernard, Sermone xxii super Cantica. Incassum proinde quis laborat in acquisitione uirtutum, si aliud ab alio petat quam a Domino uirtutum; 'it is idle to seek virtue in any life other than in the life of the king of virtues'. For he forsook the life of the world that his thoughts might rest upon the life of the Lord, and that he might be for ever drinking it in very sweet draughts. For he followed Christ in his life, by will and deed, and with a pure soul, and by having the burning embers of love for Him for ever in his heart.

6. And he understood besides the other saying of Bernard, Sermone lxi super Cantica. Tolerantia martyrii provenit quod in Christi uulneribus tota devotione uersetur, et iugi meditationem illis demoretur, 'it is from the earnest thoughts of the martyrs upon the wounds of Christ came their patience in their suffering'. For the wounds of Christ were so much in their minds that they did not feel the irons hacking and cutting their bodies.

7. And Bernard says it was not alone the martyrs that exhibited this patience, but the confessors as well. And it is clear to us that this noble confessor, to wit, Columb cille, exhibited patience in the perpetual martyrdom to which he subjected his own body, according to what is written in the end of this book setting forth his piety. And not alone was he patient in his sicknesses and troubles, but he was even happy and joyful, and returned God sincere thanks for them. And the reason was that not in himself was his soul but in the life of the Lord, so much did it wound his heart. And hence it was that he was not wont to feel the very penitential and rude pains that he inflicted upon his own body.

8. And be it known to the readers of this Life that it had gone into decay this long time, and that there remained of it only some fragments of the book that holy Adamnan had made in Latin, and a little more in Irish written very hard by the poets of the Goidil, besides still another portion in stories wide from each other apart throughout the old books of Ireland. And I think this is the reason it was so: when the Danes and foreigners first came to make conquest in Ireland, they destroyed and burned the great churches of all Ireland, and gave to havoc their shrines and Scriptures, and took with them many of the

oiris Erenn, 7 go hairite amail mebruiges an lebar dara hainm
Cogad Gall re Gaidelaib.

9. *ET* do loiscetar 7 do milletar *aird*-chella Colaim cilli go
sundradach, 7 as demin lim gorab i an uair sin do milletar 7
do loiscetar a lebair, 7 do cuaid a betha a m-bathad *acht* an
began frith re na scribad andso sis di.

10. Bidh a fhis ag lucht legtha na bethad-sa gorab é
Maghnas mac Aeda mic Aeda Ruaid mic Neill Gairb mic Toirdelbaigh an fina Hi Domhnaill do furail an cuid do bi a Laidin
don bethaid-si do cur a n-Gaidhilc, 7 do furail an chuid do bi
go cruaid a n-Gaidilc di do cor a m-buga innus go m-beith solus
sothuicsena do cach uile.

11. *ET* do thimacht 7 do tinoil an cuid do bi spreite *ar*
fedh shenlebor Erenn di, 7 do decht as a bel fein hi, *ar* fagbail
t-shaethair ro-moir uaithe, 7 *ar* caitheam aimsiri faide ria, og a
sduidear cindus do cuirfed se gach en-chuid in a hinad imcubhaid
fen, amail ata scribtha annso sis.

12. *ET ar* n-gabail baide 7 brathairsi do re na ard-naem
7 re na combrathair genelaig, 7 re na patrun gradhach fen, da
raibe se ro-duthrachtach.

13. A Caislen Puirt na tri namat umorro do dechtagh in
betha-so, an tan ba shlan da bliadain dec ar .xx. ar cuic .c. ar
.m. bliadna don tigerna.

14. *ET* sicut ex inclita prosapia 7 fulgida genirositate
parentum, aliorumque predicessorum eius, insitum ei erat a
natura, bellicosis armis suos hostes uisibiles in hoc mundo
uincere, 7 ipsos superasse, ita spiritualibus armis, uidelicet
uigiliis asiduis, crebris orationibus, continuis ieiunis, obediencia
debita, uirginali castitate necnon inenarabili lacrimarum efucione,
suos inuici(biles) hostes superauit 7 optatam contra ipsos uictoriam
atque desiderata obtinuit .i. mar bud dual don nech naemtha-sa
dar bh'ail lind labairt, o uaisli 7 o folaidhecht 7 o nert laime, a
naimte colluide do clai le harmaib cathaige, is mar sin do clai
se escaraid a anma le harmaib spiridalta, mar ata, fuirechrus
imarcoch 7 urnigthe gnathach 7 troiscthe faide 7 umlacht 7
oghacht 7 a dera do dortad go minic.

15. Sanctus Columba scola uirtutum, magisterium uite,
sanctitatis forma, iusticie norma, uirginitatis speculum, pudicicie
titulus, castitatis exemplum, penitencie uia, peccatorum uenia,

relics of the saints to their own countries, as the old historical books of Ireland relate, particularly the book called 'The wars of the Foreigners against the Irish'.

9. And they burned and destroyed the great churches of Columb cille especially. And I am sure it was then they destroyed and burned his books and that his life went to decay, except the little of it that was found to be written down here.

10. And be it known to the readers of this Life that it was Maghnas mac Aeda mic Aeda Ruaid mic Neill Gairb mic Toirdelbaigh an fina Hi Domhnaill who caused the portion of this Life that was in Latin to be turned into Irish, and caused the part that was in hard Irish to be put into easy Irish, to the end it might be clear and intelligible to everybody.

11. So he gathered and collected whatever was scattered through the old books of Ireland of it, and composed it out of his own mouth, having had very great labour upon it, and having devoted much time to it, considering how he might put each part of it in its own proper place as it is written below,

12. and having conceived affection and the regard of kinship towards his arch-saint, fellow-relative in descent and dear patron to whom he was most devoted.

13. In the Castle of Port na tri namat this Life was written when twelve and one score and fifteen hundred years was the age of our Lord.

14. Et sicut ex inclita prosapia et fulgida generositate parentum, aliorumque praedecessorum eius, insitum ei erat a natura, bellicosis armis suos hostes uisibiles in hoc mundo uincere et ipsos superasse, ita spiritualibus armis, uidelicet uigiliis assiduis, crebris orationibus, continuis ieiuniis, obedientia debita, uirginali castitate necnon inenarrabili lacrimarum effusione, suos inuisibiles hostes superauit, et optatam contra ipsos uictoriam atque desiderata obtinuit, 'as it was kind for this holy person of whom we wish to speak, from breeding, blood and might of hand, to overcome his enemies in the flesh with the arms of battle, so did he conquer the enemy of his soul with spiritual weapons; that is to say, great wariness, constant prayer, long fasting, humility, virginity and the frequent shedding of tears'.

15. Sanctus Columba scola uirtutum, magisterium uitae, sanctitatis forma, iustitiae norma, uirginitatis speculum, pudicitiae titulus, castitatis exemplum, penitentiae uia, peccatorum

fidei disciplina .i. Col*aim* naemtha scol na subhalt*i*ge, 7 maighis-
dr*echt* na beth*a* 7 foirm na naem*t*hachta, 7 riag*al* na cora, 7
speclair na hogh [fo. 1 b] achta, 7 tital na nairi, 7 esimlair na
genmaidhechta, 7 slighe na haithrige, 7 loghad na pecad, 7 tecosc
an credimh.

16. Da derbad go raibe an forbtighect-sa ag Col*aim* c*i*lli
ata sc*r*ibtha air nach tainic roime *no* na diaid, en-duine as mo
do rinde dedail do dia *ar* in cinedh daenna in*a* e; ag silad, 7
ag senmoir breithri de doib, ga tarraing docum creidme.

17. Ut d*i*x*i*t Bonauentura *ar* ngabail tr*u*aige 7 *co*mpaisi do
bo*c*t*ai*ne 7 do doghraing Crisd, *ar* n-impod on Eigeibt do: O
puer egregie 7 delicate, rex celi 7 terre, quantu*m* laborasti p*ro*
nobis, 7 quam cito hoc cepisti. O a m*a*caimh mín ro-uasail, 7 a
ri nimhe 7 talm*an*, ca med do saeth*ar* do rindis *ar* ar so*n*-ne,
7 a mocha do tindscnais e. Gonad airi si*n* adub*air*t an faid, *ag*
lab*air*t a persai*n* Crisd .i. Pauper su*m* ego et in laboribus a
iuuentute mea p*ro*p*ter* genus humanu*m* .i. ataim a m'oige, a
m-bochtaine, 7 a n-ilr*u*g*ad* gacha saethair *ar* son an ci*n*id
daen*n*a. Is demhin gor thuic Col*aim* cilli an briath*ar*-sa .i. do
bi se a m-bochtai*n*e 7 a n-imad saethair in a oige ar son de.

18. *ET* tainic an briath*ar* adub*air*t Bonauentura ag lab*air*t
do so suas do .i. O do*mi*ne teip*su*m odio habuisti amore nostro.
O a tigerna tucabair fuath dib fein *ar* ar ngr*ad*-ne. *Con*ad
a*m*laid sin tuc Col*aim* c*i*lli fuath do fein *ar* gr*a*d de.

19. Cuirfidh a betha fen a ceill duin*n* gor tuic Col*aim* c*i*lli
an focal adub*air*t an t-apst*al* ag labairt do dolass Muiri 7 na
m-ba*n* ro-naemtha eli do bi faria a n-aimsir na paisi. Socii si
pacionu*m* fuerim*us*, erimus solacionum .i. da m-bem m*ar* compá-
nachuib compaisi ag Muiri a n-aimsir na paisi, biam in ar compa-
nacha*ib* comsholais aice a ngloir flaithesa de.

20. O nach dingbala mesi d'fhagbail m'achuinge o dia,
guidhim thusa a Col*aim* c*i*lli labairt go mui*n*dterdha ris 7 gr*a*sa
d'fhagbail damh fen uadha, in*n*us go cr*i*chnuigin*n* go foirfe an
saeth*ar*-so dob ail lim do dhenam duid fen, ind*us* go n-deachaid
se an onoir dos*am*, 7 a n-*ar*dug*ad* a*n*ma duid-si, 7 a t*ar*ba dona
poiplecha*ib* leghfes 7 estfes e, 7 a tarba a*n*ma 7 cuirp dam fen,
7 a n-esonoir 7 a n-digbail imarc*ach* don diabhul.

uenia, fidei disciplina, 'holy Columb the school of virtues, the regulator of life, the form of holiness, rule of justice, mirror of virginity, title of modesty, example of chastity, way of penance, pardon of sins and the teaching of faith'.

16. For proof that Columb cille had this perfection, it is written of him, that nobody came before or after him who made greater renunciation to God for the sake of the human race than he, sowing and preaching the word of God to them, drawing them to the faith.

17. Ut dixit Bonaventura having conceived pity and compassion for the poverty and misery of Christ upon his return from Egypt: O puer egregie et delicate, rex coeli et terrae, quantum laborasti pro nobis, et quam cito hoc cepisti, 'O tender, noble boy, and king of Heaven and Earth, how much hast thou laboured for our sakes and how soon too thou didst begin it'. Wherefore the prophet said, speaking in the person of Christ, Pauper sum ego et in laboribus a iuuentute mea propter genus humanum, 'I am from youth in poverty and the tribulation of many labours for sake of the human race'. It is certain that Columb cille understood this saying, for he was in poverty and much labour in his youth for God's sake.

18. And the saying of Bonaventura speaking of the above, became him: O Domine teipsum odio habuisti amore nostro, 'O Lord, thou hast hated thyself for love of us'. And even so Columb cille hated himself for the love of God.

19. His own life will inform us that Columb cille understood the saying of the apostle speaking of the sorrow of. Mary and the other holy women who were with her in the time of the passion. Socii si passionum fuerimus, erimus solationum; 'were we companions in suffering with Mary in the time of the passion, so shall we be companions in joy with her in the glory of God's Heaven'.

20. Since I am not worthy to obtain my petition from God, I pray thee, Columb cille, speak kindly to Him, and obtain grace from Him for me, that so I may finish and perfect this work which I wish to do for thy sake, that it may tend to his honour, to the magnifying of thy name, to the profit of those who read and hear it, to my own welfare in body and soul, and to the special dishonour and hurt of the Devil.

21. Laibeoram ar tus d'uaisle 7 d'folaidhect *Colaim cilli* .i.
Colam Cilli mac Felim*the* m*i*c Fergasa cendf*ada* m*i*c Conaill
Ghulban m*i*c Neill nai-gialluig .i. aird-ri Erind 7 Alp*an* 7 Saxan
an Niall sin. 7 do bud eidir linde a geinel*ach* do lenm*ain* as
sin suas go h-Adhum munb*ed* fada lind a leinmai*n*. 7 da derbad
si*n* ni fuil *act* naenm*ar* 7 cethre .xx. ua*d* go h-Adam, am*ail*
airmid senchaide na nGaidel, 7 am*ail* ata *ar* coimed aca in a
lebruib fein.

22. *ET* fos Eithne ing*en* Dima m*i*c Nae m*i*c Eithin m*i*c
Cuirb fil*ed* m*i*c Oililla mair m*i*c Brecain m*i*c Dairi barruigh m*i*c
Cathair moir aird-*ri* Ere*nn* a math*air*. 7 ingen righ Alp*an* .i.
Erc i*n*g*en* Loair*n* a senmhath*air* .i. m*áthair* a ath*ar*. 7 ni fuil
fuil is anuaisli i*n*a fuil rigruide Ere*nn*, 7 rigr*ui*de an domain
uime go h-Adamh.

23. IS follas duin*n* nach eadh amai*n* do togh dia *Colam*
cilli a m-broind a m*átha*r m*ar* serbfoghant*id* diles do fen *act*
gor tog se a fad ria techt a m-broind a mathar e. 7 da derbad
si*n* do ba*t*ar naeimh Ere*nn* 7 Alpa*n* 7 iartair domain ga tairr(n)-
gir*e* a bh-fad ria n-a geinem*ain*.

24. Do tairr*n*gir sennser t-shagart Ere*nn* he .i. Sen-mo*ct*a
Lugmaid, da *ced* bliada*n* reme fen. 7 is mar so do tairrngir
Mochta é .i. aimser airidhe tarla Mo*ct*a i*n* Hii. Tuc a fer f*ri*-
tholma .i. *Mac* Rith a ainm, cna cuige 7 do diult Mochta na
cna, 7 as edh adub*air*t. Ni limsa, *ar* se, an fero*nn* as a tucadh
na cna sin, 7 taisidther torad an ferai*nn* no go tí a tigerna.
Ca huair ti*ct*as se? *ar* an t-oclaech. A cind da *ced* bl*iadan*, ar
Mochta. *ET* do gnathaig*ed* Mo*ct*a, ar tect a n-Eri*nn* do o Hi,
a ag*ed* bud th*uaid* ag de*n*am a urnaidhthe o sin amach. 7 do
fiarfaidis a mui*nter* fein de cred é an t-adbhar fa m-bid a aig*ed*
bu*d* th*uaid*. Is an*n* si*n* adered Mo*ct*a riu. Geinf*ider* macam san
aird tuaidh, 7 creidf*id* Ere*n*naig 7 Alpa*n*aig 7 iarthar domai*n*
uili do 7 is na onoir doberimsi m'ag*ed* budh tuaidh, *ar* se, ag
de*n*am m'urnaidh*t*e; 7 bud *Colam* c*i*lli a ainm. Gonadh airi sin
dorinde an rand-sa:

21. We shall speak at first of the nobility and gentle blood of Columb cille. Columb cille the son of Fedlimid, son of Fergus cennfada, son of Conall Gulban, son of Niall of the nine hostages. That Niall was head-king of Ireland, Scotland and England. And we could follow his descent from that up to Adam, did we not think it tedious to do so. In proof whereof, there are only eighty nine persons between him and Adam, according to the reckoning of the historians of the Goidel as preserved by them in their own books.

22. And again Ethne daughter of Dima, son of Nae, son of Eithin, son of Corb file, son of Ailill the great, son of Brecan, son of Daire barrach, son of Cathair the great head-king of Ireland, was his mother. And a daughter of the king of Scotland, to wit Erc daughter of Loarn was his grand-mother, that is, his father's mother. And no blood is more truly noble than the blood of the dynasty of Ireland, together with that of the dynasties of the world up to Adam.

23. It is clear to us that not only did God choose Columb cille from his mother's womb as his own special servant, but that he chose him a long time before his coming from his mother's womb. And in proof of that, the saints of Ireland and Scotland and of the western world used to prophesy of him a long time before his birth.

24. The senior of the priests of Ireland prophesied of him, viz. Sen-Mochta Lugmaid even two hundred years before him. This was how Mochta did prophesy of him. A certain time Mochta chanced to be in Hi. His serving man, one Mac Rith, brought hazel-nuts to him, but Mochta refused to take them saying: 'The land from which those nuts were taken belongs not to me', said he, 'and let the fruit of that land be preserved until its master comes'. 'When shall he come?' said the boy. 'In two hundred years time' said Mochta. And Mochta was accustomed to pray with his face to the North thenceforward after coming to Ireland from Hi. So the members of his convent once enquired of him why his face was to the North. Then Mochta answered: 'A child will be born in the north country, and the men of Ireland and Scotland and of the whole western world will believe in him, and it is in his honour I turn my face to the North when saying my prayers; and Columb cille will be his name' said he. Wherefore he made this rhyme:

Macam gidhnither atuaid   ag turcbail nambidh dó,
Doiridnid Eri an breo   7 Alpa dainech dó.

25. Do tairrngir dno breithem bratha fer n-Eirenn .i. naem
Patruic antí Colam cilli .i. an uair do bi Patruic ac bendachad
Conaill Gulpan 7 Fergosa cendfada mic Conaill ar Sith Aeda.
Do togaib a da laim os a cind, 7 tarla Conall ar a laim deis,
7 Fergos ar a laim cli; 7 do cuir Patruic a lam des tar Conall
ar Fergas, 7 a lam cli ar Conall. Do b'ingnad le Conall sin, 7
do haithniged gruaim in a aiged trid, 7 do fiarfaid do Patruic
cred fa tucc se an onoir sin d'Fergas tairis fein. IS andsin
adubairt Patruic. Biaid mac mic ag Fergos, or se, 7 bud mac
octa do ri nime 7 talman e, 7 bud scathan gloine ar firinde 7
ar indracus a fladnaise na n-daine e, 7 bud Calam cilli a ainm.
7 as trid gorab goire do glun d'Fherghos é ina duitsi a Conaill
do chuir mesi mo lam des ar cend Fergosa 7 mo lam cli ar do
cend-sa, go n-derna na roind-se:

Geinfid macam dia fine   bud sai bud faid bud file,
Inmain lesbairi gle   nad eibera imargae,
Bid sai 7 bid craibtech 7 budh ab   la rirath bidbuan,
Is bid bithmaith ronbia   an bithfaith dia didnad.

26. ET fos do tairrnger Patruic tect Colaim cilli ria n-a
geinemain a n-inad eli amlaid so. Fechtas do Patruic ag sibal
Erenn da bennugad, 7 tarla a n-Domnach mor Muige Hithe a
Cinel Conaill e, 7 do bendaig se an baile sin; 7 do b'ail leis
dul ar na marach do bendugad na coda eli do Cenel Conaill. 7
do cuaid in a carbad go nuice an sruth re n-abarthor an Dael,
7 ar n-dul go h-or an atha, do bris feirsde an carbaid do bi fai,
7 gach uair do daingnighthi iad 7 do teiged Patruic sa carpad
do brisdis aris, 7 do ingantar cach sin go mor. IS and sin
adubairt Patruic tre spirad faidhedoracta: na bid ingnad oraib
fá in ni se, ar se, oir ni rigend an talam ud on t-sruth sa
anund a les mesi da bendugad, oir berthar mac and a ceand
aimsiri faide o aniug, 7 bud Colam cilli a ainm, 7 as se ben-

A youth will be born in the North at the up-rising . . . for him,
Ireland will bestow a flame (?), and populous Scotland, upon him.

25. The judge of doom for the men of Ireland, that is
Saint Patrick, prophesied of Columb cille, when he was blessing
Conall Gulban and Fergus cennfada son of Conall at Sith Aeda.
He raised his hands over their heads, Conall being upon his
right and Fergus at his left hand, and Patrick put his right
hand across Conall upon Fergus and his left hand upon Conall.
Whereat Conall was surprised, and a gloom was produced upon
his countenance, and he asked Patrick why he had given that
honour to Fergus beyond himself. Then Patrick made answer:
Fergus will have a grandson who will be darling of the king
of Heaven and Earth and a mirror of purity, truth, and dignity
before the people, and Columb cille will be his name. And it
is for his being nearer by one generation to Fergus than he is
to thee, Conall, that I put my right hand upon the head of
Fergus and my left hand upon thine. And he made those verses:

A boy will be born of his tribe, he will be a sage, a prophet
                             [and a poet,
Dear is the pure light, he may not utter a falsehood.
He will be a sage, and pious, and an abbot, with great grace
                             [ever-enduring,
And ever-good it will be to him, whom the ever-prophet may
                             [console.

26. And Patrick prophesied the coming of Columb cille
before his birth in another place as follows: Once as Patrick
was travelling Ireland and blessing it he happened to be in
Domnach mor of Mag Hithe in Cenel Conaill. And he blessed
that place, and desired to bless the other portions of Cenel
Conaill on the morrow. And he went in his chariot to the
stream that is called the Dael, and on approaching the brink
of the ford the axles of the chariot in which he was being
borne broke; and as often as they were made fast and Patrick
went into his chariot they used to break again. And everybody
was greatly surprised at that. Then Patrick being filled with
the spirit of prophecy, said: 'Be ye not amazed at this thing'
said he, 'for yonder land from this stream thither does not need

deochus an talam bud tuaid. 7 as demhin corab na n-onoir do
toirmeisc dia umam sa gan mo leigen do bendugad an talaim
ud a ngenter é, 7 ata an talam ud fein bendaighte tre beith a
n-dan dó Colam cilli do genemain and. 7 do firad gach ní dib
sin amail adubairt Patruic, 7 Ath an Carbaid ar Dail ainm an
átha sin o sin alle.

27. *ET* fos do bi an oired sa do cin ag dia 7 ag Patruic
ar Colam cilli a fad re n-a geineamain gor ordaig Patruic cís
áiridhe gacha bliadna ar fer a inaid fein a n-Ard Macha fa n-a
comair. 7 fos adubairt Patruic tre spirad faidheadórachta go
raibe an oired sin do cin ag dia ar Colam cilli, nach beith cis
ag en-naem da tainec reime no da tiucfa na diaid an én-baili
do bailtib Colaim cilli act a m-beith ag Colam cilli fein innta; 7
go tibradh se an oired sin d'uaisli dó tar naemaib Erenn. 7
ata Colam cilli gá dherbadh sin sa rand so:

Do rad Patruic daingen fír   cis ó Ard Macha s ní gó,
Indeis a Baeithin aris   nocha tucassa cis do.

28. *ET* fos do fagaib Patruic an lebar darub ainm an
soiscel a timna ag Colam cilli an uair do bí se ag dul docum
bais, 7 adubairt se re Brigid naomtha do bi an aimser a bais
aicce, an lebar sin do coimed do Colam cilli. 7 dorinde Brighid
sin amail adubairt Patruic ria, ge do bi aimser fada etir sin
7 Colam cilli do geinemain. *ET* ataid lebair eli gá mebhrugad
nach mar so dorinde Patruic risin lebor sin, act co tucc se
fadera a adhnocad leis fen sa tumba in ar cuired é, d'egla go
fuigedh en-duine eli é go tect Colam cilli cuice, 7 gorab aingel
de fein tuc les e docum Colam cilli, 7 fos do fagaib Patruic a
inadh fen a n-Erinn a timna ag Colam cilli an uair sin a ponge
a bais.

29. *ET* fos do tairrngir Patruic amlaid so tect Colaim cilli
a bhfad ria n-a genemain .i. Fechtas tainic Patruic docum na
h-abond ré n-abarthor an Buill, 7 as amlaid do bi an abonn sin
fen, ni fhedaeis daine dul tairsi acht a luing no a n-ethar.

that I should bless it, for a boy shall be born there in a long time from to-day, and his name will be Columb cille, and it is he that will bless the land to the North. And surely it was in his honour that God hindered me, in not allowing me to bless the land in which he will be born; for even the land is blessed through being preordained that Columb cille should be born there. And all these things were fulfilled as Patrick had said; and the Ford of the Chariot upon Dael is the name of that ford ever since.

27. And besides Columb cille was so dear to God and to Patrick a long time before his birth that Patrick directed a certain yearly tribute to be levied on his own successor in Ard Macha against his coming. And Patrick said in a spirit of prophecy that God so loved Columb cille, that no saint of those that came before or should come after him, would have right of tribute in any of the districts of Columb cille excepting only what Columb cille himself should have in them, and that God would give him that honourable position beyond the saints of Ireland. And Columb cille corroborates that in this stanza:

Patrick gave — true the warranty — a tribute from Ard
        [Macha, and it is no lie,
Tell, O Baethin, again, I gave him no tribute.

28. And Patrick left the book called the Gospel as a bequest to Columb cille when he was about to die, and he told Saint Brigid, who was with him at the time of his death, to keep that book for Columb cille. And Brigid did as Patrick had told her although there was a long time between that and the birth of Columb cille. But other books assert that not so did Patrick act with regard to the book, but that he caused it to be buried along with himself in the same tomb for fear anybody else should get it before Columb cille came to it, and that it was an angel of God that took it to Columb cille. And furthermore Patrick left in bequest to Columb cille his own see in Ireland at the same time upon the point of death.

29. And again Patrick foretold in this wise the coming of Columb cille a long time before his birth. Once upon a time Patrick came to the river which is called the Buill, and that river was so that men might not cross it except in a ship or a

7 do cuir se fá umla *ar* an cuid soir don abain*n* isliug*ad*
[fo. 2b] 7 a h-uisce do dul a tan*act*, ind*us* go m-beith si insiub*ail*
do cois no d'ech o sin amach go brath.   7 as follas a*n* mirbuile
sin do cach aniug. Oir ata in cuid tiar don abain*n* sin mar do
bi si ó tus, 7 an cuid soir tana di.   7 do bendaig se an aband
iar si*n*, 7 tainic tor*ad* eisc go imarcach uirri do brig an ben-
duighthe si*n* P*atruic.*

30. IS and si*n* do labhair P*atruic* tre spir*ad* faidedórachta 7
is edh adub*airt.* Ticfaid m*ac* na bethadh suthaine and so, ol se
.i. Col*am* c*illi*, 7 doghena eclas onórach san inadh so, 7 biaidh
coimti*n*ol manach uada indte, 7 is na onoir do bendaig mesi an
abon*n* sa docum go m-beth a*n* t-iasc sa tainec tre mo bendachtai*n*
si uirre do cungn*am* bidh aicce fen 7 gá manch*aib*, 7 ag lucht
a oibri; 7 fos is na onoir do chuir me uisce na h-abon*n* a tanacht
7 a laghad, i*n*das go fédf*ad* lucht a oibri dul tairsi anu*nn* 7
anall do reir a riachtanuis a les fein.   7 do firudh gach ní da
n-dub*airt* P*atruic* an*n* sin, 7 Es Mac n-Eirc ar Buill ai*n*m an
inaidh sin a n-derna Col*am* c*illi* an eclus.

31. *ET* fos do tairrngeir P*atruic* aris tect Col*am* c*illi* a
bhfad ria na genemain an uair tai*n*ec se co h-Eas Ruaid, 7 do
benduig se an taeb budh thuaid de 7 do mallaig se an taeb
bvdh des re ulca re C'airbri m*ac* Neill .ix. *giallaig* nar gab
credi*m* vada.   7 adub*airt* se co ticf*ad* Col*am* c*illi*, 7 an uiresb*aid*
ben*n*aigthe do fhagaib se fen *ar* an taeb si*n* bud tuaid don es
corab fa comair Col*am* c*illi* do fagaib se an uiresbaid air 7 go
coimlinf*cd* Colam c*illi* fen hi an uair do ticf*ad* se.   7 do firudh
si*n* am*ail* advb*airt* P*atruic*, mar bus foll*us* is in scel ata a n-inad
eli sa m-bethaidh si fein air sein.

32. Do mheil im*orro* a*n* muilend ro-onórach sa .i. P*atruic,*
do bi ar sibhol 7 ar meilt o uisce ro-saidbir na ngr*as* do bi o
dia aicce, fir Er*enn* 7 a mna. Gedhedh dob' ec*en* dó o burba 7
o mísduai*m* na n-dai*n*e a tosach an creidimh mora*n* salchair 7
cogail d'fagb*ail* sa cruithnecht-sa do meil se *no* co tainec Col*am*
c*illi*, 7 no gor glan se o gach uile ní nemh-glan iad, ag sil*ad* 7
ag senmoir brei*th*ri de doib, 7 go n-derna se plur ro-glan *ar* na
pultadh, 7 ar na lecen tria sháirse na ng*ras* n-im*arcach* tuc dia
do d'Erendchaib uile 7 do mora*n* d'Alp*an*chaib.

vessel. And he caused the eastern side of the river to become shoal and its waters shallow, that so it might be fordable afoot or a-horseback from that out for ever. And that miracle is clear to everybody to-day; for the western side of the river is as it always was, whereas its eastern side is shallow. And he blessed the river after that and a great plentiness of fish came upon it by virtue of that blessing of Patrick's.

30. Thereafter Patrick spoke in a spirit of prophecy and said: 'There will come the son of everlasting life', said he, 'namely Columb cille, and he will make an honourable church in this place and he will gather an assemblage of monks in it; and it is in his honour that I blessed this river so that this fish which came through my blessing upon it might be for a convenience of food to him and his monks and to his working people. And besides it is in his honour I caused the water of the river to grow shallow and to become less so that his working people might pass it over and back according to their own necessities.' And everything Patrick then said proved true, and The Waterfall of Mac n-Eirc upon Buill is the name of that place where Columb cille made the church.

31. And also Patrick prophesied the coming of Columb cille a long time before his birth, when he came to Ess Ruad. For he blessed the northern side of it and cursed the southern side, (from a grudge against Cairbre son of Niall of the nine hostages who would not accept the faith from him). And he said that Columb cille would come; and as for the want of blessing which he had left upon that northern side of the waterfall, that it was for Columb cille he had left the want upon it, for that he should supply it when he came. And that was fulfilled as Patrick had said, as will appear in an account of it in another part of this same Life.

32. Patrick, the very noble and honourable mill, which was driven and which ground by the very rich water of the graces which he had from God, ground the men of Ireland and its women. However he had to leave a good deal of weeds and cockle in this wheat he milled, from the foolishness and want of discretion in the people at the beginning of the faith, until Columb cille came and cleansed them of all uncleanness, sowing and preaching the word of God to them, until he made pure flour bolted and sifted through the searce of the wonderful

33. Do foillsig*ed* techt *Colam cilli* a fad ria na gene*main*
do P*a*truic aml*aid* so .i. Fechtas da raibe P*a*truic ag fagb*ail*
shaethair 7 anshoc*r*ach ro-moiri oc tarrai*n*g fer n-Ere*nn* 7 a
m-ba*n* docu*m* creidmhe, 7 do bo truagh les gan a demhi*n* aicce
cind*us* do beidis fa creideam 7 fa crabadh in a diaidh fen, no
cred hi an c*r*ich do cuirfed dia orra 7 med an t-shaethair do
bi se fein d'fagail uata. 7 do bi se ag guidhe de go duthrachtach
im a fis si*n* do tab*a*irt do. Tainec an t-aing*el* cuicce iar si*n* 7
do labair ris 7 as s*ed* adub*a*irt; gorab do reir an taisbe*n*ta do
foillseochaidhe do in a cod*l*ad an oidhce si*n* do bi cuige do b*edh*
Eri re na beo fen 7 na diaid go brath aris fa creide*m*. 7 is e
taisenadh tuc*a*d do: Eiri uile d'fhaicsi*n* re d*er*glasadh, 7 an lasair
do ergedh di a*g* dul svas *con* nuice an aier, 7 na diaid si*n* docon*n*airc se an teine si*n* ar na much*a*d acht cnvic mora a bfad
o celi re teinigh, 7 na diaid sin doco*nn*airc se na cnuic fen ar
na much*a*d acht indshama*il* lochrai*n*d no coindle ar na lass*a*d
na inadh gach cnuic dib. 7 doco*nn*airc se iad si*n* ar n-dul ass
aris, 7 sm*é*roidech no aibli 7 smal orra, ge do bat*a*r beo a
n-i*n*adhaib terca a fad o ceili ar fud Ere*nn*. Tainec an t-aing*el*
cet*n*a cuige 7 do indis dó gorab iad si*n* na rechta a rach*a*id
Eri i*n* a diaid fein. *Ar* na cloisdin do P*a*truic, do cai go gér, 7
do lab*a*ir do guth mor, 7 is s*ed* adub*a*irt. A dia na n-uili cum*act*,
an e dob' ail let na daine docu*m* ar cuiris mesi da tab*a*irt eoluis ort
fén doib, do damn*a*d, 7 do troc*a*ir*e* do tarraing cugad fe*n* vatha.
Gen gor*a*b fiu mesi tu aestecht rim, a tigerna cuir h-*f*eirg ar
cul leith-riu, 7 gab luc*t* an oilein si na h-Ere*nn* at tr*o*cuiri fein.
AR c*r*ichnug*ad* na m-briathar sin do P*a*truic, do labhair an
t-aing*el* go sithcanta ris 7 as s*ed* adub*a*irt. Fech don taeb b*ud*
thuaid dit, ar se, 7 do cife tu claechlodh laimhe desi de. Dorin*n*e P*a*truic mar adub*a*irt an t-aing*el* ris; oir do fech don taeb
b*ud* tvaidh de, 7 docondaic sol*us* ag erghe andsin nar mór *ar*
tus, 7 e ag médug*ad* 7 ag sc*ri*s an dorchadais as a celi, ind*us*
gor las Eri uile de ma*r* in c*ed* lasair, 7 doco*nn*aic ag dol is na
rechtaib cedna iar sin hi. *ET* do foill [fo. 3 a] sigh an t-aing*el*
ciall na taisbenta si*n* do P*a*truic, 7 adub*a*irt go m-beith Eri ar
lasadh do creidemh 7 do crab*ad* re na lind fein, 7 go rachadh
dorchadas ar in t-soillsi si*n* re na bas. *Act* ge do beidis daeini
maithe a *n*-i*n*adaib terca a *n*-Eri*nn* in a diaid, mar do bat*a*r na

graces which God gave him for all the Irish and for many of the Scotch.

33. The coming of Columb cille was shown to Patrick a long time before his birth in this way. Once upon a time as Patrick was finding labour and great inconvenience in converting the men of Ireland and their women to the faith, he was sorry that he did not know how they would be off for faith and for piety after his own time, or how would God prosper them for all the labour he was getting from them. And he used to pray God earnestly to give him the knowledge of that. Then an angel came to him and addressed him, saying that it was according to the vision to be revealed to him in his sleep the coming night that Ireland would be as regards the faith during his own life and after him for evermore. And this is the vision that was given him: He saw all Ireland red on fire, and the flame which rose from it went up to the further aerial spaces, and afterwards he saw that fire being quenched, but only big hills on fire far from each other, and then again he saw even the hills went out except something like lamps or candles that remained alight in the place of each hill. He saw those go out again and only embers or sparks with a gloom upon them; however they smouldered in a few places far scattered throughout Ireland. The same angel came to him and told him that those were the conditions through which Ireland should go after him. Upon hearing that Patrick wept bitterly, and he spoke with a great voice and said: 'O God of all power, dost thou desire to damn and withdraw thy mercy from the people to whom thou didst send me to bring a knowledge of thyself? Though I am unworthy that thou shouldst hear me, O Lord, calm thy anger in their regard, and receive the people of this island of Ireland into thy own mercy.' Having finished those words the angel spoke reassuringly to him saying: 'Look to the North of thee' said he, 'and thou wilt behold the change of God's right hand.' Patrick did as the angel told him, for he looked to the North, and he saw a light arise there, not great at first, then waxing and tearing the darkness asunder, so that all Ireland was lighted by it as by the first flame, and he saw it go through the same stages afterwards. And the angel explained the meaning of that vision to Patrick saying that Ireland would be alight with faith and piety during his own time, but that darkness would come

cnuic sen re lasadh a b-fhad o ceile, 7 mar do gebdais na daine
maithe sin bas, go ticfad daine bud mesa ina iad féin in a
n-inad ar indshamlaid na lócarnd 7 na coinnel dar labrumar
remhe-so 7 na diaidh, 7 nach beith don chreidem ar bethugad
acu act indshamail an sméroidigh ar a raibe an smal 7 an ceo,
no go tí mac na soillsi suthaine .i. Colam cilli. 7 ge mad becc
ar tus é ag tect ar in saegal dó, go m-beith ag silad 7 ag
senmoir breithri de 7 ag medugad an credim no go lasadh Eri
re na linn, amail do las si re lind Patruic, 7 nach beith an
lasadh cedna go brath aris uiri, acht ge do beidis daeine maithe
crabaid in a diaidh. 7 fos go rachaid eclus Erenn a n-egcruth
a n-dereadh aimsire iarsen, innus nach beith beo don creidem no
don crabud indte act indshamail an smeroidigh no na n-áibhell
m-becc ar a raibe an smal 7 an dorchadas dar labrumar remhe so.

34. Do tarrngair Martain naemtha techt Colaim cilli a fad
ria na genemain a n-aimsir a bais fein. 7 as sed adubairt:
Adluicter, ol se, mo lebar fen .i. lebar na soiscel, a n-enfheacht
rim, 7 cuirter ar mh'uct fein sa tumba é, oir geinfidhir mac
naemtha bendaighte a n-Erinn, ol se, 7 is ó nem sa fidhair
doconnaic Eoin ag luidh ar Isv ag sruth Eorthanain an uair do
baisd sé é ainmneochar leth a anma, 7 is on eclais ainmneochar
an leth eli dá ainm. 7 ticfaid se annso a cinn ced bliadan ó
niugh, 7 oisceolaid sé mo tumbusa 7 dogeba sé mo lebar ann.
7 coimfhedfaidh dia fa na comhair e gan sal no dorchadus do
dul ar en-litir de, 7 béraid se go h-Erinn é, 7 bud soiscel
Martain ainm an lebair sin a n-Erinn o sin anvas.

35. Do tairrngir Brigid naemtha mar an cedna tect Colaim
cilli a fad ria na genemain, 7 as sed adubairt .i. fasfaidh slat
dom taeb sa bud tuaid d'Erinn, 7 biaid blatha na n-uili gras
uirri, 7 do déna dia crand mor di, 7 lethfaid a bharr 7 a gega
tar Erinn 7 tar Alpan, 7 tar iarthor domain uile .i. beraid
Eithne taeb-fhoda ben Feilimthe mic Fergosa cend-fhoda mic
Conaill Gulban mic Neill noi-giallaig, 7 bud Colam cilli a ainm,
7 rachaid a briathar 7 a senmoir 7 clu 7 esimlair a crabaid fo
iarthair an domain uile. 7 as deimin go mothaighim si a grasa

over that light at his death. However there would be good people here and there in Ireland after him, as were the far sundered hills on fire, but when those good people died there would come people not so good in their stead, like the lamps and candles of which we have spoken already, and that the faith would be sustained by them only as the embers that were in gloom and mist, until the son of eternal light should come, namely Columb cille. And although little at first upon coming into the world, nevertheless he would sow and preach the word of God and increase the faith so that Ireland would blaze up in his time as it did in the time of Patrick; and that it would never blaze in the same way again although there would be good, pious people after him. And that the church of Ireland would go into decay at the end of time after that, so that there would be there of faith and piety only a semblance of the embers or little sparks covered with gloom and darkness of which we have spoken already.

34. Saint Martin prophesied the coming of Colúmb cille a long time before his birth, when he was himself about to die. He said: 'Let my book, i. e. the book of the Gospels, be buried with me, and let it be placed upon my breast in the tomb. For a holy, blessed boy will be born in Ireland', said he, 'and one half of his name will be called from Heaven, in the figure that John saw resting upon Jesus in the river Jordan when he baptised him, and the other half of his name will be called from the church. He will come hither a hundred years from to-day, and he will open my tomb and find my book there. And God will preserve it for him, so that a single letter of it shall not get spot or stain; and he will take it to Ireland, and Martin's Gospel shall be the name of that book in Ireland from that out.'

35. Saint Brigid likewise prophesied the coming of Columb cille a long time before his birth, saying: 'A sapling will grow in this northern half of Ireland that will bear the blossoms of every grace; and God will make it a great tree, and its bloom and branches will spread over Ireland and over Scotland and over the entire western world. That is to say: Ethne taeb-fhoda, wife of Fedlimid son of Fergus cenn-foda, son of Conall Gulban, son of Niall of the nine hostages, will bear a son and his name will be Columb cille. And his word and his preaching,

7 a subalt*id*e do lathair **aga***m,* ge fada uaim an aimser a
nge*in*ter e, *ar* si. 7 dorin*n*e an ran*n* so:

Macam Ethne taeb-foda   sech is bol is blathug*ad,*
Colam c*illi* caidh *gan* on   nir uo romh a rathug*ad.*

36. *ET* fos do tairrng*ir* P*at*ruic com*bad* a n-aen-tumba ris
fe*n* 7 re Brig*id* a n-Dun da Lethglas do cuir*fid*e co*rp* Col*aim*
c*illi* tar eis a bais. 7 fos do tairrng*ir* Brig*id* fei*n* sin mar i*n*
ced*n*a; 7 do firad sin am*ail* indeosas a*n* betha a n-inad eli. Oir
nir b'ail leo gan an t-indm*us* ro-uasal-sa do bat*ar* fen do tairrngire 7 do gellat*ar* do tect do saidbriug*ad* na poiblech 7 na
h-eclaisi do reir na n-oibrighte n-diadha do chu*r* a n-esiml*air*
doib an*n* fei*n* do beith *ar* aen-taisc*ed* riv fein fa deoidh .i. Col*am*
c*illi* .i. a anam do beith *ar* aen-taisc*ed* re a n-a*n*mo*nn*aib a ngloir
suthain de, 7 a co*rp* do beith *ar* aen-taisc*ed* re a corp*aib* a
n-en-timpa (tumba) *ar* a*n* saeg*al*-sa. 7 fos leghtor go mi*n*ec *ar*
Colam c*illi* gor tairrng*ir* se fei*n* re na beo gorab a n-aen-tumba
riusan do beith a corp.

37. *ET* fos do tairrng*ir* Dabheoog naemtha *tect* Col*aim* c*illi*
a bfad ria na geine*main* .i. oidhce airide do bi se ar purcad*ó*ir
P*at*ruic ar Loch D*er*g, 7 doco*nn*airc se soillsi ro-mhor 7 delr*ad*
im*ar*cach don taeb b*ud* th*uaid* de, 7 do fiar*faig*etar na clerig do
bi faris de, cred b*a* ciall do*n* taisbenadh sin tug*ad* doib. Frecrais
Dabeooc iad 7 is edh adub*air*t .i. lasf*aid* dia locr*an*d do*n* taeb
sa th*uaid* dinn, 7 dobera se sol*us* d' eclais de .i. m*a*c béra*s*
Eithne taeb-fhoda be*n* Feid*l*mthe m*i*c Fergo*sa* cendf*ada* m*i*c
C*on*aill Gulban, 7 b*ud* Colam c*illi* a ainm, 7 b*ud* gein t-shochair
d'iarthair dom*ain* e, ar soillsi 7 ar ecna 7 *ar* oghacht 7 ar
faidhedoracht.

38. *ET* fos do tairrng*ir* Caillin naemtha tect Col*aim* c*illi*
a bfad ria na gene*main* [fo. 3b] .i. an uair dorin*n*e se faidedor*act*
ar slic*t* Conaill Gulban m*i*c Neill .ix. giall*aig* .i. go ngebad da
righ dec dib righ*act* Ere*nn*, 7 go ngebudh cethrar dib lan-righe

and the report and example of his piety will spread over the whole western world. And in very truth I feel his graces and his virtues present with me, though distant from me yet is the time of his birth.' And she made this stanza:

The child of Ethne taeb-foda   as being suspicious he is the
                                                   [flowering,
Chaste Columb cille without stain,   it was not too soon to notice him.

36. And again Patrick prophesied that it would be in the same tomb with himself and Brigid in Dun da Leth-glas that the body of Columb cille should be buried after his death. And Brigid herself prophesied that likewise, and it came true as the Life narrates in another place. For they desired that this truly precious treasure (of which they had prophesied, and which they promised should come to enrich the people and the church, according to the godly works whereof he gave them an example in his own person) should be in the same receptacle with themselves at last, to wit, Columb cille; for that his soul should be a-keeping with theirs in the eternal glory of God, and his body with their bodies in the same tomb in this world. And besides one often reads of Columb cille that he himself prophesied during his life, that his body would be in the same tomb with them.

37. And again saint Dabheoog prophesied the coming of Columb cille a long time before his birth. One night as he was in Patrick's Purgatory at Loch Derg, he saw a great light and wonderful effulgence to the north side of him. Now the clerics of his company asked him what was the meaning of that vision which was shown them. Dabeooc answered them saying: 'God will light a lamp on the north side of us, and it will give light to the church of God; that is, a son which Ethne taebfoda, wife of Fedilmid son of Fergus cennfada son of Conall Gulban will bear, and Columb cille will be his name. And he will be a fortunate birth for the western world, for light and wisdom, for virginity and prophecy.'

38. And again saint Caillin prophesied the coming of Columb cille a long time before his birth when he made prophecy for the race of Conall Gulban son of Niall of the nine hostages; which was, that twelve kings of them would hold kingship in

leithe Cuind, am*ail* asp*ert* sa rand-sa:

Gebtar uada fa do dec   Eri, ni ba brec an breth,
Is cethrar do sil an dui*nn*   gebas go tui*nn* luim a leth.

ET do rairrng*ir* se fos an tan nach b*ed* leo righact Er*enn* nach beith cend*us* ag righ eli orra, am*ail* asp*ert* sa ra*nn* sa:

Tan nac beid os Eri*nn* uill   ní gebaid cuing *act* a cath,
Ni beid ga*n* mal dib b*u*dei*n*   ni c*r*aidh mo ceill reim go rath.

ET do tairrng*ir* se go tiucfadh C*olam cilli ar* slict Convill Gulp*an*, 7 nach tic*fad* na diaidh go brath do clandaib na m-ban en-duine as mo i*n* a foillseochad dia a g*ras*a ina hé, a leith re faidedor*act* 7 mirbuile 7 re taisbe*n*adh aing*l*ide, 7 re cr*ua*s 7 re gloine c*r*ab*ai*d. *ET* do tairrngir se go n-dingn*ad* dia moran maithesa do*n* cuid eli do slic*t* Conaill G*ulb*an ar son C*olaim cilli* do b*eith* ar en-slic*t* riu, am*ail* asp*ert* sa rand sa:

Tic*faid* tar mh'eis Col*am* caid   fhúicfes daib briat*ar* is buaidh,
Is é sin ai*n*-fer is ferr   genfes tall go ti lá an luain.

ET da derb*ad* sin do fagaib C*olam cilli* fein mar bhua*dha* ar cin*el* Conaill, an uair nach biadh a oirbiri fei*n* orra go m-bvaideoc*h*dais re h-en-cath esbadach ar secht cathaib eli.

39. Do tairrng*ir* Brenain*n* é aml*aid* so, 7 as s*ed* adub*airt*: Beraidh Ethne taebf*ada* ben Feidlm*ithe* m*ic* Fergos*a* ce*nn*foda m*ic* Conaill G*ulb*an mac, 7 biaid g*ras*a an spi*rda* naeimh go h-im*ar*cach air, 7 ata do grad aguinne do fein 7 da gnimh*ar*th*aib* dar lind f*en* go fuil se do láth*air* againd gen co tainec se fos.

Ireland, and that four of them would enjoy royal supremacy in Conn's half, as he said in this stanza:

> From him shall Ireland be twelve times ruled, the judgment
> [will not be a lie,
> It is four of the seed of the Donn that will rule its half
> [to the bare wave.

And he prophesied furthermore that whenever the kingship of Ireland should not be theirs, no other king would exercise power over them, as he said in this stanza:

> When they rule not noble Ireland they will accept the yoke
> [only by battle,
> They shall not be without a prince from themselves a course
> [endowed with grace torments not my mind.

And he prophesied that Columb cille would come of the race of Conall Gulban, and that no one of the children of women would come after him in whom God would show forth his graces more than in him, in matter of prophecy and miracles and angelic visions and rigour and purity of piety. And he prophesied that God would show many favours to the other portion of the tribe of Conall Gulban because Columb cille belonged to their race, as he said in this verse:

> The chaste Columb will come after me who will leave with
> [you instruction and an inherent virtue,
> He is the one man that is best who will be born yonder
> [till the day of doom.

And in proof thereof Columb cille gave it as a favour to the cenel Conaill, that so long as they did not incur his displeasure, with one weakly batallion they would gain the victory over four others.

39. Brenainn prophesied his coming in this way, saying: 'Ethne taebfada, wife of Fedlimid son of Fergus cennfoda, son of Conall Gulban, will bear a son, and he will be filled with the graces of the Holy Ghost, and we love him and his deeds so much that we imagine he is already in our presence, although he has not come yet.'

40. Do tairrngir espoc Eogan Arda Sratha a tect ria na genemain amlaid so .i. la airidhe dochuaid Lugaid mac Sedna mic Ferghosa cennfada mic Conaill Gulban 7 a mac .i. Fiachra, go h-Ard Sratha, 7 fuaratar espoc Eoghain a n-dorus a mainesdrech fein.   7 tarla imresain etar Fiachraig 7 manach do manachaib espuic Eogain, cor marb se an manuch. Do fergaidh espoc Eogan trit sin, 7 do mallaig se Fiachraig 7 a slicht in a diaid, 7 adubairt go fuighedh sé fein bas fa cenn nai la, 7 nach gébadh enduine da slicht righact Erenn, no cinel Conaill go brath, 7 nach beith uimhir bud mo ina cuiger da sil a n-aeinfhect ann coidhce, 7 go m-beith bith-ainimh ar gach duine dib sin fein. Do firadh sin uile, 7 ar fagail bais d' Fiachraig mar adubairt an nech naemtha sin, do gab ecla mor a athair .i. Lugaid re faicsin na mirbol mor sin. ET tainec mar a raibhe espoc Eogan, do tabairt a brethe fen do, do cenn a benduighte, 7 do cend gan a escaine do luidhe air fein, no ar in cuid eli dá claind. Gebud-sa sin, ar espoc Eogan, 7 ni gebhaind breth ar bith uaid mona gabainn a n-onoir an mic bendaighte naemtha geinfider ar en-slict rit a cend caeca bliadna, 7 bud Colam cilli a ainm, 7 is hí Ethne taebfada ben posda Felimthe mic Fergasa cennfada mic Conaill Gulban berus an mac sin dó féin. Gonad ann dorinde an rann-sa:

Mac bearar do Feilimid   bud minn ar gach cleir,
Feilimid mac Ferghosa   mic Conaill mic Neill.

ET bud e fos, ar espoc Eogan, bus cend 7 bus posda don eclais, 7 don credem, 7 nir gein o Crisd anuas a leithéid, ar feabhus a credeim 7 a crabaid, 7 ar umhéd naeimheochar do na cinedhaib leis, 7 rachaid a ecna os cenn cleri na crisdaigechta, 7 rachaid a cogus os cenn fer n-domain. 7 nir geinedh 7 ni genfider naem bus mo d' impidech 7 do comairlech ar an trinoid ina é. 7 ni fhedand tenga daenda tect ar in molad tuc espoc Eogan ar Colam cilli an uair sin. 7 do tairrngir se comadh e Gridoir beil oir bud papa sa Roim re lind Colaim cilli, 7 go rachaid se ar cuairt cuige, 7 gomadh é Moconna naemtha bud compánuch sligid do ag dol annsin. 7 as sí breth ruc espoc Eogan ar

40. The bishop Eogan of Ard Sratha prophesied his coming before his birth in this way. One day Lugaid son of Sedna son of Fergus cennfoda, son of Conall Gulban, and his son Fiachra, went to Ard Sratha, and found bishop Eogan at the door of his monastery. And there happened a quarrel between Fiachra and one of the monks of bishop Eogan in which the monk was killed. Bishop Eogan became enraged at that, and he cursed Fiachra and his seed after him, and said that he would die in nine days, and that no one of his race nor of the cenel Conaill, should possess the kingship of Ireland for evermore, and that there should never be more than five of his race co-existing, and that even those should every one bear a perennial blemish. All that came true. Now when Fiachra had died, as that holy man had said, his father Lugaid got sore afraid on seeing that great miracle. And he came to bishop Eogan to offer him terms of submission, that he might bless him, and that the curse might not rest upon himself nor upon the remainder of his children. 'I accept that' said bishop Eogan, 'and I would not have accepted any terms from thee were it not that I did it in honour of a blessed and holy boy who will be born of the same tribe with thee in fifty years' time. And Columb cille will be his name, and it is Ethne, the spouse of Fedlimid son of Fergus cennfoda son of Conall Gulban, who will bear that son unto him.' And then he made this verse:

A son will be born unto Fedlimid   who will be the diadem
[of assemblies,
Unto Fedlimid son of Fergus   son of Conall son of Niall.

'And again' said bishop Eogan, 'he it is that will be head and prop of the church and of the faith; and his like was not born from the time of Christ until now, for the excellence of his faith and of his piety, and for the multitude of the gentiles that will be blessed through him. And his wisdom will transcend that of the clergy of christendom, and his conscience that of the men of the world. And there was not born nor will there be a saint who will be a greater beseecher and adviser of the Trinity than he.' And no human tongue can tell the praise that bishop Eogan bestowed upon Columb cille at that time. And he prophesied that it was the golden-mouthed Gregory who should be

Lugaid: screboll gacha tres bliadna vaidh fein, 7 o gach duine
dá shil in a diaidh, dó fen, 7 d' fhir a inaidh go brath, 7 gan
he fein no duine da slict da fulang esonora a baile no a eclaisi
coidhce. *ET* adubairt gorab ar son Colaim cilli do beith ar
én-slict ris nar deonaigh dia dó fein a mallugad, ina a slict in
a diaid do mallugad. 7 fos adubairt escop Eogan re Lugaid go
tibradh dia an oired sin d' onoir do ar son Colaim cilli do beith
ar enslict ris, an vair na bad le na shil righact, nach beidis go
brath gan an dara duine bud ferr a n-Erinn dib. *ET* fos
adubairt mar an cedna an vair na bad leo fen an righe [fo. 4a]
nach bud rí da righfaide ar Eirinn muna beith an duine bud
ferr acu gá rigadh. 7 adubairt go coiméoltide sin doib da coim-
lidis a cis 7 a onoir do fein 7 do Colam cilli mar an cedna.
Beatha espuic Eogain 7 Moconna naemtha adeir so uili; 7 do
fagbhamar moran da n-abraid na bethada sin ar so le na fad
lind re na scribadh.

41. Do thairrngir dno Buide mac Bronaigh é a n-aimser a
bais fen 7 adubairt ria na muinntir. Rucad san oidhce anoct,
ar se, mac uasal onorach a fiadnaise de 7 daine, 7 tiucfaid se
andso a cinn deich m-bliadna ficed ó nocht, 7 bud da fer dec a
lín a cosmailes an da esbol dec, 7 foillseochaid se m' adhnacul-
sa 7 cuimdeochaid se mo thaisi 7 mo roilec, 7 biaid ar cumann
re celi a nim 7 a talmain, 7 bud Colam cilli a ainm.

42. Ni hed amain do tairrngiretar naeim Erenn 7 a h-uasal-
aithrecha ga raibe spirad faidhedoracta ó dia tect Colaim cilli,
act do tarrngiretar na draithe 7 na daeine ag nach raibe creidem
go tiucfaid se, a fad ria na genemain. 7 da derbad sin do
tairrngir Finn mac Cumaill co ticfaid se an uair do lecc se
Bran .i. an cu oirderc do bi aicce don dam allaid ag abvind
t-Senglenda a crich cineoil Conuill ris a raiter Glend Colaim
cilli aniug. 7 nir len an cu an fiadh tar abainn glinne anvnn.
7 fa h-ingnad le cach an cu nar leicc aen-bethadach uaithe
riam dá dénum sin. IS andsin docuaid Find a muinidhin a fesa,

pope in Rome at the time of Columb cille, and that he would
go to visit him, and that it is saint Moconna who should be his
companion on the way thither. And the judgment that bishop
Eogan passed upon Lugaid was: a payment of a screpull every
third year by himself, and by everyone of his seed after him,
to him and to his successor for ever; and that neither himself
nor any of his seed should suffer his enclosure or his church
to be dishonoured for ever. And he said it was for Columb cille
being of the same race with him that God did not permit him to
curse him nor to curse his children after him. And besides bishop
Eogan told Lugaid that God would show him so great honour
for Columb cille being of the same race with him, that whenever
his seed should not possess the kingship they should never be
so that the second best man in Ireland would not be of them.
And he said furthermore that whenever the kingship should not
be theirs that no king inaugurated in Ireland should be a king
unless the best man of them was crowned. And he said that
that should be fulfilled for them if they were true to his tax
and to his honour, and to those of Columb cille likewise. It is
the Life of bishop Eogan and of saint Moconna that says all
this; and we omitted a good deal that the Lives narrate upon
this matter, it would weary us so much to copy it.

41. Buide mac Bronaigh prophesied of him when dying, and
he said to his convent: 'There was born to-night' said he, 'a
boy noble and honourable before God and men, and he will
come hither in thirty years from to-night, and twelve men will
be his company, in imitation of the twelve apostles. And he
will make known my grave and preserve my relics and cemetery,
and our mutual love will be in Heaven and in Earth, and Columb
cille will be his name.'

42. Not alone did the saints of Ireland and its patriarchs
who enjoyed the spirit of prophecy from God foretell the coming
of Columb cille, but also druids and persons who had not the
faith foretold a long time before his birth that he would come.
In proof whereof Finn mac Cumail prophesied that he would
come when he let Bran, the celebrated hound he had, after the
deer, at the river of Senglenn in the country of cenel Conuill,
that is called Glenn Coluimb cilli to-day. And the hound did
not follow the deer across the river of the glenn. Now they
all wondered that a hound that had never before let her quarry

86*

7 ro labair tre spir*u*d faidedor*ac*ta, gen co raibe creidimh aice,
7 asedh adub*air*t: Genfidher mac sa tir-si bud th*uaid* 7 bud
Col*am* c*i*lli a ai*n*m, 7 bud é an dechm*a*d glu*n* o Cormac ua
Cui*n*n e, 7 biaid se lan do rath 7 do gr*a*saib an dia ata na
aén 7 na t*r*iar, 7 itá an*n* 7 do bi, 7 bias; 7 biaidh moran do
termo*n*naib 7 do cell*aib* a n-Er*in*n 7 a n-Alb*ain* aice 7 bende-
och*aid* se a*n* talumh-sa on t-sruth ano*n*n, 7 bud termo*n*n dá
g*ach* aen rachas an*n* go brath aris é; 7 is na on*óir* tuc B*ra*n
an comairghe ud do*n* fiadh nar len si t*ar* abhai*n*n ano*n*n é. 7
Bel*ach* Damhai*n* ai*n*m an inaid si*n* a tucc Bran an c*om*airghe
si*n* don fiadh o sin ille.

43. *ET* do tairrngir*ed* fos d' Fheilm*i*d Rechtm*a*r d' aird-
righ Er*en*n tect Col*a*im c*i*lli a fad ria na genem*a*in aml*aid* so
.i. tuc se i*ng*in Righ Lochla*n*n do mnai, 7 do bui si aimser fada
aicce n*ach* t*a*rla cl*an*d eatorra, 7 fa h-olc les an righ 7 le feruib
Er*en*n uile si*n*. La ecin d*a*r ericch an ri go moch na aen*a*r ar
faithce na Temr*a*ch iarsi*n*, 7 tainec go tibra an laeich leisc
d' indlad a la*m* 7 a gnúisi 7 a aidhce. Nir cia*n* do an*n* go
faca a*n* t*r*iar da indsaig*i*d a n-edaighib ro-geala ro-soillsi ro-
delr*a*dach. 7 ba ro-ingnadh lasin rig a n-indell 7 a n-ecusc, oir
ni fhaca se a leitheid do daeinibh reime si*n*. Tancot*a*r do
lath*air* 7 do bendaiget*a*r a n-ai*n*m an athar 7 a*n* m*i*c 7 an
spir*d*a naeimh don righ. IS neamghnath*ach* linde an bendug*a*d
si*n* donithí-si dvi*n*n, ar ind *ri*g, oir ni na n-ai*n*m sen clec*t*maid-
ne bendug*a*d du*n*n act a n-ai*n*m na *n*-dee aeieoir da creidmid
fein. Do fiarf*ai*g an ri sgela dib, ca h-inadh as a t*a*ngat*ar*, no
créd iad na gnoaighte i*m*a tancvt*ar*. Do frecrat*ar* sa*n* e, 7
ass*ed* adubrat*ar*. Dia na n-uile cumh*act* .i. cruth*ui*geoir nimhe 7
talm*an* 7 na n-uile dul, 7 ata na aen-dia 7 na t*ri* persanaib do
cuir cugat-sa sind, da rada rit an recht rig-sa do bi agat go
tr*a*sda .i. suil a suil 7 cois a cois 7 lam a laim do treice*n* 7
recht nva do gab*ail* cugat bus ferr ina sin. Oir da m-be*n*ad
dr*och*-dhuine a suil *no* a chos *no* a lam do duine maith, do bo
becc an eruic andsi*n* a shuil nó a chos *no* a lamh fen; 7 da
m-be*n*adh duine maith a suil *no* a cos *no* a la*m* do droch-duine,
do bo ro-mor 7 do bo nemhimcub*aid* a shuil no a chos no a lam
do bv*ai*n* don dvine maith ar a son si*n*. *ET* o ata si*n* m*ar* sin
be*n* eraic oir 7 air*g*id cruid 7 cethra amuigh and gach en-droch-

escape from her should do such a thing. Then Finn consulted
his oracle and spoke through a spirit of prophecy, although he
had not the faith, saying: 'A child will be born in this land to
the North, and Columb cille will be his name, and he will be
tenth in descent from Cormac o Cuinn, and he will be full of
the blessing and of the graces of the triune God, who is and
who was and will be. And he shall have many sanctuaries and
churches in Ireland and in Scotland, and he will bless this land
from the stream upwards, and it will be a sanctuary for everybody that will go there for ever.' And it is in his honour that
Bran spared the deer and refused to follow him over the river.
And Belach Damhain is the name of the place where Bran
showed that clemency to the deer from that day to this.

43. And the coming of Columb cille was foretold to Fedlimid
Rechtmar the highking of Ireland a long time before his birth
in this wise: He had married the daughter of the king of
Lochlann, and, though a long time with him, they still had no
offspring; and the king and all the men of Ireland were dis-
pleased thereat. One day afterwards as the king arose early
alone upon the green of Tara, he went to Tibra an laeich leisc
to wash his hands and his face and countenance. He was not
long there till he saw three men approach him in white, shining
and very bright raiment. And the king wondered at their
apparel and quality, for he had never seen that sort of people
before. They came forward and accosted the king in the name
of the Father and of the Son and of the Holy Ghost. 'Unusual
to us is your style of address' said the king, 'for it is not in
their name we are used to salute, but in the name of the gods
of the air in whom we believe.' The king asked tidings of
them; whence came they and for what business had they come.
They made answer and said: 'The God of all might, Creator of
Heaven and Earth and of all elements, who is one God in three
persons, sent us to thee to tell thee to abandon this royal law
that thou hast followed hitherto, viz. an eye for an eye and a
foot for a foot and a hand for a hand, and to accept a new
law better than it. For if an evil person should deprive a just
man of his eye or his foot or his hand, his own eye or his foot
or his hand would be put poor compensation for that; and if a
just man should deprive an evil man of his eye or his foot or
his hand it would be excessive or improper to deprive the just

ráed bec *no* mor da n-den*t*ar fud do reir m*ar* docifidher duit
fein 7 do dainib eolcha ecn*ai*de do righa*ct*a 7 do tigernais, 7 da
n-derna tú so dobera dia luach duit *ar* a so*n* .i. do be*n* ata
ai*m*rid re fada geinf*i*der m*a*c edrad 7 hí, 7 bud la*n* Eri 7 Alba
7 Saxa 7 iarth*ar* dom*ai*n uile da clu 7 da scelaib, 7 bud Co*nn*
ced-cath*ach* a ai*n*m, 7 budh *ar* a slicht beid righraid Er*enn* go
brath. *ET* fos geinfider m*a*c ar sli*ct* an Chuind si*n*, 7 bud
Colam ci*lli* a ainm, 7 bu*d* é an d*a*ra glun déc uaid-se fein é, 7
bu*d* gen t-sochair do dainib iarth*air* doma*in* é, 7 bud dalta do
righ nimhe 7 talma*n* é, 7 doirtf*ai*d dia a gr*a*sa go h-im*a*rc*ach*
air, 7 biaidh se *ar* lassadh do gr*a*dh de, ind*us* co m-bera do
comr*a*d 7 di imacallam riss fein gacha Dard*a*éin in a flaithe*m*-
n*us* ne*m*dha fein é. 7 bidh a fhis ag*a*t, a ri Er*enn*, gorap a
n-o*n*oir *an* m*i*c sin, 7 do cend co ticfa se *ar* do slicht toilighes
dia slicht do beith ort, 7 nach ar do shon féin no ad onoir
dogeib tu hé. [fo. 4 b]

44. Do tairrng*i*r*etar* dr*ai*the Con*a*ill Gu*lban* m*i*c Neill nai-
gi*al*l*aig* techt Col*ai*m ci*lli* ria na genem*ain* amlaid so .i la da
raibe Conall ag seilg 7 ag fiadach a nG*ar*ta*n*, ni headh amhain
nach dendaeis a coin *no* a cuan dith *no* digbail do*n* fiadach,
act do bidis ac cluithe riv. Do b' ingnad le Conall *an* ní si*n*, 7
do tuig go raibe se a n-adhaidh nadúiri go mor. 7 do fiafr*ai*g
do na dr*ai*thib do bi faris cred b*u*d ciall do si*n*. Ata a fís si*n*
againde, ar na dr*ai*the .i. berthor m*a*c dot slicht-sa san inadh-so
in a bfvil tu anossa, 7 bud é an tres glun uaid-si é, 7 bud
Colam ci*lli* a ainm, 7 biaid se lan do gr*a*saib en-día na n-uile
cumhacht 7 crutaigheora na n-dul. 7 bendeochaid se an t-inad-
sa, 7 bud comairghe 7 termo*nn* da gach nech ricfas a les tect
and go brath aris é. 7 as a n-onoir *an* m*i*c sin 7 na comairghe
oirdeochas se do beith ag an ferand so tucat*ar* do coin-se a
Conaill comairge don fiadhach ud san inadh in a m-bert*ar* e,
b*ar* na dr*ai*the.

45. Amhail do derbat*ar* na se*n*-naeimh uaisli eolcha si*n* re

man of his eye or his foot or his hand for that. And since that is so, exact a fine of gold and silver, stock and cattle for every evil deed great or small that is committed under thy sway, according as shall seem good to thyself and to wise and discreet persons of thy kingdom and province. For if thou do this God will bestow upon thee a reward therefor, to wit, a son will be born between thee and thy wife, who has long been barren, and Ireland and Scotland and England and the western world will be filled with his fame and his renown, and Conn of the hundred battles will be his name, and the dynasty of Ireland will be of his family for ever. And besides a son will be born of the race of this Conn, and Columb cille will be his name, and he will be the twelfth generation from thyself, and he will be a happy birth to the people of the western world, and he will be a fosterling of the king of Heaven and Earth, and God will pour his graces plentifully upon him, and he will be aflame with the love of God, so that he will take him to his own heavenly kingdom to speak and converse with himself every Thursday. And know, thou king of Ireland, that it is in honour of that child, and because he will be of thy seed, that God allows thee to have a family and that thou receivest it not for thy own sake nor in thine honour.'

44. The druids of Conall Gulban son of Niall of the nine hostages foretold the coming of Columb cille before his birth as follows. One day as Conall was hunting and chasing at Gartan, not only did his hounds or his pack do no hurt or harm to the game but they even played with them. Conall wondered at that, for he knew it was greatly against nature. And he asked his druids who were with him, what was the reason of it. 'We know', said the druids, 'a child will be born of thy race in the spot where thou now art, and he will be the third generation from thee, and Columb cille will be his name, and he will be filled with the graces of the one God of all might and Creator of the elements. And he will bless this place, and he will be protection and sanctuary to everyone who shall require to come there for ever. And it is in honour of that child and of the virtue of protection which he ordains shall be upon this land that thy hounds, Conall, showed clemency to the game in the place where he will be born', said the druids.

45. As those wise and honourable ancient saints affirmed the

faidedor*act* o dia tect C*olaim* c*illi,* 7 m*ar* do derbot*ar* na d*r*aithe
ag nach raibe creidemh a thecht, do derbat le fisib 7 le hais-
lingibh a techt m*ar* an cedna do reir mar docondairc a mathair
fein a n-aisling .i. dar lé fen brat mor do tabairt di, 7 do bi
d' fad 7 do leithne sa m-brat go rainec o iarth*or* Erea*n*n co
hoirther Alb*an*, 7 nach raibe do dathaib an dom*ain* dath nach
raibe and. *ET* dar lé tainic ocl*ach* a n-edach taitnemhach dá
indsoig*id* 7 ruc an brat vaithe, 7 bá dub*ach* issi de sin. Tainec
an t-ocl*ach* ced*n*a cuige aris 7 adub*ai*rt an comr*ad*-sa ria. A
be*n* maith, *ar* se, ni rige a les bron na dubachas do beith ort,
act as cora duid failte 7 subachas do de*n*am, vair is é is fidhair
7 is esimlair do*n* brat u*d* docondcais, go m-bera tusa m*ac* 7 go
mba lan Eri 7 Alpa dá clu 7 da scelaib.

46. Ata Adamnan naemtha ga mebrug*ad* gor foills*ig* aing*el*
dé é fei*n* uair eli do m*á*tha*i*r C*olaim* c*illi* na codlud 7 hi torrach
ar C*olam* c*illi* fen, 7 g*ur* thaisbe*n* se tvaille di 7 ilr*ad* gacha
datha and, 7 bal*adh* gach mesa 7 gacha blatha, 7 gacha neich
degbol*aid* air. 7 do lec tamall *ar* lar na fiadn*aise*, é 7 do togaib
sé leis vaithe aris é. 7 ar m-breith an tvaille vaithe, do gab
toirrse 7 dobron mor hi, 7 adub*ai*rt risin aing*el*: cred fá rucais
adhbhar an t-sholais ro-mor do taisbenais damh comluath 7 si*n*
uai*m*. Do frecair an t-aing*el* i, 7 assedh adub*ai*rt ria: comar*d*a
neich ro-moir do taisbenadh duid, 7 ni heidir a como*n*orach do
beith at fhiadhn*aise* nias faide i*n*a sud. *Ar* c*r*ichnug*ad* an
comraid sin don aing*el*, do erigh a n-airde isin aeieor 7 an
tvaille les. D*ar* le Ethne do leth an tvaille tar Eirind 7 t*ar*
Albain 7 tar iarthar dom*ain* uile. 7 docuala si an t-aingel ga
rada do guth mor iar si*n*: a ben maith, *ar* se, bidh luthgair o*r*t
.i. berair m*ac* dot fhir posda fen 7 biaid se mar fáidh an tigerna
nemdha ag glaedhaig ar cach do munad na slig*ed* moire doib
doc*um* nimhe, 7 molf*id*er dia go ro-mor t*r*id; 7 dogeba se coroi*n*
ite*r* na faidib a flaithes de, 7 biaid se na treoraigteoir ag moran
do a*n*mo*n*nvib ga m-breith docum na cath*r*ach nemdha. *Ar*
cricnug*ad* na m-briat*ar* si*n* adub*ai*rt an t-aing*el* re h-Eithne, do
bidg si go ro-mhor, 7 do mosgail si as a codl*ud* iar sin. 7 do bi
si go curamach deisgridech umhal, ag serbis 7 ag fritolum don
toirrces si*n* do bi aice o si*n* amach, 7 do coimhed si an radarc
si*n* tuc an t-aingel di in a croide 7 in a h-inntinn g*an* foirfe.

coming of Columb cille by a power of prophecy received from God, and as the druids who had not the faith affirmed the same, so likewise was his coming established by visions and dreams as his mother herself saw in a dream. She thought a great cloak was given to her, so long and so wide that it reached from the West of Ireland to the East of Scotland, and that there was not a single colour of all those in existence that was not in it. And she thought a youth approached her in shining raiment and took the cloak from her, and she was sorrowful at that. The same youth came to her again and addressed this discourse to her: 'My good woman' said he, 'you need not be sad or sorrowful, but rather joyous and glad, for that cloak which you saw prefigures and presages that you will bear a son, and that Ireland and Scotland will be full of his name and fame.'

46. Saint Adamnan mentions that an angel showed himself another time to Columb cille's mother in her sleep while she was carrying Columb cille himself, and that he showed her a towel having every variety of colour and the odour of all fruits and flowers and of every sweet-smelling thing, and he dropped it down before her for a moment and took it away from her again. When the towel was taken from her she became very sad and sorrowful, and said to the angel: 'Why hast thou taken away from me so quickly the cause of such great joy which thou hast shown to me?' The angel answered her and said: 'The sign of something great has been shown to thee, and so honourable a thing cannot be in thy presence longer than that.' When the angel had finished that discourse he rose with the towel up into the air. It seemed to Ethne as if the towel spread over Ireland and over Scotland and over the whole western world. And afterwards she heard the angel say to her with a great voice: 'My good woman' said he, 'be joyful, for thou wilt bear a son to thy husband and he will be a prophet of the heavenly Lord calling on everybody to teach them the great way to Heaven, and God will be greatly praised through him, and he will receive a crown with the prophets in the kingdom of God, and he will be the guide of many souls taking them to the heavenly city.' When the words which the angel spoke to Ethne were finished, she started suddenly and thereupon awoke from her sleep. And she continued to serve and

47. Docondairc be*n* formaid 7 imthnuid d' Eithne aisling
.i. énach 7 ethaidedha an aeieoir 7 na tal*man*, dar le fen, do
breith inathair Eithne fo c*rí*chaib 7 fo cendadach*aib* Er*enn* 7
Alp*an*, 7 fa luthgairech le mnai an imtnvidh a faicsi*n* sen. Rug
Etne fen breth na h-aislinge si*n*, 7 asse*d* adub*airt*: berad-sa
ma*c*, ar si, 7 racha*id* a briath*ar* 7 a se*n*moir fo c*r*ichaib Er*enn*
7 Alb*an* am*ail* dorindedh a faidhed*ó*ra*ct* 7 a tairrngeri le naemaibh
Er*enn* 7 Alp*an*, 7 am*ail* docon*n*cos a fisib 7 a n-aislingi*b* dó.

48. Docondaic Finden naemtha aisling eli .i. d*ar* leis fein
dá esca d'erghe san aeier .i. esga oir 7 esca airgid, 7 an t-esca
oir d'erghe don taeb th*uaid* d'Er*inn*, 7 gor las Eri 7 Alpa 7
iarthar dom*ain* da delr*ad* 7 da shuillsi 7 da taitne*m*; 7 an t-esga
airg*id* os ci*nn* Cluana m*i*c Nóis, gor las med*ón* Er*enn* da delr*ad*
7 da soillsi. Rug Finden fen breth na h-aislinge si*n* .i. go
m-berad ben Feilim*the* m*i*c Fergosa cendf*ada* mac don taeb th*uaid*
d'Er*inn*, 7 go madh Col*am* c*illi* a ainm, 7 go racha*id* esiml*air* 7
delr*ad* a betha*d* ainglidhe 7 a gloine 7 a crab*aid*, a ecna 7 a
eolais, a breith*ri* 7 a senmora fá iarth*ar* dom*ain* uile, 7 go madh
é Ciaran mac an t-saeir an t-esca air*c*id co na subalt*ada*ib 7 go
n-deggnimh*ar*taib. [fo. 5 a]

49. Do labrum*ar* don faidhedora*ct*-sa dori*n*deta*r* naeim
Er*enn* ar thect Col*aim* c*illi*, 7 don tairrng*ir*e dorindeta*r* na
dr*a*ithe ag nach raibe creidem ar a thect, 7 don radh*ar*c tu*c*
dia a fisib 7 a n-aislingi*b* do moran do dainibh a tect mar in
ce*d*na. IS follus duin*n* asdaib so uili, nach edh amain do togh
dia Col*am* c*illi* a m-broi*n*n a máth*ar*, acht gor togh se a fad ria
tect a m-broi*n*n a math*ar* mar serbfhogant*aid* diles dó fei*n* é.
ET fos as follas duin*d* gor b'ail le dia a mol*ad* fei*n* do tect go
ro-mor as Col*am* c*illi*, ní sa mó 7 ni sa linmairi i*n*a dob'ail les
a thecht as en-naemh eli da tainec riamh *ar* a lan do ghnéthibh,
am*ail* indeos*us* an betha ó so amach, tresna gr*a*saib 7 tresna
subalt*aidib* 7 tresna tindluictib *d*iadha, 7 tresna mirbuilib ro-

to foster that child which she bore in her womb carefully, discreetly and humbly from that out. And she kept that sight which the angel had given her in her mind and heart without decay.

47. A woman who bore Ethne hatred and envy saw a vision: She thought the birds and winged things of the air and earth took the bowels of Ethne over the territories and tribes of Ireland and Scotland, and the envious woman was glad to see that. Ethne herself did rede that vision saying: 'I will bear a son' said she 'and his word and his preaching will spread over the countries of Ireland and Scotland according to the prophecy and foretelling of him which was made by the saints of Ireland and Scotland, and as was shown of him in visions and apparitions.'

48. Saint Finden saw another vision: He thought two moons arose in the air, one of them gold and the other silver. And that the golden moon arose to the North and Ireland and Scotland and the western world lighted up with its sheen and its light and its shining, and that the silver moon arose over Clonmacnoise and the middle of Ireland lighted up with its brightness and light. Finden himself explained that vision: That the wife of Fedlimid the son of Fergus cennfoda would bear a son in the North of Ireland, and that Columb cille would be his name, and that the example and brightness of his angelic life and of his purity and piety, his wisdom and knowledge, his word and his preaching, would spread over the whole western world; and that Ciaran mac an t-Saeir would be the silver moon with his virtues and good deeds.

49. We have spoken of the prophecy which the saints of Ireland made of the coming of Columb cille, and of the foretelling which the druids who had not the faith made of the same, and of the sight which God gave in visions and dreams to many people regarding his coming likewise. It is clear to us from all these that not only did God choose Columb cille in his mother's womb, but that he chose him a long time before coming into his mother's womb, as special servant to himself. And again it is clear to us, that God wished that his praise should proceed very much from Columb cille, (greater and more abundantly than he had wished it to proceed from any other saint that ever came), in a variety of ways as the Life sets

imarcacha ro-mora dob'ail les do tabairt do re na foillsivgad sa saeghal-sa. ET as follus dunn aris nach eadh amhain dob'ail le dia Colam cilli do cur a cosmuiles ris na h-uasal-aithrechaib 7 ris na naemaib eli tainec reime, act cor b'ail les a cor a cosmailes ris fen ar in modh-sa. Oir nir cvir cholainn dáenda uime aenduine ar a n-dernad oiread faidhedoracta 7 tairrngire re Colam cilli ria na gheinemain act an tigerna Isv Crisd amain.

50. Laibeorum anois do mirbuilib Colaim cilli a m-broinn a mathar amail mebraiges an nech naemtha darob ainm Mura. AR m-beith do mathair C. c. torrach air fein tainec nech naemtha darb' ainm Fergna ar cuairt cuicce ar na foillsivgad d'aingel dé dó go raibe an toirrches bendaigthe naemtha-sin aice. ET aderaid eolaig gorab derbshiur di fein mathair an Fhergna-sin IS andsin do chuir an mac bendaighte naemtha sin, do naemadh ria tect a m-broinn a mathar .i. C. c. failte reimh Fergna, 7 do cvir se a ordóg tre broinn a mathar mar comarta failte 7 luthgairi reimhe, amail isbert Mura isna randaib-si:

Dardaein cedlabhra Colaim   ria n-abrad dal gan doghaing,
Dar fer se failte go mblath   re Fergna mac rig Caisil.
Mar do fer failte re Ferghna   mac rig Caisil Mvman mvaid,
A ordain tre broinn a mháthar   gin cor gnáthach do sin vaid.

Et as follus ass so gor cuir dia C. c. a coismuiles re h-Eoin baisde an uair dorinde se luthgair a m-broind Elisdabéd reimh Muiri 7 i torrach ar Isv. 7 ni hedh amáin do cuir se a cosmailes re h-Eoin é, act do cuir se a ceim foirfidhechta os a chend é ar an modh-sa. Oir ni derna Eoin act comartha luthgara a m-broinn a mathar roimhe an tigherna, 7 do cuir C. c. a ordog tre broinn a mhathar mar comartha luthgairi reimh Ferghna, 7 gan é act na duine bec semplide. 7 fetar a rádha gorab tre mhaithes an tigherna fen táinec d'Eoin luthgairi do denamh

forth from this out, through the graces and through the virtues
and through the divine endowments and through the abundant
and very great miracles which he was pleased to give him to
perform in this world. And it is clear to us furthermore that
not alone did God wish that Columb cille should be made to
resemble the patriarchs and other saints who came before him,
but that he wished him to resemble himself in this way. For
no person ever donned a human body concerning whom so many
prophecies and foretellings were made before his birth as Columb
cille, except only our Lord Jesus Christ.

50. We shall speak now of Columb cille's miracles in his
mother's womb as they are related by the holy man whose
name was Mura. When Columb cille's mother was big of him,
there came to her a holy man named Fergna to visit her, for
an angel had revealed to him that she bore that blessed and
holy birth in her womb. And authorities say that it was a
sister of hers was mother of that Fergna. And then that blessed
and holy child, who was sanctified before he came from his
mother's womb, to wit, Columb cille, welcomed Fergna, for he
put his thumb through his mother's belly, as a sign of welcome
and rejoicing for him, as Mura said in these verses:

Of a Thursday was the first speech of Columb   which was
                        [called a meeting without sadness,
When he welcomed blithely   Fergna son of the king of Cashel;
As he welcomed Fergna   son of the king of Cashel in noble
                                                  [Munster,
His thumb through his mother's belly,   though unusual, he
                                                  [stretched forth.

And it is clear from this that God made Columb cille
resemble John the Baptist, when he rejoiced in the womb of
Elizabeth at Mary who was carrying Jesus at the time. And
not only did he make him resemble John but he put him in a
degree of perfection beyond him in this way. For John only
made a sign of rejoicing in his mother's womb at the Lord,
whereas Columb cille put his thumb through his mother's belly,
as a sign of rejoicing at Fergna, who was but a poor simple
man. And we can say that it was through the Lord's own
goodness John came to rejoice at him when he came to meet

reimhe an uair tainec se na cend; oir nirb'ingnad gach uile duil
dar cruthaidh se fein do denum luthgaire reimhe.

51. Fectus d'Eithne .i. do mathair C. c. is an inadh ré
n-abarthur Gartan; 7 an oidhce ria Colam c. do breith, do taisben
nach óg sciamach a n-edach ro-delradach é fen d'Ethne, 7
adubairt ria go m-beradh sí an mac do bi a tairrngire di do
breith ar na márach. 7 do indis di go raibe lec lethan cloiche
isin loch do bi don taeb bud des don inadh sin a raibe sí, dá
ngoirther Loch mic Ciabain aniug. 7 adubairt ria a tabairt
fodera in lec sin do breith isin inadh airithe ris an abarthur
Raith Cno, 7 go madh uirri do toileochad dia di an lenab do
breith. Cindus dogeb-sa an lec sin ata fai an loch, ar sí, nó
cindus aitheónas me hi sech na lecaib eli. Dogebair ag snam
ar uactar an locha hi, ar se. Fvair Eithne an lec ar na mairech
amail adubrad ria, 7 do furail a breith asin inadh sin adu-
brumar romaind; 7 ge do bi sí ag snamh ar uachtar an locha,
7 ge rucc muinnter Ethne gan saethar leo hi, is deimhin gor
bh'obair tricad fer a breith on loch gusin inadh a fuil sí aniugh.

An uair tra tainec teinnes lenib docum Eithne dochuaidh sí
a n-alltan uaicnech cois srotha bicc do bi a comghar di, 7 do bi
sí na svidhe in inadh airidhe and, 7 do fagaib si don fuil bud
dual do tect roimhe an lenabh san inadh sin. 7 an cre dogeibther
and ni mine 7 ni gile plvr ina hi; 7 ge be duine caithes no
imcras ní don cré sin ni loiscter 7 ni baither 7 ni marbthar
d'én-orchar an la go n-oidhce sin é, 7 ni fagand se bas gan
sagart, 7 gach ben bis re n-idhnaib caithes ní di foiridh a cedoir
hí, 7 gach nech cuires ní ar a tengaid di an ced la gabhus
fíabhrus é, ni bí blas serb in a bel ó sin amach ar fedh an
fiabruis sin, 7 as dual go foirfe si gach vili esláinte. ET is
duine ecin do duthcasachaibh an baile sin Gartán is coir do
tochailt na criadh-sa, dá tabairt do cach; 7 da derbad sin
dochuaid anduthcusach dá tochailt [fo. 5b] uair ecin 7 do teith
sí reimhe, 7 docuaidh sí astech a medon croind no bile moir do
bi dá coir, 7 ni frith na h-inadh fein hí no gor croithedh uisce
coisrectha air 7 go bendaighed e. Teid Ethne ass sin gus an
inad a ruc sí C. c. an uair dob'aeis fiche bliadna 7 cuicc ced
don tigerna.

him; for it would be no wonder that all the elements which he had created should rejoice at him.

51. Once upon a time as Ethne, the mother of Columb cille was in the place that is called Gartan, the night before Columb cille was born, a beautiful youth in shining raiment appeared to her and said that she would bring forth the child which it was foretold she should bear, on the morrow. And he told her that there was a broad flag-stone in the lake which was to the South of the place in which she was, that is called Loch mic Ciabain now. And he told her to cause that flag to be brought to a certain place called Rath Cno, for that upon it God would ordain that she should bring forth the child. 'How shall I get that flag seeing it is under the lake' said she, 'or how shall I distinguish it from the other flags?' 'You will find it floating upon the surface of the lake' said he. Ethne found the flag on the morrow as she had been told, and she caused it to be brought out of that place which we have already mentioned. And though it floated upon the surface of the lake, and though Ethne's people took it away quite easily, it is certain that it would be work for thirty men to take it from the lake to the place where it is to-day.

When the sickness of travail came upon Ethne, she retired to a lonely waste beside a little stream which was close to her, and as she was sitting there, she lost some of the blood that comes before the child, in that place. And flour is not finer nor whiter than the clay that is found there; and whoso eats or carries about with him some of that clay, he will neither be burned nor drowned nor killed by one cast for twenty-four hours afterwards, nor will he die without the priest; and any woman that eats a little of it in the pangs of childbirth is at once relieved, and whoever puts a little of it on his tongue the first day fever attacks him there will be no bitter taste in his mouth from that out during the fever, and it has the property of easing all distempers. And it is right that one of the natives of that village of Gartan should dig this clay for distribution, because a stranger went to dig it once and it fled from him, and went into the heart of a tree, or a great blessed bush that was near it, and it was not found in its own place until holy water had been sprinkled on it and it had been blessed. Ethne went thence to the place where she bore Columb cille when 520 was the year of our Lord.

52. A nGartan *umorro* a cenel Conaill G*ulban* ruc*ad* C. c.
7 Raith cno ain*m* an inaidh airide a nGartan a ruc*ad* é sa sect-
madh la do mi medhon an Gemrid. 7 tarla an lec so adubrama*r*
romaind fai ga breith, 7 do leig an lenab a crois uirri é 7 do
foscail an lec remhe ind*us* cor leic sí inad do in*nte,* 7 ata fidhair
na croise si*n* sa leic o soin ale. 7 mairidh an lec si*n* fos san
inadh si*n* ag denv*m* fert 7 mirbuile. 7 rug a m*athair* cloch
cr*uinn* *ar* dath na fola a n-enf*act* ris, 7 an cloch ruad a h-ainm,
7 do fagaib se a nGartan hí ag denam fhert 7 mirbhal, 7 ni
gaband sí a cumdach le h-or no le h-airget, ge mi*nec* do tairged
a cumdach 7 fuiln*ged* sí a cas airg*id* no óir.

Laibeoram anois do mirbailib C. c. *tar* eis a gein*eama* ar
in saeghal sa.

53: Uasal ingantach ag día 7 ag daeinib a*n* mac rug*ad*
andsin .i. m*ac* ochta rig nimhe 7 talma*n* .i. C. c. m*ac* Felim*the.*
Do baisd an t-vasal-sagart .i. Cruithnechan mac Cell*achain* e ar
na breith a ce*d*oir, 7 tuc Cr*i*mthan*n* mar ai*n*m air. 7 do oil 7
do coimeid é iarsin am*ail* adubruta*r* aingle de ris. 7 is ina*n*d
Crimtand re rada sa gaidilg 7 celgach no sindach sa laidi*n.* 7
gedheadh do condcas do dia cum*actach* nar cnesda 7 nar b'im-
cub*aid* do cailidh*ect* 7 do maithes a*n* m*acaim* naomtha si*n* an
t-ainm-si do beith air, 7 do cuir se a croidhedhaib 7 a me*n*main
na lenab 7 na m*acam* do bid ag cluiche 7 ag sugr*ad* ris Colaim
do g*airm* de. *No* is iad a aingle fen do cuir se c*uca* dá radha
riv a gairm de, am*ail* derb*as* M*ura* is na ra*n*naib-si:

Col*am* c*illi* a ainm do nimh   mac Feilim*the* ag ainglib,
Gan imroll ga*n* dalb gan dron   Cr*i*mthan a ai*n*m sa saegal.
D*ar*dai*n* nocha*r* chainge*n* cle   ag ainglibh an richidh é,
D*ar* b*en*sat*ar* Cr*i*mthan de   's dar goirsead Col*am* c*illi.*

ET adubrat*ar* gan a*n* t-ainm drochciallaidhe-se, nach ticf*ad* acht
ar drochduine, do gairm de .i. Cr*i*mthan*n.* 7 m*ar* do bi a*n*
m*acaemh* naemth*a-sa* ga oilem*ain* a m-baile cilli do bi a comghar
doib .i. Doiri Eithne, da ngoirthe*r* Cill mac Nenai*n* aniugh, do
gnathadis na leinib do bidh ag sugr*ad* ris Col*am* on Cill do rad

52. In Gartan, in the country of Conall Gulban, Columb cille was born. And Rath Cno is the name of the particular spot in Gartan in which he was born on the seventh day of December. And this flag we have already mentioned was under him as he was being born, and the child left his cross upon it, and the flag opened and made a place for him, and the sign of that cross is in the flag from that day to this. And that flag remains still there working marvels and miracles. And his mother brought forth a round stone of the colour of blood along with him, that is called the Red Stone, and she left it at Gartan to do marvels and miracles, and it refuses an ornamental covering of gold or silver, though it was often sought so to cover it, but it suffers a case of gold or silver.

We shall now speak of the miracles of Columb cille after his birth on this world.

53. Noble and wonderful before God and men was the child that was born then, to wit, the darling of the king of Heaven and Earth, Columb cille mac Fedlimthe. The priest Cruith-nechan mac Cellachain baptized him immediately after his birth and called him Crimthann. And he fostered and kept him after-wards as the angels of God had told him. And crimthann in Irish is as much as to say deceitful, or a fox in Latin. How-ever it appeared to the God of might that it was not meet nor fitting a youth of his character and goodness should bear such a name, so he inspired the hearts and minds of the children and little boys who played and frolicked with him to call him Columb. And it was his own angels he sent to them to tell them to call him so, as Mura affirms in those verses:

Columb cille mac Fedlimthe   his name from Heaven by angels,
Without error or lie or bend   Crimthan his name in the world.
Of a Thursday, it was no wrong traffic,   he was with the angels
                                          [of Heaven,
When they took Crimthan off him   and called him Columb cille.

And they forbade him to be called by that evil-meaning name Crimthann, which was becoming for nobody but an evil person. And as this holy youth was being fostered in a village that had a church not far from their house, viz. Doire Ethne, which is now called Cill mac Nenain, the children who played with him

ris. Gonadh m*ar* s*in* do an C. c. m*ar* ainm air. ⁊ ata se fen
ga derb*ad* s*in* sa rand-so:

Ann*sin* adubr*ad* on cill   leth m'a*n*ma nocha ceilim,
Cell m*ac* Nenai*n* naemhpor*t* damh   nochar aent*a* me a tregea*n*.

ET as e adbor far seol dia cuma*c*tach Cola*m* do tab*ai*rt mar
ai*n*m air, gorab fidhair ⁊ cosamlacht don spir*ud* na*em* fein an
cola*m*; ⁊ da derbadh sin is a fidhair cola*im* docu*n*nairc Eoin
baisde an spir*ad* na*em* ag luidhe ar Crisd an uair do baisd se
ag sruth Eorthanain e. ⁊ adb*ar* eli far seol dia Cola*m* do
tab*ai*rt air, oir is aml*aid* ata an colaim fei*n* o naduir ro-nemhuir-
choidech, ⁊ do bi C. c. mar sin. IN tres adbar far seol dia an
t-ainm-si do tab*ai*rt *ar* an macamh naemtha-sa da fuilmid ag
lab*ai*rt, oir t*ar* gach uile e*n* don e*n*laith ni bi domblas aei sa
cola*m*. Fétar a radha go raibe C. c. mar si*n*, oir ni raibe celg
no fvath no aingidecht no ní nemglan no serb *ar* bith na *c*roide
no na indti*n*n don taeib astoigh, ⁊ ni mó do cvi*r* se a ngnimh
don taeb amuigh e*n*-red becc *no* mór do rach*ad* a n-eso*n*oir do
dia, an fad do bvi se na beth*aid* sa saeghal-sa.

54. Tulach Dubglaisi a cinel Conoill ai*n*m an inaidh in *ar*
baisd*ed* C. c. am*ail* asper*t* an nech naemtha da na h-ai*n*m Mura:

Rug*ad* a nGarta*n* da deoin   do h-oil*ed* a Cill m*ac* n-Eoi*n*,
Do baisd*ed* m*ac* na maisi   a Tul*aig* de Dubglaisi.

ET an lec ar ar baisd*ed* é do foired gach uili eslainte da
m-berthai cuice. ⁊ fa trom le mnai comorba an baile sin a
fadhadh si do doch*ur* na dai*n*e eslan ⁊ na n-oilithrech tigedh
d'indsoig*id* na leice, ind*us* gor cuir an be*n* mall*aigth*e an lec
bendaigthe a n-dab*aig* uisce ata don taeb th*uaid* don baili, ⁊ (ni
fri)th o sin alle hi. ⁊ ata a tairrng*ir*e go fuig(ter hi) ⁊ go m-bia
in baili go maith o sin amach. ⁊ dorinde Crvithnechan a*n* mac
bendvighte d'oilem*ain* iarsi*n* do rer m*ar* adubrat*ar* aingle de ris.

used to call him Columb from the Cill. So it was that Columb cille remained his name. And he corroborates that himself in this verse:

Then half my name was called from the church, I conceal it not,
Cell mac Nenain, a heavenly rest for me, I was not willing
[to leave it.

And the reason why the God of might instructed them to call him Columb was because the dove is a figure and semblance of the Holy Ghost himself. And in proof of that it was in the figure of a dove that John the Baptist saw the Holy Ghost resting upon Christ when he baptized him in the river Jordan. And another reason why God taught that he should be called Columb was that the dove is by nature harmless, and so was Columb cille. The third reason why God instructed them to call that name upon this holy youth of whom we are speaking was, because beyond every other member of the feathered tribe, there is no gall in the dove. It can be said that Columb cille was so, for there was neither deceit nor envy, nor malice, nor any unclean or bitter thing at all in his heart or mind on the inside; neither did he perform any external act great or small, that would tend to the dishonour of God, while he was alive on this world.

54. Tulach Dub-glaise in the country of Conoll is the name of the place in which Columb cille was baptized, as said that holy man whose name was Mura:

He was born in Gartan of his will he was fostered in Cill
[mac n-Eoin,
The beautiful son was baptized in God's Tulach Dubglaise.

And the flag on which he was baptized used to succour every sick person that was brought to it. And the landlady of that village was annoyed at the amount of trouble she got from the sick and the pilgrims who used to visit the flag, so the accursed woman put the blessed flag into a deep pool of water in the northern side of the village, and it was not found (?) from that out. But it has been foretold that it will be found (?) and that it will go well with the village from that onward. And Cruith-

37*

55. Ata indam*ail* reilge bige sa m-baili-si Tulcha Dubglaisi da ngoirther *ced*imtecht C. c. .i. an ait a n-derna se a cedimtecht 7 a cedsivb*al* na lenabh, am*ail* asb*ert* Baithin nae*m*:

Reilec bec don taeb atuaidh   a Tul*aig* Dubglaisi go m-buaidh,
Col*am* c*illi* coir gan a (   )   an*n* (?) dori*n*de a cedimthecht.

56. *ET* mebr*aig*idh an nech naemta-sa darab ai*n*m Baithi*n*, [fo. 6 a] ge be duine dode*n*adh oili*tre* an inadh si*n* na b*ud* dual go tibradh sé galar no esslainte ar bith les ass; am*ail* derbus se fen isna randaibh-si:

INte timcellus gan chair   *ced*imtecht Colaim craibth*ig,*
Bud maith les a me*n*ma amuigh   ni taed a m-berna baegail.
Cred fa m-biadh galar *no* grei*m*   a smvais no a c*n*aimh no a
                                     [cuislind,
A cend no a cois *no* a n-i*n*ne   *ar* slict Colaim caimchille.

57. La airidhe do C. c. na lenub a nGartan, 7 tucc duine brec marb chuige. 7 do glac C. c. an brec 7 do cuir a tobar do bi sa bhaile é. 7 tainec anam and aris, 7 mairid an brec si*n* fos sa ri*ct* a raibe an uair sin, tre mirbuil*ib* dé 7 Col*aim* c*illi.* 7 is mi*n*ec tarla an brec si*n* a coiri uisce i*n* a m-beith feoil no iasc ga bruith, *ar* na tab*air*t da dáinib leo a soightib uisce gan fis doib. 7 da loiscthi a m-beith do condadh, no do mónaigh sna tirth*ib* fan coiri si*n* ni b*ud* móide tes an coiri si*n* nó in uisce é, *no* go m-bentai an brec ass 7 go curthai na tobor fe*n* arís é; 7 do derb*ad* sen go menic.

58. Atá lec cloiche san oilen ata *ar* Loch mac Ciabai*n* a nGartan, 7 do gnataig*ed* C. c. dul do cluiche 7 do sugr*adh* uirre an uair do bi sé na lenab. 7 na lenib eli teid uirre o si*n* alle bid aimrid, 7 ni gen*tar* vatha a com*ar*tha ogh*ac*ta 7 genmn*aide*-

nechan did foster the blessed child as the angels of God had told him.

55. There is a place like a little church-yard in this town-land of Tulach Dubglaise which is called the first walking of Columb cille; that is to say, the place where he did his first going and walking as a child, as saint Baithin said:

A little church-yard to the northern side   in Tulach Dubglaise
                                     [the endowed
Just Columb cille without . . .,   (There) he did his first walking.

56. And this holy man whose name was Baithin relates that whosoever makes a pilgrimage to that place there would be no fear that he should bring any disease or sickness with him out of it, as he himself gives assurance in these verses:

Whoso does the stations without sin in the first walk of pious
                                      [Columb,
He will have content outside,   he goes not into an occasion
                                     [of danger,
Why should there be pain or ache   in cartilage, bone or vein,
In head or foot or bowels   of the members of the tribe of
                                     [dear Columb cille.

57. A certain day as Columb cille was a child in Gartan, somebody gave him a dead trout. Columb cille took the trout and put it in a well that was in the village. And it became alive again; and that trout lives yet just as it was then through the miracles of God and Columb cille. And it is often that trout happened to be in a pot of water in which meat or fish was being boiled, having been brought by people in vessels of water unknown to themselves. And if all the fire-wood and turf in the country was burned under that pot, neither the pot nor the water would be any the hotter for it, until the trout was taken out and put in its own well again. And that was often proved.

58. There is a flag-stone in an island on Loch mac Ciabain in Gartan, and Columb cille was accustomed to go to play and frisk upon it when he was a child. And the other children who go upon it ever since become barren, and nothing is born

achta C. c. 7 do derbudh sin go minec, 7 lec na genmnaidechta ainm na leice sin aniugh.

59. O tainic aimser léginn do C. c. docuaidh Cruithnechan .i. oide C. c. mar a raibe nech naemtha do bí sa tír, da fhíarfaige de ga trath bud coir tindscna léighinn do denamh don macamh. Do labhair in nech naemtha sin tre spirad fáidhedóracta 7 assedh adubairt: 'sgríb anois aibidil do'. Do scribad iarsin aibidil do a m-bairghein. 7 is amlaid do bi C. c. an vair sin cois srota airidhe, 7 do caith sé cuid don bairgin don taeib tiar don t-sruth sin, 7 an cuid eli don taeib tair don t-sruth cedna. IS andsin do labhair an nech naemtha-sa tre rath ecna 7 fáidhedóracta 7 assedh adubairt: 'is amlaid bias feronn an mic sin ar gach taeibh don uisce .i. don fhairge .i. cuid a n-Erinn de 7 cvid eli a n-Albain; 7 caithfidh se fen cuid dá aimsir in gach inadh dib sin'. 7 do firadh sin amail derbeochas an betha o so amach.

60. Oidce airidhe do Cruithnechan ag filled on eclais ag dul d'indsoigid a tighe fein ar crichnugad seirbísi dé dó, 7 fuair se an tech lomnan do shoillsi 7 do delrad ar a chind, 7 nell tendtide os cind aighte C. c. san inad a raibe se na codludh. 7 do bi do med na soillse sin, nar féd se beith ga h-amharc. 7 iar na faicsin don t-shagart, do bidc se go mór, 7 do tuit se ar talmain tresan radharc sin do taisbenadh do. 7 ar n-eirghe do as a nell iar sin, do tuic se gorbh'iad grasa an spirda naeim do dóirtedh ar a dalta fen an uair sin, 7 go rabhatar aingle de ga coimhéd.

61. Nir fada in a diaidh sin go n-dechaid C. c. 7 a oide .i. Cruithnechan mac Cellechain ar Nodluic gosin esboc naemtha go Brugach mac n-Degadh do Raith Enaigh a tir Énna. Do furail an t-espoc ar oide C. c. sagartacht do denam do ar in sollamain sin. Do bi d'aendacht 7 do náiri a Cruithnechan og radh na trath leis in espoc gor t-saraigh an salm áiridhe-se air .i. misercordia Domini .i. an salm is faide 7 as cruaide sa saltoir. Do gab umorro an mac a raibe rath de 7 dar tidluicedh grasa an spirda naeim .i. C. c. an salm ar son a oide, 7 is deimhin nar légh se remhe sin riamh act a aibidil amháin.

from them as a token of the virginity and chastity of Columb
cille. And that was often proved, and that flag is called the
flag of chastity to-day.

59. When it was time for Columb cille to begin his studies
his tutor Cruithnechan went to a holy man that was in the
country to ask him what was the proper time for the youth to
begin his studies. The holy man spoke through a spirit of
prophecy and said: 'Write an alphabet for him now'. An
alphabet was written for him then upon a loaf. Columb cille
happened at the time to be beside a certain stream, and he
threw a portion of his loaf to the western and the other portion
to the eastern side of the same stream. Then that holy man
spoke through the grace of wisdom and prophecy and said: 'The
land of that child will be at both sides of the water, that is,
of the sea, viz. some of it in Ireland and the rest in Scotland,
and he will spend a portion of his time in each of those places.'
And that came to pass as this Life will show henceforward.

60. On a certain night as Cruithnechan was returning from
the church to his own house after finishing the service of God,
he found the house full of light and effulgence before him and
a fiery cloud above the face of Columb cille where he slept.
And so great was that light that he could not bear to continue
looking upon it. When the priest saw it he was mightily
startled and fell to the earth at that sight which was shown
him. And on recovering from his trance afterwards he understood that it was the graces of the Holy Ghost that were then
poured out upon his fosterling, and that the angels of God were
a-keeping him.

61. Not long after that Columb cille and his tutor, to wit,
Cruithnechan mac Cellechain went to spend Christmas with the
holy bishop Brugach mac n-Degach of Rath Enaigh in Tir
Enna. The bishop asked Columb cille's tutor to do priestly duty
for him during that feast. Cruithnechan felt so lonely and shy
reciting the Office with the bishop that he broke down in this
particular psalm, Misericordias Domini, that is to say, the longest
and hardest psalm in the psalter. But the youth on whom was
the blessing of God, and who had been endowed with the graces
of the Holy Ghost, Columb cille, sang the psalm for his tutor,
though it is certain he had never read anything before but only
his alphabet alone.

62. Fect docuaid Colam cilli 7 a oide .i. Cruithnechan do torrumha duine airidhe don popul fuair bas; 7 ar a filled doib ni raibe acu acht iad fen. 7 tarla tuisled don oide-sin C. c. ar in sligid gor tuit fon talmain co fuair bas fo cedoir. 7 do chuir Colam cilli benn a bruit fa cend a oide, oir do shail gorab in a codlad do bi, 7 do gab se fen ag mebrvgadh a aicepta. 7 do bi do med an mebruigthe 7 d' airde an gotha co cualatar coimtinol caillech n-dub do bi mile go leith vatha foghar a ghotha; 7 fa bes do a cluinsin an comfhad sin, amail asbert in fili:

Son a gotha Colaim cilli   mór a binde os gach cler,
Go ceann dá céd décc ceimend,   aidble remend, eadh ba reil.

ET do batar tri h-ingena do Cruithnechan fen sa coimtinol sin, 7 tancatar fa foghar gotha Colaim cilli ar na aithne, 7 fuarutar an clerech sin dob' athair doib fen 7 dob oide dósam marb aige ar an slighid. 7 mar dob' aithne doibh náemthact an macaim, do iarratar na caillecha air an cleirech do dúscad. Dochuaid C. c. d' indsoigid an cleirig 7 do bí gá dúsgadh, 7 do erigh an clerech le breithir C. c. amail do bead sé na codlad. 7 mar do tuic C. c. gorab na onoir fen do aithbeoaigh día a oide, tuc se bvidechas mor do dia ar a shon sen. 7 do chuir dia a aingel [fo. 6b] fen cuige da tegasc. 7 do labair go h-ainglidhe ris, 7 do foillsig coimairleda arda an tigerna 7 na seicréide diadha dó. 7 dochuaidh sin ar ecna 7 ar eolus sa scribtúir diada dósam, 7 dochuaid se os cinn lochta a coimleabair 7 a comaeisi go ro-mor a n-eolus an scribtúir. 7 mar do tuic 7 mar do aithin se é fen ar bisech sa tecusc ainglidhe 7 is na secreidib diadha tuc an t-aingel do, do tarruinged se é fen o truaillidhect 7 o t-salchor an t-saegail uile.

63. Ata Adhamnán ga mebrugad ge do bi C. c. ro-ócc o aeis an uair sen, go raibe croide arrsaidh eola aice; 7 ger uasal o folaidhect é gur uaisle o subaltaige 7 o besaib e, 7 gerb' imlan ó corp é gorb' imláine o creidem é. 7 fos, an gloine anma 7 cuirp fuair sé o dia, do coimheid se an méide-si hí, ge do bi

62. Once upon a time Columb cille and his tutor Cruith-nechan went to the wake of a certain parishioner who had died; and as they were returning alone it chanced that the tutor of Columb cille stumbled on the way, fell to the ground and died immediately. And Columb cille put his own cloak under his tutor's head, for he thought he only slept, and he began himself to learn his lesson. And so diligent was the memorizing and so loud the voice that a convent of nuns who where a mile and a half away from him heard the sound of his voice; for it was usual to hear him so far, as the poet said:

The sound of his voice, Columb cille's, much its melody beyond
[every choir,
For twelve hundred paces, mighty the courses, was the distance
[it was audible.

And there were three daughters of Cruithnechan in that convent, and they came towards the sound of Columb cille's voice as soon as they knew him, and they found that cleric, who was their father and his tutor, beside him dead upon the road. And because they knew the holiness of the boy, the nuns asked him to awaken the cleric. Columb cille went to the cleric and was awakening him, and the cleric arose at the word of Columb cille as if he had been asleep. When Columb cille knew that it was in his own honour that God had raised his tutor from the dead, he returned sincere thanks to God for that. And God sent him his own angel to teach him. And he spoke in an angelic way to him, and revealed to him the exalted counsels of the Lord and divine secrets. And that profited him in the wisdom and knowledge of the divine scriptures, and he surpassed those in his own class and of his own age very much in knowledge of scripture. And when he understood and knew that by so much had he an advantage, viz. the angelic teaching and the divine secrets which the angel gave to him, he used to withdraw himself from the corruption and filth of the whole world.

63. Adamnan mentions that although Columb cille was very young in age at that time he had an old and a wise heart; and that although he was noble by breeding he was nobler by virtues and manners, and that although perfect in body he was more perfect in faith. And again he preserved so well the

se na duine mailli ris na dainib a talma*in* gorub betha ainglide
7 *con*fersoid nemhdaidhe do bi aicce; 7 da derb*ad* si*n* do bi
ai*n*glidhe ó fhaicsi*n*, 7 indtlechtach o ecna, 7 naemta o oib-
rigth*ib*, 7 glic ó comairli, 7 eola isna secredib díadha, 7 dainge*n*,
documscaigthe a ng*r*ad a cruth*aigth*eora fen .i. *Isu Christ* os
ci*n*n gach uile g*r*adha.

64. Fect*us* eli do C. c. na diaidh si*n* 7 do taisbei*n* nech óg
ro-sciam*ach* é fen dó a n-edach ro-geal, ro-delru*dhach* san oidhce,
7 adub*air*t ris: D*eus* tecu*m* .i. dia mailli rit, 7 bidh laidir cobsa*id*
dainge*n*, 7 do cuir dia mesi dod coimed go siraide, suth*ain* sa
saegal-so ó gach uili cair 7 pecadh. 7 do bidg, 7 do imecl*aig*
an m*a*camh go mór les sin, 7 do fiarf*aig* de cia *he* fen. Adub*air*t
a*n* nech og: 'Mesi' ol se, 'Axal, aing*el* an tige*r*na, 7 is uime
goirt*er* Axal dim, gorab ina*n*d axal re radha 7 furtaigheoir, 7
is dot f*ur*tacht-sa ó gach uile guasocht 7 curu*m* an t-saega*il*-se
do cuir an tigerna me. 7 bidh gò calma, laid*ir*, oir ataim-si
agad am ridiri sduamdha, laidir do cathughadh 7 do comrac ta*r*
do cend a n-adhaig na locht 7 ainmia*n*a na colla, 7 na n-diab*ol*
7 na n-droch-spira*d* 7 gach uile buaidr*id* saegalta.' Do fiarf*aig*
a*n* m*a*camh naemtha-sa don aing*el*: 'I*n* a*n*nsan aibíd gleghil si*n*
no isan aeis si*n* a bfuile-si bid na huird ainglidhe a flaithes
de?' Do frecair an t-aing*el* e 7 ass*ed* adub*air*t: 'Gid aidbsech
let-sa anos med mo dealruidh-si 7 mo sholuis, bidh a fhis agat
gorub ro-mó mo dellr*a*d 7 mo solus a flaithes de i*n*a andso. 7
bidh a fís agad na fedfá fech*ain* orum sa dellrad-sa a fuilim
anois fen mun*a* beith g*r*asa dhe go hima*r*cuch agad, 7 da
coimed*air*-se do ge*n*mnaidect 7 h' ogacht sa saeghol-sa go foirfe
g*an* melludh do breith ort go c*r*ích do bais, beir co suth*ain*
siraidhe it*er* aingl*ib* a n-aibíd gleghil taitnemhaigh nach eidir a
tuaruscbail do tab*air*t amach *ar* med a taithnemaighe 7 a maisi
7 a gloiri'. Adub*air*t a*n* m*a*camh naemtha-sa andsin: 'Massed
com*ar*th*aig* 7 coisric mo c*or*p 7 mo croide ind*us* go feda*n*n
m' óghacht 7 oibr*ig*the na hoghachta do cothug*ad* 7 do crich-
nug*ad* uile go ponc mo bais'. 7 dorinde an t-aingel m*ar* adub*air*t
se ris, 7 do coisric se bruinde 7 croide 7 cliab a*n* m*a*caimh oig
naem*t*ha-sa; 7 on u*a*ir sin amach do sechai*n* 7 do ingaib an
m*a*cam-sa go maith é fen *ar* gach uile buáidre*d* 7 fís 7 aisling,
7 *ar* droch-smuai*n*tighib an t-saegail-se 7 na colla 7 an diaba*il*.
7 do diult C. c. andsi*n* do cúram 7 do deithíde an t-saega*il*-se

purity of body and soul which he had received from God that, although he was a man amongst men in the world, his life was angelic and he enjoyed heavenly conversation. In proof whereof he was angelic to look upon, intellectual in wisdom, holy in works, wise in counsel, learned in divine secrets, and firm and steadfast in the love of his own creator, Jesus Christ, who is above every grade.

64. Of another time after that a very beautiful youth in bright and shining garments showed himself to Columb cille in the night and said: 'Deus tecum' (which is, God be with thee) 'be strong, steadfast and firm, for God has sent me to keep thee for ever and always from all crime and sin in this world'. At that the boy was astounded and very much afraid, and he asked him who he was. Said the youth, 'I am Axal, an angel of the Lord', said he, 'and the reason I am called Axal is that Axal is as much as to say helper; and it is to protect thee from every danger and care of this world the Lord has sent me. And be brave and strong, for thou hast in me a discreet and brave knight to do battle and to contend for thee against the faults and lusts of the flesh, and against devils and evil spirits and every other worldly trouble.' This holy boy asked of the angel: 'Are the angelic orders in the kingdom of God clothed in that bright habit, or of the same age as thee?' The angel answered him and said: 'Though wonderful to thee now is the greatness of my shining and my light, still know that my shining and my light is far greater in the kingdom of God. And know that thou couldst not look upon me even in this brightness which is upon me now, were it not that thou art plentifully endowed with the graces of God. And if thou keepest thy chastity and thy virginity perfectly in this world, so they be never marred until thy very death, thou wilt be forever and ever amidst the angels in a bright, shining garment that may not be described for its wonderful effulgence, and beauty, and glory.' This holy boy thereupon said: 'Then sign and bless my body and my heart that so I may be enabled to nourish and perfect my virginity and all the works of virginity until the point of death'. The angel did as he had told him, and blessed the belly and heart and breast of this holy young boy, and thenceforward the boy shunned and protected himself well against every trouble and vision and dream, and against the evil thoughts of this

uile ó sin amach. Oir do thuic se an focal adubairt Pol apstal,
nach eidir le duine ar doman riderecht do denam do dia 7 don
t-saegal a n-enfhect. 7 tng se moid 7 gellad do dia go coimeolad
se gach ni adubairt an t-aingel ris ar fedh a bethad.

(To be continued.)

world and of the flesh and of the Devil. Then Columb cille renounced all the cares and troubles of this world from that out. For he remembered the saying of Paul the apostle, that nobody whatsoever can do knightly service for God and the world at the same time. And he made a vow and promise to God that he would be steadfast during his life to everything that the angel had enjoined upon him.

Washington, D.C.   R. HENEBRY.

ON A PASSAGE IN *CATH CAIRN CHONAILL*.

Bá maith iarom intí Guairi. is dó doratad tria rath féli in bó *co n*-aib ítha 7 inna sméra 'sind fulliuch, LU. 117 b 8 — 10.

My version of the above passage in this journal III, 219 is neither complete nor accurate. It should be 'Good, then, was that Guare. 'Tis to him that through grace of generosity was given the cow with livers of tallow, and the blackberries in the hiding-place.'

The explanation of this is found in pp. 52, 54 of *Imthecht na Tromdaime*, edited, from the Book of Lismore, in the fifth volume of the Transactions of the Ossianic Society, Dublin, 1860.

Brigit, wife of the poet Senchán, longs, among other things, for her fill of a red-eared bright-white cow without a liver, but having tallow in place of her liver (mo sáith ele do bhoin cluaisd*eirg* gleghil gan ai innti, acht g*eir* a n-inat a haei, Book of Lismore, 149 a 1). Such a cow is in the possession of the nine score nuns of Tuam, and supplies them by one milking. Through the aid of his holy swineherd Marbhán, Guaire obtains it in barter for nine score kine, and then kills it for Brigit.

Medb, Senchán's daughter, longs in January for a skirtful of blackberries (*lán beinne mo broit acum do smeruibh corra cirdhubha*). Marbhán tells Guaire where to find them. One day in autumn, when Guaire was hunting in Glenn in Scáil, a bush caught his mantle, which he readily let go, for he never refused a favour to any (*nir' erais nech um ní riamh*). Marbhán came up, found a quantity of berries on the bush, and spread his cloak over them, so that they were miraculously preserved till January and then given by Guaire to Medb. I am indebted to Professor Henebry for referring me to this story.

In the passage above cited from LU. 117b, as in the story of Bresal, *Lives of Saints from the Book of Lismore,* pref. XXVII, *aib* or *aeib* is the dat. pl. of *ae* 'liver' (each lobe of that organ being regarded as a separate liver), and not, as I supposed, the dat. sg. of *aeb* 'beauty'. So in Keating's *Three Shafts of Death,* ed. Atkinson, p. 45, ll. 19, 26. And *fulliuch* occurs also in LL. 244 b 13: Atracht Achil assa foluch ina fuilliuch can fis do Hectoir, 'Without Hector's knowledge, Achilles rose out of his concealment in his hiding-place.' Cf. the adj. *foilligheach* and *foillightheach* 'hidden, latent', O'Br.

Cowes.   WHITLEY STOKES.

DAS KYMRISCHE IN '*THE PLEASANT COMODIE OF PATIENT GRISILL*'.

Im Jahre 1603 erschien in London ein Drama unter dem Titel '*The Pleasant Comodie of Patient Grisill*', von dem Collier 1841 einen Neudruck für die Shakespeare Society und G. Hübsch einen weiteren in den 'Erlanger Beiträge zur Englischen Philologie', 15. Heft (Erlangen 1893), gab. Es ist schon 1600 als The Plaie of Patient Grisell auf der Londoner Buchhändlerbörse eingetragen und wahrscheinlich 1599 entstanden (s. Hübsch S. XXV ff.) als gemeinsame Arbeit der bekannten 3 Dichter Henry Chettle, W. Haughton und Thomas Dekker. Die Erzählung von der geduldigen Griseldis, wie sie bei Boccaccio zuerst sich findet, ist der Hauptvorwurf des Dramas. Auf Grund von Petrarcas lat. Nachbildung der Novelle Boccaccios hatte schon Chaucer die Erzählung in England eingeführt; sie wurde im 16. Jahrhundert mehrfach in Balladenform in England bearbeitet und erschien auch in einem oft aufgelegten Volksbuch (s. Hübsch S. VIII ff.). Eine der Balladen und die Prosaerzählung des Volksbuches sind nach Hübschs Ausführungen (S. XV bis XXIV) die Quellen des englischen Dramas. Dies letztere nun unterscheidet sich in einem wichtigen Punkt nicht nur von seinen Quellen, sondern auch von den zahlreichen übrigen Behandlungen, die der Stoff im Anschluss an Boccaccio-Petrarca in vielerlei Sprachen erfahren hat: es ist neben der Haupthandlung eine kontrastierende komische Nebenhandlung ein- und durchgeführt, wodurch das Drama überhaupt erst den Charakter eines Lustspieles bekommt. Umfang und Bedeutung dieser Nebenhandlung für die Anlage des Stückes erhellt

schon daraus, dass von den 2637 Zeilen des Dramas nicht weniger
als 865 direkt auf die Nebenhandlung oder Scenen, in denen die
Figuren derselben in die Haupthandlung verflochten sind, kommen.
Die Nebenhandlung ist ein Seitenstück zu Shakespeares *Taming
of the Shrew*, nur mit dem Unterschied, dass dem Helden der
Nebenhandlung es n i c h t gelingt, die geheiratete Witwe zu
zähmen, wie er will und sich vor dem Gatten der Griseldis
rühmt; es wird vielmehr der Versuch die Witwe zu zähmen zu
einer Kette von Geduldsproben für den zweiten Gatten, bis er
schliesslich so geduldig geworden ist wie *patient Grisill* von
Anfang ihrem Gatten gegenüber war.

Die Figuren nun dieser neben der Haupthandlung her-
laufenden, einen komischen Kontrast bildenden Nebenhandlung
sind Welsche, drei der Zahl nach: Sir Owen, der *prittish
knight* Z. 529. 650, *welsh knight* Z. 1149 genannt wird; sein
Diener, dessen Name bald Rice bald Rees geschrieben ist;
endlich die von Sir Owen geheiratete Witwe G w e n t h y a n, die
Z. 553 — vor ihrer Wiederverheiratung — *welsh widdowe*
genannt wird und nach ihren eigenen Worten (Z. 646) durch
den ersten Mann, der ein *cozen* des regierenden Grafen von
Saluce war, *from Wales* gebracht wurde. Dass die beiden
männlichen Figuren die bekannten kymrischen Namen *Owein* und
Rhys tragen, sieht man sofort; unter 'Gwenthian (Gwenthyan)'
ist der bekannte welsche Frauenname *Gwenllian* versteckt, wie
wir noch sehen werden. Alle drei Personen reden dasselbe ge-
brochene Englisch mit ähnlichen lautlichen und syntaktischen
Eigenheiten — z. B. Tenuis im Anlaut für Media wie *pie and
pie* für *by and by, prauerie* für *braverie*, oder Vorstellung von
is vor den Infinitiv statt des Verb finit nach kymr. *y mae yn*
mit Infinitiv — wie wir es aus Shakespeares 'Merry wives of
Windsor' an dem welschen Geistlichen Hugh Evans und weniger
prononziert aus Shakespeares 'Heinrich der Fünfte' an Kaptän
Fluellin, dem welschen Führer, und seinem Untergebenen Williams
kennen. Den bekannten Stolz des Kymren auf seine Muttersprache hat auch Sir Owen, denn er sagt von *prittish tongue:
for tis fine delicates tongue, I can tell her: welshe tongue is
finer as greeke tongue* (Z. 615); ebenso ist er Freund der Musik
(2397) und stolz auf die welsche Harfe: *King Tauie is well
knowne was a good musitions, as the pest fidler in aul Italie,
and King Tauie was Sir Owens countrieman, yes truly*

a prettish shentlemen porne, and did twinckle, twinckle, twinckle, out a crie upon welsh harpe, and tis knowne Tauie loue mistris Persabe, as Sir Owen loues Gwenthyan (Z. 624—629). Diese drei Personen der Nebenhandlung lassen nun in ihrer Unterhandlung unter einander und in Reden an andere Personen im Verlauf vielfach kymrische Phrasen einfliessen, deren genaueres Verständnis nicht immer ganz leicht ist. Die Scenen der Nebenhandlung und die Scenen der Haupthandlung, in welche eine der drei Personen der Nebenhandlung verflochten ist, sind Z. 425—464; 512—667; 1217—1410; 1886—2084; 2322 bis 2637. Die welschen Redewendungen, die ich im Folgenden zuerst genau nach der Überlieferung gebe, finden sich in folgenden Stellen:[1])

589—592 (S. 22, 16 ff.).

Sir Owen. Ha, Ra, Rice, goe call Gwenthyian.
Rice. I will master: dahoma, Gwenthyan, dahoma?
Sir Owen. A pogs on her, goe fedge her and call her within.
Rice. I am gone Sir.   Exit Rice.

606—613 (S. 23, 1 ff.).

Enter Gwenthyan.

Gwe. Who calls Gwenthyan so great teale of time?
Vrence. Sweet widdow, euen your countrieman heere.
Sir Owen. Belly the ruddo whee: wrage witho, Mandag eny Mou du ac whellock en wea awh.
Gwe. Sir Owen, gramarrye whee: Gwenthyan Mandage eny, ac wellock en Thawen en ryn mogh.
Farnece. Mundage Thlawen, oh my good widdow, gable that we may understand you, and have at you.

In 614 ff. wirbt nun Sir Owen um Gwenllian, und sie geht unter der Voraussetzung, dass ihr *cozen* Gualter, der regierende Herzog von Saluce, einverstanden ist, auf die Werbung ein, wobei sie jedoch ausdrücklich erklärt, dass es ihr darauf ankomme ihren Willen in der Ehe zu haben (640. 651); sie treten ab mit den Worten:

---

[1]) Die Zeilenzählung nach dem Abdruck von Hübsch; in Klammer Seitenzahl und Zeile nach Colliers Neudruck.

660—661 (S. 24, 24 ff.).

Sir Owen. Come widdow: Vn loddis Glane Gwenthyan an mondu.

Gw. Gramercie wheeh, Am a Mock honnoh.

Die Verheiratung von Sir Owen mit der Witwe Gwenllian vollzieht sich hinter der Scene; der regierende Herzog von Saluce, dessen *cozen* Sir Owen durch die Verheiratung geworden ist, stellt durch eine Reihe von Prüfungen die Geduld seiner Gattin Griseldis auf die Probe (755—1215). In einem Gespräch, das der Herzog und Sir Owen mit einander führen, bittet letzterer den Herzog, er möge die Griseldis etwas freundlicher behandeln, da Gwenllian dieserhalb aufsässig werde und ihm (Sir Owen) schlimme Scenen mache, oder er solle *tedge Sir Owen to make Gwenthians quiet and tame here.* Der Herzog geht anscheinend auf letzteres ein: er fordert Sir Owen auf, in einem in der Nähe befindlichen Korbweidengebüsch drei Ruten abzuschneiden, wie er selbst auch thut; ehe er aber imstande ist auseinander zu setzen was er meint, wird er durch die Nachricht abgerufen, dass Griseldis mit Zwillingen niedergekommen sei, und hat nur noch Zeit Sir Owen zu sagen, er solle seine drei Ruten aufbewahren, da er ihm bei späterer Gelegenheit zeigen werde *'how easily a man may tame a shrew'.* Während der Herzog nur daran dachte an dem Verhalten von frischen und trockenen Weidenruten bei ihrem Biegen zu zeigen, dass eine Zähmung der Gattin sofort mit Beginn der Ehe beginnen müsse (s. Z. 2539 ff.), überlegt Sir Owen in einem Monolog, was wohl der Herzog mit dem Rutenschneiden gemeint habe, und kommt zu der Anschauung, dass der Herzog ihm einen leisen Wink für die Behandlung Gwenllians habe geben wollen. In dem Moment *enter Gwenthian and Rice,* und Owen fährt fort:

1301—1304 (S. 46, 7 ff.).

Gods lid, here her comes. Terdawgh Gwenthian, terdawgh.

Gwe. Terdawgh whee, Sir Owen, Terdawgh whee.

Owen. Owe, looge here, fine wandes Gwenthyan, is not?

Gw. Rees, tag them and preag them in peeces.

Rice wendet sich an seinen Herren, der ihm befiehlt die Weidenruten nicht zu zerbrechen, sondern nach Hause mit-

zunehmen; es kommt zu einem lebhaften Wortwechsel zwischen
dem Ehepaare, im Verlauf dessen die geduldige Griseldis mehrfach von Sir Owen erwähnt wird. Hierüber wird Gwenllian
eifersüchtig, und Sir Owen wird gegen sie so ungehalten, dass er
ausruft, sie möge sich aufhängen (*hang her selfe*), wenn's ihr
nicht passe. Da bricht Gwenllian in Geheul aus:

1351—1362 (S. 47, 30 ff.).

*Gwe. Hang her selfe, owe, owe, owe, Gwenthyans tother
husband is scawrue to say hang her selfe: hang her selfe? owe,
owe, owe, owe.*

*Ow. Gods plude, what cannot get by prawles, is get by
owe, owe, owe, is terrible Ladie, pray be peace, and cry no more
owe, owe, owe. Tawsone Gwenthyans, God udge me, is
very furie.*

Gwen. O mon Jago, mon due, hang Gwenthyans?

*Ow. Adologo whee Gwenthyan bethogh, en Thonigh,
en moyen due.*

*Gwe. Ne vetho en Thonigh, Gna wathe gethla Tee,
hang Gwenthyans?*

Während Owen dabei ist Gwenllian zu beruhigen und ihr
verspricht nie mehr zu sagen *hang her selfe*, kommt Rice wieder
herein und meldet, dass Frau Annchen einen kostbaren Kragen
im Werte von 5 Pfund für Gwenllian gebracht habe. Sir Owen
gerät ausser sich über diese Verschwendungssucht seiner Frau
und zerreisst in der Wut die kostbare Krause (*rabato*) und
Bänder (*bonds*) der Gwenllian, während sie als Rache wertvolle
Schuldverschreibungen (*bonds*) Sir Owens, die sie in der Hand
hat, zerreisst und auf die bestürzte Frage Sir Owens *what has
her done?* antwortet:

1399—1405 (S. 49, 13 ff.).

*Gw. Goe loog, is now paide for her repatoes, ile haue her
willes & desires, ile teadge her pridle her Lady: Catho crogge,
Ne vetho, en Thlonigh gna wathee gnathla tee. Exit.*

*Owen. A breath vawer or no Tee: pridle her, sir Owen
is pridled I warrant: widdows! (were petter Gods plude marry
whoore) were petter be hang'd and quarter, then marry widdowes
as God udge me.*

Nach einer grossen Scene (1411—1885), die zahlreiche weitere Proben von der Lammesgeduld der Griseldis bringt, treten Gwenllian und Rhŷs auf. Letzterer richtet einen Schmaus her, zu dem Sir Owen den Herzog von Saluce und den ganzen Hof eingeladen hat. Gwenllian aber, die in abgerissenen Kleidern ist, hat ihrerseits einen Haufen Bettler eingeladen, die mit all den Herrlichkeiten der Tafel kurzen Prozess machen und schliesslich trunken und die Taschen voll Speisen abziehen. Da tritt Sir Owen ein, seinen Gästen etwas vorauseilend, sieht den Festsaal und seine den eben entlassenen Bettlergästen entsprechend gekleidete Frau, die ihm höhnend vorhält, wie sie ihn vor seinen bald erscheinenden Gästen blamiert habe. Sir Owen sucht sie zu besänftigen, verspricht ihr eine neue Krause und Kragen, wenn sie sich zum Empfang der Gäste nur etwas passend anziehen wolle; sie aber, in Erinnerung an Owens *hang her selfe*, ruft:

1980—1982 (S. 69, 9 ff.).

Gw. Cartho crogge, Cartho crogge, Gwenthian scornes her flatteries, her Lady goe no petter, Sir Owen hang herselfe.

Ow. O mon Jago, her Pritish plude is not indure it by Cod: a pogs on her, put on her fine coates is pest, put on, goe to, put on.

Während Rhŷs auf Befehl Owens weggegangen ist, um Feuer zu machen zu einem neuen Mahle und das Ehepaar Owen-Gwenllian sich herumzankt, tritt der Herzog, seine Schwester Julia und der Hof ein, ohne die in abgerissenen Kleidern dastehende Gwenllian zu erkennen. Auf die Frage des Herzogs, wo letztere sei, erwidert Sir Owen verlegen:

2014—2018 (S. 70, 17 ff.).

Owen. Is come pie and pie. Cod udge me, Gwenthian, pray put on your prauerie and fine knags, and shame not Sir Owen. Yes truly, Gwenthian is come out pie and pie. Man gras worthe whee cozen Marguesse, Man gras worthe whee cozen Julia, is welcome awl.

Nunmehr berichtet einer vom Gefolge des Herzogs was vorgegangen ist und wie's in der Küche aussieht. Sir Owen

muss alles zugeben, und auf die Frage, wie dies möglich sei, da
er sich doch gerühmt, die Gwenllian gezähmt zu haben, erwidert
er dem Herzog, dies sei die Rache, die Gwenllian an ihm nehme,
weil der Graf die Griseldis so schlecht behandle. Da fährt die
in schlechten Kleidern dastehende Gwenllian dazwischen:

2046—2067 (S. 71, 18 ff.).

*Gwen. Tis lye cozen Marguesse, is terrible lye: Tawsone
en Ennoh swewle,[1] tis lye, tis lye, Sir Owen teare her repatoes
and ruffes, and pridle her Latie, & bid her hang her selfe, but
is pridled I warrant her, is not Sir Owen?*

*Owe. Adologg whee bethogh en Thlonigh, en Moyen
due, Gwenthian.*

Gwe. Ne vetho en Thlonigh, Gna watha gethla Tee.

Vrc. What sayes she Sir Owen?

*Ow. I pray & pray her for Cods loue be quiet, splude!
her say her will not be quiet, do what Sir Owen can: mon due
Gwenthian, Me knocke the pen, en vmbleth, pobe des and
pobe nose.*

Gwe. Gwenogh olcha vesagh whee, en herawgh, ee.

Jul. Stand betweene them Farnese.

Far. You shall bob no nose heere.

*Gwe. En herawgh Ee? Me grauat the Legatee,
athlan oth pendee, adroh ornymee on dictar, en-
hecar Ee.*

*Ono. Doth she threaten you Sir Owen? binde her to the
peace.*

*Owe. By Cod, is threaten her indeed, her saies shee'll
scradge out Sir Owens eyes, and her frowne upon her, a pogs
on her nailes.*

Der Herzog bittet unter diesen Umständen alle Anwesenden
mit ihm zu gehen und bei ihm das Diner zu haben. Sir Owen
bittet jedoch zu bleiben, da er mit Hilfe von Rhŷs schon ein
Essen zubereiten werde, und geht ab. Hierauf geht auch
Gwenllian ab mit den Worten:

---

[1] Collier giebt *twewle.*

2080—2083 (S. 72, 18 ff.).

Gwe. Will you? Is try that pic and pie: Stethe whee lawer, Cozen Marguesse, stethe whee lawer Shentlemen, Gwenthian is not pridled so soone.

In dem grossen Schlussakt (2202—2637), in dem die geduldige Griseldis für ihre Geduld die Belohnung empfängt und in dem auch Sir Owen und Gwenllian mit den übrigen Hauptpersonen des Stückes erscheinen und zwar schliesslich ausgesöhnt, da Sir Owen einsieht, dass ihm in seinem Ehedrama nicht die Rolle des Grafen, sondern die der geduldigen Griseldis zugefallen ist, kommen noch folgende kymrische Phrasen vor:

2324 (S. 80, 20).

Owen. Tardaugh Cozen Marguesse & Lawrdes awl.

2397 (S. 83, 5).

Owen. Tawsone, Tawsone Cozens aul, and here harmonies and sol faes.

2423 (S. 84, 1).

Gwe. Fuh, fuh, is fooles Tawsone.

2636.

Sir Owen schliesst die Schlussrede des Stückes, in der er auseinandersetzt, dass ihm die Rolle der geduldigen Griseldis zugefallen ist, mit den Worten: *and so God saue you all. Man gras wortha whee, Man gras wortha whee, God night Cozens awl.*

Das genaue Verständnis der im Vorhergehenden gegebenen kymrischen Phrasen ist durch mancherlei Umstände erschwert. Einmal wird das Kymrische wie es englischem Ohr jener Zeit erklang und in englischer Orthographie gegeben; sodann sind Druckfehler und falsche Wortabtrennungen in sicheren Fällen überaus zahlreich; endlich scheint der Urheber der welschen Brocken in dem Stück das Kymrische grammatisch nicht vollständig zu beherrschen.[1] Für die beiden ersten Punkte liefert

---

[1] Von den drei Dichtern, die bei Henslowe im Dezember 1599 als die Urheber der Komödie genannt werden — Henry Chettle, William Haughton und Thomas Dekker —, ist nach dem, was wir über dieselben wissen (s.

der Name der widerspänstigen Witwe gleich einen Beleg. Derselbe wird im Text und in den Anweisungen 79 mal erwähnt, wenn ich richtig gezählt habe, und zwar in den Schreibungen *Gwenthian, Gwenthien, Gwenthians, Gwenthyan, Gwenthyans.* In allen für Engländer bestimmten Fremdenführern für Wales findet sich die Anweisung, man solle *Ll* in kymrischen Ortsnamen sprechen wie *thl,* also *Thlangóthlen* für *Llangollen,* um dem welschen Laute nahe zu kommen. So wird denn auch in den kymrischen Phrasen in unserem Text *athlan* für kymr. *allan* (2061) geschrieben; ferner *en Thlonigh* für kymr. *yn llonydd* (1401. 2050. 2052), wofür verdruckt ist *en Thonigh* (1359. 1361). Nach letzterem bessert sich *en Thawen* (611) leicht in *en Thlawen* für kymr. *yn llawen,* zumal das *Thlawen* (612) sicher ausweist, dass in dem *Thawen* 611 ein Druckfehler vorliegt. Dies alles angewandt auf den Namen der Witwe kann auch nicht den geringsten Zweifel aufkommen lassen, dass in den oben angeführten verschiedenen Formen der bekannte welsche Frauenname *Gwenllian* versteckt ist, der in der Orthographie unseres Textes sollte *Gwenthlian* geschrieben sein. — Ein weiterer Beleg für ein kymr. *ll* vertretendes *thl* in unserem Text scheint mir in einer dreimal wiederkehrenden Phrase zu liegen: *gna wathe gethla Tee* (1361) = *gna wathee gnathla tee* (1401) = *gna watha gethla Tee* (2052). Man sagt heutigen Tages in Nordwestwelsch *gora galla* (= litter. *goreu gallaf*) 'so gut ich kann'; darnach kann in der Phrase wohl ein *gna waetha galla 'ti* d. h. litter. *gwnaf waethaf gallaf iti* 'ich werde es dir treiben so schlimm (toll) ich kann'.[1])

Dictionary of National Biography unter den Namen) sicher keiner ein Walliser von Geburt oder zu Wales in Beziehung stehend. Von dem erstgenannten (H. Chettle) erfahren wir aus Henslowes Diarium, dass er 1597 ein Stück mit Drayton gemeinsam verfasst hat, das Henslow ganz allgemein nennt '*a book wherein is a part of a Welshman*'. Es ist daher wahrscheinlich, dass Henry Chettle wesentlich der Urheber der komischen Nebenhandlung ist, in der Sir Owain, Gwenllian und Rhŷs auftreten. Nach dem Dictionary of National Biographie war '*H. Chettle, son of Robert Chettle, a dyer of London*'. Es wird im letzten Viertel des 16. Jahrhunderts in London wohl ebenso leicht gewesen sein kymrisch zu lernen wie am Ende des 19. Jahrhunderts. Ich will nur daran erinnern, dass alle kymrischen Drucke bis 1600 in London erschienen.

[1]) Eine andere aus der Aussprache des kymrischen Lautes wohl verständliche Wiedergabe von *ll* liegt vor in Shakespeares *Fluellin.* In der

Auslautendes kymr. *dd* ist sicher mit *gh* gegeben in der Verbindung *en Thlonigh* (1401. 2050. 2052; 1359. 1361) = kymr. *yn llonydd* 'ruhig'. Darnach kann man *en ryn mogh* (611) fassen für kymr. *yn yr un modd?* Noch viel zweifelhafter bin ich, ob *en herawgh ee* (2058) = *en herawgh Ee* (2062) für gesprochenes *yn 'herwydd hi* d. h. litter. *yn ei herwydd hi* 'deswegen, dafür' genommen werden kann; das *a* müsste dem Setzer nach Analogie des öfters vorkommenden *terdawgh* für ein *en herwygh ee* seines Manuskriptes gekommen sein. — Auslautendes *f* in mehrsilbigen Wörtern (1. Sing. Präs., Superlativ etc.) ist im Neukymr. überall geschwunden und war dies schon um a. 1600, wie aus den Celt Llundain 1900, 27. Jan. S. 3, 3 abgedruckten Sentenzen einer Hs. jenes Jahres erhellt (*mwia gelyn i ddyn, i ffolineb i hun; mwia a sieryd y dynion ynfyta; ucha ar weithredoedd Duw yw trugaredd*). So haben wir denn auch in unserm Lustspiel *mandag eny* (608) = *mandage eny* (610) für gesprochenes *ma 'n da gcni* = litterarisch kymr. *mae yn dda genyf* 'es ist mir lieb, es freut mich'; ferner *gna waetha gathla* (1301. 1401. 2052) für *gwnaf waethaf gallaf* wie wir vorhin annahmen; auch *ne vetho* (1361. 1401. 2052) für *ni fyddaf*; endlich in *me grauat the Legatee* (2061) für *mi grafa*(f) *'th lygad di* und *me knocke the pen* (2056) für *mi gnoca*(f) *'th ben.* — Vortonige Silben sind wie heutigen Tages bis Schwund geschwächt wie in *stethe whee lawcr* (2080. 2081) gleich *'stéddwch i lawr* für litterarisches *eistéddwch i lawr* 'nehmen Sie Platz'.

Dafür dass der Urheber der kymrischen Phrasen des Welschen nicht ganz mächtig war, lässt sich vielleicht anführen, dass die vokalische Mutation in Fällen fehlt, wo man sie erwarten muss. Während nämlich *me grauat the Legatee* (2061) für *mi grafa'th lygaid di* beidemale die Mutation richtig hat (*crafu, llygad*), fehlt sie in *me knocke the pen* (2056) für *mi*

Schlacht von Azincourt spielte *Dafydd ab Llywelyn*, gewöhnlicher bekannt als *Dafydd Gam*, als Führer kymrischer Hilfstruppen thatsächlich eine Rolle. Wenn man bedenkt, dass die kymrischen Familiennamen *Williams, Edwards, Davies, Evans* etc. dadurch entstanden sind, dass die englischen Richter die *Dafydd ab Gwilym ab Owen ab Meredith* etc. oder *Richard ab Owain ab Dafydd ab Gwilym* etc. schlankweg *David Williams* oder *Richard Owen* nannten; und wenn man beachtet, dass engl. *Fluellin* die kymr. Aussprache von *Llywélyn* ziemlich gut wiedergiebt, kann man kaum zweifeln, dass in *Fluellin* in Shakespeares Heinrich V. der historische *Dafydd ab Llywelyn* vorliegt, wie schon öfters angenommen worden ist.

gnoca'th ben in beiden Stellen und ebenso in *athlan oth pendee*
für *allan o'th ben di* (2062). Dagegen wird man wohl einem
des Kymrischen Mächtigen die mir aus dem Kymrischen sonst
unbekannte, offenbar dem Englischen nachgebildete Redensart
Terdawgh (1301) = *terdawgh whee* (2302) = *tardaugh* (2324)
zutrauen dürfen. Im heutigen gesprochenen Nordwestkymrischen
sagt man regelmässig *nosdawch* 'gute Nacht' = *nos da i chwi*;
darnach ist wohl zu *tyred* 'come' (gesprochen *tyrd* und *tyd*) ein
das englische *welcome* nachahmendes oder übersetzendes *terdawgh*
(*tyrdawch*) = *tyr'd da i chwi* entstanden.[1]

Nach diesen allgemeinen Bemerkungen will ich die kymrischen Redensarten in litterarischer Sprache wiedergeben so
weit ich sie verstehe, andern überlassend mich zu berichtigen
und zu ergänzen.

590. *Dowch yma, Gwenllian, dowch yma!* ('Kommen Sie
her, Gwenllian, kommen Sie her.')
608. *B'le yr ydych chwi wraig widdow? Mae yn dda
genyf, myn Duw, eich gweled chwi yn wŷch.* ('Wo stecken Sie
Frau Witwe? es ist mir lieb Sie munter zu sehen.')[2]
610. *Sir Owen, gramercie i chwi Gwenllian! mae yn dda
genyf eich gweled chwi yn llawen yn yr un modd.* ('Sir Owen,
schön Dank Ihnen! es ist mir lieb, Sie wohl zu sehen gleichfalls.')

---

[1] Ich habe *nosdawch* weder in Sir Aberteifi — Sir Gaer noch in Sir
Forgannwg gehört und auf verschiedenes direktes Fragen von Herren, die mit
der gesprochenen Sprache in Südwales wohl vertraut sind, immer die Antwort
erhalten, diese nordkymrische Redensart finde sich nicht *ar lafar gwlad* im
Süden. Da man zudem für nordkymrisches *tyrd, tyd* 'komm' im Süden sagt
dere, so würde *terdawgh* sicher darauf hinweisen, dass der Urheber der
kymrischen Phrasen in dem Lustspiel nordwelschen Dialekt sprach oder kannte,
vorausgesetzt, dass meine Auffassung von *terdawgh* richtig ist. Auch *'rydych*
in 608 kann nur nordwelsch sein, da man im Süden sagt *'r ych*. Vielleicht
darf man auch *dowch yma* (*dahoma*) 590 für Nordwelsch anführen; ich habe
in Dyfed nur *dewch yma* gehört.

[2] Im Nordwelschen ist *yr ydych* gesprochen *'r ŏda*, was *ruddo* der
Überlieferung sein kann. Da in Wörtern wie *gwŷch* u. a. das *ch* die gutturale
Aussprache hat wie in unserm 'Loch', so stellt sich leicht zwischen dem ŷ
(*i, û*) und *ch* ein Laut ein wie im Zürcher-Deutsch in 'ich' u. a. In nkymr.
uwch, cyfuwch neben *uch, uchel, uchaf, cyfuch* kommt er auch graphisch zum
Ausdruck. So kann also *en wea awh* sehr wohl ein gesprochenes *yn wŷch*
geben. Das *eich gweled chwi* in 609 und 611 betrachte ich als ganz unsicher;
für *gweled* hört man in Nordwales gewöhnlich *gweld*.

660. *Vn* kann kymr. *yw'n, un, yn* sein; *llodes* ist in der gewöhnlichen Sprache ein Zärtlichkeitsausdruck für 'Frauenzimmer, Weibsbild'; *glan* bekanntes Adjektiv und stehendes lobendes Epitheton von 'Mädchen, Frau, Wales' etc.; *mon du* kann *myn Duw* sein. Darnach hätte Sir Owen beim Weggehen zu Gwenllian gesagt 'Komm Witwe' und zu den Umstehenden 'Gwenllian ist ein hübsches (sauberes, prächtiges) Frauenzimmer, bei Gott'. Aber ich weiss ohne Gewaltthätigkeit gegen die Überlieferung kein grammatisch richtiges Kymrisch daraus zu gewinnen.

661. *Gramercie i chwi am . . . o honoch* 'Dank (Grand' merci) Ihnen für . . . von Euch'. Etwa *am y moc ohonoch* 'für Euren Scherz'?

1301. *Tyrd dawch, Gwenllian, tyrd dawch!* ('Willkommen'.)

1302. *Tyrd dawch chwi, Sir Owen, tyrd dawch chwi!* ('Willkommen Sie, Sir Owen, Willkommen Sie'.)

1356. *Taw son* ('halt's Maul'), *Gwenllian!*

1358. *O myn Jago, myn Duw* ('bei Jakob, bei Gott').

1359. *Adolwg i chwi, Gwenllian, byddwch yn llonydd er mwyn Duw* ('ich bitte Sie, Gwenllian, seien sie ruhig [zufrieden] um Gotteswillen').

1361. *Ni fyddaf yn llonydd, gwnaf waethaf gallaf i ti* ('ich werde nicht ruhig sein, ich werde es so toll für dich treiben wie ich kann').

1400. *Gato crogi! ni fyddaf yn llonydd, gwnaf waethaf gallaf i ti* ('hänge sie sich! ich werde nicht ruhig sein, ich werde es so toll für dich treiben wie ich kann').[1]

1402. (*A breath*) *fawr arnati* ('du hast einen langen Atem').[2]

---

[1] Da Gwenllian, wenn sie Englisch redet, immer wieder das ihr schrecklich klingende, lieblose Wort Sir Owens '*hang her selfe*' wiederholt, liegt es am nächsten das *catho crogge* (1400) = *cartho crogge, Cartho crogge* (1980) so zu fassen, also *gato* als 3. Sing. Conj. zu *gadael*. Denkt man den häufigen nkymr. Ausdruck *cato Duw* 'Gott bewahre' (*caduco Duw*), so liesse sich *cato crogi* als 'behüte, hängen?' fassen; nur ist letzteres nach dem Zusammenhang weniger wahrscheinlich.

[2] So ruft Sir Owen der davonstürmenden Gwenllian nach, die offenbar Z. 1309—1402 in einem Atem herausgestürzt hat. Das engl. *breath* entsprechende kymr. *anadl* ist Feminin, daher das Femin. des Adjektivs *mawr*, wie wir ja auch sagen 'das Douceur' und 'der Likör' wegen 'das Trinkgeld' und 'der Schnaps'.

1980. *Gato crogi! Gato crogi!* ('lass sie sich hängen; s. zu 1400).

1982. *O myn Jago* ('bei Jago').

2016. *Fy ngras wrthych chwi* ('meine Gewogenheit [Huld] Euch').[1]

2046. *Taw son yn enw diawl* ('halt's Maul in Teufels Namen').

2050. *Adolwg i chwi, byddwch yn llonydd er mwyn Duw, Gwenllian!* ('Ich bitte Sie, seien Sie ruhig um Gotteswillen Gwenllian.')

2052. *Ni fyddaf yn llonydd, gwnaf waethaf gallaf i ti* ('ich werde nicht ruhig sein, ich werde es dir so toll treiben wie ich kann').

2056. *Myn Duw, Gwenllian, mi gnoca 'th ben yn wmbredd bob dydd a bob nos* ('bei Gott, Gwenllian, ich werde dir den Kopf gewaltig verhauen jeden Tag und jede Nacht').

2058. *Gwnewch! golcha 'ch visage chwi yn ei herwydd hi* ('Nur zu [thut]! ich werde Eure Visage waschen dafür').

2061. *Yn ei herwydd hi mi grafa 'th lygaid di allan o'th ben di a . . . digter . . .* ('dafür werde ich deine Augen aus deinem Kopfe kratzen und . . . Wut . . .').[2]

2080. *Eisteddwch chwi i lawr* ('setzen Sie sich nieder').

2324. *Tyrd dawch* ('Willkommen').

---

[1] *Man gras worthe whee* (2017) = *man gras wortha whee* (2636). Ob man ein altertümliches *my* für gewöhnliches *fy* noch annehmen darf, scheint mir sehr gewagt; ich weiss jedoch aus *man gras* nichts anderes zu machen, wenn es kymrisch ist. Vielleicht darf man annehmen, dass die Verfasser des Lustspiels dem Sir Owen einige französische Phrasen in den Mund legen, wie sie am Hofe gebraucht wurden, und ihn, um ihn komisch erscheinen zu lassen, *mon grâce* für *ma grâce* sagen lassen. Dann könnte auch das öfters vorkommende *mon du, mon Jago* franz. *mon dieu, mon Jago* sein und nicht *myn Duw, myn Jago*.

[2] Da sowohl im Nordwestwelsch (Sir Fon und Sir Gaernarfon) als in Südostwelsch (Sir Forgannwg) unbetonte *ai* (*au*) auslautender Silben zu *a* werden (*perffath, noswath, petha*), so fallen hier Sing. *llygad* und Plur. *llygaid* in der Form *llygad* zusammen, was zur Folge hat, dass man in Nordwestwelsch oft *llygada* (*llygadau*) für den Plural hört, welche Form in Nordostwelsch (Sir Ddinbych) und Südwestwelsch (Sir Aberteifi und Sir Gaer) nicht vorkommt, da hier litterar. *llygad : llygaid* in der gesprochenen Sprache durch *llygad : llyged* repräsentiert wird. — Da Präposition *mewn* in Nordwestwales *miawn* heutigen Tags gesprochen wird, so ist vielleicht *a . . . arni mewn digter . . .* zu schreiben.

2397. *Taw son! Taw son!* ('Still, still!')
2423. *Taw son!* ('Still.')
2636. *Fy ngras wrthych chwi* ('Meine Huld Euch.')

Eine Frage soll zum Schluss noch erwogen werden, die weder von Collier noch von Hübsch aufgeworfen ist. Wie kamen wohl die Verfasser von 'The pleasant Comodie of Patient Grisill' für die von ihnen vollständig erfundene Nebenhandlung, wodurch das Stück allein zu einer 'pleasant Comodie' erst wird, welsche Figuren zu wählen? Das Stück spielt wie die Quelle und alle sonstigen Bearbeitungen in Italien: die Hauptfigur der Haupthandlung Gualter ist Herzog von Saluce, sein Bruder Herzog in Pavia, die Namen der Nebenfiguren der Haupthandlung — selbst die von den Verfassern neu erfundenen, s. Hübsch S. XXIV — sind italienisch; das Stück spielt in Saluce am Hofe und in der Nähe bei dem armen Bauer Janicolo, dem Vater der Griseldis. In dieser Umgebung nimmt sich doch der *prittish knight* Sir Owen, seine keifende Gwenllian und sein Diener Rhŷs etwas sonderbar aus; auch dann noch, wenn man annimmt, dass für die Phantasie der Zuschauer Saluce und die Behausung Janicolos irgendwie in England liegen konnte.

Ich habe die Vermutung, dass mit der von den Dichtern nach Idee, Ausführung und Figuren vollständig neu eingeführten Nebenhandlung eine in Shakespeares Zeit verständliche Anspielung auf ein Verhältnis am englischen Königshof in früherer Zeit vorliegt. Der Held der Nebenhandlung, der als stattlicher Mann geschildert wird, heisst gewöhnlich *Sir Owen*; 1220, 1270, 2070 wird er *Sir Meredith* genannt; *cozen Meredith* nennt ihn der Herzog 2344 und *Sir Owen Meredith* 2038; *Sir Owen ap Meredith* nennt er sich selbst 1409: dies ist also sein richtiger Name. Nun, ein *Sir Owain ap Meredith* kann zwischen 1423 und 1437 am englischen Hofe eine ähnliche Rolle gespielt haben wie die Verfasser der Komödie den Sir Owen ap Meredith am Hofe des Herzogs von Saluce spielen lassen. Heinrich V. von England heiratete bekanntlich 1420 die Tochter Karls VI. von Frankreich, Katharina von Valois, die Shakespeare uns in 'Heinrich V.' dritter Akt, vierte Scene Englisch lernend vorführt (vgl. auch fünfter Akt, zweite Scene); sie gebar ihm am 6./12. 1421 den späteren Heinrich VI. Als Heinrich bald darauf (31./8. 1622) starb, über-

nahm sein Bruder Humfrey, Herzog von Gloster, die Regentschaft in England und ein anderer Bruder, der Herzog von
Bedford, die Regentschaft in Frankreich. Die Witwe Heinrichs V.
tröstete sich aber bald, indem sie, zuerst wohl heimlich, einen
am Hofe lebenden stattlichen nordkymrischen Edelmann, den
Sir Owain ap Meredydd ap Tudor von Penmynydd auf Anglesey
heiratete. Sie gebar ihm vier Kinder: drei Söhne (Edmund,
Jasper, Owen) und eine früh gestorbene Tochter; von den Söhnen
ging der jüngste Owen ins Kloster, die älteren wurden nach dem
Tode ihrer Mutter († 1437) von ihrem Stiefbruder Heinrich VI.
zu Herzögen von Richmond (Edmund) und Pembroke (Jasper)
gemacht. Der alte Owain ap Meredydd wurde, für das Haus
Lancaster kämpfend, 1461 bei Mortimers Cross gefangen genommen und hingerichtet; seines ältesten Sohnes Edmund Sohn
Heinrich, der 1456 geboren wurde, besiegte als Herzog von
Richmond Richard III. bei Bosworth (1485) und bestieg als
Heinrich VII. den englischen Thron, als dessen Enkelin zur Zeit
der Abfassung der Komödie Elisabeth auf englischem Throne
sass. Es liegen in den thatsächlichen Verhältnissen zahlreiche Berührungen mit den in der Komödie geschilderten Verhältnissen: *Sir Owain ap Meredydd* der stattliche Mann von
Penmynydd und die Figur des *Sir Owen ap Meredith* in der
Komödie kommen in erster Linie in Betracht; die von dem
historischen Sir Owen geheiratete Witwe ist zwar keine Waliserin
von Geburt, aber Englisch wird sie geradebrecht haben als ob
sie aus Wales stamme, sodass sie dem englischen Hof auch als
'welsche Witwe' gelten konnte wie Gwenllian (535), wenn auch
nicht in gewöhnlichem Sinne des Wortes 'welsh'. Gwenllian
ist, wie schon gesagt, ein häufiger kymrischer Frauenname und
von mancher in kymrischer Geschichte berühmten Person getragen, wobei ich nur an die unglückliche Gwenllian, die Tochter
des letzten kymrischen Fürsten Llywelyn zu erinnern brauche;
auch der historische Sir Owain ap Meredydd hatte in seiner
Familie eine berühmte Gwenllian: jene Gwenllian, deren Tod
zum Jahre 1190 von den welschen Annalen mit den Worten
Ac y bu uarw Gwenllian uerch Rys vlodeu a thegwch holl Gymru
('Und Gwenllian, die Tochter von Rhŷs, die Blüte und Schönheit
von ganz Wales starb') erwähnt wird, war die Gattin des
Ednyfed Fychan, des Gefährten von Llywelyn dem Grossen, also
des Sir Owain ap Meredydd ap Tudor Ahnin im sechsten Glied

(s. Heinrich VII. Stammbaum bei Carnhuanawc, Hanes Cymru S. 782 und Y Gwyddoniadur Cymreig 9, 608 s. v. *Tudur, Owain*). Es ist also wohl denkbar, dass der historische Sir Owain ap Meredydd seine Frau, die Witwe Heinrichs V., nach der berühmten Ahnin im häuslichen Verkehr Gwenllian nannte. Auch das Verhältnis, in welches Gwenllian im Drama zu den beiden Brüdern, dem Herzog von Saluce und dem Herzog von Pavia gebracht ist — sie gelten als ihre *cozen* von seiten ihres ersten Mannes — erinnert an das Verhältnis, in welchem die Gattin des historischen Owain ap Meredydd zu den beiden Brüdern, dem duke of Gloster und duke of Bedford, nach dem Tode ihres ersten Mannes stand. Über das häusliche Leben des Owain ap Meredydd und der von ihm geheirateten Witwe Heinrichs V. wissen wir nichts; wenn man ihre beiderseitige soziale Stellung vor der Ehe ins Auge fasst, ist leicht denkbar, dass das Bild in der Komödie von den vergeblichen Versuchen Sir Owens seine Gwenllian zu zähmen, den Klatsch widerspiegeln kann, der über die Ehe des Owain ap Meredydd und der verwitweten Gattin Heinrich V. (Katharina von Valois) umlief.

Zur Stütze dieser Erwägungen mag noch auf eins hingewiesen werden. Henry Chettle, einer der Verfasser unserer Komödie, hatte 1597 gemeinsam mit Drayton ein Stück verfasst 'wherein is a part of a Welshman', wie S. 581 Anm. bemerkt ist. Dieser Drayton nun ist 1599 mit Wilson, Hathway und Munday beschäftigt für Henslowe ein Stück '*Owen Tudor*' zu schreiben, worauf Henslowe nach seinem Tagebuch (p. 163) dem Vierblatt 4 Lstr. im Januar 1600 als Vorschuss zahlte (s. Dictionary of National Biography s. Drayton). Der Held dieses Stückes 'Owen Tudor' kann ganz offenkundig nur Heinrichs VII. Grossvater Owain ap Meredydd ap Tudor sein, der Gatte der Witwe Heinrichs V. Dies zeigt zum mindesten, dass dieser Stoff im Jahre 1599 bei den Londoner Dramenfabrikanten wohl bekannt war; wir dürfen aber wohl weiter gehen und eine Stütze für die vorgetragene Vermutung in dem Umstand sehen, dass von den beiden Kompagnons des Jahres 1597 — Drayton und Chettle — in demselben Jahre 1599 der eine (Drayton) mit drei anderen Gefährten ein Stück 'Owen Tudor' vor hat und der andere (Chettle) mit zwei anderen Genossen eine Komödie schreibt, in der ein Sir Owen ap Meredith eine Rolle spielt ähnlich derjenigen des historischen Owen Tudor (Owain ap Meredydd ap Tudor).

Hält man diese Erwägungen über die Figuren der Nebenhandlung nicht für ganz abwegig, dann kommt man zu einer
befriedigenden Beantwortung der Frage, wie die Verfasser von
'The pleasant Comodie of Patient Grisill' dazu kamen, für die
von ihnen vollständig neu erfundene komische Nebenhandlung
gerade kymrische Figuren zu wählen, trotzdem in dem überlieferten Stoff nichts darauf hinwies. Als die Komödie verfasst
wurde (1599/1600) und erschien (1603), beherrschte Shakespeare
mit seinen Stücken die Bühne in London. Die komische Nebenhandlung als Ganzes stellt sich nun ganz natürlich als ein be-
absichtigtes Seitenstück oder Gegenstück zu dem wahrscheinlich
(s. Elze, Shakespeare 387) zwischen 1593 und 1600 verfassten
Shakespeareschen 'Taming of the Shrew' dar und ist als solches
auch schon aufgefasst worden (s. Hübsch a. a. O. S. XXII). Dann
liegt in der Wahl des Stoffes aus der Vergangenheit des
regierenden Herrscherhauses für dies Gegenstück eine Art Paro-
dierung der Shakespeareschen Königsdramen wie Heinrich V.,
VI., Richard III. vor, die zwischen 1594 und 1599 verfasst
wurden, und in dem auf die Bühne gebrachten Kymrisch
von Owen und Gwenllian eine Übertrumpfung Shakespeares.
Letzterer führt in Heinrich V. und den 'Merry wives of Windsor'
Englisch radebrechende Kymren ein; in Heinrich IV. erster Teil
bringt er die Tochter Owen Glyndwrs auf die Bühne (3. Akt,
1. Scene), die kein Englisch versteht wie ihr Gatte Mortimer
kein Welsch: Owen Glyndwr spricht angeblich Welsch mit seiner
Tochter und verdolmetscht dann laut dem Mortimer den Inhalt,
wobei Glyndwrs Tochter in der Erregung des Abschiedes angeblich Welsch dazwischen redet, von dem Mortimer kein Wort
versteht, und schliesslich singt Owen Glyndwrs Tochter unter
Musikbegleitung angeblich ein welsches Lied. Dies alles spielt
sich auf offener Scene ab, ohne dass ein welsches Wort
gehört wird. Dem gegenüber liegt doch in der in Rede
stehenden Komödie von Shakespeares Zeitgenossen in der Art,
wie Owen ap Meredith und Gwenllian auf offener Scene aus
ihrem gebrochenen Englisch ganz natürlich immer wieder in
Kymrisch verfallen, eine Übertrumpfung Shakespeares vor und
zwar eine offenbar beabsichtigte.

Greifswald.   H. ZIMMER.

NOCH EINMAL DER DIPHTHONG *AU*.

Zs. III, 264 ff. hat W. Foy von der Vertretung des indogermanischen *au* im Inselkeltischen gehandelt. Ich sehe mich dadurch veranlasst, dieser Frage, der ich in meinem 274 ff. gedruckten Aufsatz aus dem Wege gegangen war, nun doch näher zu treten, da ich Foys Lösung nicht gut heissen kann.

Die Diphthonge *eu ou au* werden im altgallischen in älterer Zeit noch auseinander gehalten, doch künden sich im Verlauf schon Veränderungen an. *eu* und *ou* bilden dabei *au* gegenüber eine Gruppe; *eu* geht in *ou* über und dies verrät die deutliche Tendenz, monophthong zu werden. Überwiegend wird der aus *eu ou* entstandene Langvokal *o* geschrieben, vgl. *Bŏdic(c)us Bŏdica* neben *Boudicca*, *Bŏdivesus = Segovesus* zu air. *buaid* 'Sieg'; *Clŏtius* neben *Cloutius*; *Clŏta*, Ptol. *Κλώτα* 'Clyde', kymr. *Clud*; *Nŏdens* = mir. *Nuada*; *Ollotŏtis*: air. *tuath.*[1]) Es ist vielleicht kein Zufall, dass *ō* nur vor folgendem Dental bezeugt ist, man wird ja sofort daran gemahnt, dass germ. *au* im ahd. vor Dentalen zu *ō*, sonst zu *ou* geworden ist, vgl. *rōt* : got. *rauþs*, *tōd* : *dauþus*, aber *houbit* : *haubiþ* u. s. w. *u* wird sehr selten geschrieben, einmal *Nūdente* CIL. VII, 139, *Ollūdio* CIL. VII, 73. Die *Catuslūgi* des Plinius (N. h. IV, 106) ändert man meist mit Zeuss in *Catuslōgi*; vielleicht mit Unrecht, da vor Guttural der Monophthong anders gelautet haben kann, als vor Dental (vgl. das brit. *Pennocrūcium* aus dem Itin. Antonini). *au* ist bedeutend

---

[1]) Die *Nŏrici* waren gewiss Kelten, ob auch ihr Name keltisch ist, scheint mir zweifelhaft. Das *ō* ist von Alters her ganz fest. Die Identifizierung mit den *Νευροί* (Pauls Grdr. III, 782) hat daher ihre Schwierigkeiten. *Νωρ*- kehrt auf nichtindog. Gebiet wieder, z. B. in Sardinien. Mit *Brocomagus Vrocomagus* angeblich = *Breucomagus* wage ich nichts anzufangen.

fester als *eu* und *ou*, wechselt nicht eben häufig mit *ou* oder *ō*.
Man muss sich durch das Nebeneinander von ableitendem *-auno-*
und *-ouno-* nicht beirren lassen, da hier von vornherein ver-
schiedene Vokale vorliegen, z. B. *Vellaunus* neben *Vellavi*, aber
Mogounus neben *Mogovius, Carassounus* neben *Carasova*. Allein
es giebt doch einige Fälle. Neben *Alaunus, Ἄλαυνος,* sacro
Alaunarum stehen *Alounae, Alonae,* Holder, Sprsch. I, 107; neben
Causo Couso; neben *Caunus,* vgl. *Andecavi,* liegt *Counus;* neben
Lausus Lausonna : Lousius Lousonna. Mit *Nemausus* 'Nîmes'
möchte man gern das *Νεμωσσός* der Arverner, das spätere
Augustonemetum, jetzige Clermont-Ferrand, identifizieren. In
einem Fall scheint *au* zu *ū* geworden zu sein. An einer oft an-
gezogenen Stelle (Tib. 3) berichtet Sueton: *Drusus* hostium duce
Drauso comminus trucidato sibi posterisque suis cognomen in-
venit. Die gallischen Namen *Drausius Drauso* sind aus später
Zeit belegt, ziemlich früh erscheint in England der Name *Con-
draussius.* Zu diesem verhält sich äusserlich wie *Drūsus* zu
Draussus der Name der *Condrusi*[1]), eines Volkes der Gallia
Belgica (pagus *Condrustis*). Bei *Drusus* kann man vermuten,
dass es sein *ū* durch spezifisch lateinischen Lautwandel aus
älterem *ou* (Lautsubstitution für das vom lateinischen *au* irgendwie verschiedene gallische *au?*) bekommen hat. *Drŭsilla* wäre
zu *Drūsus* nach der Analogie von *pŭsillus : pūsus* gebildet worden.
Aber bei *Condrusi* versagt dieses Auskunftsmittel. Nun wissen
wir ja von dem Dialekte der *Condrusi* nichts. Es ist daher
sehr gut möglich, dass bei ihnen *au* überhaupt zu *ū* geworden
ist, und es wäre verfehlt, die vielen Beispiele des erhaltenen *au*
aus anderen Mundarten gegen diese Annahme ins Feld zu führen.
Übrigens heisst das Gebiet der *Condrusi* heute *Pays de Condroz.*
Das *o* giebt zu denken, sollte am Ende der Name mit *ŭ* anzusetzen sein? Es wäre sehr zu wünschen, dass ein Romanist
und speziell ein Kenner des Wallonischen, sich einmal zu dieser
Frage äusserte. Es bleibt *Uxellodunum, Uxama, Οὐξισάμη.* Das

---

[1]) *Condrusi* ist ein gutes Beispiel für eine ganze Kategorie von Völker-
namen, auf die jüngst erst Hirt aufmerksam gemacht hat. Es bedeutet
'*Condrusus* und Sippe'. Derartige Stammesnamen können also für ethnische
Zusammengehörigkeit nichts beweisen. Wie unhaltbar überhaupt alle Schlüsse
aus blosser Namenübereinstimmung sind, darauf hat kürzlich mit Recht
Brückner (Archiv f. slav. Phil. XXII, 238) hingewiesen und an evidenten
slavischen Beispielen erörtert.

u ist hier ganz fest, wenn wir von dem nicht über alle Zweifel erhabenen *Auxuma* des Florus absehen. *Uxama Argaela*, die Stadt der Aravaci (Plinius 3, 3, 27) ist inschriftlich eben mit *u* belegt CIL. II, 696. 2731. 2732. 2733. 2815. 2907. 3036, heute *Osma*. Ein zweites Οὐξάμα mit dem Zunamen Βάρκα (*Osma* zwischen Miranda und Orduña in Vizcaya) erwähnt Ptolemaeus 2, 6, 52. Aus England sind inschriftlich bezeugt *Uxel(l)odunum* CIL. VI, 1291 und *Uxopilli* 1222. Angesichts dieses Thatbestandes wird man Bedenken tragen, für *Uxello- Uxama* u. s. w. alten Diphthong, sei es nun *au* oder *ou*, anzusetzen. Auf *ūx-*, nicht *ax-*, deutet ferner das *o* von *Osma*; das franz. *Issoudun* = *Uxellodunum* widerspricht meines Wissens nicht. Man wird also gut thun, in *Uxello- Uxama* die Ablautsform zu italisch *Auximum*, altir. *uasal*, kymr. *uchel* zu erblicken, wie das Brugmann, Grdr. I², 200 will.

So viel ist jedenfalls klar, dass *au* im Keltischen, wie das Namenmaterial der älteren Zeit beweist, sich zwar auch auf dem Wege zum Monophthong befindet, aber hinter *eu ou* einige Etappen zurück ist. Sollte nun im weiteren Verlauf ein Stillstand oder gar eine Rückbildung erfolgt sein? Foy meint, der Diphthong *au* sei auch im Inselkelt. bis auf den heutigen Tag nicht mit *eu ou* zusammengefallen. Er lässt ihn im Irischen durch *au ó*, im Kymr. durch *au* vertreten sein, ganz wie das *au* lateinischer Lehnwörter und wie *āu*, über das er selbst in der Festschrift für Wh. Stokes 26 ff. Klarheit geschafft hat. Sein Material ist etwas dürftig, es besteht nur aus zwei Erbwörtern: mir. *au ó* 'Ohr' und mir. *tó*, kymr. *tawel* 'schweigend' (S. 268), und diesen verleiht der frühzeitige Schwund des intervokalischen *s* eine Sonderstellung. Dass *s* zu Bedas Zeit sich bereits verflüchtigt hatte, lehrt, wie bekannt, der Name des Trent, *Treanta* hist. eccl. III, 24. IV, 21 gegenüber Τρισάντωνος bei Ptol. (Pedersen, Aspir. 177). In noch weit frühere Zeit wird der Schwund gerückt durch den bretonischen Namen *Catihernus* (Loth, Chrestomathie 49). Zwischen dem Schwund des *s* und der Aufnahme von lat. Wörtern wie ir. *ór*, kymr. *aur* kann daher geraume Zeit verstrichen sein, in der sich ursprüngliches *au* so stark verändert hatte, dass es mit lat. *au* nicht mehr zusammenfallen konnte. Übrigens können *au ó* (in Komposition *u*, vgl. *unasca* 'Ohrringe' und KZ. XXVIII, 292 f.) und *tó tawel* nicht beweisen, dass *au* bis zum Schwunde des *s* völlig intakt war.

Hier kann wirklich eine Art Rückbildung vorliegen; man vergegenwärtige sich auch die Formen, die *ovi-* 'Schaf' zeigt:
au-gaire 'pastor' neben *u-gaire*, mir. *áe-gaire*.

Glücklicherweise giebt es nun ein Wort, an dem wir die
moderne kymrische Vertretung von altem *au* kennen lernen.
Alaunos Alauna ist ein mehrfach auf britannischem Boden be-
zeugter Flussname (vgl. Holder I, 76. 77). Das Kymrische hat
dafür *Alun*, schon das Buch von Llan Dâv (hgg. von Rhys und
Evans) erwähnt S. 182 ein *aper nant Alun*, 77 ein *penn Alun*.
Alun beweist, dass *au* schliesslich wirklich mit den übrigen
u-Diphthongen zusammengefallen ist. Wir haben also nicht
nötig, in altir. *uasal*, k. *uchel* aller Wahrscheinlichkeit zum
Trotz altes *ou* anzusetzen, wir dürfen ruhig mir. *guaire* mit
γαῦϱος, *cuaille* mit ϰαυλός identifizieren, in air. *lóg, óg* (ὑγιής
augeo), *uathad*[1]) ursprüngliches *au* suchen. *au* (*ѳu*) darf vielleicht
auch für kymr. *huddygl* 'Russ' vorausgesetzt werden; *huddygl*
(*ѳud-*) verhielt sich zu lit. *sū́dis*, abg. *sažda*, aisl. ae. *sót* 'Russ'
(*sāud-*), wie lat. *aureae, austium* zu *ōs*, lit. *ûstà* 'Mündung'.

Sämtliche *u*-Diphthonge sind im Kymr. mit dem geschlossenen
ō der älteren Schicht lateinischer Lehnwörter zusammengefallen,
tud uchel wie *Rhufeinydd* = *Rōmanus*, *ffurf* = *fōrma*, *llafur*
= *labōrem*, *Custennhinn* (Llan Dâv) = *Cōstantinus*. Später auf-
genommene lat. Wörter zeigen eine andere Behandlung: *hōra*
: *awr*, *nŏna* : *nawn* (Foy S. 267). *aw* ist eigentlich die Fortsetzung von offenem *ō* einheimischer (*mawr*, inschr. *Anatemori*)
und entlehnter Wörter (z. B. *cawg* = lat. *caucus*).

Zum Schluss sei noch darauf hingewiesen, dass ein Wort,
von dem man a priori sicheren Aufschluss über das Schicksal
von *au* erwarten dürfte, enttäuscht. Ich meine *Vellaunus*. Das
Buch von Llan Dâv liefert folgende Beispiele des Wortes: *Cat-
guallaun, Din-, Dun, Diuunguallaun, Idguallaun, Riuguallaun,
Liguallaun*. Später haben wir die Formen *Caswallawn, Cas-
wallon*. *au aw o* ist die reguläre Reihe der Entwicklungsformen
eines alten *ā* in unbetonter Silbe. Für das Kymr. ist also von
*Ve(a)llānos auszugehen. Es handelt sich wohl um Suffix-
vertauschung.

---

[1]) Oder wegen *hóthad* des Sanktgaller etwa **(p)ava-*?

Berlin, Friedenau.   E. ZUPITZA.

IRISCH *DUINE* 'MENSCH'.

Dieses Wort mit seinem durch die Lautung der ersten Silbe auffälligen Plural *dóini* und den Ableitungen *dóinecht dóinacht* 'humanitas', *dóinde* 'humanus' und die britannischen Entsprechungen kymr. *dyn* (Plur. *dyneðon*) korn. *den* 'Mensch' sind etymologisch noch nicht hinlänglich aufgeklärt. Aus **dunjos*, das Stokes im Urkeltischen Sprachschatz S. 154 als urkeltische Form ansetzt, sind zwar der irische Singular und die britannischen Formen herzuleiten, nicht aber ir. *dóini*. Stokes' Bemerkung, der Diphthong *ói* sei aus vortonigem *u* vor *i* regelrecht entstanden, ist mit den Thatsachen der Lautgeschichte nicht im Einklang. Vielmehr wird man nach *bó n-* Gen. Plur. 'boum', *nói n-* 'novem' u. dgl. (Verfasser Grundr. 1², S. 327) für den Plural einen Stamm wie **doṷonio- *deṷonio-* oder **doṷenio- *deṷenio-* vorauszusetzen haben (*oṷ* kann ursprüngliches *oṷ* gewesen oder aus *eṷ* hervorgegangen sein).

Stokes knüpft unser Wort an griech. ϑνητός 'sterblich', ϑάνατος 'Tod' an, die weiterhin zu ai. *dhvan-* 'sich verhüllen, sich verdunkeln', auch 'erlöschen, schwinden' (vom Zorn, RV. 8, 6, 13), Aor. *ádhvanīt*, Part. *dhvāntá-*, gehören sollen. Dass im letzten Grunde diese Wörter mit dem keltischen Wort wurzelverwandt sind, will ich nicht in Abrede stellen.[1]) Aber zunächst

---

[1]) Gegen die Zusammenstellung des griechischen Wortes mit dem indischen haben mehrere Linguisten Bedenken geäussert, weil die Formen ϑνᾱτός (ϑνητός) und τέϑνᾰμεν auf eine Wurzel ohne ṷ hinwiesen. Aber man denke an ion. delph. τετρώ-κοντα, das sich zu lat. *quadrā-gintā* wie στρωτός zu lat. *strātus* verhält und, zunächst in urgriechischer Zeit aus **τετϝρω-* abgeändert, eine idg. Grundform mit sogenannter langer Liquida sonans,

haben wir uns, wie mir scheint, nicht an jene östlichen Sprachen, sondern ans Germanische zu wenden, um Aufschluss über die keltischen Formen zu bekommen. Auf ursprüngliches *dheųonio- zurückgeführt, deckt sich nämlich dóini, wenn man von der Erweiterung durch Suffix -ịo- absieht, vollkommen mit got. diwans 'sterblich': belegt ist þata diwanō τὸ θνητόν nebst undiwanamma guþa ἀφθάρτῳ θεῷ, undiwanein ἀθανασίαν. Sollte indessen *dheųenio- die Grundform von dóini gewesen sein, so verschlägt das wenig. Denn diwans ist als Partizip zu einem Verbum *diwan, Perf. *dau *dēwum, anzusehen (Braune, Got. Gramm.⁴ § 176, Anm. 2, Streitberg, Got. Elementarb. § 208), und da bei diesen Verbalnomina zu starken Verba die Ausgänge -ono- und -eno- seit urgermanischer Zeit vielfach nebeneinander erscheinen (vgl. z. B. got. fulhans und fulgins, got. baúrans und aisl. borinn), so kann es neben *dewonas auch *dewenas gegeben haben.

Zu diwans gesellen sich im Germanischen unzweifelhaft got. dauþs 'tot', dauþus 'Tod', ahd. touwen as. dōian aisl. deyja 'sterben', wahrscheinlich auch got. af-dauiþs 'erschöpft, abgehetzt' aus *-dōwiþs, welches vom aksl. daviti 'würgen, sticken' nicht getrennt werden kann. Was weiterhin noch aus andern Sprachzweigen als urverwandt anzuschliessen ist (eventuell, wie wir oben sahen, ai. dhvan- und gr. θνῄσκω), lasse ich dahin gestellt. Die Ansichten der Etymologen gehen hier weit auseinander, wie man z. B. aus Uhlenbeck, Kurzgefasst. etym. Wörterb. der got. Sprache S. 32 und v. Grienberger, Untersuchungen zur got. Wortkunde S. 58 ersieht,[1]) und ich habe für jetzt nicht die Absicht, um unser keltisches Wort seine ganze indogermanische Verwandtschaft zu versammeln. Nur das sei bemerkt, dass — worauf mich Dr. F. Sommer aufmerksam macht — ein besonders naher Verwandter von duine dóini und dawins

---

*qᵘetu̥r̄-, voraussetzt (Verfasser Griech. Gramm.³ S. 42. 88. 214 f.). θνατός darf also lautgeschichtlich auf *θνᾱτός = uridg. *dhuₙtó-s zurückgeführt werden: es stünde mit *θάνατος = *θϝάνατος dem ai. dhvāntá-s ebenso gegenüber wie z. B. χμᾱτός (χμητός) = uridg. *km̥tó-s mit χάματος dem ai. s̓āntd-s. τέθνᾰμεν wie τέτρᾰτος aus *τετϝρατος = lit. ketvir̃tas, falls dieser Plural des Perfekts nicht erst in relativ junger Zeit nach dem Verhältnis von ἑστάμεν zu ἕστηκα neben den Singular τίθνηκα gestellt worden ist.

[1]) Wohl nur ein Versehen ist es, wenn Kretschmer, Einleitung in die griech. Sprache S. 221 Fussn. 2 got. af-dauiþs mit ai. dunṓ-ti, gr. ὀύη zusammenbringt.

vielleicht im lat. Neutrum *fūnus* 'Tod, Leiche, Leichenbestattung'
vorliegt, wozu *fūnes-tu-s* und *fūnebris* = **fūnes-ri-*. *fūnus* kann
ursprüngliches **dhūnes-* gewesen sein oder **dheunes-*, **dhounes-*
oder auch **dheu̯enes- *dheu̯ones-*, beziehentlich **dhou̯enes- *dhou̯-
ones-*. War die Stammform von Haus aus dreisilbig, so fiel
zunächst der unbetonte Vokal der zweiten Silbe weg, und *ou̯*
wurde *ū*. Als *s*-Erweiterung eines ursprünglichen *no*-Stamms
vergleicht sich *fūnus* mit *facinus, mūnus, volnus, pignus*.

Unter der Voraussetzung, dass der Singular *duine* mittels
-i̯o- aus einem Nominalstamm **dhuno-* oder **dhunā-* erweitert
war, lässt sich das zwischen ihm und *dóini* bestehende Ablaut-
verhältnis mit ai. *-puna-s* 'reinigend' : *pávana-s* 'Wind', *bhinná-s*
'gespalten' : *bhēdana-s* 'spaltend', as. *logna* 'Lohe, Flamme', aisl.
logn 'Meeres- und Windesstille' ('helles Wetter') : ai. *rōcaná-s*
'licht, hell' und ähnlichem vergleichen. Möglicherweise war
aber *duine* von einem konsonantisch schliessenden Stamm ausgegangen: vgl. etwa aksl. Gen. *din-e* 'des Tages' zum Nomin.
dĭnĭ (neben ai. *dína-m*, lat. *nūn-dinae*, ahd. *lengi-zin* = urgerm.
*-tini-, lit. *dënà* u. s. w.).

Das Nebeneinander des got. *diwans* und des durch *-i̯o-* er-
weiterten *dóini* erinnert an das Nebeneinander von ai. *márta-s*
'Sterblicher, Mensch', armen. *mard* 'Mensch' (Grundform **mr̥to-s*),
gr. μορτός· ἄνθρωπος Hesych, βροτός 'Sterblicher, Mensch' und
ai. *mártya-s* 'sterblich, Sterblicher, Mensch', apers. *martiya-*
'Mensch', und es ist leicht möglich, dass zwischen den germanisch-
keltischen und jenen ostindogermanischen Formen ein unmittel-
barer historischer Zusammenhang war, indem die letzteren
Formen aus uridg. Zeit stammten und bei der Gestaltung der
ersteren vorbildlich mitwirkten, um ihnen später das Feld zu
räumen.

Schliesslich bleibt noch zu erklären, dass im Irischen die
beiden in dieser Sprache gebrauchten Nominalbildungen auf
Singular und Plural verteilt erscheinen. Warum tritt das Wort
duine nicht auch im Plural und das Wort *dóini* nicht auch im
Singular auf? Um diesen Fall von Suppletivismus sicher beurteilen zu können, müsste man wissen, was vorläufig im Un-
klaren bleibt, von was für einem Wort *duine* mittels *-i̯o-* abgeleitet war. So müssen wir uns mit der Vermutung begnügen,
dass der Grund der in Rede stehenden Erscheinung der war,
dass *duine* einmal Kollektivbedeutung hatte; als Kollektivum

könnte es einstmals Neutrum gewesen sein. Das ai. *jána-* bedeutete 'Volk' und 'Mensch', und Delbrück, Grundr. 3, 155 nimmt wohl mit Recht an, dass die Bedeutung der Masse die ursprünglichere war, und dass sich ein Plural zu dem Wort erst einstellte, nachdem es auch zu der Bedeutung eines Einzelwesens gelangt war. Ähnlich steht es mit dem altgermanischen Wort ahd. *liut* u. s. w. (got. *jugga-lauþs*), das ebenfalls die Bedeutungen 'Menschenmasse' und 'einzelner Mensch' vereinigte. So mag also auch *duine* einstens beide Bedeutungen gehabt haben. Den kollektiven Sinn gab es im Irischen wie im Britannischen auf, und das den Sinn 'die einzelnen Menschen' ausdrückende *dóini* erhielt sich von jener Zeit her, als das Wort *duine* noch, und zwar entweder ausschliesslich oder zugleich, Kollektivum war. Ging *duine* ursprünglich nur auf die Masse, so bezeichnete natürlich auch seine Pluralform ursprünglich nur die Massen. *dóini* war dann eine notwendige Ergänzung zu ihm, wenn die einzelnen Menschen gemeint waren. Aber auch in einer Zeit, wo der Singular Masse und Einzelwesen zugleich bedeutete, der Plural also ebenfalls doppeldeutig war (gleichwie ai. *jána-* im Plural nicht nur 'die Menschen, die Leute', sondern auch 'die Stämme' ist), konnte *dóini* sich leicht als der eindeutige Ausdruck für die Einzelwesen festsetzen und als solcher bleiben, auch nachdem der Singular *duine* sich auf den Sinn der Einzelperson eingeschränkt hatte.

Leipzig.   KARL BRUGMANN.

ERSCHIENENE SCHRIFTEN.

Chr. Sarauw, Irske Studier. København, det Schuboteske Forlag 1900. 144 pp. 8⁰.

Of recent years much has been done towards clearing up the obscurities of the Irish verb, and the present work is not the least important contribution to the subject. The first twenty pages, indeed, deal with Latin loan-words in Irish, and contain acute observations on the Irish representation of some Latin sounds. But the bulk of the book treats of problems connected with the Irish verb, and in particular with *ro*-less forms and *ro*-forms, and their equivalents, which, in the terminology of Slavonic Grammar are designated as imperfective and perfective forms respectively. The writer does not define the relation of his book to the articles on the same subject by Zimmer and Thurneysen. Dr. Pedersen, however, informs me that the MS. was in his hands before the publication of Zimmer's paper. The substantial agreement between Sarauw and Thurneysen is a strong confirmation of the correctness of their theory. This portion of the work is divided as follows.

I. Perfective forms (pp. 25—49).

In the opening section the Irish tenses are enumerated, and attention is called to two peculiarities: the use of certain perfects in a present sense (but *etirgein* Ml. 24 a 19, cf. *etirgin* 102 a 22, is hardly perfect in form, and there is some difference in meaning between *rofinnadar* 'finds out' and *rofitir* 'knows'), and the difference between *bíu* and *attáu*, which I had already illustrated Trans. Phil. Soc. 1899—1901, p. 53. Then follows a discussion of the force of *ro*- in the indicative and subjunctive:

it makes the form to which it is attached perfective. With regard to the use of *ro-* in the present and future indicative and in the secondary future the writer is in most points in agreement with Thurneysen. That with the imperfect it denotes 'praeteritum consuetudinale perfectum' I doubt; in the example quoted is not *rubith* the perfect passive of *benim*? in LU. 83 b 26 *ro-* is found with the imperfect indicative, but there it clearly denotes '*posse*'. With the future *ro-* is said further to make a 'futurum exactum'. But in the example quoted the syntax demands not an indicative but a subjunctive; the form *-roima* has been repeatedly discussed. In the secondary future it is suggested that *ro-* may denote a 'futurum in praeterito perfecto', but in the single instance quoted it is much more likely that *ro-* is a scribal error for *no-*. The use of *ro-* with the preterite of the indicative is reserved for a later section. The subjunctive is somewhat superficially treated; the only thing that can be called new is that, like Thurneysen, Sarauw has seen that in the subjunctive too *ro-* may denote '*posse*'.

In the following section it is pointed out that some other prepositions may make a verb perfective. To *com-*, *ad-*, and *ess-*, with respect to which the writer is in agreement with Thurneysen, is here added *ar-* in *tesarbae*. Of *tesarbae* another explanation has been suggested, Trans. Phil. Soc. 1895—6, p. 180, and this still seems to me more probable. Then follows a list of 'neutral verbs', which do not admit of the addition of a perfective particle. With regard to verbs compounded with *ro-*, *remiriérchoil* is only so far corrupt that, with Thurneysen, we should read *remirérchoil*; *diandrerchoil* Ml. 46 c 7, *ní ruderchoin* Ml. 44 a 1 (quoted Trans. Phil. Soc. 1895—6, pp. 122, 123) have apparently escaped the writer's notice.

II. Prepositions and roots (pp. 53—88).

In the opening section of this chapter reference is first made to verbal systems consisting of more than one root. Then follows a discussion of peculiarities of *rofetar*, *rocluiniur*, *rolamur* and of the substantive verb, which I had already treated, Trans. Phil. Soc. 1895—6, p. 149, and 1899—1901, pp. 17, 61. After this come some very interesting remarks on certain orthotonic forms of verbs, and particularly of orthotonic forms resulting from wrong analysis of the enclitic forms: *dofuairc* to *to-orc-*, *-tuarc-* etc. But *dorothuus* is wrongly changed to *dorothudus*; the verb has only a sigmatic subjunctive. And might not *-*di-ro-cma* be expected to give *-*derema*? Cf. Thurneysen, KZ. XXXVII, 111, note.

In the next section there is an important discussion of certain variations of prepositions in compound verbs. The following table, which I have constructed for myself, may help to make this clearer.

Enclitic forms.	Orthotonic forms.	Non-relative forms with infixed pron. -t(n)-.[1]	Relative forms with infixed -id(n)-.
(1) -essib	assibsem	atib	
eilled	asrulensat	atlentais	
(1 a) epert	asrubart	atbeir	asidrubart
ecne	asgensu	atgéoin [2]	

These are more compounds of this kind, but the above will suffice for illustration. Different in the enclitic form is

-éicdid	adcúaid	atchúaid	assidchói
(Wb. 24 c 17)			(LL. 211 a 37)
(2) aicsiu	adcí	atchí	assidciam
airilliud	adroilliset	atroilli	assidroilliset
(3) aithgne	adgeúin	atgeóin [2]	adidgeúin
idbart	adrobart	atropart	adidnopair.

Thurneysen long ago remarked on some of these variations, Rev. Celt. VI, 136, 144. In Idg. IX, 191 he has made the very important, and to me convincing, suggestion that e. g. *epert* contains as its first element not *aith-* but *ed-*, a form developed out of *eks-* under certain phonetic conditions. This Sarauw rejects, apparently because this preposition with *c* gives in Mod. Ir. *g*, while *dc* gives Mod. Ir. *c*; but surely it cannot be assumed that *đc* (where the first letter is a spirant), and *dc* (where the first letter is an explosive) necessarily developed in the same way. In both (1 a) and (3) Sarauw thinks that the preposition is *aith-* and supposes that after '*frith, frit-*' *friss-*' '*aith- at-*', *ad-*' became '*aith- at-*' *ass-*'. But why is it that when

---

[1]) Cf. Thurneysen, Idg. Anz. IX, 192, who also points out that to *cot(n)-* the relative form is *conid(n)-*. The same holds of *frit(n)-* and *frissid(n)-*, *fort(n)-* and *forid(n)-*.

[2]) This form might belong to either compound.

the verbal noun clearly contains *aith-* we find *ad-*, *adid(n)-*,
otherwise *as-*, *assid(n)-*? Apart from phonetic difficulties (the
change of *aith-c-* to *ec-* etc.), Sarauw's theory will not explain
the distribution of the forms. It is true that in Sg. 197 b 16
we have *adrubartmar*, but that is a beginning of the later confusion, whereby the *as*-forms were gradually eliminated, and in
the enclitic forms *-epir* etc. became *-apir* etc. (So already
dianaiperr Ml. 14 d 13, *conaipred* Ml. 33 c 17, *aipert* 50 b 8.)
Sarauw has cleared away the difficulty of some verbs that
formerly were supposed to be compounded with *aith-* by pointing
out that the preposition is not *aith-* but *en-*; thus *doécai* is
rightly referred to *di-en-ces-*. (In the same way *-éicdid* to *adcuaid* can hardly be explained except from *-en-cūad-*, cf. *incuaid*
Ml. 123 d 7, *infé* Ml. 30 b 12, *infét* Ml. 14 b 12.) This leads up
to the observation of another curious variation of prepositions;
here the verbal noun is rightly taken as most surely indicating
the real compound.

esnaisse	(= *en-sn-*)	*insnadat*	*atomsnassar*	
intamil		*insamlathar*	*atasamlibid*	
insorchugud			*atobsorchaither*	
inchosc	(*écosc*)		*atcoisced*	
		in-sag-	*atobsegat*	
indarpe			*ataarban*	
ingreimm			*atamgrennat*	*asidgreinn*
ingabál			*atabgabed*	

Of this curious variation no explanation is suggested; its paralle-
lism with the former series (p. 003) is very striking. Did this
variation start from verbs beginning with *s* + consonant, where
eks + *s* + cons. and *en* + *s* + cons. would alike have given *ĕs*
+ cons.?[1]) It is clear that, where the preposition bears the accent
en- is the earlier form in composition, *ind-* the later. That this
variation should be disturbed by analogy is not to be wondered
at; thus by *ingreinn* we find *adgreinn*, by *insnadat adsnadi*, and,
conversely, by *eclim inglennat*. In this section, as we have said,
it is laid down as an axiom that the existence of a verb as a
real and independent word is best established by its nominal

---

[1]) The development in *esnaisse* etc. is like that in *cosmail* etc., cf.
Brugmann, Grundriss[2] § 418, note 3.

forms. The following section deals with such nominal forms. It is pointed out that, with few exceptions, the verbal noun goes in the same form through all compounds of a root. The principle is used in the analysis of a number of compound verbs.

III. The system *techt* and the imperfect preterite (pp. 91 —126).

This chapter treats of verbs in which the imperfective and the perfective forms come from different roots. Incidentally it contains a discussion of the syntactic uses of the imperfective and the perfective preterite. The various roots of which the verb *techt* is made up are considered at length (pp. 91—116).

Attention should be called to the happy explanation of the puzzling forms *táit* etc. p. 115. On p. 95 there are some interesting remarks on the relative forms. It is pointed out that in *téit, fil,* verbs from which there is no 3. pl., the relative forms are *téte* and *file*. From this it seems to be inferred that the relative form in the singular was originally *e* (in support of this might have been added the fact that the relative form of *birt* is *berte*). Then *beres : berte* is explained as due to the analogy of *as, *esti : ata, *senti.* The forms *as, ata* themselves are not further explained. The analogy might have operated when the copula forms were still **es, *ete* or the like. As we have said, the syntactic uses of the imperfective and perfective preterites, so far as they can be discovered from the Old Irish Glosses etc., are discussed pp. 100—112. The Saga literature, in which Zimmer made his discovery, is completely neglected. That the use of it is not free from risk cannot be denied, but it is obvious that such syntactical functions can be best studied in continuous prose. However, as I propose to deal with that elsewhere,[1] I will not discuss it here. It may be noted that on p. 109 it is pointed out in passing by that *siassair* is the imperfective preterite to *doessid*. The following sections deal with other verbs in which the system is made up of different roots: *breth,* perfective *ro-uc-; tabart* 'dare', perf. *torat-; tabart* 'afferre', perf. *to-uc-; cor,* perf. *rolā-; focerd-,* perf. *rolā-;* finally *roír* is briefly noticed. On pp. 119—122 there is an interesting discussion of *to-uc-* 'intelligere', which is very ingeniously derived from *to-uc-* 'afferre'.

---

[1] The paper has now appeared, Trans. Phil. Soc. 1900.

In the conclusion the claim of Irish to a place of honour among the languages that distinguish imperfective and perfective action (de perfektiverende sprog) is strongly asserted.

A few isolated points may be noted. On p. 29 *-rocmi* should, with Thurneysen, be corrected to *-rocmiad.* On p. 33 *ruguigter* is passive, not deponent. On p. 78 *dígal* etc. are derived from *fich-.* But the W. *dial* makes this impossible. Rather we have compounds of *gal,* which have become attached to the system of *fech-.* On the same page *-toirsitis* should be emended to *-toissitis.* On p. 95 *rosoich* is treated apparently as an orthographical variant of *rosaig,* but I do not know of e. g. *-oig* as a variant of *-aig* 'drives'. The old explanation here will, I think, be found to be the right one. On p. 87 there is a fine explanation of *don* in *dofarlaic don* etc. On p. 107 the explanation of *-torbanad* is improbable; at least such a modal use in the imperfect is unknown to me.

Finally, on pp. 136—139 are printed some emendations and explanations of Irish Glosses. Of these a great proportion are excellent, and others are deserving of consideration. Others, however, are either certainly wrong or open to grave doubt. Thus Wb. 3 b 28, would not the translation require *bed noibde*? Wb. 8 d 28 should be *cenmánom* accepisti. Wb. 27 d 13 should be *cedacht etarrobe scribent doiib.* Wb. 31 d 5, *da* is right, *ba* gives no satisfactory sense. Ml. 42 c 24, there is no reason for an Irish subjunctive. Ml. 105 c 11, there is no reason for an imperfect here; leg. with Ascoli, *dodiurgatha*? Fiacc's Hymn l. 11, but cf. Thurneysen, Rev. Celt. VI, 332. One is astonished to find here some thirty emendations or explanations which have been published before, for the most part in periodicals with which every Celtist might be supposed to be familiar.

It is impossible to conclude this notice without calling attention to the author's peculiar method of citation, or rather of non-citation, for there is hardly any reference to his predecessors. To such as have followed the course of Irish philology this matters little, but to others it might easily convey the impression that the book is more original than it really is. This is an unfortunate blemish on what is otherwise a most excellent and stimulating book.

Prestwich, near Manchester.   J. STRACHAN.

J. Rhŷs, Celtic Folklore, Welsh and Manx. Oxford at the
Clarendon Press 1901. 2 voll. XLVI + 718 pp. 8°.

Mit dem 1846 von Ambrose Merton gefundenen Worte
folklore wird ein grosses Gebiet bezeichnet, das nicht nur Sitte
und Aberglauben, sondern auch Hausmärchen und Landessagen
umfasst, als eine vergleichende Wissenschaft aber sich fast bis
ins Grenzenlose erweitert. Die celtische Volkskunde muss als
eine der reichhaltigsten und anziehendsten gelten. Das neue
Buch von J. Rhŷs behandelt ausgewählte Stücke daraus, vielfach
nach eigenen Beobachtungen in Wales und auf der Insel Man.
Ein grosser Teil des Werkes besteht aus Aufsätzen, die vor
langen Jahren im 4., 5. und 6. Bande der Zeitschrift Y Cymmrodor erschienen sind; dazu treten Erörterungen über die ver-
schiedensten Gegenstände aus dem Bereiche der celtischen
Mythenwelt, von denen manche schon in des Verfassers Celtic
Heathendom 1888, in The Arthurian Legend 1891 und in The
Welsh People 1900 besprochen sind.

Da haben wir das schon von Gualterus Mapes in der
zweiten Hälfte des 12. Jahrhunderts mitgeteilte Märchen von
der Fee, die nicht mit Eisen berührt werden darf, in einer
ganzen Reihe welscher Fassungen, die damit zum Teil jenes von
den drei unbeabsichtigten Schlägen verknüpfen; die Geschichte
des Eliodorus aus Giraldus; die des Riesen Rhito aus Galfridus
Monumetensis; die Jagd auf den Twrch Trwyth in den Mabinogion; den Afanc und die gigantischen Ochsen; die elbischen
Hasen und Hunde. Wir hören ferner von den haarkämmenden
Feeen, die die Sterblichen anlocken oder Kinder stehlen; von
den Elfen, die die Hebamme holen oder Wechselbälge unter-
schieben; von andern, die für kleine Dienste Geld auf dem
Herde niederlegen oder für eine angethane Beleidigung Rache
nehmen; von den Metten (*gwawn*), den Eidechsen, der auf-
gehängten Wäsche, den Eierschalen, in denen man Bier braut,
dem Schatz in der Höhle und auf der Brücke, dem öffnenden
und dem schliessenden Zauberwort, den drei Ratschlägen und
anderm mehr aus der Fülle der indogermanischen Märchen;
namentlich finden wir noch eine Dämonologie der Insel Man.
Auch weniger Mythisches ist eingestreut, wie die Erklärung des

caws pob 'toasted cheese', was heute Welsh rabbit oder unrichtig
rarebit heisst, und die Beobachtung, dass den Fuss des Walisers
vor dem des Engländers der hohe Spann auszeichne. Die
methodische Darstellung des mannigfaltigen Stoffes hat der Verfasser nicht versucht, wiewohl er ihn auf zwölf Kapitel verteilt,
und so ist man für den Index dankbar, der uns zurecht weisen
muss, denn das Gedächtnis nimmt die bunte Reihenfolge nicht auf.

Schätzbar bleiben die aus Y Cymmrodor wieder abgedruckten Elfenmärchen, weil es dergleichen in welscher Sprache
nicht allzuviel giebt. Crofton Croker, der 1825 zuerst mit einer
hübschen Sammlung irischer Märchen in englischem Gewande
hervortrat, hat in den andern Ländern celtischer Zunge die
erfreulichste Nachfolge gehabt, vor allem J. F. Campbell im
gälischen Schottland, F. M. Luzel in der Bretagne und zuletzt
Douglas Hyde und andere in Irland, wo man gleichfalls erkannte,
dass an der unbefangenen Überlieferung des Volksmundes alles
gelegen ist. Die Waliser haben solchen Leistungen, wenn man
von dem Büchlein Ystên Sioned des ausgezeichneten Silvan Evans
absieht, wenig an die Seite zu stellen. Eine verständige Mahnung,
die Th. Powell 1881 an die Landsleute richtete, scheint wirkungs-
los verhallt zu sein; nach Rhŷs, der nur noch 'bits of stories'
finden konnte, ist es für eine umfassendere Sammlung zu spät.
Was ihm aus einem ausgebreiteten Bekanntenkreise zugeflossen
ist, sucht der Verfasser nach den Gauen des kleinen Fürstentums
topographisch zu sondern. Das will heute nicht mehr viel bedeuten, wenn man das Ähnliche vergleicht. So ist es bei uns
noch in manches Erinnerung, wie W. Mannhardt 1865, auf die
Erforschung der ländlichen Bräuche bedacht, 'in zwölfter Stunde'
einen Aufruf in Deutschland, Österreich und die Schweiz ausgehen liess, der in unzählige Dörfer gedrungen ist und allent-
halben ein Echo geweckt hat. Seine in der Folge entstandene,
nach den Ursprungsörtern geordnete grosse und wertvolle
Sammlung ist uns ein $\varkappa\tau\tilde{\eta}\mu\alpha\ \dot{\varepsilon}\varsigma\ \dot{\alpha}\varepsilon\iota$. Am Anfange des 20. Jahrh.
ist dergleichen zu unternehmen freilich sehr schwierig; denn
das Elfenvolk hat einen Widerwillen gegen Eisenbahnen und
Zeitungen, die uralte Sitte verfällt mehr und mehr und der er-
erbte Aberglaube, wie tief er gewurzelt ist, welkt allmählich ab.

Ist schon die Aufbringung des Stoffes nicht leicht, so
scheinen bei seiner Bearbeitung ausgedehnte Belesenheit und
strenge Methode ganz unentbehrlich. Die Waliser sind früh von

dem geistigen Leben fremder Volksstämme berührt worden und
haben von den gälischen sowohl als von den sächsischen Nachbarn
angenommen, so dass es in manchem Falle der gründlichsten
Untersuchung bedarf um festzustellen, was einem jedem gehört.
So findet sich z. B. das Märchen von der Hebamme auch bei
den Iren (Jer. Curtin, Tales of the Fairies 1895, p. 42); das Bier-
brauen in den Eierschalen erzählt man nicht nur in Irland,
sondern auch in den schottischen Hochlanden (Y Cymmrodor 7, 39)
und die Brüder Grimm[1]) brachten sogleich zu Crofton Croker
überraschend Ähnliches aus noch viel fremdern Gegenden herbei;
die Elfen sind 'unable to overcome iron', berichtet Al. Carmichael
2, 257 von den Hebriden, aber W. Mannhardt (Wald- und Feld-
kulte 1, 132) weist denselben Glauben aus den erstaunlichsten
Entfernungen nach. Namentlich werden auch nordische Gebilde
auf die celtischen von Einfluss gewesen sein. Doch dergleichen
Wahrnehmungen können erst in zweiter Reihe in Betracht
kommen und dürfen uns nicht ablenken, so lange wir nicht ein
näheres Ziel erreicht haben.

Zuvörderst ist es durchaus geboten, die mythologischen
Vorstellungen der celtischen Stämme in ihrem Zusammenhange
zu erfassen. Das dem walisischen folklore hier zugesellte
manannische ist dabei von minderer Bedeutung, es steht dem

---

[1]) Die Einleitung zu den 'Irischen Elfenmärchen' von den Brüdern
Grimm 1826 war für die Zeit, in der sie geschrieben wurde, höchst vortrefflich.
Man begegnet in biographischen Darstellungen der Behauptung, sie sei vor-
waltend Wilhelm Grimms Arbeit, dem auch der Löwenanteil an den 'Kinder-
und Hausmärchen' zuerkannt wird oder wenigstens so erhebliche Verbesserungen
der Fassung zugeschrieben werden, dass sein Verdienst an dem Werke als das
überwiegende erscheinen muss. Jacob Grimm schreibt am 19. Februar 1860
an Franz Pfeiffer über seinen Anteil an den Märchen, nach einer Bemerkung
über Prioritätsfragen, denen er keine Wichtigkeit beilege, mit bestimmten
Worten wie folgt: 'Mehr liegt mir an eine andere jetzt hin und wieder auf-
tauchende Meinung nicht aufkommen zu lassen, die dass die Märchen hauptsächlich von meinem Bruder, nicht von mir ausgegangen seien. Ich habe für
den Ursprung des Werks und die ersten Ausgaben gerade so viel als er,
vielleicht noch mehr gethan (es war längst mein Plan besondere Forschungen
über die Natur der Märchen bekannt zu machen) und den Wert dieser Über-
lieferungen gleich erkannt, lebhaft auf die Treue der Sammlung gehalten und
Verzierungen abgewehrt. Die spätern Auflagen, weil ich in Grammatik
versenkt war, liess ich Wilhelm redigieren und einleiten, ohne dass meine
Sorgfalt für Sammeln und Erklären je nachgelassen hätte. Wie sollte es auch
anders sein können?' (Germania 11, 249.)

irischen nahe und näher noch dem schottischgälischen. Der
Stoff zur celtischen Volkskunde ist sehr gross, ob wir ihn in den
Sagen vergangener Jahrhunderte oder in den Märchen des Land-
mannes oder in seinen altüberlieferten Gebräuchen suchen. Man
denke über Rhŷs' Buch hinaus (um nur einiges anzuführen) an
die *dusii* der Alten; die *draci* und *dracae* des Gervasius von
Tilbury; das ganze Volk des *des side* bei den Gälen; an die
baccdnaig, die *bánánaig*, die *geniti glindi*, die *demna aeoir* in der
grossen Táin; die drei Heilrätinnen oder weird sisters in der
Schlacht von Mag Lena; an den Elfstier *Dám dili* oder *dilenn*
in den irischen Triaden; den *Torcc Dromma leithe*; den *Ech usce*
oder den Wasserhengst, der mit der Tochter des Priesters von
Glenn Dalláin jenen Unhold mit Menschenkopf und einem blase-
balgartigen Leibe zeugte (YBL. 418a); an das Völkchen der
Luchra und Lupracán und die Alpluachra oder Earcluachra; den
schottisch-gälischen *Uruisg*; dann an die walisischen *ellyllon*, die
sich von giftigen Schwämmen nähren (*bwyd ellyllon*) und deren
Handschuhe die Blütenglocken des Fingerhuts bilden (*menyg
ellyllon*); den *Gwyllt*, der dem irischen *Geilt glinne* entspricht,
einem Berggeist, wie man sagt, aber nach Dafydd ab Gwilym
sitzt er bei stürmischem Wetter oben im Mastkorbe; — überall
spuken die Wahngestalten bei Gälen und Britanniern und rufen
lauter denn je nach einer Mythologia celtica.

Der Hauptname für die walisischen Elfen ist *y tylwyth teg*
'die schöne Familie'; *tylwyth* ist zusammengesetzt aus *ty* (ir. *tech*)
'Haus' und *llwyth* (ir. *slicht*) 'Geschlecht, Stamm'. Der Ausdruck
entspricht dem irischen *sluagh sidh*, dem englischen 'the good
people', das stille Volk, was irisch gelegentlich durch *na daoine
mátha* übertragen wird (G. J. 1, 206). Der Verf. giebt keine Erklärung der welschen Bezeichnung, aber man fragt doch: wessen
Familie? Die Elfen sind die Familie des Gwyn ab Nudd, ihres
Königs, und wohnen im Nebel, im Sumpf und in der Nacht.
Dafydd ab Gwilym nennt den Nebel *gwan dalar Gwyn a'i
dylwyth* 'das öde Grenzland Gwyns und seiner Familie' 54, 52;
oder auch (mit Emendation der Lesart in den Ausgaben)

> *tyrau, uchel eu helynt,*
> *tylwyth Gwyn, talaith y gwynt —*

'die hochragenden Türme der Familie Gwyns und die Krone des
Windes' 54, 39; *y tylwyth teg* heissen die Elfen 39, 40. Vom

Morast sagt derselbe Dichter, er sei Gwyns Fischteich und die Wohnung der Gespenster und ihrer Kinder:

Pysgodlyn i Wyn yw ef,
ab Nudd, a bu 'n ei oddef:
pydew rhwng gwaun a cheunant,
plas yr ellyllon a'u plant. 133, 23 ff.

Die Eule ist Gwyns Vogel, *edn Gwyn ab Nudd ydyw* 184, 40. So wird er endlich der Böse, der den Bösen holen möge: *Gwyn ab Nudd i'm dwyn* 123, 54; *wrth Gwyn esgar, lafar lef, y du leidr y del adref* 99, 71. Ursprünglich war Gwyn vielleicht ein Dämon des Winters, der an den Kalenden des Mais, *bob duw kalan mei* (RB. 1, 113. 134), einen Kampf zu bestehen hatte. Der Name entspricht zweifellos dem irischen Finn (Celtic Heathendom p. 179). Besteht eine Verwandtschaft des welschen *tylwyth Gwyn* mit dem irischen *teglach Fhinn*, das aus der ossianischen Poesie bekannt ist? Hat auch der Mythus von Finn in Beziehung zu den Jahreszeiten gestanden? Ich erinnere an jenes Wintergedicht des Finn *Fúit co bráth* im Buche von Leinster 208a und sonst (GGA. 1887, p. 184 f.; RC. 11, 130), an das Mailied in seinen Macgnimartha (RC. 5, 201) und an die mystische Erzählung von seiner Wiedergeburt (LU. 133a). Die Kalenden des Mais (*bealtaine*) und die Winterkalenden (*samhain*) bildeten auch im Leben der Fianna Zeitabschnitte (Keating, History transl. by O'Mahony p. 345). Unter den Vorfahren Finns war Nuadha Necht, wie Keating hervorhebt: *Biodh a fhios agad a léighthóir gurab é an Fionn so an ceathramhadh glún o Nuadha Neacht righ Laighean, Muirn Muinchaomh inghean Taidhg mic Nuadhadh draoi Chathoir móir fa máthair dhó,* etc. — so nach einer Handschrift des Forus feasa vom Jahre 1659, mit Übergehung des Cumhall mac Trénmor, den O'Mahony an der Stelle einfügt. Dass Finn, der Nachkomme des Nuadha, ursprünglich mehr ein Weiser als ein Kriegsheld war und dass sich Gwyn ab Nudd erst im spätern Mittelalter zum König der Elfen entwickelt hat, ist wohl nicht zu leugnen, und dass sich in Finn mac Cumhaill Mythologisches mit Geschichtlichem verbunden hat, wahrscheinlich.

Trotzdem kann nur von einer Möglichkeit die Rede sein, denn die Identifizierung gälischer und britannischer Personennamen erheischt grosse Vorsicht. Wenn sich dergleichen nicht widerlegen, aber auch nicht bündig beweisen lässt, so führt es

40*

die Untersuchung meist auf einen toten Strang. So ergeht es
uns mit Seithenhin in dem alten Gedichte im BBC. 53b, der
hier p. 385 als der irische Setanta Beg oder Cúchulainn gedeutet
wird. Liegt es nicht näher, an *saith* (ir. *secht*) 'sieben' und an
einen Namen wie Myrddin fab Saith gudyn D. G. 113, 7, oder
aber (denn es fehlen alle Beweise) an einen Namen auf *-antinus*
zu denken? Heisst March ab Meirchion oder Amheirchion
wirklich 'steed son of steeding' (p. 231. 435. 439) und nicht
vielmehr Marcus filius Marciani oder ab Marciano? Volksetymologie ist es, wenn man den walisischen March das Schicksal
des Iren Labraid Lorc erleben lässt.

Der Verfasser verharrt (p. 569. 645) bei seiner Meinung und
knüpft weitgehende Folgerungen an die Hypothese, dass Don in
solchen Namen wie Gwydion ab Don der Name einer Frau sei,
da einerseits die Aranrot merch Don im Mabinogi dem Math
bezeichnet werde als *dy nith verch dy chwaer* 'deine Nichte, die
Tochter deiner Schwester' RB. 1, 68 (wie ähnlich Gwalchmei
mab Gwyar nei y Arthur vab y chwaer ae gevynderw Aed, 1, 114),
und andrerseits Aryanrot verch Veli in den Triaden vorkomme
(RB. 1, 298). Aber m. E. folgt daraus nicht, dass Beli Amhanogan
(Bellinus ab Minocanno), der König von Britannien, der Vater
dieser Frau und dass Don ihre Mutter sei (ein Irrtum, in den vor
Rhŷs Lady Guest 3, 258 verfallen ist), sondern jene Aranrot, die
unter eigentümlichen Verhältnissen Zwillingen das Leben schenkte
(RB. 1, 68), ist von dieser Aryanrot, der Tochter Belis, der Frau
des Lliaw und der Mutter des Gwenwynwyn und des Gwanar,
gänzlich verschieden. Die lokale Legende von Math hat mit
der pseudohistorischen von Beli mawr nicht das Mindeste zu
thun. In einem Texte der Triaden heisst denn auch des letztern
Tochter vielmehr Arauron ferch Beli (MA. 412a).

Don ist nach der regelmässigen Form der celtischen
Filiation der Vater der Aranrot, des Gwydion und seiner Brüder.
Darüber lassen die walisischen Antiquare, die dem Ursprung der
Legenden näher standen, durchaus keinen Zweifel. Die Iolo
Manuscripts p. 81 f. 471 f. widmen diesem Helden Don einen
besondern Abschnitt, der einem alten genealogischem Buche
entnommen ist. Darnach war Don *brenin Llychlyn a Dulyn*
'der König von Lochlann und Dublin', der angeblich im Jahre
267 die Iren nach Nordwales führte, wo sie 129 Jahre gesessen
haben; er war eine Geissel für das Land (IM. 78), dieser *Don Ren*

(ib. 263, 20). Und Gwydion der Ire, der Sohn des Don, war in Wissenschaften und Künsten hochberühmt; er wird genannt *Gwydion wyddel ap Don ap Dar ap Daronwy* (ib. 82. 472). Muss es nicht befremden, dass Rhŷs alles dieses dem Leser verschweigt, obwohl er den übrigen Inhalt der, früher von ihm übersehenen, Seiten der Iolo MSS. reichlich kommentiert? Er sagt nur (p. 569): 'The name, however, of the leader of the Goidels arrayed against Cadwallon may be regarded as unknown'.

Hat nun an einer britannischen Göttin Don die irische Göttin Danu keine Stütze, so ist auch die Erklärung der Tuath dé Danann als 'des Volks der Göttin Danu', die Rhŷs verteidigt, m. E. haltlos. Dass ein *día Danu* 'Göttin Danu' der gälischen Ausdrucksweise nicht entspricht, wird wohl jeder zugeben; vielmehr heisst es *in bandea Nympha* 'die Göttin Nympha', Togail Troi 84, oder *Brigit bandee* 'die Göttin Brigit', Cormac s. v. Brigit. Für König David sagt man entweder *in rí Dáibhi* oder emphatisch *Dáibhi in rí* oder gewöhnlich *Dáibhi rí* (w. *Dafydd frenin*), aber nicht *rí Dáibhi*. So muss wohl Tuath dé Danann 'das Volk Gottes von Dana' oder 'das göttliche Volk der Dana' bedeuten; und da *Dá chích Danainne* auf das ältere *Dá chích Anann* zurückzuführen ist, so schliesst man gewiss nicht unpassend, dass es ursprünglich auch Tuath dé Anann geheissen habe, 'das göttliche Volk der Göttermutter Ana' oder 'Irlands'. Ob die Göttin Ana oder, wie andere wollen, Ána mit der Feeenkönigin Áine von Limerick, die in andern Teilen Irlands Aebhinn, Aoibhell oder Eibhlinn oder Una oder Grian heisst, verwandt ist, bleibe dahingestellt.

Der Verfasser hat einige Etymologieen in sein Werk aufgenommen, die wahrscheinlich nicht allgemein überzeugen werden, wie *dim* in *penardim* = *du* (p. 225, The Welsh People p. 38); *hyspys* von der Wurzel des ir. *atchí* (p. 264, schon Cymmr. 6, 211); *ceuri*, ein gelegentlicher Plural von *cawr* 'Riese', von *cadr*, armor. *caer* (p. 280); *enw* und *enaid* (p. 625); *fenodyree* der manannische Waldschrat, pilosus satyr, aus dem Nordischen (p. 286). Die Kenning für den Ocean ist nicht Mor Neifion (p. 445), sondern Llys Neifion (IM. 89). Gwrach y rhibyn (p. 453) wird bei Croker, vermutlich nach O. Pughes mündlicher Mitteilung, als 'die Geiferhexe' erklärt.

Den alten Namen der Themse *Tamĕsis* will der Verf. *Tamēsis* sprechen und bei Dio Cassius scheint die Überlieferung

wirklich zwischen *Ταμέσα* und *Ταμήσα* zu schwanken. Dem
welschen *Tafwys* entspricht aber die mittelalterliche Nebenform
Tamensis fluvius, die bei Galfridus mehrfach (4, 3. 5, 16. 7, 4)
und sonst vorkommt, sowie w. *mwys* aus mensa, *dwys* aus densus,
pwys aus pensum entstanden sind. So ist auch das französische
Tamise aus Tamensis zu erklären, sowie *pris* aus prensus, *païs*
aus pagense, *marquis* aus marchensis. Über die Darstellung
eines lat. *ĕ* durch w. *wy* vgl. übrigens W. Meyer-Lübcke in
dieser Zeitschrift 1, 474.

Ychen bannawc RB. 1, 121 ist nach dem, was S. Evans im
Wörterbuche beibringt, kaum in *mannawc* zu verbessern (p. 580),
denn dieses bedeutet 'ein Mal habend' von *man* 'Fleck'. So
heisst Helena *Elen vannawc*, weil sie ein Mal zwischen den
Brauen hatte, 'notam inter duo supercilia habens', Dares Phrygius
c. 12, was der Waliser überträgt: *a man oed yrwg y dwy ael
ac am hynny y gelwit hi Elen vanawc*, RB. 2, 12; vgl. die Triaden
1, 297, wo man den Ausdruck falsch verstanden hat.

Die alten Wörter *oeth ac anoeth* erklärt der Verf. aus
cyfoeth = ir. *cumacht* 'Macht' und 'Nicht-Macht' (p. 619), was
gewiss möglich ist, nur stimmt die Bedeutung nicht recht zu den
Belegen, die S. Evans s. v. *anoeth* gesammelt hat. Ein kahles
Land heisst *oeth*, ein bewachsenes *anoeth* (IM. 186); was nach
aussen (*tu faes*) ist, heisst *oeth*, das nach innen gelegene (*tu
mewn*) heisst *anoeth* (IM. 187. 263); so hat eine Höhle ihr vorn
und hinten, *wyth ac annwyth* (MA. 900a); so auch eine Stadt
ihre äussern und innern versteckten Teile, *oeth ac anoeth* (RB.
1, 104. IM. 263). Arthurs Grab ist *anoeth*, geheimnisvoll (Skene
2, 32); schwer zugängliche Dinge heissen *anoetheu* (RB. 1, 125.
128. 132). Das *teulu oeth ac anoeth* (Skene 2, 31) möchte ein
Geschlecht sein, das in die Erscheinung treten und verborgen
sein konnte, von dem man nicht weiss, *puy vynt uy puy eu neges*.
Das Wort *oeth* scheint adjektivische Geltung zu haben, kann
aber sehr wohl aus einem Substantivum hervorgegangen sein.
Vielleicht entspricht es dem irischen *ucht* 'die Brust', dann 'die
Vorderseite'; *a hucht* heisst 'coram', *i nucht in tsleibe* 'am Fusse
des Berges', *re hucht in tsleibe* 'vor dem Berge' etc. Demnach
würde *oeth* das Vordere, Nähere, Offene, Zugängliche, Sichtbare,
Deutliche und *anoeth* das Hintere, Ferne, Verschlossene, Ver-
steckte, Unsichtbare, Geheimnisvolle bezeichnen. Auf Wesen
bezogen, scheinen die Ausdrücke jenem andern für die sichtbare

und die unsichtbare Welt parallel zu sein, nämlich ir. *domun* : w. **dwfn* 'die Welt' und ir. **andomun* : w. *annwfn, annwn* (aus *andwfn*) 'die Unterwelt'.

Der Verfasser billigt ausdrücklich p. 681 eine unlängst aufgestellte Lehre, die einen Ausblick in das höchste Altertum zu eröffnen scheint. Nach J. Morris Jones ist aus syntaktischen Erscheinungen in den celtischen Sprachen die Thatsache zu folgern, zu der auch anthropologische Funde gut stimmen würden, dass die britannischen Celten von den vorceltischen Bewohnern der Insel ein Satzgefüge in ihre Redeweise aufgenommen haben, das diese, namentlich die Picten, aus frühern Wohnsitzen in Nordafrika mitgebracht hätten. Er findet überraschende Übereinstimmung in der welschen Syntax mit der der alten Ägypter und der Berber. Um es an einem merkwürdigen, von Jones übrigens nicht angeführten Beispiele zu zeigen, so hat sich in der emphatischen Form des welschen Pronomens *yntev* oder *yntef* (wohl aus dem Artikel *int-* und dem Pronomen *em* zusammengesetzt) aus der Bedeutung 'er, es seinerseits' eine konjunktionale 'aber' entwickelt, z. B. *a rei yntev ysyd yn uffern* 'quae *vero* in inferno sunt', LA. 57, 5. Das Wort für 'er' heisst im Ägyptischen *entof* (aus einem pronominalen Stamme *ent-* und dem Suffix der 3. Sg. *-f*); es ist aber zugleich eine gewöhnliche Konjunktion in der Bedeutung 'dagegen'. Wer möchte nun behaupten, nicht, dass die beiden Wörter formverwandt seien, sondern dass die abgeleitete konjunktionale Bedeutung in der spätern welschen Sprache ohne eine Einwirkung der ältern ägyptischen nicht denkbar sei? Wie in diesem Falle verhält es sich in allen übrigen, wenn man der Sache auf den Grund geht. Aus gar vielen Sprachen könnte man in der Konstruktion des Subjekts und des Prädikats, in der conjugatio periphrastica, in der Art der Hervorhebung, in der Suffigierung der Pronomina, im Gebrauch der Partikeln u. s. w. ein dem celtischen ganz ähnliches Verfahren nachweisen. Wenn der Mangel oder das Absterben der Flexion die Zuflucht zu syntaktischen Mitteln zu nehmen nötigt, so ist es nicht verwunderlich, wenn sich sonst weit getrennte Sprachen in der Wahl dieser Mittel begegnen.

L. CHR. STERN.

Irische Texte mit Übersetzungen und Wörterbuch, herausgegeben von Wh. Stokes und E. Windisch. Vierte Serie,
1. Heft. Leipzig, S. Hirzel, 1900. XIV + 438 Seiten.

Dieser Teil der wertvollen Sammlung enthält eine neue,
von Stokes besorgte Ausgabe der 'Acallam na senórach' mit
Varianten und nützlichen Indices rerum, nominum et vocabulorum.
Es sind dazu die vier leider nicht vollständigen, aber sich ziemlich
ergänzenden Pergamenthandschriften des Werks benutzt. Die
älteste, Laud 610, konnte für ein Sechstel zu Grunde gelegt
werden, das Meiste beruht aber auf dem Texte des Buches von
Lismore, dessen Editio princeps mit einem gelehrten Kommentare
und einer meisterhaften Übersetzung St. H. O'Grady zu verdanken
ist. Das Werk heisst 'die Unterredung der Alten', Accallaim
na senórach, Zeile 2702, oder Imacallaim na senórach, Z. 5363,
(denn der Dativus *acallaim* tritt in der spätern Sprache an die
Stelle des alten Nominativs *acallam*), und ist seinem Inhalte nach
im Wesentlichen eine Bearbeitung des 'Dinnshenchas Érenn'
oder der irischen Heimatskunde mit durchgehender Beziehung
auf den ossianischen Sagenkreis, dem in dem ältern Dinnshenchas
nur eine kleinere Rolle zugeteilt war, und der Form nach, wie
H. Zimmer es ausdrückte, eine Rahmenerzählung. Wenn das
Werk im Dinnshenchas von Tonn Clidna nach dem Buche von
Ballymote wie auch nach den MSS. von Rennes und Edinburg
erwähnt wird, so beweist das für sein Alter, dass es in der
zweiten Hälfte des 14. Jahrhunderts vorhanden war; es ist dies
ein späterer Zusatz, der im Buche von Leinster und in Rawlinson
B. 506 noch fehlt. Nimmt man den Charakter der Sprache hinzu,
so wird man wohl sagen dürfen, dass diese Form der Sage von
den Fianna etwa am Ende des 13. oder in der ersten Hälfte des
14. Jahrhunderts entstanden ist. Keating, der andere Erzählungen
aus demselben Sagenkreise anführt, scheint diese nicht gekannt
zu haben. Man freut sich, nun ein in der gälischen Litteratur
wichtiges Werk in der Vollständigkeit, die noch erreichbar war,
und, soviel sich ohne Vergleichung der Handschriften urteilen
lässt, in zuverlässigem Abdrucke vor sich zu haben. Zu den in
der gegenwärtigen Ausgabe zum ersten Male edierten und über-
setzten Stücken seien einige Bemerkungen gestattet.

Seite 115, 227, Z. 4068 *airfitechachaib*, von *airfitech* oder *airfidech* 7720, gen. *airfidig* 7721, ist eine auffallende Form und auch kaum als eine Ableitung von *airfitid* zu erklären. Man sollte *airfitechaib* erwarten.

ib. Z. 4069 *An tuc-sam mná imda amlaid* 'And did he endow many women thus?' etc. *Tabairt* scheint hier wie oft 'vergeben, verheiraten' zu bedeuten; die Aussteuer (*coibchi*) wird besonders erwähnt.

S. 156, 228, Z. 5681 *fírchara* 'a true lover' — vielmehr (wie Keating, Three Shafts, ed. Atkinson, p. 297, und sonst *fiorchara*) 'ein Freund', dem man Geheimnisse mitteilt.

S. 157, 229, Z. 5709. Oscar erhält von Finn für seine junge Frau, eine Elfin, auf den Zeitraum von sieben Jahren das Schloss in Allen angewiesen, *7 fughaib-si féin inad ossin amach di* 'and thenceforward do thou thyself leave the place to her'. Hier hat eine Verwechselung von *fagaib* mit *fácaib* stattgefunden; der Sinn ist: 'und darnach besorge du ihr selbst eine Stätte'.

S. 158, 231, Z. 5753 *isscic* für *isidhe*, die merkwürdige Form, über die Zimmer (KZ. 32, 215) gehandelt hat.

ib. Z. 5766 '*Mochen do tiacht, a m'anum, a Fhind*', ar rí Muman, '*is tairisc linde ind fhaeilte sin*'. Welcome is thy arrival, my soul, o Find, and loyal is this greeting of ours. Hier ist etwas ausgelassen, denn die letzten Worte spricht der Angeredete. 'Sei willkommen, o Finn!' sagte der König von Munster. (Worauf Finn erwidert:) 'Das Willkommen scheint uns aufrichtig', und der König dann fortfährt: *Is tairisc ón*. 'Es ist aufrichtig'. Dieselben Worte werden Z. 6903 übersetzt: 'Dear to us is this welcome'; cf. 6106.

S. 160, 233, Z. 5825 *Dogenum, ar in maccaem*. 'We will do it, says the youth.' Lies *dogén um* 'ich werde es wirklich thun'.

S. 161, 234, Z. 5863. Von dem Orte Cuillenn heisst es: *Ocus is annseo donith in flaith Find tri catha don Fhein cacha bliadna, 7 is annseo doberthea 7 do toghtha curaid re gaisced a ninad cacha marbtha d' fhiannaib Eirenn*. 'Here too in every year the lord Find used to deliver three battles to the Fiann, and champions were brought and chosen for valour in place of all the Fiann that were killed.' Es ist nicht glaublich, dass Finn seinen eigenen Truppen alle Jahre drei Schlachten geliefert haben sollte. Es ist zu übersetzen: 'Und hier bildete Finn alljährlich drei Regimenter aus den Fianna, und daselbst wurden

herbeigeführt und ausgewählt Ritter des Waffendienstes als
Ersatz für alle (in dem vorangegangenen Zeitraume) Gefallenen'.
In Cuillenn, wo also die Rekruten gemustert und eingekleidet
wurden, gab es, wie in noch drei Örtern, ein Zeug- und Gewand-
haus (*étaigi lighda lcndmaissecha*) oder, im militärischen Kauderwelsch, ein Montierungsdépôt. Dass die Fianna drei *catha* oder
Regimenter (*tri catha na feinne* LL. 297 a 25) bildeten, wird in
der Acallaim oft gesagt, nur in Fällen der Mobilmachung wurde
ihre Zahl auf sieben erhöht.

S. 169, 218, Z. 6138. *In comfhat bias duine am degaid-si
bithí-si.* So long as any one shall follow me ye shall be ... 'So
lange jemand in meinem Gefolge ist, sollt ihr es (auch) sein.'
Die Einschiebung von *a tuilled,* eigentlich seine Zugabe, (aus
Franc. 7 *tuilled?*) hinter *bíthisi* ist vielleicht nötig.

S. 174, 243, Z. 6295. Das *bliadain quartill* 'das Quartil-
Jahr', das der h. Patrick erläutert, scheint von astrologischen
Aspekten abhängig zu sein. *Quartill* kann kaum etwas anderes
sein als engl. *quartile,* altfranz. *quartil, quarti* (Godefroy 6, 487),
gleichbedeutend mit *quadrat, quadrature,* die astronomische
Quadratur, d. h. die Stellung eines Gestirns (z. B. des Planeten
Mars) zu einem andern (etwa der Sonne) in einem Abstande von
90 Längengraden des Himmelsglobus oder um den vierten Teil
des Tierkreises. In dem fraglichen Jahre, das zwischen zwei
Jahrtausenden eintreten soll, sei, heisst es, ein Monat ohne Mond
(oder Mondschein?), ein Monat ohne Monat (oder Monatsnamen
oder Sternbild im Tierkreise?) und ein Monat mit drei verschiedenen Monden. Ob des Rätsels Lösung im 29. Februar
liegt (an welchem die Erörterung stattgefunden haben würde),
mag das *lucht áirmhe easga* entscheiden, denn diese supersubtile
Frage scheint mehr zur Kompetenz des Meisters Alcofribas als
zu der des heiligen Patrick zu gehören.

ib. Z. 6302 *i tur ar cesta reomaind,* 'in the course (?) of our
previous question'; wohl eher 'in der vorherigen Untersuchung
unserer Frage'; cf. *tur .i. iarraidh* O'Dav., *túr .i. iarraidh
sgrúdadh* O'Cl., Ir. Texte 3, 200.

S. 175, 245, Z. 6335 *ara ndentar cruinde 7 cessacht,* 'for
whom gathering and grudging are practised'; doch wohl: 'das
womit oder was zusammengescharrt und geknausert wird'.
Ceasacht ar findet sich auch Oss. 3, 122, aber es scheint ihm hier
die Bedeutung 'parvispendia' (Ir. Gl. 280) zuzukommen.

S. 184, 249, Z. 6644. *Ní maith in carpat ré roind 7 in carpat uile do Pátraic.* 'Not good is *this* chariot at breaking, and it is all for Patrick.' So sagt ein junger Mann um dem Heiligen, dessen Wagen auf der Reise zerbrochen war, den seinigen anzubieten. *Roind* bedeutet 'teilen, zuteilen', z. B. ein Haus, das mit andern geteilt wird, in dem jedem das Seine zugeteilt oder angewiesen wird. So heisst es im Gedichte des Cormacán éiges:

Adhaigh dun ind Aillinn uair . tanaic an sneachta a nairtuaidh
rob iat ar dtoighe cen roinn . ar gcochaill chorra chrocoinn.

'Als wir nachts im kalten Aillinn waren, kam der Schnee aus Nordosten. Da waren unsere absonderlichen Fellmäntel unsere Häuser ohne Zuteilung'; jeder hüllte sich in seinen Mantel. Im Sprichwort sagt man: *ni thig aontigheas gan roinn* 'Keine Hausgenossenschaft ohne Zuteilung' oder 'Mitteilung'. Daher auch die obigen Worte: 'Nicht gut ist der Wagen (mit einem andern) zu teilen (oder 'abzuteilen') und er gehört ganz Patrick.' Der Heilige belobt den jungen Mann wegen seiner eleganten und bestimmten Ausdrucksweise (*co grind*).

S. 205, 259 erwähnt der raschfüssige Cailte in einigen Strophen die Gelegenheiten, bei denen er einstmals seine drei Meisterstücke im Laufen geleistet habe. Diese werden auch sonst erwähnt, namentlich in einem alten Gedicht im Dean's book Nr. 17 mit dem Anfange *Heym tosk goskla Fynn Theigh mi tosg a dh' fhuasgladh Fhinn*, das irisch nicht vollständig erhalten zu sein scheint. Der erste Lauf, nach Laud: *dar' gabus, ba caem mo rith, lanamain gach fiadha ar bith* 'als ich ein Paar von jedem wilden Tiere fing', ist der eigentliche Gegenstand jenes merkwürdigen Gedichtes und kommt auch in einer von K. Meyer in dieser Zeitschrift 1, 458 aus dem Buche von Lecan edierten Erzählung vor. Er wird noch Z. 3615 und 4978 erwähnt, an der letztern Stelle mit dem Ausdrucke *corrimirchi,* nach O'Gradys Übersetzung, 'the odd drove', was sonst *in chorrimirgi* CZ. 1, 459 oder *a chory'mryt keilta* Rel. celt. 1, 75 geschrieben wird. Der zweite Lauf *dar cuirisa ... fa all . atha ocus muillidh Érenn* (so in Laud, wohl nicht mit Sicherheit zu lesen) entspricht den Worten in Dean's book (1, 72): *not char aggis reim linn ahah na mvllin in Eirrin* nachar fhacas re m'linn átha na muilean i nÉirinn. Cailte rühmt sich also seiner

Zerstörung der Backöfen und der Mühlen in Irland, derselben That, von der in einer andern Erzählung (S. G. 247) die Rede ist; hier heissen die Objekte *átha ocus muilte* oder *muille* (welsch *odynau a melinau*); den Plural *muilti* von *muileann* erwähnt Coneys und *muille* (cf. *muilli* Tripart. 210) oder bei Laud *muillidh* steht für *muilne*. O'Grady übersetzt *muilte* sowohl als *muille* 'millbeams', als pl. von *mol*. Der dritte Lauf Cailtes *dar léigius ldigh do buaib a nÉrinn alaind adfuair* entspricht den Worten im Dean's book: *ni leich di legin fa boyhwah doyhis sin nerrin awwor* 'die Kälber liess ich unter die Kühe', dass sie ihnen die Milch nahmen; und auch dieser Frevel wird S. G. 247 erwähnt: *ro léigsem bar laeig co becht dochum a mbuair i noinfecht.*

S. 218 f., 269. Diese Stelle ist nicht richtig verstanden. Es wird erzählt, wie der König von Connacht durch Cailte drei Figuren von dem vergrabenen Brettspiel des Goll mac Morna empfängt, da ihm drei an seinem eigenen Spiele fehlten.[1]) Z. 7815: *Ocus tucad na fir ar in fidchill arsin.* 'So then the men were put back on the board' — vielmehr: 'Die (drei von Cailte gebrachten) Figuren wurden dann auf dem Brette (des Königs) aufgestellt', denn er wollte spielen. Er kann nun ein Verlangen nach dem ganzen wertvollen Spiele Golls, dem Brett samt den Figuren (es waren 150 goldene und 150 silberne), nicht unterdrücken und sagt zu Cailte: *Dursan gan a tabairt duitsi let damsa* 'Pity he did not give it to thee for me!' Goll, der ehemalige Besitzer dieses Brettspiels, war längst verstorben und von seinem Geiste ist nicht die Rede; überhaupt hatte Cailte die drei Figuren, die er gebracht hatte, nicht bekommen, sondern aus ihrem Versteck sich genommen. Der Satz, mit dem irischen Dativus cum infinitivo, bedeutet: 'Schade, dass du es (das Spiel) mir nicht mitgebracht hast!' Cailte antwortet unwillig: *Na cuirsi ris sin, a rí!* 'Set not thyself against him, o king!' — als sei zu besorgen, dass der Eigentümer des Spieles (Goll) ungehalten sein würde. Ich fasse die Worte: 'Übertreib es nicht, o König!', denn *cuir ris* heisst 'adde, exaggera' und kann hier nicht auf eine Person bezogen werden.

---

[1]) Cailte sagt, er habe dem Könige *gein 7 aithgein* gegeben (Z. 7813), etwa 'Satz und Ersatz'; vgl. Meyers Suppl. p. 73, wo man aus dem Buche von Lecan noch hinzufügen kann: *cach diri iar naithgenib id laim bodein; cach aithgein iar nindrucus*, etc. O'Curry, Transcripts p. 1944.

Uair ní thiber in fidchill duit etir, 7 ní thibar ní bus mó da foirind. 'For I will never give thee the board! And he gave nothing more to his retinue.' Hier habe ich Bedenken gegen die Auffassung des *ní thibar* als 'er gab' oder wohl 'er giebt' (*ní thabair*), denn es ist eine Nebenform zu *ní thiber,* die 1. Sg. Fut. im Status contractus, und kommt in den spätern Texten nicht selten vor, wird auch wohl *ní thiubar* geschrieben. Die Worte heissen: 'Denn ich werde dir das Spielbrett überhaupt nicht geben und werde dir auch von seinen Figuren nicht mehr geben'. *Foirend, fairend* (welsch *gwerin*) hat hier die bekannte Bedeutung 'ein Spiel Figuren'; *fear foirne* ist 'ein Schachspieler'.

L. CHR. STERN.

Dr. Ricochon, Tablettes & formules magiques à double sens. Première série. La tablette de Poitiers et une formule byzantine. Paris, A. Picard & fils (1901). IV + 12 pp. 8⁰.

Die fünfzeilige Inschrift der 1858 gefundenen lamina argentea von Poitiers, die schon Longuemar, Pictet und Siegfried beschäftigt hat, ist den marcellischen Formeln nahe verwandt. Was dieser magische Text, vermutlich aus dem 5. oder 6. Jahrh., Celtisches enthält, ist schwer auszumachen (vgl. Stokes in TPhS. 1885—1887, p. 164 = Bezz. Beitr. 11, 140). Der Verfasser, der einen genauen Abdruck giebt, sucht ihn, wie früher D'Arbois de Jubainville (Comptes rendus de l'académie des inscriptions 1872, p. 131 ff.), aus der lingua rustica Galliens zu verstehen; er erkennt aber gleichfalls griechische Elemente darin.

J. Strachan, Action and time in the Irish verb. (Reprinted
from the Philological Society's Transactions, 1900.) 31 pp. 8⁰.

Im Anschluss an die Arbeiten Zimmers, Thurneysens und Sarauws
über die Bedeutung der verbalen Partikel *ro* gelangt der Verf. zu der
Annahme eines zwiefachen Tempus der Vergangenheit für die ältere
irische Sprache: er nennt die einfache Form als das erzählende Tempus
(passé défini) das Präteritum und die andere, die durch *ro* oder in
einigen Fällen auch durch andere Präfixe (wie *ad, do*) oder durch
besondere Wortstämme (wie *douc* und *dorat* neben *dobert*) unterschieden
wird, das Perfektum. Die Regel über den Gebrauch der beiden Formen
wird indessen durch Ausnahmen eingeschränkt.

K. Meyer, King and Hermit, a colloquy between King Guaire
of Aidne and his brother Marbán, being an Irish poem of
the tenth century edited and translated. London, Th. Wohlleben, 1901. 30 pp. 8⁰. (2 sh. 6 d.)

Im Zwiegespräch mit seinem Halbbruder, dem Könige von
Connacht Guaire († 662), preist Marbán der Eremit den Frieden und
die Freuden seiner Waldeinsamkeit so beredt und anmutig, dass der
königliche Bruder sein Reich darangeben möchte um an diesem
bescheidenen Glücke teilzunehmen. O'Curry 3, 356 f. 374. 879 hat
einige Strophen des hübschen Gedichtes mitgeteilt und besprochen, der
vollständige Text von 33 Strophen ist in dieser Zeitschrift 3, 455 aus
Harl. 5280 ediert worden und erscheint nun, als eine Gabe für einige
im *shelta* mitforschende Freunde, mit einer getreuen Übersetzung und
einem Glossar der seltenern Wörter.

E. C. Mac Giolla Eáin, C. I., Dánta amhráin is caointe Sheathrúin
Céitinn, dochtúir diadhachta. Connradh na Gaedhilge, Baile
Átha Cliath 1900. 225 pp. 8⁰.

Man kannte bisher nur einige wenige Gedichte des irischen
Theologen und Geschichtsschreibers G. Keating (1570—1650). J. C.
MacErlean in Limerick hat hier nun 18 aus den Handschriften gesammelt, einige im Dán díreach, die meisten aber in rhythmischen Vers-
massen, mit Varianten ausgestattet und durch ein sorgfältiges Glossar
erläutert. Schon die Einleitung zeigt, dass der Herausgeber in der
irischen Geschichte und Poesie bewandert ist. Mehrere der Gedichte
Dr. Keatings sind Elegieen auf den Tod einiger Männer aus der Familie
Butler; in andern erscheint er als einer der ersten und bedeutendsten
Dichter des Dirge of Ireland. Auch ein erbauliches Stück wird ihm
beigelegt: *Caoin thu féin, a dhuine bhoicht*, das zuerst aus einer
Edinburger Handschrift in A. Camerons Reliquiae Celticae 1, 126 ediert
worden ist. Der Dichter preist ferner seine Muttersprache (die beiden
Strophen sind wohl zuerst in O'Brennans Ancient Ireland 1855 p. 24
abgedruckt) und den Harfenspieler O'Coffey; er grüsst seine Heimat

aus der Fremde und feiert Frauenschönheit, weist aber auch darauf
hin, dass die Zeit zu lieben für ihn vorüber sei. Bei einigen Gedichten
ist die Autorschaft Keatings vielleicht anfechtbar. Wenn z. B. der
Dichter in Nr. 15 die Zeit der Milesier auf 3960 Jahre berechnet, so
steht er damit weder mit dem Historiker Keating noch mit den vier
Meistern im Einklang.

In gälischen Gedichten wie denen Keatings wird man immer
Wörtern begegnen, deren Bedeutung zweifelhaft ist. V. 72 *theigh* fasse
ich als ein sonst vorkommendes Präteritum von *téidhim, téighim* 'ich
gehe'. V. 97 *smól-mhala* 'thrush-coloured brow' ist gewiss richtig,
wenn unter 'thrush' nicht turdus musicus (d. i. *smólach*, alb. *smeòrach*)
verstanden wird, sondern turdus merula, die Schwarzdrossel oder Amsel
lon-dubh, deren Farbe den Dichtern zum Vergleiche dient. Ir. *smól*
(= *mér* Corm.?). ist das welsche *mwyalch* 'die Amsel' (wie ir. *smér*,
'Brombeere' = w. *mwyar*), und es ist ein hübscher Zufall, dass auch
ein welscher Dichter die Braue der Geliebten mit dem Flügel der
Amsel vergleicht: 'Asgell y fwyalch esgud Megis ei hael', sagt Dafydd
ab Gwilym. V. 1185 *trí fichid naoi gcéad gan chor*, wo cor als 'twist,
fail' erklärt wird; sollte nicht vielleicht *corr* gemeint sein, das das
Mehr und Weniger bei Rechnungen bezeichnet? z. B. *corr mór is deich
míle* 'viel mehr als 10000', Glenbard coll. 36; *corr is bliadhna* 'mehr
als ein Jahr, ib. 102. V. 1434 *caithfead beith trid i miorr gach fuarma*
'at the end of every form'. Es scheint, man müsse *im iorr* schreiben
und *iorr* als eine Nebenform für *eirr* betrachten (ähnlich wie *iorradh*
O'Rahilly 4, 7 statt *earradh*); vgl. *eirr dom andil*, O'Curry 564; *in eirr
th'aoise*, ib. 569; *o thús go eirr th'aimsire*, ib. V. 1576 *sith-leacht* 'peace-
ful monument' bezeichnet wohl 'ein längliches Grab', so wie *sithlong,
sithbarc* 'navis longa', *sithlann* 'eine lange Klinge', etc. P. 170 *míle*
'warrior', gen. *míleadh* lässt sich vielleicht nach der Analogie von *file*
statt *fili* annehmen; aber der Nominativ *milidh* ist im Mittel- und Neuirischen der gewöhnliche (wie im altir. *míl*); und der Name des Milesius
lautet gleich: *oenmac Bile .i. milid Espáine Galam a ainm díles*
LL. 12 a 52. BB. 18 b 38. 58. 19 a 18 etc. P. 177 *oscardha* 'renowned'
kann man nicht von dem ziemlich späten Namen Oscar ableiten; vermutlich bedeutet das Wort ursprünglich 'fremdartig, ausserordentlich',
wie noch in *rithim oscarda* 'der fremdartige (nicht irische) Rhythmus'
LH. 1, 14. 87. P. 207 für den Shannon muss wohl *Sionann* (vulgo
Seanuing) als Nominativ angesetzt werden, nicht *Sionna.*

Hoffen wir, dass bald mehr aus wertvollen neuirischen Manuskripten ediert wird und mit gleicher Sorgfalt. Der gälische Bund hat
kaum etwas Nützlicheres und Gefälligeres gefördert.

S. Bugge, Ølands Runeindskrifter. (Særtryk af Aarb. for nord.
Oldkynd. og Hist. 1900.) Kjøbenhavn 1900. 15 pp. 8⁰.

Von den letzthin von H. Hildebrand herausgegebenen Runen-
inschriften Schwedens bespricht der berühmte norwegische Sprachforscher
hier die wichtigsten der auf Øland gefundenen, von Sven Söterberg
edierten, namentlich den Stein von Karlevi. Dieses dem Ende des

10. Jahrh. angehörige Denkmal zeigt neben einer Runeninschrift die lateinischen Charaktere ... *NINONI ... EH* +, die etwa zu *Tumulus Ninoni fili ... eh.* zu ergänzen sind. Mit dem zweifellos celtischen Namen vergleicht der Verf. die sonst bezeugten Namen Ninnus, Ninoa, Ninnid (Nennius), Nini, Ninnine (im Félire Oengusa) und Ninnio (Genitiv *Ninnsen?* Gorman p. 387) sowie das welsche Nynnyaw (Nynia bei Beda) und Ninnianus. Auch die Buchstaben ... *eh* weisen auf einen celtischen Namen, wie z. B. das sonst vorkommende filius *Wredech*, filius *Muircholaich* u. a. in den Inschriften.

Al. Bugge, Contributions to the History of the Norsemen in Ireland. I, II. Christiania, Jac. Dybwad 1900. (Videnskabsselskabets Skrifter. II. Historisk-filosofisk Klasse, 1900, No. 4 & 5.) 17 und 32 Seiten. gr. 8⁰.

> Der Verf. teilt nicht die Ansicht, dass die Dänen infolge des Sieges, den sie 850 bei Dublin über die Norweger davontrugen, nun die Herrscher Irlands geworden seien, wie H. Zimmer aus der Darstellung der irischen Annalen geschlossen hat. Nach ihm (er legt alles Gewicht auf die 'drei Annalenfragmente' und das Cogadh Gaedhel) handelt es sich bei der nordischen Herrschaft über Irland immer nur um Norweger und die Dubliner Dynastie ist, wie aus den überlieferten Namen zu erkennen ist, eine norwegische. Das verehrte Schwert des Carlus, das in den Besitz irischer Könige überging, wäre ebenso wie der norwegische Personenname Magnus auf Karl den Grossen zurückzuführen. In einem zweiten Aufsatze legt der Verf. dar, dass sich die Erinnerung an die norwegischen Eroberer bis in die neuere Volkspoesie der Märchen und Balladen erhalten hat. Das Merkwürdigste, was man in dieser Beziehung aus der gälischen Litteratur Irlands und Schottlands anführen könnte, ist die Ballade von Seurlus an Dobhair, in der Jos. Anderson eine celtische Version der Ballade von Sorli, dem an Liebesgram gestorbenen Königssohne, erkannt hat (Highland Monthly 1, 148. 213). Das altnordische Gedicht ist verloren gegangen und nur aus einer Anspielung im sogen. Málshátta kvaedi bekannt.

J. Gwenogvryn Evans, Report on Manuscripts in the Welsh Language. Vol. I, Part II. London 1899. (Historical Manuscripts Commission.) XIX pp. + p. 297—1006.

> Diese Fortsetzung des Katalogs der welschen Handschriften (vgl. CZ. 2, 599) beschreibt 180 MS. der Sammlung in Peniarth, deren grösster Teil einstmals im Besitze des Antiquars Rob. Vaughan in Hengwrt gewesen ist. Man konnte sich aus dem kurzen Verzeichnisse, das W. W. E. Wynne in der Archaeologia Cambrensis (III, 7, 165. 15, 209. 352. IV, 1, 73. 323. 2, 101) veröffentlicht hat, einen allgemeinen Begriff vom Werte dieser Codices machen, und R. Williams hat Nützliches und Wichtiges, wenn auch nicht immer ganz genau, aus ihnen mitgeteilt. Jetzt werden sie uns mit vorzüglicher Sachkenntnis und Sorgfalt im einzelnen beschrieben, darunter die ältesten Texte der Gesetze und der Mabinogion, der heilige Graal, Geschichtswerke, Theologica, Poesie von

der frühesten Zeit bis auf die Neuzeit. Singula quid referam? nil non laudabile vidi. Dieser Katalog ist, und wird es immer mehr werden, die Fundgrube der welschen Litteratur.

J. Loth, La métrique galloise depuis les plus anciens textes jusqu'à nos jours. Tome I. La métrique galloise du XVe siècle jusqu'à nos jours. Paris, A. Fontemoing 1900. (Cours de littérature celtique, tome IX.) XIII + 388 pp. 8⁰.

> Diese welsche Verslehre behandelt im ersten Buche die Metrik des 15. bis 16. Jahrhunderts nach den Grammatikern, im zweiten Buche dieselbe nach den Dichtern, im dritten die Metrik vom 16. Jahrh. bis heute und in einem Anhange 'die freien Metra'. Der Verf. will das Buch nur als Einleitung zu einem andern Teile angesehen wissen, in dem er die Gesetze und die Wandlung der welschen Metrik vom 11. bis 15. Jahrh. darzulegen beabsichtigt.

E. Ernault, Victor Henry, Lexique étymologique des termes les plus usuels du breton moderne. Anzeige in der Revue critique XXXIV. 1900. p. 218—224.

> Der Verfasser urteilt: 'Tout en témoignant de louables efforts, le Lexique est venu trop tôt pour pouvoir être une œuvre définitive dans son ensemble. Elle ne l'est que pour certaines parties'. Vgl. CZ. 3, 439.

R. Thurneysen, Die Namen der Wochentage in den keltischen Dialecten. (Zeitschrift für deutsche Wortforschung I, 1900, p. 186—191.)

> Zu einer Abhandlung über die Namen der Wochentage bei den semitischen und einigen indogermanischen Völkern hat der Verf. die Erklärung der britannischen und gälischen beigetragen. Die erstern, durchweg mit den Namen der sieben Planeten gebildet, stammen noch aus der Zeit der römischen Herrschaft, also vor 410 n. Chr. Die Iren haben die Woche etwas später mit dem Christentum angenommen und die römische Bezeichnungsweise nur für drei Tage (*dia luain : dyw llun, dia máirt : dyw mawrth, dia sathuirn : dyw sadwrn*) von den Britanniern behalten. Einstmals hat auch der irische Name für Sonntag dem welschen *dyw sul* entsprochen. Nach Cormac lautete er *diu sról* (*sroll*) 'dies Solis', wo *sról* 'suilsi' bedeuten soll. Aber *diusrol* ist, wie ich vermute, ein alter Schreibfehler für *diussol*, denn ein ir. Wort *sról* Licht' ist sonst nicht bekannt. St.

Corrigenda, addenda.

Band II. Zu den irischen Gedichten aus dem Kopenhagener MS. trage ich einige Verbesserungen nach, die ich meist Herrn Osborn J. Bergin in Cork verdanke.

S. 832, Z. 19 *Andamh fear meine an Mancaigh* 'Selten ist ein Mann vom Sinne des Manchers'.

S. 385, Z. 3 *do claointealaigh Chuind* 'dem schrägen Hügel Conns'; vgl. RC. 16, 11. Z. 5 *gurab hi an maith gan mhaoidem ar chaith re caintibh da crod* 'dass es die Güte ohne Rühmen (oder Murren) war, was er von seiner Habe an die Dichter spendete'. Z. 9 *do Cnodba is do Cholt*, so zu ergänzen nach *Uisneach Midhe Cnódhbha is Colt* JKAS. II, 1, 847 und Oss. 5, 134; Cnodhbha ist Knowth. Z. 10 *fer bfalad* (?) zu ergänzen; *eiteach* ist hier 'zurückweisen', nicht *éitheach* 'lügen'. Z. 12 *nar geall ni acht ní do comoill* 'dass er nichts versprach, was er nicht erfüllte'. Z. 13 wohl *órnocht* 'bar an Gold', als Reim zu *mórdacht*.

S. 336, Z. 15 lies *Banba Bregh; a sgiath cabra na ccoigead* 'o Schild des Schutzes der Provinzen'. Z. 16 *toirberta d'feraib Éirend* 'die Männer Erins müssen gewähren, dass ihre Gefangenen als Unterpfand gehalten werden, als eine Schuld des Königs des schönen Hügels Fáls'; vgl. hierzu und zu S. 350 N. noch: *nucu maith ri ac na bít géill, noco maith géill cen geimle*, LL. 146 b 45. Z. 18 statt *occuind* lies *ó cCuind* 'der Enkel Conns', ebenso 344, 32. 350, 35. 349, 31. 360, 14.

S. 340, Z. 28 vielleicht *fhuairshreib* zu lesen (zu *guaillibh*).

S. 344, Z. 22 Verbinde *ní biodh ... triochacéd gan cuartughadh* 'es war keine Baronie, die er nicht umkreiste'. Z. 23 wohl *nar fegh d'omhan* zu lesen, 'der nicht Furcht beachtete'. Z. 24 *a Chú-chuloin-si*, so vielleicht als Vokativ zu lesen: 'o du, ein Cúchulainn an Waffenkünsten'. Z. 27 *ar ndrud eille h'orsgabail* 'wenn das Band deiner goldenen Rüstung befestigt ist'.

S. 346, Z, 35 *a rún fhreime Cuind* 'o Liebling vom Stamme Conns'.

S. 348, Z. 9 *ni me do thogh acht tu fein, tussa dam* 'Nicht ich wählte nur dich, sondern du (wähltest) für mich'.

S. 350, Z. 25 lies *nir thuill séd* (oder *réd*), als Korrespondenz zu *ég*.

S. 351, ult. *sgan a dhiol d'fhilidh induind* 'Es war lange meine Absicht, bis ich für die Dichtkunst vorbereitet wäre, den König vom Stamme Conns nicht zu preisen, da wir kein seiner würdiger Barde waren', d. h. da ich es nicht war.

S. 352, Z. 2 *feadh a ealadhan d'fhoglaim* 'so lange er seine Kunst lernte'. Z. 9 *do dhan d'fhoghloim is d'aithne* 'in Poesie, in Gelehrsamkeit und in Kenntnissen'. Z. 10 *flaith O'Neill* 'Fürst der O'Neills', so nach der oben 3, 611 exemplifizierten Regel. Demnach ist in Lauds Cormac s. v. Scuit *ingen rig Foraind rig Egepte* das erste *rig* (in Übereinstimmung mit LB., YBL. und LH.) zu streichen. Z. 18 *na adhaigh sin* d. h. *na aghaidh sin* 'dagegen'. Z. 25. 27. 33 *ollamh* steht für *ullamh*. Z. 26 lies *ddigh roollamhnaigh mh'fhoghluim* 'a proceeding which has perfected my learning' (Bergin). Z. 28 *beiti tend as m'oige ass* 'ich kann wohl stolz auf meine Erziehung sein'; *oige* steht hier wie Z. 34 für *aige*, was *aice .i. oileamhain* O'Cl. sein mag. Z. 32 *cend* MS., wohl *cean* zu lesen, als Korrespondenz zu *seal*.

S. 363, Z. 1 Möglich, dass *coirenel corr curaidh*, wie Bergin vermutet, einen Eigennamen enthält, etwa 'crooked colonel Currie', aber es ist unsicher, wie manches andere in diesen schwierigen Gedichten dunkel ist. Z. 4 *nertghoil* als ein Wort zu schreiben, acc. sg.

S. 335, N. 1 Man könnte daran denken, ob *teach an trír* 'das Haus der Drei' auf die drei Colla zu beziehen sei. Aber der Ausdruck ist alt und kommt schon in der Weissagung des Art mac Cuinn vor, wo er ein Anachronismus wäre: *rí Temrach in trír* LU. 119 b 10 und *mo thonach co tric a tiprait in trír* ib. 14.

Band III. S. 137, Z. 6 lies *groes*. S. 143, Z. 3 lies *los : llost*. S. 148, Z. 15 *bonheddig* mit celtischer Endung (wie *airchinnech : arbennic*) ist von *meddyg* 'medicus' mit lateinischer Endung zu trennen. S. 149, Z. 5 das w. *do* 'ja' entspricht dem ir. *tó*.

S. 156, Z. 11 Der welschen Endung -*ach*, arm. -*ac'h*, -*oc'h* entspricht im Gälischen bald -*ac* (später -*ag*), bald -*oc* (später -*og*), wie w. *gwrach*, arm. *groac'h* = ir. *fracc*; w. *deiliach* = ir. *duilleoc*, alb. *duilleag*; arm. *gaoloc'h* 'langbeinig' = ir. *gabloc*. Da in dieser Endung (wie auch sonst, vgl. Pott, Etymologische Forschungen² 1, 185. 187) die deminutive, pejorative und komparative Bedeutung vereinigt ist, so wird die von mir verglichene lettische von *labb-ak-s* 'besser' und die littauische von *did-oka-s* 'ziemlich gross' davon kaum verschieden sein. Dieselben Bedeutungen hat auch das sanskritische Suffix -*ka*; vgl. Whitney, Grammar² § 1222d.

S. 159, N. 1 *y pum llawenydd* sind die fünf Freuden (gaudia) der Jungfrau Maria, deren man später auch sieben oder funfzehn rechnet.

S. 440, Z. 17 Der Form nach entspricht dem w. *hyt* ohne Zweifel eher das ir. *sith* als *ed*. S. 442, Z. 33 w. *wybr* ist kaum ir. *eochair* (w. *ochr*), aber auch die Erklärungen des schwierigen Wortes aus lat. *vapor* oder *aequora* befriedigen nicht recht. Auch die Vermutung Z. 45 über arm. *poulc'hen* soll nicht aufrecht erhalten werden.

S. 445, Z. 3 v. u. Dies ist falsch. Die betreffenden Worte im Symbolum des Psalters der h. Salaberga lauten: 'ex patre procedentem cum patre et filio coadorandum'. Es fehlt also das *filioque*, das man später hinter *ex patre* einfügte. Im übrigen vgl. über den Codex das Neue Archiv der Ges. f. ältere deutsche Geschichte VIII. 1883, p. 341.

Dr. Henebry übersendet nachträgliche Korrekturen zum Anfange der Betha Coluimb Cille.

S. 518, Z. 4 lies *Fheilimid*, Z. 8 *tribloid*, Z. 12 *dó do*. S. 520, Z. 4 *as dimhainech*, Z. 7 *deoch*aib, Z. 12 *Tolerancia*, Z. 15 *duthrachtacha*. S. 522, Z. 5 *lebru*, Z. 11 *go mbeith si solus*, Z. 16 *en-chuid di*, Z. 36 *menic*. S. 524, Z. 22 *tuas*. S. 526, Z. 30 *Geinfid*, Z. 33 *den*[fo. 2a]*am*. S. 528, Z. 19 *bud* (statt *bid*). S. 530, Z. 8 *ria* (statt *re*), Z. 25 *adhnocul*. Ausserdem fehlen auf diesen Seiten vielfach Accent und Aspiration.   St.

ADVERTISEMFNT.

Caledonian Medical Society.
Gunning Celtic Prizes.

Through the generosity of His Excellency the late Dr. R. H. Gunning, the Caledonian Medical Society have pleasure in announcing Two Prizes, of the value of *Twenty Pounds* and *Ten Pounds* respectively, for Essays on some Celtic subject — Ethnological, Historical, Philological, or Medical, under the following conditions: —

1. The Essays shall be written in English.
2. The competition for these Prizes shall be open to all comers.
3. Within the range of Celtic subjects indicated above, competitors will be allowed perfect freedom in choice of subject. The Committee suggest the following as suitable titles: —
   (a) 'Ancient Medical Manuscripts — Gaelic or Irish.'
   (b) 'The Origin, Language, Social Habits, and Traditions of the Insular Picts.'
   (c) 'The Influence of Scenery and Climate on the Music and Poetry of the Highlands.'
4. The judgment of the Assessors and Sub-Committee shall be final.
5. The successful Essays shall become the property of the Society, and shall be published in the *Caledonian Medical Journal*.
6. Essays sent in competition shall bear a motto only, the name and address of the writer to be enclosed under seal.
7. Essays to be sent under cover to the undersigned by 1st January, 1902, endorsed 'Celtic Prize.'

S. Rutherford Mac Phail, M.D.,
Honorary Secretary, Caledonian Medical Society.

Rowditch,
Derby, *November 15th, 1900.*

Abgeschlossen am 4. Mai 1901.

Druck von Ehrhardt Karras, Halle a. S.

Ingram Content Group UK Ltd.
Milton Keynes UK
UKHW051136130623
423139UK00026B/170